HOW ARBITRATION WORKS

Fourth Edition

HOW ARBITRATION WORKS

Fourth Edition

by

FRANK ELKOURI
Cross Research Professor of Law
University of Oklahoma

and

EDNA ASPER ELKOURI
Juris Doctor With Honors
The George Washington University
Law School

The Bureau of National Affairs, Inc.
Washington, D.C.

Copyright © 1952, 1960, 1973, 1985
The Bureau of National Affairs, Inc.
Washington, D.C. 20037

Second Printing December 1985 (regular ed.)
Second Printing March 1987 (student ed.)
Third Printing April 1988 (regular and student ed.)
Fourth Printing June 1989 (regular and student ed.)

Library of Congress Cataloging in Publication Data

Elkouri, Frank.
  How arbitration works.

  Includes index.
  1. Arbitration, Industrial—United States.
I. Elkouri, Edna Asper. II. Title.
KF3424.E53 1985   344.73'018914   85-9641
ISBN 0-87179-470-5   347.30418914
ISBN 0-87179-471-3 (pbk.)

Printed in the United States of America
International Standard Book Number: 0-87179-470-5 (regular ed.)
                                     0-87179-471-3 (student ed.)

To the men and women
—labor, management, and neutrals—
who make arbitration work

Preface to Fourth Edition

The Preface to the Second Edition of *How Arbitration Works* continues to serve well and applies to the Fourth Edition, as it did to the Third Edition. Updating the book again presented a great challenge to the Authors: the increasingly prominent and relevant role of the law, the coming of age of bargaining and dispute resolution in the state and federal public sectors, and the impact of the Civil Rights Act upon arbitration, each contributed to the already demanding challenge involved in the updating process.

Frank Elkouri
Edna Asper Elkouri

Preface to Third Edition

The Preface to the Second Edition serves well for the Third Edition also. Certainly, the rapid pace of development has continued. Thus, the updating of *How Arbitration Works* again presented a great challenge to the Authors, both as to time and effort. Even so, we have expanded the scope of the book by adding two new chapters, various new topics elsewhere in the book, and of course new developments throughout the book.

Frank Elkouri
Edna Asper Elkouri

Preface to Second Edition

The period since publication of the first edition of *How Arbitration Works* has witnessed a great outpouring of arbitration decisions as well as writings by arbitrators and students of arbitration. Thus, the past few years might well be termed a "classical" period in the history of arbitration. Much new thought has emerged, much previous thinking has been modified, and some of the old has departed. This is convincing evidence of the progressive and dynamic nature of arbitration in our industrial scheme of things today. The words of John Day Larkin, speaking as President of the National Academy of Arbitrators in 1956, effectively tell the story:

> "The work of arbitrators, like that of judges, is in one sense enduring and in another sense ephemeral. That which is erroneous is sure to perish. The good remains, the foundation on which new policies, practices and procedures will be built. That which is bad will be cast off in due time. Little by little, old and outworn doctrines are undermined, both through the process of negotiation by the parties and by the sounder reasoning of those called upon to interpret the language which the parties have hammered out in the heat of economic conflict, and through long hours of patient effort to reach an agreement."*

---

*Larkin, "Introduction: The First Decade," Critical Issues in Labor Arbitration viii, xv (BNA Books, 1957).

It is with the above thoughts in mind that the Authors offer the Second Edition of *How Arbitration Works* to arbitrators, students of arbitration, and especially to employers and employees.

Frank Elkouri
Edna Asper Elkouri

Foreword to First Edition

This study is a product of the graduate and research program of the University of Michigan Law School. The subject was selected on the basis of its current and increasing importance in the field of labor-management relations and as one which, partaking of many of the characteristics of a legal institution, is suitable for examination by lawyers as well as others.

Mr. Elkouri has sought from an examination of the reported arbitration cases themselves to throw new light on the procedural and substantive aspects of the arbitration process. He has modestly, and, in my opinion wisely, refrained on the whole from attempting to pass judgment on the wisdom and soundness of particular decisions and of general principles which appear to be emerging in the cases. Perhaps a study which undertakes such a critique will emerge in time, possibly from Mr. Elkouri himself. Meanwhile, what he has done is important enough.

It is still too early to determine the full impact of arbitration on collective bargaining. The next decade should disclose whether the recorded and published decisions of arbitrators have developed some generalized thinking about collective bargaining problems which has become an important part of the utilized knowledge of bargainers and of students of the subject. If experience with other bodies of accumulated knowledge is any criterion—and I can think of no valid reason why the field of labor relations should be set apart as an exception—we are likely to see just such a development. Some may view this prospect with alarm, based on a fear of stereotyped thinking and undue reverence for precedent. This attitude seems to me to show a lack of understanding of the judicial process. It is simply contrary to every canon of progress to refuse in this field or any other to conserve the accumulated wisdom and experience of the problems as sound judgment may dictate.

Russell A. Smith
Professor of Law
University of Michigan
1952

Acknowledgment, First Edition

I wish to acknowledge my deep indebtedness to Professor Russell A. Smith of the Michigan Law School, who, as my friend and Chairman of my Research Committee, contributed in so many ways to this book. I also wish to acknowledge my special indebtedness to the following persons, each of whom, in his respective way, contributed generously to make this book possible: E. Blythe Stason, Dean of Michigan Law School; Professor Lewis M. Simes, Director of Legal Research at Michigan Law School; Professor John E. Tracy, Professor Edgar N. Durfee, Professor L. Hart Wright and Professor Burke Shartel, all of Michigan Law School; Professor Hobart Coffey, Director of the Michigan Law School Library; Professor Coffey's Staff; Judge Frank P. Douglass and Mr. Leverett Edwards, both of the National Mediation Board; U.S. Senator Mike Monroney; Professor John B. Cheadle, Professor Victor H. Kulp and Professor Maurice H. Merrill, all of the University of Oklahoma Law School; Professor Sylvester Petro of New York University Law School; Professor George Wolbert of Washington and Lee Law School; Ford Motor Company Umpire Harry Shulman; Chrysler Motor Company Umpire David A. Wolff; Arbitrator Francis J. Robertson of Washington, D.C.; John D. Stewart, Executive Editor of The Bureau of National Affairs, Inc.; and, finally, the many arbitrators whose work has provided the basic material for this study.

Frank Elkouri

Acknowledgment, Second Edition

In addition to the persons named above, the Authors wish to thank David Ross Boyd Professor George B. Fraser and Professor Mortimer Schwartz, both of the University of Oklahoma College of Law, for their valuable suggestions in connection with the Second Edition.

Frank Elkouri
Edna Asper Elkouri

Summary Table of Contents

Detailed Table of Contents

Chapter 1

Arbitration and Its Setting

The labor dispute is a natural characteristic of our enterprise system in the context of worker organization and collective bargaining. Such disputes reflect the determination of labor and capital, respectively, to receive what each considers to be its "fair share" of industrial production.

Whether such conflict is an evil, and, if so, a necessary one, is not the concern here. What is important is that society and many disputants themselves recognize that production stoppages resulting from disputes should be minimized, and that an effective means of accomplishing this end is arbitration. This is recognized, too, as a matter of national policy. While he was a Justice of the U.S. Supreme Court, Arthur J. Goldberg underscored this policy: "In the United States Arbitration Act, the Labor-Management Relations Act [LMRA] and in numerous state statutes, our legislative bodies have voiced their conviction that voluntary arbitration of disputes is favored and has an important role in a society which seeks the peaceful, prompt and just disposition of controversies involving our citizens."[1] While a member of the National Labor Relations Board (NLRB), Joseph A. Jenkins declared: "I call arbitrators 'peacemakers' because they have it within their power to contribute more to the maintenance of good relations between conflicting forces in our society than any other group, whether public or private."[2]

This book deals with the workings of labor-management arbitration and with the numerous questions and problems that have confronted the parties and their arbitrators. The most realistic picture of how arbitration works and the most practical answers to its problems, it is believed, can be obtained through analysis of actual awards. So it

---

[1]Goldberg, "A Supreme Court Justice Looks at Arbitration," 20 Arb. J. 13 at 13 (1965). In urging wider use of arbitration for certain other types of disputes, Chief Justice Warren E. Burger of the U.S. Supreme Court acknowledged that the relatively "simple and informal" arbitration procedures have made "incalculable contributions to commerce and trade and labor peace." AAA, News & Views, No. 4 (1977).

[2]Jenkins, "The Peacemakers," 47 Geo. L.J. 435, 436 (1959).

is to awards that the Authors turn for their primary source material for most of the chapters.

Arbitration Defined—Historical Background

Arbitration, to use the words of one writer, is a "simple proceeding voluntarily chosen by parties who want a dispute determined by an impartial judge of their own mutual selection, whose decision, based on the merits of the case, they agree in advance to accept as final and binding."[3]

Submission of disputes to arbitration may be made compulsory by law. However, except as otherwise indicated, the use of the term "arbitration" in this book refers to voluntary arbitration. When parties voluntarily agree to arbitrate their differences, it thereafter becomes "obligatory" upon either party to arbitrate at the request of the other. Although both parties have voluntarily agreed to arbitrate, arbitration will not be resorted to unless at least one of them thereafter so wishes.

Arbitration as an institution is not new, having been in use many centuries before the beginning of the English common law.[4] Indeed, one court has called arbitration "the oldest known method of settlement of disputes between men."[5]

King Solomon was an arbitrator,[6] and it is interesting to note that the procedure used by him was in many respects similar to that used by arbitrators today. Phillip II of Macedon, the father of Alexander The Great, in his treaty of peace with the city-states of southern Greece circa 338–337 B.C., specified the use of arbitration in disputes "between members over vexed territory."[7] Another great man of history, George Washington, was a staunch believer in arbitration. Although he exercised all possible caution in writing his last will and testament, he did not overlook the possibility of disputes as to its intent. For this eventuality he specified arbitration:

> "But having endeavored to be plain and explicit in all the Devises—even at the expense of prolixity, perhaps of tautology, I hope, and trust, that no disputes will arise concerning them; but if contrary to expectation the case should be otherwise from the want of legal expression, or the usual technical terms or because too much or too little; has been said on any of the devises to be consonant with law, my will and direction expressly is, that all disputes (if unhappily any should arise) shall be decided by three impartial and intelligent men, known for their probity and good understanding; two to be chosen by the disputants, each having the choice of one, and the third by those two.—which three men thus chosen, shall unfettered by Law, or legal constructions, declare their

---

[3]Chappell, "Arbitrate . . . and Avoid Stomach Ulcers," 2 Arb. Mag., Nos. 11–12, pp. 6, 7 (1944). For a similar definition by a court, see Gates v. Arizona Brewing Co., 95 P.2d 49, 50 (Ariz. S.Ct., 1939).

[4]For some ancient sources and early developments of arbitration, see Murray, "Arbitration in the Anglo-Saxon and Early Norman Periods," 16 Arb. J. 193 (1961).

[5]McAmis v. Panhandle Pipe Line Co., 23 LA 570, 574 (Kan. City Ct. of App., 1954).

[6]Bible, 1 Kings, 3, 16–28.

[7]Fox, The Search for Alexander, 113–114 (Little, Brown and Co., 1980).

sense of the Testator's intention; and such decision is, to all intents and purposes to be as binding on the Parties as if it had been given in the Supreme Court of the United States."[8]

Commercial arbitration has long been used as a substitute for court action in the settlement of disputes between businessmen.[9] International arbitration has been used for the settlement of differences between nations, differences which, if not removed, might lead to war; also, international commercial arbitration has been used with increasing frequency.[10] Development of labor arbitration in the United States began during the latter part of the nineteenth century, and its most rapid advance has been made since the United States became involved in World War II.[11]

The development of labor-management arbitration generally has followed the development of collective bargaining. One of the more recent examples is professional athletics, where use of arbitration quickly followed the introduction of collective bargaining.[12] Arbitration has been most successful where collective bargaining has been successful.[13]

Collective Bargaining, Mediation, Fact-Finding, and Arbitration

The distinction between collective bargaining, mediation, fact-finding, and arbitration can be seen more clearly if one considers each

---

[8]AAA, Arbitration News, No. 2 (1963), where it is also explained that the quoted lines of the will are reproduced from a document published many years ago by the Federal Government.

[9]For the historical development of commercial arbitration, see Keller, Arbitration and the Legal Profession (AAA, 1952).

[10]Regarding international commercial arbitration, in 1970 the United States ratified the United Nations Convention on the Recognition and Enforcement of Foreign Arbitral Awards, under which courts of the signatory nations are to enforce arbitration clauses and awards on the same basis as they would domestic arbitration proceedings. For explanation and discussion, see McMahon, "Implementation of the UN Convention on Foreign Arbitral Awards in the U.S.," 26 Arb. J. 65 (1971). Illustrating enforcement of an agreement to arbitrate international commercial disputes under the Convention, see Scherk v. Alberto-Culver Co., 94 S.Ct 2449 (1974), and illustrating enforcement of an award under the Convention, see Island Territory of Curacao v. Solitron Devices, 356 F.Supp. 1 (USDC, 1973). In 1976 the UN endorsed worldwide use of the UNCITRAL Arbitration Rules for international commercial arbitration. "It was felt that rules under UN sponsorship would assist international trade by promoting use of arbitration in all parts of the world and by helping to end the confusing proliferation of rules, each designed for a single region or institution." AAA, News and Views, No. 3, 1976.

[11]Commercial arbitration grew up as an alternative to court action, while labor arbitration evolved primarily as a substitute for strikes. For the historical development of labor arbitration in the United States, see Nolan & Abrams, "American Labor Arbitration: The Early Years," 35 U. Fla. L. Rev. 373 (1983); Fleming, The Labor Arbitration Process, 1–30 (U. of Ill. Press, 1965); Stessin, Employee Discipline, 8–12 (BNA Books, 1960); Witte, "The Future of Labor Arbitration—A Challenge," The Profession of Labor Arbitration, 1, 3–11 (BNA Books, 1957); Witte, Historical Survey of Labor Arbitration (U. of Pa. Press, 1952); Keller, Arbitration and the Legal Profession (AAA, 1952); Oliver, "The Arbitration of Labor Disputes," 83 U. Pa. L. Rev. 206 (1934).

[12]See Stark, "The Presidential Address: Theme and Adaptations," Proceedings of the 31st Annual Meeting of NAA, 1, 19–20 (BNA Books, 1979) (this article also notes other new uses of arbitration); Comment, "Arbitration of Grievance and Salary Disputes in Professional Baseball: Evolution of a System of Private Law," 60 Cornell L. Rev. 1049 (1975).

[13]In the full-fashioned hosiery industry, for example, where the use of collective bargaining has been highly successful, over 1500 disputes were decided over a 10-year period by the industry's impartial chairman without a single reported instance of noncompliance with or nonacceptance of an award. Millis, How Collective Bargaining Works, 460 (1942). For a comprehensive summary of the development of collective bargaining and its effect upon arbitration, see Millis, id. at 871–907.

a stage in the relationship between labor and management. Collective bargaining is the first stage and arbitration the last. Conciliation or mediation, and fact-finding, occupy intermediate stages.

Conciliation or mediation may be resorted to as an aid to negotiations.[14] Technically, conciliation is carried on without the intervention of a third party, while mediation implies the intervention of an outside person; but the two terms are commonly used interchangeably.[15] The essence of mediation and conciliation is compromise. The mediator does not make a decision. Rather, his aim is to persuade negotiators, by proposals or arguments, to come to voluntary agreement.[16]

"Fact-finding," as the term is most commonly used, refers to a method of handling labor-management disputes which prohibits strikes and lockouts until an official agency, usually a fact-finding board, has had opportunity to investigate and report. Changes in the status quo, except when made by mutual consent of the parties, are prohibited during the "cooling-off" period which runs concurrently with the period of investigation and report. The function of fact-finders is to investigate and assemble all facts surrounding disputes. After the investigation, a report is made which may include recommendations (except under the emergency dispute provisions of LMRA §§ 206–210) and which, unlike the findings of an arbitrator, the disputants have a choice of accepting or rejecting.[17]

In arbitrating, parties are compelled by their own agreement to accept the decision of an arbitrator as final and binding. The objective of arbitration is adjudication, not compromise. Resort to arbitration usually occurs after the techniques of conciliation or mediation (and possibly fact-finding) have failed to produce agreement.

Arbitration as a Substitute for Work Stoppages

It has been said that the "most important difference between civilization and savagery is the habitual willingness of civilized men and nations to submit their differences of opinion to a factual test," and that "it is a mark of civilization to present reasons rather than arms."[18] Again, "industrial peace is not a God-given product. It must

---

[14]Another possible device is the private use of independent third parties as neutral "consultants" or participants in the collective bargaining process itself. See Chamberlain, "Neutral Consultants in Collective Bargaining," Proceedings of the 15th Annual Meeting of NAA, 83–116 (BNA Books, 1962); Wirtz, "Role of Federal Government in Labor Relations," 51 LRRM 70, 78 (1962); Hildebrand, "The Use of Neutrals in Collective Bargaining," Proceedings of the 14th Annual Meeting of NAA, 135 (BNA Books, 1961).

[15]Millis & Montgomery, Organized Labor, 719 n. 2 (1945).

[16]An excellent treatise on mediation is Simkin, Mediation and the Dynamics of Collective Bargaining (BNA Books, 1971). A shorter study is Fuller, "Mediation—Its Forms and Functions," 44 S. Cal. L. Rev. 305 (1971). Also see Zirkel & Lutz, "Characteristics and Functions of Mediators: A Pilot Study," 36 Arb. J. No. 2, p. 15 (1981), citing many other articles on mediation.

[17]Boards of Inquiry under LMRA § 213 enacted in 1974 for the health care industry do make recommendations. For a discussion of fact-finding, see Simkin, "Fact-Finding: Its Values and Limitations," Proceedings of the 23rd Annual Meeting of NAA, 165 (BNA Books, 1970).

[18]Boland, "Labor Disputes: The Preventive and Cure," Arbitration in Action, 6 (Dec. 1943).

be cultivated and worked for constantly. * * * Conciliation, mediation and voluntary arbitration are the marks of civilization. They are the enemies of distrust and force. They do away with the fang and the claw."[19] Moreover, "if the rules and standards of orderly social behavior accepted for society at large are to be valid also for industrial relations, it would seem that settlement of labor disputes on rights should be sought as far as possible through judicial methods rather than through strikes and lockouts."[20] One method of settling labor-management differences without resort to strike or lockout is voluntary arbitration. As recognized by the U.S. Supreme Court, arbitration "is the substitute for industrial strife."[21]

In the United States, the right to strike is looked upon as an essential economic freedom. Like all freedoms, however, it can be abused; it can be used unwisely and without sufficient justification. Many times, for example, strikes or lockouts have occurred not because of a real difference between the parties, but because one of them could not, or would not, of his own volition recede from a position irrevocably taken.[22] Here, of course, there is no social justification for a work stoppage. Even where a real difference exists, possibilities for a peaceful solution may make resort to force uncalled for. A difference that looms large to disputants may be relatively free of complexities when viewed by a disinterested observer. A basic tenet of arbitration is that the arbitrator will be able to look at the issue objectively; accordingly, a reasonable decision based upon the true merits of the dispute can be expected.

An agreement to arbitrate effects a complete surrender of any right of the employer to determine the controversy by unilateral action and of any right of both parties to support their contentions by a show of economic strength.[23] This surrender on occasion has been the basis of distrust of arbitration. One management argument against arbitration is that it substitutes for the experienced, responsible judgment of management the judgment of an outsider who lacks the responsibility for conducting the business. Labor, in turn, sometimes feels that giving up its freedom to strike, in reliance upon the understanding of an outsider who might prove to be not so understanding, involves too great a risk.

The answer to such fears is that the initially uninformed outsider is soon elightened, for both parties have adequate opportunity to inform him as to their views, and he carries a responsibility for his decision akin to that of a judge in a court of law.

---

[19]McGrady, "Industrial Peace: A Joint Enterprise," 2 Arb. J. 339, 343 (1938). In United Steelworkers v. NLRB, 530 F.2d 266, 276, 91 LRRM 2275 (CA 3, 1976), the Court similarly stressed use of arbitration instead of "the tooth and claw of industrial warfare."
[20]Spielmans, "Labor Disputes on Rights and on Interests," Am. Econ. Rev. 299 (June, 1939).
[21]United Steelworkers v. Warrior & Gulf Navigation Co., 80 S.Ct. 1347, 1351 (1960).
[22]For views on use of arbitration for purposes of "face saving," see Eaton, "Labor Arbitration in the San Francisco Bay Area," 48 LA 1381, 1389–1390 (1967); Warren & Bernstein, "A Profile of Labor Arbitration," 16 LA 970, 979 (1951).
[23]Pan American Airways, 5 LA 590, 594–595 (Cahn, 1946).

Contracts that make arbitration the final step in the grievance procedure generally prohibit strikes and lockouts over arbitrable issues.[24] Moreover, the U.S. Supreme Court has held that a no-strike obligation is implied in those issues which are subject to binding arbitration under the agreement, and that a strike over such an issue violates the agreement despite the absence of an express no-strike clause.[25]

There is a general disposition on the part of labor and management to provide, as the final grievance step, for the arbitration of contract interpretation and application disputes. A study made by the U.S. Bureau of Labor Statistics of agreements in effect on or after July 1976 indicated that almost 96 percent of the collective bargaining agreements in the nation's important industries provided for arbitration as the terminal point of the grievance machinery.[26] Even where employees are not represented by a union, recognition of the contribution that arbitration can make toward a healthy employer-employee relationship has led some employers to provide impartial arbitration machinery for the grievances of their unorganized employees.[27]

In contrast to the overwhelming acceptance of arbitration for contract interpretation and application disputes, the proportion of collective agreements with specific provision for the arbitration of contract negotiation disputes continued to hover at about 2 percent from 1949 to 1966.[28] In some quarters, however, it is suspected that the strike is becoming outmoded even for contract negotiation disputes and that the use of voluntary arbitration with proper safeguards

[24]Of 1717 contracts analyzed in one study, 1527 contained restrictions on strikes and lockouts. Many of these specified an absolute ban, but many limited the ban to disputes subject to grievance and/or arbitration procedures; some permitted strikes after exhaustion of the grievance procedure where there was no provision for arbitration or where mutual consent was required for arbitration. Major Collective Bargaining Agreements: Arbitration Procedures (U.S. Dept. of Labor Bull. No. 1425–6, 1966), 83. A later but less detailed study revealed a 93 percent frequency of no-strike and no-lockout clauses. Characteristics of Major Collective Bargaining Agreements, July 1, 1976 (U.S. Dept. of Labor Bull. 2013, 1979), 83. That the no-strike ban and the no-lockout ban are not always coextensive is illustrated by General Electric Co., 54 LA 660, 673 (Wildebush, 1969).

[25]Local 174, Teamsters v. Lucas Flour Co., 82 S.Ct. 571, 49 LRRM 2717 (1962).

[26]Characteristics of Major Collective Bargaining Agreements, July 1, 1976 (U.S. Dept. of Labor Bull. 2013, 1979), 82. Studies made by the Bureau in 1944, 1949, 1952, and 1966 showed percentages of 73, 83, 89, and 94, respectively. Major Collective Bargaining Agreements: Arbitration Procedures (U.S. Dept. of Labor Bull. 1425–6, 1966), 5.

[27]For example, see Arbitrator Feldman in 79 LA 1, 1–2; Siegel in 70 LA 430 at 430; Leach in 52 LA 688, 690, 693, and in 48 LA 299, 301–302; Dworkin in 49 LA 370, 371–372; McKelvey in 49 LA 290, 291.

[28]Major Collective Bargaining Agreements: Arbitration Procedures (U.S. Dept. of Labor Bull. 1425–6, 1966), 95. The Bureau of Labor Statistics study of agreements in effect on July 1976, cited above, did not report on use of arbitration for contract negotiation disputes. There are marked differences between the United States and Great Britain in the use of arbitration. In Great Britain arbitration has been used less for grievances than for contract negotiation disputes. Morrison and Marjorie Handsaker, "Arbitration in Great Britain," 1 Indus. Rel. 117, 135 (1961). For more on the extent of use of arbitration in Great Britain and some European countries, see Beaumont, "Arbitration & the Extension of Terms in Britain," 34 Arb. J. 32 (1979); Blanpain, "Arbitration and Settlement of Labor Disputes in Some European Countries," Proceedings of the 29th Annual Meeting of NAA, 355 (BNA Books, 1976); Wood, "Conciliation and Arbitration in Great Britain, 1974–1975," id. at 350; Johnston, "Labor Dispute Settlement in the United Kingdom, 1972," Proceedings of the 26th Annual Meeting of NAA, 233 (BNA Books, 1974); Fairweather, "American and Foreign Grievance Systems," Proceedings of the 21st Annual Meeting of NAA, 1 (BNA Books, 1968).

may be preferable.[29] And in the public sector, many states have enacted statutes authorizing or requiring arbitration of contract negotiation disputes remaining unresolved after mediation or other bargaining aids have failed.[30]

Advantages of Arbitration Over Litigation

Arbitration claims among its advantages the expertise of a specialized tribunal and the saving of time, expense, and trouble. While it is true that the courts of some jurisdictions have recognized that parties to collective agreements have legally enforceable rights thereunder, the costly, prolonged, and technical procedures of courts are not well adapted to the peculiar needs of labor-management relations. Arbitration, on the other hand, is more satisfactory "where a speedy decision by men with a practical knowledge of the subject is desired."[31]

The U.S. Supreme Court has acknowledged that arbitration, rather than court litigation, is the superior method of resolving disputes under collective agreements:

> "The labor arbitrator performs functions which are not normal to the courts; the considerations which help him fashion judgments may indeed be foreign to the competence of courts. * * * The parties expect that his judgment of a particular grievance will reflect not only what the contract says but, insofar as the collective bargaining agreement permits, such factors as the effect upon productivity of a particular result, its consequence to the morale of the shop, his judgment whether tensions will be heightened or diminished. For the parties' objective in using the arbitration process is primarily to further their common goal of uninterrupted production under the agreement, to make the agreement serve

---

[29]See Anderson, "Lessons From Interest Arbitration in the Public Sector: The Experience of Four Jurisdictions," Proceedings of the 27th Annual Meeting of NAA, 59, 69 (BNA Books, 1975); Loewenberg, "What the Private Sector Can Learn From the Public Sector in Interest Arbitrations: The Pennsylvania Experience," id. at 69, 77; Fleming, "Interest Arbitration Revisited," Proceedings of the 26th Annual Meeting of NAA, 1, 5–7 (BNA Books, 1974); Howlett, "Contract Negotiation Arbitration in the Public Sector," 42 Cin. L. Rev. 47, 49, 74 (1973); Taylor, "Making Arbitration Work," Proceedings of the 13th Annual Meeting of NAA, 101, 104–107 (BNA Books, 1960). In 1970 the AFL-CIO announced a joint labor-management effort, under the aegis of the American Arbitration Association, to explore the possibility of voluntary arbitration as a substitute for strikes in bargaining. "Labor-Management Plans for Voluntary Arbitration Study," 75 LRR 280 (1970). In 1974 the United Steelworkers entered into the Experimental Negotiating Agreement (ENA) with ten steel companies, waiving the right to strike and agreeing to submit unresolved bargaining issues to binding arbitration. The ENA and its background are explained in Aikens v. Abel, 73 LC ¶ 14,414 (USDC, 1974); Fischer, "Updating Arbitration," Proceedings of the 26th Annual Meeting of NAA, 62, 78–79, 88 (BNA Books, 1974). As of 1978, the parties had not yet needed to resort to arbitration of bargaining issues under the ENA. Stark, "The Presidential Address: Theme and Adaptations," Proceedings of the 31st Annual Meeting of NAA, 1, 16 (BNA Books, 1979).

[30]See Chapter 2, subtopic entitled "Interest Arbitration Statutes." A study of experience in certain states disclosed that the percentage of public-sector contracts being settled by arbitration ranged from 5 percent in Iowa to a high of 28 percent in Pennsylvania (where mediation was not a required step). Anderson, "Interest Arbitration as Strike Alternative," 101 LRR 283 (1979).

[31]Webster v. Van Allen, 216 N.Y.S. 552, 554 (N.Y. S.Ct. App. Div., 1926). For detailed explanations of labor arbitration's advantages over litigation, see Edwards, "Advantages of Arbitration Over Litigation: Reflections of a Judge," Proceedings of the 35th Annual Meeting of NAA, 16 (BNA Books, 1983); Coulson, "Certification and Training of Labor Arbitrators: Should Arbitrators Be Certified," Proceedings of the 30th Annual Meeting of NAA, 173, 181–182 (BNA Books, 1978).

their specialized needs. The ablest judge cannot be expected to bring the same experience and competence to bear upon the determination of a grievance, because he cannot be similarly informed."[32]

Parties to an industrial dispute must "live with" the judgment or award rendered by the adjudicator. Courts of general jurisdiction are not often versed in labor relations problems. This recognized, some countries have established labor courts as a part of their judicial system. Scholars have noted that European labor courts serve different and broader purposes than do American arbitration tribunals, and they have advised that labor courts do not offer a ready alternative to grievance arbitration in America.[33] However, one of the similarities between the two systems should be noted: like labor courts, arbitrators are presumed to be familiar with the needs and techniques of industrial relations, so parties generally will be able to "live with" their awards.

In predicting expanded use of arbitration beyond industry to cover a broad range of conflicts in our society, Clark Kerr explained the critical role of arbitration in another light:

---

[32]United Steelworkers v. Warrior & Gulf Navigation Co., 80 S.Ct. 1347, 1352–1353 (1960). Not everyone agrees that arbitration is the superior process for grievances. In 1964 U.S. Court of Appeals Judge Paul R. Hays (a former arbitrator) launched a massive assault on the institution of labor arbitration. Hays, Labor Arbitration: A Dissenting View (Yale U. Press, 1966). For responses to the critics of arbitration, see Luskin, "The Presidential Address: Arbitration and Its Critics," Proceedings of the 21st Annual Meeting of NAA, 125 (BNA Books, 1968); Smith, "The Presidential Address: Problems of Proof in Arbitration," Proceedings of the 19th Annual Meeting of NAA, 74 (BNA Books, 1967); Straus, "Labor Arbitration and Its Critics," 20 Arb. J. 197 (1965). An overwhelming majority of union and management officials contacted in one survey prefer the arbitration process to the available alternatives as a method of ultimate resolution of grievance disputes. Jones & Smith, "Management and Labor Appraisals and Criticisms of the Arbitration Process: A Report with Comments," 62 Mich. L. Rev. 1115, 1116–1117 (1964). For a survey of opinions concerning arbitration's faults, see Graham, Heshizer & Johnson, "Grievance Arbitration: Labor Officials' Attitudes," 33 Arb. J. 21 (1978) (78 percent of union officials responding in this survey consider arbitration "the best method of resolving unsettled grievances"); Davey, "What's Right and What's Wrong With Grievance Arbitration: The Practitioners Air Their Views," 28 Arb. J. 209 (1973). Also see Abrams, "The Integrity of the Arbitral Process," 76 Mich. L. Rev. 231 (1977). Of course arbitration does not work perfectly. No human mechanism of its scope and variety of uses, confronted with such demands and challenges as arbitration faces, can function without problems. But no system has yet been offered which is capable of serving the needs of labor-management grievance settlement as well as arbitration. Any doubts concerning arbitration's acceptability and utility should be dismissed. Neither the courts nor any governmental administrative tribunal offers any realistic possibility of equaling private labor-management arbitration for the purposes it has served since World War II. It is not surprising that use of arbitration has been constantly increasing. In the latter regard, the FMCS reported that in fiscal 1978, as in every past year, requests for arbitration panels increased rapidly. Requests totaled 25,639 compared with 23,474 in fiscal 1977, a 9.2 percent increase. See "FMCS' 31st Annual Report," 102 LRR 245 (1979).

[33]Aaron, "Labor Courts: Western European Models and Their Significance for the United States," 16 U.C.L.A. L. Rev. 847, 876 (1969); Fleming, "The Presidential Address: The Labor Court Idea," Proceedings of the 20th Annual Meeting of NAA, 229, 246 (BNA Books, 1967). For other discussions of labor courts, see Handsaker, "Labor Courts in Germany," 8 Arb. J. (N.S.) 131 (1953); Lenhoff, "Some Basic Features of American and European Labor Law: A Comparison," 26 Notre Dame Law. 389 (1951). In Canada, the British Columbia Labour Court has centralized authority to administer the entire body of labor law, but parties do have the possibility of using their own private arbitration. See Weiler, "The Role of the Labour Board as an Alternative to Arbitration," Proceedings of the 30th Annual Meeting of NAA, 72 (BNA Books, 1978). For more on dispute resolution in Canada, see Woods, "The Presidential Address: Shadows Over Arbitration," id. at 1; Carrothers, "The Cuckoo's Egg in the Mare's Nest—Arbitration of Interest Disputes in Public-Service Collective Bargaining: Problems of Principle, Policy, and Process," id. at 15; Lyon, Reimer & Teple, The Labor Relations Law of Canada (BNA Books, 1977).

"The courts cannot handle all of the load now, and even if they could handle all of it well, the judicial process is too slow and too costly. Courts are better at setting principles and establishing procedures in test cases. Private mechanisms need to carry the bulk of the caseload if the whole dispute-settling process is not to break down with serious consequences. This is one of the great lessons to be derived from the handling of grievances in industrial relations."[34]

The parties can make arbitration, as compared to litigation, relatively quick and inexpensive. Sometimes it takes only a few days from the appointment of the arbitrator until the issuance of his award. For example, one Company obtained an arbitrator's reasoned and documented decision on a bargaining unit accretion question (decided by NLRA standards and decisions as the arbitrator was directed) within eleven days after the Company requested arbitration with the incumbent union by a telegram which declared that the "Company is incurring inordinate expense and potential disruption of its business as a result of NLRB scheduling of hearings re representation claim of another union."[35] However, in the bulk of the cases several weeks or even several months are required. The issues taken to arbitration have become increasingly complex and the time required for arbitration has naturally tended to increase as a result of this complexity of issues. Also, it frequently happens that the arbitrator chosen by the parties cannot be quickly available due to existing commitments to other parties. Nor are the parties themselves always quickly available for the arbitration hearing. Nonetheless, arbitration continues to be relatively speedy as compared to litigation.[36]

Since the parties arbitrate voluntarily, prompt compliance with the award is obtained in most cases. Only infrequently is court action required for the enforcement or vacation of awards.[37]

Arbitration of Public Employee Disputes

Since 1960 the tremendous growth of employee organization and collective bargaining in the public sector has been accompanied by the

---

[34]Kerr, "More Peace—More Conflict," Proceedings of the 28th Annual Meeting of NAA, 8, 14 (BNA Books, 1976). Justice William H. Rehnquist of the U.S. Supreme Court has stated: "With the increasing load on courts at all levels in state and federal judicial systems * * * the prospects of increased use of arbitration as a means of settlement of disputes must never have been better." Rehnquist, "A Jurist's View of Arbitration," 32 Arb. J. 1, 2 (1977).

[35]Hartford Jai-Alai, 71 LA 1155 at 1155 (Rubenstein, 1978). For considerations relating to finality of the decision in such situations, see Chapter 10, topic entitled "The NLRA, the Arbitrator, and the NLRB."

[36]For statistics and discussions of the time required for grievance processing and/or arbitration, see "FMCS' 31st Annual Report," 102 LRR 245 (1979) (reporting that for cases administered by the FMCS, the average number of days required from the time a grievance was filed until an arbitrator's award was rendered was 223.5 days in 1978 and 268.3 days in 1977); Davis & Pati, "Elapsed Time Patterns in Labor Grievance Arbitration: 1942–1972," 29 Arb. J. 15 (1974); Fleming, The Labor Arbitration Process 57–77 (U. of Ill. Press, 1965); "Survey of Arbitration in 1964," Proceedings of the 18th Annual Meeting of NAA, 246, 253–254 (BNA Books, 1965); Ross, "The Well-Aged Arbitration Case," 11 Indus. & Lab. Rel. Rev. 262 (1958).

[37]For statistics, see Chapter 2, Legal Status of Arbitration.

rapidly expanding use of arbitration for public employee disputes. This development has been particularly important because federal and state employees generally continue to be restricted by the traditional prohibition against strikes by public employees. Neutral dispute settlement machinery is essential in the public sector if organizational and bargaining rights are to have any real substance.[38]

Studies of grievance arbitration indicate that most issues in public sector arbitration do not differ from private sector issues and that arbitrators tend to apply the same standards in both areas.[39] The Authors have reached the same conclusion, having observed that principles and precedents from private-sector arbitration are often being considered and utilized in public-sector cases.[40]

Of course, public-sector arbitration in turn will no doubt influence future developments in the private sector.

A great many arbitration decisions from the public sector (state and federal) are cited throughout this book. For the most part the public- and private-sector cases are integrated in the book. The principal area in which material differences may exist between public- and private-sector arbitration (at least in some jurisdictions), concerns the legal status of arbitration. Accordingly, the Chapter 2 materials on legal status of arbitration deal separately and successively with the private sector, the federal sector, and the state sector. Also, in Chapter 18 some separate treatment is provided for certain aspects of interest arbitration in the public sector.

Other Important Roles of Arbitration

We have noted that arbitration is a substitute for work stoppages and for litigation. But it is much more than a substitute. Professor Harry Shulman declared:

---

[38]On the special need for neutral dispute machinery, see Zack, "Why Public Employees Strike," 23 Arb. J. 69 (1968); Triborough Bridge & Tunnel Authority, 49 LA 1212, 1224–1228 (Wolf, Feinberg & Stockman, 1968).

[39]"[T]he parties in state and local government have leaned heavily upon private industry's arbitration experience. A formidable case could be made that the parties have virtually adopted the grievance arbitration mechanism from private industry." Krislov & Peters, "Grievance Arbitration in State and Local Government: A Survey," 25 Arb. J. 196, 205 (1970). Also see Pegnetter & Hayford, "State Employee Grievances and Due Process: An Analysis of Contract Arbitration and Civil Service Review Systems," 29 S.C.L. Rev. 305, 313 (1978); DeWolf, "The Enforcement of the Labor Arbitration Agreement in the Public Sector—The New York Experience," 39 Alb. L. Rev. 393, 398 (1975) ("the law applicable to private sector labor arbitration is for the most part applicable to the public sector"); Krinsky, "Municipal Grievance Arbitration in Wisconsin," 28 Arb. J. 50, 61 (1973) ("Wisconsin municipal grievance arbitration experience shows great similarities to private sector arbitration experience both procedurally and in terms of the issues arbitrated"); Howlett, "Arbitration in the Public Sector," Southwest Legal Foundation 15th Annual Institute on Labor Law 231, 268–269 (1969).

[40]E.g., see Arbitrator Handsaker in 73 LA 1305, 1307; Hays in 73 LA 1100, 1104; Caraway in 73 LA 1074, 1083; Hauck in 73 LA 990, 991–992; Roumell in 73 LA 707, 709–711; Gerhart in 73 LA 556, 561; Ellmann in 73 LA 464, 475; LeBaron in 73 LA 455, 463; Cutler in 72 LA 1313, 1316, 1318; Smith in 72 LA 1135, 1141; Renzler in 72 LA 941, 946–947; Pieroni in 72 LA 719, 723; Kanner in 72 LA 564, 566–567; Allen in 71 LA 942, 947–948; Beck in 71 LA 314, 319–320; Cohen in 70 LA 895, 897–898; Denison in 70 LA 514, 517.

"To consider * * * arbitration as a substitute for court litigation or as the consideration for a no-strike pledge is to take a foreshortened view of it. In a sense it is a substitute for both—but in the sense in which a transport airplane is a substitute for a stagecoach. The arbitration is an integral part of the system of self-government. And the system is designed to aid management in its quest for efficiency, to assist union leadership in its participation in the enterprise, and to secure justice for the employees. It is a means of making collective bargaining work and thus preserving private enterprise in a free government."[41]

Professor George W. Taylor observed that "In a very real sense, the parties who establish their own labor arbitration machinery create a judicial procedure where none has existed."[42] In this connection, not all jurisdictions hold that collective bargaining agreements give rights which are enforceable in the courts. Moreover, the National Labor Relations Board (NLRB) lacks jurisdiction over contract-interpretation disputes which do not involve unfair labor practice aspects, and it possibly may refuse to exercise jurisdiction over interpretation disputes which do involve unfair labor practice allegations if the dispute is covered by an arbitration clause.[43]

Then, too, insofar as contract-negotiation disputes are concerned arbitration provides essentially the only available tribunal for the final and binding resolution of such disputes after negotiations and mediation have failed to produce a settlement. Thus, it is obvious that even aside from any consideration of work stoppages and their avoidance, cases are taken to arbitration simply to obtain an answer to the dispute.

Another role of arbitration was recognized by the U.S. Supreme Court in emphasizing that the "processing of even frivolous claims

---

[41]Shulman, "Reason, Contract, and Law in Labor Relations," 68 Harv. L. Rev. 999, 1024 (1955), reprinted in Management Rights and the Arbitration Process, 169, 198 (BNA Books, 1956). One observer believes that this self-government system is threatened by encroachment of laws dealing with employment relations (such as the Equal Pay Act, Title VII of the Civil Rights Act, OSHA, and ERISA), with a future fading of the "Golden Age" of arbitration as the parties' self-governance court of last resort. Feller, "The Coming End of Arbitration's Golden Age," Proceedings of the 29th Annual Meeting of NAA, 97 (BNA Books, 1976). But other observers have responded with expressions of optimism for the future of labor arbitration. See Stark, "The Presidential Address: Theme and Adaptations," Proceedings of the 31st Annual Meeting of NAA, 1, 2, 29 (BNA Books, 1979) (the "future is bright and challenging"); Smith, "The Search For Truth—The Whole Truth," id. at 40, 48; Eisenberg, "Some Recent Developments in Public-Sector Grievance Arbitration: A View From New York," id. at 240, 263–264; St. Antoine, "Judicial Review of Labor Arbitration Awards: A Second Look at Enterprise Wheel and Its Progeny," Proceedings of the 30th Annual Meeting of NAA, 29, 36 (BNA Books, 1978) ("we are actually entering a new 'golden age' for the arbitration process"); Edwards, "Labor Arbitration at the Crossroads: The 'Common Law of the Shop' v. External Law," 32 Arb. J. 65, 85–88 (1977). While the role of the courts and governmental administrative tribunals will always be critically important in our increasingly complex society, so will that of arbitration. The courts and administrative tribunals such as the NLRB and the EEOC already have overburdening caseloads and must not be further strained unnecessarily by the unrestricted and *mass* use of such forums for resolution of grievances of the type for which the contractual grievance and arbitration procedures have been designed. Furthermore, these facts remain even though we accept that some limited types of situations will arise (such as the arbitrator exceeding his jurisdiction) and some limited types of issues will exist (such as certain statutory issues) for which the contractual grievance and arbitration procedures need not be the final word and for which resort to the administrative tribunals or courts will be permitted.

[42]Statement by Professor Taylor in Preface to Freidin, Labor Arbitration and the Courts (1952).

[43]For discussion of the Board's policy and practice in regard to deferring to arbitration, see Chapter 10, subtopic entitled "The NLRA, the Arbitrator, and the NLRB."

may have therapeutic values."[44] This role was described by Professor Louis L. Jaffe in such manner as also to portray realistically the spirit of the arbitration hearing:

> "Arbitration * * * is a school, an arena, a theater. Everyone both participates and observes. The whole company of actors—arbitrator, union and employer officials, the griever, and the witnesses (mostly employees)—sits at one table. Argument, assertion, testimony, charge and countercharge, even angry abuse—sometimes spontaneous, sometimes 'for the record'—flow freely in quick, continuous intercourse. The arbitrator may let the discussion take its head for a moment, then rein it in; an occasional question, a request for clarification. Because the process is relatively free, it may assume many forms, some quiet and orderly, some volatile and discordant. The form is in fact a function of the general labor relations—of the maturity, the degree of mutual understanding and respect, the intelligence, of the opposing officials.* * *
> "Arbitration takes its stand in the very current of industrial life. The scene, the dramatis personae, the vocabulary, being familiar, raise no barriers to comprehension. The worker sees his case analyzed by his leaders, among whom I include employer as well as union officials. They reveal the clashing propositions at the heart of the grievance. The arbitrator relates his answer to basic industrial premises.* * *"[45]

Finally, it may be noted that a union might arbitrate a dispute because the employees or subordinate union officers directly involved simply could not be convinced that they were wrong; the company might do likewise in regard to its own subordinate officials. In either instance, higher officials may find it preferable to let an arbitrator make it clear to such persons that they were wrong.[46] However, while this may be justified in isolated instances, caution must be exercised against mere pretended use of the grievance procedure with possible overburdening of the arbitration machinery. A central theme at labor-management seminars conducted in 1979 by the President's Commission on Coal, was that the flood of coal industry wildcat strikes in the 1970s resulted from lost employee confidence in the grievance procedure and arbitration, caused by too little reliance upon the grievance procedure and too much reliance upon arbitration.[47]

---

[44]United Steelworkers v. American Mfg. Co., 80 S.Ct., 1343, 1346–1347 (1960). The Supreme Court again recognized the "therapy" of arbitration in Alexander v. Gardner-Denver Co., 94 S.Ct. 1011, 1021 n. 13 (1974).

[45]Jaffe, "Labor Arbitration and the Individual Worker," The Annals of the American Academy of Political and Social Science, 34, 40–41 (May, 1953).

[46]See Ahner, "Arbitration: A Management Viewpoint," Proceedings of the 11th Annual Meeting of NAA, 76, 80 (BNA Books, 1958); Killingsworth, "Arbitration: Its Uses in Industrial Relations," 21 LA 859, 865 (1953).

[47]See The President's Commission on Coal, Labor-Management Seminar III, Wildcat Strikes (April 27, 1979), 6, 26–30, U.S. Govt. Printing Office: 1979, 0–302–758; The President's Commission on Coal, Labor-Management Seminar IV, Grievance and Arbitration Procedures (June 20, 1979), 39, U.S. Govt. Printing Office: 1979, 0–302–759. Grievance and arbitration machinery in the coal industry subsequently has been revamped to correct the problem. Regarding labor arbitration in general, Arnold Zack pointed out that there "appears to be an increasing tendency by both parties to the grievance process to pass the buck to the arbitrator." Zack, "Suggested New Approaches to Grievance Arbitration," Proceedings of the 30th Annual Meeting of NAA, 105, 107 (BNA Books, 1978). Also see Seward, "The Twenty-Five Year Milestone," Proceedings of the 25th Annual Meeting of NAA, 61, 63–64 (BNA Books, 1973).

Arbitration and National War Labor Board

A great impetus in the use of arbitration was given by the National War Labor Board during World War II. The work of the Board constitutes an extensive experience in the use of arbitration. It was created by executive order in 1942 and was given statutory authority by the War Labor Disputes Act in 1943. Most of the 20,000 labor dispute cases determined by the Board during the war emergency were disputes over the terms of collective agreements. Of special importance was the Board's policy of requiring the use of clauses providing for arbitration of future disputes over the interpretation or application of the agreement. This policy of the Board laid the foundation for the popular practice today of terminating the contract grievance procedure with the final step of arbitration.[48]

Recommendations of the President's National Labor-Management Conference of 1945

The President's National Labor-Management Conference of 1945 was called for the purpose of laying the groundwork for industrial peace by studying the major causes of industrial strife and possibilities for their elimination. It was attended by delegates representing the American Federaton of Labor, the United States Chamber of Commerce, the Congress of Industrial Organizations, the National Association of Manufacturers, the United Mine Workers of America, and the Railway Brotherhoods.

In regard to the setting of new contract terms the Conference recommended that parties first undertake good-faith collective bargaining and thereafter, if necessary, conciliation and consideration of voluntary arbitration. It recommended, however, that, before voluntary arbitration is accepted, the parties should agree upon the precise issues to be decided, the terms of the submission, and principles or factors by which the arbitrator is to be governed.[49]

As to the settlement of grievances or disputes involving the interpretation or application of the agreement, the Conference recommended:

> "4. The parties should provide by mutual agreement for the final determination of any unsettled grievances of disputes involving the interpretation or application of the agreement by an impartial chairman, umpire, arbitrator, or board. In this connection the agreement should provide:
> "(a) A definite and mutually agreed-upon procedure of selecting the impartial chairman, umpire, arbitrator, or board;
> "(b) That the impartial chairman, umpire, arbitrator, or board should have no power to add to, subtract from, change, or modify any

---

[48]See Freidin & Ulman, "Arbitration and the War Labor Board," 58 Harv. L. Rev. 309 (1945).
[49]The President's National Labor-Management Conference, Nov. 5–30, 1945 (U.S. Dept. of Labor, Div. of Labor Standards, Bull. No. 77, 1946), 42–43.

provision of the agreement, but should be authorized only to interpret the existing provisions of the agreement and apply them to the specific facts of the grievance or dispute;

"(c) That reference of a grievance or dispute to an impartial chairman, umpire, arbitrator, or board should be reserved as the final step in the procedure and should not be resorted to unless the settlement procedures of the earlier steps have been exhausted;

"(d) That the decision of the impartial chairman, umpire, arbitrator, or board should be accepted by both parties as final and binding;

"(e) That the cost of such impartial chairman, umpire, arbitrator, or board should be shared equally by both parties.

"5. Any question not involving the application or interpretation of the agreement as then existing but which may properly be raised pursuant to agreement provisions should be subject to negotiation, conciliation, or such other means of settlement as the parties may provide."[50]

Compulsory Arbitration

Although there are obvious and fundamental differences between voluntary and compulsory arbitration, many of the considerations involved in the use of compulsory arbitration are helpful in an analysis of voluntary arbitration. These considerations help define the area of desirable use of voluntary arbitration. They also indicate pitfalls that may be faced in the use of arbitration generally.

Compulsory arbitration has been defined by the Department of Labor to mean a "process of settlement of employer-labor disputes by a government agency (or other means provided by government) which has power to investigate and make an award which *must* be accepted by all parties concerned."[51] Stated otherwise, compulsory arbitration "is that required by law."[52]

Thus, even where neither party wishes to arbitrate, both may be required to do so under compulsory arbitration. At times there has been agitation for legislation to subject all types of labor-management disputes to compulsory arbitration where settlement by any but a peaceful procedure would result in severe loss or hardship to third persons or the general public. While there is considerable support for use of compulsory arbitration in such situations, its use otherwise is generally opposed in the private sector by labor and management alike.[53]

---

[50]Id. at 46–47.

[51]"Should the Federal Government Require Arbitration of Labor Disputes in All Basic American Industries?" 26 Cong. Dig. 193, 195 (1947).

[52]C.C.H. Dictionary of Labor Terms. For discussions of the development of compulsory arbitration in the United States and abroad, see Northrup, Compulsory Arbitration and Government Intervention in Labor Disputes, 9–50 (Labor Policy Association, 1966); Williams, "The Compulsory Settlement of Contract Negotiation Labor Disputes," 27 Tex. L. Rev. 587 (1949).

[53]See statistics and views in Warren & Bernstein, "A Profile of Labor Arbitration," 16 LA 970, 972–973 (1951). Continued opposition was voiced to substituting compulsory arbitration for the strike in private-sector collective bargaining at the American Arbitration Association's 1977 "Arbitration Day" in New York. 95 LRR 14 (1977). The general opposition also is reflected in, for example, Farmer, "Compulsory Arbitration—A Management Lawyer's View," 51 Va. L. Rev. 396 (1965); Feller, "Compulsory Arbitration—A Union Lawyer's View," id. at 410; "Report of American Bar Association Sub-Committee on Labor Arbitration Law," 35 LA 949, 949–951 (1960).

The principal argument in favor of compulsory arbitration is that unions and industries have grown so large and our economy has become so intermeshed that one strike can paralyze a large part of the nation. This consideration is particularly urgent where the strike interferes with national defense. Moreover, local critical disputes, such as those in transportation and public utility enterprises, can severely burden the general public. Proponents of compulsory arbitration contend that in such cases governmental action is warranted to protect the general welfare; that, when collective bargaining, mediation, and all other steps have failed, the government should step in as a last resort to prevent ruinous strikes, and, as a *quid pro quo,* provide for the settlement of the issues on their merits.[54]

It has also been urged that compulsory arbitration is necessary in a relationship where workers are not free to engage in collective bargaining in its fullest sense, namely, in the area of public employment.[55] In fact, a significant number of states have legislated compulsory arbitration of contract negotiation disputes for specified classes of public employees.[56] In federal employment, the Federal Service Impasses Panel can impose settlement terms for contract negotiation disputes under the Civil Service Reform Act of 1978, and compulsory arbitration of such disputes is a possibility in the postal service under the Postal Reorganization Act of 1970.[57]

The arguments against compulsory arbitration as revealed in literature on the subject are, broadly stated, that (A) it is incompatible with free collective bargaining, (B) it will not produce satisfactory solutions to disputes, (C) it may involve great enforcement problems, and (D) it will have damaging effects upon our economic structure.[58] These arguments in more detail, again as revealed in the aforementioned literature, are:

A. That compulsory arbitration is the antithesis of free collective bargaining. Each party will be reluctant to offer compromises

[54]"Should the Federal Government Require Arbitration of Labor Disputes in All Basic American Industries?" 26 Cong. Dig. 193, 208 (1947). Also see Richberg, "Industrial Disputes and the Public Interest—I," Inst. of Indus. Rel., U. of Calif., 59, 60 (1947); Huebner, "Compulsory Arbitration of Labor Disputes," 30 J. Am. Jud. Socy. 123 (1946).

[55]Schwartz, "Is Compulsory Arbitration Necessary?" 15 Arb. J. 189, 200 (1960). "The most significant arguments against compulsory arbitration are inapplicable in the area of public employment." Id. at 194.

[56]See Chapter 2, subtopics entitled "Interest Arbitration Statutes" and "Constitutionality of Binding Interest Arbitration," where numerous articles dealing with compulsory arbitration in the public sector are also cited.

[57]5 U.S.C. § 7119; 39 U.S.C. § 1206.

[58]For writings in which various of these and related arguments are asserted or noted, see Kennedy, "Freedom to Strike is in the Public Interest," Harv. Bus. Rev., July-Aug. 1970, 45; Farmer, "Compulsory Arbitration—A Management Lawyer's View," 51 Va. L. Rev. 396 (1965); Feller, "Compulsory Arbitration—A Union Lawyer's View," id. at 410; Van de Water, "Involuntary Arbitration and National Defense," 18 Arb. J. 96 (1963); Keel, The Pros and Cons of Compulsory Arbitration, 18–24 (N.Y. Chamber of Commerce, 1961); Dash, "The Academy and Public Opinion," Proceedings of the 13th Annual Meeting of NAA, 1, 8–12 (BNA Books, 1960), summarizing arguments of George W. Taylor, John T. Dunlop, and Thomas Kennedy against compulsory arbitration; Schwartz, "Is Compulsory Arbitration Necessary?" 15 Arb. J. 189 (1960); "Should the Federal Government Require Arbitration of Labor Disputes in All Basic American Industries?" 26 Cong. Dig. 193, 203–221 (1947), where strong opposition to compulsory arbitration in the private sector was voiced by high government, labor, and management officials.

in bargaining for fear that they may prejudice its position in arbitration. Elimination of the strike from collective bargaining will eliminate the strongest incentive which the parties now have to reach agreement. One or both of the parties may make only a pretense at bargaining in the belief that more desirable terms may be obtained through the arbitration which is assured if bargaining fails. Since compulsory arbitration will be used to resolve unknown future disputes, both sides may list many demands and drop few in bargaining, believing that little will be lost if some of the "chaff" is denied by an arbitrator (who the party may believe would then be more inclined to favor that party on major issues in order to appear fair).

B. That compulsory arbitration is a dictatorial and imitative process rather than a democratic and creative one. The parties cannot select the arbitrator and cannot specify the standards or criteria for his decision. If terms of employment are determined by legislation or by arbitration required by law, rules may emerge for uniform application to all parties regardless of their individual character and needs. Compulsory arbitration means an imposed decision which will often fail to satisfy either party, rather than an acceptable settlement based upon a meeting of the minds.

C. That compulsion generates resistance and is a source of further conflict. There may be serious difficulty of enforcement of compulsory orders, with the attendant danger of divulging the impotence of government.

D. That compulsory arbitration means governmental—politically influenced—determination of wages, and will inevitably lead to governmental regulation of prices, production, and profits; it threatens not only free collective bargaining but also the free market and enterprise system.

The most extensive experience (over 70 years) with compulsory arbitration is that of Australia. Writers who have studied the Australian system are by no means in agreement as to its degree of success, but they all agree that it has not eliminated strikes.[59] Indeed,

---

[59]See Morris, "The Role of Interest Arbitration in a Collective Bargaining System," The Future of Labor Arbitration in America, 197, 209–226 (AAA, 1976); Northrup, Compulsory Arbitration and Government Intervention in Labor Disputes, 35–44 (Labor Policy Assn., 1966); Sykes, "Labor Regulation by Courts: The Australian Experience," 52 Nw. U.L. Rev. 462 (1957); Merrifield, "Wage Determination Under Compulsory Arbitration: Margins for Skill in Australia," 24 Geo. Wash. L. Rev. 267 (1956); Oxnam, "Industrial Arbitration in Australia," 9 Indus. & Lab. Rel. Rev. 610 (1956). The number of strikes in Australia in 1974 exceeded all records for that country. Isaac, "Labor Relations Developments in Australia, 1974," Proceedings of the 28th Annual Meeting of NAA, 361 (BNA Books, 1976). For a comprehensive assessment of use of compulsory arbitration in Australia, Canada, Great Britain, the United States, and Jamaica, see Loewenberg, Gershenfeld, Glasbeck, Hepple & Walker, Compulsory Arbitration (1976). Also see Forkosch, "Compulsion in Collective Bargaining and Arbitration: A Comparison of American and Australian Industrial Law," 7 U. Tol. L. Rev. 457 (1976), where the "major conclusion reached" was that "the Australian and American systems of industrial law are different, quite different, in their methods and procedures* * *."

an extensive study of compulsory arbitration experience in various countries led to the unqualified conclusion that compulsory arbitration "Does not insure industrial peace, but rather can breed strikes, especially short ones."[60]

In 1920 Kansas enacted a compulsory arbitration act which set up a court of industrial relations for disputes in industries affecting the public interest. Broad interpretation of the Kansas law led to its application to industries other than public utilities. In 1923 the U.S. Supreme Court declared the wage-fixing provisions of the statute unconstitutional as violating the "due process" clause of the Fourteenth Amendment.[61] In light of later decisions of the Supreme Court, however, it seems possible that the exercise of similar power by the states now would withstand constitutional challenge (apart from federal preemption).[62] Some of the state statutes making arbitration of public-sector disputes compulsory and binding have been challenged on constitutional grounds; the challenge sometimes has succeeded but more often has failed.[63]

Some states have enacted compulsory arbitration statutes for their public utilities. These statutes prohibit work stoppages and either provide for outright compulsory arbitration or require the use of settlement procedures which amount to compulsory arbitration. This legislation, much of which was adopted about 1947, evidenced a growing public concern over work stoppages which cause hardship to the general consuming public. However, in 1951 the United States Supreme Court held that state power in this field must fall where the state law conflicts with the Labor-Management Relations Act.[64] Thus the supremacy of federal regulation constitutes a potent barrier to the application of state compulsory arbitration laws to workers covered by the federal statute.

In 1963 Congress enacted its first peacetime compulsory arbitration law, providing for the compulsory arbitration of diesel firemen and crew consist issues in the railroad industry. The neutral members of that compulsory arbitration board expressed regrets that this Congressional action was required:

> "We write this opinion as the neutral members of a statutory arbitration board—a board whose creation was virtually forced upon

---

[60]Northrup, Compulsory Arbitration and Government Intervention in Labor Disputes, 206 (Labor Policy Assn., 1966), where Professor Northrup also stated the conclusions that compulsory arbitration does not necessarily further the economic or social policies of government, but in fact may work against such policies; that it enhances union power and growth, especially through political action; and that it discourages collective bargaining.

[61]Chas. Wolff Packing Co. v. Court of Indus. Relations of Kansas, 43 S.Ct. 630 (1923).

[62]For a survey of decisions which bear upon the matter, see Fairview Hosp. v. Hospital Employees, 22 LA 279, 282–289 (Min. S.Ct., 1954). Also see Spruck, "Compulsory Arbitration of Labor Disputes," 47 Mich. L. Rev. 242 (1948).

[63]See Chapter 2, subtopic entitled "Constitutionality of Binding Interest Arbitration."

[64]Amalgamated Assn. v. Wisconsin ERB, 71 S.Ct. 359, 27 LRRM 2385 (1951). A state "plant seizure" statute was similarly invalidated on federal preemption grounds in Division 1287 v. Missouri, 83 S.Ct. 1657, 53 LRRM 2394 (1963). For a discussion of experience under the state public utility statutes prior to these decisions, see Northrup, Compulsory Arbitration and Government Intervention in Labor Disputes, 24–33 (Labor Policy Assn., 1966). Some of the statutes have subsequently been repealed.

Congress as the only way of avoiding a nationwide railroad strike. Never before in peacetime has Congress found it necessary to take such action. We wish at the very outset to record our regret that in this case the leaders of the railroad industry and the railroad operating unions were unable to agree upon some method of resolving their differences which would avoid the need for Congressional intervention. The great virtue of arbitration as it has developed in this country's labor relations has been the fact that it was a *voluntary* procedure, created and shaped by the disputing companies and unions themselves and thus responsive to their peculiar problems, values, and needs. It is unfortunate that the parties in this case, though finally agreeing in principle to arbitration, failed to agree upon the terms and procedures of an arbitration agreement and thereby abandoned to Congress an opportunity and responsibility that should rightly have been theirs."[65]

Congress next enacted special legislation for the compulsory arbitration of a specific dispute (railroad shopcrafts) in 1967. This approach of using ad hoc compulsory arbitration by special Congressional action (and only infrequently) is viewed in some quarters as less damaging and potentially more beneficial than any general provision for compulsory arbitration.[66] A similar use of ad hoc compulsory arbitration would be to include it in a so-called "arsenal of weapons" to be made available by Congress for use within the President's discretion in critical industrial disputes.

Finally, it may be noted that Congress by LMRA § 302(c)(5)(B) has mandated the use of impartial umpires for resolving deadlocks between trustees of jointly administered employee pension or welfare plans, provided the deadlock involves administration of the plan.[67]

---

[65]Railroads v. Operating Bhds., 41 LA 673, 680 (Aaron, Healy & Seward, 1963). This dispute is discussed by Levinson, "The Locomotive Firemen's Dispute," 17 Lab. L.J. 671 (1966); Kaufman, "The Railroad Labor Dispute: A Marathon of Maneuver and Improvisation," 18 Indus. & Lab. Rel. Rev. 196 (1965).

[66]See Farmer, "Compulsory Arbitration—A Management Lawyer's View," 51 Va. L. Rev. 396, 405–406 (1965). But in other quarters the ad hoc approach is viewed as discriminatory and not to be preferred. See Wyle, "Compulsory Labor Arbitration and the National Welfare," 19 Arb. J. 98 (1964).

[67]For examples of the use of neutrals under this provision, see Umpire Hoffman in 73 LA 590 (deadlock over investment of trust funds); Koven in 72 LA 695 (removal of trust administrator); Miller in 70 LA 841 (selection of trust administrator). Another statute, ERISA, is also relevant to arbitration under LMRA § 302(c)(5)(B), as it is to certain other uses of arbitration in connection with employee benefit plans:

"Under the Employee Retirement Income Security Act of 1974 (ERISA), arbitrators may be called upon to resolve a variety of disputes involving collectively bargained employment benefit plans, including: (1) disputes between parties over a clause that affects a benefit plan; (2) disputes in which the plan trustees are deadlocked and the plan document calls for arbitration; (3) disputes between plan participants or beneficiaries and plan officials over benefit entitlement; and (4) disputes about employer liability following withdrawal from multiemployer plans."

AAA Study Time, July 1983. For discussion of arbitration under LMRA § 302(c)(5)(B) and under ERISA, see Tilove, "The Arbitration of Pension Disputes," 34 Arb. J. No. 4, p. 28 (1979); Brauer, "Limitations on Use of an Impartial Umpire to Resolve Deadlocked Disputes Between Taft-Hartley Trustees," 30 Lab. L.J. 741 (1979); Murphy, "The Impact of ERISA on Arbitration," 32 Arb. J. 123, 132 (1977); Fasser, "New Pension Reform Legislation," Proceedings of the 28th Annual Meeting of NAA, 138 (BNA Books, 1976). Dealing with the interaction of LMRA § 302(c)(5)(B) and ERISA, see Cutaiar v. Marshall, 590 F.2d 523 (CA 3, 1979). For related discussion, see Chapter 4, subtopic entitled "Arbitrator's Immunity From Civil Liability."

Arbitration Costs

A number of factors or elements may contribute to the ultimate cost of any given arbitration.[68] Some of the factors are largely within the control of the parties who, to this extent, have it within their power to reduce costs, as by avoiding unnecessary delays, making thorough preparation for the hearing, use of stipulations, nonuse of transcripts and briefs, and the like (this is not to suggest that the use of transcripts and briefs in proper cases is not justified and desirable).

The total cost of arbitration can be (and often is) considerably less than the cost of taking the dispute to court, just as the time required for arbitration can be (and often is) considerably less than would be required for court action. Of course, arbitration costs have increased with the increased complexity of issues being taken to arbitration. Then, too, arbitration costs have naturally risen along with the rise in the economic index. Nevertheless, arbitration continues to be well worth its dollar cost when considered in light of the great service (immediate and ultimate) which arbitration performs for employees and for the owners of the enterprise.

In some instances the arbitrator's fee and expenses will constitute the primary cost of arbitration. The parties and the arbitrator should always agree in advance, and usually do, as to his compensation or the basis upon which it is to be determined. Ad hoc arbitrators typically charge on a per diem basis for hearing time, travel time, and time spent studying the case and preparing the decision (permanent arbitrators may be employed on a retainer basis).[69] The idea that there should be a fixed ratio of study days to hearing days is unrealistic:

> "The ratio theory has a surface plausibility; if the hearing lasts for only one day or less, it may seem reasonable to assume that the arbitrator will need no more than one or two days to dispose of it. Unfortunately for the theory and its proponents, however, the fact is that some of the knottiest problems are most easily presented. Again, two experienced practitioners can, in a day's time, by careful preparation, use of stipulations and skillful examination of witnesses, build a record that will keep the most conscientious arbitrator working for a week."[70]

If counsel is retained, then of course counsel fees are involved. Additional costs are also entailed when a transcript of the proceedings

---

[68]For discussion and statistics regarding the cost of arbitration, see "FMCS' 31st Annual Report," 102 LRR 245 (1979); Veglahn, "Arbitration Costs/Time: Labor and Management Views," 30 Labor L.J. 49 (1979); Peterson & Rezler, "Fee Setting and Other Administrative Practices of Labor Arbitrators," 68 LA 1383 (1977). For formal rules concerning arbitrator fees or certain other expenses of arbitration, see Code of Professional Responsibility, § 11(K) (64 LA 1324–1325); AAA Voluntary Labor Arbitration Rules 43 & 44; FMCS Regulations, § 1404.16 (29 C.F.R. Part 1404). Earlier discussions and statistics regarding the cost of arbitration are cited at p. 22 of the Third Edition of this book.

[69]For related discussion, see Chapter 7, subtopic entitled "Arbitrator's Charges When Case is Cancelled."

[70]Aaron, "Labor Arbitration and Its Critics," 10 Labor L.J. 605, 645 (1959).

is desired.[71] However, there are no court costs.[72] Arbitration costs, except for counsel fees, generally are shared by the parties. Even where the parties had reached no agreement as to costs, the arbitrator required equal division since such "is common practice in arbitration."[73] Occasionally the collective agreement will provide that the loser in arbitration shall pay all of the costs. This is contrary to the recommendation of the President's National Labor-Management Conference that the cost of the neutral "should be shared equally by both parties." It is highly undesirable from the standpoint of the arbitrator and, it would seem, from the standpoint of the best interests of the parties.[74]

National Academy of Arbitrators

The National Academy of Arbitrators (NAA) is a nonprofit, professional, and honorary association of arbitrators.[75] While many of

---

[71]See Chapter 7, topic entitled "Transcript of Hearing."

[72]The American Arbitration Association has long charged parties an administrative fee for use of its services, and in 1982 the FMCS announced its expectation to commence charging parties such a fee for use of its arbitration services.

[73]P.P. Williams Co., 24 LA 587, 592 (Reynard, 1955). In Schott's Bakery, 61–3 ARB ¶ 8675 (1961), Arbitrator Angus McSwain ruled that, unlike a court, he did not have power to award costs against a party who had unnecessarily caused an increase in arbitration costs. But in certain situations some other arbitrators have awarded costs against a party or have recognized an arbitrator's power to do so in limited situations. See Arbitrator Geltman in 77 LA 999, 1001; Marlatt in 73 LA 878, 882; Harter in 72 LA 706, 712 (the power "should be reserved only for unusual cases"); Getman in 48 LA 40, 43. For related material, see Chapter 10, subtopics entitled "Attorney Fees" and "Other Avoidable Damages; Delayed Arbitration."

[74]In some instances under such provisions the arbitrator has assessed the costs against one party as the loser. See Arbitrator Cohen in 80 LA 680, 684 (but he "strongly" objected to such provisions, which he said create "ill will and animosity"); Howlett in 71 LA 1161, 1165 (if this had not been required by the agreement, he would have ordered that his fee be "shared equally" by the parties as a "fair" order in this case); Hon in 53 LA 1298, 1301; Jaffee in 52 LA 1023, 1026; Keefe in 48 LA 373, 379; Dworkin in 38 LA 385, 388–389. In other cases, however, the arbitrator divided the costs equally since neither party lost all aspects of the case. See Arbitrator Jaffee in 73 LA 138, 141; Beitner in 71 LA 994, 997; Klein in 48 LA 1058, 1065; Horvitz in 40 LA 522, 526; Pollard in 27 LA 611, 613; Emery in 22 LA 484, 489. In W.O. Larson Foundry Co., 42 LA 1286, 1293 (1964), Arbitrator Kates assessed his fee 80 percent against the union and 20 percent against the company. It may be noted that the common law has long recognized that: (1) the parties are jointly and severally liable for the arbitrator's fee, and this is so regardless of the parties' agreement concerning payment of the fee since the arbitrator is not a party or privy to that agreement; (2) a party who is compelled to pay the full fee is entitled to contribution from the other party for his proportionate share, absent any agreement to the contrary. For cases stating one or more of these points, see Alexander v. Collins, 2 Ind. App. 176, 179–180 (Ind. App. Ct., 1891); Russel v. Page, 147 Mass. 282, 286 (Mass. S.Ct., 1888); Carpenter v. Bloomer, 54 N.J. Super. 157 (N.J. Super. Ct., App. Div., 1859); Young v. Starkey, 1 Cal. 426, 427 (Cal. S.Ct., 1851). Also see Theofano Maritime Co. v. 9,551.19 Tons of Chrome Ore, 122 F.Supp. 853, 858 (USDC, 1954), a case under the Federal Arbitration Act. Discussing the above cases, see Cahn, "Who Shall Pay the Piper?" AAA Study Time, July 1980, 7–8. Also see 3 Am. Jur., Arbitration & Award, §§ 98, 99. Following the arbitration hearing in Pacific Southwest Airlines, 77 LA 320, 330 (1981), the arbitrating union was displaced by another union as bargaining representative, in view of which fact Arbitrator Edgar A. Jones, Jr. specified in the award that his fee was "a joint and several obligation of the parties for the full payment of which either is liable with a right of subrogation against the other," and that "the Company shall presently pay that sum in full with the right to reimbursement for one-half thereof against the Union."

[75]For discussion of the Academy and its history, see Killingsworth, McDermott & Myers, "Twenty-Five Years of Labor Arbitration—And the Future," Proceedings of the 25th Annual Meeting of NAA, 11–39 (BNA Books, 1973); "The National Academy After Twelve Years: A Symposium," Proceedings of the 13th Annual Meeting of NAA, 13–38 (BNA Books, 1960); Larkin, "Introduction: The First Decade," Proceedings of the 10th Annual Meeting of NAA, viii–xvi (BNA Books, 1957). The Academy's Constitution and By-Laws as amended in 1965 (there

our most experienced arbitrators are included among the NAA's members, the Academy is not an agency for the selection of arbitrators. Rather, it was founded in 1947 to establish and foster high standards of conduct and competence for labor-management arbitrators and to promote the study and understanding of the arbitration process. The Academy conducts an extensive and highly important educational program through its various committees, study groups, and annual meetings. The proceedings of the annual meetings, including all important committee reports, have been published by The Bureau of National Affairs, Inc., and thus are easily available to all persons interested in arbitration. Each of those published volumes is cited extensively throughout this book.

Government Agencies Serving Arbitration

The Federal Mediation and Conciliation Service's (FMCS) "basic arbitration function has come to be the maintenance of a roster" from which the Service can nominate arbitrators to the parties, and "the suggesting of certain procedures and guides that [the Service believes] will enhance the acceptability of arbitration as an alternative to the use of economic force in the industrial arena."[76]

The National Mediation Board (NMB) performs important functions in the promotion of arbitration and the selection of arbitrators for the railroad and airline industries under the Railway Labor Act (RLA). These functions are described in detail in Chapter 4.

The various state mediation agencies likewise perform services in the furtherance and assistance of arbitration. The New York State Board of Mediation, for instance, maintains a panel of private arbitrators, and the Board's members and staff also serve as arbitrators.

American Arbitration Association

The American Arbitration Association (AAA) is a private, non-profit organization which offers services and facilities for voluntary arbitration. It is an administrative agency solely, never acting as arbitrator. It maintains panels from which arbitrators may be selected, and it provides administrative personnel and procedures for cases being arbitrated under its rules.[77]

---

have been subsequent amendments) are published in Proceedings of the 18th Annual Meeting of NAA, 207 (BNA Books, 1965). Another organization is the Society of Professionals in Dispute Resolution (SPIDR), whose membership is not limited to neutral arbitrators but also includes mediators, fact-finders, government and private administrators, and party advocates in dispute resolution.

[76]Finnegan, "Federal Mediation and Conciliation Service," Management Rights and the Arbitration Process, 96 (BNA Books, 1956).

[77]The AAA's Labor Arbitration Rules are published in 43 LA 1292 (there have been some subsequent amendments).

The AAA is "devoted to the development and extension of the use of arbitration for the settlement of disputes in all fields of human endeavor."[78] In this connection, the AAA conducts an extensive educational program through its various publications and through its promotion of arbitration conferences nationwide.

The Labor Management Institute (a Division of the American Arbitration Association) offers services as a neutral secretariat in arranging for bargaining and advises parties on techniques for resolution of conflicts that have been developed through experience in other industries and in other parts of the country. The Institute is available to help parties evolve specialized machinery to solve their particular problem.[79]

---

[78]Braden, "Policy and Practice of American Arbitration Association," Management Rights and the Arbitration Process 84, 93 (BNA Books, 1956).

[79]For another reference to the Institute's activities, see "The Labor Management Institute," 20 Arb. J. 10 (1965).

Chapter 2

Legal Status of Arbitration

By and large the law has played a relatively limited role in labor-management arbitration in the private sector of the United States.[1] Fundamentally, such arbitration has been and still is a product of private contract between labor and management,[2] although in a significant sense arbitration in the private sector has become "federalized" as to legal status.[3]

Through the years private contract and custom have shaped the principal features of such arbitration. Having chosen arbitration as the best means of resolving their differences, the parties in the vast majority of cases have honored their agreement to arbitrate by proceeding faithfully to arbitration, by presenting their case informally but fully to the arbitrator, and by carrying out his award as the final disposition of the dispute—probably giving little or no thought to the legal status of arbitration at any time during the entire process.[4] In any event, in only a very small percentage of cases has court action been instituted in connection with any aspect of the arbitration.[5]

---

[1]Except where expressly stated otherwise, the term "arbitration" wherever used in this book refers to voluntary arbitration.

[2]"The uniqueness enjoyed by arbitration as a system of industrial jurisprudence is that it is the creature of the parties. It is created by them, and its limits, rules and regulations are established and may be changed by them." McDermott, "Arbitrability: The Courts Versus the Arbitrator," 23 Arb. J. 18, 19 (1968).

[3]See this Chapter, topic entitled "Federal Law: Private Sector." One authority concluded that court decisions have not changed "the fact that grievance arbitration is basically a private system of jurisprudence," though federal court decisions have had an important effect in making both the arbitration agreement and the award enforceable and have set the stage for the establishment of other rules by court action. Fleming, The Labor Arbitration Process, 28 (U. of Ill. Press, 1965).

[4]"The efficacy of grievance arbitration is founded on the pledge of the disputing parties that the arbitrator's award would be final and binding." Major Collective Bargaining Agreements: Arbitration Procedures, 73 (U.S. Dept. of Labor Bull. No. 1425–6, 1966). In Piggly Wiggly Warehouse v. Local 1, 103 LRRM 2646 at 2646 (CA 5, 1980), the court stated that "The relatively small number of reported cases contesting the countless arbitration proceedings convened to resolve labor-management disputes attests to the parties' general satisfaction with this method of resolving industrial problems."

[5]The Authors stated in the Third Edition of this book (p. 26) that "Over the years the percentage appears to have varied from less than 1 percent to 1.5 percent per year." That statement was based partly upon an estimate by the NAA Committee on Law and Legislation for the five-year period through 1968. See "Arbitration and Federal Rights Under Collective Agree-

In turn, the courts and the legislatures generally have honored the "private contract" nature of arbitration by wisely limiting their roles in the process.

Indeed, the role of the law for the private sector (and in varying degree for the public sector in some jurisdictions) has been largely limited to the preliminaries and the "postliminaries" of the arbitration process. That is, the law has been concerned primarily with the enforceability of agreements to arbitrate, at the outset, and with the review and enforcement of awards at the close. The heart of the arbitration process, from the time the arbitrator is selected until his award has been issued, has been left largely within the exclusive control of and determination by the parties and their arbitrator. The temperance of the law, avoiding undue interference with the arbitration process, has permitted the high degree of flexibility essential to the success of the process.

In regard to the public sector, the law has tended to play a more active role in the arbitration of disputes between public employers and employees. This is hardly a surprise, the government itself being the employer. The more surprising fact is that many jurisdictions permit public employers and employees fairly free rein to shape their labor relations, leaving much for determination by collective bargaining. Moreover, on the whole it cannot be said that arbitration (where permitted at all in the public sector) is unduly circumscribed by law. Particularly in reference to arbitration of grievances, the parties are

---

ments in 1968," Proceedings of the 22nd Annual Meeting of NAA, 187, 210 (BNA Books, 1970), the Committee's formula being a comparison of the number of relevant published court cases with the Committee's stated "quite conservative estimate that there are upwards of 10,000 labor arbitration awards issued each year by some 500 or so active arbitrators." Using a similar formula and increasing the number of relevant court cases reflected in a more recent Committee report, while also considering the constantly increasing number of cases arbitrated each year, the Authors conclude that a 1 percent to 1.5 percent figure continues to be a fair, albeit rough, estimate for the private sector. They note that a survey of NAA members in 1972 produced 227 replies representing 57 percent of the membership, and that 206 of those replies reported a total of 11,145 awards issued in 1972. McDermott, "Survey on Availability and Utilization of Arbitrators in 1972," Proceedings of the 26th Annual Meeting of NAA, 261, 262, 264 (BNA Books, 1974). Assuming the remaining members issued up to the same number of awards, and recognizing that many active arbitrators are not Academy members, a total of 20,000 to 30,000 awards per year is suggested. Furthermore, this may be an unduly conservative estimate. See the statistics and thoughts stated by Robins, "The Presidential Address: Threats to Arbitration," Proceedings of the 34th Annual Meeting of NAA, 1, 5–6 (BNA Books, 1982). Also assuming that up to 300 of the court cases reported in the NAA Committee's 1976 report are sufficiently relevant to be included in applying the aforementioned formula, the 1 percent to 1.5 percent per year figure emerges. See "Arbitration and Federal Rights Under Collective Agreements in 1976," Proceedings of the 30th Annual Meeting of NAA, 265 (BNA Books, 1978). For earlier statistics for the private sector, see Howard, "Labor-Management Arbitration: 'There Ought to Be a Law'—Or Ought There?" 21 Mo. L. Rev. 1, 18–20 (1956); "Procedural Aspects of Labor-Management Arbitration," 28 LA 933, 939 (1954 statistics). Regarding judicial review of awards, one observer described as "minuscule" the number of awards challenged in court. Adams, "Comment," Proceedings of the 30th Annual Meeting of NAA, 52, 55 (BNA Books, 1978). Another observer stated that: "[O]nly once in a blue moon has an award come down that has been successfully contested in the courts. That rare case has only served to point up how usual is the pattern of voluntary compliance by the parties with labor arbitration awards in the United States." Katz, "Comment," id. at 64. Also see Fogel, "Court Review of Discharge Arbitration Awards," 37 Arb. J. No. 2, pp. 22, 33 (1982), reporting that only "a tiny percentage" of discharge awards are challenged in court, that "only one in four of the challenged awards is vacated," and that "discharge awards of arbitration are final with only very rare exceptions."

relatively unrestricted in choosing and utilizing arbitration machinery.[6]

Collective bargaining and grievance arbitration had reached maturity and had proved their value in the private sector long before employee organization in the public sector began to find acceptance and then to grow on a broad scale in the 1960s. This maturity and this proven value are two of the reasons why many jurisdictions ultimately accepted collective bargaining and arbitration for public employment, why they permit the parties meaningful freedom of choice without undue interference by the law, and why the public jurisdictions and their parties have borrowed extensively from private-sector arbitration.

Even a limited role of law in the arbitration process does involve some complex problems. The present book deals primarily with that part of the arbitration process which falls largely within the exclusive determination of the parties and their arbitrator; it does not deal extensively with either the legal status of arbitration or the problems involved in determining that status precisely for any given case. The Authors, however, do offer an overview of these matters, and they cite numerous detailed studies for the use of persons seeking deeper insight into the legal status of arbitration.[7]

In the remainder of this chapter separate topics are utilized for coverage of the following: (1) federal law relating to the private sector; (2) state common law and state statutes relating to the private sector; (3) determining which of the foregoing categories might apply to the given private-sector case; (4) federal law relating to the federal public sector; (5) state law and municipal ordinances relating to the state public sector.

Federal Law: Private Sector

Federal statutes of significance to arbitration in the private sector are the Federal Arbitration Act (FAA), the Labor Management Relations Act (LMRA), and the Railway Labor Act (RLA). The RLA deals extensively with arbitration and is discussed elsewhere in this book.[8]

---

[6]Use of arbitration for interest disputes in the public sector has tended to be more closely regulated by statute, including some procedural details. See this Chapter, subtopic entitled "Interest Arbitration Statutes." But illustrating that public-sector arbitration often is conducted under rules widely utilized for private-sector cases, note that about one-third of the 16,669 labor cases filed with the American Arbitration Association in 1979 for administration under its Voluntary Labor Arbitration Rules were public-sector cases (this no doubt includes some interest cases). AAA Study Time, July 1980, 6. Those Rules cover various (but not all) aspects of the process from the initiation of arbitration through issuance of the award, and they apply equally to private-sector and public-sector cases. Although several of the Rules expressly envision variations "required by law," as to many aspects (particularly in grievance arbitration), public-sector parties who choose to arbitrate under the Association's Rules enjoy the same options and are bound by the same limitations that apply to private-sector parties.

[7]Throughout other parts of the book, also, the Authors refer briefly to relevant decisional and statutory law.

[8]See Chapters 3 and 4.

While the FAA (also called the United States Arbitration Act) provides significant support for arbitration, the courts have disagreed as to whether the Act applies to collective bargaining agreements. The issue is whether the Act's exclusion of "contracts of employment" applies only to individual employment contracts or also to collective agreements.[9] The Frankfurter dissent in *Lincoln Mills* construes the majority opinion as a "silent" rejection of the FAA's applicability to collective agreement arbitration clauses.[10] Even assuming that the Act is not directly applicable to labor arbitration, however, it should not be overlooked as a guide for the courts in fashioning the body of law for labor arbitration under the *Lincoln Mills* decision.[11]

The LMRA of 1947 lends policy support to arbitration by declaring in Section 203 that final adjustment by a method agreed upon by the parties is the most desirable way to settle disputes over the interpretation and application of collective agreements. Moreover, in the landmark *Lincoln Mills* case, discussed below, the United States Supreme Court held that the LMRA provides enforceable support for labor arbitration.

The Lincoln Mills *Case*

Section 301 of the LMRA authorizes suits in the federal courts for violation of collective agreements in industries affecting interstate commerce. In the *Lincoln Mills* case the U.S. Supreme Court held that § 301 authorizes the federal courts to fashion a body of federal law for the enforcement of collective agreement provisions for arbitration.[12] The Court declared that it was clear "that Congress adopted a policy which placed sanctions behind agreements to arbitrate grievance disputes, by implication rejecting the common-law rule * * * against enforcement of executory agreements to arbitrate."[13]

As to the substantive law to be applied in § 301 suits, the Court stated:

"We conclude that the substantive law to apply in suits under §301(a) is federal law which the courts must fashion from the policy of our national labor laws. * * * The Labor Management Relations Act expressly fur-

---

[9]The Act was passed in 1925 and codified in 1947. 9 U.S.C. §§ 1–14. For discussion of the Act and the conflict as to its coverage, see Burnstein, "The United States Arbitration Act—A Reevaluation" 3 Vill. L. Rev. 125; 9 Labor L.J. 511 (1958). Also see Valtin, "The Presidential Address: Judicial Review Revisited—The Search for Accommodation Must Continue," Proceedings of the 29th Annual Meeting of NAA, 1, 7 (BNA Books, 1976), noting Benjamin Aaron's conclusion that the weight of opinion is that the Act does not apply to labor disputes; Cox, "Grievance Arbitration in the Federal Courts," 67 Harv. L. Rev. 591 (1954).

[10]Textile Workers v. Lincoln Mills, dissenting opinion, 77 S.Ct. 923, 926 (1957).

[11]Illustrating such use of the FAA, see Pizzuto v. Hall's Motor Transit Co., 409 F.Supp. 427, 429 (USDC, 1976). The FAA applies directly to commercial arbitration. Furthermore, the Act gives federal substantive rights rather than merely providing federal enforcement of state-created rights. See Southland Corp. v. Keating, 104 S.Ct. 852, 858–859 (1984), stressing that "the substantive law the Act created was applicable in state and federal court," and that by the Act, "Congress declared a national policy favoring arbitration and withdrew the power of the states to require a judicial forum for the resolution of claims which the contracting parties agreed to resolve by arbitration"; Coulson, "Prima Paint: An Arbitration Milestone," 22 Arb. J. 237 (1967), discussing Prima Paint Corp. v. Flood & Conklin Mfg. Co., 87 S.Ct. 1801 (1967).

[12]Textile Workers v. Lincoln Mills, 77 S.Ct. 912, 40 LRRM 2113 (1957).

[13]77 S.Ct. at 917.

nishes some substantive law. It points out what the parties may or may not do in certain situations. Other problems will lie in the penumbra of express statutory mandates. Some will lack express statutory sanction but will be solved by looking at the policy of the legislation and fashioning a remedy that will effectuate that policy. The range of Judicial inventiveness will be determined by the nature of the problem. * * * Federal interpretation of the federal law will govern, not state law. * * * But state law, if compatible with the purpose of §301, may be resorted to in order to find the rule that will best effectuate the federal policy. * * * Any state law applied, however, will be absorbed as federal law and will not be an independent source of private rights."[14]

The Trilogy

After the *Lincoln Mills* case came the so-called *Trilogy* of 1960.[15] Some of the significant teachings of these cases may be summarized as follows:

As to compelling arbitration: Unless the parties expressly provide that the arbitrator is to dertermine arbitrability, the determination rests with the courts (if such issue is presented for judicial determination). The courts must compel arbitration where the party seeking it is making a claim which on its face is governed by the contract, even though the court might feel that the grievance is frivolous or baseless. Doubts over arbitrability should be resolved in the affirmative—arbitration should be compelled unless it may be said with "positive assurance" that the arbitration clause is not susceptible to an interpretation that covers the dispute.[16]

---

[14]Id. at 918. Included among the many articles on *Lincoln Mills* are Gregory, "The Law of the Collective Agreement," 57 Mich. L. Rev. 635 (1959); Kramer, "In the Wake of Lincoln Mills," 9 Labor L.J. 835 (1958); Bickel & Wellington, "Legislative Purpose and the Judicial Process: The Lincoln Mills Case," 71 Harv. L. Rev. 1 (1957); Feinsinger, "Enforcement of Labor Agreements—A New Era in Collective Bargaining," 43 Va. L. Rev. 1261 (1957); American Bar Association Committee on Arbitration, "Report on Labor Arbitration," 28 LA 913, 914–922 (1957).

[15]United Steelworkers v. American Manufacturing Co., 80 S.Ct. 1343, 34 LA 559 (1960); United Steelworkers v. Warrior & Gulf Navigation Co., 80 S.Ct. 1347, 34 LA 561 (1960); United Steelworkers v. Enterprise Wheel & Car Corp., 80 S.Ct. 1358, 34 LA 569 (1960). For an extensive survey of the impact of these and other Supreme Court decisions on arbitration, see Smith & Jones, "The Impact of the Emerging Federal Law of Grievance Arbitration on Judges, Arbitrators, and Parties," 52 Va. L. Rev. 831 (1966). Also see Morris, "Twenty Years of Trilogy: A Celebration," Proceedings of the 33rd Annual Meeting of NAA, 331 (BNA Books, 1981); Smith & Jones, "The Supreme Court and Labor Dispute Arbitration: The Emerging Federal Law," 63 Mich. L. Rev. 751 (1965); Aaron, "Arbitration in the Federal Courts: Aftermath of the Trilogy," 9 U.C.L.A. L. Rev. 360 (1962); Gregory, "Enforcement of Collective Agreements by Arbitration," 48 Va. L. Rev. 883 (1962); Meltzer, "The Supreme Court, Arbitrability, and Collective Bargaining," 28 U. Chi. L. Rev. 464 (1961).

[16]In Gateway Coal Co. v. United Mine Workers, 94 S.Ct. 629, 637 (1974), the Supreme Court stated that in the *Trilogy* the "Court enunciated the now well-known presumption of arbitrability of labor disputes." In Nolde Bros. v. Bakery & Confectionery Workers, 97 S.Ct. 1067, 1074 (1977), the Court reaffirmed the "strong presumption favoring arbitrability," and it expanded the scope of the presumption. *Nolde* is discussed in Chapter 3, subtopic entitled "Precontract and Post-contract Grievances." On the other hand, the presumption of arbitrability of disputes between a union and an employer does not apply in determining whether parties agreed to require arbitration of disputes between employers and trustees of employee-benefit funds. Schneider Moving & Storage Co. v. Robbins, 104 S.Ct. 1844, 1849, 115 LRRM 3641 (1984), where the U.S. Supreme

As to review and enforcement of awards: The question of interpretation of the agreement is for the arbitrator, and the courts "have no business overruling him because their interpretation of the contract is different from his." However, an award "is legitimate only so long as it draws its essence from the collective bargaining agreement. When the arbitrator's words manifest an infidelity to this obligation, courts have no choice but to refuse enforcement of the award." But the Court also indicated that a court should not reject an award unless it is clear that the arbitrator has exceeded his authority—the Supreme Court is unwilling to "assume" that an arbitrator has "abused the trust the parties confided in him" or that he "has not stayed within the areas marked out for his consideration."[17]

As to the merits of disputes: Courts should not delve into the merits of grievances. The merits are not a subject for court inquiry in actions either to compel arbitration or to enforce awards.

As to modification of awards: The Supreme Court upheld the Court of Appeals' rejection of the early common-law rule that a court action to enforce an award must be dismissed in its entirety if any deficiency exists in the award. The Supreme Court held that an award need not be set aside for incompleteness merely because the arbitrator neglected to calculate the amount of back pay due grievant; the award was returned to the parties for a determination of back pay by arbitration.[18]

Court stated:

"Arbitration promotes labor peace because it requires the parties to forego the economic weapons of strikes and lockouts. Because the trustees of employee-benefit funds have no recourse to either of these weapons, requiring them to arbitrate disputes with the employer would promote labor peace only indirectly, if at all. We conclude, therefore, that the presumption of arbitrability is not a proper rule of construction in determining whether arbitration agreements between the union and the employer apply to disputes between trustees and employers, even if those disputes raise questions of interpretation under the collective-bargaining agreements."

[17]Quoted language from *Enterprise* decision. In its 1983 *Grace* decision the Supreme Court summarized as follows (citing *Enterprise* at several points):

"Under well established standards for the review of labor arbitration awards, a federal court may not overrule an arbitrator's decision simply because the court believes its own interpretation of the contract would be the better one. When the parties include an arbitration clause in their collective bargaining agreement, they choose to have disputes concerning constructions of the contract resolved by an arbitrator. Unless the arbitral decision does not 'dra[w] its essence from the collective bargaining agreement,' a court is bound to enforce the award and is not entitled to review the merits of the contract dispute. This remains so even when the basis for the arbitrator's decision may be ambiguous."

W.R. Grace & Co. v. Rubber Workers Local 759, 103 S.Ct. 2177, 113 LRRM 2641, 2644 (1983), where the Court stated that conclusions by the arbitrator there did "draw their 'essence' from the provisions of the collective bargaining agreement," and accordingly that: "Regardless of what our view might be of the correctness of [the arbitrator's] contractual interpertation, the Company and the Union bargained for that interpretation. A federal court may not second-guess it." For more on the *Grace* decision, see Chapter 14, subtopic entitled "Contractual Seniority Rights, the Civil Rights Act, and Arbitration."

[18]For rejection of the common-law rule by the Court of Appeals, see Enterprise Wheel & Car Corp. v. Steelworkers, 269 F.2d 327, 332 (CA 4, 1959).

Post-Trilogy: *Lower Court Enforcement of Agreement to Arbitrate and Review of Award*

As to the response of the courts to these *Trilogy* teachings, thorough studies conducted by the Law and Legislation Committee of the NAA produced the following finding in 1967: "Because of the presumption favoring the arbitrability of labor disputes, courts have continued to compel arbitration in most cases where the arbitrability of the dispute has been challenged."[19] About a decade later the Committee reported that "The health of the arbitration process is graphically illustrated by the large number of cases wherein the courts hold in favor of a party who is seeking to compel arbitration or who is resisting a stay of arbitration, compared with the small number of decisions where arbitration is denied.[20]

Regarding court review of awards, the Committee stated in the later report that "in general, if the arbitration award is not [in] manifest disregard of the contract and draws its essence from the contract, it will be enforced by the courts in routine fashion."[21] Moreover, the courts in one important respect have acted to encourage voluntary compliance with arbitration awards and to discourage frivolous and unjustified postarbitration litigation. The courts may penalize an obstinate party who brings a frivolous action to set an award aside, or who without justification refuses to comply with an award and thereby forces the other party to resort to court action for its

---

[19]"Arbitration and Federal Rights Under Collective Agreements in 1967," Proceedings of the 21st Annual Meeting of NAA, 201, 214–215 (BNA Books, 1968).

[20]"Arbitration and Federal Rights Under Collective Agreements in 1976," Proceedings of the 30th Annual Meeting of NAA, 265, 280 (BNA Books, 1978). "For arbitration to be denied or stayed, the language of the contract must clearly rebut the strong presumption of arbitrability, and the courts will restrictively interpret any exclusionary clause." "Arbitration and Federal Rights Under Collective Agreements in 1975," Proceedings of the 29th Annual Meeting of NAA, 233, 251 (BNA Books, 1976).

[21]"Arbitration and Federal Rights Under Collective Agreements in 1976," Proceedings of the 30th Annual Meeting of NAA, 265, 288 (BNA Books, 1978). For other studies and views concerning court review of awards under the *Trilogy,* see Jones, "A Meditation on Labor Arbitration and 'His Own Brand of Industrial Justice,' " Proceedings of the 35th Annual Meeting of NAA, 1 (BNA Books, 1983); Morris, "Twenty Years of Trilogy: A Celebration," Proceedings of the 33rd Annual Meeting of NAA, 331, 355–372 (BNA Books, 1981); Kaden, "Judges and Arbitrators: Observations on the Scope of Judicial Review," 80 Colum. L. Rev. 267 (1980); Rothschild, Merrifield & Edwards, Collective Bargaining and Labor Arbitration, 342–361 (1979); St. Antoine, "Judicial Review of Labor Arbitration Awards: A Second Look at *Enterprise Wheel* and Its Progeny," 75 Mich. L. Rev. 1137 (1977), and in Proceedings of the 30th Annual Meeting of NAA, 29 (BNA Books, 1978) (the arbitrator is the parties' officially designated "reader" of the contract, St. Antoine states, and courts will ordinarily treat an award as final and binding because the parties have *agreed* on such treatment); Adams, "Comments," id. at 52; Katz, "Comment," id. at 61; Gorman, Basic Text on Labor Law, 584–603 (1976); articles by Christensen, Gould, and Roberts, "Judicial Review: As Arbitrators See It," Proceedings of the 25th Annual Meeting of NAA, 99–175 (BNA Books, 1973); "Panel Discussion," id. at 176–228; Meltzer, "Ruminations About Ideology, Law, and Labor Arbitration," Proceedings of the 20th Annual Meeting of NAA, 1, 7 et seq. (BNA Books, 1967); Note, "Judicial Review of Labor Arbitration Awards Which Rely on the Practices of the Parties," 65 Mich. L. Rev. 1647 (1967); Comment, "Judicial Enforcement of Labor Arbitrators' Awards," 114 U. Pa. L. Rev. 1050 (1966). For a discussion of possibilities for achieving the review of arbitration decisions short of going to court, see Jones & Smith, "Management and Labor Appraisals and Criticisms of the Arbitration Process: A Report With Comments," 62 Mich. L. Rev. 1115, 1119–1127 (1964). For actual efforts along this line by arbitrators or parties, see Arbitrator Jones in 47 LA 1075, 1078; Stix in 44 LA 1139 at 1139, and in 43 LA 824, 832; Sullivan in 42 LA 193, 212–213, 219–220.

enforcement. The obstinate party may be required to pay the other party's court costs and attorney fees in the postarbitration litigation.[22] Explaining, one court has declared that, "We refuse to countenance frivolous and wasteful judicial challenges to conscientious and fair arbitration decisions."[23]

Also acknowledging the general inclination of the courts to uphold arbitration awards, the ABA Committee on Labor Arbitration and the Law of Collective Bargaining Agreements reported in 1977 that the courts had "continued to uphold and enforce arbitration awards unless those awards conflicted with the standards set forth in the Steelworkers Trilogy."[24]

However, some uncertainty does exist in the *Trilogy* standards. In this connection, Dean Theodore J. St. Antoine stated that "Expectably, the lower courts in applying *Enterprise* have reflected the Supreme Court's ambivalence toward finality."[25] In any event, the decisions of lower courts under the *Trilogy* do not yet reflect any clearly defined (and certainly no uniformly recognized) set of grounds for vacating or refusing to enforce awards, although some individual grounds are clearly established.[26] Here we will note only some of the grounds that have been considered by the courts. It is clear that enforcement of an award ordinarily will be denied if the award sustains or orders conduct which is illegal or contrary to strong public policy, or if the court concludes that the arbitrator lacked jurisdiction

---

[22]See Machinists v. Texas Steel Co., 93 LRRM 2285, 2289 (CA 5, 1976), citing several other cases. Also see Union de Trabajadores Petroquimicos v. Union Carbide Caribe, Inc., 440 F.Supp. 310, 312 (USDC, 1977), requiring a union to so pay because it had been "obstinate" in filing its unsuccessful suit to set aside an award.

[23]Machinists v. Texas Steel Co., 93 LRRM 2285, 2289 (CA 5, 1976).

[24]"Report of the Committee on Labor Arbitration and the Law of Collective Bargaining Agreements," 1977 Labor Relations Law Committee Reports, 5, 12 (ABA, 1977).

[25]St. Antoine, "Judicial Review of Labor Arbitration Awards: A Second Look at Enterprise Wheel and Its Progeny," 75 Mich. L. Rev. 1137, 1148 (1977), and in Proceedings of the 30th Annual Meeting of NAA, 29, 40 (BNA Books, 1978).

[26]For instance, see discussion of review grounds by St. Antoine, id. at 75 Mich. L. Rev. 1146–1157, NAA Proceedings at 38–48; Kaden, "Judges and Arbitrators: Observations on the Scope of Judicial Review," 80 Colum. L. Rev. 267 (1980); Rothschild, Merrifield & Edwards, Collective Bargaining and Labor Arbitration, 342–361 (1979); Gorman, Basic Text on Labor Law, 584–603 (1976); Yarowsky, "Judicial Deference to Arbitral Determinations: Continuing Problems of Power and Finality," 23 U.C.L.A. L. Rev. 936 (1976); Note, "Judicial Review of Labor Arbitration Awards After the Trilogy," 53 Cornell L. Rev. 136 (1967). Even apart from other considerations, it may be that the total number of awards struck down over the years has not been large enough to reflect a clearly defined and generally accepted set of grounds. But consider the conclusion of one court which made an extensive survey of court decisions under the RLA, the NLRA, and the Federal Arbitration Act:

"In recognition of the limited judicial role in the arbitration process, courts have typically confined their scrutiny of awards to the broad contours of procedural fairness and arbitral impartiality. * * * It is thus firmly established that courts will not review the substance of a labor arbitration award for ordinary error and that courts will not vacate an award because a judge might have reached a different result. * * *

"The substantive grounds for vacating labor arbitral awards that do exist are extremely narrow. * * * As exposited by the courts, there appear to be three interrelated grounds for such substantive review of arbitral awards:

"(1) whether the award is irrational * * * [as, for example, where an award is 'wholly baseless and completely without reason,' or as where 'no judge, or group of judges, could ever conceivably have made such a ruling'];

"(2) whether the award draws its essence from the letter or purpose of the collective bargaining agreement * * * ; and

"(3) whether the arbitrator conformed to a specific contractual limitation upon his authority * * *."

Loveless v. Eastern Air Lines, 111 LRRM 2001, 2003–2004 (CA 11, 1982).

over the dispute. Also, more or less isolated cases have presented facts leading the court to strike down awards on grounds such as bias or partiality by the arbitrator; prejudicial exclusion of evidence; gross error of fact underlying the award; or violation of a contractual limitation on the arbitrator's authority to rule upon some particular issue, or on the arbitrator's remedy power.[27]

It appears that the most frequent basis on which lower courts refuse to uphold awards under the *Trilogy* is that the award does not draw its essence from the collective agreement. In one such case, for example, the court concluded that the arbitrator had modified a clear and unambiguous provision of the agreement, dispensing "his own brand of industrial justice," with a "clear failure to draw the essence of the award from the Agreement."[28]

Some observers believe that the courts have not exercised sufficient restraint in applying too liberally the "essence from the agreement" basis for not upholding awards. Professor William P. Murphy has stated, for instance, that "it seems fair to say that many lower courts * * * are using the 'essence' standard of *Enterprise Wheel* as the legal means to set aside awards with which they disagree strongly on the merits."[29] On the other hand, however, is the statement by the Law and Legislation Committee of the NAA to the effect that the courts have generally shown a reluctance to review the merits of arbitration awards.[30] Although the courts sometimes probably do

---

[27]See writings cited in footnote 26. Some of these grounds are similar to certain of the grounds stated in § 10 of the FAA and in many state statutes. See grounds for setting aside awards listed below in this Chapter, subtopic entitled "State Arbitration Statutes." It is reasonable to expect that many courts under the *Trilogy* would give serious consideration also to other grounds along the general lines of those specified in the FAA. Stressing the usefulness of the FAA § 10 grounds as guidelines, and advocating their greater use by lower courts under the *Trilogy*, see Yarowsky, "Judicial Deference to Arbitral Determinations: Continuing Problems of Power and Finality," 23 U.C.L.A. L. Rev. 936, 950–952, 955–962 (1976).

[28]Detroit Coil Co. v. Machinists Lodge 82, 100 LRRM 3138, 3140–3141 (CA 6, 1979). For similar examples, see Local 670 v. Kerr-McGee Refining Corp., 103 LRRM 2988, 2989 (CA 10, 1980) (in concluding that the arbitrator impermissibly "substituted his views for the express provisions of the contract," the court denied that it was considering the merits of the grievance); Federated Employers v. Local 631, 101 LRRM 2838, 2839 (CA 9, 1979). It should be noted, too, that merely basing the award upon the agreement may not be sufficient. Professor Robert A. Gorman explained that many courts "have insisted that in order to warrant judicial confirmation an award must not only be based upon the contract but must also satisfy some minimal standard of rationality." But he added: "It is only the rarest case, however, in which the court will overturn the construction of a contract because it is irrational or capricious; in such cases the court will usually find that the arbitrator has committed some error other than misconstruction. Common examples * * * are absence of jurisdiction or of remedial authority, violation of law or public policy, ambiguity or incompleteness, and fraud, bias or other misconduct." Gorman, Basic Text on Labor Law, 586 (1976).

[29]Murphy, "The Law & Arbitration," NAA, The Chronicle, Aug. 1979. Professor Thomas G.S. Christensen similarly has stated that "the bench mark that the award must 'draw its essence from the contract' has become only a basis for the very judicial review of the merits of a dispute which *Enterprise* attempted to prohibit." Christensen, "The Disguised Review of the Merits of Arbitration Awards," Proceedings of the 25th Annual Meeting of NAA, 99, 106 (BNA Books, 1973). Also see Morris, "Twenty Years of Trilogy: A Celebration," Proceedings of the 33rd Annual Meeting of NAA, 331, 355–356, 367–370 (BNA Books, 1981), charging the Sixth Circuit with "failure to heed the Supreme Court's admonition in the *Trilogy* that courts should not substitute their judgment for that of the arbitrator on the merits," but finding that "in most of the courts the *Enterprise* standard is alive and well."

[30]"Report of the Committee on Law and Legislation," Proceedings of the 32nd Annual Meeting of NAA, 257, 259 (BNA Books, 1980). In an earlier report the Committee credited the courts with being "very sensitive about not usurping the role of the arbitrator in reaching a final

delve into the merits beyond the anticipation of the *Trilogy,* most such instances probably also merely represent the exercise of "niceties of judgment," to use NLRB terminology.[31] The Supreme Court's "essence" standard is sufficiently inexact to present close cases and invite honest differences of opinion as to whether the boundary of the merits has been seriously breached. Absent any evidence of calculated intent by the courts to breach the boundaries prescribed in the *Trilogy,* the basic status of arbitration should not be impaired seriously by some unintended or chance breaches.

De Novo Litigation Following Arbitration

Under federal law, as under state common law, the issuance of an arbitration award generally bars any subsequent court action on the merits of the original claim.[32] However, some important basic exceptions have emerged.

The Alexander v. Gardner-Denver Case. In this case the U.S. Supreme Court held that an employee's statutory right to trial de novo on his discrimination claim under Title VII of the Civil Rights Act of 1964 was not foreclosed by prior submission of his claim to final arbitration under the nondiscrimination clause of a collective agreement.[33]

---

and binding decision of a contract dispute." "Arbitration and Federal Rights Under Collective Agreements in 1976," Proceedings of the 30th Annual Meeting of NAA, 265, 309 (BNA Books, 1978), citing as an example, Garment Workers Local 32 v. Melody Brassiere Co., 92 LRRM 2659, 2660–2661 (USDC, 1976). Another observer concluded that federal district court judges who were otherwise inclined usually have been required "to toe the line of imposed judicial restraint," and that the "courts of appeals have done that by interpreting the 'essence' rationale in such a manner as to implement the determined effort of the Supreme Court to surround labor arbitration and the parties' collective bargaining agreement with the strongest possible measure of insulation from the displacing intrusions of courts." Jones, "A Meditation on Labor Arbitration and 'His Own Brand of Industrial Justice,'" Proceedings of the 35th Annual Meeting of NAA, 1, 5–6 (BNA Books, 1983).

[31]See Arlan's Dept. Store of Michigan, 133 NLRB 802, 807 (1961), where the Board explained that "in the penumbral areas which are omnipresent" in labor relations, "there is no substitute for niceties of judgment." The Board quoted the U.S. Supreme Court's observation that, "However difficult the drawing of lines more nice than obvious, the statute compels the task." Protesting the vagueness of the "essence" test, see Kaden, "Judges and Arbitrators: Observations on the Scope of Judicial Review," 80 Colum. L. Rev. 267, 276 (1980).

[32]See Kaplan v. Long Island Univ., 85 L.C. ¶10, 942 (USDC, 1978); Piper v. Neco, Inc., 412 F.2d 752 (CA 6, 1969); Haynes v. United States Pipe and Foundry Co., 362 F.2d 414 (CA 5, 1966); Howard v. U.S. Rubber Co., 36 LA 62 (USDC, 1961). Extensive discussion of this subject is included in Vestal & Hill, "Preclusion in Labor Controversies," 35 Okla. L. Rev. 281 (1982).

[33]Alexander v. Gardner-Denver Co., 94 S.Ct. 1011 (1974), holding that the employee's discharge which had been upheld in arbitration could be litigated *de novo* in court under Title VII. It should be noted, however, that utilization of grievance or arbitration procedures under the collective agreement does not toll the running of the statute of limitations for filing a claim with the EEOC. Guy v. Robbins & Myers, 97 S.Ct. 441 (1976). Applicability of Gardner-Denver to rights under certain other statutes has also been considered or evaluated. In McDonald v. City of West Branch, Mich., 104 S.Ct. 1799, 1803–1804, 115 LRRM 3646 (1984), the U.S. Supreme Court held that in an action under the Civil Rights Act of 1871 a federal court should not give res judicata or collateral estoppel effect to an award in an arbitration proceeding brought pursuant to the terms of a collective agreement, the Supreme Court reiterating its *Gardner-Denver* reasoning. In Barrentine v. Arkansas-Best Freight Sys., 101 S.Ct. 1437 (1981), the Supreme Court clearly extended its *Gardner-Denver* holding to individuals who seek recovery under the Fair Labor Standards Act following an adverse decision in arbitration proceedings arising from the same event. In doing so, the Court stated that: "While courts should defer to an arbitral decision where the employee's claim is based on rights arising out of the collective-bargaining agreement,

The Court stated its conclusion to be that:

"[T]he federal policy favoring arbitration of labor disputes and the federal policy against discriminatory employment practices can best be accommodated by permitting an employee to pursue fully both his remedy under the grievance-arbitration clause of a collective-bargaining agreement and his cause of action under Title VII. The federal court should consider the employee's claim *de novo*. The arbitral decision may be admitted as evidence and accorded such weight as the court deems appropriate."[34]

In its now famous "Footnote 21" the Supreme Court indicated the terms upon which lower courts in Title VII discrimination actions

---

different considerations apply where the employee's claim is based on rights arising out of a statute designed to provide minimum substantive guarantees to individual workers." Id. at 1443. The impact of *Gardner-Denver* on arbitration in relation to OSHA and ERISA may still be uncertain. See Edwards, "Labor Arbitration at the Crossroads: The 'Common Law of the Shop' v. External Law," 32 Arb. J. 65, 83–84 (1977). It is said that the Supreme Court's *Gateway Coal* decision, decided contemporaneously with *Gardner-Denver*, "suggests that, whatever the applicability of the *Gardner-Denver* rationale to other federal statutory rights, that rationale will not extend to matters of health and safety." Id. at 83. Also see Citron, "Deferral of Employee Rights to Arbitration: An Evolving Dichotomy by the Burger Court?" 27 Hastings L.J. 369 (1975). Note, however, the Supreme Court's subsequent decision in Whirlpool Corp. v. Marshall, 100 S.Ct. 883 (1980), upholding the Secretary of Labor's OSHA regulation stating the right of an employee, with no reasonable alternative, to choose not to perform an assigned task because of a reasonable apprehension of death or serious injury. Although *Whirlpool* does not refer to grievance procedures or arbitration, it seems apparent that an arbitration award against an employee at least would not bar *de novo* litigation by the Secretary of Labor pursuant to that regulation. Regarding ERISA, see Murphy, "The Impact of ERISA on Arbitration," 32 Arb. J. 123, 126–127 (1977), discussing the possibility that some issues resolved by arbitration may be relitigated under ERISA. Also see Mahan v. Reynolds Metals Co., 569 F.Supp. 482, 489–490 (USDC, 1983), where the court stated in reference to *Gardner-Denver* and ERISA:

"When an employee brings a suit under ERISA with respect to § 1132(a)(1)(B), he is seeking to remedy alleged violations of rights accorded him under the terms of a benefit plan. Congress did not accord him any right to receive retirement or disability benefits, but simply allowed him to bring a civil action to enforce *already existing contractual rights*, much in the way other collective bargaining rights can be judicially enforced under § 301 of the LMRA. On the other hand, some provisions of ERISA itself create rights that may not exist under a collective bargaining agreement. * * *

"This Court concludes that a civil suit brought under ERISA for the purpose of vindicating an individual right created by a pension plan or collective bargaining agreement is not a claim which requires *de novo* consideration as would a claim brought under Title VII, but is instead similar to a suit brought under § 301 of LMRA and therefore must be treated as such with respect to the treatment of an arbitration decision already rendered on issues presented to the Court."

Regarding the relationship between arbitration and the NLRA since *Gardner-Denver*, see Chapter 10, subtopic entitled "The NLRA, the Arbitrator, and the NLRB."

[34] 494 S.Ct. at 1025. The Court rejected application of the doctrines of election of remedies, waiver, res judicata, and collateral estoppel. Id. at 1020–1021. (In contrast, in Kremer v. Chemical Constr. Co., 102 S.Ct. 1883, 1895, 1899 (1982), the Supreme Court did give res judicata and collateral estoppel effect to a state court decision disposing of an employment discrimination claim, thus precluding relitigation of the same question in federal court under Title VII.) The Court did suggest in *Gardner-Denver* that an employee can waive his Title VII claim if he voluntarily and knowingly accepts a settlement that provides relief that is equivalent to that provided under Title VII, and the Court also said that "if the relief obtained by the employee at arbitration were fully equivalent to that obtainable under Title VII, there would be no further relief for the court to grant and hence no need for the employee to institute suit." 94 S.Ct. at 1021. For cases applying these guides, see Strozier v. General Motors Corp., 442 F.Supp. 475 (USDC, 1978); EEOC v. McLean Trucking Co., 525 F.2d 1007 (CA 6, 1975), not precluding an EEOC action against the employer in the public interest for changes from which the employee might benefit. An employee instituting a baseless suit under Title VII risks having to pay the defendant's attorney fees. See Obin v. Machinists, 22 FEP Cases 815 (USDC, 1980), requiring an employee with a net worth of nearly $200,000 to pay $44,295 to the defendents (employer and union) for their attorney fees. Similarly, see Bugg v. Allied Indus. Workers, 28 FEP Cases 40, 44 (CA 7, 1982), where the appeal of a trial court decision against the employee was frivolous; Coleman v. General Motors Corp., 27 FEP Cases 1009, 1012 (CA 8, 1981).

"may properly accord [a prior arbitration decision] great weight."
Footnote 21 states:

> "We adopt no standards as to the weight to be accorded an arbitral
> decision, since this must be determined in the court's discretion with
> regard to the facts and circumstances of each case. Relevant factors
> include the existence of provisions in the collective-bargaining agree-
> ment that conform substantially with Title VII, the degree of procedural
> fairness in the arbitral forum, adequacy of the record with respect to the
> issue of discrimination, and the special competence of particular
> arbitrators. Where an arbitral determination gives full consideration to
> an employee's Title VII rights, a court may properly accord it great
> weight. This is especially true where the issue is solely one of fact,
> specifically addressed by the parties and decided by the arbitrator on the
> basis of an adequate record. But courts should ever be mindful that
> Congress, in enacting Title VII, thought it necessary to provide a judi-
> cial forum for the ultimate resolution of discriminatory employment
> claims. It is the duty of courts to assure the full availability of this
> forum."[35]

The Hines v. Anchor Motor Freight Case. In this case a § 301 suit
was filed by employees against their employer alleging that their

---

[35]594 S.Ct. at 1025. The Supreme Court reaffirmed Footnote 21 in its FLSA *Barrentine*
decision. 101 S.Ct. at 1446. Illustrating the willingness of courts to give significant weight to
arbitration decisions meeting the Footnote 21 terms, see Washington v. Johns-Manville Prods.
Corp., 17 FEP Cases 606, 607–608 (USDC, 1978); Burroughs v. Marathon Oil Co., 446 F.Supp. 633,
636–637 (USDC, 1978). Also regarding the possible impact of *Gardner-Denver* and its Footnote 21
upon arbitration, see Chapter 10, subtopics entitled "U.S. Supreme Court Statements Regarding
Arbitral Consideration of External Law" and "Title VII of the Civil Rights Act." For other
writings containing discussion of *Gardner-Denver,* some making special proposals regarding
arbitration in light of the decision, see Fairweather, Practice and Procedure in Labor Arbitration,
2d Ed., 643–695 (BNA Books, 1983); Fletcher, "Arbitration of Title VII Claims: Some Judicial
Perceptions," Proceedings of the 34th Annual Meeting of NAA, 218 (BNA Books, 1982); Clark,
"The Legitimacy of Arbitrating Claims of Discrimination," id. at 235; Murphy, "Arbitration of
Discrimination Grievances," Proceedings of the 33rd Annual Meeting of NAA, 285 (BNA Books,
1981), with comments by Adair and Ashmore; Jacobs, "Confusion Remains Five Years After
Alexander v. Gardner-Denver," 30 Lab. L.J. 623 (1979); Oppenheimer & LaVan, "Arbitration
Awards in Discrimination Disputes: An Empirical Analysis," 34 Arb. J. No. 1, p. 12 (1979);
Edwards, "Arbitration as an Alternative in Equal Employment Disputes," 33 Arb. J. No. 4, p. 22
(1978); Webster, "Arbitrating Title VII Disputes: A Proposal," 33 Arb. J. No. 1, p. 25 (1978); Hill &
Sinicropi, "Excluding Discrimination Grievances from Grievance and Arbitration Procedures: A
Legal Analysis," 33 Arb. J. No. 1, p. 16 (1978); Hill, "The Authority of a Labor Arbitrator to
Decide Legal Issues Under a Collective Bargaining Contract: The Situation After Alexander v.
Gardner-Denver," 10 Ind. L. Rev. 899 (1977); Robinson & Neal, "Arbitration of Employment
Discrimination Cases: A Prospectus for the Future," Proceedings of the 29th Annual Meeting of
NAA, 20 (BNA Books, 1976); Williams, "A Modest Proposal for the Immediate Future," id. at 34;
Meltzer, "The Parties' Process and the Public's Purposes," id. at 46; Jones, "Comment," id. at 85;
Feller, "The Coming End of Arbitration's Golden Age," id. at 97; Sachs, "Comment," id. at 127;
Shaw, "Comment," id. at 139; Youngdahl, "Arbitration of Discrimination Grievances: A Novel
Approach Under One Collective Agreement," 31 Arb. J. 145 (1976); Edwards, "Arbitration of
Employment Discrimination Cases: An Empirical Study," Proceedings of the 28th Annual
Meeting of NAA, 59 (BNA Books, 1976); Newman, "Post-Gardner-Denver Developments in the
Arbitration of Discrimination Claims," id. at 36; Aksen, "Post-Gardner-Denver Developments in
Arbitration Law," id. at 24; Richards, "Alexander v. Gardner-Denver: A Threat to Title VII
Rights," 29 Ark. L. Rev. 129 (1975); Citron, "Deferral of Employee Rights to Arbitration: An
Evolving Dichotomy by the Burger Court," 27 Hastings L.J. 369 (1975); Cone & Henry, "Alexander v. Gardner-Denver and Deferral to Labor Arbitration," id. at 403; Oppenheim, "Gateway
and Alexander—Whither Arbitration," 48 Tul. L. Rev. 973 (1974). In 1978 the American Arbitration Association announced its new system of rules and procedures designed especially for
arbitration of equal employment opportunity disputes. AAA President Robert Coulson stated
that the arbitration would be based not upon a collective agreement but upon "a submission
agreement drafted by an attorney representing an employee and an attorney for an employer, a
stipulation that creates a lawyer-like system of arbitration, to be used in preference to the
statutory procedures of enforcement agencies or courts"; he offered the new AAA system to
parties desiring to avoid the delays and costs of litigation in the courts. Coulson, "Fair Treatment:
Voluntary Arbitration of Employee Claims," 33 Arb. J. No. 3, p. 23 (1978).

discharge violated the collective agreement, with an accompanying complaint against their union alleging breach of its duty of fair representation. The discharges had been upheld previously by an arbitration award, and the collective agreement made the award "final and binding." The Court of Appeals held that the complaint against the union could be maintained but that the action against the employer was barred by the finality provision of the collective agreement in the absence of evidence of misconduct by the employer, or of a conspiracy between the employer and the union. The Supreme Court rejected the Court of Appeals conclusion that the award's finality was preserved by the employer's good faith. The Supreme Court said the question was "whether the contractual protection against relitigating an arbitral decision binds employees who assert that the process has fundamentally malfunctioned by reason of the bad-faith performance of the union."[36] The Court held that a breach of the union's duty of fair representation "relieves the employee of an express or implied requirement that disputes be settled through contractual grievance procedures," and that "if it seriously undermines the integrity of the arbitral process the union's breach also removes the bar of the finality provisions of the contract."[37]

Other Supreme Court Decisions Affecting Arbitration

After the *Trilogy* came other United States Supreme Court decisions directly or indirectly affecting labor-management arbitration. A brief statement concerning each of these decisions follows.

---

[36]Hines v. Anchor Motor Freight, 96 S.Ct. 1048, 1059 (1976).

[37]Id. at 1058. The Court explained: "[W]e cannot believe that Congress intended to foreclose the employee from his § 301 remedy otherwise available against the employer if the contractual processes have been seriously flawed by the union's breach of its duty to represent employees honestly and in good faith and without invidious discrimination or arbitratory conduct." Id. at 1059. The Court stated also that its *Vaca* decision had accepted the proposition that "a union may not arbitrarily ignore a meritorious grievance or process it in a perfunctory fashion." Ibid. For discussion of *Hines*, see Moss, "The Fate of Arbitration in the Supreme Court: An Examination," 9 Loy. U. Chi. L.J. 369 (1978); "Arbitration and Federal Rights Under Collective Agreements in 1975," Proceedings of the 29th Annual Meeting of NAA, 233, 235--243 (BNA Books, 1976). For related discussion, see Chapter 5, topic entitled "Grievance Adjustment by Individual Employees." The NAA Committee on Law and Legislation has reported that: "[T]here continues to be a heavy caseload of individual employee actions against employers for breach of contract and/or against unions for breach of the duty of fair representation. While these cases continue to be generally unsuccessful from the litigants' point of view, they do provide instruction for arbitrators in regard to possible areas of employee or court dissatisfaction with the arbitral process." "Arbitration and Federal Rights Under Collective Agreements in 1976," Proceedings of the 30th Annual Meeting of NAA, 265, 266 (BNA Books, 1978), with additional discussion at 297--302. Also see discussion in "Arbitration and Federal Rights Under Collective Agreements in 1975," Proceedings of the 29th Annual Meeting of NAA, 233, 235–242 (BNA Books, 1976). The ABA Subcommittee on Impact of Fair Representation on Labor Arbitration reported that in the course of its proceedings certain concerns had been expressed in response to developments in the law of fair representation, particularly the *Hines* decision. Those concerns are that: "(1) there is a greater reluctance of the parties to settle, in part because of concern as to later liabilities; (2) the arbitration process is becoming increasingly formal and expensive; (3) there is developing a greater reliance on legal counsel rather than lay representatives; and (4) there is an increasing challenge to the exclusivity of the union as bargaining agent." "Report of the Subcommittee on Impact of Fair Representation on Labor Arbitration," 1979 Labor Relations Law Committee Reports, 336, 339 (ABA, 1979). Any trends along these lines possibly will be slowed by decisions such as Hoffman v. Lonza, Inc., 108 LRRM 2311 (CA 7, 1981), which construed *Hines* as only narrowly opening the door to attacks upon the finality of the grievance procedure.

Dowd Box: LMRA § 301 did not divest state courts of jurisdiction over suits to enforce the collective agreement. State and federal courts have concurrent jurisdiction over such suits (this of course includes enforcement of the arbitration clause).[38]

Lucas Flour: Although both state and federal courts can enforce collective agreements, state courts exercising jurisdiction over cases within the purview of § 301 must apply principles of federal substantive law rather than state law. This case also held that a no-strike obligation will be implied as to those issues which are subject to arbitration.[39]

Wiley & Sons: Once it is determined that the subject matter of a dispute is arbitrable, procedural questions which grow out of the dispute and bear on its final disposition should be left to the arbitrator. The Court stated that procedural questions, such as whether the preliminary steps of the grievance procedure have been exhausted or excused, ordinarily cannot be answered without consideration of the merits of the dispute.[40]

Drake Bakeries: Section 301 suits for damages must be stayed by the court pending arbitration where the arbitration clause is sufficiently broad to contemplate submission of the issue to an arbitrator—in this instance the issue was the employer's claim for damages for breach of a no-strike clause.[41]

Atkinson v. Sinclair: An employer's damage suit for breach of a no-strike clause may not be dismissed or stayed pending arbitration where the agreement limits arbitration to employee grievances.[42]

Needham Packing: Breach of a no-strike clause was not such a repudiation of the agreement as to relieve the employer of his obligation to arbitrate grievances over discharge of the strikers.[43]

---

[38]Dowd Box Co. v. Courtney, 368 U.S. 502, 49 LRRM 2619 (1962).

[39]Local 174, Teamsters v. Lucas Flour Co., 82 S.Ct. 571, 49 LRRM 2717 (1962). The rule that there is an implied no-strike obligation as to issues subject to arbitration was held to apply to safety disputes in Gateway Coal Co. v. United Mine Workers, 94 S.Ct. 629 (1974). The Court did say it "would be unusual, but certainly permissible, for the parties to agree to a broad mandatory arbitration provision yet expressly negate any implied no-strike obligation." However, expressly rescinding no-strike clauses contained in prior agreements (leaving none in the current agreement), did not suffice to negate an implied no-strike obligation. Id. at 639–640. *Gateway Coal* also held that the *Trilogy* presumption of arbitrability does apply to safety disputes.

[40]John Wiley & Sons v. Livingston, 84 S.Ct. 909, 55 LRRM 2769 (1964). Also see Operating Engineers v. Flair Builders, 92 S.Ct. 1710 (1972). In *John Wiley,* the Court also held that under appropriate circumstances the successor employer must honor the arbitration agreement of a company acquired by merger. The successor, however, was not required to honor the entire agreement of the predecessor employer in NLRB v. Burns Intl. Sec. Servs., 92 S.Ct. 1571 (1972). Also see Howard Johnson Co. v. Hotel & Restaurant Employees, 94 S.Ct. 2236 (1974).

[41]Drake Bakeries, Inc. v. Bakery Workers Local 50, 82 S.Ct. 1346, 50 LRRM 2440 (1962).

[42]Atkinson v. Sinclair Refining Co., 82 S.Ct. 1318, 50 LRRM 2433 (1962), also holding that where a union is liable for such breach of contract, its officers and members are not liable.

[43]Packinghouse Workers Local 721 v. Needham Packing Co., 84 S.Ct. 773, 55 LRRM 2580 (1963), in which the Court implied a different result might be reached in other instances, saying that it did not decide "whether a fundamental and long-lasting change in the relationship of the parties prior to the demand for arbitration would be a circumstance which, alone or among others, would release an employer from his promise to arbitrate." As to this point, also see Drake Bakeries, Inc. v. Bakery Workers Local 50, 82 S.Ct. 1346 (1962).

Boys Markets: Strikes which breach the collective agreement no-strike clause may be enjoined despite the Norris-LaGuardia Act, but only within the bounds of certain principles which the Supreme Court adopted:

> "When a strike is sought to be enjoined because it is over a grievance which both parties are contractually bound to arbitrate, the District Court may issue no injunctive order until it first holds that the contract *does* have that effect; and the employer should be ordered to arbitrate, as a condition of his obtaining an injunction against the strike. Beyond this, the District Court must, of course, consider whether issuance of an injunction would be warranted under principles of equity—whether breaches are occurring and will continue, or have been threatened and will be committed; whether they have caused or will cause irreparable injury to the employer; and whether the employer will suffer more from the denial of an injunction than will the union from its issuance."[44]

Smith v. Evening News: NLRB authority to deal with unfair labor practice conduct which also violates a collective agreement is not displaced by § 301, but it is not exclusive and does not destroy the jurisdiction of the courts in § 301 suits. This case also held that individual employees can sue under § 301 to enforce their collective agreement rights (there was no arbitration clause); the Court overruled its prior holding that § 301 does not apply to the enforcement of "uniquely personal" rights of employees under the agreement.[45]

Maddox: An employee must attempt to exhaust the contractual grievance and arbitration procedure (if any) prior to resorting to court action under § 301.[46]

---

[44]Boys Markets, Inc. v. Retail Clerks Union Local 770, 90 S.Ct. 1583, 1594, 74 LRRM 2257, 2264 (1970), in which the Supreme Court expressly overruled its decision in Sinclair Refining Co. v. Atkinson, 82 S.Ct. 1328 (1962). The Supreme Court also has held that state courts likewise have jurisdiction over § 301 suits to enjoin strikes violating no-strike clauses of agreements containing binding settlement procedures. Arnold Co. v. Carpenters Dist. Council, 94 S.Ct. 2069 (1974), and this holds even where the strike arguably is an unfair labor practice under the NLRA. In Buffalo Forge Co. v. Steelworkers, 96 S.Ct. 3141 (1976), the Supreme Court held that a court could not issue a *Boys Markets* injunction against a sympathy strike. The agreement contained a no-strike clause and a broad arbitration clause, thus the question whether the strike violated the no-strike clause would be subject to arbitration. However, since the strike itself was not *over* any issue subject to arbitration, it could not be enjoined pending such arbitration. For discussion, see Gould, "On Labor Injunctions Pending Arbitration: Recasting Buffalo Forge," 30 Stan. L. Rev. 533 (1978); Lowden & Flaherty, "Sympathy Strikes, Arbitration Policy, and the Enforceability of No-Strike Agreements—An Analysis of Buffalo Forge," 45 Geo. Wash. L. Rev. 633 (1977); Smith, "The Supreme Court, Boys Markets Labor Injunctions, and Sympathy Work Stoppages," 44 U. Chi. L. Rev. 321 (1977).

[45]Smith v. Evening News Assn., 83 S.Ct. 267, 51 LRRM 2646 (1962).

[46]Republic Steel Corp. v. Maddox, 85 S.Ct. 614, 58 LRRM 2193 (1965). The *Maddox* rule was extended to railroad employees in Andrews v. Louisville & Nashville R.R. Co., 92 S.Ct. 1562 (1972). Cf., Glover v. St. Louis-San Francisco Ry. Co., 89 S.Ct. 548, 70 LRRM 2097 (1969). The *Maddox* rule does not apply to a seaman's wage claims, which can be taken directly to federal court under an early statute or to arbitration under §301. U.S. Bulk Carriers, Inc. v. Arguelles, 91 S.Ct. 409 (1971). Also, in *Gardner-Denver* the Supreme Court said that both the employee's statutory right to proceed in court under Title VII and his contractual right to submit a claim to arbitration "have legally independent origins and are equally available to the aggrieved employee." 94 S.Ct. at 1022. It is apparent that this is also true in regard to rights under the Fair Labor Standards Act. Barrentine v. Arkansas-Best Freight Sys., 101 S.Ct. 1437, 1443–1444 (1981).

Vaca v. Sipes: State courts have not been preempted from entertaining suits by employees against their union for refusing to arbitrate their grievance; but in such suits the state court must apply federal law, under which a breach of the statutory duty of fair representation occurs only when the union's conduct is arbitrary, discriminatory, or in bad faith. The Court noted that the courts will be compelled to decide whether there has been a breach of the duty of fair representation in the context of many § 301 breach of contract actions against the employer, and the Court suggested that in these cases both the employer and the union might be held liable.[47]

Riss: An award of a joint labor-management grievance committee, though the procedure is not styled "arbitration," is enforceable by court action under § 301 *if* the award was to be final and binding under the terms of the collective agreement.[48]

Carey v. Westinghouse: The use of arbitration to resolve work-assignment jurisdictional disputes which involve questions of representation is not barred by the superior authority of the NLRB, though the Board's processes may be invoked at any time and a Board decision would control in the event of disagreement with that of the arbitrator. In requiring the employer to arbitrate upon demand by one of the unions the Court noted "the blurred line" that often exists between work-assignment disputes and representation disputes, and the Court stated: "If it is a work assignment dispute, arbitration conveniently fills a gap and avoids the necessity of a strike to bring the matter to the Board. If it is a representation matter, resort to arbitration may have a pervasive, curative effect even though one union is not a party. * * * The superior authority of the Board may be invoked at any time. Meanwhile the therapy of arbitration is brought to bear in a complicated and troubled area."[49]

For more on these cases, see above, subtopic entitled "De Novo Litigation Following Arbitration." However, in Emporium Capwell Co. v. Western Addition Community Org., 95 S.Ct. 977, 986–987 (1975), the Court refused to sanction picketing by black employees instead of their relying upon the union's efforts as exclusive bargaining representative to resolve their complaint, involving alleged racial discrimination by the employer, in the grievance and arbitration procedures. See discussion by Citron, "Deferral of Employee Rights to Arbitration: An Evolving Dichotomy by the Burger Court?" 27 Hastings L.J. 369, 372–373 (1975).

[47]Vaca v. Sipes, 87 S.Ct. 903, 64 LRRM 2369 (1967). Also see discussion of *Hines v. Anchor Motor Freight,* above, in subtopic entitled "De Novo Litigation Following Arbitration." In I.B.E.W. v. Foust, 99 S.Ct. 2121 (1979), the Supreme Court held that punitive damages may not be assessed against a union that breaches its duty of fair representation under the RLA, and the decision was clearly intended to apply also to unions under the NLRA. In Humphrey v. Moore, 84 S.Ct. 363, 55 LRRM 2031 (1964), the Supreme Court held that federal and state courts had concurrent jurisdiction under §301 of an employee's suit for alleged breach of a collective agreement by a joint union-employer committee in dovetailing the seniority lists of two companies. The improper representation claim against the union could be resolved as part of the §301 breach of contract claim against the employer. Even if an unfair labor practice within the NLRB's jurisdiction was involved, the courts could entertain the §301 suit.

[48]General Drivers Local 89 v. Riss and Co., 83 S.Ct. 789, 52 LRRM 2623 (1963).

[49]Carey v. Westinghouse Elec. Corp., 84 S.Ct. 401, 55 LRRM 2042 (1964).

The *Strong, Acme,* and *C & C Plywood* Cases: These cases teach that while the courts and arbitrators are the principal sources of contract interpretation and enforcement, the NLRB may interpret and give effect to the terms of a collective agreement if necessary to the adjudication of an unfair labor practice.[50]

State Law: Private Sector

State arbitration law is derived either from state common law or state statute, or from both.[51] While most states have some type of arbitration statute, many of them do not apply to labor arbitration. Moreover, many of those that do apply are very general in nature, leaving many details to be supplied by court decisions under the common law. Even where the case is covered by state statute it has usually been held that the statute does not abrogate but supplements the common law.[52]

One state, Washington, has held that its statute completely supersedes the common law, but the court recognized the contractual nature of arbitration and indicated that the parties may elect to establish arbitration procedures of their own in lieu of using the statutory procedures.[53]

State Common Law

While the common law of any given jurisdiction might not always accord in all respects with that of other jurisdictions, a general summary of common law arbitration and its relation to statutory arbitration has been provided by the U.S. Department of Labor:

---

[50]NLRB v. Strong, 89 S.Ct. 541 (1969); NLRB v. Acme Indus. Co., 87 S.Ct. 565, 64 LRRM 2069 (1967); NLRB v. C & C Plywood Corp., 87 S.Ct. 559, 64 LRRM 2065 (1967). *Acme* held that the employer must furnish information to the union to aid it in deciding whether to process a grievance; the Court stated that the NLRB's action in requiring the employer to provide information "was in aid of the arbitral process," which "can function properly only if the grievance procedures leading to it can sift out unmeritorious claims." 87 S.Ct. at 569.

[51]The concept of "common law" has been explained as follows: "When [a court has] no written law [constitution or statute] on which to base its decision in a particular controversy, it decides the case on the basis of custom and general principles of right and wrong. These decisions create precedents or rules, which are applied to similar future controversies. The body of law created in this fashion is spoken of as the common law." Kagel, Anatomy of a Labor Arbitration, 139 (BNA Books, 1961).

[52]See Jones, "Judicial Review of Arbitral Awards—Common-Law Confusion and Statutory Clarification," 31 S. Cal. L. Rev. 1, 2 (1957); Gregory & Orlikoff, "The Enforcement of Labor Arbitration Agreements," 17 U. Chi. L. Rev. 233, 254–255 (1950); Williston on Contracts, § 1927 (Rev. Ed., 1938).

[53]Puget Sound Bridge & Dredging Co. v. Lake Washington Shipyards, 96 P.2d 257, 259, 261 (1939). This right of election was reaffirmed in Greyhound Corp. v. Motor Coach Employees, 22 LA 555 (Wash. Sup. Ct., 1954). In Pennsylvania the common law applies unless the parties elect to come under the statute. Guille v. Mushroom Transp. Co., 229 A.2d 903, 904 (Pa. Sup. Ct., 1967), the court noting that where neither the agreement nor the arbitration conducted pursuant thereto made any reference to the state statute, "rules governing common law arbitration are applicable * * * except to the extent that these rules themselves have been pre-empted by federal common labor law."

"Common law arbitration rests upon the voluntary agreement of the parties to submit their dispute to an outsider. The submission agreement may be oral and may be revoked at any time before the rendering of the award. The tribunal, permanent or temporary, may be composed of any number of arbitrators. They must be free from bias and interest in the subject matter, and may not be related by affinity or consanguinity to either party. The arbitrators need not be sworn. Only existing disputes may be submitted to them. The parties must be given notice of hearings and are entitled to be present when all the evidence is received. The arbitrators have no power to subpoena witnesses or records and need not conform to legal rules of hearing procedure other than to give the parties an opportunity to present all competent evidence. All arbitrators must attend the hearings, consider the evidence jointly and arrive at an award by a unanimous vote. The award may be oral, but if written, all the arbitrators must sign it. It must dispose of every substantial issue submitted to arbitration. An award may be set aside only for fraud, misconduct, gross mistake, or substantial breach of a common law rule. The only method of enforcing the common law award is to file suit upon it and the judgment thus obtained may be enforced as any other judgment. Insofar as a State arbitration statute fails to state a correlative rule and is not in conflict with any of these common law rules, it may be said that an arbitration proceeding under such statute is governed also by these rules."[54]

The common law provides very little support for executory agreements to arbitrate (executory in the sense that the arbitration has not proceeded as far as issuance of an award). Either party may repudiate or withdraw from arbitration at any time prior to issuance of an award since executory agreements to arbitrate future disputes have no binding effect and will not be enforced either by way of damages or specific enforcement, and since executory agreements to arbitrate existing disputes likewise will not be specifically enforced (although in some jurisdictions breach of the latter agreements may be the basis of suit for damages, usually nominal only).[55] This common law rule against enforceability of executory agreements to arbitrate still prevails in many states.[56]

Although executory agreements to arbitrate are not specifically enforceable at common law, once an arbitration proceeding has been conducted and an award issued the courts will take jurisdiction to enforce or vacate the award.[57] A party who is dissatisfied with an

---

[54]Ziskind, Labor Arbitration Under State Statutes, 3 (U.S. Dept. of Labor, 1943). As noted elsewhere in this Chapter, many jurisdictions hold, both under the common law and under statute, that awards ordinarily may not be set aside for a mistake of law.

[55]See Freidin, Labor Arbitration and the Courts, 2 (1952); Gregory & Orlikoff, "The Enforcement of Labor Arbitration Agreements," 17 U. Chi. L. Rev. 233, 236, 241 (1950).

[56]American Bar Association Committee on Arbitration, "Report on Labor Arbitration," 28 LA 913, 929 (1957); Gregory & Orlikoff, "The Enforcement of Labor Arbitration Agreements," 17 U. Chi. L. Rev. 233, 234, 254 (1950).

[57]Since the arbitrator's authority terminates under the common law upon issuance of his award, any review and enforcement of his award must be left to the courts, except to the extent that the parties or applicable statute give him authority to interpret or otherwise deal with the award after its issuance. Regarding termination of the arbitrator's authority, see Chapter 7, topic entitled "Clarification or Interpretation of Award," and see Updegraff, Arbitration and Labor Relations, 279–283 (BNA Books, 1970); Updegraff & McCoy, Arbitration of Labor Disputes, 1st Ed., pp. 120–124 (1946), 2d Ed., pp. 211–215 (1961), discussing also the question of power in the arbitrator to correct obvious mistakes and clerical errors in the award.

award may initiate action for court review or may challenge the award when the satisfied party seeks court enforcement.[58]

At common law the issuance of an award generally bars any subsequent action on the original claim, but suit may be filed for enforcement of the award itself to the same extent as any contract.[59]

The grounds for attacking awards at common law are generally limited to:[60]

1. Fraud, misconduct, or partiality by the arbitrator, or gross unfairness in the conduct of the proceedings.
2. Fraud or misconduct by the parties affecting the result.
3. Complete want of jurisdiction in the arbitrator. Also, failure of the arbitrator to stay within his jurisdiction or to carry it out fully—that is, he decides too much or too little.
4. Violation of public policy as by ordering the commission of an unlawful act.[61]

Under the common law awards generally will not be set aside for mistake of law or fact. As the Pennsylvania Supreme Court has stated, "Unless they are restricted by the submission, the arbitrators are the final judges of both law and fact and their award will not be disturbed for a mistake of either."[62]

State Arbitration Statutes

State arbitration statutes are of three general types: (1) general statutes designed primarily for commercial disputes, but some of which may be used for labor disputes; (2) special labor arbitration statutes, which contain some detail as to procedure; and (3) statutes which merely "promote" arbitration by charging a state agency to encourage its use.[63]

---

[58]See Justin, "Arbitration: Proving Your Case," 10 LA 955, 967 (1948); Updegraff, Arbitration and Labor Relations, 285 (BNA Books, 1970); Updegraff & McCoy, Arbitration of Labor Disputes, 1st Ed., p. 125 (1946), 2d Ed., p. 216 (1961).

[59]Williston on Contracts, §1927 (Rev. Ed., 1938). For additional discussion, see Dowell, "Judicial Enforcement of Arbitration Awards in Labor Disputes," 3 Rutgers L. Rev. 65, 70–72 (1949).

[60]See "When May an Arbitrator's Award Be Vacated?" 7 DePaul L. Rev. 236 (1958); Rothstein, "Vacation of Awards for Fraud, Bias, Misconduct and Partiality," 10 Vand. L. Rev. 813 (1957); Freidin, Labor Arbitration and the Courts, 31 (1952); Updegraff, Arbitration and Labor Relations, 275, 278, 288–289 (BNA Books, 1970); Updegraff & McCoy, Arbitration of Labor Disputes, 1st Ed., pp. 116, 120, 126–127 (1946), 2d Ed., pp. 208, 210–211, 216–217 (1961).

[61]Regarding this fourth ground, see Sturges, Commercial Arbitrations and Awards, §61, p. 202 (1930). Also see Smith & Jones, "The Supreme Court and Labor Dispute Arbitration: The Emerging Federal Law," 63 Mich. L. Rev. 751, 803–807 (1965); Cox, "The Place of Law in Labor Arbitration," The Profession of Labor Arbitration, 76, 78–79 (BNA Books, 1957).

[62]Newspaper Guild v. Philadelphia Daily News, Inc., 164 A.2d 215, 220 (1960). For large collections of cases to the same general effect, see 6 C.J.S., Arbitration and Award, §105, p. 251; 3 Am. Jur., Arbitration and Award, §92, pp. 923–924. Regarding the use of substantive law in arbitration, see Chapter 10.

[63]See Ziskind, Labor Arbitration Under State Statutes (U.S. Dept. of Labor, 1943). Also see Matto, "The Applicability of State Arbitration Statutes to Proceedings Subject to LMRA Section 301," 27 Ohio State L.J. 692 (1966); Lillard, "State Arbitration Statutes Applicable to Labor Disputes," 19 Mo. L. Rev. 280, 282–286 (1954). For extensive lists of citations to state arbitration statutes, see Bedikian, "Use of Subpoenas in Labor Arbitration: Statutory Interpretations and Perspectives," 1979 Det. C.L. Rev. 575, 576–577 (1979); Updegraff, Arbitration and Labor Relations, 385–388 (BNA Books, 1970).

One of the most detailed and most utilized statutes is that of New York, which was amended in 1940 for the specific purpose of covering labor cases, and which was revised and modernized in 1963.[64] The California statute, enacted in 1961, supplanted an earlier act and introduced a number of innovations.[65] Examples of other important industrial states with modern arbitration statutes applicable to labor arbitration are Michigan, Ohio, Massachusetts, Illinois, and New Jersey.

In 1955 a proposed Uniform Arbitration Act was promulgated by the National Conference of Commissioners on Uniform Laws.[66] As of 1978 about three fourths of the states had some sort of "modern" arbitration statute, but not all apply to labor disputes.[67] There is no absolute uniformity among these statutes, and a detailed presentation of their provisions is beyond the scope of this book. However, it may be noted that provisions along the following general lines are frequently found in the modern statutes (many of the listed provisions are included, for instance, in the New York and California statutes, and in the Uniform Act):

1. Agreements to arbitrate existing and future disputes are made valid and enforceable.
2. Courts are given jurisdiction to compel arbitration, or to stay arbitration if no agreement to arbitrate exists.
3. Courts are given jurisdiction to stay litigation when one party to an arbitrable dispute attempts to take it to court instead of arbitrating.
4. Courts are authorized to appoint arbitrators where the parties fail to provide a method for appointment.
5. Majority action by arbitration boards is authorized.
6. Provision is made for oath by the arbitrator and/or witnesses, unless waived by the parties.
7. Default proceedings (in the absence of a party) are authorized under certain circumstances.
8. Provision is made for continuances and adjournments of hearings.
9. Limitation is placed upon the effect of waivers of the right to be represented by counsel.
10. Arbitrators are given the subpoena power.

---

[64]See "An Outline of Procedure Under the New York Arbitration Law," 20 Arb. J. 73 (1965); "The New York Arbitration Law," 18 Arb. J. 132 (1963).

[65]See "Report of NAA Committee on Law and Legislation," Collective Bargaining and the Arbitrator's Role, 249, 252–253 (BNA Books, 1962).

[66]The Act is published in 24 LA 886–889. The Act as amended in 1956 is published in 27 LA 909–912. The AAA reported that as of 1978, 21 states and the District of Columbia had statutes based upon the Uniform Arbitration Act, but over half exclude coverage of labor disputes. AAA Study Time, Oct. 1979, stating that those not excluding labor disputes were Colorado, Illinois, Indiana, Maine, Minnesota, Nevada, New Mexico, South Dakota, and the District of Columbia. For discussion of court decisions under various sections of the Act, see "The Uniform Arbitration Act," 48 Mo. L. Rev. 137 (1983).

[67]Lawyers' Arbitration Letter, Vol. 2, No. 22 (AAA, 1978), listing 37 states (including those with statutes based upon the Uniform Arbitration Act), the District of Columbia, and Puerto Rico.

11. Awards are required to be in writing and signed by the arbitrator, and some limitation is stated regarding the time within which awards must be rendered.
12. Arbitrators are granted limited authority to modify or correct awards upon timely application by a party, and the Uniform Act additionally permits the arbitrator to clarify his award by application from a party.
13. A summary procedure is provided for (1) court confirmation of awards, (2) court vacation of awards on limited grounds stated by the statute, (3) court modification or correction of awards on limited grounds stated by the statute.
14. Courts are authorized to enter judgment upon awards as confirmed, modified, or corrected; the judgment is then enforceable as any other judgment.
15. Provision is made for appeals from court orders and judgments under the statute.

The limited grounds for setting aside awards under many of the state statutes (and under the FAA) are along the following general lines, which differ little from the common law grounds:[68]

1. The award was procured by corruption, fraud, or other undue means.
2. The arbitrator was guilty of evident partiality, corruption, or misconduct (some statutes expressly limit the impartiality requirement to neutrals).[69]
3. The arbitrator refused to postpone the hearing upon sufficient cause shown, or refused to hear material evidence; or otherwise so conducted the hearing as to prejudice substantially the rights of a party.
4. The arbitrator exceeded his powers, or so imperfectly executed them that a mutual, final, and definite award upon the subject matter submitted was not made.[70]
5. There was no valid agreement to arbitrate (and it has not been determined otherwise by an action to compel or stay arbitration), and objection to that fact was properly raised.

The Uniform Act and the statutes of New York, California, Florida, and some other states provide that upon vacation of an award the court may order a rehearing before new arbitrators, or in some cases before the original arbitrators.

Some state statutes, and the FAA, authorize the courts to modify or correct awards on grounds essentially as follows (some statutes also

---

[68]See Uniform Arbitration Act, 27 LA 909, 910–911; Federal Arbitration Act, 9 U.S.C. §10; Lillard, "State Arbitration Statutes Applicable to Labor Disputes," 19 Mo. L. Rev. 280, 293 (1954).

[69]The U.S. Supreme Court has stated, under the FAA, that the arbitrator "must not only be unbiased but must avoid even the appearance of bias." Commonwealth Coatings Corp. v. Continental Casualty Co., 89 S.Ct. 337, 340 (1968).

[70]Some of the statutes, such as California's, provide for vacation of the award where the arbitrator exceeded his powers and the award cannot be corrected without affecting the merits of the decision.

authorize the arbitrator to modify or correct his award on these grounds):[71]

1. Where there was an evident miscalculation of figures, or an evident mistake in the description of any person, thing, or property referred to in the award.
2. Where the arbitrators have awarded upon a matter not submitted to them, not affecting the merits of the decision upon the matter submitted.
3. Where the award is imperfect in a matter of form not affecting the merits of the controversy.

It is obvious from the above summaries that the state statutes generally provide no right of court review for errors of law or errors as to finding of fact.[72]

The Applicable Law: Private Sector

State common law and/or state statutory law governs the arbitration of labor-management disputes involving private-sector concerns not affecting interstate commerce and thus not falling within the purview of LMRA § 301. State law likewise applies to disputes involving private-sector workers who are excluded from coverage of the federal statute.[73] If such cases reach a court, it will ordinarily be a state court. Even if the case is taken to federal court, however, the case must be decided on the basis of state law when the federal court has jurisdiction only by virtue of diversity and not by virtue of any federal statute providing for arbitration; "the federal court enforcing a state-created right in a diversity case is * * * 'only another court of the State.' "[74]

The bulk of labor-management arbitrations in the private sector no doubt do fall within the purview of LMRA § 301. As we have noted, such cases are to be governed by federal substantive law, both in federal and state courts.[75] Although state courts have concurrent jurisdiction over suits covered by § 301, "Congress intended doctrines

---

[71]See Matto, "The Applicability of State Arbitration Statutes to Proceedings Subject to LMRA Section 301," 27 Ohio State L.J. 692, 713–714 (1966); Lillard, "State Arbitration Statutes Applicable to Labor Disputes," 19 Mo. L. Rev. 280, 294 (1954); Uniform Arbitration Act, 27 LA 909, 911; Federal Arbitration Act, 9 U.S.C. § 11. Courts acting only under state common law may not be permitted to modify awards. See Updegraff, Arbitration and Labor Relations, 289 (BNA Books, 1970); Updegraff & McCoy, Arbitration of Labor Disputes, 1st Ed., p. 127 (1946), 2d Ed., pp. 217–218 (1961); Enterprise Wheel & Car Corp. v. Steelworkers, 269 F.2d 327, 332 (CA 4, 1959).

[72]Also see Justin, "Arbitration: Proving Your Case," 10 LA 955, 967 (1948).

[73]For disputes covered by the Railway Labor Act, that federal statute provides the applicable law and it is treated below in Chapters 3 and 4. Regarding public-sector employment, federal law governs the federal public sector and state law governs the state public sector. These areas are treated below in this Chapter's topics entitled "Legal Status of Federal-Sector Arbitration" and "Legal Status of Arbitration in State-Sector Employment."

[74]Bernhardt v. Polygraphic Co. of America, 76 S.Ct. 273, 276, 25 LA 693, 695 (1956), holding that enforceability of agreements to arbitrate must be decided by state law in such diversity cases.

[75]See this Chapter, topic entitled "Federal Law: Private Sector." A clause stating that a contract was to be governed by New York law was held of no effect in a §301 action. Carey v. General Electric Co., 50 LRRM 2119 (USDC, 1962), modified on other grounds. 52 LRRM 2662 (CA 2, 1963). Cf., Teamsters v. Washington Employers, Inc., 96 LRRM 2096 (CA 9, 1977).

of federal labor law uniformly to prevail over inconsistent local rules."[76]

Following the *Lincoln Mills* decision the federal courts have decided many § 301 arbitration cases; thus these courts have commenced the slow process of fashioning a body of federal law for this field. By the nature of the legal process, however, decades will be required to develop a basically complete and uniform body of federal law as ordered by the Supreme Court. Only by an outpouring of decisions by that Court, or by the enactment of a detailed federal statute for labor arbitration, can the process be accelerated.[77] In the meantime, the lower courts will be free to range widely in determining what the federal labor policy is on issues which have not been resolved by the Supreme Court, and in determining what local rules are consistent with that policy.[78]

The *Lincoln Mills* decision teaches that the "federal law" of labor arbitration is to be derived from the LMRA, from other federal statutes, and from state law; it also teaches that "The range of judicial inventiveness will be determined by the nature of the problem."[79]

The principles developed under state common law to prevent abuse of powers by arbitrators have been incorporated in many state statutes; numerous other common features appear in the modern arbitration statutes, in the Uniform Arbitration Act, and in the FAA.[80] A number of states have legislated such modern statutes since *Lincoln Mills,* and some since the *Trilogy.* It is not unreasonable to expect resort to these sources by both federal and state courts in developing the federal common law under *Lincoln Mills.* In any event, there is obvious validity in the comment that the "grant of concurrent jurisdiction gives the state courts an important role in assisting in the formulation of the federal substantive law under section 301."[81]

---

[76]Local 174, Teamsters v. Lucas Flour Co., 82 S.Ct. 571, 577 (1962). Cases may be removed from state to federal court by virtue of § 301 coverage. Johnson v. England, 356 F.2d 44 (CA 9, 1966); Kracof v. Retail Clerks, 244 F.Supp. 38 (USDC Pa., 1965).

[77]In 1959 a committee of the NAA proposed a United States Labor Arbitration Act. The proposed Act is published in 34 LA 941.

[78]That significant questions may for years remain unanswered with finality is illustrated by the lower court conflict as to whether the Federal Arbitration Act applies to collective agreement arbitration clauses. This question has not been clearly resolved by the United States Supreme Court (the 1957 *Lincoln Mills* decision under LMRA § 301 has of course reduced the significance of this particular question).

[79]Textile Workers v. Lincoln Mills, 77 S.Ct. 912, 918 (1957). In UAW v. Hoosier Cardinal Corp., 86 S.Ct. 1107, 1113, 61 LRRM 2545 (1966), the range of judicial inventiveness was limited somewhat by the Supreme Court's holding that "the timeliness of a § 301 suit * * * is to be determined, as a matter of federal law, by reference to the appropriate state statute of limitations." But in DelCostello v. Teamsters, 103 S.Ct. 2281, 2290–2291, 113 LRRM 2737 (1983), the Supreme Court held that the statute of limitations to be used for suits under the *Vaca* and *Hines* decisions is the six-month statute of limitations specified by the NLRA for unfair labor practice actions; the Court pointed out that in the *Vaca* and *Hines* situations the "suit is * * * not a straightforward breach of contract suit under § 301, as was *Hoosier,* but a hybrid § 301/fair representation claim" amounting to a direct challenge to the private settlement of disputes under the collective agreement, and that "unlike the claim in *Hoosier,* it has no close analogy in ordinary state law."

[80]See this Chapter, topic entitled "State Law: Private Sector."

[81]Smith and Clark, "Reappraisal of the Role of the States in Shaping Labor Relations Law," 1965 Wis. L. Rev. 411, 421 (1965), where those authors add: "Furthermore, it may be that

As concerns reactions of state courts, there have been cases in which the state court expressly recognized that it must apply substantive rules compatible with federal policy.[82] However, while noting that "the controlling substantive law is Federal law," the Minnesota Supreme Court emphasized that "state law, if compatible with the purposes of § 301, may be resorted to in order to find the rule that will best effectuate the Federal policy."[83]

No doubt some arbitration cases will be taken to state court and resolved there without issue being raised (or if raised, without actually being resolved) as to coverage by LMRA § 301 and/or compatibility of state law with the federal labor policy.[84] Indeed, three possibilities have been recognized as to application of state statutes in cases covered by LMRA § 301: (1) per se application of the particular state statute, no attention being given to federal labor policy; (2) nonapplication, the court not applying the statute of the particular state but evaluating all state statutes in general to determine what the uniform federal rule should be; (3) prima facie application, the particular state provision being applied unless it conflicts with the federal labor policy.[85]

Legal Status of Federal-Sector Arbitration

Preliminary Observations: Federal and Private Sectors Compared

Much of the vast body of substantive and procedural principles developed by private-sector labor-management arbitration in the United States is equally applicable at the federal level and in other public-sector areas as well. While it is true that many activities and

---

procedural and remedial matters in the enforcement of labor agreements remain to be determined by the law of the forum." In Local 1416, IAM v. Jostens, Inc., 250 F.Supp. 496 (USDC Minn., 1966), the court stated that while the *Lincoln Mills* mention of resort to state law was undoubtedly referring to principles of substantive law, there should be no impediment to the use of state procedure, in the absence of a contrary or inconsistent federal statute or rule. In IAM v. Geometric Tool Co., 70 LRRM 228, 51 LA 1156 (CA 2, 1968), a 60-day time limit specified by state statute for rendering awards was deemed contrary to federal labor policy and could not be strictly enforced where the case was covered by LMRA §301. But see Huntington Alloys v. Steelworkers, 104 LRRM 2958, 2961 (CA 4, 1980). In Local 671 v. United Parcel Serv., 108 LRRM 3216, 3217 (USDC, 1981), the *Geometric Tool* reasoning was applied by the court in rejecting the applicability of a state provision regarding the arbitrator's oath.

[82]See, for example, Butchers' Union Local 229 v. Cudahy Packing Co., 428 P.2d 849 (Calif. Sup. Ct., 1967).

[83]Fischer v. Guaranteed Concrete Co., 151 N.W.2d 266, 269 (1967).

[84]It has been observed, for instance, that state courts "have not faced the problem of the applicability of their arbitration statutes to proceedings subject to section 301 to any great extent," that observer suggesting that the reason may be that "It is easy to look to the state statute and not attempt to determine what the federal policy is and whether any conflict exists." Matto, "The Applicability of State Arbitration Statutes to Proceedings Subject to LMRA Section 301," 27 Ohio St. L.J. 692, 699 (1966). This excellent article discusses certain common features of state arbitration statutes and evaluates their compatibility with the federal labor policy.

[85]Id. at 694–702, where each of the possibilities is discussed in detail. That observer recommended prima facie application because it duly notes the Supreme Court's comments concerning state law as a source of federal law and would be consistent with the federal policy of encouraging labor arbitration. Id. at 717.

fact situations in the public sector differ from those in private industry, the principles being applied in federal and other public-sector arbitration generally are the same time-tested principles that evolved through the years in private-sector arbitration. This is not surprising, even apart from the fact that quite commonly a given arbitrator serves both the public and private sectors. Nor is it surprising, human nature being as it is, that arbitration proceedings are no less adversary in nature in the public sector than in the private sector.[86]

The significant differences or variations that do exist between federal-sector and private-sector arbitration relate principally to certain aspects of legal status.[87] The scope of the duty to bargain; the status of management rights; the degree of required adherence by the arbitrator to laws, rules, and regulations; and the scope of review of the arbitrator's decision are probably the most important areas of difference or variation. (Note that differences in these areas also may affect the arbitrability of issues and the scope of the arbitrator's remedy power, in some cases making it narrower in the federal than in the private sector.) These matters are treated in the materials that follow, but the reader will quickly observe that the materials also deal with other special features of labor-management dispute settlement in the federal sector.

An understanding of the role of contractual grievance procedures and arbitration in the federal sector is aided by some knowledge of the historical and present setting within which they exist. The scope of the federal-sector materials that follow has been made more expansive with this thought in mind.

The Executive Orders and the Civil Service Reform Act of 1978

In 1962 federal employees were granted organizational and bargaining rights by President Kennedy's Executive Order 10988. These

---

[86]For an illustration of the extremely adversary nature of some public-sector grievance disputes and their handling, see National Labor Relations Board, 68 LA 279 (Sinicropi, 1977).

[87]Even regarding legal status, it is "eminently sensible" to apply existing principles of private-sector arbitration law to disputes in the public sector unless special reason exists for not doing so, as one court explained:

"The functions served by grievance and arbitration procedures in the private sector are almost identical to those served by such procedures in the public sector. In both instances, grievances and arbitration procedures provide a relatively speedy and inexpensive method of resolving labor disputes, give the employee the satisfaction of knowing that the resolution of any dispute he may have with his employer lies with a neutral party and not with his employer, and preserve judicial resources by establishing a method for resolving labor disputes independent of the courts. In the private sector, arbitration helps to maintain industrial peace by giving employees an alternative to the strike. In the public sector, arbitration helps to preserve industrial peace by giving employees some recourse when a dispute arises.

"Given all these similarities plus the existence of a well-developed body of federal common law, we conclude that it is eminently sensible to apply existing principles of arbitration law to labor disputes involving TVA. Our conclusion is reenforced by the fact that state courts increasingly are applying principles developed in the private sector to public employee labor disputes."

Salary Policy Panel v. TVA, 115 LRRM 3550, 3554 (CA 6, 1984), holding existing principles of private-sector arbitration law applicable to Tennessee Valley Authority labor disputes even though the unique TVA labor relations program is authorized by the agency's enabling Act and is not regulated by the Taft-Hartley Act or any Government-wide labor statute.

rights were further advanced by President Nixon's Executive Order 11491 of 1969, which made certain changes to coordinate, strengthen, and clarify the program.[88]

Executive Order 10988 permitted the use of advisory (not binding) arbitration; and such arbitration was in fact used for representation, bargaining unit, and grievance issues in federal employment.

Under Executive Order 11491, provision was made for representation disputes, grievances, and contract-negotiation disputes as follows:

- Provision was made for representation elections under the supervision of the Assistant Secretary of Labor for Labor-Management Relations, and this official decided questions concerning the appropriate unit.
- Negotiated procedures could provide for arbitration of employee grievances and of disputes over the interpretation or application of collective agreements between federal agencies and labor organizations. Either party could file exceptions to an arbitrator's award with the Federal Labor Relations Council.
- Arbitration or third-party fact-finding could be used to resolve negotiation impasses, but only when authorized by the Federal Service Impasses Panel (which itself could make a final decision on the impasse).

Prior to the promulgation of the Executive Orders and, indeed, throughout their periods of enforcement the United States Civil Service Commission exercised broad statutory jurisdiction over federal employment. The Commission had functions of executive, rulemaking, and judicial nature. Its judicial function related to the rights of federal employees and the protections accorded them under the merit system. Under the Civil Rights Act of 1964 and several other statutes it also had responsibility for enforcement of the policy against discrimination in federal employment. Thus, for merit-system and discrimination issues the federal employee had remedies before the Civil Service Commission. Such remedies have been called "statutory remedies," as distinguished from the "contractual remedies" of the grievance procedure and arbitration provided under collective bargaining

---

[88]For writings on the federal-sector program under E.O. 11491 as amended by subsequent Executive Orders, see Gamser, "Back-Seat Driving Behind the Back-Seat Driver: Arbitration in the Federal Sector," Proceedings of the 31st Annual Meeting of NAA, 268 (BNA Books, 1979); Porter, "Arbitration in the Federal Government: What Happened to the 'Magna Carta'?" Proceedings of the 30th Annual Meeting of NAA, 90 (BNA Books, 1978); Frazier, "Labor Arbitration in the Federal Service," 45 Geo. Wash. L. Rev. 712 (1977); Tobias, "The Scope of Bargaining in the Federal Sector: Collective Bargaining or Collective Consultation," 44 Geo. Wash. L. Rev. 576 (1976); Aronin, "Collective Bargaining in the Federal Service: A Balanced Approach," 44 Geo. Wash. L. Rev. 576 (1976); Williams, "Accommodation of Jurisdiction Over Federal Labor Disputes," 44 Geo. Wash. L. Rev. 604 (1976); Nesbitt, Labor Relations in the Federal Government Service (BNA Books, 1976); Kagel, "Grievance Arbitration in the Federal Service: How Final and Binding?" 51 Or. L. Rev. 134 (1971); Shaw & Clark, "Determination of Appropriate Bargaining Units in the Public Sector: Legal and Practical Problems," 51 Or. L. Rev. 152 (1971); Wollett, "The Bargaining Process in the Public Sector: What Is Bargainable?" 51 Or. L. Rev. 177 (1971); Weber, "Federal Labor Relations: Problems and Prospects," Proceedings of the 24th Annual Meeting of NAA, 148 (BNA Books, 1971).

agreements. Under the Executive Order program the existence of a statutory remedy for an issue preempted or foreclosed applicability of a contractual remedy for the issue. This was changed, however, by the Civil Service Reform Act of 1978.

Effective January 1979 major changes regarding federal employment were made by Presidential Reorganization Plan No. 2 of 1978 (which automatically became law when neither House of Congress disapproved within the specified time) and the Civil Service Reform Act of 1978 (CSRA). The Civil Service Commission was abolished as such and replaced by two agencies—the Office of Personnel Management and the Merit Systems Protection Board. The mechanics of this change were as follows: (1) the Civil Service Commission was "redesignated the Merit Systems Protection Board" with the "hearing, adjudication, and appeals functions" of the former Civil Service Commission (except with respect to examination ratings); and (2) the Office of Personnel Management was established to perform other functions of the former Civil Service Commission.[89]

The Federal Labor Relations Council established by Executive Order 11491 was replaced by the Federal Labor Relations Authority with statutory status.[90] The Federal Service Impasses Panel established by Executive Order 11491 was continued and given statutory status.[91] Thus, the labor-management relations and dispute-settlement program that had existed for federal employment under the Executive Orders has now been codified (with some major changes).[92]

Another significant change was made by Presidential Reorganization Plan No. 1 of 1978 (which also became law automatically when it was not disapproved by either House of Congress within

---

[89]5 U.S.C.A. §§ 1101 et seq. (Reorganization Plan No. 2 is published with the annotations to § 1101).

[90]5 U.S.C.A. §§ 7104, 7105.

[91]5 U.S.C.A. § 7119.

[92]However, 5 U.S.C. § 7135 provides that Executive Order 11491 and certain other Executive Orders "shall remain in full force and effect until revised or revoked by the President, or unless superseded by specific provisions of [the Civil Service Reform Act] or by regulations or decisions issued pursuant to [the Act]." For summaries of the codified federal-sector program, see Guide to the Federal Service Labor-Management Relations Statute (FLRA Doc. 1213, 1981); Ingrassia, "Reflections on the New Labor Law," 30 Lab. L.J. 539 (1979); Frazier, "Labor-Management Relations in the Federal Government," 30 Lab. L.J. 131 (1979). For books on the program, see Loevi & Kaplan, Arbitration and the Federal Sector Advocate, 2d Ed. (AAA, 1982); Robinson, Negotiability in the Federal Sector (Cornell U. & AAA, 1981); Burnett, Brodsky & McGovern, Labor-Management Relations, Civil Service Reforms, and EEO in the Federal Service (Fed. Bar Assn., 1980). For articles, see Haughton, "Arbitration in the Federal Sector," 38 Arb. J. No. 4, p. 55 (1983); Gentile, "Arbitration in the Federal Sector: Selected Problem Areas," 34 Lab. L.J. 482 (1983); Figenbaum, "The Relationship Between Arbitration and Administrative Procedures in the Discipline and Discharge of Federal Employees," 34 Lab. L.J. 586 (1983); McCabe, "Problems in Federal Sector Labor-Management Relations Under Title VII of the Civil Service Reform Act of 1978," 33 Lab. L.J. 560 (1982); Kagel, "Grievance Arbitration in the Federal Service: Still Hardly Final and Binding?" Proceedings of the 34th Annual Meeting of NAA, 178 (BNA Books, 1982); Reischl, "Applying Collyer in the Federal Sector: Past Due Remedy," 33 Lab. L.J. 359 (1982); Reischl, "Arbitrating Federal Sector Environmental Differential Pay Disputes," 37 Arb. J. No. 4, p. 32 (1982); Goodwin, "Federal Sector Arbitration Under the Civil Service Reform Act of 1978," 17 San Diego L. Rev. 857 (1980); Cooper & Bauer, "Federal Sector Labor Relations Reform," 56 Chi.-Kent L. Rev. 509 (1980); Smith & Wood, "Title VII of the Civil Service Reform Act of 1978: A 'Perfect' Order?" 31 Hastings L.J. 855 (1980); Clarke, "Substantial Evidence and Labor Arbitration in the Federal Sector," 31 Lab. L.J. 368 (1980); Coleman, "The Civil Service Reform Act of 1978: Its Meaning and Its Roots," 31 Lab. L.J. 200 (1980).

the specified time). This change was that responsibility for enforcement of the policy against discrimination (civil rights, age, equal pay, handicapped individuals) in federal employment was transferred from the Civil Service Commission and certain other agencies or officials to the Equal Employment Opportunity Commission.[93]

The Agencies and Their Role

Office of Personnel Management (OPM). "The Office of Personnel Management is an independent establishment in the executive branch."[94] The OPM succeeded to Civil Service Commission functions relating to recruitment, measurement, ranking, and selection of individuals for initial appointment and competitive promotion in federal employment.[95] As its name suggests, the OPM's functions are essentially executive or managerial in nature. It is the MSPB (Merit Systems Protection Board) rather than the OPM which now exercises adjudication and appeals functions relating to federal employee grievances.

Merit Systems Protection Board (MSPB). By the Civil Service Reform Act of 1978 the Merit Systems Protection Board has jursidiction over a broad range of grievance claims or issues involving federal agency actions affecting employees, including discrimination claims that are combined or mixed with merit-system claims.[96]

Also of significance is the MSPB's authority to review rules and regulations issued by the OPM, and to declare any rule or regulation invalid if the rule or regulation or its implementation would violate or lead to violation of any prohibited personnel practice adversely affecting employees (certain personnel practices are prohibited by statute because they are contrary to merit system principles).[97]

Federal Labor Relations Authority (FLRA). The Federal Labor Relations Authority succeeded the Federal Labor Relations Council and performs various important functions in federal labor-management relations.[98] In general, its functions are:

---

[93]Reorganization Plan No. 1 is published with the annotations to 42 U.S.C.A. § 2000e-4. On discrimination complaints in federal employment, see Martin, "Equal Employment Opportunity Complaint Procedures and Federal Union-Management Relations: A Field Study," 34 Arb. J. 34 (1979), where many articles on the subject are collected.

[94]5 U.S.C. § 1101.

[95]These functions are enumerated in 5 C.F.R. § 300.101.

[96]Regarding the Board's composition, its Special Counsel, and its powers and functions, see 5 U.S.C. §§ 1201-1205, 7701, 7702. For merit system principles and protections that may become involved in employee claims before the MSPB, see 5 U.S.C. §§ 2301, 2302. The MSPB was initially established by Reorganization Plan No. 2 of 1978 to exercise "the hearing, adjudication, and appeals functions" of the Civil Service Commission.

[97]See 5 U.S.C. §§ 1205(e) (review authority), 2301 (merit system principles), 2302 (prohibited personnel practices).

[98]See 5 U.S.C. §§ 7104 (appointment of FLRA members and General Counsel), 7105 (FLRA functions). Also see U.S. Supreme Court summary of FLRA's role in Bureau of Alcohol, Tobacco & Firearms v. FLRA, 104 S.Ct. 439, 442, 114 LRRM 3393 (1983), in which decision the Supreme Court considered the appropriate standard of court review of FLRA decisions interpreting the Civil Service Reform Act.

1. To "provide leadership in establishing policies and guidance relating to" labor-management relations matters under Title VII of the Civil Service Reform Act of 1978;
2. To determine appropriate units and to conduct representation elections for collective bargaining under the Act;[99]
3. To prescribe criteria and resolve issues relating to consultation rights under the Act;
4. To resolve issues relating to the duty to bargain;
5. To prescribe criteria and resolve issues relating to the determination of "compelling need" for agency rules or regulations (The duty to bargain extends to any matter which is the subject of rules or regulations of any agency or national subdivision thereof *only if* the FLRA has determined that "no compelling need" exists for the rule or regulation. This becomes an important consideration in the arbitration of some grievances.);
6. To resolve unfair labor practice complaints;
7. To resolve exceptions to arbitration awards.

Equal Employment Opportunity Commission (EEOC). The Civil Rights Act of 1964 established the Equal Employment Opportunity Commission and placed basic responsibility upon it for implementation and enforcement of the Act's prohibitions against discriminatory employment practices.[100] Also, Reorganization Plan No. 1 of 1978 transferred to the EEOC the responsibility for equal opportunity in federal employment which had been vested in the Civil Service Commission pursuant to § 717 of the Civil Rights Act of 1964; it also transferred enforcement functions for age discrimination, equal pay, and federal employment of handicapped individuals to the EEOC from the agency or official previously exercising those responsibilities.

General Accounting Office (GAO). "[I]f considered necessary by the Comptroller General, the General Accounting Office shall conduct audits and reviews to assure compliance with the laws, rules, and regulations governing employment in the executive branch and in the competitive service and to assess the effectiveness and soundness of Federal Personnel management."[101]

Federal Service Impasses Panel (FSIP). By statute the "Federal Service Impasses Panel is an entity within the [Federal Labor Relations] Authority, the function of which is to provide assistance in resolving negotiation impasses between agencies and exclusive representatives."[102] The statute provides that if an impasse is not resolved

---

[99]The NLRB rather than the FLRA handles representation matters for the Postal Service. See 39 U.S.C. §§ 1202-1204.

[100]See 42 U.S.C. §§ 2000e-4, 2000e-5.

[101]5 U.S.C. § 2304, which also specifies that the GAO shall submit an annual report to the President and Congress on MSPB and OPM activities, including an analysis of whether OPM actions conform to merit-system principles and are free from prohibited personnel practices. Also see, below, the subtopic entitled "Comptroller General's Role."

[102]5 U.S.C. § 7119. Different statutory provisions exist for the Postal Service. See 39 U.S.C. § 1207, which specifies use of a "factfinding panel" and arbitration under the auspices of the FMCS.

by the Federal Mediation and Conciliation Service or by other third-party mediation, either party may request the FSIP to consider the matter; or the parties may agree to a procedure for binding arbitration (but only if the procedure is approved by the FSIP). If the parties do not reach a settlement after assistance by the FSIP, it may conduct hearings on the matter and resolve it by action which is binding on the parties during the term of the agreement.[103]

Channels for Processing Federal-Sector Grievances

The channels for processing federal-sector grievances vary, depending upon the subject of the grievance and the grievant's choice of statutory options. Channels and options are shown in skeletal form in the chart on page 54. Relevant statutory sections are cited to indicate the statutory basis and as a source of greater detail. In the latter regard, it is stressed that the chart does not show time periods within which action is to be taken or decision rendered.

When using the chart it is imperative that the explanatory notes (*a* through *i*) be considered carefully. Also, use of the chart will be greatly aided by reading the related topics that follow.

Role and Scope of Federal-Sector Grievance Procedure and Arbitration

The basic function of the grievance procedure and arbitration in private employment is to assure compliance with the collective bargaining agreement. While this is also a key function of the grievance procedure and arbitration in the federal sector, there they have dual basic roles. The second and also very important function of the grievance procedure and arbitration in the federal sector is to review or police compliance with controlling laws, rules, and regulations by federal agency employers and employees alike.[104]

The dual role of the grievance procedure and arbitration probably was a principal factor in the congressional decision (1) to specify that each collective agreement in the federal sector "shall" provide a grievance procedure with arbitration, (2) to specify that all grievances

---

[103]A brief but informative explanation of FSIP's authority and practices is provided by Haughton, "Arbitration in the Federal Sector," 38 Arb. J. No. 4, p. 55 at 55 (1983), where in addition to other points of interest it is stated that the "statute gives rather awesome authority to the Panel"; that it "is an unfair labor practice for an agency or a labor organization to fail or refuse to cooperate in impasse procedures and impasse decisions, as required by the statute"; that "the Panel has tended to use the 'arsenal of weapons' approach"; that "med-arb has become increasingly popular"; and that "final and binding arbitration per se has still been used sparingly in federal negotiations." For a more detailed indication of FSIP operations, see Prasow, "Significant Developments in Public Employment Disputes Settlement During 1980," Proceedings of the 34th Annual Meeting of NAA, 317, 331–335 (BNA Books, 1982). For an interesting discussion regarding use of med-arb in the federal sector, see Allred, "Med-Arb and the Resolution of the SSA-AFGE Bargaining Impasse: A Case Study," 39 Arb. J. No. 2, p. 46 (1984).

[104]For cases illustrating this role of the grievance procedure and arbitration in the federal sector, see Arbitrator Goodman in 72 LA 57, 61-62; Leventhal in 72 LA 44, 45–47; Tsukiyama in 71 LA 1138, 1142, 1147; Jackson in 71 LA 463, 465; Gottlieb in 70 LA 1291, 1295; Griffin in 70 LA 360, 365; Whitman in 69 LA 1097, 1098; Dunn in 68 LA 211, 213.

"shall" be subject to the grievance and arbitration procedures except those specifically excluded by the collective agreement or statute, and (3) to define the term "grievance" very broadly.

Arbitral disposition of federal-sector grievances will often be governed or materially affected by laws, rules, and regulations apart from the collective agreement; another highly significant factor is that important areas of unilateral management control in the federal sector exist by statute. For some matters in the federal sector, the collective agreement and custom cannot be made the controlling "law of the plant."

Turning now to the detailed language of the statutes, we note first that it is required by statute that each collective bargaining agreement in the federal sector "shall provide procedures for the settlement of grievances, including questions of arbitrability."[105] The statute also requires that each agreement "shall * * * provide that any grievance not satisfactorily settled under the negotiated grievance procedure shall be subject to binding arbitration which may be invoked by either" the union or the federal agency employer.

The same statute provides, with only two exceptions, that the contractual grievance procedure *and* arbitration (since the grievance procedure must provide for arbitration) "shall be the exclusive procedures for resolving grievances which fall within its coverage."[106] The two exceptions involve certain subjects or issues for which employees are given the option of using either (but not both) the contractual grievance and arbitration procedures or certain purely statutory procedures. These issues and options are included in the chart below as Categories II and III (see also Category IV).[107]

The rule concerning "coverage" of the contractual grievance procedure is simple. All grievances are automatically covered by the grievance procedure and can go to arbitration unless excluded by

[105]5 U.S.C. § 7121. The Postal Service statute states that the collective agreement "may" provide grievance and arbitration procedures. 39 U.S.C. § 1206(b).

[106]If the union decides not to arbitrate and the issue is one which can only be taken to the contractual grievance and arbitration procedures (see Category I in the chart below), the employee may be left with no remedy unless some "duty of fair representation" issue exists. In the latter regard, the "duty of fair representation" applies in the federal sector as it does in private employment. See NTEU v. FLRA, 114 LRRM 3440, 3443 (D.C. Cir. 1983). For some issues (Category I) an employee not in the bargaining unit may have a statutory MSPB remedy not available to a unit employee. The statute recognizes the right of individual-employee grievance adjustment with representation of the individual's own choosing and with "grievance or appellate rights established by law, rule, or regulation; except in the case of grievance or appeal procedures negotiated" in the collective agreement. 5 U.S.C. § 7114(a)(5). Even if the collective agreement itself authorizes individual-employee use of the grievance procedure, the authorization may not be broad enough to include all grievances or to include the right to arbitration. For example, see Elmendorf A.F.B., 71 LA 463, 465–466 (Jackson, 1978).

[107]Actually there is a third exception to the "exclusive" status of the grievance and arbitration procedures. Another section of the Act provides that, except for certain stated matters, "issues which can be raised under a grievance procedure may, in the discretion of the aggrieved party, be raised under the grievance procedure or as an unfair labor practice under this section [7116], but not under both procedures." 5 U.S.C. § 7116(d). This provision was applied in Department of Defense Dependents Schools, 78 LA 815, 818–819 (Gilson, 1982), where issuance of an unfair labor practice decision by the FLRA precluded consideration of the merits of a grievance which had been submitted to the arbitrator. Also regarding this provision, see Arbitrator Van Wart in 74 LA 468, 474.

Channels for Processing Federal-Sector Grievances*

Grievance Subject	Processing Channels	
Category I — All subjects (issues) except those included below in Categories II, III, and IV or those the parties have excluded from the grievance procedure or which are expressly excluded by 5 U.S.C. § 7121.[a] *Statutes:* 5 U.S.C. §§ 7121, 7122, 7123.	Grievance Procedure ⟶ Arbitration ⟶ FLRA[b] (FLRA decision is final except that the U.S. Court of Appeals review of the FLRA final orders is available if an unfair labor practice issue is involved.)	
Category II — Reduction in grade or removal for unacceptable performance. Removal, suspension for more than 14 days, reduction in grade or pay, furlough of 30 days or less. *Statutes:* 5 U.S.C. §§ 4303, 7121, 7122, 7512, 7701, 7703 (court review standards stated here); 28 U.S.C. § 1295(a)(9).	Grievance Procedure ⟶ Arbitration[c] ⟶ U.S. Court of Appeals for the Federal Circuit[c] *Or,* at the employee's option (commencing one channel bars the other) MSPB ⟶ U.S. Court of Appeals for the Federal Circuit[c]	
Category III — Discrimination (race, color, religion, sex, national origin, age, sex/equal pay, handicapped condition, to the extent that any such discrimination is prohibited by federal statute)[d] *Statutes:* 5 U.S.C. §§ 2302, 7121; 42 U.S.C. §§ 2000e-5, 2000e-16[e]; Reorganization Plan No. 1 of 1978.	Grievance Procedure ⟶ Arbitration ⟶ FLRA ⟶ EEOC ⟶ U.S. District Court[e] *Or,* at the employee's option (commencing one channel bars the other, but the employee can reach the EEOC by either) Complaint to the employee's Agency ⟶ EEOC ⟶ U.S. District Court (employee has option to go directly to District Court from employee's Agency)[e]	
Category IV — Mixture of a discrimination issue and other issue.[f] *Statutes:* 5 U.S.C. §§ 7121, 7702, 7703(b)(2).	Grievance Procedure ⟶ Arbitration ⟶ FLRA[g] ⟶ MSPB[h] ⟶ U.S. District Court[i] *Or,* at the employee's option (by either channel employee can reach the MSPB and can petition the EEOC) Complaint to employee's Agency ⟶ MSPB[h] ⟶ U.S. District Court[i] (employee also has option to omit appeal to the MSPB and go directly to U.S. District Court[i])	

*See explanation of grievance-processing channels, p. 52.

Channels for Processing Federal-Sector Grievances
Chart Abbreviations

MSPB: Merit Systems Protection Board
FLRA: Federal Labor Relations Authority
EEOC: Equal Employment Opportunity Commission

Notes

[a]If the issue is excluded from the grievance procedure or if the employee is outside the bargaining unit, then any statutory remedy (such as consideration by the MSPB) would be used.

[b]What FLRA ultimately does in its review may be at least indirectly affected by the role and actions of the Comptroller General. See subtopics on Comptroller General in text.

[c]For Category II issues the arbitrator is governed by the same criteria and standards that would govern the MSPB. See 5 U.S.C. §§ 7121(e)(2), 7701(c)(1)&(2). Under 28 U.S.C. § 1295(a)(9), the U.S. Court of Appeals for the Federal Circuit, which was established in 1982 with jurisdiction limited by subject matter but not by geography, has "exclusive" jurisdiction to review MSPB decisions. By 5 U.S.C. § 7121(f), arbitration decisions in Category II cases are subject to review "in the same manner and under the same conditions as if the matter had been decided by" the MSPB; thus, the new court also has exclusive jurisdiction to review these arbitration decisions.

[d]Section 2302 also prohibits marital status or political affiliation discrimination to the extent prohibited by any law, rule, or regulation; the remedy here would be the grievance procedure or the MSPB. See § 7121(d).

[e]The U.S. District Court action specified by these sections is an original action and thus is a less restricted form of judicial proceeding than that indicated above for Category II grievances, for which the statute specifies limited grounds on which the court may disturb results reached below. Also, the U.S. District Court proceedings indicated below for Category IV grievances are similarly less restricted than the judicial review on limited grounds which applies to Category II grievances.

[f]The channels indicated for this category apply where employee's agency takes action appealable to the MSPB and the employee alleges discrimination as a basis for the agency's action. A Category III issue combined with a Category II issue would qualify, as would a Category III issue combined with any other issue appealable to the MSPB—MSPB has jurisdiction over many agency actions affecting employees in addition to those in Category II. However, if the contractual grievance procedure covers a matter not involving a Category II subject and/or discrimination, the channel indicated under Category I is the only one available.

[g]If the arbitration award involves one of the subjects included under Category II, it would not be appealable to the FLRA but would go from arbitration directly to the MSPB.

[h]Instead of going directly to court from the MSPB the employee has the option of petitioning the EEOC to consider the MSPB decision. If such request is denied, employee proceeds to U.S. District Court.[i] If the request is granted but the EEOC concurs with the MSPB, the employee then goes to U.S. District Court.[i] If the EEOC disagrees with the MSPB, the matter is returned to the MSPB; and (depending upon whether the MSPB adopts the EEOC decision) from there it goes either directly to U.S. District Court[i] or to a Special Panel and then to U.S. District Court.[i]

[i]In the U.S. District Court in these "mixed" cases the employee has the right to trial de novo. 5 U.S.C. §§ 7702(e)(3), 7703(c). Moreover, if a grievance is taken to the employee's agency and no decision issues within the statutory time limit, the employee may either proceed to the MSPB or commence an original action in U.S. District Court; if a grievance is taken to the MSPB or to the EEOC and no decision issues within the statutory time limit, the employee may commence an original action in U.S. District Court. 5 U.S.C. §§ 7702(e)(1)&(2).

agreement of the parties or unless specifically excluded by statute.[108] Regarding exclusions, the statute provides in substance that:[109]

1. Any collective bargaining agreement may exclude any matter from the application of the agreement's grievance procedure.
2. Grievances concerning the following subjects or issues are specifically excluded from the grievance procedure and arbitration: (1) political activities; (2) retirement, life insurance, or health insurance; (3) suspension or removal for national security; (4) examination, certification, or appointment; (5) classification of any position if the classification does not result in the reduction in grade or pay of an employee.

What can qualify as a "grievance" in federal employment? The term "grievance" is defined very broadly as follows:[110]

" 'grievance' means any complaint—
"(A) by any employee concerning any matter relating to the employment of the employee;
"(B) by any labor organization concerning any matter relating to the employment of any employee; or
"(C) by any employee, labor organization, or agency concerning—
"(i) the effect or interpretation, or a claim of breach, of a collective bargaining agreement; or
"(ii) any claimed violation, misinterpretation, or misapplication of any law, rule, or regulation affecting conditions of employment."

Thus, to reiterate, it is clear (1) that every collective agreement in the federal sector must provide a grievance procedure and arbitration, (2) that the door to the grievance procedure and arbitration is open wide to all grievances except those specifically excluded by the agreement or statute, and (3) that the term "grievance" is defined broadly with the result that an extremely wide variety of complaints will

---

[108]Concerning the determination of arbitrability of an issue, the fact that the CSRA states in 5 U.S.C. § 7121 that collective agreements in the federal sector "shall provide procedures for the settlement of grievances, including questions of arbitrability" indicates that in their agreement the parties are to specify who is to determine arbitrability; presumably questions of arbitrability will be decided by the arbitrator (subject to FLRA review) if the parties do not specify otherwise. For illustrative cases in which the arbitrator, in ruling upon arbitrability, clearly indicated the existence of express authority from the parties to do so, see Arbitrator Wann in 82 LA 593, 595, 597; Imundo in 77 LA 1159, 1161, 1166; Weiss in 77 LA 725 at 725, 728. For illustrative cases in which the arbitrator ruled upon arbitrability without clearly indicating the existence of express authority to do so (but also without indicating that any party had challenged the existence of such authority), see Arbitrator Gentile in 81 LA 325, 330; Rossman in 78 LA 636, 640; Bennett in 78 LA 165, 171–172; Goldman in 77 LA 518, 521; Atleson in 77 LA 136, 139; Nolan in 75 LA 712, 715–716; Dallas in 75 LA 238, 239. However, another provision that may be relevant to the determination of arbitrability in some cases is 5 U.S.C. § 7117(c), which provides that if an agency employer "alleges that the duty to bargain in good faith does not extend to any matter," the union may appeal the allegation to the FLRA under procedures specified in that subsection. As concerns procedural arbitrability, the FLRA has held that this is for the arbitrator to determine. U.S. Environmental Protection Agency, 5 FLRA No. 36, p. 3 (1981), citing the U.S. Supreme Court's *John Wiley* private-sector decision. Concerning the resolution of federal-sector grievability and arbitrability questions under Executive Orders, see Frazier, "Labor Arbitration in the Federal Service," 45 Geo. Wash. L. Rev. 712, 750–752 (1977). Also see Social Security Admin., 72 LA 359, 361–362 (Coburn, 1979).

[109]5 U.S.C. § 7121.

[110]5 U.S.C. § 7103(a)(9).

qualify for access to the grievance procedure and arbitration. From the viewpoint of the individual employee the wide open grievance and arbitration door offers the greatest assurance of fair treatment by immediate superiors in accordance with the collective agreement and governing rules and regulations. This alone is highly significant.[111]

Scope of Federal-Sector Bargaining and Management-Rights Safeguards

Although the term "grievance" is defined broadly and although the door to the grievance procedure and arbitration may be wide indeed, strong protection exists against the narrowing of federal agency management right of action and against disregard of certain laws, rules, and regulations. Both Executive Order 11491 and the Civil Service Reform Act of 1978 contain strong management-rights safeguards. Collective bargaining is prohibited on numerous important matters in the federal sector that are mandatory subjects of bargaining in the private sector. Bargaining is merely permitted and not required on certain other important matters in the federal sector that, again, are mandatory subjects of bargaining in the private sector. Nor does the duty to bargain extend to any matter which is the subject of certain rules or regulations. The end result of these prohibitions and limitations is that, although the door to the grievance procedure and arbitration may be open wide, no grievance may properly be sustained in the grievance procedure or arbitration if the grievance stands on a contract provision dealing with a subject excluded from bargaining by statute or if it stands on a contract provision which infringes upon a statutorily safeguarded management right or if sustaining the grievance would infringe upon any of certain laws, rules, or regulations. These matters are treated in the subtopics that follow.

Management Rights—Prohibited Bargaining Items. "Except as otherwise provided" by Title VII of the Civil Service Reform Act of 1978, federal-sector employees have the right "to engage in collective

---

[111]For an illustration of the fact that arbitration can be an effective means for employees to obtain compliance by field offices or installations of a federal agency with regulations of higher level authorities, see U.S. Army Communications Command, 72 LA 44, 45–47 (Leventhal, 1979), where the agreement itself made regulations of higher level authorities controlling. Also see Arbitrator Whitman in 69 LA 1097, 1098. In some cases an employee's grievance claim has been based directly upon a benefit or right claimed under the Federal Personnel Manual or under an agency regulation. See Naval Air Rework Facility, 73 LA 201, 202–203 (Livengood, 1979), where the claim was based upon the FPM and the agreement. For an interesting variation, see Arbitrator Jaffee in 73 LA 138, 141. One arbitrator construed the submission agreement as confining him to "the four corners" of the collective bargaining agreement; and although he discussed certain leave benefits for employees under the FPM and agency regulations, he was unwilling to take them into account in reaching his decision, which was that the collective agreement had not been violated since it did not provide like benefits. Social Security Admin., 72 LA 387, 390–391 (Wahl, 1979). Cf., below, subtopics entitled "Government-Wide Rules or Regulations" and "Non-Government-Wide Rules or Regulations."

bargaining with respect to conditions of employment."[112] Bargaining on certain subjects is in effect prohibited by the management-rights section of the Act, which states that "nothing" in Title VII "shall affect the authority of any management official of any agency" (the authority thus being reserved or retained in management):

"(1) to determine the mission, budget, organization, number of employees, and internal security practices of the agency; and

"(2) in accordance with applicable laws—

"(A) to hire, assign, direct, layoff, and retain employees in the agency, or to suspend, remove, reduce in grade or pay, or take other disciplinary action against such employees;

"(B) to assign work, to make determinations with respect to contracting out, and to determine the personnel by which agency operations shall be conducted;

"(C) with respect to filling positions, to make selections for appointments from—

"(i) among properly ranked and certified candidates for promotion; or

"(ii) any other appropriate source; and

"(D) to take whatever actions may be necessary to carry out the agency mission during emergencies."[113]

The statutory words "in accordance with applicable laws" do limit management rights, and this limitation would appear to be properly enforceable by contractual grievance and arbitration procedures. Apart from this, however, the statutory reservation of management

---

[112] 5 U.S.C. § 7102. "Collective bargaining" is defined by § 7103(12) to mean "the performance of the mutual obligation of the representative of an agency and the exclusive representative of employees in an appropriate unit in the agency to meet at reasonable times and to consult and bargain in a good-faith effort to reach agreement with respect to the conditions of employment affecting such employees and to execute, if requested by either party, a written document incorporating any collective bargaining agreement reached, but the obligation referred to in this paragraph does not compel either party to agree to a proposal or to make a concession."

[113] 5 U.S.C. § 7106(a). For a case illustrating arbitral recognition of the overriding force of federal-sector management rights and the fact that they cannot be bargained away, see Federal Aviation Admin., 68 LA 375, 378–379 (1977), where Arbitrator Richard A. Moore stated that while management rights may be bargained away in the private sector, the federal sector "is a different breed of cat." In considering the Executive Order 11491 counterpart to 5 U.S.C. § 7106(a), he said: "We believe this effectively limits the authority of the Agency to bargain away the matters listed in the section." Executive Order 11491 required collective agreements to contain clauses stating the same management rights stated in the Order itself, as had been done by Article 42 of the agreement before Arbitrator Moore. In this regard, he said: "The Agency's power to bargain is limited by the [Executive Order]. It has no authority to bargain away the matters retained in Article 42, Section 2. It follows that other parts of the Agreement should not be interpreted to violate that Article." Also see U.S. Railroad Retirement Bd., 71 LA 498, 501, 503 (Sembower, 1978), quoting the FLRC's statement that "implicit and co-extensive with management's conceded authority to decide to take an action under [the Executive Order] is the authority to decide *not* to take such action or to change its decision, once made, whether or not to take such action." Cf., Arbitrator Daly in 72 LA 34, 37, 42–44; Whyte in 70 LA 523, 525–526. It is to be noted that some of the subjects now excluded from bargaining were permissible subjects of bargaining under E.O. 11491. These are mission, budget, organization, number of employees, and internal security practices. On the other hand, another change that may deserve special note is that whereas § 12(b)(5) of E.O. 11491 reserves to management the right to determine the "methods" and "means" by which operations are to be conducted, the "methods" and "means" language does not appear in § 7106(a) but appears rather in § 7106(b) relating to management rights on which bargaining *is* permitted at the election of the federal agency employer (see next subtopic). For an illustration of the fact that these words may be an important basis for management action, see National Park Serv., 72 LA 314, 322 (Pritzker, 1979). Another change to be noted is that whereas § 12(b)(4) of E.O. 11491 reserves to management the right "to maintain the efficiency of * * * operations," this has become the 5 U.S.C. § 7101(b) directive that the provisions of the Civil Service Reform Act Title VII, Labor-Management Relations, "should be interpreted in a manner consistent with the requirement of an effective and efficient Government."

rights necessarily reduces the scope of grievance-procedure or arbitral authority to disturb actions taken by agency management officials.

It should be noted that in sharp contrast to the general statutory policy of safeguarding management rights in the federal sector, the Postal Reorganization Act's grant of certain specified rights to the Postal Service (similar to the statutory management rights quoted above for federal-sector agencies) is accompanied by significant words of limitation—the Postal Service has the rights *"consistent with * * * applicable laws, regulations, and collective-bargaining agreements."*[114]

Management Rights—Permitted Bargaining Items. The management-rights section's limitation on bargaining subject matter is qualified, however, by a subsection stating that nothing in the section shall "preclude" any agency and union from negotiating:

> "(1) at the election of the agency, on the numbers, types, and grades of employees or positions assigned to any organizational subdivision, work project, or tour of duty, or on the technology, methods, and means of performing work;
>
> "(2) procedures which management officials of the agency will observe in exercising any authority under this section; or
>
> "(3) appropriate arrangements for employees adversely affected by the exercise of any authority under this section by such management officials."[115]

The phrase "at the election of the agency" unequivocally applies to matters listed in paragraph 1 of the subsection.[116] On the other hand, as concerns paragraphs 2 and 3, agency management may or may not be required to bargain on *procedures* to be observed by management in exercising its rights or on the *impact* upon employees produced by the exercise of those rights.[117] Furthermore, courts have upheld the

---

[114]39 U.S.C. § 1001(e), emphasis added. For another indication of the particularly strong status of Postal Service collective agreements, see 39 U.S.C. § 1005(a)(1)(A). For a convincing example of the fact that the Postal Service management rights must be exercised in a manner consistent with the collective agreement, and illustrating the broad possibility that the Postal Service may bargain away management rights, see U.S. Postal Serv., 71 LA 1188, 1195–1197 (Garrett, 1978), where the national collective agreement did effectively impose significant restrictions on management rights.

[115]5 U.S.C. § 7106(b).

[116]Management's election not to bargain on a paragraph 1 item leaves the matter for managerial decision unless some limitation apart from the statute is found applicable. See discussion in Immigration and Naturalization Serv., 77 LA 638, 642–643 (Weckstein, 1981).

[117]As the FLRA has held in many other cases, it held in Army-Air Force Exch. Serv., Dix-McGuire Exch., 2 FLRA No. 16, pp. 2–4 (1979), that management is required to bargain on proposals concerning procedures unless their adoption would prevent management from "acting at all"; management may not refuse to bargain merely because adoption of the proposals might occasion "unreasonable delay" in the exercise of management rights protected by the Act. The "acting at all" test for determining whether bargaining is mandatory was also applied to "impact" proposals in U.S. Customs Serv., 2 FLRA No. 30, pp. 6–7 (1979), where it was held that management did not have a duty to bargain on one portion of an "impact" proposal, but did have a duty to bargain on another portion. Agency management sometimes may feel forced to walk a legality tightrope between § 7106(a) and §§ 7106(b)(2)&(3). Note in this regard the statement by Robinson, Negotiability in the Federal Sector, 189 (N.Y. Sch. Indus. Rel., 1981), that:

"[T]here exists in section 7106(a) a set of broad, ill-defined rights reserved to agency management on which substantive bargaining *is illegal*; however, impact and implementation bargaining on the exercise of these reserved rights *is mandatory*. The difficulty emerges when impact and implementation proposals move into the gray area where they become

FLRA's use of two different standards, the "acting at all" standard and the "direct interference" standard, in determining whether there is a duty to bargain on "procedures" proposals; the courts reasoned that the different standards were used for proposals that were "different in kind."[118] Of the two standards, the "direct interference" standard is of course the more favorable from the viewpoint of management. Although the FLRA has been upheld in using the "direct interference"

---

virtually indistinguishable from the exercise of the reserved management right." (Emphasis added.)

The burden of uncertainty that may exist should be eased significantly, however, upon considering all of the integrated features of regulations which the FLRA has adopted for expedited rulings on negotiability issues. See Expedited Review of Negotiability Issues, 5 C.F.R. Part 2424, §§ 2424.1–2424.11.

[118]In Air Force Logistics Command, Wright-Patterson A.F.B., 2 FLRA No. 77 (1980), a number of the union's proposals were stated in procedural language. As to several of these proposals the FLRA held (at pp. 9–11, 28) that because they would "directly interfere" with a basic management right under § 7106(a), they were "excluded from the duty to bargain"; but the FLRA held that one of this group did not "directly interfere" and thus was subject to mandatory bargaining. As to yet another proposal which was stated in procedural language, the FLRA (at pp. 21–22) quoted its *Dix-McGuire* decision and applied the "acting at all" test. The FLRA did not explain in *Wright-Patterson* why the different standards were used. An explanation did emerge when the *Wright-Patterson* and *Dix-McGuire* cases (which both involved the same international union) were consolidated for court review in Department of Defense v. FLRA, 659 F.2d 1140, 107 LRRM 2901, 2908–2910, 2914 (D.C. Cir., 1981), cert. denied, 102 S.Ct. 1443 (1982), where the Court of Appeals explained that as to each of the eight proposals being reviewed, "the management parties purport to identify some infringement of a management right protected under § 7106(a)," but that "Because its proposals are cast in procedural terms, the union finds them compulsory subjects of bargaining under the statute." The Court noted the FLRA's use of two different standards in determining whether bargaining was required:

  1. As to some of the proposals the FLRA "held that proposals structured in procedural language would be negotiable unless the effect of their adoption would be to stop management from 'acting at all,'" the FLRA rejecting the argument "that a proposal ceased to be procedural within the intent of the law if it was of such a character as to 'unreasonably delay' management action."

  2. As to other of the proposals the FLRA held that bargaining was not required despite their being expressed in procedural terms, since their adoption would "directly interfere" with reserved management rights to make decisions of substance.

Recognizing that "the distinction between procedure and substance is not always crisp," and recognizing "the inherent ambiguities of the distinction between procedure and substance, and the attendant difficulty in its application," the Court stated that it "is the task of the FLRA * * * to develop workable standards consistent with the Act's underlying policies and intent." Continuing, the Court stated:

  "In this regard, we think it appropriate to note what we perceive as a difference in kind among the cases calling for application of the statutory distinction between negotiable procedures and reserved substantive rights. There are, on the one hand, cases in which proposals cast in procedural language impinge on substantive management decisions by specifying the criteria pursuant to which decisions must be made. There are, on the other, more nearly 'pure' procedures, which have less direct substantive repercussions—for example, procedures for use in determining which employees possess characteristics identified by management as appropriate criteria for choice." 107 LRRM at 2909–2910.

Although agreeing that the "direct interference" standard is "a different test of negotiability from the 'acting at all' standard," the Court stated:

  "We find no necessary incompatibility between the two approaches. Proposals [in *Wright-Patterson*] to establish seniority as a basis for personnel assignments stand close to the uncertain border between procedure and substance. Such proposals are therefore different in kind from that involved in Dix-McGuire—a proposal that did not specify the criteria on which disciplinary action should be based, but only designated procedures for determining whether management criteria had in fact been satisfied in a particular instance. In view of the difference between the kinds of proposals under review, we cannot agree that an identical standard must be applied to both." 107 LRRM at 2914.

The Court affirmed the FLRA "in each of its holdings." In V.A. Medical Center v. FLRA, 110 LRRM 2465, 2469 (CA 11, 1982), the court stated that "we concur with the Court in Department of Defense * * * that the FLRA may distinguish between procedures that directly interfere with management rights—i.e., those procedures that specify the criteria pursuant to which management must exercise its rights—and procedures that indirectly affect management by outlining the *process* that management must follow when it exercises its rights pursuant to its own criteria."

standard in appropriate cases involving "procedures" proposals, its right to use this standard in determining whether bargaining is mandatory on "impact" proposals has been denied.[119]

If federal agency management does bargain on any elective subject, and if such bargaining does add provisions to the collective agreement, the interpretation and application of those provisions would properly fall within the scope of the contractual grievance and arbitration procedures (unless expressly excluded).[120] However, as concerns those rights on which bargaining is prohibited, "the inclusion of a clause that infringes on a 'retained management right' renders the clause null and void."[121]

Government-Wide Rules or Regulations. Under the Civil Service Reform Act of 1978 the duty to bargain does not extend to any matter which is the subject of any "Government-wide rule or regulation."[122] A saving or "grandfather" clause apparently exists under another section which makes it "an unfair labor practice for an agency * * * to enforce any rule or regulation * * * which is in conflict with any applicable collective bargaining agreement if the agreement was in effect before the date the rule or regulation was prescribed." The one stated exception relates only to discrimination; thus the basic saving clause appears equally applicable to Government-wide and non-Government-wide rules and regulations.[123]

The phrase "Government-wide rule or regulation" refers basically to rules and regulations contained in the *Federal Personnel Manual* (FPM). The source and role of the *Federal Personnel Manual* has been explained as follows:

> "The laws governing the personnel policies of federal employees are pervasive. Title 5 of the United States Code covers such matters as pay, fringe benefits, classifications, performance ratings, and incentive awards. In addition, Congress has authorized the [Civil Service] Commission to promulgate regulations implementing most of the legislation on federal personnel policies. Pursuant to statute, the President has authority to prescribe regulations for the conduct of employees in the

---

[119]U.S. Air Force v. FLRA, 115 LRRM 3490, 3494–3495 (CA 11, 1984), indicating that as concerns "impact" proposals, the "FLRA should apply the 'acting at all' standard in subsection (b)(3) cases * * *"; AFGE Local 2782 v. FLRA, 112 LRRM 3112, 3114–3116 (D.C. Cir., 1983).

[120]See Veterans Admin. Hosp., 72 LA 66, 69 (Carson, 1978).

[121]Tobias, "The Scope of Bargaining in the Federal Sector: Collective Bargaining or Collective Consultation," 44 Geo. Wash. L. Rev. 554, 557 (1976), citing FLRC decisions. In Professional Air Traffic Controllers Org., 5 FLRA No. 101, p. 5 (1981), the FLRA stated that "no arbitration award under a negotiated grievance procedure may interpret *or enforce* a provision of a collective bargaining agreement so as to deny an agency the authority to exercise its rights under section 7106 of the Statute." (emphasis added)

[122]5 U.S.C. § 7117(a)(1). Also relevant is § 7103(a)(14). Under the Act collective agreements are subject to approval by the agency head within 30 days after execution of the agreement in order to review compliance with "applicable law, rule, or regulation." 5 U.S.C. § 7114(c)(1)&(2). For an explanation that matters specifically provided for by federal statute are excluded from bargaining under the Civil Service Reform Act in the absence of a statutory exemption permitting bargaining on the particular matter, see AFGE v. FLRA, 107 LRRM 2594, 2595 (D.C. Cir., 1981). Also see discussion by Arbitrator Edmund W. Schedler, Jr., in U.S. Army III Corp., 80 LA 148, 155 (1982).

[123]5 U.S.C. § 7116(a)(7). For application of a related saving provision under Executive Orders, see Southwest Power Admin., 72 LA 31, 32, 34 (Schedler, 1978).

executive branch. These laws and regulations have been compiled in the FPM, which Executive Order 11,491 excludes from the scope of collective bargaining."[124]

Thus we have seen that under both the Civil Service Reform Act of 1978 and Executive Order 11491 the subject matter contained in the FPM is excluded from mandatory bargaining. Moreover, where as a result of voluntary bargaining or otherwise the FPM and a collective agreement provision conflict, the FPM controls.[125]

Consultation Rights. Although the duty to bargain does not apply to any matter which is the subject of any "Government-wide rule or regulation," the statute does provide, apparently in reference to agencies which issue Government-wide rules and regulations, that the union "shall be granted consultation rights by any agency with respect to any Government-wide rule or regulation issued by the agency affecting any substantive change in any condition of employment."[126] A union's statutory consultation rights include the right to receive advance notice of proposed changes in conditions of employment, opportunity to present views and recommendations, agency obligation to consider such views and recommendations before taking final action and to give the union a written statement of the reasons for taking the final action.[127] Executive Order 11491 also specified consultation rather than bargaining rights for some matters. One critic concluded that it excessively limited the issues subject to bargaining, leaving "only the right of consultation concerning many of the vital

---

[124]Tobias, "The Scope of Bargaining in the Federal Sector: Collective Bargaining or Collective Consultation," 44 Geo. Wash. L. Rev. 554, 555–556 (1976). The former Civil Service Commission's function of maintaining and updating the FPM (which comprises ten or more volumes) is now shared by the OPM, the MSPB, and the FLRA, each in its respective area of operations. The sheer bulk of the FPM and other regulation handbooks may leave an arbitrator at least momentarily appalled. See U.S. Dept. of HUD, 69 LA 961, 961–962 (Comey, 1977).

[125]It was stressed by the FLRC under Executive Order 11491 that "Arbitrators should consider appropriate regulations, such as those in the Federal Personnel Manual, and ensure that their awards are consistent with them." Frazier, "Labor Arbitration in the Federal Service," 45 Geo. Wash. L. Rev. 712, 733 (1977). For an illustration of the overriding authority of the FPM as a limitation upon federal agency collective bargaining, and of an arbitrator's alertness to the fact that disregard of that authority renders the award vulnerable "as an abuse of the Arbitrator's [own] authority," see General Servs. Admin., 71 LA 860, 864 (Leeper, 1978). For other cases illustrating the close attention given by arbitrators to Government-wide rules and regulations, often those in the FPM, see Arbitrator Alsher in 80 LA 1342, 1343, 1346; Wann in 80 LA 403, 411; Schedler in 80 LA 148, 155; Jones in 79 LA 231, 236; Mount in 78 LA 630, 631; Shister in 74 LA 977, 980; Peck in 73 LA 1110, 1113–1114. The obligation to consider regulations may require the arbitrator to interpret and determine the scope of the regulations. See, for instance, Arbitrator Garman in 74 LA 1117, 1120–1121; Peck in 73 LA 1110, 1113–1114; Harkless in 71 LA 1018, 1019–1020. The FPM and other regulations cited by a federal agency employer did not control where they were construed not to be directly applicable to the narrow issue before the arbitrator; literal language of the agreement covered the issue and the arbitrator stated that "the parties are obligated to live with its literal meaning to the extent it is not inconsistent with existing laws or regulations." Patent and Trademark Office, 71 LA 39, 41–42 (Gentry, 1978). In another case the FPM provisions relied upon by the employer were found to be "nondispositive" of the issue before the arbitrator, whereas past practice of the parties was clear and controlling. Norfolk Naval Shipyard, 72 LA 364, 365–366 (Moran, 1979).

[126]5 U.S.C. § 7117(d)(1). Another section dealing with consultation rights is § 7113.

[127]5 U.S.C. § 7117(d)(2)&(3). Regarding the distinction between the duty to consult and the duty to negotiate under the Act, see Robinson, Negotiability in the Federal Sector, 38–39 (N.Y. Sch. Indus. Rel., 1981).

conditions of employment."[128] However, a Civil Service Commission official stressed that it should not be concluded from the limitations on the scope of federal-sector bargaining that the content of negotiated agreements had been meaningless, and he offered a sizeable list of important matters that had been negotiated.[129]

   Non-Government-Wide Rules or Regulations.[130] No general "yes" or "no" answer is available for the question of whether the duty to bargain under the Civil Service Reform Act of 1978 extends to matters which are the subject of any non-Government-wide rule or regulation or for the related question of whether a non-Government-wide rule or regulation will control over a conflicting collective agreement provision. Rather, the answer to these questions appears to depend upon (1) the agency level at which the rule or regulation is issued, (2) the level and scope of the bargaining unit which has produced the collective agreement provision, and (3) in certain situations, an FLRA determination that "no compelling need" exists for the rule or regulation.

   The substance of two directly relevant statutory subsections construed together is that the duty to bargain extends to matters which are the subject of any rule or regulation "issued by any agency or issued by any primary national subdivision of such agency" if, but "only if," the FLRA has determined that "no compelling need (as determined under regulations prescribed by the Authority) exists for the rule or regulation."[131] However, the statute states an exception. The "no compelling need" finding must be made as a condition prece-

---

   [128]Tobias, "The Scope of Bargaining in the Federal Sector: Collective Bargaining or Collective Consultation," 44 Geo. Wash. L. Rev. 554, 555 (1976). For an illlustration of the fact that (contractual) consultation rights may be inadequate from the viewpoint of employees, see Social Security Admin., 70 LA 699, 700–701 (Atleson, 1978), where the agreement drew a distinction between the obligation to "confer" and the obligation to "consult." Also see Arbitrator Shearer in 74 LA 687, 690–691.
   [129]Aronin, "Collective Bargaining in the Federal Service: A Balanced Approach," 44 Geo. Wash. L. Rev. 576, 602 (1976), stating that: "Within the limitations [on the scope of bargaining], parties have negotiated merit promotion procedures, evaluation procedures, evaluation criteria to be used in promotions, and union participation on promotion panels. They have negotiated on environmental pay differentials, overtime distribution, and procedures relating to assignments. Negotiated agreements contain provisions relating to all matters of health and safety, to equal employment opportunity, and to leave administration. Working rules, codes of discipline, and performance standards have been established. These agreements provide for employee facilities, parking spaces, reimbursement for travel, and, most important, comprehensive grievance systems with binding arbitration."
   [130]As used in this material, the term "non-Government-wide" refers to Government rules and regulations which are not Government-wide in application.
   [131]5 U.S.C. § 7117(a)(2)&(3). Also relevant is § 7103(a)(14). Section 7117(b) specifies detailed procedures, to be expedited to the extent practicable, for obtaining an FLRA determination regarding compelling need. Executive Order 11491 also made "compelling need" a controlling factor. One authority explained that under criteria adopted by the FLRC, "regulations may bar negotiations below the level of issuance only if issued at the agency headquarters level or at the level of a primary national subdivision and if they meet the criteria issued by the Council." Aronin, "Collective Bargaining in the Federal Service: A Balanced Approach," 44 Geo. Wash. L. Rev. 576, 601 (1976), where it is also stated that: "These criteria require that before any published personnel policy can bar negotiations below the level of issuance, the policy must be essential to the agency's mission or management, required for the protection of merit principles, mandated by a nondiscretionary policy issued outside the agency, or designed to achieve uniformity in personnel policies over a substantial segment of the agency."

dent to any duty to bargain, "unless an exclusive representative represents an appropriate unit including not less than a majority of the employees in the issuing agency or primary national subdivision, as the case may be, to whom the rule or regulation is applicable."[132]

The statute does not state any limitation upon the duty to bargain on matters which are the subject of any rule or regulation issued below the level of primary national subdivision of an agency. It thus appears clear that rules and regulations issued at such lower levels of an agency have a status at the opposite extreme from that of Government-wide rules or regulations. That is, there is a duty to bargain on matters (assuming they are otherwise proper subjects for bargaining) which are the subject only of a rule or regulation issued below the level of primary national subdivision of an agency; and a collective agreement provision would control over such lower level rules or regulations where they conflict.

Between the two extremes stand those rules and regulations "issued by any agency [no doubt this means issued at the top level or headquarters of the agency] or issued by any primary national subdivision of such agency." For ready reference, these may be termed "intermediate" rules and regulations as distinguished from "Government-wide" rules and regulations or from "lower level" rules and regulations issued below the level of primary national subdivision of an agency.

As noted above, the duty to bargain extends to matters which are the subject of any "intermediate" rule or regulation only if the FLRA has determined that "no compelling need" exists for the rule or regulation, or if, under the statutory exception, the union "represents an appropriate unit including not less than a majority of the employees in the issuing agency or primary national subdivision, as the case may be, to whom the rule or regulation is applicable." It appears that the following results are produced by this statutory scheme:

1. A rule or regulation issued at the top level or headquarters of an agency, or issued by any primary national subdivision of the agency, will control over any conflicting collective agreement negotiated below the primary national subdivision level unless the FLRA has determined that "no compelling need" exists for the rule or regulation; if the FLRA has made such determination, the collective agreement will control.[133]

2. A rule or regulation issued at the top level or headquarters of an agency, or issued by any primary national subdivision of the agency, will not control over any conflicting collective agree-

---

[132]5 U.S.C. § 7117(a)(3). Also relevant is § 7103(a)(14).

[133]On the basis of a 1980 statistical summary it appears likely that the great bulk of federal-sector bargaining units exist at a level below the primary national subdivision level. The statistics reveal that within 59 national agencies in the federal sector which have at least 2,600 employees each, there were 1,848 collective agreements for 2,159 "Recognitions Covered." Union Recognition in the Federal Government, 20–21 (Office of Personnel Management, OLMR–81–9). The statistics identify 90 unions holding federal-sector representation rights (49 are independent unions and the others are AFL unions). Id. at 22–23.

ment if the agreement was negotiated by a union which "represents an appropriate unit including not less than a majority of the employees in the issuing agency or primary national subdivision, as the case may be, to whom the rule or regulation is applicable."

The policy underlying this statutory scheme is both obvious and reasonable. At the upper levels of the agency, where top management makes the bargaining judgments with a union speaking for at least a large segment of the agency's employees, the union has a statutory right to bargain (assuming the matter is otherwise a proper subject for bargaining) without regard to the agency's rules and regulations; and those rules and regulations will not control over the collective agreement if they conflict. On the other hand, stability of agency operations and of management-employee relations as well requires that rules and regulations issued at upper levels for broad application and for which "compelling need" exists must control over conflicting collective agreements negotiated by the agency's lower level bargaining units.[134] Meanwhile, at opposite extremes, justification is equally strong (1) for not permitting collective agreements to prevail against a rule or regulation issued for "Government-wide" application, but (2) for permitting collective agreements to prevail against a rule or regulation issued at lower levels of an agency, applying only at the limited "local" level and concerning matters appropriate for local determination.

Review of Arbitration Awards

All arbitration awards in the federal sector are subject to some type of review. The "Processing Channels" chart provided above indicates categories of issues and the processing channels for each category. If a grievance does not involve any adverse-action issue listed under Category II, and does not involve any discrimination issue, an arbitration award resolving the grievance is subject to review only by the Federal Labor Relations Authority as indicated in the Category I segment of the chart (and the FLRA decision is final unless an unfair labor practice issue is involved). Category I grievances also have been called "pure grievances."[135] No doubt a high percentage of all federal-sector grievances will fall into Category I. Thus for many arbitration awards the only possibility for review will be by the FLRA (what the FLRA ultimately does in its review may be at least indirectly affected

---

[134]Similar considerations may underlie the general dominance of a master agreement over a local agreement in the federal sector. See Bureau of Prisons, 73 LA 435 (Fitch, 1979), dealing with the relationship between a master agreement negotiated at the national level and agreements negotiated at the local level.

[135]Devine v. White, 112 LRRM 2374, 2392 (D.C. Cir., 1983), defining a "pure grievance" as one "that does not involve a reduction in grade or removal for unacceptable performance; a removal, suspension for more than 14 days, reduction in grade or pay, or furlough of 30 days or less; or a complaint of discrimination."

by the related role and actions of the Comptroller General[136]). In addition, the FLRA has an intermediate review role for awards involving discrimination issues, provided no Category II issue is also involved.

Under the Civil Service Reform Act of 1978 either party may file exceptions to any arbitration award with the FLRA (unless the award involves any issue listed under Category II of the chart above). After so providing, the statute continues:[137]

> "If upon review the Authority finds that the award is deficient—
>   (1) because it is contrary to any law, rule, or regulation; or
>   (2) on other grounds similar to those applied by Federal courts in private sector labor-management relations;
> the Authority may take such action and make such recommendations concerning the award as it considers necessary, consistent with applicable laws, rules, or regulations.
> "(b) If no exception to an arbitrator's award is filed under subsection (a) of this section during the 30-day period beginning on the date of such award, the award shall be final and binding. An agency shall take the actions required by an arbitrator's final award. The award may include the payment of backpay (as provided in section 5596 of this title)." [By 1984 amendment to this subsection the 30-day period for filing exceptions to an award begins "on the date the award is served on the party," rather than "on the date of such award."]

The FLRA regulations are no more specific than is the statute regarding grounds for review of awards, the regulations stating that the FLRA will review an award to determine if it is deficient because "it is contrary to any law, rule or regulation," or on "other grounds similar to those applied by Federal courts in private sector labor-management relations."[138]

The foregoing statutory grounds for review are essentially a codification of the review grounds adopted by the Federal Labor Relations Council under Executive Order 11491, which did not state grounds but authorized the Council to do so. The Council adopted the following grounds for review:[139]

1. The award violates applicable law.
2. The award violates an "appropriate regulation."

---

[136]See the next subtopic entitled "Comptroller General's Role."

[137]5 U.S.C. § 7122(a). The fact that exceptions to the award can be filed may result in expanded coverage of the facts and parties' positions in the federal-sector arbitrator's written opinion. An illustration is San Antonio Air Logistics Center, 73 LA 455, 463 (LeBaron, 1979).

[138]5 C.F.R. Part 2425, § 2425.3. For some indication of grounds utilized by federal courts in reviewing private-sector awards, see subtopic entitled "Post-*Trilogy:* Lower Court Enforcement of Agreement to Arbitrate and Review of Award," above in this Chapter.

[139]Frazier, "Labor Arbitration in the Federal Sector," 45 Geo. Wash. L. Rev. 712, 717–750 (1977), where decisions are cited to illustrate the scope and application of the grounds for review. Also see discussion by Gamser, "Back-Seat Driving Behind the Back-Seat Driver: Arbitration in the Federal Sector," Proceedings of the 31st Annual Meeting of NAA, 268, 273–276 (BNA Books, 1979), indicating 15 percent of federal-sector awards had been appealed to the FLRC (the FLRA appeal rate is indicated below in this subtopic). For a comprehensive survey of federal-sector arbitration decisions and FLRC disposition of those reviewed, see the publication of U.S. Civil Service Commission Office of Labor-Management Relations entitled Grievance Arbitration in the Federal Service (Principles, Practices and Precedents), issued in 1977.

3. The award violates Executive Order 11491.[140]

Additionally, the Council adopted the following grounds, said to be "similar to those on which courts sustain challenges to arbitration awards in the private sector":

1. The arbitrator exceeded his authority.
2. The award does not draw its essence from the collective bargaining agreement.
3. The award is incomplete, ambiguous, or contradictory, making implementation of the award impossible.
4. The award is based on a "nonfact."
5. The arbitrator was biased or partial.
6. The arbitrator refused to hear pertinent and material evidence.

Early in its history the FLRA, successor to the FLRC, had occasion to consider most of the just-noted grounds which the FLRC had recognized as being similar to private-sector grounds, and each ground considered was expressly recognized also by the FLRA as a ground on which it might find an arbitration award deficient under the statute.[141]

The Federal Labor Relations Council's executive director, Henry B. Frazier III, subsequently a member of the Federal Labor Relations Authority, believed that the "value and strength of labor dispute arbitration depend upon the finality of the arbitrator's decision" and that "courts and agencies authorized to review the decision must be reluctant to interfere with it."[142] He summed up the teaching of Council reports and decisions:

> "As in the private sector, federal sector arbitration is a creation of the parties and their collective bargaining agreement. The Council has emphasized, through its reports and decisions, that it will intervene in the arbitration process only to the limited extent that an award comes within one of the Council's grounds for review. The Council patterned its philosophy of limited review in large part on that in the private sector. The Council also recognizes, as do courts in the private sector, that

---

[140]For example, "an award may not erode rights designed to protect the public interest that are reserved to management by the Order." Frazier, "Labor Arbitration in the Federal Sector," 45 Geo. Wash. L. Rev. 712, 734 (1977). Similarly, under the Civil Service Reform Act the FLRA has stated that "no arbitration award under a negotiated grievance procedure may interpret or enforce a provision of a collective bargaining agreement so as to deny an agency the authority to exercise its rights under section 7106 of the Statute. Accordingly, the rights reserved to management may not be waived or relinquished by an award of an arbitrator." Professional Air Traffic Controllers Org., 5 FLRA No. 101, p. 5 (1981).

[141]On arbitrator exceeding authority, see Department of the Air Force, 3 FLRA No. 38, p. 3 (1980); on award not drawing its essence from the collective agreement, see U.S. Army Missile Materiel Readiness Command, 2 FLRA No. 60, p. 5 (1980); on award being incomplete, ambiguous, or contradictory, making implementation of award impossible, see Veterans Admin. Hosp., 5 FLRA No. 12, p. 3 (1981); on award being based on a nonfact, see U.S. Army Missile Materiel Readiness Command, 2 FLRA No. 60, p. 6 (1980); on arbitrator refusal to hear pertinent and material evidence, see National Border Patrol Council, 3 FLRA No. 62, p. 4 (1980). It goes without saying that the other ground recognized by the FLRC as a private-sector ground, i.e., arbitrator bias or partiality, is also a proper ground on which the FLRA may find an award deficient.

[142]Frazier, "Labor Arbitration in the Federal Sector," 45 Geo. Wash. L. Rev. 712, 721 (1977).

arbitrators need leeway in formulating remedies. In the federal sector, however, arbitrators must take into account and act consistently with applicable federal laws, appropriate regulations, and the [Executive] Order."[143]

General continuation of the Council's limited review policy by the Federal Labor Relations Authority was indicated in late 1978 by statements of the FLRA Director of Arbitration Services, and has been further indicated by subsequent developments. That speaker stated that awards have not been and will not be overturned merely because of disagreement with the arbitrator's findings of fact, reasoning and conclusion, or conclusions drawn from the evidence. However, he reminded that in the vast majority of instances in which the Council had set aside or modified an award, it was done on the ground that the award violated applicable law or a Government-wide regulation, and he cautioned that: (1) the federal-sector arbitrator must consider and conform to relevant laws and regulations in deciding cases and for-mulating remedies—primarily the provisions of Title 5 of the United States Code and the rules and regulations contained in the *Federal Personnel Manual;* (2) the parties have an obligation to bring relevant laws and regulations to the arbitrator's attention, and the arbitrator should request it if they have not done so; (3) in many instances the critical review area concerns the remedy directed by the arbitrator and its conformance with law and regulation.[144]

Turning now to the review of arbitration awards involving Cate-gory II issues, we recall that the FLRA has no jurisdiction over Cate-gory II cases (called "adverse action" cases); nor does it have authority

---

[143]Id. at 755–756. "[The cases] illustrate a basic difference between private sector and federal sector arbitration. In the private sector, the negotiated terms of the collective bargaining agree-ment govern the resolution of grievances. Arbitrators in the federal sector, however, must consider not only the terms of the parties' agreement, but also the provisions of statutes and regulations that may apply to the grievance with which they are presented. Federal sector agencies and unions are generally more aware than arbitrators of statutes and regulations applicable in a given situation and should advise arbitrators of the statutes and regulations that might apply to a particular grievance." Id. at 730.

[144]Transcript of Discussion on Problems of Arbitration in the Federal Sector (NAA, 1979). The discussion occurred on December 29, 1978; and the transcript was disseminated for discus-sion purposes only by the National Academy of Arbitrators Subcommittee on Seminars. After four years of FLRA operations, FLRA Member Ronald W. Haughton pointed out that:
- "The Authority has sent out clear signals that it will modify or set aside an award only with great reluctance. In fiscal 1982, for example, of 127 arbitration awards considered by the Authority, only 11 were set aside on the merits and nine modified."
- "As a matter of policy, the Authority has tried consistently to avoid substituting its judgment for that of an arbitrator. It has repeatedly held that the arbitrator's interpreta-tion or application of the agreement, and the arbitrator's reasoning, are not subject to challenge."
- "The most frequent exception [to an award] is that the award is contrary to law or contrary to regulation. A finding of support for this contention has been the most common basis for finding an award deficient."

Haughton, "Arbitration in the Federal Sector," 38 Arb. J. No. 4, pp. 55, 56 (1983), where it is stated that:

"During the first three years of the statute, the parties filed exceptions with the Authority in about 17 percent of the arbitration awards issued each year [the FLRC appeal rate was 15 percent, as indicated above in this subtopic]. The projection for 1983, however, is that around 30 percent of all federal sector arbitration awards will have exceptions filed with the Authority. What accounts for this dramatic increase is, as yet, unclear. What is clear is that the rate of exceptions in the federal sector is substantial compared to a maximum of about 1½ percent appeals in the private sector."

to review arbitration awards involving any Category II issue (i.e., reduction in grade or removal for unacceptable performance; removal, suspension for more than 14 days, reduction in grade or pay, furlough of 30 days or less). However, the Civil Service Reform Act does provide for court review of such awards (with a broader right of review for employees than for the employer), as is explained by the U.S. Court of Appeals, District of Columbia Circuit:

> "Appeals *by aggrieved employees* from decisions of arbitrators or the MSPB in adverse action cases are governed by section 7703(c), which requires the court to set aside any actions, findings, or conclusions found to be
>
>> (1) arbitrary, capricious, an abuse of discretion, or otherwise not in accordance with law;
>>
>> (2) obtained without procedures required by law, rule, or regulation having been followed; or
>>
>> (3) unsupported by substantial evidence.
>
> "* * * In applying this standard to arbitral decisions, Congress has, it seems clear, departed somewhat from the private sector tradition of deference in order to promote some uniformity of process and to ensure that the statutory procedures adequately protect the rights of government employees. But, consistent with private sector precedent, it has done so in a manner that leaves arbitrators' interpretations of collective bargaining agreements themselves largely unreviewable.
>
> "The limited nature of this departure becomes clear when we examine the standards governing appeals by the OPM, which can be implied from the grounds on which that entity may seek judicial review of decisions of the MSPB or arbitrators. It would make nonsense of Congress' statutory scheme to allow a court considering such an appeal to consider either the sufficiency of the evidence or the arbitrator's interpretation of the collective bargaining agreement. Only if the court determines that the arbitrator erred as a matter of law in interpreting a civil service law, rule, or regulation can it upset his decision—a standard of review that is at least as deferential as the standard governing review of arbitral decisions in the private sector.
>
> "We conclude, therefore, that (1) the policies favoring extremely limited judicial review of arbitrators' decisions are fully applicable in the federal sector; (2) Congress recognized the advantages of arbitration, but effected a limited departure from the private sector's tradition of deference to ensure that arbitrators' decisions, like the decisions of the MSPB, adequately protect federal employees' rights; and (3) courts should promote arbitral resolution of disputes arising out of federal employment by considering OPM petitions for review only when the demonstrated need for review outweighs the damage to arbitration inherent in the appellate process."[145]

Finally, the reader is directed to the aforementioned "Processing Channels" chart for tribunals with review functions where a Category III or IV grievance is involved.

---

[145]Devine v. White, 697 F.2d 421, 439–440, 112 LRRM 2374, 2387–2388 (D.C. Cir., 1983). For related discussion, see White, "The Review Process for Labor Arbitration in the Federal Sector," 35 Lab. L.J. 35 (1984). In proceedings for court review of an award under the Act, the arbitrator was required to file a record of the arbitration proceedings with the court when requested by the appellant. Devine v. Goodstein, 109 LRRM 2385, 2386 (D.C. Cir., 1981).

Comptroller General's Role

The right and responsibility of the Comptroller General to review awards issued in federal-sector arbitration during the period of Executive Order programs was explained by that official in a 1977 General Accounting Office publication as follows:

"The Comptroller General has a statutory responsibility to review awards in which agency officials question the propriety of Federal expenditures ordered by a third party. Under 31 U.S.C. 74 and 82(d), disbursing officers, certifying officers, and heads of Government departments or establishments have the right to apply for and obtain advance decisions from the Comptroller General on any question of law involved in the expenditure of Federal funds, including those ordered by a binding arbitration award, Assistant Secretary of Labor decision, or Federal Labor Relations Council decision."[146]

Comptroller General views and actions in reviewing federal-sector arbitration awards was sometimes strongly criticized. It was charged that the Comptroller General "has directly involved himself in the determination of the merits" of some cases and that his decisions "thus pose a difficult obstacle if arbitration is to be an effective process in federal labor relations."[147] Another critic declared that the "Comptroller General has constricted the scope of bargaining beyond the limitations designated by the FLRC" and has "undermined [the federal-sector] arbitration process by accepting agency appeals from arbitration awards in direct conflict with FLRC rulings." This critic urged that statutory reforms "should eliminate entirely [the Comptroller General's] role in federal labor relations."[148]

The Federal Labor Relations Council sometimes requested rulings from the Comptroller General, and its acknowledgment of the authority of Comptroller General rulings was reflected in the FLRC executive director's comments concerning Comptroller General application of the Back Pay Act of 1966 to federal agency violations of

---

[146]The quoted statement appears on the cover of the Manual on Remedies Available to Third Parties in Adjudicating Federal Employee Grievances. There it is also stated that "GAO prepared this manual to assist third parties in fashioning remedies consistent with Federal statutes and regulations," and that the manual "details the available remedies for the most common cases requiring make-whole remedies."

[147]Kagel, "Grievance Arbitration in the Federal Service: How Final and Binding?" 51 Or. L. Rev. 134, 148–149 (1971). For similar criticism see Gamser, "Back-Seat Driving Behind the Back-Seat Driver: Arbitration in the Federal Sector," Proceedings of the 31st Annual Meeting of NAA, 268, 276–279 (BNA Books, 1979); Porter, "Arbitration in the Federal Government: What Happened to the 'Magna Carta'?" Proceedings of the 30th Annual Meeting of NAA, 90, 98–102 (BNA Books, 1978).

[148]Tobias, "The Scope of Bargaining in the Federal Sector: Collective Bargaining or Collective Consultation," 44 Geo. Wash. L. Rev. 554, 570–572 (1976). Regarding his first point Tobias explained that under the authority to review requests concerning expenditure of government funds, the Comptroller General "reserves the right to review clauses in collective bargaining agreements and declare them null and void." Regarding his second point Tobias quoted the Comptroller General's statement [54 Comp. Gen. 921, 927 (1975)] that whether the agency "does or does not file [exceptions to an arbitration award] with the Council the agency at any time has the right to request a decision of the Comptroller General in matters relating to the expenditure of Government funds," and the Comptroller General's decision "is binding on the agency, the Council and the Assistant Secretary of Labor." Id. at 557, 572.

collective agreements—comments which also underscore the "but for" test or limitation upon the remedy power of federal-sector arbitrators:

> "Overruling his previous decisions to the contrary, the Comptroller General declared [in his 1974 *NLRB* decision] that the Back Pay Act was appropriate statutory authority for compensating the employee for pay, allowances, or differentials he would have received *but for* violation of the agreement.
>
> "In accordance with the Comptroller General's interpretation of the Back Pay Act in NLRB and subsequent decisions, the Council has upheld backpay awards which met NLRB requirements, including the *but for* test. In some situations, however, notably 'failure to consult' cases, a grievant is unlikely to satisfy the *but for* standard."[149]

Contrary to the urging of some critics, Congress did not eliminate the Comptroller General's role in labor relations when the Civil Service Reform Act of 1978 was enacted. This is evident from the fact that the Act does not expressly state any intent to modify those provisions of Title 31 of the United States Code which give heads of agencies and certifying and disbursing officers the right to request Comptroller General decisions concerning the expenditure of appropriated funds.[150] Furthermore, in the Act Congress now gave the Comptroller General express statutory authority to "conduct audits and reviews to assure compliance with the laws, rules, and regulations governing employment" in the federal sector.[151]

---

[149]Frazier, "Labor Arbitration in the Federal Service," 45 Geo. Wash. L. Rev. 712, 723 (1977). For some instances in which arbitrators, too, gave careful attention to Comptroller General decisions in order to comport with that Official's views, see Arbitrator Keltner in 73 LA 429, 432–433, 435; Wahl in 72 LA 1044, 1046; Robertson in 71 LA 869, 872; Merrifield in 70 LA 365, 368. Also see Arbitrator Lipton in 77 LA 793, 800 n. 13; Sherman in 75 LA 623, 624–625; Kaplan in 69 LA 1149, 1150 n. 1, 1153; Doyle in 69 LA 800, 803. The Back Pay Act specifies back pay for employees "affected by an unjustified or unwarranted personnel action which has resulted in the withdrawal or reduction of all or part of the pay, allowances, or differentials of the employee." The Comptroller General's Manual on Remedies, Appendix I, stresses that the employee's loss must have resulted "directly" from the unjustified or unwarranted personnel action (an interpretation which in effect interpolates the word "directly" into the statute), and the manual states the "but for" requirement as follows: "A direct causal relationship must be established between the unjustified or unwarranted personnel action and the loss of pay, allowances, or differentials. Remedies under the Back Pay Act are not available unless it is established that 'but for' the wrongful action, the withdrawal of pay, allowances, or differentials would not have occurred." Although the Back Pay Act was amended by the Civil Service Reform Act of 1978, no change was made in the above-quoted language on which the Comptroller General's "but for" test is based.

[150]The Comptroller General has stressed this fact. See Samuel R. Jones, 61 Comp. Gen. 20, 24 (1980). Also see General Accounting Office, "Supplementary Information," 45 Fed. Reg. No. 164, p. 55689 (Aug. 21, 1980), where it is stated that:

"GAO's jurisdiction is based upon * * * 31 U.S.C. 74 and 82d. Section 74 provides that balances certified by GAO upon the settlement of public accounts shall be final and conclusive upon the Executive Branch of the Government. Section 74 also gives heads of Federal agencies and disbursing officers the right to request a decision from GAO on any question involving the expenditure of appropriated funds. Section 82d extends the same right to certifying officers." It is then pointed out there that the Civil Service Reform Act "did not amend 31 U.S.C. 74 and 82d." Title 31 was recodified in 1982, §§ 74 and 82(d) now being codified in 31 U.S.C. §§ 3526, 3529, 3541.

[151]5 U.S.C. § 2304. For additional authority given the Comptroller General under this statute, see the subtopic entitled "General Accounting Office (GAO)," above. It may be noted that the General Accounting Office Personnel Act of 1980 gives the GAO full control over its internal personnel and labor relations systems (GAO employees no longer being under the jurisdiction of executive branch agencies such as the OPM and MSPB). The General Accounting Office Personnel Appeals Board has been established, with provision for court review of its decisions. Additional detail on this special program is provided by Prasow, "Significant Developments in Public Employment Disputes Settlement During 1980," Proceedings of the 34th Annual Meeting of NAA, 317, 328–329 (BNA Books, 1982).

Nonetheless, other provisions of the Civil Service Reform Act affect or may affect the role and actions of the Comptroller General in connection with review of federal-sector arbitration awards:

1. The statute now expressly provides that an arbitrator's award "shall be final and binding" if no exceptions are filed with the FLRA within 30 days, and that the agency "shall take the actions required by an arbitrator's final award."[152]

2. The statute now expressly provides that an arbitrator's award "may include the payment of backpay" as provided by the Back Pay Act, and the Back Pay Act was amended making it expressly applicable in the disposition of grievances under collective agreements (see the next subtopic, entitled "The Back Pay Act").[153]

3. The statute provides that FLRA may request from OPM "an advisory opinion concerning the proper interpretation of rules, regulations, or policy directives issued by the Office of Personnel Management in connection with any matter before the Authority."[154]

---

[152] 5 U.S.C. § 7122(b).

[153] 5 U.S.C. §§ 5596, 7122(b). As noted above, however, the Back Pay Act language on which the Comptroller General's strict "but for" interpretation has been based was not changed. The FLRA does in fact recognize the "but for" requirement for back pay. See discussion by FLRA Member Ronald W. Haughton, "Arbitration in the Federal Sector," 38 Arb. J. No. 4, pp. 55, 57 (1983), stating that:

"Awards can be subject to exceptions on the contention that they are not compatible with the Federal Back Pay Act. For example, under this act, the remedy of retroactive promotion and back pay is only available when the aggrieved employee would have received the promotion if he or she had not suffered an unjustified or unwarranted personnel action. Accordingly, in order for a retroactive promotion and back pay to be authorized under the act, there must be not only a determination by the arbitrator that the employee suffered an unwarranted personnel action, but also a determination that such action directly resulted in the denial of a promotion that otherwise would have been received. This is because relief under the Back Pay Act is intended only to make the aggrieved employee whole, that is, to place the employee in the position the employee would originally have achieved but for the unwarranted action."

Also see discussion by Hayford, "The Impact of Law and Regulation upon the Remedial Authority of Labor Arbitrators in the Federal Sector," 37 Arb. J. No. 1, pp. 28, 30–32 (1982). For illustrative cases in which arbitrators made the requisite "but for" inquiry in determining back pay entitlement, see Arbitrator Goldsmith in 79 LA 367, 371–372; Phelan in 78 LA 740, 748; Clarke in 74 LA 217, 223 (placing the burden of proof on the employer to establish that the grievant would not have gotten the disputed work even if the employer had not violated the agreement).

[154] 5 U.S.C. § 7105(i). Although this arguably produces an implied exclusion or limitation of the Comptroller General's role, it would seem that an express provision would be required for that result. One writer has criticized the FLRA for obtaining advisory opinions from OPM under this statutory authorization, since, that critic asserted, it is "not unlike letting the fox into the hen house" when the FLRA relies "upon the invited opinions of management's principal executive." Kagel, "Grievance Arbitration in the Federal Service: Still Hardly Final and Binding?" Proceedings of the 34th Annual Meeting of NAA, 178, 188–189 (BNA Books, 1982), where it is also stated, however, that a "much greater threat to the arbitration process in the federal service continues to come from the Comptroller General." Also voicing concern regarding the Comptroller General, the Associate General Counsel of the National Treasury Employees Union, Alan S. Hersch, stated in 1980 that he "was distressed that the FLRA is asking the Comptroller General for advisory opinions." "Report on Activity at ALRA Conferences," 104 LRR 337, 347 (1980). In regard to a related but different aspect, it has been explained that the "decisions of the FLRA have generally been consistent with GAO decisions and sometimes explicitly rely upon them." Blatch, "The General Accounting Office's Jurisdiction and Federal Labor Relations since Passage of the Civil Service Reform Act," 39 Arb. J. No. 1, pp. 31, 41 n. 43 (1984). For an example of FLRA citation and reliance upon Comptroller General decisions, see United States Department of Labor, 10 FLRA No. 82, p. 493 (1982), where an arbitration award was set aside.

It has been explained that when the Civil Service Reform Act was enacted, "the GAO reevaluated its statutory authority and its labor-management procedures"; that this reevaluation revealed that "Almost every term and condition of employment of federal employees that involves the payment of appropriated funds was still under the GAO's statutory jurisdiction"; but that the "Comptroller General did, however, as a matter of policy, restrict the GAO's jurisdiction in certain respects."[155] In the latter connection, the General Accounting Office in 1980 adopted amended regulations specifying "Procedures for Decisions on Appropriated Fund Expenditures which are of Mutual Concern to Agencies and Labor Organizations."[156] Some excerpts from the GAO regulations are quoted here to indicate certain salient features of the role performed by the Comptroller General:

"§ 22.5 Request for an advisory opinion.

"(a) Arbitrators and other neutral parties authorized to administer 5 U.S.C. Chapter 71 may request an advisory opinion on any matter involving the expenditure of appropriated funds which is of mutual concern to Federal agencies and labor organizations. * * *

"(b) Service of a request for an advisory opinion on the parties to the dispute or on other interested parties is discretionary with the requesting party. * * *"[157]

---

[155]Blatch, "The General Accounting Office's Jurisdiction and Federal Labor Relations since Passage of the Civil Service Reform Act," 39 Arb. J. No. 1, pp. 31, 36 (1984).

[156]The regulations in question, along with "Supplementary Information" explaining more fully their intent, were originally published in 45 Fed. Reg. No. 164, pp. 55689–55692 (Aug. 21, 1980), as 4 C.F.R. Part 21, §§ 21.1–21.9; they were redesignated and published in 1983 as 4 C.F.R. Part 22, §§ 22.1–22.9. A detailed explanation of the intent and background history of the regulations, and indeed of the past and present role of the Comptroller General, is provided by Maralyn G. Blatch, a GAO senior attorney, in "The General Accounting Office's Jurisdiction and Federal Labor Relations since Passage of the Civil Service Reform Act," 39 Arb. J. No. 1, p. 31 (1984). Statements from the GAO "Supplementary Information" and from the Blatch article have been included at various points of the present subtopic.

[157]The underlying purpose and intent of this regulation has been explained:

"The GAO recognized that although binding arbitration now had a statutory basis, many of the issues submitted to arbitration would still be controlled by other statutes and governmentwide implementing regulations. As required by Article 1 of the Constitution, there must be a law to authorize every expenditure and, therefore, all forms of pay, pay differentials, leave, and travel and relocation benefits are governed by higher law. In the federal sector, these conditions of employment are governed by many different laws and regulations. The collective bargaining agreement can fill in the gaps left by these laws and regulations, but the basic entitlements of federal employment are still governed by a maze of law and regulations.
* * *

"The GAO has over 60 years of decisions interpreting and applying this maze of law and regulations. The provisions of 4 C.F.R. § 22.5 (1983) make this expertise available to arbitrators and other neutrals on a risk-free basis. Advisory opinions are signed by the General Counsel of the GAO and, therefore, are not binding on agency officials or any other party."

Blatch, "The General Accounting Office's Jurisdiction and Federal Labor Relations since Passage of the Civil Service Reform Act," 39 Arb. J. No. 1, pp. 31, 40–41 (1984). However, Arbitrator John Kagel has reminded that "arbitrators are bound to assume full personal responsibility for the decision in each case," and that limitations exist upon use of information not obtained at the hearing; Arbitrator Kagel questioned whether an arbitrator may use the advisory opinion process without violating the Code of Professional Responsibility, particularly if the arbitrator does not utilize the "service" procedures available under the regulation. See Kagel, "Grievance Arbitration in the Federal Service: Still Hardly Final and Binding?" Proceedings of the 34th Annual Meeting of NAA, 178, 190 n. 62 (BNA Books, 1982).

"§ 22.7 Deference to grievance and arbitration procedures established pursuant to 5 U.S.C. Chapter 71.

"(a) *Final and binding arbitration awards.* Payments made · pursuant to an arbitration award which is final and binding under 5 U.S.C. 7122 (a) or (b) will be considered conclusive on GAO in its settlement of the accounts involved, and the Comptroller General will not review or comment on the merits of such an award. However, payments made pursuant to such an award do not constitute precedent for payment in other instances not covered by the award.

"(b) *Matters subject to a grievance procedure.*The Comptroller General will not issue a decision or comment on the merits of a matter which is subject to a negotiated grievance procedure authorized by 5 U.S.C. 7121, except upon the request of an authorized certifying or disbursing officer, or the joint request of an agency and labor organization. Requests will be considered joint for purposes of this subsection when the other party has been served pursuant to § 22.4 and has not objected to submission of the matter to GAO."[158]

"§ 22.8 Discretion to decline issuance of a decision.

"The Comptroller General will not issue a decision on (a) any matter which the Comptroller General finds is more properly within the jurisdiction of the Federal Labor Relations Authority or other administrative body or court of competent jurisdiction, or (b) on a matter which the Comptroller General finds is unduly speculative or otherwise not appropriate for decision."[159]

The role of the Comptroller General has been and likely will remain a controversial subject. One respected arbitrator has urged, for

---

[158]The GAO's "Supplementary Information" states that "§ 21.7(a) [changed to § 22.7(a) in 1983] * * * makes it clear that we will not review or comment on the merits of an arbitration award which is final and binding pursuant to 5 U.S.C. § 7122(a) or (b). * * * However, § 21.7(a) also makes it clear that payments made pursuant to a final and binding arbitration award do not serve as precedent for payment in similar situations not covered by the award. Questions as to how to treat other employees similarly situated but not covered by the award may be submitted by anyone authorized to request a decision from GAO." 45 Fed. Reg. at p. 55690 (Aug. 21, 1980). The provision in § 22.7(a) that "payments made pursuant to such an award do not constitute precedent for payment in other instances not covered by the award" was condemned by one critic, who stated:

"Consider the impact of these regulations: Ideally, parties in the traditional collective bargaining setting try to do two things. The first is to settle as many grievances as they can short of arbitration, and, second, if they go to arbitration, generally they will use the arbitration award to resolve and give guidance in like cases that arise between them in the future—at least until their collective bargaining agreement is amended through negotiations. With its historic antipathy to arbitration and its tradition of interference in the federal service collective bargaining process, the Comptroller General has expressed a view that will continue to thwart these goals. As seen, the Comptroller General has only begrudingly acceded to Congress's will as to actual arbitration awards themselves, contrary to what a grievance and arbitration system is intended to accomplish—to provide means of peaceful and final dispute resolution which thereby reduce employer-employee tensions."

Kagel, "Grievance Arbitration in the Federal Service: Still Hardly Final and Binding?" Proceedings of the 34th Annual Meeting of NAA, 178, 190–191 (BNA Books, 1982). Next, in regard to § 22.7(b), which formerly was § 21.7(b), the GAO's "Supplementary Information" states that:

"As evident from subsection § 21.7(b), we have determined that since the negotiated grievance procedure is an integral part of the arbitration process, it would be inappropriate for GAO to respond to requests from either management or union to review any matter which is subject to a negotiated grievance procedure if the other party objects. * * * As stated in subsection (b), however, GAO may provide a response to requests from certifying and disbursing officers, or to requests from management or union if the other party does not object to our review. Arbitrators and other neutral parties may also request an advisory opinion on such matters pursuant to § 21.5."

45 Fed. Reg. at p. 55690.

[159]The GAO's "Supplementary Information" states that the "determination to decline to issue a decision pursuant to § 21.8 [changed to § 22.8 in 1983] will be made on a case-by-case basis, with due regard to the impact our action may have on the procedures established by" the Civil Service Reform Act. 45 Fed. Reg. at pp. 55690–55691.

instance, that the "Comptroller General should be finally and fully eliminated as a factor in grievance and arbitration determinations,"[160] while another respected arbitrator, finding this suggestion "unrealistic," responded that:

> "Even if law, rule, and regulation did not dominate the arbitration process, the Comptroller General has the legal obligation to guard the public purse against the ordering by an arbitrator of an illegal expenditure. It would take bold action by Congress, that might raise interesting constitutional questions, to exempt expenditures ordered by arbitrators from the general legal requirements."[161]

As for the Comptroller General, that official apparently believes that "the combination of a restrained jurisdictional policy by the GAO, and full access to the GAO under procedures specifically designed to meet the needs of the labor relations community has permitted the reasonable accommodation of labor law and appropriations law in the federal sector."[162]

The Back Pay Act

The Back Pay Act of 1966 was amended in 1978 to make it expressly applicable in the disposition of grievances under collective bargaining agreements. In view of its significance to the arbitrator's remedy power, the following subsection of the Act is reproduced here for the reader:[163]

> "(b)(1) An employee of an agency who, on the basis of a timely appeal or an administrative determination (including a decision relating to an unfair labor practice or a grievance) is found by appropriate authority under applicable law, rule, regulation, or collective bargaining agreement, to have been affected by an unjustified or unwarranted personnel action which has resulted in the withdrawal or reduction of all or part of the pay, allowances, or differentials of the employee—
> "(A) is entitled, on correction of the personnel action, to receive for the period for which the personnel action was in effect—
> "(i) an amount equal to all or any part of the pay, allowances, or differentials, as applicable which the employee normally would have earned or received during the period if the personnel action had not occurred, less any amounts earned by the employee through other employment during that period; and
> "(ii) reasonable attorney fees related to the personnel action which, with respect to any decision relating to an unfair labor practice or a grievance processed under a procedure negotiated in accordance with chapter 71 of this title, shall be awarded in accordance with standards established under section 7701(g) of this title; and
> "(B) [Here it is provided that annual leave in excess of the maximum leave accumulation permitted by law shall be credited to a

---

[160]Kagel, "Grievance Arbitration in the Federal Service: Still Hardly Final and Binding?" Proceedings of the 34th Annual Meeting of NAA, 178, 196 (BNA Books, 1982).

[161]Shearer, "Comment," id. at 211, 216. Also see statement by Harkless, "Comment," id. at 206, 210.

[162]Blatch, "The General Accounting Office's Jurisdiction and Federal Labor Relations since Passage of the Civil Service Reform Act," 39 Arb. J. No. 1, p. 31, 42 (1984).

[163]5 U.S.C. § 5596(b).

     separate leave account for the employee who has undergone an unjustified or unwarranted personnel action that has caused annual leave loss.]

     "(2) This subsection does not apply to any reclassification action nor authorize the setting aside of an otherwise proper promotion by a selecting official from a group of properly ranked and certified candidates.

     "(3) For the purpose of this subsection, 'grievance' and 'collective bargaining agreement' have the meanings set forth in section 7103 of this title, 'unfair labor practice' means an unfair labor practice described in section 7116 of this title, and 'personnel action' includes the omission or failure to take an action or confer a benefit."

The statutory provision for "reasonable attorney fees" applies where the employee is the prevailing party and payment of attorney fees by the agency "is warranted in the interest of justice, including any case in which a prohibited personnel practice was engaged in by the agency or any case in which the agency's action was clearly without merit."[164]

For important additional material on the Back Pay Act, and particularly as concerns the "but for" rule that is applied under the Act, see the preceding subtopic entitled "Comptroller General's Role."

A Recapitulation From the Arbitrator's Viewpoint

It would appear from foregoing materials that the federal-sector arbitrator's task is to enforce the collective bargaining agreement and decide the grievance on the basis of the agreement, *unless*

1. The grievance involves one of the matters specifically excluded from the grievance procedure and arbitration by statute or by the parties themselves; or
2. The collective agreement contravenes a management right which is excluded from bargaining by statute or one on which management is permitted but not required to bargain (and management has elected not to bargain); or
3. The collective agreement contravenes an applicable law or a "Government-wide" rule or regulation; or contravenes a rule or regulation issued at the top level or headquarters of an agency or issued by any primary national subdivision of an agency, unless the FLRA has determined that "no compelling need" exists for the rule or regulation, or unless the collective agreement was negotiated by a union which "represents an appropriate unit including not less than a majority of the employees in the issuing agency or primary national subdivision, as the case may be, to whom the rule or regulation is applicable."

---

    [164]5 U.S.C. § 7701(g), the stated basis for awarding attorney fees applying also to MSPB decisions. The Comptroller General's Manual on Remedies takes the position that punitive damages may not be awarded, and that this is true also of interest on back pay since the statute does not authorize interest. Also holding that interest on back pay cannot be awarded, Portsmouth Naval Shipyard, 7 FLRA No. 9 (1981). For related discussions, see Chapter 10, subtopics entitled "Punitive Damages," "Interest on Award," and "Attorney Fees."

Finally, in the event of a sustaining award the arbitrator's remedy should comport with and meet any limitations imposed by the Back Pay Act and any other controlling law, rule, or regulation.

Legal Status of Arbitration in State-Sector Employment

This topic and its subtopics deal with collective bargaining and arbitration for employees of state or local government, public school boards, and public colleges and universities. Accordingly, as used below the terms "state sector," "public sector," "public employees," "public employers," and "public employment," refer only to such employment and not to the federal sector.

The labor relations problems of state and local government employees often are not covered by federal statutes or regulations, and a constitutionality issue likely will exist whenever Congress moves to cover such employees by any given federal law.[165] Following the federal lead, however, many states and municipalities have authorized organizational, bargaining, and dispute-resolution activities by public employees. But employees in both the state and federal sectors generally continue to be restricted by the traditional prohibition against strikes by public employees.[166]

One informed writer has spoken of the "crazy-quilt pattern of state legislation and decisional law" relating to bargaining and arbitration in state-sector employment, and of the "mercurial" char-

---

[165]At one point, application of the Fair Labor Standards Act to state and local government employment was held unconstitutional on the basis that the states are free "to structure integral operations in areas of traditional governmental functions." National League of Cities v. Usery, 96 S.Ct. 2465, 2474, 22 WH Cases 1064 (1976). Operation of a railroad was not such an area in United Transportation Union v. Long Island R.R., 102 S.Ct. 1349 (1982), holding that the RLA could be applied to a state-owned railroad. Furthermore, in EEOC v. Wyoming, 103 S.Ct. 1054, 31 FEP Cases 74, 79–80 (1983), the U.S. Supreme Court upheld the coverage of state and local government employees by the Age Discrimination in Employment Act, the Court distinguishing *Usery* on the basis of the ADEA's lesser "degree of federal intrusion" and the absence of "either a direct or an obvious negative effect [by ADEA] on state finances." Then, by a 5–4 vote, the Supreme Court expressly overruled *Usery* in Garcia v. San Antonio Metropolitan Transit Auth., 27 WH Cases 65 (1985), the Court majority stating that the "traditional governmental functions" test "is not only unworkable but is inconsistent with established principles of federalism"; one dissenting Justice stated that the majority "opinion apparently authorizes Federal control, under the auspices of the Commerce Clause, over the terms and conditions of employment of all state and local employees," but another dissenter tersely served notice that the "principle" underlying *Usery* will "in time again command the support of a majority of this Court." Congress had power to extend Title VII of the Civil Rights Act of 1964 to state and local government employment since that Act was enacted pursuant to § 5 of the Fourteenth Amendment, which gives Congress power to enact legislation to implement the Amendment. Fitzpatrick v. Bitzer, 96 S.Ct. 2666 (1976). Federal application of temporary wage controls to such employment was upheld in Fry v. United States, 95 S.Ct. 1792 (1975), involving the Economic Stabilization Act of 1970, an emergency measure to counter severe inflation that threatened the national economy.

[166]"Eight states provide a right to strike, as an adjunct to negotiation, to some or all of their public employees, limited by considerations such as a threat to public health or safety." Staudohar, "The Grievance Arbitration and No-Strike Model in Public Employment," 31 Arb. J. 116, 117 (1976). Minnesota's Public Employment Labor Relations Act § 179.64 was amended in 1980 to extend the right to strike to nonessential public employees, if their employer refuses to submit a bargaining impasse to arbitration or to implement an arbitration award. Discussing one state's statute, see Chvala & Fox, "Final Offer Mediation-Arbitration and the Limited Right to Strike: Wisconsin's New Municipal Employment Bargaining Law," 1979 Wis. L. Rev. 167 (1979). The prohibition of strikes by public employees has been held constitutional. For state-sector cases see City of New York v. De Lury, 295 N.Y.S.2d 901, 907–908 (N.Y. Ct. App., 1968), citing other cases. Prohibition of strikes by federal employees was held constitutional in United Fedn. of Postal Clerks v. Blount, 325 F.Supp. 879 (USDC, 1971), affd. without opinion, 92 S.Ct. 80 (1971).

acter of state-sector labor relations.[167] In a similar vein other writers
have cautioned that "[t]he decentralized nature of public sector labor
relations, as evidenced by the variety of legislation, court decisions,
opinions of Attorney Generals and local ordinances and resolutions,
makes the identification of patterns and trends most difficult."[168]

The objective of the present Authors is merely to present an
overview of the legal status of bargaining and arbitration in state-
sector employment, the Authors leaving readers to look elsewhere for
more detailed coverage or for the statutory and decisional law of any
particular state.[169]

Sovereignty Doctrine

Sovereignty concepts, such as the *nondelegable* responsibility of
public officials to determine policy and to exercise official judgment
and discretion in determining matters of government, led many public
employers and courts (and probably some legislatures) to conclude
that it would be improper and illegal to share such responsibility by
collective bargaining and arbitration. Since 1960, however, cracks
and then gaping holes have appeared in the sovereignty-doctrine dam.

Some states have gone far in legalizing collective bargaining and
arbitration by public employers, no longer being deterred by sovereignty concepts. Other states have moved in this direction but do
apply the sovereignty doctrine in some matters. In yet other states the
sovereignty doctrine still holds undiminished, or virtually so.[170] The
varied standing of the doctrine is apparent in the sections that follow.

State-Sector Collective Bargaining

Roughly two thirds of the states have enacted statutes relating to
collective bargaining in public employment.[171] Many of these states

---

[167]Eisenberg, "Some Recent Developments in Public-Sector Grievance Arbitration: A View
From New York," Proceedings of the 31st Annual Meeting of NAA, 240, 241, 266 (BNA Books,
1979). In particular reference to school-district bargaining, he stated that it "has succeeded in
producing a rapidly growing body of case law that is astonishing for its variety and its inconsistencies." Id. at 243.

[168]Sinicropi & Gilroy, "The Legal Framework of Public Sector Dispute Resolution," 28 Arb.
J. 1 (1973).

[169]There has been a flood of informative writings on various aspects of the subject, some of
which are cited in the sections that follow. Also note that informative summaries of state statutes
and litigation on collective bargaining and arbitration in public employment have been provided
in the annual proceedings of the National Academy of Arbitrators (published by The Bureau of
National Affairs, Inc.), including: Proceedings of the 34th Annual Meeting (1981), 317–363;
Proceedings of the 33rd Annual Meeting (1980), 414–451; Proceedings of the 32nd Annual
Meeting (1979), 215–256; Proceedings of the 31st Annual Meeting (1978), 357–393; Proceedings of
the 30th Annual Meeting (1977), 311–356; Proceedings of the 29th Annual Meeting (1976),
287–325; Proceedings of the 28th Annual Meeting (1975), 297–334; Proceedings of the 27th
Annual Meeting (1974), 291–327.

[170]Firm continuation of the sovereignty doctrine is urged by Petro, "Sovereignty and Compulsory Public-Sector Bargaining," 10 Wake Forest L. Rev. 25 (1974).

[171]Thirty-four states with such statutes are listed along with statutory citations and classes
of employees covered, in Blair, "State Legislative Control Over the Conditions of Public Employ-

give statutory bargaining rights to all or most public employees.[172] Other states have given statutory bargaining rights only to limited classes of employees, an example being teachers and firefighters in Idaho. One state, North Carolina, has a statute expressly prohibiting collective bargaining by public employers. The remaining states have no statute relating to collective bargaining by any class of public employee, but some cities in these states have charter provisions or ordinances granting bargaining rights to their employees.[173]

Courts of several states have held by various lines of reasoning that statutory authority is required to legalize bargaining by public employers.[174] A contrary result was reached by the Ohio Supreme Court in rejecting the argument of "improper delegation" of school board powers; the court held that even though Ohio had no statute authorizing public employers to bargain, "a board of education is vested with discretionary authority to negotiate and to enter into a collective bargaining agreement with its employees."[175]

---

ment: Defining the Scope of Collective Bargaining for State and Municipal Employees," 26 Vand. L. Rev. 1, 3–4 (1973). Under collective bargaining statutes for the public sector, the nature of the employer's bargaining obligation may vary. The employer's obligation under the so-called "collective negotiations" statutes is similar to that of private employers under the NLRA. Under pure "meet and confer" statutes, on the other hand, the public employer is required to meet and discuss but the outcome of the discussions may be largely determined by the employer; or the outcome may be a nonbinding memorandum of understanding with employee representatives. It has been explained, however, that "most states have adopted either a *modified* meet-and-confer statute, which gives unions more bargaining power than the pure model, or a *modified* collective-negotiations statute, which is more restrictive from the union's viewpoint than its private sector counterpart;" and for this reason alone, "it is often difficult to distinguish between meet-and-confer and collective-negotiations as viable working concepts in the public sector." Edwards, "The Emerging Duty to Bargain in the Public Sector," 71 Mich. L. Rev. 885, 896 (1973), also stating that "the recent history of collective bargaining in the public sector suggests that there is relatively little difference in bargaining tactics or techniques under these two models," and that under many meet-and-confer statutes "it is no longer accurate to say that the parties * * * do not meet as 'equals.' " For a panoramic view of public employee organization and bargaining in democratic countries throughout the world, see Morse, "Labor in the Public Sector: An International Perspective," 33 Arb. J. 16 (1978).

[172]For a list of 27 states with statutes covering all or most public employees, see Edwards, Clark & Craver, Labor Relations Law in the Public Sector, 259 (1979).

[173]Phoenix, Arizona is an example. Illinois had no statute relating to public-employee bargaining until 1981, but state employees were given bargaining rights in 1973 by Executive Order (the 1981 statute is noted in the next footnote). It has been held that labor relations statutes covering the private sector do not cover public employers unless the statute expressly provides for it. See Westly v. Bd. of City Commrs. of Salt Lake City, 97 LRRM 2580, 2581 (Utah S.Ct., 1978), citing other states in accord.

[174]See Commonwealth of Virginia v. County Bd. of Arlington County, 232 S.E.2d 30, 94 LRRM 2291 (Va. S.Ct., 1977). Other cases holding statutory authorization necessary are collected in Chicago Div. of Ill. Educ. Assn. v. Chicago Bd. of Educ., 222 N.E.2d 243, 251 (Ill. App. Ct., 1966), itself holding, however, that the Chicago Board of Education did not need "legislative authority to enter into a collective bargaining agreement" and that "such an agreement is not against public policy." Illinois' first statute relating to bargaining by public-sector employees was enacted in 1981 and states only that school boards "may enter into agreements with employees or representatives of employees to resolve disputes and grievances by binding arbitration before disinterested third parties." 122 Ill. Ann. Stat. § 10–22.4a.

[175]Dayton Teachers Assn. v. Board of Educ., 323 N.E.2d 714, 717, 88 LRRM 3053 (1975), also holding the school employer legally bound by the provision for grievance arbitration contained in the agreement negotiated by the board. Likewise holding that statutory authorization was not required to legalize bargaining by school boards, see Littleton Educ. Assn. v. Arapahoe County School Dist., 553 P.2d 793 (Colo. S.Ct., 1976).

Grievance Arbitration With and Without Statutory Authorization

Many states have statutory provisions for establishment of grievance and arbitration procedures in public-sector employment.[176] In one case statutory support for grievance arbitration was found even though the particular arbitration statute did not expressly cover the class of public employees asserting arbitration rights.[177] And in California, with several statutes covering most other classes of public employees, a statute was ultimately enacted covering employees in the higher education system.[178]

There now appears to be little reason to doubt the validity of binding grievance arbitration in the public sector if authorized by statute.[179]

---

[176]"As of September 1975 some 28 states permitted the establishment of grievance mechanisms culminating in arbitration." Note, "Public Sector Grievance Procedures, Due Process, and the Duty of Fair Representation," 89 Harv. L. Rev. 752, 753 (1976), citing an unpublished report by Benjamin Aaron. Also see Staudohar, Grievance Arbitration in Public Employment, 30–32 (U. of Calif. Press, 1977). In fact, some of the states *require* that collective agreements contain . grievance procedures and binding arbitration provisions (Alaska and Florida are examples). Under the Massachusetts statute authorizing grievance arbitration but not expressly making it mandatory, the Massachusetts Labor Relations Commission could not require arbitration where neither party had sought it under their collective agreement. Director of Div. of Employee Relations v. Labor Relations Commn., 346 N.E.2d 852 (Mass. S.Ct., 1976). Regarding prevalence of grievance arbitration, 75 percent of the 400 public-sector agreements examined in one survey contained provisions for binding or advisory arbitration of grievances (56 percent of the agreements specified binding arbitration). See Staudohar, "The Grievance Arbitration and No-Strike Model in Public Employment," 31 Arb. J. 116, 122 (1976), reproducing 1974 data reported in U.S. Bureau of Lab. Stat. Bull. No. 1861, Characteristics of Agreements in State and Local Governments, p. 41. In Metuchen Bd. of Educ., 70 LA 944, 945–946 (Handsaker, 1978), the collective agreement specified binding arbitration for one category of grievances and advisory arbitration for another category; it became necessary for the arbitrator to rule on the binding effect of his decision. From an arbitrator's viewpoint, a carefully reasoned opinion is equally warranted even in advisory arbitration. See, for example, Vacaville Unified School Dist., 71 LA 1026 (Brisco, 1978), where a denial award was issued in advisory arbitration, making it binding in actual fact. Similarly, see Arbitrator Staudohar in 78 LA 1294; Lubow in 73 LA 1259; Rule in 73 LA 274. Discussing one of the more extensive experiences with grievance arbitration in the public sector, see Krinsky, "Municipal Grievance Arbitration in Wisconsin," 28 Arb. J. 50 (1973), a concluding statement being that "[t]he Wisconsin municipal grievance arbitration experience shows great similarities to private sector arbitration experience both procedurally and in terms of the issues arbitrated."

[177]Providence Teachers Union v. School Comm. of City of Providence, 276 A.2d 108 (R.I. S.Ct., 1971). Also see Community College of Beaver County v. Society of the Faculty, 375 A.2d 1267, 1276 (Pa. S.Ct., 1977); Gary Teachers Union v. School City of Gary, 284 N.E.2d 108, 113–114 (Ind. Ct. App., 1972). Cf., Westly v. Board of City Commrs. of Salt Lake City, 97 LRRM 2580, 2581 (Utah S.Ct., 1978), cited above in subtopic entitled "State-Sector Collective Bargaining."

[178]In California an Executive order established grievance procedures for academic personnel in higher education; the term "grievance" was defined broadly and grievances were made subject to binding arbitration. See California State Univ., 71 LA 647, 648–650 (Staudohar, 1978). Subsequently becoming effective in 1979 was California's Higher Education Employer-Employee Relations Act, giving organizational rights to academic and nonacademic employees in the higher education system. Some features of the Act are that it preserves the "principle of peer review of appointment, promotion, retention, and tenure for academic employees" (§ 3561(b)); it excludes from scope of bargaining such matters as course content and criteria for faculty appointment, tenure, and promotion, but the academic senate and the trustees share responsibility in all of these areas except course content (§ 3562(q)&(r)); it authorizes agreements for binding arbitration of rights disputes (§ 3589); it specifies impasse procedures (mediation and advisory fact-finding) for interest disputes (§§ 3590–3594).

[179]See West Fargo Public School Dist. No. 6 v. West Fargo Educ. Assn., 259 N.W.2d 612, 97 LRRM 2361 (N.D. S.Ct., 1977); Note, "Legality and Propriety of Agreements to Arbitrate Major and Minor Disputes in Public Employment," 54 Cornell L. Rev. 129, 129–136 (1968). In Garner v. City of Tulsa, 651 P.2d 1324, 113 LRRM 3613, 3615–3616 (Okla. S.Ct., 1982), the court stated that "courts generally look with favor upon arbitration statutes and contracts as a shortcut to

Moreover, significant judicial support has been expressed for its validity even in the absence of statutory authorization. The State of Ohio, although at the time having no statutory authorization either for collective bargaining or grievance arbitration by public employers, upheld a provision for binding grievance arbitration contained in a collective agreement negotiated by a school board. Lower courts had held that the arbitration clause unlawfully delegated the board's responsibilities and was, therefore, invalid. In disagreeing and holding the school employer bound by its agreement to arbitrate, the Ohio Supreme Court said:

"Arbitration is favored because its purpose is 'to avoid needless and expensive litigation.' * * *
"We also recognize that the availability of arbitration may contribute to more harmonious relations between a school board and its employees, and that factor fosters the public policy of keeping the schools open. Although teacher strikes are illegal in practically every state, during the period July 1960 through June 1971, teacher strikes numbered 631 nationwide and 72 in Ohio, resulting in lost time of 5,955,689 and 51,434 man-days, respectively.
"Against that backdrop, and finding no statutory prohibition against the subject arbitration clause, we reject [the] contention that such clause is invalid and unenforceable."[180]

Although the Vermont statutes authorizing collective bargaining by public employers are silent on arbitration, the Vermont Supreme Court compelled a school employer to arbitrate pursuant to the provision for binding grievance arbitration contained in its collective agreement. The court said the school employer had "failed to demonstrate the existence of a statutory provision which limited its authority to enter into the [collective agreement] and the arbitration provisions incorporated in it."[181]

Interest Arbitration Statutes

Many states provide by statute for use of mediation and/or fact-finding in the resolution of interest disputes (contract negotiation

---

substantial justice with a minimum of court interference"; in this public-sector case the state's high court assumed original jurisdiction and, under the facts and circumstances, enforced the arbitrator's award by issuing a writ of mandamus (the lower court thus being bypassed).
[180]Dayton Teachers Assn. v. Board of Educ., 323 N.E.2d 714, 718, 88 LRRM 3053 (1975). In 1983 Ohio did enact a comprehensive statutory program for collective bargaining and dispute settlement in public-sector employment. 41 Ohio Revised Code §§ 4117.01–4117.23. In its *Dayton Teachers* decision the Ohio Supreme Court cited decisions of other states upholding grievance arbitration without statutory authorization, including a Wisconsin Supreme Court decision which rejected the contention that "to require the city to submit to binding [grievance] arbitration is an unlawful infringement upon the legislative power of the city council and a violation of its home-rule powers." However, a provision adopted by the Virginia State Board of Education for binding grievance arbitration between local school boards and their employees was struck down by the Virginia Supreme Court, the court saying the provision divested school boards of their constitutional authority over application of local policies, rules, and regulations adopted for the day-to-day management of a teaching staff. School Bd. of Richmond v. Parham, 243 S.E.2d 468, 472 (1978). In 1978 the State of Virginia, though still not authorizing collective bargaining, did enact statutory grievance procedures (including binding tripartite panel decisions) for state, county, and city employees. It appears clear that such express statutory authorization of binding grievance arbitration would be required to legalize it in any state which does not permit collective bargaining by public employers. In the latter regard, also see City of Fairmont, 73 LA 1259, 1261–1262 (Lubow, 1979).
[181]Danville Bd. of School Directors v. Fifield, 315 A.2d 473, 476, 85 LRRM 2939 (1974).

disputes) in public-sector employment, and frequently these statutes provide for use of arbitration for disputes that have not been resolved by mediation or fact-finding.[182] There are also local ordinances and charter provisions dealing with use of mediation, fact-finding, and arbitration for interest disputes involving municipal employees.[183]

Coverage of employees in these statutes and ordinances relating to interest disputes varies widely. Some apply only to limited classes of employees such as police and/or firefighters, or teachers, or hospital employees, or mass transit employees; others apply much more broadly, such as to coverage of most employees of the state or municipality.[184] Some states have two or more statutes, with different coverage.

Frequent and significant variations in features exist in interest arbitration statutes and ordinances from state to state (and indeed sometimes from statute to statute or ordinance within the same jurisdiction). Variations in features of statutes and ordinances include, but are not limited to, the following:[185]

---

[182]For one state's generally satisfactory experience with fact-finding, see Wolkinson & Stieber, "Michigan Fact-Finding Experience in Public Sector Disputes," 31 Arb. J. 225 (1976). Also see Bierman, "Factfinding: Finding the Public Interest," 9 Rut.-Cam. L. Rev. 667 (1978).

[183]Some states have statutory provisions expressly permitting local governments to adopt their own procedures. For discussion of the New York City procedures adopted under such authorization, see Anderson, MacDonald & O'Reilly, "Impasse Resolution in Public Sector Collective Bargaining—An Examination of Compulsory Interest Arbitration in New York," 51 St. John's L. Rev. 453, 482–493 (1977).

[184]"Iowa is the first state to grant final and binding arbitration of interest disputes * * * to every nonsupervisory public employee of the state and its political subdivisions." Loihl, "Final-Offer Plus: Interest Arbitration in Iowa," Proceedings of the 31st Annual Meeting of NAA 317, 318 (BNA Books, 1979). "The statute provides for mediation, fact-finding, and a modified form of final-offer-by-issue arbitration, with the fact-finder's recommendation an alternate selection for the arbitrator on each issue. The arbitration proceeding is moderately rigid and judicial, not permitting amendment of final offers or mediation by the arbitrator. The results [for the first three years] are encouraging, particularly when viewed as the first full-blown experiment with legislated arbitration for public employees other than those in the 'essential' services. Low usage of arbitration, particularly among teachers and other educational employees, has left a high proportion of voluntary settlements, although the time parameters have resulted in an overuse of mediation. Fact-finding shows a surprisingly high success ratio both in resolving disputes prior to arbitration and reducing the number of arbitrated issues. * * *" Id. at 340. For additional discussion of the Iowa program, see Hoh, "The Effectiveness of Mediation in Public Sector Arbitration Systems: The Iowa Experience," 39 Arb. J. No. 2, p. 30 (1984); Lund, "Impasse Resolution under the Iowa Public Employment Relations Act: A Defense of Factfinding," 30 Drake L. Rev. 561 (1981). A result of the Urban Mass Transportation Act of 1964 has been conversion of many mass transit systems from private to public ownership. States receiving federal funds under the Act must preserve the rights enjoyed by organized mass transit workers under private ownership. "In response to the requirements of the Act, a number of states, having no similar law for any other group of public employees, have passed binding interest arbitration statutes covering transit employees." Comment, "Binding Interest Arbitration in the Public Sector: Is it Constitutional?" 18 Wm. & Mary L. Rev. 787, 796 (1977). Also see Jackson Transit Auth. v. Local Div. 1285, 102 S.Ct. 2202 (1982), discussing Congressional intent in enacting the Act and holding that the Act envisions state rather than federal remedies as concerns collective agreements between transit employees and local government entities. The mere denial of binding arbitration or other dispute settlement rights to teachers while granting them to police and firefighters was held not to violate constitutional equal protection requirements where the difference in treatment was based upon substantial distinctions making one class different from another. Hortonville Educ. Assn. v. Hortonville Joint School Dist., 225 N.W.2d 658, 88 LRRM 3075 (Wis. S.Ct., 1975).

[185]For publications listing states with interest arbitration statutes for public-sector employment, see Craver, "The Judicial Enforcement of Public Sector Interest Arbitration," 21 B.C.L. Rev. 557, 558–560 (1980); Edwards, Clark & Craver, Labor Relations Law in the Public Sector, 588–591 (1979), updating an earlier publication by Gilroy & Sinicropi; Anderson, MacDonald & O'Reilly, "Impasse Resolution in Public Sector Collective Bargaining—An Examination of Compulsory Interest Arbitration in New York," 51 St. John's L. Rev. 453, 455 (1977); Comment,

1. Arbitration may be made (1) entirely voluntary, or it may be made mandatory in the sense that it is either (2) obligatory upon a nonvoluntary party if the other party desires arbitration, or (3) compulsory even if neither party desires arbitration.

2. Arbitration decisions may be made either (1) binding, or (2) merely advisory. Sometimes binding decisions are specified for some matters or classes of employees while advisory decisions are specified for other matters (such as monetary issues) or classes of employees. A number of statutes make interest arbitration both compulsory and binding.

3. Arbitrators may be left unconfined in drafting their award or they may be confined to accepting the "final offer" of one party or the other. If "final offer" arbitration is specified, the arbitrators may be required to accept a single party's final offers as to all issues or they may be permitted to choose final offers on an "issue-by-issue" rather than "total package" basis.[186]

"Binding Interest Arbitration in the Public Sector: Is it Constitutional?" 18 Wm. & Mary L. Rev. 787 at 787 (1977); Morris, "The Role of Interest Arbitration in a Collective Bargaining System," The Future of Labor Arbitration in America, 197, 227–250 (AAA, 1976); Dunham, "Interest Arbitration in Non-Federal Public Employment," 31 Arb. J. 45, 54–57 (1976); Howlett, "Contract Negotiation Arbitration in the Public Sector," 42 U. Cin. L. Rev. 47, 65–66 (1973). For other discussions of the subject, see articles by Rehmus, Newman, Tener, Murray, Anderson, Greer, and Sink in "Interest Arbitration in the Public Sector," 37 Arb. J. No. 4, pp. 3–30 (1982); articles by Ellman, Gershenfeld, Loihl, and Torosian in "Decision-Making in Public-Sector Interest Arbitration," Proceedings of the 31st Annual Meeting of NAA, 291–350 (BNA Books, 1979); Feuille, "Selected Benefits and Costs of Compulsory Arbitration," 33 Indus. & Lab. Rel. Rev. 64 (1979); Bornstein, "Interest Arbitration in Employment: An Arbitrator Views the Process," 29 Lab. L.J. 77 (1978); Kochan, "The Politics of Interest Arbitration," 33 Arb. J. 5 (1978); Attia, "Public Sector Interest Arbitration: Threat to Local Representative Government?" 9 Pac. L.J. 165 (1978); Grodin, "Political Aspects of Public Sector Interest Arbitration," 64 Calif. L. Rev. 678 (1976); Coughlin & Rader, "Right to Strike and Compulsory Arbitration: Panacea or Placebo?" 58 Marq. L. Rev. 205 (1975); Summers, "Public Sector Bargaining: Problems of Governmental Decisionmaking," 44 U. Cin. L. Rev. 669 (1975); articles by Anderson, Loewenberg, Rehmus & Stern, "Lessons From Interest Arbitration in the Public Sector," Proceedings of the 27th Annual Meeting of NAA, 59–105 (BNA Books, 1975); Barr, "The Public Arbitration Panel as an Administrative Agency: Can Compulsory Interest Arbitration Be an Acceptable Dispute Resolution Method in the Public Sector?" 39 Alb. L. Rev. 377 (1975); McAvoy, "Binding Arbitration of Contract Terms: A New Approach to the Resolution of Disputes in the Public Sector," 72 Colum. L. Rev. 1192 (1972); Seinsheimer, "What's so Terrible About Compulsory Arbitration?" 26 Arb. J. 219 (1971); Garber, "Compulsory Arbitration in the Public Sector: A Proposed Alternative," 26 Arb. J. 226 (1971). For intense examination of New York experience, see Kochan, Mironi, Ehrenberg, Baderschneider & Jick, Dispute Resolution Under Fact-Finding and Arbitration: An Empirical Analysis (AAA, 1979).

[186]For discussion of "final offer" arbitration, see Feuille, "Final-Offer Arbitration and Negotiating Incentives," 32 Arb. J. 203 (1977); Anderson, MacDonald & O'Reilly, "Impasse Resolution in Public Sector Collective Bargaining—An Examination of Compulsory Interest Arbitration in New York," 51 St. John's L. Rev. 453, 495–499 (1977); Holden, "Final-Offer Arbitration in Massachusetts: One Year Later," 31 Arb. J. 26 (1976); Nelson "Final-Offer Arbitration: Some Problems," 30 Arb. J. 50 (1975); Zack, "Final Offer Selection—Panacea or Pandora's Box?" 19 N.Y. L.F. 567 (1974). A particularly flexible variety of final-offer compulsory arbitration exists under a New Jersey statute for police and firefighter interest disputes. See Weitzman & Stochaj, "Attitudes of Arbitrators toward Final-Offer Arbitration in New Jersey," 35 Arb. J. 25 (1980). Evaluations of "final offer" arbitration often reveal that it has potential utility but that both of its basic forms have problems and critics. For example, the "total package" variety carries greater danger of unreasonable awards on some issues. Note, for example, the lament expressed on this score by Arbitrators Witney and Dworkin in City of Indianapolis, 58 LA 1302, 1315 (1972). Also see Arbitrator Golob in Ridgefield Park Bd. of Educ., 68 LA 163, 164 (1976), where final-offer arbitration on a single issue left the arbitrator without flexibility. The "issue-by-issue" variety reduces incentive to settle more issues prior to arbitration (a basic goal of final-offer statutes is

4. Variations exist in procedural provisions such as those relating to hearings, use of transcripts, written findings of fact, and written opinions.
5. Specific criteria or standards may or may not be specified for consideration by the arbitrators or for their guidance.[187]
6. Safeguards against budgetary problems resulting from monetary awards may or may not be specified. Where safeguards are specified, variations exist as to what is required (such as requiring completion of arbitration prior to the last day on which appropriations can be made, or delaying the effective date of monetary awards until the next fiscal year).
7. The arbitration tribunal's membership may be tripartite (a common requirement in public-sector interest arbitration), or it may be limited to neutrals.

Constitutionality of Binding Interest Arbitration. Binding interest arbitration has been challenged on constitutional grounds in a number of states. The challenge has succeeded in some cases but more often has failed.[188]

In holding binding interest arbitration for firefighters to be unconstitutional, the Utah Supreme Court explained:

"[T]he act authorizes the appointment of arbitrators, who are private citizens with no responsibility to the public, to make binding determinations affecting the quantity, quality, and cost of an essential public service. The legislature may not surrender its legislative authority to a body wherein the public interest is subjected to the interest of a group which may be antagonistic to the public interest.

"Although it is not dispositive of the delegation issue, in this case the legislature failed to provide any statutory standards in the act or any protection against arbitrariness, such as, hearings with procedural safeguards, legislative supervision, and judicial review."[189]

The Colorado Supreme Court similarly struck down a city charter provision for binding arbitration of police interest disputes, the Court holding it an unconstitutional delegation of legislative power since "governmental decision-making (e.g., setting budgets, salaries, and other terms and conditions of public employment) must be accountable to the citizens," the court stating further that "[b]inding arbitra-

---

less arbitration) since a party may believe a favorable award on favored issues will be more assured if the party offers additional issues which the arbitrators may resolve against in formulating a balanced award on all issues.

[187]For more on standards, see Chapter 18, topic entitled "Standards in Public-Sector Disputes." It has been observed that: "When a statute does not prescribe rules for decision, arbitrators will presumably apply 'general standards.' In these circumstances, articulation of the rationale underlying the award is important to forestall a charge of arbitrariness by a disgruntled party. Similarly, decisions that demonstrably correspond to prevailing wages, terms, and conditions of employment in comparable jurisdictions will be more readily accepted by the parties." Edwards, Clark & Craver, Labor Relations Law in the Public Sector, 620 (1979).

[188]For collection and discussion of the cases, see Attia, "Public Sector Interest Arbitration: Threat to Local Representative Government?" 9 Pac. L.J. 165, 170 et seq. (1978); Comment, "Binding Interest Arbitration in the Public Sector: Is it Constitutional?" 18 Wm. & Mary L. Rev. 787 (1977); Staudohar, "Constitutionality of Compulsory Arbitration Statutes in Public Employment," 27 Lab. L.J. 670 (1976).

[189]Salt Lake City v. Firefighters, 563 P.2d 786, 789, 95 LRRM 2383 (1977).

tion removes these decisions from the aegis of elected representatives, placing them in the hands of an outside person who has no accountability to the public."[190]

On the other hand, the New Jersey Supreme Court held a statutory provision for binding interest arbitration to be constitutional, and in doing so the court surveyed decisions of other states also upholding binding interest arbitration against constitutional challenge:

> "The concept of compulsory and binding arbitration of labor negotiation as well as grievance disputes in the public sector has been coming more and more into favor. * * * The New Jersey Legislature has not only adopted this procedure in the statutory section under consideration [applying to mass transit employees], but also has recently imposed compulsory arbitration for resolution of such disputes between municipal bodies and their police and firemen. * * *
>
> "The principal objection made to compulsory and binding arbitration of labor negotiation disputes in the public sector is that it constitutes an unlawful delegation of public authority and responsibility to a private person or persons. However, most of the cases that have dealt with the question have sustained the concept as an innovative way to avoid the morass of deadlocked labor disputes in the public sector. Nevertheless, in doing so, there must be excluded from the arbitration process matters involving governmental policy determinations which involve an exercise of delegated police power.
>
> "Some of the cases reason that there is no improper delegation involved as the arbitrator is deemed a public official when performing functions which are public in nature. * * * Others hold that legislative delegation is not illegal as long as adequate standards and safeguards are provided. * * * Still other decisions hold that statutory provisions for compulsory arbitration of labor disputes in the public sector do not really entail the delegation of a governmental function at all, but rather in the exercise of that function, merely utilize a well-established procedure for the resolution of deadlocked labor disputes. * * * Some authorities are critical of the standards rule as applied to delegation of power. They suggest that procedural safeguards and judicial review are more important than a requirement of standards."[191]

---

[190]Greeley Police Union v. City Council of Greeley, 553 P.2d 790, 792 (1976). The arbitration was compulsory, but it is apparent that it was the binding status of the award (rather than the mere fact that use of arbitration was compulsory) that led to the holding of unconstitutionality. The Colorado Supreme Court reaffirmed its *Greeley* views in City and County of Denver v. Denver Firefighters, 663 P.2d 1032, 1037–1040 (1983), but the court distinguished binding grievance arbitration and upheld its constitutionality when limited to questions of contract interpretation.

[191]Division 540, Amalgamated Transit Union v. Mercer County Improvement Auth., 386 A.2d 1290, 1293, 98 LRRM 2526 (N.J. S.Ct., 1978), citations omitted. The court said that the statute contained sufficient standards to guide arbitrators in exercising their authority and contained clear procedural requirements, and that absence of an express provision for judicial review meant that one should be implied since arbitration was made compulsory. 386 A.2d at 1294. As of July 1979 constitutional challenges to compulsory and binding arbitration statutes for public-sector interest disputes had failed in Maine, Massachusetts, Minnesota, New Jersey, New York, Pennsylvania, Rhode Island, and Washington, but had succeeded in Colorado, South Dakota, and Utah. Anderson, "Interest Arbitration as Strike Alternative," 101 LRR 283 (1979). The constitutionality of compulsory interest arbitration was upheld by Michigan in Detroit v. Police Officers Assn., 294 N.W.2d 68, 105 LRRM 3083 (Mich. S.Ct., 1980), discussed in Chapter 18, topic entitled "Standards in Public-Sector Disputes." For discussion of compulsory arbitration in general, see Chapter 1, topic entitled "Compulsory Arbitration."

Determining Arbitrability and Compelling Arbitration

Arbitrability issues in the public sector may reach court in the same ways as in the private sector, i.e., one party asks the court to compel or enjoin arbitration, or to review an arbitration award that already has been issued.[192]

Under federal law applicable to the private sector the question of substantive arbitrability is for the court unless the arbitration clause clearly specifies that the arbitrator shall make the determination; a similar rule applies in the public sector.[193] Also as in the private sector, questions of procedural arbitrability are for the arbitrator and not for the courts.[194]

A number of states also have adopted for public-sector arbitration a rule similar to the rule of presumptive arbitrability which applies to the private sector under federal law, i.e., doubts are to be resolved in favor of arbitrability.[195] But New York has held that for public-sector cases under that state's Taylor Law, the courts in determining arbitrability "are to be guided by the principle that the agreement to arbitrate must be express, direct and unequivocal as to the issues or disputes to be submitted to arbitration; anything less will lead to a denial of arbitration."[196]

---

[192]See Chapter 6, topics entitled "Where Arbitrability Challenge Might Be Lodged" and "Determination by the Courts."

[193]See Chapter 6, topic entitled "Determination by the Courts"; Glendale Professional Policemen's Assn. v. Glendale, 264 N.W.2d 594, 599 (Wis. S.Ct., 1978); Policemen's and Firemen's Retirement Bd. v. Sullivan, 376 A.2d 399, 402 (Conn. S.Ct., 1977) (the court said the parties may manifest their intent that the arbitrator determine arbitrability either by an express provision or by use of a broad arbitration clause); West Fargo Public School Dist. v. West Fargo Educ. Assn., 259 N.W.2d 612, 619 (N.D. S.Ct., 1977). "Where parties to a negotiated agreement expressly authorize the arbitrator to make a final and binding resolution of arbitrability questions, reviewing courts will generally defer to the arbitrator's decision regarding that issue. However, if the clause does not indicate the parties' intent that the arbiter's resolution will be final, or the contractual arbitration provision is narrowly drawn, reviewing courts will frequently not feel bound by the arbitrator's determination." Edwards, Clark & Craver, Labor Relations Law in the Public Sector, 702 (1979). In Teachers Local 958 v. School Comm., 112 LRRM 2998, 2999–3000 (R.I. S.Ct., 1981), both private and public-sector cases were cited by the court in stating that: "Courts should not equate the issue of arbitrability with the deference due the arbitrator's interpretation of the contract. * * * Rather, a reviewing court must decide the question of arbitrability de novo."

[194]See School Dist. v. Duquesne Educ. Assn., 380 A.2d 353, 356 (Pa. S.Ct., 1977); West Fargo Pub. School Dist. v. West Fargo Educ. Assn., 259 N.W.2d 612, 618–619 (N.D. S.Ct., 1977).

[195]See Chapter 6, topic entitled "Determination by the Courts"; Westbrook School Comm. v. Teachers Assn., 102 LRRM 2396, 2398 (Me. S.Ct., 1979); Joint School Dist. v. Jefferson Educ. Assn., 253 N.W.2d 536, 545 (Wis. S.Ct., 1977); Policemen's and Firemen's Retirement Bd. v. Sullivan, 376 A.2d 399, 403–404 (Conn. S.Ct., 1977); West Fargo Pub. School Dist. v. West Fargo Educ. Assn., 259 N.W.2d 612, 619 (N.D. S.Ct., 1977); Kaleva-Norman-Dickson School Dist. v. Kaleva-Norman-Dickson School Teachers' Assn., 227 N.W.2d 500, 505–506 (Mich. S.Ct., 1975). But note that in the public sector some matters may be held excluded from public-employer bargaining and arbitration by statutes and public policy considerations; a dispute over such matters is not arbitrable, regardless of what the collective agreement says. See below, subtopic entitled "Statutory and Public Policy Limitations on Scope of Bargaining and Arbitration."

[196]Acting Superintendent v. United Liverpool Faculty Assn., 369 N.E.2d 746, 747, 96 LRRM 2779 (N.Y. Ct. App., 1977). The court reasoned that arbitration is not as well established and proven in the public sector as in the private sector, so stronger proof of intent to arbitrate is required. In Liverpool the arbitration clause was narrow and the question whether the disputed matter fell within, or without, the clause was debatable. The court said the matter was not arbitrable since it did not fall "clearly and unequivocally within the class of claims agreed to be referred to arbitration." 369 N.E.2d at 750. Shortly after Liverpool was decided the court did uphold arbitrability in a case involving a broad arbitration clause, even though the clause did not specifically mention the particular matter in dispute. South Colonie Central School Dist. v. South

Court Review of Arbitration Awards

Because arbitration is used in the public sector, as in the private sector, to settle disputes between employers and employees without extended use of time and resources, it is not surprising that states have tended to view the matter of court review of awards along lines similar to the private-sector pattern. It is apparent that the states by their statutes and by the decisions of their respective highest court have tended to adopt a policy of only limited judicial review of arbitration awards in the public sector.[197]

The Minnesota Supreme Court, for example, has stated that "only when it is established that an arbitrator has clearly exceeded his powers under the agreement to submit to arbitration must a court vacate an award."[198] In reviewing a public-sector arbitration award the Wisconsin Supreme Court explained:

> "The standard of review of an award under both [the Wisconsin statute] and common law is substantially the same. The court will not relitigate issues submitted to arbitration. The parties contracted for the arbitrator's decision, not the court's. Under common law rulings, an award may be set aside for fraud or partiality or gross mistake by the arbitrator. [The statute] sets forth similar standards. If these standards were not violated by the arbitrator's award, the trial court should confirm the award."[199]

Colonie Teachers Assn., 400 N.Y.S.2d 798 (N.Y. Ct. App., 1977). Furthermore, in New York Bd. of Educ. v. Glaubman, 112 LRRM 2094, 2095 (N.Y. Ct. App., 1981), the court stated: "Although we noted in [*Liverpool*] that the choice of the arbitration forum should be 'express' and 'unequivocal' we did not mean to suggest that hairsplitting analysis should be used to discourage or delay demands for arbitration in public sector contracts* * *."

[197]One observer has pointed out, for instance, that courts "rarely will overturn the factual conclusions of an arbitrator and they will accord contractual interpretations similar respect"; also, that "Remedial orders of arbitrators usually are accorded similar judicial respect." Craver, "The Judicial Enforcement of Public Sector Grievance Arbitration," 58 Tex. L. Rev. 329, 346–347 (1980). That observer concluded that "critical differences between grievance arbitration and interest arbitration militate in favor of a somewhat stricter standard of judicial review pertaining to interest arbitration awards." Craver, "The Judicial Enforcement of Public Sector Interest Arbitration," 21 B.C.L. Rev. 557, 571 (1980).

[198]Minnesota v. Berthiaume, 259 N.W.2d 904, 910, 96 LRRM 3240 (1977), in which the Uniform Arbitration Act was considered equally applicable to the public and private sectors. Similarly, see Bridgeport Bd. of Educ. v. Bridgeport Educ. Assn., 377 A.2d 323, 325 (Conn. S.Ct., 1977) (court's role in reviewing award is only to inquire whether the award conforms to the submission). For examples of clear approval for applying to the public sector the U.S. Supreme Court's narrow scope of review for private-sector cases, see Local 1147 v. Scranton School Dist., 113 LRRM 3296, 3299 (Pa. S.Ct., 1982); Westbrook School Comm. v. Teachers Assn., 102 LRRM 2396, 2399 (Me. S.Ct., 1979). Again concerning Minnesota, although that State has reiterated that its courts will not interfere with the arbitration process pursuant to a collective agreement, it nonetheless recognizes the limitation that arbitrators may not decide constitutional issues regardless of the scope of the arbitration agreement. McGrath v. State of Minnesota, 312 N.W.2d 438, 442 (Minn. S.Ct., 1981).

[199]Joint School Dist. v. Jefferson Educ. Assn., 253 N.W.2d 536, 547, 95 LRRM 3117 (1977), where the court also said: "The decision of an arbitrator cannot be interfered with for mere errors of judgment as to law or fact. Courts will overturn an arbitrator's award if there is a perverse misconstruction or if there is positive misconduct plainly established, or if there is a manifest disregard of the law, or if the award itself is illegal or violates strong public policy." Agreeing that awards are not impeachable for errors of law, see Employees Assn. v. City of Milford, 106 LRRM 2383, 2384 (Conn. S.Ct., 1980); Port Jefferson Station Teachers Assn. v. Brookhaven-Comsewogue Union Free School Dist., 383 N.E.2d 553, 555 (N.Y. Ct. App., 1978); Belanger v. Matteson, 346 A.2d 124, 138 (R.I. S.Ct., 1975), reaffirmed in Smithfield Educ. Assn. v. Smithfield School Comm., 386 A.2d 1093, 1094 (R.I. S.Ct., 1978). In Providence Teachers Local 958 v. McGovern, 319 A.2d 358, 362 (1974), the Rhode Island Supreme Court held that lack of funds was no defense to the enforcement of an arbitration award requiring payment of severance pay by the

Of special interest is the fact that New York's high court, whose *Liverpool* decision adopted a particularly cautious approach for determining arbitrability in public-sector cases, has subsequently reaffirmed the following rules of that state regarding court review of arbitration awards in the public sector:

1. "[O]nce the issue is properly before the arbitrator, questions of law and fact are merged in the award and are not within the power of the judiciary to resolve."
2. Reviewing courts are not to review the merits, for the "fact that a different result might have been reached had the dispute been resolved in the courts is of no moment and does not empower a court to substitute its judgment for that of the arbitrator."[200]

The court did say that "a small number of areas, interlaced with strong governmental or societal interests, restrict the power of an arbitrator to render an otherwise proper award."[201]

Even where arbitration of public-sector disputes has been made compulsory, the states have not generally tended toward broad judicial review of awards.[202] Some statutes actually deny any right to appeal from the award.[203] Several statutes are silent on the matter of judicial review of awards.[204] Although a New Jersey statute for compulsory and binding arbitration of interest disputes was silent regarding judicial review of awards, the New Jersey Supreme Court held judicial review to be implied; the court added that "because the

---

public employer. In Antonopoulou v. Beame, 296 N.E.2d 247, 251 (N.Y. Ct. App., 1973), a grievance procedure settlement awarded back pay to a teacher who had been placed on forced maternity leave but the city comptroller refused to pay, finding it unconstitutional and against public policy to pay for time not worked. The New York Court of Appeals disagreed, stating that a collective agreement creates legal obligations which contemplate continuing adjustment through the grievance mechanism; since the public employer had lawfully contracted, any settlement or arbitration award would be legally binding if relating to a term or condition of employment and it could not be considered a "gift."

[200]Binghamton Civil Serv. Forum v. City of Binghamton, 374 N.E.2d 380, 382–383, 97 LRRM 3070 (N.Y. Ct. App., 1978). The *Liverpool* decision on determining arbitrability is discussed above, subtopic entitled "Determining Arbitrability and Compelling Arbitration."

[201]Id. at 383. But in the court's view the matter being appealed was not one of these areas. The award being reviewed had modified the discharge penalty assessed by a municipal employer against an employee who accepted a bribe but who had not been convicted of any crime. In confirming the award, the court said that the employer had bargained to arbitrate the question of just cause for discipline or discharge of the employee, and that "[t]he bargain, having been struck, must now be honored." Ibid.

[202]See Comment, "Compulsory Arbitration: The Scope of Judicial Review," 51 St. John's L. Rev. 604, 618–625 (1977), where some of the approaches are indicated: the statute may specify that compulsory arbitration awards are subject to the limited review associated with voluntary arbitration (Alaska is an example); an "arbitrary or capricious" standard of review may be specified (Washington is an example); or the statute may specify broader grounds for court review (Michigan is an example, making the award vulnerable if "unsupported by competent, material and substantial evidence on the whole record," or if procured by fraud, or if it exceeds the arbitrator's jurisdiction). In Union Local 1296 v. City of Kennewick, 542 P.2d 1252, 1256 (Wash. S.Ct., 1975), the "arbitrary or capricious" standard was strictly enforced.

[203]Pennsylvania is an example, but the Pennsylvania Supreme Court nonetheless did recognize limited grounds for review. City of Washington v. Police Dept., 259 A.2d 437, 440–441 (1969).

[204]"[T]he absence of a specific provision usually will not prevent judicial review on grounds such as fraud, lack of impartiality or wrongful assumption of power by the panel." McAvoy, "Binding Arbitration of Contract Terms: A New Approach to the Resolution of Disputes in the Public Sector," 72 Colum. L. Rev. 1192, 1204 (1972).

arbitration process is imposed by law, the judicial oversight available should be more extensive than the limited judicial review had under [another statute for] parties who voluntarily agree to submit their dispute to binding arbitration."[205]

Statutory and Public Policy Limitations on Scope of Bargaining and Arbitration

Regarding collective bargaining and arbitration in the federal sector, we have seen that under the Civil Service Reform Act significant limitations exist on permitted scope of bargaining and arbitration by virtue of the overriding status of (1) certain laws, rules and regulations, and (2) certain areas of exclusive management rights.[206] In some states similar limitations exist on scope of bargaining and arbitration in the public sector.

Three authorities on labor relations in the public sector explain that:

"Courts appear to be more willing to declare a dispute non-arbitrable in the public sector than in the private sector. This phenomenon has probably resulted because governmental employers are generally considered to retain broader discretion and 'management rights' to control the employment relationship than are their private sector counterparts. In addition, collective agreements in the public sector are likely to exclude in specific terms more subjects from arbitration, and statutes and public policy considerations often reserve other areas for final decision by management alone."[207]

In its *Liverpool* decision the New York Court of Appeals stated that two questions are to be answered in determining arbitrability in public-sector cases: (1) whether the law *permits* arbitration of the disputed matter, and, if so, (2) whether the parties have agreed to arbitrate the disputed matter.[208] The Maine Supreme Court also has

---

[205]Division 540, Amalgamated Transit Union v. Mercer County Improvement Auth., 386 A.2d 1290, 1294, 98 LRRM 2526 (1978). In City of Buffalo v. Rinaldo, 364 N.E.2d 817, 818, 95 LRRM 2776 (1977), the New York Court of Appeals similarly held a right of judicial review to be implied under a compulsory and binding interest arbitration statute; that court reaffirmed the view that judicial review is limited to determining whether the award is "rational or arbitrary and capricious."

[206]See above, topic entitled "Legal Status of Federal-Sector Arbitration."

[207]Edwards, Clark & Craver, Labor Relations Law in the Public Sector, 693 (1979). Similarly, see Staudohar, "Contract and Law in Public Sector Grievance Arbitration," 30 Arb. J. 212, 216 (1975). On the scope of bargaining see Edwards, "The Emerging Duty to Bargain in the Public Sector," 71 Mich. L. Rev. 885, 908–923 (1973); Blair, "State Legislative Control over the Conditions of Public Employment: Defining the Scope of Collective Bargaining for State and Municipal Employees," 26 Vand. L. Rev. 1 (1973).

[208]Acting Superintendent v. United Liverpool Faculty Assn., 369 N.E.2d 746, 749, 96 LRRM 2779 (1977). In connection with the first question the court spoke of "overarching and fundamentally nondelegable" responsibilities of elected representatives of the public. Ibid. In a subsequent decision the same court indicated a narrow scope for the public policy limitation on arbitration: "[A] small number of areas, interlaced with strong governmental or societal interests, restrict the power of an arbitrator to render an otherwise proper award * * *. In the public sector, this policy limitation has arisen with respect to school matters and is derived from the statutory scheme implicit in the Education Law * * *." Binghamton Civil Serv. Forum v. City of Binghamton, 374 N.E.2d 380, 383 (N.Y. Ct. App., 1978). However, one author has expressed concern that in state courts the question is arising too frequently "whether the dispute in question is within the scope of bargaining under the applicable collective bargaining statute." Toole, "Judicial Activism in Public Sector Grievance Arbitration: A Study of Recent Developments," 33 Arb. J. 6, 7 (1978).

stated two questions, to be considered in determining whether a matter is subject to public-sector interest arbitration: (1) "whether the matter is within the statutorily defined scope of bargaining," and, if so, (2) "whether the matter is limited by any other existing statutory enactments."[209]

Mandatory, Prohibited, and Permitted Subjects of Bargaining. Matters which are mandatory subjects of bargaining in the public sector can ordinarily be made arbitrable by agreement of the parties. However, some subject matter may fall outside the legal bargaining authority of public-sector employers because either: (1) a collective bargaining statute expressly removes it from the scope of bargaining; or (2) the subject matter is regulated by some controlling statutory law, preempting regulation by bargaining; or (3) public policy requires that responsibility over the matter, because of its nature, be exercised exclusively by the public employer. Such matters thus are not proper subjects of bargaining and in this sense may be classified as prohibited or nonnegotiable subjects. A matter is not arbitrable if it is not negotiable, regardless of whether or not the parties have agreed to arbitrate.[210]

As to still other matters, public-sector employers may be permitted but not required to bargain. Management can elect to retain control over such permissible subjects of bargaining merely by refraining from bargaining or agreeing on provisions which share management's control. If a public employer does elect to bargain on a permissible subject of bargaining and a clause on the subject is negotiated, grievances involving application of the clause may be made subject to arbitration.[211] But at least one state has not given general recognition to the "permissible subjects of bargaining" category for the public sector. New Jersey has held that in the public sector except for police and firefighters there are only two categories of issues, "mandatorily negotiable terms and conditions of employment and non-negotiable matters of governmental policy."[212]

---

[209]Superintending School Comm. v. Winslow Educ. Assn., 363 A.2d 229, 232, 93 LRRM 2398 (1976).

[210]Arbitrability in the public sector has been challenged on "scope of bargaining" grounds both in suits to compel arbitration and in suits to vacate arbitration awards. Cases are collected and discussed by Toole, "Judicial Activism in Public Sector Grievance Arbitration: A Study of Recent Developments," 33 Arb. J. 6 (1978). Also note the cases cited below in this topic.

[211]See, for example, Rochester City School Dist. v. Rochester Teachers Assn., 362 N.E.2d 977, 982, 95 LRRM 2118 (N.Y. Ct. App., 1977). The Massachusetts Supreme Court has held that both mandatory and permissible subjects of bargaining may be submitted to interest arbitration, with the qualification that educational policy matters cannot be arbitrated. School Comm. of Boston v. Boston Teachers Union, 363 N.E.2d 485, 95 LRRM 2855 (Mass. S.Ct., 1977).

[212]Ridgefield Park Educ. Assn. v. Board of Educ., 393 A.2d 278, 287, 98 LRRM 3285 (N.J. S.Ct., 1978). The police and firefighter exception resulted from a 1977 statutory amendment and has been narrowly construed. Patterson Police v. Patterson, 432 A.2d 847, 854 (N.J. S.Ct., 1981). Regarding education, in Board of Educ. v. Englewood Teachers Assn., 311 A.2d 729, 732 (1973), the New Jersey Supreme Court stated that "major educational policies which indirectly affect the working conditions of teachers remain exclusively with the Board and are not negotiable whereas items which are not predominantly educational policies and directly affect the financial and personal welfare of the teachers do not remain exclusively with the Board and are negotiable." For Discussion, see Gidding, "In re Patterson Police Benevolent Association—The New Jersey Supreme Court Fails to Solve the Lingering Problem of Permissive Bargaining in the Public Sector," 34 Rutgers L. Rev. 378 (1982); Westerkamp, "Obscure Lines: The New Jersey Courts' Response to Public Sector Bargaining," 35 Arb. J. No. 2, p. 8 (1980).

Express Statutory Removal of Matter From Bargaining. Statutes providing for collective bargaining in the public sector often expressly remove some subject matters from the scope of bargaining, particularly specified areas of management rights.[213]

Contractual Terms Versus Statutory Law Covering Similar Matters. Collective bargaining statutes for the public sector vary regarding the relationship between contractual terms and statutory law covering similar matters. Some of the variations are:

1. Often the collective bargaining statute is silent regarding the relationship between contract terms and statutory law covering the subject matter. This leaves to the courts the ultimate determination of any nonbargainable subject.[214]

---

[213]For example, see Wisconsin State Employment Labor Relations Act, §§ 111.90 and 111.91, prohibiting bargaining on various specified matters, including listed management rights (except that management is permitted but not required to bargain on certain of the rights). The Hawaii Act, which covers most public employees in the state, provides in § 89–8(d)(7) that: "The employer and the exclusive representative shall not agree to any proposal which would be inconsistent with merit principles or the principle of equal pay for equal work pursuant to [statute], or which would interfere with the rights of a public employer [to exercise any of the extensive list of management rights listed in the statute]."

[214]In Glendale Professional Policemen's Assn. v. Glendale, 264 N.W.2d 594, 602, 98 LRRM 2362 (1978), the Wisconsin Supreme Court was confronted with such a task since the state's Municipal Employment Relations Act (unlike the State Employment Labor Relations Act in this regard) was silent on the relationship between agreement and statutory law. The court said: "The relationship between public sector bargaining agreements and other statutes governing terms and conditions of employment can be one of the most difficult issues in public sector labor law. As one commentator has pointed out, a rule giving automatic priority to the statute can reduce the statutory duty to bargain into insignificance, while a rule giving automatic priority to the agreement can result in effective repeal of state law. * * * In the absence of * * * a legislative resolution of the problem * * * we have held that collective bargaining agreements and statutes also governing conditions of employment must be harmonized whenever possible. When an irreconcilable conflict exists, we have held that the collective bargaining agreement should not be interpreted to authorize a violation of law." Also see Krinsky, "Municipal Grievance Arbitration in Wisconsin," 28 Arb. J. 50, 58 (1973). In Jefferson County Bd. of Educ., 69 LA 890, 895 (Render, 1977), a board of education contended that statutes vesting it with broad administrative discretion precluded arbitrability of a compulsory retirement grievance, to which the Arbitrator responded: "The existence of statutes dealing with the same subject matter does not necessarily preclude an arbitrator from concluding that contractual violations may also exist. * * * If the Board was allowed to successfully forestall arbitration in this case, few, if any, Association complaints could ever be resolved through the contractual grievance procedure." Also see Leechburg Area School Dist. v. Leechburg Educ. Assn., 380 A.2d 1203, 1206, 97 LRRM 2133 (Pa. S.Ct., 1977); Arbitrators Kramer in 71 LA 1051, 1054, and Lipson in 70 LA 1185, 1187. Sometimes the collective agreement itself will clearly indicate the parties' intent concerning the relationship between agreement provisions and external law. See, for example, Metuchen Bd. of Educ., 70 LA 944, 949 (Handsaker, 1978), where the agreement provided that teachers would not be deprived of any rights conferred by a specified statute; those statutory rights were held to be rights under the agreement by reference. Also see Arbitrator Lipson in 78 LA 493, 498; Witney in 78 LA 176, 181, 183, 185; Gratz in 70 LA 387, 394; LeWinter in 68 LA 1235, 1236–1237. Where neither the collective bargaining statute nor the collective agreement is definitive and unequivocal on the relationship between contract terms and external law covering similar matters, the arbitrator will at times be confronted with the question. In this situation arbitrators have disagreed on the question of considering external law in public-sector cases, just as they have disagreed in private-sector cases (for the latter see Chapter 10, topic entitled "Range of Views as to Application of 'Law' "). Often in such cases in the public sector the arbitrator readily delved into and considered external law in deciding the case. For example, see Arbitrator Witney in 75 LA 504, 511; Gomberg in 73 LA 927, 928; Drotning in 71 LA 1219, 1222–1223; Yarowsky in 71 LA 286, 287; Caraway in 69 LA 541, 544–545; Sinicropi in 69 LA 842, 846; Elbert in 69 LA 102, 108–112; Yaffe in 68 LA 644, 648; Tamoush in 68 LA 85, 86–88. But in some cases the arbitrator refused to do so and considered only the collective agreement. For example, see Arbitrator McCrary in 76 LA 333, 334; Coyle in 74 LA 697, 699; Belsky in 70 LA 143, 145–146, and Kornblum in 69 LA 344, 349–350. And in some public sector cases the arbitrator has been particularly unwilling to determine the legality of a contract provision (see Arbitrator Siegel in

2. The statute may provide that where the agreement conflicts with statutory law, the statutory law prevails.[215]
3. Some collective bargaining statutes specifically prohibit bargaining over specified subjects covered by statutory law.[216]
4. The collective bargaining statute may provide that the agreement shall prevail against statutory law insofar as areas of legal bargaining are concerned.[217]

Some Matters Sometimes Held Nonbargainable. In this section we will note some of the matters which might be held to fall outside the scope of bargaining. The reader will observe quickly that most of the matters concern education, an area that has produced much of the litigation.[218] Each of the matters listed below has been held nonbargainable in at least one state (or at least the court held the matter not to be a mandatory bargaining subject and the general tenor of the court's opinion implied that the matter could not be submitted to bargaining), even though the collective bargaining statute applicable to the particular public-sector employer did not expressly prohibit bargaining on the matter. The reader is cautioned that variable factors such as those discussed above in preceding sections may be critical to the result reached in any given case. Furthermore, cases cited below illustrate the split of legal authority on the question of what matters are nonbargainable in the public sector.

Some of the matters which have been held outside the scope of bargaining by at least one state in public-sector litigation are (again note, however, the split of legal authority as to many items):

---

69 LA 869, 870, and Rauch in 68 LA 608, 612), or to administer statutes which impose affirmative duties or make conduct illegal in an affirmative sense (see Arbitrator Larkin in 69 LA 563, 565). Finally, it should be noted that where substantive provisions of a collective agreement are uncertain as to intent, arbitrators generally do not hesitate to consider external law as an aid in determining that intent. See, for example, Garner v. City of Tulsa, 651 P.2d 1324, 113 LRRM 3613, 3615 (Okla. S.Ct., 1982).

[215]An example is the Vermont State Employee Labor Relations Act, § 904. In holding statutory authorization not to be required for school-employer bargaining, the Colorado Supreme Court added that, in the absence of specific statutes to the contrary, collective bargaining agreements "must not conflict with existing statutes concerning the governance of the state school system." Littleton Educ. Assn. v. Arapahoe County School Dist., 553 P.2d 793, 797 (1976). A similar limitation imposed by the Ohio Supreme Court was honored by Arbitrator Cohen in Berea City School Dist., 71 LA 679, 682, 685 (1978). In some public-sector cases an arbitrator's basic task becomes one of interpreting statutory language. See Fort Wayne State Hosp., 70 LA 253, 255–257 (Witney, 1978). Also see Arbitrator Daniel in 73 LA 717, 721; Rule in 73 LA 274, 277.

[216]An example is the New Hampshire Public Employee Labor Relations Law, § 273–A:3, ¶III.

[217]For example, see Connecticut State Employee Relations Act, § 5–278(e). The Wisconsin State Employment Labor Relations Act, §§ 111.90, 111.91 & 111.93(3), does this by specifically indicating areas of mandatory bargaining, areas of permissible bargaining, and areas where bargaining is prohibited, and by providing that: "If a labor agreement exists between the state and a union representing a certified or recognized bargaining unit, the provisions of such agreement shall supersede such provisions of civil service and other applicable statutes related to wages, hours and conditions of employment whether or not the matters contained in such statutes are set forth in such labor agreement."

[218]For related discussion, see Holden, "The Clash Over What Is Bargainable in the Public Schools and Its Consequences for the Arbitrator," Proceedings of the 31st Annual Meeting of NAA, 282–290 (BNA Books, 1979); Matthew, "The Arbitration of Faculty Status Disputes in Higher Education," 30 Sw. L.J. 389 (1976).

1. Tenure—grant or denial (but procedural steps preliminary to the employer's final action on tenure are ordinarily held bargainable and arbitrable).[219]
2. Discharge of probation officers.[220]
3. Right to inspect teacher personnel files.[221]
4. Class size.[222]
5. Curriculum (courses of study).[223]

---

[219]A number of states have held that tenure decisions or decisions not to renew a nontenured teacher's contract are nonbargainable and nonarbitrable. See, for example, Moravek v. Davenport Community School Dist., 262 N.W.2d 797 (Iowa S.Ct., 1978); Cohoes City School Dist. v. Cohoes Teachers Assn., 358 N.E.2d 878 (N.Y. Ct. App., 1976) (but procedural steps are bargainable and enforceable); Superintending School Comm. v. Winslow Educ. Assn., 363 A.2d 229 (Maine S.Ct., 1976), discussing numerous other cases on the subject. But reaching the contrary result, Kaleva-Norman-Dickson School Dist. v. Kaleva-Norman-Dickson School Teachers' Assn., 227 N.W.2d 500 (Mich. S.Ct., 1975); Board of Educ. v. Philadelphia Teachers Local No. 3, 346 A.2d 35 (Pa. S.Ct., 1975); Danville Bd. of School Directors v. Fifield, 315 A.2d 473 (Vt. S.Ct., 1974). Also see Hawaii Supreme Court decisions covering three disputes between the University of Hawaii Professional Assembly and the University of Hawaii, 659 P.2d 717, 720, 729 (Hawaii, S.Ct., 1983). Regarding the arbitrator's function in tenure-denial cases, and contrasting arbital review of tenure denial with arbitral review of just cause for discharge in industrial employment, see Wayne State Univ., 68 LA 1085, 1089–1090 (St. Antoine, 1977). Discharge of a teacher who *had* tenure could be submitted to arbitration in Board of Educ. v. Associated Teachers of Huntington, 282 N.E.2d 109 (N.Y. Ct. App., 1972), where the agreement authorized arbitration of tenured teacher discharge for misconduct or incompetency. The Court said: "[This provision] assures teachers with tenure that no disciplinary action will be taken against them without just cause and that any dispute as to the existence of such cause may be submitted to arbitration. It is a provision commonly found in collective bargaining agreements in the private and public sectors and carries out Federal and State policy favoring arbitration as a means of resolving labor disputes." Id. at 113. In School Dist. of Colfax, 73 LA 697, 698, 702 (Honeyman, 1979), nonrenewal of a teacher's contract was held to be without just cause and the school employer was ordered to offer the teacher a contract; pursuant to statute the collective agreement would have barred the grievance had it involved a probationary teacher.

[220]Council No. 23 v. Recorder's Court Judges, 248 N.W.2d 220, 222, 226 (Mich. S.Ct., 1976) (the court stressed that a sensitive judicial official was involved). Apart from special classes of employees, however, discharge of public employees may be a proper subject of bargaining and arbitration. See Rhinelander City Employees v. City of Rhinelander, 151 N.W.2d 30, 36 (Wis. S.Ct., 1967). For illustrations of arbitral review of discharge of police officers, see Arbitrators Ellmann in 73 LA 464, 477, and Taylor in 72 LA 1248, 1250, both overruling discharge.

[221]Board of Educ. v. Areman, 362 N.E.2d 943, 947–948 (N.Y. Ct. App., 1977), holding that "a board of education cannot bargain away its right to inspect teacher personnel files and that a provision in a collective bargaining agreement which might reflect such a bargain is unenforceable as against public policy"; the court cautioned that "any inspection must be related to legitimate board purposes and functions."

[222]Kenai Peninsula Borough School Dist. v. Kenai Peninsula Educ. Assn., 97 LRRM 2153 (Alaska S.Ct., 1977) (the court provided a list of nine nonnegotiable matters and a list of 38 negotiable matters). Also see N.E.A.-Topeka v. USD 501, Shawnee County, 592 P.2d 93, 98, 101 LRRM 2611 (Kan. S.Ct., 1979). But see West Hartford Educ. Assn. v. DeCourcy, 295 A.2d 526, 537 (Conn. S.Ct., 1972) (class size and teacher load held mandatory subjects of bargaining). New York has held that although class size is not a mandatory bargaining subject, if a school employer voluntarily contracts on the subject, a dispute over the provision may be arbitrable. Susquehanna Valley Central School Dist. v. Susquehanna Valley Teachers Assn., 376 N.Y.S.2d 427, 430 (N.Y. Ct. App., 1975). Arbitration of class-size issues is illustrated by Swartz Creek Community Schools, 70 LA 1185 (Lipson, 1978). The *impact* of class size as it bears on teacher work loads was held a mandatory subject of bargaining in West Irondequoit Teachers Assn. v. Helsby, 358 N.Y.S.2d 720, 723 (N.Y. Ct. App., 1974); City of Beloit v. WERC, 92 LRRM 3318, 3325 (Wis. S.Ct., 1976). In the *Beloit* case the Wisconsin Supreme Court said mandatory bargaining subjects are those which are "primarily related" to wages, hours, and working conditions. Id. at 3321, where the court noted various tests of other states for determining what are mandatory subjects of bargaining. Under its "primarily related" test, the court classified the following subjects as mandatory subjects of bargaining: teacher evaluation procedures; teacher access to their personnel files; seniority in teacher layoffs (without restricting school employer right to determine curriculum and to retain teachers qualified to teach particular subjects); school calendar and in-service days; impact of class size; impact of reading program. Id. at 3322–3326.

[223]Board of Educ. v. Rockaway Township Educ. Assn., 81 LRRM 2462, 2465 (N.J. Super. Ct., 1972). The court said that "if the contract is read to delegate to a teacher or to a teacher's union the

6. School calendar.[224]
7. Hours of work of teachers.[225]
8. Abolition of positions.[226]
9. Teacher transfers.[227]
10. Faculty workload.[228]
11. Sabbatical leave.[229]
12. Hiring of teachers.[230]

---

subject of courses of study, the contract in that respect is *ultra vires* and unenforceable," and the court held nonarbitrable a grievance alleging interference with "academic freedom" (teacher was prohibited from conducting debate in seventh grade class on the subject of abortion) even though the agreement recognized that "academic freedom is essential to the fulfillment of the purposes" of the school. A contractual guarantee of academic freedom was reconciled with the school employer's role in making decisions relating to curriculum, evaluation of students, and other matters of educational policy, in Endicott College, 71 LA 355 (Shapiro, 1978). In Joint School Dist. v. WERB, 155 N.W.2d 78, 82–83 (Wis. S.Ct., 1967), court dictum indicated that curriculum would not be bargainable.

[224]West Hartford Educ. Assn. v. DeCourcy, 295 A.2d 526, 534–535 (Conn. S.Ct., 1972) (the actual holding was that school calendar was not a mandatory subject of bargaining; the court's general discussion reasons that the legislature did not intend such matters to be subjected to bargaining). Also see Burlington County College Faculty Assn. v. Board of Trustees, 311 A.2d 733 (N.J. S.Ct., 1973). School calendar was held bargainable in Joint School Dist. v. WERB, 155 N.W.2d 78, 81–82 (Wis. S.Ct., 1967), but the court said many items in the calendar are fixed by statute (such as the school year), and these items "cannot be changed by negotiation."

[225]West Hartford Educ. Assn. v. DeCourcy, 295 A.2d 526, 534 (Conn. S.Ct., 1972) (held not a mandatory subject of bargaining and the court's general discussion reasons that the legislature did not intend such matters to be subjected to bargaining). But hours of work of teachers was held bargainable in Board of Educ. v. Englewood Teachers Assn., 311 A.2d 729, 732 (N.J. S.Ct., 1973).

[226]School Comm. of Hanover v. Curry, 343 N.E.2d 144, 145 (Mass. S.Ct., 1976). Also see Dunellen Board of Educ. v. Dunellen Educ. Assn., 311 A.2d 737, 744 (N.J. S.Ct., 1973) (consolidation of chairmanships of two departments held nonbargainable). But see Board of Educ. v. Yonkers Fedn. of Teachers, 92 LRRM 3328, 3330 (N.Y. Ct. App., 1976). Elimination of certain departmental chairmanships was a mandatory subject of bargaining in Barrington School Comm. v. Rhode Island SLRB, 388 A.2d 1369, 1374–1375 (R.I. S.Ct., 1978) (it thus could be arbitrable).

[227]Ridgefield Park Educ. Assn. v. Board of Educ., 393 A.2d 278, 288–289 (N.J. S.Ct., 1978). Also see Tippecanoe Educ. Assn. v. Board of School Trustees, 429 N.E.2d 967 (Ind. Ct. App., 1981). In Minneapolis Fedn. of Teachers v. Minneapolis Special School Dist., 258 N.W.2d 802, 806 (Minn. S.Ct., 1977), the court held: "1. The decision to transfer a number of teachers is a managerial decision and not a subject for negotiation. 2. The adoption of the criteria by which individual teachers may be identified for transfer is a proper subject for negotiation and, as such, is properly included in the collective bargaining contract. 3. To insure that individual teacher transfers conform to the negotiated contract, each individual transfer is a proper subject of grievance arbitration." A limited contractual provision on teacher transfers was held enforceable through arbitration in Bradley v. School Comm. of Boston, 364 N.E.2d 1229, 1233 (Mass. S.Ct., 1977). For an illustration of arbitral review of forced transfer of a Pennsylvania teacher, see Intermediate Unit I Bd. of Directors, 73 LA 80, 84 (Duff, 1979). For an illustration of arbitration of teacher transfer under a collective agreement seniority/relative ability clause, see Cincinnati Bd. of Educ., 72 LA 524 (Ipavec, 1979).

[228]Metropolitan Educ. Assn. v. Community College, 281 N.W.2d 201, 102 LRRM 2142, 2146 (Neb. S.Ct., 1979), stating that certain decisions of other states were distinguishable. The allocation of nonprofessional chores to teachers was held nonbargainable and nonarbitrable in Kenai Peninsula Educ. Assn. v. Kenai Peninsula School Dist., 628 P.2d 568, 569 (Alaska S.Ct., 1981).

[229]Board of Educ. v. Murphy, 372 N.E.2d 899, 901 (Ill. App. Ct., 1978). But see Board of Educ. v. Bridgeport Educ. Assn., 377 A.2d 323, 326 (Conn. S.Ct., 1977); Associated Teachers of Huntington v. Board of Educ., 306 N.E.2d 791 (N.Y. Ct. App., 1973). In Peekskill City School Dist., 72 LA 127, 129 (Dennis, 1979), a school employer's control over sabbatical leave was largely displaced by the collective agreement into the hands of a faculty committee.

[230]School Dist. 36 v. Teachers Assn., 428 A.2d 419, 110 LRRM 3361, 3364 (Me. S.Ct., 1981). Also see School Comm. v. New Bedford Educ. Assn., 108 LRRM 3201, 3204–3205 (Mass. App. Ct., 1980).

Relationship Between Contractual and Statutory Grievance Channels

Often statutory provisions for collective bargaining and arbitration in public employment are silent regarding the relationship between contractual grievance procedures and statutory procedures such as those under civil service laws.[231] Where a statute does deal expressly with the question, one possibility is that the employee will be given an option to use either the contractual grievance procedure or a statutory procedure.[232] However, some statutes make the contractual grievance procedure exclusive if it covers the grievance. For example, Massachusetts provides that, if there is an applicable contract grievance procedure, such procedure shall "be exclusive and shall supersede any otherwise applicable grievance procedure provided by law."[233]

States that authorize collective bargaining and arbitration in the public sector generally permit employees to adjust their grievance with the employer without intervention of the union, but the adjustment must be consistent with the terms of the collective agreement and the union is entitled to be present.[234]

---

[231]For general discussion of the subject, see Hayford & Pegnetter, "A Comparison of Rights Arbitration and Civil Service Appeals Procedures," 35 Arb. J. No. 3, p. 22 (1980); Pegnetter & Hayford, "State Employee Grievances and Due Process: An Analysis of Contract Arbitration and Civil Service Review Systems," 29 S.C.L. Rev. 305 (1978); Comment, "Public Sector Grievance Procedures, Due Process, and the Duty of Fair Representation," 89 Harv. L. Rev. 752, 757–764 (1976); Ullman & Bergin, "The Structure and Scope of Appeals Procedures for Public Employees," 23 Indus. & Lab. Rel. Rev. 323 (1970).

[232]An example is the Minnesota Public Employment Labor Relations Act, § 179.70.

[233]Mass. Gen. Laws, Chapter 150E, §8. Another example is the Maine State Employees Labor Relations Act, § 979-K. In City of Ontario, Oregon, 72 LA 1089, 1091–1092 (Conant, 1979), the public employer was upheld in reprimanding an employee who bypassed the contractual grievance procedure, which was construed to provide the exclusive remedy, and carried his complaint to a city councilman; the arbitrator said that in public sector labor relations, " 'end-runs' to city officials can disrupt and impair the functioning of the bargaining process." In Pontiac Police Officers Assn. v. City of Pontiac, 246 N.W.2d 831, 835 (Mich. S.Ct., 1976), it was held that establishment in a home-rule city's charter of a civilian board to review discipline of police officers did not relieve the city of its obligation to bargain on grievance procedures for disciplined officers.

[234]For example, see Delaware Code, Title 19, § 1306.

Chapter 3

Scope of Labor Arbitration

While many labor disputes are clearly suitable for arbitration, one of the potential hazards of labor arbitration has been said to be an "overoptimistic estimate" of its effective scope, "which tends to consider it an all-purpose tool or panacea for the resolution of any and all disputes which the parties fail to settle privately."[1]

Even if a dispute is of a type generally suitable for arbitration and is arbitrable under the collective agreement, judgment must be exercised in deciding whether to arbitrate the particular dispute. Included among the factors to be considered in this regard are the merits of the case, the importance of the issue, the effect of winning or losing, the possibilities of settlement, internal policies and politics within the union and the company, psychological and face-saving considerations, and the like.[2]

Certainly, not all disputes are equally suitable for arbitration. The most popular use of labor arbitration concerns disputes involving the interpretation or application of the collective agreement. There is much less enthusiasm for its use, even on a voluntary basis, as a means of resolving disputes over terms of new or renewal contracts.[3]

There are some matters, too, which are so delicate or are considered to belong so intimately to one or the other of the parties, that they are not too readily submitted to arbitration.[4] This has been suggested

---

[1]Davey, "Hazards in Labor Arbitration," 1 Indus. & Lab. Rel. Rev. 386, 387 (1948). For related discussion, see Chapter 1, topic entitled "Other Important Roles of Arbitration."

[2]See "Prehearing Arbitration Problems: A Panel Discussion," Proceedings of the 20th Annual Meeting of NAA, 341–352 (BNA Books, 1967); Fleming, The Labor Arbitration Process, 205–208 (U. of Ill. Press, 1965); Kagel, Anatomy of a Labor Arbitration, 14–15, 23 (BNA Books, 1961).

[3]For extent of acceptance of the various uses of arbitration, see Chapter 1, topic entitled "Arbitration as a Substitute for Work Stoppages." For earlier data, see "Basic Patterns in Labor Arbitration Agreements," 34 LA 931, 939 (1960); Warren & Bernstein, "A Profile of Labor Arbitration," 16 LA 970, 971–973 (1951).

[4]See Moore & Mix, "Arbitration Provisions in Collective Agreements," 76 Monthly Lab. Rev. 261–264 (1953); Lapp, Labor Arbitration, 44 (1942). For surveys of matters which might be excluded from the collective agreement arbitration clause, see Characteristics of Major Collective Bargaining Agreements, July 1, 1976, 82 (U.S. Dept. of Labor Bull. 2013, 1979). Major Collective Bargaining Agreements: Arbitration Procedures, 6–22 (U.S. Dept. Labor Bull. No. 1425–6, 1966); "Basic Patterns in Labor Arbitration Agreements," 34 LA 931, 939 (1960).

as a reasonable explanation for many of the specific exclusions from arbitration clauses studied by the U.S. Department of Labor in one survey:

> "The reasons for such exclusions usually were not indicated by the agreements and, although they may have been fully understood by the parties, they are not always clear to outsiders reading the agreements. Some exclusions undoubtedly were intended to preserve certain management prerogatives, others to preserve union prerogatives. Some were necessary because the parties had agreed upon other methods of handling certain problems, and possibly some were motivated by a mutual desire not to overburden the arbitration machinery with trivialities. Exclusions in some cases appeared to represent a signal to workers in the bargaining unit that it would be pointless to raise a grievance over the designated issue. It seems reasonable to assume, however, that underlying many exclusions was a strongly held belief of one or both parties that the issue in question was too important or too subtle to be entrusted to a decision of a third party."[5]

Management naturally hesitates to submit to arbitration issues involving its normal prerogatives in the conduct of the business, such as the determination of methods of operation, operation policies, and finances. Labor usually considers that the settlement of an internal union conflict is "a matter in which management should not be permitted to participate, and it would be undesirable to permit the company to become involved in this question indirectly or in any manner whatsoever."[6] Improper activities of union officials in the administration of grievances have been held to be improper subjects for arbitration, since a contrary approach "might well result in a form of policing of internal union affairs by a third party who clearly was not intended nor competent to accomplish such a purpose. * * * The remedy lies with the union membership, which has the ultimate power, through democratic means, to control the selection of their representatives."[7]

It may be noted, however, that internal union disputes do sometimes reach arbitration between company and union.[8] Furthermore, internal union disputes may be arbitrated without management involvement,[9] and such arbitration has been used widely for inter-

---

[5]Major Collective Bargaining Agreements: Arbitration Procedures, 11 (U.S. Dept. Labor Bull. No. 1425–6, 1966).

[6]Babcock & Wilcox Co., 8 LA 58, 61 (Dworkin, 1947).

[7]Spencer Kellogg & Sons, 1 LA 291, 294 (Miller, 1945). Cf., North American Aviation, 17 LA 199, 204 (Komaroff, 1951).

[8]See Publishers' Assn. of N.Y. City v. New York Mailers' Union, 317 F.2d 624 (CA 2, 1963), involving union action against a member who as company foreman had disciplined another union member. Similarly, Houston Chronicle Publishing Co. v. Houston Typographical Union, 272 F.Supp. 974 (USDC, 1966). Both of these cases involved broad arbitration clauses.

[9]See Arbitrator Nathan in 71 LA 1057; Johnson in 51 LA 642; Bernstein in 46 LA 169. Some unions utilize public review boards for such arbitration. "In the context of UAW governance, the public review board represents essentially a group of arbitrators in whom the union has reposed ultimate authority to interpret its constitution and ethical practices codes and to decide disputes arising thereunder." Klein, "The Public Review Boards: Their Place in the Process of Dispute Resolutions," Proceedings of the 27th Annual Meeting of NAA, 189, 191 (BNA Books, 1975). Also see Linn, "The American Federation of Teachers Public Review Board," id. at 205; Feller, "The Association of Western Pulp and Paper Workers Public Review Board," id. at 221.

union jurisdictional disputes.[10] Similarly, intermanagement disputes may be arbitrated without labor involvement.[11]

Labor ordinarily would not consider its statutory right to strike a proper subject for arbitration. However, the right to strike is frequently arbitrated in construing contractual no-strike clauses, and in such proceedings the question of the right to strike under statute may be brought into play.[12]

Some doubt exists as to the suitability of labor-management arbitration for resolving racial discrimination grievances, but proposals have been made to adapt it to the needs of such grievances.[13]

While it has been suggested that "Arbitration is most effective when used sparingly,"[14] it has also been suggested that "it would hardly be right to judge the effectiveness or worth of an arbitration system or the health of a labor-management relationship by the number of cases" arbitrated each year.[15]

Disputes on Rights and Interests

The distinction between "rights" and "interests" is basic in the classification of labor disputes and in views as to arbitrability. Disputes as to rights involve the interpretation or application of laws, agreements, or customary practices, whereas disputes as to interests involve the question of what shall be the basic terms and conditions of employment. This nomenclature is derived from the Scandinavian countries, which have treated the distinction between rights and interests as basic in their labor legislation. Sweden, for instance, established permanent national labor courts with jurisdiction carefully restricted to disputes concerning rights under collective agreements.[16]

The U.S. Supreme Court has explained the fundamental distinction between interest disputes and rights disputes:

---

[10]E.g., Arbitrator Cole in 46 LA 28; Taft in 45 LA 69; Cole in 23 LA 827. For discussion, see Krislov & Mead, "Arbitrating Union Conflicts: An Analysis of the AFL-CIO Internal Disputes Plan," 36 Arb. J. No. 2, p. 21 (1981); Stark, "The Presidential Address: Theme and Adaptations," Proceedings of the 31st Annual Meeting of NAA, 1, 28 (BNA Books, 1979); Cole, Feinsinger & Dunlop, "Arbitration of Jurisdictional Disputes," Arbitration Today, 149–165 (BNA Books, 1955). The U.S. Supreme Court has upheld the use of arbitration for resolving representation disputes; "the therapy of arbitration" may thus be brought to bear, though any subsequent decision by the NLRB would take precedence over that of the arbitrator. Carey v. Westinghouse Elec. Corp., 84 S.Ct. 401, 409 (1964).

[11]Plumbing, Heating and Piping Employers Council, 39 LA 513 (Ross, 1962).

[12]See General Elec. Co., 42 LA 1255, 1264–1266 (Koretz, 1964).

[13]See discussion of *Alexander v. Gardner-Denver* in Chapter 2, subtopic entitled "De Novo Litigation Following Arbitration," where other writings are also cited.

[14]Davey, "Labor Arbitration: A Current Appraisal," 9 Indus. & Lab. Rel. Rev. 85, 90 (1955).

[15]Comment by Harry H. Platt in "The Chrysler-UAW Umpire System," Proceedings of the 11th Annual Meeting of NAA, 111, 142–143 (BNA Books, 1958), where Umpire Platt asserted that labor relations at Ford were "at least as good as at Chrysler" even though Ford arbitrated many more cases than Chrysler; Umpire Platt offered explanations and justifications for the heavier caseload at Ford.

[16]Spielmans, "Labor Disputes on Rights and on Interests," 29 Am. Econ. Rev. 299 (1939).

"The first relates to disputes over the formation of collective agreements or efforts to secure them. They arise where there is no such agreement or where it is sought to change the terms of one, and therefore the issue is not whether an existing agreement controls the controversy. They look to the acquisition of rights for the future, not to assertion of rights claimed to have vested in the past.

"The second class, however, contemplates the existence of a collective agreement already concluded or, at any rate, a situation in which no effort is made to bring about a formal change in terms or to create a new one. The dispute relates either to the meaning or proper application of a particular provision with reference to a specific situation or to an omitted case. In the latter event the claim is founded upon some incident of the employment relation, or asserted one, independent of those covered by the collective agreement * * *. In either case the claim is to rights accrued, not merely to have new ones created for the future."[17]

Disputes as to rights are adjudicable under the laws or agreements on which the rights are based, and are readily adaptable to settlement by arbitration. Disputes as to interests, on the other hand, involve questions of policy which, for lack of predetermined standards, have not been generally regarded as justiciable or arbitrable. Yet, many interest disputes are settled by arbitration, and, as was seen in Chapter 1, some states have concluded that public utility interest disputes involve such serious risk of public harm that a requirement of compulsory arbitration of such disputes is justified. Also, as was seen in Chapter 2, many states provide by statute for use of mediation and/ or fact-finding in the resolution of interest disputes in public-sector employment, and frequently these statues provide for use of arbitration (some making it compulsory) for disputes that have not been resolved by mediation or fact-finding.

It is highly important that the distinction between these two basic types of disputes be recognized and preserved in considering methods of settlement. This distinction was recognized early in the full-fashioned hosiery industry, which adopted one method of procedure for rights disputes and another for interest disputes. This has been explained:

"The jurisdiction of the Impartial Chairman does not extend to disputes regarding the general level of wages in the industry. Since decisions of this type would involve changing all the rates specified in the Agreement, they are excluded from his jurisdiction by the provision which denies him the right to change any of the terms of the contract. Furthermore, the parties have established in the Agreement a special procedure for handling disputes over general wage-level changes. The 'flexibility clause' permits either party to seek a change in the general wage level at any time during the life of the agreement and provides for

---

[17]Elgin, J. & E. Ry. v. Burley, 65 S.Ct. 1282, 1290, 16 LRRM 749 (1945), involving the Railway Labor Act. The Court noted that the two basic types of disputes are traditionally called "major" and "minor" disputes in the railroad industry. Ibid. The Railway Labor Act is discussed below in this topic.

the establishment of a special wage tribunal in case the parties cannot agree on the percentage change to be made."[18]

The industry considered that, because there is no uniformly accepted body of principles for determining wage levels, one or both of the parties will be likely to feel that a given interest decision is grossly inequitable. Recognition of this fact gives special point to the use of one set of machinery for the arbitration of rights disputes and another for interest disputes in permanent umpire or permanent chairman systems. Ill feeling against an arbitrator after an interest decision may be so general and so severe that one decision will destroy his usefulness to the industry.

Of the first six arbitrators chosen to determine general wage-level changes under the flexibility clause in the hosiery industry, not one was invited to serve a second time. Since it is not easy to find a person who combines the specialized knowledge of the industry and the type of personality which is necessary for success as an Impartial Chairman, the parties decided not to risk the loss of a good Impartial Chairman by asking him to decide general wage-level cases which can be handled by other arbitrators.[19] The same problem is recognized in respect to other new contract issues.[20]

Railroad labor legislation of the United States also recognizes the distinction between rights disputes and interest disputes. The first three federal acts did not differentiate between them,[21] but the Transportation Act of 1920 provided for special treatment of the two types of disputes. Since then the distinction has been sharpened.

The Railway Labor Act of 1926, as amended in 1934, created the National Railroad Adjustment Board (NRAB), which, upon submission of a complaint by either party, takes jurisdiction over "disputes between an employee or group of employees and a carrier or carriers growing out of grievances or out of the interpretation or application of agreements concerning rates of pay, rules, or working conditions * * *" after they have been "handled in the usual manner up to and including the chief operating officer of the carrier designated to handle such disputes." On the other hand, disputes concerning "changes in rates of pay, rules, or working conditions not adjusted by the parties in conference" and "any other dispute not referable to the National Railroad Adjustment Board and not adjusted in conference between the parties or where conferences are refused" are handled by the National Mediation Board.

The function of the NRAB is to interpret and apply collective agreements, not to make or modify them. The NMB, on the other hand, is directed to help the parties, through mediation, to reach agreement

---

[18]Kennedy, Effective Labor Arbitration, 37 (1948). This is a comprehensive treatise on the Impartial Chairmanship of the Full-Fashioned Hosiery Industry. As to this industry, also see Fleming, The Labor Arbitration Process, 10–11 (U. of Ill. Press, 1965).
[19]Kennedy, Effective Labor Arbitration, 38–39 (1948).
[20]Id. at 39.
[21]Acts of 1888, 1898, and 1913.

on the terms of collective agreements and, upon failure to bring about an agreement, to attempt to induce the parties to submit their dispute to voluntary arbitration.[22]

Recognizing the important distinction between the arbitration of rights disputes and interest disputes, the various appointing agencies consider the type of dispute when requested by the parties to provide assistance in the selection of an arbitrator.[23]

While most disputes clearly fall into one of the two categories, basically involving "rights" or basically involving "interests," some disputes involve elements of both and cannot be clearly classified as falling exclusively within either of the categories. Arbitrability of the latter cases depends, as in other cases, upon whether the arbitration clause or submission is broad enough to cover the dispute.

Purpose and Subjects of Interest Arbitration

It is generally believed that the best labor-management contracts are those that are negotiated through collective bargaining without outside assistance. There are frequent instances, however, where the parties find it difficult or impossible to reach agreement by direct negotiation. In these instances, they may choose to settle the conflict by a test of strength, making use of the strike or lockout. But this can be costly and injurious to both parties. Moreover, a suspension of operations may bring great hardship upon others, as in the case of a cessation of public utility activities, for which neither labor nor management may wish to risk public censure.

In these situations voluntary arbitration is a way out of the dilemma.[24] One arbitration board, which was itself determining the provisions to be included in a utility renewal contract, stated the case for arbitration as follows: "Arbitration should be a last resort and not an easy pillow on which to fall just because difficulties are encountered. There is some evidence that in the transit industry there has not been the fullest utilization of collective bargaining just because there has existed a ready alternative. But, on the other hand, it cannot be denied that even some minor overuse of arbitration is preferable to

---

[22]For additional discussion see Chapter 4, topic entitled "Tribunals Under Railway Labor Act"; Lecht, Experience Under Railway Labor Legislation (1955); Jones, Handling of Railroad Labor Disputes 1888–1940 (1941). "[V]irtually every major carrier and labor organization in the railroad industry has participated in at least one major interest arbitration. The same is true in the airline industry." Stark, "The Presidential Address: Theme and Adaptations," Proceedings of the 31st Annual Meeting of NAA, 1, 16 (BNA Books, 1979).

[23]For instance, see policy statement of the United States Conciliation Service, U.S. Dept. of Lab. Rel. S. 47–152 (1946).

[24]For studies of interest arbitration and recommendations concerning its use, see Chapter 1, topic entitled "Arbitration as a Substitute for Work Stoppages"; Chapter 2, subtopic entitled "Interest Arbitration Statutes." Also see Morris, "The Role of Interest Arbitration in a Collective Bargaining System," The Future of Labor Arbitration in America, 197 (AAA, 1976); Handsaker, "Arbitration and Contract Disputes," Proceedings of the 13th Annual Meeting of NAA, 78 (BNA Books, 1960). For an extensive survey of past use of voluntary interest arbitration and its acceptability to the parties, see Stieber, "Voluntary Arbitration of Contract Terms," Proceedings of the 23rd Annual Meeting of NAA, 71 (BNA Books, 1970).

long and costly strikes in this vital utility."[25] With this comment the arbitration board denied the request of one party for deletion of a provision, contained in the prior agreement, for arbitration of new contract terms.[26] However, it is now well established by rulings of the NLRB and the U.S. Court of Appeals that inclusion of an interest arbitration provision in the collective agreement is not a mandatory subject of bargaining; a party may not legally insist upon inclusion of such provisions in the agreement and an existing interest arbitration clause may not be used to perpetuate itself.[27]

Arbitration of interest disputes may be viewed more as an instrument of collective bargaining than as a process of adjudication. In this connection it may be noted that this kind of arbitration is most frequently found in industries where collective bargaining is well established.

An objection commonly urged against the arbitration of interest issues is the absence of definite principles or standards to govern the decision. This belief is not entirely justified, however. There are a number of standards which, while not as adequate as may be desired, are available and applied in the arbitration of such disputes. These standards are discussed in Chapter 18. Moreover, it is not uncommon for parties to agree upon general principles to be observed by the arbitrator (in the public sector such criteria may be specified by statute), leaving to him only the task of applying these principles in the light of evidence. And if they choose, the parties by use of "final offer" arbitration can limit the arbitrator's leeway still more.[28]

The subject matter of interest arbitration can be as extensive and varied as the parties choose to make it. Any subject comprehended by collective bargaining can be placed in the agreement by arbitration. In determining over 20,000 labor-management disputes, most of which were over the terms of new agreements, the National War Labor Board of World War II traversed practically the entire range of collective bargaining issues.

---

[25]Reading St. Ry., 6 LA 860, 871 (Simkin, 1947).

[26]Id. at 872. Also denying such a request, Arbitrator Scheiber in 27 LA 309, 318. However, in a newspaper industry case Arbitrator Platt refused to continue a contractual provision for interest arbitration against the wishes of one party, Arbitrator Platt stating that to rule otherwise would in effect order compulsory arbitration contrary to our system of free collective bargaining. Pacific Neo-Gravure, 51 LA 14, 25 (1968). Accord, Arbitrator Haughton in 13 LA 125. The Platt view was not always followed by subsequent arbitrators in that industry. See Bacheller, "The Value of Old Negotiated Language in an Interest Dispute," Proceedings of the 26th Annual Meeting of NAA, 48, 48–49 (BNA Books, 1974). Seven experts have discussed the long history of using interest arbitration in the local transit and newspaper industries. See "Arbitration of Interest Disputes in the Local Transit and Newspaper Publishing Industries," id. at 8–61. Regarding continued use of interest arbitration for mass transit systems that have been converted to public ownership, see Chapter 2, subtopic entitled "Interest Arbitration Statutes."

[27]Communications Union Local 23 v. Newspapers, 99 LRRM 3033 (CA 7, 1978), citing decisions of four additional Circuits and the NLRB in general accord. In Sheet Metal Workers v. Employers Assn., 95 LRRM 2149 (USDC, 1977), enforcement of an arbitration award was refused where it had been used pursuant to an interest arbitration clause which the union illegally forced upon the employer. For a discussion in favor of imposing a duty to bargain over interest arbitration clauses, see Scharman, "Interest Arbitration in the Private Sector," 36 Arb. J. No. 3, p. 14 (1981).

[28]For more on "final offer" arbitration, see Chapter 2, subtopic entitled "Interest Arbitration Statutes."

Wage issues, as would be expected, constitute the most common subject of interest arbitration.[29] Among other interest issues that have been submitted to arbitration or to emergency boards are those involving: holidays,[30] vacations,[31] sick leave,[32] health and hospitalization benefits,[33] life insurance plans,[34] pension and retirement benefits,[35] automation layoffs,[36] benefits to curb the impact of automation,[37] overtime,[38] merit increases,[39] meal periods,[40] rest periods,[41] seniority rules,[42] job classification,[43] work schedules and shifts,[44] length of workday or workweek,[45] paid bargaining time,[46] separation pay,[47] subcontracting restrictions,[48] union shop,[49] check-off,[50] length of contract term,[51] management rights,[52] pay period,[53] size of grievance committee,[54] and use of permanent arbitrator.[55]

The frequency of submitting issues to interest arbitration is no doubt affected by the economic conditions of the times and by the prevailing political climate. The nature of the issue and the current relations of the parties are of obvious significance. Some of the above issues have been submitted to interest arbitration fairly frequently, but others only infrequently. Then, too, there have been periods of scanty use of interest arbitration, though wage issues have been submitted rather consistently.

Indiscriminate use of interest arbitration is to be avoided, for such use may impede healthy development of the labor-management relationship. In particular, parties who abdicate to arbitrators the responsibility of writing the bulk of the collective agreement risk serious disappointment.

---

[29]For many cases involving the arbitration of wage issues, see Chapter 18.

[30]E.g., 71 LA 271, 69 LA 1041, 68 LA 1097, 48 LA 289, 47 LA 482, 37 LA 3, 27 LA 728, 25 LA 352, 18 LA 290, 16 LA 933.

[31]E.g., 70 LA 850, 70 LA 793, 69 LA 1041, 63 LA 71, 48 LA 289, 45 LA 905, 39 LA 249, 28 LA 182, 24 LA 835, 21 LA 494, 17 LA 353.

[32]E.g., 70 LA 1258, 69 LA 1041, 58 LA 1302, 52 LA 233, 48 LA 289, 47 LA 482, 17 LA 559, 16 LA 749, 14 LA 574, 13 LA 103, 11 LA 450.

[33]E.g., 71 LA 271, 69 LA 1041, 68 LA 454, 57 LA 1000, 44 LA 514, 26 LA 303, 25 LA 352, 22 LA 392, 21 LA 356, 16 LA 933, 11 LA 450.

[34]71 LA 271, 28 LA 600, 22 LA 392, 21 LA 310, 16 LA 749, 13 LA 46.

[35]E.g., 69 LA 1041, 52 LA 233, 37 LA 719, 33 LA 862, 29 LA 101, 25 LA 54, 19 LA 538, 18 LA 5, 14 LA 321, 13 LA 702, 11 LA 1037.

[36]69 LA 1041.

[37]36 LA 44.

[38]65 LA 557.

[39]65 LA 557.

[40]47 LA 482, 17 LA 353, 16 LA 749, 11 LA 166, 9 LA 577, 4 LA 548, 2 LA 663.

[41]17 LA 353, 7 LA 845, 6 LA 98, 2 LA 227.

[42]63 LA 1087, 32 LA 945.

[43]72 LA 383, 68 LA 1064.

[44]11 LA 501, 6 LA 860, 5 LA 269, 3 LA 804, 2 LA 10.

[45]E.g., 47 LA 482, 43 LA 875, 39 LA 249, 28 LA 600, 27 LA 343, 25 LA 54, 21 LA 307, 19 LA 538, 18 LA 903.

[46]71 LA 271.

[47]71 LA 271.

[48]33 LA 451.

[49]E.g., 45 LA 801, 18 LA 112, 16 LA 611, 14 LA 574, 13 LA 620, 11 LA 501.

[50]69 LA 1041, 65 LA 248, 17 LA 833, 14 LA 574, 11 LA 501, 8 LA 149.

[51]E.g., 71 LA 271, 69 LA 1041, 68 LA 1064, 47 LA 482, 45 LA 905, 45 LA 58, 33 LA 451, 27 LA 468, 21 LA 356, 18 LA 174, 15 LA 871.

[52]65 LA 248.

[53]71 LA 271, 68 LA 628, 58 LA 1302.

[54]69 LA 1041.

[55]69 LA 1041.

Leaving too many interest issues to be resolved by neutrals has been severely criticized by the neutrals themselves[56] and has produced some pronounced disappointments of dispute settlement efforts.[57]

Arbitrator's Function in Interest Disputes

While various authorities have expressed generally similar views about the arbitrator's function in interest disputes, there are nuances which are worthy of note and which are illustrated by the comments quoted below.

In a definite sense the function of an interest arbitrator is to legislate for the parties. As explained by Arbitrator Emanuel Stein:

"The task is more nearly legislative than judicial. The answers are not to be found within the 'four corners' of a pre-existing document which the parties have agreed shall govern their relationship. Lacking guidance of such a document which confines and limits the authority of arbitrators to a determination of what the parties had agreed to when they drew up their basic agreement, our task here is to search for what would be, in the light of all the relevant factors and circumstances, a fair and equitable answer to a problem which the parties have not been able to resolve by themselves."[58]

In a similar sense, the function of the interest arbitrator is to supplement the collective bargaining process by doing the bargaining for both parties after they have failed to reach agreement through their own bargaining efforts. Possibly the responsibility of the arbitrator is best understood when viewed in that light. This responsibility and the attitude of humility that appropriately accompanies it

---

[56]See Consumers Power Co., 18 LA 686, 688–689 (Fact-Finding Board, 1952); Pan American World Airways, 17 LA 878, 881 (Emergency Board, 1952). Similar criticism has been voiced in the public sector. See Ellman, "Legislated Arbitration in Michigan—A Lateral Glance," Proceedings of the 31st Annual Meeting of NAA, 291, 302 (BNA Books, 1979) (stating that some parties "have brought 40 or 50 unresolved issues to the arbitration panel," and that in such circumstances "strong chairmen have often told the parties they will simply not entertain such a multitude of issues and directed them to get back to the table and sort out the critical points of dispute"); Anderson, "Lessons from Interest Arbitration in the Public Sector: The Experience of Four Jurisdictions," Proceedings of the 27th Annual Meeting of NAA, 59, 66 (BNA Books, 1975). Worthy of note is the manner in which Arbitrator David E. Feller and the parties handled the disposition of many interest issues in Air New Zealand Ltd., 77 LA 667, 669 (1981), where in addition to wages, "there were in all a total of almost thirty other issues," regarding which Arbitrator Feller stated:

"As the [hearing] meetings progressed, and with some assistance from me when I indicated how I would probably decide, the parties were able to negotiate settlement of most of these issues. As to most of them no explanatory opinion is necessary. As to at least a few, however, I believe that the rationale for the agreement should be set forth at length. There also remained, of course, a few which proved intractable and which I was compelled to decide as an arbitrator. * * * This award, therefore, will set forth my decisions as to the award provisions which remained unresolved and the rationale for the agreement of the parties on some of the stickier issues which were settled during the conciliation process."

[57]New England Transp. Co., 15 LA 126, 133 (Company Dissent, 1950); Duquesne Light Co., 6 LA 470, 487, 492, 498 (Company and Union Dissents, 1947).

[58]New York Shipping Assn., 36 LA 44, 45 (1960). Expressing agreement, see Arbitrator Johannes in 72 LA 383, 386. Contrast the function as viewed by Arbitrator Flagler in Des Moines Transit Co., 38 LA 666, 671 (1962).

have been described by one arbitration board speaking through its chairman, Whitley P. McCoy:

"Arbitration of contract terms differs radically from arbitration of grievances. The latter calls for a judicial determination of existing contract rights; the former calls for a determination, upon considerations of policy, fairness, and expediency, of what the contract rights ought to be. In submitting this case to arbitration, the parties have merely extended their negotiations—they have left it to this board to determine what they should, by negotiation, have agreed upon. We take it that the fundamental inquiry, as to each issue, is: what should the parties themselves, as reasonable men, have voluntarily agreed to? * * * We believe that an unusual demand, that is, one that has not found substantial acceptance in other properties, casts upon the union the burden of showing that, because of its minor character or its inherent reasonableness, the negotiators should, as reasonable men, have voluntarily agreed to it. We would not deny such a demand merely because it had not found substantial acceptance, but it would take clear evidence to persuade us that the negotiators were unreasonable in rejecting it. We do not conceive it to be our function to impose on the parties contract terms merely because they embody our own individual economic or social theories. To repeat, our endeavor will be to decide the issues as, upon the evidence, we think reasonable negotiators, regardless of their social or economic theories might have decided them in the give and take process of bargaining. We agree with the company that the interests of stockholders and the public must be considered, and consideration of their interests will enter into our conclusions as to what the parties should reasonably have agreed on."[59]

In concluding its opinion, the board said:

"We render this award not with pride but with some humility. The parties have placed upon us a tremendous task. In judging the results reached and deciding whether the award as a whole is fair, we invite the parties to consider whether, if an offer embodying this entire award had been made in bargaining, it would have been accepted as a reasonable compromise of many demands. If it would have been, we have performed the function we set for ourselves at the outset, namely, to determine what the parties, as reasonable men, should themselves have agreed to at the bargaining table."[60]

A highly realistic statement of the interest arbitrator's function has been offered by Arbitrator Harry H. Platt:

---

[59]Twin City Rapid Transit Co., 7 LA 845, 848 (1947). Similar views have been expressed by other highly respected arbitrators. See North American Aviation, 19 LA 76, 77 (Cole, Aaron, and Wirtz, 1952). Cf., statement of Arbitrator Ables in 71 LA 838, 840.

[60]Twin City Rapid Transit Co., 7 LA 845, 858 (1947). Arbitrator McCoy also used "reasonable compromise" terminology in 29 LA 7, 10 (1957). Professor Charles O. Gregory suggested that the compulsory arbitration of interests should be called "compulsory collective bargaining" rather than arbitration. Gregory, "The Enforcement of Collective Labor Agreements by Arbitration," 13 U. Chi. L. Rev. 445, 469–470 (1946). For various possible uses of neutrals in bargaining negotiations, see "Current Problems of Arbitration," 35 LA 963, 965–966 (1961). In respect to combining or alternating mediation and arbitration functions in an interest-dispute neutral, see Gershenfeld, "Perceptions of the Arbitrator and the Parties," Proceedings of the 31st Annual Meeting of NAA, 305, 314–315 (BNA Books, 1979) (speaking of (1) "med-arb," in which the neutral moves from mediation into arbitration, and (2) "arb-med," in which the neutral moves from arbitration into mediation); Howlett, "Contract Negotiation Arbitration in the Public Sector," 42 U. Cin. L. Rev. 47, 70 (1973).

"[A]rbitrators in private wage disputes do not always conceive their function to be merely to discover what the parties would have agreed upon in negotiations and to decide accordingly. Quite often they view their function to be to fix a wage rate that will be fair and equitable to all concerned. Indeed, it is questionable whether any practical objective method exists of measuring the parties' bargaining strength—even when they bargain to a conclusion. In reality, an arbitrator's determination of what the parties would have agreed upon in negotiations if they had not arbitrated is his own opinion of what they should have agreed upon."[61]

Sometimes it is possible for the parties to agree upon the criteria to be observed by an arbitrator in deciding the issues submitted to him. (In the public sector, criteria may be specified by statute.) But even with agreed-upon points of reference, the discretion of the arbitrator ordinarily can be expected to be quite broad.[62] Interest arbitration, as part of the collective bargaining process, is essentially dynamic and fluid. The aggressor seeks to move into a new field, to expand the limits of an old area, or to reduce rights previously granted. It can be expected that something new will come from the arbitrator and that there will be some substitution of his judgment for that of the respective parties. It must be recognized that if the strike is to be relegated to a position of being the "very last resort, reasonable innovations must be possible through the arbitration process. Otherwise either progress would be unduly slowed or strikes invited, or both."[63] This should also apply to the public sector, where progress is no less needed. Nor does the interest arbitrator's role in the public sector appear to be generally different from the private-sector role, although in specific jurisdictions some distinctions or limitations concerning the interest arbitrator's role will be produced by public-sector statutes.[64]

Of course, in carrying out his function as "legislator" or "bargainer" for the parties, the interest arbitrator must strive to achieve a workable solution. It has been well said:

"[The arbitrator is] not a superior sort of dictator, dispensing justice from on high, but an agent of the two sides to the collective bargain. His job is to reach a solution that will be satisfactory enough to both sides to be workable. He has to take into consideration their relative strength and their relative necessities. He has to remember not to depart so far from a possible compromise, consistent with the respective power and desires of the parties, that one or the other of them will be likely next

---

[61]Port Authority of Allegheny County, 50 LA 1103, 1109 (1968). For a similar view, see Arbitrator Heliker in 33 LA 451, 454.

[62]"Final offer" arbitration is an obvious exception.

[63]San Diego Elec. Ry., 11 LA 458, 461 (Kerr, 1948).

[64]See Chapter 2, subtopic entitled "Interest Arbitration Statutes." And the public interest will tend to be of greater concern for the public sector. In this regard, note the thoughts expressed by Gershenfeld, "Perceptions of the Arbitrator and the Parties," Proceedings of the 31st Annual Meeting of NAA, 305, 316 (BNA Books, 1979) ("public-sector interest-arbitrators are moving away from a pure 'creature of the parties' approach to a recognition of some public-interest role"); Morse, "Comment," Proceedings of the 29th Annual Meeting of NAA, 175, 178–179 (BNA Books, 1976) ("with regard to the politics of arbitration, it is quite probable that arbitrators will become legislators in the public sector," and "we in public management find it difficult to accept this sort of control outside the normal public-policy process").

time to prefer open hostility to peaceful settlement. He has also to remember that a decision is useless if it cannot be enforced and that the power and ability of the respective parties to administer a decision successfully is an integral part of the decision itself.

"A decision which cannot be carried into effect or which will create lasting dissatisfaction is not really a decision at all. On this account a wage arbitration is not an exercise in pure reason, and a summary of merely logical arguments, accompanied by the opinion accompanying the decision, does not tell the whole story. Arbitrators frequently do not, of course, fully understand these limitations, but the more successful ones do so."[65]

Finally, we note that distinctions may be drawn between the role of emergency boards and that of the interest arbitrator. One emergency board, for instance, explained:

"The present Board, comprised solely of neutrals, is not empowered to make a final and binding award. Its Report, including recommendations, is designed to facilitate the subsequent and further collective bargaining of the parties. This Report is not intended to write the precise language of the collective bargaining agreement nor to determine the exact terms of settlement of the disputes between the parties. Rather, it is designed to suggest a relatively narrow area of settlement which the parties should explore constructively. The purpose of the Board is to present the facts, appropriate standards, and suggestions, in the hope that these will persuade the parties voluntarily to reach an agreement."[66]

Interest Arbitration and Contract Clauses

Specific Provision for Interest Arbitration

Occasionally, a collective agreement will provide specifically for arbitration, at its expiration, of unsettled disputes over the terms of a new agreement.[67] A collective agreement clause providing for arbitration of future interest disputes may, for example, be as follows:

"Any differences that may arise between the company and the local union concerning wage reviews at dates specified in the agreement, or

---

[65]Soule, Wage Arbitration, 6–7 (1928). While this statement was made in reference to wage issues, it would appear equally applicable to other interest matters.

[66]Railroads v. Nonoperating Unions, 34 LA 517, 522 (Dunlop, Aaron, and Sempliner, 1960). The Board also emphasized its responsibility to clarify the public interest in the dispute, to explain the dispute to the public, and thus "to bring to the bargaining table a further measure of public interest." Ibid. Another board explained that some emergency boards make recommendations only on the major subjects in dispute, while other boards deal with each submitted item. "Whatever technique is used, however, the underlying assumption is the same. The parties, following receipt of the Board's report, will be in a position to enter into a new collective bargaining contract which finally disposes of all requests of both employer and union." Pan American World Airways v. Flight Engineers, 36 LA 1047, 1051 (Dash, Lynch, and Stark, 1961).

[67]For example, see Oxmoor Press, 68 LA 1064 at 1064 (Williams, 1977). Of 1717 agreements covered by one study, less than 2 percent provided for arbitration of such disputes. Major Collective Bargaining Agreements: Arbitration Procedures, 95 (U.S. Dept. Labor Bull. No. 1425–6, 1966). Five hundred of the agreements contained "reopening" clauses, and of these about 15 percent provided for arbitration if negotiations failed. Id. at 101. For related discussion, see Chapter 1, topic entitled "Arbitration as a Substitute for Work Stoppages"; Chapter 2, subtopic entitled "Interest Arbitration Statutes."

concerning amendments to the agreement at any termination date, which the representatives of the company and the local union are unable to settle, shall be submitted at the request of either party to a Board of Arbitration to be selected in a manner as specified hereinafter. The company and the local union agree that the majority decision of such Board shall be final and binding on both parties."[68]

More often, however, parties do not reach any agreement to arbitrate new contract terms until the old contract has expired and an impasse in negotiations has been reached.[69]

It may be noted that court decisions are in conflict as to whether LMRA § 301 covers agreements to arbitrate future interest disputes so as to empower the courts to enforce collective agreement provisions for such arbitration.[70]

Clauses Equivocal as to Interest Disputes

Some collective agreements contain provisions which on their face indicate a very broad scope of arbitration, without providing a clue as to whether the process was intended to be limited to disputes involving the interpretation of the agreement or was intended to include also disputes not arising under the agreement. Such provisions may state that "any grievance or complaint" or "any difference" or "any dispute over wages, hours, or other conditions of employment" may be arbitrated. In some instances arbitrators have held interest type disputes to be arbitrable under such *broad* arbitration clauses,[71] but in other instances arbitrators have ruled to the contrary.[72]

In one case the arbitrator held that while a provision for arbitration of "all" unsettled disputes made a demand for amendment of the contract arbitrable in the procedural sense that the arbitrator could rule upon it, the fact that granting the demand would alter the contract was good reason for its denial, since it would be unsound and

---

[68]Agreement between San Diego Gas & Elec. Co. and IBEW (agreement has expired). For other examples, see Major Collective Bargaining Agreements: Arbitration Procedures, 98–103 (U.S. Dept. Labor Bull. No. 1425–6, 1966).

[69]For the type of instrument that may be used in such cases, see Arbitrator Oppenheim in 63 LA 621, 622–623; Cluster in 45 LA 801, 806–807; Blair in 3 LA 245, 246. In Stur-Dee Health Prods., 104 LRRM 1012 (NLRB, 1980), a collective agreement barred the election petition of an outside union although the economic terms had not been set, since the employer and incumbent union had left them for determination by binding interest arbitration.

[70]Cases pro and con are collected in Mayo, "The Enforceability of Interest Arbitration Agreements Under Section 301(a) of the Labor Management Relations Act," 27 Syracuse L. Rev. 985, 986–987 (1976), indicating that of the circuits of the U.S. Court of Appeals that have ruled on the question, a majority favor enforcement.

[71]See Arbitrator Kates in 49 LA 40, 44; Duff in 48 LA 600, 603; Joseph in 48 LA 425, 427; Pope in 7 LA 685, 686; Brissenden in 6 LA 639, 641. For court decisions holding interest type disputes arbitrable under such broad clauses, see Laundry Workers Local 93 v. Mahoney, 491 F.2d 1029 (CA 8, 1974), where an evenly divided court upheld a lower court order for arbitration; Beech Nut Packing Co., 23 LA 125 (N.Y. Sup. Ct., 1954); Textile Workers Union v. Cheney Bros., 22 LA 512 (Conn. Sup. Ct., 1954); Northland Greyhound Lines v. Amalgamated Assn., 3 LA 887 (USDC, 1946).

[72]See Arbitrator Gregory in 41 LA 1169, 1174–1176; Wallen in 12 LA 475, 478; Lehoczky in 9 LA 656, 657.

unwise for him to impose his judgment where the appropriate course of action is bilateral negotiation and agreement.[73]

Efforts of a party to arbitrate pure interest issues under *narrow* arbitration clauses have often failed. For instance, under a clause providing only for arbitration of disputes involving the interpretation or application of the agreement, the fact that the agreement permitted reopening for consideration of general wage adjustments did not oblige the parties to agree on wage increases or, upon failing to agree, to permit an arbitrator to decide for them.[74]

But the fact that a contract excepts general wage increases from arbitration does not prevent arbitration of the question of whether the wage reopening clause permits more than one reopening during the contract term, since this issue involves the interpretation of the contract, rather than a general wage increase as such.[75]

Subject Matter of Rights Arbitration

The sources of the subject matter of rights disputes are usually agreements, laws, and customary practices. Among the infinite number of matters that may be the subject of rights arbitration are questions with respect to seniority rights, vacations, holidays, discharge and discipline, layoffs, job classification, and the like.

But not all issues that are taken to arbitrators fall into such commonly recognized categories. This is illustrated by the historic "Case of the Lady in Red Slacks." A Ford Motor Company employee was reprimanded and docked one-half hour because she wore slacks described as bright red in color. The objection was to the color, not to the slacks, which female employees were required to wear. The issue was whether a lady's red slacks constituted a production hazard because of a tendency to distract male employees. Umpire Shulman stated that "it is common knowledge that wolves, unlike bulls, may be attracted by colors other than red and by various other enticements in the art and fit of female attire." The reprimand was expunged and the employee was reimbursed for the pay that she had been docked.[76]

---

[73]Dictograph Prods., Inc., 8 LA 1033, 1038 (Kaplan, 1947). Also see Chapter 7, topic entitled "Recommendations by Arbitrator."

[74]In re Berger, 9 LA 1048 (N.Y. Sup. Ct., 1948), aff'd, 10 LA 929 (N.Y. App. Div., 1948). Accord, Arbitrator Aaron in 36 LA 1125, 1128; McCoy in 24 LA 741, 744; Livingston in 10 LA 528, 530. Also see Reynard in 24 LA 587, 589–591. Cf., Kerr in 20 LA 106, 107–108; Donnelly in 14 LA 1055, 1058.

[75]F.H. Hill Co., 8 LA 223, 225 (Blair, 1947). To similar effect, Arbitrator Piercey in 22 LA 261, 263–264; Stein in 7 LA 748, 749.

[76]Shulman, Opinions of the Umpire, Opinion A-117 (1944). Other disputes about female attire were resolved by Arbitrator Ryder in 45 LA 1071, 1073 (female could not be punished for wearing "short shorts"); Davis in 28 LA 83, 87. In later years personal appearance has emerged as a frequently arbitrated subject. See Chapter 17, topic entitled "Personal Appearance: Hair and Clothes."

Arbitrator's Function in Rights Disputes

The function of the rights arbitrator in the interpretation and application of collective agreements is treated in detail in Chapter 9 of this book, particularly in the topic entitled "Ambiguity" and the subtopic entitled "Legislation v. Interpretation." The reader is urged to consult those topics concerning the arbitrator's function in rights disputes.

Observers will probably agree that, on the whole, the function of the rights arbitrator is quite similar to that of a court in construing contracts.[77] The function is basically that of adjudication rather than legislation. Indeed, the parties very frequently provide that the arbitrator shall have no power to add to, subtract from, or modify any provision of the agreement.[78] Nonetheless, the boundary line between interpretation and legislation cannot be drawn absolutely, and it is inevitable that the line will be crossed, in greater or lesser degree, fairly often. As is true of a court, an arbitrator may apply either a liberal or a strict construction to the provisions of an agreement, depending upon the question and circumstances involved, the attitude of the parties, and, of course, the general attitude of the arbitrator.

Helpful insight into rights arbitration, and in particular in regard to the function of the arbitrator, is provided by observing one of the nation's most extensive experiences in such arbitration—the NRAB. The RLA gives the Adjustment Board jurisdiction over "disputes between an employee or group of employees and a carrier or carriers growing out of grievances or out of the interpretation or application of agreements concerning rates of pay, rules, or working conditions * * *." While the word "Adjustment" in the Board's name might suggest that under this grant of jurisdiction the Board was intended to serve as an extension and continuation of the bargaining process,[79] in actual practice the function of the Board is much like true adjudication:

> "In hearing and deciding the cases which come before the Board [the Board members] do not act as negotiators or adjusters. Whatever may have been the intent of the law in setting up an Adjustment Board, there has been no trace in the history of the Board of any view on its part that its function is to iron out differences by taking into account the situation and needs of the parties and the practical effect of their respective demands, and on the basis of such consideration making concessions to

---

[77]One survey revealed general (but not unanimous) agreement regarding this similarity. See Eaton, "Labor Arbitration in the San Francisco Bay Area," 48 LA 1381, 1383, 1391 (1967).

[78]Of 400 agreements included in one study, 88 percent so restricted the arbitrator. See "Basic Patterns in Labor Arbitration Agreements," 34 LA 931, 939 (1960).

[79]The labor members of the Board at one time expressed the view that this was the intended function of the Board. See statement of labor members submitted to the Attorney General's Committee on Administrative Procedure, in Railway Labor, 9–10 (1940), reprinted in Jones, National Railroad Adjustment Board, 226 (1941). Those "who were mainly responsible for the statutory creation of the Board in 1934 hoped and doubtless believed that the Board would grow up to live chiefly as a collective bargaining agency * * * rather than as a real arbitration tribunal of last resort. * * * this hope has not been fulfilled for many years * * *." Daugherty, "Arbitration by the National Railroad Adjustment Board," Arbitration Today, 93, 94 (BNA Books, 1955).

one party in return for concessions by it for the good of the industry as a whole. The Board has never taken this view of its function. Instead it has assumed with the strictest legalistic viewpoint that the loosely drawn and often vague terms of the schedules and agreements which come before it have a rigid technical meaning, and that this meaning is to be discovered by a process of purely technical reasoning. The most cursory examination of the nature of the arguments put up to the Board and the grounds of its decisions, where these are given, conclusively demonstrates that it regards its function as one of strict legal interpretation rather than compromise and adjustment."[80]

Probably most persons familiar with the activities of the NRAB would agree that the just-quoted statement is basically accurate and applies with equal force today. Certainly, when a referee is called in to sit as a member of the Board in deadlocked cases, the function of the Board is adjudication. But even in adjudication some rule making is inevitable:

"Even on the assumption that the Adjustment Board is strictly confined to the interpretation and application of existing rules, it is inescapable, particularly in deadlocked cases, that it will exercise a greater or less influence on the nature and scope of agreements between carriers and labor organizations. The Constitution of the United States is a small compact document; but one can gain no appreciation of its meaning and scope without examining the thousands of decisions in which the Supreme Court, in its interpretation, has molded and modified it. In a similar manner, it is inevitable that the Adjustment Board, subject to judicial review, will mold and modify railway collective agreements."[81]

In industries that use the permanent umpire or chairman device, the function varies. The jurisdiction of the Impartial Umpire for the Ford Motor Company and the United Auto Workers (UAW) has been limited generally to "alleged violations of the terms" of the parties' agreements. By specific provision he has been denied the power to "add to or subtract from or modify any of the terms of any agreement"; or to "substitute his discretion for the company's discretion in cases where the company is given discretion" by any agreement; or to "provide agreement for the parties in those cases where they have in their contract agreed that further negotiations shall or may provide for certain contingencies to cover certain subjects."[82] The General Motors-UAW agreement states that the Umpire "shall have no power to add to or subtract from or modify any of the terms" of the agreement; the agreement further states that "Any case appealed to the Umpire on which he has no power to rule shall be referred back to the parties

---

[80]Railway Labor, ibid. The quotation is the statement of a carrier spokesman before the Attorney General's Committee.

[81]Spencer, The National Railroad Adjustment Board, 31 (1938), reprinted in Jones, National Railroad Adjustment Board, p. 181 of appendix (1941).

[82]See Ford Motor Co., 6 LA 952, 953 (Shulman, 1944). The quoted provisions have been continued in subsequent Ford-UAW agreements. The jurisdiction of the Chrysler Appeal Board is somewhat similar to that of the Ford umpire. See Wolff, Crane & Cole, "The Chrysler-UAW Umpire System," Proceedings of the 11th Annual Meeting of NAA, 111, 114 (BNA Books, 1958).

without decision." However, the agreement gives the Umpire "full discretion" in certain discipline cases.[83]

On the other hand, the Impartial Chairman of the full-fashioned hosiery industry has been given authority to determine all disputes except those involving new or renewal contract terms.[84]

This subject should not be discussed without noting the view, as expressed by George W. Taylor, former Chairman of the National War Labor Board and a former Impartial Chairman of the full-fashioned hosiery industry, that grievance settlement often becomes an integral part of agreement-making. In an address before the NAA, he said:

> "A third important characteristic of grievance arbitration should be mentioned. Contrary to the views of many arbitrators, grievance settlement is not simply a process of contract interpretation. * * * [T]he difficult grievances arise because the labor contract reflects only a partial or an inconclusive meeting of minds. It doesn't give the reasonably clear answer to a dispute. In such cases, grievance settlement becomes an integral part of agreement-making. At any event, the manner in which the grievances are settled provides understandings that are as durable, or more so, than the actual terms of the labor contract themselves. No one need amplify to this audience the weight of 'established practices.' "[85]

The Taylor view has been approved by some but severely criticized by others.[86]

In one utterance the U.S. Supreme Court appears to have considered arbitration a part of "the continuous collective bargaining process":

> "Apart from matters that the parties specifically exclude, all of the questions on which the parties disagree must therefore come within the scope of the grievance and arbitration provisions of the collective agreement. The grievance procedure is, in other words, a part of the continuous collective bargaining process. It, rather than a strike, is the terminal point of a disagreement.

---

[83]The quoted provisions were adopted years ago and have been continued in subsequent agreements. One General Motors Umpire has commented that General Motors and the UAW have "needed and expected a so-called 'legalistic' approach to arbitration." Alexander, "Impartial Umpireships: The General Motors-UAW Experience," Arbitration and the Law, 157 (BNA Books, 1958).

[84]Kennedy, Effective Labor Arbitration, 34–36 (1948). In this industry, all disputes arising during the life of the contract "including but not limited to the interpretation, construction or application of the terms of this agreement" are "submitted to the Impartial Chairman for final and binding decision by him." He is denied the power to "alter, modify, or change" the "Agreement or any of the terms or provisions thereof," but there is no denial of power to add to the agreement, and the grant of power to decide issues not covered by the agreement can be viewed as giving him authority to add, by decisions, to the agreement. Ibid.

[85]Taylor, "Effectuating the Labor Contract Through Arbitration," The Profession of Labor Arbitration, 20, 21 (BNA Books, 1957). In Standard Gravure Corp., 62-3 Arb ¶8927 (1962), the company urged that the arbitrator's function was adjudication while the union urged that it was an instrument of collective bargaining. Arbitrator Platt responded: "But in the Chairman's opinion, neither approach alone adequately represents the arbitration function in manning cases; together they mark the bounds within which an award should fall."

[86]For various reactions to the Taylor view, see O'Connell, "Should the Scope of Arbitration Be Restricted," Proceedings of the 18th Annual Meeting of NAA, 102, 103–110 (BNA Books, 1965); Garrett, "Some Potential Uses of the Opinion," Proceedings of the 17th Annual Meeting of NAA, 114, 122 (BNA Books, 1964); Garrett, "The Role of Lawyers in Arbitration," Proceedings of the 14th Annual Meeting of NAA, 102, 115–122 (BNA Books, 1961).

"The labor arbitrator performs functions which are not normal to the courts; the considerations which help him fashion judgments may indeed be foreign to the competence of courts. * * *

"The labor arbitrator's source of law is not confined to the express provisions of the contract, as the industrial common law—the practices of the industry and the shop—is equally a part of the collective bargaining agreement although not expressed in it. The labor arbitrator is usually chosen because of the parties' confidence in his knowledge of the common law of the shop and their trust in his personal judgment to bring to bear considerations which are not expressed in the contract as criteria for judgment. * * * The ablest judge cannot be expected to bring the same experience and competence to bear upon the determination of a grievance, because he cannot be similarly informed."[87]

But in another utterance, contemporaneous with the statement quoted above, the Supreme Court bluntly confined arbitrators to the function specified by the parties:

"When an arbitrator is commissioned to interpret and apply the collective bargaining agreement, he is to bring his informed judgment to bear in order to reach a fair solution of a problem. This is especially true when it comes to formulating remedies. * * * Nevertheless, an arbitrator is confined to interpretation and application of the collective bargaining agreement; he does not sit to dispense his own brand of industrial justice. He may of course look for guidance from many sources, yet his award is legitimate only so long as it draws its essence from the collective bargaining agreement. When the arbitrator's words manifest an infidelity to this obligation, courts have no choice but to refuse enforcement of the award."[88]

In apparently denying that there can be "a single generalized concept of the arbitration process which would be valid for all purposes," Impartial Chairman Sylvester Garrett explained:

"There is infinite variety among arbitrators and arbitration systems, just as there are all kinds of judges and other tribunals. What one man will believe proper and practical in the interpretation of language will seem visionary to another under the same circumstances. One man's flair for mediation can be matched by another's distaste for it."[89]

Chairman Garrett explained further that some judges, like some arbitrators, have sought to induce settlements; he stated that critics of the "judicial process" theory of grievance arbitration have proceeded on the false assumption that all judges take a mechanical and sterile approach to agreement interpretation.[90]

Rights Arbitration Contract Clauses

Broad arbitration clauses utilize terminology such as "all disputes" or "any difference" between the parties. Such clauses often

---

[87]United Steelworkers v. Warrior & Gulf Navigation Co., 80 S.Ct. 1347, 1352–1353 (1960). For extensive discussion of past practice in arbitration, see Chapter 12, particularly the topic entitled "Custom and Practice as Part of the Contract."

[88]United Steelworkers v. Enterprise Wheel & Car Corp., 80 S.Ct. 1358, 1361 (1960).

[89]Garrett, "The Role of Lawyers in Arbitration," Proceedings of the 14th Annual Meeting of NAA, 102, 122 (BNA Books, 1961).

[90]Id. at 114, 120, 122.

expressly exclude stated types of interest disputes, and sometimes exclude stated types of rights disputes.[91] Apart from express exclusions, *broad* clauses permit the arbitration of a wide variety of rights disputes, including those which do not involve the interpretation or application of the agreement.[92]

Of 1609 collective agreements studied by the U.S. Department of Labor in one survey, about one fourth contained *broad* arbitration clauses, while about three fourths contained *narrow* clauses restricting arbitration to disputes involving interpretation or application of the agreement.[93]

Narrow clauses restrict arbitration to disputes involving the interpretation or application of the agreement. Agreements with narrow clauses typically restrict the arbitrator's authority further by expressly prohibiting him from adding to, subtracting from, or altering the agreement. Sometimes additional restrictions are added by the express exclusion of stated types of interpretation or application disputes.

Under narrow arbitration clauses a dispute may be held nonarbitrable unless it involves rights traceable to the agreement.[94] However, disputes are sometimes held arbitrable under such clauses even though the agreement contains no specific provision on the subject of

---

[91]A clause excluding disputes concerning the "general subject of wages, hours and working conditions" was construed to exclude interest disputes but not rights disputes. Standard Oil Co., 52 LA 151, 153 (Koven, 1968).

[92]Examples of disputes held arbitrable though not involving interpretation or application of the agreement are: *claim against employer for assault upon employee by employer's agent,* Goldstein v. Corbin, 63 LRRM 2248 (N.Y. Sup. Ct., 1966); *compulsory retirement,* Communications Workers v. Southwestern Bell Tel. Co., 415 F.2d 35 (CA 5, 1969); *claim based upon alleged oral agreement,* United Eng'g. & Foundry Employees Assn. v. United Eng'g. and Foundry Co., 389 F.2d 479 (CA 3, 1967); *issue of contract termination by abandonment,* Local 1176 v. Bay Area Sealers, 99 LRRM 2313 (CA 9, 1978); *safety dispute,* Gateway Coal Co. v. Mine Workers, 94 S.Ct. 629 (1974); *right to Christmas bonus,* Newspaper Guild v. Tonawanda Corp., 55 LRRM 2222 (N.Y. Sup. Ct., 1964); *damage claim for secondary boycott,* Old Dutch Farms, Inc. v. Teamsters, 59 LRRM 2745 (USDC, 1965). For other examples, but involving arbitrability rulings by arbitrators, see Arbitrator Handsaker in 22 LA 482, 483–484; Ryder in 22 LA 769, 771; Jaffee in 19 LA 872, 874; Gilden in 17 LA 81, 84; Lane in 8 LA 306; Abernethy in 7 LA 202, 217; Whiting in 6 LA 661, 662–663. In Operating Eng'rs. v. Flair Builders, Inc., 80 LRRM 2441 (1972), the U.S. Supreme Court broadly interpreted the term "any difference." However, in Atkinson v. Sinclair Ref. Co., 82 S.Ct. 1318 (1962), the Supreme Court held that employer grievances were not included within a clause defining grievances as "any difference regarding wages, hours or working conditions between the parties hereto or between the employer and an employee"; the Court held that since the employer's claim for damages for breach of a no-strike clause would not be arbitrable, he could seek damages in court.

[93]Major Collective Bargaining Agreements: Arbitration Procedures, 6, 10 (U.S. Dept. Labor Bull. No. 1425–6, 1966). Of the 433 broad clauses, 93 excluded one or more issues from arbitration. Of the 1173 narrow clauses, 255 expressly excluded one or more issues. A subsequent survey provides statistics on subjects excluded from arbitration but does not provide data to indicate the relative use of *broad* and *narrow* arbitration clauses. See Characteristics of Major Collective Bargaining Agreements, July 1, 1976, 82 (U.S. Dept. of Labor Bull. No. 2013, 1979).

[94]For example, see WJLA v. Broadcast Employees, 88 LC ¶11,856 (USDC, 1980); Safeway Stores, 71 LA 102 (Stephens, 1978). Where arbitration was limited to "alleged violation of the terms of the agreement," and where the agreement was silent on subcontracting, a grievance protesting subcontracting was not arbitrable. Independent Petroleum Workers v. American Oil Co., 324 F.2d 903 (CA 7, 1963), aff'd. by equally divided Court, 379 U.S. 130 (1964). Where the agreement limited arbitration to grievances involving "the interpretation and application of the specific provisions of this agreement," a grievance over the employer's decision to discontinue the distribution of Christmas turkeys was held nonarbitrable. Boeing Co. v. Auto Workers, 349 F.2d 412 (CA 3, 1965). For cases in which arbitrators have denied or dismissed grievances as being beyond the scope of their authority, see Chapter 7, topic titled "Recommendations by Arbitrator."

the alleged right, as where the claimed right may be inherent in clauses on other subjects.[95] Furthermore, the "presumptive arbitrability" standard of the U.S. Supreme Court must be kept in mind in considering whether a court or an arbitrator might hold any given dispute to be arbitrable.[96]

Precontract and Postcontract Grievances

Under the narrow "interpretation and application" arbitration clauses, disputes which arise prior to execution of the agreement have been held nonarbitrable, even though the grievance is filed after execution of the agreement.[97]

Regarding grievances that arise in the interim between the expiration of one collective agreement and the execution of a new one, the situation as it stood prior to the U.S. Supreme Court's decision in the *Nolde* case was summarized as follows:

> "[M]ost courts have held that a grievance which arises after a contract terminates is not subject to the expired arbitration provisions of that contract, and that the court must thus determine whether the contract on which suit is brought has indeed expired. * * *
>
> "When the grievance arises during the contract term but arbitration is not demanded until after its termination, the theory just developed might point toward denying arbitration, but the few cases on the issue hold to the contrary * * *. In effect, the right of access to the grievance procedure is deemed 'vested' as of the date the alleged grievance arises."[98]

In its 1977 *Nolde* decision the Supreme Court recognized that grievances which arise during the life of the collective agreement, and are arbitrable under the agreement, would not become nonarbitrable merely because the agreement is terminated before arbitration is requested or commences. But the Court went further and held a grievance arbitrable although it arose after termination of the collective agreement, where the grievance was based on a right that argua-

---

[95]See Arbitrator Marshall in 23 LA 228; Donnelly in 13 LA 747; Wallen in 9 LA 757. Also see Arbitrator Goodstein in 69 LA 1; Shister in 25 LA 50; Kaplan in 3 LA 259. In Camden Indus. Co. v. Carpenters Union, 60 LRRM 2183 (USDC, 1965), the court took the view that arbitration should be ordered if there is a possibility that an arbitrator may be able to resolve the dispute by interpreting existing provisions of the agreement; if the arbitrator subsequently finds that the dispute cannot be resolved by interpreting existing provisions, it is his responsibility then to hold the dispute to be nonarbitrable.

[96]See Chapter 2, subtopic entitled "The *Trilogy*," and Chapter 6, topics entitled "Determination by the Courts" and "Determination by the Arbitrator." Matters which are expressly excluded from the arbitration clause will ordinarily be held nonarbitrable. See United Mine Workers v. Chris-Craft Corp., 385 F.2d 946 (CA 6, 1967). In Local 4-449 v. Amoco Chem. Corp., 100 LRRM 2646 (CA 5, 1979), the collective agreement made the employer's decision on a certain matter "final" and this was held to constitute a specific exclusion of the matter from arbitration. Cf., Los Angeles Paper Bag Co. v. Printing Specialties and Paper Prods. Union, 345 F.2d 757 (CA 9, 1965).

[97]See Arbitrator Wettach in 25 LA 772, 773; Platt in 20 LA 850, 851–852; Millar in 20 LA 207, 210; McCoy in 8 LA 66, 67; Marshall in 6 LA 460, 461. Cf., Shister in 33 LA 390. Similarly, a promise made to persons before they became covered by the collective agreement was not arbitrable under an "interpretation and application" clause. Ranco, Inc., 50 LA 269, 273 (Klein, 1968).

[98]Gorman, Basic Text on Labor Law, 563–564 (1976). Also see summary in City of Detroit, 71 LA 340, 341 (Munger, 1978), where illustrative cases are cited.

bly had "accrued" or become "vested" under the agreement prior to its termination. Thus, where (1) the severance-pay grievance in *Nolde* would clearly have been arbitrable under the broad "all grievances" clause had it arisen during the life of the agreement, and (2) the union alleged that the claimed severance benefits had accrued or become vested during the term of the agreement (though payable only when employment terminates), the Court held the grievance arbitrable even though it arose from an event, plant closure, which occurred after the union terminated the agreement.[99]

The Court stated that the dispute, "although arising *after* the expiration of the collective-bargaining contract, clearly arises *under* that contract."[100] And stating strong policy reasons for holding the dispute arbitrable, the Court concluded that "where the dispute is over a provision of the expired agreement, the presumptions favoring arbitrability must be negated expressly or by clear implication."[101]

Professor Harry Edwards (subsequently a federal judge) suggested that *"Nolde Brothers'* extension of arbitrability after contract termination will likely be limited to cases in which the union can formulate a plausible argument that management has violated a right 'accrued' or 'vested' by the lapsed agreement."[102] Taking a like view

---

[99]Nolde Bros., Inc. v. Local No. 358, Bakery & Confectionery Workers Union, 97 S.Ct. 1067, 94 LRRM 2753 (1977). The employer had paid accrued vacation pay under the expired agreement but refused to pay severance pay. Since the union promptly sought arbitration, the Court said it "need not speculate as to the arbitrability of posttermination contractual claims which, unlike the one presently before us, are not asserted within a reasonable time after the contract's expiration." 97 S.Ct. at 1074 n. 8. For related discussion, see Chapter 5, topic entitled "Time Limitations."

[100]97 S.Ct. at 1071, where the Court explained: "Of course, in determining the arbitrability of the dispute, the merits of the underlying claim for severance pay are not before us. However, it is clear that * * * the resolution of that claim hinges on the interpretation ultimately given the contract clause providing for severance pay. The dispute, therefore, although arising *after* the expiration of the collective-bargaining contract, clearly arises *under* that contract." In Bunn-O-Matic Corp., 70 LA 34, 39–40 (Talent, 1977), a postcontract claim for severance pay was sustained, the Arbitrator discussing *Nolde* along with arbitral precedents in which severance pay had been held to be accrued benefits surviving the agreement's expiration. Regarding court action to preserve employer assets pending arbitration, see Teamsters Local 71 v. Akers Motor Lines, 99 LRRM 2601 (CA 4, 1978). On a union's right to arbitrate grievances after it has lost its majority status or has been decertified, see ILWU Local 142 v. Land & Constr. Co., 86 LRRM 2874 (CA 9, 1974); Machinists v. International Aircraft Servs., 49 LRRM 2976 (CA 4, 1962); Trumbull Asphalt Co., 38 LA 1093 (Elson, 1962). Also see Note, "Union's Right to Assert Grievances Subsequent to Its Decertification and Change of Corporate Employers," 16 Kan. L. Rev. 552 (1968). In Chemical Workers v. Du Pont & Co., 103 LRRM 3111 (CA 5, 1980), an employer was compelled to arbitrate with a successor union under the predecessor union's agreement.

[101]97 S.Ct. at 1074. In Typographical Union v. Madison Newspapers, 97 LRRM 2950 (USDC, 1978), certain matters raised by the union after the agreement expired were held nonarbitrable, the Court stating that, unlike *Nolde*, it was not alleged that the matters "arose" out of the agreement. And a postcontract discharge was nonarbitrable where evidence negated any mutual intent to keep the terms of the old agreement in effect during negotiations. Mid-Hudson Publications, 103 LRRM 2050 (USDC, 1980). Similarly, see Westwood Prods., 77 LA 396, 398–399 (Peterschmidt, 1981). Intent not to extend the arbitration procedure beyond the life of the agreement was adequately indicated where the agreement defined grievances subject to the grievance procedure as those "arising under *and during* the term of the agreement." Local 636 v. J.C. Penney Co., 103 LRRM 2618, 2622 (USDC, 1980), emphasis added. On the other hand, actions of the parties after the term of the agreement has expired may be important to a finding of arbitrability. See Arbitrator Griffin in 77 LA 399, 400–401; Heath in 73 LA 1264, 1269 (parties recognized continued existence of the grievance procedure by their conduct); Allen in 70 LA 234, 237–238; Dennis in 68 LA 921, 922 (parties had continued the contract on a day-to-day basis).

[102]Edwards, "The Coming Age of the Burger Court: Labor Law Decisions of the Supreme Court During the 1976 Term," 19 B.C.L. Rev. 1, 52 (1977). Also discussing arbitrability of postcontract grievances, see Feldwisch, *"Nolde* and Arbitration of Post-Contract Disputes," 40

on *Nolde,* Arbitrator Thomas T. Roberts held nonarbitrable the discharge of employees for strike misconduct occurring after the collective agreement expired; he rejected the union's heavy reliance upon *Nolde* and explained that that decision "does not disturb the existing concept that grievances not involving claims of 'vested' rights are not arbitrable if they arise after an agreement has expired."[103] However, it should be noted that *Nolde* has been applied quite broadly in some cases,[104] and that *Nolde* has substantially influenced NLRA doctrine.[105]

Another situation which may be noted involved employees who returned to work after a new agreement was executed and who were then discharged for alleged misconduct as strikers during the interim between agreements; the discharges could be arbitrated since the grievance was the action of the employer in discharging the employees, not the employer's reason for that action.[106]

Ohio St. L.J. 187 (1979); Decker, "Arbitrability of Public Sector Grievances after Expiration of a Contract," 7 J. of Collective Negotiations in the Public Sector 287 (1978); Goetz, "Arbitration after Termination of a Collective Bargaining Agreement," 63 Va. L. Rev. 693 (1977).

[103]Bell Foundry Co., 73 LA 1162, 1166 (1979).

[104]For example, in UAW v. Tri-State Plastic Moulding Co., 95 LRRM 2116 (USDC, 1977), arbitration of a severance-pay dispute was ordered under an expired agreement even though the arbitration clause of the agreement was narrow and the agreement did not expressly include the employer's severance-pay plan. In Service Employees Local 6 v. Guthrie, 105 LRRM 3499, 3500 (USDC, 1980), the court stated that the "rationale of Nolde is equally applicable to *interest* arbitration provisions"; there the employer was ordered to comply with an interest arbitration clause in an expired collective agreement to determine provisions of a successor agreement. Also see reference to court enforcement of interest arbitration clauses in subtopic entitled "Specific Provision for Interest Arbitration," above.

[105]On the basis of *Nolde,* an NLRB panel revised the prior NLRB view concerning the duty to bargain in relation to union demands for arbitration during the interim between agreements. American Sink Top & Cabinet Co., 242 NLRB 408, 101 LRRM 1166 (1979). Also, *Nolde* influence was strong in Goya Foods, Inc., 238 NLRB 1465, 99 LRRM 1282, 1283 (1978), holding that a no-strike obligation exists to the extent that an arbitration obligation continues on issues created by an expired agreement; the NLRB said that in *Nolde* "the Supreme Court adopted the rule that the contractual duty to arbitrate disputes arising out of or during the term of a collective-bargaining agreement extends beyond the date of expiration of that agreement, unless negated expressly or by clear implication." Regarding the relationship between the collective agreement, bankruptcy, and *Nolde,* see Bohack Corp. v. Truck Drivers Local 807, 431 F.Supp. 646 (USDC, 1977). For later developments in this case, see Truck Drivers v. Bohack Corp., 541 F.2d 312 (CA 2, 1976), aff'd. by full court, 567 F.2d 237 (CA 2, 1977), cert. denied, 99 S.Ct. 95 (1978). Also see In re F&T Contractors, Inc., 649 F.2d 1229 (CA 6, 1981). In considering these cases the reader also should consider the U.S. Supreme Court's 1984 *Bildisco* decision and the subsequent legislation affecting it, discussed below in Chapter 18, topic entitled "Ability to Pay."

[106]Boeing Co. v. Machinists, 381 F.2d 119 (CA 5, 1967).

Chapter 4

The Arbitration Tribunal

Several types of tribunals are available for parties who wish to arbitrate. Also available are a variety of methods for selecting the arbitrator. Parties may choose in general between the use of a "temporary" arbitrator or the use of a "permanent" arbitrator. They also have a choice as to the number of arbitrators to be used, either single or multiple. The choice exercised in these matters may be of great importance to the success of the arbitration.

Single Arbitrator Versus Arbitration Board

The parties have a choice as to the number of arbitrators to be used for their case. Overall, the most common practice is to use a single neutral arbitrator, though in a given industry the most common practice may be to use arbitration boards.[1] When an arbitration board is used, it may be composed entirely of neutrals or it may be tripartite in its membership. Of the two types of boards, the tripartite board is used much more frequently than the board of neutrals.[2]

When a board of neutrals is used it will ordinarily have three members. Sometimes an alternate is also designated.[3] Under one variation in the use of neutral boards, only one member hears the case and makes findings of fact; then a decision based upon such findings is made by the full board.[4] Under another arrangement the case is heard

---

[1]Of 1609 agreements studied in one survey by the United States Department of Labor, 858 specified use of a single arbitrator, 670 specified a tripartite board, 42 gave the parties an option to use one or the other, 26 specified use of a single arbitrator for some issues and a board for others, and 13 were silent on the matter. Major Collective Bargaining Agreements: Arbitration Procedures, 33 (U.S. Dept. Labor Bull. No. 1425–6, 1966). Also see statistics in "Basic Patterns in Labor Arbitration Agreements," 34 LA 931, 938 (1960 survey); "Procedural Aspects of Labor-Management Arbitration," 28 LA 933, 934–935 (1954 survey).

[2]For discussion of tripartite boards, see "Tripartite Arbitration Board," below.

[3]As in Southern Bell Tel. & Tel. Co., 25 LA 85, 86 (Alexander, McCoy, Schedler & Whiting, 1955).

[4]Ibid.

by a board of two neutrals, with a third neutral to be selected subsequently if the first two cannot agree on a decision.[5]

"Temporary" or "Ad Hoc" Arbitrators

The "temporary" or "ad hoc" arbitrator is selected after the dispute arises.[6] He is named to arbitrate a specific dispute or a specific group of disputes, and there is no commitment to select him again. Most interest arbitrations involve temporary arbitrators. In a high percentage of rights arbitrations, too, temporary arbitrators are used. Most of the latter arbitrations are conducted pursuant to an arbitration clause in the collective agreement. The details of such clauses vary considerably from agreement to agreement, but it is customary to state at least: (1) what grievances may be submitted to arbitration; (2) the procedure for selecting the arbitrator; and (3) the scope of the arbitrator's jurisdiction and the binding effect of his award.

Advantages

The possibility of easy change of arbitrators is one of the chief advantages of the use of temporary arbitrators. At the same time, as long as an arbitrator continues to be satisfactory to the parties, he can be selected again and again, if available, for cases as they arise. When parties first begin to arbitrate, the use of temporary arbitrators makes experimentation possible. Thus, they may become acquainted with arbitration and, at the same time, better determine their particular needs in regard to its use. Later, the parties might graduate to the use of a permanent system.

For those parties who find themselves in the happy situation of having relatively few disputes, the appointment of arbitrators only as needed generally is more satisfactory, and especially so from the standpoint of economy.

Use of temporary arbitrators permits the selection, in each case, of an arbitrator who has special qualifications for deciding that particular dispute. While the use of a specialist, as such, may not be required often, some issues are of such technical nature that it is advisable to select an arbitrator who has special training or knowledge in regard thereto.

Finally, it is probable that a temporary arbitrator, not being personally acquainted with either party, will not be swayed too far by the personalities of the parties. In other words, brief tenure in office makes it unlikely that a temporary arbitrator will acquire a bias in favor of either party.

---

[5]As in Fairmont Auto Supply Co., 43 LA 369 at 369 (Lugar & Furbee, 1964), where the two neutrals who heard the case did agree on a decision.

[6]Over four fifths of the agreements in the aforementioned survey by the Department of Labor provided for selection of the arbitrator on an ad hoc basis. Major Collective Bargaining Agreements: Arbitration Procedures, 33 (U.S. Dept. Labor Bull. No. 1425–6, 1966).

Disadvantages

The selection of an arbitrator after dispute has arisen may involve as much difficulty as the dispute itself. Much time and effort may be lost because parties who are no longer friendly find themselves unable to agree upon an arbitrator, or even upon a method of selecting one. In the meantime the dispute remains unsettled, which may result in additional damage to the parties' relationship.

The arbitrator who is chosen for only one dispute, or a specific group of disputes, usually will not be familiar with the general circumstances of the parties. He will know little of the background of the dispute or the setting in which the collective agreement operates. At best, the parties may seek to educate him as to these matters, and even if additional hearing time is spent in his enlightenment, the arbitrator's knowledge of the parties' relationship will be shallow. The most successful arbitration is that which sets a smooth course for future operations. Thorough knowledge of the past relationship of the parties is an invaluable aid to one who would pursue this end. Moreover, since temporary arbitrators sometimes are selected on something of an emergency basis, the parties may not have adequate opportunity to check the qualifications of the arbitrator. Thus, there is additional hazard that the parties may have to accept a decision which leaves their relationship in a weaker condition than existed prior to the rendition of the award.

Another disadvantage of the use of temporary arbitrators is that when several arbitrators render interpretations of the same contract, there is a real danger that conflicting decisions may create more differences than have been settled. In fact, it is not uncommon for a losing party to take the very same issue to arbitration again if it is thought that there is any possibility of obtaining a different ruling. An award by one temporary arbitrator may have so little precedential force as viewed by a subsequent arbitrator that the latter will decide contra.

Because it is easy to change temporary arbitrators, losing parties frequently will demand a change of arbitrators even though there may be no reasonable cause for a change. Thus, the parties may be deprived of future valuable service of the eliminated arbitrator. Moreover, frequent and indiscriminate change of arbitrators permits none to become truly acquainted with the needs of the parties. This means that the parties may deprive themselves of the best possible arbitration services.[7]

"Permanent" Arbitrators

A "permanent" arbitrator is one who is selected to serve for a period of time, rather than for just one case or specific group of cases.

---

[7]For an excellent discussion of the advantages and disadvantages of using temporary arbitrators, see Simkin & Kennedy, Arbitration of Grievances (U.S. Dept. of Labor, Div. of Labor Standards, Bull. No. 82, 1946). Also see Warren & Bernstein, "A Profile of Labor Arbitration," 16 LA 970 (1951); "Labor Arbitration Today: Accomplishments and Problems," 16 LA 987 (1951).

He may be selected to serve for the term of the collective agreement, for some other specific period, or even at the pleasure of the parties.[8] His responsibilities and functions are determined by the contract by which his office is created. (The terms of permanent-arbitrator contracts vary widely, especially as to the precise jurisdiction of the arbitrator, since each such contract is carefully tailored to meet the special needs and wishes of the parties.) He may be employed on a full-time basis, but more often he is employed on a part-time basis, subject to call when needed. The use of a permanent arbitrator in an industry is evidence that labor-management relations have reached a relatively high degree of maturity.

The permanent arbitrator usually is called either "Impartial Umpire" or "Impartial Chairman." The Impartial Umpire usually sits alone. His function is similar to that of the temporary arbitrator, except that he is appointed to consider all arbitrable disputes which arise during his tenure. The Umpire generally is not commissioned to mediate, his function being quasi-judicial in the sense that it is one of contract interpretation and application.[9]

The Impartial Chairman, on the other hand, usually sits as the only impartial member of an arbitration board. Often the Impartial Chairman is commissioned to be something more than an arbitrator, although his functions vary considerably from industry to industry. He may be authorized to mediate, and, where such is the case, he will arbitrate only after other methods fail, making it a last-resort solution. But when the Impartial Chairman does find it necessary to assume the role of an arbitrator, he too may then be restricted to contract interpretation and application.

The type of situation to which use of the permanent arbitrator is especially well adapted is indicated in the recommendation of a fact-finding board appointed by the Secretary of Labor to serve in connection with an International Harvester Company dispute:

> "While the Board believes that a permanent umpire system of arbitration would be more desirable here because of the complexity of the issues involved in the numerous grievances which have arisen under the recently expired contract, as witnessed by cases involving these grievances which have come before the National War Labor Board, we hesitate to recommend provision for a permanent umpire system in the contract unless by agreement of the parties. We recommend that the

---

[8]The permanent umpire under the 1979 General Motors-UAW agreement "shall serve during the term of his contract for as long as he continues to be acceptable to both parties." The Ford-UAW agreement has provided that the umpire "shall continue to serve only so long as he continues to be acceptable to both parties." For factors which might affect the tenure or "survival" of a permanent arbitrator, see Fleming, The Labor Arbitration Process, 219–220 (U. of Ill. Press, 1965). In Greater N.Y. Health Care Facilities Assn., Inc. v. Service Employees' Local 144, 88 LC ¶12,044 (USDC, 1980), the collective agreement defined the permanent arbitrator's jurisdiction very broadly, and the court held that he was the proper arbitrator to interpret the agreement's termination-of-arbitrator clause and rule upon one party's effort to terminate him against the wishes of the other party. The court rejected the contention that his pecuniary interest in continued employment disqualified him from ruling upon his own termination.

[9]An interesting variation is the "Impartial Advisor," whose authority is not only restricted to agreement interpretation but is also limited to making findings and recommendations only. New York City Transit Auth., 27 LA 838 (Stark, 1955).

parties give serious consideration to naming an arbitrator in the contract, whose term of office would extend for the life of the agreement unless otherwise changed by mutual agreement. We believe that the value of the services of an arbitrator to the industrial relations welfare of the parties may be considerably enhanced by the experience gained through more frequent contact with the shop practices prevailing in the various International Harvester plants and the characteristics of the company's wage and incentive system than would be possible under an ad hoc arrangement."[10]

Accepting the above recommendation, the parties established a permanent umpire system at International Harvester, and one informed observer has been quoted as saying that it "proved to be the turning point in bringing order out of chaos in the field of contract interpretation."[11]

The use of permanent labor-management arbitrators is not new in the United States. Some industries have had umpire systems since the turn of the century. The anthracite coal industry, for instance, established a permanent system in 1903. Increase in the use of permanent arbitrators was gradual at first, but since 1935 it has been fairly rapid. Permanent-arbitrator provisions occur most frequently in collective agreements within the automobile, aircraft, meat-packing, steel, rubber, apparel, and transportation equipment industries.[12] Sometimes a permanent arbitrator has been selected for an entire industry, as, for instance, in the full-fashioned hosiery industry.[13]

The Chrysler Corporation uses an Appeal Board which consists of two representatives of each of the parties and an Impartial Chairman. The partisan members of the Appeal Board first attempt to settle all grievances properly referred to the board. If the partisan members are unable to settle a matter, it is decided by the Impartial Chairman.[14]

Sometimes permanent umpire panels are maintained, as, for instance, in the case of the Bethlehem and United States Steel com-

---

[10]International Harvester Co., 1 LA 512, 522 (Marshall, Spencer & Holly, 1946).
[11]Reilly, "Arbitration's Impact on Bargaining," 16 LA 987, 990 (1951).
[12]See Major Collective Bargaining Agreements: Arbitration Procedures, 33 (U.S. Dept. Labor Bull. No. 1425–6, 1966); Arbitration Provisions in Union Agreements, 3 (U.S. Dept. Labor Bull. No. 780, 1944). Comparing percentages of cases under permanent and ad hoc appointments, see McDermott, "Survey on Availability and Utilization of Arbitrators in 1972," Proceedings of the 26th Annual Meeting of NAA, 261, 297 (BNA Books, 1974). For extensive discussion of some permanent arbitrator systems, see Killingsworth & Wallen, "Constraint and Variety in Arbitration Systems," Proceedings of the 17th Annual Meeting of NAA, 56–81 (BNA Books, 1964); Davey, "The John Deere-UAW Permanent Arbitration System," Critical Issues in Labor Arbitration, 161–192 (BNA Books, 1957); Arbitration of Labor-Management Grievances (U.S. Dept. Labor Bull. No. 1159, 1954), a study of the Bethlehem Steel system.
[13]See Kennedy, Effective Labor Arbitration, 20, 24 (1948).
[14]For a detailed discussion of the Appeal Board, see Wolff, Crane & Cole, "The Chrysler-UAW Umpire System," Proceedings of the 11th Annual Meeting of NAA, 111–136 (BNA Books, 1958), which discussion is followed by comments comparing the Ford and General Motors umpire systems with that at Chrysler. Id. at 141–148. Also see Killingsworth & Wallen, "Constraint and Variety in Arbitration Systems," Proceedings of the 17th Annual Meeting of NAA, 56, 62–69 (BNA Books, 1964), comparing Ford, Chrysler, and General Motors; "Chrysler Procedure," 29 LA 885 (1958). In 1963 the Chrysler procedure of using only signed written statements as evidence was changed to receive evidence in manner customary in most arbitration proceedings. See Jones & Smith, "Management and Labor Appraisals and Criticisms of the Arbitration Process: A Report With Comments," 62 Mich. L. Rev. 1115, 1129 (1964).

panies.[15] Umpires are called in turn from these panels. Sometimes, too, recommended decisions are made by individual members of a panel, subject to approval by another member thereof.[16]

Advantages

Many persons active as arbitrators or as students of arbitration feel that great value is to be realized from the use of the permanent arbitrator. Dr. George W. Taylor, for instance, urged that ad hoc arbitration should be looked upon, at best, as a transitory method and as entailing comparative disadvantages. "As a support for industrial relations stability, a permanent arbitrator is a prime requisite. Out of the continuing relationship, consistent policy and mutually acceptable procedures can gradually be evolved."[17]

Since the permanent arbitrator is appointed in advance, no time need be lost in selecting one after a dispute arises. Moreover, the advance selection of the arbitrator permits time for careful consideration of his qualifications of impartiality, skill, and knowledge of labor-management relations. The permanent arbitrator usually is selected by the highly desirable method of mutual choice of the parties, rather than by some outside person or agency.

The permanent arbitrator becomes familiar with the provisions of the parties' agreement. He comes to know the day-to-day relationships of the parties, their circumstances, their personalities, and their customary practices. The importance of this knowledge was emphasized by Umpire Harry Shulman:

> "An opportunity should be provided, if possible, for the arbitrator by continuous association with the parties, or at least by repeated association with the parties, to get to know them better. A good many disputes that come to arbitration are deceptive.*** Some are deceptive even because they don't really portray what the parties are concerned about. They seem to be fighting about one thing, and actually it is something

---

[15]See Fischer, "The Steelworkers Union and the Steel Companies," Proceedings of the 32nd Annual Meeting of NAA, 198 (BNA Books, 1980); Killingsworth, "Arbitration: Its Uses in Industrial Relations," 21 LA 859, 860 (1953).

[16]For instance, see United States Steel Corp., 68 LA 1094 (Rimer, Garrett, 1977); Bethlehem Steel Co., 47 LA 270 (Gill, Seward, 1966). In certain circumstances the parties waive the review and approval requirement. See Bethlehem Steel Co., 37 LA 143, 144 (Valtin, 1961). The newspaper industry has utilized a procedure for appellate review of local arbitrators' awards. See Stark, "The Presidential Address: Theme and Adaptations," Proceedings of the 31st Annual Meeting of NAA, 1, 12–13 (BNA Books, 1979); McLellan, "The Appellate Process in the International Arbitration Agreement Between the American Newspaper Publishers Association and the International Printing Pressmen," Proceedings of the 26th Annual Meeting of NAA, 53 (BNA Books, 1974); Newspaper Agency Corp., 43 LA 1233 (Platt, 1964). The coal industry similarly has utilized arbitral appellate review procedures. See Selby, "The United Mine Workers and Bituminous Coal Operators' Association," Proceedings of the 32nd Annual Meeting of NAA, 181 (BNA Books, 1980); Valtin, "The Bituminous Coal Experiment," 29 Lab. L.J. 469 (1978). However, that industry ultimately abandoned use of its Arbitration Review Board. Valtin, The Coal Mediation Experiment: What's It About and What's Happened? (Proceedings of Fourth Annual Seminar, Arbitration in the Coal Industry, 4, 1981), examining the grievance mediation experiment that was subsequently commenced by some areas of the industry.

[17]Taylor, "Effectuating the Labor Contract Through Arbitration," The Profession of Labor Arbitration 20, 40 (BNA Books, 1957).

else which is bothering them. That kind of thing happens, at least in my experience, quite frequently. A grievance is filed partly as a sort of pressure technic. It is filed partly in order to lay a foundation for a claim subsequently to be made. An arbitrator who doesn't know and doesn't sense what he is getting into, what a decision one way or the other will lead to in the developing strategy, might find himself regretting subsequently, when he finds out what the parties were really after—regretting he made that kind of determination. And so an arbitrator who is in continuous association with the parties may be in a better position to realize what the parties are really fighting for rather than what they appear to be fighting for."[18]

In respect to the matter of costs, if the parties have a large number of disputes so as to require frequent resort to arbitration, the use of a permanent arbitrator is a definite advantage. Moreover, with increased knowledge of the parties' relationship, the permanent arbitrator is able to shorten hearings; from the outset, many details already will be known to him. He needs less time for making investigations since he is familiar with the parties and the industry in which they operate. For the same reason time is saved in the preparation of opinions. Naturally, the saving of time means a reduction of costs.

Permanent arbitrators make their awards available for the guidance of the parties. Cases which do not involve new issues or new situations are likely to be settled at early stages of the grievance procedure since the parties know how the arbitrator has decided similar disputes. Thus, one effect of a decision covering a disputed point may be its application by the parties themselves to other disputes involving the same issue. The awards of a permanent arbitrator generally will be consistent with one another, thus avoiding the confusion that sometimes results from having two or more temporary arbitrators rule on similar issues.

The permanent arbitrator has special reason for concern regarding the ultimate effect of each decision. He expects to continue to serve the parties after each decision is rendered and expects to be confronted time and again by his own decisions. The situation is somewhat different with a temporary arbitrator, who, while in good conscience is eager to render a sound award, serves with the realization that he may never again have contact with the parties.

Disadvantages

The difficulty of finding enough mutually acceptable and available grade "A" arbitrators is a problem, at least, if not a disadvantage, to be faced in the use of permanent arbitrators. Any arbitrator given tenure of office should be able to inspire a high degree of confidence in both parties and should be experienced. The field of choice is necessarily limited.

---

[18]Conference on Training of Law Students in Labor Relations, Vol. III, Transcript of Proceedings, 710–711 (1947).

There is always a danger that the parties will be too quick to turn to the permanent arbitrator.[19] Once selected, he is easily available. There is temptation to take a short-cut route to dispute settlement. Arbitration should not be substituted for negotiation—harm results when the parties fail to exhaust all possibilities of settlement at the prearbitration steps of the grievance procedure. Moreover, there is a danger that some cases will be sent to the arbitrator just to make him earn his salary.

The use of a permanent arbitrator obligates the parties in advance of need to some expense. The arbitrator's retainer fee must be paid regardless of whether his services prove to be needed.[20]

Danger of Favoritism or of "Splitting" Awards

In deciding whether to use permanent or temporary arbitrators another matter should be considered. Both labor and management should be quick to disown any arbitrator who appears to be playing favorites or appears to have the faintest taint of prejudice in favor of either party. Permanent value can be had from arbitration only if decisions are rendered on the merits. In this regard there are two potential dangers. First, the arbitrator might acquire a bias in favor of one side or the other. Second, the arbitrator might go to the other extreme and, in his desire to please both parties, render approximately the same number of awards for each side. In common parlance this is known as "splitting" awards.[21]

Some persons believe that a temporary arbitrator is less likely to acquire a bias in favor of either side and is in a better position to decide cases impartially on the merits. On the other hand, it is argued that the relative stability of the permanent arbitration relationship is the best insurance for decisions on the merits. It is recognized, however, that each of these conclusions is debatable.[22]

---

[19]Concerning the serious effort by the UAW to screen grievances headed for the umpire at GM, see Dunne, "The UAW Board of Review on Umpire Appeals at General Motors," 17 Arb. J. 162 (1962). Also see Stark, "The Presidential Address: Theme and Adaptations," Proceedings of the 31st Annual Meeting of NAA, 1, 5 (BNA Books, 1979), explaining that many of the grievances that are processed on to arbitration by the UAW are settled in an "unwritten 'shakeout' step" at which GM and UAW staff representatives and officers "whittle away at the arbitration docket"; in one year 214,000 grievances were filed, of which 1150 were processed to arbitration and fewer than 50 were actually arbitrated.

[20]Sometimes a retainer is provided plus a certain sum per case. For a discussion of the pros and cons of the use of permanent arbitrators, see Simkin & Kennedy, Arbitration of Grievances (U.S. Dept. of Labor, Div. of Labor Standards, Bull. No. 82, 1946).

[21]Arbitrators as a group reject any suggestion of splitting awards, though the possibility has been recognized. See comments by Jones & Smith, "Management and Labor Appraisals and Criticisms of the Arbitration Process: A Report With Comments," 62 Mich. L. Rev. 1115, 1148–1149 (1964).

[22]Davey, "Hazards in Labor Arbitration," 1 Indus. & Lab. Rel. Rev. 386, 394 n. 22 (1948). One survey indicated that among those parties who do believe that cases are not always decided on their merits, "the fear of excessive compromise is greatest in a series of cases tried in succession before the same arbitrator, or where there is a permanent arbitrator." Eaton, "Labor Arbitration in the San Francisco Bay Area," 48 LA 1381, 1387 (1967). Danger of splitting awards has been rejected as grounds for resisting the simultaneous arbitration of several grievances before the same arbitrator. Koehring Div., 46 LA 827, 830 (King, 1966).

Possibly there has been too much concern over this matter. Faith in the integrity and sound judgment of arbitrators generally and in their ability to "see through" attempts to obtain decisions not based on the merits should be sufficient to eliminate initial concern at least. If adequate evidence is produced showing that an arbitrator is not deciding issues on the merits, the parties need lose no time in terminating his services. This matter was given special consideration by the late Harry Shulman. His splendid analysis and expression of views leaves little more to be said:

"Another, and perhaps less lofty thought, should be expressed. There seems to be a feeling on the part of some that a party can win a greater number of cases if it presents a greater number for decision, the assumption being that some purposeful percentage is maintained. There are many reasons why this point of view is wholly unsound. No Umpire should be retained in office if he is really believed to be making decisions on such a basis. An Umpire should be employed only so long as he renders decisions on the basis of his best and honest judgment on the merits of the controversies presented, and only so long as both parties believe that he does so. If he is believed to be making his decisions on a percentage basis, the remedy is to put him out of office rather than to give him more cases for arbitrary decision.

"Moreover, as anyone concerned with industrial relations thoroughly knows, there is a great deal of room in the relation between a company and its employees for honest and reasonable differences of opinion on important questions of interpretation and application. If only such questions were brought to an Umpire, their normal, honest determination could fairly be expected in proper course to fall on both sides of the line. A purposeful percentage would be as unnecessary as it would be dishonest.

"From the selfish point of view of a party, there is a great advantage in appealing only cases believed to be entirely good rather than appealing indiscriminately many cases for the purpose of winning a percentage. When a party brings only strong cases, it breeds in others a feeling of confidence in its judgment and in its reasonableness which may tip the scales in cases of doubt and give it a considerable advantage at the start. If, on the other hand, a party brings cases carelessly, without substantial evidence and without apparent judgment in selection, it tends to breed in others a lack of confidence in its judgment which starts it off with a considerable disadvantage. This is particularly true in the 'did or didn't he' type of case here mentioned. For in such cases, [speaking of cases in which the evidence is not conclusive] as already stated, there is little to go on except the conflicting testimony of witnesses and the confidence in the parties developed over a period of time as a result of the record of their own selections."[23]

---

[23]Ford Motor Co., 1 ALAA ¶67,274, p. 67,620 (1945). Also see comments by Arbitrator Amis in 69 LA 966, 969; Ferguson in 1 LA 163, 165. Summarizing the results of a study by Geoffrey R. King to determine the extent of union success in arbitration, see Note, "Union Success in Arbitration," 33 Arb. J. 45 (June, 1978), indicating that of 4990 cases reported between 1960 and 1970 in LA Reports and germane to the study (interest disputes, split decisions, and interunion disputes were excluded as not germane), the union won 42.7 percent. For a broad discussion of the need for joint acceptability of arbitrators by the parties and its influence upon the arbitration process, see Ryder, "The Impact of Acceptability on the Arbitrator," Proceedings of the 21st Annual Meeting of NAA, 94–124 (BNA Books, 1968), where the subject is also discussed by other observers.

Mediation by Permanent Arbitrators

As we have noted, Impartial Chairmen often are commissioned to try to bring about settlement of differences through mediation. Sometimes an Impartial Umpire also exercises this function. The Impartial Chairman for the full-fashioned hosiery industry has acted as a mediator as well as an arbitrator.[24] The Impartial Chairman for the men's clothing industry in New York City has had the duty of continuing negotiations concerning disputes brought to him and of deciding issues only if agreement is not reached through such negotiations.[25]

During his tenure with the Ford Motor Company, Umpire Harry Shulman performed some mediation functions, as he once explained:

> "The Umpire's contractual jurisdiction is limited to the interpretation, application or alleged violation of the terms of the parties' written agreements, with few exceptions. But, as the parties and I came to know each other better, my actual functions were greatly expanded. With the full consent of both sides, I conferred with the parties separately and jointly on diverse problems outside that contractual jurisdiction, sat with them as mutual friend and adviser in their negotiations of amendments and supplements, spoke at educational classes and other union meetings, and was generally available for such help as a well-intentioned mutual friend could give in the interest of the total enterprise."[26]

Umpire Shulman also observed that sometimes the parties may press the umpire to decide issues which might be left undecided or at least delayed until time and experience provide greater assurance of wise judgment; in "cases of this character, and others in which the arbitrator conscientiously feels baffled, it may be much wiser to permit him to mediate between the parties for an acceptable solution."[27]

One of the strongest advocates of mediation by permanent arbitrators was Dr. George W. Taylor. It was his belief that collective bargaining should be carried on through the arbitration step and that the essential task of most chairmen is to bring about a meeting of minds if possible.[28] His view of the Impartial Chairman's office was expressed as follows:

---

[24]Kennedy, Effective Labor Arbitration, 57 (1948).

[25]Morgan, Arbitration in the Men's Clothing Industry in New York City, 1, 5 (1940).

[26]Shulman, Opinions of the Umpire, Preface, 3 (1943–1946). Describing the varied role of Permanent Arbitrator Richard Mittenthal and his close relationship with the parties, see Meyer, "The Teamsters and Anheuser-Busch," Proceedings of the 32nd Annual Meeting of NAA, 174, 179 (BNA Books, 1980). Stressing the value of neutrals who have been "mediator-arbitrator-advisers to the parties," John T. Dunlop expressed concern that "the rise of professional staff in labor and management organizations, and the growing legalisms of many aspects of industrial relations, have led to much more limited roles for most neutrals" in recent years. Dunlop, "The Industrial Relations Universe," Proceedings of the 29th Annual Meeting of NAA, 12, 15 (BNA Books, 1976).

[27]Shulman, "Reason, Contract, and Law in Labor Relations," 68 Harv. L. Rev. 999, 1022–1023 (1955), reprinted in Management Rights and the Arbitration Process 169, 195–197 (BNA Books, 1957).

[28]Taylor, "Effectuating the Labor Contract Through Arbitration," The Profession of Labor Arbitration 20, 35 (BNA Books, 1957).

"An impartial chairman, then, is first of all a mediator. But he is a very special kind of mediator. He has a reserve power to decide the case either by effectuating his own judgment or by joining with one of the partisan board members to make a majority decision, depending upon the procedure designated by the agreement. A new reason for labor and management to agree is introduced—to avoid a decision. By bringing in a fresh viewpoint, moreover, the impartial chairman may be able to assist the parties in working out their problem in a mutually satisfactory manner. To me, such a result has always seemed to be highly preferable to a decision that is unacceptable to either of the parties. What's wrong per se about an agreement when agreeing is the essence of collective bargaining?"[29]

Dr. Taylor recognized the widespread belief among industrial relations people that an arbitrator should not mediate, and he hastened to warn that the Impartial Chairman approach is not universally applicable; "it is only usable when both parties see eye-to-eye on the point."[30] It is interesting to note that over one third of all problems presented to Dr. Taylor as Impartial Chairman of the full-fashioned hosiery industry were settled by agreement of the parties.[31] A criticism of that office since Dr. Taylor stepped down has been in regard to the decreased number of such voluntary settlements.[32]

Combination of arbitration and mediation functions has been criticized by those who believe that there should be a clear distinction between the two and that the arbitrator's usefulness is reduced when he attempts to mediate.[33]

In some umpire systems neither party wishes the umpire to act as a mediator at any time.[34] Furthermore, an umpire system might utilize mediation for a time but the parties might ultimately come to favor the adjudication approach to decision-making rather than the mediation approach, as has been said to be true both at General Motors and at Ford.[35]

As concerns temporary arbitrators, it appears reasonably clear that the majority of parties ordinarily prefer that the arbitrator not attempt mediation.[36]

---

[29]Ibid.

[30]Id. at 36.

[31]Kennedy, Effective Labor Arbitration, 28 (1948).

[32]Id. at 216.

[33]For a collection of views expressed in opposition to Dr. Taylor's, see Braden, "The Function of the Arbitrator in Labor-Management Disputes," 4 Arb. J. (N.S.) 35 (1949). For very strong criticism of the Taylor view, see O'Connell, "Should the Scope of Arbitration Be Restricted," Proceedings of the 18th Annual Meeting of NAA, 102, 103–104 (BNA Books, 1965).

[34]See, for instance, Davey, "The John Deere-UAW Permanent Arbitration System," Critical Issues in Labor Arbitration, 161, 162, 185 (BNA Books, 1957).

[35]See Killingsworth & Wallen, "Constraint and Variety in Arbitration Systems," Proceedings of the 17th Annual Meeting of NAA, 56, 64, 68, 75–76 (BNA Books, 1964).

[36]For statistical surveys of views on the desirability of mediation by arbitrators, see Eaton, "Labor Arbitration in the San Francisco Bay Area," 48 LA 1381, 1384 (1967); Warren & Bernstein, "A Profile of Labor Arbitration," 16 LA 970, 981–982 (1951). For further discussion of the pros and cons of mediation by arbitrators, see Simkin, Mediation and the Dynamics of Collective Bargaining, 301–312 (BNA Books, 1971); Panel Discussion, "The Arbitration Hearing—Avoiding a Shambles," Proceedings of the 18th Annual Meeting of NAA, 75, 94–101 (BNA Books, 1965); Fuller, "Collective Bargaining and the Arbitrator," Proceedings of the 15th Annual Meeting of NAA, 8, 24–54 (BNA Books, 1962); Raffaele, "Needed: A Fourth Party in Industrial Relations," 13 Lab. L.J. 230 (1962).

The Code of Professional Responsibility for arbitrators recognizes that (1) an arbitrator may be appointed on the basis that some mediation role is expected, and (2) an arbitrator may undertake mediation after arbitration has been "invoked" if neither party objects, either at the request of a party or at the arbitrator's own suggestion provided it can be discerned that both parties are likely to be responsive.[37]

Tripartite Arbitration Board

The tripartite arbitration board, which may be either temporary or permanent, is one made up of one or more members selected by management, an equal number selected by labor, and a neutral member who serves as chairman.[38] The labor and management members generally are partisans and act as advocates for their respective sides.[39] The Code of Ethics for Arbitration did not impose an obligation of strict neutrality upon the party members of tripartite boards, and the Code of Professional Responsibility which superseded it "does not apply to partisan representatives on tripartite boards."[40]

Thus, the impartial member is in some respects a single arbitrator, and it is something of a misnomer to call the partisan members "arbitrators." Some writers believe it would be more realistic to call

[37]See Code § II(F), 64 LA 1322. Attempts at mediated settlements are certainly not rare, but many arbitrators appear reluctant to undertake mediation. See "Survey of Arbitration in 1962," Proceedings of the 17th Annual Meeting of NAA, 292, 314 (BNA Books, 1964). For arbitration-mediation techniques that have been generally successful for one highly regarded arbitrator, see Zack, "Suggested New Approaches to Grievance Arbitration," Proceedings of the 30th Annual Meeting of NAA, 105, 112–117 (BNA Books, 1978). Many state agencies established primarily to mediate interest disputes also provide mediation assistance for grievances. See O'Grady, "Grievance Mediation Activities by State Agencies," 31 Arb. J. 125 (1976). In Canada, the British Columbia Labour Board with centralized authority to administer the entire body of labor law, has an arbitration procedure primarily utilizing mediation rather than adjudication. Weiler, "The Role of the Labour Board as an Alternative to Arbitration," Proceedings of the 30th Annual Meeting of NAA, 72, 79 (BNA Books, 1978). Regarding the potential for greater use of grievance mediation in the United States, see Goldberg, "The Mediation of Grievances Under a Collective Bargaining Contract: An Alternative to Arbitration," 77 Nw. U.L. Rev. 270 (1982).

[38]For discussion of tripartite boards, see articles by Zack, Rehmus, Gromfine & Schnapp in "Tripartite Interest and Grievance Arbitration," Proceedings of the 34th Annual Meeting of NAA, 273–301 (BNA Books, 1982); Smith, "The Search for Truth—The Whole Truth," Proceedings of the 31st Annual Meeting of NAA, 40, 57–59 (BNA Books, 1979); Davey, "The Uses and Misuses of Tripartite Boards in Grievance Arbitration," Proceedings of the 21st Annual Meeting of NAA, 152–179 (BNA Books, 1968). For the views of other observers, see "The Uses and Misuses of Tripartite Boards in Grievance Arbitration: Workshop Sessions," id. at 180–197.

[39]Sometimes they even present the evidence and argument for their respective sides, no other representatives being used. As in Pfeiffer Brewing Co., 16 LA 89, 90 (Smith, 1951). When they thus serve as counsel, they might agree to make the neutral the sole arbitrator. As in United Tavern, 16 LA 210, 211 (Slavney, 1951). In Edmund E. Garrison, Inc. v. Operating Eng'rs., 283 F.Supp. 771 (USDC, 1968), the employer's appointees to the arbitration board were himself and his attorney (who the court said was as closely related to the dispute as the employer). The union would not voluntarily accept such complete merger of roles and the court would not compel it to do so. The court said that party arbitrators need not be neutral, but a party could not appoint himself. Even aside from the fact that one of the relevant agreements prohibited parties to the dispute from serving on the board, the court believed that such a limitation applies by arbitration custom.

[40]See 15 LA 961, 962–963, 965 (Code of Ethics); 64 LA 1319 (Scope of Code of Professional Responsibility). Some state arbitration statutes expressly limit the impartiality requirement to neutrals. Similarly, party members of tripartite boards under the Railway Labor Act "are not in legal contemplation, or in fact, supposed to be neutral arbitrators." Arnold v. United Air Lines, 296 F.2d 191, 195, 49 LRRM 2072 (CA 7, 1961).

them "representatives in arbitration" or use some other such title to acknowledge that the dispute is to be submitted to the neutral member, who is to act as sole arbitrator.[41] In this connection, some agreements provide that the party representatives shall be "advisory" members without voting rights, thus leaving the decision solely to the neutral.[42]

Tripartite boards do not often reach unanimous decisions.[43] In this regard, the collective agreements, statutes, and other instruments under which tripartite boards are established usually provide that a majority award of the board shall be final and binding.[44] The side whose position is favored by the neutral member generally joins the neutral in a majority award.

Some agreements give the neutral member the right and responsibility of making the final decision, regardless of whether it is a majority award.[45] Even where the agreement does not give the neutral this right, the parties may agree at the hearing that he alone shall write the opinion and award and that same shall be final and binding upon the parties (the right to dissent may be reserved);[46] or they may agree that if no majority award is reached, the award of the neutral shall be final and binding.[47] Indeed, when arbitration commences the parties frequently agree to waive the collective agreement provision for a tripartite board, and they agree that the neutral is to act as sole arbitrator from the outset.[48]

---

[41]Updegraff & McCoy, Arbitration of Labor Disputes, 27 (1946). Also see Reynard, "Drafting of Grievance and Arbitration Articles of Collective Bargaining Agreements," 10 Vand. L. Rev. 749, 757 (1957).

[42]See "Tri-Partite Arbitration: Comment From Readers," 15 Arb. J. 49, 95 (1960). Also see Fleming, "Reflections on the Nature of Labor Arbitration," 61 Mich. L. Rev. 1245, 1267–1268 (1963).

[43]See statistics in "Procedural Aspects of Labor-Management Arbitration," 28 LA 933, 935 (1954 statistics).

[44]Thus, in most cases the common law rule requiring a unanimous decision does not apply. Furthermore, the U.S. Supreme Court has held that the common law unanimity rule does not apply "when the submission is one which concerns the public." City of Omaha v. Omaha Water Co., 30 S.Ct. 615, 616 (1909). In La Stella v. Garcia Estates, Inc., 331 A.2d 1, 5 (N.J. S.Ct., 1975), the common law unanimity rule was rejected for the private sector in New Jersey, the court holding a majority award sufficient unless the agreement to arbitrate specifies otherwise. AAA Rule 25 specifies awards by majority vote unless unanimity is expressly required. Of course, all members of a tripartite board are entitled to full participation in its deliberations and no member should be excluded without fault on its part. See Simons v. New Syndicate, 152 N.Y.S.2d 236 (N.Y. S.Ct., 1956).

[45]For views on this, see Warren & Bernstein, "A Profile of Labor Arbitration," 16 LA 970, 977 (1951). Similarly, a fairly common provision is that the decision of a majority of the board, or of the neutral member if a majority decision cannot be reached, shall be final and binding. See, Major Collective Bargaining Agreements: Arbitration Procedures, 76 (U.S. Dept. Labor Bull. No. 1425–6, 1966).

[46]See Arbitrator Bothwell in 51 LA 41, 42; Hebert in 46 LA 140 at 140; Reynard in 24 LA 116, 117; Ferguson in 20 LA 684 at 684; Feinsinger in 16 LA 501 at 501; Ralston in 15 LA 608 at 608.

[47]See Arbitrator Maggs in 35 LA 249, 250; Howard in 23 LA 429, 430; Livengood in 21 LA 456, 457.

[48]See Arbitrator Johannes in 70 LA 683, 685; Dworkin in 68 LA 101, 103; Geissinger in 46 LA 115, 116; Yagoda in 46 LA 111, 112; King in 46 LA 70 at 70; Stutz in 42 LA 446 at 446; Abernethy in 19 LA 658, 659; Slavney in 16 LA 210, 211. This was also done in Food Employers Council, 20 LA 724, 725, 730 (Van de Water, 1953), but the neutral was also authorized to call upon counsel for the parties for a joint discussion of the issues brought out at the hearing. Where the agreement called for a tripartite board but where the neutral acted throughout as sole arbitrator without a waiver of the board requirement, a court refused to enforce the award of the neutral as sole arbitrator. Local 227, Hod Carriers v. Sullivan, 221 F.Supp. 696 (USDC, 1963). A waiver was found and the

When the neutral member of a tripartite board is not given authority to render a binding award without a majority vote, he might be faced with the necessity of compromising his own views or even accepting the extreme position of one side or the other in order to have a majority award.[49] Sometimes neither party will vote with the neutral in favor of an award based upon the true merits of the case.

Advantages

One advantage of using a tripartite board is that the neutral member may get valuable advice and assistance from the partisan members.[50] The usual practice is for the parties to select persons from their own ranks who are familiar with the background of the dispute. The technical assistance that such persons may give to the neutral member may be of special value. Moreover, use of the tripartite board gives the parties a better opportunity to keep the neutral arbitrator informed as to their real positions, which may not be exactly the same as their formal positions.

The tripartite board has its greatest utility in the arbitration of interest disputes.[51] In this regard, the tripartite composition of the National War Labor Board was considered in reality to be a substitute for the lack of completely satisfactory guiding principles and points of reference.[52] In the arbitration of interest disputes, it is of the utmost importance that clear understanding of the underlying needs and requirements of the parties be obtained. To this end the neutral

---

award of the neutral as sole arbitrator was upheld in Builders Supply Co. v. Teamsters Local 123, 112 LRRM 3300, 3303 (CA 8, 1983). In Amalgamated Meat Cutters v. Cross Bros. Meat Packers, 518 F.2d 1113, 1121 (CA 3, 1975), the court held that factual issues regarding waiver of a tripartite board are for the arbitrator, and the neutral's award was upheld although it was silent concerning such waiver. In Houston Publishers Assn., 71 LA 667 at 667 (1978), the agreement specified arbitration by a joint standing committee (two union members and two company members) and an impartial chairman, but based upon the manner in which the case was submitted to him, Arbitrator Duane L. Traynor "presumed" that: (1) the parties had waived the contractual provision for a tripartite board, and (2) his decision was to be final. As a precaution he added: "In the event these presumptions are incorrect then there should be appended to this award by the parties a statement as to their concurrence or non-concurrence with the award signed by the members of the joint standing committee."

[49]In Publishers' Assn. of N.Y. City, 36 LA 706, 711–712 (1961), Arbitrator Seitz thus had to compromise his own best judgment. In Remington Rand, Inc., 20 LA 799, 800 (1953), Arbitrator Lehoczky withdrew his first proposed award (reported in 20 LA 271) and issued an amended award which attained a majority vote.

[50]See, for instance, Arbitrator Seward in Diamond State Tel. Co., 32 LA 200, 212 (1959); Arbitrator Day in Bell Aircraft Corp., 13 LA 813, 820–821 (1950).

[51]See discussion by Freidin, Labor Arbitration and the Courts, 44–46 (U. of Pa. Press, 1952). Stating that a "vital characteristic of successful" interest arbitration is "tripartite determination," Attorney Herman Sternstein explained: "The tripartite executive session produces the result that can come no other way." Sternstein, "Arbitration of New Contract Terms in Local Transit: The Union View," Proceedings of the 26th Annual Meeting of NAA, 10, 19 (BNA Books, 1974). Interest arbitration statutes for the public sector commonly specify use of tripartite boards. For an indication of how such boards may function in executive session, see Anderson, MacDonald & O'Reilly, "Impasse Resolution in Public Sector Collective Bargaining—An Examination of Compulsory Interest Arbitration in New York," 51 St. John's L. Rev. 453, 472, 481, 513 (1977).

[52]See Taylor, "The Arbitration of Labor Disputes," 1 Arb. J. (N.S.) 409, 413 (1946).

member of a tripartite board has the assistance of the partisan members, which may serve to prevent serious errors of judgment.[53]

Awards of tripartite boards, when they are unanimous, tend to be more acceptable than awards by single arbitrators. As one workshop discussion concluded:

> "A principal feature of the tripartite system, as expressed during the workshop discussion, is that it promotes acceptability of the award on the part of both management and union and provides an opportunity for practical compromise. This result was not viewed as objectionable, and several responsible industry and union representatives voiced the opinion that compromise is not improper in some cases. It guards against an award which, although correct, may be impracticable for reasons not readily apparent to the neutral member."[54]

Disadvantages

Tripartite boards often cause delay not only in the initial appointment of the partisan members, but also both at hearings and afterwards.[55] The members selected by the parties may insist upon complete reargument of the case after the hearing is concluded, which can lead to unduly extended sessions. Also, time may be lost in waiting for dissenting opinions to be written. Any additional time required necessarily adds to the costs.

The task of the impartial member can be unhappy and difficult. Too frequently he must act as conciliator for the other members, and, as has been seen, he may be forced to compromise his own best judgment in order to secure a majority vote, where such vote is required.

Because of such disadvantages, many parties prefer not to use tripartite boards for rights disputes. Although a survey of 1609 agreements indicated that roughly one third specified use of tripartite boards,[56] there is evidence that the actual ultimate use of tripartite boards does not reach nearly so high a percentage.[57]

---

[53]See Davey, "Hazards in Labor Arbitration," 1 Indus. & Lab. Rel. Rev. 386, 399 (1948). The same precaution is served by tripartite boards for grievances. See Davey, "The Uses and Misuses of Tripartite Boards in Grievance Arbitration," Proceedings of the 21st Annual Meeting of NAA, 152, 190–192 (BNA Books, 1968), where other advantages of tripartite boards for grievances are enumerated.

[54]"The Uses and Misuses of Tripartite Boards in Grievance Arbitration: Workshop Sessions," Proceedings of the 21st Annual Meeting of NAA, 180, 193 (BNA Books, 1968).

[55]Regarding the problem of delay and possibilities of minimizing it, see Bell Aircraft Corp., 13 LA 813, 820–821 (Day, 1950).

[56]Major Collective Bargaining Agreements: Arbitration Procedures, 41 (U.S. Dept. Labor Bull. No. 1425–6, 1966).

[57]See Davey, "The Uses and Misuses of Tripartite Boards in Grievance Arbitration," Proceedings of the 21st Annual Meeting of NAA, 152, 155–157 (BNA Books, 1968). Davey in his article is generally critical of the use of tripartite boards for grievances, though he did offer suggestions for improving their workings. Id. at 172–174. Some other observers, however, see real utility in tripartite boards for grievances. See "The Uses and Misuses of Tripartite Boards in Grievance Arbitration: Workshop Sessions," id. at 180–197. Strong criticism of use of tripartite boards for grievances has been voiced by Reynard, "Drafting of Grievance and Arbitration Articles of Collective Bargaining Agreements," 10 Vand. L. Rev. 749, 755–760 (1957); Braden, "Recurring Problems in Grievance Arbitration," Preparing and Presenting Arbitration Cases, 28, 33–34 (1954).

Procedure Following the Hearing

The inherent nature of tripartite boards brings certain procedural matters into special consideration, particularly in regard to the extent of consultation and discussion between the impartial chairman and the partisan members following the arbitration hearing.[58]

The members of tripartite boards in many cases meet in executive session to discuss the case sometime after the hearing has been completed.[59] There is no fixed approach to be taken by the neutral in conducting executive sessions. Rather, he is free to choose the course of procedure and to vary his approach in accordance with his evaluation of the parties, the circumstances of the case, and the time when the session is held.[60]

Customarily the impartial chairman of the board will inquire as to the wishes of the partisan members in regard to meeting in executive session. In some cases it will be specifically agreed that there will be no executive session and that the neutral will write the opinion and award with each party reserving the right to file a dissent.[61] Another procedure is for the neutral to prepare a tentative opinion and award, the executive session then to be held to review the tentative decision.[62] Or it may be agreed that an executive session will be held only if a party requests one after the neutral has issued a tentative award.[63]

Often tripartite boards meet in executive session prior to the preparation of any proposed award. But while the session ordinarily gives the neutral a better insight into the dispute, only infrequently does it produce a unanimous decision. Often when the executive session fails to resolve the dispute, it will be understood that the neutral will prepare a proposed award without further conference or communication with the partisan members other than to submit the award to them for concurrence or dissent.[64]

---

[58]For discussion of arbitration procedure generally, see Chapter 7.

[59]Sometimes it is agreed that counsel for the parties may attend the session, as in Safeway Stores, 22 LA 466, 467 (Hildebrand, 1954).

[60]See explanations by Arbitrators Stein, Haughton, Platt, and Wallen in "Procedural Problems in the Conduct of Arbitration Hearings: A Discussion," Proceedings of the 17th Annual Meeting of NAA, 1, 14–16 (BNA Books, 1964).

[61]As in Texas Co., 24 LA 240, 241 (White, 1955). Upholding this procedure, see Davey Tree Surgery Co. v. Electrical Workers Local 1245, 94 LRRM 2905 (Cal. Ct. App., 1976). When this procedure is followed it also may be agreed that if the award prepared by the neutral does not receive a majority vote, the board will then meet in executive session to discuss the case further. See Kraft Foods Co., 15 LA 38, 39 (Updegraff, 1950). Similarly, Hillbro Newspaper Printing Co., 48 LA 1304, 1321 (Jones, 1967).

[62]As in Northwest Airlines, 41 LA 360, 361 (Rohman, 1963). Such tentative decision by the neutral is not final and binding. See Air Line Pilots Assn. v. Northwest Airlines, 498 F.Supp. 613, 618–619 (USDC, 1980). Nonetheless, where this procedure is used, "the neutral obviously has committed himself and normally it will take a good deal of persuasion to induce him to change his mind." Smith, "The Search for Truth—The Whole Truth," Proceedings of the 31st Annual Meeting of NAA, 40, 58 (BNA Books, 1979). In City of Renton, 71 LA 271, 272 (Snow, 1978), the neutral's tentative award covering a police interest dispute was announced in a conference telephone call (which he would not permit to be recorded), and this was followed by written comments from the party members and then by issuance of the final award.

[63]As in Chevron Oil Co., 70 LA 572, 573 (Davis, 1978).

[64]See, for example, Arbitrator Tatum in 26 LA 477, 478; Dworkin in 21 LA 367, 369; Larkin in 17 LA 335, 341.

Usually the neutral prepares an opinion to accompany his proposed award but it is commonly understood that a partisan member in signing an award does not necessarily indicate concurrence with any or all of the statements made by the neutral in his opinion.[65] Even where an executive session produces a unanimous decision, the responsibility for preparing a supporting opinion may be placed solely in the neutral member.[66]

Under some circumstances, at least, the neutral member of a tripartite board might not be compelled to meet in executive session with the partisan members even though the latter members have not expressly waived such session. For instance, in arbitration by a tripartite board under the Railway Labor Act, a U.S. District Court declared that the provisions of said Act "necessarily recognize that the partisan members [of the tripartite board] will champion the position of their respective employers," and where all members of the board attended the arbitration hearing the court held that the failure of the neutral member to call the board together after his proposed findings had been submitted to them should, at most, "be considered as a mere irregularity and not sufficient to vitiate the action of the majority of the Board." There was no showing that the members of the board ever conferred or consulted together as to the findings or as to the award to be made, nor that such consultation was requested by either party. About this the court said:

> "The amenities of the situation might well have suggested to the Chairman that the other two members be advised that he would call the Board together for a conference if it was deemed desirable after the draft of the findings and award had been submitted to them. But, realistically considered, it must be recognized that such gesture would have accomplished nothing."

The neutral's findings and award, when submitted to the partisan members, were concurred in by the company member and accordingly became the binding award by a majority of the board.[67]

Neither the refusal of a partisan member of a tripartite board to attend the board's executive session nor the resignation or withdrawal of a partisan member prior to issuance of the award has been held to

---

[65]Sometimes the neutral himself emphasizes the latter fact. See Arbitrator Seitz in 48 LA 705 at 705; Davey in 44 LA 1057, 1059, 1089; Dash in 23 LA 177 at 177; Smith in 20 LA 625 at 625; Pension in 17 LA 152, 153.

[66]As in Shenango Valley Transit Co., 21 LA 356, 357 (Brecht, 1953).

[67]In re Duluth, Missabe and Iron Range Ry., 124 F.Supp. 923, 928–929 (D. Minn., 1954). Also see Railroad Trainmen v. Chicago, M., St.P. & P. R.R., 237 F.Supp. 404, 423–424 (D.C.D.C., 1964). The opposite result was reached under state law in Simons v. News Syndicate, Inc., 26 LA 281 (N.Y. Sup. Ct., 1956). Failure of the neutral to call an executive session prior to issuance of his proposed award was strongly criticized by one party in Northwest Airlines, 29 LA 541, 545–546 (Schedler, 1957). In Jones v. St. Louis-San Francisco Ry., 115 LRRM 2905, 2909–2910 (CA 6, 1984), the court stated that "although an arbitration board need not be impartial, certain minimal procedural considerations must be afforded the parties"; this requirement was not met where two of the three members of a special board of adjustment which issued an award under the RLA failed both to "*hear* the proof in evidence submitted by the parties and to consult with each other for the purpose of determining the proper resolution."

defeat the proceedings or prevent the issuance of a binding majority award by the other members of the board.[68]

Even if the common law which permits either party to withdraw from arbitration at any time prior to issuance of an award is otherwise applicable, it is said that where an arbitrator orally "announces what his decision will be, it is doubtful whether a party could withdraw between the time of that announcement and the formal written rendition."[69]

Methods of Selecting Arbitrators

Selection of an arbitrator satisfactory to both parties often entails difficulties. No part of the arbitration process is more important than that of selecting the person who is to render the decision. Fortunately, a variety of selection methods are available.

It is generally assumed that selection by mutual agreement of the parties is the most desirable method. This may be true in terms of insuring acceptance of the award, although there is no inherent reason why an equally if not more competent arbitrator might not be selected by a third party. However, there does appear to be more justification for mutual selection of permanent arbitrators since they ordinarily have some tenure of office.

Collective agreements often provide for selection by the parties[70] and, at the same time, alternative methods to be used if they fail to agree within a specified time. Provision for alternative methods of appointment always should be made in the agreement. Otherwise, proposed arbitration might be defeated for want of an effective means of selecting the arbitrator.[71] This need not be the result, however, under the modern arbitration statutes which specify court appoint-

---

[68]See Publishers' Assn. of N.Y. City v. Stereotypers Union, 181 N.Y.S.2d 527 (N.Y. Sup. Ct., 1959); Shoeworkers Assn. v. Federal Shoe, Inc., 24 LA 573, 576 (Me. Sup. Ct., 1955); Street Ry. Employees v. Connecticut Co., 24 LA 107, 108–110 (Conn. Sup. Ct., 1955). Cf., Fromer Foods, Inc. v. Edelstein Foods, Inc., 181 N.Y.S.2d 352 (N.Y. Sup. Ct., 1959), involving death of a partisan member. Also see West Towns Bus Co. v. Division 241, 168 N.E.2d 473 (Ill. App. Ct., 1960); Consumers Power Co., 24 LA 581, 582 (Smith, Howlett & Sorensen, 1955). For a related discussion, see Chapter 7, topic entitled "Default Awards in Ex Parte Proceedings." In Sheet Metal Workers Local 416 v. Helgesteel Corp., 80 LRRM 2113 (USDC, 1971), the agreement specified three union and three company members for the arbitration board, but an award by three union members and only two company members was upheld since the two company members were given one and one-half votes each and the three union members were given only one each; there being no substantive voting disparity, the technical violation of the agreement did not invalidate the award.

[69]Updegraff & McCoy, Arbitration of Labor Disputes, 122 (1946). To similar effect, Updegraff, Arbitration and Labor Relations, 280 (BNA Books, 1970). For related matter, see Chapter 2, Legal Status of Arbitration.

[70]Under some circumstances this step may be held to have been waived. See Werner-Continental, 72 LA 1, 7 (LeWinter, 1978); Barbet Mills, 16 LA 563 (Livengood, 1951). But see Hartford Gas Co., 49 LA 630, 631–633 (Summers, 1967).

[71]See discussion by board of inquiry in Rochester Transit Corp., 19 LA 538, 558 (Tolley, McKelvey & Turkus, 1952). For a survey of collective agreement provisions on selecting the arbitrator, see Major Collective Bargaining Agreements: Arbitration Procedures, 36–46 (U.S. Dept. Labor Bull. No. 1425–6, 1966). While many agreements provide alternative methods of appointment, this precaution is by no means universal. Id. at 36.

ment of an arbitrator if the parties cannot agree upon one or upon a method of appointment.[72]

The neutral member, or members, of tripartite boards may be selected by the members appointed by the parties. Agreements often provide that each party shall choose one or more arbitrators and that those so chosen shall select a neutral chairman. The partisan members, however, may fail to agree upon the neutral, so here too the agreement should provide alternate methods of selection.[73]

Aid from an outside agency, whether requested at the outset or after the parties have failed to agree upon an arbitrator, generally takes one of two forms: (1) A list is submitted from which, often by a process of elimination, the parties select an arbitrator;[74] or (2) direct appointment of the arbitrator by the agency. An agreement may designate the FMCS, a state agency, the AAA, a judge, some public official, or any other impartial agency.[75]

Federal Mediation and Conciliation Service rules relating to the selection and appointment of arbitrators provide in § 1404.13 that:

> "(a) The parties should notify the OAS [Office of Arbitration Services] of their selection of an arbitrator. The arbitrator, upon notification by the parties, shall notify the OAS of his selection and willingness to serve. Upon notification of the parties' selection of an arbitrator, the Service will make a formal appointment of the arbitrator.
>
> "(b) Where the contract is silent on the manner of selecting arbitrators, the parties may wish to consider one of the following methods for selection of an arbitrator from a panel:
>
> "(1) Each party alternately strikes a name from the submitted panel until one remains.
>
> "(2) Each party advises the Service of its order of preference by numbering each name on the panel and submitting the numbered list in writing to OAS. The name on the panel that has the lowest accumulated numerical number will be appointed.

---

[72]For example, the New York statute provides: "If the arbitration agreement does not provide for a method of appointment of an arbitrator, or if the agreed method fails or for any reason is not followed, or if an arbitrator fails to act and his successor has not been appointed, the court, on application of a party, shall appoint an arbitrator." 75 CPLR § 7504. Also see Uniform Arbitration Act, § 3. In Bethlehem Mines Corp. v. Mine Workers, 80 LRRM 3069 (USDC, 1972), the court concluded that it had authority under LMRA § 301 to determine how an arbitrator shall be selected if the parties cannot agree.

[73]In Sam Kane Packing Co. v. Meat Cutters Local 171, 477 F.2d 1128 (CA 5, 1973), the employer arbitrator refused to participate in the selection of a neutral and the union arbitrator thereupon issued an award; the court vacated the award, stating that the proper remedy was an action to secure appointment of a neutral rather than an ex parte award by a party member.

[74]Explaining how the FMCS and the AAA decide which names to place on the list for a given case, see Jones & Smith, "Management and Labor Appraisals and Criticisms of the Arbitration Process: A Report and Comments," 62 Mich. L. Rev. 1115, 1138–1139 (1964). Also see FMCS Regulations, § 1404.12(c), providing a 1979 summary of factors the FMCS considers when selecting names for inclusion on a panel; "Report by FMCS, AAA on Arbitration Panels," 1967 Labor Relations Yearbook, 225, 226 (BNA Books, 1968).

[75]For statistics as to the use of various appointing agencies, see "Survey of Arbitration in 1964," Proceedings of the 18th Annual Meeting of NAA, 243, 245, 251–252 (BNA Books, 1965); "Survey of Arbitration in 1962," Proceedings of the 17th Annual Meeting of NAA, 292, 296 (BNA Books, 1964); Warren & Bernstein, "A Profile of Labor Arbitration," 16 LA 970, 974–975 (1951). In one survey, 203 arbitrators reported that 55.1 percent of their ad hoc appointments came from appointing agencies, 42.5 percent came directly from the parties, and 2.5 percent came from other sources. McDermott, "Survey on Availability and Utilization of Arbitrators in 1972," Proceedings of the 26th Annual Meeting of NAA, 261, 297 (BNA Books, 1974).

"(3) Informal agreement of the parties by whatever method they choose.

"(c) The Service will, on joint or unilateral request of the parties, submit a panel or, when the applicable collective bargaining agreement authorizes, will make a direct appointment of an arbitrator. * * *"

Regarding access to additional panels, § 1404.12(c)(5) states that:

"(5) In almost all cases, an arbitrator is chosen from one panel. However, if either party requests another panel, the Service shall comply with the request providing that an additional panel is permissible under the terms of the agreement or the other party so agrees. Requests for more than two panels must be accompanied by a statement of explanation and will be considered on a case-by-case basis."

Similarly, under the rules of the AAA the parties may select an arbitrator as they please. Also, in order to facilitate selection, the Association sends lists of names to the parties. They have the privilege of crossing off names objected to. The Association then makes the appointment from the names remaining on the lists, in order of preference.[76] If the parties fail to agree upon any of the names submitted, they may request additional lists. If they still cannot agree, the Association appoints an arbitrator whose name has not appeared on the lists.[77]

While the rules of the FMCS and the AAA provide for direct appointments by the agency,[78] both agencies prefer selection by the parties. It has been said that the agencies will make the selection "only when the parties are adamant."[79]

Arbitrator's Acceptance or Withdrawal

The Code of Ethics for Arbitrators included the following statement on acceptance, refusal, or withdrawal from office: "The arbitrator, being appointed by voluntary act of the parties, may accept or decline the appointment. When he accepts he should continue in office until the matter submitted to him is finally determined. When there are circumstances which, in his judgment, compel his withdrawal, the parties are entitled to prompt notice and explanation."[80] The Code of

---

[76]AAA Rule 12. The Association may aid in the selection of the arbitrator even where it is not administering other aspects of the case, as in Celotex Corp., 24 LA 369, 370 (Reynard, 1955).

[77]Labor Arbitration, 14–15 (AAA, 1957). The Association's formal rules have not actually provided for additional lists. See 43 LA 1292, 1293 (1965 Rules); 28 LA 908, 909 (1952 Rules).

[78]See FMCS Regulations, § 1404.13(c), above. Rule 12 of the AAA regulations states: "If the parties fail to agree upon any of the persons named or if those named decline or are unable to act, or if for any other reason the appointment cannot be made from the submitted lists, the Administrator shall have power to make the appointment from other members of the Panel without the submission of any additional lists."

[79]"Basic Patterns in Labor Arbitration Agreements," 34 LA 931, 939 (1960), where it is also noted that the FMCS makes the selection in less than 3 percent of the cases which it handles. The direct appointment percentage for the AAA is also low, being only about 5 percent in some years. See "Procedural Aspects of Labor-Management Arbitration," 28 LA 933, 935 (1957). Also see Murphy, "Free Choice of Arbitrators Is Still the American Way in Labor Arbitration," 3 Arb. J. (N.S.) 234 (1948).

[80]Part I, § 6, 15 LA 961, 963.

Professional Responsibility which succeeded the Code of Ethics has no general provision on acceptance or withdrawal, but does state that an invitation to serve "should be declined if the arbitrator is unable to schedule a hearing as soon as the parties wish," unless "the parties, nevertheless, jointly desire to obtain the services of the arbitrator" and arrangements can be agreed upon "that the arbitrator confidently expects to fulfill."[81]

American Arbitration Association Rule 18 provides that if any arbitrator should resign, die, withdraw, refuse, or be unable or disqualified to perform the duties of his office, the AAA shall declare the office vacant and the vacancy shall be filled in the same manner as that governing the original appointment, the matter to be reheard by the new arbitrator.[82]

Arbitrators and Their Qualifications

Background, Training, and Supply of Arbitrators

With the rapid expansion of labor-management arbitration during and since World War II, there has emerged a large group of persons experienced and available for arbitration service. No special educational or technical training is required for arbitrators except as may be specifically required by the parties. It is not surprising, then, that arbitrators come from a wide variety of backgrounds. Indeed, the group includes professors, lawyers, judges, public office holders, ministers, accountants, economists, professional arbitrators, and others.[83]

---

[81]Sec. II(J)(2)(b), 64 LA 1323. The Code also provides that: "An arbitrator must decline appointment, withdraw, or request technical assistance when he or she decides that a case is beyond his or her competence." § I(B)(1), 64 LA 1320.

[82]43 LA 1292, 1293.

[83]Arbitrators Ralph T. Seward, Eva Robins, and Clare B. McDermott each answered "no" when asked the following question: "Most of today's arbitrators entered the profession by way of highly diverse paths. Do you believe it is beneficial to standardize a method of training future arbitrators?" Arbitrator Seward answered in part: "Most emphatically not. The wide variety of background and training that arbitrators have brought to the process has immeasurably enriched it. * * *" "An Interview with Three Distinguished Arbitrators," The Chronicle (NAA, May, 1980) 12. For "vital statistics" concerning arbitrators (education, background, arbitration training, arbitration income, and the like), see Herrick, "Profile of a Labor Arbitrator," 37 Arb. J. No. 2, p. 18 (1982); Proceedings of the 29th Annual Meeting of NAA, 376–381 (BNA Books, 1976); "Survey of the Arbitration Profession in 1969," Proceedings of the 24th Annual Meeting of NAA, 275–303 (BNA Books, 1971); "Survey of the Arbitration Profession," The Profession of Labor Arbitration, 176–182 (BNA Books, 1957); "Survey of Arbitration in 1962," Proceedings of the 17th Annual Meeting of NAA, 292–294, 304–316 (BNA Books, 1964); "Procedural Aspects of Labor-Management Arbitration," 28 LA 933, 936 (1954 statistics); Warren & Bernstein, "A Profile of Labor Arbitration," 16 LA 970, 973–974 (1951). For general discussions of arbitrators and the qualities essential to their success, see Lawson, "Arbitrator Acceptability: Factors Affecting Selection," 36 Arb. J. No. 4, p. 22 (1981); Kelliher, "The Presidential Address," Proceedings of the 18th Annual Meeting of NAA, 66, 68–71 (BNA Books, 1965); Loucks, "Arbitration—A Profession?" Proceedings of the 13th Annual Meeting of NAA, 20–31 (BNA Books, 1960); Cole, Freidin & Oliver, "The Status and Expendability of the Labor Arbitrator," The Profession of Labor Arbitration, 42–65 (BNA Books, 1957). Suggesting that "we have moved from expendability to interchangeability of arbitrators," see Killingsworth, "Twenty-Five Years of Labor Arbitration—And the Future," Proceedings of the 25th Annual Meeting of NAA, 11, 21 (BNA Books, 1973).

Although there are many experienced arbitrators who are readily acceptable to the parties, there sometimes has been a shortage of such arbitrators. The problem was stated by a committee of the NAA:

"Since experience is unquestionably the best teacher in this field, as in so many others, and since there are many potentially able arbitrators whose services are not being used, the problem of maintaining an adequate supply of arbitrators now and in the future is to a large extent a problem of promoting the acceptability of newcomers * * *."[84]

Subsequently a committee of the American Bar Association (ABA) noted the absence of any institution comparable to the National War Labor Board, which served as the training ground for many arbitrators, and the committee added that both management and labor "are understandably reluctant to permit unknown men to experiment with their affairs."[85]

To help alleviate the problem, the AAA, the FMCS, and the NAA have cooperated in programs to aid in giving training, experience, and acceptability to new arbitrators.[86] In this regard, FMCS Regulations expressly state that one of the factors considered "when selecting names for inclusion on a panel," is "the need to expose new arbitrators to the selection process."[87]

---

[84]"Report on the Education and Training of New Arbitrators," The Profession of Labor Arbitration, 170, 173 (BNA Books, 1957). For related discussion, see McDermott, "Survey on Availability and Utilization of Arbitrators in 1972," Proceedings of the 26th Annual Meeting of NAA, 261 (BNA Books, 1974), stating at p. 290 that "the conclusion to be reached with respect to the overall availability and utilization of acceptable and experienced arbitrator time is that no critical shortage exists"; Davey, "Restructuring Grievance Arbitration Procedures: Some Modest Proposals," 54 Iowa L. Rev. 560, 561–564 (1969). "Even if there is no need for more arbitrators, in general the caseloads are growing and the ranks of mainline arbitrators who started during World War II are thinning, therefore, there is a need for new arbitrators to fill the gap of 'acceptable arbitrators.' " "A Need for New Arbitration * * * Revisited," The Chronicle (NAA, Dec. 1978) 1, 8. The problems of gaining acceptance for a "first case" are depicted by Nordlund, "The Arbitrator Development Process: An Outsider View," 30 Arb. J. 34 (1975).

[85]"Report of the Committee on Labor Arbitration," Proceedings of the 15th Annual Meeting of NAA, 242, 243 (BNA Books, 1962).

[86]Descriptions and explanations of these and other training programs, sometimes with indications of their degrees of success, are provided in the proceedings of the annual meetings of the NAA which are published by the Bureau of National Affairs, Inc. See Proceedings of 32nd Annual Meeting of NAA, 275–282 (1980); 31st Annual Meeting, 397–402 (1979); 30th Annual Meeting, 357–362 (1978); 29th Annual Meeting, 327–344 (1976) (this report is particularly interesting in that it indicates how persons admitted to NAA membership between 1970 and 1975 had initially gotten into arbitration); 28th Annual Meeting, 335–355 (1976) (another particularly interesting report); 27th Annual Meeting, 329–346 (1975); 26th Annual Meeting, 247–259 (1974); 25th Annual Meeting, 331–346 (1973). Reports on earlier proceedings are cited in the Third Edition of this book, p. 91. For other discussions of programs for training new arbitrators, see articles, respectively, by Sinicropi, Cahn, Robins & Seitz, and Douglas in 37 Arb. J. No. 3, pp. 24–51 (1982). A training program manual is that by Barreca, Miller & Zimny, Labor Arbitrator Development: A Handbook (BNA Books, 1983). In 1977 Montana by statute authorized the establishment of a course of study for training arbitrators and fact-finders. The Code of Professional Responsibility provides that experienced arbitrators "should cooperate in the training of new arbitrators." § I(C)(2), 64 LA 1320. Regarding arbitrator use of assistants, see Code § II(H), 64 LA 1323. Also see Dorr, "Labor Arbitrator Training: The Internship," 36 Arb. J. No. 2, p. 4 (1981). For an explanation of how the steel industry obtained many new arbitrators for its expedited arbitration program, see Fischer, "Updating Arbitration," Proceedings of the 26th Annual Meeting of NAA, 62, 70–71 (BNA Books, 1974).

[87]Sec. 1404.12(c).

Qualifications Set Forth in Agreement or by Regulation

The collective agreement may specify qualifications which must be possessed by the arbitrator.[88] The selection of an arbitrator may be hampered seriously, however, by an attempt to fix qualifications rigidly in the agreement. It may be impossible to secure an arbitrator who meets the qualifications so specified. Although the determination of qualifications generally is left to the parties, a few state arbitration statutes do prescribe qualifications designed to insure impartiality. Also, the Code of Professional Responsibility states that essential general qualifications of an arbitrator "include honesty, integrity, impartiality and general competence in labor relations matters."[89]

The suggestion that arbitrators should be licensed has been discussed thoroughly by informed students of arbitration, and serious doubts have been raised against such a step.[90]

Impartiality

No qualification is more important than that of impartiality. It may well be that no person can be absolutely free from bias or prejudice of any kind, but it is not too much to expect an arbitrator to be able to divest himself of any personal inclinations, and to be able to stand between the parties with an open mind. This does not mean, however, that an arbitrator should decide contrary to his own best judgment. Indeed, the element of honesty is not satisfied unless the arbitrator fully believes that he is doing what is right. To be an arbitrator worthy of the name, one must always be able and ready to "call 'em as he sees 'em." As long as both parties believe that an arbitrator is doing just that, they will respect him whether or not they "see 'em" the same way he does.[91]

Integrity

The integrity of arbitrators generally can be expected to be of the highest. Appointed judges sometimes are criticized for allegedly

---

[88]This is not the usual practice. See Major Collective Bargaining Agreements: Arbitration Procedures, 50–51 (U.S. Dept. Labor Bull. No. 1425–6, 1966).

[89]Sec. I(A)(1), 64 LA 1320. Asked whether there should "be significant differences in the type of qualifications required of arbitrators as between the private and public sectors," over two thirds of the respondents in an extensive ABA survey tended to believe or strongly believed that there should not be. "Report of Subcommittee on Qualifications and Training of Arbitrators," Section of Labor and Employment Law Committee Reports, 303, 309 (ABA, 1979).

[90]See Coulson, "Certification and Training of Labor Arbitrators: Should Arbitrators Be Certified?" Proceedings of the 30th Annual Meeting of NAA, 173 (BNA Books, 1978); Barreca, "Comment," id. at 192; Gilliam, "Comment," id. at 199; Greenbaum, "Comment," id. at 202; Aaron, "Should Arbitrators Be Licensed or 'Professionalized'?" Proceedings of the 29th Annual Meeting of NAA, 152 (BNA Books, 1976).

[91]Some parties remain unconvinced that the typical arbitrator always "calls 'em as he sees 'em." See Jones & Smith, "Management and Labor Appraisals and Criticisms of the Arbitration Process: A Report With Comments," 62 Mich. L. Rev. 1115, 1146–1147 (1964). However, many parties apparently believe that awards are generally fair and objective. See Eaton, "Labor Arbitration in the San Francisco Bay Area," 48 LA 1381, 1387 (1967).

receiving political "plums." Elected judges sometimes are accused of being politicians. Arbitrators generally are not open to such criticism since they are selected by free choice of the parties or their agent. But how may a prospective arbitrator be tested for integrity and impartiality? Careful consideration of personal and business background and affiliations is enlightening in this respect. Has the arbitrator any financial or business interest in the affairs of either party?[92] Has there been any such interest in the past? Does he have any personal affiliations, either directly or indirectly, with either of the parties?[93] Does he have strong opinions in favor of either labor or management?[94] What has been his past record as an arbitrator?[95] The parties may review some past awards of the arbitrator, but the number of awards rendered in favor of each side should not be used as a test of impartiality.[96] An arbitrator who deliberately tries to please both sides by "splitting" awards is not one who decides cases objectively. It is the arbitrator's fairness and good judgment, as indicated by his past awards and by his general reputation, that the parties should be concerned with.

Ability and Expertise

Naturally, extensive arbitration experience is one indication of ability. But at the outset a labor-management arbitrator should have a broad background of social and economic study or experience. He should have an analytical mind and should be able to orient himself quickly when dealing with new subject matter. Maturity of judgment is indispensable. Diplomacy helps too.

---

[92]Arbitrators must disclose to parties any dealings that might create an impression of possible bias. Commonwealth Coatings Corp. v. Continental Casualty Co., 89 S.Ct. 337 (1968). The Code of Professional Responsibility requires disclosure of "any current or past managerial, representational, or consultative relationship with any" party to the case; of "any pertinent pecuniary interest"; and of "any close personal relationship or other circumstance *** which might reasonably raise a question as to the arbitrator's impartiality." § II(B), 64 LA 1321, which also provides that: "After appropriate disclosure, the arbitrator may serve if both parties so desire. If the arbitrator believes or perceives that there is a clear conflict of interest, he or she should withdraw, irrespective of the expressed desires of the parties." For an extensive survey of views concerning the scope of the arbitrator's duty to disclose information concerning his background, associations, previous and current contacts with a party, and the like, see Sherman, "The Duty of Disclosure in Labor Arbitration," 25 Arb. J. 73 (1970). Also see Sherman, "Arbitrator's Duty of Disclosure—A Sequel," Proceedings of the 24th Annual Meeting of NAA, 203–233 (BNA Books, 1971); Elson, "Ethical Responsibilities of the Arbitrator," id. at 194–203.

[93]The degree of formality in the arbitrator's personal relationships with the parties is essentially a matter of joint choice by the parties themselves. See Code of Professional Responsibility, § II(D), 64 LA 1322.

[94]A New York court was upheld in removing an arbitrator it had appointed but who, the court later learned, was partisan toward labor, although his integrity and honesty were not questioned. Western Union v. Selly, 2 LA 688 (N.Y. Ct. App., 1946). Also see In re Steuben, 14 LA 541 (N.Y. Sup. Ct. 1950); In re Culinary Bar & Grill Employees, 11 LA 1119 (N.Y. Sup. Ct., 1949). An award was vacated on the ground of bias on the part of the arbitrator in Holodnak v. Avco Corp., 387 F.Supp. 191, 88 LRRM 2950 (CA 2, 1975). The *Holodnak* decision is strongly criticized in Valtin, "The Presidential Address: Judicial Review Revisited—The Search for Accommodation Must Continue," Proceedings of the 29th Annual Meeting of NAA, 1, 5–9 (BNA Books, 1976).

[95]For helpful suggestions to aid parties in obtaining information concerning any particular arbitrator and suggestions to aid in evaluating his thinking and methods, see Jaffee, "Have Gavel, Will Travel," 18 Arb. J. 235 (1963).

[96]For instance, see General Contractors Assn. v. Teamsters Local 282, 98 LRRM 2135 (USDC, 1978).

Must an arbitrator be something of a specialist in the subject matter which he is to consider? Generally speaking, no. While neither side cares to appoint persons completely unfamiliar with industrial matters, an arbitrator generally will not be disqualified merely because he is not an expert in the subject of the dispute. An acceptable expert may be difficult or impossible to secure. Moreover, the parties often prefer an arbitrator who has general business or financial experience or who is versed in law. Arbitrators, as judges, generally should be selected for their ability to understand all sorts of problems. But in some disputes a specialist may be considered essential.[97] Thus, the parties may seek an industrial engineer, or a doctor, or some other type of specialist, depending upon the technical matter involved.

The desire of appointing agencies to accommodate the special needs of parties is illustrated by the following statement in an FMCS memorandum (seeking to establish a roster of arbitrators experienced in public employee disputes) sent to all arbitrators on the FMCS National Roster:

> "[We are] anxious to insure that our arbitration services continue to be responsive to the particular needs of those who normally utilize our services. For example, we make every effort to accommodate the parties when it comes to an arbitrator's geographical location, his experience or educational background or his particular specialty. Our national roster of arbitrators is maintained in such a way that we can now provide this tailored service. We now wish to refine our service even more by establishing a separate list of arbitrators who have had some experience in the public sector."[98]

Legal Training

Persons trained in law often make able arbitrators, although legal training is not indispensable. Many labor-management arbitrators are lawyers. Many parties prefer lawyers as arbitrators,[99] and lawyers are considered especially desirable for the position of neutral chairman of arbitration boards.[100]

Legal training helps an arbitrator to be objective. It improves the ability to analyze and evaluate facts. This means that the arbitrator who has had legal training may be less likely to be moved by personal

---

[97]For pros and cons as to use of arbitrators with "specific expertise" for the given dispute, see Eaton, "Labor Arbitration in the San Francisco Bay Area," 48 LA 1381 at 1381 (1967). Regarding need for technical expertness of arbitrators, see Warren & Bernstein, "A Profile of Labor Arbitration," 16 LA 970, 975 (1951). Also see Code of Professional Responsibility § II(J)(2)(b), quoted above in subtopic entitled "Arbitrator's Acceptance or Withdrawal." Some agreements provide for specialists for certain types of cases, or for employment of technical experts to assist the arbitrator when needed. See Major Collective Bargaining Agreements: Arbitration Procedures, 47–50 (U.S. Dept. Labor Bull. No. 1425–6, 1966).

[98]January 10, 1969, Memorandum from the FMCS General Counsel to all arbitrators on the National Roster. FMCS Regulations state that: "A brief statement of the issues in dispute should accompany the request [for a panel of arbitrators] to enable the Service to submit the names of arbitrators qualified for the issues involved." § 1404.10(c). Also see § 1404.12(c)(4). AAA Rules 7 and 9 require parties seeking arbitration to indicate "the nature of the dispute."

[99]See Eaton, "Labor Arbitration in the San Francisco Bay Area," 48 LA 1381 at 1381 (1967).

[100]See Gotshal, "The Lawyer's Place in Arbitration," 1 Arb. J. (N.S.) 367 (1946).

bias or by extraneous evidence. By no means, however, do all lawyers make good arbitrators. Especially ineffective is the lawyer who is so concerned with technical rules of evidence and procedure that the arbitration process is made unduly complicated. Such concern also may result in an award which fails to give sufficient consideration to the real merits of the dispute. Legal training alone is not enough to make an able arbitrator, but if a person possesses the other qualifications, legal training will make an even better arbitrator.[101]

Arbitrator's Immunity From Civil Liability

An arbitrator acting in his official capacity performs quasi-judicial duties and, like a judge, is immune from civil liability for acts done in his arbitral capacity.[102] In recognizing this immunity, it is considered that arbitrators "must be free from the fear of reprisals" and "must of necessity be uninfluenced by any fear of consequences for their acts."[103] Indeed, in light of the national policy which encourages arbitration it is said that the common-law rule protecting arbitrators from liability "ought not only to be affirmed, but, if need be, expanded."[104]

It may be noted that when neutrals serve as umpires under LMRA § 302(c)(5)(B) for the purpose of resolving deadlocks between the trustees of employee benefit trusts, the provisions of ERISA become relevant, as they also are relevant in some other types of disputes

---

[101]Cf., Raffaele, "Lawyers in Labor Arbitration," 37 Arb. J. No. 3, p. 14 (1982).

[102]Larry v. Penn Truck Aids, 100 LC ¶10,095 (USDC, 1983); Calzarano v. Liebowitz, 550 F.Supp. 1389 (USDC, 1982); Locomotive Eng'rs. v. New York Dock R.R., 94 LC ¶13,704 (USDC, 1981); Yates v. Yellow Freight Sys., 106 LRRM 2438 (USDC, 1980); Merchants Despatch Transp. Corp. v. Systems Fedn., 97 LRRM 2644 (USDC, 1977), dismissing RLA Special Board of Adjustment members and referee (as parties defendant) in a suit to review an award; Cahn v. ILGWU, 51 LRRM 2186 (CA 3, 1962). The U.S. Supreme Court strongly reaffirmed the doctrine of judicial immunity in Stump v. Sparkman, 98 S.Ct. 1099 (1978).

[103]Babylon Milk & Cream Co. v. Horvitz, 26 LA 121, 122 (N.Y. S.Ct., 1956). The AAA Legal Department has defended suits against arbitrators and has helped arbitrators fend off moves to involve them in postarbitration litigation. See Page, "Representing the Arbitrator," The Chronicle (NAA, Aug. 1978) 12; AAA Study Time, Jan. 1977, 1. Based upon an extensive examination of court decisions, the AAA has offered the following summary:

"The cases are unaminous in holding that arbitrators are quasi-judicial officers and as such are immune from civil liability when acting in their official capacity. This concept has been expanded by one federal court to include challenges to the authority of the arbitrators to hear the dispute. [Tamari v. Conrad, 552 F.2d 778 (CA 7, 1977).]

"In general, the courts have held that an arbitrator may not be deposed or required to testify in order to impeach, clarify or otherwise show that the award resulted in an unintended outcome. [For example, see Fukaya Trading Co., S.A. v. Eastern Marine Corp., 322 F.Supp. 278 (USDC, 1971).] There have been only a few exceptions to this rule such as the admissibility of testimony of a dissenting arbitrator or admissibility of testimony to show arbitrator misconduct. However, in those cases the testimony was admitted primarily to show what matters were considered or to show misconduct by the arbitrators. Therefore, while a few jurisdictions have allowed the limited use of arbitrators' testimony, none have allowed it for the express purpose of impeaching the award through a general inquiry into the manner in which the award was arrived at."

"Arbitrators' Immunity From Civil Liability—Deposition of Arbitrators," Lawyers' Arbitration Letter (AAA, Dec. 1977) 6.

[104]Hill v. Aro Corp., 263 F.Supp. 324 (USDC, 1967). For related discussion, see Douglas, "The Scope of Arbitrator Immunity," 36 Arb. J. No. 2, p. 35 (1981); Domke, "The Arbitrator's Immunity From Liability: A Comparative Survey," 3 U. Tol. L. Rev. 99 (1971); Glick, "Bias, Fraud, Misconduct and Partiality of the Arbitrator," 22 Arb. J. 161 (1967).

involving employment benefit plans;[105] opinion has differed regarding the possibility that, in certain arbitration cases under ERISA, the neutral may be subject to liability as a fiduciary.[106] In any event, it has been suggested that arbitrators "may be more willing to serve on ERISA cases as the result of" the 1983 *Greyhound Lines* decision in which the U.S. Court of Appeals concluded that immunity did extend to an arbitrator who performed functions that arguably come within ERISA's definition of a fiduciary.[107]

The Arbitrator's Accountability

Ordinarily a person must possess at least minimal qualifications in order to get a "first case" as an arbitrator. Regardless of qualifications at the outset, the more important ultimate consideration is how well has the person performed as an arbitrator. As is no doubt generally typical of the appointing agencies, it is the policy of the FMCS to maintain on its roster only those arbitrators who "conform to the ethical standards and procedures" of the Code of Professional Responsibility," and who:

"(1) Are experienced, competent and acceptable in decision-making roles in the resolution of labor disputes; or
"(2) Have extensive experience in relevant positions in collective bargaining; and
"(3) Are capable of conducting an orderly hearing, can analyze testimony and exhibits and can prepare clear and concise findings and awards within reasonable time limits."[108]

The FMCS Arbitrator Review Board is guided by the above criteria not only when it reviews applications for listing on the FMCS Roster of Arbitrators *but also when it reviews the status of arbitrators whose eligibility for continued listing on the Roster has been questioned.*[109]

The arbitrator is indeed accountable, as was emphasized by a president of the NAA:

"The arbitrator functions in a glass bowl. The conduct of the hearing is closely observed by sophisticated, knowledgeable advocates. An arbitrator who exhibits a lack of understanding of the process and who fails to conduct a hearing in an orderly fashion will usually find himself unacceptable to the parties for a subsequent hearing. The *ad hoc* arbitrator has no tenure; an umpire has limited tenure, and nothing is so

---

[105]For more on arbitration under § 302(c)(5)(B) and on ERISA see Chapter 1, topic entitled "Compulsory Arbitration."

[106]By memorandum of Dec. 14, 1979, to members of its Roster of Arbitrators, the FMCS cautioned that the U.S. Department of Labor had taken the position that in deciding the issue of a participant's entitlement to benefits under a pension trust plan, the umpire would in fact be acting as a fiduciary within the meaning of ERISA. The AAA and the FMCS have questioned that position, outlining the differences between the roles of a fiduciary and an arbitrator, and arguing that imposition of fiduciary liabilities will deter neutrals from serving. "Arbitrators in Pension Disputes," AAA Study Time, Jan. 1980.

[107]"An Arbitrator's Fiduciary Responsibility in Pension Cases," AAA Study Time, July 1983, referring to UAW v. Greyhound Lines, 701 F.2d 1181 (CA 6, 1983).

[108]FMCS Regulations, §§ 1404.4(b), 1404.5(a).

[109]FMCS Regulations, § 1404.3(c).

impermanent as the permanent arbitrator. The arbitrator is selected by
the parties either directly or through the offices of the AAA, the FMCS,
or state mediation agencies. His decisions are read and reread, not only
by the parties, but by hundreds of company and union representatives
who have access to his awards through their own systems of distribution.
Awards that are not based upon logical, sound interpretation of the
provisions of the agreement will very quickly make the arbitrator
responsible unacceptable to companies and unions alike.

"Sophisticated companies and unions do not keep a box score. They
are primarily concerned with the quality of decisions. The companies
and unions which submit a dispute to arbitration have complete freedom
of choice in the selection of the arbitrator. The arbitrator is almost never
foisted upon the parties. We are all aware of the fact that unions and
companies, and those who represent them, effectively utilize their private pipelines of information. An arbitrator's reputation precedes him,
and a series of poorly reasoned or poorly written decisions will very
quickly read that arbitrator out of the profession. Major companies and
major unions have their own 'don't use' list. That is a fact of
life * * *."[110]

Data on Arbitrators

Information concerning the qualifications of some of the more
active arbitrators may be had by consulting the "Directory of Arbitrators" prepared by The Bureau of National Affairs, Inc., or the
"Who's Who" (of arbitrators) prepared by Prentice-Hall, Inc. This
information includes the name, age, address, education, occupation,
affiliations, experience, articles or books written, awards published,
and other miscellaneous information concerning the arbitrator.

The FMCS provides biographical data on the arbitrators whose
names are supplied to the parties for selection, and most other designating agencies follow the same practice.

The Code of Professional Responsibility has prohibited arbitrators from advertising.[111] Opinion among labor and management
representatives is divided on the question of arbitrator advertising.[112]

---

[110]Luskin, "The Presidential Address: Arbitration and Its Critics," Proceedings of the 21st
Annual Meeting of NAA, 125, 134 (BNA Books, 1968). Also see the very interesting comments
and information offered by Jones, "A Meditation on Labor Arbitration and 'His Own Brand of
Industrial Justice,' " Proceedings of the 35th Annual Meeting of NAA, 1, 8–11 (BNA Books, 1983).
For various factors which parties might consider in accepting or rejecting an arbitrator, see
Eaton, "Labor Arbitration in the San Francisco Bay Area," 48 LA 1381, 1382 (1967); Fleming, The
Labor Arbitration Process, 209–210 (U. of Ill. Press, 1965). One study based on in-depth interviews with labor and management representatives regularly involved in arbitrator selection revealed that: "[E]xperience of an arbitrator is the single most important factor in selection.
However, it is closely followed by the consideration of the arbitrator's suitability to the issue involved in the case. Familiarity with the arbitrator ranked third. All other factors lagged far
behind the first three criteria, with the combined background of the arbitrator and his availability being fourth and fifth. Obviously, the geographical proximity of the arbitrator, a factor of
overall costs, and the arbitrator's fee do not carry much weight in the selection process." Rezler &
Petersen, "Strategies of Arbitrator Selection," 70 LA 1307, 1315 (1978).
[111]Sec. I(C)(3), 64 LA 1320. Discussing the legality and propriety of this prohibition, see
Bloch, "Arbitrator Advertising," 35 Arb. J. No. 2, p. 21 (1980).
[112]See Petersen & Rezler, "Views on Arbitrator Advertising," 34 Arb. J. No. 3, p. 9 (1979).

Tribunals Under Railway Labor Act

One of the nation's most extensive experiences in labor-management arbitration has resulted from the arbitration provisions of the Railway Labor Act of 1926.[113]

Since it sometimes has been suggested that arbitration tribunals of the RLA variety be used for other industries, consideration is given here to the basic features of those tribunals. As was seen in Chapter 3, the present railroad labor legislation of the United States recognizes the distinction between disputes as to "rights" and those as to "interests." The NMB is concerned primarily with interest disputes, while the NRAB is concerned with rights disputes.

Railroad Interest Disputes

The NMB has jurisdiction over any "dispute concerning changes in rates of pay, rules, or working conditions not adjusted by the parties in conference," or any "other disputes not referable to the National Railroad Adjustment Board and not adjusted in conference between the parties or where conferences are refused." Either party may invoke the services of the NMB, or the NMB may proffer its services if a labor emergency is found to exist. The primary function of the NMB is to help the parties, through mediation, to reach agreement. Upon failure to bring about an amicable settlement through mediation, however, the Board seeks to induce the parties to submit the controversy to voluntary arbitration.

Section 7 of the Act provides details for the organization of the arbitration tribunal. It provides that, whenever a controversy is not settled "either in conference between representatives of the parties or by the appropriate adjustment board or through mediation," it may, by agreement of the parties, be submitted "to the arbitration of a board of three (or, if the parties to the controversy so stipulate, of six) persons * * *." If the parties choose a board of three, then each party selects one member and the two so selected choose the neutral member. If a board of six is desired, each side selects two members, and the four so selected choose the two neutral members. If the members selected by the parties cannot agree upon the neutral or neutrals, they are appointed by the NMB. The board of arbitration selects one of its members to serve as chairman and makes such rules as are necessary for conducting hearings. The members selected by the parties need not

---

[113]45 U.S.C. §§ 151–163, 181–188; 1 LRRM 843. The arbitration provisions of the 1926 Act (44 Stat. 577) were amended and expanded in 1934 (48 Stat. 1185), in 1936 (49 Stat. 1189), and in 1966 (80 Stat. 208). For extensive discussion of the Act, see Gohmann, Arbitration and Representation: Applications in Air and Rail Labor Relations (1981); Gohmann, Air and Rail Labor Relations: A Judicial History of the Railway Labor Act (1979); Rehmus, The Railway Labor Act at Fifty: Collective Bargaining in the Railroad and Airline Industries (1976); Lecht, Experience Under Railway Labor Legislation (1955). Also, Roukis, "Should the Railway Labor Act Be Amended?" 38 Arb. J. No. 1, p. 16 (1983); "Procedures Under the Railway Labor Act: A Panel Discussion," Proceedings of the 18th Annual Meeting of NAA, 27 (BNA Books, 1965).

be impartial. Each party compensates its appointees and the NMB compensates neutrals.

The award of the board, when signed by a majority of the members, may be filed with the clerk of the federal district court for the district in which the controversy arose or the arbitration is entered into. When so filed, it is conclusive on the parties as to the merits and facts of the controversy, and, unless within ten days a petition to impeach it on grounds specifically set out in the Act is filed with the court, judgment will be entered on the award.

National Railroad Adjustment Board

Upon submission of a petition by either side, the National Railroad Adjustment Board takes jurisdiction over "disputes between an employee or group of employees and a carrier or carriers growing out of grievances or out of the interpretation or application of agreements concerning rates of pay, rules, or working conditions," after they have been "handled in the usual manner up to and including the chief operating officer of the carrier designated to handle such disputes." Thus, it is seen that the NRAB handles rights disputes. It assumes jurisdiction only if at least one of the parties wishes it to do so.[114]

The NRAB is strictly bipartisan. It is composed of 34 members, 17 of whom are selected and compensated by the carriers and 17 by the railroad labor organizations.[115] The NRAB is organized into four Divisions, each Division having jurisdiction over specified classes of railroad employees. The NRAB functions almost entirely through the individual Divisions, and each Division for all practical purposes is independent of the others. Each Division really amounts to a distinct arbitration tribunal, bipartisan in nature, with equal representation from the carriers and the labor organizations. The First Division has eight permanent members, the Second and Third Divisions have 10 each, and the Fourth Division has six.

When a dispute is referred to one of the Divisions, a hearing is held, unless waived. At the hearing the parties may be heard either in person, by counsel, or by other representatives. After the hearing, the Division proceeds to decide the case. As a matter of practice the Divisions frequently hold successive hearings on a group of cases, then hold sessions for deliberation and decision of the cases. Since each Division is equally represented by labor and management and since the representatives of each side almost always tend to vote the same

---

[114]Railroad employees no longer have any option to take their grievance under the collective agreement to court without exhausting the NRAB remedy. Andrews v. Louisville & Nashville R.R., 92 S.Ct. 1562 (1972). Cf., Glover v. St. Louis-San Francisco Ry., 89 S.Ct. 548 (1969).

[115]Prior to amendment of the RLA in 1970 the Board had 36 members, 18 selected by each side. The 1970 amendment, Public Law 91–234, reduced from 10 to 8 the number of members on the Board's First Division. This was made necessary by the merger of four unions representing the trainmen, firemen, conductors, and switchmen into a single union, the United Transportation Union. Although each side now has four members on the First Division, only two members from each side are entitled to vote.

way, a unanimous vote generally is necessary to decide a case. While many cases do receive the required vote, numerous others do not. Deadlocks are inevitable and frequent. The RLA provides for the selection of referees in such cases. The referee sits with the Division as a temporary member and decides the cases for which he is appointed. Usually a referee's appointment will be for a group of cases. Deadlocked cases are set aside until a sufficient number have accumulated to warrant calling in a referee.

Initial responsibility for the selection of referees is upon the Divisions. If a Division, however, is unable to agree upon a neutral person to serve as referee, one is selected by the NMB. Within ten days after a Division certifies to the NMB the fact of inability to agree upon a referee, the NMB makes the appointment. The Divisions, generally speaking, have not been able to agree upon referees, so the primary responsibility for appointment of referees has been with the NMB. All referees are compensated by the NMB.

Cases assigned to a referee are presented to the referee by Division members. Occasionally, if request is made, some Divisions permit oral argument by the parties before the referee. Generally, however, the referee's knowledge of a case comes from the parties' written submissions and from briefs and arguments of Division members.[116] Each Division has both labor and management members highly skilled in presenting cases to the referees. The referee is given opportunity to study case records prior to meeting with Division members. Division members often present written briefs to the referee and always give him opportunity to ask questions.

The referee then takes the cases under advisement, makes his findings, and writes the proposed opinions and awards. Practice varies as to the length of opinions. The Third Division, for instance, has expected its referees to write relatively long opinions. The First Division has preferred brevity. The referee discusses proposed awards with the Division and voting follows. The side in whose favor an award is rendered generally will vote with the referee to provide the required majority vote.[117]

The RLA as amended in 1966 provides that Adjustment Board awards "shall be final and binding upon both parties to the dispute" (though, as noted hereinbelow, limited right of court review does now exist).[118] If a dispute arises over the interpretation of an award, the

---

[116]The NRAB is essentially an appellate tribunal. Rejecting a due process challenge related to one aspect of this fact, see Edwards v. St. Louis-San Francisco Ry., 361 F.2d 946 (CA 7, 1966).

[117]For other studies and discussions of the Adjustment Board, see Lazar, Due Process in Disciplinary Hearings: Decisions of the National Railroad Adjustment Board (UCLA Inst. of Indus. Rel., 1980); Gohmann, Air and Rail Labor Relations: A Judicial History of the Railway Labor Act, 141 et seq. (1979); Mangum, "Railroad Grievance Procedures," 15 Indus. & Lab. Rel. Rev. 491 (1962); Kaufman, "Grievance Arbitration in the Railroad Industry," 9 Lab. L.J. 244 (1958); Daugherty, Whiting & Guthrie, "Arbitration by the National Railroad Adjustment Board," Arbitration Today, 93–127 (BNA Books, 1955); Lecht, Experience Under Railway Labor Legislation, 10–11, 83, 163, 171, 191–192 (1955); Jones, National Railroad Adjustment Board (1941); Spencer, The National Railroad Adjustment Board (1938); Garrison, "The National Railroad Adjustment Board; A Unique Administrative Agency," 46 Yale L.J. 567 (1937). NRAB Rules of Procedure are published in 29 C.F.R. Part 301.

[118]Sec. 3(m). As to the permissible scope of court review under the language of the Act prior to the 1966 amendments, see Gunther v. San Diego & Arizona E. Ry., 86 S.Ct. 368 (1965).

Act directs the Division to interpret the award upon request by either party.

If an award is in favor of the employees, the Division is directed by the Act to issue an order requiring the carrier to make the award effective. After such order is issued, the Division has nothing to do with its enforcement. When a denial award is issued, the Division is directed by the Act to issue an order to the petitioner stating such determination.

Prior to the 1966 amendments only the winning party could take the award to court, which it could do for the purpose of seeking court enforcement. Under the amendments the loser, too, has a right to take the award to court, for review. In either instance the court may not set the award aside except on limited grounds.

If a carrier does not comply with an order implementing an award, the party in whose favor it stands may within two years sue upon it for enforcement by the appropriate federal district court. In such suit the findings and order of the Adjustment Board Division "shall be conclusive on the parties."[119] The court may, however, set the Division's order aside for any of the following reasons: (1) failure of the Division to comply with requirements of the Act, (2) failure of the Division to confine itself to matters within the scope of its jurisdiction, or (3) fraud or corruption by a member of the Division making the order.[120]

Under the 1966 amendments any party who is aggrieved by an NRAB award (that is, a loser, whether an employee or carrier) may obtain review thereof by petitioning the appropriate federal district court. Here again, the action must be instituted within two years and the findings and order of the Adjustment Board Division "shall be conclusive on the parties," except that the court may set the order aside or remand it to the Division for any of the three reasons noted in the paragraph immediately hereinabove.[121] The U.S. Supreme Court has stressed that judicial review is limited to these three specific grounds.[122]

---

[119]Sec. 3(p). The two-year limitation is stated in § 3(r).

[120]Sec. 3(p). These three grounds for setting awards aside are part of the 1966 amendments. As to the court's right to "interpret" awards, see Sweeney v. Florida E. Coast Ry., 67 LRRM 2263 (CA 5, 1968). The burden of seeking court enforcement of awards is reduced by a provision of the Act which relieves the petitioner from some of the court costs and which allows a petitioner who prevails in his action a reasonable attorney's fee.

[121]Sec. 3(q). Prior to the 1966 amendments the party against whom an award was directed had no right to take it to court for review. Essentially the only way an award could be tested was for it to be in favor of the employees, for the carrier to refuse to comply with the award, and for the employees then to take it to court for enforcement. Theoretically, the carrier needed no right to go to court on its own initiative since it could refuse to comply with an award in favor of employees and let them take it to court. However, employees at times chose to strike instead of suing to force carrier compliance, thus depriving the carrier of opportunity for court review. The carrier's right of court review was ultimately assured by the Supreme Court ruling that strikes cannot be used to enforce Adjustment Board awards, Brotherhood of Locomotive Eng'rs. v. Louisville & Nashville R.R., 83 S.Ct. 1059 (1963), and by the 1966 amendment giving any party aggrieved by an NRAB award the right to take it to court for review.

[122]Union Pacific Ry. v. Sheehan, 99 S.Ct. 399, 402 (1978). In Curtis v. United Transp. Union, 102 LRRM 2961, 2963 (USDC, 1979), the District Court concluded that the doctrine specified by the Supreme Court in Hines v. Anchor Motor Freight applies also under the RLA. For that doctrine, see Chapter 2, subtopic entitled "De Novo Litigation Following Arbitration."

Finally, it should be noted that sometimes neither party to a dispute will submit it to the Adjustment Board even though the dispute is a "rights" or "minor" dispute of the type for which the Board was established. The U.S. Supreme Court has held that railroad employees may not strike over disputes that are actually pending before the NRAB, and that the federal courts may enjoin such strikes.[123] However, strikes over such disputes apparently may not be enjoined if the dispute is not actually pending before the NRAB.[124]

Existing differences which neither party will submit to the Board may plague the parties year after year until finally a sufficient number will have accumulated to cause a strike. At this point the National Mediation Board sometimes induces the parties to accept arbitration by a three-member or six-member board, or to establish a special board of adjustment for the cases in question.

Railroad Special Boards of Adjustment

Even prior to the 1966 amendments the Railway Labor Act authorized the establishment of system, group, or regional boards of adjustment by mutual consent of the parties.[125] The 1966 amendments added a provision for establishment of special boards of adjustment, at the request of either party, "to resolve disputes otherwise referable to the Adjustment Board, or any dispute which has been pending before the Adjustment Board for twelve months from the date" when the dispute was submitted to the NRAB. Thus, disputes in some instances may be withdrawn from the NRAB and submitted to a special board.

The RLA directs the National Mediation Board to aid in the establishment of these special boards (which have three members) and in the designation of the neutral member.[126] The Act makes awards of

---

[123]Brotherhood of R.R. Trainmen v. Chicago R. & I.R. R.R., 77 S.Ct. 635, 39 LRRM 2578 (1957). The carriers sometimes submit disputes to the Board as a means of avoiding strikes. While strikes may thus be enjoined, however, the Supreme Court has held that the district court may impose conditions requiring maintenance of the status quo as the "price of relief" when the injunctive powers of the court are invoked; thus the employees would be protected against a harmful change in working conditions during pendency of the dispute before the Adjustment Board. Brotherhood of Locomotive Eng'rs. v. M-K-T R.R., 80 S.Ct. 1326, 46 LRRM 2429 (1960).

[124]A state court injunction against one such strike was vacated by the U.S. Supreme Court where the dispute was not pending before the Adjustment Board. Manion v. Kansas City Terminal Ry., 77 S.Ct. 706, 39 LRRM 2641 (1957).

[125]Discussing such private, mutually voluntary boards, and holding their awards to be subject to judicial review, see Merchants Despatch Transp. Corp. v. Systems Fedn., 551 F.2d 144 (CA 7, 1977).

[126]The NMB's rules for setting up special boards of adjustment under the 1966 amendments are published in 29 C.F.R. Part 1207. The Mediation Board calls the special boards "PL Boards" under Public Law 89–456. For discussion of these special boards, see Atchison, Topeka & Santa Fe Ry., 50 LA 1057 (Jones, 1968), which also contains rulings as to procedural matters before PL Boards; Western Pac. R.R., 50 LA 1013 (Wyckoff, 1968). It has been held that a special board considering a case that has been withdrawn from the NRAB should not be limited to a consideration of the evidence contained in the parties' submissions to the NRAB—the parties may proffer such oral testimony or written evidence as they wish, and the special board may request additional evidence from either party. Illinois N. Ry., 53 LA 767, 769–770 (Sembower, 1969). It has been pointed out, however, that "[a]lthough the public law boards now hear witnesses, the underlying concept remains that of an appellate rather than a *de novo* proceeding." Stark, "The Presidential Address: Theme and Adaptations," Proceedings of the 31st Annual Meeting of NAA, 1, 15 (BNA Books, 1979).

the special boards of adjustment "final and binding upon both parties," and provides that the awards shall be enforceable in federal district courts in the same manner as awards of the NRAB.[127]

Airline System Boards of Adjustment

Amendment of the Railway Labor Act in 1936 made provision for the establishment of a national board of adjustment for the airlines when it shall be necessary "in the judgment of the National Mediation Board." Pending establishment of such national board, the airlines and their employees are directed to establish system boards of adjustment for the resolution of grievances. System boards of adjustment have been established by each airline pursuant to this mandate and have functioned very effectively on the whole.[128] Awards of these airline boards are governed and enforceable by federal law, in the federal courts.[129]

The National Mediation Board aids in the designation of neutrals for service with airline system boards of adjustment. The parties compensate the neutrals who serve with airline system boards. In sharp contrast, the Railway Labor Act provides that the National Mediation Board shall compensate the neutrals who serve with the National Railroad Adjustment Board or with railroad special boards of adjustment. Requiring the parties to compensate the neutrals tends to reduce the number of meritless grievances that will be taken to arbitration, and this in turn contributes significantly to the success of any dispute settlement program or tribunal.[130]

Statutory Tribunals for Critical Industrial Disputes

Both the RLA and the LMRA of 1947 contain provisions for special tribunals for critical industrial disputes, and both Acts contain provisions for requiring the parties to maintain the status quo without work stoppages pending investigation and report by the special tribunal. These tribunals should be noted briefly in passing even though, technically speaking, they are not arbitration tribunals.

Section 10 of the RLA provides that if a dispute between a carrier and its employees is not settled by use of the Act's other machinery, and if the NMB finds that the dispute threatens a substantial interruption of interstate commerce, the President may in his discretion create an Emergency Board to investigate and report the facts and

---

[127]Awards of these boards are subject to judicial review. United Transp. Union v. Indiana Harbor Belt R.R., 540 F.2d 861 (CA 7, 1976).

[128]For general discussion of these boards, see Kahn, "Airline Grievance Procedures: Some Observations and Questions," 35 J. Air L. & Com. 313 (1969).

[129]International Assn. of Machinists v. Central Airlines, 83 S.Ct. 956 (1963).

[130]For related discussion, see Vernon, "Public Funding for the Arbitration of Grievances in the Railroad Industry," 38 Arb. J. No. 3, p. 22 (1983); Fletcher, "Backlog Not the Issue—Public Funding Is; User Fees Questioned," id. at 34; Hopkins, "Public Funding Not the Issue—Backlog Is; Cost Sharing Supported," id. at 38.

circumstances of the dispute and make recommendations as to its settlement.[131]

Section 206 of the LMRA of 1947 provides that in national emergency disputes imperiling the national health or safety the President may appoint a Board of Inquiry to inquire into the issues involved in the dispute and to make a written report which "shall include a statement of the facts with respect to the dispute, including each party's statement of its position but shall not contain any recommendations."[132]

Section 213 of the LMRA was added in 1974 and authorizes the Director of the FMCS to establish a Board of Inquiry, whose report shall contain findings of fact together with recommendations, when "a threatened or actual strike or lockout affecting a health care institution" threatens to "substantially interrupt the delivery of health care in the locality concerned."[133]

Boards of Inquiry may also be established under state statute. The function of one such board, which had authority to make recommendations, was deemed by its members to "contain elements both of mediation and arbitration," since:

> "Like a mediator, the Board must think about the acceptability of its proposals. Like an arbitrator, it is concerned with the weight of the evidence and with the merits of the questions before it. As a statutory Board appointed by the State of New York, the Board has the additional function of serving a public interest which is not necessarily present in private proceedings."[134]

While the parties are not legally compelled to accept the findings of emergency boards and boards of inquiry, public pressure may strongly motivate them to do so, especially where the board has authority to make recommendations and actually does so.

---

[131]For detailed discussion of these boards, see Railroads v. Nonoperating Unions, 17 LA 833, 841, 843 (Cole, Horvitz & Osborne, 1952); Kaufman, "Emergency Boards Under the Railway Labor Act," 9 Lab. L.J. 910 (1958); Lecht, Experience Under Railway Labor Legislation, 6, 11–12, 53–54, 176, 190–191 (1955). For statement of the functions of emergency boards, see Chapter 3, topic entitled "Arbitrator's Function in Interest Disputes." In 1981 the RLA was amended to provide special emergency board procedures for disputes "between a publicly funded and publicly operated carrier providing rail commuter service (including the Amtrak Commuter Services Corporation) and its employees." At one stage a second emergency board may be established to receive and select between the "final offers" of the parties. Employees refusing to honor the board's final-offer selection become ineligible for certain statutory unemployment benefits. Employers refusing to honor the board's selection become ineligible to "participate in any benefits of any agreement between carriers which is designed to provide benefits to such carriers during a work stoppage." 45 U.S.C. § 159.

[132]For the reports of some of these boards, see Board of Inquiry Members Taylor, Perkins & Lehoczky in 33 LA 236; Farmer, Frankenthaler & Sembower in 33 LA 255; Cole, Carman & Comey in 21 LA 189 and in 21 LA 489; Harris, Cheney & Levy in 19 LA 532. For general discussion, see Dunlop, Dispute Resolution: Negotiation and Consensus Building, 147–172 (1984); Cole, "Major Labor Disputes—Reexamination and Recommendations," The Profession of Labor Arbitration, 90 (BNA Books, 1957). Also see Foster, "Final Offer Selection in National Emergency Disputes," 27 Arb. J. 85 (1972).

[133]For discussion, see Sinai Hosp. of Baltimore v. Horvitz, 104 LRRM 2171, 2174 (CA 4, 1980), holding that the FMCS Director's decision to establish a health-care Board of Inquiry is not subject to judicial review.

[134]Rochester Transit Corp., 19 LA 538, 542 (Tolley, McKelvey & Turkus, 1952). Also see statement of functions by Board of Inquiry in Steel Industry, 33 LA 236 at 236 (Taylor, Perkins & Lehoczky, 1959).

Chapter 5

Grievances—Prelude to Arbitration

Arbitration generally is the last step or terminal point of dispute settlement under union contracts. A happy situation exists when the preliminary steps of dispute-settlement machinery function effectively, resulting in settlement of a high percentage of disputes prior to the arbitration stage. If the preliminary steps do not function smoothly, the arbitration tribunal may be overburdened with cases, which overburdening in turn may lead to a breakdown of the system. It is generally agreed that no dispute should be taken to arbitration until all possibilities of settlement at the negotiation stages of the grievance procedure have been exhausted. However, once the preliminary steps have been exhausted without success, resort to arbitration should be prompt.

The Grievance Procedure

It is said that collective bargaining is not confined to the making of an agreement once a year but is a day-to-day process in which the grievance procedure has a very important role.[1] "The grievance procedure is, in other words, a part of the continuous collective bargaining process."[2] Some writers declare the grievance procedure to be the core of the collective bargaining agreement.[3] Professor Harry Shulman expressed a similar view:

"In labor negotiations there are factors peculiar to them which affirmatively press for almost deliberate incompleteness and uncertainty in the agreement; but, even if it were otherwise, it surely is true that no collective agreement has been or can be written which covers in detail all the exigencies with which the parties may be confronted in the contract period, or which makes crystal-clear its meaning with respect

---

[1]Chrysler Corp., 10 War Lab. Rep. 551, 554 (1943).
[2]United Steelworkers v. Warrior & Gulf Navigation Co., 80 S.Ct. 1347, 1352 (1960).
[3]Hill & Hook, Management at the Bargaining Table, 199 (1945).

to the matters that it does cover. * * * It is this that makes collective bargaining an unending process in labor relations, and it is this that makes the grievance procedure the heart of the collective agreement."[4]

The extreme importance of a good grievance procedure in large companies was emphasized by Arbitrator Michael I. Komaroff, who called the grievance machinery the "life-blood of a collective bargaining relationship."[5] In the coal mining industry the grievance procedure was said "to be the 'safety-valve' in industrial relations, the procedure which gives a vital flexibility to the whole system of collective bargaining."[6] When parties in that industry ceased to make serious effort to utilize the grievance procedure properly, a flood of wildcat strikes ensued.[7]

The President's National Labor-Management Conference of 1945 recommended that every collective bargaining agreement contain provision for an effective grievance procedure. The Conference outlined some of the standards which a grievance procedure, to be "effective," should meet:

"1. Collective bargaining agreements should contain provisions that grievances and disputes involving the interpretation or application of the terms of the agreement are to be settled without resort to strikes, lockouts, or other interruptions to normal operations by an effective grievance procedure with arbitration as its final step.

"2. To be effective, the procedure established for the settlement of such grievances and disputes should meet at least the following standards:

"(a) The successive steps in the procedure, the method of presenting grievances or disputes, and the method of taking an appeal from one step to another should be so clearly stated in the agreement as to be readily understood by all employees, union officials, and management representatives.

"(b) The procedure should be adaptable to the handling of the various types of grievances and disputes which come under the terms of the agreement.

"(c) The procedure should be designed to facilitate the settlement of grievances and disputes as soon as possible after they arise. To this end:

"(1) The agreement should provide adequate stated time limits for the presentation of grievances and disputes, the rendering of decisions, and the taking of appeals.

"(2) Issues should be clearly formulated at the earliest possible moment. In all cases which cannot be settled in the first informal discussions, the positions of both sides should be reduced to writing.

"(3) Management and union should encourage their representatives to settle at the lower steps grievances which do not

---

[4]Conference on Training of Law Students in Labor Relations, Vol. III, Transcript of Proceedings, 669 (1947). The U.S. Supreme Court expressed a similar view in *Warrior & Gulf*, supra at 1352.

[5]North Am. Aviation, 16 LA 744, 747 (1951).

[6]Somers, Grievance Settlement in Coal Mining, 43 (W. Va. U. Bull. Series 56, No. 12–2, 1956).

[7]See reports of The President's Commission on Coal, cited above in Chapter 1, topic entitled "Other Important Roles of Arbitration."

involve broad questions of policy or of contract interpretation and should delegate sufficient authority to them to accomplish this end.

"(4) The agreement should provide adequate opportunity for both parties to investigate grievances under discussion.

"(5) Provision should be made for priority handling of grievances involving discharge, suspension, or other disciplinary action.

"(d) The procedure should be open to the submission of grievances by all parties to the agreement.

"3. Managements and unions should inform and train their representatives in the proper functioning of the grievance procedure and in their responsibilities under it. In such a program it should be emphasized:

"(a) That the basic objective of the grievance procedure is the achievement of sound and fair settlements and not the 'winning' of cases;

"(b) That the filing of grievances should be considered by foremen or supervisors as aids in discovering and removing causes of discontent in their departments;

"(c) That any tendency by either party to support the earlier decisions of its representatives when such decisions are wrong should be discouraged;

"(d) That the willingness of management and union officials to give adequate time and attention to the handling and disposition of grievances and disputes is necessary to the effective functioning of the procedure;

"(e) That for the sound handling of grievances and disputes both management and union representatives should be thoroughly familiar with the entire collective bargaining agreement."[8]

Most collective bargaining agreements give recognition to some, at least, of these standards, and arbitrators of interest disputes have been known to direct the parties to "spell out" the details of their grievance procedures in accordance with the recommendations of the National Labor Management Conference.[9]

Grievances Defined

What is a "grievance"? Comprehensively, it is that which the parties to a particular collective agreement say it is. Such a definition, of course, does no more than apprise one of the fact that labor relations authorities disagree widely as to the precise meaning of the term and that collective agreements reflect this lack of accord. The term connotes conflict and irritation, and thus could be defined as any "gripe" or any type of complaint by an employee or a union against the employer or by an employer against his employee or the union. It is

---

[8]The President's National Labor-Management Conference, Nov. 5–30, 1945 (U.S. Dept. of Labor, Div. of Labor Standards, Bull. No. 77, pp. 45–46, 1946).

[9]See New York Shipping Assn., 1 LA 80, 84, 87–88 (Davis, 1945). Also see comments of Arbitrator Maurice H. Merrill in 20 LA 211, 212. For general discussion of grievance procedures, see The Grievance Process (Mich. State U. Lab. & Indus. Rel. Center, 1956); Reynard, "Drafting of Grievance and Arbitration Articles of Collective Bargaining Agreements," 10 Vand. L. Rev. 749 (1957).

generally understood, however, that disputes involving demands for changes in the terms of a collective bargaining agreement ("interests" disputes) and disputes arising out of representation issues are not grievances.

Grievances may arise from an infinite number of causes, which may be either real or imaginary. This suggests inquiry as to what determines when a person has a grievance. Must there have been a wrong done? One employer has urged that a grievance does not come into existence so as to be subject to the grievance procedure until some harmful or disciplinary action has been taken against the complainant. The arbitrator who considered this view rejected it as being too narrow. He said: "Whether a man has a grievance or not is primarily his own feeling about the matter. Generally speaking, if a man thinks he has a grievance, he has a grievance."[10]

From a more technical standpoint, however, Arbitrator Charles O. Gregory has stated that the term "grievance" as it appears in the average contract refers to "a formal complaint" by persons who believe they have been wronged.[11]

Attitude of Parties to the Grievance Procedure

The parties' attitude in handling grievances, probably more than in any other aspect of the labor-management relationship, indicates their good faith. Nowhere in that relationship is mutual good faith more important.[12] The attitude of the parties is even more important than the type of grievance provisions contained in the agreement. This view has been shared by unions and management alike in most cases in which the grievance procedure has been considered successful and in the majority of cases in which the procedure has broken down.[13] Good grievance machinery is important, but such machinery alone will not insure success. The attitude, judgment, experience, and training of the individuals involved are of prime importance. Moreover, a desire to settle grievances, rather than to win them, is essential.

No grievance should be presented unless there is a real basis for complaint or need for decision. Much responsibility belongs directly to the union stewards, and indirectly to the union, to screen out com-

---

[10]Cudahy Packing Co., 7 LA 645, 646 (Fisher, 1947). "A grievance, real or imaginary, is nevertheless a grievance." Vulcan Mold & Iron Co., 41 LA 59, 61 (Brecht, 1963). Inchoate harm from a new management policy sufficed for a "grievance." Northwest Airlines, 45 LA 565, 569–570 (Shister, 1965). Also see Arbitrator Coffey in 62–3 ARB ¶8885; Wollett in 35 LA 783, 786–787. Cf., Komaroff in 16 LA 744, 747–748. In Forrest Indus. v. Woodworkers Local 3–436, 381 F.2d 144, 146 (CA 9, 1967), the court explained that "a liberal and broad construction should be given to the term 'grievance' in the interest of encouraging the use of machinery which the parties themselves have set up for the peaceful settlement of disputes."

[11]E.I. DuPont de Nemours & Co., 29 LA 646, 650 (1957). But cf., Braniff Airways, 27 LA 892, 896–898 (Williams, 1957).

[12]Also see comments by Arbitrator Luskin, "The Presidential Address: Arbitration and Its Critics," Proceedings of the 21st Annual Meeting of NAA, 125, 133 (BNA Books, 1968), and by Arbitrator Jenkins in Hunt Foods & Indus., 44 LA 664, 669 (1965).

[13]"Grievance Procedure Under Collective Bargaining," 63 Monthly Lab. Rev. 175 (U.S. Dept. of Labor, 1946).

plaints that have no real merit. The United States Department of Labor has suggested that persons responsible for the preparation of stewards' manuals give serious thought to the inclusion of the following instructions to stewards:

> "* * * *Use your best judgment in deciding whether or not a grievance is justified.*—If you are convinced that the worker does not have a real case it is better to tell him so right from the beginning. Taking up a lot of poor cases will cost you the respect of all concerned. On the other hand, don't forget that you are the worker's representative. If the case is a borderline one but you feel that the worker has considerable justice on his side, tell him frankly that you are not sure what is the correct answer. Then take the case up and get a definite ruling through the grievance procedure."[14]

Suggestions have been made, too, concerning the responsibility of foremen:

> "Greater emphasis should be placed on training foremen in the human relations aspects of their jobs. Many times a man simply wants a relief hour or perhaps a sympathetic listener. Foremen must be given better training, on the importance of fully hearing out rather than prematurely debating with their employees. They must acquire the ability of [noting] *what* is being said, rather than the manner in which the problem is being presented. Only in this way can gripes be separated from grievances, or can gripes be kept from becoming grievances."[15]

Both parties should make every effort to settle grievances at the lowest step. Grievances become magnified in importance and increasingly difficult to settle as they progress toward the top.[16]

Settlements at the first steps of the grievance procedure often will be facilitated by honest and open disclosure of each party's position and its basis.[17] Moreover, the U.S. Supreme Court has held that a company had a legal duty to provide information to explain certain of its actions and thus enable the union to determine whether to process a grievance, the Court explaining: "Arbitration can function properly only if the grievance procedures leading to it can sift out unmeritorious claims. For if all claims originally initiated as griev-

---

[14]Preparing a Steward's Manual, 7 (U.S. Dept. of Labor, Div. of Labor Standards, Bull. No. 59, 1943). Also see Arbitrator Sembower in 41 LA 185, 188.

[15]Comments of management spokesman Harry W. Lacey, Proceedings of the Conference on Improving the Relations Between the Parties, 29 (U. of Notre Dame Press, 1960). Also see Mills, Labor Relations for Supervisors—A Manual for Day-to-Day Living With Employee Organizations (1977); Walker & Robinson, "The First-Line Supervisor's Role in the Grievance Procedure," 32 Arb. J. 279 (1977); Grievance Handling: 101 Guides for Supervisors (AAA, 1970). The BNA Editorial Staff offers a useful guide for stewards and supervisors alike, in Grievance Guide, 6th Ed. (BNA Books, 1982).

[16]For discussion, see Fischer, "Updating Arbitration," Proceedings of the 26th Annual Meeting of NAA, 62, 64–65 (BNA Books, 1974); statement of G.A. Moore in "25 Years of Labor Arbitration—And the Future," Proceedings of the 25th Annual Meeting of NAA, 11, 42 (BNA Books, 1973).

[17]See comments of Arbitrator Seitz in Sperry-Rand Corp., 46 LA 961, 965–966 (1966). Also see Zack, "Suggested New Approaches to Grievance Arbitration," Proceedings of the 30th Annual Meeting of NAA, 105, 110–111 (BNA Books, 1978).

ances had to be processed through to arbitration, the system would be woefully overburdened."[18]

When approached with the proper attitude, grievance machinery serves the mutual advantage of employer, employees, and the union. It helps management discover and correct sore spots in plant operations before they cause serious trouble. Grievances constitute a channel of communication, informing top management of things concerning which employees or the union feel strongly.[19] It is to the employer's advantage to make it as easy as possible to present grievances, and employees should be encouraged, not only to present their complaints, but also to present them while they are still "warm." Grievance machinery provides the union a mechanism for enforcing the rules which it has worked for and achieved through collective bargaining.

Moreover, through use of grievance machinery the union performs a service to the employees, thereby increasing their loyalty to the union. "To the individual worker, grievance procedure provides the means of enforcing the terms of the contract and * * * a democratic method of appeal against any one person's arbitrary decision affecting his wages or working conditions. It protects the democratic rights of the individual in industry in the same way that our judicial system protects his democratic rights in civil life."[20]

Abuse and Misuse of Grievance Procedure

It has been said that an "irresistible impulse to file grievances" is not a dischargeable offense, though the purposeful filing of deliberately untruthful grievances may be.[21]

The more serious threat to the health and integrity of the grievance procedure (including arbitration) comes from other causes. A valuable study of distressed grievance procedures and their rehabilitation was made by Arbitrator Arthur M. Ross. This study reveals various impediments to a healthy grievance procedure, including such factors as: failure to screen grievances; factional strife

---

[18]NLRB v. Acme Indus. Co., 87 S.Ct. 565, 569 (1967). In Vickers, Inc., 43 LA 1256, 1261 (Bothwell, 1964), the provisions of the grievance procedure were held to imply an obligation by the company to provide the union with certain minimum information relevant to the validity of a grievance. For related discussion, see Chapter 8, topic entitled "Requiring the Production of Evidence."

[19]Hill & Hook, Management at the Bargaining Table, 199 (1945).

[20]Settling Plant Grievances, 1 (U.S. Dept. of Labor, Div. of Labor Standards, Bull. No. 60, 1943).

[21]National Lead Co. of Ohio, 37 LA 1076, 1079 (Schedler, 1962). Also illustrating the strong inclination of arbitrators to protect employees against reprisals for filing grievances, see Arbitrator Altrock in 72 LA 118, 119; Beitner in 71 LA 994, 997; Helburn in 70 LA 504, 513–514; Larkin in 52 LA 1221, 1226 (persistent filing of grievances was annoying to supervision but not cause for discipline). Cf., Bradley in 54 LA 206, 211–213. Such protection also exists under the NLRA. See Welco Indus., Inc., 237 NLRB 294 (1978), enforced, 653 F.2d 231, 108 LRRM 2428 (CA 6, 1980); Ernst Steel Corp., 212 NLRB 78 (1974). Cf., Square D Co., 204 NLRB 154 (1973). Filing a deliberately untruthful grievance justified discharge in Chrysler Corp., 32 LA 719, 738–739 (Wolff, 1959). Discharge for filing grievances and a court suit in bad faith to harass the employer was upheld under the NLRA in Leviton Mfg. Co. v. NLRB, 84 LRRM 2670 (CA 1, 1973).

within the union; desire of union shop committee to perpetuate itself (indiscriminate filing of grievances); poor investigation of grievances; poor steward training; company hard line on practically all grievances; failure of top management to back up industrial-relations personnel, who become inclined to pass the buck to an arbitrator; overgenerous grievance pay; availability of free or subsidized arbitration.[22] Identifying another impediment, a management spokesman stated that foremen are generally well trained but that they should be better trained in the human-relations aspects of their job and should not automatically assume a defensive attitude in favor of the company.[23]

Remedies for Distressed Grievance Procedures

Some of the remedial devices frequently mentioned by persons consulted in the aforementioned Ross study include mass grievance settlements, screening of grievances, direct negotiations between management and union officials at higher levels of authority, and procedural changes.[24] It is generally agreed that screening of grievances is a most beneficial remedy, though this remedy may not be fully available due to internal union politics and union fears of legal liability to employees for failure to process grievances.[25]

A caveat as to repair of the grievance procedure was offered by William E. Simkin while speaking as Director of the Federal Mediation and Conciliation Service:

---

[22]Ross, "Distressed Grievance Procedures and Their Rehabilitation," Proceedings of the 16th Annual Meeting of NAA, 104, 107–108 (BNA Books, 1963).

[23]Comments of Harry W. Lacey, Proceedings of the Conference on Improving the Relations Between the Parties, 29 (U. of Notre Dame Press, 1960).

[24]For the pros and cons of these and other suggested remedies, see Ross, "Distressed Grievance Procedures and Their Rehabilitation," Proceedings of the 16th Annual Meeting of NAA, 104, 111 et seq. (BNA Books, 1963). Also dealing with revival of distressed procedures, see Luskin, "The Presidential Address: Arbitration and Its Critics," Proceedings of the 21st Annual Meeting of NAA, 125, 132–134 (BNA Books, 1968). Warning against "grab bag" settlements where some individual employee grievances of possible merit are abandoned by the union in exchange for the allowance of other grievances, see Summers, "The Individual Employee's Rights Under the Collective Agreement: What Constitutes Fair Representation," Proceedings of the 27th Annual Meeting of NAA, 14, 27–28 (BNA Books, 1975).

[25]See Jones & Smith, "Management and Labor Appraisals and Criticisms of the Arbitration Process: A Report With Comments," 62 Mich. L. Rev. 1115, 1152–1153 (1964). As to extent of concern, by union officials, regarding possible legal liability, see Kleeb, "Comment," Proceedings of the 27th Annual Meeting of NAA, 41, 42 (BNA Books, 1975); panel discussion, "A Colloquium on the Arbitration Process," Proceedings of the 17th Annual Meeting of NAA, 100–102, 106, 109 (BNA Books, 1964). UMW counsel Harrison Combs explained that even when a union is convinced that an employee's grievance is meritless, "when you get to the question of onsite settling of grievances, it isn't as free as you might think"; that the union "may get slapped with a charge of failure to fairly represent"; and that "it's a real danger." Thus, the meritless grievance may be taken to arbitration because of overcaution by the union. The President's Commission on Coal, Labor-Management Seminar I, Collective Bargaining (Mar. 21, 1979) 71, U.S. Govt. Printing Office, 1979, 0–302–756. He pointed in particular to the U.S. Supreme Court's *Hines* decision on the duty of fair representation. Discussing *Hines* and related decisions, see Chapter 2, subtopic entitled "De Novo Litigation Following Arbitration," and see this Chapter's topic entitled "Grievance Adjustment by Individual Employees." Although, as noted above, the Supreme Court in *Acme* emphasized the necessity of sifting out unmeritorious claims, it is apparent that other considerations may impede the attainment of this objective. Nonetheless, some parties have been very successful in resolving grievances short of arbitration. See Chapter 4, topic entitled " 'Permanent' Arbitrators," noting the successful efforts of GM and the UAW.

"Grievance procedure repair is not a simple process. It is not a good subject matter for crisis bargaining. It can only be handled adequately in a noncrisis atmosphere, by a great deal of hard work and with an approach designed to correct the differing faults of each specific situation. The basic job of correction in the collective bargaining process must be done by the parties themselves * * *."[26]

Failure to Comply Strictly With Technical Requirements of Grievance Procedure

As a general proposition arbitrators expect parties to comply with the technical requirements of the grievance procedure.[27] While arbitrators have sometimes ruled that substantial compliance will suffice,[28] or have accepted some special justification for a nonprejudicial failure to meet a technical requirement,[29] wholesale disregard of grievance procedure requirements will not be tolerated.[30]

Where parties have been very informal in past handling of grievances, clear notice must be given if a party intends to insist upon strict future compliance with the previously ignored procedural requirements.[31]

Should Grievance Machinery Be Open to All Complaints?

There is no strong reason why parties should place limitations upon the subject matter that may be taken to the grievance procedure, even though a complaint is ultimately rejected as constituting an attempt to amend the agreement. Complaints often shrink in importance and are easily disposed of once they are brought into the open, while employees who have no outlet for their complaints tend to magnify them far beyond their true importance. Harry Shulman urged that every grievance should be received, heard, and considered seriously and sympathetically and that, to the extent possible, every grievance should be made the occasion for additional education of the

---

[26]Quotation from National Acad. of Arb. Newsletter, Jan. 1968, p. 3.

[27]This fact is apparent from cases cited throughout this Chapter. Also see comments of Arbitrator Koven in Fibreboard Paper Prods. Corp., 39 LA 691, 695 (1962).

[28]See Arbitrator Boles in 45 LA 502, 504; Kates in 44 LA 507, 510–512; Berkowitz in 41 LA 182, 183. In Great Lakes Pipe Line Co., 34 LA 617, 622–623 (Howard, 1959), alleged procedural defects were held waived by failure to object until arbitration was scheduled. A party who fails to comply fully with agreed procedures may not be permitted to protest noncompliance by the other party. See Empire Steel Castings v. Steelworkers, 99 LRRM 2728, 2731 (USDC, 1978); Union Fork & Hoe Co., 68 LA 432, 436 (Ipavec, 1977), concluding that procedural requirements "were in effect waived by both parties."

[29]See National Park Serv., 72 LA 314, 320, 326 (Pritzker, 1979). Also see Arbitrator Taylor in 65 LA 1195, 1199.

[30]See Arbitrator Nichols in Byrd Plastics, 51 LA 79, 82–83 (1968).

[31]Whiteway Stamping Co., 41 LA 966, 968 (Kates, 1963). To similar effect, Arbitrator Sembower in 49 LA 817, 820–821. Contra, Arbitrator Koven in 39 LA 691, 695.

parties and for a little more smoothing out of the wrinkles in their relationship.[32]

Some agreements do open the door of the grievance machinery to any complaint. The clause to this effect may take the following form:

> "In the event of any complaints, grievances, difficulties, disagreements or disputes arising between the Company, its employees within the collective bargaining unit hereinabove defined, or the Union, there shall be no suspension of plant operations but an earnest effort shall be made to settle such difference, complaints, grievances, difficulties, disagreements, or disputes forthwith in the following manner [grievance procedure then described]."[33]

Many agreements, however, limit the grievance procedure to complaints involving the "interpretation or application" of the agreement, or otherwise state exclusions from the grievance procedure.[34] Agreements which limit the subject matter that may be taken to the grievance procedure are most commonly found in newly organized industries, where the parties have not acquired sufficient mutual confidence to open the door to any and all complaints. Some agreements define "grievance" in a restrictive way, limiting the types of complaints that will be considered. Or the types of complaints that will be heard may be listed specifically, thus excluding those not listed. Some agreements spell out specific types of complaints which may *not* be taken to the grievance procedure, as, for instance, matters within the field of exclusive management functions.

The complexities of social insurance and pension plans have led some parties to require complaints arising out of their administration to be processed separately from the usual grievance procedure.[35]

The question whether a given complaint is subject to the grievance procedure may itself be processed through the grievance procedure and arbitration.

The right of former employees to utilize the grievance procedure for grievances based upon their previous employment status has sometimes been at issue. In one such instance, Arbitrator Mark L. Kahn declared that the union not only has a right but also a duty to utilize the grievance procedure in behalf of the former employee.[36] But the right of former employees to use the grievance procedure has not always been upheld.[37]

---

[32]Conference on Training of Law Students in Labor Relations, Vol. III, Transcript of Proceedings, 702–703 (1947). Regarding the scope of the right of public-sector employees to express complaints to their employer under the First Amendment, see Givhan v. Western Line Consol. School Dist., 99 S.Ct. 693 (1979).

[33]From an agreement between Windsor Mfg. Co. and Textile Workers Union.

[34]See Major Collective Bargaining Agreements: Arbitration Procedures, 6, 9 (U.S. Dept. Labor Bull. No. 1425–6, 1966); Major Collective Bargaining Agreements: Grievance Procedures 2, 6 (U.S. Dept. Labor Bull. No. 1425–1, 1964).

[35]"Basic Patterns in Labor Arbitration Agreements," 34 LA 931 at 931 (1960); Southwestern Bell Tel. Co., 44 LA 545, 547–548, 551 (Altieri, 1965), where the initial complaint was held subject to the grievance procedure and the company was ordered to cooperate in its processing.

[36]Hudson Tool & Mach. Co., 21 LA 431, 433–434 (1953). A former employee could use the grievance procedure for rights allegedly accrued prior to his resignation in Dover Corp., 48 LA 965, 968 (Volz, 1966). In accord on this point, Arbitrator Murphy in 52 LA 837, 840–841.

[37]See Van Dyne-Crotty, Inc., 46 LA 338, 343–345 (Teple, 1966); Kelly v. Adler, Inc., 25 LA 214 (N.Y. Sup. Ct., 1955).

The widow of an employee was not herself an "employee" with the right to use the grievance procedure, so she could not process her grievance concerning accrued vacation pay of her deceased husband even though the grievance was filed by the union.[38]

Company Grievances

Express provision is sometimes made for the initiation of management grievances at some stage of the grievance procedure.[39] Absent an express provision on the matter, the company's right to submit grievances depends upon the interpretation of the particular agreement.[40] The presence of a no-lockout clause may be a very significant factor in an arbitrator's conclusion that company grievances are permitted where the agreement does not deal expressly with the question.[41]

Some management spokesmen urge that every contract which provides for arbitration as the final step of the grievance procedure should include machinery available to management for presenting grievances against the union.[42]

Identification and Signature of Individual Grievants; Group Grievances

Sometimes an agreement will require, either specifically or by implication, that employee grievances be signed or otherwise pre-

---

[38]United States Steel Corp., 34 LA 306 at 306 (Sherman, 1960). The agreement was subsequently amended to permit the processing of such claims. See Pittsburgh Steel Co., 43 LA 860, 863 (McDermott, 1964). For a case involving the right of the union to use the grievance procedure in behalf of a supervisor who was discharged instead of being returned to the bargaining unit, see Tin Processing Corp., 16 LA 48, 51 (Emery, 1951).

[39]Of 400 agreements examined in one survey, 18 percent provided for company grievances. "Basic Patterns in Labor Arbitration," 34 LA 931, 936 (1960).

[40]See Meletron Corp., 36 LA 315, 317–319 (Jones, 1961). Also see Chase Bag Co., 42 LA 153, 154 (Elkouri, 1963). Earlier cases appeared to require clear language authorizing company grievances in order to open the grievance procedure to the company. See Bassick Co. v. Bassick Local 229, 24 LA 59 (USDC, 1954); Hinson Mfg. Co., 20 LA 688, 690 (Davey, 1953). In contrast, Arbitrator Lloyd H. Bailer would require "clear and unambiguous language" in the collective agreement to bar federal agency management from filing grievances. Navy Exchange, Naval Station, 73 LA 1016, 1019–1020 (1979). A similar result for the private sector, at least for some cases, may be indicated by Eberle Tanning Co. v. Section 63L, 110 LRRM 3136, 3139 (CA 3, 1982). By discussing a company grievance through the grievance procedure up to arbitration the union waived any right to object that the contract made no provision for company grievances in Whitlock Mfg. Co., 19 LA 234, 236 (Stutz, 1952).

[41]See Arbitrator Duff in 45 LA 225, 226–227; Elkouri in 42 LA 153, 154–155; Jones in 36 LA 315, 317–319.

[42]Hill & Hook, Management at the Bargaining Table, 216 (1945). Employer access to the grievance procedure determines whether claims against the union for breach of no-strike clause shall be taken to court or to an arbitrator. See Atkinson v. Sinclair Ref. Co., 82 S.Ct. 1318, 50 LRRM 2433 (1962); Drake Bakeries, Inc., v. Local 50, 82 S.Ct. 1346, 50 LRRM 2440 (1962). Subsequent lower court decisions are collected in Bliss & Laughlin Indus. v. Machinists Local Lodge 2040, 88 LRRM 3531 (CA 7, 1975). An employer's right to discipline individual employees for work stoppages does not preclude his right to file a grievance against the union where the agreement authorizes company grievances. Wallace-Murray Corp., 53 LA 1171, 1173 (Kabaker, 1969).

sented by the aggrieved employee or employees.[43] One purpose of such requirements is to aid the employer in evaluating and responding to the grievance.[44]

Where such requirements have been strictly enforced by arbitrators, complaints signed only by a union steward could not qualify as grievances.[45] In some of these cases the grievance was of a personal nature (as distinguished from a "policy" or a "general" grievance), but even policy grievances were held covered by the requirement for employee signatures in some cases.[46]

On the other hand, some arbitrators have viewed the provision for employee signatures or initiation of grievances as a mere formality,[47] or have otherwise indicated a strong inclination to find in favor of the union's right to initiate grievances.[48] For example, although agreement language implied that the grievance procedure applied only to individually authorized grievances, Arbitrator Philip E. Marshall held that grievances not personal in nature and those involving the whole of the bargaining unit could be filed by the union without specific authorizations. Arbitrator Marshall asserted that "industrial practice generally recognizes the fact that certain types of grievances involving conflicting interpretations of contractual provisions are frequently brought by union representatives in behalf of the entire membership."[49]

Somewhat conversely, under a clause permitting the union to file grievances which apply to "employees as a group," Arbitrator

---

[43]However, in many contracts it is not clear whether it is the employee or the steward who is authorized to launch the formal complaint. "Basic Patterns in Labor Arbitration Agreements," 34 LA 931 at 931 (1960). A requirement for the signatures of individual employees on grievances has been held not to be a mandatory subject of bargaining. Bethlehem Steel Co., 136 NLRB 1500 (1962), enforcement denied on other grounds, 320 F.2d 615 (CA 3, 1963).

[44]See comments by Arbitrator Morvant in Geigy Chem. Corp., 34 LA 102, 104–105 (1960), and by Arbitrator Updegraff in John Deere Harvester Works, 10 LA 778, 782 (1948). Where this purpose is otherwise adequately achieved an arbitrator might feel less strictly bound by the employee signature requirement. See Republic Steel Corp., 11 LA 691, 694–695 (McCoy, 1948).

[45]See Arbitrator von Rohr in 80 LA 644, 645–646 (union president's signature not sufficient); Gentile in 72 LA 1156, 1159; Erbs in 54 LA 1118, 1120; Eigenbrod in 53 LA 1230, 1233–1234; Dybeck in 49 LA 278, 279–280; Lennard in 44 LA 76, 82; Seinsheimer in 41 LA 947, 952; Kahn in 38 LA 580, 582–583; Larkin in 37 LA 659, 661; Updegraff in 10 LA 778, 782; Shulman in 3 LA 840, 841. Also see Cole in 23 LA 64, 65. Where there are multiple grievants, each may be required to sign to be included. See Arbitrator Conway in 68 LA 325, 330–331; Eigenbrod in 53 LA 1230, 1233–1234; Lennard in 44 LA 76, 82; Morvant in 34 LA 102, 104–105; Howlett in 28 LA 633, 634; Updegraff in 10 LA 778, 782. As to any need to verify the grievant's signature, see American Airlines, 46 LA 440, 442–443 (Sembower, 1966). In Sohio Chem. Co., 52 LRRM 1390 (1963), the NLRB strictly construed a provision for signature by "the employee or the employee and his steward" to require the assent of the aggrieved employee to the filing of a grievance.

[46]See Arbitrator Seinsheimer in 41 LA 947, 952; Kahn in 38 LA 580, 582–583; Larkin in 37 LA 659, 661.

[47]See Von Weise Gear Co., 51 LA 714, 715 (Bernstein, 1968); Industrial Gasket & Packing Co., 45 LA 847, 848–849 (Coffey, 1965), holding omission of employee signature not be a defect as to substance and holding that signature by a union representative will suffice.

[48]See Arbitrator Berkowitz in 73 LA 347, 349; Dworkin in 55 LA 709, 714; Leach in 45 LA 1039, 1044; Willingham in 42 LA 376, 384; Seligson in 40 LA 652, 658 (stating that under public policy there is a presumption of union right to initiate grievances). Also see Anderson in 69 LA 164, 167–168; Di Leone in 69 LA 48, 51; Greco in 62 LA 149, 151–153.

[49]Timken-Detroit Axle Co., 6 LA 926, 934 (1947). To similar effect, Arbitrator Warns in 32 LA 516, 518–519. Of course the parties may agree to arbitral resolution of an interpretation dispute without identification of any individual grievant or even without submission of any grievance, as in Western Employers Council, 49 LA 61 at 61 (McNaughton, 1967).

Maurice H. Merrill held that the union could file the grievance of an individual employee since the situation was one which could occur to any employee, and therefore the grievance did affect the employees as a group.[50]

In many cases the agreement has been construed to permit the union to file "group," "class," and/or "policy" grievances without the signatures of all specific individuals covered by the grievance (sometimes without any of their signatures), and, in some instances, without identification of all individuals covered by the grievance (sometimes without identification of any specific individual).[51]

Financial or other benefits under the award in such cases might apply to all affected employees though not identified in the grievance,[52] but this is not always so.[53] A grievance is more likely to be held to cover employees not specifically identified if the group nature of the claim is evident on its face or if the matter was treated as a group grievance in the parties' handling of the dispute.[54]

Waiver of Employee Rights or Signature Requirement

The questions arise (1) whether individual employees may waive their rights under the collective agreement, and (2) whether the employer may waive a contractual requirement that grievances be signed by the aggrieved employee or a requirement that he be named.

---

[50]Jonco Aircraft Corp., 22 LA 887 (1954).

[51]For cases reflecting these variations, see Arbitrator Caraway in 72 LA 47, 52; Cocalis in 72 LA 619, 621; Solomon in 49 LA 718, 721; Whyte in 49 LA 33, 36–37; Murphy in 46 LA 289, 290; Blumrosen in 42 LA 392, 402; Teple in 40 LA 13, 17; Peck in 37 LA 496, 498–499; Jaffee in 37 LA 458, 463; Thompson in 29 LA 518, 520; Wolff in 27 LA 448, 452–453; Stutz in 27 LA 386, 388–389; Williams in 25 LA 748, 749–750; Lennard in 25 LA 644, 648–649; Dworkin in 23 LA 481, 482; Kelliher in 14 LA 1049, 1053. Even where the contract called for specific identification of the individual grievants, the requirement was not strictly enforced for a grievance which was basically of a "group" nature and where the company "knew full-well who the grievants were and what the Union was driving at." Folding Carrier Corp., 53 LA 784, 788 (Gorsuch, 1969). In Ohio State Univ., 69 LA 1003, 1009 (Bell, 1977), 43 identically affected employees signed a grievance which the union sought to process as a group grievance. The agreement expressly contemplated union initiation of grievances "which cannot be appropriately resolved through the filing of individual grievances." Rejecting the employer's contention that this applied only to university-wide policy matters, the Arbitrator declared: "To invite, to encourage, the initiation of 43 separate, individual, grievances for the resolution of this single dispute would retard, if not emasculate, the objective of constructive labor-management relations—the expeditious resolution of labor disputes." Regarding group processing at a lower grievance step, see Arbitrator Taylor in 65 LA 1195, 1199.

[52]See Arbitrator Cocalis in 72 LA 619, 621; Caraway in 72 LA 47, 52; Yaffe in 68 LA 644, 650; Solomon in 49 LA 718, 721, 726; Blumrosen in 42 LA 392, 402–403; Gill in 37 LA 134, 137; Wolff in 27 LA 448, 453; Lennard in 25 LA 644, 657; Dworkin in 23 LA 481, 487; Davey in 17 LA 330, 333. This was the result, even though the agreement expressly required identification of all grievants, where the employer had refused to provide the names of all affected employees. Jeffrey Mfg. Co., 34 LA 814, 821 (Kuhn, 1960).

[53]See Greer Steel Co., 50 LA 340, 343 (McIntosch, 1968); St. Louis Newspaper Publishers' Assn., 33 LA 471, 477 (Green, 1959), holding that additional names could not be added at the arbitration hearing. Also see Arbitrator Coburn in 72 LA 501, 502; Hotel Employees v. Michelson's Food Servs., 94 LRRM 2014, 2019 (CA 9, 1976).

[54]See Arbitrator Caraway in 72 LA 47, 52; Spencer in 69 LA 674, 677; Jaffee in 37 LA 458, 463; Duff in 30 LA 441, 444; Dworkin in 23 LA 481, 482; Updegraff in 20 LA 243, 245; Davey in 17 LA 330, 333; Grant in 11 LA 312, 314.

As to the latter question, waiver results from failure to make timely objection to noncompliance with the requirement.[55] Similarly, the requirement may be held unenforceable (for the case under advisement) by virtue of loose past practice.[56]

As to waiver of agreement rights by individual employees, even where affected employees refused to file or prosecute a grievance,[57] or where they wished to withdraw after they had instituted their grievance,[58] the right of the union to file or prosecute the grievance was not denied.

Arbitrators have recognized a strong right of the union to police the agreement and have recognized that the interests of the union and of an individual employee do not always dovetail.[59] Thus, it has been considered that an employee may waive a purely personal right under the agreement (such as the right to a promotion), but that the employee may not waive other rights (which affect the interests of other employees or the union) against the wishes of the union.[60]

Steps in Grievance Procedure

Grievance machinery usually consists of a series of procedural steps to be taken within specified time limits.[61] The nature of the procedure will depend upon the structure of the company and on the needs and desires of the parties, but there is a tendency to follow a fairly definite pattern. Grievances ordinarily are taken by the aggrieved employee, either with or without a union representative, to the foreman,[62] and, if no settlement is reached, may be appealed through successive steps of the management hierarchy and, in most cases, to arbitration. The aggrieved may be represented successively

---

[55]See Arbitrator Dolnick in 50 LA 167, 169–170; Kates in 49 LA 1095, 1096–1097; Larkin in 43 LA 140, 144–145. But see Gentile in 72 LA 1156, 1159.

[56]See Arbitrator Dolnick in 50 LA 167, 169–170; Sembower in 49 LA 817, 818, 820–821; Fisher in 47 LA 224, 226; Larkin in 43 LA 140, 144–145.

[57]Atlantic Seaboard Corp., 42 LA 865, 869 et seq. (Lugar, 1964). Also see Arbitrator Bernstein in 51 LA 714, 715; Garrett in 44 LA 168, 174.

[58]Whiteway Stamping Co., 41 LA 966, 968 (Kates, 1963); Baur Bros. Bakery, 36 LA 1422, 1423 (Joseph, 1961). Cf., Arbitrator Perry in 74 LA 1296 at 1296; Graham in 73 LA 185, 187.

[59]See Eastern Shore Pub. Serv. Co., 39 LA 751, 756–758 (Frey, 1962), recognizing right to police; Great W. Sugar Co., 40 LA 652, 658 (Seligson, 1963), recognizing possible diverse interests. The agreement in both of these cases could be construed to authorize union grievances.

[60]United States Borax & Chem. Corp., 41 LA 1200, 1203 (Leonard, 1963). As to personal rights, also see Arbitrator Graham in 73 LA 185, 187; as to other rights, also see Belshaw in 73 LA 72, 73; Koven in 47 LA 8, 10. For related discussion, see Chapter 10, topic entitled "Waiver and Estoppel."

[61]Precise pleadings in moving from step to step ordinarily should not be required. See Henry Vogt Mach. Co., 46 LA 654, 657 (Stouffer, 1966). One arbitrator has taken the view that a grievance alleging violation of a prior agreement but filed during the term of the subsequent agreement is to be processed under the procedures designated in the prior agreement. Dover Corp., 48 LA 965, 968 (Volz, 1966).

[62]The absence of a readily accessible "first step" may lead an employee to resort to self-help. See Millage Produce, 45 LA 211, 214–215 (Miller, 1965), where discharge for insubordination was set aside. For related discussion, see subtopic entitled "Right to Union Representation at Early Stage," below.

by the shop steward, the business agent, the union shop committee, and international union representatives.[63]

Small companies can be expected to have short, simple grievance procedures, sometimes with only one or two steps. Larger companies usually have multistep procedures. Three-step and four-step procedures probably are most common,[64] but procedures with five or six steps are sometimes used, especially in plants which are units of a multiplant company.[65] The employee often is represented by the union grievance committee at the intermediate steps and by an international union representative at the next to last step and also at the last step.[66] The more steps in a grievance procedure, the more formal it can be expected to be. There is such variation in multistep procedures that no one plan may be said to be really typical. An indication, however, of what might be found in a multistep procedure is provided by the following illustration:

> "Should any employee, subject to this agreement, believe he has been unjustly dealt with, or that any of the provisions of this agreement have been violated, he shall present his alleged grievance to the Foreman of his department within five (5) days of the occurrence of such grievance.
>
> "In case the grievance is not adjusted by the foreman it shall be reduced to writing upon forms provided by the Company and signed and dated by the aggrieved employee and his department committeeman and three copies furnished the foreman. The foreman will have inserted in the proper place on the form his disposition of the matter and will sign and date the same returning one (1) copy to the aggrieved employee and one (1) copy to the department committeeman representing the employee within five (5) days.
>
> "If satisfactory adjustment is not made the department committeeman or his representative shall then take up the grievance with the General Foreman and General Superintendent in their respective order, within ten (10) days.
>
> "If no satisfactory adjustment is then reached it shall be submitted for consideration and handling to the Manager of Works, or his representative, by the duly authorized General Committee or their representative, within ten (10) days.
>
> "If after such consideration by the General Committee and the management, the grievance shall be unsettled, then the question shall be jointly submitted to the Chief Executive of the Company and the Chief Executive of the Brotherhood of Railway Carmen of America (or their representative) for joint conference within ten (10) days."[67]

Advanced Step Filing

There are certain issues which by nature are not capable of being settled at the preliminary stages of the procedure. Fundamental

---

[63]Also see "Basic Patterns in Labor Arbitration Agreements," 34 LA 931, 932 (1960). It has been suggested that the representative of each party at each succeeding step should be a different person, with higher authority than the representative at the preceding step. Manning, Maxwell & Moore, Inc., 37 LA 475, 480 (Stutz, 1961).

[64]See "Basic Patterns in Labor Arbitration Agreements," 34 LA 931, 934 (1960).

[65]"Grievance Procedure Under Collective Bargaining," 63 Monthly Lab. Rev. 175, 179 (U.S. Dept. of Labor, 1946).

[66]Id. at 180.

[67]From an agreement between the Pullman-Standard Car Mfg. Co. and Brotherhood of Ry. Carmen.

issues concerning company policies, for instance, are of this type
Provision sometimes is made for filing such grievances at an advanced
step of the procedure.[68]

The question might be raised whether, in the absence of such
provision, it should be permissible to file grievances at an advanced
step where it is obvious that they cannot be settled at preliminary
steps. The view has been expressed that there should be strict conformity with the agreement lest the exception be used to short-circuit the
first steps in all cases.[69]

But Arbitrator Robert J. Wagner expressed a different view,
holding that a grievance concerning veterans' vacation rights was
properly initiated at the third step of the grievance procedure without
presentation to the foreman at an earlier step. While he denied the
union's contention that it had the right to enter an advanced step "at
any time they choose," nevertheless he held that it could do so in
proper cases. He stated that it is well recognized in the practice of
industrial relations that certain disputes of a general nature can only
be resolved at a high union-management level. "Then, again, particular circumstances may make it impractical to begin processing a
grievance at the first step." Arbitrator Wagner concluded: "It would
seem to be quite proper for this grievance to be processed at the third-
step level, for only at this level are all negotiators of the contract, those
officers of company and union who knew the meaning and intent of the
language of the contractual provision controlling, required to
appear."[70]

In any event, the right to object to the lack of discussion of a
grievance at a preliminary step may be held waived by failure to make
a timely objection.[71]

Grievance Mediation

Some parties add a "grievance mediation" step to the grievance
procedure.[72] When this is done, a neutral is called in to discuss the
case with the parties immediately prior to the arbitration stage. This

---

[68]Bypassing of one or more steps in certain cases is permitted by 35 percent of the 400
agreements covered by one survey. "Basic Patterns in Labor Arbitration Agreements," 34 LA 931,
935 (1960), where types of cases included in these provisions are also indicated.

[69]Lapp, How to Handle Labor Grievances, 95–96 (1945). Holding that all grievances must go
the prescribed route, including group and policy grievances, Arbitrator Byron Abernethy stated
that it is not for the arbitrator to say that required steps can be ignored. Tenneco Oil Co., 40 LA
707, 710–712 (1963).

[70]Manion Steel Barrel Co., 6 LA 164, 168 (1947). For similar comments, see Arbitrator
Markowitz in 44 LA 212, 215; Kates in 43 LA 695, 699. Advanced step filing under proper
circumstances was also permitted by Arbitrator Eagle in 79 LA 351, 355–356; O'Neill in 73 LA
540, 542; Gorsuch in 53 LA 784, 788–789; Prasow in 50 LA 645, 655, and in 27 LA 153, 155–156;
Gibson in 48 LA 1234, 1237; Murphy in 46 LA 289, 290; Dworkin in 42 LA 449, 453; Kelliher in 14
LA 1049, 1053. Also see Flagler in 72 LA 479, 483–484.

[71]See Arbitrator Rothchild in 68 LA 1373, 1378; Callaghan in 28 LA 659, 663; Donnely in 28
LA 621, 622; Kelliher in 20 LA 618, 619; Jaffe in 17 LA 187, 189–190.

[72]As to the apparent extent of this practice, see "Basic Patterns in Labor Arbitration
Agreements," 34 LA 931, 936–937 (1960), where it is also noted that grievance mediation was
more extensively used prior to the broad emergence of arbitration, and that a few agreements still
specify conciliation instead of arbitration as the final step of the grievance procedure.

process can dispose of some cases that otherwise must be arbitrated, and it may well deserve more experimentation as an intermediate device in the future.[73]

Time for Holding Hearings

Agreements vary as to the time prescribed for holding hearings on grievances. Some agreements provide that differences are to be taken up "as soon as possible"; others simply provide that "grievances shall be first taken up by the grievant and the foreman," without specifying a time; still others provide that grievances may be adjusted with the foreman "at the end of the working day." Reason should be exercised in determining when to present grievances. It has been held, for instance, that when the number of employees involved in a grievance is so great that their absence from the job would interfere with production and upset morale and discipline, the shop steward has a clear duty to give management an opportunity to adjust the grievance without an interruption of work. Accordingly, a shop steward who took six or seven men off the job to discuss a grievance, without having made advance arrangements with management, was held to have been properly admonished not to do so again.[74]

Similar results have been reached in other such cases where employees or their representative interfered with production and disregarded the need for orderly presentation of grievances in seeking to rush the hearing of their complaint.[75]

Advanced-step hearings generally are scheduled more definitely. Many plants hold regularly scheduled meetings at specified intervals to negotiate appealed grievances.[76] Such meetings are usually held weekly during working hours, but may be held monthly or at other intervals.

---

[73]For informative discussion of grievance mediation, see McPherson, Grievance Mediation Under Collective Bargaining (U. of Ill. Inst. of Lab. & Indus. Rel. Reprint Series No. 44, 1956); "Grievance Mediation," The Grievance Process, 53–54, 59 (Mich. State U. Lab. & Indus. Rel. Center, 1956).

[74]Dwight Mfg. Co., 10 LA 786, 792 (McCoy, 1948). Where the agreement was silent on the matter, it was held that management could schedule grievance meetings after working hours and was not bound by its past practice of scheduling them during working hours. Oshkosh Truck Corp., 67 LA 103, 107–108 (Karlins, 1976). Also see Arbitrator Purcell in 68 LA 517, 521.

[75]See Arbitrator Jones in 49 LA 944, 947; Platt in 21 LA 220, 221–222; Komaroff in 21 LA 67, 70–71; Shister in 17 LA 230, 232. Also see Kossoff in 79 LA 225, 230–231. Cf., Beadles in 70 LA 333, 335. In Terry Poultry Co., 109 NLRB 1095 (1954), an employee could be punished where he left his post to present a grievance in violation of a reasonable and nondiscriminatory plant rule. But spontaneous work stoppages to present grievances under the NLRA have been held protected under the facts of some cases. See NLRB v. Serv-Air, 69 LRRM 2476 (CA 10, 1968); NLRB v. Kennametal, Inc., 182 F.2d 817 (CA 3, 1950). Also see NLRB v. Washington Aluminum Co., 82 S. Ct. 1099 (1962). Regarding employee resistance to management's effort to terminate a grievance meeting, compare Container Corp., 107 LRRM 1126 (NLRB, 1981), with U.S. Postal Serv. v. NLRB, 107 LRRM 3249 (CA 5, 1981). As to the right of management to specify a specific location within the plant for union representatives to interview grievants and write up their grievances, see Walker Mfg. Co., 41 LA 1288, 1299 (Whelan, 1963).

[76]"Basic Patterns in Labor Arbitration Agreements," 34 LA 931, 936 (1960); "Grievance Procedure Under Collective Bargaining," 63 Monthly Lab. Rev. 175, 183 (U.S. Dept. of Labor, 1946).

Sometimes, however, these meetings are not regularly scheduled, but are made subject to "call," to be held whenever necessary. "Call" meetings may be preferred because they provide the necessary flexibility for more prompt disposition of complaints, and the number of meetings can be adjusted to the number of cases. On the other hand, some parties prefer regularly scheduled meetings because of the assurance that grievances will be considered within a definite period. Moreover, regular meetings provide better opportunity for the discussion of mutual problems of policy and for the anticipation of difficulties, thus preventing future grievances.[77] When the agreement provides for regularly scheduled meetings, it might also provide for emergency meetings when either party feels that consideration of a grievance should not be delayed.[78]

Grievance Representatives

Unless restricted by the agreement, both the union and the company are generally free to determine the kind and number of representatives they wish to use,[79] and are likewise free to select the individuals who are to serve as their grievance representatives.[80]

Limitation of the number of representatives who may appear at various hearings or negotiations is a common feature of collective agreements. Such limitation is said to be both legitimate and proper, and to be a proper subject for negotiation between the parties.[81] Sometimes, too, the agreement will impose a limitation upon the right of a party to select its representatives.[82]

---

[77]"Grievance Procedure Under Collective Bargaining," 63 Monthly Lab. Rev. 175, 183 (U.S. Dept. of Labor, 1946).

[78]"Basic Patterns in Labor Arbitration Agreements," 34 LA 931, 936 (1960); Cudahy Packing Co., 7 LA 645, 646 (Fisher, 1947).

[79]Ford Motor Co., 1 ALAA ¶67,045 (Shulman, 1944).

[80]For the general right of each party under the NLRA to select its representatives for the purpose of collective bargaining (which of course includes grievance processing) and for some of the situations in which a party might be entitled to veto the other party's selection, see Fitzsimons Mfg. Co., 105 LRRM 1083 (NLRB, 1980); General Elec. Co., 71 LRRM 2418 (CA 2, 1969); NLRB v. David Buttrick Co., 62 LRRM 2241 (CA 1, 1966); Standard Oil Co. of Ohio v. NLRB, 54 LRRM 2076 (CA 6, 1963); Slate Belt Apparel Contractors' Assn., 45 LRRM 2626 (CA 3, 1960). For arbitral recognition of this general right, see Arbitrator Tsukiyama in 71 LA 1138, 1147; Hayes in 53 LA 972, 973–974; Kabaker in 50 LA 634, 636; Kates in 36 LA 682, 685. Where an agreement provided for third-step grievance meetings between the employer and "an International Union Representative," the arbitrator reasoned that use of "the word 'an' rather than 'the' indicates that there is no specific individual who fulfills the role of 'International Union Representative,'" thus the International could designate the local union president as its representative at third-step meetings. St. Mary Corwin Hosp., 76 LA 1142, 1145 (Aisenberg, 1981), where past practice also supported this result.

[81]Ford Motor Co., 1 ALAA ¶67,045 (Shulman, 1944).

[82]In Kahala Hilton Hotel Co., 44 LA 453, 457 (Burr, 1965), the agreement contained an express limitation. In Corry-Jamestown Corp., 36 LA 682, 685 (Kates, 1961), the agreement was interpreted to prevent the union from designating a representative to serve outside his own department. Also see Arbitrator Daniel in 80 LA 521, 523–524. But no such restriction was found by Arbitrator Tsukiyama in 71 LA 1138, 1147; Kabaker in 50 LA 634, 636. Also see Arbitrator Berkowitz in 55 LA 901, 904. In Holan Div., 52 LA 1078, 1081 (Stouffer, 1969), the agreement was interpreted to restrict participation by the company's attorney at a prearbitral stage of the grievance procedure.

Unions most often use "shop stewards" and grievance "commit-teemen." The steward represents the employee at the initial stages of the grievance procedure. The steward who performs successfully the responsibilities with which he is entrusted is an asset to management as well as to the employees whom he represents. As an employee spokesman he has the responsibility of policing the collective agreement, but he also has the responsibility of dissuading employees from pursuing complaints that are without merit.[83] In dealing with management he seeks to effectuate general union policies. Union grievance committeemen usually represent employees in the intermediate stages of the grievance procedure. The grievance committee frequently has the responsibility of determining union policy in connection with grievances.

The management representative closest to the employees and their work is the foreman. The foreman's effectiveness in grievance settlement is determined largely by his own capability and the amount of authority given him; if he is able and sufficient authority is given him, better settlements as a rule will be obtained at the foreman level than at later steps, since the foreman often understands shop problems better than those above him.[84] "Foremen trained by experience, observation, and study of labor and industrial psychology are able to prevent and to rectify most of the ordinary grievances of the workers."[85] Of course, to state this is to state the ideal only. Unfortunately, in numerous plants foremen lack authority, or fail to use it, and "pass the buck" to higher management officials.[86] Many employers, however, conduct training courses for foremen for the purpose of enabling them better to deal with grievances and acquaint them with the applicable company policies.

Many unions and companies conduct training programs for all their representatives. Such training usually covers the provisions of the collective agreement and basic union or company policy. Proper training should develop a feeling of mutual respect and confidence between stewards and foremen; one of its primary purposes should be to foster the attitude that grievances are problems to be solved, not arguments to be won. Training, too, increases employee understanding of the use and objectives of the grievance procedure.[87]

---

[83]For related discussion, see this Chapter, topic entitled "Attitude of Parties to the Grievance Procedure." Quoting an AFL-CIO statement of steward responsibilities, see Bowater Carolina Co., 77 LA 336, 341 (Holley, 1981).

[84]"Grievance Procedure Under Collective Bargaining," 63 Monthly Lab. Rev. 175, 179 (U.S. Dept. of Labor, 1946).

[85]Lapp, How to Handle Labor Grievances, 109–110 (1945).

[86]"Grievance Procedure Under Collective Bargaining," 63 Monthly Lab. Rev. 175, 179 (U.S. Dept. of Labor, 1946). Some reasons why the "ideal" of foreman-steward settlement often is not attained include personality clashes between foreman and steward, fear by both management and unions that such settlements may establish undesirable precedents, and fear by both the foreman and the steward that they will be reversed by their superiors. The Grievance Process, 57–58 (Mich. State U. Lab. & Indus. Rel. Center, 1956).

[87]These points regarding training programs are stated and discussed in "Grievance Procedure Under Collective Bargaining," 63 Monthly Lab. Rev. 175, 177–183 (U.S. Dept. of Labor, 1946).

Many plants have industrial relations departments to handle labor relations. Generally it is the function of this department to centralize and unify the company's policy and dealings with the union. Some industrial relations departments handle grievances. Opinion differs as to whether this is desirable. While some feel that it is an aid to grievance processing, others feel that it forces more grievances to the higher stages of the procedure because it cuts into the authority of the foreman.[88]

Right to Union Representation at Early Stage

Unions and management frequently disagree as to whether, in the interest of better relationships, employee grievances should be taken directly to the foreman or first to the union steward and then by the steward to the foreman.

Management often holds the view that the aggrieved employee should go to his foreman alone before going to his steward and that the union should not enter the picture until after the first step of the grievance procedure. It is argued that better relationships are fostered if the individual employee and the foreman discuss the grievance alone. The presence of the steward, it is thought, tends to make the grievance appear more serious than it really is. Management's right to act pursuant to these beliefs, however, is limited by the bargaining duty under the NLRA.[89]

On the other hand, unions often take the position that the steward should handle grievances from the start. The employee is believed to need the assistance and moral support of the steward to insure recognition of all of the employee's rights. Unions wish to be able to "push"

---

[88]Id. at 184.

[89]The NLRB has held that settlements at the first step of the grievance procedure are "adjustments" within the meaning of the § 9(a) proviso and that the union must have an opportunity to be present. Bethlehem Steel Co., 25 LRRM 1564 (1950). The right to be present may be waived. Globe-Union, Inc., 29 LRRM 1198 (1952). In Westinghouse Elec. Corp., 52 LRRM 1385 (1963), the NLRB held that the employer modified the contractual grievance procedure and thus violated the duty to bargain by inviting employees to take grievances directly to their foreman before consulting their union steward. A court disagreed, holding the employer's statement to be only a suggestion that the grievance procedure would operate more smoothly if employees discussed possible complaints with their foreman before a formal grievance arose. Westinghouse Elec. Corp. v. NLRB, 54 LRRM 2696 (CA 7, 1963). In Smith v. Arkansas State Highway Employees, 99 S.Ct. 1826, 1828, 101 LRRM 2091, 2092 (1979), the public-sector employer required aggrieved employees to submit a written complaint directly to the employer and refused to consider grievances submitted by their union (which did represent its members, however, at all grievance steps subsequent to the filing of a written grievance). The Supreme Court said the fact that this "might well" be unlawful for a private employer is immaterial in deciding whether the public employer's actions violated the First Amendment of the U.S. Constitution. The Court said the First Amendment "is not a substitute for the national labor relations laws," and "does not impose any affirmative obligation on the government to listen, to respond or, in this context, to recognize the association and bargain with it." Then in Minnesota Bd. for Community Colleges v. Knight, 104 S.Ct. 1058, 1067, 115 LRRM 2785 (1984), the Supreme Court upheld a statute which required public employers to "meet and confer" only with the union on questions relating to employment but outside the scope of mandatory bargaining, the Court stating:

"The conduct challenged here is the converse of that challenged in *Smith*. There the government listened only to individual employees and not to the union. Here the government 'meets and confers' with the union and not with individual employees. The applicable constitutional principles are identical to those that controlled in *Smith*."

grievances of employees who are too timid to approach the foreman alone. Moreover, unions say that management benefits by the union's screening of grievances, a process which eliminates complaints that have no merit. Finally, unions feel that settlements by individuals make it possible for foremen to play favorites and that uniform settlements can be had only if the union is present from the outset.

A related matter over which unions and management have disagreed concerns union representation of employees at investigatory interviews conducted by the employer. Through the years this matter has been considered by many arbitrators, the NLRB, and the courts. In 1975 the U.S. Supreme Court issued its *Weingarten* decision on the subject. In *Weingarten* the Supreme Court upheld the NLRB position (which had been rejected by the Court of Appeals), that individual employees have the right under the NLRA to refuse to submit without union representation to an investigatory interview which the employee reasonably believes may result in disciplinary action.[90] The Court explained that the NLRB also had "shaped the contours and limits of the statutory right," which "contours and limits" are outlined (and apparently endorsed by the Court) in the following excerpt from the Court's opinion:

> "*First,* the right inheres in § 7's guarantee of the right of employees to act in concert for mutual aid and protection. * * *
>
> "*Second,* the right arises only in situations where the employee requests representation. In other words, the employee may forego his guaranteed right and, if he prefers, participate in an interview unaccompanied by his union representative.
>
> "*Third,* the employee's right to request representation as a condition of participation in an interview is limited to situations where the

---

[90]NLRB v. J. Weingarten, Inc., 95 S.Ct. 959, 963, 965 (1975), holding that NLRA § 8(a)(1) is violated if the employer requires the employee to submit to the interview and denies the employee's request for union representation. Simultaneously the Court issued its decision in ILGWU v. Quality Mfg. Co., 95 S.Ct. 972 (1975), holding unlawful the discharge of an employee for refusing to submit to an investigatory interview without union representation where she reasonably feared disciplinary action, and also holding unlawful the discharge of a union steward for insisting on representing the employee pursuant to her request. In Montgomery Ward & Co. v. NLRB, 109 LRRM 2005, 2007 (CA 8, 1981), the court concluded that two employees were discharged for admitted theft rather than because they had rightfully refused to participate in an investigative interview without union representation; in refusing to uphold the NLRB's order for reinstatement and back pay, the court stated that "the employees effected their own discharge by stealing and the section 8(a)(1) violation was simply incidental to the investigation which preceded the firing." Cf., Arbitrator House in 78 LA 409, 415–417. For discussion of union representation at investigative interviews, see Hill, "We Only Promised You a Weingarten," 51 Okla. Bar Assn. J. 1823 (1980), collecting many post-*Weingarten* decisions of the NLRB and the lower courts; Wireman, "Union Representation at Investigatory Interviews: The Subsequent Development of *Weingarten*," 28 Clev. St. L. Rev. 127 (1979); Erickson & Smith, "The Right of Union Representation During Investigatory Interviews," 33 Arb. J. No. 2, p. 29 (1978); Craver, "The Inquisitorial Process in Private Employment," 63 Cornell L. Rev. 1, 16–28 (1977); Nelson, "Union Representation During Investigatory Interviews," 31 Arb. J. 181 (1976); Kurtz & Murphy, "Arbitration and Federal Rights Under Collective Agreements in 1974," Proceedings of the 28th Annual Meeting of NAA, 243, 259–260 (BNA Books, 1976); Gorman, Basic Text on Labor Law, 395–398 (1976), stating that: "While the Supreme Court has thus determined that Section 8(a)(1) will normally guarantee the presence of the union at an investigatory interview when that is requested by the interviewed employee, it has not considered whether the union is independently entitled under Section 8(a)(5) to be informed of an interview and given an opportunity to appear, as is the case when a 'grievance' has already come into existence." In *Weingarten* the Supreme Court made only a brief and inconclusive reference to the § 8(a)(5) question. See 95 S.Ct. at 967. For the NLRB's treatment of this aspect prior to *Weingarten,* see the Erickson & Smith article cited above.

employee reasonably believes the investigation will result in disciplinary action. * * * [The Board] 'would not apply the rule to such run-of-the-mill shop-floor conversations as, for example, the giving of instructions or training or needed corrections of work techniques. In such cases there cannot normally be any reasonable basis for an employee to fear that any adverse impact may result from the interview * * *.'

"*Fourth*, exercise of the right may not interfere with legitimate employer prerogatives. The employer has no obligation to justify his refusal to allow union representation, and despite refusal, the employer is free to carry on his inquiry without interviewing the employee, and thus leave to the employee the choice between having an interview unaccompanied by his representative, or having no interview and foregoing any benefits that might be derived from one. * * *

"*Fifth*, * * * The employer has no duty to bargain with the Union representative at an investigatory interview. 'The representative is present to assist the employee, and may attempt to clarify the facts or suggest other employees who may have knowledge of them. The employer, however, is free to insist that he is only interested, at that time, in hearing the employee's own account of the matter under investigation.' "[91]

The Court concluded that the Board had reached "a fair and reasoned balance upon a question within its special competence," and the Court added:

"The statutory right confirmed today is in full harmony with actual industrial practice. Many important collective-bargaining agreements have provisions that accord employees rights of union representation at investigatory interviews. Even where such a right is not explicitly provided in the agreement a 'well established current of arbitral authority' sustains the right of union representation at investigatory interviews which the employee reasonably believes may result in disciplinary action against him. Chevron Chemical Co., 60 L.A. 1066, 1071 ([Merrill] 1973)."[92]

The line of arbitration cases referred to by the Supreme Court will no doubt carry added stature as a guide for future arbitrations. Moreover, it is understandable that arbitrators in arriving at their decisions since *Weingarten* have given due consideration to *Weingarten* itself in accordance with the arbitrator's understanding of what it does and does not require.[93]

---

[91] 95 S.Ct. at 963–965. Regarding the extent to which the employer may properly regulate the representative's participation at an investigatory interview, also see Southwestern Bell Tel. Co. v. NLRB, 109 LRRM 2602 (CA 5, 1982); Texaco, Inc., 105 LRRM 1239, 1243 (NLRB, 1980), where the employer improperly conditioned a representative's right to attend by requiring that he remain silent throughout the investigatory interview. Regarding employee awareness of *Weingarten* rights, it sometimes has been contended that the employer has an obligation to apprise the employee of those rights. The NLRB rejected such a contention in Montgomery Ward & Co., 269 NLRB No. 156 (1984). Similarly, see Arbitrator Garrett in 78 LA 921, 926.

[92] 95 S.Ct. at 968–969. The Court cited additional arbitration decisions in accord, but also recognized that other arbitrators had held contra. Regarding arbitrability where the agreement does not expressly deal with the right, see Humble Oil & Ref. Co. v. IIWU, 337 F.2d 321 (CA 5, 1964).

[93] For example, see Arbitrator Sergent in 81 LA 368, 371; White in 80 LA 1140, 1142; House in 78 LA 409, 415–417; Daniel in 76 LA 379, 383; Peterschmidt in 72 LA 437, 439, 441; Williams in 71 LA 740, 743; Wolff in 71 LA 174, 177; Marlatt in 68 LA 1305, 1308–1309; Markowitz in 67 LA 352, 353–354; Clarke in 67 LA 349, 351; Gibson in 64 LA 668, 671–672. For related considerations, see Chapter 10, subtopic entitled "The NLRA, the Arbitrator, and the NLRB," and topic entitled "Court Decisions." Concerning the applicability of *Weingarten* to federal-sector employ-

Sometimes an employer meets with an employee to inform the individual of a previously made disciplinary decision. Overruling its previous position to the contrary, the NLRB has held that "an employee has no Section 7 right to the presence of his union representative at a meeting with his employer held solely for the purpose of informing the employee of, and acting upon, a previously made disciplinary decision."[94] However, in respect to instances in which the employer engages an employee in an interview or discussion which the employee reasonably believes may result in disciplinary action, the Board has stated that "an employee's Weingarten rights, with all its attendant safeguards, matures at the commencement of the interview, be it on the production floor or in a supervisor's office."[95]

Finally, *Weingarten* indicates that the "reasonableness" of an employee's belief that discipline might result, will be determined "'by objective standards under all the circumstances of the case.'"[96] The

---

ment prior to enactment of the Civil Service Reform Act of 1978, see discussion in Dept. of the Air Force, 75 LA 994, 997 (Hart, 1980). The latter Act expressly provides that: "An exclusive representative of an appropriate unit in an agency shall be given the opportunity to be represented at * * * any examination of an employee in the unit by a representative of the agency in connection with an investigation if * * * the employee reasonably believes that the examination may result in disciplinary action against the employee * * * and the employee requests representation." 5 U.S.C. § 7114(a)(2). Also see Internal Rev. Serv., 78 LA 1016, 1018, 1021 (Render, 1982). Regarding applicability of *Weingarten* to the state public sector, see Lancaster City Schools, 81 LA 1024, 1028 (Abrams, 1983); City of Sterling Heights, 80 LA 825, 829 (Ellmann, 1983).

[94]Baton Rouge Water Works Co., 103 LRRM 1056, 1058 (NLRB, 1980), where the Board cautioned that:

"[I]f the employer engages in any conduct beyond merely informing the employee of a previously made disciplinary decision, the full panoply of protections accorded the employee under Weingarten may be applicable. Thus, for example, were the employer to inform the employee of a disciplinary action and then seek facts or evidence in support of that action, or to attempt to have the employee admit his alleged wrongdoing or to sign a statement to that effect, or to sign statements relating to such matters as workmen's compensation, * * * the employee's right to union representation would attach. In contrast, the fact that the employer and employee thereafter engage in a conversation at the employee's behest or instigation concerning the reasons for the previously determined discipline will not, alone, convert the meeting to an interview at which the Weingarten protections apply."

The Board overruled its *Certified Grocers* decision to the extent that it was inconsistent with *Baton Rouge*, but reaffirmed the *Certified Grocers* conclusion that no longer should any distinction be drawn between "investigatory" and "disciplinary" interviews. "Thus, the full purview of protections accorded employees under Weingarten apply to both 'investigatory' and 'disciplinary' interviews, save only those conducted for the exclusive purpose of notifying an employee of previously determined disciplinary action." Ibid. The *Baton Rouge* exception to *Weingarten* was applied in Allied Aviation Serv. Co. of New Eng., 77 LA 455, 459 (Turkus, 1981).

[95]Roadway Express, 103 LRRM 1050, 1052 (NLRB, 1979), where the Board indicated that the employer may specify the place of the interview. In this case the Board also indicated that the range of acceptable representatives should not be too narrowly drawn, the Board stating that *Weingarten* does not "state or suggest that an employee's interest can only be safeguarded by the presence of a *specific* representative sought by the employee." Id. at 1053. Also see Crown Zellerbach, 100 LRRM 1092 (NLRB, 1978); Anchortank, Inc., 99 LRRM 1622, 1623 (NLRB, 1978). The NLRB has been upheld in holding that *Weingarten* rights are not restricted to unionized plants; both unionized and nonunion employees are entitled to representation at management interviews they reasonably believe may result in discipline. Du Pont Co. v. NLRB, 115 LRRM 2153, 2156 (CA 3, 1983). For a later development concerning the requirement that activity be "concerted" in order to be protected, see Du Pont Co. v. NLRB, 116 LRRM 2343 (CA 3, 1984). Regarding a fair opportunity to consult with the representative before the interview, see Pacific Tel. & Tel. Co. v. NLRB, 113 LRRM 3529, 3531 (CA 9, 1983), where the court stated that "the securing of information as to the subject matter of the interview and a pre-interview conference with a union representative" are also rights of the employee; Climax Molybdenum Co. v. NLRB, 99 LRRM 2471, 2473 (CA 10, 1978), where the court concluded that the date of a scheduled investigatory interview left the employee adequate opportunity to consult union representatives on his own time prior to the interview, so the employer was not required to permit such consultation on company time before the interview.

[96]95 S.Ct. at 964 n. 5, the Court quoting the NLRB.

employee risks the possibility that his belief may be found unreasonable. If an employee disobeys an order in the erroneous belief that he is entitled to union representation, discipline for insubordination may be upheld.[97]

Grievance Adjustment by Individual Employees

Much has been written concerning individual employee rights in grievance adjustment and arbitration, and concerning the employee's right of fair representation. It is the purpose here to deal only briefly with these matters.[98]

The NLRA as amended by the LMRA of 1947 provides in § 9(a) that the majority union shall be the "exclusive representative" of all employees in the bargaining unit, and provides in § 8(d) that the duty of the employer and union to bargain includes the duty to confer in good faith with respect to questions arising under the collective agreement. However, a proviso to § 9(a) states that "any individual employee or a group of employees shall have the right at any time to present grievances to their employer and to have such grievances adjusted, without the intervention of the bargaining representative, as long as the adjustment is not inconsistent with the terms of a collective-bargaining contract or agreement then in effect," and as long as "the bargaining representative has been given opportunity to be present at such adjustment." The enactment of this proviso in 1947 generated much discussion, reflecting two widely differing interpretations.

---

[97]For example, in General Elec. Co., 100 LRRM 1248, 1250 (NLRB, 1979), an employee was lawfully suspended for insubordination when he disobeyed an order not to leave his work station in order to consult a union steward; although faced with questions concerning his work, his foreman had told him that he would not be disciplined for faulty work, and this fact along with other circumstances made his belief that he might be disciplined unreasonable. Also see Spartan Stores v. NLRB, 105 LRRM 2293 (CA 6, 1980); Arbitrator Sergent in 81 LA 368, 371; Williams in 71 LA 740, 743; Chaffin in 69 LA 307, 310; Marlatt in 68 LA 1305, 1308–1309.

[98]For more intense coverage, the reader is directed to the writings cited throughout the present topic. For some of the many other writings in this general area, see Jacobs, "The Duty of Fair Representation: Minorities, Dissidents and Exclusive Representation," 59 B.U.L. Rev. 857 (1979); Leffler, "Piercing the Duty of Fair Representation: The Dichotomy Between Negotiations and Grievance Handling," 1979 U. Ill. L.F. 35 (1979); Gross & Bordoni, "Reflections on the Arbitrator's Responsibility to Provide a Full and Fair Hearing: How to Bite the Hands that Feed You," 29 Syracuse L. Rev. 877 (1978); Rabin, "The Impact of the Duty of Fair Representation Upon Labor Arbitration," id. at 851; McKelvey, The Duty of Fair Representation (1977), a collection of articles by Aaron, Vladeck, Jones, Lipsitz, Summers, Rabin, Klein, & Donahue; Murphy, "Due Process and Fair Representation in Grievance Handling in the Public Sector," Proceedings of the 30th Annual Meeting of NAA, 265 (BNA Books, 1978), followed by comment and discussion by other speakers; Gorman, Basic Text on Labor Law, 695–728 (1976); Note, "Public Sector Grievance Procedures, Due Process, and the Duty of Fair Representation," 89 Harv. L. Rev. 752 (1976); Summers, "The Individual Employee's Rights Under the Collective Agreement: What Constitutes Fair Representation," Proceedings of the 27th Annual Meeting of NAA, 14 (BNA Books, 1975), followed by comment and discussion by other speakers; Friedman, "Individual Rights in Grievance Arbitration," 27 Arb. J. 252 (1972); Fleming, The Labor Arbitration Process, 107–133 (1965); Rosen, "The Individual Worker in Grievance Arbitration: Still Another Look at the Problem," 24 Md. L. Rev. 233; Williams, "Intervention: Rights and Policies," Proceedings of the 16th Annual Meeting of NAA, 266–295 (BNA Books, 1963); Aaron, "Some Aspects of the Union's Duty of Fair Representation," 22 Ohio St. L.J. 39 (1961).

Under one interpretation individual employees have a statutory right to settle their grievances directly with the employer and no agreement between the union and the employer can deprive them of this right; individual employees have a right to use the grievance and arbitration procedure without the union's assistance or over its veto.[99]

Under a second interpretation the § 9(a) proviso permits (as an exception to the duty to deal exclusively with the union) but does not require the employer to adjust grievances with individual employees. Under this interpretation the statute places a right of control in the employer, who can keep control or who can relinquish it in the collective agreement either (1) by giving individual employees a right to adjust their grievances directly with the employer, or (2) by placing the right of grievance adjustment solely in the union.[100]

Some of the uncertainty as to the scope of individual employee rights in grievance adjustment was removed by the U.S. Supreme Court's *Maddox* decision in 1965 and by its *Vaca* decision in 1967, though neither decision expressly discusses the § 9(a) proviso.[101] A third decision of particular significance in regard to individual employee rights, is the Court's *Hines* decision of 1976.

In *Maddox* the Supreme Court held that an employee who had not attempted to use the contractual grievance procedure to enforce his right to benefits under the collective agreement was precluded from instituting court suit against the employer for this purpose. The court explained:[102]

> "As a general rule in cases to which federal law applies, federal labor policy requires that individual employees wishing to assert contract grievances must *attempt* use of the contract grievance procedure agreed upon by employer and union as the mode of redress. If the union refuses to press or only perfunctorily presses the individual's claim,

---

[99]See Summers, "Individual Rights in Collective Agreements and Arbitration," 37 N.Y.U. L. Rev. 362 (1962); Lenhoff, "The Effect of Labor Arbitration Clauses Upon the Individual," 9 Arb. J. 3, 14–16 (1954); Donnelly v. United Fruit Co., 190 A.2d 825 (N.J. S.Ct., 1963); Arbitrator Bauder in 40 LA 780, 783; Arbitrator Volz in 37 LA 356, 358. In the *Donnelly* case, supra, the court recognized a right of individual employees to intervene, with independent representation, in arbitration proceedings between union and employer. For arbitration cases involving attempts of third parties or minority groups of employees to intervene in cases being processed by the union, see Arbitrator Jones in 45 LA 1115, 1122–1123; Sembower in 27 LA 353, 354–355. Also see Youngdahl, "Uneasy Second Thoughts on the Independent Participation by Employees in Labor Arbitration Proceedings," 33 Ark. L. Rev. 151 (1979). Related discussion is found in Chapter 7, topic entitled "Bilateral Arbitration of Trilateral Conflicts." For a case involving a union's right to complete an arbitration instituted prior to the union's decertification, see Trumbull Asphalt Co., 38 LA 1093, 1097–1098 (Elson, 1962). Also see Arbitrator Snow in 71 LA 66, 69.

[100]See Cox, "Rights Under a Labor Agreement," 69 Harv. L. Rev. 601, 621–624 (1956); Black-Clawson Co. v. Machinists Lodge 355, 313 F.2d 179 (CA 2, 1962); Arbitrator Frey in 39 LA 751, 756; Arbitrator Hays in 20 LA 443, 444–445. Also see Larkin in 73 LA 715, 717. In North Am. Aviation, 44 LA 1102, 1107–1108 (1965), Arbitrator Ross held that a separate "employee grievance procedure" in which employees could represent themselves violated the collective agreement, stating that while § 9(a) of the statute permits the employer to maintain a separate employee grievance procedure in absence of any contrary commitment, the agreement may require (as this one did) that grievances be processed exclusively through the contract grievance procedure.

[101]Indeed, only in *Maddox* did the Court make even a passing reference expressly to the proviso. That reference is noted hereinbelow.

[102]Republic Steel Corp. v. Maddox, 85 S.Ct. 614, 616, 58 LRRM 2193 (1965). Somewhat conversely, it was held in Vickers Petroleum Corp., 73 LA 399, 400 (Miller, 1979), that the fact that a retiring employee may have a right to institute court proceedings on a pension-plan issue, does not deny the right to utilize the grievance procedure to which the issue otherwise could be taken.

differences may arise as to the forms of redress then available. * * * But unless the contract provides otherwise, there can be no doubt that the employee must afford the union the opportunity to act on his behalf. * * * Union interest in prosecuting employee grievances is clear. Such activity complements the union's status as exclusive bargaining representative by permitting it to participate actively in the continuing administration of the contract."[103]

Vaca directly involved an employee's suit against his union in which he alleged that the union had arbitrarily and capriciously failed to take his case to arbitration. In the wide-ranging majority opinion in this case the Supreme Court recognized that because the contractual grievance and arbitration remedies "have been devised and are often controlled by the union and the employer, they may well prove unsatisfactory or unworkable for the individual grievant."[104] Furthermore, the Court expressly rejected the notion that the individual employee has an absolute right to have his grievance taken to arbitration regardless of the provisions of the collective agreement:[105]

"Though we accept the proposition that a union may not arbitrarily ignore a meritorious grievance or process it in perfunctory fashion, we do not agree that the individual employee has an absolute right to have his grievance taken to arbitration regardless of the provisions of the applicable collective bargaining agreement. In L.M.R.A. §203(d), Congress declared that 'Final adjustment by a method agreed upon by the parties is * * * the desirable method for settlement of grievance disputes arising over the application or interpretation of an existing collective-bargaining agreement.' In providing for a grievance and arbitration procedure which gives the union discretion to supervise the grievance machinery and to invoke arbitration, the employer and the union contemplate that each will endeavor in good faith to settle grievances short of arbitration. Through this settlement process, frivolous grievances are ended prior to the most costly and time-consuming step in the grievance procedures. Moreover, both sides are assured that similar complaints will be treated consistently, and major problem areas in the interpretation of the collective bargaining contract can be isolated and perhaps resolved. And finally, the settlement process furthers the interest of the

---

[103]In its footnote to the first sentence of the just-quoted passage, the Court said: "The proviso of § 9(a) of the LMRA * * * is not contra; Black-Clawson Co. v. Machinists Local, 2 Cir., 313 F.2d 179." Also to be noted from *Maddox* is the Court's comment that "The federal rule would not of course preclude Maddox' court suit if the parties to the collective bargaining agreement expressly agreed that arbitration was not the exclusive remedy." 85 S.Ct. at 619. The Supreme Court has extended its *Maddox* rule to claims of railroad employees under the Railway Labor Act, but has refused to apply it to a seaman's wage claims, to claims under Title VII of the Civil Rights Act, or, it appears clear, to claims under the FLSA. See Chapter 2, subtopic entitled "Other Supreme Court Decisions Affecting Arbitration," where *Maddox* and cases on its scope of applicability are noted. In Clayton v. Automobile Workers, 101 S.Ct. 2088, 107 LRRM 2385 (1981), the union refused to arbitrate a discharge grievance and the time limit for arbitration expired; since the internal union appeals procedure could neither reactivate the grievance nor award complete relief (it could not order reinstatement), exhaustion of the internal union appeals procedure was not required with respect to either the employee's § 301 suit against the employer on the agreement or his suit against the union for alleged breach of the duty of fair representation.

[104]Vaca v. Sipes, 87 S.Ct. 903, 914, 64 LRRM 2369 (1967).

[105]87 S.Ct. at 917.

union as statutory agent and as coauthor of the bargaining agreement in representing the employees in the enforcement of that agreement."[106]

The Court stated that an employee may seek judicial enforcement of his contractual rights if the union has sole power under the agreement to invoke the higher stages of the grievance procedure and if the employee has been prevented from exhausting the contractual remedies by the union's wrongful refusal to process the grievance.[107] As to what is a "wrongful" refusal, the Court stated that "A breach of the statutory duty of fair representation occurs only when a union's conduct toward a member of the collective bargaining unit is arbitrary, discriminatory, or in bad faith."[108]

In the Court's 1976 *Hines* decision, where the union had arbitrated an employee's grievance but allegedly had breached its duty of fair representation by the manner in which it processed the grievance, the Court said the question was "whether the contractual protection against relitigating an arbitral decision binds employees who assert that the process has fundamentally malfunctioned by reason of the bad-faith performance of the union."[109] The Court held that if a breach of the duty of fair representation "seriously undermines the integrity of the arbitral process," the award is not final and binding upon the employee, who may sue the employer under § 301 notwithstanding the award.[110]

In *Hines* the Court reiterated its *Vaca* standards, including the *Vaca* reference to "arbitrary" or "perfunctory" handling of grievances as a basis for finding a breach of the union's duty (the Court also saying, however, that "this involves more than demonstrating mere errors in judgment").[111] Yet later, the Court explained that: "In particular, a union breaches its duty when its conduct is 'arbitrary, discriminatory or in bad faith,' as, for example, when it 'arbitrarily

---

[106]The Court did not fear for the interests of the individual employee: "Nor do we see substantial danger to the interests of the individual employee if his statutory agent is given the contractual power honestly and in good faith to settle grievances short of arbitration. For these reasons, we conclude that a union does not breach its duty of fair representation, and thereby open up a suit by the employee for breach of contract, merely because it settled the grievance short of arbitration." Id. at 918. Insofar as the Railway Labor Act is concerned, the Supreme Court indicated in the *Burley* cases that in order for a union to bind individual employees in grievance settlements before the National Railroad Adjustment Board it must appear that the employees authorized the union in some "legally sufficient manner," which may be by custom, by union rules in the case of union members, or by the failure of an individual employee with notice of proceedings to assert his rights. See Elgin, Joliet & E. Ry. v. Burley cases in 325 U.S. 711, 16 LRRM 749 (1945); 327 U.S. 661, 17 LRRM 241 (1946). In Isaacson, "Labor Arbitration in State Courts," 12 Arb. J. 179, 188 (1957), it was suggested that the *Burley* decisions apply only to cases under the RLA. It may be noted that the Supreme Court did not refer to these decisions in *Vaca*.

[107]87 S.Ct. at 914.

[108]87 S.Ct. at 916.

[109]Hines v. Anchor Motor Freight, 96 S.Ct. 1048, 1059, 91 LRRM 2481 (1976).

[110]96 S.Ct. at 1058. For additional discussion of *Hines*, see Chapter 2, subtopic entitled "De Novo Litigation Following Arbitration." Regarding violation of Title VII of the Civil Rights Act by discriminatory failure to represent an employee properly in contractual grievance proceedings, see McDonald v. Santa Fe Trail Transp. Co., 96 S.Ct. 257 (1976).

[111]96 S.Ct. at 1059–1060. In the interim between *Vaca* and *Hines*, the Court decided Motor Coach Employees v. Lockridge, 77 LRRM 2501, 2512 (1971), which some lower courts have construed to require a showing of bad faith or hostility for a breach of the duty of fair representation.

ignore[s] a meritorious grievance or process[es] it in a perfunctory fashion.' "[112]

Based upon their respective understanding of U.S. Supreme Court doctrine, the circuits of the U.S. Court of Appeals have reached divergent conclusions regarding the *minimal* showing that must be made in order to establish a breach of the duty of fair representation.[113]

---

[112]IBEW v. Foust, 99 S.Ct. 2121, 2125, 101 LRRM 2365 (1979), quoting *Vaca* and holding that punitive damages may not be assessed against a union for breach of its duty of fair representation by failing properly to pursue a grievance.

[113]At one extreme stands the view that bad faith or hostility by the union must be shown. At the other extreme, some decisions can be construed as having required only negligence, or conduct no worse than negligence, in order to establish a breach. An intermediate view, which appears to have the greatest following, is that a breach of the duty may be established by showing arbitrary action even though the union did not act in bad faith or with hostility, but that a mere showing of negligence or conduct no worse than negligence will not suffice. Some cases appear at first glance to fall within the intermediate category but do not do so in fact, for although the court denies that negligence will suffice, it nonetheless will classify as "arbitrary" some type of conduct which other courts would classify only as negligence. For articles collecting and discussing cases reflecting these and other views, see Vandervelde, "A Fair Process Model for the Union's Fair Representation Duty," 67 Minn. L. Rev. 1079 (1983); Morgan, "Fair is Foul, and Foul is Fair— *Ruzicka* and the Duty of Fair Representation in the Circuit Courts," 11 U. Tol. L. Rev. 335 (1980); McGuire, "The Individual Employee in Breach of Contract and Duty of Fair Representation Cases: Exhaustion of Remedies," 34 Arb. J. No. 4, p. 31 (1979); Swedo, "*Ruzicka v. General Motors Corporation:* Negligence, Exhaustion of Remedies, and Relief in Duty of Fair Representation Cases," 33 Arb. J. No. 2, p. 6 (1978); Hill, "The Union's Duty to Process Discrimination Claims," 32 Arb. J. 180 (1977). For later decisions, see Curtis v. UTU, 112 LRRM 2864, 2865 (CA 8, 1983), holding the duty of fair representation was not breached where the union chairman represented the employee conscientiously and with enthusiasm—to hold lay union representatives to the standard of care applied to a trained trial lawyer would defeat the aims of informality and speedy resolution contemplated by labor-management grievance agreements; Dutrisac v. Caterpillar Tractor Co., 113 LRRM 3532, 3534–3535 (CA 9, 1983), concluding that the union's oversight in performing a ministerial function went beyond simple negligence—it rather constituted "reckless disregard" of the employee's rights and violated the duty of fair representation; Harris v. Schwerman Trucking Co., 109 LRRM 3135, 3137 (CA 11, 1982), stating that neither negligence on the part of the union nor a mistake in judgment is sufficient to support a claim that the union acted in an arbitrary and perfunctory manner—"[n]othing less than a demonstration that the union acted with reckless disregard for the employee's rights or was grossly deficient in its conduct will suffice to establish such a claim"; Hoffman v. Lonza, Inc., 108 LRRM 2311, 2314 (CA 7, 1981), requiring "substantial evidence of fraud, deceitful action or dishonest conduct" to establish a breach of the duty of fair representation; Ruzicka v. General Motors Corp., 107 LRRM 2726 (CA 6, 1981), where the Sixth Circuit may have softened its view (but if so, only slightly) concerning union vulnerability to charges of unfair representation. In Kleban v. Hygrade Food Prods. Corp., 102 LRRM 2773, 2777–2778 (USDC, 1979), the court concluded that the circumstances surrounding negligent action can transform it into arbitrary action, that the circumstances surrounding the union's negligence were not such as to make the union's action "arbitrary," and that the duty of fair representation had not been breached. The court quoted a 1979 NLRB General Counsel Memorandum on breach of the duty of fair representation as an unfair labor practice, the Memorandum stating that "the mere fact that the union is inept, negligent, unwise, and insensitive, or ineffectual, will not, *standing alone,* establish a breach of the duty." Id. at 2778, emphasis added by court. In United Steelworkers Local 2869, 100 LRRM 1073, 1074 (NLRB, 1978), the NLRB explained:

"It is well settled that Section 8(b)(1)(A) of the [NLRA] prohibits unions, when acting in a statutory representative capacity, from taking action against any employee upon consideration or upon the basis of classifications that are irrelevant, invidious, or unfair. It is, however, equally well settled that a wide range of reasonableness must be allowed a statutory bargaining representative in serving the unit it represents, subject always to complete good faith and honesty of purpose in the exercise of its discretion. Thus it is not every act of disparate treatment or negligent conduct which is proscribed by Section 8(b)(1)(A), but only those which, because motivated by hostile, invidious, irrelevant, or unfair considerations, may be characterized as 'arbitrary conduct.'"

Regarding breach of the duty of fair representation as a breach of the collective agreement, Hotel Employees v. Michelson's Food Serv., 94 LRRM 2014 (CA 9, 1976), held that a claimed breach of the duty of fair representation was not an arbitrable issue under the collective agreement, since the agreement was between the union and the employer, and not between the employee and the union.

Finally, it is to be noted that in *Vaca* the Court indicated that an employee bringing suit against the union for alleged breach of the duty of fair representation may and probably should join his § 301 action against the employer in the same suit, the employer to be liable for damages attributable to the employer's breach of the collective agreement and the union to be liable for any increase in those damages caused by the union's refusal to process the grievance.[114]

It is now apparent that individual employees have no inherent right to independent grievance processing and/or arbitration with the employer. However, opportunity for independent processing may be given to employees by the employer (if he has not bargained away his right to do so); and the right to independent processing may be given to employees by the collective agreement. Of course, even apart from the two just-noted possibilities, the union does not always resist an employee's desire for independent processing even though the union may have a contractual right to do so.[115]

Many agreements do appear to give the individual employee a right to present and adjust his grievance independently of the union.[116] Whether a given agreement actually does give such right is of course a matter of construction. Some tribunals no doubt will find the right only if it is clearly indicated by the language of the agreement.[117]

---

[114]87 S.Ct. at 920–921. In Bowen v. United States Postal Serv., 103 S.Ct. 588, 595, 112 LRRM 2281 (1983), the union was held primarily liable for the increase in damages caused by its arbitrary refusal to take a discharge grievance to arbitration. "Although the number of Section 301 LMRA breach of contract/breach of the duty of fair representation suits continues to swell, plaintiffs have had relatively little success in meeting the 'arbitrary, discriminatory or bad faith' conduct standard enunciated in *Vaca* * * * ." Report of the Committee on Labor Arbitration and the Law of Collective Bargaining Agreements, 52 (ABA, 1978). For related discussion see Chapter 2, subtopic entitled "De Novo Litigation Following Arbitration," where it is also indicated that in certain respects these individual suits nonetheless may be having significant impact upon the arbitration process itself.

[115]See, for example, Maier Brewing Co., 49 LA 14, 18 (Roberts, 1967), where the union and company agreed that the contract had not been violated but where these parties nonetheless gave individual grievants full opportunity, through counsel of their own choosing, to establish otherwise. Of course, where the union is the moving party against an employee there should be no union objection to his representation by counsel of his own choosing. See Pacific Mercury Elec., 34 LA 91, 92 (Aaron, 1960). Also see Arbitrator Wren in 42 LA 292, 293–294. In Wirtz, "Due Process of Arbitration," Proceedings of the 11th Annual Meeting of NAA, 1, 25 (BNA Books, 1958), it is said that arbitrators have generally refused to permit the grievant to be represented by counsel of his own choosing rather than by the union. For instances of such refusal, see Arbitrator Kerrison in 41 LA 736, 737; Short in 38 LA 1076, 1079–1080. It is also said that "[a]s a general rule, the courts hold that the employee or grievant is not entitled to his or her own counsel where the contract does not provide for such representation and the employer or the union objects." Kurtz, "Arbitration and Federal Rights Under Collective Agreements in 1976," Proceedings of the 30th Annual Meeting of NAA, 265, 283–284 (BNA Books, 1978), citing cases. Regarding individual adjustment of grievances and individual choice of counsel by federal-sector employees, see 5 U.S.C. § 7114(a)(2) and (5).

[116]See Major Collective Bargaining Agreements: Arbitration Procedures, 29 (U.S. Dept. Labor Bull. No. 1425–6, 1966); "Basic Patterns in Labor Arbitration Agreements," 34 LA 931, 932 (1960). For the results of union and company efforts to rectify their initial disregard of the individual grievant's contractual right to attend and participate in grievance sessions, see Flambeau Valley Farms Coop., 39 LA 724, 727–729 (Anderson, 1962). With an individual employee's contractual right to file grievances may go the burden of meeting contractual time limits. Publishers' Assn. of N.Y. City, 39 LA 379, 382 (Schmertz, 1962). As to how arbitrators might dispose of settlements between employer and individual employee which conflict with the collective agreement, see Arbitrator Koven in 44 LA 431, 433–434; Schedler in 38 LA 909, 911–912; Blumrosen in 36 LA 251.

[117]For an example of a court's reasoning process in interpreting the agreement in this regard, see Black-Clawson Co. v. IAM, 313 F.2d 179, 183 (CA 2, 1963). Cf., Riley Stoker Corp., 7 LA

Privileges and Protection of Grievance Representatives

In order to facilitate the operation of the grievance machinery, collective agreements frequently give special privileges and protection to union grievance representatives. Also, an area of protection for grievance representatives exists under arbitration decisions recognizing a certain immunity from discipline for their actions in performing their duties as such.

Superseniority

Many agreements provide superseniority for union representatives, assuring their continued employment as long as they hold office.[118] The underlying purpose of superseniority provisions often is to assure the fullest possible union representation at the plant by experienced representatives, and arbitrators have construed superseniority clauses liberally to achieve this objective.[119]

Apart from this objective, however, there is considerable arbitral authority for the principle that superseniority benefits to union representatives are limited to those rights and privileges which are clearly stated in the agreement.[120] Arbitrator Edwin R. Teple has explained:

> "Superseniority obviously is a contradiction of the basic principle of seniority * * * and should be carefully limited to the terms by which it is created. It is clearly an exception to the rule which seniority demands, that older employees in point of service are entitled to preference."[121]

Furthermore, significant limitations upon superseniority for union representatives have emerged under the NLRA. In the *Dairylea* case an NLRB majority ruled that:

> (1) "[Union] steward superseniority limited to layoff and recall is proper * * * . The lawfulness of such restricted superseniority is * * * based on the ground that it furthers the effective administration of bar-

---

764 (Platt, 1947). In Local Union No. 12405, UMW v. Martin Marietta Corp., 328 F.2d 945 (CA 7, 1964), the court interpreted the word "union" in the agreement as referring to the international, and the court held that the local union could not compel arbitration over the objection of the international.

[118]For statements by the U.S. Supreme Court and by the War Labor Board in support of such superseniority, see U.S. Plastics Prods. Corp., 36 LA 808, 810–811 (Tischler, 1961). The union has a responsibility to notify the employer as to which employees hold union office with entitlement to superseniority. Rex Windows, Inc., 41 LA 606, 607 (Lehoczky, 1963). Also see Arbitrator Gentile in 76 LA 1264, 1267.

[119]See Arbitrator Wolk in 74 LA 987, 991; Ipavec in 67 LA 741, 745; Updegraff in 39 LA 587, 589–590; Tischler in 36 LA 808, 812; Valtin in 35 LA 304, 305. In U.S. Plastics Prods. Corp., 36 LA 808, 811–812 (Tischler, 1961), the agreement was construed to prevent the employer from transferring committeemen, during reduction in force, out of departments they had been representing. But see Arbitrator Teple in 37 LA 396, 399–400; Shister in 25 LA 856, 857; Lehoczky in 17 LA 291, 293. Express contractual restrictions against transfer of union representatives from their department or shift were enforced by Arbitrator Santer in 73 LA 13, 15; Cohen in 64 LA 1080, 1082.

[120]See Arbitrator Aronin in 80 LA 317, 320; Jones in 69 LA 157, 161; Dworkin in 45 LA 1109, 1114–1115; McCoy in 40 LA 675, 679; Teple in 40 LA 323, 326; Cahn in 37 LA 1017, 1018; Mueller in 37 LA 991, 996; Jaffee in 37 LA 458, 464; Fisher in 33 LA 655, 661. Cf., Roberts in 41 LA 275, 278; Cole in 40 LA 208, 214.

[121]American Monorail Co., 40 LA 323, 326 (1963).

gaining agreements on the plant level by encouraging the continued presence of the steward on the job."

(2) "[S]uperseniority clauses which are not on their face limited to layoff and recall are presumptively unlawful, and * * * the burden of rebutting that presumption (i.e., establishing justification) rests on the shoulders of the party asserting their legality."[122]

In another case the NLRB considered the legality of layoff superseniority for a union officer (a recording secretary) who was not also a steward and who had no "steward-type" duties. An NLRB majority stated that the "administration of the collective-bargaining agreement" is not "limited solely to grievance processing or other 'steward-type' duties performed at the workplace." The superseniority was upheld since the union made the showing required by the Board majority, i.e., that the officer's responsibilities "bear a direct relationship to the effective and efficient representation of unit employees."[123] However, the NLRB subsequently overturned this decision and held that it was impermissible to give superseniority to officers not involved in grievance processing or other on-the-job administration of the agreement.[124]

Finally, it must be stressed that an employee ordinarily should not be deprived of normal seniority rights by virtue of service as a union representative. Thus, an employer improperly refused to award a vacant job to a union representative (who was entitled to the job by seniority and qualifications) on the ground that her necessary absences from the job to attend to union matters would result in inefficient operations. In this case Arbitrator Ralph C. Hon stated that seniority provisions characteristically involve a compromise with efficiency, and that the need for competent union representatives requires that employees not be prejudiced by reason of their union position.[125]

---

[122]Dairylea Coop., Inc., 219 NLRB 656, 658, 89 LRRM 1737, 1738–1739 (1975), enforced, 531 F.2d 1162 (CA 2, 1976). Also see NLRB v. Teamsters, Local 443, 101 LRRM 2622 (CA 2, 1979). For examination of many post-*Dairylea* cases, see Kaplan, "Superseniority for Union Representatives as Unfair Labor Practice," 41 ALR Fed 309 (1979). "[T]he cases disclose a distinction between superseniority provisions designed to achieve 'continuity' and those which are not necessary to insure the effective presence of the union representative on the job, but which, rather, provide preferences for the representative as a reward for union activity, or to make such an office as that of steward more desirable, thereby assisting the union in maintaining its own organization by means of on-the-job benefits, the latter constituting an unfair labor practice." Kaplan, id. at 312. For cases upholding superseniority provisions prohibiting transfer or reassignment of union representatives out of their particular shift, department, or job assignment, see Kaplan, id. at 325–328. An example is United Carbide Corp., 95 LRRM 1068 (NLRB, 1977). Legality of superseniority provisions granting union representatives a *preference* as to shifts has depended "upon the relationship of the shift to the particular duties which the union representative performs relative to insuring effective enforcement of the collective bargaining agreement." Kaplan, id. at 328. An example is NLRB v. Teamsters Local 443, 101 LRRM 2622, 2624 (CA 2, 1979).

[123]Limco Mfg., 95 LRRM 1343, 1345 (NLRB, 1977), enforced sub nom. D'Amico v. NLRB, 99 LRRM 2350 (CA 3, 1978).

[124]Gulton Electro-Voice, 112 LRRM 1361 (NLRB, 1983), enforced in Electrical Workers Local 900 v. NLRB, 115 LRRM 2760 (D.C. Cir., 1984).

[125]American Lava Corp., 42 LA 117, 119–120 (1964). Similarly, see Arbitrator Marshall in 54 LA 1123, 1124. Cf., Arbitrator Kaplan in 69 LA 1149, 1153.

Plant Access

Many agreements give representatives access to the plant for the purpose of investigating grievances.[126] Furthermore, some arbitrators have considered that such right inheres under a collective agreement even if not expressly given.[127] Thus, nonemployee union representatives, such as the union business agent, may be given reasonable access to the plant. It is essential that union representatives be given opportunity, as management is, to examine all circumstances surrounding grievances.[128]

In one case, under an agreement permitting union officers to enter the plant for the purpose of assisting in the adjustment of grievances, the word "plant" was interpreted to mean the "entire working area where employee grievances may arise."[129] Under another agreement giving union representatives the right to investigate grievances in the plant the company had no right to determine unilaterally that a grievance was not bona fide and use that determination to deny access to the plant.[130]

But certain limitations must be observed. In one of the cases just considered, for instance, Arbitrator James C. Hill held that under this type of provision the employer is entitled to know the subject of the grievance for which the union representative seeks entry to the plant.[131] Speaking of the right of entrance, Arbitrator Hill said:

> "There should be a legitimate reason for entering a specific area of the plant. It does not give the Union representative the right to roam the plant at will, and it would be a clear violation of the agreement for the Union to use this opportunity to engage in organizational activities."[132]

---

[126]Of course, grievance investigation is not the only purpose for which an agreement may authorize plant access by nonemployee union representatives. For example, the broad purpose stated by one agreement was "to carry on Association business." Fort Wayne Community Schools, 68 LA 1256 at 1256 (Eagle, 1976).

[127]See Collins Radio Co., 36 LA 815, 820–822 (Rohman, 1961), in which the employer was directed to grant union access to a building in which disputed duties were performed; Librascope, Inc., 30 LA 358, 363–364 (Jones, 1958). Contra, Wheland Co., 32 LA 1004, 1006–1007 (Tatum, 1959). As to a right to plant access for the purpose of investigating grievances under the NLRA, compare Adolph Coors Co., 150 NLRB 1604 (1965), with Westinghouse Elec. Corp., 113 NLRB 954 (1955). Also see Peerless Food Prods., 98 LRRM 1182 (NLRB, 1978).

[128]For a discussion of the respective obligations of the parties in the investigation of grievances, see Jonco Aircraft Corp., 20 LA 211, 212 (Merrill, 1953). For an example of the intense emotions and turmoil that may be generated by plant access disputes, see Waycross Sportswear, Inc., 53 LA 1061 (Marshall, 1969).

[129]Standard Motor Prods., 11 LA 1147, 1153 (Hill, 1949). Also see Buddy-L Corp., 41 LA 185, 188–189 (Sembower, 1963). But in Avco Mfg. Corp., 40 LA 476, 480–481 (Stouffer, 1963), the agreement confined stewards to their own department.

[130]Aluminum Co. of Am., 23 LA 317, 320–321 (Prasow, 1954).

[131]Standard Motor Prods., Inc., 11 LA 1147, 1152 (1949). In Farah Mfg. Co., 65 LA 654, 658 (Cohen, 1975), the agreement was construed to require the union to identify the specific grievance which it intended to investigate. In Naval Air Rework Facility, N. Island, 72 LA 129, 132 (1979), Arbitrator Walter N. Kaufman said that "bad faith should not be presumed" in considering whether a plant-access request was made "for a proper purpose."

[132]11 LA 1147, 1153. Also see Arbitrator Albert in 66 LA 506, 509–511; Cahn in 39 LA 393, 394. As to plant access by nonemployee union organizers under the NLRA, see NLRB v. Babcock & Wilcox Co., 67 S.Ct. 679 (1956). It is under the NLRA rather than the First Amendment that labor may have a right of access to the private property of another person. See Hudgens v. NLRB, 96 S.Ct. 1029 (1976), and, on remand, Scott Hudgens, 230 NLRB 414 (1977). Regarding the scope of the company's obligation to make records available to union representatives under plant access "investigation" clauses, see North Am. Aviation, 19 LA 385, 389–390 (Komaroff, 1952).

As to procedural formalities and requirements, an employer could not require union agents to make advance appointments for plant visits or to give advance notice as to the reason for visits where the agreement gave the right to plant access "for the purpose of ascertaining whether or not this agreement is being observed."[133] Another case held that management could require the union president-steward, while on leave for union business, to sign in at the plant main gate as a "visitor," but could not restrict him to talking to only one employee at a time.[134]

Special Immunity

Many arbitrators have recognized that union representatives have some immunity, though it is by no means unlimited, against punishment by the employer for their actions in performing their duties as such. There have been numerous cases in which discipline of an employee was set aside or reduced because the "cause" for the discipline (often abusive language in heated exchange with supervision) emerged from or was related to the employee's activities as union steward.[135] However, there have been numerous other cases in which steward status did not shield the individual from discipline even though the incidents leading to it (abusive language, threats, or worse) were directly or indirectly related to the individual's status as union representative and might never have occurred but for such status.[136]

The cases in this area of study do not always fall into neat and reconcilable categories. Indeed, for the most part each case appears to have been decided on its own merits. However, various generalizations have been offered by arbitrators and some of these are noted here to illustrate possible lines of arbitral thought.[137]

In overruling the suspension of a union committeeman for insulting remarks to a foreman, Arbitrator John P. McGury explained:

> "If a committeeman, when attempting to discuss pending grievances, while not even on Company time, is given a disciplinary suspen-

---

[133]Associated Hosps. of the E. Bay, Inc., 47 LA 858, 860–861 (Koven, 1966). Cf., Arbitrator Albert in 66 LA 506, 510.

[134]Manning, Maxwell & Moore, Inc., 37 LA 475, 482–483 (Stutz, 1961).

[135]See Arbitrator Brown in 77 LA 172, 179–180; Kossoff in 73 LA 1028, 1036; Witney in 73 LA 663, 669; Larkin in 49 LA 1111, 1114; Teple in 49 LA 346, 350; Solomon in 45 LA 751, 756; Giles in 45 LA 258, 261; Kadish in 39 LA 277, 280–281; Reynolds in 18 LA 772, 773; Komaroff in 17 LA 199, 204; Dwyer in 3 LA 497, 498. Also see Kleinsorge in 46 LA 73, 75; McGury in 44 LA 858, 861. In Bradlees Family Circle Stores, 47 LA 567, 574 (House, 1966), the employer was not permitted to punish a steward for failure to return to work immediately as instructed since he was engaged in legitimate steward duties and had not used excessive time. For other cases involving alleged time infractions, see Arbitrator Holly in 49 LA 269, 271; Komaroff in 17 LA 199, 204.

[136]See Arbitrator Penfield in 74 LA 889, 895; Imundo in 73 LA 1244, 1247; Cyrol in 73 LA 610, 613–614; Caraway in 71 LA 1148, 1150; Maroney in 71 LA 164, 169; McLeod in 69 LA 1220, 1223; Ables in 69 LA 917, 919; Ipavec in 68 LA 432, 437–438; Turkus in 51 LA 766, 767; Nichols in 47 LA 672, 674–675; Roberts in 46 LA 486, 489; Luskin in 42 LA 948, 950; Rock in 42 LA 746, 749–750; Murphy in 42 LA 563, 566; Miller in 42 LA 568, 571; Roman in 41 LA 360, 365; Trotta in 38 LA 1226, 1229–1230; Kates in 36 LA 947, 950; Bothwell in 28 LA 543, 547–548.

[137]For related discussions, see Seidman, "Discipline of Union Officers by Public Management," 32 Arb. J. 256 (1977); Leahy, "Grievances Over Union Business on Company Time and Premises," 30 Arb. J. 191 (1975).

sion for improper language, the Union and Unionism are being penalized, as well as the committeeman. The danger is that committeemen will become inhibited in their dealings with management, by fear of discipline. * * * Discipline should not be upheld solely on the basis that insulting remarks were made to a foreman. There should be a further showing that due to the surrounding circumstances, the remarks had an adverse effect on production or managerial authority."[138]

Arbitrator Alex Elson emphasized the dual status of union stewards and noted that it requires a delicate balancing of the duties and responsibilities as steward and those to the employer as an employee. Arbitrator Elson explained that the steward "must be free to express himself vigorously and indeed militantly, if the employees are to have an adequate advocate," but, important as is the steward's function, "he is a creature of the collective agreement" and has an "overriding responsibility" to maintain the agreement; discipline may be in order if this responsibility is disregarded.[139] In this particular case Arbitrator Elson held, as have other arbitrators, that a steward is not immune from discipline for encouraging work stoppages in violation of the agreement.[140]

Also emphasizing the dual status characteristic, Arbitrator Byron R. Abernethy accepted that an individual serving in the dual capacity "is properly subject to discipline for his actions as an employee, but is immune from discipline when acting clearly within the scope of his recognized Union duties and responsibilities."[141] Arbitrator Abernethy added, however, that the line between permissible conduct as a union representative and that not permitted an employee is not always so clear that a new and inexperienced steward (as in the case before him) should be expected to recognize it unmistakably, when acting in good faith.[142] It has also been consid-

---

[138]Bucyrus-Erie Co., 44 LA 858, 861 (1965). Also see Arbitrator Klein in 68 LA 124, 128.

[139]Sinclair Ref. Co., 42 LA 131, 134 (1964). In Arden Farms Co., 45 LA 1124, 1130–1131 (1965), Arbitrator Tsukiyama similarly spoke in terms of the "two hats" worn by employees who also serve as stewards. Regarding Arbitrator Elson's statement that stewards have an "overriding responsibility" to maintain the agreement, other arbitrators similarly have stressed the responsibility of stewards to maintain the agreement, or their responsibility to set a proper example for other employees. See Arbitrator Caraway in 71 LA 1149, 1150; Ipavec in 68 LA 432, 437–438; Ray in 59 LA 385, 390. Discipline of union officers for abusing or intimidating other employees, in an effort to obtain compliance with union wishes, was upheld by Arbitrator Helburn in 73 LA 241, 249–250; Leeper in 72 LA 583, 587–588; O'Shea in 64 LA 698, 700.

[140]42 LA at 135–136. For other cases upholding discipline for encouraging work stoppages, see Arbitrator Sabo in 75 LA 774, 784; McDermott in 68 LA 618, 624–625 (upholding discharge of union president although he was on leave of absence when he acted); Miller in 50 LA 562, 564; Roberts in 48 LA 855, 860–861. In Reynolds Metals Co., 52 LA 936, 939–940 (Porter, 1969), a union president could be punished for conducting a union committee meeting during scheduled work hours without permission, since the meeting amounted to a small-scale walkout in violation of the no-strike clause.

[141]Bates Lumber Co., 65-1 ARB ¶8222 (1964).

[142]Id. at 3801. For instances in which immunity was denied for infractions pertaining to the individual's service as an employee, see Arbitrator Tsukiyama in 45 LA 1124, 1130–1132; Kornblum in 43 LA 838, 842. In General Elec. Co., 40 LA 1126, 1156–1157 (1963), Arbitrator Davey sustained the discharge of a union officer for writing an article in the union newspaper maliciously disparaging the employer's product—the misconduct was viewed as that of an employee. In Linn v. UPGWA Local 114, 86 S.Ct. 657, 61 LRRM 2345 (1966), the Supreme Court held the states are not preempted from giving damages for false and defamatory statements (if

ered that punishment for an individual's actions as an employee is subject to modification if it is tainted by ill will carried over from the individual's activities as a union steward.[143]

A "rule of reason" for determining immunity of union stewards was advanced by Arbitrator Eli Rock in upholding discharge of a steward for threats and blackmail in connection with grievance handling:

> "Obviously, the right of a steward to do his job properly must be strictly protected, without fear of retaliation of any kind for the performance of that proper role. Mere militancy or zealousness can never justify punishment; nor can a steward be limited to the language or behavior of the parlor. And as the Union points out, the steward is certainly entitled to be wrong in the issues that he presses or fights over, on behalf of his constituents.
>
> "If the latter were all that was involved here, there would obviously be no problem. Much more is contained, however. Even the average, extremely zealous steward knows that there are some limits on his behavior. He cannot, for example, assault foremen, or call wildcat strikes or counsel employees to disobey Company orders, or do other things which are recognized as being outside the sphere of proper activity for this position. Clearly, a rule of reason is recognized and accepted on the subject, and few, if any, are the stewards who would regard the office as conferring on them the right to resort to the *combination* of extreme activities which were followed by this particular grievant."[144]

In turn, Arbitrator Burton B. Turkus, in upholding the discharge of a union steward for a series of insubordinate acts designed to embarrass and humiliate management in front of other employees, declared:

> "Probably no area in disciplinary disputes may pose a more troublesome problem to the parties to a labor agreement than keeping the balance true between the right of Union shop stewards and representatives to be accorded a sound and realistic latitude in the method and attitude adopted in presenting grievances to management and their

---

made with malice) during union organizational campaigns conducted under the NLRA. Then in Letter Carriers v. Austin, 94 S.Ct. 2770, 86 LRRM 2740 (1974), the Supreme Court ruled that: (1) the *Linn* principles apply also where federal-sector employment is involved; (2) "malice" under *Linn* requires knowledge of falsity or reckless disregard of the truth; and (3) the union's characterization of nonmembers as "scabs" during an organizational campaign was not a false or defamatory statement (thus, the state was preempted from awarding damages) since one of the generally accepted definitions of "scab" is "one who refuses to join a union." In General Motors Corp. v. Mendicki, 367 F.2d 66 (CA 10, 1966), accusations uttered at a *grievance hearing* were held unqualifiedly privileged and immune from liability for damages. For views of other courts on the extent of privilege carried by communications made in grievance or arbitration proceedings, see Spivey, "Libel—Privilege in Labor Grievance Matter," 60 ALR3d 1041. Regarding NLRA protection from discipline, in Hawthorne Mazda, 105 LRRM 1057 (NLRB, 1980), an employee was unlawfully discharged for repeated statements that members of management were either incompetent or idiots, where the statements were made during a grievance hearing in which the employee was acting as informal spokesperson for fellow employees. Also see Crown Cent. Petroleum Corp., 177 NLRB 322 (1969). But in Hotel St. Moritz, 105 LRRM 1116 (NLRB, 1980), a steward's conduct was "so opprobrious" that it was unprotected under the NLRA.

[143]Lawndale Indus., 46 LA 220, 223 (McGury, 1966). However, the mere fact that an employee's misconduct occurs at grievance or union meetings will not necessarily immunize him from employer punishment. See Lone Star Brewing Co., 45 LA 817, 821 (Merrill, 1965), involving fighting by an employee (not a steward) at a union meeting on company premises; Special Metals Inc., 39 LA 1, 3 (Shister, 1962), involving discipline of an employee (not a steward) for false testimony at a grievance meeting.

[144]Singer-Fidelity, Inc., 42 LA 746, 749 (1963).

concomitant responsibility and obligation as Union officials to scrupulously refrain from the abuse of such status to cloak patent insubordination and defiant challenge of management's right to manage and direct the work force."[145]

In this case the steward's actions were triggered in part at least by his being sent home early with loss of overtime earnings. As to this, Arbitrator Turkus stated:

> "In return for assuming a steward's responsibilities an employee does not receive the right to be high-handedly insubordinate or to urge others not to work as directed by their supervisors. And this is particularly so when a steward is prosecuting his own grievance—one that arises from his own conduct or misconduct in the work place. In these circumstances, his conduct when pressing the grievance must be judged by the same standards that govern the conduct of any other employee."[146]

Pay for Grievance Time

Many employers compensate union representatives and other employees for time spent in handling grievances during working hours.[147] In some large plants it is the practice of management to pay for full-time union stewards.[148]

Unions take the position that the activity of union grievance representatives benefits management as much as employees. Of course, both parties will agree that it is to the advantage of both if only

---

[145]Calmar, Inc., 51 LA 766, 767 (1968). In Department of the Air Force, 75 LA 170, 177 (Dash, 1980), the Arbitrator stated that two union officers, in using that status "as a cloak to test the propriety of a supervisory order, improperly concluded that Union positions would protect them from any potential discipline."

[146]51 LA at 769. In Trans World Airlines, 39 LA 1131, 1134 (Gilden, 1962), a steward had no immunity for misbehavior in acting on his own behalf at a grievance meeting. Also see Arbitrator Steese in 72 LA 84, 87. In Reynolds Metals Co., 39 LA 584, 587 (1962), Arbitrator Sembower cautioned that a steward should hesitate to represent himself as to his own grievance.

[147]As to variations of this practice, see "Basic Patterns in Labor Arbitration Agreements," 34 LA 931, 935–936 (1960); "Grievance Procedure Under Collective Bargaining," 63 Monthly Lab. Rev. 175, 184 (U.S. Dept. of Labor, 1946). A high percentage of federal-sector agreements contain some provision for paid grievance and arbitration time. See A Survey of Negotiated Grievance Procedures and Arbitration in Federal Post Civil Service Reform Act Agreements, 52 (OPM, 1980). The Civil Service Reform Act's requirement that federal agencies grant "official time" to employee representatives in negotiations was construed by the Supreme Court in Bureau of Alcohol, Tobacco & Firearms v. FLRA, 104 S.Ct. 439, 114 LRRM 3393 (1983).

[148]Under a proviso to NLRA §8(a)(2) an employer may permit employees to confer with him during working hours without loss of time or pay. Under LMRA § 302 employer payments to employee representatives are prohibited, with the express exception of compensation for services as an employee. It is accepted that management may pay union representatives for time spent discussing grievances with management, but question exists as to whether payment may be made for grievance activities other than those of "conferring" with management. Several carefully reasoned arbitral opinions (some after the 1959 amendment of § 302) have concluded that employer payments to union representatives for time spent in processing grievances and administering the agreement are legal, though some of these opinions recognized that a court might disagree. See Arbitrator Seibel in 44 LA 866, 867–871; Stark in 36 LA 351, 364–371; Beatty in 36 LA 291, 297–300; Dworkin in 35 LA 228, 234–235; Gregory in 10 LA 471, 473–474. Also see Arbitrator Williams in 70 LA 1007, 1008; Willcox in 23 LA 21, 23; Kelliher in 16 LA 734, 735–736. In Iron Workers v. Bechtel Power Corp., 106 LRRM 2385 (CA 6, 1981), employer contributions to an industry steward fund violated § 302; the steward, with the function of overseeing employer compliance with the collective agreement, was found to be under the real control of the union, the court rejecting the union's contention that the steward was an employee of the employers and that payments to the steward represented compensation for services as an employee.

persons of responsibility act as grievance representatives. Payment for time spent in handling grievances is one way to secure the services of such persons. Grievance pay also facilitates prompt settlement, thereby improving morale and plant efficiency.

Emphasizing that the basic purpose of pay for grievance time is to compensate union officials who help management resolve differences with employees, an arbitrator construed a contractual provision to pay grievance representatives for time lost as not applying to the grievant himself; that arbitrator stated that "it might be very unwise to offer to pay employees for time lost while settling their own grievances."[149] But even where the agreement did not specifically require pay for time spent by employees in discussing their conduct with management prior to possible assessment of discipline, they were held entitled to pay for all time lost from work, the arbitrator stating that they should have been called in during nonworking time.[150] In the latter regard, pay for nonworking time utilized by employees on their own grievances has been denied.[151]

Some arbitrators have held that past practice should determine whether grievance time is to be compensated where the agreement is silent or ambiguous on the matter.[152]

In some cases the employer has not been required to pay union representatives for time spent at arbitration hearings in the absence of a clear and specific contractual requirement for such pay.[153] However, so definite a provision for such pay has not been required in all

---

[149]American Car & Foundry Co., 2 LA 644, 645–646 (Larkin, 1945).

[150]Bethlehem Steel Co., 19 LA 261, 262–264 (Shipman, 1952).

[151]Allied Chem. Corp., 47 LA 686, 690 (Hilpert, 1966); Bethlehem Steel Co., 17 LA 436, 439 (Killingsworth, 1951). For reasons why an interest arbitrator refused to approve a public-sector union's request for compensated off-duty bargaining time, see City of Renton, 71 LA 271, 274–275 (Snow, 1978).

[152]See Arbitrator Hardy in 49 LA 415, 417–418; Seibel in 41 LA 1042, 1044–1045; Dworkin in 35 LA 228, 233–234; Lehoczky in 27 LA 187, 188; McCoy in 16 LA 240, 241–242; Hepburn in 13 LA 418, 422. Also see Owen in 69 LA 247, 250. Cf., Karlins in 67 LA 103, 107–108.

[153]See Arbitrator May in 68 LA 20, 25; Updegraff in 50 LA 1025, 1027, and in 36 LA 1044, 1046; Bothwell in 50 LA 230, 231; Bennett in 43 LA 331, 332; Begley in 38 LA 319, 320; Marshall in 28 LA 107, 108; Campbell in 25 LA 700, 707–708; Spaulding in 21 LA 763, 768; Fulda in 14 LA 775, 780; Coogler in 12 LA 1021, 1022; Gorder in 8 LA 945, 946–948; Lehoczky in 8 LA 33, 35. In some of these cases the arbitrator noted the absence of any clearly established practice to pay for arbitration time. Although recognizing employer and public benefit from labor-management activities of union representatives, Arbitrator Stuart Rothman advocated strict construction of contractual provisions relating to employer payment for the time involved: "[T]he substitution through collective bargaining of employer-paid-for (whether in the public sector or in the private sector) time for an employee to conduct Union (labor-management) activities in place of the normal duties to which the employee has been assigned ought not to be lightly inferred. * * * In case of doubt or ambiguity in the contract language used, the doubt or ambiguity should in the view of the arbitrator militate against the interests and the side claiming that the government as an employing agency has waived the requirement that an employee perform his normal duties. It can be done, but the contract should be clear and convincing." Social Sec. Admin., 73 LA 789, 797 (1979). But believing that a federal agency employer's interpretation of a provision relating to pay for representational work would "operate as a penalty against" a shop steward, with the "larger effect" being "to chill this shop steward and all others who might follow him from accepting the job," Arbitrator Robert J. Ables rejected the employer's interpretation (which could have jeopardized some of the employee's fringe benefits, such as sick leave and retirement credits) and he concluded "that an action by management which undermines union representation—where an alternative is available—was not intended in establishing collective bargaining relationships between the federal government and its employees." Marine Corps Dev. Command, 71 LA 726, 730 (1978).

cases,[154] especially where there was an established practice for the employer to pay union representatives for arbitration time.[155]

Under an agreement providing that union representatives shall be paid for time spent "conferring with management," time spent researching company records (relevant to grievances) in the absence of management was held to be compensable if the amount of time is "relatively slight and of an incidental nature."[156]

Payment for grievance work is generally made on a straight-time basis.[157] Some agreements, however, provide that grievance representatives "shall not lose pay for time spent" in grievance meetings with management. Under such a provision one arbitrator held that representatives had to be paid a special differential which they would have received had they not been called from work for grievance meetings, even though another provision of the agreement stated that the differential was to be paid only in case of actual performance of differential work.[158] But under a similar provision in an agreement which also provided that grievance conferences should be held during working hours, a minimum of four hours' pay at straight time, in accordance with call-in pay provisions, was held to be sufficient for less than four hours of grievance work performed after working hours; the arbitrator rejected the union demand for payment at the overtime rate.[159]

Various means of control have been used to prevent abuse of grievance-pay practices. Some agreements limit the amount of time that may be spent in such activity;[160] others contain no specific limit, but state that a "reasonable amount" of time will be paid for.[161] Management has been held entitled to require the union to fill out forms, giving a general account of grievance services performed and the time involved.[162] This right is said to accompany management's contractual obligation to pay for such services.[163] Use of such report

---

[154]See Arbitrator Feldman in 69 LA 862, 864; Smith in 62 LA 469, 471; McIntosh in 53 LA 866, 866–867; Porter in 23 LA 243, 245.

[155]See Arbitrator Smith in 46 LA 637, 639; Dunau in 38 LA 49, 51; Jones in 31 LA 240, 242–243; Dworkin in 22 LA 352, 357; Brown in 21 LA 529, 532.

[156]Standard Oil Co., 16 LA 734, 735–736 (Kelliher, 1951).

[157]"Grievance Procedure Under Collective Bargaining," 63 Monthly Lab. Rev. 175, 184 (U.S. Dept. of Labor, 1946). But see International Harvester Co., 22 LA 196, 197–198 (Cole, 1954). As to applicability of cost-of-living adjustments to grievance time pay see Bethlehem Steel Co., 33 LA 632, 636–637 (Feinberg, 1959).

[158]Bethlehem Steel Co., 10 LA 284, 287–288 (Dodd, 1948).

[159]Ford Roofing Prods. Co., 5 LA 182, 184 (Wardlaw, 1946).

[160]Similarly, the agreement may expressly limit the pay for grievance activity, or limit the number of individuals who may collect grievance pay. See "Basic Patterns in Labor Arbitration Agreements," 34 LA 931, 935 (1960).

[161]Where the agreement by implication provided pay for grievance handling but did not state any limitation, and where past practice was to pay for all time so spent, it was held that the employer could not unilaterally limit the amount of paid time but could challenge in specific instances the reasonableness of the amount of time claimed for grievance activity. Goss Co., 44 LA 824, 826–827 (Pedrick, 1964). The burden of demonstrating use of excessive time similarly was placed on the employer in Houdaille Indus., 73 LA 872, 874–875 (Frost, 1979), where the agreement stated no specific limit on allowable time but did prohibit abuse.

[162]See Arbitrator Cahn in 50 LA 909, 914–915; Seinsheimer in 36 LA 166, 169 (merely saying "union business" did not suffice); Wolff in 33 LA 112, 123; Jaffe in 11 LA 729, 730–731; Shulman in 2 LA 382, 383.

[163]Bell Aircraft Corp., 11 LA 729, 730–731 (Jaffe, 1948).

forms is not considered to be espionage or interference with union activity.[164]

Many companies require union representatives to report to their foreman before leaving work to handle grievances. Where an agreement provided that stewards were to be compensated for earnings lost in handling grievances but did not spell out a procedure to be followed by stewards, Arbitrator Peter Di Leone held that management could require stewards to notify their supervisor when leaving work to handle grievances, and to clock out and in for the period of time away from the steward's work station; provided, that prior notification should not be required in emergencies or if the foreman is not readily available.[165]

Another means of protecting grievance-pay practices from abuse is to provide, in the agreement, that management may inaugurate a grievance at an advanced step of the grievance procedure if abuse is believed to exist.[166] Then, too, such abuse may lead directly or indirectly to the proper warning or punishment of the grievance representative.[167]

Written Statement of Grievance

There are various reasons why grievances should be presented in writing at an early stage of the grievance procedure, and to do so is the general practice. The written complaint establishes a record of the grievance. By putting the grievance in writing it is less likely to become distorted as it is processed through the grievance procedure.[168] Then, too, if grievances must be stated in writing, those that lack merit often are dropped.

Some persons consider it important to have a written grievance filed at the beginning, or "first step," of the grievance procedure in view of the value of a complete written record.[169] However, many parties prefer informal oral discussion at the first step, considering written grievances to be best suited to the later steps of the procedure. These parties may oppose written presentation of grievances at the first step on the ground that it makes the procedure too inflexible and

---

[164]Ford Motor Co., 2 LA 382, 383 (Shulman, 1944).

[165]Picker X-Ray Corp., 44 LA 463, 465–466 (1965). Arbitrator Di Leone also stated that the prior practice of not requiring stewards to do these things when the union business was within their own department did not preclude management from establishing reasonable procedures to guard against abuse of the right to conduct union business on company time. Id. at 465. In Active Prods. Corp., 67-1 ARB ¶8261 (Seinsheimer, 1967), a plant rule requiring stewards to clock out and in was held reasonable and enforceable by discipline. In Jenkins Bros., 11 LA 432, 434–435 (Donnelly, 1948), management (with some contractual basis) could require stewards to clock out and in when leaving work to process grievances, but the Arbitrator stated that such action by management may be shortsighted in view of the dissatisfaction which it may cause.

[166]See Fact-Finders Van Fossen, Humphrey & Prifrel in 2 LA 227, 241; Marshall, Spencer & Holly in 1 LA 512, 521–522.

[167]See Arbitrator Hon in 73 LA 636, 640; Levy in 69 LA 831, 838; Teple in 48 LA 1345, 1348–1349; Cahn in 39 LA 1185, 1185–1186; Wolff in 33 LA 112, 123.

[168]For a related discussion, see Chapter 7, topic entitled "Extent of Permissible Deviation From Prearbitral Discussion of a Case."

[169]Updegraff, Arbitration and Labor Relations, 138 (BNA Books, 1970); Updegraff & McCoy, Arbitration of Labor Disputes, 53 (1946).

cumbersome, discourages employees from voicing their complaints, and impedes prompt settlement.[170] Indeed, the more common practice in all sectors probably is well illustrated by the federal-sector practice of utilizing oral grievances at the first step of the grievance procedure but written grievances at the second step.[171]

One interest arbitrator, recognizing that the presentation of grievances in writing is a well-established practice in industry, granted an employer's request for a provision requiring grievances carried beyond the employee's immediate superior to be presented in writing on simple forms provided by the company.[172] In this connection, a clause requiring that grievances be "filed" at the second step within a specified time was interpreted to require that grievances be stated "in writing" at that step.[173]

In some instances the discussion of grievances not filed in writing as required by the agreement has been held to waive the "written grievance" requirement.[174] One arbitrator, in placing the burden upon management to raise the issue promptly, stated that if management desires to insist upon strict compliance with "written grievance" requirements, it should express its disapproval of oral grievances at the time when they first become a subject of discussion between the parties. "The company's failure to raise the objection at that time constitutes a waiver of that requirement."[175] But another arbitrator ruled otherwise, declaring that "if there is any place in the interpretation of collective bargaining agreements where strict or technical construction is necessary it is in that which provides for the grievance machinery and procedure."[176]

Time Limitations

Promptness is one of the most important aspects of grievance settlement. Failure to settle grievances with dispatch is sure to lead to

---

[170]For a most interesting program by one company and union for speedy and informal handling of most complaints "at the level of the shop floor, without written grievances," see Ross, "Distressed Grievance Procedures and Their Rehabilitation," Proceedings of the 16th Annual Meeting of NAA, 104, 128 (BNA Books, 1963).

[171]See A Survey of Negotiated Grievance Procedures and Arbitration in Federal Post Civil Service Reform Act Agreements, 25–26 (OPM, 1980), indicating that of the 452 agreements surveyed, 90 percent specified oral process at the first step but all of the agreements required the grievance to be in writing at the second step.

[172]New York City Omnibus Corp., 7 LA 794, 820–821 (Cole, 1947).

[173]Jones & Laughlin Steel Corp., 16 LA 788, 789 (Cahn, 1951). To similar effect, Ranco, Inc., 48 LA 974, 977 (Gibson, 1967). Cf., John Morrell & Co., 69 LA 264, 266–267, 276 (1977), where Arbitrator Conway concluded that a writing was not required where he found no contractual "reference to a grievance * * * being a written instrument."

[174]See Arbitrator Teple in 45 LA 196, 201; Wolf in 44 LA 107, 109; Greene in 10 LA 567, 568; Gilden in 3 LA 327, 332–333. Also see Dworet in 40 LA 788, 789. The contractual time limit for filing a written grievance was held waived by proceeding without objection in Beaunit Fibers, 44 LA 1040, 1042 (McCoy, 1965).

[175]Lapham-Hickey Co., 3 LA 327, 333 (Gilden, 1946). To similar effect, Royal Paper Prods., 48 LA 636, 638 (Seitz, 1966).

[176]Firestone Tire & Rubber Co., 9 LA 518, 522 (Rader, 1948). Also see statement in Pressmen's Union v. International Paper Co., 107 LRRM 2618, 2621 (CA 3, 1981). For related material, see this Chapter, subtopic entitled "Failure to Comply Strictly With Technical Requirements of Grievance Procedure."

labor unrest. All parties agree that promptness in the settlement of grievances leads to better labor-management relationships; opinion differs, however, as to the best means of insuring such promptness. While many agreements provide time limits for taking complaints to the grievance procedure as well as time limits for processing grievances through the various steps of the procedure, other agreements contain no such provisions. Some parties feel that time limits provide a safeguard against stalling, and against the accumulation of cases and pressing of stale claims. On the other hand, others believe that the setting of specific time allowances permits a party to stall to the maximum allowable time.[177] Even worse, it sometimes operates to bar grievances which should be settled for the sake of improving the relations of the parties.

In the final analysis, prompt settlement of grievances depends, not upon the presence of contractual time limits, but upon a sincere desire of the parties to settle differences. But that time limits do have definite value may be presumed from the fact that numerous agreements contain them. Without question, such limits provide an additional element of order to the grievance procedure.[178]

No set formula is available for the establishment of time limits. Rather, the special circumstances of the parties should determine, in each instance, the nature of the time-limit provisions of their agreement. The agreement may fix time limits for each step of the procedure, or an overall time limit for complete processing of a grievance, or simply forbid delay. Any of these forms might be coupled with a time limit for the initial submission of grievances. Different limits may be prescribed for the submission of different types of grievances. This was done, for instance, by a fact-finding board recommendation of a 5-day limit for filing discharge and pay adjustment disputes, and a 30-day limit for all other grievances.[179]

Some cases hold there is no time limit for filing grievances where the agreement does not specify any.[180] But some arbitrators have held

---

[177]It has been emphasized, however, that grievance processing should not be rushed to the extent that snap judgments are prompted. Lehigh Portland Cement Co., 46 LA 132, 134–135 (Duff, 1965), where the agreement was viewed as anticipating a brief time lapse between filing time and answering time; time limits could not be shortened by employer insistence upon giving immediate answers.

[178]For general discussion of advantages of using time limits, see The Grievance Process, 60 (Mich. St. U. Lab. & Indus. Rel. Center, 1956). Of 400 agreements included in one survey, 81 percent contained time limits for filing grievances and 53 percent contained limits for later stages of the procedure. "Basic Patterns in Labor Arbitration Agreements," 34 LA 931, 932–933 (1960), where variations in time limit provisions are also noted. Time limits also are common in federal-sector agreements. See A Survey of Negotiated Grievance Procedures and Arbitration in Federal Post Civil Service Reform Act Agreements, 35–36 (OPM, 1980), noting that: "In the majority of agreements, failure to meet specified time limits will either advance the grievance to the next procedural step (management failure) or terminate it (union or employee failure). However, 2 percent of the agreements state that management's failure to work within the negotiated time limits would result in the Union winning the grievance."

[179]Minneapolis-Moline Power Implement Co., 2 LA 227, 241 (Van Fossen, Humphrey & Prifrel, 1946).

[180]See Arbitrator Siegel in 66 LA 1271, 1273–1274; Larkin in 66 LA 443, 445; Shister in 47 LA 601, 602; Gundermann in 44 LA 585, 589 (but recognizing an exception where undue hardship results to the other party from delayed filing); Gilden in 6 LA 238, 260 (grievance may be filed at any time during the contract term), and in 3 LA 327, 333; Whiting in 5 LA 477, 478.

that even though the contract does not state a time limit for filing, a requirement for filing within a reasonable time is inferred by the establishment of a grievance procedure.[181] It has been held also that where the contract states no time limit for filing grievances but does state specific time limits for taking grievances to the various steps of the procedure once they have been filed, the evident intent of the contract is that grievances must be filed with reasonable promptness.[182]

Where the absence of strict time limits results in the acceptance of grievances notwithstanding delayed filing, the arbitrator may make the grievance adjustment retroactive only to the date on which the grievance was filed or to some other date short of full retroactivity.[183] In particular, arbitrators can be expected to deny that part of a claim which, if allowed, would result in a loss to one party caused by the negligent delay of the other party in asserting the claim. Whether the arbitrator calls such delay laches, acquiescence, or sleeping on one's rights, the principle involved appears to be generally recognized and applied.[184]

If the agreement does contain clear time limits for filing and prosecuting grievances, failure to observe them generally will result in dismissal of the grievance if the failure is protested.[185] Thus, the

---

Also see Havinghurst in 26 LA 688, 692; Copelof in 21 LA 788, 792. Where an agreement did not contain any time limit for filing grievances, it was held that a grievance which was dismissed on procedural grounds could be refiled and processed to arbitration. Local 616, IUE v. Byrd Plastics, 74 LRRM 2550 (CA 3, 1970). Cases relating to delay as grounds for finding a waiver of contractual right to arbitration are collected in Spain v. Houston Oilers, 593 S.W. 2d 746 (Tex. Ct. Civ. App., 1979).

[181]See Arbitrator Killion in 47 LA 1153, 1156–1157 (where an unreported decision by Edgar A. Jones is quoted to the same effect); Scheiber in 43 LA 129, 134–137; Somers in 24 LA 324, 330. Also see Cox in 49 LA 837, 840–841.

[182]See Arbitrator Traynor in 47 LA 767, 775–776; Greenwald in 66-1 ARB ¶8185; Williams in 26 LA 505, 507; Maggs in 19 LA 677, 681, and in 12 LA 311, 316. But see Smith in 32 LA 274, 276. A requirement for reasonably prompt filing was held to exist under a provision calling for expeditious grievance settlement. Kennecott Copper Corp., 35 LA 412, 413–414 (Ross, 1960). In American Bakeries Co., 44 LA 156, 160–161 (1965), Arbitrator Harold D. Jones held that the union could file a grievance and hold its further processing in abeyance pending the occurrence of a similar incident, since the contract did not set time limits for processing grievances from step to step.

[183]See Arbitrator Dworkin in 45 LA 812, 816; Larkin in 45 LA 517, 521–522; Markowitz in 37 LA 140, 143; Lockhart in 16 LA 156, 160–161; Davey in 9 LA 139, 140; Brandschain in 7 LA 785, 787; Gilden in 2 LA 655, 659–660. Also see cases cited in next footnote. But see Appleby in 20 LA 183, 188–189. Of course the agreement may expressly limit retroactivity. See Arbitrator Cole in 39 LA 1148, 1153; Crawford in 37 LA 1046, 1047.

[184]See extensive statement by Arbitrator Lockhart in Lavoris Co., 16 LA 156, 160–161 (1951). For other arbitrators applying the principle, see Kates in 47 LA 1045, 1048; Dworkin in 45 LA 812, 816; Dolnick in 45 LA 357, 361; Markowitz in 37 LA 140, 143; Ross in 32 LA 713, 719; Kelliher in 31 LA 219, 220; Cornsweet in 12 LA 482, 483–484; Wolff in 10 LA 288, 293–294; Lehoczky in 9 LA 659, 660; Brandschain in 7 LA 785, 787; Gilden in 2 LA 608, 612. Also see Gibson in 69 LA 697, 705; Seitz in 49 LA 197, 199; Bauder in 40 LA 780, 784; Stouffer in 37 LA 231, 234. Cf., Murphy in 38 LA 1031, 1040–1041.

[185]E.g., Arbitrator Dworkin in 76 LA 798, 802; Christopher in 75 LA 1179, 1182; Eigenbrod in 72 LA 52, 57; Feldman in 70 LA 904, 908; Gibson in 70 LA 52, 57–58; Kuvin in 69 LA 1188, 1191–1192; Stouffer in 53 LA 79, 82; Gibson in 51 LA 837, 840; Nathanson in 50 LA 1220, 1222; Krinsky in 48 LA 594, 597; Porter in 47 LA 1057, 1059; Tatum in 47 LA 563, 566; Boothe in 47 LA 336, 339; Strongin in 46 LA 767, 768; Teple in 46 LA 338, 345; Roberts in 46 LA 59, 61; Small in 45 LA 257, 258; Loucks in 37 LA 588, 590; Scheiber in 64-3 ARB ¶9041; Livengood in 27 LA 157, 159; Morvant in 26 LA 732, 735–736; Prasow in 25 LA 225, 228–230; Maggs in 19 LA 677, 680; Cahn in 17 LA 277, 280; Handsaker in 16 LA 369, 372; Holden in 13 LA 387, 390; McCoy in 11 LA 98, 100; Rader in 7 LA 595, 597–598. Also see Peter Trippey v. Rock Island Motor Transit Co., 78 LC ¶11,249 (USDC, 1976). An award was vulnerable to court challenge where the arbitrator disregarded clear time limitations because he believed time limitations may damage labor relations. Detroit Coil Co. v. Machinists Lodge 82, 100 LRRM 3138 (CA 6, 1979).

practical effect of late filing in many instances is that the merits of the dispute are never decided.[186]

It has been held that doubts as to the interpretation of contractual time limits or as to whether they have been met should be resolved against forfeiture of the right to process the grievance.[187] Moreover, even if time limits are clear, late filing will not result in dismissal of the grievance if the circumstances are such that it would be unreasonable to require strict compliance with the time limits specified by the agreement.[188]

If both parties have been lax as to observing time limits in the past, an arbitrator will hestitate to enforce them strictly until prior notice has been given by a party of intent to demand strict adherence to the contractual requirements.[189]

Of course time limits may be extended or waived by a special agreement in writing. Oral agreements have also sufficed for this purpose.[190] Even where an agreement expressly required time limit waivers to be in writing, it was held that the parties' actions may produce a waiver without a writing.[191]

In many cases time limits have been held waived by a party in recognizing and negotiating a grievance without making clear and timely objection.[192] But there are some cases holding to the con-

---

[186]For discussion, see Benewitz, "On Timely Grievances and Arbitrability," 34 Arb. J. No. 2, p. 6 (1979). One of the relatively few cases in which the merits were reached by the arbitrator in spite of his ruling against the grievant on the time issue is Northeast Airlines, 37 LA 741, 745 (Wolff, 1961), where a ruling on the merits was issued in the belief that the parties would be aided by the Arbitrator's views. Also see Arbitrator Foster in 76 LA 626, 631 (dismissing the grievance because of time limitations but issuing an "advisory opinion" on the merits). In American Zinc Co., 46 LA 645, 650 (Abernethy, 1966), the company asserted late filing but nonetheless agreed to have a ruling on the merits first, the time limit issue to be ruled upon only if the company should lose on the merits. In Hoffman v. Lonza, Inc., 108 LRRM 2311, 2314 (CA 7, 1981), arbitration of a grievance was barred because the union forgot to file a notice of intent to arbitrate within the time limit specified by the agreement; the court held that an action for breach of the duty of fair representation "cannot be based soley on an allegation that a union unintentionally failed to file" a notice within the specified period. Also finding no breach of the duty of fair representation where the union forgot to act within the time specified by the agreement, Graf v. Elgin, Joliet & E. Ry., 112 LRRM 2462, 2466–2468 (CA 7, 1983). But see Dutrisac v. Caterpillar Tractor Co., 113 LRRM 3532, 3535 (CA 9, 1983); Ruzicka v. General Motors Corp., 107 LRRM 2726 (CA 6, 1981). For related discussion, see this Chapter, topic entitled "Grievance Adjustment by Individual Employees."

[187]See Arbitrator Fiering in 79 LA 207, 214–215; Foster in 73 LA 819, 823; Dworkin in 70 LA 917, 919; Teple in 69 LA 599, 601; LaDriere in 36 LA 148, 151; Sanders in 33 LA 553, 555. In Miami Indus., 50 LA 978, 984 (1968), Arbitrator Howlett stated that in raising time issues a party raises an affirmative defense which he has the burden of proof to establish by a preponderance of the evidence.

[188]See Arbitrator Kruger in 75 LA 948, 951; Hardin in 74 LA 1229, 1236; Ziskind in 73 LA 670, 671; Sloane in 71 LA 302, 303; King in 69 LA 1016, 1021; Jewett in 68 LA 188, 191; Schedler in 63 LA 1196, 1202; Porter in 47 LA 524, 525; Klein in 42 LA 1076, 1082; Hardy in 66-2 ARB ¶8699; Duff in 63-3 ARB ¶9060; Reid in 23 LA 135, 136; Sturges in 16 LA 794, 800; Maggs in 15 LA 934, 935.

[189]See Arbitrator Roberts in 75 LA 789, 792; Sembower in 73 LA 959, 960; Doyle in 50 LA 1157, 1158; Kesselman in 42 LA 884, 888; Biscoe in 9 LA 595, 596; Cornsweet in 9 LA 625, 626; Rauch in 4 LA 170, 173. Also see Killingsworth in 19 LA 186, 187.

[190]See Arbitrator Howlett in 50 LA 978, 984; Seinsheimer in 42 LA 740, 745; Dworet in 41 LA 303, 304. Also see Feldman in 74 LA 1058, 1060.

[191]Jackson Elec. Instrument Co., 42 LA 740, 745 (Seinsheimer, 1964). Similarly, see Arbitrator Greer in 75 LA 612, 614; Caraway in 71 LA 1244, 1246. Also see Eaton in 68 LA 876, 880.

[192]E.g., Arbitrator Valtin in 79 LA 999, 1003–1004; Herman in 75 LA 449, 453; Eyraud in 72 LA 1178, 1180; Goodstein in 69 LA 1, 5; Carson in 68 LA 240, 241; Keefe in 50 LA 453 at 453;

trary.[193] Where clear and timely objection is made to time-limit violations, no waiver will result from subsequent processing of the grievance on the merits.[194] Indeed, it has been suggested that upon making timely objection to delayed filing, the objecting party ordinarily should then discuss the grievance on the merits so that all issues will be ready for presentation to an arbitrator if the case reaches that stage.[195] Under a less expeditious procedure the objecting party may refuse to entertain the grievance on the ground that it is null and void, forcing the grievant to file a second grievance involving the time issue alone; discussion of the original dispute on the merits would thus be delayed pending final resolution of the time issue.[196]

The particular contractual provision would appear to determine whether Saturdays, Sundays, holidays, and the day of the occurrence are to be counted in computing time.[197] An arbitrator might be inclined toward flexibility in applying a short time limit within which a holiday falls, provided the basic objective of prompt grievance processing is not seriously jeopardized.[198] Also, an arbitrator similarly believed that flexibility was needed where the agreement required grievances to be signed by the grieving employee and be filed within two "working days"; there Arbitrator Leo Weiss said the definition of the term "working days" may vary depending "on who it is that is being required to" act.[199]

Grievances are not always discovered at the time they occur. Some agreements provide specifically that grievances are to be filed

---

Wagner in 49 LA 1036, 1039; Roberts in 49 LA 214, 218; Dybeck in 48 LA 1085, 1087; Krimsly in 48 LA 802, 805–806; Merrill in 47 LA 1120, 1125; Fallon in 45 LA 271, 275–276; Teple in 45 LA 196, 201; Anderson in 44 LA 66, 72; Rice in 44 LA 16, 18; Stouffer in 63-1 ARB ¶8358; Willingham in 62-2 ARB ¶8464; Gorsuch in 41 LA 200, 203–205; Davey in 43 LA 453, 458; Autrey in 38 LA 400, 403; Wood in 32 LA 216, 219; Whiting in 28 LA 398, 400; Platt in 27 LA 685, 687; Klamon in 24 LA 869, 873; Ross in 24 LA 857, 859; Day in 22 LA 775, 778. Cf., Sharnoff in 75 LA 353, 361–362; Davey in 18 LA 497, 504. While parties gave persistent and prolonged consideration to a grievance over a period of three years, the contractual time limit was held not to bar the claim. Grace Lines, Inc., 39 LA 633, 635–636 (Shaughnessy, 1962). Similarly, see Arbitrator Roberts in 55 LA 210, 216–217. As long as the parties are still discussing the possibilities of settling a grievance at a given step, the time for proceeding to the next step of the grievance procedure might be held not to have started running. See Montgomery Ward & Co., 48 LA 1171, 1172–1173 (Updegraff, undated). However, management's expression of opinion that employees had no valid basis for complaint did not suffice to relieve them of the contractual time limit for filing their grievance. Kroger Co., 36 LA 270, 272 (Stouffer, 1960).

[193]See Arbitrator Tatum in 47 LA 563, 566; Sembower in 44 LA 304, 306–307; Schmertz in 39 LA 379, 381–382.

[194]See Arbitrator Boothe in 47 LA 336, 339; Scheiber in 43 LA 129, 136; Elkouri in 42 LA 153, 156.

[195]North Am. Aviation, 17 LA 715, 719 (Komaroff, 1951).

[196]Square D Co., 25 LA 225, 230 (Prasow, 1955).

[197]See Arbitrator Raffaele in 65 LA 894, 895; Ralston in 15 LA 640, 642–643; Ebeling in 11 LA 732, 737; Shulman in 1 ALAA ¶67,040. In Belknap, Inc., 69 LA 599, 601 (1977), Arbitrator Edwin R. Teple stated that he was "convinced that the 10-day period [specified by the agreement] was meant to indicate calendar days, which is the normal construction of 'day' unless the word is limited in some way, as when the labor contract refers to 'working days'."

[198]See Eimco Corp., 41 LA 1184, 1186–1187 (Dykstra, 1963). In Kent County, Mich., 75 LA 948, 951 (1980), Arbitrator Daniel H. Kruger applied a "rule of reason" in counting time during the Christmas holiday season.

[199]Indian Head, Inc., 71 LA 260, 262 (1978), where an employee was disciplined on Saturday and filed his grievance the following Wednesday, which was his next regularly scheduled workday. In holding the grievance timely, Arbitrator Weiss stated: "[T]he contract places the obligation on the grieving employee. He instigates the complaint and is required to sign it. The term 'working days' must then apply to his own work schedule."

within a certain number of days after they "occur or are discovered."[200] Even without such specific provision, arbitrators have
held that one cannot be expected to file a grievance until he is aware or
should be aware of the action upon which the grievance is based.[201]
But time limits "cannot be extended by the excuse that the grievant
just didn't think of it sooner."[202] Furthermore, where the employee
had knowledge of adverse action but did not speak up, the union will
not be heard to say that the time limit should be extended because the
union did not know.[203]

A party sometimes announces its intention to do a given act but
does not do or culminate the act until a later date. Similarly, a party
may do an act whose adverse effect upon another does not result until a
later date. In some such situations arbitrators have held that the
"occurrence" for purposes of applying time limits is at the later
date.[204] For example, where a company changed a seniority date on its
records as a correction, a grievance protesting the change was held
timely though not filed until nine months later; the arbitrator stated
that the basis of the grievance would be the employee's frustrated
attempt to exercise seniority rights based upon the old date, rather
than the mere change in the company's records.[205]

In this general connection, too, where a grievance protesting a
layoff was filed seven days after the employer signed the layoff notice,
the filing was held timely although the contract placed a five-day limit
on filing grievances; it was said to be reasonable to assume that two
days were required for the notice to reach the grievant.[206] In another
case the agreement required the company to give its answer to a
grievance within 10 days, but the arbitrator refused to determine the
allowed period on an "hour and minute" basis where the parties had
not previously applied their time limits so exactly.[207] The arbitrator
in this case also stated that delivery of the company's answer to the

[200]As in International Minerals & Chem. Co., 3 LA 405, 406 (Dwyer, 1946). Also see
Bethlehem Steel Corp., 46 LA 767, 768 (Strongin, 1966).

[201]See Arbitrator Flagler in 72 LA 479, 483; Goldstein in 69 LA 1, 5; Dennis in 68 LA 921,
923; Block in 48 LA 2, 8–9; Altieri in 42 LA 781, 784; Geissinger in 40 LA 1182, 1183; Donahue in
26 LA 501, 502–503; Holly in 24 LA 268, 271; Platt in 24 LA 141, 143; Willcox in 23 LA 21, 23;
Maggs in 19 LA 647, 649; Komaroff in 17 LA 715, 718. Also see Dworkin in 48 LA 83, 86; McCoy in
20 LA 416, 419.

[202]General Fireproofing Co., 48 LA 842, 848 (Teple, 1967). Also see Arbitrator Herman in 65
LA 368, 370.

[203]Ekco Prods. Co., 40 LA 1339, 1341 (Duff, 1963). Also see Arbitrator Christopher in 75 LA
1179, 1182 (grievant's desire to avoid "stirring things up" did not excuse late filing).

[204]See Arbitrator Berman in 75 LA 131, 133; Chandler in 73 LA 174, 177; Barnhart in 71 LA
1178, 1179; Caraway in 70 LA 930, 934; Swain in 69 LA 493, 497; Teple in 68 LA 1347, 1349;
Krimsly in 55 LA 14, 16; Dworkin in 46 LA 1021, 1027; Solomon in 46 LA 993, 997–999 (here the
"occurrence" was at an intermediate point); Tatum in 44 LA 373, 375; Schedler in 38 LA 259, 261;
Grant in 37 LA 1044, 1046; Komaroff in 26 LA 622, 626; Warren in 18 LA 662, 663–664. Cf.,
Sembower in 44 LA 304, 307; Komaroff in 19 LA 385, 387. In Square D Co., 25 LA 225, 228–229
(1955), Arbitrator Prasow held that an act occurred on the day it was announced, but there the
union itself had clearly recognized the existence of a grievance as of that day.

[205]Dayton Tire & Rubber Co., 46 LA 1021, 1027 (Dworkin, 1966). Also see Arbitrator Larkin
in 52 LA 633, 635–636.

[206]Torrington Co., 13 LA 323, 325 (Stutz, Mottram & Sviridoff, 1949).

[207]E.W. Bliss Co., 45 LA 1000, 1002–1003 (Lehoczky, 1965).

U.S. mail was equivalent to delivery to the union.[208] The combined effect of these two cases is that a time limit does not start running against a party until he is actually informed as to the other party's position, and his response will be timely if it is thereafter deposited in the mails within the time limitations period. This is consistent with the above-noted view that doubts as to the interpretation of contractual time limits or as to whether they have been met should be resolved against disposition of grievances by forfeiture.

Under some circumstances a party may be permitted to toll the running of time limits by giving notice to the other party of reasonable basis for delaying the filing of a grievance.[209]

Many arbitrators have held that "continuing" violations of the agreement (as opposed to a single isolated and completed transaction) give rise to "continuing" grievances in the sense that the act complained of may be said to be repeated from day to day—each day there is a new "occurrence"; these arbitrators have permitted the filing of such grievances at any time, this not being deemed a violation of the specific time limits stated in the agreement (although any back pay ordinarily runs only from the date of filing).[210] For example, where the agreement provided for filing "within ten working days of the occurrence," it was held that where employees were erroneously denied work, each day lost was to be considered a new "occurrence" and that a grievance presented within ten working days of any such day lost would be timely.[211]

Sometimes an agreement will provide that any grievance not appealed from one step to the next within a specified time shall be considered settled on the basis of the last answer. On one occasion this type of provision was applied strictly with the result that a grievance

---

[208]Id. at 1003. For other cases in which delivery to the U.S. mail of a grievance or an answer to a grievance within the time-limit period was held equivalent to delivery to the addressee, see Arbitrator Johannes in 75 LA 597, 601; Duff in 73 LA 80, 83; Goodstein in 72 LA 892, 895, and Lightner in 64 LA 428, 429 (in both of which cases the time limit was met by mailing although company testified it did not receive the document); Watkins in 63 LA 49, 50; Heilbrun in 61 LA 613, 616; Block in 61 LA 44, 51. But in a case involving notice for wage reopening, the arbitrator held the notice must be received by the specified date, and that the "presumption of the timely delivery in due course to the addressee of a letter properly posted" was rebutted by the evidence. Covington Furniture Mfg., 71 LA 105, 108 (Murphy, 1978).

[209]See American Smelting & Ref. Co., 29 LA 262, 265 (Ross, 1957). Also see Arbitrator Gibson in 69 LA 697, 704; Pierson in 13 LA 782, 786.

[210]E.g., Arbitrator Rotenberg in 81 LA 41, 48; Daniel in 74 LA 196, 198; Richman in 73 LA 405, 409; Abrams in 72 LA 470, 473; Cushman in 71 LA 412, 418; Morgan in 70 LA 1243, 1245; Eischen in 69 LA 1115, 1121; Boothe in 55 LA 23, 25; Slavney in 49 LA 1028, 1033–1034; Shister in 49 LA 480, 481–482; Williams in 48 LA 44, 45–46; Kates in 47 LA 1045, 1048; Altrock in 47 LA 408, 413; Teple in 46 LA 1106, 1109–1110; Murphy in 46 LA 289, 290–291; Dolnick in 45 LA 357, 360–361; Fallon in 45 LA 271, 275; Hayes in 44 LA 701, 703; Handsaker in 64-2 ARB ¶8789; McNaughton in 43 LA 1165, 1167; Kornblum in 43 LA 765, 767–768; Stouffer in 62-2 ARB ¶8504; Gillingham in 39 LA 567, 570; Gorsuch in 33 LA 135, 137; Warns in 28 LA 424, 428; Platt in 27 LA 262, 264–265; Cahn in 26 LA 649, 650–651; Seward in 23 LA 538, 540; Justin in 17 LA 303, 309; Gregory in 15 LA 147, 149; Hepburn in 14 LA 387, 388. Cf., Larkin in 47 LA 382, 383–384; Livengood in 27 LA 157, 159; Feinberg in 26 LA 550, 551–552; Aaron in 12 LA 786, 793–794. Retroactivity is not always limited to the date of filing. See Blaw-Knox Co., 50 LA 1086, 1089 (Meltzer, 1968). Also see Arbitrator Brown in 69 LA 897, 899–900.

[211]Pacific Mills, 14 LA 387, 388 (Hepburn, 1950).

which, by error, had been left unappealed until the time limit had expired was held to have been settled.[212]

Similarly, agreements sometimes contain express provision for granting grievances by default if the company fails to answer or take other required action within a stated time, and these "company default" provisions also have been strictly enforced.[213] However, in the absence of such express provision the failure of the foreman to answer within the prescribed time will not be interpreted as an admission of the grievance by default, since the grievant has the burden and right to carry the complaint to the next step following the lapse of the specified time.[214] But it has been emphasized that the foreman should make a decision or comment on each grievance.[215]

Observance of Grievance Procedure

Arbitrators recognize that the grievance procedure, when adhered to, advances peaceful and constructive industrial relations, with resultant benefits to labor, management, and the public. Moreover, arbitrators realize that the success of arbitration itself may be jeopardized if the grievance procedure is not carefully followed.

Arbitration awards show that arbitrators expect the parties to pay due respect to the grievance procedure, not only by using it, but also by observing its formal requirements. Such respect is in the nature of a "condition precedent." In some cases it is a condition precedent to an award of requested relief. In these cases the arbitrator takes jurisdiction but, upon learning of the grievant's failure to fulfill the condition precedent, denies relief, in whole or in part. In other cases it is a condition precedent to the assumption of jurisdiction by the arbitrator. The requirement that these conditions precedent be met is somewhat analogous to the requirement by the courts that the administrative remedy, if any, be exhausted before the court will give relief.

---

[212]Chrysler Corp., 1 ALAA ¶67,017 (1945). In several other cases, too, such "default" type provisions have been strictly enforced. See Arbitrator Dworkin in 44 LA 878, 882–883; Ryder in 41 LA 8, 10 (nor could the issue be revived by filing another grievance, based upon the same incident, in the name of another employee); Platt in 25 LA 437, 438. Where the union on two occasions told the employer a discharge grievance was being withdrawn from the grievance procedure, it could not be reintroduced later. Associated Grocers of Colo., 74 LA 141, 143 (Finston, 1980). Also see Arbitrator LeWinter in 74 LA 37, 39.

[213]See Arbitrator Roberts in 81 LA 149, 155–156; Feldman in 75 LA 137, 140–141; Culley in 69 LA 912, 916; Allen in 63 LA 542, 544; Duff in 25 LA 534, 537–538. Cf., Sanders in 33 LA 553, 555–556.

[214]See Arbitrator Johnston in 69 LA 604, 608–609; Conant in 68 LA 663, 668; Steele in 60 LA 1291, 1295; Sembower in 43 LA 165, 168; Emery in 37 LA 1103, 1104; Seligson in 26 LA 393, 394; Boles in 24 LA 295, 299; Updegraff in 3 LA 737, 742–743. The "authority" to refer a grievance to the next step is said to rest with the grievant, not with the foreman. Ford Motor Co., 3 LA 840 at 840 (Shulman, 1946).

[215]Ford Motor Co., 3 LA 840, 841 (Shulman, 1946). Also see Bethlehem Steel Co., 19 LA 521, 522 (Feinberg, 1952). Some agreements require the foreman's response to be in writing. "Basic Patterns in Labor Arbitration Agreements," 34 LA 931, 933 (1960). Absent such provision, an oral response to a grievance within the contractual five-day time limit was held to suffice and not to be invalidated by a written response after that time limit. Warren Co., 39 LA 395, 398 (Woodruff, 1962).

Use of Grievance Procedure Versus Self-Help

Arbitrators often deny or limit requested relief, notwithstanding the merits of the original complaint, where the grievant has resorted to self-help rather than to the grievance procedure. Many arbitrators have taken the position that employees must not take matters into their own hands but must obey orders and carry out their assignments, even if believed to violate the agreement, then turn to the grievance procedure for relief.[216]

The fact that employees acted by "advice of counsel" has been held not to provide a defense or justification for self-help.[217] Nor is a refusal to obey management's orders immunized by the fact that the employee was "caught in the middle" between company and union, though this fact might be reason for reducing the penalty.[218] In regard to reducing the penalty, the offense of disobeying orders has sometimes been considered to have been mitigated somewhat where the initial refusal to obey was followed by obedience.[219]

An important exception to the general rule against resorting to self-help exists where obedience to orders would involve an unusual health hazard or similar sacrifice.[220] This exception is discussed in detail in this book's chapter on Safety and Health.[221]

Some arbitrators have recognized other possible exceptions to the duty to obey orders, as where the order commands the performance of an immoral or criminal act;[222] or where the employee has a right to

---

[216]For many cases, see p. 155 of Third Edition of this book. For some of the many later cases, see Arbitrator Dash in 75 LA 170, 175; O'Neill in 74 LA 99, 105; Friedman in 74 LA 15, 17; Maroney in 73 LA 1273, 1277; Jedel in 73 LA 581, 587; Dawson in 73 LA 86, 89; Cromwell in 73 LA 549, 551; Wallace in 72 LA 1093, 1095; Doyle in 72 LA 1033, 1035; Cohen in 72 LA 824, 828; Gootnick in 72 LA 735, 736; Chalfie in 72 LA 668, 674; Daniel in 72 LA 591, 594; Kanner in 72 LA 564, 566; Craver in 72 LA 405, 407; Ferguson in 72 LA 164, 167, 169; McDonald in 71 LA 1199, 1202; Caraway in 71 LA 1148, 1150; Madden in 71 LA 555, 566; Spritzer in 71 LA 222, 226; Robins in 70 LA 1144, 1147; Ipavec in 70 LA 1058, 1060; Talent in 70 LA 335, 337; Turkus in 70 LA 285, 287; Roberts in 70 LA 278, 282; Norman in 70 LA 1, 3; Letson in 69 LA 792, 794; Hunter in 69 LA 727, 731; Rimer in 69 LA 582, 586; Beck in 69 LA 502, 506; Lipson in 69 LA 93, 99; Mullaly in 69 LA 64, 67; Simon in 68 LA 1010, 1014; Fox in 68 LA 773, 778; Purcell in 68 LA 517, 521–526; Sabo in 68 LA 391, 396; Boals in 68 LA 291, 295–296. In most of the above cases the grievant's action in taking matters into his own hands was a significant factor in the arbitrator's decision to deny the grievance or to grant relief in part only. However, the fact that employees may be penalized for resorting to self-help does not constitute a waiver of the union's right to arbitrate the issue which had led to the self-help. Mansfield Tire & Rubber Co., 36 LA 1348, 1351 (Teple, 1961), where the propriety of a contested work assignment was held arbitrable.

[217]Robertshaw-Fulton Controls Co., 36 LA 4, 9 (Hilpert, 1961). Accord, Arbitrator Rimer in 73 LA 921, 923–924; LeBaron in 73 LA 455, 463. Cf., Hebert in 39 LA 419, 430.

[218]See Safeway Stores, 51 LA 413, 416–417 (Gillingham, 1967). Contra, Costa Readymix, 38 LA 200, 204–205 (Koven, 1962).

[219]For example, see Arbitrator Kanner in 69 LA 787, 789; Stutz in 28 LA 255, 257; Reynard in 24 LA 66, 71.

[220]This exception was expressly noted by many of the arbitrators cited hereinabove as authority for the general rule.

[221]See Chapter 16, topics entitled "Refusal to Obey Orders—The Safety Exception," and "Employee Complaints of Specific Hazards."

[222]This possible exception was recognized but did not apply in Temco Aircraft Corp., 29 LA 693, 696 (Boles, 1957). In Univac Div., 48 LA 619, 620–621 (1967), Arbitrator Cahn stated that an employee's personal moral or religious beliefs do not excuse a refusal to obey orders. Also see Arbitrator Kelliher in 63 LA 251, 252. But see Krislov in 61 LA 14, 15. Exceptions to the general rule might exist as to an order which would humiliate the employee (see Arbitrator McCoy in 34 LA 689 at 689) or which would invade some personal right which the arbitrator considers inviolable (see Arbitrator Williams in 52 LA 57, 59).

union representation which would be denied by obedience to the order;[223] or where the order violates the rights or domain of the union itself by interfering with the union's contractual right to investigate and process grievances;[224] or where an order interferes with the employee's proper use of the grievance procedure;[225] or where the order commands a skilled craftsman to perform work wholly unrelated to his craft;[226] or where the order "is *quite clearly and indisputably* beyond the authority of" the company.[227] In certain other situations, too, arbitrators have recognized an exception to the general duty to obey management's orders.[228]

Although disobedience to orders or work assignments may be immunized as to those employees who are directly covered by one of the aforementioned exceptions and who are acting individually, this does not mean that otherwise improper group or concert action to force concessions from the employer will be permitted.[229] Even where a fact situation brings one of the exceptions into play, the exception might be deemed to give only personal and individual immunity to employees.[230] Similarly, some actions which may properly be taken by indi-

---

[223]See Arbitrator Peterschmidt in 72 LA 437, 439, 441; Block in 61 LA 453, 463; Teple in 39 LA 784, 788–789; Anderson in 33 LA 769, 771. For related discussion see this Chapter's subtopic entitled "Right to Union Representation at Early Stage."

[224]See Arbitrator Klein in 68 LA 124, 127–128; Kinyon in 35 LA 873, 880; McCoy in 16 LA 307, 310–311; Shulman in 10 LA 213, 214. Also see Whelan in 41 LA 1288, 1297–1299; Mittenthal in 39 LA 238, 241; Maguire in 36 LA 1193, 1195–1196. Cf., Porter in 50 LA 1140, 1142; Williams in 39 LA 934, 936–937.

[225]See Arbitrator McNaughton in 40 LA 1100, 1102; Williams in 27 LA 892, 900; Rosenfarb in 18 LA 418, 428. In Nuclear Fuel Servs., 53 LA 252, 255–256 (King, 1969), another exception was found where the refusal to obey an order resulted from the company's own failure to honor the grievance procedure. In Goodyear Atomic Corp., 71 LA 619, 622 (Gibson, 1978), the fact that the grievance procedure was burdened by a large backlog did not excuse the refusal to obey an order instead of turning to the grievance procedure.

[226]See Ironrite, Inc., 28 LA 394, 397 (Haughton, 1956); Ford Motor Co., 3 LA 782, 783 (Shulman, 1946). However, Arbitrator Shulman declared that this exception would apply in rare cases only, in 19 LA 237, 238–239, and this limitation was again emphasized by Arbitrator Platt in 30 LA 46, 55. In Sheller Mfg. Corp., 34 LA 689, 692 (McCoy, 1960), a related exception was recognized as to orders which have no reasonable relation to the employee's job duties. Also see Arbitrator Block in 55 LA 690, 693–694. Here again, however, the exception may be viewed as a narrow one. See Arbitrator Solomon in 42 LA 1, 11–12.

[227]Dwight Mfg. Co., 12 LA 990, 996 (McCoy, 1949). Also see Ross Clay Prods. Co., 43 LA 159, 163–164 (Kabaker, 1964), permitting self-help where the employer acted directly contrary to an arbitration award which had just been issued. Some arbitrators have held that employees need not obey orders to work overtime where the contract permits them to refuse such work. See Arbitrator Sembower in 48 LA 492, 497; McCoy in 48 LA 61, 63; Begley in 27 LA 458, 461–463; Maggs in 17 LA 606, 609–610. Also see Burr in 37 LA 275, 277. Cf., Seitz in 53 LA 200, 202–203; Geissinger in 50 LA 181, 185; Mullins in 44 LA 141, 144; Hilpert in 36 LA 4, 8–10; Wollet in 34 LA 925, 927–928; Young in 21 LA 145, 150; Fuchs in 15 LA 645, 651. In Equitable Bag Co., 52 LA 1234, 1237–1238 (Hayes, 1969), an employee could not be punished for refusing to attend fire-fighting training on overtime, the Arbitrator stating that an employee cannot be punished for refusing to train for a job which he cannot be required to perform (fire fighting as distinguished from fire prevention). Cf., Arbitrator Rothschild in 80 LA 601, 604–605. In Marion Power Shovel Div., 72 LA 417, 420 (1979), Arbitrator Kates found an "unmistakable specific right of refusal" of temporary transfer, so an employee could not be disciplined for disobeying an order to accept one.

[228]See Arbitrator Weiss in 76 LA 921, 922; Jones in 72 LA 747, 749–750; Dallas in 70 LA 28, 33; Duff in 55 LA 862, 864–865; Sembower in 55 LA 731, 743; Krimsly in 54 LA 604, 606; Lennard in 54 LA 574, 575–576.

[229]See Arbitrator Mullin in 47 LA 848, 854, and in 44 LA 141, 144; Altrock in 47 LA 621, 627–628; Volz in 43 LA 849, 853–854; Platt in 41 LA 609, 615.

[230]Ibid. To illustrate, employees not affected by a safety hazard would not be justified in using self-help instead of the grievance procedure. Metal Specialty Co., 43 LA 849, 853–854 (Volz, 1964).

viduals for individual reasons might be improper when taken as a group or concert action for a group objective. For example, where employees as a group refused to report for early morning "start up" work, Arbitrator Saul Wallen held the group action improper even assuming that the work was voluntary to the extent that individual employees, for individual reasons, could refuse the work:

> "Such individual right to refuse work as may be inherent in the Agreement was intended to be motivated by purely individual reasons, not by a desire to join with others to compel a solution to a problem by group action—or inaction. The settlement of grievances or other disputes during the life of the Agreement is supposed to be accomplished by means of the grievance procedure and arbitration, not by group refusals to perform work. And if the problem is one not compassable by those procedures, it must remain to be handled in negotiations at expiration time."[231]

Union representatives should not instruct employees to disobey management's orders.[232] Indeed, many arbitrators have recognized a special responsibility on the part of union leaders to uphold the agreement and to take affirmative action to persuade employees to use the grievance procedure for matters subject thereto in lieu of taking matters into their own hands (as by refusing to obey orders or by striking in violation of a no-strike obligation).[233] However, while many arbitrators have recognized the special responsibility, they have disagreed (at least prior to the U.S. Supreme Court's 1983 *Metropolitan Edison* decision) as to what discipline, if any, may be assessed against union officers for failure to fulfill that special responsibility. Arbitrators have generally agreed that union officers may be disciplined more severely than other employees where the officers have urged or led other employees to engage in misconduct under the agreement. The disputed question has been whether officers who have participated in misconduct, but not as an instigator or leader, should

---

[231]Fitchburg Paper Co., 47 LA 349, 352 (Wallen, 1966). Similar results were reached in Pratt & Whitney, 53 LA 69, 71–72 (Feinberg, 1969).

[232]See Arbitrator Guenther in 73 LA 551, 555–556; Strong in 39 LA 1080, 1081–1082; Abrahams in 37 LA 76, 81–82; Abersold in 37 LA 62, 71–74; Feinberg in 19 LA 43, 46–47; Kerr in 11 LA 219, 221–222; Scheiber in 7 LA 3, 4–7; Shulman in 3 LA 779, 780. An exception has been recognized, however, as to "action falling primarily within the Union's domain." Ford Motor Co., 10 LA 213, 214 (Shulman, 1948). The existence of a grievance procedure, and particularly the availability of arbitration, for resolving a dispute implies a no-strike obligation even if there is no express no-strike clause in the contract (or if such a clause is too narrow to cover the dispute). See Ingersoll-Rand Co., 51 LA 83, 88 (Teple, 1968); Trailways of New Eng., 46 LA 369, 371 (Wallen, 1965); Teamsters v. Lucas Flour Co., 369 U.S. 95, 49 LRRM 2717 (1962).

[233]See Arbitrator Wolff in 77 LA 1038, 1040–1042; Madden in 71 LA 555, 565; Elbert in 69 LA 102, 114; Lipson in 69 LA 93, 101; Byars in 65 LA 1245, 1248; Stashower in 64 LA 425, 428; Karasick in 60 LA 109, 117; Belcher in 53 LA 154, 157–158; Oppenheim in 52 LA 1047, 1050; Graff in 50 LA 1029, 1032–1034; Turkus in 50 LA 691, 692–694; King in 49 LA 27, 33; Schmertz in 47 LA 1100, 1100–1102; Summers in 47 LA 369, 370; Kennedy in 45 LA 976, 979; Larkin in 45 LA 81, 85; Koven in 43 LA 644, 649; Dworet in 43 LA 608, 609; Davis in 43 LA 182, 189; Markowitz in 41 LA 732, 735; Platt in 41 LA 609, 613–615; Burr in 39 LA 688, 690–691; Volz in 37 LA 401, 406; Koretz in 37 LA 36, 42; Crawford in 36 LA 214, 215; Wallen in 34 LA 325, 328; Bothwell in 33 LA 594, 601; Kelliher in 29 LA 622, 623–624; Howlett in 29 LA 495, 497; Sembower in 25 LA 774, 777; Feinberg in 21 LA 421, 424; Laskin in 18 LA 919, 923–924; Seward in 14 LA 986, 988–989; Gilden in 8 LA 758, 769–770; Shipman in 2 LA 194, 198–199. Contra, McCoy in 33 LA 807, 808.

be more vulnerable to discipline than other offenders because of the officer's special responsibility.[234]

Under the NLRA, opinion also was divided on the latter question prior to the U.S. Supreme Court's 1983 *Metropolitan Edison* decision. The Supreme Court decided the question in favor of union officials, although it did recognize that their statutory protection can be waived by the union. The decision teaches that under the NLRA:

- A general no-strike clause does not impose a higher duty upon union officials than upon other employees to prevent illicit work stoppages, and NLRA § 8(a)(3) protects union officials against being disciplined more severely than other employees for like misconduct.
- This NLRA protection can be waived by the union, but any waiver of the statutory right must be "explicitly stated," or "More succinctly, the waiver must be clear and unmistakable."[235]

The Supreme Court stated in *Metropolitan Edison* that the case did "not present the question whether an employer may impose stricter penalties on union officials who take a leadership role in an unlawful strike," but the Court noted that where presented in other cases the NLRB had answered the question in the affirmative.[236]

The overall necessity for observing the grievance procedure is effectively explained in the following statement of Umpire Harry Shulman:

---

[234]Examination of the cases cited in the preceding footnote reveals that many arbitrators answered this question in the affirmative, but some disagreed. For example, in Stokley-Van Camp, 60 LA 109, 117 (1973), Arbitrator Karasick upheld the more severe discipline of union officers, explaining that they "had the duty of setting an example for their fellow employees," and if the employees "could not be induced to return to work, the union officers should have gone back to their jobs." Illustrating the other view, however, Arbitrator Stashower stated in Stevens Air Sys., 64 LA 425, 428 (1975), that "a Union official bears a higher responsibility * * * [but] is entitled to the same treatment as any other employee, and cannot be singled out." For cases involving claims against the union for alleged failure to make reasonable effort to prevent or terminate unauthorized work stoppages, see Arbitrator Eigenbrod in 75 LA 189, 196; Goodstein in 72 LA 1127, 1130; Scheib in 52 LA 74, 78; Kabaker in 50 LA 683, 689–690; Turkus in 50 LA 691, 692–694; Kelliher in 47 LA 610, 613; House in 47 LA 567, 572–574; Platt in 43 LA 785, 788. In Carbon Fuel Co. v. United Mine Workers, 100 S.Ct. 410, 413, 416 (1979), the U.S. Supreme Court held an international union not liable under the LMRA for failure to use reasonable efforts to prevent or end "wildcat" strikes by local unions where it was not shown that the International was "responsible according to the common-law rule of agency." Here there was no evidence that the International had instigated, supported, ratified, or encouraged any of the work stoppages. The employer's reliance upon the arbitration and "integrity" clauses of the national agreement was rejected, the bargaining history showing that the parties "purposely decided not to impose" the alleged obligation upon the International. Also see United Mine Workers v. Gibbs, 86 S.Ct. 1130 (1966).

[235]Metropolitan Edison Co. v. NLRB, 103 S.Ct. 1467, 1475, 1477–1478, 112 LRRM 3265 (1983). For more on the *Metropolitan Edison* decision, see Chapter 11, subtopic entitled "Temporary Arbitrators."

[236]103 S.Ct. at 1472. Regarding the NLRB's view on this aspect, the Court stated:

"The Board has held that employees who instigate or provide leadership for unprotected strikes may be subject to more severe discipline than other employees. * * * In making this factual determination the board has recognized that a remark made by a union official may have greater significance than one made by a rank-and-file member."

In the latter regard, also see statement of Arbitrator Cromwell in General Shale Corp., 80 LA 375, 377 (undated).

"Some men apparently think that, when a violation of contract seems clear, the employee may refuse to obey and thus resort to self-help rather than the grievance procedure. That is an erroneous point of view. In the first place, what appears to one party to be a clear violation may not seem so at all to the other party. Neither party can be the final judge as to whether the contract has been violated. The determination of that issue rests in collective negotiation through the grievance procedure. But, in the second place, and more important, the grievance procedure is prescribed in the contract precisely because the parties anticipated that there would be claims of violations which would require adjustment. That procedure is prescribed for all grievances, not merely for doubtful ones. Nothing in the contract even suggests the idea that only doubtful violations need be processed through the grievance procedure and that clear violations can be resisted through individual self-help. The only difference between a 'clear' violation and a 'doubtful' one is that the former makes a clear grievance and the latter a doubtful one. But both must be handled in the regular prescribed manner."[237]

Umpire Shulman observed further that:

"When a controversy arises, production cannot wait for exhaustion of the grievance procedure. While that procedure is being pursued, production must go on. And someone must have the authority to direct the manner in which it is to go on until the controversy is settled. That authority is vested in supervision. It must be vested there because the responsibility for production is also vested there; and responsibility must be accompanied by authority. It is fairly vested there because the grievance procedure is capable of adequately recompensing employees for abuse of authority by supervision."[238]

Company Obligation to Honor Grievance Procedure

In a number of cases arbitrators have emphasized management's obligation to preserve the integrity of the grievance procedure.[239] For example, in view of the obligation to utilize fully the possibilities of settlement inherent in the grievance procedure, an employer was held to have acted improperly in bypassing the union committee which represented certain grievants and communicating an offer of settlement directly to the grievants themselves.[240]

The company in another case was held to have an obligation to furnish information to the union, upon request, as to how the company

---

[237]Ford Motor Co., 3 LA 779, 780–781 (1944).

[238]Id. at 781. However, Umpire Shulman recognized the "unusual health hazard or similar sacrifice" exception to the duty to obey orders. Id. at 782. The Shulman reasoning regarding the "work now and grieve later" concept was quoted in Amax Lead Co., 70 LA 1, 3 (1978), where Arbitrator Norman stressed that the reasoning "is not new, neither is it out of date." Also see Arbitrator Archibald Cox in 60 LA 78, 83. For a very strong statement as to the obligation of both parties to observe the grievance procedure and preserve its integrity, see Arbitrator Healy in Gregg & Sons, 45 LA 981, 984–985 (1965).

[239]For a very strong statement as to the company's duty in this regard, see Arbitrator Healy in Gregg & Sons, 45 LA 981, 984–985 (1965).

[240]Central Franklin Process Co., 17 LA 142, 145 (Marshall, 1951).

had complied with a settlement reached in the grievance procedure so the union could determine if the settlement was carried out.[241]

In another situation, where an arbitrator found that management had a contractual obligation to exhaust the negotiation machinery before resorting to disciplinary action, management's failure to do so was held to be sufficient basis for reinstating discharged employees, although the discharges were otherwise justified.[242] However, absent such contractual requirement the employer need not resort to the grievance procedure before punishing an employee for misconduct.[243]

In a "slowdown" case the arbitrator condemned the company for taking "the law into its own hands" by assessing a wage cut for the slowdown instead of utilizing the "adequate grievance provisions" or other remedies available under the contract (including the right to discipline or lockout employees engaged in the slowdown).[244]

It may be noted that some agreements require maintenance of the status quo pending grievance settlement, both parties being obligated to maintain the conditions prevailing immediately prior to some stated point (such as prior to the incident or prior to filing the grievance).[245]

Exhaustion of Grievance Procedure as Condition Precedent for Arbitration

A limitation by arbitrators of their jurisdiction to cases which the parties have made bona fide efforts to settle can be expected to result in improved handling of grievances at the lower levels. The National War Labor Board learned from experience that settlements through negotiations are encouraged when arbitrators refuse to take jurisdiction over grievance issues until the parties show that they have exhausted all chances of settlement through negotiations.[246] Arbitrators can do this unless the agreement permits direct resort to arbitration.[247] A New York court, in granting an employer's motion

---

[241]North Am. Aviation, 17 LA 121, 124–125 (Komaroff, 1951). For related material, see this Chapter, topic entitled "Attitude of Parties to the Grievance Procedure."

[242]Gloucester, Mass. Fisheries, 1 ALAA ¶67,340 (1946). Also see Arbitrator Miller in 35 LA 757, 780. In San Angelo Packing Co., 52 LA 261, 263 (Sartain, 1969), an otherwise justified discharge was set aside because the employer refused to participate in meetings on the discharge grievance as required by the agreement. Similarly, see Arbitrator Daly in 52 LA 306, 309.

[243]Falls Stamping & Welding Co., 48 LA 107, 113 (Dworkin, 1967). Nor was the employer required to use the grievance procedure instead of direct punishment by virtue of the added fact that the actions for which the employee was punished might have been done in his role as a union officer. Beckett Paper Co., 51 LA 936, 939–940 (Gibson, 1968). Accord, Arbitrator Wolff in 33 LA 112, 123. Contra, Arbitrator Gray in 31 LA 144, 145.

[244]Jacobs Mfg. Co., 29 LA 512, 517–518 (Scheiber, 1957). Similarly, see Arbitrator Roberts in 69 LA 623, 630.

[245]See McCall Corp., 43 LA 951, 954, 956 (Layman, 1964). Regarding the employer's obligation concerning the photographic preservation of evidence for the grievance procedure, see Airco Alloys & Carbide, 63 LA 395, 398–399 (Sembower, 1974).

[246]Aluminum Co. of Am., 12 War Lab. Rep. 446, 455 (1943).

[247]For instance, where the grievance procedure had not been exhausted the dispute was held to be nonarbitrable by Arbitrator Goldberg in 46 LA 1131, 1138; Blair in 39 LA 760, 762–763; Feinberg in 20 LA 675, 678; Komaroff in 19 LA 729, 731–733. Also see Nichols in 51 LA 79, 82–83; Dworkin in 46 LA 941, 945. For related discussion, see Chapter 7, topic entitled "Extent of Permissible Deviation From Prearbitral Discussion of Case."

for a stay of arbitration, spoke of the requirement that conditions precedent be performed prior to arbitration:

> "One of the preliminary steps, viz. submission to the grievance committee of the association, was omitted entirely as were other steps in connection with some of the issues tendered for arbitration. No explanation is here given for such omission or neglect. It was incumbent upon the union, under the terms of the contract, to exhaust all other methods of conciliation as provided for therein before it could invoke the remedy of arbitration. Until it complies with the conditions of the contract in respect to all the essential acts on its part to be performed or offers a reasonable and just excuse for non-performance, the union will be enjoined from proceeding with the arbitration."[248]

The critical nature of some disputes leads the parties to stipulate that all prearbitral steps are waived and that the dispute is to be taken directly to arbitration.[249] The agreement itself may provide for the direct appeal of such disputes to arbitration, but this type of provision has been held inapplicable to ordinary employee grievances.[250]

A party who refuses to comply or fails to comply properly with the negotiation steps of the grievance procedure will not be permitted to prevent arbitration on the ground that the grievance procedure has not been exhausted.[251] Nor must the grievance procedure be exhausted where to do so would be "futile,"[252] or a "useless and idle gesture,"[253] or where compliance with the prearbitral grievance procedure has been rendered unrealistic or impossible by plant closure or removal.[254]

Then, too, if an agreement provides only an informal type of grievance procedure, the arbitrator may not be exacting as to the preliminaries necessary to give him jurisdiction. Arbitrator William E. Simkin has stated, for instance, that to give an arbitrator jurisdiction in such a case it is necessary only that the issue be one on which the parties have had some prior discussion and on which the

---

[248]In re Picture Frame Workers Union, 8 LA 1063, 1064 (N.Y. Sup. Ct., 1947). If the federal law applies to the case, questions of procedural arbitrability (such as whether the preliminary steps of the grievance procedure have been exhausted or excused) are to be decided by the arbitrator. John Wiley & Sons v. Livingston, 84 S.Ct. 909, 918–919, 55 LRRM 2769 (1964). But note the situation involved in Philadelphia Newspapers, 68 LA 401, 405 (Jaffee, 1977). For related discussions, see Chapter 6, Determining Arbitrability.

[249]See Arbitrator Simon in 68 LA 797, 799; Hayes in 47 LA 449 at 449; Smith in 25 LA 663, 664.

[250]Ford Motor Co., 1 ALAA ¶67,030 (1944). The agreement also provided for direct appeal in New Orleans S.S. Assn., 45 LA 1099, 1101 (Oppenheim, 1965).

[251]City of Meriden, 48 LA 137, 140–141 (Summers, 1967), involving improper compliance with lower steps. Also, Glass Bottle Blowers v. Arkansas Corp., 35 LA 153, 46 LRRM 2950 (USDC, 1960), and Brynmore Press, 8 LA 511, 512–514 (Rains, 1947), involving refusal to comply with lower steps.

[252]Barbet Mills, Inc., 16 LA 563, 565 (Livengood, 1951). Also, In re Roto Supply Sales Co., 28 LA 657, 658 (N.Y. Sup. Ct., 1957).

[253]In re Greenstone, 29 LA 161, 162 (N.Y. Sup. Ct., 1957). To similar effect, General Tire & Rubber Co. v. Rubber Workers, 37 LA 496, 49 LRRM 2001 (USDC, 1961). In Avco Corp., 65 LA 1195, 1199–1200 (Taylor, 1975), the union requested a default judgment based upon the employer's refusal to participate in separate step-two hearings on each of 37 identical grievances, but the request was denied since the grievants were not unduly prejudiced by the procedure utilized by the employer, though it did not comply literally with that specified in the agreement.

[254]H.K. Porter Co., 49 LA 147, 153–154 (Cahn, 1967); Sidele Fashions, 36 LA 1364, 1369 (Dash, 1961).

"realistic possibilities" of settlement at the lower grievance steps have been exhausted.[255]

Finally, the right to object that the grievance procedure has not been exhausted may be held waived by agreeing to arbitrate the dispute without raising any issue as to exhaustion of prearbitral steps.[256]

Grievance Settlements as Binding Precedents

It is to be expected that a mutual settlement of a grievance by the parties ordinarily will be held binding upon them insofar as the particular instance is involved.[257] It also seems obvious that where a grievance has been settled by mutual agreement of the parties, the same issue that is involved in such "settled" grievance, though appearing in the guise of another grievance, should not ordinarily be subject to arbitration at the request of only one party (or, if the issue does reach arbitration, the prior settlement should constitute a binding precedent). "It is essential to good labor-management relations * * * that grievance settlements not be disturbed in the absence of a conclusive showing of changed conditions."[258] One arbitrator would add that settlements are open to investigation on substantial charge of fraud or grievous error.[259] Another arbitrator would not consider a

---

[255]Reading St. Ry., 8 LA 930, 933 (1947).

[256]United Tavern, 16 LA 210, 214 (Slavney, 1951).

[257]See Arbitrator Marcus in 73 LA 194, 195–196; Bloch in 59 LA 235, 238; Kates in 48 LA 1361, 1364. Where necessary, a subsequent grievance may be filed on the question of the other party's compliance with the prior settlement. Lockheed Aircraft Serv. Co., 44 LA 51, 58–59 (Roberts, 1965). Of similar essence, Arbitrator Morgan in 47 LA 756, 759; Turkus in 40 LA 504, 506. Another possible means of enforcing grievance settlements is court action under LMRA § 301. See General Drivers Local 89 v. Riss & Co., 83 S.Ct. 789 (1963); Amalgamated Meat Cutters & Butcher Workmen v. M. Feder & Co., 224 F. Supp. 739 (USDC, 1963). Also see Mine Workers v. Barnes & Tucker Co., 96 LRRM 2144 (CA 3, 1977). Regarding the NLRB's policy of deferring under certain circumstances to voluntary settlements, see Roadway Express, Inc. v. NLRB, 107 LRRM 2155 (CA 4, 1981).

[258]Standard Oil Co. (Ind.), 13 LA 799, 800 (Kelliher, 1949). In general accord, Arbitrator McCoy in 49 LA 82, 83; Barnhart in 45 LA 300, 301; Emery in 19 LA 812, 814; Wallen in 17 LA 36, 39–40; Blumer in 7 LA 378, 380. Essentially contra, Raimon in 36 LA 621, 625 (particularly as to lower step settlements); Brandschain in 15 LA 672, 673. Arbitrator J.K. Hayes found no binding precedent in a prior settlement since, he stated, "one settlement does not make for a past practice." Consolidated Aluminum Corp., 53 LA 122, 124 (1969). In Vulcan Mold & Iron Co., 41 LA 59, 60–61 (1963), Arbitrator Brecht held that even where an issue has been arbitrated, the award cannot constitute a bar to the arbitration of similar issues—the earlier award would influence the subsequent arbitrator but would not bar the issue from arbitration. Regarding the latter view, see discussion in Chapter 11, topic entitled "Authoritative Prior Awards."

[259]Tennessee Coal, Iron & R.R., 7 LA 378, 380 (Blumer, 1947). No precedent will exist where it is uncertain whether any settlement was ever reached. See National Cash Register Co., 47 LA 248, 250–251 (Nichols, 1966). And of course a settlement will not bind future cases if it was reached with the understanding that it not establish a precedent for any future case. For example, see Arbitrator Roumell in 73 LA 1129, 1132; Hunter in 69 LA 727, 728; Gilden in 50 LA 300, 302. In an effort to encourage settlement of grievances short of arbitration, the coal industry adopted a contractual provision in 1978 placing settlements reached at the first step of the grievance procedure on a nonprecedential basis. See discussion in The President's Commission on Coal, Labor-Management Seminar I, Collective Bargaining (Mar. 21, 1979) 11–12, 26, 52, U.S. Govt. Printing Office: 1979, 0–302–756; The President's Commission on Coal, Labor-Management Seminar IV, Grievance and Arbitration Procedures (June 20, 1979) 23, 43 ("non-precedential effect of settlements or withdrawals at step one has encouraged resolution of complaints" there) 53 (the provision "is working fine at some member company mines, and at other company mines, it does not work that well"), U.S. Govt. Printing Office: 1979, 0–302–759.

prior grievance settlement to be a binding precedent where "the basis for the joint disposition of the previous grievance is sufficiently clouded to preclude its automatic application" when the same issue reaches him.[260]

Aside from any effect of mutual settlements as binding precedents, such settlements may be accepted by an arbitrator as indicating the proper interpretation of ambiguous contract language. It has been observed, in this regard, that "Where the parties themselves settle a grievance the evidence of intent as to the meaning of a provision carries special weight."[261]

Somewhat different considerations are involved, however, where a grievance has not been mutually settled, but simply has been denied by management at some prearbitral step of the grievance procedure and, for various possible reasons, has not been appealed further. If management's denial of a grievance is "accepted" by the union so as to provide the elements of a "settlement" an arbitrator might consider it a binding precedent.[262] But numerous arbitrators have held that the mere failure to appeal a grievance is not per se acquiescence in the disposition of the issue on the basis of management's final answer so as to bar the issue from arbitration in a subsequent case.[263] This is particularly so where withdrawal of a case from the grievance procedure is done "without prejudice,"[264] or where the withdrawing party indicates that it intends ultimately to seek an arbitral ruling on the issue.[265] To insure against the possibility of a binding precedent, a party apparently is well advised to state some such condition in deciding not to appeal a grievance further.[266]

Sometimes the collective agreement deals specifically with this matter. For example, under a clause providing that grievances not appealed to arbitration were "to be considered settled on the basis of the decision last made," Arbitrator Harry H. Platt refused to decide an

---

[260]Neches Butane Prods. Co., 70 LA 1251, 1253 (Bailey, 1978). Similarly, in Federal Aviation Admin., 68 LA 1213, 1217 (Yarowsky, 1977), settlement of a similar grievance at another location of the federal agency employer was held to "have no binding precedential effect because only the *result* of the informal grievance [settlement] is known." That Arbitrator believed that "it would be necessary to analyze the totality of circumstances before one could gain a perspective" regarding the settlement; "no record was made of [the settlement conferences] and as a result they lack binding effect on a subsequent grievance arbitration." Ibid.

[261]Bendix-Westinghouse Automotive Air Brake Co., 23 LA 706, 710 (Mathews, 1954). Similarly, see Washington Hosp. v. Hospital Employees, 97 LRRM 2485, 2486 (USDC, 1978); Arbitrator Winton in 78 LA 401, 404; Block in 61 LA 453, 459–460; Ray in 50 LA 265, 267. But a prior settlement could not operate to amend a clear and unambiguous provision of the agreement in Lukens Steel Co., 35 LA 246, 248 (Crawford, 1960). Similarly, see Arbitrator McKenna in 72 LA 96, 100–101. As to a matter not treated by the collective agreement, a settlement may amount to a special agreement governing future rights of the parties. See Peoples Gas Light & Coke Co., 39 LA 224, 225–226 (Davis, 1962).

[262]See U.S. Steel Corp., 21 LA 26, 30 (Garrett, 1953).

[263]See Arbitrator Anderson in 75 LA 53, 55; Merrill in 52 LA 179, 180–181; Stein in 49 LA 288, 289; Dash in 48 LA 314, 316; Teple in 46 LA 1106, 1110; Stouffer in 46 LA 578, 581–582; Autrey in 45 LA 783, 787; Jenkins in 45 LA 696, 702; Fallon in 45 LA 271, 275, 277; Williams in 44 LA 5, 6; Peck in 39 LA 1249, 1251; L. Smith in 23 LA 289, 291; Gilden in 16 LA 811, 816; Blumer in 6 LA 426, 429. Cf., Ryder in 41 LA 8, 10.

[264]Ohio Steel Foundry Co., 36 LA 445, 446 (Dworkin, 1961); Greer Hydraulics, Inc., 29 LA 706, 708 (Friedman, 1957).

[265]Lion Oil Co., 25 LA 549, 552 (Reynard, 1955).

[266]See Kaiser Aluminum & Chem. Corp., 28 LA 439, 440 (McCoy, 1957).

issue which had been involved in two prior grievances which had been withdrawn:

> "The present grievance appears plainly to be an attempt to reinstate the former grievances which had already been withdrawn by the Union. To permit this, in the absence of proof that the earlier withdrawal was induced by the Company through fraud, misrepresentation, intentional concealment of facts, overreaching or through mutual mistake, would encourage the relitigation of grievances after they had been disposed of by the parties in the proper exercise of their discretion. This would indeed undermine the grievance procedure and the Umpire system. Here, there is no claim or proof that the Company had anything to do with the Union's decision to withdraw the earlier grievances from the procedure and from arbitration. It was a voluntary action presumably taken with full knowledge of all the facts, and must be held binding on the Union."[267]

Other arbitrators have reached similar results,[268] one of the arbitrators stating that the only exception "would be a situation in which the 'new' grievance would embrace factors and changed conditions which would clearly distinguish the latter grievance from the former."[269] However, some cases have reached a contrary result on the basis that the contractual language did not clearly indicate an intention that the underlying issue as well as the individual grievance be deemed settled.[270] One arbitrator believed that the question whether the underlying issue as well as the specific grievance are both to be considered settled should be answered on a case-by-case basis.[271]

Notice of Intent to Arbitrate

Collective agreements frequently provide that parties who wish to arbitrate disputes not settled by the negotiation steps of the grievance procedure must give notice of desire and intent to arbitrate

---

[267]Republic Steel Corp., 25 LA 437, 438 (1955).

[268]See Arbitrator Murphy in 52 LA 869, 874–875; R. Smith in 39 LA 624, 627–629; Duff in 31 LA 297, 299–300; Dworkin in 24 LA 541, 547–548; Myers in 15 LA 417, 419.

[269]Babcock & Wilcox Co., 24 LA 541, 548 (Dworkin, 1955).

[270]See Arbitrator Merrill in 52 LA 179, 180–181; Barnhart in 45 LA 300, 301–302; May in 25 LA 157, 162.

[271]Kansas City Power & Light Co., 71 LA 381, 385 (Elkouri, 1978), stating that: "[W]here the provision does not expressly state that the underlying issue as well as the specific grievance which the Union failed to carry forward are both to be considered settled in the Company's favor (or in the Union's favor if the Company fails to give its decision within the specified time), it would seem that the fact of such foreclosure could be determined only on a case by case basis. The answer to be reached in any given case would depend in significant part upon how thoroughly the particular prior grievance was treated in the grievance discussions and, of paramount importance, upon a clear showing that the specific nature and scope of the prior grievance are precisely the same as the specific nature and scope of the subsequent grievance which the Company is seeking to bar by the operation of the [provision]." Although the required showings for a bar were not made in that case, the fact that the prior grievances were dropped by the union was relevant to the question of damages where the underlying issue was again raised. Id. at 386. In UMW Dist. 5 v. Consolidated Coal Co., 109 LRRM 2001, 2003–2004 (CA 3, 1981), a lower court was held to have erred in applying a prior settlement to a subsequent grievance, the prior settlement having lacked specificity and the earlier grievance having differed from the subsequent grievance.

within a specified period of time.[272] Arbitrators often have held that failure to give the required notice, unless waived by the other party or otherwise excused, renders the dispute nonarbitrable.[273]

The obvious fact that many arbitrators consider a contractual provision for notice of appeal to arbitration to be far more than a mere formality, and indeed to be in effect a statute of limitations, is particularly significant in view of the fact that questions of procedural arbitrability (including time-limit compliance) are to be decided by the arbitrator if the federal law applies to the case.[274]

Under an agreement which required written notice of intent to arbitrate, a timely oral announcement of intention was held not to be sufficient.[275] However, a timely oral announcement of intent to arbitrate was held sufficient where the agreement did not specifically require written notice.[276] Unless the agreement expressly requires the notice to be in some particular form or requires the use of some particular terminology, substance should govern over form and a notice should be held sufficient if it clearly and unequivocally advises the other party within the time limit that the grievance is being taken to arbitration.[277]

Some agreements provide that within a specified time after notice of intent to arbitrate has been given, a joint request is to be submitted asking that an arbitrator act on the dispute. Failure of parties to act within the specified time may be held to render the dispute nonarbitrable.[278] But if one party fails to meet its obligation in some ma-

---

[272]See Major Collective Bargaining Agreements: Arbitration Procedures, 30–31 (U.S. Dept. Labor Bull. No. 1425–6, 1966). Many agreements also state time limits on the selection of the arbitrator. Id. at 51–52. Where an issue is in arbitration, some agreements toll the time limits for similar grievances pending decision of the representative or "test" case. Id. at 70.

[273]See Arbitrator Donoghue in 75 LA 14, 16; Wolff in 69 LA 85, 86; Mueller in 68 LA 933, 937; Hebert in 51 LA 384, 387–389; Stouffer in 49 LA 338, 341–342; Stark in 47 LA 606, 607 (dispute not arbitrable where notice was mailed one day late as indicated by postmark); Feinberg in 46 LA 1185, 1188 (notice must be unequivocal, a conditional notice not sufficing); Geissinger in 44 LA 1190, 1192; Ellmann in 41 LA 97, 99–100; Keeler in 39 LA 772, 776; Burr in 39 LA 668, 670; Seinsheimer in 36 LA 1460, 1463; McCoy in 20 LA 34, 34–35; Emery in 20 LA 865, 866; Handsaker in 16 LA 369, 371; Abersold in 13 LA 266, 267–269; Levy in 6 LA 397, 399–403; Dodd in 5 LA 742, 744–746; Updegraff in 4 LA 458, 461. Where the agreement did not state a time limit for proceeding to arbitration, an implied requirement that a party act within a reasonable time was found by Arbitrator Dworkin in Cleveland Pneumatic Tool Co., 43 LA 869, 872–874 (1964), and in Hydraulic Press Mfg. Co., 39 LA 1135, 1138–1139 (1962).

[274]In John Wiley & Sons v. Livingston, 84 S. Ct. 909, 918–919, 55 LRRM 2769 (1964), the U.S. Supreme Court noted that the lower courts were disagreed as to whether the court or the arbitrator should decide if "procedural" conditions to arbitration have been met. Some of the cases cited by the Court as evidencing the conflict involved compliance with time limits. The Supreme Court held that questions of procedural arbitrability are for the arbitrator rather than the court. Also see Teamsters Local 765 v. Stroehmann, 104 LRRM 3005, 3007 (CA 3, 1980). For related discussion, see Chapter 2, Legal Status of Arbitration, and Chapter 6, Determining Arbitrability.

[275]Bethlehem Steel Co., 5 LA 742, 746 (Dodd, 1946). Also see Arbitrator Mittenthal in 44 LA 469, 472.

[276]See Ironrite, Inc., 28 LA 398, 400 (Whiting, 1956); Lincoln Indus., Inc., 19 LA 489, 491 (Barrett, 1952). Also see Arbitrator Roberts in 42 LA 589, 592.

[277]See Arbitrator Anderson in 44 LA 66, 72; Elkouri in 42 LA 153, 156; Mueller in 38 LA 307, 310. Of course, the notice must be given by a party who has a contractual right to take the grievance to arbitration. Fibreboard Paper Prods. Corp., 46 LA 59, 61–62 (Roberts, 1966).

[278]See Arbitrator Cocalis in 70 LA 180, 182; Teple in 50 LA 1207, 1210–1211; Updegraff in 10 LA 778, 781–782. Cf., Teple in 42 LA 995, 998. A court insisted upon strict application of a contractual notice requirement in Detroit Coil Co. v. Machinists, 100 LRRM 3138, 3140–3141 (CA 6, 1979).

terial respect, that party cannot prevent arbitration on the ground that the other party alone referred the case to arbitration.[279] Where the agreement states no time limit for proceeding to the selection of an arbitrator after notice of intent to arbitrate has been given, considerable delay in selecting an arbitrator might occur without rendering the dispute nonarbitrable,[280] particularly when both parties have been guilty in respect to the delay.[281]

Although arbitrators are compelled to apply contractual limitations, they may do so with apparent displeasure. Witness, for example, the statement of Arbitrator Bert W. Levy:

> "It should be frankly noted that the umpire reaches his conclusion with real regret. 'A time limitation is a summary bar. Its imposition precludes application of principles of equity, of fairness, and of justice, regardless of merit * * * .' But the company in these cases has carefully refrained from any conduct which could properly be deemed a waiver of the strict procedural requirements * * * . There is nothing here to buttress the liberal interpretation which the umpire would much prefer to adopt, no peg upon which he can 'hang his hat.' These grievances must be choked off at this point. It is ruled that they have all been appealed too late * * * ."[282]

As might be expected, reasonable excuse for failure to meet notice requirements or the presence of other justification for the arbitrator not to enforce such requirements strictly may prevent a forfeiture of the right of arbitration. In such cases jurisdiction will be assumed and the dispute will be decided on the merits.[283] This was true where the parties in the past had mutually accepted loose interpretation of their

---

[279]See Arbitrator Eigenbrod in 75 LA 189, 196; Bothwell in 52 LA 1035, 1039–1040; Wardlaw in 5 LA 443, 445–446. Waivers were found by Arbitrator Roberts in 73 LA 781, 786; Oberdank in 70 LA 86, 88–89. Arbitration was not defeated where both parties were responsible for delay in selecting an arbitrator. American Air Filter Co., 54 LA 1251, 1253 (Dolnick, 1970). Similarly, see Arbitrator Heneman in 72 LA 1302, 1305. Nor was arbitration defeated where a party made a timely request to the appointing agency but its response was delayed. Sprague Devices, 72 LA 376, 378 (Cox, 1979).

[280]See Magma Copper Co., 40 LA 45, 48–49 (Gorsuch, 1962), and cases cited there. Chase Bag Co., 42 LA 153, 155–156 (Elkouri, 1963), held that notice of intent to arbitrate need be given only to the other party within the prescribed time limit, with notice to the appointing agency to be given within a reasonable time thereafter. Also see Arbitrator White in 81 LA 157, 158; Cohen in 71 LA 574, 578–579 (660-day delay in requesting arbitration panel was unreasonable); Swain in 69 LA 493, 497–498 (nine-month delay was reasonable where the parties met regarding the grievance during the interim); Koven in 52 LA 805, 807–809. Where timely notice of intent to arbitrate is given, a reasonable time will then be permitted for filing any necessary court action to compel arbitration. Local 198, URCLPW v. Interco, Inc., 415 F.2d 1208 (CA 8, 1969).

[281]See Arbitrator Nelson in 81 LA 318, 321–322; Roberts in 42 LA 589, 592; Gilden in 38 LA 1251, 1254.

[282]Bethlehem Steel Co., 6 LA 397, 402 (1947). Also see Arbitrator Hebert in 51 LA 384, 387–389; Sembower in 49 LA 302, 309–310.

[283]See Arbitrator Seidenberg in 69 LA 884, 885; Cahn in 49 LA 147, 153–154; Bender in 45 LA 545, 547; Lehoczky in 26 LA 633, 634; Stutz in 19 LA 234, 236; Abruzzi in 18 LA 193, 195–196; Prasow in 17 LA 205, 206; Selekman in 17 LA 7, 8; McCoy in 8 LA 883, 884; Trotta in 8 LA 844, 845; Simkin in 7 LA 276, 278; Brandschain in 4 LA 509, 510–513; Wardlaw in 3 LA 500, 503–504. But see Arbitrator Stouffer in 49 LA 338, 342. In some cases dispute centers upon *when* the time limit started running. In Newspaper Agency Corp., 43 LA 1233, 1235 (Platt, 1964), the contract stated a time limit for giving notice of intent to appeal from awards of local arbitrators to an appeals board (within 5 days after the award has been "rendered"); the time limit was held not to have started running until receipt of an award some 10 days after its date. For related material see this Chapter, topic entitled "Time Limitations."

contractual time limits.[284] A reasonable excuse may be a good-faith mistake or difference of opinion,[285] or it may be the unavoidable absence of an essential party, so as to make the observance of time limits impracticable.[286] Furthermore, a reasonable excuse may be said to exist if it would be futile to request arbitration within the time limit.[287] In one case a request for an extension of time was held adequate to preserve the union's right to appeal a grievance to arbitration where the delay was not unreasonable under the circumstances.[288]

In an estoppel situation, a commitment made but later repudiated by one party was held to be a reasonable excuse for the failure of the other party to comply literally with the notice requirement.[289] Finally, the right to enforce time limits may be waived, as by signing a submission agreement to arbitrate and failing to raise the time issue until the arbitration hearing.[290]

---

[284]See Arbitrator Wolf in 49 LA 681, 682; Sembower in 48 LA 492, 496; Lehozcky in 26 LA 633, 634. Also see Abruzzi in 18 LA 193, 195–196. Where each party had "sinned" as to observing contractual procedural requirements the arbitrator refused to hold the union strictly to the time limit for proceeding to arbitration. Penn Jersey Boiler & Constr. Co., 50 LA 177, 179 (Buckwalter, 1967). Arbitrators have disagreed as to whether the time limit for proceeding to arbitration is extended by continued negotiations toward settlement of the grievance. A "yes" answer was given by Arbitrator Dworkin in 70 LA 917, 919–920; Carson in 69 LA 87, 92; Updegraff in 49 LA 271, 272–273. But it was "no" by Geissinger in 44 LA 1190, 1192; Ellmann in 41 LA 97, 99–100.

[285]See Bethelem Steel Co., 7 LA 276, 278 (Simkin, 1947); International Shoe Co., 3 LA 500, 503–504 (Wardlaw, 1946).

[286]Ohmer Corp., 5 LA 278, 280 (Lehoczky, 1946).

[287]Forse Corp., 39 LA 709, 716 (Dworkin, 1962); Manhattan Transit Co., 8 LA 844, 845 (Trotta, 1947).

[288]Carpenter Steel Co., 44 LA 1185, 1186–1187 (Kerrison, 1965).

[289]B.F. Goodrich Co., 8 LA 883, 884 (McCoy, 1947).

[290]See Arbitrator Dolnik in 73 LA 297, 299; Kenaston in 68 LA 638, 643; Smith in 23 LA 289, 291; Marshall in 14 LA 310, 311. But see Seinsheimer in 36 LA 1460, 1463.

Chapter 6

Determining Arbitrability

When an existing dispute is taken to arbitration by a joint submission of the parties there ordinarily is no problem of arbitrability since by the submission the parties identify the dispute and agree to its arbitration. A different situation may be presented, however, when one party invokes the arbitration clause of a collective agreement by a demand or notice of intent to arbitrate a dispute which has arisen during the term of the agreement. Here arbitration may be resisted by the other party on the ground that the dispute is not arbitrable.[1] It may be asserted, for instance, that the case does not involve any of the types of disputes that are covered by the arbitration clause,[2] or that while covered by the arbitration clause the dispute is not arbitrable because some condition precedent to arbitration, such as exhaustion of the grievance procedure or timely notice of intent to arbitrate, has not been met.[3]

Where Arbitrability Challenge Might Be Lodged

Challenges to arbitrability are presented either to the arbitrator or to the courts. If an appointing agency is named in the arbitration clause, the challenge may be filed with it. There is no uniformity of policy of the various agencies in regard to processing cases and

---

[1]For extensive categorization and discussion of specific grounds upon which arbitrability might be challenged, see Smith & Jones, "The Impact of the Emerging Federal Law of Grievance Arbitration on Judges, Arbitrators, and Parties," 52 Va. L. Rev. 831, 839 et seq. (1966); Smith & Jones, "The Supreme Court and Labor Dispute Arbitration: The Emerging Federal Law," 63 Mich. L. Rev. 751, 780 et seq. (1965). For additional discussions of arbitrability issues and the roles of courts and arbitrators in the determination of arbitrability, see Fairweather, Practice and Procedure in Labor Arbitration, 29–78, 97–132 (BNA Books, 1983); McDermott, "Arbitrability: The Courts Versus the Arbitrator," 23 Arb. J. 18 (1968); Pirsig, "Arbitrability and the Uniform Act," 19 Arb. J. 154 (1964); Smith, "Arbitrators and Arbitrability," Proceedings of the 16th Annual Meeting of NAA, 75 (BNA Books, 1963); Cornfield, "Developing Standards for Determining Arbitrability," 14 Lab. L.J. 564 (1963).

[2]For related discussion, see Chapter 3, topics entitled "Interest Arbitration and Contract Clauses" and "Rights Arbitration Contract Clauses."

[3]See Chapter 5 for discussion of these conditions precedent.

appointing an arbitrator where one party files a challenge to arbitrability. Some of the agencies do appoint an arbitrator in such instances, at least where a minimal showing of an arbitration clause is made, and the party protesting arbitrability is permitted to raise that issue before the arbitrator or the courts.[4]

In deciding where to lodge the challenge to arbitrability, the challenger may be influenced in varying degree by the particular language of the arbitration clause, by the state or federal law that governs the case,[5] and, possibly most important, by the challenger's general attitude toward the arbitration process. Then, too, he might take a passive attitude, forcing the other party to seek enforcement of the arbitration clause by a court or arbitrator, at which stage the challenger will raise the issue of arbitrability.

Determination by the Courts

Although the parties often leave arbitrability questions in the hands of the arbitrator, such questions may be involved when the courts are drawn into the arbitration process. The nature and extent of court participation may depend largely upon the applicable law and the language of the arbitration clause.

The courts may become concerned with arbitrability questions in several ways:[6]

1. The party challenging arbitrability may seek a temporary injunction or "stay of arbitration" pending determination of arbitrability.

2. The party demanding arbitration may seek a court order compelling the other party to arbitrate where the applicable law upholds agreements to arbitrate future disputes; the latter party then raises the issue of arbitrability.

3. The issue of arbitrability may be considered when an award is taken to court for review or enforcement, unless the parties have clearly vested the arbitrator with exclusive and final right of determining arbitrability, or unless the right to challenge arbitrability is held by the court to have been otherwise waived under the circumstances of the case.[7]

---

[4]For discussion of the policy and procedures of the various appointing agencies (state, federal, and private) where arbitrability is questioned, see Justin, "Arbitrability and the Arbitrator's Jurisdiction," Management Rights and the Arbitration Process, 1, 11–15 (BNA Books, 1956). For additional discussion of American Arbitration Association and Federal Mediation and Conciliation Service policy (the rules of both agencies provide for ex parte proceedings), see McDermott, "Arbitrability: The Courts Versus the Arbitrator," 23 Arb. J. 18, 31–33, 37 (1968). Also see "Arbitrability," 18 LA 942, 951 (1951).

[5]See, generally, Chapter 2, Legal Status of Arbitration.

[6]See Chapter 2, Legal Status of Arbitration; McDermott, "Arbitrability: The Courts Versus the Arbitrator," 23 Arb. J. 18, 20 (1968); Smith & Jones, "The Supreme Court and Labor Dispute Arbitration: The Emerging Federal Law," 63 Mich. L. Rev. 751, 753 (1965); Pirsig, "Arbitrability and the Uniform Act," 19 Arb. J. 154 (1964). Also see Note, "Judicial Review of Labor Arbitration Awards After the Trilogy," 53 Cornell L. Rev. 136, 139–144 (1967).

[7]Regarding waiver of right to court review of arbitrability, see this Chapter, topic entitled "Delay in Contesting Arbitrability."

When a court is asked to stay or compel arbitration the question of arbitrability ordinarily becomes involved. If such a case is covered by federal law, the court's function is delimited by teachings of the *Trilogy*.[8] Two of the *Trilogy* decisions deal with substantive arbitrability (whether the subject matter of the dispute is arbitrable).[9] In *American Manufacturing* the Supreme Court stated:

> "The function of the court is very limited when the parties have agreed to submit all questions of contract interpretation to the arbitrator. It is then confined to ascertaining whether the party seeking arbitration is making a claim which on its face is governed by the contract. Whether the moving party is right or wrong is a question of contract interpretation for the arbitrator. In these circumstances the moving party should not be deprived of the arbitrator's judgment, when it was his judgment and all that it connotes that was bargained for."[10]

In *Warrior and Gulf* the Court stated that "arbitration is a matter of contract and a party cannot be required to submit to arbitration any dispute which he has not agreed so to submit." In its next sentences, however, the Court declared:

> "Yet, to be consistent with congressional policy in favor of settlement of disputes by the parties through the machinery of arbitration, the judicial inquiry under § 301 must be strictly confined to the question whether the reluctant party did agree to arbitrate the grievance or agreed to give the arbitrator power to make the award he made. An order to arbitrate the particular grievance should not be denied unless it may be said with positive assurance that the arbitration clause is not susceptible to an interpretation that covers the asserted dispute. Doubts should be resolved in favor of coverage."[11]

In *American Manufacturing* the Supreme Court expressly rejected the *Cutler-Hammer* doctrine that a contract cannot be said to provide for arbitration if the meaning of the provision sought to be arbitrated is beyond dispute.[12] In rejecting that doctrine the Supreme Court stated that the courts are not to weigh the merits of grievances:

---

[8]As to coverage of the federal law and applicability of state law, see Chapter 2, topic entitled "The Applicable Law: Private Sector." For a summary of the significant teachings of the *Triology* and other Supreme Court decisions affecting arbitration, see Chapter 2, topic entitled "Federal Law: Private Sector." Concerning the public sector, federal and state, respectively, see Chapter 2, subtopics entitled "Role and Scope of Federal-Sector Grievance Procedure and Arbitration" and "Determining Arbitrability and Compelling Arbitration."

[9]The Supreme Court ruled as to procedural arbitrability in *Wiley & Sons,* treated hereinbelow.

[10]United Steelworkers v. American Mfg. Co., 80 S.Ct. 1343, 1346, 34 LA 559, 560 (1960).

[11]United Steelworkers v. Warrior & Gulf Navigation Co., 80 S.Ct. 1347, 1353, 34 LA 561, 564–565 (1960). The Supreme Court subsequently explained that the quoted language "established a strong presumption favoring arbitrability." Nolde Bros. v. Bakery & Confectionery Workers, 97 S.Ct. 1067, 1074 (1977). The party resisting arbitration might claim that bargaining history shows the parties intended to exclude the disputed matter from arbitration. Courts of Appeals disagree as to whether they should consider such evidence. Conflicting decisions on the question are collected in Local 13, Professional & Technical Eng'rs. v. General Elec. Co., 531 F.2d 1178, 1183 n. 13 (CA 3, 1976); Communications Workers v. Southwestern Bell Tel. Co., 415 F.2d 35, 40 n. 10 (CA 5, 1969). For additional material concerning the presumption of arbitrability, see Chapter 2, subtopic entitled "The *Trilogy*."

[12]This New York doctrine has since been repudiated there by statutory amendment. N.Y. Civ. Prac. Law §7501 (1963). But concerning arbitrability of public-sector disputes in New York, see Chapter 2, subtopic entitled "Determining Arbitrability and Compelling Arbitration."

"The courts therefore have no business weighing the merits of the grievance, considering whether there is equity in a particular claim, or determining whether there is particular language in the written instrument which will support the claim. The agreement is to submit all grievances to arbitration, not merely those the court will deem meritorious. The processing of even frivolous claims may have therapeutic values which those who are not a part of the plant environment may be quite unaware."[13]

Under the federal law the question of substantive arbitrability is for the court when asked to stay or compel arbitration, unless the arbitration clause clearly specifies that the arbitrator shall make the determination.[14] However, even though the agreement does not expressly leave the determination of arbitrability to the arbitrator and in spite of the fact that the parties have gone first to the court, the court might leave the initial determination to the arbitrator. This was the result, for instance, where arbitrability could not be determined without delving into the merits, the court stating:

"In these circumstances we believe the matter should proceed to arbitration, where the arbitrator may determine the subsidiary facts upon which depend both the merits of the controversy and his jurisdiction to decide it. A finding of jurisdiction, unlike a finding on the merits when jurisdiction is not in question * * * will not be insulated from subsequent judicial review. * * * We believe full recognition of the role of labor arbitration requires court intervention in a case such as this only when it has become absolutely necessary, viz., on a petition to vacate or enforce the award."[15]

But in another case a district court was held to have erred in delegating to an arbitrator the determination of arbitrability.[16]

In respect to the determination of procedural arbitrability, the Supreme Court has ruled that questions of procedural arbitrability are for arbitrators to decide and not for the courts. When a court has determined that the subject matter of a dispute is arbitrable (substan-

---

[13]United Steelworkers v. American Mfg. Co., 80 S.Ct. 1343, 1346, 34 LA 559, 560–561 (1960), the Court adding: "The union claimed in this case that the company had violated a specific provision of the contract. The company took the position that it had not violated that clause. There was, therefore, a dispute between the parties as to 'the meaning, interpretation and application' of the collective bargaining agreement. Arbitration should have been ordered."

[14]The concurring opinion to the *Trilogy* states: "Since the arbitration clause itself is part of the agreement, it might be argued that a dispute as to the meaning of that clause is for the arbitrator. But the Court rejects this position, saying that the threshold question, the meaning of the arbitration clause itself, is for the judge unless the parties clearly state to the contrary." 34 LA 572, 573. On this also see Bakery & Confectionery Workers v. Nolde Bros., 530 F.2d 548, 552–553 (CA 4, 1975), and Nolde Bros. v. Bakery & Confectionery Workers, 97 S.Ct. 1067, 1074 n. 8 (1977). In Atkinson v. Sinclair Ref. Co., 82 S.Ct. 1318, 1320 (1962), the Supreme Court stated that under its decisions "whether or not" a party is "bound to arbitrate, as well as what issues it must arbitrate, is a matter to be determined by the Court on the basis of the contract entered into by the parties."

[15]Camden Indus. Co. v. Carpenters Local 1688, 353 F.2d 178, 180 (CA 1, 1965). Subsequently this same court did stress that a court in reviewing an arbitrator's conclusion on arbitrability, "must make its own independent determination" on the question. Mobil Oil Corp. v. Local 8-766, 101 LRRM 2721, 2723 (CA 1, 1979). For other instances in which courts have found it difficult to consider arbitrability without penetrating the merits, see McDermott, "Arbitrability: The Courts Versus the Arbitrator," 23 Arb. J. 18, 27–29 (1968), where it is also noted that attorneys arguing arbitrability will frequently have difficulty in doing so without delving into some aspect of the merits.

[16]Westinghouse Broadcasting Co. v. State Employees, 103 LRRM 2798, 2799 (CA 3, 1980).

tive arbitrability), the arbitrator is to decide all procedural questions which grow out of the dispute and bear on its final disposition. The Supreme Court stated that procedural questions, such as whether the preliminary steps of the grievance procedure have been exhausted or excused, ordinarily cannot be answered without consideration of the merits of the dispute.[17]

Determination by the Arbitrator

The determination of arbitrability is often left by the parties to the arbitrator. There are sound reasons for this. The delay and expense of court proceedings are avoided. Moreover, the arbitrator can be expected to exercise the industrial relations expertise which the parties contemplated when they provided for arbitration.

The collective agreement itself may specifically provide that the arbitrator is to rule on questions of arbitrability as well as upon the merits of the dispute.[18] This provides the surest method for parties to minimize court involvement in the arbitration process.

Further, the parties by special submission or stipulation may authorize the arbitrator, either specifically or impliedly, to rule both on questions of arbitrability and on the merits of the dispute.[19] Where it is clear that the parties have authorized the arbitrator to determine arbitrability, the courts will not readily overturn his ruling on that issue.[20]

Most significant, however, is the fact that even where the parties have not clearly authorized the arbitrator to determine arbitrability, he often does so (as an inherent part of his duty) and they generally accept his conclusions without resort to litigation.

Arbitrators appear generally agreed that the legitimate interests of the parties are adequately served by submitting arbitrability issues to the arbitrator.[21] Furthermore, the hundreds of substantive arbitrability issues that have been decided by arbitrators would appear to indicate general concurrence by arbitrators in the view that "an agreement to arbitrate future disputes of a specified kind vests in a duly appointed arbitrator power to determine whether a particular

---

[17]John Wiley & Sons v. Livingston, 84 S.Ct. 909, 918–919, 55 LRRM 2769 (1964), in which the Court also noted that a different ruling would produce frequent duplication of effort by court and arbitrator, and needless delay. In Operating Eng'rs. v. Flair Builders, Inc., 80 LRRM 2441 (1972), the Supreme Court refused to narrow the scope of this ruling as to the arbitrator's jurisdiction to decide procedural questions.

[18]It is not uncommon for the collective agreement to provide expressly for determination of arbitrability by the arbitrator, although a few agreements specify court determination. See A Survey of Negotiated Grievance Procedures and Arbitration in Federal Post Civil Service Reform Act Agreements, p. 11 (OPM, 1980); Major Collective Bargaining Agreements: Arbitration Procedures, 24–26 (U.S. Dept. Labor Bull. No. 1425–6, 1966).

[19]An example is Park-Pitt Bldg. Co., 47 LA 234, 235 (Duff, 1966).

[20]See, for instance, Metal Prods. Workers Union v. Torrington Co., 358 F.2d 103, 62 LRRM 2011 (CA 2, 1966); United Steelworkers v. North Range Mining Co., 249 F.Supp. 754 (USDC, 1966); Wiese Rambler Sales Co. v. Teamsters Local 43, 47 LA 1152, 64 LRRM 2139 (Wis. Cir. Ct. 1966).

[21]Smith, "Arbitrators and Arbitrability," Proceedings of the 16th Annual Meeting of NAA, 75 (BNA Books, 1963).

dispute, with respect to which one party invokes arbitration, is a dispute of that kind."[22]

An American Bar Association committee has stated that "the function of the arbitrator to decide whether or not an allegation of non-arbitrability is sound could be compared to that of a trial judge who is asked to dismiss a complaint on motion for a directed verdict or for failure to state a cause of action. This analogy indicates that a preliminary decision relating to arbitrability by the arbitrator *is an inherent part of his duty*."[23] That arbitrators are capable of self-restraint is evidenced by the committee's conclusion, based upon examination of many awards, that "arbitrators generally are well aware of the limitations of their authority and scrupulously try to avoid any transgression of those limitations."[24]

The question arises whether substantive arbitrability must be determined by a court in the first instance where a party, without going to court, challenges the arbitrator's jurisdiction to determine arbitrability. Arbitrator Thomas J. McDermott has concluded that he should not refuse to rule on arbitrability in such case:

> "[An arbitrator] would be remiss in his responsibilities as an arbitrator, if he were to refuse to rule on the arbitrability of a given dispute, where the arbitration provisions are of an all inclusive nature and where one party requests that such ruling be made. Obviously, any ruling that he makes is not self-enforcing, and court action will be required for such enforcement, if either party refuses to abide by the award. Should such action take place all parties are well aware that the Courts will be the final source of determining arbitrability."[25]

With regard to procedural arbitrability, it should be recalled that even where challenge to arbitrability is first lodged in the courts, the Supreme Court has held that questions of procedural arbitrability are for the arbitrator rather than the court.[26]

Trilogy *Arbitrability Criteria and the Arbitrator*

Several arbitrators have emphasized that when parties go to an arbitrator on the question of substantive arbitrability, he should

---

[22]Barbet Mills, Inc., 19 LA 737, 738 (Maggs, 1952). Also see comments of Abritrator Whitley P. McCoy in West Penn Power Co., 24 LA 741, 742 (1955).

[23]"Arbitrability," 18 LA 942, 950 (1951), emphasis added. The Committee's view was relied upon by Arbitrator Gorsuch in Sandia Corp., 40 LA 879, 886 (1963). Also note the statement of the U.S. Supreme Court in W.R. Grace & Co. v. Rubber Workers Local 759, 103 S.Ct. 2177, 113 LRRM 2641, 2644 (1983), as follows: "Because the authority of arbitrators is a subject of collective bargaining, just as is any other contractual provision, the scope of the arbitrator's authority is itself a question of contract interpretation that the parties have delegated to the arbitrator."

[24]"Arbitrability," 18 LA 942, 951 (1951).

[25]Master Builders' Assn. of W. Pa., 45 LA 892, 896 (1965). He cited court decisions supporting his conclusion that he need not wait for a court to rule first as to arbitrability, but other court decisions were cited to the contrary. Id. at 895. For other expressions on this question, see Arbitrator Mittelman in 81 LA 1, 8–9; Helfeld in 68 LA 633, 635–636; Summers in 48 LA 137, 139; Hilpert in 32 LA 1013, 1022. For related discussion, see McDermott, "Arbitrability: The Courts Versus the Arbitrator," 23 Arb. J. 18 (1968).

[26]See this Chapter, topic entitled "Determination by the Courts." Also see Local 765 v. Stroehmann Bros., 104 LRRM 3005, 3007 (CA 3, 1980).

exercise his own judgment on the question; that he is not restricted to the criteria established for the courts by the *Trilogy*, and should not decide the issue slavishly on the basis of how a court might decide it.[27] Some other arbitrators, in holding that doubts concerning arbitrability should be resolved in the affirmative, appear to have their eye on the basic *Trilogy* standard of presumptive arbitrability.[28]

May an arbitrator determine a dispute to be nonarbitrable after a court has ordered arbitration under the *Trilogy*? Arbitrator Edgar A. Jones has expressed belief that an arbitrator may do so (though he did not do so in the case before him) since there may be surface indication of arbitrability to justify a court in ordering arbitration whereas the arbitrator in delving deeper into the case may conclude that it was not intended to be arbitrable.[29] Court decisions go both ways on this question.[30]

Procedural Techniques for Ruling on Arbitrability

Sometimes arbitrability is the sole question before the arbitrator, but probably more often he is called upon to rule both on the preliminary issue of arbitrability and, if he finds the dispute arbitrable, also on the merits.[31]

Where the arbitrator is to rule on both arbitrability and the merits, evidence and argument on the question of arbitrability will be *heard* before the presentation on the merits. But the procedural question remains as to whether the arbitrator should *rule* on arbitrability before any presentation is made on the merits, or whether he should reserve his ruling on arbitrability until the full case has been presented.

One school of thought holds that a ruling on arbitrability should be made before the presentation on the merits. This view was elaborated by Arbitrator Harry J. Dworkin:

---

[27]See Arbitrator Turkus in 43 LA 1287, 1289; Roberts in 39 LA 1191, 1203–1205; Aaron in 36 LA 1125, 1129. Similarly, Arbitrator Dugan in 46 LA 1018, 1021.

[28]See Arbitrator Tanaka in 77 LA 467, 470; Sinicropi in 75 LA 420, 426; Caraway in 75 LA 113, 116; Feldman in 74 LA 1058, 1060; LeBaron in 73 LA 455, 456–457; Carson in 72 LA 66, 70; Roberts in 71 LA 730, 736; Rule in 69 LA 1167, 1170; Morris in 53 LA 246, 248; Kates in 51 LA 741, 742; Ray in 51 LA 284, 286; Yagoda in 48 LA 1040, 1043; Warns in 36 LA 380, 381. Many arbitrators have denied that the 1960 *Trilogy* has made them more inclined to decide in favor of arbitrability. Smith, "Arbitrators and Arbitrability," Proceedings of the 16th Annual Meeting of NAA, 75 (BNA Books, 1963). An early study supports this denial. See Report of Research & Education Committee, "The Steelworkers' Trilogy and the Arbitrator." Id. at 360–363. For an extensive survey of views of arbitrators and parties concerning the impact of *Trilogy* arbitrability teachings upon arbitrators, see Smith & Jones, "The Impact of the Emerging Federal Law of Grievance Arbitration on Judges, Arbitrators, and Parties," 52 Va. L. Rev. 831, 866 et seq. (1966), where numerous decisions by arbitrators are also examined for indications as to *Trilogy* influence. Authors Smith and Jones concluded that "The total impact upon arbitrators, although real, is difficult to evaluate fully at this time." Id. at 912.

[29]Zoological Soc. of San Diego, 50 LA 1, 7 (1967). A like view is elaborated by Arbitrator Milton O. Talent in Bunn-O-Matic Corp., 70 LA 34, 37–38 (1977). Also see Arbitrator Holly in 36 LA 695, 697 (company contention). Cf., Arbitrator Feldman in 70 LA 904, 908–909.

[30]See "Arbitration and Rights Under Collective Agreements," Problems of Proof in Arbitration, 377–378 (BNA Books, 1967); Smith & Jones, "The Supreme Court and Labor Dispute Arbitration: The Emerging Federal Law," 63 Mich. L. Rev. 751, 761 (1965).

[31]Some statistics are provided in "Substantive Aspects of Labor-Management Arbitration," 28 LA 943, 944 (1957).

"The Chairman is of the opinion that when a party raises the issue of arbitrability, it is better practice to pass upon this issue at the time it is presented, and before hearing the dispute on the merits, for the reason that whenever possible parties should have the right to an interim decision or ruling on any question presented during the course of the hearing, and that this procedure is preferable to the reservation of the ruling until after the conclusion of the hearing."[32]

Under this procedure only one hearing might prove to be required,[33] but two hearings often are required.[34]

Another view holds that the ruling on arbitrability may be reserved until the full case has been heard. As elaborated by Arbitrator Douglass B. Maggs:

"The arbitrator may properly reserve his ruling upon arbitrability until after he has heard evidence and argument upon the merits. A contrary rule would cause needless delay and expense, necessitating two hearings whenever the arbitrator needed time to consider the question of arbitrability. Furthermore, in many cases, it is only after a hearing on the merits has informed the arbitrator of the nature of the dispute that he is in a position to determine whether it is of the kind covered by the agreement to arbitrate.

"* * * This procedure does not, of course, preclude the party who loses from obtaining any judicial review of the arbitrator's decision to which it is entitled by law; to reassure the Company about this I explicitly ruled that its participation in the hearing upon the merits would not constitute a waiver of its objections to arbitrability."[35]

It would seem that the choice between these two procedures should be dictated by consideration of all the circumstances of the particular case. Such a flexible procedure has been used by the Connecticut State Board of Mediation:

"The Board will inform the party protesting arbitrability that it will be permitted to raise that issue at the hearing. The Board will then first hear arguments on arbitrability before it proceeds to the merits of the dispute. The Board makes clear that at the hearing both parties must be

---

[32]Babcock & Wilcox Co., 22 LA 456, 460 (1954). For other instances in which this procedure was used (sometimes by specific agreement of the parties), see Arbitrator Carson in 72 LA 66, 67; Duff in 48 LA 600, 603; Bennett in 45 LA 90, 91; Anrod in 45 LA 34 at 34; Kornblum in 43 LA 765, 766; Dworkin in 39 LA 1135 at 1135; Howard in 34 LA 617, 618. The interim ruling as to arbitrability might be verbal, in which case it will later be restated in a written opinion which also covers the merits. As in Dynamic Mfrs., Inc., 36 LA 635, 636 (Crane, 1960).

[33]As in Hercules Powder Co., 47 LA 336, 338–339 (Boothe, 1966). In Lockheed Aircraft Serv. Co., 44 LA 51, 59 (Roberts, 1965), the arbitrator held the grievance to be arbitrable and remanded it to the parties, to be heard on the merits only if the parties could not resolve it.

[34]See Arbitrator Oberdank in 70 LA 86, 89; Helfeld in 68 LA 633, 634, 638; McCoy in 45 LA 1055, 1056, and in 46 LA 1063 at 1063; Jones in 45 LA 633, 635, and in 45 LA 635, 640; Anrod in 45 LA 34 at 34; Stark in 44 LA 1150, 1154, and in 47 LA 91, 92.

[35]Barbet Mills, Inc., 19 LA 737, 738 (1952). Arbitrator Maggs explained his view in greater detail in Caledonia Mills, Inc., 15 LA 474, 476–477 (1950). For other instances in which the ruling on arbitrability was reserved until the merits had been heard (the arbitrator sometimes saying this would minimize delay and costs), see Arbitrator Gentile in 72 LA 1156, 1156–1157; Mewhinney in 71 LA 852, 853; Munger in 71 LA 340, 340–341; Cantor in 69 LA 794, 799; Oppenheim in 52 LA 1164, 1168–1169; Gibson in 51 LA 837, 838; Bender in 45 LA 545 at 545; Boles in 45 LA 502, 503; Singletary in 45 LA 261, 262; Schedler in 35 LA 499 at 499. This approach is suggested also in "Arbitrability," 18 LA 941, 950–951 (1951). For an instance where it was necessary to get into the merits before the arbitrability issue could be decided, see Chesapeake & Potomac Tel. Co., 46 LA 321, 322 (Seward, 1965). Also see Arbitrator Freund in 75 LA 537, 539.

prepared to proceed on the merits after the Board has heard them on arbitrability.

"After the issue on arbitrability has been presented, 'the Board will assess the circumstances then obtaining to determine if it will proceed directly to the merits.'

"Under its policy, the Board reserves the right either to require the parties 'to go forward directly on the merits' at the same hearing or to determine that 'the decision on arbitrability should be made first before proceeding on the merits.' "[36]

Some agreements expressly give the arbitrator the option of hearing the arbitrability issue and the merits either together or in separate proceedings.[37] Even without such contractual provision, however, the arbitrator might require a party (against its wishes) to proceed to the merits before the ruling is made on arbitrability.[38] What should an arbitrator do when a party insists, against the opposition of the other party, upon a ruling as to arbitrability before proceeding to the merits? A panel discussion by the National Academy of Arbitrators indicated that some arbitrators would issue an oral ruling as to arbitrability at the hearing, while some would proceed to the merits (possibly ex parte) despite the objections of one party.[39]

Finally it may be noted that regardless of *when* the ruling on arbitrability is made, it will often be placed in the arbitrator's written decision of the case at a point prior to his discussion of the merits.[40]

Delay in Contesting Arbitrability

The right to contest arbitrability before the arbitrator is not waived merely by failing to raise the issue of arbitrability until the arbitration hearing.[41]

---

[36]Justin, "Arbitrability and the Arbitrator's Jurisdiction," Management Rights and the Arbitration Process, 1, 12 (BNA Books, 1956).

[37]Major Collective Bargaining Agreements: Arbitration Procedures, 25 (U.S. Dept. Labor Bull. No. 1425–6, 1966), where it is also noted that most agreements specify use of the same arbitrator for determining arbitrability and merits.

[38]As under the policy of the Connecticut State Board, noted hereinabove, or as the arbitrator did in Union Carbide Nuclear Co., 35 LA 499 at 499 (Schedler, 1960). Also see Arbitrator Gentile in 72 LA 1156, 1156–1157. A "special appearance" to contest arbitrability did not prevent a ruling on the merits where the submission was broad enough to include the merits. Lake Mills Redi-Mix, Inc., 38 LA 307, 312 (Mueller, 1962).

[39]"Procedural Problems in the Conduct of Arbitration Hearings: A Discussion," Proceedings of the 17th Annual Meeting of NAA, 1–2, 21–22 (BNA Books, 1964), where all participants indicated, however, that their choice of action might vary with the situation. Also see Arbitrator Merrill in 47 LA 339, 340; Lennard in 46 LA 746, 747, 749–750, and in 46 LA 750 at 750. For discussion as to proceeding ex parte, see Chapter 7, topic titled "Default Awards in Ex Parte Proceedings"; McDermott, "Arbitrability: The Courts Versus the Arbitrator," 23 Arb. J. 18 (1968). The arbitrator did proceed ex parte to the merits in Velsicol Chem. Corp., 52 LA 1164, 1168–1169 (Oppenheim, 1969), and issued a default award against the company, which had refused to introduce evidence or cross examine as to the merits. In North Clackamas School Dist. No. 12, 68 LA 503, 504 (Snow, 1976), the union submitted evidence on both arbitrability and merits but the employer declined to participate in the portion of the hearing relating to the merits. The Arbitrator held the dispute arbitrable in an initial award and he then followed a procedure involving use of briefs to obtain the positions of both parties on the merits.

[40]As Arbitrator Dworkin did in Babcock & Wilcox Co., 22 LA 456, 460 (1954), and Arbitrator Maggs in Barbet Mills, Inc., 19 LA 737, 739 (1952).

[41]For example, Arbitrator Gentile in 72 LA 1156, 1159–1160; Mallon in 71 LA 699, 701; Robertson in 70 LA 71, 74; Williams in 48 LA 44, 46; Dugan in 46 LA 1018, 1021; Young in 20 LA

Whether participation in an arbitration hearing on the merits constitutes a waiver of the right to court review of arbitrability may depend upon the terms of an applicable statute or upon the view of the particular court. No uniform rule exists as to this question.[42] As a precaution against such waiver, a participant in an arbitration hearing on the merits may expressly reserve the right to court review of arbitrability.[43] Likewise, an arbitrator who calls for evidence and argument on the merits of a dispute before he rules on a challenge to arbitrability may emphasize that "participation in the hearing upon the merits would not constitute a waiver of objections to arbitrability."[44]

289, 292; Kerr in 11 LA 219, 220; Rader in 7 LA 595, 598. Cf., Di Leone in 69 LA 48, 51; Peterschmidt in 69 LA 34, 38; Greene in 47 LA 282, 283. As to how far into the arbitration hearing a party may wait before first contesting arbitrability, see Arbitrator McDonald in 74 LA 2, 4; Layman in 45 LA 417, 421–422; Sembower in 39 LA 534, 537.

[42]The different results on the question are reflected in Humble Oil & Ref. Co. v. Teamsters Local 866, 65 LRRM 3016 (USDC, 1967); Ficek v. Southern Pac. Co., 57 LRRM 2573 (CA 9, 1964), cert. denied, 60 LRRM 2284 (U.S. S.Ct. 1965); National Cash Register Co. v. Wilson, 35 LA 646 (N.Y. Ct. App., 1960). Also see Piggly Wiggly Warehouse v. Local 1, 103 LRRM 2646, 2649 (CA 5, 1980). For other material relevant to this question, see Chapter 2, Legal Status of Arbitration.

[43]Under many statutes this precaution would suffice. But under the New York statute it might be inadequate. See McNamara v. Air Freight Haulage Co., 46 LA 768, 61 LRRM 2424 (N.Y. S.Ct., 1966). In George Day Constr. Co. v. Carpenters Local 354, 115 LRRM 2459, 2462 (CA 9, 1984), a suit under LMRA § 301, the Court explained:

"Had the employer objected to the arbitrator's authority, refused to argue the arbitrability issue before him, and proceeded to the merits of the grievance, then, clearly the arbitrability question would have been preserved for independent judicial scrutiny. The same result could be achieved by making an objection as to jurisdiction and an express reservation of the question on the record. However, where, as here, the objection is raised, the arbitrability issue is argued along with the merits, and the case is submitted to the arbitrator for decision, it becomes readily apparent that the parties have consented to allow the arbitrator to decide the entire controversy, including the question of arbitrability."

[44]Barbet Mills, Inc., 19 LA 737, 738 (Maggs, 1952). Also see Arbitrator Wolff in 74 LA 432 at 432; Helfeld in 68 LA 633, 638.

Chapter 7

Arbitration Procedures and Techniques

Source of Procedural Rules

It is difficult to generalize concerning arbitration procedures since rarely do the procedures followed in any given case spring from a single source. Indeed, it frequently happens that in a given case some of the procedure utilized is based upon legal requirements, some upon agreement of the parties, and some upon directive of the arbitrator. Then, too, if the parties have agreed to arbitrate under the rules of some administrative agency, such as the American Arbitration Association, many procedural matters will be governed by the rules of the agency. Accordingly, the reader should bear in mind that the procedures outlined in this chapter do not necessarily apply in all cases, but may be varied significantly for some cases by the applicable law,[1] administrative agency rules, special agreement of the parties, or by the views of the particular arbitrator.[2]

It is highly desirable that arbitration procedures be based, to the extent reasonably possible, upon the wishes of the parties and the judgment of their arbitrator. In this regard, it is significant that most arbitration statutes contain very little detail regarding that part of the arbitration process from the time the arbitrator is selected until

---

[1]See Chapter 2 for various topics and subtopics relating to federal and state law applicable to private-sector employment, to law applicable to federal-sector employment, and to law applicable to state-sector employment.

[2]For helpful discussions of various aspects of arbitration procedure, in addition to the discussions cited elsewhere in this Chapter, see St. Antoine, "Arbitration Procedure," Labor Arbitrator Development: A Handbook, 55 (BNA Books, 1983); Schmertz, "Evidentiary Considerations," id. at 78; Anderson, "Public Sector Arbitration," id. at 93; Zack, "Decision-Making," id. at 111; Fairweather, Practice and Procedure in Labor Arbitration, 10–28, 160–198, 557–637 (BNA Books, 1983); Zirkel, "A Profile of Grievance Arbitration Cases," 38 Arb. J. No. 1, p. 35 (1983); Herrick, "Labor Arbitration as Viewed by Labor Arbitrators," id. at 39; Seitz, "Delay: The Asp in the Bosom of Arbitration," 36 Arb. J. No. 3, p. 29 (1981); Mittenthal, "Making Arbitration Work: Alternatives in Designing the Machinery," id. at 35.

his award has been issued.[3] Then, too, even where statutes deal with this part of the process, the parties may be permitted to waive statutory requirements.[4] Likewise, the procedural rules of administrative agencies ordinarily may be waived by the parties by proceeding without objection when the rules are not observed.[5]

It is the function and responsibility of the arbitrator to determine procedural matters which are not covered by any applicable law or administrative agency rule and upon which the parties have not reached agreement. It is also to be noted that, as between court and arbitrator, the U.S. Supreme Court has stated that when a court has determined that the subject matter of a dispute is arbitrable, procedural questions "which grow out of the dispute and bear on its final disposition should be left to the arbitrator."[6]

In actual practice arbitrators frequently determine what procedure shall be followed in regard to many aspects of the arbitration process.[7] It must be emphasized, however, that the arbitrator should and ordinarily will endeavor to comply with the wishes of the parties whenever they agree on procedural matters.[8] Such agreement may of course be reached at the hearing, but it may have been reached earlier in the submission or the collective agreement.[9]

Control of Arbitration Proceedings

It is generally accepted that the conduct of arbitration proceedings is under the jurisdiction and control of the arbitrator, subject to

---

[3]See Chapter 2 for the general content of arbitration statutes.

[4]For instance, see In re Aranson, 6 LA 1033 (N.Y. Sup. Ct., 1946). Also see Chapter 2.

[5]Such waiver is permitted, for instance, by American Arbitration Association Rule 33, 43 LA 1292, 1295. Under FMCS Regulations, § 1404.6, parties have the right "jointly to select any arbitrator or arbitration procedure acceptable to them."

[6]John Wiley & Sons v. Livingston, 84 S.Ct. 909, 918–919, 55 LRRM 2769 (1964). For related discussion, see Chapter 6, Determining Arbitrability.

[7]The cases and materials throughout this Chapter illustrate this function of the arbitrator. In this regard, too, American Arbitration Association Rule 46 empowers the arbitrator to interpret its rules insofar as they relate to the arbitrator's powers and duties. 43 LA 1292, 1296.

[8]See subtopic entitled "Control of Arbitration Proceedings," below. Also see report of tripartite committee, "Problems of Proof in the Arbitration Process," Problems of Proof in Arbitration, 86, 87–88 (BNA Books, 1967). Where arbitrators failed to follow a procedural requirement specified by the agreement, a federal court remanded the case to them for compliance with the contractual procedure. Smith v. Union Carbide Corp., 60 LRRM 2110, 45 LA 703 (CA 6, 1965). On the other hand, it has been stressed that the arbitrator has the responsibility to provide "a full and fair hearing to employers, unions, *and* grievants," and that this "would, when necessary, require an arbitrator to assert an independence of the parties in order to fulfill arbitral obligations that transcend or even conflict with the intentions of the employer and/or union parties to the contract." Gross & Bordoni, "Reflections on the Arbitrator's Responsibility to Provide a Full and Fair Hearing: How to Bite the Hands that Feed You," 29 Syracuse L. Rev. 877, 879–880 (1978). Also see discussion by Aaron, "The Role of the Arbitrator in Ensuring a Fair Hearing," Proceedings of the 35th Annual Meeting of NAA, 30 (BNA Books, 1983).

[9]The submission stated procedural details, for instance, in A.S. Abell Co., 45 LA 801, 806–807 (Cluster, 1965). Of 416 agreements analyzed in one survey, 33 percent contained provisions concerning arbitration procedures (either by stating procedural rules in the agreement, or by stipulating that the procedural rules of the American Arbitration Association, of a specified state, or as established by the arbitrator, are to govern). Major Collective Bargaining Agreements: Arbitration Procedures, 59–61 (U.S. Dept. Labor Bull. No. 1425-6, 1966), where it is also noted that the FMCS has set only a few rules for the conduct of the proceedings. The latter remains true under FMCS Regulations as revised in 1979. See 29 C.F.R. Part 1404.

such rules of procedure as the parties may jointly prescribe.[10] As to this control by the arbitrator, the reporter of one survey has observed that:

> "In the absence of strict procedural guidelines the arbitrator necessarily has had to assume wide discretion in conducting hearings and in deciding cases. This broad role has been affirmed by the United States Supreme Court. But the arbitrator, it is clear from this survey, has not become a tyrant as a consequence."[11]

Of course a fair hearing is generally the ultimate objective of procedural rules. However, an efficient and orderly hearing is also important to the success of arbitration proceedings. Thus, the arbitrator must give the parties a fair chance to present their case, must satisfy himself that he is being adequately informed by the parties to enable him to decide the case, and at the same time he must provide procedural efficiency to keep the hearing from getting out of hand.[12] This is not always an easy task.[13]

---

[10]See FMCS Regulations, § 1404.14, 29 C.F.R. Part 1404; Code of Professional Responsibility, § V(A)(1) & (1)(a), 64 LA 1325–1326. Section II(J)(2)(c) of the Code states that "An arbitrator may properly seek to persuade the parties to alter or eliminate arbitration procedures or tactics that cause unnecessary delay."

[11]Eaton, "Labor Arbitration in the San Francisco Bay Area," 48 LA 1381, 1391 (1967). For the possibility of court relief where procedural unfairness is found, see Harvey Aluminum, Inc. v. Steelworkers, 263 F.Supp. 488 (USDC, 1967). Also see Comment, "Appealing the Procedural Decisions of Arbitrators," 59 Minn. L. Rev. 109, 145–153 (1974).

[12]Regarding these objectives, see Smith, "The Search for Truth," Proceedings of the 31st Annual Meeting of NAA, 40, 48–49 (BNA Books, 1979); Davey, "What's Right and What's Wrong With Grievance Arbitration: The Practitioners Air Their Views," 28 Arb. J. 209, 215, 223–224 (1973); panel discussion, "The Arbitration Hearing—Avoiding a Shambles," Proceedings of 18th Annual Meeting of NAA, 75 (BNA Books, 1965); Jones & Smith, "Management and Labor Appraisals and Criticisms of the Arbitration Process: A Report With Comments," 62 Mich. L. Rev. 1115, 1127 (1964). Also see workshop discussions, "Procedural Rulings During the Hearing," Proceedings of the 35th Annual Meeting of NAA, 138 (BNA Books, 1983). In Rose Con, 70 LA 972, 975 (Walsh, 1978), the arbitrator explained that "Because of the inexperience and the lack of expertise of the parties in presenting their positions in arbitration cases, the arbitrator permitted this case to be presented by the parties in a very informal manner." At one stage he "permitted the parties to openly discuss the facts in an open forum manner."

[13]In one case a party charged Arbitrator Peter Seitz with partiality toward the other party by the manner in which the hearing was being conducted, and submitted a motion that he withdraw as arbitrator in the case. Arbitrator Seitz explained various considerations that must be balanced by an arbitrator in conducting a hearing. He then added the following explanation:
   "Practice and procedure in arbitration has not developed the relative uniformity that exists in judicial tribunals under codes or procedure and court rules. In my judgment it is fortunate that it has not. The parties, with the assistance of the arbitrator, are left relatively free (excepting for the demands of procedural due process) to run their arbitration according to the style which they prefer. Difficulties arise when one party insists on a particular style of procedure and the other party's preference is in opposition to it—or the arbitrator believes that what is occurring will not furnish him with the kind of record that will enable him, ultimately, to discharge his own duties properly.
   "Apparently, this was such a case. * * * [T]he Arbitrator, in an effort to ensure that the Company's rights to fair hearing be not transgressed and that his own duties be properly discharged, made procedural suggestions * * * [which] were the basis for the personal attack on the arbitrator."
Upon due consideration Arbitrator Seitz found the charge to be without merit and he explained that to grant the motion for his withdrawal, which he refused to do, would be unfair and damaging not only to the other party "but to the arbitration process, generally." Westinghouse Elec. Corp., 73 LA 256, 257–258 (1979). Also see Arbitrator LeWinter in 72 LA 1, 6.

The Code of Professional Responsibility and the Code of Ethics

Although the Code of Professional Responsibility for Arbitrators of Labor-Management Disputes was intended to supersede the Code of Ethics and Procedural Standards for Labor-Management Arbitration, there are various aspects of arbitral practice which were covered in some detail in the latter code but upon which the Code of Professional Responsibility is silent (or touches upon only vaguely). In some such instances the Authors consider that the Code of Ethics and Procedural Standards nevertheless provides possible guidance and, where appropriate, they accordingly call its provisions to the attention of the reader.

Initiating Arbitration: Submission Versus Arbitration Clause

Arbitration may be initiated either (1) by a "submission" or (2) by a demand or notice invoking a collective agreement arbitration clause. Sometimes both instruments are used in a case.

A submission (sometimes called a "stipulation" or an "agreement to arbitrate") is used where there is no previous agreement to arbitrate. The submission, which must be signed by both parties, describes an existing dispute; it often also names the arbitrator (or the method of appointment) and it sometimes contains considerable detail regarding the arbitrator's authority, the procedure to be used at the hearing, and other matters which the parties wish to control.[14]

Since collective agreements generally do not provide for the arbitration of "interest" disputes that might arise in the future, the agreement to arbitrate such disputes most often is entered into after the dispute has materialized and at a time when the issues can be defined. In such cases the parties will use one instrument only, which will contain full provision for the arbitration.[15]

However, most collective agreements do provide for arbitration of "rights" disputes involving the application or interpretation of the agreement. Thus, there is an "agreement to arbitrate" future disputes that may arise under and during the term of the collective agreement. If a dispute is covered by such an arbitration clause, arbitration may be initiated unilaterally by one party by serving upon the other a written demand or notice of intent to arbitrate; the latter party may reply with a statement covering its position, but the arbitration pro-

---

[14]For example, see the submission in Goodyear Eng'g Corp., 24 LA 360, 361–362 (Warns, 1955).

[15]For examples of the instrument used in such instances, see A.S. Abell Co., 45 LA 801, 806–807 (Cluster, 1965); River Valley Tissue Mills, 3 LA 245, 246 (Blair, 1946). Also see submission instruments in 28 LA 477, 478–479; 26 LA 904, 904–905; 25 LA 54, 55.

ceeds regardless of whether any such reply is made.[16] Use of a demand only, with no joint submission, has long been common practice where the collective agreement contains an arbitration clause.[17] Moreover, in such cases no submission will be required to make arbitration enforceable by the courts if the case is covered by state or federal law under which agreements to arbitrate future disputes are specifically enforceable.[18]

Even where the collective agreement contains an arbitration clause covering a dispute, the parties may choose also to execute a submission after the dispute has materialized. Some reasons for doing this are:

1. To expand or diminish the authority of the arbitrator more than provided by the collective agreement.[19]
2. To state precisely the issue to be decided by the arbitrator, and thus to indicate the scope of his jurisdiction more precisely.[20]
3. To state procedural details where the parties desire to control them and the collective agreement contains little or no detail in regard thereto.
4. In arbitration under a statute, to complete any statutory requirements not met by the arbitration clause of the collective agreement.
5. In cases not covered by state or federal law making agreements to arbitrate future disputes specifically enforceable, to provide

---

[16]See American Arbitration Association Rules 7 and 8, 43 LA 1292. The FMCS "prefers to act upon a joint request," but the FMCS Regulation adds that: "In the event that the request is made by only one party, the Service will submit a panel; however, any submission of a panel should not be construed as anything more than compliance with a request and does not necessarily reflect the contractual requirements of the parties." FMCS Regulations, § 1404.10(a), 29 C.F.R. Part 1404.

[17]See "Procedural Aspects of Labor-Management Arbitration," 28 LA 933, 934 (1954 statistics); Updegraff, Arbitration and Labor Relations, 138–139 (BNA Books, 1970); Updegraff & McCoy, Arbitration of Labor Disputes, 53 (1946). AAA Rule 7 provides for initiation of arbitration under an arbitration clause in a collective agreement, and AAA Rule 9 provides for initiation under a submission. Under FMCS Regulations, § 1404.10(c), requests for arbitration "should also include a current copy of the arbitration section of the collective bargaining agreement *or* stipulation to arbitrate." Emphasis added. One survey revealed that: "Opinion on use of the submission agreement varied from 'always,' 'absolutely,' and 'usually prefer it,' to 'almost never,' and 'never had one.' Use of the submission agreement seems to depend more than anything else on the relationship between the parties. Opposition to its use was most frequently based on the ground that it leads to interminable haggling over phraseology, with each side jockeying for a favorable statement. * * * Despite these difficulties, a majority of those interviewed preferred a submission agreement, and stated that they arrive at one successfully in most cases." Eaton, "Labor Arbitration in the San Francisco Area," 48 LA 1381, 1386 (1967). Also see Davey, "What's Right and What's Wrong With Grievance Arbitration: The Practitioners Air Their Views," 28 Arb. J. 209, 220 (1973).

[18]See Chapter 2, Legal Status of Arbitration. Illustrating such arbitration by court order, see B & K Investments, 71 LA 366, 367 (Turkus, 1978); Amoco Oil Co., 70 LA 979, 981 (Britton, 1978), an instance in which the court narrowly confined the arbitrator's jurisdiction.

[19]For example, see International Shoe Co., 21 LA 550, 550–551 (Rader, 1953). In E.K. Porter Co. v. United Saw, File & Steel Prods. Workers, 406 F.2d 643 (CA 3, 1969), the subsequently adopted submission controlled over the collective agreement in reference to the arbitrator's jurisdiction. Also see District Council v. Anderson, 104 LRRM 2188, 2189 (CA 8, 1980).

[20]See E.I. du Pont de Nemours & Co., 39 LA 1083, 1084 (Begley, 1962); North Am. Cement Corp., 28 LA 414, 417–418 (Callaghan, 1957). The desired clarity is not always achieved in the submission, and the burden may fall upon the arbitrator to make the initial interpretation of an ambiguous submission in order to determine the scope of his jurisdiction. See Eagle Rubber Co., 35 LA 256, 261–262 (Dworkin, 1960).

a contract after the dispute has materialized. Contracts to arbitrate existing disputes are the basis of damage actions under the common law of some jurisdictions and sometimes are made specifically enforceable by statute even where agreements to arbitrate future disputes are not.[21]

6. To confirm the arbitrability of the particular dispute.[22]
7. To provide an additional opportunity to settle the dispute—in negotiating on a submission the parties may find that they are not too far apart for a negotiated settlement of the basic dispute.[23]

It is obvious from the above discussion that any use of a submission depends upon the particular case, and that the particular contents and form of submissions which are used will vary greatly from case to case. Some submissions are very brief, while others are quite detailed.

The arbitration clause of the collective agreement and/or the submission define the limits of the arbitrator's jurisdiction. An award may be subject to court challenge if it decides any issue or matter not submitted to the arbitrator by at least one of these instruments, and court relief might be available also if the award fails to decide all issues and matters so submitted.[24] Obviously, care should be exercised by the parties in drafting these instruments and by the arbitrator in responding to them.

Stating the Issue

Arbitration does not utilize formal pleadings similar to those used by courts to determine the precise issue or issues to be resolved. Such formal pleadings would destroy at least some of the simplicity and utility of arbitration. But somewhere in the course of an arbitration proceeding the issue to be resolved by the arbitrator must be specifically stated or pinpointed.

If the parties jointly initiate the arbitration by a submission agreement the issue will ordinarily be stated clearly in that instrument. However, as noted above, frequent practice is to use only a

---

[21]See Chapter 2, topic entitled "State Law: Private Sector." Also see Updegraff, Arbitration and Labor Relations, 142–145 (BNA Books, 1970); Updegraff & McCoy, Arbitration of Labor Disputes, 56–58 (1946).

[22]As in Kraft Foods Co., 15 LA 336 at 336 (Elson, 1950).

[23]See Kagel, Anatomy of a Labor Arbitration, 55 (BNA Books, 1961).

[24]Illustrating the possibility of court remedies in these situations, see Chapter 2, topic entitled "State Law: Private Sector"; Rye Police Assn. v. City of Rye, 100 LRRM 3115, 3116 (N.Y. S.Ct., 1979); Delta Lines, Inc. v. Teamsters Local 85, 93 LRRM 2037, 2038 (USDC, 1976); Amalgamated Food & Allied Workers v. Great Atl. & Pac. Tea Co., 415 F.2d 185 (CA 3, 1969); Carr v. Kalamazoo Vegetable Parchment Co., 354 Mich. 327, 331–332 (Mich. S.Ct., 1958); In re MacMahon, 4 LA 830, 831 (N.Y. S.Ct., 1946). Also see Arbitrator Begley in 39 LA 1083, 1084; Howlett in 38 LA 808, 817. But if a party proceeds through the entire arbitration proceedings without questioning arbitrability of an issue under consideration until after an award has been issued, the right to raise the question may be lost. See Piggly Wiggly Warehouse v. Local 1, 103 LRRM 2646, 2649 (CA 5, 1980). For related material see Chapter 6, topic entitled "Delay in Contesting Arbitrability."

demand for arbitration where the collective agreement contains an arbitration clause covering the dispute.[25]

Although no submission is used, the arbitrator will have jurisdiction of a dispute if it is covered by an arbitration clause in the collective agreement. To illustrate, if the arbitration clause covers disputes over the application or interpretation of the collective agreement, then any such dispute becomes arbitrable when either party serves the other with a demand or notice of intent to arbitrate. This demand or notice will identify the case in general terms at least, but often it does not state the precise issue in dispute.[26] The arbitrator selected for the case has jurisdiction to decide the dispute since it involves the application or interpretation of the collective agreement; but the question remains, what is the precise issue to be resolved by him? The issue, or issues, must be identified or pinpointed. This may be achieved in any of several ways where the parties have not done so sometime prior to the hearing.

Use of Original Grievance

The grievance statement as processed through the grievance procedure often serves as the statement of the issue, especially if the grievance statement is carefully worded.[27] The parties sometimes specifically stipulate that the written grievance is to be the statement of the issue,[28] particularly after they have tried but failed to agree on a specific statement of the issue.[29] The arbitrator himself might turn to the original grievance when the parties have not agreed upon a specific statement of the issue.[30]

---

[25]It may be noted that most collective agreements are silent as to statement of the issue in arbitration, but some do deal expressly with the matter by providing that the parties shall submit a joint statement of the issue or by calling for separate statements from each party (implying that ultimate determination of the issue is for the arbitrator). See Major Collective Bargaining Agreements: Arbitration Procedures, 61–64 (U.S. Dept. Labor Bull. No. 1425-6, 1966). Even where the agreement expressly provided that the issue "shall be mutually agreed upon," a federal court held that arbitration would not be defeated by inability of the parties to agree upon a statement of the issue. Socony Vacuum Tanker Men's Assn. v. Socony Mobil Co., 63 LRRM 2590 (CA 2, 1966).

[26]For instance, one Bethlehem Steel arbitrator noted that it had "not been the practice under the Bethelem Agreement for the parties to formulate 'submissions' defining precisely and exclusively the issues to be resolved." Bethlehem Steel Co., 17 LA 295, 300 (Selekman, 1951). Also see Davy, "The John Deere-UAW Permanent Arbitration System," Critical Issues in Labor Arbitration, 161, 190 (BNA Books, 1957). Where no joint submission is used, American Arbitration Association Rule 7 requires the unilateral demand for arbitration (a copy of which goes to the Association) to state "the nature of the dispute and the remedy sought," but this gives only one party's version, which may or may not contain an accurate statement of the issue. 43 LA 1292. The parties sometimes send a joint letter to the Association, in which the issue might be stated. As in Public Serv. Co., 52 LA 639 at 639 (Klein, 1969).

[27]As in Borden Mfg. Co., 25 LA 629, 630 (Wettach, 1955); Lukens Steel Co., 15 LA 408, 409 (D'Andrade, 1950).

[28]As in Texas Gas Transmission Corp., 27 LA 413 at 413 (Hebert, 1956).

[29]As in Johnson Bronze Co., 34 LA 365 at 365 (McDermott, 1960); New Haven Clock & Watch Co., 18 LA 203 at 203 (Stutz, 1952). The collective agreement called for a similar approach in Bowaters S. Paper Corp., 52 LA 674, 675 (Oppenheim, 1969).

[30]As did Arbitrator Roadely in 75 LA 249, 250; Sisk in 68 LA 1006, 1007; Johnson in 48 LA 1357, 1358; Davey in 43 LA 453, 455; Donnelly in 19 LA 690, 691.

Too often, however, the original grievance is too poorly worded to provide a key to the precise issue in dispute.[31] Also, the discussion at the prearbitral grievance steps sometimes develops the issue in different or modified channels. To a limited extent this may happen also at the arbitration stage, as in the case wherein Arbitrator Meredith Reid noted that "at the hearing the broad issue suggested by the grievance was narrowed very substantially as a result of testimony and argument."[32]

Parties Stipulate Issue at the Hearing

At the commencement of the arbitration hearing the parties may execute a stipulation or submission precisely stating the issue.[33]

The view has been expressed that the issue should be framed as soon as possible, preferably by the parties even prior to the arbitration hearing.[34] As we have noted, the parties sometimes do agree to a statement of the issue either prior to the hearing or at its commencement. Unfortunately, however, the parties frequently are unable to agree upon any specific statement of the issue, and sometimes attempts to do so tend to generate more dispute. Indeed, the parties themselves do not always know precisely what the issue is at the outset of the hearing.[35] Moreover, even when the parties have signed a submission stating the issue, it may be ambiguous and in need of clarification.[36]

Likewise, the issue as stated by the parties may be too narrow to dispose of the entire dispute; in such instances the arbitrator may so inform the parties in order that they might authorize him to resolve the dispute fully.[37]

---

[31]Then, too, cases sometimes reach arbitration without any formal written grievance ever having been submitted. For example, see White Motor Co., 43 LA 682, 683 (McGury, 1964).

[32]Heppenstall Co., 22 LA 84, 85 (1954). For other cases in which the issue as developed at the hearing governed over the grievance statement, see Arbitrator Mathews in 74 LA 224, 235; Garrett in 71 LA 1188, 1193–1194; Dworkin in 45 LA 897, 901–902; McCoy in 45 LA 630, 633. In City of Southfield, 78 LA 153 at 153 (Roumell, 1982), the neutral "held numerous pre-trial conferences in an attempt to set the ground rules for proceeding with the hearing and to narrow the issues"; as "finally narrowed, there were ten issues" to be decided.

[33]See Arbitrator Woolf in 75 LA 701, 703; Roberts in 46 LA 486, 487; Whelan in 23 LA 126, 127; Kelliher in 15 LA 363, 364. Reference to such stipulations does not always reveal the stage of the hearing at which the issue is defined. See Arbitrator Craver in 74 LA 89 at 89; Helburn in 70 LA 518, 519; Jones in 53 LA 165, 167; Abernethy in 50 LA 760 at 760 (parties agreed to substance of the issue and arbitrator thereafter stated it in his own words); Wagner in 46 LA 81, 82. Sometimes the stipulation is oral. See Arbitrator Roberts in 46 LA 486, 487; Aaron in 16 LA 165, 166.

[34]See Heath, "Defining the Issue and the Remedy," Proceedings of the 20th Annual Meeting of NAA, 352–359 (BNA Books, 1967). Also see comments by Jones & Smith, "Management and Labor Appraisals and Criticisms of the Arbitration Process: A Report With Comments," 62 Mich. L. Rev. 1115, 1130–1132 (1964).

[35]See Mundet Cork Corp., 18 LA 254, 255 (Reynolds, 1952).

[36]See Zia Co., 52 LA 89, 90 (Cohen, 1969), where both parties signed a reworded submission to clarify the issue; McKinney Mfg. Co., 19 LA 291, 292 (Reid, 1952), where the arbitrator had implied authority to restate the issue contained in the submission.

[37]See American Smelting & Ref. Co., 29 LA 262, 264 (Ross, 1957). Absent such broadened authority from the parties, the arbitrator will feel confined to the narrowly stipulated issue. See Arbitrator Simon in 68 LA 797, 802; Roberts in 49 LA 121, 122, 125; Fallon in 48 LA 12, 15–16.

Sometimes the parties agree to a statement of the issue during the course of the hearing.[38] After some testimony has been received the dispute often appears in sharper focus. At an opportune moment the arbitrator may call for a discussion to clarify the issue. Such discussion may produce an agreed statement of the issue—perhaps one worded by the arbitrator and accepted by the parties.

Of course the arbitrator has the privilege at the hearing of calling for discussion or statements to clarify the issue and its scope. Whether he will choose to do this (and if so, at what stage of the hearing) will depend upon his evaluation of its necessity and upon his impression as to whether it will expedite or retard the proceedings. In any event, it has been suggested that arbitrators should not press the parties unduly to arrive at an exact statement of the issue.[39]

Issue Pinpointed by Arbitrator

In many cases the burden of clarifying or pinpointing the issue settles upon the arbitrator. Ordinarily the general nature of the issue or issues underlying the dispute becomes apparent to the arbitrator before the hearing has progressed very far, and he usually has no difficulty in discerning the precise issue or issues after he has studied the entire case.

The parties may specifically request that the arbitrator determine what the issue is.[40] A similar result may be produced by the collective agreement itself, as where the agreement provided that if the parties "fail to agree on a joint submission each shall submit a separate submission and the arbitrator shall determine the issue or issues to be heard."[41]

Often the burden of pinpointing the issue falls to the arbitrator after the parties have attempted without success to agree upon a statement thereof at the hearing.[42] In these instances the parties' discussion and/or separate statements from each may aid the arbitrator in stating the issue.[43]

---

[38]As in Marblehead Lime Co., 48 LA 310 at 310 (Anrod, 1966); Republic Oil Co., 15 LA 895 at 895 (Klamon, 1951).

[39]Sembower, "Halting the Trend Toward Technicalities in Arbitration," Critical Issues in Labor Arbitration, 98, 101 (BNA Books, 1957). Of possible applicability here is the very general statement in the Code of Professional Responsibility that an arbitrator "may restate the substance of issues or arguments to promote or certify understanding." § V(A)(1)(b), 64 LA 1326.

[40]See Arbitrator Elbert in 69 LA 102, 107; Daugherty in 46 LA 1049, 1049–1050; Hildebrand in 28 LA 769, 775.

[41]Lockheed Aircraft Corp., 23 LA 815, 815–816 (Marshall, 1955). Also see Arbitrator Abernethy in 42 LA 988, 989; Dworkin in 29 LA 29, 31, 35.

[42]E.g., Arbitrator Hyman in 75 LA 733 at 733; May in 75 LA 346, 351; Gentile in 74 LA 590 at 590, 593; Talent in 74 LA 80, 81–82; Howell in 72 LA 421, 423; Weiss in 71 LA 260, 262; Waite in 71 LA 141 at 141; Springfield in 70 LA 788, 789; Taylor in 69 LA 782, 782–783; Spencer in 69 LA 674, 674–675; Rule in 69 LA 136 at 136. In some of these cases the parties expressly requested that the arbitrator frame the issue after they had been unable to agree on it. In Borden Co., 46 LA 1175 at 1175 (Bellman, 1966), the parties declined to attempt a joint statement of the issue—this left it to the arbitrator. In C & D Batteries, 31 LA 272, 273, 275–276 (Jaffee, 1958), a party could not defeat the arbitration by walking out upon failure to achieve a joint statement of the issue.

[43]See Arbitrator Conway in 68 LA 325, 325–326; Abernethy in 51 LA 9, 10; Burr in 36 LA 1132, 1133; Smith in 27 LA 251, 253. Also see Larkin in 46 LA 39, 40.

In many cases there is no discussion by either the arbitrator or the parties at the hearing specifically directed toward pinpointing the issue, even where it has not been previously defined clearly.[44] In these cases the arbitrator arrives at a precise statement of the issue or issues after he has studied the entire record of the case, including, if available to him, such matters as the original grievance statement and the grievance procedure minutes, the demand for arbitration and any reply of the other party, correspondence of the parties, the transcript of the hearing (or the arbitrator's notes), the parties' exhibits, and the parties' briefs.

Frequently the arbitrator finds that the issue is clearly and accurately stated in a single one of these sources. Again, the arbitrator may conclude that one party's wording of the issue is an accurate statement thereof.[45]

Simultaneous Arbitration of Several Grievances

The question has often arisen whether one party may be compelled by the other to arbitrate several grievances before the same arbitrator in one proceeding. Simultaneous arbitration of grievances has been said to reflect "the best ideals of the whole arbitration process, which are devoted to efficiency, expeditious disposition and economy."[46] A large number of arbitrators obviously agree, for a very strong line of arbitral authority holds that such simultaneous arbitration of all grievances which reach the arbitration stage at the same time can be compelled by either party unless the arbitration clause of the collective agreement clearly and unambiguously provides otherwise.[47]

---

[44]For some cases which appear to fall within this category and in which the arbitrator pinpointed the issue, see Arbitrator Belkin in 70 LA 300, 300–301; Krimsly in 47 LA 518, 520–521; Rezler in 46 LA 1073, 1074; Kates in 45 LA 153, 154; Marshall in 25 LA 480, 481; Dworkin in 24 LA 73, 74; Cole in 22 LA 868, 869; Merrill in 20 LA 727, 731; Bailer in 19 LA 257, 259; Prasow in 17 LA 25, 26; Healy in 15 LA 764, 765; Gregory in 15 LA 420, 424.

[45]See Magma Copper Co., 51 LA 9, 10 (Abernethy, 1968); Gisholt Mach. Co., 23 LA 105, 108 (Kelliher, 1954).

[46]Stewart-Warner Corp., 12 LA 305, 306 (Gregory, 1949). For discussions of the various arguments for and against multiple grievance arbitration, with the "for" arguments prevailing, see Arbitrator Traynor in 51 LA 1001, 1004–1005; Solomon in 50 LA 1070, 1074–1080; King in 46 LA 827, 829–830; Ray in 46 LA 210, 212–214. If the agreement deals expressly with this matter, its terms will of course govern. See Arbitrator Shister in 47 LA 601, 602; Schedler in 40 LA 95, 96.

[47]See Arbitrator Dworkin in 53 LA 239, 244–245; Bothwell in 52 LA 1035, 1041–1043; Traynor in 51 LA 1001, 1004–1005; Solomon in 50 LA 1070, 1074–1080; Cahn in 47 LA 330, 332; King in 46 LA 827, 829–830; Ray in 46 LA 210, 212–214; Singletary in 44 LA 1154, 1156–1158; Holly in 43 LA 570, 572; Hebert in 42 LA 1232, 1237–1239; Jaffee in 41 LA 1017, 1019–1020; Stouffer in 41 LA 424, 426–427; Horlacher in 41 LA 252, 254; Haughton in 39 LA 943, 947; Fisher in 37 LA 724, 725–726; Hawley in 36 LA 751, 752–753; Sembower in 36 LA 96, 98–99; Luskin in 33 LA 859, 860; Fleming in 32 LA 442, 444; Warns in 28 LA 586, 588–589; Feinberg in 23 LA 588, 589–590; Williams in 23 LA 13, 14–15; Rader in 20 LA 441, 442–443; Trotta in 13 LA 878, 879; Gregory in 12 LA 305, 306–307. Federal courts have ruled that the question whether grievances are to be resolved in a single or in multiple proceedings should be decided by the arbitrator rather than the courts. American Can Co. v. Papermakers Local 412, 82 LRRM 3055, 3057 (USDC, 1973), citing other cases in accord; Avon Prods., Inc. v. Auto Workers Local 710, 67 LRRM 2001 (CA 8, 1967). Cf., Local 2–477 v. Continental Oil Co., 90 LRRM 3040, 3041–3042 (CA 10, 1975).

In adhering to this general rule, many arbitrators have expressly considered and rejected the contention that a different result is required by the contract's use of the singular term "grievance."[48] However, the right to require multiple grievance arbitration has been denied where the contract speaks in the singular *and* there is an adequately established past practice of arbitrating only one grievance at a time.[49] Furthermore, Arbitrator Samuel H. Jaffee recognized that there may be special circumstances justifying other exceptions to the aforementioned general rule, such as in the following situations: (1) individual grievances involving widely separated plants, with separate contracts, with witnesses located in many places; (2) inordinately large number of grievances; or (3) grievances of a special nature requiring an arbitrator with corresponding specialized experience.[50] Arbitrator Harry J. Dworkin discerned that multiple grievance arbitration would not be required if "it is clearly shown that to do so would result in confusion, prejudice or substantial detriment to either party."[51]

Once an arbitrator has been selected a party has little basis for submitting additional grievances to the arbitrator without his consent and agreement by the other party.[52] In this regard, for instance, American Arbitration Association Rule 7 provides that "After the Arbitrator is appointed, no new or different claim may be submitted to him except with the consent of the Arbitrator and all other parties."[53]

---

[48]Of the arbitrators listed in the prior footnote, all who were confronted with this contention rejected it. Also see IBEW Local 2188 v. Western Elec. Co., 108 LRRM 3027, 3028 (CA 5, 1981).

[49]See Arbitrator Marshall in 51 LA 215, 220; Lockhart in 42 LA 65, 66–67; Turkus in 39 LA 814, 819–820; Wissner in 38 LA 1045, 1047–1048.

[50]American Brake Shoe Co., 41 LA 1017, 1019–1020 (1963). These possible exceptions have been recognized by other arbitrators. See Arbitrator Bothwell in 52 LA 1035, 1041–1043; Duff in 49 LA 355, 356 (where there was a backlog of 52 cases he limited the number to be heard by a single arbitrator at a hearing to 5); Seinsheimer in 44 LA 97, 101 (nature of different cases might require different arbitrators); Taylor in 7 LA 112, 112–113 (simultaneous arbitration of grievances under separate contracts not required). Where an agreement separated grievances into "general" and "technical" categories, separate arbitration was required for each category. Cambridge Tile Mfg. Co., 66–1 ARB ¶8098 (Nichols, 1966).

[51]Apex Smelting Co., 53 LA 239, 244 (1969). In Appalachian Power Co., 53 LA 1012, 1013 (Reid, 1969), the arbitrator would hear only one of four grievances where the other three had not been processed in accordance with the agreement and hearing them would be "unreasonably burdensome" since the employer was not prepared on them and had no witnesses.

[52]See discussion by Arbitrator Bert L. Luskin in Maremont Automotive Prods., 25 LA 171, 172–173 (1955). Accord, Arbitrator Nathan in 70 LA 1091, 1096; Dworkin in 53 LA 239, 245, and in 41 LA 961, 965. Stressing the requirement of agreement by the other party, see Local 2–477 v. Continental Oil Co., 90 LRRM 3040, 3041–3042 (CA 10, 1975). It has also been held that simultaneous arbitration can be required only as to those grievances which can be grouped together in the same letter to the FMCS. Harshaw Chem. Co., 44 LA 97, 101 (Seinsheimer, 1965); Stauffer Chem. Co., 44 LA 41, 42 (Griffin, 1964).

[53]43 LA 1292. But see Sylvania Elec. Prods., 24 LA 199, 201–205, 210 (Brecht, 1954), where under Rule 7 grievances filed at the start of the arbitration hearing were accepted against the objection of one party where they added no new issue, arose from the same action as the grievance specifically identified in the demand for arbitration, and were fully anticipated in that demand. Also, Allied Chem. Corp., 43 LA 996, 997 (Cahn, 1964), would permit cases to be added for a limited period after the parties have exchanged lists of acceptable arbitrators.

Advisory Opinions

Arbitrators generally are reluctant to issue advisory opinions or "declaratory judgments."[54] In one case Arbitrator D. Emmett Ferguson ruled, for example, that it was premature to submit to arbitration "a hypothetical question" and that "each case must be judged on its own merits when, and if, it arises."[55] Arbitrator Harry H. Platt elaborated:

"Grievance determination, in order to be effective, should rest on facts or conclusions drawn from facts and not on speculative and hypothetical situations. Especially in cases like this [challenge as to reasonableness of revised company rule concerning the status of any flight hostess who becomes pregnant or adopts a child], factual differences weigh heavily. The question of whether a rule is fair and reasonable cannot be confidently determined except in the context of a concrete case and upon consideration of the specific circumstances of a particular case in which the rule is invoked and applied. Even a so-called policy grievance should be made as concrete as possible in terms of an actual case rather than in vague and general terms. For, as has often been said, general principles do not decide concrete cases. And equally important is the fact that where a decision is made on a specific grievance or a concrete factual setting, the chances are minimized of the Board reaching unintended conclusions or indulging in generalization."[56]

An arbitrator may be more inclined to issue an advisory opinion if the requesting party demonstrates that it is necessary to protect the party's interests under the contract,[57] or if the arbitrator is convinced that both parties desire one.[58]

The parties may specifically provide by contract for advisory opinions. The Chrysler Corporation, for instance, adopted "an Agreement-provided 'declaratory judgment' procedure for securing deter-

---

[54]See Arbitrator Jones in 70 LA 833, 834–835; Platt in 61 LA 1205, 1212, and in 47 LA 1127, 1130–1131; Kamin in 50 LA 1093, 1096; Purdom in 50 LA 940, 947 (he refused to issue a "bush whacking broadside" ruling and confined himself to the narrow issue presented by the evidence); Kabaker in 50 LA 683, 691; Duff in 45 LA 225, 227–229; Scheiber in 44 LA 929, 936; Howlett in 44 LA 827, 829 (no ruling on moot question), and in 29 LA 495, 501; Turkus in 64–3 ARB ¶9161 (no ruling on moot question); Kates in 41 LA 937, 942; Crawford in 35 LA 453, 454 (no ruling on moot question); Dworkin in 35 LA 237, 240–241; Eckhardt in 29 LA 861, 862; Ferguson in 27 LA 640, 642; Marshall in 26 LA 74, 78. Also see Alpha Beta Co. v. Retail Clerks Local 428, 110 LRRM 2169, 2171 (CA 9, 1982). Cf., Stouffer in 40 LA 898, 901; Seitz in 37 LA 1034, 1036–1037; Haughton in 33 LA 543, 545. For a related discussion, see Shulman, "Reason, Contract, and Law in Labor Relations," 68 Harv. L. Rev. 999, 1022–1023 (1955), reprinted in Management Rights and the Arbitration Process, 169 (BNA Books, 1956).

[55]Monarch Mach. Tool Co., 27 LA 640, 642 (1956).

[56]Trans World Air Lines, 47 LA 1127, 1130 (1967), refusing to issue a declaratory judgment. But in National Airlines, 42 LA 1206, 1208–1209 (Black, 1964), a company grievance seeking a declaration that management had the right to adopt a rule requiring employees to wear safety caps was successful. Also see Northwest Airlines, 45 LA 565, 570 (Shister, 1965).

[57]See Arbitrator Dworkin in 49 LA 922, 926–927; Williams in 39 LA 1051, 1054; Kharas in 25 LA 755, 758.

[58]See Arbitrator Levy in 71 LA 909, 910; Dworkin in 68 LA 101, 101–102; Barnhart in 47 LA 596, 598–600; Klamon in 25 LA 830, 835. However, even where both parties wanted a declaratory judgment for future cases, Arbitrator Samuel S. Kates did not render one. D-V Displays Corp., 41 LA 937, 942 (1963).

minations of basic issues in advance of actual grievance situations."[59] A disadvantage of such provisions has been said to be that "an actual grievance may present an issue of contract interpretation in sharper focus than a claim stated in general terms."[60]

Another situation, similar in substance to requests for advisory opinions, is that in which the evidence is inadequate to enable the arbitrator to make an informed ruling on an issue that has been presented in a case involving an actual grievance. In such a situation Arbitrator Frank Elkouri ruled that the "issue accordingly must be left open and unresolved by the award in the present case, without prejudice to the rights of either Party in the event either of the Parties raises the issue in the future."[61]

Extent of Permissible Deviation From Prearbitral Discussion of Case

Occasionally one party to an arbitration objects to an alleged attempt by the other party to enlarge the scope of the case by unilaterally injecting new issues, arguments, or claims for the first time at the arbitration stage. In disposing of these objections arbitrators tend to emphasize substance over form in seeking to uncover the real merits of the case.

An arbitrator may refuse to confine the parties rigidly to what occurred prior to the arbitration if the deviation from the prearbitral stage does not amount to the addition of new issues, but merely involves a modified line of argument, an additional element closely related to the original issue, the refinement or correction of an ineptly stated grievance, or the introduction of new evidence.[62]

To this extent, new aspects of the dispute may be aired initially at the arbitration stage, unless the arbitration tribunal is serving purely in an "appellate" capacity. For example, in overruling a party's objection to the consideration of an element which was relevant to the dispute but which had not been discussed by the parties prior to arbitration, Arbitrator Benton Gillingham stated that the objection was "based upon an unreasonably and unjustifiably limited and restrictive concept of arbitration" as it is generally conceived and

---

[59]Wolff, Crane & Cole, "The Chrysler-UAW Umpire System," Proceedings of the 11th Annual Meeting of NAA, 111, 118 (BNA Books, 1958).

[60]Id. at 147 (discussion by a General Motors Umpire, Nathan P. Feinsinger). Where evidence was in fact presented on the merits of an actual grievance, but the grievance had to be dismissed on procedural grounds, Arbitrator Sidney A. Wolff did render an advisory opinion on the merits in response to an invitation from the parties. Chase Bag Co., 69 LA 85, 86 (1977).

[61]Kansas City Power & Light Co., 71 LA 381, 393 (1978).

[62]For discussion of use of new evidence at the arbitration stage, see Chapter 8, topic entitled " 'New' Evidence at Arbitration Hearing." Also see Chapter 15, subtopic entitled "Postdischarge Conduct or Charges." Permitting a reasonable amount of deviation at the arbitration stage also enhances the possibility of settlement. See topic entitled "Settlements at Arbitration Stage," below. The general subject of new issues and evidence at the arbitration stage is also treated by Fleming, The Labor Arbitration Process, 144–153 (U. of Ill. Press, 1965).

applied in the field of labor relations.[63] Arbitrator Gillingham explained further:

> "[A]rbitration is not strictly comparable to the appeal process in the courts, or in any system of judicial or quasi-judicial agencies, where the appeal process involves a review by a higher authority of a judgment already rendered by a subordinate or inferior agency. To the contrary, arbitration is a process involving the use of a third party to resolve a dispute where the primary parties have been unable to resolve the disagreement. Thus it would appear that arbitration is much more nearly analogous to the litigation of a controversy in a judicial or quasi-judicial agency of *initial jurisdiction* * * *."[64]

Arbitrator Robert Feinberg stated that contentions which do not change the issue should always be available to the parties, although he indicated that he would reject attempts to broaden the scope of the grievance for the first time in arbitration.[65] In turn, Arbitrator Walter Boles declared that "any arbitrator would be derelict in his duty if, in considering whether or not a given section of a contract was applicable to a matter before him, he limited his inquiry only to points of argument raised before the matter came on to hearing."[66]

Nor will a grievant be bound rigidly at the arbitration stage by an ineptly worded grievance statement, or one which gives an incorrect contractual basis for the claim or cites no contractual provision at all.[67] Formal and concise pleadings are not required in arbitration. A possibly typical view is that which was expressed by Arbitrator Marion Beatty:

> "Employees or their Union officers cannot be expected to draw their grievances artfully. If they have sufficiently apprised the Company of the nature of their complaint and if it is found that the Company has violated any portion of the contract, the employees, in my opinion, are entitled to relief."[68]

A more extensive expression was provided by Arbitrator A. Langley Coffey:

---

[63]Washington Motor Transp. Assn., 28 LA 6, 9 (1956).

[64]Ibid., emphasis added.

[65]Mergenthaler Linotype Co., 15 LA 707, 708 (1950). Also see Arbitrator Doyle in 39 LA 489, 492.

[66]Temco Aircraft Corp., 22 LA 826, 828 (1954), wherein Arbitrator Boles distinguished a prior case in which he refused to hear "an entirely new issue."

[67]See Arbitrator Gallagher in 79 LA 1151, 1153; Nolan in 75 LA 712, 714–715; Leahy in 73 LA 882, 884; Hamby in 73 LA 771, 772; Rothman in 72 LA 1109, 1111; Cohen in 71 LA 1171, 1173–1174; Rice in 71 LA 509, 512; Pritzker in 68 LA 658, 661–662; Kates in 51 LA 1098, 1100; Dunau in 50 LA 236, 238–239; Hayes in 48 LA 524, 528; Gorsuch in 48 LA 429, 436; Howard in 48 LA 379, 382; Altieri in 41 LA 47, 48–49; Sembower in 40 LA 1266, 1271; Beatty in 39 LA 1226, 1230; Hebert in 37 LA 42, 46; Miller in 35 LA 757, 778; Hale in 34 LA 827, 833–834; Griffin in 33 LA 847, 850; Jaffee in 27 LA 844, 854; Gorder in 20 LA 880, 882; Coffey in 17 LA 125, 129; McCoy in 16 LA 775, 776. While a grievant will be permitted to rely upon a contractual provision not relied upon prior to arbitration, the possibility should be noted that his failure to cite the provision in the grievance statement might be taken as some indication that he did not then believe the provision supported his case. For example, see Wyandotte Chems. Corp., 41 LA 230, 235–236 (Howlett, 1963). If a jointly signed submission states a precise issue, the arbitrator ordinarily will feel strictly limited to answering that question. E.I. du Pont de Nemours & Co., 39 LA 1083, 1084 (Begley, 1962). But see Western Elec. Co., 42 LA 1316, 1319–1320 (Altieri, 1964).

[68]Armour & Co., 39 LA 1226, 1230 (1963). In American Bosch Arma Corp. v. IUE Local 794, 243 F.Supp. 493 (USDC, 1965), the court noted that it has never been required that grievances be submitted in language comparable to that used in formal court proceedings.

"Neither is it acceptable as a valid objection, that, because the Union in its written protest, and in claiming that the aggrieved employee has been discriminated against, cites provisions of the contract other than the one upon which jurisdiction rests, it has foreclosed its right to enlarge upon its claim that the discharge was in violation of the contract. Such objections admittedly have standing in places where the record means more than it does in arbitrations. However, where there is no requirement by contract, or otherwise, that either party submit or stand on any formal written protest or answer, formalities are dispensed with in hearings of this kind, and technical objections are brushed aside in an endeavor to get at the facts of a given case, and to do equity and complete justice to the rights of all parties, without let or hindrance, or the entanglements of formal pleadings, procedures or techniques."[69]

If a party materially changes its position from the grievance procedure to the arbitration stage in such a way that the other party is taken by surprise and finds it difficult or impossible to present its case adequately, the arbitrator may take some appropriate action (such as granting a continuance or remanding the case to the parties for further negotiations).[70]

Moreover, if a deviation from what occurred at the prearbitral stage actually constitutes the addition of a new issue or dispute that has not been previously discussed by the parties, or the addition of a claim that has not been filed as required by the collective agreement, and if this bypassing of the grievance procedure is objected to by one of the parties, the arbitrator will ordinarily refuse to dispose of the new matter in his award.[71] In this regard, a General Motors Umpire has stated:

"It is the function of the Umpire to decide questions which the parties themselves have tried to settle without success. New contentions presented for the first time at the Fourth Step are untimely, for their late presentation defeats the avowed aim of the grievance procedure—to settle disputes by collective bargaining whenever possible and to refer to

---

[69]Charles Eneu Johnson Co., 17 LA 125, 129 (1950). Even where the agreement limits the arbitrator's authority to a ruling on the specific provision relied upon prior to the hearing, strict enforcement of such limitation might result at most in a postponement of the ultimate consideration of the merits of the dispute. See statement by Arbitrator Seward in Bethlehem Steel Co., 36 LA 441, 442 (1961), and by Arbitrator Stark in Bethlehem Steel Co., 33 LA 285, 290–291 (1959). Also see Arbitrator Nolan in 75 LA 712, 714–715.

[70]See comments of Arbitrator Cahn in Jones & Laughlin Steel Corp., 23 LA 397, 398 (1954); Emery in Texas-New Mexico Pipe Line Co., 17 LA 90, 93 (1951). Also see Arbitrator Allen in 70 LA 805, 808. Even apart from material *changes* in position, an arbitrator will take appropriate action where the grievance statement is too vague to inform the other party as to what is alleged. See Caterpillar Tractor Co., 39 LA 875, 878–879 (Dworkin, 1962). Arbitration proceeded, however, where the employer "was not in fact in the dark or uninformed as to what [the] grievance was all about at the time it came to arbitration." Black, Sivalls & Bryson, Inc., 42 LA 988, 991 (Abernethy, 1964).

[71]See Arbitrator Gentile in 76 LA 450, 456; Barsamian in 74 LA 278, 280; Andrews in 71 LA 519, 523–524; Swain in 69 LA 493, 502; Dworkin in 51 LA 645, 656; Seward in 50 LA 1214 at 1214, and in 17 LA 537, 540; Hayes in 47 LA 421, 422–423; Alexander in 46 LA 184, 186–187; Bothwell in 45 LA 141, 143–144; Grant in 38 LA 153, 156; Meltzer in 27 LA 580, 584; Wolff in 27 LA 448, 453; Rosenfarb in 21 LA 22, 23; Davey in 20 LA 844, 849; Piper in 18 LA 801, 806; Selekman in 17 LA 295, 300. Cf., Dallas in 75 LA 238, 240; Koven in 54 LA 677, 680; Brecht in 24 LA 199, 204–206. Also see AAA Rule 7(b) which appears to touch upon this matter. 43 LA 1292.

the Umpire only those cases in which collective bargaining has been tried and has failed."[72]

Preparing Cases for Arbitration

Thorough preparation of cases for arbitration is of paramount importance. Ordinarily most or all of the arbitrator's knowledge and understanding of the case is based upon the evidence and arguments presented at the arbitration hearing. Moreover, a party must fully understand its own case in order to communicate it effectively to the arbitrator, and full understanding depends upon thorough preparation.

What is necessary for thorough preparation of any given case will depend largely upon the nature of the case. For instance, in some cases the facts are especially important and each party will concentrate upon proving, largely through testimony of witnesses, that the facts are as that party sees them. In other cases the facts may be less important or not disputed, the controversy being centered upon some other matter, such as the proper interpretation of the collective agreement. Here each party's case may be devoted largely to arguments about how the agreement should be interpreted. In still other cases, economic and statistical data may be especially important.

Thus, the nature of the case should be considered in determining which items of the following "preparation" checklist should be emphasized in any particular case. Since not all items are pertinent to every case, no significance lies in the order in which they are listed.

a. Review the history of the case as developed at the prearbitral steps of the grievance procedure.
b. Study the entire collective agreement to ascertain all clauses bearing directly or indirectly on the dispute. Also, comparison of current provisions with those contained in prior agreements might reveal changes significant to the case.
c. In order to determine the general authority of the arbitrator, and accordingly the scope of the arbitration, examine the instruments used to initiate the arbitration. (See topics entitled "Initiating Arbitration: Submission Versus Arbitration Clause" and "Stating the Issue," above.)

---

[72]Umpire Decision No. E-276 (1949). Also, Decision No. E-295 (1949). However, where an ambiguous grievance statement was interpreted in fact to encompass certain claims or issues, they were not barred from the arbitration merely because they were not discussed at the prearbitral steps, since (1) the company's reply to the grievance was both terse and stated in very general language, and (2) the company in grievance discussions quickly gave the union the impression that the company had closed its mind on the grievance, so the entire spectrum of the grievance was not discussed. Kansas City Power & Light Co., 71 LA 381, 384–385 (Elkouri, 1978). In the latter case, however, still another issue was barred from the arbitration since it neither was encompassed within the written grievance statement, nor had been discussed at the prearbitral steps.

d. Talk to all persons (even those the other party might use as witnesses) who might be able to aid development of a full picture of the case, including different viewpoints. You will thus better understand not only your own case but your opponent's as well; if you can anticipate your opponent's case you can better prepare to rebut it.[73]

e. Interview each of your own witnesses (1) to determine what they know about the case, (2) to make certain they understand the relation of their testimony to the whole case, and (3) to cross-examine them to check their testimony and to acquaint them with the process of cross-examination. Make a written summary of the expected testimony of each witness; this can be reviewed when the witness testifies to insure that no important points are overlooked. Some parties outline in advance the questions to be asked each witness.

f. Examine all records and documents that might be relevant to the case. Organize those you expect to use and make copies for use by the arbitrator and the other party at the hearing. If needed documents are in the exclusive possession of the other party, ask that they be made available before or at the hearing. (For other possible means of obtaining such evidence, and for the significance of the other party's refusal to produce it, see Chapter 8.)

---

[73]Concerning the need for such prearbitration interviews, and their general propriety and benefits to the arbitration process, note the following statement by Arbitrator Edgar A. Jones, Jr., in Pacific Sw. Airline, 70 LA 205, 213 (1977):

"It is almost routine for a union or an employer advocate—lawyer or not—to go to the locale of a pending arbitration a day or two before a scheduled hearing in order to interview witnesses and plan the details of the morrow's presentation. It is not at all unusual for that prehearing occasion to be the first time that the advocate has had the chance to get first-hand accounts of witnesses, to identify possible discrepancies among their accounts, to press them as a cross-examiner is apt to, to observe their demeanor and evaluate their credibility, to assess the potential influence on the course of the hearing of what they have to say and how they are apt to say it in the context of the hearing.

"Contrary to the impression expressed by the Union representatives and the potential witnesses in this case, that kind of encounter immediately before a hearing is simply not in itself a "dirty pool" situation. Instead, it is an important part of the administration of the grievance procedure. It is by no means unusual for cases to be settled on the day—or even the hour—before the hearing is to convene based on the advocate's last-minute, eye-opened assessment of the significance of these prehearing contacts.

"Of course, this otherwise proper investigative pre-hearing procedure may be converted to an improper one if the advocate or a colleague with authority somehow acts improperly in a material way in the course of it. The parameters of legitimate inquiry are set by the employment relationship. Job-related conduct of the employee and fellow workers is within the area of the permissible, whereas prying into subjects of a personal nature or concerning conduct that is not job-related is foreclosed. Nor is there any license to conduct interviews in a manner coercive or demeaning to the employee."

In this case two employees were discharged for refusing to answer prearbitration questions by the employer's attorney. Arbitrator Jones held their refusal to be "contractually unprotected and, presumably, statutorily unprotected as well," and although the penalty was reduced in this instance, he stated that "Future refusals to cooperate in like circumstances will render an employee subject to discharge. * * *" Id. at 215–216. In Cook Paint & Varnish Co. v. NLRB, 106 LRRM 3016 (D.C. Cir., 1981), Arbitrator Jones was quoted with approval by the court, which held that under the NLRA employers may interview employees in preparation for a pending arbitration, provided certain limitations are observed. For more on the Cook Paint case along with related material, see Chapter 8, subtopic entitled "Interviewing Employees in Preparation for Arbitration." For other related material, see Chapter 5, subtopic entitled "Right to Union Representation at Early Stage."

g. Visit the physical premises involved in the dispute to better visualize what occurred and what the dispute is about. Also, consider the advisability of asking at the hearing that the arbitrator (accompanied by both parties) also visit the site of the dispute.

h. Consider the utility of pictorial or statistical exhibits. One exhibit can be more effective than many words, if the matter is suited to the exhibit form of portrayal. However, exhibits which do not "fit" the case, and those which are inaccurate or misleading, are almost certain to be ineffective or to be damaging to their proponent.

i. Consider what the parties' past practice has been in comparable situations. (For the significance of past practice, see Chapter 12.)

j. Attempt to determine whether there is some "key" point upon which the case might turn. If so, it may be to your advantage to concentrate upon that point.

k. In "interpretation" cases prepare a written argument to support your view as to the proper interpretation of the disputed language. (For the standards or rules used by arbitrators in interpreting contract language, see Chapter 9.)

l. In "interest" or "contract writing" cases collect and prepare economic and statistical data to aid evaluation of the dispute. (For the standards or guides used by arbitrators in interest disputes, see Chapter 18.)

m. Research the parties' prior arbitration awards and the published awards of other parties on the subject of the dispute for an indication of how similar issues have been approached in other cases. (Regarding the use of prior awards, see Chapter 11.)

n. Prepare an outline of your case and discuss it with other persons in your group. This insures better understanding of the case, and will strengthen it by uncovering matters that need further attention. Then, too, it will tend to underscore policy and strategy considerations that may be very important in the ultimate handling of the case. Use of the outline at the hearing will facilitate an organized and systematic presentation of the case.

Thorough preparation involves the use of ingenuity to illuminate all the possibilities of the case.[74] Certainly, the arbitrator needs a full

---

[74]For other discussions relating to case preparation, see Baer, Winning in Labor Arbitration, Chapter 6 (1982); Seward, "The Quality of Adversary Presentation in Arbitration: A Critical View," Proceedings of the 32nd Annual Meeting of NAA, 14 (BNA Books, 1980); Robins, "Comment," id. at 30; Rubenstein, "Comment," id. at 47; Oliver, "Comment," id. at 51; Harrison, Preparing and Presenting Your Arbitration Case: A Manual for Union and Management Representatives (BNA Books, 1979); Liebes, "Preparing the Case for Arbitration," Proceedings of the 20th Annual Meeting of NAA, 359–366 (BNA Books, 1967); Kagel, Anatomy of a Labor Arbitration, 37–54 (BNA Books, 1961).

picture of the case and he will be interested in all its possibilities to aid him in reaching a sound decision.

Fact Stipulations

An agreed statement of facts can serve well to expedite the arbitration hearing by reducing the number of necessary witnesses and by permitting concentration upon the disputed aspects of the case. This recognized, the parties may come to the hearing with a fact stipulation, or they may enter into one at the hearing.[75]

Sometimes fact stipulations are entered into at the suggestion of the arbitrator, who may recess the hearing to permit the parties to determine whether any facts can be stipulated.[76]

Need for Hearing

A hearing in the presence of the arbitrator is deemed imperative in virtually all cases. In giving each party full and fair opportunity to be heard, the arbitration hearing simultaneously serves to inform the arbitrator fully regarding all material aspects of the dispute. However, in some cases the parties believe that the arbitrator can be adequately informed without a hearing in his presence, so they submit the dispute for decision entirely on the basis of stipulated facts, written briefs, and sometimes affidavits.[77]

Even where the parties agree to submit their case without a hearing, the arbitrator may not always agree that the case can be properly resolved without a hearing. For instance, where the facts were in issue but the parties nonetheless wanted to submit the case without a hearing (the arbitrator being directed to investigate the facts by interviewing the affected persons), Arbitrator David M.

---

[75]See Arbitrator Grether in 76 LA 446, 447; Merrifield in 72 LA 691, 691–692; Mansfield in 69 LA 14, 15–16 (parties came to hearing with fact stipulation *and* a stipulation as to what the testimony of certain persons would be if called as a witness, while some other persons did testify in person); McCoy in 46 LA 1078, 1078–1079; Updegraff in 44 LA 1028, 1029–1030; Kagel in 38 LA 500, 502; Ryan in 17 LA 800 at 800.

[76]As in Inland Container Corp., 28 LA 312 at 312 (Ferguson, 1957). The Code of Professional Responsibility confirms the utility of fact stipulations, stating in Code § V(A)(1)(b) that "An arbitrator may * * * encourage stipulations of fact. * * *"

[77]For instances where the dispute was submitted to the arbitrator for decision without a hearing, see Arbitrator McDonald in 76 LA 81 at 81; Fieger in 68 LA 1154 at 1154; McDermott in 59 LA 195, 196 (illustrating that waiver of hearing may result in a narrower ruling by the arbitrator); Merrill in 47 LA 635 at 635; Platt in 18 LA 160, 160–161 and in 16 LA 379 at 379; Komaroff in 16 LA 489, 494. For a detailed procedure which has been suggested for use when parties choose to submit their case to an arbitrator without a hearing, see Kagel, Anatomy of a Labor Arbitration, 122–124, 137–138 (BNA Books, 1961). American Arbitration Association Rule 34 provides that when parties agree to waive the oral hearing but are unable to agree as to the substitute procedure, "the AAA shall specify a fair and equitable procedure."

Helfeld convinced the parties that the benefits and safeguards of a hearing were indispensable.[78]

Representatives in Arbitration

It is generally agreed that each party has the right to be represented in arbitration proceedings by persons of its own choosing.[79] As Arbitrator Morton Singer declared, neither side "may compel the other side to retain or consult with any person other than one of their own free will and choice."[80]

Some parties prefer to be represented in arbitration by the person who served as their spokesman in the prearbitral stages of the grievance procedure, since he is thoroughly familiar with the dispute. That person, however, may lack the skill needed to present the case clearly to an outsider who has no background knowledge of the parties or their dispute. Therefore, other representatives such as higher union or company officials may be used to present the case at the arbitration stage. Then, too, attorneys often are used by one or both parties.[81]

Regarding use of attorneys, Arbitrator Benjamin Aaron aptly observed that an attorney, if he is well-trained and if he understands the nature of collective bargaining and the purposes of arbitration, will have the ability to outline the dispute clearly and simply, to come directly to the point at issue, to present his evidence in an orderly fashion, and to sum up his arguments and relate them to the record made at the hearing.[82] Legal training may be especially important in still other respects if the case is covered by any detailed arbitration statute.

---

[78]San Juan Star, 43 LA 445, 445–446 (1964). Also see statement of Willard Wirtz disapproving the omission of hearings. The President's Commission on Coal, Labor-Management Seminar IV, Grievance and Arbitration Procedures (June 20, 1979) 69, U.S. Govt. Printing Office: 1979, 0-302-759.

[79]For related discussion, see Chapter 5, topic entitled "Grievance Representatives," where the generally broad scope of this right under federal law is also noted.

[80]Bronx County Pharmaceutical Assn., 16 LA 835, 838 (1951), where Arbitrator Singer proceeded without one of the parties, who refused to appear in the same room with counsel for the opposition.

[81]See statistics in "Survey of Arbitration in 1964," Proceedings of the 18th Annual Meeting of NAA, 243, 245, 252 (BNA Books, 1965); Fleming, "The Labor Arbitration Process: 1943–1963," Proceedings of the 17th Annual Meeting of NAA, 33, 39–40 (BNA Books, 1964); "Survey of Arbitration in 1962," id. at 292, 296, 314; "Procedural Aspects of Labor-Management Arbitration," 28 LA 933, 936–937 (1954 statistics). In some situations both parties may prefer *not* to use attorneys. For instance, this was indicated for expedited arbitration in the steel industry. See comments of Fischer in "Updating Arbitration," Proceedings of the 26th Annual Meeting of NAA, 62, 90–91 (BNA Books, 1974). Use of laymen, however, will not necessarily simplify the hearing. For instance, Arbitrator John F. Leahy stated of the coal industry: "It seems strange that this industry's grievance procedure, which excludes lawyers from representing the parties at the hearings, is on its way to becoming the most technical of all industries." T & S Coal Co., 73 LA 882, 884 (1979).

[82]Aaron, "Some Procedural Problems in Arbitration," 10 Vand. L. Rev. 733, 748 (1957). Also see Feinsinger, "Collective Bargaining, Labor Arbitration and the Lawyer," id. at 761; Merrill, "A Labor Arbitrator Views His Work," id. at 789, 794; Garrett, "The Role of Lawyers in Arbitration," Proceedings of the 14th Annual Meeting of NAA, 102 (BNA Books, 1961), summarized in "Current Problems of Arbitration," 35 LA 963, 966 (1961).

Of course, some laymen possess the ability and experience to present cases very skillfully and effectively. Indeed, as one union consultant has been quoted, "a good union representative" may be "more than an even match for a company attorney."[83] This does not mean, however, that a grievant should undertake to present his own case in arbitration or to share that function with the representative designated by the union, particularly where the grievant has not had meaningful experience in labor representation matters.[84]

Some arbitration statutes expressly state that either party has a right to be represented by an attorney and that waivers of this right are subject to limitations stated in the statute. However, if either party plans to be represented by an attorney, the other party as a courtesy may be so informed.[85]

Privilege to Attend Hearing

Arbitration is a private proceeding and the hearing is not, as a rule, open to the public. However, all persons having a direct interest in the case ordinarily are entitled to attend the hearing.[86] Other persons may be permitted to attend with permission of the arbitrator,[87] or the parties. Where *both* parties object to attendance by given individuals, the following provision in the Code of Professional Responsibility becomes particularly relevant:

"Attendance at hearings by persons not representing the parties or invited by either or both of them should be permitted only when the parties agree or when an applicable law requires or permits. Occasionally, special circumstances may require that an arbitrator rule on such

---

[83]Warren & Bernstein, "A Profile of Labor Arbitration," 16 LA 970, 981 (1951). In V.E. Anderson Mfg. Co., 43 LA 174, 175 (King, 1964), the grievant personally expressed concern that the company was represented by an attorney while he was not, but his concern apparently faded when the arbitrator explained that grievant's union representatives were capable and experienced in the presentation of arbitration cases. A union ordinarily does not breach its duty of fair representation merely because it uses a union representative rather than an attorney to represent the grievant at the arbitration hearing. Grovner v. Georgia-Pacific Corp., 105 LRRM 2706, 2708 (CA 5, 1980); Walden v. Teamsters, 81 LRRM 2608, 2609 (CA 4, 1972). But the union was required to provide an attorney of grievant's choice under the situation involved in Teamsters Local 186 (United Parcel Serv.), 90 LRRM 1227 (NLRB, 1975). Does representation in arbitration by a layman constitute the unauthorized practice of law? One bar association study committee stated its conclusion on this question as follows: "The Committee is of the opinion that representation by a nonlawyer from another jurisdiction is not the unauthorized practice of law. Even if it is held to be the practice of law, there are sound and overriding policy reasons for permitting such nonlawyer representation in the labor arbitration field." AAA News and Views, No. 6 (1975), quoting the Committee on Labor and Social Security Legislation of the Association of the Bar of the City of New York.

[84]For a convincing demonstration that this limitation ordinarily should be observed, see Western Union Int'l., 70 LA 285, 285–286 (Turkus, 1978).

[85]Advance notice of intent to use an attorney formerly was specified by AAA Rule 20, but this is no longer required. 30 LA 1088; 43 LA 1294.

[86]For example, AAA Rule 22 expressly provides that "Persons having a direct interest in the arbitration are entitled to attend hearings." 43 LA 1294. The problem of what an arbitrator should do when a second union wishes to attend the hearing as observer against the wishes of grievant union in work jurisdiction cases is treated briefly by discussion panel in "Procedural Problems in the Conduct of Arbitration Hearings," Proceedings of the 17th Annual Meeting of NAA, 1, 24–25, 32 (BNA Books, 1964). Related discussion is found in topic entitled "Bilateral Arbitration of Trilateral Conflicts," below.

[87]Again, AAA Rule 22 states that "It shall be discretionary with the Arbitrator to determine the propriety of the attendance of any other persons."

matters as attendance and degree of participation of counsel selected by a grievant."[88]

Limiting Attendance by Witnesses

The arbitrator customarily has authority to require witnesses (except those who are direct parties) to leave the hearing room during the testimony of other witnesses.[89] This is explained by Arbitrator Maurice H. Merrill:

"One of the traditional methods for preserving the purity of testimony, 'the rule' that witnesses be excluded from the hearing chamber during the reception of others' testimony, frequently is invoked in arbitration. Whenever it is sought, I grant it, except, of course, as to the parties. On several occasions, I have observed the effectiveness of this safeguard against the possibility that one witness may be influenced in his testimony by what he has heard some one else say."[90]

Another aspect concerns the possibility that production will be impaired if too many employees miss work in order to attend an arbitration hearing. In one case employees were held entitled to "excused absences" from their job while attending a hearing as potential witnesses, but not if they attend merely as "observers"; moreover, Arbitrator Irwin M. Lieberman recognized that under the agreement involved there an improper work stoppage possibly might result if too many employees leave their job to attend even as potential witnesses.[91]

---

[88]§ II(C)(1)(a), 64 LA 1321. § II(C)(1)(e) states that: "Applicable laws, regulations, or practices of the parties may permit or even require exceptions to the above noted principles of privacy." For some instances in which arbitrators have been confronted with the need to rule upon attendance questions, see Arbitrator McDonald in 76 LA 81, 85–86 (applicability of open meeting statute to grievance meetings conducted by school board); Moore in 72 LA 490, 493–494 (attendance by the attorney of a nonemployee witness during testimony of such witness against whom grievant had filed civil suit); Belcher in 71 LA 359, 361 (attendance by grievant's wife and children). Regarding secret recordings of what transpires at grievance meetings, see views of Arbitrator James C. Vadakin in 75 LA 243, 247 (1980), which views also may be relevant to arbitration hearings. In Los Angeles Unified School Dist., 76 LA 804, 808 (Christopher, 1981), a grievance was dismissed because the grievant had "leaked" information to the news media in violation of the agreement, which stated: "In order to encourage a professional and harmonious disposition of grievances, it is agreed that from the time a grievance is filed until it is finally resolved, neither [the union, the employer] nor the grievant shall make public the grievance or evidence regarding the grievance."

[89]See AAA Rule 22. Also see Douglas Aircraft Co., 28 LA 198, 203–204 (Jones, 1957). A survey of its members by the National Academy of Arbitrators revealed that many would grant motions for exclusion of witnesses from the hearing in disciplinary cases, but they would not exclude the grievant. "Procedural Problems During Hearings," The Chronicle (NAA, April 1981), indicating that only a few would exclude the grievant. In Economy Forms Corp., 45 LA 430, 432 (Bauder, 1965), it was held that where the arbitration concerns discipline against several employees, all of them are entitled to hear all of the testimony. Even where the contract expressly provided for exclusion of witnesses except when testifying, the discharged employee's presence at the hearing could not be limited. International Smelting & Ref. Co., 45 LA 885, 886 (Kornblum, 1965).

[90]Merrill, "A Labor Arbitrator Views His Work," 10 Vand. L. Rev. 789, 795 (1957). Also see Updegraff & McCoy, Arbitration of Labor Disputes, 97–98 (1946). An arbitrator's failure to exclude witnesses as requested by a party apparently will not render his award vulnerable, since it is for the arbitrator to determine the credibility of witnesses. See Transport Workers v. Philadelphia Transp. Co., 283 F.Supp. 597 (USDC, 1968).

[91]Monterey Coal Co., 79 LA 1107, 1111–1112 (1982), where Arbitrator Lieberman reasoned that "it is well nigh impossible in many arbitration disputes for a definitive decision to be made concerning which employees will testify prior to the opening of the hearing," but that "a modicum of concern for continued operation of the business" is required of the Union and "an undisciplined or extreme position with respect to the number of witnesses required * * * cannot be tolerated."

Time, Place, and Notice of Hearing

No fixed rule exists for setting the date and locale of arbitration hearings. Ordinarily the arbitrator will meet at any time and place agreed to by the parties, if he can be available. If the parties cannot agree upon these matters, the arbitrator or the administering agency must set them.[92] In this regard, it has been generally accepted that the "arbitrator [or agency] should consult the convenience of the parties in fixing the time and place for the hearing but should not allow one party to delay unduly the fixing of a date for the hearing. Written and timely notice of the date, time and place of the hearing should be given."[93]

Under some arbitration statutes the time and place for the hearing are fixed by the arbitrator, who may also be responsible for giving timely notice thereof. In any case, the arbitrator should always take action to insure adequate notice to the parties.[94]

The hearing room itself is ordinarily selected by the parties or by an administering agency. Frequently some "neutral ground" such as a hotel suite is used; this may minimize interruptions that sometimes occur when the hearing is held at the plant.[95] However, some parties prefer to use a conference room at the company since this may reduce costs, will make records and witnesses more quickly available, and will require less time for any visit by the arbitrator to the site of the dispute.

A conference table arrangement (with the arbitrator at the head of the table) is most satisfactory if there are not too many participants. A "courtroom" arrangement tends to be more formal, but it may be preferred if there are numerous participants.

It goes without saying that the hearing room should be well lighted and ventilated, but unfortunately this ideal is not fulfilled in all cases.

---

[92]For one agency's rules relating to these matters, see AAA Rules 10 & 19. For factors considered by Arbitrator William S. Rule in specifying the location of the hearing pursuant to request by the parties when they could not agree on location, see Immigration & Naturalization Serv., 76 LA 180, 184 (1981). Regarding insistence upon the location for arbitration hearings and its relation to the duty to bargain under the NLRA, see Indiana Bell Tel. Co., 105 LRRM 1325 (NLRB, 1980).

[93]Code of Ethics and Procedural Standards for Labor-Management Arbitration, Part II, §2. 15 LA 961, 964. The Code of Professional Responsibility which was intended to supersede the Code of Ethics does not cover these aspects. Regarding failure to have all cases heard promptly, see Davey, "What's Right and What's Wrong With Grievance Arbitration: The Practitioners Air Their Views," 28 Arb. J. 209, 213, 220–221 (1973), indicating that delays in scheduling are not always due to delayed availability of the arbitrator.

[94]For actions taken by Arbitrator Robert G. Howlett to assure due process to a grievant who did not receive notice of the arbitration hearing, see Eaton Corp., 73 LA 403, 404–405 (1979). It has been reported that arbitrators (considering that the agreement is basically one between the company and the union, subject only to the union's duty of fair representation) generally are not disturbed by absence of notice to other employees who might be adversely affected if the grievance being processed by the union for some employee or employees is sustained. Fleming, "Due Process and Fair Procedure in Labor Arbitration," Proceedings of the 14th Annual Meeting of NAA, 69, 71 (BNA Books, 1961), summarized in "Current Problems of Arbitration," 35 LA 963, 964 (1961).

[95]In Safeway Stores, 65 LA 1177, 1178 (1975), Arbitrator Jerome Smith concluded that "Neither the collective agreement, nor practice thereunder, nor any principle of arbitration law requires that arbitrations be held at a neutral site at equally shared expense."

Default Awards in Ex Parte Proceedings

Arbitrators sometimes feel compelled to render default awards, akin to the "default judgments" of courts. The justification for ex parte proceedings was explained by Arbitrator Liston Pope in commenting that: "A general arbitration clause in a contract would be rendered meaningless if its implementation depended on the willingness of each party to the contract to present its case, as the party desiring no change in relationships could nullify arbitration simply by refusing to make an appearance."[96]

However, it also was observed by Arbitrator Joseph Rosenfarb that "our judicial system looks askance at the finality of decisions based on default appearances. The Arbitration process is no exception. Only an unexplained failure to appear, not a delay in appearance, can justify an ex parte proceeding."[97] In this case one party was tardy and the other party requested that the hearing proceed without the tardy party under American Arbitration Association Rule 27 (quoted below); this request was refused by the arbitrator, who rescheduled the hearing for a later date at which time both parties participated.[98]

In cases of willful or deliberate default by one party after due notice, arbitrators have heard testimony and rendered awards as if both parties had participated.[99] Some but not all of these cases have involved state arbitration statutes providing for default awards, or collective agreements which specifically provided for default awards in the event of willful or deliberate default by one of the parties, or application of a provision such as American Arbitration Association Rule 27.[100] Rule 27 provides:

> "*Arbitration in the Absence of a Party*—Unless the law provides to the contrary, the arbitration may proceed in the absence of any party, who, after due notice, fails to be present or fails to obtain an adjournment. An award shall not be made solely on the default of a party. The

---

[96]Velvet Textile Corp., 7 LA 685, 691 (1947). For similar comment, see McDermott, "Arbitrability: The Courts Versus the Arbitrator," 23 Arb. J. 18, 34–35 (1968). A few agreements expressly authorize the issuance of default awards. See Major Collective Bargaining Agreements: Arbitration Procedures, 71 (U.S. Dept. Labor Bull. No. 1425–6, 1966).

[97]Busch's Jewelry Co., 19 LA 365, 367 (1952).

[98]Ibid. In Flinkote Co., 51 LA 74, 75 (Hardy, 1968), the employer delayed two months in choosing an arbitrator from an FMCS list but he did not thus forfeit his right to show just cause for the disputed discharge.

[99]See Arbitrator Gentile in 74 LA 377, 380–381; Katz in 71 LA 1238, 1241 (default award issued against State of New Jersey); Feller in 70 LA 526, 527–528 (employer had commenced but refused to complete its presentation); Lennard in 62 LA 276, 278–279, and in 59 LA 119, 123 (default award issued against federal agency employer, whose representatives attended the hearing but only as observers); Kagel in 52 LA 1189 at 1189; Oppenheim in 52 LA 1164, 1168–1169; Bennett in 44 LA 1174, 1175; Kerrison in 42 LA 62, 62–63; Vadakin in 33 LA 412, 414; Cole in 24 LA 529, 531; Singer in 16 LA 835, 838; Jaffee in 15 LA 715, 720–721; Pope in 7 LA 685, 691; Baskind in 4 LA 719, 720. Cf., Prasow in 39 LA 614, 621.

[100]In Thompson Fuel Serv., 42 LA 62 at 62 (1964), Arbitrator Kerrison had no doubt that he could issue a default award where law did not provide to the contrary. But in A.B.C. Cartage & Trucking Co., 42 LA 55, 58–59 (1963), Arbitrator Whelan refused to issue a default award where the case was not covered by American Arbitration Association rules or by any statute expressly authorizing such awards.

Arbitrator shall require the other party to submit such evidence as he may require for the making of an award."[101]

Federal Mediation and Conciliation Service regulations also provide for ex parte proceedings—the Service has a rule which is very similar in wording to the above-quoted Rule 27 and is identical to it as to substance.[102]

The Code of Professional Responsibility in turn specifies that:

"1. In determining whether to conduct an ex parte hearing, an arbitrator must consider relevant legal, contractual, and other pertinent circumstances.

"2. An arbitrator must be certain, before proceeding ex parte, that the party refusing or failing to attend the hearing has been given adequate notice of the time, place, and purposes of the hearing."[103]

An indication of how an arbitrator might proceed in the absence of one party is provided by Arbitrator Samuel H. Jaffee's approach under American Arbitration Association Rule 27:

"The hearing then proceeded in the absence of * * * any Company representative or of any Company observer. Counsel for the Union remained with his clients and witnesses. These witnesses were sworn in normal course and testified in the usual way, but without the benefit of any cross-examination and in response only to questions of Union counsel, though the arbitrator took it upon himself to ask a substantial number of questions of some of them.

"The findings which follow, and the conclusions based on such findings, of necessity, then, are based upon the evidence received pursuant to the procedure described above. Because of the absence of Company counsel I have examined the evidence with extreme care. The fact that such evidence was uncontradicted did not necessarily mean that it was accepted. Some has been rejected. In evaluating such evidence I have done all I could, within the limitations of the procedure described, to apply such tests and criteria as are applied in courts generally. But the evaluation was of necessity handicapped by the absence of Company counsel, especially, of course, since I had no knowledge of the facts in these cases until evidence was received concerning them."[104]

As Arbitrator Jaffee stated, evaluation of one party's testimony is "of necessity handicapped" by the absence of the other party. This handicap possibly could be diminished by making the evidence and argument submitted at the hearing subsequently available to the other party (unless some other procedure is specified by statute or the collective agreement) for its comments thereon within a reasonable time.[105]

---

[101]43 LA 1294. For statistics regarding the number of ex parte proceedings under Rule 27, see "Procedural Aspects of Labor-Management Arbitration," 28 LA 933, 937 (1954 statistics).

[102]FMCS Regulations, § 1404.14, 29 C.F.R. Part 1404.

[103]Sec. V(C), 64 LA 1326.

[104]Aleo Mfg. Co., 15 LA 715, 721 (1950). For another example as to how Arbitrator Jaffee has proceeded ex parte, see C & D Batteries, 31 LA 272, 273–274 (1958), where the defaulting union said it would not honor a default award. It changed heart, however, and participated in a subsequent hearing as to the interpretation of the award. C & D Batteries, 32 LA 589, 591 (Jaffee, 1959).

[105]A similar approach was suggested by a group of arbitrators in the Philadelphia area. See Guides for Labor Arbitration, 5–6 (U. of Pa. Press, 1953).

Court Enforcement of Default Awards

Court enforcement of default awards may depend upon a variety of factors, such as how the arbitration tribunal was selected, due process considerations, and the applicable law.

Obviously, no arbitration tribunal is entitled to issue a binding decision, ex parte or otherwise, unless the tribunal has been duly vested with jurisdiction over the dispute. Some possible methods for vesting an arbitration tribunal with jurisdiction are (1) joint action by the parties specifically designating the tribunal for a case, a group of cases, or as permanent arbitrator of stated tenure; (2) collective agreement provisions for the designation of the arbitration tribunal, as by specifying the procedures of some appointing agency; or (3) designation of an arbitration tribunal pursuant to court decree compelling arbitration. In proper circumstances a tribunal established by any of these methods can issue enforceable default awards under federal law and under modern arbitration statutes.[106]

However, there are ramifications as to method number two. If the collective agreement specifies a procedure for designation of the arbitration tribunal without the participation of both parties, a tribunal so designated can issue an enforceable default award. For instance, a default award was enforced in an action under LMRA § 301 where the neutral was appointed by the Maine State Board of Conciliation and Arbitration under a procedure specified by the collective agreement for use in the event the parties failed to agree upon a neutral within 10 days—the court emphasized that the arbitration tribunal was designated according to the procedure upon which the parties had agreed in their contract.[107] However, where the agreement makes no provision for designating an arbitration tribunal without the participation of both parties, or where the agreement expressly requires cooperation by both parties, a court may refuse to enforce the default award of an arbitration tribunal designated without the cooperation of both parties (the court usually explaining in

---

[106]As to these areas of law and the common law, and as to the applicable law, see Chapter 2. A court enforced a default award by a tribunal established by method number one in Retail Clerks v. Seattle Dept. Stores Assn., 62 LRRM 2706 (USDC, 1966), and in Simons v. New York Herald Tribune, 26 LA 282 (N.Y. Sup. Ct., 1956). Also see Local 480 v. Bowling Green Express, 113 LRRM 2683 (CA 6, 1983); Teamsters Union v. Purity Food Co., 14 LA 934 (Conn. Super. Ct., 1950). The default award of a tribunal established by method number three was enforced in Teamsters Local Unions v. Braswell Motor Freight Lines, 392 F.2d 1 (CA 5, 1968). Cases on method number two are cited below.

[107]Meat Cutters v. Penobscot Poultry Co., 49 LRRM 2241 (USDC, 1961), in which the court also observed that a party is not required to seek a court order to compel arbitration unless the contract specifies no procedure for designating the arbitrator without the participation of a defaulting party. For other cases in which default awards were enforced where the arbitrator was designated by a procedure specified in the collective agreement without cooperation by a defaulting party, see Providence Teachers Local 958 v. McGovern, 319 A.2d 358, 363 (R.I. S.Ct., 1974), enforcing a default award against a public-sector employer, the court declaring that "Neither party may prevent the rendition of a binding arbitration award by his default in appearing at the proceedings"; Steelworkers v. Danville Foundry Corp., 52 LRRM 2584 (USDC, 1963). Also see Local 480 v. Bowling Green Express, 113 LRRM 2683, 2685 (CA 6, 1983).

such cases that the proper remedy of the party not in default is a suit to compel arbitration).[108]

Furthermore, it is unlikely that a default award even by a properly established tribunal will be upheld by a court if the absent party was not given adequate notice or if other due process considerations were not satisfied.[109] Court enforcement will also be unavailable if the case is covered by the common law rule that executory agreements to arbitrate are unenforceable, but in an increasingly large number of cases that rule will have been displaced by more modern state law or by the federal law under LMRA § 301.[110]

Regardless of whether a given default award is legally enforceable, another important consideration lies in the possibility that the award may impose a moral obligation on the losing party and may give the other party a significant moral and psychological victory.

Withdrawal of Cases From Arbitration

Related to the matter of default awards is the withdrawal of the case from arbitration. While the parties may withdraw a case through agreement, we have observed the rendition of default awards in some cases wherein the charged party refused to participate in the hearing.[111] But it is not always the charged party who avoids the case. Sometimes the aggrieved party seeks to withdraw it from arbitration.

It has been suggested that the complainant usually may withdraw the case at any point prior to the arbitration hearing, but that after the hearing has commenced he may not withdraw the case over the objection of the other party unless permitted by the arbitrator.[112]

---

[108]As in Sam Kane Packing Co. v. Meat Cutters Union, 477 F.2d 1128 (CA 5, 1973); Fuller v. Pepsi-Cola Bottling Co., 63 LRRM 2220 (Ky. Ct. App., 1966); In re Masters, Mates & Pilots, 52 LRRM 2392 (N.Y. S.Ct., 1963). In two "pre-*Trilogy*" cases the court held that it did not suffice that the neutral member of a tripartite board was designated by an appointing agency specified by the agreement (AAA in one case and FMCS in the other) where the defaulting party refused to appoint its member of the board as also specified by the agreement. Industrial Union v. Dunn Worsted Mills, Inc., 36 LRRM 2629 (USDC, 1955); Food Handlers Local 425 v. Pluss Poultry, Inc., 43 LRRM 2090 (CA 8, 1958). In light of the *Trilogy* teachings, doubt has been expressed as to the soundness of these two decisions. See McDermott, "Arbitrability: The Courts Versus the Arbitrator," 23 Arb. J. 18, 31–35 (1968); Smith, "Arbitrators and Arbitrability," Proceedings of the 16th Annual Meeting of NAA, 75, 78–82 (BNA Books, 1963), both authors discussing court enforcement of awards rendered in ex parte proceedings.

[109]See Farkach v. Brach, 52 LRRM 2334 (N.Y. Sup. Ct., 1963); Goldman Bros., 28 LA 589 (N.Y. Sup. Ct., 1957).

[110]See Chapter 2. Also see B.Z. Wesche Elec. Co., 20 LA 216 (Sembower, 1953), which accurately forecast later developments.

[111]See preceding topic.

[112]See Guides for Labor Arbitration, 6 (U. of Pa. Press, 1953). For similar views, see Discussion Panel, "Procedural Problems in the Conduct of Arbitration Hearings," Proceedings of the 17th Annual Meeting of NAA, 1, 22–23 (BNA Books, 1964). In Harry S Truman Memorial Veterans Hosp., 74 LA 1021, 1022 (Hoffmeister, 1980), the union was not permitted to withdraw its grievance from arbitration after it had joined the employer in selecting an arbitrator. For court decisions holding that the complainant may not withdraw from arbitration proceedings, see Old Dutch Farms, Inc. v. Milk Drivers & Dairy Employees Union Local 584, 222 F.Supp. 125 (USDC, 1963); Simons v. New York Herald Tribune, 26 LA 282 (N.Y. Sup. Ct., 1956). In United Aircraft Corp. v. Canel Lodge 700, 77 LRRM 3167 (USDC, 1971), the court ordered arbitration at the employer's request where the union had requested arbitration but then had attempted to withdraw the case "without prejudice."

Of course, the collective agreement will govern the matter of withdrawal if it deals with it. Agreement provisions concerning withdrawal of cases after reaching arbitration are in fact fairly common, generally permitting withdrawal only by mutual consent of the parties.[113]

From a strictly legal standpoint, the common law rule that either party may withdraw from arbitration at any time prior to issuance of an award will not apply if the case is covered by the federal law or if the particular state has modified the common law rule.[114]

Aside from legal or express contract considerations, the privilege of the complainant to withdraw the case from arbitration may depend upon the peculiar circumstances.[115] For example, a union which submitted an issue to arbitration but then learned that the company had not taken the action complained of was held under such circumstances to be entitled to withdraw the issue "without prejudice" prior to its consideration by the arbitrator.[116] Another union was permitted to withdraw its grievance after the hearing where it offered to do so "with prejudice," Arbitrator Robert J. Ables considering such withdrawal to be equivalent to a decision on the merits against the withdrawing party.[117]

Arbitrator's Charges When Case Is Cancelled

It was aptly observed by the Federal Mediation and Conciliation Service General Counsel (the thoughts being equally applicable to cases not administered by the FMCS) that "A real problem for arbitrators today is the cancellation of a case after he has been selected and a date for hearing set."[118] While emphasizing that efforts by the parties to settle cases "should be seriously pursued right up to the time set for the hearing," that observer straightforwardly recognized that too many cases are scheduled for arbitration with little expectation that they will actually be heard:

> "[FMCS] service is free. It is provided by the federal government to those who wish to use it. Accordingly, many companies and many unions have

---

[113]Major Collective Bargaining Agreements: Arbitration Procedures, 71 (U.S. Dept. Labor Bull. No. 1425–6, 1966), also indicating variations as to the precise point after which mutual consent is required. Cases which have reached the umpire at Ford and at Chrysler may not be withdrawn without mutual consent. See discussion panel, "Procedural Problems in the Conduct of Arbitration Hearings," Proceedings of the 17th Annual Meeting of NAA, 1, 22 (BNA Books, 1964); Wolff, Crane & Cole, "The Chrysler-UAW Umpire System," Proceedings of the 11th Annual Meeting of NAA, 111, 121 (BNA Books, 1958).

[114]Thus, a federal court and a state court denied the right of unilateral withdrawal in the *Old Dutch Farms* and *Simons* cases cited hereinabove.

[115]For related discussion, see Chapter 5, subtopic entitled "Waiver of Employee Rights or Signature Requirement" and topic entitled "Grievance Adjustment by Individual Employees."

[116]Princeton Worsted Mills, 25 LA 587, 588 (Hill, 1955). Hess Oil & Chem. Corp., 51 LA 445, 448 (Gould, 1968), held that a demand for arbitration could be resubmitted after having been withdrawn where all contractual time limits were still met and where the contract did not deal expressly with withdrawal and resubmission of grievances.

[117]Loewenthal, Walker & Heimberg, 72 LA 578, 580 (1979).

[118]Address of April 8, 1969, by General Counsel Richard P. McLaughlin, entitled "Labor Arbitration Today" and published in 70 LRR 428 (quotation from p. 430) under the title "Cost, Time, Training Factors in Labor Arbitration."

built our easy availability into their dispute-settling machinery and strategy. There is nothing like a threat— 'we'll take you to court'—to persuade a recalcitrant party to settle on the courthouse steps. I'm afraid this threat is being used with some regularity. As a result, it is not too uncommon for us or the arbitrator to be notified that a case has been worked out at the eleventh hour—just prior to its scheduled hearing.

"This situation, which you must admit places a great burden on labor arbitrators, all of whom have scheduling problems just like we do, is recognized in our regulations."[119]

Under FMCS regulations as revised in 1979, arbitrators are permitted "to charge a per diem fee and other predetermined fees for services, the amount of which has been certified in advance to the Service," and in furnishing panels of arbitrators to the parties, FMCS includes information of each arbitrator's per diem fee and "other fees such as cancellation, postponement, rescheduling or administrative fees."[120]

The Code of Professional Responsibility also recognizes the propriety of postponement and cancellation charges, by providing that arbitrators should establish in advance "the basis for charges, if any, for * * * postponement or cancellation of hearings by the parties and the circumstances in which such charges will normally be assessed or waived * * *."[121]

Of course the arbitrator is equally inconvenienced regardless of whether the withdrawal or cancellation of a case could be anticipated by the parties from the outset. It is not surprising, then, that in many cases the arbitrator bills the parties where the arbitration is cancelled after a hearing date has been set.[122] However, in many instances his charges will not in any sense adequately recompense the arbitrator for the full loss of working time and inconvenience suffered by him.[123]

Bilateral Arbitration of Trilateral Conflicts

Underlying some grievances are the conflicting interests of two different groups of employees represented by different unions. These are trilateral situations, with the employer in the middle. Usually the matter involves conflicting work-assignment claims, but not

---

[119]Ibid., where he suggested that "perhaps a one-day fee" would be a fair administrative charge where the case is settled a short time before the scheduled hearing date, and where he also suggested that arbitrators give parties advance notice as to the arbitrator's policy concerning such charges. Regarding the views of party representatives, see Davey, "What's Right and What's Wrong With Grievance Arbitration: The Practitioners Air Their Views," 28 Arb. J. 209, 216, 222 (1973).

[120]FMCS Regulations, §§ 1404.12(a) and 1404.16(a), 29 C.F.R. Part 1404. Also § 1404.16(b) provides that: "In cases involving unusual amounts of time and expenses relative to pre-hearing and post-hearing administration of a particular case, an administrative charge may be made by the arbitrator."

[121]Sec. II(K)(1)(b)(1)(d), 64 LA 1324.

[122]For statistics on the practice of arbitrators in this regard, see Peterson & Rezler, "Fee Setting and Other Administrative Practices of Labor Arbitrators," 68 LA 1383, 1391–1393 (1977); Proceedings of the 18th Annual Meeting of NAA, 243, 247–248 (BNA Books, 1965); Proceedings of the 17th Annual Meeting of NAA, 292, 311 (BNA Books, 1964).

[123]Also see Elkouri, "Informal Observations on Labor Arbitration Today," 35 Arb. J., No. 3, p. 41 (1980).

always.[124] Final resolution of trilateral conflicts will be greatly facilitated, of course, if all three affected parties agree to the use of one arbitration proceeding for that purpose. Too often, however, one of the unions rejects this procedure.

In *Carey v. Westinghouse* the U.S. Supreme Court held that the employer was required to arbitrate a work assignment jurisdictional dispute upon demand by only one of the unions. In so holding, the Court said:

> "To be sure, only one of the two unions involved in the controversy has moved the state courts to compel arbitration. So unless the other union intervenes, an adjudication of the arbiter might not put an end to the dispute. Yet the arbitration may as a practical matter end the controversy or put into movement forces that will resolve it."[125]

The dissenting opinion responded that the majority decision "not only permits but compels Westinghouse to arbitrate the dispute with only one of the two warring unions" and that this could not bring about a final resolution of the conflict.[126]

Where only one of two affected unions is a party to a pending arbitration proceeding, arbitrators are in disagreement as to whether the arbitrator may invite the second union to participate in the proceeding against the wishes of the union which filed the grievance.[127]

---

[124]Conflicting seniority interests were involved, for instance, in American Sterilizer Co. v. Local 832, 67 LRRM 2894 (USDC, 1968). Also see Associated Brewing Co., 40 LA 680, 682–683 (Kahn, 1963), where trilateral arbitration of a seniority dispute was arranged by all affected parties.

[125]Carey v. Westinghouse Elec. Corp., 84 S.Ct. 401, 406, 55 LRRM 2042 (1964). In holding that a lower court erred in enjoining a scheduled arbitration, the U.S. Court of Appeals reasoned in In re MEBA, Pac. Coast Dist., 114 LRRM 3431, 3436 (D.C. Cir., 1983), that "If the Supreme Court in Carey was willing to *compel* arbitration even though one of the contesting unions might not be a party before the arbitrator, it was an abuse of discretion for the District Court to *enjoin* an arbitration merely because of the presence of such a risk."

[126]84 S.Ct. at 410. That bilateral arbitration indeed may not resolve the conflict, see Radio Corp. of Am., 43 LA 762, 764 (Dunau, 1964). The Supreme Court has indicated that an employer who is not a party to any agreement to arbitrate cannot be forced into a jurisdictional dispute arbitration proceeding agreed to by the disputing unions. The Court explained: "Although this Court has frequently approved an expansive role for private arbitration in the settlement of labor disputes, this enforcement of arbitration agreements and settlements has been predicated on the view that the parties have voluntarily bound themselves to such a mechanism at the bargaining table." NLRB v. Plasterers' Local 79, 92 S.Ct. 360, 370–371 (1971), in which decision the actual holding was that the employer has a right to participate in NLRB proceedings to determine jurisdictional disputes under § 10(k) of the NLRA. Jurisdictional disputes may be finally resolved by an NLRB award of the work to one of the unions under § 10(k). UAW v. Rockwell Intl. Corp., 104 LRRM 2050, 2052 (CA 6, 1980), holding that such an NLRB award controlled over a prior arbitration award which conflicted with it, and also holding that the employer was not liable in damages for failing to comply with the arbitration award. However, "Before the Board may proceed with the determination of a dispute pursuant to Section 10(k) of the Act, it must be satisfied that (1) there is a reasonable cause to believe that Section 8(b)(4)(D) has been violated, and (2) that the parties have not agreed upon a method for the voluntary adjustment of the dispute." Mine Workers Local 1269 (Ritchey Trucking, Inc.), 100 LRRM 1496, 1497 (NLRB, 1979). When have the parties agreed to a voluntary method of adjustment sufficient to foreclose NLRB jurisdiction under § 10(k)? See *Mine Workers*, id. at 1498.

[127]Holding that the arbitrator has no authority to extend an invitation to the second union, see Arbitrator Najita in 81 LA 214, 218–219; Helbling in 51 LA 902, 903–905 (citing numerous articles dealing with the pros and cons of the question); Block in 46 LA 865, 868–870 (also citing articles and discussing Supreme Court decisions touching on the question); Koven in 44 LA 1049, 1052; Schedler in 41 LA 665, 666. Also see Lazarus in 42 LA 604, 606. Other arbitrators, however, have concluded that they could extend the invitation. See Lockheed-California Co., 49 LA 981, 985–987 (Francis E. Jones, 1967); Mayfair Mkts., 42 LA 14, 21–24 (Edgar A. Jones, 1964). In any

Similarly, the efforts of the second union to intervene in the pending arbitration have produced varied results.[128]

Where the union which initiated the arbitration does not oppose its expansion into a trilateral proceeding, arbitrators likewise have had varying views as to whether the arbitrator should take steps beyond a mere invitation to induce the absent union to participate in the proceedings.[129]

In the special circumstances of one trilateral conflict, the consolidation of pending but separate arbitration proceedings into one trilateral proceeding was required through court action under LMRA § 301. Since each of the two unions had a bilateral arbitration pending with the employer, and since the arbitration clause in each of the two contracts was sufficiently broad to permit the employer to submit disputes to arbitration, the employer's motion to consolidate the two proceedings was granted in order to avoid duplication of effort and the possibility of conflicting awards.[130]

In the area of the Railway Labor Act, the U.S. Supreme Court has held that when a union brings a work assignment jurisdictional dispute to the National Railroad Adjustment Board, the Board must dispose of the entire dispute by joining the other union in the proceedings and by considering the contracts (and practices thereunder) of both unions.[131]

---

event, even where only one union is before an arbitrator and the decision is accordingly to be governed basically by that union's agreement, this does not necessarily mean that the arbitrator will not examine and comment upon the second union's agreement with the employer, and possibly suggest how the two agreements may be reconciled. For example, see Walter S. Johnson Bldg. Co., 75 LA 543, 547–548 (Denson, 1980); Grower-Shipper Vegetable Assn., 70 LA 350, 354 (Ross, 1978).

[128]See Sinclair-Koppers Co., 52 LA 648, 651–652 (Leonard, 1968); Stardust Hotel, 50 LA 1186, 1188 (Edgar A. Jones, 1968).

[129]Compare Arbitrator R.W. Fleming in E.R. Wagner Co., 43 LA 210, 211–212 (1964), with Arbitrator Edgar A. Jones in National Steel & Shipbuilding Co., 40 LA 625, 630–631, and 40 LA 838, 840–842 (1963). Also see Bernstein, "Nudging and Shoving All Parties to a Jurisdictional Dispute into Arbitration: The Dubious Procedure of National Steel," 78 Harv. L. Rev. 784 (1965); Jones, "On Nudging and Shoving the National Steel Arbitration into a Dubious Procedure," 79 Harv. L. Rev. 327 (1965). In Marvel-Schebler Div., 54 LA 24, 28–30 (1969), Arbitrator Sembower directed the complaining union to arrange with the other union a schedule for hearing the work assignment dispute; he stated that if the other union fails to cooperate and the complaining union does not seek or get court enforcement of an arbitral interpleader, then a hearing on the merits shall proceed between the company and the complaining union and an award shall be issued.

[130]Columbia Broadcasting Sys., Inc. v. American Recording & Broadcasting Assn., 414 F.2d 1326, 72 LRRM 2140 (CA 2, 1969). Where an employer failed to seek a court order compelling trilateral arbitration until after the employer became subject to conflicting arbitration awards under separate agreements with two different unions, the request for such an order came too late in Louisiana-Pacific Corp. v. Electrical Workers, 102 LRRM 2070, 2074–2075 (CA 9, 1979), the court stating that the employer should have initially contracted with each union for tripartite arbitration of jurisdictional disputes, or should have sought a possible court order for such arbitration before arbitrating separately with either of the unions (the court pointing to the Columbia Broadcasting System decision). But the employer was not held to conflicting arbitration awards, and trilateral arbitration was ordered, in Machinists Local 850 v. T.I.M.E.-DC, Inc., 113 LRRM 2677 (CA 10, 1983); Edmos Corp. v. Textile Workers, 80 LRRM 3225 (USDC, 1972); Textile Workers v. Scottex Corp., 80 LRRM 2899 (USDC, 1972). Trilateral arbitration has sometimes been ordered between one union and two employers, as in United Steelworkers v. Crane Co., 456 F.Supp. 385 (USDC, 1978).

[131]Transportation-Communication Employees Union v. Union Pac. R.R., 385 U.S. 157, 63 LRRM 2481 (1966). Arbitrators have concluded that special boards estalished under the 1966 amendments to the Act similarly must act to dispose of the entire matter in jurisdictional dispute cases. Western Pac. R.R., 50 LA 1013, 1015–1017 (Wyckoff, 1968); Southern Pac. Co., 49 LA 1052, 1054–1058 (Mann, 1967).

Continuances

Arbitrators may grant continuances or adjourn the hearing from time to time upon their own motion or upon joint request of the parties. Moreover, arbitrators do not hesitate to do so upon the application of only one party for good cause shown.[132] Indeed, failure to grant a continuance for good cause may make the proceedings vulnerable to court challenge.[133]

The "good cause" showing is essential since, as Arbitrator David L. Cole declared, if arbitration proceedings "are to have dignity and command respect, then no party to a dispute can be allowed to decide when, where and how the hearings are to be conducted."[134] Arbitrator Cole emphasized, however, that for "good cause" he would "always try to accommodate the parties and meet their convenience within reason."[135] In that case one continuance had been granted the absent party, whose request for another continuance was denied as not being for "good cause"; that party's absence from the hearing resulted in a default award.[136]

Not infrequently continuances are requested because of the absence of witnesses. In such instances a continuance ordinarily will be granted, though opposed by the other party, if the arbitrator is convinced that the request for a continuance was made in good faith and that the absence of the witness was without fault on the part of the requesting party.[137]

If a continuance on the ground of absence of witnesses or evidence is requested after the hearing has commenced, in particular where the participants are numerous and have traveled long distances to attend the hearing or where it would otherwise be difficult to arrange a satisfactory time for reconvening the hearing, arbitrators sometimes use a procedure akin to that commonly used by courts. That is, no continuance will be granted upon the ground of absence of evidence (either documentary, witnesses, or otherwise) except upon a statement or affidavit showing the materiality of the evidence and also showing: (1) that due diligence has been exercised and the evidence

---

[132]AAA Rule 23 provides: "The Arbitrator for good cause shown may adjourn the hearing upon the request of a party or upon his own initiative, and shall adjourn when all the parties agree thereto." The Code of Professional Responsibility, § II(J), 64 LA 1323–1324, deals with "Avoidance of Delay," but it does not deal expressly with the granting or denial of continuances requested by one party. For a difference of opinion on application of § II(J) to such requests, see Smith, "The Search for Truth—The Whole Truth," Proceedings of the 31st Annual Meeting of NAA, 40, 47–48 (BNA Books, 1979); McFall, "Comment," id. at 152, 155.

[133]See Chapter 2, topic entitled "State Law: Private Sector"; Friedman, "Correcting Arbitrator Error: The Limited Scope of Judicial Review," 33 Arb., J. 9, 14–15 (1978); Allendale Nursing Home v. Local 1115 Joint Bd., 87 LRRM 2498 (USDC, 1974).

[134]Textile Workers (CIO) v. Upholsterers' Union (AFL), 24 LA 529, 531 (1955).

[135]Ibid.

[136]For some situations in which an arbitrator was charged with abuse of discretion in refusing to grant a continuance, but where a court found otherwise, see Grahams Serv., Inc. v. Local 975, 111 LRRM 2916 (CA 8, 1982); Painters Local 171 v. Williams & Kelley, 102 LRRM 2321 (CA 10, 1979); Warehouse Union v. Greater Living Enter., 90 LRRM 2767 (USDC, 1975); Teamsters Local 251 v. Narragansett Co., 87 LRRM 2279 (CA 1, 1974).

[137]For example, see Bethlehem Steel Co., 17 LA 676, 677 (Shipman, 1951).

still has been unavailable, (2) where the evidence is, (3) the probability of securing it within a reasonable time, and (4) that the party making the statement or affidavit believes the evidence to be true. After this is submitted, the opposing party still may avoid a continuance by agreeing to accept the evidentiary facts alleged in the statement or affidavit as having been proved for purposes of the case. Then, too, in arbitration it is sometimes simply agreed that absent evidence may be submitted within a stated time after the hearing (if testimony, in the form of an affidavit or deposition). The opposing party is then given a reasonable opportunity to reply.

In the event the submission or other agreement specifies time limits within which action must be taken, no continuance should be granted which would overreach any applicable time limit (unless extended by agreement of the parties).

Split Hearings

In some cases the parties and the arbitrator agree that the hearing should be divided into two parts, the arbitrator to hear and rule upon some aspects of the case before completing the hearing as to other aspects. For instance, where an alleged contract violation, if established, would have involved possible losses by numerous employees whose individual factual situations were not identical, it was agreed that a decision on the proper interpretation of the contract would be reached "before taking further testimony upon the detailed rights and possible losses of each individual employee * * * because of the length of time which seemed likely to be consumed in testimony upon the individual situations, which time would prove to be wasted if the Board should hold that the Company had not breached the Agreement."[138]

Also, the arbitrator (often on his own) may rule upon some aspects of the case and refer other aspects back to the parties for further negotiations, to be heard and ruled upon ultimately by him only if negotiations fail.[139] Similarly, if an arbitrator concludes after the hearing that additional information is necessary to enable him to reach a decision, he might return the case to the parties for additional fact-finding, or for some other action designed to produce the needed

---

[138]Fruehauf Trailer Co., 19 LA 159, 160 (Spaulding, 1952). Similarly, Color Corp. of Am., 25 LA 644, 651, 657 (Lennard, 1955). Also see Publishers' Assn. of N.Y. City, 66-1 ARB ¶8284 (Turkus, 1966). In American Totalsator Co., 74 LA 377, 388 (Gentile, 1980), a default award was issued stating that the union violated the agreement and calling for another hearing to determine damages.

[139]See Arbitrator Belshaw in 73 LA 1087, 1092; Carson in 73 LA 599, 603; Belkin in 72 LA 881, 889–890; LeWinter in 72 LA 102, 109; Gentile in 71 LA 762, 771; Lipson in 70 LA 1185, 1189; Kates in 52 LA 396, 403; Porter in 50 LA 33, 35; Jones in 48 LA 1304, 1305; Begley in 44 LA 1212, 1215; Garrett in 44 LA 168, 174–175; Valtin in 38 LA 1166, 1170; Dworkin in 37 LA 323, 330; Rohman in 36 LA 815, 820–822 (the case was returned to him in 36 LA 938); Marshall in 36 LA 71, 78; Shipman in 21 LA 387, 391.

information (or to develop the matter to the point that a final decision may be made).[140]

Use of Interim Award

Where the case is divided into phases, as in some of the above situations, the arbitrator may use what he calls an "Interim Award" in disposing of the first phase and a "Supplemental Award" or "Final Award" in disposing of the later phase.[141]

From the legal standpoint, use of "interim" or "partial" awards may be subject to challenge under state law unless authorized by the parties.[142] It would seem, however, that any requirement of authorization might be waived by the parties if they proceed to the issuance of a final award without objection.[143]

Furthermore, if the federal law applies to the case there is some indication in a federal court decision that the arbitrator may have authority to utilize an interim award procedure even without agreement by both parties.[144] Also, there are cases upholding an arbitrator's retention and use of jurisdiction to determine the amount of back pay due an employee whose contractual rights the arbitrator has found to have been violated by the employer.[145]

---

[140]See Arbitrator Williams in 75 LA 939, 940 (grievance held arbitrable but hearing on the merits postponed pending conclusion of related court proceeding); Kossoff in 74 LA 604, 607; Markowitz in 74 LA 58, 64; Jones in 73 LA 742, 745 (interim award directed the parties to seek a federal-agency ruling on a relevant aspect of the case, the hearing being continued pending the results of that effort); Mullin in 72 LA 1073, 1075 (grievant to undergo psychiatric examination, the case to be returned to arbitrator if parties cannot then agree on final disposition); Dunn in 71 LA 63, 66; Roumell in 70 LA 1061, 1065–1066; Dybeck in 53 LA 1215, 1216; Griffin in 53 LA 453, 463–464; Garrett in 53 LA 40, 44; Rohman in 64–1 ARB ¶8209; Smith in 36 LA 1018, 1023; Seitz in 36 LA 86, 91; Warns in 27 LA 290, 293. Another possibility is that he will deny the grievance without prejudice, as in Jones & Laughlin Steel Corp., 23 LA 33, 37 (Cahn, 1954). Also see topic entitled "Reopening the Hearing," below.

[141]See Arbitrator Bickner in 77 LA 1021, 1024; Lennard in 53 LA 464, 470, and in 25 LA 644, 651, 657; King in 48 LA 518, 524; Crawford in 41 LA 844, 856; Rohman in 64–1 ARB ¶8209; Warns in 27 LA 290, 293; Shipman in 21 LA 387, 391.

[142]See discussion in Updegraff, Arbitration and Labor Relations, 280–281 (BNA Books, 1970); Updegraff & McCoy, Arbitration of Labor Disputes, 1st Ed., 122 (1946), 2d Ed., 213 (1961). But see Local 1147 v. Scranton School Dist., 113 LRRM 3296, 3300 (Pa. S.Ct., 1982), where the court noted that nothing in the collective agreement or applicable statute prohibited the procedure that had been followed, the court concluding that mere judicial disfavor with bifurcated proceedings was insufficient to overturn the arbitrator's decision. For related material, see Chapter 2, topic entitled "State Law: Private Sector," and see topic entitled "Clarification or Interpretation of Award," below.

[143]See Updegraff and McCoy citations, ibid.

[144]Local 246, ILGWU v. Evans Mfg. Co., 53 LRRM 2455, 40 LA 864 (CA 3, 1963), upholding an arbitrator's authority to issue an interim award directing the company to permit inspection of certain records by the union. The court compared the decision of the U.S. Supreme Court in United Steelworkers v. Enterprise Wheel & Car Corp., 80 S.Ct. 1358, 34 LA 569 (1960), which held that an award need not be set aside for incompleteness merely because the arbitrator neglected to calculate the amount of back pay due the grievant, the Supreme Court ordering that the award be returned to the parties for a determination of back pay by arbitration. In Electric & Gas Co. v. System Council U-2, 112 LRRM 333 (CA 3, 1983), the parties agreed to use two separate hearings, one for the merits and another for the remedy; a finding against the Company on the merits was held not to be a final order and thus not subject to court review before any hearing had been held on the remedy. For related material, see Chapter 2, topic entitled "Federal Law: Private Sector."

[145]Belo Corp. v. Typographical Union, 82 LRRM 2574, 2575 (USDC, 1972); District 50, UMW v. James Julian, Inc., 80 LRRM 2260, 2263 (USDC, 1972), where the court said: "Since we view

Arbitrator's Express Retention of Jurisdiction

Sometimes the parties jointly request or stipulate the retention of jurisdiction by the arbitrator after issuance of his award, for use in the event the parties are unable to agree as to some specified matter (such as the amount of damages or back pay, or even as to the appropriate remedy for contract violation).[146] Without indicating any request or stipulation by the parties, numerous arbitrators have stated an express reservation of jurisdiction in rendering their award, to be used if the parties are unable to agree as to the amount of back pay,[147] as to the damages or proper remedy for the contract violation,[148] as to which employees are entitled to payments under the award,[149] or for use if needed for the disposition of other problems which might arise in connection with the execution or implementation of the award.[150] In many of these instances the arbitrator fixed a time limit within which

the second hearing and the subsequent opinion and award as an integral part of the first, no specific agreement of both parties was necessary before the arbiter could act as he did. But, assuming that such agreement was necessary we find that such agreement [existed under the facts].* * *" Also see U.F.I. Razor Blades, Inc. v. Distributive Workers, 85 L.C. ¶ 11,123 (USDC, 1978).

[146]See Arbitrator Weiss in 75 LA 1298, 1300; Shanker in 75 LA 1163, 1168; House in 75 LA 628, 632; Beck in 75 LA 6, 12; Kanowitz in 74 LA 1095, 1101; Serot in 71 LA 897, 898 (the retained jurisdiction was being used); Walter in 69 LA 388, 389; Jackson in 68 LA 682, 683, 687; Roberts in 45 LA 929, 932; Wolff in 44 LA 944, 947; Tongue in 44 LA 475 at 475; Cohen in 43 LA 114, 115; Altieri in 41 LA 47, 52; Benewitz in 39 LA 14, 18–19; Wood in 38 LA 148, 149.

[147]See Arbitrator Wollett in 75 LA 255, 258; Rutherford in 74 LA 241, 247; Alexander in 70 LA 425, 426; Blackmar in 69 LA 1179, 1182; Chalfie in 68 LA 129, 143; Sembower in 51 LA 582, 589; Jones in 51 LA 421, 428; Howlett in 49 LA 728, 731; Emery in 49 LA 403, 405; Erbs in 49 LA 229, 231; Lugar in 48 LA 463, 478; Davis in 48 LA 441, 445; Lee in 48 LA 353, 364; Bellman in 47 LA 899, 902; McKelvey in 45 LA 1034, 1039; Kabaker in 43 LA 159, 165; Maggs in 33 LA 694, 700. As noted in the preceding subtopic, there are court cases upholding an arbitrator's retention of jurisdiction for the determination of back pay.

[148]See Arbitrator Belcher in 80 LA 742, 747–748; Prasow in 50 LA 645, 657; Leonard in 47 LA 661, 666; Leach in 46 LA 897, 902; Anderson in 43 LA 65, 76; Scheiber in 42 LA 483, 490; Black in 42 LA 325, 327; Warns in 41 LA 905, 909; Seligson in 40 LA 540, 544, Shaughnessy in 39 LA 633, 636.

[149]Halle Bros. Co., 42 LA 705, 709 (Kabaker, 1964).

[150]Here a wide assortment of reasons for retaining jurisdiction have been stated by arbitrators, but often the arbitrator has spoken in general terms, such as reserving jurisdiction "for problems arising in the implementation of the award," or "over any question which may arise from the administration of the award." See Arbitrator Richman in 74 LA 923, 927; Talent in 74 LA 80, 88; Belcher in 74 LA 69, 75; Ross in 73 LA 1036, 1040–1041; Petersen in 71 LA 43, 48; Ruben in 69 LA 944, 959; Brown in 69 LA 897, 901; Ellmann in 69 LA 811, 816; Jones in 68 LA 1343, 1347; Nicolau in 68 LA 271, 279; Cahn in 67 LA 869, 871; Eaton in 53 LA 633, 637; Teple in 53 LA 334, 338; Howlett in 52 LA 997, 1002; Koven in 52 LA 659, 663; Sembower in 52 LA 268, 278; Rauch in 49 LA 627, 630; Peck in 47 LA 739, 744; Marshall in 43 LA 1118, 1126 (retained jurisdiction used in 43 LA 1137); Seligson in 42 LA 902, 910; Sherman in 42 LA 683, 685; Seitz in 36 LA 86, 91. Such reservation of jurisdiction for problems arising in the implementation of the award, unless approved by both parties or done with statutory support, in the given case may be more vulnerable to court challenge than reservation of jurisdiction for some of the other purposes. See in particular the *Westvaco* case treated in the topic entitled "Clarification or Interpretation of Award," below. Under the "functus officio" doctrine this may also be true of reservations of jurisdiction to clarify or to interpret the award. Again, see topic on "Clarification or Interpretation of Award." Occasionally jurisdiction has been reserved for such purposes. See Arbitrator Eaton in 75 LA 1086, 1092; Roadley in 75 LA 249, 255; Roumell in 71 LA 589, 592; Kanner in 70 LA 295, 300; Maslanka in 70 LA 173, 176; Bailey in 69 LA 294, 303, in none of which instances did the reservation expressly purport to be by agreement of the parties or with statutory support. On the other hand, in Southwestern Bell Tel. Co., 75 LA 57, 63 (Allen, 1980), the parties were given advance notice by the award that differences regarding its interpretation would be settled by the arbitrator at the request of "both" parties. In this regard, the Code of Professional Responsibility states that "No clarification or interpretation of an award is permissible without the consent of both parties." § VI(D)(1), 64 LA 1327.

the matter might be returned to him by the unilateral action of a party.

In considering this subject it should be noted that from the strictly legal standpoint there may be some question of the effectiveness of an arbitrator's effort to reserve jurisdiction in light of the possible application of the doctrine that the arbitrator's power is ended in a given case when his award is issued.[151] More often this question is not reached, since under the more frequent practice the award is issued without any mention of reserving jurisdiction.[152] Moreover, it has been observed that where the arbitrator does reserve jurisdiction it usually meets with the approval of the parties and no question is raised.[153]

The latter possibility (that is, that the reservation of jurisdiction usually meets with the approval of the parties) seems stronger when we consider the views of Arbitrator Peter Seitz. Arbitrator Seitz expressed doubt that the "functus officio" doctrine applies to terminate the arbitrator's jurisdiction where he has issued only an interim or partial award, and he suggested that arbitrators should not hesitate to retain jurisdiction or delay the closing of hearings where the arbitrator believes his adjudicatory function cannot be responsibly discharged on the kind of presentation made by the parties; he added, however, that arbitrators retaining jurisdiction might be well advised to label their awards as interim or partial and in their accompanying opinion to state the circumstances which justify a piecemeal approach to fulfillment of their duty.[154] But taking issue with the Seitz view, Arbitrator Louis A. Crane was equally persuasive in arguing against issuance of interim awards and retention of jurisdiction, Arbitrator Crane stating, in part:

> "An arbitrator, especially one in an ad hoc situation, is not empowered to monitor the parties' future activities or to exercise continuing jurisdiction over a matter after it has been submitted to him for decision. Call it *functus officio* or what you will, but the parties have a right to expect an arbitrator to decide the question as they have pre-

---

[151]See topic on "Clarification or Interpretation of Award," below, and subtopic on "Use of Interim Award," above; Updegraff, Arbitration and Labor Relations, 278, 281 (BNA Books, 1970); Updegraff & McCoy, Arbitration of Labor Disputes, 1st Ed., 120, 123 (1946), 2d Ed., 211, 213 (1961); Textron, Inc., 48 LA 1373, 1377 (Altrock, 1967); New Orleans S.S. Assn., 45 LA 1099, 1104 (Oppenheim, 1965).

[152]For instance, American Arbitration Association statistics indicate that jurisdiction is retained by the arbitrator "only occasionally" in cases which it administers. "Retaining Jurisdiction," AAA Study Time, July 1980, 1, 2, 4. Usually an arbitrator simply remains silent on the matter when not acting to retain jurisdiction, but sometimes arbitrators have expressly disclaimed further jurisdiction. See Arbitrator Gibson in 76 LA 286, 292; Dobry in 74 LA 252, 257; Young in 73 LA 421, 429; Platt in 61 LA 1205, 1213; Dunau in 50 LA 236, 239.

[153]Updegraff, Arbitration and Labor Relations, 281 (BNA Books, 1970); Updegraff & McCoy, Arbitration of Labor Disputes, 1st Ed., 123 (1946), 2d Ed., 213–214 (1961), where agreement by the parties for reservation of jurisdiction is recommended, however, to guard against a possible challenge. In Ohio Power Co., 45 LA 1039, 1049 (Leach, 1965), the company dissent questioned the right of the board to retain jurisdiction.

[154]Seitz, "Problems of the Finality of Awards, or Functus Officio and All That," Proceedings of the 17th Annual Meeting of NAA, 165, 170–171, 174–175 (BNA Books, 1964). Still holding such views, see Seitz, "Substitution of Disciplinary Suspension for Discharge (A Proposed 'Guide to the Perplexed' in Arbitration)," 35 Arb. J. No. 2, pp. 27, 30–31 (1980).

sented it and then to go his own way unless and until they ask him to
resolve another dispute between them."[155]

Appearing to stand somewhere between the views of Arbitrators
Seitz and Crane, the following statement by the American Arbitration
Association in any event merits serious consideration:

> "A strong case can be made, based on a long legal history in this
> area, that arbitration has been, and should be, a final and binding
> process. But if one takes the position that, on occasion, under special
> circumstances, justice is better served by a more complete record and
> that jurisdiction should be retained, what is the danger in making such a
> request of the parties? One must assume that they also seek justice and
> that if the evidence falls clearly on the side of retention, they will grant
> it.
>
> "Should they not, however, the decision to override their wishes can
> then be made. This, of course, is a major step and one that most
> arbitrators would not take lightly. In all fairness (and in keeping with
> the basic proposition that the parties 'own' the arbitration process), the
> argument can be made that the advocates should be consulted and
> allowed to consider the purpose for which retention of jurisdiction is
> being requested."[156]

Transcript of Hearing

A formal written record of the hearing is not always necessary.
Use of a reporter appears to be the less frequent practice.[157]
Whether the expense and additional time involved in use of a
transcript are justified depends upon the case (and of course the
general view of the parties concerning transcripts). In simple cases the

---

[155]Crane, "The Use and Abuse of Arbitral Power," Proceedings of the 25th Annual Meeting
of NAA, 66, 67–70 (BNA Books, 1973), quotation from p. 68. Also disagreeing with Arbitrator
Seitz, Alexander C. Mekula of the Ford Motor Co. explained that: "It has been our experience at
Ford that interim decisions, in nearly every instance, prove unsatisfactory to the parties and
foster discord between them." Mekula, "The Ford Experience," Proceedings of the 24th Annual
Meeting of NAA, 118, 121 (BNA Books, 1971).

[156]"Retaining Jurisdiction," AAA Study Time, July 1980, 1, 4–5. The Association's discussion of this subject was continued in subsequent issues of Study Time.

[157]See statistics reported in FMCS Mini Memo No. 81–2 (1981), reporting that of the 7539
FMCS "award cases" in 1980, transcripts were taken in 2062, none was taken in 5149, and no
indication was given for the remaining 328 cases; Edwards, "Arbitration of Employment Discrimination Cases: An Empirical Study," Proceedings of the 28th Annual Meeting of NAA, 59, 77
(BNA Books, 1976); Krinsky, "Municipal Grievance Arbitration in Wisconsin," 28 Arb. J. 50, 60
(1973); Proceedings of the 18th Annual Meeting of NAA, 245, 252 (BNA Books, 1965); "Procedural Aspects of Labor-Management Arbitration," 28 LA 933, 937–938 (1954 statistics). But
"Most [federal-sector] agreements make some provision for transcripts of the arbitration proceedings." A Survey of Negotiated Grievance Procedures and Arbitration in Federal Post Civil
Service Reform Act Agreements, 50 (OPM, 1980). Also on the use of transcripts, see Anderson,
MacDonald & O'Reilly, "Impasse Resolution in Public Sector Collective Bargaining—An Examination of Compulsory Interest Arbitration in New York," 51 St. John's L. Rev. 453, 464 (1977);
Peterson & Rezler, "Fee Setting and Other Administrative Practices of Labor Arbitrators," 68 LA
1383, 1396 (1977), reporting that a majority of arbitrators retain the transcript, exhibits, and
briefs for one to four years; Davey, "What's Right and What's Wrong With Grievance Arbitration:
The Practitioners Air Their Views," 28 Arb. J. 209, 215 (1973), survey indicating a "clean split"
over use of transcripts and/or briefs, management representatives generally favoring and union
representatives generally disfavoring their use; Jaffee, "Battle Report: The Problem of Stenographic Records in Arbitration," 20 Arb. J. 97 (1965), not encouraging the ordinary use of
reporters; Kagel, Anatomy of a Labor Arbitration, 68–69 (BNA Books, 1961), stating strong
arguments in favor of using a reporter; Braden, "Problems in Labor Arbitration," 13 Mo. L. Rev.
143, 162 (1948).

arbitrator can take adequate notes. Likewise, in cases involving contract interpretation only, there being no disputed facts, the arbitrator's notes and the parties' exhibits and/or briefs ordinarily make a transcript unnecessary. However, in complicated or lengthy cases stenographic records may be very helpful, if not indispensable; the transcript will aid not only the arbitrator in studying the case, but also the parties in preparing briefs.[158] The transcript may be invaluable in any court review of the arbitration proceedings.[159] It is said that the palest ink is more accurate than the most retentive memory.

American Arbitration Association Rules as amended effective January 1, 1979, contain the following provision on transcripts:

> "21. **Stenographic Record**—Any party may request a stenographic record by making arrangements for same through the AAA. If such transcript is agreed by the parties to be, or in appropriate cases determined by the arbitrator to be the official record of the proceeding, it must be made available to the Arbitrator, and to the other party for inspection, at a time and place determined by the Arbitrator. The total cost of such a record shall be shared equally by those parties that order copies."

Federal Mediation and Conciliation Service Regulations as revised in 1979 contain no express provision on transcripts but do state in § 1404.4(b) that arbitrators on the FMCS Roster are "expected to conform to the ethical standards and procedures set forth in the Code of Professional Responsibility for Arbitrators of Labor Management Disputes," which Code was promulgated in 1975 by the NAA, the AAA, and the FMCS. Section V(B) of the Code provides:

> "B. Transcripts or Recordings*
> 1. Mutual agreement of the parties as to use or non-use of a transcript must be respected by the arbitrator.
> "a. *A transcript is the official record of a hearing only when both parties agree to a transcript or an applicable law or regulation so provides.*
> "b. An arbitrator may seek to persuade the parties to avoid use of a transcript, or to use a transcript if the nature of the case appears to require one. *However, if an arbitrator intends to make his or her appointment to a case contingent on mutual agreement to a transcript, that requirement must be made known to both parties prior to appointment.*
> "c. If the parties do not agree to a transcript, an arbitrator may permit one party to take a transcript at its own cost. The arbitrator may also make appropriate arrangements under which the other party may have access to a copy if a copy is provided to the arbitrator.
> "d. Without prior approval, an arbitrator may seek to use his or her own tape recorder to supplement note taking. The arbitrator should not insist on such a tape recording if either or both parties object."

The following broad *generalizations* appear to hold under the just-quoted AAA and Code of Professional Responsibility provisions:

---

[158]In Williams U.S. Super Mkt., 39 LA 558, 560 (Granoff, 1962), the arbitrator stated that his note taking "necessarily curtailed his desire to concentrate on observing witnesses' demeanor." In Gregory Galvanizing Metal Processing, 46 LA 102, 104 (Kates, 1966), a party's brief and the arbitrator's notes and recollection presented conflicting versions as to testimony given at the hearing—the arbitrator relied upon his notes and recollection.

[159]See In re Ruppert, 26 LA 283, 284 (N.Y. Sup. Ct., 1956).

1. Ordinarily any party is entitled to have a reporter present to record the proceedings.[160]
2. Generally a transcript will be the official record of the hearing only when both parties agree (note that the AAA and Code provisions recognize possible exceptions).[161]
3. A party ordinarily will not be required to contribute to the cost of a transcript if the party does not order any copy, but even in such cases the party ordinarily should have some *access* to the transcript if it is being provided to the arbitrator.[162]

Equal sharing of the transcript cost was advocated by Arbitrator Clarence M. Updegraff,[163] and it seems likely that this in fact has

---

[160]Also see Maremont Corp., 71 LA 333, 333–334 (Coven, 1978), where the union's objection to the presence of a reporter for this purpose was overruled. In contrast to this general right in arbitration, a party to collective bargaining under the NLRA does not have a similar right. NLRB v. Bartlett-Collins Co., 106 LRRM 2272, 2275 (CA 10, 1981), the court accepting the NLRB's conclusion that any advantages from the stenographic recording of negotiations are outweighed by the negative effects on the bargaining process of allowing one side to insist upon a court reporter. The court drew a distinction between collective bargaining and adjudicatory hearings: "Court reporters are an integral part of an adjudicatory hearing because they facilitate the main goal of adjudication, ascertaining the truth. Collective bargaining, on the other hand 'cannot be equated with an academic collective search for truth—or even with what might be thought to be the ideal one.'" Ibid. In Chicago Cartage Co. v. Local 710, 108 LRRM 2567, 2569–2570 (CA 7, 1981), a hearing by a grievance committee composed only of union and company members (no neutral) was considered "analogous to a collective bargaining session," and a party accordingly had no right to have the hearing recorded.

[161]Compare the results of a survey of National Academy of Arbitrators members as reported in "Procedural Problems During Hearings," The Chronicle (NAA, April 1981):

"[Questions:] A court reporter has been requested by the Company and the Company indicates that you will be provided with a copy of the transcript. The Union insists it cannot afford a copy of the transcript and objects to the use of a court reporter. What would you do? Assume you decide to allow a transcript to be made and the Union asks that it be provided a copy or be allowed to use your copy. What would you do?

"[Reports on responses:] * * * Five members would sustain the Union's objection and would not allow a transcript. Another four members would permit the Company to have a transcript made for its purposes, but these members would refuse the Company's offer to provide them with a transcript. They take the position that their notes will constitute the official record of the hearing. One member notes that he insists upon a transcript and if the parties, in one fashion or another, do not provide him with a transcript, he will refuse to take the case. Another member responded that he would 'order' the Union to share the cost with the Company.

"All but four of the remaining members who responded to this question would allow a transcript to be made. One hundred sixteen of them would place no restrictions or conditions on the making of the transcript. Seventy-eight members, however, would allow the transcript to be made but with the condition that the Union be given access to the transcript. * * *

"When asked directly if they would allow the Union access to the transcript, 49 members responded that they would not do so. The remaining members would permit the Union to have access to the transcript, but often under some limitation; that is, only if the transcript is used in the arbitrator's office, in the offices of the Company, etc. However, 19 members would not permit the Union to use the transcript if the Company objected to the procedure."

[162]Compare the NAA survey results reported in the preceding footnote. For cases involving disputes over payment of transcript costs (some but not all of which cases comport with the just-stated generalization), see Arbitrator Holman in 79 LA 102, 103; Flagler in 75 LA 764, 770; Moore in 72 LA 490, 493; Coburn in 72 LA 359, 362–363; Coven in 71 LA 333, 334; Miller in 63 LA 692, 701; Platt in 61 LA 1205, 1213; Archer in 61 LA 849, 851; Leventhal in 56 LA 701, 703; Dworkin in 42 LA 722, 727–729; Roberts in 19 LA 270, 271. Also see Grovner v. Georgia-Pacific Corp., 105 LRRM 2706 (CA 5, 1980), relating to transcripts and the duty of fair representation, which was not breached in this case; Machine Workers v. Markle Mfg. Co., 94 LRRM 2766 (USDC, 1975), affirmed, 94 LRRM 2781 (CA 5, 1976); Stenzor v. Leon, 24 LA 306, 309 (Calif. Dist. Ct. App., 1955). It has been suggested that if sharing of cost is mandatory, "one side may be obliged to curtail its testimony in the interests of economy, while the other might be inclined to prolong the case in order to discourage future arbitration proceedings." Guides for Labor Arbitration, 2 (U. of Pa. Press, 1953), authored by a group of Philadelphia area arbitrators.

[163]Updegraff, "Preparing for Arbitration," 22 LA 889, 890 (circa 1954).

been and remains the most common practice, with each party paying for extra copies it orders. In any event, only rarely have disputes on transcripts reached arbitration, which may indicate that parties generally reach a mutually acceptable understanding on transcript use and costs (the arbitration cases cited above on transcript costs constitute a large portion of all transcript disputes appearing in volumes 1–76 of LA Reports).

One means of mitigating expenses is for one party to provide stenographic services or a tape recorder, in lieu of a formal transcript, to record substantially what transpires.[164] Another possibility is that the parties may have the hearing recorded with the understanding that if the arbitrator finds need for all or portions of the record, it shall be transcribed.[165] One arbitrator himself recorded the entire proceedings on tape, in addition to taking notes, where no official reporter was being used.[166]

Obviously, the bulk of the transcript will be composed of (1) the opening statements, if any, (2) the testimony of the witnesses, and (3) closing arguments, if any. Certain other matters, however, should be included in the record so the transcript will reflect a complete picture of the case. Thus, the arbitrator or tribunal clerk will open the hearing by putting such information as the following into the record:

a. Names of the parties;
b. If there is a special agreement, submission, or stipulation for arbitration, identify it by date and read it into the record (the latter may be done by handing a copy to the reporter with instructions that it be written into the record at that point);
c. The date, hour, and place of the hearing;
d. The name of the arbitrator or arbitrators, and how selected (as by agreement of the parties, appointment by a neutral agency, etc.);
e. Name of the Chairman, if it is an arbitration board (the Chairman is ordinarily selected by the board in executive session immediately prior to opening the hearing—the manner in which the Chairman was designated should be indicated in the record);
f. Announcement of appearances for the parties, that is, the attorneys or other representatives who are to present the case for the parties (state the name, title, and address of each

---

[164]Moog Indus., 15 LA 676, 677 (Klamon, 1950). Similarly, see Arbitrator Gibson in 49 LA 1115 at 1115; Roberts in 44 LA 51, 52. Of course such a record probably will not be accepted by the arbitrator as an official record unless both parties agree to such use. See discussion in "Procedural Problems in the Conduct of Arbitration Hearings," Proceedings of the 17th Annual Meeting of NAA, 1, 31 (BNA Books, 1964).

[165]American Potash & Chem. Corp., 17 LA 364, 370 (Grant, 1951).

[166]Mobil Oil Co., 46 LA 140 at 140 (Hebert, 1966). Also tape recording the proceedings, see Arbitrator Stix in 75 LA 574, 585; Stokes in 74 LA 756, 758; Levy in 69 LA 831, 834 (where the Arbitrator refused to make the tape recording available to either party after the union objected to the company's request for a copy); Taylor in 68 LA 559, 562. "Many members" of the National Academy of Arbitrators consider tape recordings of arbitration proceedings "to be of little value." "Procedural Problems During Hearings," The Chronicle (NAA, Apr. 1981).

person and state the party for whom he appears—all of this
information may be written on a sheet of paper to be handed to
the reporter for inclusion in the record, or it may be stated
orally by the parties);

g. Name of the reporter;
h. Hours for the hearing, if it is likely to require several days;
i. Any other material information, especially such items as fact
   stipulations.

After the above information has been read into the record the hearing
generally proceeds to the opening statements and on to the introduction of evidence.

In order to avoid cluttering the record, the arbitrator or parties
may go "off the record" for comment or discussion which promises to be
not material to the record, or for matter on which the spokesman
desires not to be committed. It may be then decided that any such
matter or any understanding growing out of the discussion should be
placed in the record; the hearing would then go "on the record" for this
purpose and for continuing with the introduction of evidence.

Both delay and errors in preparation of the transcript can be
avoided if parties who intend to read or quote lengthy passages at the
hearing furnish extra copies of the material for use by the reporter.[167]

Where witnesses are to be sworn, each witness may be sworn
individually immediately prior to his initial testimony, or all persons
scheduled to testify may be sworn (if present) when the hearing is
opened. Under the latter procedure the reporter should indicate, at the
outset of the testimony of each witness, that the witness has been
sworn.

Exhibits

Even where no reporter is used, a portion of the evidence will
ordinarily be presented and preserved in written form as exhibits.
Each party may submit its own exhibits and the parties may also
submit exhibits jointly.[168]

Sound observations concerning the use of exhibits have come from
Arbitrator Samuel H. Jaffee, who has suggested that parties should
"put as much of the evidence as possible in black and white, as simply
and plainly and logically as possible," since visible evidence "is often
far more persuasive than evidence which one hears and may forget."[169] He also noted that:

---

[167]For other suggestions for more effective use of the reporter, see Jaffee, "Battle Report: The
Problem of Stenographic Records in Arbitration," 20 Arb. J. 97 (1965).

[168]As in Republic Steel Corp., 16 LA 618 (Selekman, 1951), where 19 exhibits were submitted—10 jointly, 1 by the union, and 8 by the company. In Alameda County Superintendent of
Schools, 76 LA 566 at 566 (Anderson, 1981), the parties submitted eight joint exhibits and agreed
that this would be the only evidence to be presented.

[169]Jaffee, "Need for Exhibits in Labor Arbitration," 15 Arb. J. 203, 205 (1960).

"This is usually the best way of 'educating' an arbitrator. Moreover, it enables the arbitrator to understand the case more quickly and to write the decision faster, and this should reduce arbitration costs."[170]

In offering an exhibit as evidence a party must be prepared to use a witness to identify the exhibit and to put in enough evidence to show its accuracy, in the event that the other party does not indicate a willingness to accept the exhibit for what it purports to be.[171]

Exhibits customarily are introduced into evidence at the point of the hearing where the data in the exhibit are most relevant. While the parties may number their exhibits in advance, the more common practice is to number them when introduced into evidence since the parties do not always know in advance the order in which their exhibits will be submitted. Thus, exhibits generally are numbered in numerical or alphabetical order of introduction. A separate series is used for each party, as well as for joint exhibits. The first exhibit submitted by the company would be identified as Company Ex. #1, the next as Company Ex. #2, and so on. The union's exhibits would be identified as Union Ex. #1, and so on. To avoid confusion parties may choose to use alphabetical designations, A, B, C, etc., to identify one party's exhibits, and to use numbers 1, 2, 3, etc., to identify the other party's exhibits.

Several copies of each exhibit should be prepared in advance to insure a copy for each party, one for personal use by the arbitrator during the hearing, and a copy to be handed to the reporter, if one is used, to be incorporated by reference into the record.

Oath by Arbitrator and Witnesses

Acceptable practice regarding the arbitrator's oath of office and the swearing of witnesses is effectively summarized by American Arbitration Association Rule 24, which provides:

"Oaths—Before proceeding with the first hearing, each Arbitrator may take an Oath of Office, and if required by law, shall do so. The Arbitrator may, in his discretion, require witnesses to testify under oath administered by any duly qualified person, and if required by law or requested by either party, shall do so."

Even where the arbitrator's oath is required by statute (it is not required under the common law) it ordinarily may be waived by the parties, and very often is.[172] Moreover, where a case was covered by LMRA § 301 the award was not subject to being vacated merely

---

[170]Ibid.

[171]Ibid. As stressed by Arbitrator Feldman in U.S. Air Force Logistics Command, 78 LA 1092, 1093 (1982), parties in offering an exhibit should explain its relevance and identify the specific parts believed to be significant.

[172]Even without an express waiver, one will be implied by participating in the hearing without objection. Robinson v. Navajo Freight Lines, 49 LRRM 3048, 38 LA 321 (N.M. Sup. Ct., 1962). For statistics on extent of use of arbitrator's oath, see "Procedural Aspects of Labor-Management Arbitration," 28 LA 933, 936 (1954 statistics).

because the arbitrator's oath was not administered in accordance with a statute of the state in which the hearing was held (the oath was administered by a person not authorized by the state to administer oaths); the court stated that the party challenging the award had "cited no federal rule regarding oath-taking in labor arbitrations," that to "adopt the various state rules on this issue * * * would lead inevitably to disuniformity in the resolution of labor disputes," and that "In any event, the public interest in oath-taking and in the probity of arbitrators has been vindicated because the arbitrator did take an oath" and "there is no claim that he failed to act entirely in accordance with the oath."[173]

When the oath of office is taken, the arbitrator swears that he will faithfully and fully hear and examine the matters in controversy and make a just award according to the best of his understanding.[174] Under the practice of some appointing agencies the oath of office is written into the instrument of appointment and is affirmed by the arbitrator by signing the instrument in accepting the case.[175]

In adversary proceedings such as arbitration the swearing of witnesses is often preferred, whether required by statute or not (it is not required under the common law). In swearing witnesses, the arbitrator or hearing clerk asks the witness if he solemnly swears that the testimony he is about to give in the case is the truth, the whole truth, and nothing but the truth, so help him God. The witness, with right hand raised, answers, "I do."[176]

Participation by Arbitrator in Hearing

Arbitrators should be informed as fully as possible about the disputes they are to resolve. Accordingly, the arbitrator must feel free to participate personally in the hearing by asking questions, seeking information, and exploring all angles to the extent reasonably necessary to satisfy himself that he has in fact been informed as fully as possible. Arbitrator Harry Shulman emphasized, in this regard, that the arbitrator "should be satisfied that he knows enough to be able to decide the case" and that he "cannot simply sit back and judge a

---

[173]Local 671 v. United Parcel Serv., 108 LRRM 3216, 3217–3219 (USDC, 1981).

[174]"Procedural Aspects of Labor-Management Arbitration," ibid; Code of Ethics and Procedural Standards, Part II, §3, 15 LA 961, 964. The Code of Professional Responsibility which superseded the Code of Ethics is silent on the matter.

[175]See "Procedural Aspects of Labor-Management Arbitration," 28 LA 933, 936 (1957).

[176]Regarding the procedural point at which witnesses are sworn, see topic on "Transcript of Hearing," above. In Aristocrat Travel Prods., 52 LA 314, 316–317 (Koven, 1968), it was held that an employee could be discharged for giving perjured testimony in a prior case involving the earlier discharge of the employee. For related discussion, see Tidwell, "The Effects of Perjury Committed at an Arbitration Hearing," 38 Arb. J. No. 3, p. 44 (1983).

debate. He must seek to inform himself as fully as possible and encourage the parties to provide him with the information."[177]

Similarly, it has been emphasized that while the arbitrator obviously should not take sides, he must be free to ask questions and to explore all angles which he deems necessary to a full understanding of the case "even if they have not occurred to either one or both of the parties."[178]

It has been observed that:

"Where testimony is controverted, it is quite proper for the Arbitrator to take the initiative, if necessary, in reconciling apparent contradictions, or in seeking insight into the motives of those whose testimony is at odds. It is the parties' primary responsibility to present facts and to rebut contrary testimony, but the Arbitrator may also use his office to elicit information or to secure insights where, in his opinion, such procedure is made necessary by the critical nature of the controverted testimony."[179]

Likewise, some arbitrators have felt justified in making an independent study of the entire collective agreement to insure consideration of all provisions that might be relevant to the disposition of the case.[180] However, other arbitrators have disapproved of independent

[177]Shulman, "Reason, Contract, and Law in Labor Relations," 68 Harv. L. Rev. 999, 1017–1018 (1955), also reported in Management Rights and the Arbitration Process, 169, 190–191 (BNA Books, 1957). If the arbitrator does not take the initiative where necessary to adequately explore relevant aspects at the hearing, he may later feel some regret for not having done so. See Halstead Metal Prods., Inc., 49 LA 325, 331 (Wagner, 1967). Even where an arbitrator felt constrained to ask some "pointed questions" in an effort to bring out the facts more fully, he later expressed doubt that the whole truth ever came out at the hearing. Gulf Oil Corp., 36 LA 207, 209–210 (Reid, 1960).

[178]Guides for Labor Arbitration, 11–12 (U. of Pa. Press, 1953). Also see Seitz, "Some Observations on the Role of an Arbitrator," 34 Arb. J. No. 3, pp. 3, 6–7 (1979); Smith, "The Search for Truth—The Whole Truth," Proceedings of the 31st Annual Meeting of NAA, 40, 45–46 (BNA Books, 1979); Murphy, "Due Process and Fair Representation in Grievance Handling in the Public Sector," Proceedings of the 30th Annual Meeting of NAA, 121, 138 (BNA Books, 1978), stating that the *Hines* decision by the U.S. Supreme Court "supports the wisdom and propriety of the active role" of arbitrators "in the adducement of evidence"; Eaton, "Labor Arbitration in the San Francisco Bay Area," 48 LA 1381, 1382–1383 (1967); "Procedural Problems in the Conduct of Arbitration Hearings: A Discussion," Proceedings of the 17th Annual Meeting of NAA, 1, 12–13 (BNA Books, 1964); Aaron, "Some Procedural Problems in Arbitration," 10 Vand. L. Rev. 733, 745 (1957). Sec. V(A)(1)(b) of the Code of Professional Responsibility states that: "An arbitrator may * * * restate the substance of issues or arguments to promote or certify understanding; question the parties' representatives or witnesses, when necessary or advisable, to obtain additional pertinent information; and request that the parties submit additional evidence, either at the hearing or by subsequent filing." Sec. V(A)(1)(c) states that *"An arbitrator should not intrude into a party's presentation so as to prevent that party from putting forward its case fairly and adequately."*

[179]Guides for Labor Arbitration, 8 (U. of Pa. Press, 1953). For examples of how an arbitrator might participate in the interrogation of a witness, see Allied Chem. Corp., 49 LA 773, 778–780 (Davey, 1967); Booth Newspapers, 43 LA 785, 789–790 (Platt, 1964).

[180]See Arbitrator Elkouri in 68 LA 304, 309–310 (illustrating that the arbitrator's evaluation may be aided significantly by examining the agreement to determine the presence or absence of express provisions relating to a relevant aspect of the case); Stephens in 66 LA 941, 943; Erbs in 50 LA 744, 750; Moore in 37 LA 119, 121; Boles in 22 LA 826, 828. Arbitrator Maxwell Copelof vigorously defended this practice against the charge that it helped the other party make out its case in West Virginia Pulp & Paper Co., 20 LA 385, 391–393 (1953). In Perma-Line Corp. v. Painters Local 230, 106 LRRM 2483, 2486 (CA 2, 1981), the court said: "An arbitrator need not determine the facts in a vacuum. He must have freedom to consider and decide the submitted issues in light of all relevant data, which in this case includes the collective bargaining agreement. * * * [W]e think the arbitrator * * * could look to the collective bargaining agreement as a whole for further enlightenment on the meaning of just cause. * * * Even though we believe that the arbitrator misconstrued the agreement, * * * he was entitled to examine it."

studies of the agreement by the arbitrator.[181] The present Authors believe that an arbitrator may be justified in making an independent study of the agreement, that only rarely should need exist for such a study, and that added care obviously should be exercised in relying upon *any* provision not discussed *fully* at the hearing or in briefs.

Order of Presenting Case

There is no rigid order in which the parties must present their case in arbitration.[182] The party asserting a claim usually presents its case first, or at least a preliminary or introductory case, but this practice may not be followed where the nature of the issue makes a different procedure preferable. In the latter regard, American Arbitration Association Rule 26 provides:

> "The Arbitrator has discretion to vary the normal procedure under which the initiating party first presents his claim, but in any case shall afford full and equal opportunity to all parties for presentation of relevant proofs."

Logically, "the determination of the order of presentation in an arbitration case should depend exclusively on how the facts can best be developed in an orderly way."[183] If the arbitrator can see at the outset of a hearing that one of the parties possesses the basic facts of the case and that the case of the other party will consist primarily of a rebuttal, the arbitrator upon his own initiative or at the request of a party may suggest or require that the party in possession of the basic facts present its case first. This is not uncommon, for instance, in discharge and discipline cases.[184]

A related matter involves the efforts of a company to call a union member or representative as its first witness or of a union to call a

---

[181]The question whether "the arbitrator is justified in making a totally independent study of the contract" was presented to 24 arbitrators selected at random by the American Arbitration Association, and the views of the 17 who responded to the question were summarized by the Association as follows:

"Most of those replying indicated either that arbitrators were not justified in doing so * * * or that they should do so only upon request of the parties or when they have given the parties an opportunity to respond to the arbitrator's findings. Several people cited the danger that clauses may have meanings for the parties that are not apparent to an outsider.

"One arbitrator said, however, that in some instances he would automatically review the contract, while two others indicated that when a provision in dispute was ambiguous, they would examine the entire contract to determine the interest or intent of the parties."
AAA Study Time, Apr. 1978, 3. Also see Crane, "The Use and Abuse of Arbitral Power," Proceedings of the 25th Annual Meeting of NAA, 66, 71–72 (BNA Books, 1973), disapproving of independent studies.

[182]For related discussion, see Chapter 8, topic entitled "Burden of Proof."

[183]Aaron, "Some Procedural Problems in Arbitration," 10 Vand. L. Rev. 733, 739 (1957). Also see discussion by Smith, "The Search for Truth—The Whole Truth," Proceedings of the 31st Annual Meeting of NAA, 40, 52–54 (BNA Books, 1979).

[184]See Aaron, id. at 739–740; Eaton, "Labor Arbitration in the San Francisco Area," 48 LA 1381, 1385 (1967); Douglas Aircraft Co., 28 LA 198, 202–203 (Jones, 1957); Armstrong Cork Co., 18 LA 651 at 651 (Pigors, 1952). But see Latrobe Steel Co., 38 LA 729, 734 (Wood, 1962); Sealtest Dairy Prods. Co., 35 LA 205, 208–209 (1960).

foreman.[185] In this connection, a survey of its members by the National Academy of Arbitrators presented the following questions:

> "You are hearing a discharge case and the Company calls a Union member as its first witness. The Union objects to the procedure. How would you rule and why? What would you do if the grievant is called as the first witness?"

A large majority of the responding members would permit the company to call a union member as its first witness in the discharge case over the union's objection, and a somewhat smaller majority would permit the company to call the grievant.[186]

After both parties have presented their basic case, each party in turn will be given full opportunity to present its rebuttal case. Indeed, the hearing will not be adjourned until each party has nothing further to add.[187]

Opening Statements and Closing Arguments

Opening statements are brief, generalized statements in clear language designed to acquaint the arbitrator with each party's view of what the dispute is about and what the party expects to prove by its evidence.[188] Occasionally a party will prepare its opening statement in written form, with copies to be handed to the arbitrator and the

---

[185]See discussion in "Procedural Problems in the Conduct of Arbitration Hearings," Proceedings of the 17th Annual Meeting of NAA, 1, 3–4 (BNA Books, 1964). Stating that the arbitrator has the authority to regulate the proceedings and the order of proof, a court held that an arbitrator's refusal to uphold the employer's attempt to call the grievant in a discharge case as its first witness was not basis for refusing to enforce an award reinstating the grievant. Local 560, IBT v. Eazor Express, Inc., 65 LRRM 2647 (N.J. Super. Ct., 1967), where the union had made it clear that it would call the grievant and that the employer would not have to limit its cross-examination to the scope of the union's direct examination. For related discussion, see Chapter 8, subtopic entitled "Use of Adverse Witnesses."

[186]"Procedural Problems During Hearings," The Chronicle (NAA, Apr. 1981), where some of the details reported are as follows: "154 members would overrule the objection and only 19 would sustain it. Another 50 members were ambivalent." Many of those who would overrule the objection explained that "arbitration is a civil matter and either side may call as a witness anyone they please." As to the grievant, "63 members would sustain the Union's objection if the grievant were called as the first witness, 115 would overrule the objection, and 44 would rule according to the circumstances * * *. Those who refuse to permit the grievant (or a Union member in some cases) to be called as the first witness reason, primarily, that the Company has the obligation to establish at least a *prima facie* case through its own witnesses." Most of the responding members indicated that in the event they did not permit the company to call a union member as its first witness, they would permit a supervisor to testify as to what the member told him concerning the discharge incident. "Almost all respondents note that such testimony would be hearsay and the arbitrator would have to determine the weight to be given the testimony. * * * Clearly, the reason for permitting such testimony is that in many relationships it is not considered good practice for the Company to call a bargaining unit member or the grievant as the first witness. Thus, permitting such testimony obviates the problem of one side calling a witness from the other side."

[187]The arbitrator should not restrict or limit the rebuttal case of either party. In Harvey Aluminum, Inc. v. Steelworkers, 67 LRRM 2580 (USDC, 1967), an award was vacated because of the arbitrator's refusal to consider certain testimony on the grounds that it should have been presented as part of the employer's case-in-chief and was not proper rebuttal; the employer had the right to assume that the arbitrator would permit the presentation of all material evidence before closing the hearing.

[188]For more extensive comment as to what might be included in opening statements, see Bornstein, "The Opening Statement in Arbitration Advocacy: An Arbitrator's Perspective," 38 Arb. J. No. 1, p. 49 (1983); Roberts & Dash, "How to Get Better Results From Labor-Management Arbitration," 22 Arb. J. 1, 3, 8–9 (1967).

other party. Even when this is done, however, the statement will be presented orally for purposes of emphasis and more effective communication.

Use of opening statements is ordinarily optional with the parties, but often the arbitrator specifically requests that each party make one.[189]

Sometimes both parties make opening statements at the outset of the hearing, before any evidence is introduced by either party. This is especially helpful to the arbitrator since it enables him to grasp more quickly what the dispute is about. Another possibility is that each party will make its opening statement immediately prior to presenting its initial evidence; thus, one party will have made its opening statement and presented its evidence before the other party makes its opening statement. Ordinarily the arbitrator will follow whatever procedure the parties desire, unless he is convinced that some particular procedure is essential for proper presentation of the case.

By making closing arguments after all the evidence of both parties has been presented, the parties

> "can render a real service to the arbitrator as well as to themselves by carefully analyzing and synthesizing the important aspects of the case, emphasizing the facts they feel they have proved and placing them in proper relation to the ultimate conclusion at which they seek to persuade the arbitrator to arrive."[190]

The arbitrator will always permit the parties to make closing arguments (though he may limit the amount of time), and he sometimes requests specifically that they do so. Closing arguments and posthearing briefs sometimes serve much the same purpose, and while the parties sometimes choose to use both they more frequently choose to use either one or the other.[191]

Examining Witnesses

The manner in which witnesses are used, both in direct and cross-examination, may either promote or impede a party's case; and it will also affect the character of the arbitration proceeding generally. In this regard, an excellent guide was offered by Arbitrator Clarence M. Updegraff:

> "Prove your case by your own witnesses. Do not try to establish it by evidence gleaned from people put on the stand by your opponent. They are there to oppose you, not to help you.
> "If you cross-examine the other parties' witnesses, *make it short*. Do not unduly prolong cross-examination in attempts to get damaging admissions. The more questions you ask on cross-examination, the more opportunity you give a hostile witness to repeat the adverse testimony

---

[189]As in Inland Container Corp., 28 LA 312 at 312 (Ferguson, 1957).
[190]Howard, "Informing the Arbitrator," 10 Vand. L. Rev. 771, 786–787 (1957).
[191]As in William Brooks Shoe Co., 19 LA 65, 67 (Dworkin, 1952).

he came to give. Choose most carefully the inquiries you make of such parties. Make them as few as possible.

"Each party has the right to ask leading questions [so worded as to suggest an answer] when cross-examining hostile witnesses. Each party should save time by asking its own witnesses leading questions, excepting at points where disputed facts are involved. Testimony on controverted matters should be brought out by questions which do not suggest the answer, if possible."[192]

In contrast to the question-answer method of examining witnesses, it is sometimes best to request that one's own witness tell his story in his own way. Obviously, the latter method is not advisable for the examination or cross-examination of adverse witnesses.

Objections to Evidence

Each party is entitled to object when it believes the other party is seeking to introduce improper evidence or argument at the arbitration hearing. Such objections, when based upon some plausible grounds, can serve a useful function even if overruled, for the arbitrator will have been cautioned to examine the challenged evidence or argument more closely before giving it weight. A party is also entitled to object to evidence he considers irrelevant, for the record should not be burdened with a mass of material having little or no bearing on the issue.

However, objections which have no plausible basis, and those which are repetitious, should be avoided, as was advised by Arbitrator Clarence M. Updegraff:

"Do not make captious, whimsical or unnecessary objections to testimony or arguments of the other party. Such interruptions are likely to waste time and confuse issues. The arbitrator, no doubt, will realize without having the matter expressly mentioned more than once, when he is hearing weak testimony such as hearsay and immaterial statements."[193]

Plant Visits by Arbitrator

Sometimes the arbitrator's understanding of the case can be greatly improved if he personally visits the physical site directly involved in the dispute. Indeed, in some types of cases, such as job evaluation, a plant tour is virtually indispensable.[194]

---

[192]Updegraff, "Preparation for Arbitration," 22 LA 889, 890 (1954). For another informative discussion, see Friedman, "Problems of Cross-Examination in Labor Arbitration," 34 Arb. J. No. 4, p. 6 (1979), commented upon by Kaufman, "Cross-Examination," 35 Arb. J. No. 1, p. 3 (1980).

[193]Updegraff, "Preparation for Arbitration," 22 LA 889, 890 (1954). For another statement as to use of objections in arbitration, see Kagel, Anatomy of a Labor Arbitration, 98 (BNA Books, 1961).

[194]For some indication of the practical significance of actually viewing the job in its setting, see Arbitrator Hunter in 69 LA 727, 731; Rubin in 47 LA 577, 579; Bothwell in 42 LA 145, 148; Forrester in 16 LA 264, 266.

The values of a plant visit were elaborated by Arbitrator William E. Simkin:

> "The eye is better than the ear in many aspects of disputes, or at least is a valuable supplement to oral or written evidence. A plant visit is a simple device by which the arbitrator can secure a better understanding of the background of a case. In some instances a plant visit either before or during the hearing will serve to avoid voluminous testimony. The award may be more realistic and therefore acceptable because the plant visit fills part of the gap in the arbitrator's knowledge."[195]

Frequently the parties suggest a plant visit by the arbitrator. However, the arbitrator may suggest one if he feels it essential. For instance, Arbitrator Paul Prasow sought and obtained permission from the parties to make first-hand observations where evidence submitted at the hearing failed to reveal clearly the distinction between two job classifications involved in the dispute; as a result of the plant visit much of the confusion caused by the apparently conflicting contentions of the parties was eliminated.[196]

The arbitrator has discretionary authority to make plant visits in cases governed by American Arbitration Association Rule 30, which provides:

> "Whenever the Arbitrator deems it necessary, he may make an inspection in connection with the subject matter of the dispute after written notice to the parties who may, if they so desire, be present at such inspection."

Even if the case is not being administered by the American Arbitration Association, it now appears to be generally agreed that consent of both parties is not essential for plant visits by the arbitrator. This appears evident from the Code of Professional Responsibility provision on plant visits:

> "An arbitrator should comply with a request of *any* party that he or she visit a work area pertinent to the dispute prior to, during, or after a hearing. An arbitrator may also initiate such a request."[197]

---

[195]Simkin, Acceptability as a Factor in Arbitration Under an Existing Agreement, 24 (U. of Pa. Press, 1952).

[196]Procter & Gamble Mfg. Co., 1 LA 313, 314 (1945).

[197]Sec. V(D)(1), 64 LA 1326, emphasis added. The Code adds in § V(D)(1)(a) that "Procedures for such visits should be agreed to by the parties in consultation with the arbitrator." A survey of its members by the National Academy of Arbitrators presented the following question:
"At the beginning of the hearing, one party requests that you make an onsite inspection. The other party strongly objects to such an inspection, claiming that such an inspection is unnecessary and will unduly prolong the hearing. What would you do?"
A summary of the responses states, in part:
"Eighty members would make the inspection as a matter of course. * * * Sixty members would inquire as to the need and/or purpose for the inspection and if the member believes a valid purpose exists for making the inspection, they would do so. Seventy-nine members would proceed with the hearing with the understanding that the inspection will be made later if it is deemed necessary. Three members would not make the inspection and another seven indicate they would make the inspection only with mutual consent * * *.
"The responses clearly indicate that most members lean toward making the inspection, either initially or later in the hearing, if a request is made. The reasons vary but three are cited most frequently: (1) desire for all information obtainable; (2) belief that a party has the right to decide how to present its case; and (3) in technical cases, inspections often provide

Settlements at Arbitration Stage

Sometimes disputes are settled by the parties after arbitration has been initiated. Some settlements occur prior to the arbitration hearing, and possibilities of settlement may be even stronger after the hearing is commenced.[198] The parties sometimes see the dispute in new light during arbitration, especially upon participating at the hearing. Umpire Harry H. Platt observed in this regard:

> "Under a system in which grievances are heard by the umpire *de novo* and in the presence of all interested parties to the controversy, it is not unusual for the hearing to disclose an underlying misunderstanding that may have blocked an earlier settlement or uncover new thoughts, new facts, and occasionally new areas of agreement that provide real opportunities for constructive settlements. At Ford, these opportunities are usually not ignored, even though it may be thought that this tends to encourage appeals to the umpire."[199]

Likewise, other parties and arbitrators do not ignore real possibilities for constructive settlements. Some of the available procedures for accommodating further negotiations between the parties include the following:

a. The hearing may be recessed for direct negotiations at the request of the parties or at the arbitrator's suggestion, if accepted by the parties.[200]

b. The hearing may be closed with the understanding that the award will be delayed pending negotiations by the parties for a specified time, an award to be issued thereafter only if no settlement is reached.[201]

c. It may be agreed that the arbitrator will rule or comment by an interim decision upon some aspects of the case, referring the unresolved matters back to the parties for further negotiations, to be ruled upon ultimately in a supplemental award by the arbitrator only if the negotiations fail.[202]

---

valuable information."
"Procedural Problems During Hearings," The Chronicle (NAA, Apr. 1981). Also see Justin, "Arbitration: Proving Your Case," 10 LA 955, 964 (1948), deeming plant visits by the arbitrator improper unless consented to by both parties. In Stefano Berizzi Co. v. Krausz, 146 N.E. 436, 437–438 (N.Y. Ct. App., 1925), an award was vacated because the arbitrator following the hearing and without notice to the parties made an independent investigation concerning facts which were both material and reasonably disputable. For related material, see Chapter 8, topic entitled "Testimony by Persons From Outside."

[198]For related material, see topic entitled "Extent of Permissible Deviation From Prearbitral Discussion of a Case," above, and subtopic entitled "Arbitrator's Charges When Case Is Cancelled," also above.

[199]Comments of Umpire Platt in Proceedings of the 11th Annual Meeting of NAA, 141, 144 (BNA Books, 1958), in response to statement by the Chairman of the Chrysler Appeal Board, which at the time had basically appellate jurisdiction, that cases were not often referred back to the parties for settlement efforts after reaching the Impartial Chairman, but that many cases had been settled by the prearbitral meetings of the Appeal Board. See "The Chrysler-UAW Umpire System," id. at 111, 124, 133.

[200]For discussion of this and other settlement procedures, see Simkin, Acceptability as a Factor in Arbitration Under an Existing Agreement, 57–65 (U. of Pa. Press, 1952).

[201]See Victor Chem. Works, 22 LA 71, 72 (Dworet, 1953), where the parties requested this procedure. Also see Arbitrator Boals in 69 LA 238 at 238.

[202]See topic entitled "Split Hearings," above.

Whatever procedure is used, it should be undertaken only by sanction of the parties. If they show no interest in an arbitrator's suggestion for further negotiations he should not attempt to force acceptance. Concededly, an arbitrator

"should not undertake to induce a settlement of the dispute against the wishes of either party. If, however, an atmosphere is created or the issues are so simplified or reduced as to lead to a voluntary settlement by the parties, a function of his office has been fulfilled."[203]

Ordinarily the settlement negotiations themselves are carried on only by the parties, without participation by the arbitrator. However, in some situations the arbitrator may perform a mediation role. In this regard, the Code of Professional Responsibility provides that:

"a. Once arbitration has been invoked, either party normally has a right to insist that the process be continued to decision.

"b. If one party requests that the arbitrator mediate and the other party objects, the arbitrator should decline the request.

"c. An arbitrator is not precluded from making a suggestion that he or she mediate. To avoid the possibility of improper pressure, the arbitrator should not so suggest unless it can be discerned that both parties are likely to be receptive. In any event, the arbitrator's suggestion should not be pursued unless both parties readily agree."[204]

Attempts at mediation by ad hoc arbitrators are certainly not rare,[205] and mediation by permanent arbitrators has long been a fairly common practice.[206]

It was well stated by Robert Coulson, President of the American Arbitration Association, that:

"The arbitrator is free to suggest settlement or, in appropriate cases, to attempt to mediate. The Code of Professional Responsibility is flexible in this regard. Few labor awards are challenged because a labor arbitrator has attempted to mediate. In practice, a 'bionic neutral' frequently sets the parties upon the road toward settlement."[207]

---

[203]Code of Ethics and Procedural Standards for Labor-Management Arbitration, Part I, §5, 15 LA 961, 963. The Code of Professional Responsibility which was intended to supersede the Code of Ethics does not contain an identical provision, but it does provide that: "A direct settlement by the parties of some or all issues in a case, at any stage of the proceedings, must be accepted by the arbitrator as relieving him or her of further jurisdiction over such issues." § II(E)(2).

[204]Sec. II(F)(2)(a, b, & c), 64 LA 1322–1323.

[205]See surveys reported in Proceedings of the 18th Annual Meeting of NAA, 243, 245, 252 (BNA Books, 1965); Proceedings of the 17th Annual Meeting of NAA, 292, 296, 314 (BNA Books, 1964), indicating that such attempts often are successful. For some arbitral efforts toward a settlement, see Arbitrator Platt in 50 LA 1103, 1104 (interest dispute); Aaron in 15 LA 162, 168 (rights dispute). In Fairbanks, Morse & Co., 32 LA 278, 281 (1959), Arbitrator Howlett resisted the temptation to try mediation, but he recalled Arbitrator Platt's observation that arbitrators are criticized both for having a tendency to mediate and for seldom trying to mediate.

[206]For full discussion of mediation by permanent arbitrators, and citation of articles discussing whether or in what circumstances ad hoc arbitrators should undertake to mediate a settlement, see Chapter 4, topic entitled "Mediation by Permanent Arbitrators."

[207]Coulson, "Certification and Training of Labor Arbitrators: Should Arbitrators Be Certified?" Proceedings of the 30th Annual Meeting of NAA, 173, 182 (BNA Books, 1978). In Mobil Oil Corp., 72 LA 143, 143–144 (Herman, 1980), the arbitrator requested the parties to attend a mediation session after the hearing and this was one of the grounds for the company's request that the AAA remove him from the case; the AAA transmitted the request to the arbitrator, who dismissed the "mediation" objection as "patently without merit," the company being "free to decline at all times."

Putting Settlement in Form of Award

When parties settle their dispute during the course of arbitration they often request that the arbitrator set forth the terms of the settlement in an award. Concerning such requests, AAA Rule 39 states that the arbitrator "may set forth the terms of the agreed settlement in an award."[208] The Code of Professional Responsibility provision on this aspect is more detailed:

> "Prior to issuance of an award, the parties may jointly request the arbitrator to include in the award certain agreements between them, concerning some or all of the issues. If the arbitrator believes that a suggested award is proper, fair, sound, and lawful, it is consistent with professional responsibility to adopt it."[209]

Briefs

Practice varies considerably regarding use of briefs in arbitration. In some cases no briefs of any type are used. However, use of posthearing briefs is quite common,[210] and sometimes prehearing (or hearing) briefs or statements are submitted.[211] Then, too, in some cases both prehearing (or hearing) and posthearing briefs are used,[212]

---

[208]43 LA 1292, 1295. In Chase Bag Co., 53 LA 612 at 612 (Larson, 1969), the withdrawal of an AAA case "with prejudice" was confirmed by an award.

[209]Sec. II(I)(1), 64 LA 1322. Amplifying, § II(I)(1)(a) provides:

"a. Before complying with such a request, an arbitrator must be certain that he or she understands the suggested settlement adequately in order to be able to appraise its terms. If it appears that pertinent facts or circumstances may not have been disclosed the arbitrator should take the initiative to assure that all significant aspects of the case are fully understood. To this end, the arbitrator may request additional specific information and may question witnesses at a hearing."

This no doubt applies also to the related situation of the so-called agreed case in which the arbitrator is made aware that the company and union have a common view as to the merits of the case but want a hearing for the record, or for some other purpose such as arbitral review of their proposed solution or arbitral consideration of the different view of some individual or group. Some arbitrators do not care to participate in such proceedings but others will do so as long as they remain satisfied that it will serve some useful purpose and that it is neither intended nor to be anticipated that it will work an injustice. For discussions of this matter and indications as to views, see Fleming, "Due Process and Fair Procedure in Labor Arbitration," Proceedings of the 14th Annual Meeting of NAA, 69, 87–90 (BNA Books, 1961); Fleming, "Reflections on the Nature of Labor Arbitration," 61 Mich. L. Rev. 1245, 1271 (1963); "Current Problems of Arbitration," 35 LA 963, 965 (1961). Also see Eaton, "Labor Arbitration in the San Francisco Bay Area," 48 LA 1381, 1389 (1967); "Survey of Arbitration in 1964," Proceedings of the 18th Annual Meeting of NAA, 243, 252 (BNA Books, 1965). Where there was "prima facie indication of conspiracy" between the company and union in reaching a grievance settlement by which "the Local Union threw the Grievant to the wolves," the settlement could not be justified by the "otherwise laudable goal" of easing a strain on their relationship. Gordon Wyman Co., 68 LA 997, 999–1000 (Keefe, 1977), where Arbitrator Keefe in substance rescued the employee from the consequences of the settlement.

[210]See statistics reported in FMCS Mini Memo No. 81–2 (1981), reporting that of the 7539 FMCS "award cases" in 1980, briefs were filed in 5275, none were filed in 2176, and no indication was given for the remaining 88 cases; "Procedural Aspects of Labor-Management Arbitration," 28 LA 933, 938 (1954 statistics).

[211]As in 47 LA 270 at 270; 29 LA 635, 638; 17 LA 412 at 412; 15 LA 792 at 792.

[212]As in 22 LA 251, 252; 18 LA 20, 21; 16 LA 955 at 955.

and still other possibilities include use of rebuttal and supplemental briefs.[213]

Hearing or prehearing briefs outline the party's view of the case as it stands before the hearing; one of their chief advantages is that the hearing may be shortened by their use.[214] The purpose of posthearing briefs is "summarization of the evidence presented at the hearing, together with the arguments of the parties and their comments on the evidence."[215]

No new evidence should be included in posthearing briefs.[216] However, expanded discussion regarding the proper interpretation of the agreement, and citation and discussion of precedents, articles, and the like for the first time in posthearing briefs is not unusual.[217] Occasionally arbitrators find it necessary to confer with the parties or to call them together again for additional hearing when some point of critical importance develops as a result of filing briefs.

Briefs can be of valuable assistance to the arbitrator.[218] Sometimes the arbitrator deems briefs sufficiently advisable that he specifically requests them.[219]

From the standpoint of the parties, the privilege of submitting briefs may be considered essential to a "fair hearing."[220] However, an arbitrator's refusal to accept posthearing briefs was declared by a Pennsylvania court not to warrant vacating the award either at common law or under the statutes of that state.[221]

---

[213]See 48 LA 1304, 1306; 47 LA 142, 143; 23 LA 706, 707; 16 LA 149 at 149. After initial briefs are in, additional argument should not be transmitted to the arbitrator without prior agreement by the parties or consent by the arbitrator after notice to the other party. For the trouble that may result when this rule is violated, see Bendix-Westinghouse Automotive Air Brake Co., 36 LA 724, 731 (Schmidt, 1961).

[214]For discussion of the advantages and disadvantages of using prehearing and posthearing briefs, see Simkin, Acceptability as a Factor in Arbitration Under an Existing Agreement, 21–23 (U. of Pa. Press, 1952). For additional discussion of briefs, see Roberts & Dash, "How to Get Better Results From Labor-Management Arbitration," 22 Arb. J. 1, 4–5, 19–21 (1967); Eaton, "Labor Arbitration in the San Francisco Bay Area," 48 LA 1381, 1386 (1967); Fleming, The Labor Arbitration Process, 74–75 (U. of Ill. Press, 1965); Jones & Smith, "Management and Labor Appraisals and Criticisms of the Arbitration Process: A Report With Comments," 62 Mich. L. Rev. 1115, 1128, 1131 (1964); "A Colloquium on the Arbitration Process," Proceedings of the 17th Annual Meeting of NAA, 82, 95–97, 107 (BNA Books, 1964).

[215]Code of Ethics and Procedural Standards for Labor-Management Arbitration, Part III, §6, 15 LA 961, 966. The Code of Professional Responsibility which was intended to supersede the Code of Ethics is silent on the purpose of briefs. Sometimes a "short short" brief is submitted, as by one party in Owens-Illinois, 50 LA 871, 872 (Klamon, 1968), but briefs more often detail the major facets of the dispute.

[216]Code of Ethics and Procedural Standards, ibid. Also see Arbitrator Cohen in 74 LA 1276, 1278; Snow in 71 LA 271, 272; Rock in 43 LA 833, 836; Dworkin in 36 LA 491, 492–493; Sembower in 29 LA 67, 73. Cf., Jenkins in 45 LA 696, 697 n. 1, 702. Again, the Code of Professional Responsibility is silent on this aspect.

[217]As to advancement of entirely new theories of the case in briefs, see discussion by Fleming, The Labor Arbitration Process, 154–157 (U. of Ill. Press, 1965). Matters which were first mentioned in a party's posthearing brief and which were not related to any proofs submitted at the hearing were not considered by Arbitrator Stouffer in Tibbetts Plumbing-Heating Co., 46 LA 124, 126 (1966). Similarly, see Arbitrator Bernstein in 71 LA 903, 908; Keefe in 44 LA 530, 537.

[218]See comments of Arbitrator Turkus in 49 LA 798, 801; Mathews in 23 LA 706, 707; McCoy in 16 LA 1, 2. A strong case for use of posthearing briefs appears in Arbitrator Paul Prasow's statement that he had "found posthearing briefs nearly always helpful, and in many cases indispensable." Prasow, "Comment," Proceedings of the 26th Annual Meeting of NAA, 184, 188 (BNA Books, 1974).

[219]See Merrill, "A Labor Arbitrator Views His Work," 10 Vand. L. Rev. 789, 796–797 (1957).
[220]See Updegraff, "Preparation for Arbitration," 22 LA 889, 890 (1954).
[221]Technical Employees v. U.S. Steel Co., 22 LA 62, 64–65 (Pa. Com. Pleas Ct., 1954). The

Sometimes the question of what briefs, if any, may be submitted is handled by stipulation of the parties.[222] Such stipulations will be enforced by the arbitrator unless modified by mutual agreement.[223] That mutual agreements of the parties on briefs do control the arbitrator is expressly confirmed by the Code of Professional Responsibility, but the Code otherwise recognizes considerable discretion in the arbitrator concerning briefs:

> "1. An arbitrator must comply with mutual agreements in respect to the filing or nonfiling of post hearing briefs or submissions.
> "a. An arbitrator, in his or her discretion, may either suggest the filing of post hearing briefs or other submissions or suggest that none be filed.
> "b. When the parties disagree as to the need for briefs, an arbitrator may permit filing but may determine a reasonable time limitation.
> "2. An arbitrator must not consider a post hearing brief or submission that has not been provided to the other party."[224]

Where there is no agreement regarding briefs, the arbitrator ordinarily will accept and consider the brief of either party desiring to submit one, and the other party may be allowed time to submit a reply brief.[225]

Either party desiring to file a posthearing brief should give notice at the hearing; if notice is first given after the hearing is closed, the arbitrator may be more reluctant to accept a brief filed over the opposition of the other party.[226]

An arbitrator may take unusual steps to permit consideration of briefs. For instance, where one party requested permission to file a brief but, because of a misunderstanding by the arbitrator the award was issued prior to receipt of the brief, the arbitrator secured agreement by the parties to permit issuance of a supplement to the award to allow consideration of the brief.[227]

When briefs are to be used, a time limit within which they can be filed will be set by stipulation of the parties or by the arbitrator. A very common arrangement is for both parties to file (mail) briefs simultaneously on a specified date.[228] If either party fails to submit a brief

---

court observed that it "is not at all unusual" for judges to "decline to accept post-hearing briefs and make an immediate decision." Id. at 65. In Local 139 v. Anchor Hocking Corp., 84 LRRM 3000 (USDC, 1973), an award was enforced even though it was issued before the timely filing of the union's brief, the court finding that the brief added nothing to the positions of the parties in the transcript.

[222]As in McInerney Spring & Wire Co., 20 LA 642, 643 (Smith, 1953); Cedartown Textiles, 15 LA 573, 574 (Hawley, 1950).

[223]See Sayles Biltmore Bleacheries, 24 LA 408 at 408 (Livengood, 1955).

[224]Sec. VI(A), 64 LA 1326–1327.

[225]See Steinway & Sons, 17 LA 31 at 31 (Justin, 1951). In Angelus Sanitary Can Mach. Co., 68 LA 973, 975 (1977), Arbitrator Julian L. Ashe explained that the "filing of a brief with numerous citations of prior arbitration decisions by one side and no brief by the other, made it incumbent on the Arbitrator to research several texts as well as arbitration decisions themselves."

[226]Of course, it goes without saying that neither the grievant, the union, nor the company should seek to communicate their views or evidence to the arbitrator on an ex parte basis. See comments of Arbitrator Jones in Wilshire Mfg. Jewelers, 49 LA 1079, 1082–1083 (1967).

[227]Crook Paper Box Co., 27 LA 836 at 836 (Compton, 1957); the supplement to the award did not change the result.

[228]As in Needham Packing Co., 44 LA 1057, 1059 (Davey, 1965).

within the specified time, the arbitrator may proceed to decide the case without waiting for the brief,[229] especially if no request is made for more time.[230] However, for reasonable cause the arbitrator may grant a request for more time, especially if the other party after due notice does not object.[231] It also appears that many arbitrators would be inclined to consider a brief even where it is properly classified as being "late."[232]

Copies of all briefs submitted to the arbitrator should always be submitted simultaneously to the other party.

Closing the Hearing and Time Limit for Rendering Award

Customarily arbitration hearings are deemed "closed" when all evidence and arguments of the parties have been received and the hearing is ready for adjournment with no additional days of hearing being contemplated. However, where briefs or other documents are to be filed after final adjournment of the hearing, it appears clear that the hearing will be deemed "closed" as of the final date for receipt of these items.[233] The point at which an arbitration hearing is deemed "closed" is significant in determining the time within which the award is to be rendered since ordinarily the time commences to run at the point where the hearing is deemed "closed."

---

[229]See Beech-Nut Packing Co., 20 LA 575, 576 (Davis, 1953).

[230]See Pan Am. Ref. Corp., 15 LA 464, 465 (Klamon, 1950).

[231]See Needham Packing Co., 44 LA 1057, 1059 (Davey, 1965); Great Lakes Carbon Corp., 16 LA 918, 919 (Livengood, 1951).

[232]In Sheller Mfg. Co., 40 LA 890, 891 (Davey, 1963), the arbitrator rejected the union's request to consider the company brief as "null and void" where it was filed one day late, the arbitrator stating that briefs are only an "aid" to the arbitrator and that the union was not prejudiced by the late filing. A survey of its members by the National Academy of Arbitrators presented the following question:

"A fixed date is set for the direct exchange of posthearing briefs between the parties with a copy to the arbitrator. One party is late in filing its brief and offers no good excuse for being late. The other party objects to your consideration of the late brief. What do you do?"

The reported response of 90 members was that they "would disregard the objection, accept the brief and give it full consideration." Sixty other responding members indicated they would exclude the brief. "Procedural Problems During Hearings," The Chronicle (NAA, Apr. 1981), where the varied responses of still other members were also summarized. A May 16, 1981 Advisory Opinion by the NAA Committee on Professional Responsibility and Grievances stated that:

"Where the parties agree to a certain date for the filing of posthearing briefs, and also agree that the arbitrator should not consider a posthearing brief filed after that date, Part 6–A–1 [§ VI(A)(1) of the Code of Professional Responsibility, quoted above] precludes the arbitrator from considering a posthearing brief filed by a party after that date, without the consent of the other party. However, where the parties agree only that posthearing briefs are to be filed by a certain date, without agreeing as to what the effect of a late filing is to be, Part 6–A–1 does not preclude the arbitrator from considering a posthearing brief filed after the agreed date."

Applying the just-noted distinction, the Advisory Opinion concluded that an arbitrator did not violate the Code by considering a brief that was filed over four months late, but the Opinion concluded that the arbitrator did violate § II(J)(2) of the Code "by failing to make any inquiry or taking any action concerning the late brief until several months after the agreed upon filing date." Code § II(J)(2) states: "An arbitrator must cooperate with the parties and with any administrative agency involved in avoiding delays."

[233]See AAA Rules 31, 37. Also, Arbitrator Gill in 46 LA 513 at 513; Geissinger in 46 LA 115 at 115; Graff in 44 LA 237, 239; Schmidt in 36 LA 724, 728. As noted below, § 1404.15 of the FMCS Regulations speaks of the "closing of the record as determined by the arbitrator."

Some collective agreements expressly state time limits, often unrealistic, for rendering the award.[234] Also, time limits for rendering awards are specified by some state arbitration statutes. The AAA specifies 30 days for rendering the award after close of the hearing or transmittal of final statements, unless otherwise agreed to or required by law; the somewhat less strict FMCS rule specifies that arbitrators "are encouraged to render awards not later than 60 days from the date of closing of the record as determined by the arbitrator, unless otherwise agreed upon by the parties or specified by law."[235]

The Code of Professional Responsibility in turn provides in § II(J)(3) that:

"3. Once the case record has been closed, an arbitrator must adhere to the time limits for an award, as stipulated in the labor agreement or as provided by regulation of an administrative agency or as otherwise agreed.
"a. If an appropriate award cannot be rendered within the required time, it is incumbent on the arbitrator to seek an extension of time from the parties.
"b. If the parties have agreed upon abnormally short time limits for an award after a case is closed, the arbitrator should be so advised by the parties or by the administrative agency involved, prior to acceptance of appointment."

In the absence of a mandatory time limit, the award may be made within a reasonable time.[236]

Tardy Awards

If by agreement of the parties or by the applicable law an award is to be rendered within a specified time, the award might be held invalid if not made within that time and the parties have not agreed to an extension.[237] Under some state statutes the right to object to a tardy award is waived by failure to object prior to its issuance.[238]

---

[234]See Major Collective Bargaining Agreements: Arbitration Procedures, 80–82 (U.S. Dept. Labor Bull. No. 1425–6, 1966).

[235]AAA Rule 37, 43 LA 1295 (AAA's amendment of its rules in 1979 left Rule 37 unaltered as to substance); FMCS Regulations, § 1404.15, 29 C.F.R. Part 1404. The FMCS regulation adds that an arbitrator's "failure to render timely awards may lead to his removal from the FMCS roster." Concerning the 30-day limit which AAA and FMCS were then using (FMCS now specifies 60 days), it was surmised that "there are doubtless many instances in which the arbitrator requests and receives from the parties an extension of time, and there may even be instances of deliberate ignoring of time limits." Jones & Smith, "Management and Labor Appraisals and Criticisms of the Arbitration Process: A Report With Comments," 62 Mich. L. Rev. 1115, 1140–1141 (1964), where other pertinent observations are also made on the subject.

[236]See Danbury Rubber Co. v. Rubber Workers, 29 LA 815, 817–818 (Conn. Sup. Ct., 1958), and authorities there cited. Also see Local 508 v. Standard Register Co., 103 LRRM 2212, 2214 (USDC, 1979), dealing with removal of an arbitrator who has failed to issue an award within a reasonable time.

[237]For extensive discussion, with citation of authorities going both ways under the common law and under state statutes, see Givens, "The Validity of Delayed Awards Under Section 301, Taft-Hartley Act," 16 Arb. J. 161 (1961). Collecting both commercial and labor cases on tardy awards, see Korpela, "Construction and Effect of Contractual or Statutory Provisions Fixing Time Within Which Arbitration Award Must Be Made," 56 ALR 3rd 815 (1974).

[238]The Uniform Arbitration Act so provides, for instance. § 8(b), 27 LA 909, 910.

Where a case is covered by LMRA § 301 there appears to be relatively little likelihood that the award will be invalidated merely because it is rendered late. Consider the view of one federal appellate court, for instance, that where there has been no objection to the delay until after an award is issued and there is no showing of harm due to the delay, the failure to meet a time limit specified either by state statute or by the collective agreement should not be held to invalidate the award.[239] That court explained:

> "In adopting a uniform federal standard, we ought not to accept an arbitration rule which encourages post-award technical objections by a losing party as a means of avoiding an adverse arbitration decision. Rather, we believe it to be a better rule that any limitation upon the time in which an arbitrator can render his award be a directory limitation, not a mandatory one, and that it should always be within a court's discretion to uphold a late award if no objection to the delay has been made prior to the rendition of the award or there is no showing that actual harm to the losing party was caused by the delay."[240]

Similarly, a court refused to invalidate an award rendered after expiration of the contractual time limit since there was no protest prior to its issuance,[241] and a like result was reached even where there was a timely protest but where there was no showing of prejudice from the delay.[242]

The latter court stated that if the parties "desire to bind themselves to a more drastic rule [than the FMCS rule applying to the case], they must clearly and unequivocally provide for the automatic invalidity of the award on the expiration of the [contractually] prescribed time."[243] Where an agreement did provide expressly that no arbitration decision shall be "conclusive and binding" unless delivered within the time specified by the agreement, and where the employer did protest prior to issuance of the award, an award not delivered within that time was held not binding upon the employer; surprisingly, the appellate court reached this result (disagreeing with the trial court) even though the employer's attorney had agreed to use the FMCS 60-day period rather than the contract's 30-day period, the court stating that this was "Short of a specific agreement that this provision [against "conclusive and binding" effect] be waived."[244]

---

[239]IAM v. Geometric Tool Co., 406 F.2d 284, 286–287, 70 LRRM 2228 (CA 2, 1968). This result under § 301 was predicted by Givens, "The Validity of Delayed Awards Under Section 301, Taft-Hartley Act," 16 Arb. J. 161, 181 (1961).

[240]406 F.2d at 286, citations omitted. Tardy awards are not necessarily or even usually a result of procrastination by the arbitrator. See Elkouri, "Informal Observations on Labor Arbitration Today," 35 Arb. J., No. 3, pp. 41, 44–45 (1980).

[241]IAM v. Mooney Aircraft, 71 LRRM 2121 (CA 5, 1969).

[242]Teamsters v. Anchor Motor Freight, Inc., 71 LRRM 3205, 3208–3209 (CA 3, 1969).

[243]71 LRRM at 3208. In Inland Container Corp., 74 LA 110, 114 (1980), Arbitrator Bruce R. Boals stated (apparently as dictum): "The arbitration clause requires an award to be rendered within 30 days. * * * Perhaps the restriction should be made to the arbitrator as a condition of his acceptance; otherwise, the arbitrator will follow the 60-day requirement of the appointing agency [FMCS]."

[244]Huntington Alloys v. Steelworkers, 104 LRRM 2958, 2960 (CA 4, 1980).

Reopening the Hearing

Under accepted practice the arbitrator on his own motion, or upon request of a party for good cause shown, may reopen the hearing at any time before the award is rendered. American Arbitration Association Rule 32 so provides, but cautions that if the agreement states a mandatory time limit for rendering the award and reopening would prevent issuance of the award within that time, the hearing may not be reopened unless the parties agree to extend the time limit.[245]

The Code of Ethics and Procedural Standards for Labor-Management Arbitration provided:

> "When hearings are concluded, parties should not attempt to communicate any additional information to the arbitrator. If new evidence becomes available, written application for the re-opening of the proceeding with the reasons therefor should be made to the arbitrator and a copy transmitted simultaneously to the other party."[246]

The reopening of hearings for introduction of new evidence was discussed by Arbitrator Edward A. Levy in reopening a hearing for this purpose:

> "Ordinarily where a hearing has been had in which all parties have participated, and have presented all evidence, and have stated on the record that they have nothing further to offer, the matter is deemed to be officially closed for the taking of evidence. However, where certain evidence is evidentiary and of material import and the admission thereof will probably affect the outcome of a cause, is unavailable at the time of the hearing, and if the same is produced subsequently without seriously affecting any substantial right, and it is shown that reasonable grounds existed for its non-production at the time of the hearing, the arbitrator may, in his discretion, reopen the arbitration for the introduction of such evidence only. The reason for this rule is to afford to each of the parties full opportunity to present such material evidence as will assist the arbitrator in ascertaining the truth of all matters in controversy."[247]

In one case, Arbitrator George H. Hildebrand refused to reopen the hearing to receive new evidence where the party requesting

---

[245]43 LA 1292, 1295. Also see Guides for Labor Arbifration, 15 (U. of Pa. Press, 1953). For related discussion, see topic entitled "Closing the Hearing and Time Limit for Rendering Award," above.

[246]Part III, §6, 15 LA 961, 966. The Code of Professional Responsibility which was intended to supersede the Code of Ethics is silent on reopening the hearing.

[247]Madison Inst., 18 LA 78, 81 (1952), an arbitration administered by the New Jersey State Board of Mediation. Also see statements by Arbitrator Gibson in 81 LA 365, 366; Krimsly in 51 LA 745, 748; McCoy in 40 LA 727, 730 (reopening to receive data essential for compliance with court order); Morvant in 33 LA 302, 307. The arbitrator's action in reopening the hearing was held not to constitute an abuse of discretion under the facts in Local Lodge 1746 v. United Aircraft Corp., 77 LRRM 2596, 2598 (USDC, 1971). Discussing reopenings, see Smith, "The Search for Truth—The Whole Truth," Proceedings of the 31st Annual Meeting of NAA, 40, 56–57 (BNA Books, 1979); Problems of Proof in Arbitration, 330–332 (BNA Books, 1967).

reopening could not show that the new evidence could be clearly established.[248]

Sometimes the arbitrator, without reopening the hearing, will simply call upon one or both of the parties for additional information,[249] or he might invite further written arguments regarding some aspect of the case.[250]

The Award and Opinion

The award is the arbitrator's decision of the case. Awards usually are short, and they "should be definite, certain, and as concise as possible."[251]

Except in rare instances awards are issued in writing.[252] Even when an oral award is rendered, the arbitrator usually later reduces it to writing.[253] The written award must be signed by the arbitrator. Awards of arbitration boards must be signed by all members where a unanimous decision is required, otherwise they must be signed by at

---

[248]Safeway Stores, 22 LA 466, 467 (1954). In Harmony Dairy Co., 51 LA 745, 748 (1968), Arbitrator Krimsly could not see that any useful purpose would be served by a reopening so the request for one was denied. The arbitrator's refusal to reopen was held not to constitute an abuse of discretion under the facts in Local 169 v. Acme Mkts., 105 LRRM 3206, 3209 (USDC, 1980); Northwest Airlines v. ALPA, 88 LRRM 2052, 2055 (USDC, 1974); Shopping Cart, Inc. v. Food Employees, 82 LRRM 2107, 2109 (USDC, 1972). In Bridgeport Rolling Mills Co. v. Brown, 53 LRRM 2589, 40 LA 1024 (CA 2, 1963), the court held that evidence discovered after the award had been issued came too late for consideration. Of similar substance, see Newspaper Guild Local 35 v. Washington Post Co., 76 LRRM 2274, 2277 (D.C. Cir., 1971), upholding the arbitrator's refusal to reopen for additional evidence.

[249]As in Paragon Bridge & Steel Co., 45 LA 833 at 833 (Vines, 1965); Full-Fashioned Hosiery Mfrs., 15 LA 452, 454 (Taylor, 1954). For related discussion, see Chapter 8, topic entitled "Evidence Submitted After Hearing."

[250]As did Arbitrator Louisell in Donaldson Co., 21 LA 254, 255 (1953).

[251]Code of Professional Responsibility, § VI(C)(1), 64 LA 1327.

[252]Awards may be oral unless a written award is required by the parties or by statute. Oral awards are sufficient under the common law, but if in writing they must be signed. See Chapter 2, subtopic entitled "State Common Law." Illustrating court enforcement of oral awards, where their terms are adequately established by the evidence, see Mine Workers v. Peggs Run Coal Co., 80 LRRM 2736 (USDC, 1972). The collective agreement often will require the award to be in writing. See Major Collective Bargaining Agreements: Arbitration Procedures, 76–77 (U.S. Dept. Labor Bull. No. 1425-6, 1966).

[253]See discussion of oral awards in Guides for Labor Arbitration, 14 (U. of Pa. Press, 1953). Sometimes it is expressly agreed that an oral ruling will be issued at the hearing or as soon thereafter as possible, to be followed later by a written opinion and award. As in Cleveland Transit Sys., 45 LA 905, 905–906 (Kates, 1965); Quaker Oats Co., 35 LA 535, 536 (Valtin, 1960). In Aerosol Techniques, 48 LA 1278, 1280 (Summers, 1967), an arbitration board directed the immediate reinstatement of the grievant without waiting for issuance of the formal award. Relevant here is § V(E) of the Code of Professional Responsibility, which provides:

"E. Bench Decisions or Expedited Awards

"1. When an arbitrator understands, prior to acceptance of appointment, that a bench decision is expected at the conclusion of the hearing, the arbitrator must comply with the understanding unless both parties agree otherwise.

"a. If notice of the parties' desire for a bench decision is not given prior to the arbitrator's acceptance of the case, issuance of such a bench decision is discretionary.

"b. When only one party makes the request and the other objects, the arbitrator should not render a bench decision except under most unusual circumstances.

"2. When an arbitrator understands, prior to acceptance of appointment, that a concise written award is expected within a stated time period after the hearing, the arbitrator must comply with the understanding unless both parties agree otherwise."

Discussing bench decisions, see Stark, "The Presidential Address: Theme and Adaptations," Proceedings of the 31st Annual Meeting of NAA, 1 (BNA Books, 1979). For related material, see topic entitled "Expediting the Arbitration Machinery," below.

least a majority unless the agreement or a stipulation expressly permits issuance of an award by the neutral alone.[254]

Often the arbitrator accompanies his award with a written opinion stating the reasons for his decision. The award ordinarily is stated separately from the opinion to indicate clearly where the opinion ends and the award begins;[255] in agreeing in advance to accept the arbitrator's award the parties do not necessarily promise to agree with all of his reasoning.

Attitudes vary as to the desirability of reasoned opinions, but a large majority of parties and of arbitrators favor their use.[256]

A well-reasoned opinion can contribute greatly to the acceptance of the award by the parties by persuading them that the arbitrator understands the case and that his award is basically sound. The U.S. Supreme Court emphasized this function of opinions in encouraging their use by arbitrators:

"Arbitrators have no obligation to the court to give their reasons for an award. To require opinions free of ambiguity may lead arbitrators to play it safe by writing no supporting opinions. This would be undesirable for a well-reasoned opinion tends to engender confidence in the integrity of the process and aids in clarifying the underlying agreement."[257]

Opinions indeed can have significant educational value to the parties and can aid them in adjusting future related problems. In the latter regard Arbitrator Whitley P. McCoy explained in one case:

"In explanation of my having discussed issues and contentions upon which the ultimate decision is not to be based, I may say that parties do not spend many days of preparation, three days of hearings, and thousands of dollars worth of the time of important officers and attorneys, for the purpose of finding out whether one girl should or should not have got a trivial promotion. They are interested in principles. They are entitled,

---

[254]For full discussion, see Chapter 4, topic entitled "Tripartite Arbitration Board."

[255]See Code of Ethics and Procedural Standards for Labor-Management Arbitration, Part II, §5(b), 15 LA 961, 965. The Code of Professional Responsibility which was intended to supersede the Code of Ethics is silent on this aspect. Where the nature of a case made it difficult to spell out a formal award without considerable repetition of the opinion, the award merely stated that its substance was as indicated in the opinion. C & D Batteries, 32 LA 589, 595 (Jaffee, 1959).

[256]One survey, revealing a demanding task for arbitrators to fulfill the desires of the parties concerning opinions, indicated that: (1) most parties want opinions—"management and union practitioners have a strong *desire to know why,*" (2) they want "shorter opinions," and (3) there is at the same time a general "insistence upon the arbitrator's reasoning being set forth fully and unambiguously." Davey, "What's Right and What's Wrong With Grievance Arbitration: The Practitioners Air Their Views," 28 Arb. J. 209, 215, 226 (1973). For additional statistics, see "Survey of Arbitration in 1964," Proceedings of the 18th Annual Meeting of NAA, 243, 246, 254 (BNA Books, 1965); Warren & Bernstein, "A Profile of Labor Arbitration," 16 LA 970, 983 (1951). A "bare award" may be held to have no force as a precedent even for the same parties. See John J. Nissen Baking Co., 48 LA 12, 17 (Fallon, 1966).

[257]United Steelworkers v. Enterprise Wheel & Car Corp., 80 S.Ct. 1358, 1361, 34 LA 569, 571 (1960). For cases applying the Supreme Court's statement that arbitrators "have no obligation to the court to give their reasons for an award," see V.I. Nursing Assn. v. Schneider, 109 LRRM 2323, 2324–2325 (CA 3, 1981); Air Line Pilots v. Eastern Air Lines, 106 LRRM 2104, 2106 (CA 5, 1980). Also see Bylund v. Safeway Stores, Inc., 86 LRRM 2686, 2687 (USDC, 1974). However, frequently the collective agreement will require that awards be accompanied by an opinion. See Major Collective Bargaining Agreements: Arbitration Procedures, 76 (U.S. Dept. Labor Bull. No. 1425-6, 1966). Another possibility is that an opinion may be required by statute, as in City of Burlington, Iowa, 68 LA 454 at 454 (Witner, 1977), where a statute specified that public-sector arbitrators "shall give written explanation for" selecting party proposals in "final offer" arbitration.

for their future guidance in various respects, to the arbitrator's findings upon the evidence and the various contentions."[258]

On the other hand, Arbitrator Samuel L. Chalfie explained that an arbitrator is not obligated to respond in the opinion to every argument presented by a party, and that in order to avoid an unduly lengthy opinion, he would "focus his attention only on those matters which he deems necessary to a correct, proper and fair decision of the dispute."[259]

Furthermore, some parties prefer not to have an opinion for fear that the arbitrator might make comments not germane to the issue and thus possibly stimulate future disputes. Also, reasoned opinions require more of the arbitrator's time, increasing the cost of arbitration and the period required for issuance of decisions to the parties. In view of the cost factor, one arbitrator asked the parties to indicate specifically whether they wanted an opinion.[260] More formally, President Gerald A. Barrett of the National Academy of Arbitrators asserted to that organization that it "may well be time for us to reconsider our common assumption that every award must be accompanied by an opinion."[261]

Thought Processes of the Arbitrator

In a general sense much of this book deals with the decision-making process or the thought processes of the arbitrator. The

---

[258]Southern Bell Tel. & Tel. Co., 16 LA 1, 9 (1951). Also relating to (and some discussing) such matters as the functions of opinions, the mechanics of writing opinions, criticisms of opinions, hazards of dicta, the advancement in the opinion of new theories for deciding the case, and the like, see: Code of Professional Responsibility, § VI(C)(1)(a), 64 LA 1327; articles by Bernstein, Cames & Mittenthal, "The Art of Opinion Writing," Proceedings of the 35th Annual Meeting of NAA, 68, 80, 89 (BNA Books, 1983); Petersen & Rezler, "Arbitration Decision Writing: Selected Criteria," 38 Arb. J. No. 2, p. 18 (1983); Stark, "Arbitration Decision Writing: Why Arbitrators Err," id. at 30; Vladeck, "Comment," Proceedings of the 25th Annual Meeting of NAA, 81, 83–84 (BNA Books, 1973); Eaton, "Labor Arbitration in the San Francisco Bay Area," 48 LA 1381, 1387–1388 (1967); Roberts & Dash, "How to Get Better Results From Labor-Management Arbitration," 22 Arb. J. 1, 14–16 (1967); Fleming, The Labor Arbitration Process, 157–163, 216–217; 220–221 (U. of Ill. Press, 1965); "Problems in Opinion Writing: A Panel Discussion," Proceedings of the 18th Annual Meeting of NAA, 1 (BNA Books, 1965); Garrett, "Some Potential Uses of the Opinion," Proceedings of the 17th Annual Meeting of NAA, 114 (BNA Books, 1964); Editorial, "The Hazards of Dicta in Labor Arbitration," 19 Arb. J. 65 (1964); Syme, "Opinions and Awards," 15 LA 953, 956–958 (1950).

[259]Cincinnati Post & Times Star, 68 LA 129, 138 (1977).

[260]See Trailmobile, 28 LA 710, 711 (Coffey, 1957). In 1963 the American Arbitration Association drafted a waiver-of-opinion form for use where both parties desire an award without a written opinion. This action followed an association survey in which many parties indicated that they would not ordinarily waive the opinion but that an easy opportunity should be available to do so when desired. Arb. News, No. 2 (1963). AAA Rule 38 states that "The parties shall advise AAA whenever they do not require the Arbitrator to accompany the award with an opinion." Also see Gill, "The Presidential Address: The Role of the Arbitrator's Wife," Proceedings of the 25th Annual Meeting of NAA, 1, 7 (BNA Books, 1973), urging that parties should not hesitate to tell their arbitrator whether they want an opinion, and, if so, how long or short. Illustrating that arbitrators seek to comply with the mutual desires of the parties on such matters, see Library of Congress, 72 LA 691, 693 (Merrifield, 1979), where brevity was ordered and brevity was delivered!

[261]Barrett, "The Presidential Address: The Common Law of the Shop," Proceedings of the 26th Annual Meeting of NAA, 95, 97–98 (BNA Books, 1974), where he also asserted that "awards without opinions or awards accompanied by simple per curiam opinions may now better serve the purpose in some cases." Also see comments by Rehnquist, "A Jurist's View of Arbitration," 32 Arb. J. 1, 6–7 (1977); Valtin, "The Presidential Address: Judicial Review Revisited—The Search for Accommodation Must Continue," Proceedings of the 29th Annual Meeting of NAA, 1, 8 (BNA Books, 1976).

Authors do not undertake to deal more specifically with this matter, but they call attention to the writings of others who have touched directly upon the thought processes of arbitrators.[262]

Clarification or Interpretation of Award

It has been said to be "a general rule in common law arbitration that when arbitrators have executed their awards and declared their decision they are functus officio and have no power to proceed further."[263] A detailed statement of this common law rule explains:

> "The authority and jurisdiction of arbitrators are entirely terminated by the completion and delivery of an award. They have thereafter no power to recall the same, to order a rehearing, to amend, or to 'interpret' in such manner as may be regarded as authoritative. But they may correct clerical mistakes or obvious errors of arithmetical computation."[264]

The general common law rule is also the apparent basis for the following provision in the Code of Professional Responsibility: "No clarification or interpretation of an award is permissible without the consent of both parties."[265]

---

[262]See Jones, "The Decisional Thinking of Judges and Arbitrators as Triers of Fact," Proceedings of the 33rd Annual Meeting of NAA, 45 (BNA Books, 1981); Elson, "Decisional Thinking, Chicago Panel Report," id. at 62; Block, "Decisional Thinking, West Coast Panel Report," id. at 119; Christensen, "Decisional Thinking, New York Panel Report," id. at 173; Valtin, "Decisional Thinking, Washington Panel Report," id. at 209; Mittenthal, "The Presidential Address: Joys of Being an Arbitrator," Proceedings of the 32nd Annual Meeting of NAA, 1 (BNA Books, 1980); Dworkin, "How Arbitrators Decide Cases," 25 Lab. L.J. 200 (1974); Linn, "Comment," Proceedings of the 26th Annual Meeting of NAA, 176 (BNA Books, 1974); Davey, "How Arbitrators Decide Cases," 27 Arb. J. 274 (1972); Alexander, "Discretion in Arbitration," Proceedings of the 24th Annual Meeting of NAA, 84 (BNA Books, 1971); Fleming, The Labor Arbitration Process, 78–106, 159–164, 211 (U. of Ill. Press, 1965); Garrett, "Some Potential Uses of the Opinion," Proceedings of the 17th Annual Meeting of NAA, 114 (BNA Books, 1964); Teele, "The Thought Processes of the Arbitrator," 17 Arb. J. 85 (1962); Seitz, "How Arbitrators Decide Cases: A Study in Black Magic," Proceedings of the 15th Annual Meeting of NAA, 159 (BNA Books, 1962).

[263]Mercury Oil Ref. Co. v. Oil Workers, 187 F.2d 980, 983 (CA 10, 1951). Accord, Devine v. White, 697 F.2d 421, 433 (D.C. Cir., 1983), indicating that the rule is applicable also to federal-sector arbitration; Salt Lake Pressmen v. Newspaper Agency, 485 F.Supp. 511, 515 (USDC, 1980); Indigo Springs, Inc. v. Hotel Trades Council, 59 LRRM 3024 (N.Y. Sup. Ct., 1965); Jannis v. Ellis, 308 P.2d 750 (Calif. Dist. Ct. App., 1957), citing Sturges, Commercial Arbitrations and Awards §220. Numerous other cases, some going back many years, are cited by Updegraff & McCoy, below. The term "functus officio" is literally translated to mean "a task performed." Black's Law Dictionary, 4th Ed.

[264]Updegraff, Arbitration and Labor Relations, 116 (BNA Books, 1970), where numerous cases are cited. The same statement is contained in Updegraff & McCoy, Arbitration of Labor Disputes, 1st Ed., 33 (1946), 2d Ed., 75–76 (1961).

[265]Sec. VI(D)(1), 64 LA 1327. By memorandum of March 3, 1980, to persons on its Roster of Arbitrators, the Federal Mediation and Conciliation Service reminded them of this Code provision and the Service stated: "The submission of a Decision removes an arbitrator from further authority for a particular matter. Absent a *joint* request, any response by an arbitrator to both parties [should] be limited to stating the function of the office ceases with the Decision submission. Even an abbreviated explanation is too much." A few collective agreements expressly provide for interpretation of awards by the arbitrator. See Major Collective Bargaining Agreements: Arbitration Procedures, 75 (U.S. Dept. Labor Bull. No. 1425-6, 1966); Paragon Bridge & Steel Co., 48 LA 995, 999 (Gross, 1967). When proceeding under such an agreement, the arbitrator is required by the Code of Professional Responsibility to "afford both parties an opportunity to be heard." § VI(D)(2). More often any agreement to request an interpretation by the arbitrator will be reached after the need for an interpretation arises, as in Brass-Craft Mfg. Co., 36 LA 1438 at 1438 (Kahn, 1961). Sometimes the parties at that time select a different

The common-law doctrine of "functus officio" has been modified by statute in some states to permit the arbitrator to modify or correct his award, to the limited extent stated in the statute, upon submission by a court or upon direct application to him by one of the parties.[266] In addition to the more commonly stated grounds for such action by the arbitrator, the Uniform Arbitration Act also permits him to modify or correct his award "for the purpose of clarifying the award."[267] The Act specifies that the application shall be made within 20 days after delivery of the award to the applicant, that prompt notice of the application shall be given to the other party, and that the notice shall inform the latter that he has 10 days within which to serve any objections to the application.[268]

Under the federal law as developed under LMRA § 301 the courts may return an award to the arbitrator for clarification or intepretation where it is ambiguous.[269] However, the fact that a court may have power to return an award to an arbitrator for interpretation does not necessarily mean that he may undertake to render an interpretation on his own.[270] Furthermore, the courts themselves refuse to return an award to the arbitrator where the court believes the disagreement over its implementation constitutes a new dispute which would

---

arbitrator to interpret the original arbitrator's award. See Dispatch Printing Co., 70 LA 104, 105 (Kanner, 1978); Newspaper Guild Local 25 v. Hearst Corp., 83 LRRM 2728, 2730, 2732 (CA 5, 1973), where the parties jointly selected a second arbitrator whose clarification award was upheld, but where the court stated as dictum that the preferable procedure is clarification by the original arbitrator. One survey indicated that labor, management, and arbitrators alike appear generally to favor giving arbitrators power to interpret their awards. See Warren & Bernstein, "A Profile of Labor Arbitration," 16 LA 970, 979 (1951).

[266]See Chapter 2, subtopic entitled "State Arbitration Statutes." For an example of a proceeding based upon a motion for modification of award under state statute, see Reserve Mining Co., 55 LA 648 (Sembower, 1970).

[267]Sec. 9, 27 LA 909, 910. This provision is discussed by Dilts, "Award Clarification: An Ethical Dilemma?" 33 Lab. L.J. 366 (1982). For states adopting the Uniform Act, see Chapter 2, ibid. The New York statute does not list "clarification" as one of the grounds, but this ground is possibly included in the intent of the statute. See "An Outline of Procedure Under the New York Arbitration Law," 20 Arb. J. 73, 90–91 (1965).

[268]Sec. 9, ibid.

[269]Electrical Workers Local 2222 v. New England Tel. & Tel. Co., 105 LRRM 2211, 2214–2215 (CA 1, 1980), where the parties disagreed on computation of a wrongfully discharged employee's loss of earnings, and where (1) the court cited numerous cases recognizing the power of courts to resubmit awards "to the original arbitrators for 'interpretation' or 'amplification,' " and (2) the court held that as "an issue falling directly within the scope of the parties' submission to the Arbitration Board, * * * the partly resolved matter of remedy was properly returned to the Board [by the district court] for further consideration"; United Steelworkers v. Interpace Corp., 97 LRRM 3189, 3192 (USDC, 1978); United Steelworkers v. W.C. Bradley Co., 95 LRRM 2177 at 2177 (CA 5, 1977); IBEW v. Olin Corp., 82 LRRM 2338, 2341 (CA 6, 1972); IBEW v. Brewery Proprietors, 69 LRRM 2292, 2295 (USDC, 1968); Metal Trades Council v. General Elec. Co., 61 LRRM 2004, 2008 (CA 9, 1965).

[270]In Union Local 679 v. Richmond-Chase Corp., 36 LA 881, 882 (Calif. Dist. Ct. App., 1961), the court under the California statute ordered a rehearing by an arbitration board to clarify its award, but the court denied that the board itself had authority to order the rehearing. And a court under § 301 reaffirmed the principle under prior cases that an arbitrator's powers on remand are limited to the specific matter remanded for clarification. Paperhandlers v. U.S. Trucking Corp., 96 LRRM 2535, 2539–2540 (USDC, 1977). In Printing Indus. of Washington, D.C., 40 LA 727, 728–729 (1963), Arbitrator Whitley P. McCoy stated that upon rendering his award he had lost all power over the case and that the court order subsequently returning the case to him must be looked to for determining the scope of his new authority. The "functus officio" doctrine was also acknowledged by Arbitrator Lumbley in 81 LA 282, 283–284; Abrams in 78 LA 1156, 1157 (refusing to reconsider his decision on the basis of newly discovered evidence); Dworkin in 68 LA 1082, 1084; Purdom in 51 LA 919, 920–924; Sembower in 37 LA 673, 674; Bothwell in 36 LA 979, 980. Cf., Arbitrator Kates in 53 LA 619, 623, and in 43 LA 625, 633; Platt in 47 LA 289, 316.

require the arbitrator to pass upon issues beyond the scope of the original submission—such new disputes are to be remedied by filing a new grievance under the grievance/arbitration provisions of the collective agreement.[271]

Where an arbitrator is not fully satisfied that he has authority to issue an interpretation of his award at the request of one party, he will have good cause to consider the suggestion that "he should refuse to comply, but should indicate that he will give consideration to the request if made by both parties."[272]

Remedy Power and Its Use

The remedy power in arbitration has often been considered from two standpoints: (1) whether the arbitrator has the power to utilize the given remedy, and (2) whether the given remedy should be used in the particular case even assuming that the arbitrator has the power to use it.[273] These two matters are the basic concern of the present topic. Discussion of specific types of remedies and remedies for specific types of violations is found throughout this book.[274]

---

[271]Papermakers Local 675 v. Westvaco Corp., 105 LRRM 2360, 2362 (USDC, 1978); IAM Local 1893 v. Aerojet-General Corp., 65 LRRM 2421, 2423 (USDC, 1966); District 50, UMW v. Revere Copper, Inc., 51 LRRM 2033, 2034 (USDC, 1962). The *Westvaco* court stated (105 LRRM at 2362):

> "[R]emand is particularly inappropriate where a collateral dispute has arisen from an award which is not self-executing. * * * These awards often impose upon the parties the need to take additional actions which, in turn, give rise to new disputes. The implementation of these awards may constitute new grievances which can be remedied only by resort to the established grievance procedure."

Stating that it had such a case before it, the *Westvaco* court then classified the dispute additionally as one involving the "application" of the award as distinguished from the "interpretation" of the award (ibid):

> "It is crucial to distinguish between disputes arising from the application of the award and those which concern the interpretation of an award. * * * Whereas the latter may be remanded to permit clarification of the arbitrator's decision, the former present entirely new issues upon which the arbitrator has not ruled. * * * The question of whether the Company adhered to the guidelines established by the arbitrator is a subsequent, albeit related, matter. This new dispute can be remedied only by resort to the grievance procedures contained in the collective bargaining agreement."

[272]Guides for Labor Arbitration, 15 (U. of Pa. Press, 1953).

[273]For discussions of the remedy power in arbitration, see Feller, "Remedies in Arbitration: Old Problems Revisited," Proceedings of the 34th Annual Meeting of NAA, 109 (BNA Books, 1982); Sinicropi, "Remedies: Another View of New and Old Problems," id. at 134; Katz, "Comment," id. at 171; Hill & Sinicropi, Remedies in Arbitration (BNA Books, 1981); Harter, "Tenure and the Nonrenewal of Probationary Teachers," 34 Arb. J. No. 1, p. 22 (1979); Note, "Protecting Intangible Expectations Under Collective Bargaining Agreements—Overcoming the Proscription of Arbitral Penalties," 61 Minn. L. Rev. 127 (1976); Stevens, "Arbitrability and the Illinois Courts," 31 Arb. J. 1 (1976), relating to the public sector; Wolff, "The Power of the Arbitrator to Make Monetary Awards," Proceedings of the 17th Annual Meeting of NAA, 176 (BNA Books, 1964); Sirefman, "Rights Without Remedies in Labor Arbitration," 18 Arb. J. 17 (1963); Stutz, "Arbitrators and the Remedy Power," Proceedings of the 16th Annual Meeting of NAA, 54 (BNA Books, 1963); Fleming, "Arbitrators and the Remedy Power," 48 Va. L. Rev. 1199 (1962); Stein, "Remedies in Labor Arbitration," Proceedings of the 13th Annual Meeting of NAA, 39 (BNA Books, 1960).

[274]For instance, the remedy of damages and remedies for mistake are treated in Chapter 10; the injunction remedy is treated elsewhere in Chapter 7; remedies in discharge and discipline cases are treated in Chapter 15; and so on.

Scope of Remedy Power

In its *Enterprise* decision the U.S. Supreme Court spoke of the remedy power of arbitrators:

> "When an arbitrator is commissioned to interpret and apply the collective bargaining agreement, he is to bring his informed judgment to bear in order to reach a fair solution of a problem. This is especially true when it comes to formulating remedies. There the need is for flexibility in meeting a wide variety of situations. The draftsmen may never have thought of what specific remedy should be awarded to meet a particular contingency. Nevertheless, an arbitrator is confined to interpretation and application of the collective bargaining agreement; he does not sit to dispense his own brand of industrial justice. He may of course look for guidance from many sources, yet his award is legitimate only so long as it draws its essence from the collective bargaining agreement. When the arbitrator's words manifest an infidelity to this obligation, courts have no choice but to refuse enforcement of the award."[275]

This statement of broad but nonetheless restricted remedy power obviously fails to provide a clear and unequivocal guide. This is further illustrated by the fact that one federal court has acted on the view that arbitrators have power to use a given type of remedy unless it is expressly precluded by the agreement,[276] while another federal court does not appear willing to go nearly so far to find remedial authority in the arbitrator.[277]

In the realm of state law broad remedial authority exists in the arbitrator under the Uniform Arbitration Act, which specifies certain grounds for court vacation of awards but which expressly adds that "the fact that the relief was such that it could not or would not be granted by a court of law or equity is not ground for vacating or refusing to confirm the award."[278]

The views of arbitrators themselves differ widely as to how broad their remedial power is or should be.[279] The expressions or actions of some arbitrators reflect the belief that broad remedy power is implied in the arbitrator. For instance, in awarding an increased rate for a changed job, Arbitrator James J. Willingham explained:

> "As arbitration is a process to resolve industrial differences without resort to work stoppage, lockout and other economic measures, it necessarily implies power in the arbitrator, exclusive of specific contractual

---

[275]United Steelworkers v. Enterprise Wheel & Car Corp., 80 S.Ct. 1358, 1361 (1960).

[276]Local 369, Bakery & Confectionery Workers v. Cotton Baking Co., 514 F.2d 1235, 1237 (CA 5, 1975), cert. denied, 423 U.S. 1055 (1976); IAM v. Cameron Iron Works, 292 F.2d 112, 119 (CA 5, 1961), cert. denied, 368 U.S. 926 (1961). Also see General Tel. Co. of Ohio v. Communications Workers, 107 LRRM 2361, 2364–2365 (CA 6, 1981); Lynchburg Foundry Co. v. Steelworkers, 404 F.2d 259, 261 (CA 4, 1968).

[277]Luggage Workers v. Neevel Co., 325 F.2d 992, 993–994 (CA 8, 1964); Truck Drivers & Helpers v. Ulry-Talbert Co., 330 F.2d 562, 565 (CA 8, 1964). Also see Local 782 v. Sav-On Groceries, 88 LRRM 3205, 3206–3207 (CA 10, 1975). Cf., Capital City Tel. Co. v. CWA, 98 LRRM 2438, 2440 (CA 8, 1978).

[278]Sec. 12(a)(5), 27 LA 909, 911. For some states that have adopted the Uniform Act, see Chapter 2, subtopic entitled "State Arbitration Statutes."

[279]For related discussion, see Chapter 9, subtopic entitled " 'Legislation' v. 'Interpretation.' "

prohibitions, to settle and dispose of the corpus of the grievance. In this case the corpus of the grievance is, in essence, what pay grade is applicable to the jobs with changed content resulting from the banking of machines. Accordingly, the answer to the third issue is that the arbitrator is empowered to establish the Labor Grade applicable to the grievance herein."[280]

In rather sharp contrast, consider the view of Arbitrator Harold W. Davey, stated in response to a suggestion that arbitrators have power under the *Trilogy* to achieve justice in situations not contemplated by or not adequately covered by the collective agreement:

> "The present arbitrator does not share this expansive view of arbitral jurisdiction. Arbitrators are constrained by contracts in the same manner as the parties themselves. I do not believe in blank check arbitration of the 'philosopher king' type, as I have made clear in numerous decisions and journal articles.
>
> "I am fully aware that denial of these grievances, while required on contractual grounds, does not solve the equitability question that both management and the Union recognize in their earlier efforts to work out some mutually satisfactory treatment of the seniority problem posed by the two groups of employees now working in the same warehouse. My authority as arbitrator, however, does not extend to development of a Solomon-like solution to be imposed upon both parties as final and binding. My authority is limited to deciding whether the grievances have contractual merit. The ruling must be that they do not."[281]

If a given type of remedy has been widely used by arbitrators, an exceedingly strong case may be made in support of an arbitrator's right to use the remedy (absent express denial of such right by the agreement or submission). Compensatory damages to employees who have suffered financial loss from the employer's violation of their rights under the agreement provides the most prominent illustration.[282] Arbitrator Alfred Kuhn declared in this regard:

---

[280]U.S. Slicing Mach. Co., 41 LA 1076, 1081–1082 (1963). For other assertions of broad remedy power, see Arbitrator Kramer in 80 LA 457, 463 (stating that "it cannot be gainsaid, given a violation, that the remedy should be as broad as justice dictates, provided of course, that the Arbitrator's conclusions are drawn from the intent of the collective agreement"); Wolff in 78 LA 772, 776; Kanner in 70 LA 104, 107; Chalfie in 68 LA 129, 142; Somers in 51 LA 822, 836; Summers in 48 LA 760, 763; Turkus in 46 LA 607, 608, and in 44 LA 1219, 1221–1222. Also see actions by Gill in 46 LA 513, 517; Howlett in 42 LA 678, 680–682. Stating that it "is ultimately for the arbitrator to frame a remedy if the parties are unable to agree upon a resolution of their differences," Arbitrator David F. Sweeney "rejected the employer argument that for the arbitrator to grant a remedy other than sought in the grievance form constitutes an amendment or altering of the collective bargaining agreement." Nassau County School Bd., 76 LA 1044, 1045, 1048 (1981).

[281]Lagomarcino-Grupe Co., 43 LA 453, 460 (1964), holding that employees of Company A who were terminated when its warehouse was closed had no right to carry their seniority with them when they were hired at Company B's warehouse, even though both companies could be regarded as one from a labor relations standpoint and the same union had contracts with both companies. For other arbitrators taking a similarly narrow "contractual" view of the remedy power, see Arbitrator Brisco in 77 LA 424, 427–428; Williams in 69 LA 334, 336; Marshall in 53 LA 1061, 1062; McIntosh in 48 LA 1121, 1121–1122; Shister in 43 LA 1228, 1231 (the arbitrator derives his authority from the contract, is a prisoner of the contract, and is not freed from this imprisonment by the *Trilogy*); Ross in 42 LA 353, 355 (it remains true that grievance arbitration is essentially contractual interpretation—the *Warrior & Gulf* decision "does not enthrone the arbitrator as a law maker nor permit him to impose new obligations or restrictions which cannot fairly be wrung from the contract as the parties negotiated it").

[282]For full discussion of the damages remedy, see Chapter 10, topic entitled "Principles of Damages."

"Many—perhaps most—labor-management contracts in this nation do not specifically authorize an arbitrator to award damages. But in hundreds of such contracts year after year arbitrators do, in fact, award damages. This is done with full knowledge of the parties, who in many cases have had decades in which to rewrite their contracts if they did not so intend them. The Arbitrator submits that under those circumstances the authority of an arbitrator to award damages is as truly and integrally a part of the contract as if it were written there in unmistakable English and boldface type."[283]

As just stated, many agreements are silent as to the arbitrator's remedy power where he has found a violation of the agreement.[284] Of course the parties can deal with the matter in the agreement, the submission, or by stipulation at the hearing. While they sometimes act to restrict the arbitrator's remedy power,[285] likely as not any express action that they may take will be to recognize discretionary remedial authority in the arbitrator by authorizing him to determine "what shall the remedy be" in the event a violation is found.[286]

Should the Given Remedy Be Used?

Even some of the arbitrators who believe the remedy power should be very broad are quick to caution that there is "a great difference between the possession of power and the occasion for its exercise," and that arbitrators should proceed with great caution particularly in devising new remedies.[287] Arbitrator M.S. Ryder expressed the view that absent restrictive contract language broad remedial power should be deemed to inhere in the arbitrator, but he also offered the following standards for confining the use of remedies to a proper form and scope:

"1. In form the remedy should be one that would appear to most directly effectuate the intent and purposes of that provision in the labor agreement in connection with which the right was contracted.

---

[283]Jeffrey Mfg. Co., 34 LA 814, 825 (1960). Similarly as to compensatory damages, see Arbitrator Dworkin in Aetna Portland Cement Co., 41 LA 219, 222 (1963).

[284]One of the apparently few aspects of the remedy power (apart from the common prohibition against adding to, subtracting from, or modifying the agreement) fairly commonly treated in the collective agreement concerns the retroactive application of the award. See Major Collective Bargaining Agreements: Arbitration Procedures, 77–80 (U.S. Dept. Labor Bull. No. 1425-6, 1966). Where the agreement did specify a remedy for a given type of violation, the arbitrator used it and rejected a request for an additional remedy. Ralphs Grocery Co., 70 LA 1001, 1003 (Roberts, 1978). But see General Tel. Co. of Ohio v. Communications Workers, 107 LRRM 2361, 2364–2365 (CA 6, 1981).

[285]As in Lone Star Steel Co., 48 LA 1095, 1098 (Jenkins, 1967), where the arbitrator utilized a footnote to suggest what remedy he would have awarded had his authority not been limited. In Globe-Union, 42 LA 713, 721 (Prasow, 1963), the arbitrator outlined choices open to the parties as to the remedy power, including reservation of the power to themselves.

[286]See Arbitrator Woolf in 75 LA 701, 703; Craver in 74 LA 89 at 89; Jedel in 69 LA 707 at 707; Helburn in 69 LA 181, 183; Helfeld in 65 LA 453, 455, 467; Yagoda in 49 LA 823, 826; Rohman in 47 LA 1178 at 1178; Daugherty in 47 LA 554 at 554; Gray in 46 LA 1146 at 1146; Teele in 46 LA 215 at 215, 218. In Taystee Bread Co., 52 LA 677 at 677, 680–681 (Purdom, 1969), the parties stipulated that the arbitrator was free to fashion a remedy as he saw fit based upon the merits and that he was not bound by the restrictive language of the agreement.

[287]Stein, "Remedies in Labor Arbitration," Proceedings of the 13th Annual Meeting of NAA, 39, 45–47 (BNA Books, 1960). Similarly, see Arbitrator Turkus in Shell Oil Co., 44 LA 1219, 1221–1222 (1965) (power is a heady wine which carries with it an equally potent obligation to exercise care in its use).

"2. The party called upon to give remedy should not be subjected to well-founded surprise by the form, nature, extent and degree of the remedy. What is awarded should be within the realm of conceivable and reasonable remedial expectation by the party in error or by other parties were they to be similarly circumstanced.

"3. Remedies that are punitive in monetary or exemplary nature should be avoided, on the ground that parties bargaining collectively in a more or less perpetual relationship should not seek that one or the other partner be punished for a mistake. To so seek and to obtain punishment is putting a mortgage on the future happiness of the joint relationship. * * *

"4. Remedies that are novel in form should be avoided, again for reasons of unexpectedness or possible well-based surprise. A novel remedy might bring with it unforeseen contractual and other impacts on one or both of the parties and create uncertainty as to what may result from future submissions to arbitration. The concept of the arbitrator having an 'arsenal' of forms of relief, with the parties in a position of uncertainty rather than expectation, should be avoided in what is a private litigation seeking to resolve a dispute. Suspense in a private relationship might subvert the efficacy of that relationship."[288]

Of course, not every case will fit into some existing mold or is capable of disposition by some relatively simple formula. Thus, a remedy sometimes will be complex, multifaceted, or otherwise uniquely fashioned by the arbitrator in one or more of its major aspects.[289]

In some cases the arbitrator finds a violation of the agreement but he returns the case to the parties for negotiations as to the remedy. One arbitrator deemed this procedure essential where he had "received no guidance at the hearing with respect to a remedy should the grievance be sustained."[290] In another case the arbitrator offered the parties a contingent remedy, to be used unless they could agree

---

[288]Comments by Arbitrator Ryder in Proceedings of the 16th Annual Meeting of NAA, 68–69 (BNA Books, 1963). Also see Arbitrator Beck in 68 LA 1146, 1152–1153 (refusing to order any "extraordinary" remedy); Jackson in 68 LA 682, 683, 686 (although he had been expressly authorized to determine "what should be the remedy," and although he stated that regarding "the form of remedy, the arbitrator's authority is broader than a court's," he stated also that the "remedy that is most suitable and equitable is that which was in the contemplation of the parties"). In Madison Bus Co., 52 LA 723, 727–728 (Mueller, 1969), the arbitrator stated that although the Union was subjected to arbitration costs as a result of the Company's violation of the agreement, an award for such costs would constitute a novel remedy not within the reasonable expectations of the parties and accordingly would not be granted. But such an award was made by Arbitrator Marlatt in 73 LA 878, 882; Helfeld in 65 LA 453, 468–469; Getman in 48 LA 40, 43.

[289]Illustrating the use of a complex and multifaceted award, see George Ellis Co., 68 LA 261, 270–271 (Sacks, 1977). Illustrating that a situation can arise in which the arbitrator feels that a novel remedy is "peculiarly appropriate," see Gamble-Skogmd, 71 LA 1151, 1154 (Weiss, 1978). Also see Arbitrator Grossman in 77 LA 633, 636; Florey in 77 LA 693, 694; Rothschild in 76 LA 1028, 1033; Lubow in 66 LA 446, 449.

[290]United States Steel Corp., 45 LA 104, 107 (Florey, 1965). Also see Arbitrator Rothschild in 75 LA 1112, 1119; Witney in 71 LA 969, 977; Young in 69 LA 1159, 1167; Gregory in 69 LA 1050, 1056–1057; Platt in 55 LA 170, 182; Talent in 52 LA 93, 97; Feinberg in 45 LA 161, 174. In some cases the arbitrator concluded that the appropriate remedy *was* negotiations, which the arbitrator ordered. See Arbitrator Wiggins in 74 LA 770, 775; Garrett in 69 LA 740, 751; Caraway in 65 LA 178, 182. Cf., Typographical Union v. Newspapers, Inc., 106 LRRM 2317, 2322–2323 (CA 7, 1981). In Weyerhaeuser Co., 64 LA 869, 874 (1975), Arbitrator Raph C. Barnhart's award stated:
"The grievance is sustained. The Union is requested to submit a more particularized request for relief than is presented by the suggested formula in its brief.
"The request for interest and for damages will be ruled upon when the Arbitrator perfects a final award."
For related discussion, see topic entitled "Split Hearings," above.

"upon an alternative solution" within 60 days from the date of the award.[291]

Recommendations by Arbitrator

Many "rights" arbitrators are authorized only to interpret and apply the collective agreement and are denied the power to add to or modify the agreement. In these instances the award must be based upon what is or is not required by the agreement and there is only limited room, if any at all, for application of "equity."[292] For instance, in refusing to follow a prior award based upon equitable grounds Arbitrator Whitley P. McCoy declared:

"I cannot agree with that decision, which was based on so-called 'equitable' grounds. When it becomes customary and legitimate for arbitrators to amend and add to contracts according to their sense of equity, i.e., what the contract *ought* to provide, then I shall fall in line."[293]

However, arbitrators occasionally do make purely advisory recommendations based upon equitable considerations. In some such cases where the grievance could be sustained only by adding to or modifying the agreement or by otherwise exceeding the arbitrator's authority, but where the arbitrator is convinced that the grievance has merit from the standpoint of equity, he will deny the grievance (or he might dismiss it) and at the same time make an advisory recommendation as to how he thinks it should be disposed of for the best interests of both parties.[294]

In doing this Arbitrator Joseph Shister explained:

"Since the Arbitration Board must rule according to the so-called 'contractual approach' to the issue, it has no alternative but to deny the grievance. But while the Board's authority to *rule* is so circumscribed, its powers of *recommendation* are considerably broader. For in making such

---

[291]Lehman Bros., 51 LA 1063, 1067 (Hill, 1968). In Ulene v. Murray Millman, Inc., 33 LA 531, 534–535 (Cal. Dist. Ct. App., 1959), an award was not rendered unenforceable merely because it contained an election provision in respect to the remedy.

[292]See Arbitrator Siegel in 71 LA 1044, 1046–1047; Ludlow in 68 LA 1191, 1194–1195; Brent in 68 LA 337, 342; Conway in 68 LA 325, 330; Davis in 48 LA 938, 940, and in 46 LA 970, 972; Cole in 48 LA 481, 485; Lugar in 48 LA 463, 478; C.L. McCoy in 46 LA 11, 15; W.P. McCoy in 45 LA 1165, 1166; Kagel in 65–2 ARB ¶8774; Hebert in 45 LA 131, 139, and in 29 LA 469, 473; Autrey in 43 LA 1066, 1070; Davey in 43 LA 453, 460; Dworkin in 43 LA 120, 125–126, and in 21 LA 133, 139; Barrett in 16 LA 466, 472. Cf., Grooms in 68 LA 992, 994; Cantor in 68 LA 469, 472; Sembower in 41 LA 631, 635–636; Handsaker in 15 LA 209, 210. Certainly, the parties generally want the agreement applied as written. See Eaton, "Labor Arbitration in the San Francisco Bay Area," 48 LA 1381, 1390 (1967).

[293]Esso Standard Oil Co., 16 LA 73, 75 (1951).

[294]This approach was taken by Arbitrator Bell in 69 LA 1003, 1011; Wyman in 69 LA 871, 876; Simon in 68 LA 797, 804; Kerrison in 51 LA 761, 764; Reid in 50 LA 951, 955; Stouffer in 47 LA 443, 448; Davis in 46 LA 970, 972; Autrey in 43 LA 1066, 1070; Prasow in 42 LA 1067, 1071; Russell in 41 LA 913, 917; Hebert in 29 LA 469, 476; Roberts in 28 LA 470, 477; Davey in 25 LA 394, 397; Kelliher in 21 LA 444, 446; Anrod in 20 LA 653, 658; Aaron in 15 LA 162, 168. Also see Cox in 69 LA 822, 824; Sinicropi in 66 LA 602, 604; Copelof in 15 LA 229, 233. Similarly, where the grievance is sustained the arbitrator may suggest that the winner not demand the full measure of its rights under the award. See Arbitrator Carson in 72 LA 288, 293; Shister in 49 LA 791, 797; Johnson in 48 LA 835, 837; Summers in 48 LA 760, 762–763.

recommendations it can avail itself of the guideposts afforded by what one might term, 'Industrial relations equity.' "[295]

Similarly, where an arbitrator concludes that the dispute essentially involves "interests" rather than "rights" under the existing agreement so that a sustaining award would in effect be legislating for the parties, he may deny the claim, or remand it, with the suggestion that the matter be negotiated by the parties.[296] But the arbitrator may undertake to decide the dispute by "legislating" for the parties if he believes both parties want and have authorized him to do so.[297]

Injunctions by Arbitrators

A type of relief included in some arbitration awards is an injunction ordering a party not to do (or to cease doing) some specified act which the arbitrator has ruled violative of the collective agreement; although arbitral use of injunctions was relatively infrequent in the past, use of this remedy does appear to be increasing.[298]

The New York Court of Appeals has recognized significant authority in arbitrators to grant such injunctive relief in proper circumstances, the court observing that "Traditionally, arbitrators have been licensed to direct such conduct of the parties as is necessary to the settlement of the matters in dispute."[299] The court upheld an award containing an injunction where the collective agreement did not directly affirm or deny power in the arbitrator to use such remedy, and where nothing short of an injunction would have accomplished the

---

[295]General Aniline & Film Corp., 25 LA 50, 54 (1955). Cf., Arbitrator Shister in National Carbon Co., 23 LA 263, 264 (1954).

[296]This approach was taken by Arbitrator Seward in 26 LA 646, 648; Klamon in 26 LA 48, 54; Copelof in 18 LA 486, 489; Kelliher in 16 LA 394, 396; Komaroff in 16 LA 303, 307. Cf., Gill in 46 LA 513, 515–517; Dworkin in 46 LA 9, 11. Also see Chapter 9, topic entitled "Ambiguity" and subtopic entitled " 'Legislation' v. 'Interpretation' "; Chapter 10, topic entitled "Contract Principles."

[297]See Colonial Provision Co., 16 LA 176, 178–179 (Copelof, 1951). For related discussion, see Chapter 3, topic entitled "Rights Arbitration Contract Clauses."

[298]For some instances in which arbitrators in giving relief have spoken literally in terms of injunction or cease and desist, see Arbitrator Ross in 76 LA 576, 579; Cantor in 75 LA 369, 376 (ordering a federal-sector employer to cease and desist); Nathan in 74 LA 934, 939 (ordering a state-sector employer to cease and desist); LeBaron in 73 LA 455, 463 (federal sector); Kaufman in 72 LA 129, 133 (federal sector); Gibson in 69 LA 697, 705; Roberts in 69 LA 623, 630; Bailey in 68 LA 893, 897–898; Yaffe in 68 LA 644, 651 (state-sector); Jaffee in 68 LA 401, 405; Helfeld in 65 LA 453, 471 (agreement expressly authorized such remedy); Fisfis in 62 LA 743, 748–749; Kornblum in 52 LA 771, 772, and in 35 LA 384, 386; Burns in 47 LA 873, 888; Turkus in 66–1 ARB ¶8284; Scheiber in 40 LA 954, 958; Williams in 37 LA 824, 830. Discussing injunctions by arbitrators, see Crane, "The Use and Abuse of Arbitral Power," Proceedings of the 25th Annual Meeting of NAA, 66, 72–74 (BNA Books, 1973), arguing against such remedy; Bernstein, "Comment," id. at 76, 79–80; Vladeck, "Comment," id. at 81, 84–85, defending use of such remedy; Stein, "Remedies in Labor Arbitration," Proceedings of the 13th Annual Meeting of NAA, 39, 47 (BNA Books, 1960), arguing against such remedy. The reluctance of many arbitrators to issue injunctions or cease-and-desist orders is illustrated by Arbitrator Platt in 61 LA 1205, 1213; Holly in 53 LA 226, 227–228; Hilpert in 47 LA 686, 691; Bernstein in 42 LA 931, 935; Gill in 34 LA 176, 178. Also see Kates in 50 LA 191, 194. Foreseeably, there will be even greater reluctance by arbitrators to issue a temporary restraining order pending determination of the merits of a dispute. See Armour & Co., 68 LA 1076, 1077 (Goetz, 1977). For related discussion, see topic entitled "Remedy Power and Its Use," above.

[299]In re Ruppert, 29 LA 775, 776–777 (1958).

intent of the parties for speedy relief against the prohibited activity.[300] Moreover, the court also held that the New York Anti-Injunction Act did not forbid injunctions by arbitrators even though that Act severely limited the jurisdiction of the courts to issue injunctions in labor disputes.[301]

It is clear that under the federal law the courts can enforce injunctions issued by arbitrators to halt strikes in breach of the collective agreement.[302] Any doubt that the federal courts have jurisdiction to do so in proper cases can no longer have real substance in view of the U.S. Supreme Court's holding in *Boys Markets* that the Norris-LaGuardia Act does not bar court injunctive relief against such strikes.[303]

Where an arbitrator issues an order commanding the employer to cease and desist from some procedure which the arbitrator has found to violate the collective agreement, the cease and desist order may not necessarily bind a subsequent arbitrator faced with the same substantive issue under the agreement.[304]

While arbitrators do not often issue awards which prohibit a party from carrying out some specified act, awards in the nature of "mandatory injunctions" which command a party to take some affirmative action, such as an award ordering the employer to reinstate an employee, are very common in arbitration.[305]

---

[300]Ibid. An arbitrator's cease-and-desist order was also enforced in F. & M. Schaefer Brewing Co., 53 LA 676 (N.Y. Sup. Ct., 1969). The New York arbitration statute does not deal specifically with injunctions by the arbitrator. An arbitrator's injunction was enforced by a court in Illinois, a Uniform Arbitration Act state. In re Ford Motor Co., 41 LA 621 at 621 (Ill. Cir. Ct. Cook County, 1963). In Cranston Teachers Assn. v. School Comm., 416 A.2d 1180, 1183 (R.I. S.Ct., 1980), the court said that a contempt motion is "an appropriate means by which a party may seek another's compliance with a judgment conforming to a confirmed arbitration award [containing an injunction]," but the court held that an arbitrator's award ordering the company to "cease any implementation of the agreement contrary to this award," did not have the effect of an injunction subject to enforcement by contempt proceedings since it did not indicate precisely what was expected of the company in "clear, certain and specific terms."

[301]In re Ruppert, 29 LA 775, 777 (N.Y. Ct. App., 1958). To similar effect, In re Griffin, 42 LA 511 (N.Y. Sup. Ct., 1964).

[302]See General Dynamics Corp. v. Marine Workers, 81 LRRM 2746 (CA 1, 1972); Pacific Maritime Assn. v. Longshoremen, 454 F.2d 262 (CA 9, 1971); New Orleans S.S. Assn. v. Longshoremen, 389 F.2d 369 (CA 5, 1968); Philadelphia Marine Trade Assn. v. Longshoremen, 365 F.2d 295 (CA 3, 1966), reversed on other grounds, 88 S.Ct. 201 (1967). The arbitrator's injunction may not be a feasible remedy where quick action is needed unless the agreement provides for an expedited arbitration procedure. See comments of Owen Fairweather to N.Y.U. 18th Annual Conference on Labor, 58 LRR 240 (1965).

[303]Boys Mkts., Inc. v. Retail Clerks Union Local 770, 90 S.Ct. 1583, 74 LRRM 2257 (1970). For more as to the substance of this decision, see Chapter 2, subtopic entitled "Other Supreme Court Decisions Affecting Arbitration." For a comprehensive discussion of court enforcement of arbitrator injunctions (written prior to *Boys Mkts.* but still very useful), see Meyer, "Enforcement of Arbitrator's Labor Injunctions in the Federal Courts," 7 How. L.J. 17 (1961). Also see Stutz, "Arbitrators and the Remedy Power," Proceedings of the 16th Annual Meeting of NAA, 54, 65–66 (BNA Books, 1963).

[304]See Connecticut Light & Power Co. v. Local 420, 114 LRRM 2770, 2775 (CA 2, 1983). For related discussion, see Chapter 11, subtopic entitled "Temporary Arbitrators."

[305]For other illustrations of the use of mandatory injunctions, see Arbitrator Barone in 71 LA 524, 535; Barrett in 70 LA 1159, 1168; Gootnick in 69 LA 808, 811; Allen in 50 LA 522, 529; Prewett in 50 LA 344, 347; Teple in 48 LA 819, 825; Keefe in 48 LA 373, 379; Howlett in 46 LA 879, 881–882; Hon in 46 LA 769, 773; Cahn in 46 LA 195, 198; Somers in 43 LA 414, 426; Gross in 42 LA 339, 343.

Common Errors in Arbitration

On the basis of its extensive experience in administering arbitration proceedings the American Arbitration Association has concluded that a party may harm its case by the following practices:

"1. Using arbitration and arbitration costs as a harassing technique.
"2. Over-emphasis of the grievance by the union or exaggeration of an employee's fault by management.
"3. Reliance on a minimum of facts and a maximum of arguments.
"4. Concealing essential facts; distorting the truth.
"5. Holding back books, records and other supporting documents.
"6. Tying up proceedings with legal technicalities.
"7. Introducing witnesses who have not been properly instructed on demeanor and on the place of their testimony in the entire case.
"8. Withholding full cooperation from the arbitrator.
"9. Disregarding the ordinary rules of courtesy and decorum.
"10. Becoming involved in arguments with the other side. The time to try to convince the other party is before arbitration, during grievance processing. At the arbitration hearing, all efforts should be concentrated on convincing the arbitrator."[306]

Expediting the Arbitration Machinery

In limited situations, particularly where there is a large accumulation of grievances, the parties may be able to expedite arbitration procedures to their mutual satisfaction and benefit.

For example, an expedited procedure was adopted by one union and employer to cut the costs and time involved in arbitrating a backlog of grievances. Under the expedited procedure: (1) Each party prepares a written statement of the grievance and facts, and submits a copy to the other party. (2) Each party states its thinking as to how the facts fit the contract, again with a copy to the other party. (3) Both parties seek to arrive at a joint statement. Failing that, their diverse views are submitted to the arbitrator. (4) The arbitrator holds a hearing where he asks questions and listens to statements limited to facts and opinions submitted in the aforementioned statements. No posthearing briefs are filed and no opinion accompanies the award unless the arbitrator feels that comments are needed (an award without an opinion would not serve as a precedent under their plan but could be used "as a basis for conversation").[307]

Another example is the program of the steel industry, which has provided one of the most extensive experiences with expedited arbitra-

---

[306]Labor Arbitration Procedures and Techniques, 20–21 (AAA, 1961). For other suggested "don'ts" in arbitration, see Gill, "Gamesmanship in Labor Arbitration," Proceedings of the 15th Annual Meeting of NAA, 148 (BNA Books, 1962).
[307]Ingersoll-Rand Co., 42 LA 965, 966–967 (Scheiber, 1964), where it is also noted that 25 grievances were settled during preparation of joint statements and the parties were able to agree upon a statement of facts in 18 of the 19 remaining cases. The arbitrator did write short opinions on most of the 19 cases. No doubt a significant factor in the success of the plan was the fact that Arbitrator Scheiber had long served the parties prior to use of the expedited procedure.

tion. Some features of the steel program are reflected in the following evaluation by one of its founders:

> "Expedited arbitration, first started in steel in 1972, is designed to get prompt disposition of grievances and sharply reduce delay. It would not have been accepted if the regular procedures had not been plagued by too much delay and the resulting dissatisfaction with arbitration.
>
> "However, expedited arbitration as used in steel and other industries by the steel union would not be acceptable if it were not for the basically successful experience with regular arbitration. That experience has helped give arbitration a good name. Despite constant carping by management and union people at various levels, on balance, the institution of arbitration, as they know it, enjoys a reputation for integrity, competence, and usefulness.
>
> "As a result, expedited arbitration is viewed as a quicker, less expensive method of getting the same kinds of results. The qualms that do exist over the use of relatively untried, untested arbitrators with a waiver of many procedural safeguards tend to be quieted by the knowledge that the expedited arbitrators operate within the parameters already established by regular arbitration. While expedited arbitration does not establish precedents, the panelists are committed to accept the precedents already established by the regular process. * * *
>
> "To reinforce the no-precedent nature of expedited arbitration, the parties do not distribute the awards beyond the plant and cannot cite them in any further proceeding.
>
> "Expedited arbitration as used by the United Steelworkers has worked."[308]

Some of the above-noted possibilities for expediting arbitration proceedings are included among the following possibilities enumerated by Arbitrator Harold W. Davey: (1) dry run arbitration, (2) prehearing statements, (3) avoidance of "brinkmanship" prior to actual arbitration, (4) greater use of submission agreements, (5) more effective use of factual stipulations and consequent reduced use of witnesses, (6) elimination of transcripts, except under special circumstances, (7) elimination of posthearing briefs, (8) drastic shortening of opinions, (9) early issuance of award with brief statement of reasoning, followed later by full opinion, (10) greater use of memorandum opinions or even the equivalent of bench rulings, (11) increased

---

[308]Fischer, "The Steelworkers Union and the Steel Companies," Proceedings of the 32nd Annual Meeting of NAA, 198, 201 (BNA Books, 1980). Also discussing the steel program, see Cohen, "The Search for Innovative Procedures in Labor Arbitration," 29 Arb. J. 104 (1974); Fischer, "Updating Abitration," Proceedings of the 26th Annual Meeting of NAA, 62 (BNA Books, 1974); St. John, "Comment," id. at 73; Stoner, "Comment," id. at 80; Fischer, "Comment," id. at 86 (explaining that, in what appears to be isolation award arbitration, the arbitrators in the program "can't read each other's decisions, nor can they learn what they are," that it "becomes improper for anybody to tell what was decided in a case last week," that to some extent there is "a built-in lack of predictability," that the parties "have accepted this because that's what the system is," and that the parties "have weighed the pros and cons of that situation"); Fischer, "The Steel Industry's Expedited Arbitration: A Judgment After Two Years," 28 Arb. J. 185 (1973). In 1973 the American Arbitration Association adopted a special set of rules for expedited arbitration. For discussion and statistics concerning AAA expedited arbitration programs, see McDermott, "Evaluation of Programs Seeking to Develop Arbitrator Acceptability," Proceedings of the 27th Annual Meeting of NAA, 329, 336–346 (BNA Books, 1975). Regarding expedited arbitration in the federal sector, see A Survey of Negotiated Grievance Procedures and Arbitration in Federal Post Civil Service Reform Act Agreements, 41 (OPM, 1980), reporting that: "Expedited arbitration or mini-arbitration has been adopted in 20 of the [323] agreements sampled. This device is not a substitute for, but a supplement to existing arbitration procedures."

use of "instant" arbitration, (12) expanded use of the hearing officer technique for routine cases under guidance of senior arbitrators.[309]

One or more of the above possibilities may have real utility in a particular case. Judgment obviously must be exercised by the parties and their arbitrator in determining which, if any, of the possibilities are desirable and of beneficial promise for the given parties or for the given case.[310] Expedited arbitration without question does have benefits, but it has limitations and can carry significant liabilities as well.[311]

Tripartite Board Procedures

Tripartite arbitration boards are made up of one or more members selected by management, an equal number selected by labor, and a neutral who serves as chairman. While most of the material in this Chapter applies equally to tripartite boards and to arbitration tribunals composed only of one or more neutrals, the tripartite composition of the former tribunals raises certain other procedural questions. Both tripartite boards and the procedural questions which are particularly applicable to such boards are discussed in detail in Chapter 4.

Procedure of Boards Under Railway Labor Act

Under the Railway Labor Act, boards exist or may be established for both "rights" and "interests" disputes. The procedures of these boards, which are of tripartite composition, are likewise discussed in detail in Chapter 4.

---

[309]Davey, "Restructuring Grievance Arbitration Procedures: Some Modest Proposals," 54 Iowa L. Rev. 560, 565 (1969). Each of these suggestions was discussed by Arbitrator Davey. Id. at 566–577.

[310]Regarding the scope of an arbitrator's obligation to expedite, see § V(E) of the Code of Professional Responsibility, quoted above in topic entitled "The Award and Opinion." Arbitration proceedings sometimes are greatly expedited by court order, as in Philadelphia Newspapers, 68 LA 401, 402, 405 (Jaffee, 1977).

[311]For discussions relating to the benefits, limitations, and/or liabilities of expedited arbitration, in addition to the articles cited above, see Sandver, Blaine & Woyar, "Time and Cost Savings Through Expedited Arbitration Procedures," 36 Arb. J. No. 4, p. 11 (1981); Selby, "The United Mine Workers and Bituminous Coal Operators' Association," Proceedings of the 32nd Annual Meeting of NAA, 181, 187–188 (BNA Books, 1980); The President's Commission on Coal, Labor-Management Seminar III, Wildcat Strikes, 26–30 (Apr. 27, 1979), U.S. Govt. Printing Office, 1979, 0-302-758; Murray & Griffin, "Expedited Arbitration of Discharge Cases," 31 Arb. J. 263 (1976); Miller, "Presidential Reflections," Proceedings of the 28th Annual Meeting of NAA, 1 (BNA Books, 1976); Seitz, "Some Thoughts on the Vogue for Instant Arbitration," 30 Arb. J. 124 (1975); Schlager, "Expedited Arbitration on the LIRR," 30 Arb. J. 273 (1975).

Chapter 8

Evidence

Strict Observance of Legal Rules of Evidence Usually Not Required

It is widely agreed that unless expressly required by the parties in submitting their case to an arbitrator, strict observance of legal rules of evidence is not necessary. As stated by one federal court:

> "In an arbitration the parties have submitted the matter to persons whose judgment they trust, and it is for the arbitrators to determine the weight and credibility of evidence presented to them without restrictions as to the rules of admissibility which would apply in a court of law."[1]

Another federal court, in reviewing an arbitration award within the court's jurisdiction under § 301(a) of the Labor Management Relations Act, stated that "It is well established that rules of evidence as applied in court proceedings do not prevail in arbitration hearings."[2] This has long been the rule under common law,[3] and it is the rule under most of the state statutes which deal with the matter.[4] Where a

---

[1]Instrument Workers v. Minneapolis-Honeywell Co., 54 LRRM 2660, 2661 (USDC, 1963).

[2]Harvey Aluminum, Inc. v. Steelworkers, 64 LRRM 2580, 2581 (USDC, 1967). As persuasive guides to this effect the court quoted a state court decision and AAA Rule 28. The court recognized that the parties can require use of legal rules of evidence. Id. at 2582–2583. In Meat Cutters Local 540 v. Neuhoff Bros. Packers, Inc., 481 F.2d 817, 820 (CA 5, 1973), the court in upholding an arbitrator's refusal to consider the results of polygraph tests as evidence of guilt, said that "Viewed as a question of admissibility of evidence, the arbitrator has great flexibility and the courts should not review the legal adequacy of his evidentiary rulings."

[3]See cases cited in 6 C.J.S. 203 n. 52.

[4]See Justin, "Arbitration: Proving Your Case," 10 LA 955, 962–963 (1948). For example, the Indiana Arbitration Act of 1969 provides in § 34-4-2-6(b) that the parties "are entitled to be heard, to present any and all evidence material to the controversy regardless of its admissibility under judicial rules of evidence." The 1981 procedural rules of the Connecticut State Board of Mediation and Arbitration provide in § 31-91-37 that "Conformity to legal rules of evidence shall not be necessary." One of the few states which have changed the common law rule by statute is Georgia, whose arbitration statute provides in § 7-214 that the "examination of witnesses and the admission of testimony shall be governed by the rules of the superior courts * * *." However, restrictive statutes such as this would be inapplicable to any case covered by LMRA § 301. See Chapter 2, topic entitled "The Applicable Law: Private Sector."

case is covered by a state arbitration statute which is either silent or not specific on a point, the common law ordinarily applies.[5]

Tripartite committees, set up by the National Academy of Arbitrators to study evidence problems, agreed that the observance of rules of evidence should not be strictly required in arbitration proceedings.[6]

While the parties may expressly require the arbitrator to observe legal rules of evidence, they seldom do so. In fact, they sometimes specifically provide that strict observance of such rules shall not be required.[7]

Parties arbitrating under the rules of the American Arbitration Association are subject to its Rule 28, which provides, in part: "The Arbitrator shall be the judge of the relevancy and materiality of the evidence offered and conformity to legal rules of evidence shall not be necessary."[8] Likewise, the National Railroad Adjustment Board does not require strict adherence to the rules of evidence used by judicial tribunals.[9]

The net result is that in a majority of cases, "any evidence, information, or testimony is acceptable which is pertinent to the case and which helps the arbitrator to understand and decide the problem before him."[10]

In regard to the flexible application of legal rules of evidence in arbitration proceedings, Arbitrator W. Willard Wirtz concluded that:

> "[Arbitrators] have established the pattern of ordered informality; performing major surgery on the legal rules of evidence and procedure but retaining the good sense of those rules; greatly simplifying but not eliminating the hearsay and parole evidence rules; taking the rules for the admissibility of evidence and remolding them into rules for weighing it; striking the fat but saving the heart of the practices of cross-examination, presumptions, burden of proof, and the like."[11]

---

[5]See Chapter 2, topic entitled "State Law: Private Sector."

[6]Problems of Proof in Arbitration, 149–150, 163, 296 (BNA Books, 1967). This volume contains extensive discussion, with a wide variety of viewpoints, as to the precise extent to which the various legal rules of evidence should be applied in arbitration. One committee reached a consensus upon some general precepts to aid in gauging the extent of desirable resort to rules of evidence in a given case. Id. at 163–166. Another committee summarized the basic rules of evidence used by courts and made suggestions as to their applicability in arbitration proceedings. Id. at 249–260. For other books dealing with various aspects of evidence in arbitration, see Zack & Bloch, Labor Agreement in Negotiation and Arbitration, 13–24 (BNA Books, 1983); Fairweather, Practice and Procedure in Labor Arbitration, 265–435 (BNA Books, 1983); Hill & Sinicropi, Evidence in Arbitration (BNA Books, 1980). For workshop discussions of various aspects of evidence in arbitration, see "Admissibility of Evidence," Proceedings of the 35th Annual Meeting of NAA, 107 (BNA Books, 1983); "Procedural Rulings During the Hearing," id. at 138.

[7]As in Goodyear Eng'g. Corp., 24 LA 360, 361 (Warns, 1955).

[8]30 LA 1086, 1089.

[9]Jones, National Railroad Adjustment Board, 24 (1941). This is a finding of the Attorney General's Committee on Administrative Procedure. The NRAB's formal rules contain the general statement that the parties in their submissions "must clearly and briefly set forth all relevant, argumentative facts, including all documentary evidence submitted in exhibit form." § 301.5(d) and (e), 29 C.F.R. Part 301.

[10]Simkin & Kennedy, Arbitration of Grievances (U.S. Dept. of Labor, Div. of Labor Standards, Bull. No. 82, p. 25, 1946).

[11]Wirtz, "Due Process of Arbitration," Proceedings of the 11th Annual Meeting of NAA, 1, 13 (BNA Books, 1958).

Flexible arbitral application of formal rules of evidence is particularly justified in regard to those rules of proof which come from the criminal law. The application of these principles of proof in the field of arbitration, which deals with intraplant employer-employee relations, probably should not be accepted in all cases without some consideration of the appropriateness of their use in the determination of rights under collective agreements by arbitrators.[12]

Liberal Admission of Evidence

Although strict observance of legal rules of evidence usually is not required, the parties in all cases must be given adequate opportunity to present all of their evidence and argument. Arbitrators are usually extremely liberal in the reception of evidence, giving the parties a free hand in presenting any type of evidence thought to strengthen and clarify their case. Indeed, Arbitrator Harry Shulman has observed that "the more serious danger is not that the arbitrator will hear too much irrelevancy, but rather that he will not hear enough of the relevant."[13]

An interesting view was expressed by Arbitrator William E. Simkin in justification of the free reception of evidence:

> "One of the fundamental purposes of an arbitration hearing is to let people get things off their chest, regardless of the decision. The arbitration proceeding is the opportunity for a third party, an outside party, to come in and act as a sort of father confessor to the parties, to let them get rid of their troubles, get them out in the open, and have a feeling of someone hearing their troubles. Because I believe so strongly that that is one of the fundamental purposes of arbitration, I don't think you ought to use any rules of evidence. You have to make up your own mind as to what is pertinent or not in the case. Lots of times I have let people talk for five minutes, when I knew all the time that they were talking it had absolutely nothing to do with the case—just completely foreign to it. But there was a fellow testifying, either as a worker or a company representative, who had something that was important for him to get rid of. It was a good time for him to get rid of it."[14]

It should be noted that the liberal reception of evidence is not as extreme a departure from traditional judicial practice as many persons might believe; it is not unusual for judges who are trying cases

---

[12]For a similar view with extensive discussion, see Edwards, "Due Process Considerations in Labor Arbitration," 25 Arb. J. 141 (1970).

[13]Shulman, "Reason, Contract, and Law in Labor Relations," 68 Harv. L. Rev. 999, 1017 (1955).

[14]Conference on Training of Law Students in Labor Relations, Vol. III, Transcript of Proceedings, 636–637 (1947). The "therapeutic" approach has many adherents, but also some critics. See Problems of Proof in Arbitration, 244–247 (BNA Books, 1967). There have been some party complaints about the looseness of arbitration proceedings in the matter of presentation of evidence. See Smith & Jones, "Management and Labor Appraisals and Criticisms of the Arbitration Process: A Report and Comments," 62 Mich. L. Rev. 1115, 1127–1130 (1964).

without a jury to receive evidence very freely, on the basis that they can determine its weight and relevancy after all the case is in.[15]

The Code of Ethics and Procedural Standards for Labor-Management Arbitration provided that: "The arbitrator should allow a fair hearing, with full opportunity to the parties to offer all evidence which they deem reasonably material. He may, however, exclude evidence which is clearly immaterial."[16] The need is to achieve a satisfactory balance between procedural efficiency and other interests:

> "At the hearing the arbitrator must provide for procedural efficiency, and at the same time assure himself that he is getting all that he needs to decide the case. To be successful at this he must bear in mind simultaneously a number of complex considerations. The attorneys must be allowed to present their cases fully as they see them. Witnesses should be allowed to say what they feel is important, sometimes even when it is technically irrelevant. It is sometimes necessary to be aware of political considerations within the union or among management people involved in the case, or between union and management in the plant or industry."[17]

Some excursions into extraneous matter may help the arbitrator get the background of the case or may help him understand the viewpoints of the parties. Moreover, the relevance of evidence offered in arbitration, though it may appear at first glance not to be germane to the case, cannot always be determined accurately until the entire case has been unfolded.[18] Accordingly, from a procedural standpoint arbitrators often accept evidence while reserving their response thereto until the challenged evidence can be evaluated in the light of the whole record.[19] The objection to the evidence, even if overruled, will serve to caution the arbitrator to examine the challenged evidence more closely before giving it weight.[20]

Actually, the liberal admission of evidence is much less likely to render the proceedings vulnerable to court challenge than is the rejection of competent evidence.[21] Moreover, under some statutes an arbitrator's refusal to hear all relevant evidence is a ground for vacating the award.[22]

---

[15]Also in this regard see comments by McDermott, "The Presidential Address—An Exercise in Dialectic: Should Arbitration Behave as Does Litigation?" Proceedings of the 33rd Annual Meeting of NAA, 1, 13, 16–17 (BNA Books, 1981); Smith, "The Search for Truth—The Whole Truth," Proceedings of the 31st Annual Meeting of NAA, 40, 50 (BNA Books, 1979).

[16]Part II, Rule 4(e). The Code of Professional Responsibility which was intended to supersede the Code of Ethics is less specific concerning the exclusion of evidence, only stating generally that an arbitrator "must provide a fair and adequate hearing which assures that both parties have sufficient opportunity to present their respective evidence and argument." § V(A)(1), 64 LA 1325.

[17]Eaton, "Labor Arbitration in the San Francisco Bay Area," 48 LA 1381, 1391–1392 (1967).

[18]As to this, see an interesting discourse in "Procedural Problems in the Conduct of Arbitration Hearings: A Discussion," Proceedings of the 17th Annual Meeting of NAA, 1, 10–11 (BNA Books, 1964). Also see Smith, "The Search for Truth—The Whole Truth," Proceedings of the 31st Annual Meeting of NAA, 40, 49 (BNA Books, 1979).

[19]For example, see Arbitrator Ruben in 69 LA 944, 947; Sembower in 44 LA 593, 599–600; Seinsheimer in 40 LA 1048, 1052; Garrett in 16 LA 32.

[20]For further discussion, see Chapter 7, topic entitled "Objections to Evidence."

[21]See Harvey Aluminum, Inc. v. Steelworkers, 67 LRRM 2580 (USDC, 1967). But also see Meat Cutters Local 540 v. Neuhoff Bros. Packers, Inc., 481 F.2d 817, 820 (CA 5, 1973); Newspaper Guild Local 35 v. Washington Post Co., 76 LRRM 2274, 2278 (D.C. Cir., 1971).

[22]The Uniform Arbitration Act so provides. 27 LA 909, 910. Also see Chapter 2, Legal Status of Arbitration.

But an arbitrator may properly refuse to admit evidence that lacks revelance or probative value, for if no limitation is placed upon the reception of evidence the hearing can too easily go far afield. Moreover, under some circumstances an award may be properly rendered even though certain relevant evidence has not been formally received by the arbitrator. For instance, where data requested by an arbitrator was not submitted within the specified time, the issuance of the award prior to receipt of the requested data was held not to be ground for vacating the award where the court found that the arbitrator had in fact been fully informed as to the facts and issues of the case.[23]

Evidence to Be Heard by Entire Board

It is a general requirement that, where there is a board of arbitration, all evidence must be taken in the presence of all of the arbitrators. This requirement prevails in common-law arbitration[24] and in arbitration under state statutes.[25] It is also a general requirement under American Arbitration Association Rule 28.[26]

It has been held under a state statute, for instance, that an agreement to arbitrate entitles the parties to the considered judgment of arbitrators based upon evidence submitted in the presence of all the arbitrators, and that participation at proceedings at which only three of six arbitrators were present did not constitute a waiver of the requirement that all arbitrators be present for a binding award.[27] However, where it had been agreed that the partisan members of a board of arbitration could be substituted at any time, the award was held binding although one of the arbitrators who signed it had been substituted after the hearing and had not heard the evidence.[28]

It should be noted that the deliberate refusal by a party and its representatives on a tripartite board to attend the hearing may result in the issuance of a default award.[29]

What Type of Evidence Should Be Used

Of course the specific evidence introduced in individual cases will vary greatly from case to case according to the question involved. It is

---

[23]In re Aranson, 6 LA 1033 (N.Y. S.Ct., 1946). Also see Northwest Airlines v. ALPA, 88 LRRM 2052, 2055 (USDC, 1974), stating that it is for the arbitrator to determine at what point the evidence submitted is sufficient. But cf., Excel Pharmacal Co., 21 LA 831 (N.Y. S.Ct., 1954). For related discussion, see Chapter 7, topics entitled "Default Awards in Ex Parte Proceedings," and "Reopening the Hearing."

[24]Ziskind, Labor Arbitration Under State Statutes, 3 (U.S. Dept. of Labor, 1943).

[25]Id. at 15. While still providing that the hearing shall be conducted by all the arbitrators, some statutes provide that a majority may determine any question and render a final award. As, for instance, under the Uniform Arbitration Act, 27 LA 909, 910.

[26]30 LA 1086, 1089.

[27]Buitoni Prods., Inc. v. Nappi, 12 LA 667 (N.Y. S.Ct., 1949).

[28]West Towns Bus Co. v. Division 241, 35 LA 145, 148 (Ill. App. Ct., 1960).

[29]See Chapter 7, topic entitled "Default Awards in Ex Parte Proceedings." Also, Uniform Arbitration Act, 27 LA 909, 910.

likewise obvious, however, that each general type of case requires a more or less specific type of evidence. In disputes over the setting of general wage rates, for instance, the most important type of evidence is documented statistical and economic data on such matters as prevailing practice, cost of living, ability to pay, and the like.[30]

In discharge or discipline cases the most important evidence generally comes in the form of testimony of witnesses, the facts which led to the disciplinary action being of great importance. If, however, there is no disagreement as to these facts and if the primary issue is one concerning proper punishment, then the past record of the employee and evidence of past disciplinary action taken in similar cases enter the picture in a major capacity.

In contract interpretation cases the history of precontract negotiations and the past practice of the parties in applying the disputed provision may be of great importance.

In some cases visual or pictorial evidence is useful. The arbitrator's understanding of the dispute may be greatly improved, for instance, by his visiting the physical site directly involved in the case.[31] Pictorial evidence may also be provided at the hearing room, as where photographs of employees operating machines were submitted to the arbitrator in a job-rating dispute.[32] In another case a videotape purporting to show strike misconduct was relied upon by Arbitrator James C. Duff.[33]

Indeed, as long as evidence "fits" and is relevant to the case the unusual nature of the evidence should not bar its admission and consideration. Thus, in one case a significant type of evidence was sound and time recordings of the movements of a diesel locomotive to indicate the extent to which it was being utilized in a certain operation and to compare its efficiency with that of a steam locomotive.[34]

Ordinarily each party has the right to decide in what form it shall present its evidence; thus, one arbitrator refused to require a party to present its evidence through witnesses rather than statements and exhibits.[35]

---

[30]In one such case, "No witnesses were heard but counsel for each party argued their positions and commented on the exhibits." Pensacola News-Journal, 49 LA 433 at 433 (King, 1967). Documentary evidence in the form of joint exhibits was the only evidence presented in the "rights arbitration" interpretation case of Alameda County Superintendent of Schools, 76 LA 566 at 566 (Anderson, 1981).

[31]For full discussion, see Chapter 7, topic entitled "Plant Visits by Arbitrator."

[32]Brown & Sharpe Mfg. Co., 21 LA 461, 464–469 (Waite, 1953). Also see Arbitrator Larkin in 75 LA 118, 120; Simkin in 26 LA 836, 842.

[33]Pennzoil Co., 76 LA 587, 589 (1981).

[34]Republic Steel Corp., 24 LA 336, 339 (Platt, 1955).

[35]Sewanee Silica Co., 47 LA 282, 283 (Greene, 1966). Sometimes a party has offered no direct evidence at all, relying entirely upon cross-examination of the opponent's witnesses. See topic entitled "Unsupported Allegations," below.

"New" Evidence at Arbitration Hearing

Evidence is sometimes presented at the arbitration hearing which was not disclosed at the prearbitral grievance steps.[36] Some of the considerations involved in an arbitrator's decision to accept or reject such evidence include his great need for all the facts relevant to the case, the need to protect the integrity of the prearbitral grievance machinery, and general concepts of fairness. Thus, it is not surprising that, in balancing these considerations, such evidence has been accepted in some cases but rejected in others.

It should be emphasized that whatever element of unfairness may be involved in the use of new evidence, it is largely mitigated or eliminated by the fact that arbitrators who accept newly submitted evidence will take any reasonable steps necessary to insure the opposite party adequate opportunity to respond thereto, regardless of whether the evidence had been withheld in good or bad faith.[37] If the arbitrator deems it necessary, for instance, he may return the case to the parties for further consideration in the light of the new evidence or he may recess the hearing for whatever time necessary to give the surprised party opportunity to prepare or revise its defense.[38] Such interruptions of the arbitration hearing can be avoided if parties using new evidence will submit it to the other party prior to the hearing whenever the nature of the evidence makes it reasonably foreseeable that the other party will need time to prepare a response.[39]

A survey conducted by Arbitrator W. Willard Wirtz indicated that "unless some deliberate attempt to mislead the other party is disclosed, and particularly if the 'new' evidence or argument appears substantially material, most arbitrators will be disinclined to rule the matter out of the proceedings."[40] In this regard, Arbitrator Ralph Seward explained that many prearbitral grievance meetings "are informal and deal with the surface of a problem without in any sense taking real evidence,"[41] and Arbitrator Wirtz observed that the "company, for its part, may very reasonably not have made the thorough

---

[36]For a related discussion, see Chapter 7, topic entitled "Extent of Permissible Deviation From Prearbitral Discussion of Case"; Chapter 15, subtopic entitled "Postdischarge Conduct or Charges." As to how frequently surprise evidence is encountered, see Eaton, "Labor Arbitration in the San Francisco Bay Area," 48 LA 1381, 1385 (1967).

[37]As to the reaction of surprised parties, "there is no evidence that they feel that the procedural steps which arbitrators have taken to protect their rights to respond to surprise materials have been less than satisfactory." Fleming, The Labor Arbitration Process, 153–154 (U. of Ill. Press, 1965).

[38]See Wirtz, "Due Process of Arbitration," Proceedings of the 11th Annual Meeting of NAA, 1, 16 (BNA Books, 1958). In Pittsburgh Steel Co., 48 LA 585, 587 (Valtin, 1967), the arbitrator received the new material into evidence and gave the surprised party an election to have the case remanded or to proceed with it; the party chose to proceed.

[39]See suggestions of Arbitrator Maurice H. Merrill in Jonco Aircraft Corp., 22 LA 819, 823 (1954). Also see Smith, "The Search for Truth—The Whole Truth," Proceedings of the 31st Annual Meeting of NAA, 40, 46 (BNA Books, 1979).

[40]Wirtz, "Due Process of Arbitration," Proceedings of the 11th Annual Meeting of NAA, 1, 15 (BNA Books, 1958). Also see Arbitrator Kaplan in 62 LA 616, 620; Marcus in 60 LA 536, 537; Livengood in 47 LA 1170, 1171–1172; Kesselman in 46 LA 65, 70; Komaroff in 17 LA 183, 185–186.

[41]Wirtz, "Due Process of Arbitration," Proceedings of the 11th Annual Meeting of NAA, 1, 15 (BNA Books, 1958).

investigation it will properly consider warranted if the union ultimately decides to take the case seriously enough to go to arbitration."[42]

Also justifying the admission of new evidence, a tripartite committee reasoned:

"In some situations * * * it is the practice of the parties not to present all the evidence during the grievance procedure. In other situations the parties may recognize from the outset that a particular grievance must be arbitrated and pass quickly through the steps of [the] grievance procedure. In cases like these, evidence not disclosed prior to the hearing should be admitted. In general, evidence discovered after the grievance was processed should also be admitted. The arbitrator, however, should grant adjournments or take other measures to insure a fair hearing and to protect a party taken by surprise as to evidence concerning a material issue."[43]

The absence of any contract provision restricting acceptance of new evidence has sometimes been emphasized by arbitrators in receiving evidence presented for the first time at the arbitration hearing.[44] But even where an agreement provided that "the facts concerning the case shall be made available to both parties" at an early stage, facts acquired later could be introduced at subsequent steps of the grievance procedure or at the arbitration hearing.[45]

Also, under a contract requiring the employer to furnish all available evidence to the union "and/or" the arbitrator, the withholding of evidence until the arbitration hearing was held not to be improper where the union was granted 10 days to consider the evidence; sufficient time for consideration of evidence was deemed the basic purpose of the provision.[46]

While stating that "it is understandable that the evidence which comes out at the arbitration hearing is more detailed and more complete than that which is produced in the preliminary steps of the grievance machinery," Umpire I. Robert Feinberg considered that delay in presenting evidence "mitigates its relative importance."[47] Moreover, he refused to accept evidence offered by a party for the first time at the arbitration stage where the evidence was known to the party at the earlier grievance stages and would have expanded the party's claim if admitted at the arbitration stage.[48]

[42]Ibid. Also see Arbitrator Sembower in San Gamo Elec. Co., 44 LA 593, 600 (1965).

[43]"Report of the New York Tripartite Committee," Problems of Proof in Arbitration, 295, 302–303 (BNA Books, 1967). Other tripartite committees were likewise in general agreement that new evidence should be admitted into evidence, and that the arbitrator should take reasonable steps to protect the other party. Id. at 104, 142–143, 260–261.

[44]See North Am. Aviation, 17 LA 183, 185–186 (Komaroff, 1951); Carbon Fuel Co., 1 ALAA ¶67,327 (1946). The above-quoted tripartite committee took the position that to the extent that the contract specifically requires full disclosure, new evidence should be rejected by the arbitrator. "Report of the New York Tripartite Committee," Problems of Proof in Arbitration, 302, (BNA Books, 1967). But see Zinsco Elec. Prods., 64 LA 107, 109 (Caraway, 1975), where the parties in their contract expressly agreed not to withhold evidence but did not expressly state any penalty for withholding evidence or authorize its exclusion from arbitration.

[45]American Steel & Wire Co., 5 LA 193, 206–207 (Blumer, 1946).

[46]Texas Co., 7 LA 735, 739 (Carmichael, 1947).

[47]Bethlehem Steel Co., 21 LA 655, 656 (1953).

[48]Bethlehem Steel Co., 18 LA 366, 367 (1951).

It is the intentional, calculated, withholding of evidence that arbitrators criticize most severely. In this regard, the view of Umpire Gabriel N. Alexander is no doubt shared by many arbitrators:

> "[S]ound collective bargaining requires frank and candid disclosure at the earliest opportunity of all the facts known to each party. There will undoubtedly be times when facts are not discovered, and therefore not disclosed, until after the grievance has been partially processed, and problem enough is created by those instances. There is not a scintilla of justification for the withholding of information by either party from and after the time it is discovered."[49]

But the calculated withholding of evidence did not result in its rejection by the arbitrator where, from the outset, the attitude of the party from whom it was withheld was such as to put all prearbitral steps on an adversary basis, "with both sides primarily pointed at an ultimate arbitration instead of mutual ascertainment of fact, compromise, or some other solution based upon general collective bargaining considerations."[50]

If the arbitration tribunal is serving essentially in an appellate capacity there is obviously strong reason to confine the evidence to what was considered below. In this regard, the rules of the National Railroad Adjustment Board require that "all data submitted in support" of the party's position "must affirmatively show the same to have been presented to the [other party] and made a part of the particular question in dispute."[51]

Requiring the Production of Evidence

Parties covered by the NLRA have a statutory duty, though by no means unlimited, to provide information needed by a requesting party in connection with grievance processing.[52] When this duty is not

---

[49]General Motors Umpire Decision No. F-97 (1950). Arbitrator Peter Seitz chastised both parties for calculated withholding of evidence in Sperry-Rand Corp., 46 LA 961, 966 (1966), and he noted that such practice can be "self-defeating." Also suggesting that the practice "is likely to boomerang," Davey, "The John Deere-UAW Permanent Arbitration System," Critical Issues in Labor Arbitration, 161, 170 (BNA Books, 1957).

[50]Bethlehem Steel Co., 6 LA 617, 619 (Wyckoff, 1947).

[51]Sec. 301.5(d) and (e), 29 C.F.R. Part 301. Also, § 301.7(b) charges the parties "with the duty and responsibility of including in their original written submission all known relevant, argumentative facts and documentary evidence."

[52]In NLRB v. Acme Indus. Co., 87 S.Ct. 565, 569, 64 LRRM 2069 (1967), the U.S. Supreme Court recognized an employer obligation to provide information to the union to enable it to evaluate grievances that had been filed, the Court stating that the NLRB's action in requiring the employer to provide information "was in aid of the arbitral process," which "can function properly only if the grievance procedures leading to it can sift out unmeritorious claims." In Machinists Lodge 78 (Square D Co.), 92 LRRM 1202, 1203 (NLRB, 1976), the NLRB majority stated that assuming, without deciding, that a union's duty to furnish information is "parallel" to that of the employer, there is "no statutory obligation on the part of either to turn over to the other evidence of an undisclosed nature that the possessor of the information believes relevant and conclusive with respect to its rights in an arbitration proceeding." For other cases relating to the scope of the duty to provide information in connection with grievance processing, see C&P Tel. Co. v. NLRB, 111 LRRM 2165 (CA 2, 1982), where the union successfully utilized unfair labor practice proceedings to obtain information after the company had declined to comply with an arbitrator's subpoena for its production; Communication Workers Local 1051 v. NLRB, 106 LRRM 2960 (CA 1, 1981), holding that the employer improperly refused to furnish the union photocopies of grievance-related documents—requiring the union to hand copy the documents impeded the

complied with, use of unfair labor practice proceedings of course may be available to obtain access to needed information but often would be prohibitively slow.[53] In addition to possible NLRB proceedings, some of the other methods that possibly may be available for requiring the production of evidence in appropriate situations are arbitral issuance of subpoenas and direct requests by the arbitrator to the party possessing it. The latter methods and certain related matters are treated in the subtopics that follow.

Use of Subpoenas

It has been generally accepted that unless authorized by applicable statute or by the agreement, the arbitrator has no subpoena power.[54] However, there is a clear indication that a variance some-

---

contractual grievance procedure; Procter & Gamble Mfg. Co. v. NLRB, 102 LRRM 2128 (CA 8, 1979), holding that the employer improperly refused the union's request for information regarding a job evaluation plan needed by the union to evaluate two grievances alleging discriminatory job evaluation (this case is also useful for its collection of other cases dealing with various aspects of the duty to provide information); Machinists v. United Aircraft Corp., 90 LRRM 2272, 2303 (CA 2, 1975), holding that the employer could require the union to pay the cost of furnishing information where the amount of material requested was substantial. Under the facts in United States Steel Corp., 79 LA 249, 252–253 (Neyland, 1982), the Company's "assessment of a service fee for the furnishing of relevant information to the Union was improper."

[53]Limitations of NLRB proceedings in this regard were asserted by Heinsz, Lowry & Torzewski, "The Subpoena Power of Labor Arbitrators," 1979 Utah L. Rev. 29, 34 (1979), as follows:

"Although the *Acme* holding is noteworthy for its recognition of the importance of full and reliable data prior to invoking the arbitral process, it is of limited value due to the time-consuming procedure required to enforce its right of access to information. On the average it takes approximately one and one-half years from the time an unfair labor practice charge is filed in an NLRB regional office until the Board renders its decision. In the meantime, the arbitration is postponed while the tensions and pressures that arbitration was designed to quickly eliminate continue to build. Thus, the remedy provided by *Acme,* though useful in the proper context (e.g., collective bargaining), simply cannot meet the paramount need of the arbitral process—timely and efficient access to information." (footnotes omitted)

[54]Problems of Proof in Arbitration, 99, 140, 258 (BNA Books, 1967). The American Arbitration Association, whose labor arbitration Rule 28 states that the arbitrator is permitted to subpoena witnesses and documents when "authorized by law," reported in regard to arbitration in general (and not merely in reference to labor arbitration) that "Arbitration statutes in 40 states, the District of Columbia and Puerto Rico give the arbitrator the power to issue subpoenas." "Arbitrator Subpoena Power," Law. Arb. Letter, Vol. 3, No. 26, p. 1 (AAA, 1979), listing the 40 states with such statutes and also listing the remaining 10 states as not giving the arbitrator subpoena power (named in the latter group are Iowa, Michigan, Mississippi, Montana, Nevada, North Dakota, Tennessee, Vermont, Virginia, and West Virginia). The report also states:

"In some instances where the arbitrations are held in a state which does not provide for subpoenas, arbitrators may issue subpoenas if the Federal Arbitration Act is applicable to the dispute. It should also be noted that in some states there are statutes other than the arbitration statute which authorize the arbitrator to issue subpoenas. For example, Vermont's statute covering public sector labor disputes gives the arbitrator subpoena power although there is no comparable provision in the arbitration statute." Ibid.

It must be stressed, however, that *by no means do all of the 40 states* (having statutes giving arbitrators subpoena power) *apply their statute to labor contracts.* See Chapter 2, subtopic entitled "State Arbitration Statutes." Furthermore, the courts have disagreed on applicability of the Federal Arbitration Act to collective bargaining agreements. See Chapter 2, topic entitled "Federal Law: Private Sector." In the federal sector the Civil Service Reform Act of 1978 specifies subpoena power for FLRA members, the FLRA General Counsel, the FSIP, and administrative law judges, but it is silent regarding subpoena power for arbitrators. 5 U.S.C.A. § 7132. Finally, it may be noted that some agreements do expressly grant the arbitrator power to call witnesses and to require production of documentary evidence. Major Collective Bargaining Agreements: Arbitration Procedures, 66–67 (U.S. Dept. Labor Bull. No. 1425–6, 1966). For extensive and informative discussions of arbitral subpoena power, see Bedikian, "Use of Subpoenas in Labor

times exists between a formal legal limitation to this effect and actual arbitral practice.[55] One observer has pointed to LMRA § 301 and has suggested "the idea that because the arbitration process is now federal" an argument can be made that even in states which do not authorize arbitrators to issue subpoenas an arbitrator may do so.[56] Another view asserts that adoption of contractual grievance and arbitration procedures carries with it an implied contractual duty to provide information in appropriate situations, and that this provides a proper basis for an arbitrator to issue a subpoena or an "arbitral discovery order."[57]

Where a subpoena had been issued by an arbitrator pursuant to state statute, a federal court responded as follows when asked to enforce the subpoena:

> "Had the arbitrator and plaintiff's counsel utilized the enforcement procedures prescribed by the Federal Arbitration Act, * * * we would not be confronted with the hybrid question of defendant's compliance with a state subpoena. The plaintiff elected to proceed through avenues afforded by state process; it is not now within this Court's prerogative to intervene and enforce that process.
>
> "Procedural niceties and technical obstructionism, however, with rare exception, should not be judicially nurtured; especially, is this true when lawful arbitration procedural remedies are already in progress. * * * This federal Court does have concurrent enforcement jurisdiction and possesses the necessary statutory authority [citing the Federal Arbitration Act] to enforce the procedures attendant upon the orderly consummation of this arbitration hearing. * * * Under this aegis, it will act *sua sponte* to sever the Gordian knot which created the impasse. The defendant shall produce forthwith the disputed file material for an *in camera* inspection by the arbitrator.

Arbitration: Statutory Interpretations and Perspectives," 1979 Det. C.L. Rev. 575 (1979), strongly endorsing subpoena power for arbitrators; Heinsz, Lowry & Torzewski, "The Subpoena Power of Labor Arbitrators," 1979 Utah L. Rev. 29 (1979), stating that "thus far the judiciary has failed to fashion an arbitral subpoena process," and urging that it be done (id. at 29, 55). Also informative, see "Report of the Subcommittee on Labor Arbitration Procedures," ABA Section of Labor and Employment Law Committee Reports, 322–328 (1979).

[55]See the results of the National Academy of Arbitrators survey quoted below in this subtopic.

[56]Comment of T.L. Tolan, Problems of Proof in Arbitration, 143–144 (BNA Books, 1967). For more detailed suggestions along similar lines, see Heinsz, Lowry & Torzewski, "The Subpoena Power of Labor Arbitrators," 1979 Utah L. Rev. 29, 48–55 (1979), concluding at p. 55 that a "strong argument can be made that the proper basis of an arbitral subpoena is section 301 of the Labor Management Relations Act and the collective bargaining agreement," and that "the federal courts should establish the proper guidelines for the granting of arbitral subpoenas to insure the uniformity so necessary in labor cases"; Matto, "The Applicability of State Arbitration Statutes to Proceedings Subject to LMRA Section 301," 27 Ohio St. L.J. 692, 705–708 (1966). One court in fact did conclude that "pursuant to the authority embodied in section 301, subpoenas issued by labor arbitrators are, in appropriate circumstances, enforceable in the federal district courts"; but the court refused to enforce the subpoenas in question "until the arbitrator is given the opportunity to consider the relevance of the information sought and to rule on the Company's objections." Wilkes-Barre Publishing Co. v. Local 120, 113 LRRM 3409, 3414–3415 (USDC, 1982). For related discussion, see Chapter 2, topic entitled "The Applicable Law: Private Sector."

[57]See Bedikian, "Use of Subpoenas in Labor Arbitration: Statutory Interpretations and Perspectives," 1979 Det. C.L. Rev. 575, 598–601 (1979); Jones, "The Accretion of Federal Power in Labor Arbitration—The Example of Arbitral Discovery," 116 U. Pa. L. Rev. 830, 836–838 (1960). In E & G Eng'rs., 71 LA 441, 445 (1978), Arbitrator Edgar A. Jones, Jr., used both the term "subpoena" and the term "arbitral order of discovery" in connection with his view that an implied contractual obligation exists and supports arbitral commands for the production of information in proper circumstances.

"Such a procedure will, of course, deny to the plaintiff-Union its claim of a carte blanche discovery privilege, to peruse the employer's file. Arbitration has never afforded to litigants complete freedom to delve into and explore at will, the adversary party's files under the pretense of pre-trial discovery. * * *

"It must be assumed that the presiding arbitrator is an experienced person well versed in evaluating the alleged claims of the employer, that some files contain classified security information involving national defense or plant security, personal health records and other similar confidential data. All of this should be screened from the file, except where the arbitrator determines it to be relevant evidence in the dispute. Even in the latter instances, proper safeguards should be ordered, such as sealing the record or limiting its access to counsel only, so that no unnecessary harm or prejudice or unnecessary embarrassment may be caused to anyone."[58]

One group expressed the view that "Even assuming its legality, the use of the subpoena is not to be encouraged. Demands for relevant information by either party should be honored without the formality of a subpoena."[59] However, in replying to that group and in urging that arbitrators should have subpoena power, some other commentators denied that this would inject undue formality into the arbitration process, and they explained that adequate safeguards against abuse of arbitral subpoena power exist by virtue of court superintendence of the exercise of that power.[60]

In fact, many arbitrators are willing to issue subpoenas. This was clearly shown by a National Academy of Arbitrators survey of its members, who were asked the following question:

---

[58]Machinists v. Pratt & Whitney Div., 329 F.Supp. 283, 286–287 (USDC, 1971), the court also upholding the arbitrator's authority to reopen the arbitration hearing in order to issue a subpoena which by oversight the arbitrator had failed to issue earlier in the arbitration proceedings. Also see Great Scott Supermarkets v. Local 337, 84 LRRM 2514, 2515–2516 (USDC, 1973). In Local 757, IBT v. Borden, Inc., 78 LRRM 2398 (USDC, 1971), the court refused to enforce a subpoena obtained by a union from a state court, where an arbitrator had already taken the union's request for production of the desired books and records under advisement.

[59]Report of Pittsburgh Tripartite Committee, Problems of Proof in Arbitration, 258 (BNA Books, 1967). The Chicago Tripartite Committee agreed. Id. at 99. This Committee deemed use of subpoenas justified in some situations (as where an employee is reluctant to take time off to testify) but of doubtful wisdom in others (as where an employee is required to testify against a fellow employee). Id. at 100.

[60]Heinsz, Lowry & Torzewski, "The Subpoena Power of Labor Arbitrators," 1979 Utah L. Rev. 29, 40–42 (1979), where they stated, in part:

"Most courts and labor arbitrators have appropriately resisted any attempt to create an arbitral discovery process that would include interrogatories, depositions, and related procedures. Such procedures are expensive and technical. Their implementation would unduly delay the arbitration and would lessen the utility of arbitration as a prompt and inexpensive method of resolving disputes.

"But these are not real dangers to granting an arbitral subpoena power. * * * Empowering labor arbitrators to subpoena relevant evidence and witnesses, without adding a full scale pre-arbitration discovery process, will neither slow nor change the nature of arbitration. The grant of arbitral subpoena power will simply increase the facts available to the decision-maker.

"* * * A labor arbitrator * * * has the expertise to determine whether claimed information is material. Further, arbitral subpoenas are in the nature of administrative subpoenas. The subpoenas are neither self-executing nor self-enforcing, nor can an arbitrator compel compliance with a subpoena by a contempt citation or other enforcement mechanisms. If compliance is not forthcoming, the party who sought the arbitral subpoena must apply to a court for its enforcement. Similarly, the party who objects to a subpoena may apply to a court to quash it. Thus, upon proper motion by either party a court will review the matter and act as a judicial check on arbitral subpoena power to insure that only relevant evidence is being required and that the legal rights of the parties are adequately protected." (footnotes omitted)

"You are requested by a party to issue a subpoena for the testimony of a person who is outside the parties' relationship and lives in a city distant from the hearing location. You have no information as to the substantive nature of the case. What do you do: (a) in a state which has a subpoena statute; (b) in a state which has no subpoena statute; and (c) if the request for the subpoena is under the Federal Arbitration Act?"

The responses revealed that "a majority of members under all three conditions will issue a subpoena without qualification or concern in regard to its enforcement."[61]

When a subpoena is to be issued, a procedure along the following lines might be utilized: The requesting party will prepare the subpoena and submit it to the arbitrator for his signature; then the arbitrator or the requesting party will cause it to be served (by anyone other than a party to the case); the subpoena may thereupon be challenged as to scope, materiality, or reasonableness.[62]

---

[61]"Procedural Problems During Hearings," The Chronicle (NAA, Apr. 1981), reporting also that:

"The size of the majority declines considerably, however, if the request for a subpoena is made in a state without a statute and somewhat less if the request is made under the Federal Arbitration Act. The concern here is whether the subpoena can be enforced. * * *

"There are a number of members who may ultimately issue a subpoena but only after certain steps are taken. Among these steps are: (1) insisting upon supporting arguments and/or disclosure of the reasons for requesting the subpoena before issuing the subpoena; (2) insisting that the other party be notified prior to issuing the subpoena; (3) cautioning the party requesting the subpoena as to possible liability for the expense of the witness; and (4) attempting to persuade the party to use other means to obtain the presence of the witness. * * *

"In part, the reasons for establishing conditions or refusing to issue a subpoena prior to the hearing is concern that the parties may be improperly requesting a subpoena and concern that the use of a subpoena may damage the arbitration process. Many of those members who do issue subpoenas upon request do so, however, with some qualms."
Also see statements by several arbitrators quoted in Bedikian, "Use of Subpoenas in Labor Arbitration: Statutory Interpretations and Perspectives," 1979 Det. C.L. Rev. 575, 592–597 (1979). There Arbitrator Harry H. Platt stated, in part:

"The matter of subpoenaing witnesses or requiring the production of books and records is really a matter for the courts, unless there is a clear provision to the contrary granting such activity to an arbitrator. Although as an arbitrator, I have signed subpoenas upon request, the legality or validity is something I do not vouch for. There is no warranty, and certainly there are no contempt powers."
And Arbitrator Robert G. Howlett stated, in part:

"I have, on a number of occasions, issued subpoenas in private sector cases under the United States Arbitration Act. I have never had a case where the subpoena has not been obeyed. I also note there is nothing in the public sector similar to the United States Arbitration Act authorizing an arbitrator to issue a subpoena. Clearly, the Act does not apply to any public sector situation. I have issued subpoenas in public sector cases—patently, without authority. However, they have always been obeyed."
[62]See Automatic Elec. Co., 42 LA 1056, 1057, 1060–1064 (Sembower, 1964); Schultz & Burch Biscuit Co., 42 LA 280, 281–282, 290 (Solomon, 1964). These two cases also recognize that use of subpoenas may present troublesome time problems, sometimes requiring adjournment of the hearing to a later date. In the latter regard, also see Arbitrator Bickner in 77 LA 1021, 1024, utilizing an "interim award" relative to subpoenas. The Uniform Arbitration Act, §7, authorizes the arbitrator to issue (or cause to be issued) subpoenas and provides for court enforcement. 27 LA 909, 910. The New York statute in addition authorizes issuance of subpoenas by the attorneys of record. New York CPLR §§ 2308(b), 7505. In Local 757, IBT v. Borden, Inc., 78 LRRM 2398, 2399 (USDC, 1971), the court observed that "Under the United States Arbitration Act it is clear that only an arbitrator can issue a subpoena while under state law an attorney of record may issue a subpoena."

Evidence Requested by Arbitrator

In a significant sense the absence of the subpoena power is not very important, since the parties usually are willing to provide any data or evidence requested by the arbitrator.[63]

Arbitrators do not hesitate to request the production of data or information if they have reasonable basis to believe that it will be germane to the case.[64] While the arbitrator himself often initiates the request for the production of evidence,[65] in other instances he may make the request on the motion of the party who otherwise does not have access to the evidence in question.[66]

One arbitrator declared that "neither the Company nor the Union should be allowed to withhold relevant and material testimony or other evidence except possibly in special circumstances * * * such as possible criminal incrimination, trade secrets and classified Defense matters."[67] As concerns the "relevant and material" qualification, arbitrators have refused to order the production of evidence for the purpose of uncovering grievances as distinguished from testing the validity of specific claims.[68]

In one case the arbitrator issued "an interim award," during the course of the hearing, "directing the Company to submit certain payroll information to the Union for its use in connection with" the case.[69] Prior to the hearing in another case, an arbitration board of three neutrals issued the following order:

> "Each party shall produce, at least three working days in advance of the hearing, for the use of the other party such specific documents or information in the employment history of either the challenging striker or the challenged replacement on which it expects to rely at the hearing. Further, at the demand of either party made at least five working days in advance of the hearing the other party shall produce such pertinent specific documents as the demanding party believes to be in the possession of the other party."[70]

---

[63]See, for example, Clay City Pipe Co., 20 LA 538, 542 (Young, 1952). Also see comments by Arbitrator Fleming, The Labor Arbitration Process, 175 (U. of Ill. Press, 1965).

[64]See discussion by Arbitrator Harry J. Dworkin in Chesapeake & Potomac Tel. Co. of W. Va., 21 LA 367, 369–371 (1953). AAA Rule 44 provides that "the expenses of any witnesses or the cost of any proofs produced at the direct request of the Arbitrator, shall be borne equally by the parties unless they agree otherwise, or unless the Arbitrator in the award assesses such expenses or any part thereof against any specified party or parties."

[65]See Arbitrator Jones in 71 LA 441, 443; Snow in 71 LA 271, 272; Smith in 43 LA 193, 200; Levy in 19 LA 761, 762.

[66]See Arbitrator Barnhart in 64 LA 869, 873; Jones in 29 LA 372, 373; Justin in 24 LA 44, 47; Dworkin in 21 LA 367, 369–371; Feinberg in 18 LA 55, 56.

[67]Tectum Corp., 37 LA 807, 810 (Autrey, 1961).

[68]See Santa Clara County & Cent. Cal. Meat Processors' Assn., 36 LA 42, 43–44 (Wyckoff, 1961); Chrysler Corp., 22 LA 128, 138 (Wolff, 1954). Also see Arbitrator Garrett in 63 LA 98, 100.

[69]News Syndicate Co., 18 LA 55, 56 (Feinberg, 1952). Similar action by an arbitrator was upheld in Local 246, ILGWU v. Evans Mfg. Co., 53 LRRM 2455, 40 LA 864 (CA 3, 1963).

[70]Yale & Towne Mfg. Co., 39 LA 1156, 1160 (Hill, Horlacher & Seitz, 1962). Also see Arbitrator Volz in 68 LA 1314, 1318. In E & G Eng'rs., 71 LA 441, 444–445 (1978), Arbitrator Edgar A. Jones, Jr., stated that although insufficient cause had been shown "for the issuance of an arbitral order of discovery," parties in arbitration may be "subject to arbitral discovery," in that the "obligation of disclosure to a proper degree and in proper circumstances is implicit in the contractual grievance procedure." However, it seems unlikely that wide support would exist for

While the National Railroad Adjustment Board does not have the subpoena power,[71] its rules of procedures provide that the parties are charged "with the duty and responsibility of including in their original written submission all known relevant, argumentative facts and documentary evidence."[72]

Significance of Failure to Provide Evidence

The significance of a refusal or failure to provide requested data or evidence is indicated by a statement of Arbitrator Saul Wallen:

> "An arbitrator has no right to compel the production of documents [it might be otherwise if the arbitration is carried out under an arbitration statute] by either side. He may, however, give such weight as he deems appropriate to the failure of a party to produce documents on demand. The degree of weight to be attached to such failure will depend upon the relevancy of the documents requested to the issues at hand. If the information withheld appears to be strongly pertinent, the withholding of it may be vital in the making of a decision. If it is of doubtful relevancy and merely represents an attempt by one party to probe through the files of another on the mere chance that its position may be generally strengthened thereby, then the failure to produce such records should be disregarded."[73]

The failure of a party to use a person as a witness who should be in a position to contribute informed testimony may create some sort of

---

arbitral use of the full panoply of pretrial "discovery" procedures used by courts to enable a party to obtain information for use in preparing for trial (the term "discovery" as generally used in a technical sense in relation to court litigation concerns the acquisition of information in advance of trial as distinguished from requiring witnesses or documents first to be made available at the trial). For federal court rules relating to discovery, see 28 U.S.C.A., Federal Rules of Civil Procedure, Rules 26–37. Rule 26 states the following methods of obtaining discovery: "depositions upon oral examination or written questions; written interrogatories; production of documents or things or permission to enter upon land or other property, for inspection and other purposes; physical and mental examinations; and requests for admission." Rule 45 deals with use of subpoenas to command the presence of persons or the production of "books, papers, documents or tangible things" at hearings or trials, or (as concerns discovery) at the taking of depositions. For pros and cons of arbitral use of court discovery procedures, see Problems of Proof in Arbitration, 170–171, 218–227, 304, 333–334 (BNA Books, 1967); Fleming, The Labor Arbitration Process, 61–63 (U. of Ill. Press, 1965); Sembower, "Halting the Trend Toward Technicalities in Arbitration," Critical Issues in Labor Arbitration, 98, 102 (BNA Books, 1957). Also see Arbitrator Merrill in 20 LA 211, 212; Komaroff in 19 LA 385, 390. But see McFall, "Comment," Proceedings of the 31st Annual Meeting of NAA, 152, 154 (BNA Books, 1979). Urging voluntary exchange by the parties of full information prior to the hearing, see Smith, "The Search for Truth—The Whole Truth," id. at 40, 46; Zack, "Suggested New Approaches to Grievance Arbitration," Proceedings of the 30th Annual Meeting of NAA, 105, 110–111 (BNA Books, 1978). In Westinghouse Transp. Leasing Corp., 69 LA 1210, 1215 (1977), Arbitrator Stanley H. Sergent, Jr., considered that a party who has reason to believe that information which it lacks will be relevant at the hearing and is in the possession of the other party, should ask the latter to provide it prior to the hearing and should not be permitted to claim surprise if no request was made and the information is introduced into evidence at the hearing.

[71]Jones, National Railroad Adjustment Board, 25 (1941).

[72]Sec. 301.7(b), 29 C.F.R. Part 301.

[73]American Tel. & Tel. Co., 6 LA 31, 43 (1947). A Pittsburgh Tripartite Committee stated that "an arbitrator should be free to draw conclusions from an individual's failure to testify." Problems of Proof in Arbitration, 258 (BNA Books, 1967). Cf., statement of Arbitrator Kornblum, id. at 328–329; Dworkin in 21 LA 367, 371. For some instances in which a party's refusal to submit requested data or evidence created an inference against the party, see Arbitrator Jacobson in 74 LA 1107, 1110; Carter in 73 LA 623, 625; Gootnick in 70 LA 383, 387.

inference against the party or at least cause the arbitrator to wonder why the person was not called to testify.[74]

Preservation of Evidence

Parties may have an obligation to cooperate in the preservation of evidence for use in grievance processing. In this regard, Arbitrator John F. Sembower ruled that where the parties fail to agree on what pictures should be taken at the scene of accidents, the scene must be "frozen"—left undisturbed—until a neutral can decide whether pictures are justified "with due regard to securing to the company full protection of any and all trade secrets concerning materials and equipment."[75]

Interviewing Employees in Preparation for Arbitration

Of course each party ordinarily should be free to interview any person who may have information relevant to a given grievance, provided the person voluntarily cooperates in the interview and the information sought is germane and appropriate to the proper preparation of the party's case. A more difficult question concerns the right of an employer to *require* employees to cooperate in the interview.

In *Cook Paint & Varnish* the U.S. Court of Appeals held that "As part of a contractual arbitration procedure, an employer may conduct a legitimate investigatory interview in preparation for a pending arbitration," with the basic limitation that the interview "may not pry into protected union activities." Quoting with approval the views of Arbitrator Edgar A. Jones, Jr., regarding the need for prearbitration interviews, the court refused to enforce an NLRB ruling that the employer violated the NLRA when its attorney told two employees they could be disciplined if they did not answer questions relating to a discharged co-worker's grievance that was to be arbitrated. Rejecting the NLRB's apparently per se rule that an employer may never threaten an employee with discipline for refusing to cooperate in prearbitration interviews, the court said:

> "The method in which disputes are resolved through a grievance-arbitration process is a contractual matter to be determined by the parties. The Board may not construct an inflexible rule that any compulsory interview conducted in preparation for a pending arbitration violates the Act.
>
> "In so holding, we do not suggest that limits do not exist on the permissible scope of a legitimate pre-arbitration interview. An employer may in certain cases be forbidden from inquiring into matters

---

[74]See Arbitrator Gowan in 75 LA 625, 628; Schor in 74 LA 578, 580–581; LeWinter in 72 LA 102, 106–107; Gootnick in 69 LA 808, 811; Bowles in 67 LA 598, 600; Kahn in 36 LA 1177, 1184; Burris in 25 LA 32, 36. For related discussion, see subtopic entitled "Failure of Grievant to Testify," below. In Van Haaren Specialized Carriers, Inc., 247 NLRB 1185 (1980), the NLRB refused to defer to an arbitration award since the company had failed to call as a witness an official whose testimony would be crucial to the NLRA issue.

[75]Airco Alloys & Carbide, 63 LA 395, 398–399 (1974).

that are not job-related. An employer also may be prohibited from prying into union activities, or using the interview as an excuse to discover the union strategies for arbitration."[76]

Use of Adverse Witnesses

Except for one limitation, noted below, it appears accepted that the arbitrator should not limit the right of parties to call witnesses from the other side.[77]

The limitation referred to above concerns the grievant in discipline cases. There is a definite split of opinion as to whether the company should have any right to call the grievant as a witness.[78]

Question has been raised as to whether a party calls an adverse witness as its peril; opinion differs as to how strictly such party should be held bound by the testimony of an adverse witness.[79]

A related aspect is involved in the following question included in a survey of its members by the National Academy of Arbitrators:

> "The testimony is clear that there is a witness in regard to an important controverted fact but, upon your inquiry, neither party intends to call that witness. What would you do?"

Not surprisingly, the responses indicated a division of opinion on this aspect. Those members "who hold the view that it is the obligation of the parties to present the evidence and the role of the arbitrator to decide the issue upon the facts presented will take no action. Those members who believe that a full and fair hearing depends upon the

---

[76]Cook Paint & Varnish Co. v. NLRB, 106 LRRM 3016, 3023–3024 (D.C. Cir., 1981). For related discussion including the statement by Arbitrator Jones, see Chapter 7, topic entitled "Preparing Cases for Arbitration."

[77]See results of a 1981 survey by NAA noted in Chapter 7, topic entitled "Order of Presenting Case"; Problems of Proof in Arbitration, 99, 258, 324 (BNA Books, 1967). However, it has been suggested that the calling of witnesses from the other side should not be encouraged. Problems of Proof in Arbitration, 99 (BNA Books, 1967). As a matter of policy, some companies never call bargaining unit members as witnesses. Id. at 233, 328. On the other hand, a party making no effort to call a person to testify might have little standing to complain that the other party failed to use the person as a witness. F.M. Stamper Co., 51 LA 533, 537 (Eaton, 1968). In Jaeger Mach. Co., 55 LA 850, 852 (High, 1970), inferences adverse to the union's case were created when the union refused to permit its representative to testify when the employer attempted to call him as a witness.

[78]See results of a 1981 survey by NAA noted in Chapter 7, topic entitled "Order of Presenting Case"; Problems of Proof in Arbitration, 201–202, 228–229, 258, 324–325 (BNA Books, 1967). Also see panel discussion, "Procedural Problems in the Conduct of Arbitration Hearings: A Discussion," Proceedings of the 17th Annual Meeting of NAA, 27 (BNA Books, 1964). For related material, see the next subtopic, entitled "Failure of Grievant to Testify," and see Chapter 7, topic entitled "Order of Presenting Case."

[79]See panel discussion, "Procedural Problems in the Conduct of Arbitration Hearings: A Discussion," Proceedings of the 17th Annual Meeting of NAA, 28 (BNA Books, 1964). "Ordinarily, a party may not impeach its own witness through his own testimony, except where he is a hostile witness or his testimony can be shown to constitute surprise." Problems of Proof in Arbitration, 302 (BNA Books, 1967), where it is also stated that "A hostile witness is one who manifests so much hostility or prejudice under examination that the party who has called him is allowed to cross-examine him, i.e., to treat him as though he had been called by the opposite party." In A-T-O Inc., 72 LA 408, 410 (1979), Arbitrator Joseph Shister refused to permit the union to impugn the credibility of a company official it had called as a witness. On the other hand, the testimony of an employer's official who testified pursuant to subpoena was "especially persuasive" upon an arbitrator where it supported the union's case. Hempstead Pub. Schools Bd. of Educ., 69 LA 808, 809, 811 (Gootnick, 1977).

presentation of all evidence will take some action ranging from calling the witness to discussing the matter with the parties."[80]

Failure of Grievant to Testify

The individual grievant is often able to cast light upon the dispute and ordinarily takes the witness stand. Indeed, the arbitrator prefers that he do so, as explained by Arbitrator Russell A. Smith: "* * * I would like to see the grievant on the stand at some point during the proceeding, and I feel a little uncomfortable, frankly, when he is not. I don't know how many other people share that feeling."[81]

It is not unexpected that the failure of a grievant to appear and testify at the hearing of his grievance has in some cases been one of the factors leading to the arbitrator's conclusion that the grievance lacked merit.[82] However, arbitrators sometimes have expressly stated that the failure of a grievant to testify creates no inference against him;[83] even so, an arbitrator may pointedly note that the grievant's failure to testify has left the case against him unrefuted.[84] The latter situation assumes, of course, that the company has adequately established its case by probative evidence.[85]

In most cases a grievant's testimony will be beneficial to his case. It has sometimes happened, however, that "the chief witness against

---

[80]"Procedural Problems During Hearings," The Chronicle (NAA, Apr. 1981), where the following details are reported:
"Eighty-one members would not take any action whatsoever; another six would do nothing unless there was a due process question or problem, and another six members would call the witness only if it appeared that the case would turn on this testimony. Twenty members would call the witness on their own motion. Another 24 members might call the witness depending on the circumstances; that is, they would determine if there is a valid reason why the party does not wish to call the witness. The remaining members would take a variety of actions such as discussing the matter with the parties and urging that the witness be called or warning the parties that the testimony is crucial and noting what inference could be drawn by the failure of the witness to testify. However, these members would leave to the party the final decision as to whether the witness should be called."

[81]This statement was made in a National Academy of Arbitrators' discussion; a poll was taken in response to Arbitrator Smith's statement, revealing that a "very large majority" of those present shared his feeling. Problems of Proof in Arbitration, 232 (BNA Books, 1967). For later discussion of this matter by Arbitrator Smith, see Smith, "The Search for Truth—The Whole Truth," Proceedings of the 31st Annual Meeting of NAA, 40, 54–56 (BNA Books, 1979), where he still expressed the belief that "grievant ought to give his version," but where he also acknowledged that "the notion that an employee ought not to have to testify when a disciplinary penalty assessed against him is being reviewed has some appeal."

[82]See Arbitrator Hall in 60 LA 506, 508; Carmichael in 52 LA 469, 473; Teple in 51 LA 177, 181; Hardy in 48 LA 1036; 1038 (grievant was present but did not testify); Turkus in 41 LA 575, 576 (but Turkus viewed the grievant's silence differently in 45 LA 1050, 1051–1052, since criminal charges were still pending against the grievant); Maggs in 22 LA 761, 764; Klamon in 16 LA 461, 465–466. Also see Grabb in 72 LA 949, 950–951; Cole in 23 LA 64, 65.

[83]See Arbitrator McIntosh in 50 LA 504, 506; Kesselman in 49 LA 692, 696; Altieri in 43 LA 400, 405; Foster in 40 LA 1311, 1313. It has been noted that there may be innocent explanations of failure to testify, as where the individual is "inarticulate, unintelligent, or easily confused." Problems of Proof in Arbitration, 201 (BNA Books, 1967). Also see Arbitrator Vause in 74 LA 806, 809. Parties sometimes stipulate that the nonappearance of the grievant shall not be prejudicial to his interests. As in U.S. Rubber Co., 25 LA 417, 418 (Hall, 1955).

[84]See Arbitrator McIntosh in 50 LA 504, 506; Kesselman in 49 LA 692, 696; McCoy in 26 LA 742, 745–746. In Pepsi Cola Bottling Co., 70 LA 434, 435 (Blackmar, 1978), the grievant *did* testify regarding a transaction between himself and his supervisor, but the supervisor did not testify, so it was deemed "proper to conclude that he would not dispute the grievant's testimony" concerning the transaction. Similarly, see Arbitrator Shanker in 68 LA 13, 15.

[85]See Phillips Painting Contractors, 72 LA 16, 20 (Brisco, 1978).

the grievant was the grievant."[86] Futhermore, if the grievant does take the witness stand, he has an "obligation to testify frankly and fully."[87]

A question thus arises whether an employee may refuse to testify in arbitration by the exercise of a privilege against self-incrimination. One survey has indicated that "there is a fairly clear consensus in the arbitration opinions" that the privilege against self-incrimination, "established in the criminal law, has no place, at least as such, in the arbitration of grievance cases (invariably discharge or disciplinary cases)."[88] However, Arbitrator Nathan P. Feinsinger spoke in that survey as follows: "My evaluation of a discharged employee's not testifying has depended on the circumstances. * * * I don't think one can generalize here." Arbitrator R.W. Fleming proposed a set of rules whose effect would appear to give at least minimal application in arbitration to the privilege against self-incrimination.[89] Furthermore, Arbitrator Edgar A. Jones urged that arbitrators should give consideration to all Fifth Amendment principles, including the privilege against self-incrimination.[90] Arbitrator Jones' view was severely criticized, however, by Professor Harry T. Edwards.[91]

It should be noted that employee discipline for "refusal to cooperate" has been upheld in some court and arbitration cases, even though the employee based his position on privilege against self-incrimination.[92] This was so, for instance, where an arbitrator upheld the discharge of an employee for refusal to be fingerprinted in connection with an investigation into the theft of company products.[93]

---

[86]Diebold, Inc., 48 LA 893, 900 (Bradley, 1967). To similar effect, Capitol Mfg. Co., 46 LA 633, 636 (Gibson, 1966).

[87]Clark Grave Vault Co., 47 LA 381, 382 (McCoy, 1966). Also see Arbitrator MacDonald in 72 LA 391, 403–404.

[88]Wirtz, "Due Process of Arbitration," Proceedings of the 11th Annual Meeting of NAA, 1, 19–20 (BNA Books, 1958), where several unreported arbitration decisions are noted. Also see comments of Arbitrator McGury in 44 LA 658, 662–663; Maggs in 27 LA 709, 712–713; Klamon in 16 LA 461, 465–466.

[89]Fleming, The Labor Arbitration Process, 185–186 (U. of Ill. Press, 1965). Arbitrator Fleming discussed the constitutional privilege against self-incrimination in some detail. Id. at 181–185. Discussing the Fleming proposal, see Carlson & Phillips, "Due Process Considerations in Grievance Arbitration Proceedings," 2 Hast. Const. L.Q. 519, 538–541 (1975).

[90]See Thrifty Drug Stores Co., 50 LA 1253, 1260–1263 (Jones, 1968); Problems of Proof in Arbitration, 199–200 (BNA Books, 1967). In the circumstances of one case Arbitrator Turkus gave strong recognition to the privilege against self-incrimination. United Parcel Serv., 45 LA 1050, 1051–1052 (1965). In Phillips Painting Contractors, 72 LA 16, 19–20 (1978), Arbitrator C. Chester Brisco pointed out that California statutes make the privilege against self-incrimination applicable in arbitration proceedings, but that the privilege had not been properly invoked as concerned a question which posed "no real or substantial danger of incrimination."

[91]Edwards, "Due Process Considerations in Labor Arbitration," 25 Arb. J. 141, 151, 154–155, 157, 165 (1970). The Jones view is said to be "unrealistic in terms of providing a reasonable guide for harmonious collective bargaining between the parties." Id. at 154. The "standard of 'fairness,' which has traditionally been employed by arbitrators as the more flexible replacement for due process, seems far better suited to the composite needs of all of the parties to the tripartite collective bargaining relationship." Id. at 169. For other discussions relating to arbitral application of constitutional concepts, see Getman, "What Price Employment? Arbitration, the Constitution, and Personal Freedom," Proceedings of the 29th Annual Meeting of NAA, 61 (BNA Books, 1976); Dunsford, "Comment," id. at 71; Jones, "Comment," id. at 85. Also see statement of Arbitrator Marlatt in 73 LA 878, 881; Maslanka in 72 LA 968, 971.

[92]See Fleming, The Labor Arbitration Process, 182–184 (U. of Ill. Press, 1965).

[93]Colgate-Palmolive Co., 50 LA 441, 443–444 (Koven, 1968). In Exact Weight Scale Co., 50 LA 8, 8–9 (1967), Arbitrator Whitley P. McCoy held that an employee could not be discharged for

The Lie Detector

Under the overwhelming weight of arbitral authority employees are not to be penalized for refusal to take lie detector tests; and where an employee does submit to lie detector testing, the test results should be given little or no weight in arbitration.[94] Indeed, in his exhaustive examination and discussion of the polygraph, its degree of reliability, and court and arbitration decisions regarding its use, Arbitrator Edgar A. Jones, Jr., declared that "the conclusion is compelling that no matter how well qualified educationally and experientially may be the polygraphist, the results of the lie-detector tests should routinely be ruled inadmissible."[95]

Emphasizing the reluctance of arbitrators to rely upon lie detectors, certain specific cases may be noted. Thus, an employee may not be

refusing to say whether or not he had violated a company rule, but that back pay should be denied since the employee could have mitigated damages by answering promptly (he had finally answered "no," but not until the arbitration hearing). In Trans World Airlines, 46 LA 611, 612 (Wallen, 1965), the company was held entitled to require a hostess to demonstrate that she was not wearing a wig in connection with enforcement of regulations as to length of hair. Another arbitrator upheld a broadcasting company's right to require members of its news staff to fill out a financial interests questionnaire (to prevent conflict of interest problems) against the charge that the requirement subjected the employee to self-incrimination. National Broadcasting Co., 53 LA 312, 318–319 (Scheiber, 1969). Also see Arbitrator Johnson in 56 LA 52, 53–54. For cases involving self-incrimination arguments in connection with use of blood tests in determining sobriety, see Arbitrator Newmark in 72 LA 198, 205 (private employer would not be violating employee's constitutional rights in requiring sobriety test); Ellmann in 69 LA 811, 815 ("profound issues of constitutional law" would be raised in requiring public authority employees to submit to sobriety test); Simon in 68 LA 421, 426. An employer's refusal *to give* a blood test requested by an employee left inadequate proof of intoxication, so reinstatement was ordered in Continental Conveyor & Equip. Co., 69 LA 1143, 1149 (Tucker, 1977).

[94]See Arbitrator Weizenbaum in 79 LA 977, 986; Dolnick in 77 LA 380, 383–385, and in 75 LA 331, 336–337; Hon in 76 LA 857, 862–865; Rimer in 75 LA 233, 237; Fish in 71 LA 1202, 1204; Pinkus in 70 LA 909, 912; Kramer in 70 LA 869, 873–875 (describing how the polygraph purports to work); Seward in 68 LA 581, 582–583 (stating that the "courts have generally—indeed, almost universally—rejected polygraphic evidence unless offered with the consent of all parties concerned," and concluding that "wisdom suggests that the Impartial Umpire's office should follow this judicial approach"); Murphy in 59 LA 283, 286–290 (stating that "until the accuracy of the state of the polygraph art is generally recognized by substantial scientific, judicial and arbitral authority, and the criteria for evaluating the polygraph technique is fully available at the arbitration hearing, * * * the arbitrator should move with great caution in this area"); Gross in 46 LA 756, 761; Epstein in 45 LA 1155, 1158; Eiger in 66-1 ARB ¶8359; Carmichael in 66-1 ARB ¶8310; Kornblum in 44 LA 709, 710–711; Sembower in 44 LA 405, 409; Rice in 44 LA 16, 18–19; Miller in 63-1 ARB ¶8179; Kelliher in 63-1 ARB ¶8106; Walter in 41 LA 442 at 442; Ryder in 39 LA 470, 479; Lewis in 39 LA 332, 335; Duncan in 39 LA 125, 127; Simkin in 33 LA 44, 48. But see discussion by Arbitrator Charles V. Laughlin in Bowman Transp., 61 LA 549, 551–556 (1973), sustaining the employer's action in disciplining an employee for refusal to take a lie detector test.

[95]Jones, " 'Truth' When the Polygraph Operator Sits as Arbitrator (or Judge): The Deception of 'Detection' in the 'Diagnosis of Truth and Deception,' " Proceedings of the 31st Annual Meeting of NAA, 75, 151 (BNA Books, 1979), where he also stated that in fact, with "relatively rare exceptions," arbitrators and courts do continue "to reject polygraph proof." Arbitrator Jones did note that in addition to gaining acceptability with some courts and several arbitrators, the polygraph had done so with some law-review commentators and "perhaps" with the NLRB. Id. at 90–92. In Bunker Ramo Corp., 76 LA 857, 862 (1981), Arbitrator Ralph C. Hon stated concerning the polygraph that by virtue of Arbitrator Jones' article and the 1977 report to the President and Congress by the Privacy Protection Study Commission, "there is now a much wider recognition of its serious deficiencies." Among other arbitrators stating reasons for questioning the use of the polygraph and for doubting the reliability of its results, see Arbitrator Seward in 68 LA 581, 582; Murphy in 59 LA 283, 286–290; Ryder in 36 LA 552, 558. Regarding the NLRA, there are cases holding that under the circumstances that existed, the employer did not violate the Act by disciplining employees for refusal to take polygraph tests. Shoppers Drug Mart, 226 NLRB 901, 906 (1976); American Oil Co., 76 LRRM 1506 (NLRB, 1971). In Medicenter, Mid-South Hosp., 90 LRRM 1576 (NLRB, 1975), an NLRB panel majority adopted without comment the Administrative Law Judge's finding that polygraph testing is a mandatory subject of bargaining.

bound by his employment application promise to submit to lie detector tests.[96] Even where an accused employee agrees to take a lie detector test and does so, an arbitrator will prefer to rely upon other types of evidence, though the test results may be noted as to their corroborating effect.[97] Efforts to strengthen the testimony of other persons against an employee, by causing the accuser to take a lie detector test, have not impressed arbitrators.[98]

Right of Cross-Examination

Arbitrators uphold the right of cross-examination, but probably not as strongly as do courts of law. An arbitrator ordinarily will not accept an offer of evidence if it is conditioned upon nondisclosure to the other party. Thus, for instance, disciplinary action based solely on the charge of an employee whose identity the employer was unwilling to reveal was set aside by Arbitrator David A. Wolff, who stated that no matter how meritorious the reasons for nondisclosure may be, it results in a lack of competent proof.[99] Like reasoning applies to employer reliance on allegedly confidential records not available as proof,[100] and to an employee's defense assertions supported by evidence which the union is unwilling to disclose.[101]

In certain limited situations, however, nondisclosure has not resulted in rejection of evidence. For example, Arbitrator George H. Hildebrand accepted reports of professional "spotters," although the bus driver against whom the reports were used was not permitted to

---

[96]Lag Drug Co., 39 LA 1121, 1122–1123 (Kelliher, 1962). Accord, Arbitrator Dolnick in 77 LA 380, 383–385. But an employer was held entitled to require plant guards to take lie detector tests under their agreement in Warwick Elecs., 46 LA 95, 97–98 (Daugherty, 1966). Similarly, see Grocers Supply Co., 75 LA 27, 29 (Williams, 1980), noting, however, that the "eventual use of the test results, and whether or not they would be admissible in an arbitration hearing, are not involved in the present grievance." In Meat Cutters v. Neuhoff Bros. Packers, 83 LRRM 2652 (CA 5, 1973), an arbitrator's refusal to consider the results of polygraph tests was upheld even though the collective agreement reserved to the employer the right to require polygraph tests of any employee suspected of theft, the court pointing out that the agreement did not mention use of the test results in arbitration proceedings.

[97]See Owens-Corning Fiberglas Corp., 48 LA 1089, 1091 (Doyle, 1967), where the test corroborated other evidence of innocence; Westinghouse Elec. Corp., 43 LA 450, 452–453 (Singletary, 1964), where the test corroborated other evidence of guilt. Also see Arbitrator Brown in 75 LA 293, 294; Moore in 72 LA 490, 495; High in 70 LA 100, 103; Laughlin in 65 LA 1157, 1162. In Trans-City Terminal Warehouse, 77 LA 11, 14 (Seidman, 1981), the arbitrator enforced the employer's promise to reinstate the grievant and make him whole if he passed a polygraph test.

[98]See Arbitrator Curry in 73 LA 1148, 1152; Powell in 70 LA 146, 149; Walter in 41 LA 442 at 442; Maxwell in 39 LA 883, 885; Porter in 39 LA 745, 746–747.

[99]Murray Corp. of Am., 8 LA 713, 714 (1947). To similar effect, Arbitrator Burwell in 69 LA 589, 592; Glushien in 59 LA 879, 881; Forsythe in 53 LA 511, 513; Haughton in 52 LA 832, 834; Doyle in 48 LA 1089, 1091 (involving anonymous tip); Koven in 42 LA 803, 805; Kates in 36 LA 857, 859; Scheiber in 24 LA 538, 540–541; Bowles in 22 LA 320, 323; Aaron in 13 LA 433, 434. Also see discussion of "absentee evidence" in Wirtz, "Due Process of Arbitration," Proceedings of the 11th Annual Meeting of NAA, 1, 16–17 (BNA Books, 1958). Where he did confront grievant at the arbitration hearing, failure to identify the accuser at the grievance meeting was held not to be improper. Cleaners Hangers Co., 39 LA 661, 664, 667 (Klein, 1962). To similar effect, Arbitrator Jones in 61 LA 886, 889–890; Sembower in 55 LA 731; 735–737, and in 53 LA 841, 844. Also see Johnston in 75 LA 716, 720.

[100]Problems of Proof in Arbitration, 204 (BNA Books, 1967), view of West Coast Tripartite Committee.

[101]Berg Airlectro Prods. Co., 46 LA 668, 672, 675–676 (Sembower, 1966).

confront the spotters or otherwise know their identity, considering that (1) control over bus drivers is essential for the safety of the public and protection of company property, and the spotter system provides the only practical means by which supervision can exert its responsibility in the transit industry; (2) open identification of the spotters would destroy the effectiveness of the system; (3) the spotters, unlike ordinary employees, were trained observers taught to be accurate and objective, having no personal contacts with the employees and having no incentive to falsify facts; (4) the spotters' reports were prepared before the decision to discharge was made; and (5) there was no tangible basis for believing that the company was biased against the grievant.[102]

Arbitrator Hildebrand added a very important qualification, however: "the necessity for the system would not justify its sloppy or unfair use in disciplinary procedure."[103] Thus, even where spotters were identified and testified, Arbitrator Frank Elkouri could not place strong weight on their testimony or written reports since the testimony was shaky and the reports had not been written up promptly.[104]

Some arbitrators are unreceptive to suggestions that the arbitrator interview spotters or other accusers in private,[105] and one arbitrator insists that the spotter be produced, if he is to be relied upon, "even though the consequence would be to destroy his usefulness to the company."[106]

---

[102]Los Angeles Transit Lines, 25 LA 740, 744–746 (1955). In general accord are the views of Arbitrator Brecht in 23 LA 362, 365. Also see Levinson in 37 LA 748, 750, 754; Oppenheim in 29 LA 291, 292; Seward in 19 LA 210, 211. In Muskegon County Bd. of Comm'rs., 71 LA 942, 948 (1978), the discharge of grievant based upon complaints received by grievant's fellow staff employees from many clients of the county employer's drug rehabilitation program was sustained by Arbitrator A. Dale Allen, Jr., despite the hearsay and essentially anonymous character of the evidence, where (1) there was no animosity between grievant and his fellow employees, and (2) federal HEW regulations prevented disclosure of identity of the clients without their written consent. Believing the employer justified in not seeking consent for disclosure of identity because to do so could undermine the entire program, Arbitrator Allen stated that "when one hears such complaints fed to several counsellors by many clients at different times and under different circumstances, it is logical to assume that there is substance in the accusations, and it is not the result of a mass conspiracy against an employee singled out for some unapparent reason." In Wayne County Juvenile Court, 68 LA 369, 370–371 (Forsythe, 1977), involving discharge of employees for alleged abusive treatment of children in custody, a child protection statute preserved the anonymity of persons reporting child abuse; the reports of such persons were admitted into evidence "to comply with the intent of" the statute.

[103]Los Angeles Transit Lines, 25 LA 740, 745 (1955). Arbitrator Levinson adds still another qualification: "in assessing the degree of discipline," the sworn denial of the accused should be given "the benefit of the doubt" as against the written report of the undisclosed spotter. Twin City Rapid Transit Co., 37 LA 748, 754 (1961).

[104]Twin City Transit, 65-2 ARB ¶8438 (1965). Where the grievant is confronted with the spotter at the arbitration hearing, the spotter's testimony and report will be accepted into evidence. See Arbitrator Nathanson in 51 LA 120, 126; Scheiber in 48 LA 812, 816 (also holding that delayed confrontation of accused by spotter is not improper, since premature confrontations impair future usefulness of spotter).

[105]Discussion Panel, "Procedural Problems in the Conduct of Arbitration Hearings: A Discussion," Proceedings of the 17th Annual Meeting of NAA, 21 (BNA Books, 1964).

[106]Id. at 19. In one case a spotter was placed behind a screen where he was visible only to the arbitrator and counsel for the parties. Fleming, "Due Process and Fair Procedure in Labor Arbitration," Proceedings of the 14th Annual Meeting of NAA, 69, 85 (BNA Books, 1961); Fleming also discussed confrontation cases in general (pp. 82–87). Sometimes the collective agreement itself will indicate the extent to which testimony or proof by professional investigators may be used and the extent to which it must be subjected to cross-examination, as in Bee Line, 20 LA 675, 676 (Feinberg, 1953).

Even where an accuser's identity is known to the grievant, if the accuser does not appear at the hearing to testify and be subject to cross-examination it is still likely that the accuser's statement will be given reduced weight or will not be admitted into evidence at all.[107] For example, a statement signed by numerous employees making certain assertions as to fact in a disciplinary case was admitted into evidence, over strenuous objections of the company, but could be given "very little weight" since most of the signers did not testify and were not subject to cross-examination.[108] However, the mere fact that a party presented its nondisciplinary case by written statements and exhibits, rather than through use of witnesses subject to cross-examination, was held not to deprive the opponent of a fair hearing where adequate opportunity to respond to the evidence did exist.[109]

The admission of hearsay evidence denies the opposing party opportunity for complete cross-examination. Courts of law ordinarily refuse hearsay testimony for this reason. While arbitrators admit hearsay evidence, they seek to offset the effects of incomplete cross-examination by admitting it only "for what it is worth."[110]

Since the arbitrator has a paramount interest in securing all of the facts, he may refuse to restrict cross-examination to matters brought out in the examination-in-chief, and he can be expected not to place strict limitation upon the number of re-cross or re-direct examinations. As to the first of these points, arbitral consensus appears to be that reasonably wide latitude should be permitted in cross-examination.[111] It has been suggested, however, that the cross-examiner who seeks to go beyond the direct examination area should call the witness as an adverse or hostile witness.[112]

While the parties are allowed considerable latitude in cross-examining witnesses, to reveal conflicts in their testimony and to challenge credibility, arbitrators will not condone use of personal invectives against witnesses.[113]

---

[107]See Arbitrator Johannes in 75 LA 597, 602; Keenan in 75 LA 155, 167; Curry in 73 LA 1148, 1155; Elson in 72 LA 780, 783; Roumell in 70 LA 614, 618; Bowles in 69 LA 351, 354; Seward in 68 LA 581, 584; Buckwalter in 50 LA 177, 180; Block in 46 LA 154, 161. Cf., Marlatt in 77 LA 721, 722–723; Penfield in 75 LA 592, 596.

[108]Rich Mfg. Co., 46 LA 154, 161 (Block, 1966). Customer accusations of employee disrespect carried less significance where the customers, though identified, were absent from the arbitration hearing. Penn Jersey Boiler & Constr. Co., 50 LA 177, 180 (Buckwalter, 1967).

[109]Sewanee Silica Co., 47 LA 282, 283 (Greene, 1966), involving change in job classification.

[110]See this Chapter, topic entitled "Hearsay Evidence."

[111]Problems of Proof in Arbitration, 102, 147, 259, 301 (BNA Books, 1967). Apart from confining the subject matter of cross-examination within proper limits, a related concern is unduly protracted cross-examination. In both respects, the fact that latitude often is permitted carries a concomitant responsibility of self-restraint by the parties. In this regard, it has been urged that "[s]ince there is relatively little that an arbitrator can actually do to curtail wastefully protracted cross-examination, training advocates in that area would produce better presentations of evidence and shorter hearings." Friedman, "Problems of Cross-Examination in Labor Arbitration," 34 Arb. J. No. 4, pp. 6, 11 (1979), adding that "if nothing else, nonlawyer advocates particularly could profit by reading a book like Francis Wellman's The Art of Cross-Examination."

[112]Discussion Panel, "Procedural Problems in the Conduct of Arbitration Hearings: A Discussion," Proceedings of the 17th Annual Meeting of NAA, 1, 9 (BNA Books, 1964).

[113]See Friden Calculating Mach. Co., 27 LA 496, 500–501 (Justin, 1956).

Evidence Submitted After Hearing

While ordinarily no new data or evidence may be presented after the hearing, in briefs or otherwise, there are exceptions.[114] Sometimes discussion at the hearing indicates need for additional data which are not quickly available, and if the parties desire not to recess or otherwise delay the hearing, they may agree to the submission of the data to the arbitrator after the hearing has been completed. Likewise, the arbitrator during or after the hearing has been completed may request posthearing data or information.[115]

Then, too, important evidence sometimes is discovered or first becomes available after the hearing.[116]

Such posthearing data often will be jointly prepared and submitted by the parties. If the data are individually prepared each party ordinarily must be furnished a copy of the other party's data so that comment may be made thereon or so that a further hearing can be requested in case of gross discrepancies.[117]

Weight and Credibility of Evidence

It is within the province of the arbitrator to determine the weight, relevancy, and authenticity of evidence. The general approach of arbitrators in giving weight and credibility to evidence is effectively illustrated by a statement made by Arbitrator George Cheney in reviewing the discharge of an employee. He noted that the case was illustrative of the type of situation in which the facts are to a large extent determined by the weight and credibility accorded to the testimony of the witnesses and to the documentary evidence offered by the parties. He pointed out that, in arriving at the truth in such a case, an arbitrator must consider whether conflicting statements ring true or false; that he will note the witnesses' demeanor while on the stand; and that he will credit or discredit testimony according to his impressions of the witnesses' veracity. Arbitrator Cheney also pointed out that, in determining where the preponderance of the evidence lies with respect to any material point, the arbitrator will take into consideration whether the witness speaks from first-hand information or whether his testimony is largely based on hearsay or gossip. In summarizing, Arbitrator Cheney stated that the duty of the arbitrator is simply to determine the truth respecting material matters in contro-

---

[114]See Chapter 7, topics entitled "Briefs" and "Reopening the Hearing."

[115]For instance, after receiving posthearing briefs, Arbitrator Russell A. Smith requested additional data in McInerney Spring & Wire Co., 20 LA 642, 643 (1953). In City of Renton, 71 LA 271, 272 (1978), Arbitrator Carlton J. Snow during the hearing requested that additional data be submitted after the hearing.

[116]See discussion in Chapter 7, topic entitled "Reopening the Hearing." Also see discussion by Hill & Sinicropi, Evidence in Arbitration, 114–115, 117–120 (BNA Books, 1980).

[117]See Northeast Airlines, 37 LA 741, 743 (Wolff, 1961); McInerney Spring & Wire Co., 20 LA 642, 643 (Smith, 1953); Simkin, Acceptability as a Factor in Arbitration Under an Existing Agreement, 59–60 (U. of Pa. Press, 1952); Updegraff & McCoy, Arbitration of Labor Disputes, 103 (1946). For related considerations, see this Chapter, topic entitled "Right of Cross-Examination."

versy, as he believes it to be, based upon a full and fair consideration of the entire evidence and after he has accorded each witness and each piece of documentary evidence, the weight, if any, to which he honestly believes it to be entitled.[118]

Arbitrator Clair V. Duff, in turn, has offered some considerations relevant in evaluating testimony:

"Any attempt to sort credible testimony from that which is not worthy of belief is very difficult for at least four basic reasons. They may be briefly stated:

"INTEREST. While having an interest or stake in the outcome does not disqualify a witness, it renders his testimony subject to most careful scrutiny. * * * Few witnesses will deliberately falsify but there is a common tendency to 'put your best foot forward.' This tendency, either consciously or subconsciously, leads many witnesses to remember and express testimony in a way favorable to the result which they hope the Hearing will produce.

"PERCEPTION. Frequently the initial observation is faulty or incomplete because the observer has no prior knowledge that a dispute will develop concerning what he has seen or heard and his casual sensory impression is not sharp and keen.

"MEMORY. The remembrance of an event weeks or months after it occurred is frequently dim and inaccurate and a witness may be confused as to facts which initially he correctly perceived. By lapse of time precise details may elude his memory.

"COMMUNICATION. The manner in which a witness expresses what he saw and heard may fail to communicate exactly his initial perception of the occurrence, so that after listening to the testimony and the cross-examination of the witnesses, the fact-finder may not have had transmitted to him a completely accurate impression of the facts, even though they were initially observed carefully and well remembered by the witness."[119]

Arbitrator Joseph Rosenfarb cautioned that while "both sides might be subject to the unconscious influences of self-interest, personal predilection or antipathy," it is the duty of the arbitrator "to examine the testimony of each witness on its own merits"—Arbitrator Rosenfarb considered that union members are not necessarily prejudiced witnesses any more than are supervisors.[120] Arbitrator Samuel Krimsly cautioned that if grievant's testimony "is colored by bias,"

---

[118]Andrew Williams Meat Co., 8 LA 518, 519 (1947). Also see Arbitrator Klein in 68 LA 792, 795; Sabo in 68 LA 391, 395; Gorsuch in 40 LA 45, 55; Coffey in 28 LA 710, 715. "Demeanor and the spirit of responses are factors in credibility. Reliability or unreliability never lies wholly in the *words* said." Karnish Instruments, 45 LA 545, 548 (Bender, 1965). "Demeanor" was a significant factor in the thinking of Arbitrator Robertson in 73 LA 316, 323; Brooks in 72 LA 351, 354; Jedel in 69 LA 707, 712. But see Sisk in 73 LA 915, 917; Sherman in 68 LA 1279, 1281 ("there are suspicious looking, nervous witnesses who are clearly telling the truth and just as surely there are out-and-out liars who can look you in the eye and tell a most convincing story"); Jaffee in 68 LA 1232, 1235 (stating the belief that "the 'attitude and demeanor' of witnesses is almost always a shaky foundation on which to rest conclusions").

[119]South Penn Oil Co., 29 LA 718, 720 (1957). Also see discussion by Arbitrator Edgar Jones in 28 LA 198, 204–205. Applying Arbitrator Duff's criteria, see Arbitrator Darrow in 72 LA 206, 209. In Mark VII Sales, 75 LA 1062, 1066 (1980), Arbitrator Richard P. O'Connell utilized a "check list of factors" offered by California statute for consideration in evaluating testimony.

[120]Poloron Prods. of Pa., 23 LA 789, 793 (1955).

employees used as company witnesses also may have "a bias by reason of their employment."[121]

Widely differing versions of the facts are too frequently presented by the parties. Where the testimony is highly contradictory it ordinarily "becomes incumbent upon the Arbitrator to sift and evaluate the testimony to the best of his ability, and reach the best conclusion he can as to the actual fact situation."[122] However, sometimes "It is unnecessary to resolve the substantial conflict in the evidence to obtain an unobstructed view of the scene. By piecing together the parts, the broad outlines of the whole picture emerges."[123] Arbitrator Sidney L. Cahn observed that, in discipline cases, the truth often "lies somewhere between" the widely conflicting versions of the facts.[124]

In any event, as Arbitrator R.W. Fleming aptly observed:

> "Arbitrators are not equipped with any special divining rod which enables them to know who is telling the truth and who is not where a conflict in testimony develops. They can only do what the courts have done in similar circumstances for centuries. A judgment must finally be made, and there is a possibility that that judgment when made is wrong."[125]

It seems clear that inconsistencies in the testimony of any witness will ordinarily detract much from the testimony's credibility.[126]

Finally, it is recognized that testimony often may conflict even where all witnesses have testified honestly and in good faith.[127] Thus,

---

[121]Billingsley, Inc., 48 LA 802, 807 (1967), where he added, however, that "nothing in either of these relationships to a matter in arbitration can be taken to mean there is any presumption any witness will lie."

[122]Texas Elec. Steel Casting Co., 28 LA 757, 758 (Abernethy, 1957). Also see Arbitrator Kates in 71 LA 1082, 1083; Kaufman in 69 LA 776, 778–779; Manson in 69 LA 737, 739; Williams in 49 LA 210, 212; Klein in 46 LA 974, 977; Wood in 46 LA 75, 80; Morvant in 41 LA 1327, 1329–1330 (stating that it was his "job to unravel this maze of contradictions and extract the core of truth"). Sometimes the burden-of-proof concept becomes of critical significance when severe conflict exists in the evidence, as in TRW, Inc., 69 LA 214, 216–217 (Burris, 1977).

[123]Sampsel Time Control, 18 LA 453, 456 (Gilden, 1951). In Borg-Warner Corp., 47 LA 903, 906 (1966), Arbitrator Larkin suggested that "Where the testimony of two witnesses is directly opposite, the Arbitrator must consider the surrounding circumstances to determine which story can be corroborated."

[124]Republic Aviation Corp., 17 LA 577, 579 (1951).

[125]General Cable Co., 28 LA 97, 99 (1957). Also see Arbitrator Forrester in 72 LA 761, 764–765. In Overly-Hautz Co., 51 LA 518, 524 (1968), Arbitrator Jerome A. Klein declared: "Considering the incredibly conflicting nature of the testimony, one might feel that the parties might have decided to use a ouija board rather than an arbitrator to resolve their impasse."

[126]See Arbitrator Randall in 71 LA 1247, 1252, stating that inconsistencies in the grievant's testimony "make it highly suspect"; Tsukiyama in 43 LA 1218, 1225; Gorder in 2 LA 633, 635–636. But this is not always so. In Tampa Elec. Co., 73 LA 98, 102–103 (1979), Arbitrator J. Thomas Rimer, Jr., stated that much of the evidence centered "on the credibility of the grievant's explanation that he was suddenly confronted with a snake in the cab of the vehicle just before the accident," and that the company regarded the discrepancies, contradictions, and inconsistencies in the grievant's testimony to be " 'tainted with deception' to exonerate the grievant from the charge made against him." Arbitrator Rimer then stated:
"We find them to reflect little more than the bewilderment and panic brought about by the sight of the snake. Rational behavior and precise recall of detail cannot be reasonably expected in these circumstances under repeated interrogations. It is one thing to find a degree of inconsistency by questioning in hindsight; it is something else to have experienced an incident such as this and retain a clear and logical recollection of what and why one did as he did. Truth is often obscured by the distraction of inconsistency."

[127]In Covington Furniture Mfg. Corp., 75 LA 455, 459 (Holley, 1980), Arbitrator Richard Mittenthal was quoted as follows:
"Experience has taught (Arbitrators) that, in this kind of situation, neither (witness)

arbitrators sometimes have explained that in resolving conflicts in testimony, "we do not mean to cast the slightest doubt on the veracity or good faith of any witness appearing before us."[128]

Special Considerations in Discipline Cases

Special considerations are involved in weighing testimony in discharge and discipline cases. Thus, Umpire Harry Shulman recognized that an accused employee has an incentive for denying the charge against him, in that he stands immediately to gain or lose in the case, and that normally there is no reason to suppose that a plant protection man, for example, would unjustifiably pick one employee out of hundreds and accuse him of an offense, although in particular cases the plant protection man may be mistaken or in some cases even malicious. Umpire Shulman declared that, if there is no evidence of ill will toward the accused on the part of the accuser and if there are no circumstances upon which to base a conclusion that the accuser is mistaken, the conclusion that the charge is true can hardly be deemed improper.[129]

Similarly, the testimony of a foreman was accepted over that of the employee whom he accused where the foreman had many years of satisfactory service as against seven months' service by the accused and the foreman had never discharged an employee before.[130] Obviously, however, the testimony of the accuser will be subject to

---

may be consciously lying. When two people are involved in a highly emotional confrontation, their recollection of the facts is far from reliable. Each tends to repress whatever wrong he'd done. Each quickly recasts the event in a light most favorable to himself. As time passes, the distorted view of the event slowly hardens. By the time the arbitration hearing is held, each (person) is absolutely certain that his account of what happened is true. Perhaps neither (person) is then telling a deliberate untruth. Their own self-interest and self-image operate to limit their capacity for reporting the truth."

An NAA panel report expressed the opinion that "the principal reason for testimonial conflicts is not the result of a reluctance to tell the truth, but is caused by marked differences in the capacity of individuals to *observe, hear, recollect,* and *communicate* external reality." "Decisional Thinking—West Coast Panel Report," Proceedings of the 33rd Annual Meeting of NAA, 119, 121 (BNA Books, 1981). Discussing factors that affect communication in testifying, see Fraser, "The Role of Language in Arbitration," id. at 19, 23–41.

[128]Coordinating Committee Steel Companies, 70 LA 442, 454 (Aaron, Garrett & Seward, 1978). Similarly, see Arbitrator Manson in 69 LA 737, 739 (although classifying it as a "You did—I didn't" case, he concluded that "from their demeanor" the witnesses "spoke the truth as they saw it"); Mansfield in 68 LA 565, 569. On the other hand, an arbitrator sometimes will conclude that one witness or another necessarily testified untruthfully, as in Stansteel Corp., 69 LA 776, 779 (Kaufman, 1977).

[129]Ford Motor Co., 1 ALAA ¶67,274, p. 67,620 (1954). In general accord, Arbitrator Roumell in 75 LA 83, 90; Rothschild in 75 LA 32, 35; Spencer in 74 LA 25, 27; Leeper in 72 LA 960, 965; Vadakin in 72 LA 784, 786; Roberts in 70 LA 1110, 1114; Gundermann in 70 LA 1017, 1020; Wyman in 64 LA 988, 991; Seward in 19 LA 210, 211. Also see Marlatt in 73 LA 705, 706; Jewett in 70 LA 318, 319–320; Griffin in 69 LA 965, 966; Chaffin in 69 LA 307, 309; Casselman in 68 LA 702, 705; Crawford in 40 LA 1084, 1086–1087. Cf., Feldman in 72 LA 1144, 1150; Sherman in 68 LA 1279, 1281–1282. Arbitrator Scheiber agreed that a discharged employee has "a strong incentive for denying" guilt (48 LA 812, 814) but Arbitrator Krimsly reminded that interest in the outcome does not raise any presumption that a discharged employee is lying (48 LA 802, 807). On the latter point, also see Roumell in 73 LA 707, 710–711. In Martin Marietta Aerospace, 80 LA 115, 118 (1982), Arbitrator J.A. Raffaele expressed strong disagreement with use of the Shulman principle in arbitration.

[130]Jenkins Bros., 11 LA 432, 434 (Donnelly, 1948). For similar results, see Arbitrator Leonard in 48 LA 1187, 1190; Abernethy in 28 LA 757, 758–759; Coffey in 28 LA 710, 715.

doubt and careful scrutiny if there is evidence of ill will on his part against the accused.[131] The same is true if the factual situation otherwise casts doubt on the accuser's version,[132] or if his testimony on its face is not reasonably credible.

Another factor which might be considered by an arbitrator in weighing testimony in discharge and discipline cases is the so-called code which inhibits one member of an organization and frequently one member of an unorganized working force from testifying against another.[133]

The Best Evidence

A worthy view as to application of the "best evidence" concept in arbitration has been offered by a New York area tripartite committee:

> "*Best Evidence*—Where objection is made to the introduction of evidence of a secondary nature on the ground that it is not the best evidence, the original document should be produced unless it is shown, for reasons satisfactory to the arbitrator, that it is not available. Reproductions of original documents shall be deemed the best evidence unless the authenticity of the purported original document is significantly in question."[134]

A West Coast area tripartite committee suggested that "Failure, without adequate explanation, to produce a more reliable form of evidence should itself be recognized to have evidentiary weight adverse to the profferer of the lesser valued proof."[135]

Formal Versus Informal Records

Business records are a frequent source of proof in arbitration. Complete data taken directly from original business records will ordinarily be given more weight than estimates or informal records.[136] However, even informal records kept by the union or by the employees themselves may be given significant weight if the company has kept no formal records of the activity in question.[137]

---

[131]As in Bethlehem Steel Co., 2 LA 187, 190–191 (Dodd, 1945).

[132]See FMC Corp., 45 LA 293, 295 (McCoy, 1965). In V.A. Medical Center, 74 LA 830, 832 (Ludolf, 1980), the accusers were mental patients and the arbitrator stated that their testimony accordingly "must be viewed with caution" as against accused staff personnel, whose testimony "must be considered as more authentic and weighed more heavily." Also regarding the competence, weight, and evaluation of the testimony of mental patients, see Friedman, "Arbitration of Discipline for Abuse of Mental Patients," 33 Arb. J. 16 (1978).

[133]General Motors Corp., 2 LA 491, 502 (Hotchkiss, 1938). To similar effect, American Smelting & Ref. Co., 48 LA 1187, 1190 (Leonard, 1967). Also see assertions by McFall, "Comment," Proceedings of the 31st Annual Meeting of NAA, 152, 154 (BNA Books, 1979); Problems of Proof in Arbitration, 234 (BNA Books, 1967).

[134]Problems of Proof in Arbitration, 299–300 (BNA Books, 1967). Other tripartite committees expressed similar views. Id. at 92, 252. The West Coast Committee referred to the best evidence rule at law as "a rather narrowly drawn prescription which mandates that 'no evidence other than the writing itself is admissible to prove the content of a writing.' " Id. at 189.

[135]Id. at 189. Also discussing application of the "best evidence" concept in arbitration, see Hill & Sinicropi, Evidence in Arbitration, 28–29 (BNA Books, 1980).

[136]See Jonco Aircraft Corp., 22 LA 819, 823 (Merrill, 1954).

[137]See Bethlehem Steel Co., 16 LA 926, 927–928, 931–932 (Feinberg, 1951).

Burden of Proof

It is very difficult to generalize on the application of the doctrine of "burden of proof" in the field of arbitration.[138] The burden of proof may depend upon the nature of the issue, the specific contract provision, or a usage established by the parties. In many cases the arbitrator simply gets the facts and decides the issue without any express indication that he is thinking in terms of burden of proof.

Arbitrators have written specifically in terms of burden of proof much more frequently in some types of cases than in other types. For instance, burden of proof considerations have been stressed fairly often in discharge and discipline cases, as well as in cases involving seniority clauses which require consideration of the fitness and ability of employees.[139] In contrast, for example, Arbitrator Harry Shulman emphasized that "notions of burden of proof are hardly applicable to issues of interpretation."[140]

It is probable that in arbitration the "burden of proof" concept is usually more important in its substantive than in its procedural significance. There is, for instance, no required order of presenting evidence in arbitration cases. While the party asserting a claim usually presents his proof first, or at least a preliminary or introductory case, this practice may not be followed where the nature of the issue makes a different procedure preferable.[141]

It may be noted that the burden of going forward with the evidence may shift during the course of the hearing; after the party having the burden of persuasion presents sufficient evidence to justify

---

[138]For helpful discussions of the "burden of proof" concept at law, with comments as to its application in arbitration, see Tenneco Oil Co., 44 LA 1121, 1122 (Merrill, 1965); Fleming, The Labor Arbitration Process, 68–73 (U. of Ill. Press, 1965). Arbitrator Fleming noted: "Part of the difficulty in talking about burden of proof is that the term means several different things and is often used without careful definition. It can mean the burden of pleading [which does not apply in arbitration], the burden of producing evidence, and the burden of persuasion. When used in the sense of burden of persuasion, it involves further questions as to the quantum of evidence, or standard of proof, which will be required to prevail in the particular case." Id. at 68.

[139]See Chapter 15, topic entitled "Burden and Quantum of Proof"; Chapter 14, topic entitled "Review of Management's Determination: Evidence and Burden of Proof." For some other types of issues in which an arbitrator has spoken specifically in terms of burden of proof, see Arbitrator McIntosh in 52 LA 1026, 1027; Small in 46 LA 1077, 1078; Bothwell in 43 LA 1256, 1262–1263; Pollock in 37 LA 60, 62; Duff in 24 LA 715, 717; Reynard in 24 LA 369, 372–373; Holly in 24 LA 268, 273; Loucks in 24 LA 81, 84; Reid in 19 LA 291, 294; Livengood in 19 LA 205, 207; Cheney in 8 LA 187, 188; Cole in 3 LA 723, 724. For a related discussion, see this Chapter, topic entitled "Unsupported Allegations."

[140]Shulman, "Reason, Contract, and Law in Labor Relations," 68 Harv. L. Rev. 999, 1018 (1955). Also see Arbitrator Holley in 74 LA 330, 332. Arbitrator Benjamin Aaron spoke vigorously against use of "burden of proof" concepts in arbitration (except in certain types of discharge cases), and in this regard declared: "To insist that the complaining party carries the burden of proof is manifestly absurd. Neither side has a burden of proof or disproof, but both have an obligation to cooperate in an effort to give the arbitrator as much guidance as possible." Aaron, "Some Procedural Problems in Arbitration," 10 Vand. L. Rev. 733, 740–742 (1957). Illustrating that some arbitrators do hold the view that the complaining party generally carries the burden of proof, see Arbitrator Fox in 73 LA 330, 333; Heneman in 72 LA 1302, 1303; Bell in 69 LA 682, 685. Discussing these various views, along with other aspects of burden of proof in arbitration, see Smith, "The Search for Truth—The Whole Truth," Proceedings of the 31st Annual Meeting of NAA, 40, 50–54 (BNA Books, 1979).

[141]For full discussion, see Chapter 7, topic entitled "Order of Presenting Case."

a finding in its favor on the issue, the other party has the burden of producing evidence in rebuttal.[142]

Unsupported Allegations

Too often a party goes to arbitration with nothing but allegations to support some of its contentions or even its basic position. But allegations or assertions are not proof, and mere allegations unsupported by evidence are ordinarily given no weight by arbitrators.[143] Similarly, where neither party has provided sufficient evidence for an informed ruling on an issue or aspect of the case, the arbitrator will decline to rule upon it.[144]

Sometimes, too, a party will present no direct case at all, but will rely entirely upon cross-examination of the other party's witnesses, or will simply contend that the other party has the burden of proof and has not proved its case. This practice has been severely criticized by arbitrators.[145]

Hearsay Evidence

Evidence of a hearsay character is often presented at arbitration hearings. Arbitrators generally admit such evidence, but qualify its reception by informing the parties that it is admitted only "for what it is worth."[146] One general survey of labor arbitration revealed the following responses as to hearsay evidence:

"On the admission of hearsay into arbitration proceedings the consensus can be described as a collective shrug, a throwing-up of the hands, and a proclamation that it is inevitable. Many responses of both sides indicated that hearsay 'has to come in,' and that the arbitrator 'can't

---

[142]See Arbitrator Whyte in 51 LA 428, 434; Shipman in 42 LA 343, 344; Sembower in 39 LA 341, 346. Also, Problems of Proof in Arbitration, 196, 211 (BNA Books, 1967).

[143]See Arbitrator Rule in 74 LA 64, 68; Yarowsky in 74 LA 55, 57; Ellmann in 73 LA 1083, 1087; Foltman in 69 LA 865, 869; Hardy in 49 LA 415, 417; Crawford in 47 LA 971, 973, and in 29 LA 837, 841; Sherman in 46 LA 187, 189 (mere surmise or speculation is not evidence); McDermott in 40 LA 487, 488; Beatty in 39 LA 1226, 1231; Justin in 24 LA 45, 47; DiLeone in 16 LA 613, 615; Barrett in 16 LA 466, 468.

[144]For example, see Norfolk Naval Shipyard, 70 LA 779, 786 (Margolin, undated).

[145]See John Deere Waterloo Tractor Works, 20 LA 583, 584–585 (Davey, 1953); Felsway Shoe Corp., 17 LA 505, 509–510 (Justin, 1951). In Southern Can Co., 68 LA 1183, 1187 (Jedel, 1977), the arbitrator voiced no objection to such reliance upon cross-examination by the company. For related discussion, see Chapter 7, topic entitled "Default Awards in Ex Parte Proceedings."

[146]For general discussion of the hearsay rule *and its many exceptions* at law, with suggestions as to treatment of hearsay evidence in arbitration, see Problems of Proof in Arbitration, 90–91, 187–189, 212, 249–250, 272–279, 297–298 (BNA Books, 1967). "Hearsay consists of testimony given by a person who states, not what he knows of his own knowledge, but what he has heard from others." Id. at 249. A more comprehensive definition states: " 'Hearsay evidence' is evidence of a statement that was made other than by a witness while testifying at the hearing and that is offered to prove the truth of the matter stated. A statement offered for some purpose other than to prove the fact stated by it is not hearsay." Id. at 212. Also see Arbitrator Roumell in 70 LA 614, 618. For one of the relatively infrequent instances in which an arbitrator sustained the objection to hearsay evidence, giving no consideration at all to it, see Warner Robins Air Logistics Center, 74 LA 217, 220 (Clarke, 1980). For related discussion, see this Chapter, topic entitled "Right of Cross-Examination."

keep it out.' Admission of hearsay is justified to keep arbitration from becoming too cumbersome through procedural wrangling, or by the requirement that every witness who might be brought in be required to appear. It is agreed that the arbitrator must have wide latitude, and that he should let a witness with a grievance 'get it out.' Though the parties should feel that they have had their say in an informal manner, hearsay should be carefully weighed, once admitted, for its probative value. Despite the general fatalism expressed about the admission of hearsay evidence, there was still substantial opposition to its use."[147]

It is impossible to say just what the arbitrator in an individual case will consider hearsay evidence to be "worth." Arbitrator Arthur R. Lewis observed that "the reasons calling for the existence of a hearsay rule in common law jury actions should at least guide the judgment of the arbitrator in the evaluation of the weight, if any, to be attributed to such evidence in an arbitration proceeding."[148] In many cases very little weight is given to hearsay evidence, and it is exceedingly unlikely that an arbitrator will render a decision supported by hearsay evidence alone.[149] Then, too, hearsay evidence will be given little weight if contradicted by evidence which has been subjected to cross-examination.[150]

A pertinent observation concerning the weight of hearsay evidence was made by Arbitrator Benjamin Aaron:

"[A] competent arbitrator may be depended upon substantially to discount some kinds of hearsay evidence that he has admitted over objection. He will do so selectively, however, and not on the assumption that hearsay evidence, as such, is not to be credited. If, for example, a newly appointed personnel manager, or a recently elected business agent, offers a letter to his predecessor from a third party, the arbitrator is likely to ignore the fact that the evidence is hearsay; if satisfied that the document is genuine, he will give it such weight as its relevancy dictates. On the other hand, hearsay testimony about statements allegedly made by 'the boys in the shop' or by executives in the 'front office,' though

---

[147]Eaton, "Labor Arbitration in the San Francisco Bay Area," 48 LA 1381, 1385 (1967). In Walden v. Teamsters, 81 LRRM 2608, 2609 (CA 4, 1972), the court held that a union's failure to object to hearsay evidence in arbitration did not constitute a breach of its duty of fair representation, the court declaring that: "An arbitration hearing is not a court of law and need not be conducted like one. Neither lawyers nor strict adherence to judicial rules of evidence are necessary complements of industrial peace and stability—the ultimate goals of arbitration."

[148]Continental Paper Co., 16 LA 727, 728 (1951). On the other hand, the reason underlying an applicable exception to the hearsay rule was likewise considered by Arbitrator Nathan Lipson in admitting hearsay statements as technically competent evidence (not given reduced weight as hearsay). Faribault State Hosp., 68 LA 713, 719 (1977), involving *res gestae* declarations of a deceased employee whose discharge was the subject of the arbitration, Arbitrator Lipson stating that the "reason for the exception is the assumption that statements made contemporaneously with a crucial event, or while the declarant is excited are more likely to be true."

[149]In the latter regard, see Arbitrator Brisco in 72 LA 16, 19; Schmidt in 35 LA 77, 80; Gorder in 20 LA 880, 885–886; Klamon in 19 LA 571, 574; Cheney in 8 LA 518, 522. Cf., Siegel in 35 LA 103, 108–109. In Air France, 71 LA 1113, 1116 (1978), the only evidence presented against the grievant was the record of testimony against him in a court case; Arbitrator Burton B. Turkus gave such evidence "no probative value" because he "did not hear any of the witnesses whose testimony is now presented by way of the trial record, and was in no position to evaluate their credibility." In Berberich Delivery Co., 79 LA 277, 283–284 (Kubie, 1982), discharge for burglary was upheld on the basis of hearsay evidence where it was corroborated by evidence of grievant's flight from a law officer, by his failure to deny his involvement when questioned by his employer, and by his failure to testify in his own defense at the arbitration hearing.

[150]See, for instance, Howell Ref. Co., 27 LA 486, 492 (Hale, 1956). Also see Arbitrator LeWinter in 72 LA 102, 106–107; Rubin in 20 LA 483, 484.

perhaps not excluded from the record by the arbitrator, probably will have no effect on his decision."[151]

Affidavits

Affidavits are sometimes used in arbitration but are subject to the same limitations as other forms of hearsay evidence.[152] In this connection, American Arbitration Association Rule 29 provides that arbitrators may receive and consider the evidence of witnesses by affidavit but should give it only such weight as they deem it entitled to after consideration of any objections made to its admission.[153] A similar approach was taken by the Code of Ethics and Procedural Standards for Labor-Management Arbitration, with the added qualification that the arbitrator "should afford the other side an opportunity to cross-examine the persons making the affidavits or to take their depositions or otherwise interrogate them."[154]

Circumstantial Evidence

Arbitrators sometimes decide cases on the basis of circumstantial evidence. For instance, such evidence was used to sustain the discharge of an employee charged with violation of a no-smoking rule; Arbitrator Jean McKelvey noted that the evidence was purely circumstantial but said that the proof, circumstantial as it was, indicated beyond a reasonable doubt that no person other than the accused could have been responsible for the smoke in the men's room.[155]

In another case the circumstances did not point so definitely to guilt, but a web of circumstances did exist to support the discharge of several employees for instigating an unauthorized strike; the reasoning of Arbitrator Whitley P. McCoy indicates how circumstantial evidence may be found sufficient to support a finding of guilt:

> "Because of the secret nature of the offense of these men, proof is extremely difficult. It does not follow from this that proof may be dispensed with or that mere suspicious circumstances may take the place of proof, as I have indicated in sustaining the grievances of four men. But I think it does follow that something less than the most direct and the most positive proof is sufficient; in other words, that, just as in cases of

---

[151]Aaron, "Some Procedural Problems in Arbitration," 10 Vand. L. Rev. 733, 744 (1957).

[152]See, for instance, South Haven Rubber Co., 54 LA 653, 654–655 (Sembower, 1970); Borden Co., 20 LA 483, 484 (Rubin, 1953).

[153]30 LA 1086, 1089. A physician's statement was received and given some weight under this Rule in Karnish Instruments, Inc., 45 LA 545, 550 (Bender, 1965).

[154]Part II, § 4(e). The Code of Professional Responsibility, which was intended to supersede the Code of Ethics, does not deal expressly with use of affidavits.

[155]Columbian Rope Co., 7 LA 450, 455 (1947). As to circumstantial evidence of smoking, cf., Arbitrator Foster in 70 LA 270, 276–278; Kates in 44 LA 507, 512–513. Circumstantial evidence was given significant weight by Arbitrator Roumell in 76 LA 213, 219; Daniel in 75 LA 642, 644; Gentile in 74 LA 377, 387; Gibson in 73 LA 868, 871–872; Gilson in 71 LA 1224, 1232; Mueller in 69 LA 1182, 1185; Christopher in 66 LA 1165, 1169; Platt in 47 LA 1015, 1016–1017; Gilden in 47 LA 966, 970; Larkin in 47 LA 903, 906; Sembower in 47 LA 890, 896 (but he stated that "if there is a shred of doubt it should be taken into account"); Boles in 42 LA 954, 958–959; Reid in 38 LA 749, 751; Marshall in 22 LA 573, 575; Klamon in 16 LA 461, 466.

fraud and conspiracy, legitimate inferences may be drawn from such circumstances as a prior knowledge of the time set for the strike. Unusual actions in circulating among the employees just prior to 9:30, communication of the time set to employees, and signals, however surreptitious, given at that hour. Mere prior guilty knowledge of the time set would not alone be sufficient since presumably many of the employees must have been told the time a half hour, an hour, or several hours in advance. Nor would merely being the first in a department to quit at the stroke of 9:30, standing alone, be sufficient. A wave of the hand, which might as reasonably be interpreted as a signal of good-bye as a signal to the others to go out, as in the case of Hollingsworth, would of itself be insufficient. But these or other suspicious circumstances, in combination, and especially in case of known leaders in the union's affairs, may be sufficient to convince the reasonable mind of guilt."[156]

Arbitrator Joseph A. Jenkins stated that "Circumstantial evidence is often far more persuasive than direct testimony, particularly when action 'in the nature of a conspiracy' is involved."[157] In this unauthorized work stoppage case, Arbitrator Jenkins found that circumstantial evidence made out a "prima facie case" of guilt, leaving a burden on each individual employee to offer evidence of excuse (such as illness) for not reporting to work.[158]

As a basic safeguard, Arbitrator Clair V. Duff emphasized that an arbitrator in using circumstantial evidence "must exercise extreme care so that by due deliberation and careful judgment he may avoid making hasty or false deductions. If the evidence producing the chain of circumstances pointing to [guilt] is weak and inconclusive, no probability of fact may be inferred from the combined circumstances."[159]

Or, as Arbitrator Paul M. Hebert stated, use of circumstantial evidence "does not eliminate in any sense the requirement that there must be clear and convincing proof to establish that the offense charged was committed."[160] Certainly, mere suspicion is not enough to establish wrongdoing.[161]

While expressly rejecting for use in arbitration the criminal law rule that circumstantial evidence is inadequate unless its excludes

---

[156]Stockham Pipe Fittings Co., 4 LA 744, 746–747 (1946). For reliance upon circumstantial evidence in other work-stoppage cases, see Arbitrator Gentile in 74 LA 377, 387 (the arbitrator could "not accept the unified action of some 30 to 40 employees statewide as individual judgments, but concluded that it must be characterized as 'in concert' "); Mueller in 69 LA 1182, 1185; Jenkins in 48 LA 949, 950–951; Pollack in 42 LA 142, 143; Harter in 7 LA 239, 240.

[157]Lone Star Steel Co., 48 LA 949, 950–951 (1967). Agreeing that circumstantial evidence may have more probative value than direct testimony, see Arbitrator Gibson in 73 LA 868, 871; Christopher in 66 LA 1165, 1169; Scheiber in 48 LA 812, 815.

[158]Lone Star Steel Co., 48 LA 949, 951 (1967). Accord, see Arbitrator Forrester in 72 LA 761, 764–765; Mueller in 69 LA 1182, 1185.

[159]South Penn Oil Co., 29 LA 718, 721 (1957). Also see similar statements by Arbitrator Sembower in 44 LA 593, 601–603; Duff in 44 LA 577, 578.

[160]Reed Roller Bit Co., 29 LA 604, 606 (1957). Also see Arbitrator Block in 55 LA 1221, 1227; Gross in 46 LA 756, 762–763; Bennett in 45 LA 247, 249; Bowles in 24 LA 761, 764; Kadish in 24 LA 102, 104–105; Platt in 21 LA 428, 429. In Collins Foods Intl., 77 LA 483, 485 (Richman, 1981), circumstantial evidence did suggest an employee's guilt, but this did not justify the employer's failure to make a thorough investigation at the physical site of the alleged misconduct.

[161]See Enterprise & Century Undergarment Co., 24 LA 63, 64 (Donnelly, 1955). Also see comments of Arbitrator Petersen in 71 LA 949, 952–953; Prasow in 23 LA 317, 321; Updegraff in 19 LA 413, 416. Cf., actions of Arbitrator Davis in 48 LA 199, 200.

every reasonable theory except guilt, Arbitrator Ralph Roger Williams concluded that the work involved in the case before him was so complicated and the opportunity for errors so broad that circumstantial evidence did not suffice for a charge of deliberate production of defective work.[162]

Evidence Obtained by Allegedly Improper Methods

Labor and management representatives have disagreed as to the admissibility in arbitration of evidence obtained by breaking into an employee's locker, forcible search of his person, secret surveillance, and other such means.[163] The broad question for the arbitrator is said to be that "absent a constitutional right or a right specified in the contract, may the arbitrator reject evidence because the manner in which it has been obtained is reprehensible or distasteful to him or because it is his opinion that sound labor-management relations would be better served by such exclusion."[164]

As will be noted from the following discussion, reported arbitration cases reveal that the views of arbitrators, too, may differ significantly as to the use of such evidence, though the inclination to accept and rely upon it appears to be fairly strong.

In a case involving the discharge of a female employee for violating a rule against possession of dangerous knives on company premises, Arbitrator Joseph D. Lohman emphasized that the company guard had obtained knowledge of the employee's possession of the knife through unilateral entry and search of her locker and purse, that she was escorted to the guard office and asked to empty her purse without being told the reason for the inquiry, and that the guard had been instructed not to disclose the reason for the inquiry. Arbitrator Lohman said that this tactic bordered on entrapment, and that the employee's locker and purse continued inviolate as the private realm of the individual even though the entire episode was confined to the premises of the company.[165]

Arbitrator Lohman concluded that "Knowledge, even though incriminating, if acquired through such illegitimate procedures, is of questionable validity in bringing action against the individual." The

---

[162]Westinghouse Elec. Co., 48 LA 211, 212–213 (1967). Many arbitrators would no doubt agree with Arbitrator Williams' rejection of said criminal law rule for use in arbitration. But see Arbitrator Wildebush in 44 LA 1143, 1149.

[163]See Problems of Proof in Arbitration, 105–106, 129–134, 138–139 (BNA Books, 1967). Labor spokesmen have emphasized the individual's right to privacy and human dignity; management spokesmen have pointed to the necessity for investigative power and they comment that when an employee takes a job, he does so with the knowledge that he must adhere to plant rules and that he may also be required to give up certain rights which he has on the outside. Id. at 106, 108. For additional discussion of the matters treated in the present topic, see Craver, "The Inquisitorial Process in Private Employment," 63 Cornell L. Rev. 1 (1977).

[164]Id. at 106.

[165]Campbell Soup Co., 2 LA 27, 31 (1946).

evidence obtained through such procedures was held inadmissible, and consequently the discharge was held unjustified.[166]

However, even where a court had refused to admit certain illegal search and seizure evidence in a criminal action against an employee, the discharge of the employee on the basis of that evidence (which clearly indicated guilt) was upheld.[167] In this case the arbitrator stated that "The company is manifestly entitled to inquire into facts which suggest their employees are involved in the theft of Company property."[168]

Charges of entrapment and improper surveillance have not been readily accepted by arbitrators. In one case employees complained of entrapment where a night foreman, being reasonably suspicious that a poker game was in progress, returned to the plant after he had previously driven away. Arbitrator Harold M. Gilden rejected the contention of entrapment, stating that the foreman's action must be deemed within his general line of duty, and that the situation was to be distinguished from one where a carefully devised plan is formulated and bait is set or invitations extended for the express purpose of capturing persons in the commission of a wrongful act.[169]

A carefully devised plan was formulated and bait was set in one case to apprehend a locker-room thief. The bait (identifiable money) was placed in a locker which was kept under surveillance. Discharge of the thus apprehended employee was sustained.[170]

Evidence obtained by various forms of secret surveillance has been admitted by arbitrators and, where reliable, has been given

---

[166]Ibid. Also see Ross-Meehan Foundries, 55 LA 1078, 1080 (King, 1970). In accepting evidence obtained by a locker search in General Elec. Co., 72 LA 391, 397–398 (1979), Arbitrator Eleanor S. MacDonald acted on the view that past practice and employee expectations should determine the propriety of locker searches: "if employee lockers have not been considered private and personal property of the employees involved and if employees have not reasonably expected the lockers to be inviolate, then a search of an employee locker" is not improper; but a search is improper "if employees at a plant have long believed and relied upon the circumstance that their lockers were considered private areas and that these could not be opened without the personal consent of the owner of the locker."

[167]Hennis Freight Lines, 44 LA 711, 713–714 (McGury, 1964). Also recognizing the admissibility in arbitration of evidence rejected by a court as having been obtained by some unpermitted method such as entrapment or illegal search and seizure, see Arbitrator Simon in 76 LA 387, 391; Ray in 73 LA 304, 308; Dolnick in 61 LA 663, 665–666; Doppelt in 60 LA 1260, 1262–1263. But compare Arbitrator McGury's decision in 58 LA 1213, 1215–1216. In Jones & Laughlin Steel Corp., 29 LA 778, 779 (Stark, 1957), an employee was escorted to the guard office and told to empty his pockets, which he did. The incriminating evidence thus obtained was a factor in his discharge, which was upheld. No contention of illegal search and seizure was apparent in the latter case. Where such contention was made in Lockheed Aircraft Corp., 27 LA 709, 712–713 (Maggs, 1956), the arbitrator stated that constitutional rights as to search and seizure can only be asserted against the government in criminal cases and are not available to employees in discharge cases. Similarly, see Arbitrator O'Grady in 79 LA 1045, 1049–1051; Feldman in 78 LA 1092, 1102–1103; Peck in 72 LA 1075, 1078; Dolnick in 61 LA 663, 665–666; Doppelt in 60 LA 1260, 1262–1263. But see Williams in 52 LA 57, 59. For discussion of search and seizure in arbitration and at law, see Fleming, The Labor Arbitration Process, 186–190 (U. of Ill. Press, 1965). He likewise discusses wiretapping. Id. at 190–194.

[168]Hennis Freight Lines, 44 LA 711, 714 (McGury, 1964). Also see Arbitrator Yaffe in 78 LA 89, 100; Newmark in 76 LA 421, 424 (employee suspected of chewing tobacco in violation of OSHA rules could be disciplined for refusing to show what he had in his mouth); Draznin in 74 LA 518, 521; Casselmen in 68 LA 702, 705 (order that grievant unbutton his sweater was not improper where company had probable cause to believe he was committing a serious violation).

[169]Borg-Warner Corp., 3 LA 423, 432 (1944).

[170]United States Steel Corp., 49 LA 101, 102–105 (Dybeck, 1967). Also see Arbitrator Babiskin in 74 LA 299, 300; Jewett in 70 LA 318, 318–319; Hildebrand in 68 LA 1224, 1228–1229; Hill in 55 LA 226, 228–230; Alexander in 53 LA 1279, 1280.

weight.[171] A justification for covert procedures in certain circumstances was stated by Arbitrator M. David Keefe:

> "It is, indeed, distasteful that management should have to check on the honesty of employees. Nevertheless, when suspicions are kindled it seems better to bring the matter to a head, one way or the other, rather than to risk the greater harm of misdirected doubts smoldering to char the esteem in which an innocent person might be held. In any event, the Company has an undeniable right to protect itself against the type of offense herein involved."[172]

Also he denied that a procedure becomes "entrapment simply because it must be planned."[173]

Recordings made by one party to a telephone conversation without the knowledge of the other party were not admitted into evidence, the arbitrator requiring the person who made the recordings to testify on a recollection basis.[174] Another arbitrator permitted use of evidence obtained against an employee by tape recorder, the arbitrator stating that "the legality of the means by which information has been gathered is for other authorities to determine."[175]

The right to use a closed circuit television camera to observe employees in a room from which the company believed it was losing material through theft was upheld by Arbitrator Richard Mittenthal, who stated, however, that he did not need to decide whether evidence obtained by this method would be admissible in a disciplinary dispute.[176]

It is said that "Arbitrators know that industrial pilferage is a major problem, and there is no disposition to interfere with proper

---

[171]See Michigan Bell Tel. Co., 45 LA 689, 694–696 (Smith, 1965), in which evidence obtained by listening in on telephone operators could be used, with possible limitations; Du Mont Laboratories, 44 LA 1143, 1146, 1149 (Wildebush, 1965), in which "peephole" evidence was admitted but found unreliable since the peephole was too small to permit accurate observation; Keystone Asphalt Prods. Co., 3 LA 789, 793 (Hampton, 1946), in which management made secret visits to the plant to catch employees sleeping on duty and in which the employees were not confronted until conclusive evidence of guilt had been obtained—the discharges were upheld though the arbitrator considered the employer's actions "beneath the dignity of management"; Douglas Aircraft Co., 1 LA 350, 353 (Courshon, 1945), in which employees were caught "red-handed" through surveillance by guards—the offense was thus established but the discharges were set aside due to past laxness in enforcement of plant rules. For general discussion of surveillance, see Black, "Surveillance and the Labor Arbitration Process," Proceedings of the 23rd Annual Meeting of NAA, 1 (BNA Books 1970).
[172]Attwood Corp., 48 LA 331, 334 (1967).
[173]Ibid.
[174]Needham Packing Co., 44 LA 1057, 1095 (Davey, 1965).
[175]Sun Drug Co., 31 LA 191, 194 (Marcus, 1958). Use of tape-recorded evidence was also permitted by Arbitrator Smith in 82 LA 414, 418.
[176]FMC Corp., 46 LA 335, 338 (1966). Accord, Arbitrator Elson in 62 LA 586, 591; Kelliher in 61 LA 697, 699–700. Arbitrator W. Willard Wirtz stated that situations of the television camera/ pilferage type "present clear 'due process' questions, not constitutional or legal due process, but obvious demands that individual and enterprise interests be balanced * * *." Wirtz, "Due Process of Arbitration," Proceedings of the 11th Annual Meeting of NAA, 1, 17 (BNA Books, 1958). In Casting Eng'rs., 76 LA 939, 941 (Petersen, 1981), the employer's installation of videotaping equipment for surveillance of the time-clock area, of which the union and employees were aware, was held not to violate state law barring use of any "eavesdropping device" to "hear or record oral conversation"; the arbitrator's viewing of videotapes along with his examination of time cards led to the "inescapable conclusion" that the grievants were guilty of stealing time. In Eico, Inc., 44 LA 563, 564 (Delany, 1965), the employer was held to have violated a maintenance of working conditions clause by installing a closed circuit television system on the production floor; no problems of supervision or operations existed to warrant the employer's action.

rules to control it."[177] For instance, in one case the right of the company to inspect large purses of female employees as they leave the plant was upheld.[178]

The use of "spotters" in some industries and the admission of their reports and testimony as evidence of rule violations by employees is discussed above in this Chapter under the topic entitled "Right of Cross-Examination."

Confessions

An arbitrator may ordinarily be expected to give little or no weight to a signed "confession" if the signature was obtained through inducements, commitments, or threats.[179] One arbitrator explained:

"Such methods of obtaining confessions of guilt are patently wrong. A confession, to be valid in prosecuting a case must be statements given by the suspected person of his own free will and choice. Inducements and threats invalidate such documents as evidence."[180]

However, where the evidence showed neither "physical nor mental duress procuring the grievant's admissions of guilt, nor promises of leniency or reward in exchange for such admissions," the admissions could be used even though statements by security officers that grievant could be arrested helped induce the admissions.[181] Nor would a confession be deemed the product of duress or coercion merely because it was made under the pressure of circumstances.[182]

An employee's plea of guilty in public criminal proceedings ordinarily can be accepted in arbitration as an indication of guilt.[183] A

---

[177]Fleming, The Labor Arbitration Process, 188 (U. of Ill. Press, 1965).

[178]Aldens, Inc., 51 LA 469, 470 (Kelliher, 1968).

[179]See Arbitrator Heinsz in 71 LA 989, 991; Jacobs in 55 LA 1195, 1202; Babb in 29 LA 272, 277; Blair in 12 LA 1065, 1067. In Thrifty Drug Stores Co., 50 LA 1253, 1262 (Jones, 1968), confession statements made by an employee in admitting guilt, but also implicating other employees, were regarded with skepticism; the question was "whether the statements are so tainted by compulsions created by the manner of their taking as to make it too speculative for a trier of fact * * * to give them credence as evidence against those whom they would implicate." But as to the Thrifty Drug decision, see comments by Edwards, "Due Process Considerations in Labor Arbitration," 25 Arb. J. 141, 150–151 (1970). In Casting Eng'rs., 71 LA 949, 951–952 (Petersen, 1978), an employee's confession supported his discharge but was insufficient to incriminate other employees whom he also named in the confession.

[180]Kroger Co., 12 LA 1065, 1067 (Blair, 1949).

[181]Weirton Steel Co., 50 LA 103, 104–105 (1968), Arbitrator Samuel S. Kates stating that he did "not subscribe to the doctrine that purity must always envelop those engaged in attempting to ascertain the truth, or that subterfuge or pretence is always improper in a truth-seeking endeavor." Also see Arbitrator Garrett in 78 LA 921, 928. In Lucky Stores, 53 LA 1274, 1276 (Eaton, 1969), confessions were used although the employees had not been notified of any right to remain silent, the arbitrator stating that rules of the criminal law under the Constitution "do not necessarily apply in the same way to private investigations where there is no agent of the state present, which is the case here."

[182]Eastern Air Lines, 46 LA 549, 555 (Seidenberg, 1965). An employee's spontaneous or impromptu remark to a detective, "you got me fair and square," was admitted into evidence as "a damaging admission against interest" in the arbitration of the employee's discharge although it had been excluded in a criminal action against the employee. Dannon Milk Prods., 76 LA 133, 137, 139 (Kramer, 1980).

[183]See Department of the Air Force, 74 LA 949, 952 (Ward, 1980). Although a grievant

plea of nolo contendere is neither an indication of guilt nor of innocence.[184]

The mere fact that a "confession" is purely voluntary does not always endow it with validity. Thus, a confession of strike leadership was given no weight where there was no evidence surrounding the confession to indicate that the employee was in fact a "leader."[185]

Offers of Compromise and Admissions

Offers of compromise and admissions made in attempting settlement of rights disputes prior to submission to arbitration may be received but probably will be given very little, if any, weight by arbitrators.[186] It is recognized that a party to a dispute may make an offer with the hope that a compromise can be reached and the dispute ended.[187] Even the mere introduction of such evidence may impair future attempts at dispute settlements. Thus, it has been strongly urged that offers of compromise should not even be admitted into evidence.[188]

While admissions and statements against interest other than those made in settlement attempts may be considered by an arbitrator, the arbitrator can be expected to recognize that as a matter of law they are not conclusive.[189]

---

testified that he had pleaded guilty to criminal charges only upon advice of an attorney as "the easiest way out" and the way to obtain a suspended sentence, Arbitrator John F. Sembower declared that "it is not possible to go behind such a plea." Northwest Airlines, 53 LA 203, 206 (1969). Similarly, see Arbitrator Kleeb in 69 LA 987, 988. In American Airlines, 68 LA 1245, 1247 (Harkless, 1977), a jury's "guilty" verdict was conclusive against the grievant in subsequent arbitration proceedings.

[184]Akers Motor Lines, 41 LA 987, 990–991 (Woodruff, 1963). But in sustaining a discharge in Great Scot Food Stores, 73 LA 147, 148 (1979), Arbitrator Arthur R. Porter, Jr., stated that although a "no contest" plea "is not identical with a technical conviction, the grievant by his plea, admitted to the facts." Similarly, see Arbitrator McDonald in 80 LA 596, 600.

[185]Union Tank Car Co., 49 LA 383, 388–389 (Crawford, 1967).

[186]See Arbitrator Prasow in 25 LA 398, 403–404; Marshall in 24 LA 430, 436; Cornsweet in 14 LA 494, 497. Also see Chapter 9, topic entitled "No Consideration to Compromise Offers."

[187]Universal Milking Mach. Co., 2 LA 399, 402 (Elson, 1946).

[188]Problems of Proof in Arbitration, 93–94, 190, 253, 287–288 (BNA Books, 1967).

[189]Harley-Davidson Co., 6 LA 395, 397 (Lappin, 1947). Regarding *grievance meeting* admissions and statements against interest other than offers of compromise, the question has been debated whether, from a policy standpoint, they should be considered by arbitrators. "Yes," stated General Electric Labor Relations Counsel Earl F. Jones, Jr., in "Letter to the Editor," AAA Study Time (Oct. 1979), noting that an earlier Letter to the Editor from Arbitrator Sidney L. Cahn had advocated the exclusion of such evidence. To this view Jones replied: "unless the parties agree that grievance discussions are not to be brought up at hearings, the arbitrator should not impose such a prohibition"; if "a need is seen to protect the integrity of the grievance procedure by a blanket exclusion of evidence relating to offers of settlement and compromise, there is no basis for broadening the policy to apply to statements helpful in resolving questions of fact, especially in discipline cases." In rebuttal, Arbitrator Cahn explained: "The difficulty that I envision with this proposal is that once the 'door is opened' to admit testimony relating to admissions against interest or prior inconsistent statements, opposing counsel would have the evidentiary if not the legal right to introduce testimony of everything discussed by the parties during such grievance meetings." "Letters to the Editor," AAA Study Time (Jan. 1980), where a separate letter from Arbitrator Peter Seitz discouraged arbitral use against a party of statements made during grievance sessions, Arbitrator Seitz believing that "acceptance of such testimony will have long-range damaging effects on the dispute-resolving system" of the parties.

Admissions made by the grievant in the presence of union representatives during prearbitral grievance hearings may be given significant weight.[190] This is true also of grievant's admissions at the arbitration hearing itself.[191]

Admissions which have been acted on by others and those that appear in the record of prior proceedings so as to partake of the nature of judicial admissions may be held by arbitrators to be weighty evidence against the party making them.[192] Thus, where a party assumed a position in an arbitration case which was inconsistent with the position of that party in a prior arbitration case involving the same contract clause, the position taken in the prior case was one of the reasons for a decision against the party in the subsequent case.[193]

While the record of proceedings before a state workers' compensation commission was ruled inadmissible in a subsequent arbitration hearing as to the employee's capability of performing his job, the arbitrator nevertheless permitted statements made by the employee in the compensation proceedings to be used by the employer at the arbitration hearing for purposes of impeaching the employee as a witness.[194]

Testimony from other proceedings must be evaluated with special care and in the full setting of the prior proceeding. Moreover, Arbitrator Bertram F. Willcox observed that sometimes even in the same case an apparently damaging admission by a witness will have resulted from a momentary confusion and that the arbitrator should exercise care not to overemphasize any single item of testimony, especially if it is inconsistent with other testimony of the witness and with the rest of the party's case.[195]

Testimony by Persons From Outside

The nature of some cases makes the use of impartial technicians helpful. In such cases, arbitrators sometimes request permission to bring in specialists for impartial study of the disputed matter. This was done by Arbitrator David Wolff who consulted an electrical engineer, in the presence of both parties, as to whether a power failure

[190]Diebold, Inc., 48 LA 893, 900 (Bradley, 1967); Problems of Proof in Arbitration, 93 (BNA Books, 1967), where a Chicago Area Tripartite Committee "agreed that admissions of the grievant during the grievance procedure present no problem," the Committee stating: "These certainly should be admitted in evidence. Admissions by other employees in the bargaining unit in the grievance procedure, and particularly the representatives of the union, fall into a different category. It is here the arbitrator should exercise the utmost caution."

[191]Bethlehem Steel Co., 42 LA 307, 309–310 (Hughes, 1964).

[192]For instance, see Arbitrator Komaroff in 21 LA 248, 251; McCoy in 6 LA 681, 684. Also see Meltzer in 28 LA 303, 308.

[193]Goodyear Tire & Rubber Co. of Ala., 6 LA 681, 684 (McCoy, 1947). The prior case was also heard by Arbitrator McCoy. Goodyear Tire & Rubber Co., 4 LA 231 (1946). Also see Arbitrator Kates in 58 LA 1111, 1116, where a term used by a party was "construed as a declaration against interest" and was given weight against the party in the same case.

[194]Vulcan Mold & Iron Co., 42 LA 734, 736–737, 739 (Sembower, 1964). In St. Joe Minerals Corp., 70 LA 1110, 1114 (Roberts, 1978), admissions against interest made in unemployment compensation proceedings were similarly admissible in arbitration for impeachment purposes.

[195]General Elec. Corp., 16 LA 554, 559 (1951).

was a cause beyond the employer's control (so as to relieve him of any obligation for call-in pay).[196] It has also been done in the determination of proper incentive rates for new operations.[197] Likewise, Arbitrator Peter M. Kelliher was authorized to secure the services of a handwriting expert in fixing responsibility for errors in shipping orders.[198]

In some cases in which arbitrators consulted outside sources the arbitrator's opinion did not expressly indicate whether he obtained advance permission to do so.[199] In another case the arbitrator's request that the parties procure the services of an outside expert (to study and express an opinion as to a safety-crew size issue) was virtually an order that they do so.[200]

It was the union that took the initiative where it "evoked a promise from the Arbitrator that he would check with competent medical authority, as well as law enforcement officials," regarding the reliability of blood tests in determining whether a person is intoxicated or under the influence of alcohol.[201]

Arbitrator Arthur M. Ross emphasized that "While an arbitrator may obtain technical assistance, he cannot delegate the decision-making authority which has been conferred upon him individually."[202]

A limitation upon the use of outside testimony was defined by Arbitrator Willard E. Hotchkiss, who accepted but refused to consider testimony of outsiders to the effect that a discharged employee had admitted his guilt to them; Arbitrator Hotchkiss urged that testimony of outsiders, whether or not relevant, should not generally be admitted since the frequent admission of such testimony would tend to retard the growth of healthy industrial relations and would encourage the calling of character witnesses to refute or support the testimony of the outsiders, the building of technical alibis, and other legalistic prac-

---

[196]Chrysler Corp., 21 LA 573, 577 (1953). One group expressed the view that the arbitrator should always advise the parties when seeking expert advice and should give them opportunity to comment on the expert's opinion before reaching his decision. View of Chicago Area Tripartite Committee, Problems of Proof in Arbitration, 108 (BNA Books, 1967).

[197]Container Co., 6 LA 218, 220 (Whiting, 1946). Similarly, see Simmons Co., 33 LA 725, 727 (Ross, 1959).

[198]Hiram Walker & Sons, 18 LA 447, 448 (1952). Similarly, see Seaview Indus., 39 LA 125, 127–130 (Duncan, 1962).

[199]See Arbitrator Vines in 45 LA 833, 837–838; Ross in 33 LA 725, 727; Lehoczky in 32 LA 481, 482. Arbitrator Ross appointed an industrial engineer to make technical studies on disputed matter; the engineer "received excellent cooperation from both parties." Simmons Co., 33 LA 725, 727 (1959).

[200]American Oil Co., 51 LA 484, 489 (Barnhart, 1968). In Naval Air Rework Facility, 73 LA 644, 644–645 (Flannagan, 1979), the arbitrator gave the union "the opportunity, if it so desired," of having tests made by an outside specialist after the union had failed to meet its burden of proof on a safety issue at an initial hearing; a specialist was utilized and his conclusions were given serious consideration by the arbitrator. Also see Arbitrator Livengood in 73 LA 201, 205–206, where a specialist similarly was utilized to examine and report as to alleged safety and health hazards.

[201]Tennessee River Pulp & Paper Co., 68 LA 421, 425 (Simon, 1976).

[202]Simmons Co., 33 LA 725, 727 (1959). In this instance Arbitrator Ross received "a confidential report in full detail" from the technical assistant whom he had appointed; Arbitrator Ross found the report "most helpful" in reaching a decision, which he emphasized was solely his own. Ibid.

tices which would prolong hearings at great expense but to no useful purpose.[203]

Opinion Evidence by Expert Witnesses

"The function of a witness is to relate what he has seen and heard, not to draw inferences from these observations or from other facts. This rule does not apply to the 'expert.' The 'expert' is allowed to draw inferences and conclusions because, in theory, his knowledge is superior to that of the person having to resolve the issue, be it judge, jury, or arbitrator."[204]

In addition to the admission of opinion evidence by expert witnesses (generally admitted by courts of law), it is suggested that arbitrators may in their discretion admit any opinion testimony from knowledgeable persons if such testimony might be helpful.[205]

Medical Evidence

A frequent use of medical evidence in arbitration concerns the physical fitness or qualifications of employees for some given type of work or, indeed, for any continued employment at all with the company.[206] Another use of medical evidence concerns verification of illness by doctors' certificates.

Written Statements Versus Oral Testimony

While doctors sometimes testify in person, their testimony is more often offered in the form of written statements or affidavits. It is understandable that where one party's doctor testifies in person, his opinion may carry greater weight with the arbitrator in contrast to the other party's use of only written statements.[207] Of course, the parties may stipulate that written statements of doctors (though not subject to

---

[203]General Motors Corp., 2 LA 491, 497, 503 (1938). Cf., Continental Paper Co., 16 LA 727, 728–729 (Lewis, 1951).

[204]"Report of the Pittsburgh Tripartite Committee," Problems of Proof in Arbitration, 253 (BNA Books, 1967). Related statements by other tripartite committees are also available. Id. at 94–95, 114–115, 298.

[205]View of the New York Area Tripartite Committee, id. at 298.

[206]For related material, see Chapter 13, topic entitled "Disqualifying Employees for Physical or Mental Reasons"; Chapter 16, topic entitled "Physical or Mental Condition as a Safety Hazard"; Chapter 14, subtopic entitled "Employee's Physical and Psychological Fitness." For general discussion of medical and psychiatric testimony in arbitration, see "The Use of Experts in Arbitration," Proceedings of the 22nd Annual Meeting of NAA, 135–145, 151–161 (BNA Books, 1970). For other informative discussions of these or related aspects, see Wolkinson, "Arbitration and the Employment Rights of the Physically Disadvantaged," 36 Arb. J. No. 1, p. 23 (1981); Cramer, "Arbitration and Mental Illness: The Issues, the Rationale, and the Remedies," 35 Arb. J. No. 3, p. 10 (1980); Hill & Sinicropi, Evidence in Arbitration, 29–34 (BNA Books, 1980); Volz, "Medical and Health Issues in Labor Arbitration," Proceedings of the 31st Annual Meeting of NAA, 156 (BNA Books, 1979).

[207]See Arbitrator Kates in 43 LA 61, 64; Stockman in 41 LA 449, 453–454; Russell in 40 LA 229, 230–231. Arbitrators sometimes have stressed the unsatisfactory aspects of presenting medical evidence by written statements. See Arbitrator Leonard in 48 LA 1187, 1190; Boles in 43 LA 484, 487.

cross-examination) shall be given the same effect as if the doctors had testified.[208] Even without such stipulation the arbitrator might give the statements "full weight" in the absence of other evidence minimizing their significance.[209]

Shall Medical Evidence Be Weighed?

Often both parties submit medical evidence concerning the grievant's physical qualifications, and it is not surprising that the opinion of the grievant's doctor and that of the employer's medical adviser do not always agree. In many cases the arbitrator has not attempted to resolve such conflicts in medical evidence, but has been inclined to uphold the employer if he acted in good faith pursuant to good-faith medical advice from his doctor (some of these arbitrators spoke in terms of upholding the employer's action unless his doctor's advice or its application was unreasonable, capricious, or arbitrary).[210] Arbitrator W. Willard Wirtz, for instance, stated that the arbitrator can only decide "whether the medical determination was made in a manner and by * * * a procedure indicating that it was fairly and reasonably made."[211] And Arbitrator James A. Doyle explained:

"The judgment of the plant physician is entitled to great weight. He is conversant with the requirements of the occupation involved and the risks inherent in such work. It is generally held that where there is a

---

[208]As in Southern Cotton Oil Co., 26 LA 353, 356 (Kelliher, 1956).

[209]As in White Motor Co., 28 LA 823, 829 (Lazarus, 1957). Also see Arbitrator Roumell in 73 LA 952, 953–954; Moberly in 69 LA 644, 649 (involving use in arbitration of depositions of doctors previously taken in workers' compensation proceedings). The weight of written statements was greatly reduced by other evidence in American Iron & Mach. Works Co., 19 LA 417, 420 (Merrill, 1952).

[210]See Arbitrator Nelson in 78 LA 499, 503; Creo in 78 LA 437, 443; Barrett in 66 LA 433, 438–439; Fleischli in 62 LA 351, 353–354; Guse in 50 LA 476, 486–487; Doyle in 49 LA 535, 539; Cayton in 47 LA 254, 256; Elkouri in 47 LA 12, 14; Kerrison in 45 LA 724, 726; Stouffer in 66-1 ARB ¶8030; Kates in 43 LA 61, 64; Autrey in 41 LA 519, 523; Stockman in 41 LA 449, 453–454; Russell in 40 LA 229, 230–231; May in 38 LA 1049, 1054; Thompson in 37 LA 581, 584; Kelliher in 37 LA 175, 176 (involving psychiatric opinion); Quinlan in 33 LA 141, 145; Hoel in 31 LA 256, 259–260 (holding also that if the employer has the employee examined by several doctors and receives conflicting opinions, the employer may decide which opinion to follow in absence of error or unreasonableness); Prasow in 24 LA 732, 738 (quoting Arbitrator Gregory); Abernethy in 24 LA 290, 298; Wirtz in 24 LA 274, 275. By the same token, if a doctor selected by the employer makes findings that support an employee, the employer should not lightly disregard those findings. Thus, where an orthopedic specialist selected by the employer had given the grievant a medical clearance, Arbitrator Seymour Strongin declared that "the Company cannot make a medical judgment contrary to that formally expressed by the specialist selected by the Company itself." Bethlehem Steel Corp., 70 LA 332, 333 (1978). Also see Arbitrator Keefe in 74 LA 744, 747–748. Then, too, an employee under postoperative care of his personal physician has a right to rely upon that doctor's opinion that he is *not yet able* to return to work. International Harvester Co., 22 LA 138, 139 (Platt, 1954). Also see Arbitrator Blackmar in 72 LA 238, 240; Draper in 68 LA 78, 81–82; McConnell in 37 LA 575, 580.

[211]International Harvester Co., 24 LA 274, 275 (1955). In Erie Forge & Steel Corp., 47 LA 629, 633–634 (1966), Arbitrator Mullin stated that while the company doctor's opinion is normally controlling it will not be so where that opinion or its application is arbitrary or capricious. Also see Arbitrator White in 68 LA 498, 501–502; Traynor in 64 LA 293, 298–300. In Crane Co., 47 LA 227, 231–233 (1966), Arbitrator Mullin held that the employer should have had the employee examined again where the employer was confronted with conflicting opinions from company and employee doctors, the most recent examination (by the employee's doctor), having indicated the employee to be fit. Compare, however, Goss Co., 43 LA 640, 643 (Epstein, 1964), where the employer acted upon the opinion of the employee's first doctor but the employee sought to stand on the opinion of his second doctor.

conflict in the views of qualified physicians, whose veracity there is no reason to question, the Company is entitled to rely on the views of its own medical advisers."[212]

In some cases the arbitrator has undertaken to weigh conflicting medical evidence.[213] In thus searching for a preponderance of the evidence, the arbitrator's role has been compared "to that of a lay jury which must decide between conflicting expert testimony."[214]

Although Arbitrator Maurice H. Merrill apparently would to some extent weigh conflicting medical testimony, he has held that where there is "direct conflict in the medical testimony, with nothing to swing the balance preponderantly on one side or the other," the company "is entitled to rely on the views of its own medical advisers, if it has given" the grievant "fair notice and opportunity to overcome those views before reaching a final decision."[215]

Special Factors in Considering Medical Evidence

Whether the arbitrator weighs the medical evidence or only assumes to decide whether the employer's determination was fairly and reasonably made, certain factors or considerations may be present and of special significance to the arbitrator in the given case. For instance, a stale diagnosis may fare poorly against one that is current;[216] medical opinion based upon extensive examination of the employee and observation over a period of time will carry added weight;[217] medical opinion based only upon the notes of another doctor (who examined the employee) may carry limited weight;[218] the opinion of a medical specialist will usually carry added weight,[219] but will not necessarily control over the opinion of a general practitioner.[220] In some types of cases it is imperative that the doctor direct his evalua-

---

[212]Hughes Aircraft Co., 49 LA 535, 539 (1967).

[213]See Arbitrator R. Roberts in 70 LA 1110, 1114–1115; Traynor in 69 LA 254, 262–264; Purdom in 54 LA 1041, 1044–1047; Dworkin in 46 LA 719, 723–724; Boles in 43 LA 734, 737–738, and in 43 LA 484, 487; Wallen in 38 LA 395, 398–399. For instances of at least limited weighing of such evidence, see Leonard in 48 LA 1187, 1191–1192; T. Roberts in 48 LA 1175, 1178–1179. Also see Moberly in 69 LA 644, 651–652.

[214]United States Steel Corp., 38 LA 395, 399 (Wallen, 1962). Also see Arbitrator Traynor in 69 LA 254, 262–263; Purdom in 54 LA 1041, 1047.

[215]Ideal Cement Co., 20 LA 480, 482 (1953). Also see Arbitrator Merrill in 19 LA 417, 420; Kelliher in 26 LA 353, 356.

[216]See North Shore Gas Co., 40 LA 37, 43–44 (Sembower, 1963). Also see Arbitrator McDermott in 62-1 ARB ¶8223.

[217]See Pennsylvania Tire & Rubber Co., of Miss., 69-1 ARB ¶8395 (Williams, 1969). Also see Arbitrator Allen in 50 LA 1152, 1155; Guthrie in 62-2 ARB ¶8369. In A.M. Castle & Co., 41 LA 391, 400 (1963), Arbitrator Sembower relied upon "the clearest, most succinct and unequivocal opinion" from the doctor closest to the case.

[218]See U.S. Pipe & Foundry Co., 36 LA 481, 484 (King, 1960). Also see Arbitrator Mallon in 69 LA 303, 305. Cf., Daly in 59 LA 425, 428.

[219]See Arbitrator Teple in 66 LA 647, 654; Roberts in 48 LA 1175, 1178–1179; Cahn in 42 LA 1042, 1044; Wallen in 38 LA 395, 399.

[220]See Gulf States Utilities Co., 44 LA 1252, 1260 (Murphy, 1965). Even the testimony of lay witnesses may be relevant and competent in reference to an employee's physical ability for work. See North Shore Gas Co., 40 LA 37, 43 (Sembower, 1963). However, a medical doctor's opinion that grievant might not "psychologically be a good employee" carried little weight with the arbitrator, who commented that the doctor was not a psychiatrist. Whitaker Cable Corp., 50 LA 1152, 1156 (Allen, 1968).

tion to the specific work requirements and environment of the employee's job. Where the employee's doctor failed to do this, his opinion stood up poorly against "the judgment of the Company physician and of the Company officials with their knowledge of the job to be done and the hazards involved."[221]

Use of "Neutral" Doctors

Some agreements provide that if the company's doctor and the employee's doctor disagree as to the employee's physical condition, these two doctors shall jointly select a third doctor whose findings shall be controlling.[222] This course of action also might be taken pursuant to an arbitrator's suggestion in the course of the hearing.[223] In a case where there was insufficient evidence to warrant a finding as to the grievant's physical fitness for continued employment, the arbitrator by his award specified a detailed procedure for securing impartial determination of the employee's physical condition.[224]

Doctor's Certification of Illness

A frequent use of medical evidence concerns written certificates from doctors stating that employees named in the certificates were examined on a stated date and were found to be ailing. Arbitrators have held that these certificates, although not conclusive, should be given significant weight in determining whether the absence from

---

[221]Gulf States Utilities Co., 47 LA 42, 46–48 (Murphy, 1966). To similar effect, Arbitrator Abernethy in 46 LA 645, 653. But an employer did not prevail where it relied solely upon the lay judgment of company officials as against the opinion of the employee's "medical experts." Texlite, Inc., 48 LA 509, 512 (Ray, 1966). Also illustrating that lay opinion ordinarily will not fare as well as professional medical opinion, see Arbitrator Ipavec in 72 LA 956, 959; DiLeone in 70 LA 899, 903–904; Klein in 69 LA 922, 926.

[222]For example, see Lone Star Indus., 74 LA 1049, 1050–1051 (Cohen, 1980). Even where the parties in agreeing to use of a third doctor do not expressly agree that such doctor's findings shall be controlling, an arbitrator understandably will give very careful consideration to those findings. See Arbitrator Strongin in 75 LA 169, 170; Das in 72 LA 1131, 1134–1135. Furthermore, where the agreement specified use of a third doctor to resolve conflicts in medical opinion, Arbitrator William T. Rutherford in substance insisted that such procedure be utilized as the means of resolving the medical issue. Jno. H. Swisher & Sons, 68 LA 947, 951–953 (1977). For the responses of other arbitrators where parties disregarded their agreement to use a third doctor for resolving medical conflicts, see Arbitrator May in 70 LA 954, 955–956; Naehring in 65 LA 666, 670–671. In Colgate-Palmolive Co., 64 LA 293, 298 (1975), the agreement contained no provision for resolving conflicts in medical opinion, but Arbitrator Duane L. Traynor took the parties to task for resorting to arbitration without first trying to resolve the matter by using an "agreed-upon physician"; he recommended that they agree upon a neutral doctor, "give him a detailed description of the duties the Grievant would be required to perform, or even let him observe the duties, then give the Grievant a full and complete examination and agree that they will abide by his decision." Also see Arbitrator Teple's statement in 77 LA 113, 120.

[223]As in Dayton Malleable Iron Co., 43 LA 959, 960 (Stouffer, 1964).

[224]New Tronics Corp., 46 LA 365, 368 (Kates, 1966). The procedure was: (1) the grievant shall cause herself to be examined by professionals of her own choosing; (2) the company, which had not yet had her examined, may have her examined by professionals of its choice; (3) if the above procedure produces a conflict of medical opinion, neutral medical experts are to be selected by the parties, or by the arbitrator if the parties cannot agree; (4) the neutral findings shall be controlling; (5) the expense of neutral experts shall be shared by the parties. In Ideal Cement Co., 33 LA 141, 143, 145 (Quinlan, 1959), medical testimony was sharply divided but sufficient to warrant a finding as to grievant's condition; the arbitrator noted that no provision of the agreement authorized him to appoint a neutral doctor as requested by one of the parties.

work is to be excused due to illness.[225] Such certificates, however, may be impeached if shown to have been given as a favor, to have been obtained through misrepresentation, or to have been based upon mistake.[226]

The right of management to *require* a doctor's certificate as proof of illness is discussed in Chapter 17, subtopic entitled "Sick Leave."

Protecting Witnesses

In some situations giving testimony in arbitration proceedings may subject the witness to varied risks of retaliation. For instance, employees and supervisors alike may incur the displeasure of the employer as a result of their testimony. Likewise, employees may jeopardize their relations with fellow workers for testifying at the employer's request. When feeling the need, the arbitrator may seek to protect the interests of persons facing this predicament by reminding the parties of the risks involved.[227]

Although the arbitrator cannot insure definite protection if the person does testify, there may be firm basis for a valid grievance or unfair labor practice charges in some situations of retaliation for giving testimony.[228]

A union's action in fining four members for testifying in the employer's favor at an arbitration hearing violated a clause stating that "either party to this agreement shall be permitted to call employee witnesses at each step of the grievance and arbitration

---

[225]See Arbitrator Crawford in 73 LA 1227, 1229; Witney in 59 LA 635, 642; Elbert in 42 LA 582, 584–585; Oppenheim in 29 LA 291, 292; Livengood in 20 LA 451, 453; Seward in 11 LA 909, 912; Griffin in 1 LA 281, 282. Arbitrator Larkin expressed doubt that such certificates are too reliable, especially if submitted to the employer after extensive time has elapsed. Midland-Ross Corp., 49 LA 283, 287 (1967).

[226]See Arbitrator Shister in 59 LA 869, 870; Oppenheim in 29 LA 291, 292; Livengood in 20 LA 451, 453; Courshon in 2 LA 509, 513. Also see Garman in 76 LA 441, 445–446 (certificate inadequate not because the signature was stamped or affixed by a nurse, but because it did not state that the doctor himself had examined the employee); Duff in 74 LA 22, 24 (medical slip was equivocal and was not signed by the doctor himself). In discussing the company's "suggestion" that a doctor's *medical release for returning to work* was his response to grievant's economic needs and her desire to return to work rather than to her physical condition, Arbitrator Jerry R. Andersen reasoned that even though the doctor was concerned about the employee's personal problems, "it is also true that his potential liability if he recommended that a patient be returned to work and that patient could not perform without re-injuring herself would logically preclude his giving such a release solely to help the patient out financially." St. Regis Paper Co., 75 LA 737, 740 (1980).

[227]See Guides for Labor Arbitration, 9 (U. of Pa. Press, 1953). In Max Factor Co., 61 LA 886, 890 (Jones, 1973), the arbitrator denied the union's request for the addresses of certain witnesses against whom threats had been made. Also see Kaiser Permanente, 77 LA 66, 71 (Draznin, 1981), where delay in revealing the identity of grievant's accuser was necessitated by concern for his safety.

[228]See comments of Arbitrator Sembower in Berg Airlectro Prods. Co., 46 LA 668, 675–676 (1966), and of Arbitrator Jones in Western Insulated Wire Co., 45 LA 972, 975 (1965). Also see NLRB v. Scrivener, 92 S.Ct. 798, 79 LRRM 2587 (1972); Ebasco Servs., 181 NLRB 768 (1970). On the other hand, in Public Serv. Elec. & Gas Co., 115 LRRM 1006, 1007 (NLRB, 1983), the NLRB distinguished between punishing an employee for the act of giving testimony and punishing the employee for misconduct revealed by that testimony; thus the employer could "discipline employees for their misconduct even though the misconduct was discovered as a result of their testimony at an arbitration hearing."

procedure." Furthermore, in so ruling Arbitrator Edgar J. Nathan declared:

> "Even apart from such a contract provision, it would seem that any arbitration agreement would necessarily secure the right of both sides to freely call witnesses. Maturity in relations between responsible people and organizations can result in no other course of conduct."

Arbitrator Nathan's award enjoined the union from enforcing any discipline against the four members and ordered it to revoke the fines.[229]

---

[229]New York Twist Drill Mfg. Corp., 39 LA 167, 169 (1962).

Chapter 9

Standards for Interpreting Contract Language

Ambiguity

Probably no function of the labor-management arbitrator is more important than that of interpreting the collective bargaining agreement. The great bulk of arbitration cases involve disputes over "rights" under such agreements. In these cases the agreement itself is the point of concentration, and the function of the arbitrator is to interpret and apply its provisions.

There is no need for interpretation unless the agreement is ambiguous. If the words are plain and clear, conveying a distinct idea, there is no occasion to resort to technical rules of interpretation and the clear meaning will ordinarily be applied by arbitrators.[1]

An agreement is not ambiguous if the arbitrator can determine its meaning without any other guide than a knowledge of the simple facts on which, from the nature of language in general, its meaning depends.[2] But an agreement is ambiguous if "plausible contentions may be made for conflicting interpretations" thereof.[3] Moreover, it is recognized that whether a document is or is not ambiguous is a matter of impression rather than of definition; and this is obviously so, because each provision "may be as clear and definite as language can make it, yet the result of the whole be doubtful from lack of harmony in its various parts."[4]

---

[1]See, for instance, Arbitrator McCoy in 51 LA 1023, 1025; Pollock in 36 LA 391, 392; Klamon in 15 LA 676, 682; Kelliher in 15 LA 46, 49. Cf., Arbitrator Tischler in 33 LA 919, 922. Where the arbitration is subject to court review on matters of law the court may apply this principle. See cases discussed in Marceau, "Are All Interpretations 'Admissible'?" 12 Arb. J. 150 (1957).

[2]13 Corpus Juris, Sec. 481, p. 520.

[3]Armstrong Rubber Co., 17 LA 741, 744 (Gorder, 1952). Similarly, see Arbitrator Goetz in 71 LA 375, 378–379; Wolf in 70 LA 1303, 1305.

[4]Butte Water Co. v. Butte, 138 P. 195, 197 (Mont., 1914). In denying that a contractual provision was clear and unambiguous as one party contended, Arbitrator Neil N. Bernstein explained: "The law recognizes the existence of two types of ambiguities in contracts. The first type is the 'patent ambiguity,' in which language is unclear on its face—a mere reading of the

Most persons experienced in collective bargaining recognize the collective agreement as a comprehensive, but necessarily flexible, instrument which governs the relations between the parties. The very fact that almost all such agreements provide for the arbitration of grievances concerning agreement interpretation suggests that the parties recognize the impossibility of foreseeing and providing for all questions which may arise during the life of the agreement.[5]

As Arbitrator Martin Raphael stated, language cannot be tailored to fit precisely the variant meanings which parties to an agreement may have in their minds; language is frequently used which is general in nature and flexible enough to include those meanings which future experience necessitates being filled in. This arbitrator quoted Mr. Justice Holmes: "A word is not a crystal, transparent and unchanged; it is the skin of a living thought and may vary greatly in color and content according to the circumstances and the time in which it is used."[6]

The primary goal of the "rights" arbitrator is to determine and carry out the mutual intent of the parties. An ambiguity in a contract usually means that the parties have failed to express that intent with clarity. Sometimes, however, an ambiguity may mean more. It may mean that there never was any meeting of the minds. When this has been found to be the case, arbitrators have taken various courses of action as indicated in the next subtopic.

Accepting, then, that the basic function of the "rights" arbitrator is agreement interpretation, an inquiry should be made concerning the techniques, standards, or rules used by arbitrators in executing this function. An analysis of these techniques and standards should be of much value to contract negotiators as well as to parties preparing cases for arbitration. Such analysis will provide guides which, if observed in the drafting of collective agreements, will tend to protect the parties against pitfalls in the use of language.

This study may suggest the desirability of the use by negotiators of skilled counsel in rephrasing the agreement after mutual understanding is reached. While the agreement should be stated in simple language, understandable by the employees, negotiators are not

---

contract discloses the confusion. However, there is also the category of the 'latent ambiguity,' where the language appears clear on its face but becomes unclear when an effort is made to apply it to a given situation." Midwest Rubber Reclaiming Co., 69 LA 198, 199 (1977).

[5]Loew's, Inc., 10 LA 227, 232 (Aaron, 1948). Republic Steel Corporation's Director of Labor Relations, W.C. Stoner, acknowledged that: "Even the most experienced negotiators cannot anticipate all the conditions and variations which can arise under a particular provision of the labor agreement, and often arbitration is the only way to fill in the gaps to arrive at a reasonable interpretation of the contract language." Stoner, "Comment," Proceedings of the 26th Annual Meeting of NAA, 80, 81 (BNA Books, 1974). In Marine Corps Dev. Command, 71 LA 726, 728 (Ables, 1978), the parties had knowingly left a gap in a contractual provision where "the difficulty in coming to a full agreement" led them "to leave to working groups the way in which to develop the mechanics" of implementing the provision; it was those "mechanics" which ultimately brought the parties to arbitration.

[6]Yale & Towne Mfg. Co., 5 LA 753 (1946). Illustrating that the social attitudes and mores of the times may underlie an expansive interpretation of a term, see Pacific Sw. Airlines, 73 LA 634, 635 (Jones, 1979), where the term "regular parent-child relationship" was interpreted to include a stepdaughter.

always capable of expressing their true intent, either in simple language or otherwise. Moreover, negotiators are inclined to read into that which they have written, however ambiguous on its face, the meaning which they have agreed upon, and to lose sight of the problem which may exist for a third party who must read the contract.

It should be emphasized that the courts, when called upon to construe collective agreements, use accepted standards of interpretation of general application.[7]

Arbitrators likewise use these standards of construction. In other words, it should be recognized that all written instruments, constitutions, statutes, and contracts are interpreted by the same general principles, although the specific subject matter may call for strictness or liberality.[8] Accordingly, collective agreements should be drafted with the same care and precision exercised in drafting commercial contracts.[9]

On the other hand, the standards of construction as used by arbitrators are not inflexible. They are but "aids to the finding of intent, not hard and fast rules to be used to defeat intent."[10] Parties probably expect arbitrators to be less circumscribed by rigid rules of construction than the courts, and this helps to protect against harsh and unworkable results.

Sometimes two or more of the rules of interpretation conflict in a given case. Where this is so, the arbitrator is free to apply that rule which he believes will produce the better result.[11] Sometimes, however, a combination of two or more of the standards may be consistently applied in construing an ambiguous word or clause. The statement of Mr. Justice Holmes, that "it is not an adequate discharge of duty for courts to say: We see what you are driving at, but you have not said it, and therefore we shall go on as before,"[12] would appear to express the attitude of the many arbitrators who strive to determine what the parties were driving at and to effectuate their intent.

It is recognized that there are dangers to collective bargaining both in a mere literal, mechanical approach to agreement interpretation and, at the other extreme, in the indirect rewriting of the agreement by the substitution of the arbitrator's views under the guise of interpretation.[13]

---

[7]See Smith v. Bowen, 121 N.E. 814 (Mass., 1919); Mueller v. Chicago & N.W. Ry., 259 N.W. 798 (Minn., 1935); Reichert v. Quindazzi, 6 N.Y.S. 2d 284 (N.Y., 1938). Citing additional legal authorities and offering a summarized list of interpretation standards, see Tri-County Metro. Transp. Dist. of Or., 68 LA 1369, 1370–1371 (Tilbury, 1977).

[8]See Moran Towing & Transp. Co., 1 ALAA ¶67,012, p. 67,015 (Kidd, 1944). This view is practiced by many arbitrators, but there have been occasional expressions of doubt, as in Crescent Warehouse Co., 10 LA 168, 171 (Aaron, 1948). Some parties expressly provide that in reaching a decision the arbitrator shall use the standards of interpretation used by courts. Even without such express provision, use of those standards by arbitrators is proper and often will strengthen the award. See Smith Steel Workers v. A.O. Smith Corp., 105 LRRM 2044, 2045–2046 (CA 7, 1980); Johnson Bronze Co. v. UAW, 104 LRRM 2378, 2380 (CA 3, 1980).

[9]For valuable guides to aid the draftsman, see Marceau, Drafting a Union Contract (1965).

[10]Republic Steel Corp., 5 LA 609, 614 (McCoy, 1946).

[11]See, for instance, Arbitrator Block in Inspiration Consol. Copper Co., 50 LA 58, 62 (1968).

[12]Johnson v. United States, 163 Fed. 30, 32 (CA 1, 1908).

[13]National Tube Co., 11 LA 378, 380 (Seward, 1948).

There are, at the extremes, arbitrators who take a strict legalistic view of interpretation and those who recognize few limitations; but it may be safely said that most arbitrators take an intermediate approach, refusing to pay slavish deference to legalisms but also seeking to give effect to the contract which the parties themselves have made.

"Legislation" Versus "Interpretation"

Regardless of the approach taken by the arbitrator, it is to be expected that something of his personality will creep into his decision. The award of the arbitrator is based upon *his interpretation,* not that of somebody else.[14]

The line between "interpretation" and "legislation" cannot be drawn absolutely and it is inevitable that this line will be crossed frequently. One arbitrator openly declared that although the arbitration of a dispute must be confined within the scope of the existing agreement, its adjudication necessitates some *legislating* and interpreting to clarify and remove the uncertainties, obscurities, and ambiguities which exist in the agreement.[15]

Some gap-filling is a natural part of the interpretative process. Situations unforeseen when the agreement was written, but falling within its general framework, often arise. Where reasonably possible, arbitrators considering these situations must decide what the parties would have agreed upon, within the general framework of the agreement, had the matter been specifically before them.[16] As to such situations, one survey of labor arbitration suggests:

> "In such cases there is no true 'intent' of the parties expressed in the agreement itself. What is asked of the arbitrator is that he conceive, or adopt from the arguments of counsel, a theory of the agreement which explains his solution to the matter not covered by the agreement, and

---

[14]Kendall Mills, 8 LA 306, 309 (Lane, 1947). Also see comments of Arbitrator Levy in 70 LA 1296, 1299; Boehm in 47 LA 667, 668.

[15]Borg-Warner Corp., 3 LA 423, 428–429 (Gilden, 1944). Also see Arbitrator Rice in 8 LA 586, 588–589.

[16]See Arbitrator Williams in 76 LA 968, 974; Dworkin in 72 LA 337, 339–340, and in 46 LA 9, 11; Hadlick in 69 LA 547, 550; Bernstein in 69 LA 198, 201; Katz in 68 LA 249, 253–254; E. Jones in 48 LA 1304, 1317–1318; Merrill in 44 LA 1121, 1123; Seitz in 44 LA 259, 262; Block in 43 LA 97, 101; Smith in 42 LA 517, 522–523; H. Jones in 35 LA 686, 690; Dash in 33 LA 925, 948; McKelvey in 25 LA 94, 99; Abernethy in 21 LA 129, 131; Hampton in 18 LA 581, 583; Handsaker in 3 LA 383, 389. Also see Mueller, "The Law of Contracts—A Changing Legal Environment," Proceedings of the 31st Annual Meeting of NAA, 204, 213–214 (BNA Books, 1979); Fleming, "Reflections on the Nature of Labor Arbitration," 61 Mich. L. Rev. 1245, 1250–1252 (1963); Killingsworth, "Arbitration: Its Uses in Industrial Relations," 21 LA 859, 861–862 (1953). Dean Theodore J. St. Antoine stated that the arbitrator as the parties' designated "reader" of the contract "is their joint alter ego for the purpose of striking whatever supplementary bargain is necessary to handle the anticipated unanticipated omissions of the initial agreement." St. Antoine, "Judicial Review of Labor Arbitration Awards: A Second Look at Enterprise Wheel and Its Progeny," Proceedings of the 30th Annual Meeting of NAA, 29, 30 (BNA Books, 1978), also published in 75 Mich. L. Rev. 1137. Quoting this view with clear approval, see Boise Cascade Corp. v. Local 7001, 100 LRRM 2481, 2483 (CA 5, 1979). But stressing that "the admonition that 'the arbitrator will not add to, subtract from, or modify this agreement' has meaning," and warning that there will be a "loss of confidence in the arbitration process" if arbitrators fail to exercise caution about filling gaps, see Adams, "Comment," Proceedings of the 30th Annual Meeting of NAA, 52, 61 (BNA Books, 1978).

which does no violence to the general spirit and intent which have been expressed in the agreement. The arbitrator's task might be described as having to find out what the parties would have intended had they thought to deal with the particular item under dispute, or if they had had time to deal with it. How to accomplish this procedurally becomes a cardinal task of arbitration."[17]

In one such case the agreement expressly specified rail transport for orchestra members, no thought being given to air travel when the agreement was negotiated. When asked to decide whether the musicians could be *required* to fly on overseas trips, Arbitrator Lewis M. Gill declared:

> "[T]he arbitrator's responsibility here is not merely limited to searching for a mutual intent. He is not to throw up his hands and declare himself without authority to decide the case if he concludes that there is not any mutual intent on the point at issue. * * *
> "This contract has the common definition of matters which are subject to arbitration, describing them as 'disputes regarding the interpretation *or application* of the provisions of this Agreement' [emphasis added]. The provisions must be *applied* to the dispute at hand, in a fair and sensible manner—the only restriction on the arbitrator is the usual admonition that his decision must not 'have the effect of modifying or amending any provision of this Agreement.' "[18]

In holding that the members (with certain exceptions) could be required to fly, Arbitrator Gill denied that he was "adding something" to the agreement, but the Union argued otherwise.[19]

A similar approach was taken by Arbitrator Russell A. Smith when confronted with the question whether seniority rights would survive closure of a plant and transfer of its operations to the employer's other plant, where the employer was covered by a multi-employer contract defining "seniority" as "length of service with the employing company in the plant involved." Arbitrator Smith noted three possible dispositions of the case:[20]

1. Give the contract language literal meaning, though the negotiators never thought of the consolidation situation. Under this approach the employees of the closed plant would have no more seniority.
2. View the contract as silent with respect to the consolidation situation and hold the arbitrator to be without jurisdiction to resolve it since he could supply a definite solution only by violating the prohibition against adding to the agreement; he would have to remand the matter to the parties.
3. Consider it incumbent upon the arbitrator to give meaning to the term "plant" in the event of consolidation, though the present situation was not specifically contemplated in negotia-

---

[17]Eaton, "Labor Arbitration in the San Francisco Bay Area," 48 LA 1381, 1390 (1967).
[18]Philadelphia Orchestra Assn., 46 LA 513, 515 (1966).
[19]Id. at 517. The award withstood court challenge. Local 77. American Fedn. of Musicians v. Philadelphia Orchestra Assn., 252 F.Supp. 787 (USDC, 1966).
[20]Superior Prods. Co., 42 LA 517, 522–523 (1964).

tions; this the arbitrator could do as a matter of contract interpretation and application. Under this approach it would be reasonable to derive from use of the "plant" seniority concept a basic intent to grant seniority rights relating to types of plant operations then existing, and not to presume that parties contemplated eradication of seniority rights through consolidation.

Arbitrator Smith utilized the latter approach.[21] In doing so he stated:

"Arbitrators are constantly required and expected to give meaning to contract provisions which are unclear, in situations which were not specifically foreseen by the contract negotiators. So long as this is done by application of principles reasonably drawn from the provisions of the Agreement, and not by treating of a subject not covered at all by the Agreement, arbitral authority is not being improperly assumed."[22]

However, an arbitrator may refuse to fill "gaps" where he is convinced that to do so "would constitute contract-making" rather than contract interpretation or application.[23] In such cases arbitrators have concluded that the dispute should be resolved by the parties through negotiations; some of these arbitrators in refusing to rule on the merits have spoken in terms of "no meeting of the minds" of the parties.[24]

Which approach is best where an arbitrator is confronted with an issue growing out of an unforeseen situation? Obviously, no given approach is necessarily best for all cases. The arbitrator is justified in ruling upon the merits where a plausible solution is available within the general framework of the agreement or on the basis of an adequately defined past practice. However, where no such solution is available and the arbitrator is convinced that a ruling on the merits would cross the line too far into the area of legislation, or would involve too much guesswork or "shooting in the dark," he is likewise justified in remanding the case to the parties for negotiations. In any

---

[21]It is significant that the plants involved in the projected consolidation had distinctive types of operations; and under Arbitrator Smith's decision, the term "plant" as used in the seniority provision would be construed as establishing two seniority groups, one relating to the type of operations previously performed only at the L plant and one relating to the type of operations previously performed only at the G plant. Thus, employees from the L plant (to be closed) would carry with them what would amount to departmental seniority to perform in the G plant the same type of operations that they had performed in the former location, while the employees who had seniority at the G plant would continue to have a preferential right to the G plant type of operations.

[22]Superior Prods. Co., 42 LA 517, 523 (1964). Also see Arbitrator Smith in 48 LA 213, 218–219.

[23]Labor Standards Assn., 50 LA 1009, 1012 (Kates, 1968).

[24]See Arbitrator Lubow in 67 LA 257, 260; Dennis in 64 LA 1221, 1226; Sembower, in 54 LA 292, 297–298; Sweeney in 29 LA 188, 191; Garman in 20 LA 199, 201–202; Killingsworth in 12 LA 709, 714, and in 7 LA 70, 74; Copelof in 7 LA 507, 510, and in 6 LA 667, 669. Also see Arbitrator Cox in 75 LA 822, 824; Rayl in 70 LA 633, 635; Johannes in 20 LA 362, 363–364; Brandschain in 9 LA 239, 241; McCoy in 1 LA 556, 560. Cf., Arbitrator Lehoczky in 19 LA 766, 767. The NLRB held that there was no binding agreement without a meeting of the minds in Computer Sciences Corp., 108 LRRM 1233 at 1233 (NLRB, 1981); McKinzie Enters., 104 LRRM 1321, 1322 (NLRB, 1980). The "meeting of the minds" requirement is questioned by Arbitrator Sylvester Garrett, "The Role of Lawyers in Arbitration," Proceedings of the 14th Annual Meeting of NAA, 102, 121 (BNA Books, 1961). For related discussion, see Chapter 7, topics entitled "Remedy Power and Its Use" and "Recommendations by Arbitrator"; Chapter 10, topic entitled "Contract Principles."

case, the arbitrator must give due consideration to contractual limitations upon his authority, for gap-filling would then be improper (unless authorized by the parties for the particular case) if it results in a basic addition to, subtraction from, or modification of the agreement.[25]

Intent of the Parties

The rule primarily to be observed in the construction of written agreements is that the interpreter must, if possible, ascertain and give effect to the mutual intent of the parties. The collective agreement should be construed, not narrowly and technically, but broadly and so as to accomplish its evident aims.[26]

In determining the intent of the parties, inquiry is made as to what the language meant to the parties when the agreement was written.[27] It is this meaning that governs, not the meaning that can be possibly read into the language.[28]

The "intent of the parties" rule has been elaborated as follows:

"Whatever may be the inaccuracy of expression or the inaptness of words used in an instrument in a legal view, if the intention of the parties can be clearly discovered, the court will give effect to it and construe the words accordingly. It must not be supposed, however, that an attempt is made to ascertain the actual mental processes of the parties to a particular contract. The law presumes that the parties understood the import of their contract and that they had the intention which its terms manifest. It is not within the function of the judiciary to look outside of the instrument to get at the intention of the parties and then carry out that intention regardless of whether the instrument contains language sufficient to express it; but their sole duty is to find out what was meant by the language of the instrument. This language must be sufficient, when looked at in the light of such facts as the court is entitled to consider, to sustain whatever effect is given to the instrument."[29]

Language Which Is Clear and Unambiguous

If the language of an agreement is clear and unequivocal, an arbitrator generally will not give it a meaning other than that expressed. As Arbitrator Fred Witney has stated, an arbitrator cannot

---

[25]For cases in which the parties did give special authorization for the particular case, see Arbitrator Dworkin in 70 LA 917, 923; Beatty in 24 LA 424, 425; Ryder in 22 LA 769, 771.

[26]Rentschler v. Missouri Pac. R.R., 253 N.W. 694 (Neb. S.Ct., 1934). Also see Arbitrator Krimsly in 48 LA 1359, 1361.

[27]Brampton Woolen Co. v. Local Union 112, 61 A.2d 796 (N.H. S.Ct., 1948). Also see Arbitrator Gowan in 75 LA 625, 627; Winton in 71 LA 892, 896–897; Platt in 13 LA 126, 131. Cf., Boles in 20 LA 227, 231. In Globe Newspaper Co., 74 LA 1261, 1268 (1980), Arbitrator Samuel S. Kates stated that "To determine the mutual intention of the parties from the language they used, that language should be construed in the light of the purpose clearly sought to be accomplished, giving consideration to the negotiations leading to the adoption of that language."

[28]Autocar Co., 10 LA 61, 63 (Brecht, 1948). Also see Arbitrator Davey in 21 LA 139, 144.

[29]12 American Jurisprudence, § 227, pp. 746–748 (citations omitted).

"ignore clear-cut contractual language," and he "may not legislate new language, since to do so would usurp the role of the labor organization and employer."[30] Even though the parties to an agreement disagree as to its meaning, an arbitrator who finds the language to be unambiguous will enforce the clear meaning.[31]

An arbitrator, as a neutral, is less likely than the parties to commit the error of seeing what one would like to find in written language rather than what is actually there. Even when both parties declare a provision to be ambiguous, the arbitrator may find it not so.[32] On the other hand, language which appears on the surface to be clear sometimes will prove to have a latent or hidden ambiguity.[33]

Arbitrators apply the principle that parties to a contract are charged with full knowledge of its provisions and of the significance of its language.[34] Arbitrator W. Herman Rauch explained:

> "One of the most important facts about the collective bargaining process is that the parties involved are familiar with the employee and the business problems in respect to which they seek agreement. Therefore, when a tentative agreement is reached, both of them know what it was expected to accomplish. Probably more important, however, is the fact that the entire Union membership reviews the terms of tentative commitments and, based on the knowledge which the individual employee has of the matter in question, decides whether those terms are acceptable."[35]

Thus, the clear meaning of language may be enforced even though the results are harsh or contrary to the original expectations of one of the parties.[36] In such cases the result is based upon the clear language of

---

[30]Clean Coverall Supply Co., 47 LA 272, 277 (1966). The courts, too, are obligated to apply clear provisions of collective agreements as intended by the parties. UMW Health & Retirement Fund v. Robinson, 102 S.Ct. 1226, 1230, 1234, 109 LRRM 2865 (1982), the Supreme Court stating that "when neither the collective bargaining process nor its end product violates any command of Congress, a federal court has no authority to modify the substantive terms of a collective bargaining contract." Where evidence indicated that the contracting union could not be held responsible for the refusal of its members to cross another union's picket line, that refusal was held not covered by a contractual provision prohibiting strikes or stoppages "on the part of the Union" and lockouts "on the part of the Company," Arbitrator A.J. Wann explaining: "In such highly controversial cases, the arbitrator long ago concluded that it is best to try to interpret the words of the contract in as literal, exact, and limited a way as possible so as not to read into the contract, or inadvertently add to it, meanings which were not intended by the parties and which should not reasonably be inferred from the words used." Continental Oil Co., 69 LA 399, 404 (1977).

[31]See Arbitrator Weiss in 69 LA 10, 13; Daniel in 68 LA 54, 55; Leonard in 47 LA 661, 665; Traynor in 47 LA 193, 194–195; Daugherty in 46 LA 95, 98; Autrey in 45 LA 783, 786, 788; Scheiber in 44 LA 883, 887; Shipman in 9 LA 716, 718; Blumer in 5 LA 378, 382; Rader in 4 LA 497, 502; Epstein in 3 LA 412, 414; Updegraff in 2 LA 469, 472; Peifer in 2 LA 66, 67.

[32]As in Andrew Williams Meat Co., 8 LA 518, 524 (Cheney, 1947). Also see Arbitrator Scheiber in 40 LA 152, 154–155.

[33]As in Carlile & Doughty, 9 LA 239, 241 (Brandschain, 1947). Similarly, see Arbitrator Bernstein in 69 LA 198, 199.

[34]See Arbitrator Sacks in 71 LA 983, 988; Rauch in 51 LA 561, 565; Kerrison in 45 LA 530, 531; Platt in 7 LA 708, 711; Updegraff in 3 LA 229, 232 (citing law cases), and in 2 LA 469, 472.

[35]Wyman-Gordon Co., 51 LA 561, 565 (1968).

[36]See Arbitrator Hedges in 80 LA 591, 595–596; Feldman in 76 LA 1256, 1258; Doyle in 76 LA 1164, 1167; Shaw in 76 LA 1136, 1137; Harr in 76 LA 581, 582; Cohen in 74 LA 1049, 1051; Tamoush in 72 LA 1180, 1184; Laybourne in 72 LA 138, 143; Berkeley in 71 LA 1029, 1030; Moran in 70 LA 1041, 1042; Boals in 68 LA 672, 676; Moore in 66 LA 1002, 1005; McDermott in 49 LA 1157, 1159; Erbs in 49 LA 229, 230–231; Stouffer in 46 LA 578, 583; Small in 45 LA 775, 777; Abernethy in 44 LA 183, 188; Ross in 28 LA 557, 558; Shipman in 20 LA 756, 758–759; Copelof in 13 LA 110, 114; Potter in 7 LA 724, 729; Cheney in 6 LA 962, 965; Marshall in 6 LA 838, 843; Prasow in 6 LA 540, 543; Carmichael in 1 ALAA ¶67,096. Cf., Seitz in 32 LA 513, 516.

the contract, not upon the equities involved.[37]

Nonetheless, where very broad language has been used an arbitrator might refuse to apply it literally, but apply it restrictively so as to produce the intended result.[38] Also, if an arbitrator finds that as a result of mutual mistake or typographical error the parties used language or punctuation which does not express their true intent, a reformation may be granted so as to effectuate the true intent of the parties.[39]

Interpretation in Light of the Law

Arbitrators strive to give effect to the collective agreement rather than to dismember it, and, whenever two interpretations are possible, one making the agreement valid and lawful and the other making it unlawful, the former will be used. The parties are presumed to have intended a valid contract.[40] Similarly, the public interest may be a relevant factor in contract interpretation.[41]

When parties use language in their agreement which is the same as language of a statute, the meaning given to that language by courts and administrative tribunals may be persuasive upon arbitrators as indicating the proper interpretation of the language.[42]

Normal and Technical Usage

Arbitrators give words their ordinary and popularly accepted meaning in the absence of anything indicating that they were used in a different sense or that the parties intended some special colloquial

---

[37]See Arbitrator Boals in 69 LA 238, 240; Marcus in 68 LA 838, 841; Altrock in 61 LA 1061, 1063; Davis in 48 LA 938, 939–940; Hayes in 48 LA 276, 280; Marshall in 6 LA 838, 843.

[38]See Arbitrator Edes in 74 LA 1063, 1065; Cushman in 71 LA 412, 420 (read literally, the contested overtime equalization clause "applies to any kind of work performed by members of the bargaining unit"; but in view of the new and unusual features of the off-site project which produced the overtime in question, and since the contract was entered into before there ever had been any off-site work, it was concluded that the clause "was not intended to apply to off-site work"); Rutherford in 69 LA 406, 408, 410; R.C. Seitz in 65 LA 762, 763–764; McCoy in 49 LA 255, 256; P. Seitz in 46 LA 961, 963–964 (declaring that it "is not difficult to make an ass of the law by a too literal reading of words used by the parties in expressing their bargain"); Roberts in 45 LA 291, 292–293; Warns in 36 LA 380, 381; Updegraff in 33 LA 629, 631–632; Lehoczky in 9 LA 656, 657. Also see Loveless v. Eastern Air Lines, 111 LRRM 2001, 2004–2007 (CA 11, 1982); Arbitrator Gibson in 46 LA 598, 601. The switch to daylight savings time has produced a pair of contrasting cases in which the arbitrator's attitude toward literal application of contractual language is worthy of note. See Arbitrator Abernethy in 51 LA 9, 12, and Arbitrator Roberts in 33 LA 752, 753.

[39]See Arbitrator Anderson in 43 LA 730, 732–733; Compton in 27 LA 829, 831; Willcox in 23 LA 21, 24. Also see Taylor in 70 LA 1148, 1151–1152; Emery in 20 LA 865, 867; McCoy in 3 LA 257, 259. Cf., Sembower in 43 LA 722, 726–727. For further development of this matter, see Chapter 10, topic entitled "Remedies for Mistake."

[40]See Arbitrator Shearer in 75 LA 1038, 1040; Snow in 71 LA 109, 112–113; Gorder in 20 LA 880, 889; Horvitz in 9 LA 702, 703; Tischler in 5 LA 282, 283; Shake in 2 LA 445, 452.

[41]Maritime Serv. Comm. Inc., 49 LA 557, 562 (Scheiber, 1967). Also see Arbitrator Kramer in 71 LA 1051, 1054.

[42]See Arbitrator Rogosin in 75 LA 827, 829; Handsaker in 73 LA 1305, 1307; Reeves in 20 LA 564, 566; Horvitz in 20 LA 318, 320; Platt in 19 LA 457, 458. For extensive discussion of use by arbitrators of substantive rules of law, see Chapter 10.

meaning.[43] For instance, the word "may" has been given its ordinary "permissive" meaning in absence of strong evidence that a mandatory meaning was intended.[44] The words "day" or "workday" ordinarily must be construed as a calendar day, from midnight to midnight.[45]

Trade or technical terms will be interpreted in a trade or technical sense unless clearly used otherwise. For instance, the term "union shop" was applied in the sense commonly used in labor circles instead of in a special sense (which would not have required maintenance of membership) urged by management; the arbitrator declared that if the employer did not intend that which was meant by the term in the parlance of organized labor or did not understand the term, he should not have let it be used in the contract.[46] Under similar reasoning, the term "regular hourly rate" was given its generally accepted meaning in industry.[47] However, an arbitrator gave a medical term its popular meaning after he "conducted his own 'Gallup Poll' " with laymen, who all agreed as to the meaning of the disputed term; he assumed, absent proof to the contrary, that the negotiators were laymen.[48]

Any term not characteristically a trade or technical term will be construed in its natural, usual sense unless the context or evidence indicates that a technical meaning was intended by the parties.[49]

It is said to be "a well recognized rule of construction that a word used by parties in one sense is to be interpreted, in the absence of countervailing reasons, as employed in the same sense throughout the writing."[50] On the other hand, use of two different terms might be held to imply different meanings.[51]

It is also stated that when parties have changed the language of their agreement there is a presumption that they intended a changed

---

[43]See Arbitrator McDonald in 76 LA 569, 571; Britton in 74 LA 964, 965; Waters in 70 LA 320, 322; Simon in 69 LA 687, 694; Roberts in 48 LA 978, 980; Anrod in 48 LA 310, 312–313; Summers in 48 LA 137, 142; Shipman in 46 LA 1053, 1056; Slavney in 28 LA 532, 534; Prasow in 27 LA 40, 45; Feinberg in 18 LA 227, 231; Shulman in 12 LA 949, 954; McCoy in 12 LA 650, 652; Lewis in 6 LA 202, 203; Kelliher in 5 LA 409, 410; Rader in 3 LA 605, 607. Illustrating that parties do not always intend that a term shall carry its ordinary meaning, see Vlasic Foods, 74 LA 1214, 1217–1218 (1980), where Arbitrator Nathan Lipson drew a distinction between (1) situations in which parties allegedly have amended clear language by past practice, and (2) situations in which the parties in negotiating their agreement never intended that certain words were to carry their ordinary meaning; he concluded that in the case before him, "where the evidence is overwhelming that something other than the ordinary meaning was intended, the application of the words in said [special] sense does not manifest an infidelity to the contract but indeed carries out the agreement of the parties."

[44]See Arbitrator McDonald in 76 LA 569, 571; Hogan in 25 LA 243, 246; Reynard in 22 LA 880, 881.

[45]See AMF W. Tool, 49 LA 718, 723 (Solomon, 1967), and cases cited therein. In Pratt & Lambert, 76 LA 685, 690 (Denson, 1981), the word "month" was given its ordinary meaning of "calendar" month.

[46]Safeway Stores, 1 ALAA ¶67,096, p. 67,169 (Carmichael, 1944). Also applying a term in its technical sense, Arbitrator Merrill in 47 LA 1120, 1125. Cf., Sullivan in 39 LA 791, 794–795. In Southern New Eng. Tel. Co., 61 LA 184, 187 (1973), Arbitrator Arnold M. Zack reasoned that the term "hired" should be viewed in its labor relations context and not in its ordinary dictionary usage.

[47]R.M.F., Inc., 50 LA 789, 790 (Sherman, 1968).

[48]American Synthetic Rubber Co., 50 LA 25, 30 (Kesselman, 1967).

[49]Walton Laboratories, 47 LA 375, 377 (Yagoda, 1966); Great Lakes Dredge & Dock Co., 5 LA 409, 410 (Kelliher, 1946).

[50]Vickers, 15 LA 353, 356 (Platt, 1950). Also see Arbitrator Platt in 48 LA 1213, 1215.

[51]As in Hanz Trucking, 46 LA 1057, 1062 (Anderson, 1966), where the contract used two different terms in setting up hourly pay rates for the same work performed under different circumstances. Cf., Arbitrator Morvant in 36 LA 496, 500–501.

meaning.[52] By the same token, continued use of certain key terms in successive agreements justified a party's assumption that no change in meaning was intended by the other party who had failed to state otherwise in negotiations.[53]

Use of Dictionary Definitions

Arbitrators have often ruled that in the absence of a showing of mutual understanding of the parties to the contrary, the usual and ordinary definition of terms as defined by a reliable dictionary should govern.[54] In any event, dictionary definitions may be considered "as an aid" in reaching the arbitrator's decision.[55]

Trade or technical terms of a particular industry may be given meaning by resort to a special dictionary for that industry,[56] and a labor relations dictionary may be used for general industrial terms.[57]

However, an examination of the entire agreement and its application to the subject matter being considered by the arbitrator may result in the interpretation of words not in the general dictionary sense but in a mutually agreed sense.[58]

Furthermore, it sometimes happens that dictionary definitions can be found to cover opposing contentions.[59] In such situations (and indeed ordinarily) it is desirable that interpretations not rest upon dictionary definitions alone but be additionally supported by other considerations, especially where the persons drafting the agreement were laymen untrained in the precise use of words.[60]

Agreement to Be Construed as a Whole

It is said that the "primary rule in construing a written instrument is to determine, not alone from a single word or phrase, but from

---

[52]See Arbitrator Kates in 46 LA 715, 717, and in 44 LA 861, 865; Prasow in 40 LA 201, 204; Emery in 20 LA 865, 867. In Lakeside Malleable Casting Co., 48 LA 1104, 1106 (Anderson, 1967), the deletion of an express exception was deemed a clear indication of intent to abolish the exception. Cf., Arbitrator Barnhart in 71 LA 1178, 1180. Where two provisions of a contract were contradictory, the one adopted later in point of time was held controlling. National Distillers Prods. Co., 53 LA 477, 479 (Jones, 1969).

[53]Coordinating Comm. Steel Cos., 70 LA 442, 454 (Aaron, Garrett & Seward, 1978).

[54]For example, see Arbitrator Hayes in 72 LA 788, 794; Traynor in 47 LA 193, 195; Gibson in 46 LA 633, 635–636; Murphy in 46 LA 289, 292; Cahn in 29 LA 597, 603; Hebert in 23 LA 497, 500; Gorder in 20 LA 880, 888; Luskin in 18 LA 459, 461.

[55]Cincinnati Post & Times Star, 68 LA 129, 138 (Chalfie, 1977). Also illustrating this common practice, see Arbitrator Teple in 69 LA 599, 601; Roberts in 69 LA 286, 289; Weiss in 69 LA 10, 13. Where the dictionary gives several definitions for the word in question, the arbitrator of course will select the one which is most applicable and appropriate to the subject matter of the grievance, as in Area Educ. Agency 13, 70 LA 555, 558 (Smith, 1978).

[56]Columbian Carbon Co., 47 LA 1120, 1125 (Merrill, 1967).

[57]National Can Corp., 70 LA 1268, 1269 (Boner, 1978); Wisconsin Porcelain Co., 36 LA 485, 487 (Anderson, 1961).

[58]See Fran Jom, 75 LA 97, 99 (Siegel, 1980); Moran Towing & Transp. Co., 1 ALAA ¶67,012 (Kidd, 1944).

[59]As in Atlanta Newspapers, 20 LA 809, 817 (Dworet, 1953). Similarly, see Arbitrator Cole in 61 LA 745, 749.

[60]See comments of Arbitrator Lockhart in 16 LA 173, 175; McCoy in 12 LA 650, 652, and in 5 LA 492, 494.

the instrument as a whole, the true intent of the parties and to interpret the meaning of a questioned word or part with regard to the connection in which it is used, the subject matter and its relation to all other parts or provisions."[61]

Similarly, "Sections or portions cannot be isolated from the rest of the agreement and given construction independently of the purpose and agreement of the parties as evidenced by the entire document. * * * The meaning of each paragraph and each sentence must be determined in relation to the contract as a whole."[62] This standard requiring the agreement to be construed as a whole is applied very frequently.[63]

Giving Effect to All Clauses and Words

If an arbitrator finds that alternative interpretations of a clause are possible, one of which would give meaning and effect to another provision of the contract, while the other would render the other provision meaningless or ineffective, he will be inclined to use the interpretation which would give effect to all provisions.[64] In the words of one arbitrator:

"It is axiomatic in contract construction that an interpretation which tends to nullify or render meaningless any part of the contract should be avoided because of the general presumption that the parties do not carefully write into a solemnly negotiated agreement words intended to have no effect."[65]

Ordinarily all words used in an agreement should be given effect. The fact that a word is used indicates that the parties intended it to have some meaning, and it will not be declared surplusage if a reasonable meaning can be given to it consistent with the rest of the agreement.[66] However, if no reasonable meaning can be given to a word or clause, either from the context in which it is used or by examining the

[61]Riley Stoker Corp., 7 LA 764, 767 (Platt, 1947). Also see Arbitrator Horowitz in 70 LA 1003, 1006.

[62]Great Lakes Dredge & Dock Co., 5 LA 409, 410 (Kelliher, 1946). Also see statement by Arbitrator Gowan in 74 LA 345, 347.

[63]E.g., Arbitrator Dunham in 77 LA 377, 379; Abrams in 76 LA 739, 743; Gowan in 74 LA 345, 347; Maggiolo in 72 LA 700, 701; Greco in 70 LA 725, 728; Richman in 69 LA 751, 756; Rutherford in 69 LA 406, 410; Tongue in 49 LA 443, 445; Geissinger in 47 LA 748, 751–752; Erbs in 47 LA 475, 477; Krimsly in 47 LA 159, 161; Anrod in 45 LA 738, 741; Turkus in 40 LA 1248, 1250; Merrill in 29 LA 334, 339–342; Scheiber in 26 LA 117, 120; Ryder in 20 LA 337, 340; Maggs in 11 LA 992, 993; Hampton in 10 LA 487, 493; McCoy in 5 LA 609, 613; Gilden in 1 ALAA ¶67,315. Might the particular placement or location of a word or clause possibly be given any significance? See Arbitrator Fogelberg in 71 LA 116, 119; Traynor in 70 LA 963, 966.

[64]E.g., Arbitrator Richman in 76 LA 635, 638; Ordman in 75 LA 1288, 1292; Elkouri in 71 LA 381, 395; Gratz in 70 LA 387, 394; Witney in 50 LA 535, 538; Summers in 48 LA 137, 140; Leonard in 47 LA 661, 665; Merrill in 46 LA 1044, 1047; Layman in 45 LA 417, 424–425; Fraker in 42 LA 1073, 1075; Rohman in 40 LA 1217, 1221; Hale in 39 LA 310, 314; Hebert in 29 LA 469, 473; Kelliher in 27 LA 798, 800; Coffey in 12 LA 1117, 1120; Merrill in 11 LA 25, 30; Aaron in 10 LA 227, 233; McCoy in 4 LA 310, 313. Cf., Platt in 9 LA 91, 94.

[65]John Deere Tractor Co., 5 LA 631, 632 (Updegraff, 1946). Also see Arbitrator Scheiber in 49 LA 557, 562–563.

[66]Beatrice Foods Co., 45 LA 540, 543 (Stouffer, 1965); Borden's Farm Prods., 3 LA 401, 402 (Burke, 1945).

whole agreement, it may be treated as surplusage and declared to be inoperative.[67]

Words may be implied into an agreement with as much force and effect as if expressed therein if, from a consideration of the agreement as a whole, such inclusion by implication is called for.[68] Thus, in one instance the arbitrator decided that the words "job classification" were impliedly meant to precede the phrase "hourly rates of pay."[69]

Avoidance of Harsh, Absurd, or Nonsensical Results

When one interpretation of an ambiguous contract would lead to harsh, absurd, or nonsensical results, while an alternative interpretation, equally consistent, would lead to just and reasonable results, the latter interpretation will be used.[70] Where the extreme positions of both parties would have produced absurd results, an arbitrator rejected both and arrived at his own interpretation of the disputed provision.[71]

To illustrate application of this standard, a provision for paid vacations for employees in the "active employ" of the company on a specified date, provided they met other requirements, would not be interpreted so as to produce the "absurd" result of disqualifying employees absent on such date due to illness or any other valid reason.[72] Likewise, an interpretation was rejected which, if applied, would have placed a premium on contract violation by encouraging unauthorized strikes.[73]

Arbitrator Harry H. Platt found arbitral surgery justified where necessary to prevent absurd results:

"Experience teaches that contracting parties are not always absolutely precise, nor can they be expected to be, in their agreement formulations. Not infrequently, words or phrases are unthinkingly included which, if construed according to their literal meaning would produce results in opposition to the main purpose and object of a provision. This is often true when, as here, some of the language used was drafted by others in a different context and in response to other circumstances and policies. In such a case, there can be no doubt as to the right of an interpreter to modify and mitigate—in effect excise—the unpremeditated, unintended language in order to prevent an absurd result and to give effect to the true intention of the parties."[74]

---

[67]American Shearer Mfg. Co., 6 LA 984, 985–986 (Myers, 1947). Also see Arbitrator McNaughton in 49 LA 61, 62–63.
[68]J.M. Huber, 5 LA 100, 103 (Shipman, 1946). Also see Arbitrator Platt in 15 LA 352, 356.
[69]J.M. Huber, 5 LA 100, 103 (Shipman, 1946).
[70]See Arbitrator Nathan in 76 LA 1017, 1022; Sembower in 76 LA 909, 911; Roberts in 74 LA 998, 1004; Ables in 71 LA 726, 730; Bernstein in 69 LA 198, 200; Block in 50 LA 58, 62; Duff in 48 LA 513, 516; Anrod in 48 LA 310, 314; Kates in 45 LA 641, 643; Robertson in 37 LA 220, 225; Dworkin in 23 LA 481, 486; Platt in 15 LA 353, 355; Merrill in 11 LA 25, 29; Raphael in 5 LA 753, 757; McCoy in 2 LA 367, 370; Gilden in 1 LA 417, 419.
[71]D-V Displays Corp., 41 LA 937, 942 (Kates, 1963).
[72]Rockwell Spring & Axle Co., 23 LA 481, 486 (Dworkin, 1954). Also see Arbitrator Elkouri in 68 LA 304, 310.
[73]A.D. Julliard & Co., 2 LA 140, 141 (Copelof, 1946).
[74]Evening News Assn., 50 LA 239, 245 (1968).

To Express One Thing Is to Exclude Another

Frequently arbitrators apply the principle that to expressly include one or more of a class in a written instrument must be taken as an exclusion of all others.[75] To expressly state certain exceptions indicates that there are no other exceptions.[76] To expressly include some guarantees in an agreement is to exclude other guarantees.[77] Similarly, where an employee had 20 years of service with the company but less than one year in the bargaining unit, the fact that the agreement specifically allowed credit for all service with the company in determining entitlement to vacation benefits was held to indicate that only bargaining unit service could be credited for earning sick leave.[78]

The hazards of this rule of construction, known as *"expressio unius est exclusio alterius,"* in some instances leads parties to use general rather than specific language,[79] or to follow a specific enumeration with the statement that the clause is not to be restricted necessarily to the things specifically listed.

Doctrine of *"Ejusdem Generis"*

It is axiomatic under the doctrine of *ejusdem generis* that where general words follow an enumeration of specific terms the general words will be interpreted to include or cover only things of the same general nature or class as those enumerated, unless it is shown that a wider sense was intended.[80] Arbitrators apply this doctrine.[81]

For instance, it was held that a clause providing that seniority shall govern in all cases of layoff, transfer, "or other adjustment of personnel" should not be construed to require allocation of overtime work on the basis of seniority.[82] The doctrine has been held inapplicable, however, where the specific words preceding the general words embrace all objects of their class since, except for this qualification, the general words that follow the specific enumeration would be meaningless.[83]

---

[75]See Arbitrator Lipson in 77 LA 107, 112–113 (discussing the principle in some detail); Tamoush in 76 LA 1040, 1043; Collins in 70 LA 662, 663; Malkin in 51 LA 1266, 1268; Turkus in 49 LA 155, 158; Sembower in 46 LA 430, 435; Rosenfarb in 18 LA 418, 423; Copelof in 16 LA 685, 688; Hobbs in 10 LA 541, 549; Hampton in 10 LA 487, 494; Potter in 7 LA 81, 84; McCoy in 3 LA 257, 259. Cf., Holly in 24 LA 268, 271; Maggs in 22 LA 761, 762; Gilden in 15 LA 345, 349.

[76]See Arbitrator Roberts in 70 LA 475, 479; Dworkin in 47 LA 654, 661; Jaffee in 44 LA 1045, 1049.

[77]Great Atl. & Pac. Tea Co., 46 LA 372, 374 (Scheiber, 1966).

[78]A.S. Abell Co., 46 LA 327, 329 (Horvitz, 1966).

[79]Loew's Inc., 10 LA 227, 232 (Aaron, 1948).

[80]See 12 Am. Jur. 799–780 (Contracts § 244).

[81]See Arbitrator House in 77 LA 561, 568; Gibson in 62 LA 558, 560; Hilpert in 46 LA 752, 755; Leach in 43 LA 888, 890–891; McCoy in 39 LA 530, 533; Bradley in 37 LA 9, 13; Mueller in 35 LA 912, 914; Rohman in 34 LA 781, 784. Also see Larney in 74 LA 909, 915; Sembower in 43 LA 722, 728; Sullivan in 39 LA 791, 794.

[82]Canadian Indus. Ltd., 19 LA 170, 172 (Hanrahan, 1951).

[83]St. Louis Terminal Warehouse Co., 19 LA 807, 808–809 (Treiman, 1952). Also see Publishers' Assn. of N.Y. City, 46 LA 388, 394 (Moskowitz, 1966).

Specific Versus General Language

Where there is conflict between specific language and general language in an agreement, the specific language will govern.[84]

For example, where a contract contained a general provision stating that the Company should "continue to make reasonable provisions for the safety and health of its employees" and another provision stating that "wearing apparel and other equipment necessary properly to protect employees from injury shall be provided by the Company in accordance with practices now prevailing * * * or as such practices may be improved from time to time by the Company," it was held that the employer was not obligated to furnish rain clothes to employees where such had not been furnished or required in the past; the arbitrator said that had the general clause stood alone he would have been required to determine whether the furnishing of rain clothes was reasonably necessary for the safety and health of the employees.[85]

Arbitrators also may be expected to rule that, when an exception is stated to a general principle, the exception should prevail where it is applicable.[86]

Construction in Light of Context

Definite meaning may be given to ambiguous or doubtful words by construing them in the light of the context.[87] "*Noscitur a sociis* is an old maxim which summarizes the rule both of language and of law that the meaning of words may be controlled by those with which they are associated."[88]

Avoidance of a Forfeiture

If an agreement is susceptible of two constructions, one of which would work a forfeiture and one of which would not, the arbitrator will be inclined to adopt the interpretation that will prevent the forfeiture.[89] This principle was elaborated by Arbitrator George Cheney:

> "A party claiming a forfeiture or penalty under a written instrument has the burden of proving that such is the unmistakable intention

---

[84]See Arbitrator Shister in 74 LA 977, 979; Lipson in 74 LA 489, 493; Nicholas in 73 LA 573, 578; Cohen in 71 LA 781, 783; Petersen in 71 LA 43, 47; Holly in 69 LA 231, 234; Seidenberg in 48 LA 1005, 1010; Geissinger in 47 LA 748, 751; Kates in 46 LA 715, 717; Abernethy in 44 LA 183, 187; Sembower in 39 LA 534, 538; McKelvey in 29 LA 376, 380; Fleming in 28 LA 554, 556; McCoy in 12 LA 530, 531; Wyckoff in 12 LA 462, 469.

[85]Tennessee Coal, Iron & R.R., 12 LA 530, 531 (McCoy, 1949).

[86]Fulton-Sylphon Co., 8 LA 983, 984 (Greene, 1947). In Verniton Corp., 77 LA 349, 352 (Shipman, 1981), where the agreement also stated a general rule and an exception, the arbitrator stated that the exception would "be strictly though, to be sure, properly construed and applied."

[87]See Arbitrator Gorder in 20 LA 880, 888; Merrill in 11 LA 25, 31; Wallen in 6 LA 179, 182.

[88]Williston, Contracts, § 618.

[89]See Arbitrator Edes in 76 LA 986, 993; Mueller in 35 LA 912, 914; Kelliher in 27 LA 798, 800; Cheney in 1 LA 490, 494.

of the parties to the document. In addition, the courts have ruled that a contract is not to be construed to provide a forfeiture or penalty unless no other construction or intepretation is reasonably possible. Since forfeitures are not favored either in law or in equity, courts are reluctant to declare and enforce a forfeiture if by reasonable interpretation it can be avoided."[90]

In that case a clause requiring retroactive pay for employees unjustly discharged was interpreted by Arbitrator Cheney as an indemnity (rather than forfeiture) clause not requiring retroactive pay where employees suffer no loss of earnings while off the company payroll.

Precontract Negotiations

Precontract negotiations frequently provide a valuable aid in the interpretation of ambiguous provisions. Where the meaning of a term is not clear, it will be deemed, if there is no evidence to the contrary, that the parties intended it to have the same meaning as that given it during the negotiations leading up to the agreement.[91] In such case, consideration will be given to all of the circumstances leading up to the making of the contract.[92]

The arbitrator must place himself, to the extent possible, in the situation of the parties at the time of the negotiations so as to view the circumstances as the parties viewed them and to judge the meaning of the agreement accordingly. In this regard, the arbitrator might make a special request for complete detail as to bargaining history.[93] Recordings and minutes of bargaining meetings provide important evidence,[94] and in one case a union's "Negotiations Bulletin" was

---

[90]Mode O'Day Corp., 1 LA 490, 494 (1946), wherein numerous court cases were cited.

[91]See Arbitrator Boyer in 81 LA 438, 442; Babiskin in 74 LA 17, 19–20; Teple in 47 LA 438, 440; Whyte in 47 LA 26, 30; Bouwhuis in 1 ALAA ¶67,025, p. 67,041. Sometimes, however, little may actually have been said on a provision during the negotiations, and even where it is accepted that there were discussions, there may be little evidence of what was actually said at the time. In City of Williamsport, 68 LA 99, 100 (1976), the absence of extensive discussion when new language was placed into the agreement was a factor leading to a narrow construction of the language; rejecting an interpretation which would have broadly expanded the prior coverage of certain medical benefits, Arbitrator R.D. Kreitler stated that if the parties had intended a broad extension of coverage, "normally there would have been discussion to such effect" during negotiations. Of course, this does not mean that arbitrators ever will lightly treat contractual language as surplusage. Thus, where words were deliberately added to a provision by the parties in the course of their negotiations, the addition of the words could not be taken to have been a meaningless gesture. Kansas City Power & Light, 71 LA 381, 395 (Elkouri, 1978).

[92]Kohlenberger Eng'g. Corp., 12 LA 380, 384 (Prasow, 1949). Also see Arbitrator Liebowitz in 77 LA 493, 495.

[93]See, for instance, Detroit Edison Co., 43 LA 193, 200–210 (1964), in which the parties prepared a comprehensive exhibit at Arbitrator Russell A. Smith's request.

[94]See Arbitrator Shister in 74 LA 977, 979; Sickles in 71 LA 1009, 1012–1013; Grant in 21 LA 704, 706; Komaroff in 19 LA 138, 143; Blumer in 7 LA 512, 514; Blair in 5 LA 446, 448. In W.R. Grace & Co., 68 LA 966, 969 (1977), the union protested that the company's bargaining history exhibits were "excerpts pulled from the composite minutes, and that the documents may be self-serving"; in relying upon the exhibits, Arbitrator James C. Oldham explained that they "contain the only material in the company files bearing on the contract provision in question," and that the union had failed to submit evidence to support any inference that the exhibits were "distorted out of context," or, with regard to "the self-serving nature of the documents," to challenge their accuracy. In Blue Cross of N. Cal., 73 LA 352, 357 (Barrett, 1979), "shorthand notes" backed by a witness's sworn testimony that they were "notes which he had made in an across-the-table presentation," were accepted as bargaining history evidence.

found to provide a "useful clue" in reference to bargaining history.[95] Even where no stenographic record is kept and no notes are taken, the history of negotiations may be relied upon if the arbitrator is satisfied as to the accuracy of the oral testimony of persons who attended the negotiations.[96] Not all evidence as to what occurred in negotiations is competent, however; there may be privileged communcations not admissible into evidence.[97]

Furthermore, if an agreement is not ambiguous, it is improper to modify its meaning by invoking the record of prior negotiations.[98]

The intent manifested by the parties during negotiations, rather than any undisclosed intent, is considered by arbitrators to be most important. If one party to negotiations is negligent or unreasonable in permitting the use of a term which does not clearly express the meaning intended by that party and if the other party is thus reasonably misled as to the first party's intentions, a contract may be held to exist in accordance with the second party's understanding.[99]

If a party attempts but fails, in contract negotiations, to include a specific provision in the agreement, many arbitrators will hesitate to read such provision into the agreement through the process of interpretation.[100] Arbitrator Edgar A. Jones explained that "there is a hazard" in making a specific contract demand in negotiations:

"If the provision gets caught up in a grievance, the Party who proffers the language will have to bear the burden of demonstrating in a later arbitration proceeding that its omission ought not to be given its normal significance. Normally, of course, the plain inference of the omission is that the intent to reject prevailed over the intent to include."[101]

---

[95]Los Angeles Herald Examiner, 45 LA 860, 862 (Kadish, 1965). Also see Arbitrator Phelan in 77 LA 535, 539, where a "handout prepared by the Company for the Union's use in its ratification meeting," likewise provided a clue to the parties' intent.

[96]See Arbitrator Roberts in 74 LA 75, 79; Babiskin in 74 LA 17, 20; Bell in 69 LA 682, 686; Dolnick in 46 LA 426, 428–429; Hebert in 42 LA 458, 465; Burke in 3 LA 401, 402–403. In Manitowoc Eng'g. Co., 69 LA 336, 338 (Yaffee, 1977), the recollection testimony was not sufficiently precise to be relied upon. Also see Arbitrator Stix in 69 LA 1057, 1061; Silver in 68 LA 412, 413 (he could place "no reliance on such recollections [of the negotiators], beset as they are with faulty recall and self-serving statements of a conclusory nature").

[97]See Air Reduction Chem. & Carbide Co., 41 LA 24, 26 (Warns, 1963), in which statements of mediators in assisting parties to reach agreement were held privileged. Accord, Arbitrator Glushien in 55 LA 1130, 1135. For similar results under the NLRA, see NLRB v. Joseph Macaluso, Inc., 104 LRRM 2097 (CA 9, 1980).

[98]See Arbitrator Cole in 18 LA 916, 918; Blair in 3 LA 753, 756; Whiting in 3 LA 482, 486. For further discussion, see Chapter 10, topic entitled "Parol Evidence."

[99]See Arbitrator Kossoff in 71 LA 624, 629; Calhoon in 68 LA 572, 573; Merrill in 46 LA 503, 505, and in 11 LA 25, 31; Emery in 17 LA 632, 635; Wolff in 8 LA 452, 458; Blair in 4 LA 110, 111; McCoy in 1 LA 165, 167. Also see Turkus in 49 LA 155, 158; Bender in 43 LA 263, 266; Garrett in 15 LA 834, 838. Cf., McKenna in 76 LA 456, 461 (illustrating that a party has a responsibility to be reasonably alert to what it is accepting in negotiations—the union was held bound by a dental plan which it accepted without reading and without being misled by the company); Brandschain in 5 LA 164, 166; McCoy in 1 LA 556, 560. For related discussion, see Goetz, "Comment," Proceedings of the 31st Annual Meeting of NAA, 218, 225–227 (BNA Books, 1979).

[100]For numerous cases, see p. 314 of Third Edition of this book. For some later cases, see Arbitrator McDonald in 76 LA 811, 815; Cole in 76 LA 368, 372; Heath in 73 LA 1264, 1269; Merrifield in 72 LA 691, 693; Nutt in 71 LA 1235, 1237; Nitka in 71 LA 809, 812; Aisenberg in 71 LA 637, 645, 647; Yarowsky in 71 LA 473, 475; Johannes in 70 LA 1269, 1272; Kennedy in 70 LA 1217, 1224; Nathan in 70 LA 1091, 1096; Megley in 70 LA 925, 929; Collins in 70 LA 662, 663; Owen in 69 LA 247, 250; Oldham in 68 LA 966, 969; Volz in 68 LA 51, 54.

[101]Progress-Bulletin Publishing Co., 47 LA 1075, 1077 (1966). Also see Arbitrator Jones in 48 LA 1304, 1319.

However, where a proposal in bargaining is made for the purpose of clarifying the contract, the matter may be viewed in a different light. Arbitrator Sidney A. Wolff explained:

> "[I]t is fundamental that it is not for the Labor Arbitrator to grant a party that which it could not obtain in bargaining.
> "This restriction, however, has its limitations. If, in fact, the parties were in dispute, on the proper interpretation of a contract clause and one of them unsuccessfully sought in collective bargaining to obtain clarification, it would not necessarily follow that the interpretation sought by the unsuccessful party was wrong."[102]

Then, too, a party's unsuccessful attempt to obtain a clause severely restricting the other party does not compel the conclusion that a limited restriction does not inhere in the contract.[103]

The withdrawal or rejection during contract negotiations of a proposed clause spelling out a right has been held not to be an admission that the right did not exist without the clause, where the proponent stated at the time that it would stand firm on the position that the right existed even without the proposed clause.[104] A similar result was reached where withdrawal of a proposal was encouraged by the other party's statement that the proposal was not necessary.[105]

No Consideration to Compromise Offers

In the interpretation of an ambiguous agreement no consideration will be given to compromise offers or to concessions offered by one party and rejected by the other during negotiations which precede arbitration.[106] "[It] is clear that any offer made by either party during the course of conciliation cannot prejudice that party's case when the case comes to arbitration. It is the very essence of conciliation that compromise proposals will go further than a party may consider itself bound to go on a strict interpretation of its rights."[107]

---

[102]Hospital Serv. Plan, 47 LA 993, 993–994 (1966). For similar or even strong statements of this limitation, see Arbitrator Richman in 75 LA 1189, 1194; Feller in 73 LA 976, 981; Carter in 73 LA 623, 626; Di Leone in 70 LA 774, 776; Anderson in 69 LA 164, 168; Krinsky in 54 LA 824, 828; Valtin in 48 LA 797, 799; Traynor in 46 LA 53, 57; Cole in 36 LA 753, 759. Arbitrator Shister rejected the Company's contention that it merely had been seeking clarification where he found that "the Company was reaching for something radically different from a clarification; it was attempting to change the language of the provision, and was unsuccessful." Sterilon Corp., 40 LA 531, 532 (1963). Also see Arbitrator Robertson in 70 LA 71, 75.

[103]See Arbitrator Gibson in 76 LA 286, 290; Bailer in 50 LA 1270, 1272; Dash in 33 LA 925, 950.

[104]See Arbitrator Myers in 42 LA 269, 271 (rejection); Peck in 39 LA 1249, 1252 (withdrawal); Wolff in 21 LA 436, 439 (withdrawal). As to the effect of withdrawal without such assertion of right, contrast the view of Arbitrator Talent in 50 LA 1061, 1068, with that of Teple in 43 LA 338, 341.

[105]Philadelphia Orchestra Assn., 46 LA 513, 514 (Gill, 1966).

[106]See Arbitrator Kates in 39 LA 20, 22; Garrett in 26 LA 812, 824; Prasow in 25 LA 398, 403–404; Gorder in 25 LA 202, 205; Davey in 20 LA 737, 742; O'Rourke in 10 LA 417, 419; Greene in 8 LA 993, 996; Elson in 2 LA 399, 402. Also see Sembower in 41 LA 391, 397. For related discussion, see Chapter 8, topic entitled "Offers of Compromise and Admissions."

[107]Fulton-Sylphon Co., 8 LA 993, 996 (Greene, 1947).

Experience and Training of Negotiators

Whether or not an arbitrator will apply a strict interpretation to an ambiguous agreement may to some extent depend upon the training and experience of the negotiators. If the arbitrator finds that they were laymen untrained in the precise use of words and if the contract on its face bears evidence of a lack of precision, he may refuse to apply a strict construction.[108] Under such circumstances the arbitrator might conclude that the writing "should be considered as a somewhat imperfect attempt to embody rules which were better understood than it was possible to express in words."[109]

A less liberal approach is likely to be taken if the arbitrator knows that the negotiators for both parties were experts in drafting collective agreements;[110] or, to state it in other ways, if the arbitrator believes that the negotiators were "capable and shrewd,"[111] or were "sophisticated veterans" of negotiations.[112]

In applying a strict interpretation to a contested provision, Umpire Harry Shulman emphasized that: "The negotiators were not tyros in the art. They were skilled hands who worked hard, intelligently, and alertly. The agreement was not negotiated in a hurry or under pressure. Careful scrutiny was given to the language after agreement was reached on the substance."[113]

Custom and Past Practice of the Parties

One of the most important standards used by arbitrators in the interpretation of ambiguous contract language is that of custom or past practice of the parties. For extensive discussion of this standard of interpretation the reader is directed to Chapter 12, topic entitled "Role of Custom and Practice in Interpretation of Ambiguous Language."

Industry Practice

Reference to custom and practice of the industry in which the parties operate may shed light upon the intended meaning of an

[108] As in U.S. Pipe & Foundry Co., 5 LA 492, 494 (McCoy, 1946). Also see Arbitrator Dolnick in 46 LA 426, 429; McCoy in 11 LA 556, 560. Similar liberal construction was utilized in interpreting a strike settlement agreement drafted by a citizens committee in Yale & Towne Mfg. Co., 39 LA 1156, 1157–1158 (Hill, Horlacher & Seitz, 1962).

[109] Moran Towing & Transp. Co., 1 ALAA ¶67,012, p. 67,015 (Kidd, 1944).

[110] See Arbitrator Gootnick in 70 LA 383, 386; Marcus in 69 LA 1076, 1079; Garrett in 69 LA 740, 749; Burr in 36 LA 1132, 1135; Morvant in 26 LA 526, 528; Anderson in 20 LA 910, 911; Margulies in 19 LA 683, 686; Lane in 8 LA 306, 308.

[111] Carnation Co., 3 LA 229, 232 (Updegraff, 1946). Also see Arbitrator Updegraff in 2 LA 469, 472.

[112] Hilo Transp. & Terminal Co., 36 LA 1132, 1135 (Burr, 1961).

[113] Ford Motor Co., 1 ALAA ¶67,126, p. 67,265 (1945).

ambiguous provision.[114] An even stronger guide is supplied when the same agreement has been entered into by one employer with several unions or by one union with several employers. In this situation, practice of any of the pairs of parties operating under the agreement may be taken as some indication of the intended meaning of the language used,[115] but the arbitrator would not be bound by such practice.[116]

Where past practice of the parties in the plant and industry practice differ, the plant practice will ordinarily govern.[117] However, if the industry practice is well established, while the plant practice is not adequately established, the arbitrator may follow the industry practice as the better guide.[118]

Custom and practice of an industry other than that in which the parties operate may be accorded little if any weight. A practice which may be necessary and reasonable in one industry might be meaningless or foolish in another industry.[119] However, this is not always so.[120] In some instances a possible guide is practice by industry in general, either in the locality[121] or over a broader area.[122]

Of course, evidence of industry practice will not be given weight if too meager to furnish a reliable guide.[123] Moreover, while evidence of industry custom will be permitted for the purpose of clarifying the meaning of an ambiguous contract, it must not be given weight where the contract is clear and unambiguous.[124]

Prior Settlements as Aid to Interpretation

Sometimes light is shed upon ambiguous provisions by prior settlements by the parties of grievances involving those provisions. It has been suggested, in this regard, that "Where the parties them-

---

[114]See Arbitrator Williams in 76 LA 968, 975; Nutt in 71 LA 1235, 1237; Sherman in 68 LA 953, 957; Duff in 48 LA 513, 515–517; Fallon in 48 LA 12, 16; Foley in 46 LA 989, 992; McDermott in 46 LA 774, 782; Roberts in 45 LA 291, 292–293; Kornblum in 35 LA 384, 385; Hill in 11 LA 1081, 1082; Wallen in 6 LA 1017, 1022; Wagner in 6 LA 292, 293. Also see Bauder in 46 LA 712, 714; Zimring in 46 LA 411, 413; Young in 21 LA 278, 282.

[115]See Arbitrator Ross in 74 LA 92, 95; Finston in 71 LA 233, 237; Grabb in 70 LA 765, 766; Brown in 58 LA 852, 853–854; Geissinger in 48 LA 1011, 1013–1014; Marshall in 20 LA 297, 299; Sherbow in 17 LA 524, 526; McCoy in 1 ALAA ¶67,186. Also see McDermott in 53 LA 725, 729; Turkus in 46 LA 1112, 1115; Seitz in 43 LA 277, 283–288; Emery in 20 LA 458, 459–460. Cf., Di Leone in 70 LA 899, 902; Wolff in 38 LA 242, 244–245.

[116]Sidney Wanzer & Sons, 47 LA 708, 711 (Kamin, 1966).

[117]See Arbitrator Alleyne in 76 LA 916, 919; Oldham in 74 LA 884, 886; Cahn in 24 LA 601, 603. Also see Bowles in 76 LA 1273, 1275 (practice varied among the company's several plants, so the arbitrator considered only the practice at the plant involved in the case).

[118]As did Arbitrator Loucks in 24 LA 81, 84, 87–88; Maggs in 17 LA 451, 454.

[119]Certain-Teed Prods. Corp., 1 LA 354, 358 (Gorder, 1946).

[120]See Arbitrator Seinsheimer in 73 LA 15, 19; Rose in 70 LA 420, 422; Dolson in 46 LA 1158, 1159–1160.

[121]See Carnation Co., 38 LA 270, 272 (Peck, 1962).

[122]See Arbitrator Raimon in 48 LA 87, 90; Whyte in 47 LA 26, 29; Stein in 45 LA 1073, 1074. Also see McCoy in 32 LA 643, 644.

[123]Lehigh Portland Cement Co., 42 LA 458, 466 (Hebert, 1964).

[124]Western Union Tel. Co. v. American Communications Assn. CIO, 79 N.Y.S.2d 545 (N.Y., 1949). Industry practice was properly considered by the arbitrator where the contract was ambiguous in Aircraft Mechanics v. Ozark Air Lines, 101 LRRM 2358 (CA 8, 1979).

selves settle a grievance the evidence of intent as to the meaning of a provision carries special weight."[125] In effect, mutual settlements often constitute binding precedents for the parties.[126]

Similarly, even oral agreements of the parties as to the application of ambiguous language may subsequently be given significant weight by an arbitrator in interpreting that language if such oral agreements are clearly proven.[127]

If the agreement is not ambiguous, however, a past settlement which is inconsistent with the clear language of the agreement may be disregarded by an arbitrator in subsequent cases involving that language.[128]

Interpretation Against Party Selecting the Language

It is incumbent upon the proponent of a contract provision either to explain what is contemplated or to use language which does not leave the matter in doubt.[129] Where doubt exists, any ambiguity not removed by any other rule of interpretation may be removed by construing the ambiguous language against the party who proposed it.[130] It is reasoned that the draftsman, by exactness of expression, can more easily prevent doubts as to meaning.[131]

Courts of law, however, apply this rule only if a satisfactory result cannot be reached by any other rule of construction,[132] and it would seem that arbitrators should observe the same limitation.[133] Moreover, the rule will not be applied if there is no ambiguity,[134] or if there are special reasons for refusal to apply it, as where the clause finally used differed substantially from the one originally prepared unilaterally, and both parties approved the final draft.[135]

---

[125]Bendix-Westinghouse Automotive Air Brake Co., 23 LA 706, 710 (Mathews, 1954). Also see Arbitrator Emery in 19 LA 812, 814–815; Wallen in 17 LA 36, 39.

[126]For discussion, see Chapter 5, topic entitled "Grievance Settlements as Binding Precedents."

[127]See Autocar Co., 19 LA 89, 92 (Jaffee, 1952). Also see Arbitrator Gundermann in 46 LA 520, 522.

[128]International Harvester Co., 19 LA 812, 815 (Emery, 1953).

[129]See Arbitrator McKelvey in 73 LA 846, 850; Barone in 71 LA 524, 532; Dyke in 71 LA 89, 92; Kahn in 44 LA 1196, 1201; Morvant in 36 LA 496, 502; Smith in 21 LA 196, 198. Also see Emery in 17 LA 632, 635.

[130]See Arbitrator Bard in 75 LA 1119, 1128; Speroff in 74 LA 861, 864; McKelvey in 73 LA 846, 850; Shaw in 73 LA 569, 573; Richman in 68 LA 1132, 1138; Anrod in 49 LA 988, 990; Sales in 47 LA 1078, 1080; Jenkins in 45 LA 696, 702; Kahn in 44 LA 1196, 1201; Small in 41 LA 370, 372; Haughton in 39 LA 943, 947; Smith in 21 LA 196, 198; Healy in 11 LA 228, 233; Merrill in 11 LA 25, 32; Wolff in 8 LA 452, 458; Elson in 2 LA 399, 403. Cf., Scheiber in 48 LA 663, 667.

[131]Brown & Sharpe Mfg. Co., 11 LA 228, 233 (Healy, 1948). To similar effect, Arbitrator Small in 41 LA 370, 372.

[132]For cases, see 13 Corpus Juris 545 n. 44.

[133]The limitation was stated in Deep Rock Oil Corp., 11 LA 25, 32 (Merrill, 1948). To similar effect, Arbitrator Kates in 46 LA 317, 320; Krimsly in 42 LA 311, 314. For a suggestion of a stronger justification for using the rule where commercial rather than labor contracts are involved, see U-Brand Corp., 72 LA 1267, 1270–1271 (Ruben, 1979).

[134]John Deere Tractor Co., 2 LA 469, 472 (Updegraff, 1945).

[135]Crescent Warehouse Co., 10 LA 168, 171 (Aaron, 1948).

Further, it has been held that ambiguous language need not be interpreted against the party who proposed it where there is no showing that the other party was misled.[136]

Company Manuals and Handbooks

Company-issued booklets, manuals, and handbooks which have not been negotiated or agreed to by the union are said to constitute "merely a unilateral statement by the Company and [are] not sufficient to be binding upon the Union."[137] It can be expected that arbitrators ordinarily will be inclined to give such publications little or no weight in the interpretation of disputed contractual language.[138]

Relationship of Insurance Policy to Collective Agreement

Sometimes a group insurance contract entered into by the employer with an insurance carrier will conflict or otherwise not comport with the collective agreement between the employer and the union. Arbitrators confronted with this type of situation frequently have concluded that the insurance contract did not constitute a part of the collective agreement, and they have held that the collective agreement must control over the insurance contract (thus, the scope of the employer's obligation to the employees has been determined by the collective agreement).[139] In so holding, Arbitrator John F. Sembower stated:

---

[136]International Harvester Co., 13 LA 133, 135 (McCoy, 1949). Also see Arbitrator Mulhall in 76 LA 1033, 1036; Goetz in 71 LA 375, 381; Block in 58 LA 912, 917.

[137]Greer Steel Co., 50 LA 340, 343 (McIntosh, 1968). Also see Arbitrator Roberts in 71 LA 1123, 1125. The term "manual" as used in this topic does not relate to the Federal Personnel Manual, which is highly relevant in federal-sector arbitration. Regarding that Manual, and regarding other special considerations relating to the federal sector, see Chapter 2, subtopics entitled "Government-Wide Rules or Regulations," and "Non-Government-Wide Rules or Regulations."

[138]See comments of Arbitrator McIntosh in Greer Steel Co., 50 LA 340, 343 (1968), and those of Arbitrator Hebert in Westinghouse Elec. Corp., 45 LA 131, 140 (1965). A company's interoffice memorandum was held not binding on the company where it had not been adopted as a contract between the parties either by formal amendment or past practice. Tenn Flake of Middlesboro, 55 LA 256, 258 (May, 1970). The right of an arbitrator to consider a company pamphlet and a bulletin containing company rules in interpreting the collective agreement was upheld in United Furniture Workers v. Virgo Mfg. Corp., 257 F.Supp. 138 (USDC, 1966).

[139]See Arbitrator Rezler in 77 LA 256, 262–264; Sweeney in 76 LA 1044, 1047; Wolff in 75 LA 602, 607 (it was "the obligation of the employer to obtain an insurance contract which would provide coverage and benefits which were * * * provided for in the" collective agreement, and if the "insurance contract does not measure up to those benefits, the Company is required to make the grievant whole for the benefits contracted for by the Company and the Union"); Foster in 75 LA 380, 382; High in 72 LA 1013, 1015; Johannes in 71 LA 843, 846 (the "contract between the Company and the insurance carrier was not made a part of the collective bargaining agreement, therefore the Arbitrator may interpret and apply only the contract with the Union"); Williams in 71 LA 794, 796; Roomkin in 71 LA 796, 798 ("the employer is the purchaser of the contract with the carrier, and, as such, holds the ultimate liability for the subcontractor's performance"); Barone in 71 LA 134, 139–140; Porter in 70 LA 660, 662; Knudson in 67 LA 290, 292; Sembower in 66 LA 352, 353–354; Blum in 64 LA 995, 996 (employee rights under the collective agreement "cannot be compromised by the non-payment of premiums by the employer and/or oversights and mistakes of the insurance company"); Shanker in 63 LA 997, 1006–1007; Volz in 61 LA 864, 866; Larkin in 58 LA 815, 817; Teple in 56 LA 1308, 1312; Howlett in 53 LA 1302, 1303–1304; Holly in

"In innumerable arbitration and court decisions it has been held that the union-company contract always controls in these instances, and that the Company is acting as an agent of the parties to secure insurance coverage consistent with the terms of the Agreement so that the Agreement always controls and if the insurance policy is inconsistent therewith, it is subordinate. The unfortunate and regrettable result of this is that often the Company, in innocently trying to carry out its obligation is stuck with liability because the insurance carrier has inserted into its policy terms which are inconsistent with the labor-management agreement which is the entire basis for the obtaining of the policy in the first instance."[140]

However, the insurance contract has been held binding upon both the employer and the union where it was incorporated into the collective agreement by reference or where they were found otherwise to have agreed upon the insurance contract.[141]

Some collective agreements have been construed to require the employer merely to maintain insurance coverage in force without assuming an obligation to assure performance by the insurance carrier.[142]

In construing provisions of the collective agreement relating to insurance benefits for employees, arbitrators sometimes have given a broad construction to general contract language, and they require an express exception or limitation if a benefit or claim deemed to fall within the general language is to be excluded.[143]

---

53 LA 18, 20 (although the collective agreement provided that insurance benefits shall be determined by regulations established in the insurance contract, such regulations could not remove a benefit clearly provided by the collective agreement).

[140]Georgia-Pacific Corp., 66 LA 352, 353–354 (1976). But the employer sometimes is benefited by the rule that the collective agreement is the controlling document. See Masonite Corp., 72 LA 1013, 1015 (High, 1979), where the employer's obligation under the collective agreement was narrower than the obligation which arguably would have existed under the insurance contract.

[141]See Arbitrator Lipson in 74 LA 489, 493; Archer in 71 LA 786, 789; Matthews in 68 LA 780, 783; Cohen in 68 LA 396, 400; Simon in 66 LA 786, 792–793; Witney in 66 LA 13, 17–18; Strashower in 42 LA 372, 374. Also see Chapman in 73 LA 117, 123; Duff in 69 LA 1112, 1115. Where the employer and union are found to have agreed upon the level of benefits but not upon a particular policy or carrier, the employer's obligation is to provide the agreed level of benefits but not necessarily to continue use of a particular carrier. See Arbitrator Randall in 78 LA 533, 535; Chapman in 73 LA 117, 122–123; Marshall in 65 LA 1208, 1211; Karlins in 59 LA 1294, 1296.

[142]See Celotex Corp., 62 LA 752, 755 (Ray, 1974). Similarly, see Arbitrator Dworkin in 78 LA 973, 978; Handsaker in 75 LA 405, 408; King in 63 LA 779, 781–782. In this general type of situation a dispute based upon the insurance carrier's failure to pay benefits allegedly due under the insurance policy may be held nonarbitrable as not involving a dispute arising under the collective agreement. In this regard, a distinction has been recognized between (1) disputes concerning the question whether the employer has met its obligation to furnish insurance coverage (this would involve interpretation of the collective agreement), and (2) disputes concerning an insurance carrier's failure to pay benefits allegedly due under the insurance policy (this would not involve interpretation of the collective agreement unless the parties in some manner have made the policy a part of their agreement). See Arbitrator Nicholas in 79 LA 1308, 1311; Handsaker in 75 LA 405, 408; LeWinter in 67 LA 264, 265–267; Volz in 63 LA 165, 167–168; and in 57 LA 479, 481–482; Larkin in 54 LA 931, 932; Ryder in 49 LA 1128, 1131; WJLA, Inc. v. Broadcast Employees, 103 LRRM 2952 (USDC, 1980).

[143]See Arbitrator Roumell in 74 LA 569, 572–573; Williams in 71 LA 794, 796; Di Leone in 70 LA 899, 902–903; Sembower in 62 LA 360, 363; Klein in 53 LA 304, 311–312. Also see Foster in 75 LA 380, 381; Jones in 73 LA 634, 635; Traynor in 70 LA 767, 771; Ross in 59 LA 189, 193. Cf., Neal in 75 LA 1129, 1138–1141; Flannagan in 69 LA 928, 930; Carson in 68 LA 240, 244; Howlett in 57 LA 572, 576–577. Where the collective agreement was ambiguous regarding coverage of a claim but an insurance booklet was "very clear and definitive" against it, the claim was held not covered. Barber Colman Co., 78 LA 433, 436–437 (Holley, 1982).

Reason and Equity

It is widely recognized that if a contract "is clear and unambiguous it must be applied in accordance with its terms despite the equities that may be present on either side."[144] Arbitrators strive where possible, however, to give *ambiguous* language a construction which is reasonable and equitable to both parties rather than one which would give one party an unfair and unreasonable advantage.[145]

The arbitrator, it has been said, should "look at the language in the light of experience and choose that course which does the least violence to the judgment of a reasonable man."[146]

---

[144]Firestone Tire & Rubber Co., 29 LA 469, 473 (Hebert, 1957). See similar views by Arbitrator Abernethy in 51 LA 9, 13; Erbs in 49 LA 229, 230–231. For other cases and discussion of this principle, see this Chapter, topic entitled "Language Which Is Clear and Unambiguous," and Chapter 7, topic entitled "Recommendations by Arbitrator."

[145]See Arbitrator Maggs in 17 LA 606, 609; Broadwin in 12 LA 478, 481; Stein in 11 LA 1019, 1020. For arbitrators construing ambiguous provisions in such manner as to minimize possible harm to the parties and their relationship, see Arbitrator Wyman in 69 LA 871, 874; Cyrol in 68 LA 165, 171. For related discussion, see Goetz, "Comment," Proceedings of the 31st Annual Meeting of NAA, 218, 227–228 (BNA Books, 1979).

[146]Clifton Paper Bd. Co., 11 LA 1019, 1020 (Stein, 1949).

Chapter 10

Use of Substantive Rules of Law

General Considerations

In agreeing to resolve disputes by arbitration, parties choose to substitute a private solution for litigation in courts of law. Since the appointment and authority of the arbitrator are under the control of the parties, they can by the submission agreement expressly regulate (but do not often do so) the extent to which the arbitrator is to consider applicable law. Thus, for instance, they may expressly direct that the case be decided consistent with applicable law,[1] or they may restrict the arbitrator's authority to interpret the law.[2] Likewise, the parties can provide in the submission agreement the extent to which the decision is to be final. Thus, for instance, they may provide that the award is to be final only with respect to limited areas, such as questions of fact,[3] or they may provide that it is to be final except in case of "gross mistake of law or fact."[4]

Unless the parties specifically limit the powers of the arbitrator in deciding various aspects of the issue submitted to him, it is often presumed that they intend to make him the final judge on any questions which arise in the disposition of the issue, including not only questions of fact but also questions of contract interpretation, rules of interpretation, and questions, if any, with respect to substantive law.

Over a century ago the U.S. Supreme Court emphasized that arbitration awards are not generally subject to being set aside for errors of law:

> "Arbitrators are judges chosen by the parties to decide the matters submitted to them, finally and without appeal. As a mode of settling disputes, it should receive every encouragement from courts of equity. If the award is within the submission, and contains the honest decision of

---

[1]See Arbitrator Helfeld in 65 LA 453, 463–465; Cluster, Gallagher & Kraushaar in 45 LA 801, 807; Stark in 44 LA 997, 1001.

[2]See Ingalls Shipbuilding Corp., 54 LA 484, 487 (Boothe, 1970).

[3]See submission in Food Employers Council, Inc., 20 LA 724, 725 (Van de Water, 1953), which specifically made the award reviewable as to law by the courts.

[4]As in Goodyear Eng'g. Corp., 24 LA 360, 362 (Warns, 1955).

366

the arbitrators, after a full and fair hearing of the parties, a court of equity will not set it aside for error, either in law or fact. A contrary course would be a substitution of the judgment of the chancellor in place of the judges chosen by the parties, and would make an award the commencement, not the end, of litigation."[5]

In a 1953 case involving the Federal Arbitration Act, the U.S. Supreme Court stated that: "In unrestricted submissions * * * the interpretations of the law by the arbitrators in contrast to manifest disregard are not subject, in the federal courts, to judicial review for error in interpretation."[6]

As concerns the private sector, the continued vitality of the general rule that awards are not impeachable for errors of law has been recognized by federal and state courts in both statutory and common law arbitration (the applicability of this rule in public-sector arbitration is treated in the footnote).[7]

However, it must be added that the courts, under statute or under the common law, are not likely to honor any award which directs a party to commit an act or engage in conduct clearly prohibited by law, or which is found to be contrary to a strong public policy.[8]

---

[5]Burchell v. Marsh, 58 U.S. 344; 17 Howard 344 (1854).

[6]Wilko v. Swan, 74 S.Ct. 182, 187 (1953), citing the Court's 1854 *Burchell v. Marsh* decision. In evaluating this statement, the Ninth Circuit stated that "manifest disregard of the law must be something beyond and different from a mere error in the law or failure on the part of the arbitrators to understand or apply the law"; a manifest disregard of the law "might be present when arbitrators understand and correctly state the law, but proceed to disregard the same." San Martine Co. de Navegacion, S.A. v. Saguenay Terminals Ltd., 293 F.2d 796, 801 (CA 9, 1961). For subsequent reference to Wilko v. Swan and its theme of limited judicial review of awards, see Justice Harlan's concurring opinion in U.S. Bulk Carriers, Inc. v. Arguelles, 91 S.Ct. 409, 414 (1971). Where an arbitrator chose between two conflicting lines of cases on a question of law, the award withstood court challenge even though the view which the arbitrator followed was subsequently rejected by the U.S. Supreme Court in proceedings involving other parties. OPEIU Local 2 v. Transit Auth., 115 LRRM 2210, 2217 (D.C. Cir., 1984), stating that the arbitrator is not required to "have the ability to predict future Supreme Court decisions."

[7]For cases under the LMRA, see Perma-Line Corp. v. Painters Local 230, 106 LRRM 2483, 2485 (CA 2, 1981); Hod Carriers v. Pennsylvania Pipeline, 108 LRRM 2550, 2553 (Cal. Ct. App., 1980), stating that findings "on questions of law or fact by the arbitrator are final and conclusive"; Bell Aerospace Co. Div. of Textron, Inc. v. Local 516, 356 F.Supp. 354, 356 (USDC, 1973); Transport Workers v. Philadelphia Transp. Co., 283 F.Supp. 597, 599 (USDC, 1968); Dallas Typographical Union v. A.H. Belo Corp., 372 F.2d 577, 581, 583 (CA 5, 1967). Under the Federal Arbitration Act, see Raytheon Co. v. Rheem Mfg. Co., 322 F.2d 173, 182 (CA 9, 1963). Under state common law, see Guille v. Mushroom Transp. Co., 229 A.2d 903, 905 (Pa. S.Ct., 1967). Under state statute, see In re Dist. 2, Marine Eng'rs., 51 LRRM 2561, 2564 (N.Y. S.Ct., 1962); Kesslen Bros. v. Board of Conciliation, 32 LA 859 at 859 (Mass. S.Ct., 1959). For many other cases, see 6 Corpus Juris Secundum, Arbitration and Award, § 105, p. 251. For general discussion as to the limited scope of review of arbitration awards in the private sector, see Chapter 2, private-sector subtopics entitled "The *Trilogy*," "Post-*Trilogy*: Lower Court Enforcement of Agreement to Arbitrate and Review of Award," "State Common Law," and "State Arbitration Statutes" (very few of the private-sector statutes grant any right of review for mistake of law). Regarding arbitration in the federal public sector, awards are subject to challenge if they conflict with controlling laws, rules, or regulations. See Chapter 2, federal-sector subtopics entitled "Role and Scope of Federal-Sector Grievance Procedure and Arbitration," "Government-Wide Rules or Regulations," "Non-Government-Wide Rules or Regulations," and "Review of Arbitration Awards." In the state public sector, a number of states have expressly endorsed the rule that awards are not impeachable for errors of law, but of course both the applicability of this rule and the general relationship between external law and arbitration in the state public sector must be determined on a state-by-state basis. See Chapter 2, state-sector subtopics entitled "Court Review of Arbitration Awards" and "Contractual Terms v. Statutory Law Covering Similar Matters."

[8]Again, see the subtopics cited in the preceding footnote. Also see Local 540 v. Great W. Food Co., 114 LRRM 2001, 2003 (CA 5, 1983), stating that "the public policy of preventing people from drinking and driving is embodied in the case law, the applicable regulations, statutory law, and pure common sense"—to enforce "an award which compels the reinstatement to driving duties of

Furthermore, while arbitration awards are generally final insofar as the application of the agreement is concerned, there are some statutory issues (at least including those under the NLRA, the FLSA, and Title VII of the Civil Rights Act) which the award may not undertake to dispose of or concerning which the award may not be the final word even if it does assume to dispose of the issue.[9]

On the whole, relatively wide discretion is left to arbitrators to deal with the law according to their best judgment. A principal inquiry in this Chapter concerns the extent to which arbitrators do in fact have recourse to substantive law and to decisions of courts and administrative agencies on questions similar to the one before the arbitrator.

The reader will observe that many arbitrators do give consideration to "the law," but the extent of adherence thereto may vary considerably from case to case depending largely upon the source, form, and status of the legal rule or principle before the arbitrator. Thus, specific requirements and restrictions contained in codified law may be given greater weight by an arbitrator than general substantive law principles of agency, contracts, damages, and the like (although these will not be slighted). Clearly defined law will be given more consideration than unsettled and uncertain law or rules based upon controversial views as to what should be the public policy. Decisions by courts of final jurisidiction normally carry more weight than those of lower courts.

Then, too, the extent to which an arbitrator will consider any factor outside the collective agreement may depend upon the degree to which the parties have restricted his authority to the interpretation

---

a truck driver who admittedly drank while on duty, would violate this public policy"; Postal Workers v. Postal Serv., 110 LRRM 2764, 2768 (CA 9, 1982), stating that an award "will not be vacated because of erroneous findings of fact or misinterpretations of law," but "the courts cannot enforce an arbitrator's award if it requires the performance of an illegal act"; Perma-Line Corp. v. Painters Local 230, 106 LRRM 2483, 2487 (CA 2, 1981), stating that "an award may be set aside if it compels the violation of law or is contrary to a well accepted and deep rooted public policy"; Local P-1236 v. Jones Dairy Farm, 108 LRRM 2128, 2132–2133 (USDC, 1981), collecting cases invalidating awards found to conflict with public policy; Cook County Bd. of Trustees v. Local 1600, 100 LRRM 2723, 2727 (Ill. S.Ct., 1979); World Airways v. Teamsters, 99 LRRM 2325, 2327–2328 (CA 9, 1978); Goodyear Tire & Rubber Co. v. Sanford, 540 S.W.2d 478, 482–485 (Tex. Ct. Civ. App., 1976), collecting federal and state cases invalidating awards found to conflict with public policy. But in Local 1309 v. Aztec Bus Lines, 108 LRRM 2412, 2413 (CA 9, 1981), the court cautioned that "Public policy should not be turned into 'a facile method of substituting judicial for arbitral judgment.'" Similarly, in the New York public-sector case of Port Jefferson Station Teachers Assn. v. Brookhaven-Comsewogue Union Free School Dist., 383 N.E.2d 553, 554 (N.Y. Ct. App., 1978), the court declaired that: "Incantations of 'public policy' may not be advanced to overturn every arbitration award that impairs the flexibility of management of a school district. * * * Only when the award contravenes a strong public policy, almost invariably involving an important constitutional or statutory duty or responsibility, may it be set aside." The U.S. Supreme Court is similarly restrictive, stating in W.R. Grace & Co. v. Rubber Workers Local 759, 103 S.Ct. 2177, 113 LRRM 2641, 2645 (1983), that to refuse under public policy to enforce a contract as interpreted by an arbitrator, the public policy "must be well defined and dominant, and is to be ascertained 'by reference to the laws and legal precedents and not from general considerations of supposed public interests.'" For more on the latter decision, see Chapter 14, subtopic entitled "Contractual Seniority Rights, the Civil Rights Act, and Arbitration."

[9]See the discussion in this Chapter, subtopics entitled "U.S. Supreme Court Statements Regarding Arbitral Consideration of External Law," "Some Ramifications or Consequences of Arbitrator's Choice Respecting External Law," "Title VII of the Civil Rights Act," and "The NLRA, the Arbitrator, and the NLRB"; Chapter 2, subtopic entitled "De Novo Litigation Following Arbitration."

and application of the agreement, and upon his view as to the effect of that restriction insofar as consideration of "law" is concerned. It is also to be noted that many arbitrators have viewed the role of public enforcement agent to be beyond their authority and function; these arbitrators believe that the *enforcement* of statutes which impose affirmative duties or make conduct illegal in an affirmative sense should be left to the courts or statutory agency which was established for that purpose.

As to fundamental rules of law, in arbitration cases (just as in litigated matters) there frequently is one primary legal basis for the decision, such as a rule of agency, a principle of waiver or estoppel, or some other rule of law. It is true that arbitrators do not often cite legal decisions, but they do take cognizance—in essence judicial notice—of the legal principle concerning the issue under consideration. In the informality of arbitration it seems natural for arbitrators to state such principles without deeming it necessary to cite specific supporting authority.

It should be apparent from the materials contained in the remainder of this Chapter that parties preparing cases for arbitration, and indeed parties concerned with the initial negotiation of collective agreements, may be well advised to take into consideration pertinent laws, legal principles, and court and administrative rulings.

The Authors do not propose to show in this Chapter every situation in which arbitrators have observed or deviated from "the law." Rather, the objective will be to examine the views and practice of arbitrators in sufficient instances to indicate some of the more likely possibilities.

Range of Views as to Application of "Law"

In the present topic the Authors first will note the individual views of a number of arbitrators to indicate the range of arbitral thinking as to the extent to which arbitrators should consider "law" in resolving private-sector disputes (material relating to this question as concerns public-sector arbitration is provided in the footnote).[10] The readers in turn may reach their own conclusions as to the degree to which the various views overlap and/or conflict. It does seem reasonably clear from the materials in the remainder of this Chapter, how-

---

[10]Arbitrators in the federal public sector are required to deal with external law, and awards are subject to challenge where they conflict with controlling laws, rules, or regulations. See the Chapter 2 federal-sector subtopics entitled "Role and Scope of Federal-Sector Grievance Procedure and Arbitration" and "Review of Arbitration Awards." The relationship between external law and arbitration in the state public sector of course must be determined on a state-by-state basis, and has in fact varied depending upon the contents of the particular state arbitration statute and the views of the state's courts. See the Chapter 2 state-sector subtopic entitled "Contractual Terms v. Statutory Law Covering Similar Matters," where it is noted also that in cases where neither the collective bargaining statute nor the collective agreement is definitive and unequivocal on the relationship between contract terms and external law covering similar matters, arbitrators in state-sector cases have disagreed, just as have those in private-sector cases, on the question of considering external law.

ever, that each of the arbitrator views noted in the present topic has some if not considerable support in arbitral practice.

After noting the range of arbitral thinking as to consideration of external law, the Authors will note some statements (often dictum or essentially so) by the U.S. Supreme Court relevant to the consideration or application of external law by arbitrators. Then, as concerns the legal finality of an award and its de facto effect of concluding adversary proceedings on the matter in dispute, the Authors will suggest *some* possible ramifications or consequences that may result depending upon the arbitrator's views and actions in respect to consideration of external law.

In the remainder of the Chapter the Authors will then note the actual actions of arbitrators in respect to consideration or application of statutory law, court decisions, administrative rulings, and fundamental principles of the common law.

Views of Arbitrators

At the outset it may be observed that probably most arbitrators would agree with the following three points presented by Arbitrator Bernard D. Meltzer at a meeting of the National Academy of Arbitrators, to wit: (1) where the contractual provision being interpreted or applied has been formulated loosely, the arbitrator may consider all relevant factors, including relevant law; (2) where a contractual provision is susceptible to two interpretations, one compatible with and the other repugnant to an applicable statute, the statute is a relevant factor—arbitrators should seek to avoid a construction that would make the agreement invalid; and (3) where the submission makes it clear that the parties want an advisory opinion as to the law, such opinion would be within the arbitrator's role.[11]

However, Arbitrator Meltzer also presented a fourth point, upon which arbitrators have disagreed. He urged that where there is clear

---

[11]Meltzer, "Ruminations About Ideology, Law, and Labor Arbitration," Proceedings of the 20th Annual Meeting of NAA, 1, 15, 31 (BNA Books, 1967). Regarding Arbitrator Meltzer's first point, it is of interest to note that even where a given statute does not cover the parties, or does not apply directly to the case, or permits variations through the collective agreement, an arbitrator may find the statute (or cases construing it) a helpful guide if the agreement is ambiguous or contains no method of determining the issue. See Arbitrator Larkin in 47 LA 513, 517 (Presidential Executive Order was persuasive though it did not cover the parties); Anderson in 47 LA 356, 364; Moskowitz in 46 LA 388, 394; Dworkin in 45 LA 897, 904; Quinlan in 42 LA 626, 628–630; Aaron in 22 LA 249, 250–251; Ralston in 21 LA 381, 385; Myers in 7 LA 1, 2. Regarding Arbitrator Meltzer's second point, see Chapter 9, topic entitled "Interpretation in Light of the Law." Regarding his third point, note that where arbitrators have been specifically authorized by the submission to determine the validity or application of a contract provision under statutory law, or in other cases where it was clear that the parties anticipated that the arbitrator would do so, arbitrators have undertaken to make such a determination. See Arbitrator Bogue in 76 LA 883 at 883, 888; Ward in 76 LA 834, 838–839; Berman in 76 LA 158, 159; Fitch in 74 LA 214, 215–216; Williams in 72 LA 819, 820, 823; Conant in 72 LA 505, 508; Dunsford in 70 LA 1131, 1135; Davis in 69 LA 660, 663–664 (the contract provided for amendment of any clause found to be in violation of the law); Dworkin in 68 LA 101, 109, 112. For earlier cases see p. 329 of the Third Edition of this book. In Aro, Inc., 54 LA 453, 456 (Caraway, 1970), a court mandate required the arbitrator to review federal and state law to ascertain the legality of an unusual union shop agreement that was being requested; the arbitrator made an extensive review of relevant law as the basis of his ruling. Also see Arbitrator Flagler in 71 LA 427, 432–433; Jackson in 68 LA 682, 683, 685.

conflict between the agreement and law, the arbitrator "should respect the agreement and ignore the law." He reasoned that parties call upon an arbitrator to construe their agreement rather than to destroy it, and that there is no reason to credit arbitrators with special expertise with respect to the law as distinguished from the agreement. Thus, arbitrators should respect "the agreement that is the source of their authority and should leave to the courts or other official tribunals the determination of whether the agreement contravenes a higher law. Otherwise, arbitrators would be deciding issues that go beyond not only the submission agreement but also arbitral competence."[12]

In sharp contrast to Arbitrator Meltzer's fourth point, Arbitrator Robert G. Howlett insisted that: "Arbitrators, as well as judges, are subject to and bound by law, whether it be the Fourteenth Amendment to the Constitution of the United States or a city ordinance. All contracts are subject to statute and common law; and each contract includes all applicable law."[13] Furthermore, Arbitrator Howlett asserted that:

> "There is a responsibility of arbitrators, corollary to that of the General Counsel and the NLRB, to decide, where relevant, a statutory issue, in order that the NLRB, consistent with its announced policy, may avoid a decision on the merits, and the statutory policy of determining issues through arbitration may be fulfilled."[14]

---

[12]Meltzer, supra note 11 at 16–17. Professor Theodore J. St. Antoine has commented: "I don't wish to seem perverse in urging arbitrators to issue awards that may fly in the face of applicable law. But I just can't see any source of arbitral power to exercise a more extended jurisdiction unless the parties themselves have so provided." St. Antoine, "Discussion," Proceedings of the 21st Annual Meeting of NAA, 75, 79 (BNA Books, 1968). He explained: " * * * the arbitrator in the usual case remains just the 'reader' of the instrument before him. And if, after giving due weight to the presumption of legality, he cannot reconcile the contract and the law, he should render the award compelled by the contract." Id. at 82. He reiterated his views in Antoine, "Judicial Review of Labor Arbitration Awards: A Second Look at Enterprise Wheel and Its Progeny," Proceedings of the 30th Annual Meeting of NAA, 29, 34–36 (BNA Books, 1978), where he also indicated that he had modified his view in one important respect (p. 36):

> "It has previously been assumed, by others as well as by me, that insofar as an arbitrator's award construes a statute, it is advisory only, and the statutory question will be examined de novo if the award is challenged in the courts. I no longer think this is the necessary result. As between the parties themselves, I see no impediment to their agreeing to a final and binding arbitral declaration of their statutory rights and duties. Obviously, if an arbitrator's interpretation of an OSHA requirement did not adequately protect the employees, or violated some other basic public policy, a court would not be bound by it. But if the arbitrator imposed more stringent requirements, I would say the award should be enforced. The parties agreed to that result, and their agreement should be accorded the same finality as any other arbitration contract.

> "Whatever damage may be done to the pristine purity of labor arbitration by this increased responsiblity for statutory interpretation, I consider an expanded arbitral jurisdiction inevitable. Such recent statutes as Title VII of the Civil Rights Act, the Pension Reform Act (ERISA), and OSHA are so interwoven in the fabric of collective bargaining agreements that it is simply impracticable in many cases for arbitrators to deal with contractual provisions without taking into account statutory provisions."

[13]Howlett, "The Arbitrator, the NLRB, and the Courts," Proceedings of the 20th Annual Meeting of NAA, 67, 83 (BNA Books, 1967).

[14]Id. at 78–79. He also stated the arbitrator has a duty to "probe" to determine whether a statutory issue is involved. Id. at 92. In 1982 Arbitrator Howlett stated that: "In federal, state, and local government arbitration, arbitrators must consider what has been improperly called 'external law.' More than in the private sector, statutes and government regulations are part of the collective bargaining contracts." Howlett, "Observations on Labor Arbitration," AAA News & Views, No. 1, p. 6 (1982). Also see Gross, "The Labor Arbitrator's Role: Tradition and Change," 25 Arb. J. 221 (1970).

Having given extensive thought to the views of Arbitrators Meltzer and Howlett, Arbitrator Richard Mittenthal advanced the intermediate view that "although the arbitrator's award may *permit* conduct forbidden by law but sanctioned by contract, it should not *require* conduct forbidden by law even though sanctioned by contract."[15] Arbitrator Mittenthal emphasized that arbitrators are "part of a private process for the adjudication of private rights and duties," and that they "should not be asked to assume public responsibilities and to do the work of public agencies."[16]

Other arbitrators also have emphasized that they would not interpret or apply an agreement in a way that would require a party to commit an illegal act.[17] For instance, Arbitrator George H. Young stated that "he cannot bring himself to render an opinion and award, which, if carried out, would result in both parties to the arbitration being guilty of unlawful conduct," and he refused to order the employer to discharge an employee as requested by the union where such discharge would place both the employer and the union in violation of the NLRA.[18] Moreover, in refusing to award a union security provision which would be illegal under state statute, Arbitrator Clarence M. Updegraff touched on the question of constitutionality and explained that the validity of the statute must be assumed:

---

[15]Mittenthal, "The Role of Law in Arbitration," Proceedings of the 21st Annual Meeting of NAA, 42, 50 (BNA Books, 1968). Cf., Arbitrator Altieri in 45 LA 1025, 1027.

[16]Mittenthal, id. at 58. Asked to comment on the Mittenthal view, Arbitrators Meltzer and Howlett each reiterated his own view. See Meltzer, "The Role of Law in Arbitration: Rejoinders," id. at 58–64; Howlett, "A Reprise," id. at 64–75. Still a fourth view, similar to Mittenthal's but with distinctions of consequence to some cases, was presented to the National Academy of Arbitrators at a later meeting. See Sovern, "When Should Arbitrators Follow Federal Law?" Proceedings of the 23rd Annual Meeting of NAA, 29 (BNA Books, 1970). At yet later Academy meetings the discussion continued, as did the disagreement, as to the extent to which arbitrators should concern themselves with law and public policy in resolving disputes. See Proceedings of the 24th Annual Meeting of NAA, 1–83 (BNA Books, 1971), presenting the views of Arbitrators McKelvey, Wirtz, Jones, Morris, and Feller. A questionnaire sent to 200 Academy members was answered by 79, the answers reflecting an almost equal division in support for the two basic views. Young, "The Authority and Obligation of a Labor Arbitrator to Modify or Eliminate a Provision of a Collective Bargaining Agreement Because in His Opinion It Violates Federal Law," 32 Ohio St. L.J. 395, 396 (1971), also indicating how those who responded rate themselves as to knowledge of specific federal statutes. One third of the arbitrators responding to a later survey conducted by Professor Harry T. Edwards "indicated that they believed a collective bargaining agreement must be read to include by reference all public law applicable thereto," and about two thirds of the responding arbitrators "stated that they believed that an arbitrator has no business interpreting or applying a public statute in a contractual grievance dispute." Edwards, "Arbitration of Employment Discrimination Cases: An Empirical Study," Proceedings of the 28th Annual Meeting of NAA, 59, 79 (BNA Books, 1976), stating also that "nearly one half of the responding arbitrators did indicate that an arbitrator should be free to *comment* on the relevant law if it appears to conflict with the collective bargaining agreement."

[17]See Arbitrator Barone in 71 LA 524, 531; Draznin in 70 LA 338, 341; Stein in 44 LA 965, 966–967; Smith in 41 LA 65, 71–72; Young in 40 LA 833, 835; Dworkin in 37 LA 638, 646–647; Anderson in 22 LA 470, 473; Abernethy in 8 LA 62, 65.

[18]Buckstaff Co., 40 LA 833, 835 (1963). In making it clear that he would not render an award which would require the performance of illegal acts, Arbitrator Russell A. Smith stated in Globe-Democrat Publishing Co., 41 LA 65, 75 (1963):

"I recognize, however, that the authority to decide these legal questions is vested in the Board and the courts, not in the Arbitrator. The parties have agreed that my task has been to interpret their agreement. This I have done. My only concern, with respect to the legal issues (aside from their relevance in the matter of contract interpretation) has been whether my award will have the effect of ordering the Company to perform an illegal act."

"No award of this board can give validity to any contract which contravenes the law of any state. If it is indeed true that the Kansas law is ineffective because unconstitutional, that result has not yet been authoritatively declared by a court of last resort. The act must be assumed effective until otherwise determined."[19]

Regarding Arbitrator Mittenthal's statement that arbitrators "should not be asked to assume public responsibilities and to do the work of public agencies," a similar idea has been vigorously asserted by Arbitrator Peter Seitz:

"If arbitration begins to do the business of the NLRB and the courts, interpreting legislation, effecting national rather than private goals as a kind of subordinate tribunal of the Board, that voluntarism which is the base of its broad acceptance could be eroded and its essential objectives changed. Arbitration can be weakened by freighting it with public law questions which in our system should be decided by the courts and administrative agencies. Arbitration should not be an initial alternative to Board adjudication. It has been (and should be) a separate system of judicature respecting *private* rights and duties resulting in final decisions—not decisions on *public* matters reviewable by the Board and deferred to if not repugnant to the Labor Act."[20]

Turning next to the matter of arbitral reliance upon fundamental principles of the common law, while not all arbitrators will agree fully, probably most do share the view that "long and generally accepted judicial principles" can serve well in the forum of arbitration.[21] In this regard, Arbitrator John F. Sembower commented:

"This arbitrator long has been intrigued by how parties to labor arbitrations, while naturally eschewing all intentions of being 'legalistic,' nevertheless so often tread the same time-worn paths of the development of the great common law. Nor should this be surprising, because after all the vaunted Ango-American common law consists of the vast heritage of experience—the accumulated customs, viewpoints, and usages of ordinary people just like ourselves."[22]

Finally, the Authors call attention to the fact that there have been numerous other expressions by individual arbitrators falling at vari-

---

[19]Kansas City Pub. Serv. Co., 8 LA 149, 159 (1957), an "interest" arbitration. Also see Arbitrator Callaghan in 32 LA 661, 663–664. If a contract adopts one of two alternatives permitted by statute, the agreement does not conflict with the statute but simply limits the parties to one of two possibilities under the law. Wilson & Co., Inc., 1 LA 367, 378 (Lohman, not dated).

[20]Seitz, "The Limits of Arbitration," 88 Monthly Lab. Rev. 763, 764 (1965). Also see Arbitrator Siegel in 76 LA 729, 731–732 (he would "not assume functions which belong in the courtroom or before a public agency and which are not rightfully his"); Barrett in 72 LA 898, 903; Laybourne in 72 LA 367, 369 (it is "not within the authority or jurisdiction of the arbitrator to enforce laws enacted by a legislative body"); Roberts in 71 LA 1123, 1126 (if the employer "breaches a statutory obligation the recourse of the victimized employee must be to the appropriate agency or court"); Larkin in 69 LA 563, 565.

[21]The latter thought was expressed by Arbitrator Israel Ben Scheiber in applying a basic principle of agency law. Trubitz Hardware & Elec. Co., 32 LA 930, 935 (1959), stating also that "the avoidance of procedural legalism should not be accompanied by a disregard for such principles of law as have long been our guiding stars."

[22]Caterpillar Tractor Co., 39 LA 534, 537 (1962).

ous points within the broad range of views noted hereinabove.[23] In evaluating these expressions the reader of course should keep in mind that consideration of external law is a multifaceted matter—there are different purposes for considering external law and any given arbitrator quite properly may feel justified in doing so for one purpose or in one situation while declining to do so for some other purpose or in some other situation.[24] In this general regard, the following statement by Arbitrator Peter Seitz is of particular interest:

> "The extent to which external law should be a factor in the arbitration of a dispute between parties to a collective agreement presents a difficult and thorny question. Many who have pontificated on the subject have regretted their words when faced with the arbitration of the next case. The only thing of which it is possible to be certain is that it would not be prudent to lay down broad rules on the subject without a degree of tentativeness and caution."[25]

U.S. Supreme Court Statements Regarding Arbitral Consideration of External Law

We have noted above the view of Arbitrator Meltzer that where there is clear conflict between the agreement and law, the arbitrator "should respect the agreement and ignore the law." His reasoning in support of this view included consideration of certain language of the U.S. Supreme Court in the *Enterprise Wheel* case, wherein the Court stated of the award involved there:

> "It may be read as based solely upon the arbitrator's view of the requirements of enacted legislation, which would mean that he exceeded the scope of the submission. Or it may be read as embodying a construction of the agreement itself, perhaps with the arbitrator looking to 'the law' for help in determining the sense of the agreement."[26]

The Supreme Court subsequently spoke expressly of the arbitrator's function where the agreement conflicts with external law. In the course of its opinion in *Gardner-Denver*, the Court stated that an arbitrator "has no general authority to invoke public laws that conflict with the bargain between the parties," that arbitration is "a comparatively inappropriate forum for the final resolution of rights cre-

---

[23]See Arbitrator McCrary in 76 LA 333, 334; Lipson in 76 LA 295, 298; Hardin in 76 LA 278, 283–284; Berman in 76 LA 158, 159; Coyle in 74 LA 697, 699; Gomberg in 73 LA 927, 928; Hon in 73 LA 636, 637; Randall in 71 LA 889, 892; Barone in 71 LA 524, 531; Rice in 71 LA 509, 512–513; Flagler in 71 LA 427, 432–433; Yarowsky in 71 LA 286, 287; Snow in 71 LA 109, 112–113; Ross in 70 LA 350, 353; Richman in 70 LA 266, 269; Rutherford in 70 LA 257, 262; Roberts in 69 LA 930, 934–935; Siegel in 69 LA 869, 870; Caraway in 69 LA 540, 545; Kornblum in 69 LA 349, 350; Di Leone in 69 LA 48, 52; Ipavec in 68 LA 887, 893; Bloch in 68 LA 31, 33–34. For earlier cases, see p. 328 of the Third Edition of this book. The disagreement among arbitrators over consideration of external law also exists where state law is concerned. See cases cited at p. 333 of the Third Edition of this book.

[24]For example, compare the approach of Arbitrator Edgar A. Jones, Jr., in Max Factor & Co., 73 LA 742, 744–745 (1979), with his approach in Pacific Sw. Airlines, 70 LA 833, 837 (1978).

[25]Ellenville Cent. School Dist., 74 LA 1221, 1222 (1980). As noted in the second subtopic below, Arbitrator Seitz in 1981 reiterated his general belief that it is undesirable for arbitrators to decide statutory issues. However, the present case involved a different purpose for consideration of external law, and he did note certain external law in determining the sense of the agreement.

[26]United Steelworkers v. Enterprise Wheel & Car Corp., 80 S.Ct. 1358, 1361, 46 LRRM 2432 (1960).

ated by Title VII" of the Civil Rights Act, that the arbitrator's "task is to effectuate the intent of the parties rather than the requirements of enacted legislation," and that "[w]here the collective-bargaining agreement conflicts with Title VII, the arbitrator must follow the agreement."[27]

However, in no sense has the Supreme Court stated that an arbitrator should not examine external law in interpreting and applying the collective agreement. Indeed, as noted above, the Court in *Enterprise Wheel* expressly recognized the propriety of "the arbitrator looking to 'the law' for help in determining the sense of the agreement."[28] Furthermore, by *Gardner-Denver's* now famous "Footnote 21" the Court in a sense invited arbitrators to examine external law. More specifically, the Supreme Court indicated the terms upon which lower courts in Title VII discrimination actions "may properly accord [a prior arbitration decision] great weight." Footnote 21 states:

> "We adopt no standards as to the weight to be accorded an arbitral decision, since this must be determined in the court's discretion with regard to the facts and circumstances of each case. Relevant factors include the existence of provisions in the collective-bargaining agreement that conform substantially with Title VII, the degree of procedural fairness in the arbitral forum, adequacy of the record with respect to the issue of discrimination, and the special competence of particular arbitrators. *Where an arbitral determination gives full consideration to an employee's Title VII rights*, a court may properly accord it great weight. This is especially true where the issue is solely one of fact, specifically addressed by the parties and decided by the arbitrator on the basis of an adequate record. But courts should ever be mindful that Congress, in enacting Title VII, thought it necessary to provide a judicial forum for the ultimate resolution of discriminatory employment claims. It is the duty of courts to assure the full availability of this forum."[29]

---

[27]Alexander v. Gardner-Denver Co., 94 S.Ct. 1011, 1022, 1024 (1974). The actual holding in *Gardner-Denver* was that an employee's statutory right to trial de novo on his discrimination claim under Title VII was not foreclosed by prior submission of his claim to final arbitration (where the award was adverse to the employee) under the nondiscrimination clause of a collective agreement. For citation of many articles discussing *Gardner-Denver* and its possible impact upon arbitration, see Chapter 2, subtopic entitled "De Novo Litigation Following Arbitration." In extending the *Gardner-Denver* holding to individuals who seek recovery under the FLSA following an adverse decision in arbitration proceedings arising from the same event, the Court in Barrentine v. Arkansas-Best Freight Sys., 101 S.Ct. 1437, 1446–1447 (1981), reiterated that an arbitrator "has no general authority to invoke public laws that conflict with the bargain between the parties," and the Court stated also that "the arbitrator is required to effectuate the intent of the parties, rather than to enforce the statute." As concerns conflict between agreement and statute, it is interesting to note that Congress in the Railway Labor Act expressly provided that certain provisions of the Act are "made a part of the contract of employment between the carrier and each employee, and shall be held binding upon the parties, regardless of any other express or implied agreements between them." RLA § 2, Eighth. For arbitral recognition of this requirement, see Texas Intl. Airlines, 68 LA 244, 248 (Gruenberg, 1976).

[28]When the arbitrator upon considering external law finds conflict between law and agreement, it is only then that the court calls for the arbitrator to disregard the law to the extent that it is contrary to the agreement.

[29]94 S.Ct. at 1025, emphasis added. For additional material regarding *Gardner-Denver* and its Footnote 21, see Chapter 2, subtopic entitled "De Novo Litigation Following Arbitration." For other related discussion, see this Chapter, below, subtopic entitled "Title VII of the Civil Rights Act." In its FLSA *Barrentine* decision the Supreme Court quoted with obvious reaffirmance *Gardner-Denver's* Footnote 21 factors relevant in a court's determination of the weight to be accorded an arbitral decision, and the Court also quoted the Footnote 21 statement that "Where an arbitral determination gives full consideration to an employee's [statutory] rights, a court may properly accord it great weight." 101 S.Ct. at 1446 n. 22, bracketed word "statutory" supplied by Supreme Court.

Capability of Arbitrators to Deal With External Law

Doubt concerning arbitral expertise to deal with external law has been voiced by some arbitrators and judges, including some members of the U.S. Supreme Court. On the other hand, many arbitrators do believe that they possess the requisite capability. Furthermore, qualified observers in the field of labor law and arbitration have expressed the belief that the requisite capability is in fact possessed by many if not most arbitrators. For instance, while Arbitrator Peter Seitz stated that he did "not regard it as desirable for arbitrators to make final and binding decisions on the meaning and application of public statutes * * * except in public sector cases where such action is wholly unavoidable," he nonetheless stated that his "own view is that most arbitrators are at least as competent and as qualified as most judges to decide employment discrimination or fair labor standards cases."[30] In the latter regard, Dean James E. Westbrook stated in a 1980 speech that:

> "[I]t is a mistake to assume that more cases will be decided right if we multiply the levels of review. Courts aren't right more often than arbitrators and the parties because they are wiser. They are 'right' because they have the final say. There is no such thing as a perfect decision."[31]

As Arbitrator Seitz indicated, the question whether arbitrators are *capable* of deciding statutory issues and the question whether they *should* do so are two different questions. Another different question concerns the finality of arbitral decisions on statutory issues. Concerning *capability* of arbitrators (as distinguished from the "should they" and the "finality" questions, which are not addressed here), the present Authors, having studied thousands of arbitration opinions and a great many court opinions, believe that arbitrators on the whole *are* capable of dealing with statutes and other external law bearing upon problems which the parties have brought to the arbitrator. Moreover, the Authors believe that this capability probably equals and sometimes exceeds that of many courts, including some federal courts. Of course, few if any arbitrators, or judges, are or have any logical need to be walking encyclopedias of the law. Arbitrators, as do judges, usually must rely to a greater or lesser extent upon current research, and upon the representatives of the parties to explore the relevant law and argue it to the adjudicator. The capacity to comprehend and to evalu-

---

[30]Seitz, "Render unto Caesar (Arbitrators and Public Laws)," AAA Study Time, Oct., 1981, a Letter to the Editor. Also see statements by Edwards, "Advantages of Arbitration Over Litigation: Reflections of a Judge," Proceedings of the 35th Annual Meeting of NAA, 16, 21, 27–28 (BNA Books, 1983). Compare the conclusions stated in the discussion of this subject by Bartlett, "Employment Discrimination and Labor Arbitrators: A Question of Competence," 85 W. Va. L. Rev. 873, 907–909 (1983).

[31]Westbrook, "The End of an Era in Arbitration: Where Can You Go if You Can't Go Home Again," (1980), unpublished.

ate weighty subject matter, and to apply it to the specific case, is the critical requirement, and here most arbitrators are qualified.[32]

Some Ramifications or Consequences of Arbitrator's Choice Respecting External Law

In a large percentage of arbitrations the award actually constitutes a final disposition of the disputed matter in that the award is accepted and there are no subsequent arbitration, court, or administrative agency proceedings involving the disputed activity or incident. However, this obviously is not true of every arbitration. All arbitration awards are subject to the possibility of at least limited review by a court and/or administrative agency. Furthermore, some activities or incidents involve both statutory and contractual rights, and a grievant after arbitrating may be able to pursue statutory rights in other tribunals. In such respects as these, developments after an award is issued may be affected by the arbitrator's views and course of action in regard to consideration of external law.

Arbitrators in private-sector cases are *not required* to consider external law unless to do so is clearly mandated by the submission agreement, under which the arbitrator accepts and is vested with jurisdiction, or by the collective agreement itself. Arbitrators in the federal public sector do have a responsibility by statute to consider external law. Arbitrators in the state public sector may or may not have a responsibility to do so, the applicable state arbitration statute, the submission agreement, and the collective agreement being relevant in this regard. Certainly many if not most arbitrators of cases in the private sector, and some arbitrators of cases in the state public sector, do have an option or choice to consider or not to consider external law.

The following paragraphs contain summaries or statements of some possible postaward developments that may be affected by the arbitrator's views and course of action in regard to consideration of external law. The Authors *stress* that the summaries or statements are neither definitive nor exclusive of other possibilities, and are intended to serve merely as a preliminary aid in connection with the reader's own evaluation.

A. *Private-sector cases in which the arbitrator does not consider external law.* The arbitrator may choose to consider only the collective agreement and give no consideration to external law. Here the award usually will draw its essence from the agreement and, if the award also does not command the per-

---

[32]If confronted with an issue beyond the competence of the individual arbitrator, a safeguard is provided by the Code of Professional Responsibility mandate that: "An arbitrator must decline appointment, withdraw, or request technical assistance when he or she decides that a case is beyond his or her competence." § 1(B)(1), 64 LA 1320.

formance of an illegal act and is not contrary to some strong
public policy, it likely would withstand court review. However, there may be statutory issues growing out of the same
matter and on which proceedings before other tribunals still
would be possible unless foreclosed by considerations other
than an arbitration award adverse to the grievant. For
instance, where the arbitrator did not consider any NLRA
issue, the NLRB would not defer to the award; and issues
under the FLSA or Title VII of the Civil Rights Act would be
subject to de novo court proceedings regardless of whether the
arbitrator considered them in rendering an award adverse to
the grievant.[33]

B. *Private-sector cases in which the arbitrator does consider external law.* The arbitrator may choose to consider external law
along with the collective agreement. Here, if the agreement
and the external law are reasonably reconciled, with no clear
conflict between them, and if the arbitrator merely looks to
the law for help in determining the sense of the agreement, it
is likely that the award will draw its essence from the agreement; and, provided it does not order the performance of an
illegal act and is not contrary to a strong public policy, the
award likely would withstand court review. The mere fact
that the arbitrator may have misconstrued the law used as an
aid in determining the sense of the agreement likely would
not invalidate the award in view of the generally recognized
rule that awards are not impeachable for errors of law. However, if the agreement and external law do conflict, and if the
award is based, to use the Supreme Court's *Enterprise Wheel*
words, "solely upon the arbitrator's view of the requirements
of enacted legislation, which would mean that he exceeded the
scope of the submission," the award would not withstand court
review unless both parties authorized the arbitrator to decide
the case in conformity with external law. Furthermore, there
may be statutory issues growing out of the same matter and on
which proceedings before other tribunals still may be possible
unless foreclosed by considerations other than an arbitration
award adverse to the grievant. For instance, even if the
arbitrator did consider and rule against a grievant's Title VII
or FLSA claim, the claim still would be subject to de novo court
proceedings. The court could not "defer" to the award by
accepting its results as conclusive on the statutory issue and
thus deny the grievant access to the court (as the NLRB
sometimes does under its policy where an arbitrator has con-

---

[33]For discussions relevant to the foregoing summary, see this Chapter, topic entitled "General Considerations," and subtopics entitled "U.S. Supreme Court Statements Regarding
Arbitral Consideration of External Law" and "The NLRA, the Arbitrator, and the NLRB";
Chapter 2, subtopics entitled "Post-*Trilogy*: Lower Court Enforcement of Agreement to Arbitrate
and Review of Award" and "De Novo Litigation Following Arbitration."

sidered an NLRA issue). Rather, the court must hear the Title VII or FLSA issue anew and reach its own decision on the issue, though in reaching that decision the court under *Gardner-Denver*'s footnote 21 or *Barrentine*'s footnote 22 has discretion to accord some weight and sometimes great weight to the arbitrator's decision.[34]

C. *Private-sector cases governed by state arbitration law.* In paragraphs A and B, above, the Authors contemplate that the arbitration is covered by LMRA § 301. They do not offer such a summary for private-sector cases governed by state law, where the possible results must be evaluated on a state-by-state basis; but it is to be expected that results reached in private-sector cases under state law generally would not vary significantly from the results suggested above under § 301 doctrine. Furthermore, even if the arbitration itself is not covered by § 301 and rather is governed by state law, the FLSA and/or Title VII of the Civil Rights Act may apply to the given employment and, if so, the grievant's right to court litigation of any FLSA or Title VII rights would not be foreclosed by an arbitration award adverse to the grievant, and this would be so regardless of the particular state's doctrine.

D. *Federal public-sector cases.* Arbitrators in the federal public sector are required by the Civil Service Reform Act to deal with external law and their awards are subject to challenge where they conflict with controlling laws, rules, or regulations.[35]

E. *State public-sector cases.* The relationship between external law and arbitration in the state public sector must be evaluated on a state-by-state basis, and has in fact varied among the states. The Authors here offer no summary statement of possible results, but do offer some discussion elsewhere in this book.[36] It should be noted that Title VII of the Civil Rights Act applies to states and their subdivisions, as does the FLSA (see *Garcia* and *Fitzpatrick* decisions cited in Chapter 2, note 165). Thus, here again there may be rights under these statutes which could be litigated in court and would not be foreclosed by an arbitration award adverse to the grievant, and this would be so regardless of the particular state's doctrine.

---

[34]For discussion relevant to the foregoing summary, see this Chapter, topic entitled "General Considerations," and subtopics entitled "U.S. Supreme Court Statements Regarding Arbitral Consideration of External Law," and "The NLRA, the Arbitrator, and the NLRB"; Chapter 2, subtopic entitled "De Novo Litigation Following Arbitration."

[35]See Chapter 2, federal public-sector subtopics entitled "Channels for Processing Federal-Sector Grievances," "Review of Arbitration Awards," and "A Recapitulation From the Arbitrator's Viewpoint."

[36]See Chapter 2, state public-sector subtopics entitled "Court Review of Arbitration Awards" and "Contractual Terms v. Statutory Law Covering Similar Matters."

Finally, the Authors suggest that regardless of whether the case falls within the private sector, the federal public sector, or the state public sector, the validity of an award ordinarily should not be jeopardized merely because, to use the words of the Supreme Court in the § 301 *Enterprise Wheel* decision, the arbitrator pursued a course of "looking to 'the law' for help in determining the sense of the agreement," as distinguished from the situation in which an award is "based solely upon the arbitrator's view of the requirements of enacted legislation."

Statutory Law

The present topic notes the actions of arbitrators in respect to consideration or application of specific statutes. Several statutes are treated in the first subtopic, while the two succeeding subtopics deal, respectively, and exclusively, with Title VII of the Civil Rights Act and with the NLRA.

Some Specific Statutes

Arbitrator David L. Cole explained that "in any conflict between a collective bargaining agreement and the law with reference to the rights of a returning veteran, it has repeatedly been held that the law must prevail."[37] In a similar note, Arbitrator Thomas P. Whelan held that regulations under the National Security Act were as a matter of public policy superimposed upon the collective agreement when the employer entered into a "security agreement" with the Department of Defense, and that they took precedence over any provisions of the collective agreement that might have conflicted with them.[38]

In times of wage stabilization arbitrators have taken steps to avoid transgression upon wage stabilization legislation.[39] In one case

---

[37]International Harvester Co., 22 LA 583, 585 (1954). Accord, Arbitrator Blackmar in 75 LA 696, 697, 699; Hebert in 46 LA 624, 633; Parker in 23 LA 44, 47. For other cases in which arbitrators took note of the statutory rights of veterans, see Arbitrator Margolin in 74 LA 449, 454, 457; Bothwell in 54 LA 1055, 1058–1059; Dworkin in 46 LA 1021, 1025–1026; McCoy in 41 LA 716, 717; Updegraff in 37 LA 1009, 1013; Justin in 23 LA 113, 119–124. But see discussion by Mittenthal, "The Role of Law in Arbitration," Proceedings of the 21st Annual Meeting of NAA, 42, 47, 51–55 (BNA Books, 1968); Meltzer, "The Role of Law in Arbitration: Rejoinders," id. at 58, 59–60. For summary and analysis of court decisions on veterans' reemployment rights, see United States Steel Corp., 51 LA 1244, 1248–1249; 51 LA 1253, 1255–1256 (Garrett, 1968). Also see Arbitrator Wolff in 56 LA 312, 314–315. Later decisions of interest regarding veterans' employment rights include Monroe v. Standard Oil Co., 101 S.Ct. 2510 (1981); Coffey v. Republic Steel Corp., 100 S.Ct. 2100 (1980); Personnel Admr. of Mass. v. Feeney, 99 S.Ct. 2282 (1979).

[38]Wisconsin Tel. Co., 26 LA 792, 806 (1956). As to limitations on statutory regulation of employment in national defense facilities, see United States v. Robel, 88 S.Ct. 419 (1967), involving the Subversive Activities Control Act.

[39]See Arbitrator Keefe in 57 LA 1090, 1091; Donnelly in 17 LA 748, 750–751; Warren in 17 LA 353, 354, 361; Lesser in 16 LA 881, 882; Justin in 16 LA 399, 404. Also see Rose in 19 LA 303, 306. For related discussion, see Chapter 18, topic entitled "Governmental Wage Stabilization."

an overtime claim was rejected because its allowance would have resulted in a clear violation of the Wage Stabilization Act.[40] However, an arbitrator emphasized that while wage stabilization regulations should be considered in determining wage adjustments, the influence of wage stabilization on an arbitrator's decision should vary "in direct ratio to the certainty, clarity and stage of its evolution."[41]

In the past, arbitrators disagreed as to whether the agreement or the Fair Labor Standards Act should control where they conflict. Arbitrator Emanuel Stein held that where the statute is clear, the agreement must be construed and applied in a manner consistent with the statute.[42] However, where a party argued that an adverse decision would conflict with the Fair Labor Standards Act, Arbitrator Harold S. Burr declared that it is the contract language upon which he must focus and rule.[43] Subsequent to the 1981 decision of the U.S. Supreme Court in *Barrentine*, arbitrators of course will evaluate the teachings of that decision whenever the FLSA is in some manner relevant to the dispute under consideration.[44]

The Federal Occupational Safety and Health Act of 1970 (OSHA) often has been a factor (sometimes a particularly strong factor) in the disposition of safety and health issues by arbitrators.[45]

Title VII of the Civil Rights Act

Prior to the U.S. Supreme Court's decision in *Alexander v. Gardner-Denver* arbitrators were in disagreement as to what consideration, if any, an arbitrator should give to Title VII of the Civil Rights

---

[40]Monsanto Chem. Co., 1 ALAA ¶67,089 (1944). Also see Arbitrator Stark in 57 LA 1115, 1118. In Clarkstown Cent. School Dist., 58 LA 191, 193 (Markowitz, 1972), the arbitrator refused to rule as to the validity of an increase under wage stabilization, having concluded that the question must be decided by the stabilization agency.

[41]Merchants Bank of N.Y., 16 LA 901, 904 (Rosenfarb, 1951).

[42]Pennsylvania Elec. Co., 47 LA 526, 527 (1966), where Arbitrator Stein rejected the argument that "Fair Labor Standards Act questions should be resolved in another forum." In accord as to the controlling effect of the statute, Youngstown Sheet & Tube Co., 14 LA 752, 756 (Updegraff, 1950). Also see Arbitrator Allen in 73 LA 103, 105; Gillingham in 66 LA 131, 133. Cf., Strasshofer in 74 LA 1042, 1044; Krimsly in 47 LA 518, 523. In Mason & Hanger-Silas Mason Co., 75 LA 1038, 1040 (Shearer, 1980), the FLSA rather than past practice was followed as the controlling guide for interpreting an ambiguous agreement. Heavy reliance was placed upon FLSA and Portal-to-Portal Act doctrine where the contract did not deal expressly with a claim for travel time in Chevron USA, 78 LA 1241, 1248–1251 (Killion, 1982).

[43]Hilo Transp. & Terminal Co., 33 LA 541, 543 (1959). Accord, Arbitrator Seward in 17 LA 29, 30; Marshall in 16 LA 335, 337. Also see Arbitrator Feller in 70 LA 526, 528–529. A number of arbitrators have considered the question whether an increase in the minimum wage under the FLSA may be relied upon by the employer toward fulfilling his obligation to grant a periodic wage increase specified by the agreement. For example, see Arbitrator Andersen in 52 LA 430, 433–435; Merrill in 52 LA 145, 147–148; Gershenfeld in 48 LA 816, 818; Owen in 42 LA 250, 251.

[44]Regarding *Barrentine* and the likewise relevant *Gardner-Denver* decision, see this Chapter's subtopic entitled "U.S. Supreme Court Statements Regarding Arbitral Consideration of External Law."

[45]See Chapter 16, subtopic entitled "OSHA Considerations."

Act of 1964 in deciding grievances.[46] Arbitral opinion has remained divided on the question of considering Title VII since the *Gardner-Denver* decision was issued. However, while some arbitrators subsequently dealing with discrimination issues did not consider Title VII,[47] a significantly greater number of arbitrators have considered Title VII doctrine in deciding the case.[48]

---

[46]Arbitral opinion appeared to be fairly evenly divided on this matter. See cases cited at pp. 331–332 of the Third Edition of this book. In addition to its basic holding in *Gardner-Denver* that a denial award in arbitration under the collective agreement did not foreclose the grievant from subsequently proceeding in court by trial de novo on his Title VII discrimination claim, the Supreme Court recognized that: "a contractual right to submit a claim to arbitration is not displaced simply because Congress also has provided a statutory right against discrimination. Both rights have legally independent origins and are equally available to the aggrieved employee." Alexander v. Gardner-Denver Co., 94 S.Ct. 1011, 1022 (1974). For discussion of the *Gardner-Denver* decision under Title VII, see this Chapter, subtopic entitled "U.S. Supreme Court Statements Regarding Arbitral Consideration of External Law," and Chapter 2, subtopic entitled "De Novo Litigation Following Arbitration." The latter subtopic cites many articles discussing the *Gardner-Denver* decision and its possible impact upon arbitration. For other related discussion of Title VII, see Chapter 14, subtopic entitled "Contractual Seniority Rights, the Civil Rights Act, and Arbitration." For some general studies on employment discrimination law, see Schlei & Grossman, Employment Discrimination Law, 2d Ed. (BNA Books, 1983); Lorber, McGovern & Sampson, Equal Employment Practice Guide—1981 (BNA Books, 1981); Levin-Epstein, Primer of Equal Employment Opportunity (BNA Books, 1984).

[47]See Arbitrator Sergent in 74 LA 369, 372–373 (although the agreement's nondiscrimination clause provided that the parties would "comply with all State and Federal Laws and Regulations regarding Equal Employment Opportunity," he did not examine Title VII doctrine but rather quoted the *Enterprise Wheel* statement that an award is legitimate only so long as it draws its essence from the agreement); Porter in 73 LA 729, 732 (stating that the agreement did not authorize him to consider the union's Title VII arguments, which must be left to "a duly authorized federal or state quasi-judicial or judicial body"); Marlatt in 73 LA 705, 707 (stating that the evidence did not deal adequately with the alleged discrimination, and that the "ultimate responsibility for pursuing legal remedies for Title VII discrimination falls upon the employee himself and not the Union"); Belsky in 70 LA 143, 145–146 (pointing to *Gardner-Denver*, he stated that "the arbitrator has no general authority to invoke public laws that may be or may not be in conflict with" the collective agreement); Gregory in 69 LA 1050, 1056 (stating that he would decide "in accord with" the terms of the agreement, "leaving to the courts the interpretation and appropriateness of the various federal anti-discrimination laws, rulings and sanctions"); Turkus in 68 LA 527, 535 (declining to judge a discharge under Title VII criteria, he stated that as "made clear in *Gardner-Denver*, grievant's Title VII rights can only be decided by the Federal Courts"); Edelman in 64 LA 816, 819–821 (stating that national policy on conflicts between seniority systems and federal anti-discrimination laws was "not yet clear enough to give the requisite guidance to the arbitrator"). Also see Arbitrator Russell in 75 LA 1145, 1146; Cohen in 71 LA 1171, 1177–1178; Chaffin in 69 LA 307, 311 (this is one of the infrequent instances in which the arbitrator in disposing of a discrimination issue remained totally silent regarding any possible consideration of external law); McKenna in 67 LA 709, 714.

[48]In addition to the arbitrators cited in the next three footnotes, see Arbitrator Marx in 76 LA 680, 683–684 (both parties cited Title VII); Ross in 76 LA 101, 103; Goldstein in 76 LA 32, 42–43; Wolff in 75 LA 1300, 1301; Randall in 75 LA 1273, 1280 (the agreement was silent regarding external law and did not clearly conflict with it, thus "the parties are presumed to have known and to have intended to comply with the law, and * * * the arbitrator should construe the agreement in a manner which is compatible with external law"); Petrie in 75 LA 439, 443–444; Griffin in 74 LA 1248, 1253, and in 69 LA 439, 448, 459 (stating that a charge of racial discrimination requires "the most meticulous consideration," and that he had considered the evidence "with an eye to" the teachings of *Gardner-Denver*); Vause in 74 LA 806, 809–810; Markowitz in 74 LA, 58, 61–62; Carnes in 71 LA 1215, 1216, 1219 (by a settlement agreement the parties had established special arbitration procedures for Title VII issues, and in the present case the arbitrator found a Title VII violation notwithstanding the EEOC's earlier investigation indicating lack of probable cause for further proceedings); Yarowsky in 71 LA 286, 287 (federal and state laws on equal employment opportunity "must be read into the parties agreement as if specifically incorporated therein"); Richman in 70 LA 266, 268–269; Shister in 70 LA 110, 112; Taylor in 69 LA 857, 861 (the company "was justified in failing to observe the specific terms of the Agreement" in taking an affirmative action step required under Title VII); Rehmus in 68 LA 171, 174; Weiss in 67 LA 159, 162 (grievant's discharge violated both the agreement and Title VII); Gould in 64 LA 620, 625 (the parties expressly commissioned him to decide the Title VII issue); Marshall in 64 LA 187, 192 (he stated that *Gardner-Denver* does not confine the arbitrator "to the precise terms of the collective bargaining agreement, without regard to the law of the land, court decisions, and applicable administrative rulings," and he reiterated his belief "that applicable

In some of the cases in which the arbitrator considered Title VII doctrine, the agreement either expressly stated that the parties would comply with antidiscrimination law,[49] or it expressly provided for voiding any clause to the extent that it conflicts with federal or state law.[50]

In one case Arbitrator George T. Roumell, Jr., pointed to the agreement's prohibition of "discrimination as to age, sex, marital status, race, color, creed, national origin or political affiliation," and he stated that:

> "Because the contract does not define the word 'discrimination,' one must look to the law as it is being developed under applicable statutes by the courts of the land for a definition. When the parties use a phrase such as 'discrimination as to * * * creed,' they presumably are incorporating the applicable law on that subject into their contract. As to the issue of religious discrimination in employment, the law is set forth in Title VII of the Civil Rights Act."[51]

Other arbitrators similarly have pointed to the existence of a non-discrimination clause in the agreement as sufficient basis for arbitral consideration of Title VII.[52]

Where the collective agreement did not contain a nondiscrimination clause and the employer contended that the arbitration board lacked authority to decide an issue of religious discrimination in reviewing a discharge, Arbitrator Geraldine M. Randall stated:

> "The contract involved in the case at hand contains a typical provision prohibiting the discharge or discipline of an employee 'except for just and sufficient cause.' * * * The principle that discriminatory acts by employers violate such clauses long predates Title VII; for decades, labor arbitrators have overturned employer actions taken for reasons such as those now prohibited by law. Surely, an arbitrator should not sustain an action taken by an employer because of an employee's race, sex or nationality. Similarly, a discharge for reasons which constitute religious discrimination should not be found to be for 'just and sufficient'

provisions of state and federal law impress themselves upon the labor contract, not only *may,* but *must,* be given consideration in any arbitration proceeding which arises thereunder."

[49]See Arbitrator Bothwell in 77 LA 553, 555, 559–561 (the employer's action was held to violate both Title VII and the agreement); Goodman in 73 LA 497, 506; Novak in 68 LA 1309, 1314.

[50]See Arbitrator Davis in 69 LA 660, 663–664 (he amended a clause to conform to Title VII requirements); Foster in 66 LA 1, 7 (he would not honor a provision not conforming to Title VII); Dunn in 64 LA 310, 313–314 (the company was not required to meet a contractual obligation where compliance would result in a Title VII violation); Heliker in 63 LA 1057, 1059; Foster in 62 LA 849, 852–853.

[51]Hurley Hosp., 70 LA 1061, 1062–1063 (1978).

[52]See Arbitrator Owen in 73 LA 215, 223 (the seniority clause in the agreement conflicted with the nondiscrimination clause, and he resolved the conflict in such manner as to avoid conflict between the agreement and Title VII); Kramer in 72 LA 1223, 1227–1230; Matthews in 70 LA 4, 16–17; Boals in 68 LA 755, 758, 760 (stating that the inclusion of a nondiscrimination clause in the agreement "is tantamount to the incorporation of applicable statutory and adminstrative law into the Agreement"); Yaffe in 68 LA 644, 648; Bloch in 68 LA 31, 34; Platt in 64 LA 316, 326 (stating that "there can no longer be any real question that an arbitrator has both the authority and the obligation to consider Federal equal employment opportunity laws in the arbitration of grievances concerning alleged discriminatory employment practices" and this "is particularly true where the collective bargaining agreement contains an anti-discrimination clause"). Also see Koven in 79 LA 1171, 1175–1176, holding the Arbitrator may consider the Rehabilitation Act of 1973 in interpreting the contractual nondiscrimination clause before him.

cause. Thus, while this Board has no authority to enforce Grievant's statutory or Constitutional rights, the issue of 'religious discrimination' is necessarily involved in its determination of whether there has been a contract violation. Moreover, it is proper for the Board to consider outside legal authorities in making that determination."[53]

Finally, it should be noted in passing that in the past many arbitrators gave serious consideration to state statutes regulating the employment of female workers (to protect their health), but that ultimately some of these statutes were invalidated by courts as being in conflict with Title VII of the Civil Rights Act.[54] In any event, the dearth of recent arbitration decisions making any reference to female-employee protective statutes suggests that such statutes no longer constitute a significant factor in arbitration.

The NLRA, the Arbitrator, and the NLRB

Where a dispute involves both statutory issues under the NLRA and interpretation issues under the collective agreement, dual jurisdiction exists in the NLRB and the arbitrator. This dual jurisdiction as reflected by decisions of the U.S. Supreme Court was summarized by then NLRB member Gerald A. Brown:

"(1) the availability of arbitration does not preclude Board exercise of jurisdiction over unfair labor practices, (2) the availability of a Board remedy does not bar arbitration, and (3) the Board has discretion to refuse to exercise its jurisdiction when in its judgment federal policy would best be served by leaving the parties to contract remedies."[55]

In its *Carey* decision (involving a jurisdictional dispute between two unions and an employer) the Supreme Court held that an arbitrator could act, but should the Board disagree with the arbitrator its ruling would take precedence. The Court also stated that "The superior authority of the Board may be invoked at any time. Meanwhile the therapy of arbitration is brought to bear in a complicated and troubled area."[56]

Arbitrators themselves have long considered that they are not prevented from acting upon contract issues merely because the dis-

---

[53]Alameda-Contra Costa Transit Dist., 75 LA 1273, 1280 (1980). In Kaiser Found. Hosps., 48 LA 1138, 1142 (1967), Arbitrator Edgar A. Jones stated that the "coincident existence of the proscriptions of the Civil Rights Act superimposes no discrimination policy of the bargaining relationships which has not already been rather widely recognized for some time by arbitrators to be an incident of the employment relationship to be vindicated through the arbitral tribunal created by the parties."

[54]For arbitration cases in which such "protective" statutes were given consideration, and for some court decisions finding conflict between state statute and Title VII, see pp. 333–334 of the Third Edition of this book. Also see Homemakers, Inc. v. Division of Ind. Welfare, 509 F.2d 20 (CA 9, 1974); Manning v. International Union, 466 F.2d 812 (CA 6, 1972); Sail'er Inn, Inc. v. Kirby, 485 P.2d 529 (Cal. S.Ct., 1971). The potential for conflict also exists between such "protective" statutes and the state's own antidiscrimination statute (most states do have a statute prohibiting discrimination on the basis of sex, race, religion, color, or national origin).

[55]Brown, "The National Labor Policy, the NLRB, and Arbitration," Proceedings of the 21st Annual Meeting of NAA, 83, 84 (BNA Books, 1968). Relevant decisions include NLRB v. Strong, 89 S.Ct. 541 (1969); NLRB v. Acme Indus. Co., 87 S.Ct. 565 (1967); NLRB v. C & C Plywood Corp., 87 S.Ct. 559 (1967); Carey v. Westinghouse Elec. Corp., 84 S.Ct. 401, 55 LRRM 2042 (1964); Smith v. Evening News Assn., 83 S.Ct. 267 (1962). Also see discussion in Painters Dist. Council v. Maloney Specialties, 106 LRRM 2183 (CA 9, 1980).

[56]Carey v. Westinghouse Elec. Corp., 84 S.Ct. 401, 409, 55 LRRM 2042 (1964).

pute may also involve statutory issues that can be taken to the NLRB.[57] Similarly, the mere fact that the NLRB had dismissed unfair labor practice charges has not deterred arbitrators from subsequently taking jurisdiction over contract issues involved in the dispute.[58]

When an arbitrator takes jurisdiction of a dispute that involves issues under both the agreement and the NLRA, he may be confronted with the question as to whether or not he should confine himself primarily to the agreement and leave statutory issues to the NLRB. In many cases arbitrators have considered NLRA issues (often with an express finding that there has or has not been conduct of a type which would violate the Act), or they have at least considered the Act and NLRB doctrine in deciding contractual issues.[59] Particularly where the NLRB has deferred to arbitration, many arbitrators have addressed the statutory issue and have expressed a conclusion on it.[60]

---

[57]See Arbitrator Gentile in 76 LA 228, 229, and in 73 LA 1313, 1317; Aisenberg in 69 LA 1023, 1030; Helfeld in 68 LA 633, 635; Lennard in 46 LA 746, 747–749; Johnson in 45 LA 1182, 1183 (unfair labor practice charge involves breach of law whereas grievance involves breach of the agreement); Rohman in 42 LA 1308, 1310–1311; Miller in 35 LA 757, 783 (filing of unfair labor practice charges does not constitute an election of remedies or waiver of rights under the agreement asserted in grievance filed at same time); Schmidt in 35 LA 455, 457; Stutz, Mottram & Curry in 22 LA 651, 652; Kaplan in 22 LA 201, 207; Updegraff, Klamon & Raymond in 19 LA 609, 611–612. In National Radio Co., 60 LA 78, 81, 84 (1973), Arbitrator Archibald Cox suspended arbitration proceedings pending completion of NLRB proceedings, but two years later the NLRB deferred to arbitration; he then considered the statutory issue and found no unfair labor practice.

[58]See Arbitrator Harter in 72 LA 706, 710; McCoy in 51 LA 309, 310; Schedler in 42 LA 345, 346; Sembower in 37 LA 308, 312; Cole in 24 LA 332, 335.

[59]Most of the cases cited in the next two footnotes are applicable here. Also fully applicable, see Arbitrator Peterschmidt in 77 LA 396, 398; Hearne in 77 LA 32, 37; Kossoff in 76 LA 300, 307; Gibson in 75 LA 1011, 1013–1014; Talent in 75 LA 689, 694; Roumell in 75 LA 83, 91–96; Ross in 74 LA 633, 637–639; Kreimer in 74 LA 601, 604; Fitch in 74 LA 214, 215–216; Belcher in 74 LA 69, 73; Williams in 73 LA 1292, 1296; Witney in 73 LA 663, 669 ("the Arbitrator must be mindful of the policies established by" the NLRB since it "may reverse an arbitrator's decision should it be repugnant to its construction and application of" the NLRA); Ellmann in 72 LA 804, 806–807; Harter in 72 LA 706, 711; Morris in 72 LA 333, 336–337; Dyke in 71 LA 89, 92–93; Koven in 68 LA 1288, 1293–1294; Fields in 68 LA 448, 453; Maniscalco in 67 LA 439, 441; Barsamian in 67 LA 45, 50. For earlier cases see p. 335 of the Third Edition of this book. Where the NLRB has already made findings on an issue, an arbitrator will likely honor those findings. See Arbitrator Barnhart in 71 LA 579, 581; Lennard in 46 LA 746, 747–749; Larkin in 44 LA 580, 584–585. Cf., Finston in 68 LA 1022, 1032; Hebert in 68-1 ARB ¶8175. In Ernst Steel Corp., 89 LRRM 1233 at 1233 (NLRB, 1975), the NLRB stated that issues concerning compliance with a previous NLRB reinstatement order constituted "a matter clearly inappropriate for determination by an arbitrator." In A.S. Abell Co., 75 LA 537, 539 (Freund, 1980), a grievance was held nonarbitrable where it was found to involve the interpretation of an NLRB order rather than the collective agreement.

[60]See Arbitrator Lieberman in 77 LA 545, 546, 552; Rothman in 76 LA 1120, 1124–1125; Hannan in 76 LA 817, 819, 821; Foster in 76 LA 761, 769–770; Keefe in 76 LA 699, 700, 705; Eisler in 76 LA 516, 517, 520; Bognanno in 76 LA 499, 500, 504; Morris in 75 LA 975, 981–984; Boetticher in 75 LA 917, 920; Flagler in 75 LA 764, 765, 770; Vadakin in 75 LA 243, 245, 249; Goldberg in 74 LA 388, 395–396 (stating a conclusion on the statutory bargaining issue which the NLRB had deferred, but refusing to consider a statutory issue which had not been deferred to arbitration); Marlatt in 73 LA 1252, 1254, 1256; Ross in 73 LA 1036, 1037, 1040; Kaplan in 72 LA 1186, 1188–1189; Brooks in 72 LA 865, 872–873; Seidman in 72 LA 594, 596–598 (stating that the parties asked him to consider the NLRA charges "and apply the applicable federal law thereto in accordance with the usual practice under a Collyer referral"); Howell in 72 LA 421, 430–431 (stating that the NLRB having deferred, it was his "responsibility" to make a determination on the NLRA charge); Mikulina in 72 LA 73, 77, 81; Traynor in 71 LA 667, 670, 673–674; Ipavec in 71 LA 488, 489, 493; Roberts in 71 LA 325, 326, 329; Foster in 71 LA 244, 248; Dyke in 68 LA 1142, 1146. In some of the above cases the arbitrator indicated either that both parties had expressly authorized arbitral consideration of the statutory issue or that one party had opposed it, but in the other cases the arbitrator offered no comment on this aspect. Obviously, in all of the cases the arbitrator believed that jurisdiction did exist to address the statutory issue. For a good illustration that an arbitrator's ordinary jurisdiction to resolve disputes over the interpretation and application of the collective agreement may reasonably be found to cover issues identical to discrimination or bargaining-duty issues which the NLRB has deferred to arbitration, see the

Also, arbitrators appear to be particularly disposed to look to the NLRA and to consider NLRB doctrine when confronted with bargaining unit and union security questions under the agreement.[61]

On the other hand, in some other cases arbitrators have refused to consider NLRA issues (or have disclaimed authority to do so), or to consider the Act and NLRB doctrine in deciding contractual issues.[62] Even where the parties had provided, in submitting discharges to arbitration, that the arbitrators "shall consider the standards of strike misconduct as contained in adjudications under the National Labor Relations Act," Arbitrators Alexander, McCoy, Shedler, and Whiting declared that while the word "shall" required them to give decisions under said Act "considerable weight," it did not require them "to follow any of such decisions blindly."[63]

Particularly in regard to allegations of refusal to bargain, many arbitrators have taken the view that their function is to interpret and apply the agreement rather than to enforce affirmative duties under the statute, and they have refused to decide whether the statutory duty to bargain had been violated.[64] Here again, however, where the

---

reasoned analysis of Arbitrator Archibald Cox in National Radio Co., 60 LA 78, 81–85 (1973). Another example is provided by Arbitrator Charles J. Morris, finding that he had jurisdiction over a bargaining-duty issue in Keebler Co., 75 LA 975, 981–983 (1980), where he cautioned, however, that NLRB deferral "cannot vest the Arbitrator with any authority he does not have under the collective agreement," and where he recalled the U.S. Supreme Court's *Gardner-Denver* statement that arbitrators have "no general authority to invoke public laws that conflict with the bargain between the parties." However, even where the NLRB has deferred to arbitration some arbitrators have found the issue involved to be nonarbitrable. See Arbitrator Hardin in 76 LA 278, 283–284; Jones in 70 LA 833, 837 (even though the company had concurred in the union's statement of the issue as being whether the company violated the agreement and/or federal labor statutes, he ruled on the contract issue but stated that a violation of the NLRA "is a matter for the NLRB to determine" since the agreement did not "vest the Arbitrator with the responsibility so to determine"); Summers in 65 LA 816, 820–825 (even under a broad arbitration clause, he argued forcefully for a presumption against arbitrability of alleged NLRA violations, which presumption "can be rebutted by a showing that [the parties] considered and consciously agreed that arbitration was preferable to Board procedures for deciding the particular category of cases").

[61]See Arbitrator Kossoff in 78 LA 283, 286–287; McCurdy in 76 LA 1197, 1199–1200; Seldin in 75 LA 1074, 1075; Ross in 74 LA 633, 637–639; Matthews in 73 LA 751, 754; P.M. Williams in 72 LA 971, 974; Martin in 72 LA 684, 688–689; Maslanka in 72 LA 628, 630; Grossman in 72 LA 370, 372–373; Katz in 71 LA 1238, 1242; Flagler in 71 LA 427, 435–436; Marcus in 71 LA 228, 230–231; Gibson in 70 LA 230, 232–233; J.E. Williams in 70 LA 58, 64, 66–67; Lucas in 69 LA 394, 399; Bolte in 68 LA 343, 344–345; Porter in 61 LA 1259, 1271–1274. For earlier cases see p. 336 of the Third Edition of this book. However, as explained below in the present subtopic, the NLRB has taken the position that "questions of representation, accretion, and appropriate unit" are matters "for decision of the Board rather than an arbitrator." Recognizing NLRB decisions in this regard, bargaining unit accretion issues were held nonarbitrable in Alcolac, 75 LA 110, 112–113 (Chernick, 1980); White Motor Corp., 64 LA 1028, 1032–1034 (Perry, 1975). But see Arbitrator Kaplan in 80 LA 82, 85–86.

[62]See Arbitrator Taylor in 78 LA 1235, 1240; Marlatt in 77 LA 721, 724; Hardin in 76 LA 278, 283–284; Gentile in 76 LA 228, 229, 232; Cantor in 76 LA 89, 94; Lumbley in 75 LA 1224, 1226; Lipson in 74 LA 489, 492; Kossoff in 71 LA 204, 214; Jones in 70 LA 833, 837; Ross in 70 LA 350, 352–353; Whyte in 68 LA 957, 961; Schatzki in 68 LA 414, 416; Beck in 68 LA 386, 391; Summers in 65 LA 816, 822–824. For earlier cases see p. 336 of the Third Edition of this book. Some years ago a survey of 2300 cases administered by the American Arbitration Association revealed 338 with issues which also fell within the NLRB's scope of activities, but in only 54 of the latter cases did the arbitrator in some manner acknowledge NLRB policies. Waks, "The 'Dual Jurisdiction' Problem in Labor Arbitration: A Research Report," 23 Arb. J. 201, 205–207, 226 (1968).

[63]Southern Bell Tel. & Tel. Co., 25 LA 85, 86–87 (1955).

[64]See Arbitrator Lipson in 74 LA 489, 492; Kossoff in 71 LA 204, 214; Jones in 70 LA 833, 837; Schatzki in 68 LA 414, 416; Beck in 68 LA 386, 391; Summers in 65 LA 816, 822–824; Marshall in 54 LA 1295, 1297–1298; McDermott in 53 LA 470, 474–477; Gould in 51 LA 752, 758–759; Larkin in 50 LA 109, 111; Malinowski in 48 LA 1257, 1258–1259; Darragh in 46 LA 310, 315; Hilpert in 45

NLRB had deferred an NLRA bargaining duty issue to arbitration, many arbitrators have considered and expressed a conclusion on it.[65]

Now turning our attention more fully to the subject of NLRB deferral to arbitration, we should stress that this is a matter which has been controversial both within and outside the NLRB, and that Board policy on deferral has been neither constant nor always clearly defined.[66] Regarding this situation, former NLRB General Counsel John S. Irving, Jr., stated that:

> "There are simply not enough hours in the day to recount all the legal arguments that have been made about how much or how little deference to arbitration is required by the NLRA. And there is no need to, because no conclusion, one way or the other, is compelled by the statute. Rather, there is plenty of room in the act to argue for or against deferral. One either believes that private means of dispute resolution should be emphasized and encouraged, even where unfair labor practices may be involved, or that the NLRB's obligation to enforce the NLRA comes first."[67]

In its *Adams Dairy* decision the NLRB recognized that statutory refusal-to-bargain issues may not fall within the scope of an arbitrator's authority. In holding that a union's failure to resort to arbitration did not warrant dismissal of a refusal-to-bargain complaint under the NLRA, the Board explained:

> "The contract subjects to its arbitration procedures only such disputes as concern 'the interpretation or application of the terms of this Agreement.' But in the instant case, the precise union claim, which is the subject of the complaint before us, does not relate to the meaning of any established term or condition of the contract, or to any asserted

---

LA 651, 652–654, and in 38 LA 267, 268–270; Roberts in 44 LA 1109, 1114–1115; Kelliher in 43 LA 267, 269; Smith in 43 LA 193, 209–210; Warns in 41 LA 905, 908; Seidenberg in 41 LA 314, 315; Graff in 38 LA 869, 877; Ross in 35 LA 695, 697; Dworkin in 35 LA 237, 241. For related discussion, see Chapter 13, subtopic entitled "The Duty to Bargain: Right of Unilateral Action."

[65]See Arbitrator Lieberman in 77 LA 545, 546, 552; Hannan in 76 LA 817, 819, 821; Eisler in 76 LA 516, 517, 520; Morris in 75 LA 975, 981–984; Goldberg in 74 LA 388, 395–396; Ross in 73 LA 1036, 1040; Seidman in 72 LA 594, 596–598; Howell in 72 LA 421, 430–431; Traynor in 71 LA 667, 670, 673–674; Ipavec in 71 LA 488, 489, 493; Roberts in 71 LA 325, 326, 329; Foster in 71 LA 244, 248.

[66]For discussions of NLRB policy and cases in reference to deferring to arbitration where no award has yet been issued and also in reference to honoring awards that have been issued, see Morris, The Developing Labor Law, 2d Ed. 914–991 (BNA Books, 1983); Alleyne, "Courts, Arbitrators, and the NLRB: The Nature of the Deferral Beast," Proceeding of the 33rd Annual Meeting of NAA, 240 (BNA Books, 1981); Gregorich, "The NLRB and Deferral to Awards of Arbitration Panels," 38 Wash. & Lee L. Rev. 124 (1981); Irving, "Arbitration and the National Labor Relations Board," 35 Arb. J. No. 1, p. 5 (1980); Edwards, "Labor Arbitration at the Crossroads: The 'Common Law of the Shop' v. External Law," 32 Arb. J. 65, 71–76 (1977); Gorman, Basic Text on Labor Law, 751–765 (1976); Teple, "Deferral to Arbitration: Implications of NLRB Policy," 29 Arb. J. 65 (1974); Nash, Wilder & Banov, "The Development of the Collyer Deferral Doctrine," 27 Vand. L. Rev. 23 (1974); Getman, "Collyer Insulated Wire: A Case of Misplaced Modesty," 49 Ind. L.J. 57 (1973); Isaacson & Zifchak, "Agency Deferral to Private Arbitration of Employment Disputes," 73 Colum. L. Rev. 1383 (1973); Brown, "The National Labor Policy, the NLRB, and Arbitration," Proceedings of the 21st Annual Meeting of NAA, 83 (BNA Books, 1968); Ordman, "The Abitrator and the NLRB," Proceedings of the 20th Annual Meeting of NAA, 47 (BNA Books, 1967); Cushman, "Arbitration and the Duty to Bargain," 1967 Wis. L. Rev. 612 (1967); McCulloch, "The Arbitration Issue in NLRB Decisions," 19 Arb. J. 134 (1964).

[67]Irving, "Arbitration and the National Labor Relations Board," 35 Arb. J. No. 1, pp. 5, 6 (1980), where he also predicted (p. 9) that "the future will see the board placing more, not less, reliance on arbitrators for the very practical reason that the board will find it more profitable to channel its scarce resources in other directions."

misapplication thereof by Respondent. It is directed instead at Respondent's denial to it of a statutory right guaranteed by §8(d) of the Act, namely, the right to be notified and consulted in advance, and to be given an opportunity to bargain, about substantial changes in the working conditions of unit employees in respects *not covered by the contract.* As the particular dispute between the Union and Respondent now before us thus involves basically a disagreement over statutory rather than contractual obligations, the disposition of the controversy is quite clearly within the competency of the Board, and not of an arbitrator who would be without authority to grant the Union the particular redress it seeks and for which we provide below in our remedial order."[68]

In the *Schlitz* case the NLRB did defer to arbitration by refusing to exercise its jurisdiction where (1) the collective agreement provided for arbitration; (2) the union was challenging a unilateral action by the employer which was not patently erroneous or designed to undermine the union, but rather was based on a substantial claim of contractual privilege; and (3) it appeared that arbitration would resolve both the contract interpretation issue and the intertwined unfair labor practice issue in a manner compatible with the purposes of the NLRA.[69]

In 1971 the latter case was reaffirmed in the "strikingly similar" *Collyer* case, in which the NLRB adopted a policy of deferring to arbitration in unilateral action cases where such conditions are met, but the Board in deferring to arbitration expressly retained jurisdiction over the dispute

> "for the purpose of entertaining an appropriate and timely motion for further consideration upon a proper showing that either (a) the dispute has not, with reasonable promptness after the issuance of this decision, either been resolved by amicable settlement in the grievance procedure or submitted promptly to arbitration, or (b) the grievance or arbitration procedures have not been fair and regular or have reached a result which is repugnant to the Act."[70]

The NLRB extended its *Collyer* deferral policy to discrimination cases in 1972 but again restricted it to unilateral action cases in 1977.[71] The NLRB did continue its *Dubo* policy under which the Board defers discrimination cases if the charging party is processing the same matter through arbitration either voluntarily or by court order.[72]

Then in 1984 the NLRB (1) recalled that "Despite the universal judicial acceptance of the Collyer doctrine" the Board itself in 1977 had "abruptly changed course and adopted a different standard for arbitral deferral," and (2) the NLRB stated that the *Collyer* doctrine had "worked well because it was premised on sound legal and prag-

---

[68]Cloverleaf Div. of Adams Dairy Co., 147 NLRB 1410, 1415, 56 LRRM 1321 (1964).
[69]Jos. Schlitz Brewing Co., 175 NLRB 141, 70 LRRM 1472 (1969).
[70]Collyer Insulated Wire, 192 NLRB 837, 77 LRRM 1931, 1936, 1938 (1971), in which two members dissented to the deferral to arbitration and in which the majority opinion reviewed the history of the Board's accommodation to the arbitration process.
[71]See National Radio Co., 80 LRRM 1718 (NLRB, 1972); General Am. Transp. Corp., 94 LRRM 1483 (NLRB, 1977).
[72]See Dubo Mfg. Corp., 53 LRRM 1070 (NLRB, 1963). The scope of the *Dubo* policy is explained by Nash, Wilder & Banov, "The Development of the Collyer Deferral Doctrine," 27 Vand. L. Rev. 23, 71–72 (1974). For an explanation that the *Dubo* policy remained intact, see Irving, "Arbitration and the National Labor Relations Board," 35 Arb. J. No. 1, p. 5 (1980).

matic considerations," and that it "deserves to be resurrected and infused with renewed life"; the Board indicated that, accordingly, it would defer not only unilateral action cases but also cases alleging violation of the interference, restraint or coercion, and discrimination provisions of the Act.[73]

Where an award has already been rendered the NLRB under its *Spielberg* doctrine will honor the award if it is found that the arbitration proceedings were fair and regular, that all parties had agreed to be bound, and that the award was not clearly repugnant to the purposes and policies of the Act.[74] But after long adhering to a policy of not deferring to the award unless the unfair labor practice issue before the Board was passed upon by the arbitrator,[75] the Board in 1984 adopted the standard that it "would find that an arbitrator has adequately considered the unfair labor practice if (1) the contractual issue is factually parallel to the unfair labor practice issue, and (2) the arbitrator was presented generally with the facts relevant to resolving the unfair labor practice."[76]

The courts have recognized broad discretion in the NLRB in respect to deferring to arbitration, but they nonetheless have reviewed NLRB decisions in unfair labor practice cases for possible abuse of that discretion.[77]

Finally, it may be noted that in its *Raley's* decision the NLRB also appeared to adopt a policy for representation cases of honoring arbitration awards under certain conditions, but under subsequent decisions it appears unlikely that the NLRB in representation cases will defer to arbitration (either by prearbitral deferral or by honoring an award).[78]

---

[73]United Technologies, 115 LRRM 1049, 1051 (NLRB, 1984).

[74]Spielberg Mfg. Co., 112 NLRB 1080, 1082, 36 LRRM 1152 (1955).

[75]See Suburban Motor Freight, Inc., 103 LRRM 1113 (NLRB, 1980); Raytheon Co., 52 LRRM 1129 (NLRB, 1963). Sometimes arbitrators expressly indicate that they have not undertaken to pass upon NLRA issues. See Arbitrator Jones in 70 LA 833, 837; Platt in 50 LA 239, 248; Larkin in 50 LA 109, 111; Casselman in 44 LA 361, 372; Bowles in 23 LA 812, 814.

[76]Olin Corp., 115 LRRM 1056, 1058 (NLRB, 1984), where the Board also stated (1) that it no longer would be required that the award "be totally consistent with Board precedent"; (2) that the award will be honored unless it "is 'palpably wrong,' i.e., unless the arbitrator's decision is not susceptible to an interpretation consistent with the Act"; and (3) that "the party seeking to have the Board ignore the determination of an arbitrator has the burden of affirmatively demonstrating the defects in the arbitral process or award."

[77]First, note that the U.S. Supreme Court inferentially approved the NLRB's *Collyer* policy in Arnold Co. v. Carpenters Dist. Council, 94 S.Ct. 2069, 2072, 86 LRRM 2212 (1974). Also see NLRB v. City Disposal Sys., 104 S.Ct. 1505, 1515, 115 LRRM 3193 (1984). Many lower court decisions have dealt directly with NLRB deferral in unfair labor practice cases. Those that are cited below collect additional decisions, discuss the changing policy of the Board on deferral, and serve to illustrate some of the possible results in court review of NLRB deferral actions. On prearbitral deferral, see Wheeling-Pittsburgh Steel Corp. v. NLRB, 104 LRRM 2054 (CA 3, 1980), upholding the Board's failure to defer to arbitration; NLRB v. Northeast Okla. City Mfg. Co., 105 LRRM 2618 (CA 10, 1980), holding that the Board did not abuse its discretion in refusing to defer to arbitration. On deferral to awards, see Distillery Workers Local 2 v. NLRB, 107 LRRM 3137 (CA 2, 1981), holding that the Board abused its discretion in refusing to defer to an award; Ad Art, Inc. v. NLRB, 106 LRRM 2010 (CA 9, 1980), holding that the Board did not abuse its discretion in refusing to defer for an award; Bloom v. NLRB, 102 LRRM 2082 (D.C. Cir., 1979), upholding the Board's deferral to an award; Stephenson v. NLRB, 94 LRRM 3224 (CA 9, 1977), holding that the Board abused its discretion in deferring to an award.

[78]See Raley's, Inc., 143 NLRB 256, 53 LRRM 1347 (1963); Ortiz Funeral Home, 105 LRRM

Court Decisions

An arbitrator's willingness to follow a judicial precedent on a question (assuming that the arbitrator has concluded that "law" should be considered in deciding the case) will depend to a large extent upon the level of the court rendering the decision and upon the unanimity of other decisions on the point. Arbitrators naturally feel constrained to follow decisions of courts of last resort. When the U.S. Supreme Court or the highest tribunal of the state in which the parties operate has ruled on a point, it is likely that an arbitrator will give very serious consideration to the ruling.[79]

On the other hand, if an arbitrator does not agree with a decision handed down by a court other than one of last resort, he may refuse to follow it. Where one arbitrator, for instance, felt that an opinion by a federal district court was contrary to all accepted rules of statutory construction, he refused to follow it, declaring that since it was not a decision of a court of last resort he was not bound thereby.[80]

Moreover, arbitrators are less likely to honor conflicting lower court decisions. Thus, where two federal district courts had ruled one way and two others had ruled otherwise, an arbitrator declared that the parties were without the benefit of authoritative judicial decisions, and he decided the issue without reliance upon any of the precedents.[81]

Regardless of whether an arbitrator feels any obligation to follow court decisions, he may seek assistance from them in his disposition of contract issues.[82]

Administrative Rulings

The weight to be given by arbitrators to rulings of administrative and executive agencies of the government may be determined by a

---

1094, 1095 (NLRB, 1980), refusing to defer to an arbitration award and citing several NLRB decisions including Marion Power Shovel Co., 95 LRRM 1339 (NLRB, 1977). In the latter case prearbitral deferral was refused, the Board stating (95 LRRM at 1341–1342):
    "The determination of questions of representation, accretion, and appropriate unit do[es] not depend upon contract interpretation but involve[s] the application of statutory policy, standards, and criteria. These are matters for decision of the Board rather than an arbitrator."
In Hershey Food Corp., 208 NLRB 452, 457 (1974), the Board stated that its *Raley's* decision must be deemed superseded where it is inconsistent with certain later cases. Holding that the court lacked jurisdiction to review the NLRB's refusal in a representation case to defer to an arbitration award, see Teamsters Local 748 v. Haig Berberian, Inc., 105 LRRM 2172 (CA 9, 1980).

[79]See Arbitrator Seifer in 75 LA 1261, 1264–1265; Avins in 74 LA 514, 518; Goodstein in 72 LA 1127, 1129; Belkin in 72 LA 881, 885–887; Williams in 69 LA 368, 375; Oppenheimer in 69 LA 325, 328; Rehmus in 68 LA 1195, 1197. For earlier cases see p. 339 of the Third Edition of this book. Illustrating, however, that even where the U.S. Supreme Court has spoken on a matter, an arbitrator will exercise care to determine the real import of the decision and the limits of its application, see County of Los Angeles, 68 LA 1132, 1136–1137 (Richman, 1977). Also see Arbitrator Jackson in 68 LA 682, 685–686; Yaffe in 68 LA 644, 648–649; Helfeld in 68 LA 633, 636–638.

[80]Dow Chem. Co., 1 LA 70, 74–75 (Whiting, 1945). Also see Arbitrator Smedley in 75 LA 936, 938; Witney in 70 LA 253, 255–256; Edelman in 37 LA 487, 490–491; Seering in 22 LA 108, 110.

[81]Bell Aircraft Corp., 2 LA 22, 24 (Sharkey, 1946). Regarding conflicting court decisions, also see Arbitrator Aisenberg in 69 LA 1024, 1027; Schedler in 46 LA 697, 698–699; Willingham in 40 LA 173, 177; Howlett in 39 LA 449, 454–455; Sanders in 21 LA 180, 181.

[82]For example, see Arbitrator Eyraud in 73 LA 1144, 1145; Tucker in 69 LA 1143, 1147–1148; Seward in 68 LA 581, 582–583; Sembower in 47 LA 414, 419; McMahon in 47 LA 393, 395; Feinberg in 46 LA 1129, 1130–1131.

variety of factors, the most important of which is the authority of the agency making the ruling. For instance, rulings and regulations of wage stabilization agencies are likely to be given serious consideration, possibly prevailing over a conflicting collective agreement provision[83] and over bulletins of other government agencies or officials.[84]

While administrative opinions by the Bureau of Veterans Reemployment Rights were given weight by some arbitrators,[85] another arbitrator gave no weight to advice from the Bureau to an employer, the arbitrator emphasizing that the Bureau's only function was to "render aid" to former servicemen.[86]

Official interpretations by executive departments of the government are given significant weight where relevant. Thus, arbitrators have respected statutory interpretations by the U.S. Department of Justice[87] and interpretations by the U.S. Department of Labor.[88]

Moreover, executive and administrative rulings or interpretations in cases similar to the one being considered by the arbitrator may be relied upon as persuasive, though not controlling, even though the statute to which the ruling applies does not cover the parties before the arbitrator. For instance, the interpretation that had been given the word "day" by officials enforcing the Walsh-Healey Act was persuasive upon an arbitrator in a subsequent case not covered by that statute.[89]

An interesting view regarding the weight to be given to administrative rulings was expressed by Arbitrator L.F. Sharkey in considering an interpretation of the Selective Service Act made by the Director of Selective Service:

> "The interpretation of an administrative agency is entitled to weight, but it is not decisive especially when it is a newly formulated one and one not long in effect, one on which the actions of men have not been based over a long period of time. In this instance, the opinion of the Director is one man's opinion entitled to respect. It may be persuasive,

---

[83]As in Libby, McNeill & Libby, 5 LA 564, 569 (Prasow, 1946). Also see this Chapter's subtopic entitled "U.S. Supreme Court Statements Regarding Arbitral Consideration of External Law"; Chapter 18, topic entitled "Governmental Wage Stabilization."

[84]As in Peabody Coal Co., 5 LA 18, 23 (Fries, 1946).

[85]See Hancock Steel Co., 23 LA 44, 45 (Parker, 1954); Pet Milk Co., 21 LA 180, 181–182 (Sanders, 1953). Also see Arbitrator Garrett in 25 LA 778, 781–782.

[86]Archer-Daniels-Midland Co., 26 LA 561, 564 (Lindquist, 1955).

[87]See Arbitrator Platt in 54 LA 12, 17; Ruckel in 36 LA 1138, 1140; Boles in 23 LA 93, 97–98; Barrett in 17 LA 53, 55; Komaroff in 11 LA 395, 397. Rulings by the state Attorney General were relied upon by Arbitrator Zack in 54 LA 857, 858–859; Kotin in 52 LA 1065, 1067. Also see Snow in 68 LA 503, 506–507; Quinlan in 42 LA 1089, 1092. But see Hoffman in 76 LA 267, 272.

[88]F.C. Thornton Co., 50 LA 254, 256–258 (Gross, 1967), interpretation of statute; Warren Foundry & Pipe Corp., 5 LA 282, 283 (Tischler, 1946), interpretation of executive order. Also see Arbitrator Gillingham in 66 LA 131, 133–134. Cf., Kleingartner in 62 LA 891, 892, 894. Stating that arbitrators should give weight to administrative interpretations when the meaning of a statute is in doubt, Arbitrator James F. Bell nonetheless refused to follow a "clearly erroneous" opinion by the Secretary of Labor. BBC Manufactured Bldgs., 77 LA 1132, 1134 (1981). In W.M. Chace Co., 48 LA 231, 232–236 (1966), Arbitrator Erwin B. Ellmann refused to adhere strictly to a state department of labor guide, which he said was not "law." In Keystone Consol. Indus., 75 LA 608, 612 (Fish, 1980), company witnesses testified that they had been advised by Illinois Department of Labor personnel to avoid a certain practice, but this "oral testimony, unsupported by any written regulation or interpretation" of the law, carried little weight with the arbitrator.

[89]Corn Prods. Ref. Co., 7 LA 125, 131–132 (Updegraff, 1947). Also see Arbitrator Elson in 39 LA 1210, 1212. But see Coffey in 49 LA 1195, 1197.

but it is not controlling. It has not the authority of law. It has not the power to change the provisions of a statute or a contract."[90]

Arbitrator Sharkey thereupon declared that the interpretation of the Director had raised doubts in the minds of honest men and he refused to rely upon it.

Finally, it may be noted that the conclusions and actions of state unemployment compensation commissions have been given very little weight (often none at all) in arbitration proceedings.[91]

Agency Principles

Arbitrators place strong reliance upon the generally recognized principles of agency. Thus, parties are held responsible for the acts of their authorized agents.[92] For instance, the employer has been required to compensate an employee for lost earnings due to the erroneous diagnosis by the employer's doctor of the employee's condition.[93] A union which authorized its vice president to settle a grievance was held bound by the settlement even though it was rejected by the union membership when submitted for their approval.[94] Commitments made by past union officials have bound their successors.[95]

---

[90]Bell Aircraft Corp., 2 LA 22, 24 (1946). Also see Arbitrator Lindquist in 26 LA 561, 564. In Millinocket School Comm., 65 LA 805, 810 (1975), Arbitrator Harry B. Purcell declared:
"Whatever might be the leanings of the Equal Employment Opportunity Commission regarding the pregnancy-sick leave question, they are not binding upon this or any other arbitrator. The interpretative bulletins of such governmental agencies do not constitute law. Such opinions are transitory, and subject to sudden and frequent changes due to the tendency of governmental agencies towards the broadest kind of preemption and authority. Their reach is always greater than their grasp in the belief that the courts are always there to correct any excesses in which they might indulge themselves. In any event, it is not the function of such agencies *nor even of the courts*, to interpret the collective bargaining agreement. That is the peculiar authority of the arbitrator."
[91]See Arbitrator Feldesman in 76 LA 705, 709–710; LeWinter in 76 LA 232, 239; Flagler in 75 LA 764, 768–769; Witney in 73 LA 663, 666; Brooks in 72 LA 865, 873; Gilson in 71 LA 1224, 1231; Imundo in 68 LA 677, 681. For earlier cases see p. 341 of the Third Edition of this book. In Yellow Cab Co., 44 LA 445, 446 (1965), Arbitrator Edgar A. Jones pointed out that the procedures, functions, and issues in the two proceedings are different, and he stated that there is "no functional incongruity" in contradictory decisions from the two proceedings. In Union Fork & Hoe Co., 68 LA 432, 439 (Ipavec, 1977), a decision by the Ohio Bureau of Employment Services carried little weight with the arbitrator, as did a decision by the Indiana State Employees' Appeal Commission in Fort Wayne St. Hosp., 70 LA 253, 255 (Witney, 1978).
[92]See Bethlehem Steel Co., 26 LA 646, 647 (Seward, 1956). Also see Arbitrator Yarowsky in 77 LA 14, 18–19. For cases dealing with the possibility that one may be the "alter ego" of another so as to impose responsibilities toward third parties on that basis, see Arbitrator Gentile in 81 LA 133, 139–140; Jones in 79 LA 1312, 1313–1316; Anderson in 46 LA 1057, 1060; Howlett in 43 LA 514, 518–519, 524–525. Also see Sinclitico in 63 LA 263, 265. In Sterling Regal, 69 LA 513, 537 (1977), Arbitrator David M. Kaplan in placing responsibility for certain incidents upon an international union as principal, declared that any discussion of the authority of its local union was irrelevant since the international "not only devised the game plan, acted as coach and called the signals from the bench, but also ran with the ball on every play."
[93]Arbitrator Bothwell in 27 LA 404, 406–407; Bowles in 26 LA 370, 373; Anderson in 24 LA 756, 758–759. In Pickands Mather & Co., 74 LA 1, 2 (Kahn, 1980), the negligence of an employee in grading a company road was imputed to the employer, who then became liable under the agreement for damage resulting to another employee's car.
[94]Kendall Cotton Mills, 24 LA 684, 687–688 (Dworet, 1955). Also see Arbitrator Dworkin in 49 LA 974, 979–980; McNaughton in 41 LA 1345, 1347; Wallen in 38 LA 522, 523; Rock in 37 LA 465 at 465.
[95]See Arbitrator Kates in 48 LA 865, 867; Morvant in 33 LA 302, 305–306; Shister in 25 LA 50, 53.

A principal may be held responsible for the act of his agent within the scope of the agent's general authority even though the principal has not specifically authorized the act in question; it is enough if the principal empowered the agent to represent him in the general area within which the agent acted.[96] On this basis, employers have been held responsible for or bound by various actions of supervisors.[97] Of course, the employer will not be bound by an act of a supervisor or other management representative if no basis exists to establish authority for the act.[98] Thus, an employer was held not bound by an agreement reached between the plant superintendent and the union committee where both the committee and the superintendent knew that it was subject to the approval, never received, of company officials.[99]

Even where no agency authority exists at the time of an act, it may be supplied retroactively by subsequent ratification. Ratification may be express, but it also may be implied by silence after knowledge of the unauthorized act[100] or by actual operation under an unauthorized agreement.[101]

Arbitrators have often been strict in requiring a showing of authorization or ratification by the union membership of any action of a union committee which changes the terms of the collective agreement. "To hold otherwise would mean that a local Union committee meeting with management could dissipate the contractual benefits of its membership without its approval."[102]

---

[96]Sunset Line & Twine Co., 79 NLRB 1487, 1509 (1948), citing the Restatement of Agency.

[97]See Arbitrator Smith in 73 LA 280, 283; Bernstein in 71 LA 903, 908; Moore in 68 LA 1048, 1053; Cantor in 54 LA 1011, 1018; Jones in 54 LA 820, 823–824; Kates in 48 LA 773, 775; McNaughton in 37 LA 958, 960. Also see Newmark in 76 LA 946, 952; Graff in 37 LA 1108, 1111. Cf., Beatty in 48 LA 1123, 1124; Horlacher in 41 LA 252, 255. In Rust Eng'g. Co., 77 LA 488, 490 (Williams, 1981), responsibility was traced to a union where certain actions of its steward in connection with illicit picketing were found to be within the steward's "scope of authority."

[98]See Arbitrator Herman in 73 LA 962, 964 (stating that a "foreman has no authority to bind his employer to make payments which are not required by" the agreement); Stewart in 73 LA 928, 932; Griffin in 68 LA 1326, 1328; Kates in 48 LA 606, 608; Daugherty in 25 LA 426, 429. Cf., Kuhn in 69 LA 437, 439 (employer was bound by foreman's interpretation of the agreement where the interpretation was not clearly erroneous and grievant had relied upon it); Wagner in 68 LA 254, 256. The mere fact that a person undertakes to act for another or claims authority to do so is not sufficient, without more, to establish agency. See Arbitrator Aisenberg in 73 LA 680, 683 (the union president "was not authorized to speak on behalf of" the company when he "took it upon himself to go to the gate and not let the employees in the plant" after a fire had occurred); Ruben in 69 LA 944, 957–958.

[99]Kempsmith Mach. Co., 5 LA 520, 530 (Marshall, 1946). Cf., Arbitrator Lee in 70 LA 839, 841. If a company representative is found to have had authority to commit the company to a settlement, the company will be bound. General Tel. Co. of Ill., 49 LA 493, 499 (Kesselman, 1967).

[100]Pacific Am. Shipowners Assn., 10 LA 736, 746 (Miller, 1948). Also see Arbitrator Weiss in 67 LA 159, 162–163; Kennedy in 45 LA 30, 33; Cox in 28 LA 677, 690.

[101]Lafe Pharmacy, 1 ALAA ¶67,469 (1946). Also see Arbitrator Williams in 66 LA 962, 964; Marshall in 47 LA 97, 101.

[102]Flintkote Co., 9 LA 976, 977 (Naggi, 1948). In accord with the general proposition, Arbitrator Dean in 72 LA 1220, 1222–1223; Altrock in 50 LA 845, 850; Witney in 44 LA 624, 628–629; Schedler in 34 LA 860, 861; Thompson in 23 LA 89, 91; Platt in 12 LA 161, 164, and in 11 LA 805, 808; Donnelly, Curry & Clark in 10 LA 55 at 55. Also see Witney in 71 LA 969, 973–975; Lennard in 49 LA 76, 80–81. Cf., Valtin in 79 LA 999, 1005–1006; Anrod in 29 LA 848, 852–854; Warns in 28 LA 424, 427–428. In Eagle Mfg. Co., 51 LA 970, 979 (Lugar, 1968), it was held, somewhat in converse, that a majority of the employees could not excuse employer action contrary to the collective agreement where the employer's action was not approved by the union as the contracting party. Also see Arbitrator Belshaw in 73 LA 1087, 1091. For related discussion, see Chapter 5, topic entitled "Grievance Adjustment by Individual Employees."

The Connecticut State Board of Mediation and Arbitration has held that, in view of the customary procedure of collective bargaining by which all matters of high importance, such as annual wage increases, must be submitted to the membership for final approval, a presumption exists against the validity of action taken by a union committee in respect to these matters until proof of authorization or ratification is shown.[103]

Likewise, a shop steward has no authority to bind the union by an agreement altering or creating an exception to the collective agreement, nor has he authority to waive strict performance of the agreement.[104] Nor does a union field representative have authority to change the collective agreement unless such authority is clearly vested in him by the membership.[105]

Such a strict rule, however, would not apply to an action taken in grievance settlements which does not have the effect of changing the terms of the agreement.[106] Moreover, an oral agreement between the company and a union president was held binding though it involved deviation from the seniority provisions of the collective agreement since he had made numerous such agreements in the past without objection from the union.[107]

An arbitrator will hold a party bound by the act of its agent, though unauthorized, if the party is found to have clothed the agent with "apparent" or "ostensible" authority to act.[108] For instance, a company was so bound where it held out an employers association as its agent by permitting one of its officers to sit on the association's bargaining committee without disclosing an intent not to be bound by the agreement being negotiated on behalf of the association's mem-

---

[103]Russell Mfg. Co., 10 LA 55 at 55 (Donnelly, Curry & Clark, 1948). Also see Arbitrator Platt in 40 LA 1089, 1090. Cf., Winton in 71 LA 892, 895–897. In Southern Mich. Cold Storage, 80 LA 53, 64–65 (1982), Arbitrator Malcolm G. House granted the Company's request that the written agreement "be reformed to reflect the oral agreement reached between the parties at the bargaining table," since union bargaining representatives failed to speak up when they realized the Company had made an error, but rather one of them by "bad faith and inequitable conduct" then "knowingly misled an uninformed membership to ratify the Company's written proposal which was in error and inconsistent with the truth."

[104]Valley Metal Prods. Co., 25 LA 83, 84 (Ryder, 1955); Pacific Mills, 2 LA 545, 548 (McCoy, 1946). Also see Arbitrator Whelan in 33 LA 902, 909.

[105]McLouth Steel Corp., 11 LA 805, 808 (Platt, 1948).

[106]See Arbitrator Williams in 45 LA 727, 729, 731; Dykstra in 41 LA 1184, 1188–1189; Morvant in 41 LA 288, 292–293; Kates in 39 LA 327, 332; Valtin in 30 LA 967, 969; Platt in 12 LA 161, 164. Also see Gibson in 74 LA 854, 856; Dworkin in 40 LA 1042, 1047; Wallen in 38 LA 522, 523; Kesselman in 28 LA 434, 436.

[107]Lockheed Aircraft Corp., 23 LA 815, 820–821 (Marshall, 1955). Also see Arbitrator Epstein in 45 LA 146, 149–150; Kennedy in 45 LA 30, 33. The union president's waiver of a contractual prohibition against plant removal did not bind the employees in Douwe Egberts Superior Co., 78 LA 1131, 1137 (Ellmann, 1982).

[108]See Arbitrator Talarico in 76 LA 854, 856; Goodstein in 69 LA 329, 332–333; Sacks in 68 LA 735, 737; Sembower in 54 LA 1265, 1267–1268; Krimsly in 52 LA 1125, 1128–1130; Madden in 52 LA 506, 509; Jarvis in 52 LA 197, 199–200; Dworkin in 49 LA 974, 979–980; Roberts in 48 LA 1166, 1170–1171; Fallon in 45 LA 85, 88–89; Anrod in 29 LA 848, 852–853; Cox in 28 LA 677, 690; Marshall in 23 LA 815, 820–821; Myers in 16 LA 584, 585. In Western Condensing Co., 37 LA 912, 915 (Mueller, 1962), an employee was held bound by actions of his wife under this concept. In Maier Brewing Co., 45 LA 1115, 1123 (Jones, 1965), an employer was not permitted to challenge or "probe behind" the apparent authority, upon which the employer could rely, of union representatives to enter into a collective bargaining agreement.

bers.[109] A union was held bound by actions of its officer where the officer, with the union's knowledge, appeared to be speaking for the union and the union failed to openly disavow that action.[110]

The rule that knowledge of an agent is imputed to the principal has been applied by arbitrators. Knowledge held by a union regarding the existence and nature of a grievance settlement may be charged to the employee affected, and the employer relieved from making good any loss suffered by the employee as a result of the union's failure to notify him of the settlement.[111]

Knowledge held by a management representative may be imputed to the employer,[112] and that of a union agent may be charged to the union.[113] In some cases, however, arbitrators have pointed to the limited authority of the agent and have refused to impute his knowledge to the principal.[114]

As to imputing knowledge of the individual employee to the union, one arbitrator has taken the view that knowledge of individual union members concerning the employer's policy and practices under the agreement "cannot be without more charged to the Union, for members of a Union are not necessarily agents of the Union."[115] But another arbitrator has declared that as to knowledge of company policy, "the knowledge of the employee must be the knowledge of the Union."[116]

As to the principal's obligation to indemnify his agents, an arbitrator resorted to basic principles of agency law in determining whether an employee was entitled to be indemnified by his employer for monetary loss which the employee suffered in defending legal actions against him growing out of certain things which he did allegedly in the employer's interest.[117]

---

[109]Pope and Talbot, 1 ALAA ¶67,157, p. 67,324 (1942). Also see Arbitrator Roberts in 49 LA 14, 19; Mintzer in 38 LA 1171, 1172.
[110]Carmen v. BRT, 44 LA 540, 543 (Wallen, 1965). Also see Arbitrator Yarowsky in 77 LA 14, 18. Cf., Finley in 69 LA 175, 176.
[111]Ford Motor Co., 1 LA 409, 410 (Shulman, 1945). Also see Arbitrator Warns in 27 LA 179, 182. But see Aisenberg in 77 LA 880, 882–883. In Newspaper Agency Corp., 43 LA 1233, 1235 (Platt, 1964), notice to union representatives who resided at points distant (in different states) from the local union and who were not known to be authorized to receive the notice (copies of arbitration decision), was not notice to local union.
[112]See Arbitrator Sergent in 74 LA 369, 373; Moore in 68 LA 1048, 1053; Dworkin in 40 LA 87, 90.
[113]Anheuser-Busch, 33 LA 752, 753 (Roberts, 1959); Boys & Men's Shop, 8 LA 214, 217–218 (Rosenfarb, 1947).
[114]See Arbitrator Gowan in 71 LA 344, 348; Kates in 52 LA 557, 560; Hilpert in 36 LA 1169, 1172. Cf., Shanker in 68 LA 13, 19.
[115]Boys & Men's Shop, 8 LA 214, 218 (Rosenfarb, 1947). As to union responsibility for employee actions in breach of the no-strike clause, see National Homes Mfg. Co., 72 LA 1127, 1130 (Goodstein, 1979), stating that the union "is responsible for the actions of its members, at least until it has made a good faith effort to get the members to honor their Contract." Similarly, see Arbitrator Pollack in 42 LA 142, 144. But see Platt in 43 LA 785, 790.
[116]Chattanooga Box & Lumber Co., 44 LA 373, 376 (Tatum, 1965). Accord, imputing to the union an employee's knowledge that the agreement was being violated by the employer, Sinclair Mfg. Co., 49 LA 310, 313–314 (Nichols, 1967). In Tri-State Eng'g Co., 69 LA 980, 984 (Brown, 1977), the arbitrator stated that company policy regarding proof of illness must be "communicated to all employees," and that an "informal discussion with the plant shop committee cannot be said to be proper notice."
[117]Trubitz Hardware & Elec. Co., 32 LA 930, 934–935 (Scheiber, 1959).

Contract Principles

Arbitrators may be expected to recognize fundamental principles of contract law, such as those concerning the need for consideration to produce a binding contract,[118] those concerning offer and acceptance,[119] those concerning anticipatory breach,[120] and those concerning the obligation to perform contractual commitments in spite of hardship.[121]

The principle that there can be no binding contract without a meeting of the minds has been applied by arbitrators.[122] Where the arbitrator finds that there has been no meeting of the minds on a matter he may recommend further negotiations by the parties,[123] unless he construes his authority to be broad enough to empower him to decide the dispute on the merits.[124]

Remedies for Mistake

The remedy of reformation to correct a mutual mistake in a contract is well established at law, and it has been recognized by

---

[118]See Dixie-Portland Flour Mills, 46 LA 838, 840 (Hon, 1966); United Drill & Tool Corp., 28 LA 677, 685–686 (Cox, 1957). Discussing the application in arbitration of this and various other principles of contract law, see Mueller, "The Law of Contracts—A Changing Legal Environment," Proceedings of the 31st Annual Meeting of NAA, 204 (BNA Books, 1979); Goetz, "Comment," id. at 218; Meiners, "Comment," id. at 229.

[119]See Arbitrator Peterschmidt in 77 LA 396, 399; Kelliher in 54 LA 647, 648; Eaton in 54 LA 478, 482–483; Hays in 20 LA 406, 408. Also see Solomon in 42 LA 280, 288.

[120]See Metro E. Journal, 47 LA 610, 612 (Kelliher, 1966).

[121]See American Iron & Mach. Works Co., 18 LA 285, 287 (Horton, 1952). Also see Seng Co., 51 LA 928, 931–932 (Sembower, 1968), in accord as to hardship and also noting that only in extreme cases will impossibility of performance be accepted as an excuse for not performing a contract. Regarding impossibility of performance, also see Arbitrator Flannagan in 72 LA 1293, 1296 (time was extended where it was impossible to perform within time specified by agreement); Lubow in 69 LA 847, 851 (contractual obligation would be modified only as justified by impossibility of performance); Gibson in 69 LA 697, 703 (employer failed to act timely in claiming impossibility of performance); Snow in 68 LA 503, 506–507. Regarding federal-sector agreements, see Arbitrator Moore in 68 LA 375, 378–379. The U.S. Supreme Court recognized impossibility as a possible defense to breach of contract but rejected economic necessity as a defense in W.R. Grace & Co. v. Rubber Workers Local 759, 103 S.Ct. 2177, 113 LRRM 2641, 2645 n. 10, 2646 n. 12 (1983), which case is discussed generally in Chapter 14, subtopic entitled "Contractual Seniority Rights, the Civil Rights Act, and Arbitration."

[122]See Arbitrator Kaplan in 78 LA 842, 847; Sharnoff in 76 LA 308, 311; Cox in 75 LA 822, 824; Rayl in 70 LA 633, 635; Bowles in 68 LA 1110, 1121–1122; Render in 68 LA 57, 62; Lubow in 67 LA 257, 260; Garman in 58 LA 1084, 1087, and in 20 LA 199, 201–202; Sembower in 54 LA 292, 297–298; Shipman in 46 LA 885, 886; Johannes in 20 LA 362, 363; Brandschain in 9 LA 239, 241; Copelof in 8 LA 475, 478; McCoy in 1 LA 556, 560. The NLRB held that there was no binding agreement without a meeting of the minds in Computer Sciences Corp., 108 LRRM 1233 at 1233 (NLRB, 1981); McKinzie Enters., 104 LRRM 1321, 1322 (NLRB, 1980). The "meeting of the minds" requirement is questioned in Garrett, "The Role of Lawyers in Arbitration," Proceedings of the 14th Annual Meeting of NAA, 102, 121 (BNA Books, 1961). Fraud in the inducement of a contract was basis for voiding it in Hastings Mfg. Co., 49 LA 297, 299–300 (Howlett, 1967); but the fact that a contractual promise was given under coercive circumstances did not excuse its performance in City of New Haven, 50 LA 661, 663 (Summers, 1968).

[123]For example, see Arbitrator Sembower in 54 LA 292, 297–298; Johannes in 20 LA 362, 364; Brandschain in 9 LA 239, 241; Copelof in 8 LA 475, 478. Also see Strasshofer in 76 LA 697, 699.

[124]See Arbitrator Beatty in 24 LA 424, 425; Ryder in 22 LA 769, 771; Wallen in 6 LA 286, 288; Rice in 8 LA 586, 589. For related discussion and other cases, see Chapter 9, subtopic entitled " 'Legislation' v. 'Interpretation' "; Chapter 7, topic entitled "Recommendations by Arbitrator."

arbitrators.[125] In fact, a reformation may be granted even where the evidence falls short of what a court of equity would require for contractual reformation if upon consideration of all the evidence the arbitrator is persuaded that fairness and justice, even though not strictly "equity" as it is administered in the courts, requires this kind of relief.[126]

However, arbitrators, like courts, will grant relief only in case of *mutual* mistake; unilateral mistake is not sufficient.[127]

The common prohibition against adding to, subtracting from, or modifying the terms of the agreement by the arbitrator would seem to provide special justification for the refusal to grant a reformation solely on the basis of unilateral mistake. Moreover, this same prohibition dictates against the setting aside of the terms of an agreement merely because its operation has not been up to the expectations of one of the parties or because, at the time of signing the agreement, the full implications of its provisions may not have been realized by one of the parties.[128]

Like reformation of contract, the remedy of rescission for mistake ordinarily is available only under limited circumstances.[129] In particular, a unilateral mistake is not sufficient basis for rescission unless the mistake was basic and the other party knew and took advantage of it.[130]

Another type of "mistake" situation that has arisen in arbitration has involved the payment of money. In one case, for instance, employees recovered sums which their employer owed them but had mistakenly failed to pay.[131]

---

[125]For instance, see Arbitrator Anderson in 43 LA 730, 732–733; Whyte in 41 LA 555, 558–559; Tatum in 34 LA 406, 409; Willcox in 23 LA 21, 24. Also see statements by Arbitrator Christensen in 46 LA 789, 797; Seinsheimer in 35 LA 409, 411; Compton in 27 LA 829, 830–831; Duff in 25 LA 534, 536; Tilford in 20 LA 446, 447; Emery in 17 LA 632, 635; Forrester in 17 LA 592, 594.

[126]See Huntsville Mfg. Co., 6 LA 515, 516–517 (McCoy, 1947). Where an arbitrator was not so persuaded, he insisted that "Only under rare, unusual and compelling circumstances should a labor arbitrator exercise authority not expressly conferred upon him by modifying or reforming a labor agreement of long standing." Sidney Wanzer & Sons, 47 LA 708, 710–711 (Kamin, 1966).

[127]See Arbitrator Boyer in 80 LA 96, 102–103; Gentile in 76 LA 345, 347; Hardin in 74 LA 1229, 1235; Goodman in 71 LA 1128, 1133–1134; Perry in 68 LA 1294, 1299; Marcus in 68 LA 838, 841; Hebert in 66 LA 517, 520; Sembower in 54 LA 1265, 1268; Erbs in 51 LA 606, 611–612; Gould in 50 LA 877, 881; Williams in 48 LA 1185, 1186; Koven in 48 LA 164, 167; Seward in 47 LA 549, 551; Holly in 67–2 ARB ¶8452; Howlett in 43 LA 913, 917–918; Bowles in 23 LA 746, 749; Platt in 7 LA 708, 711–712; McCoy in 3 LA 257, 259. A reformation may be granted to effectuate the true intent of the parties where that intent is not reflected in the agreement as a result of typographical error. See Mohawk Beverages, 50 LA 298, 300 (Moran, 1968). Also see Arbitrator House in 80 LA 53, 64–65. For related discussion, see Chapter 9, topic entitled "Language Which Is Clear and Unambiguous."

[128]For cases, see Chapter 9, topic entitled "Language Which Is Clear and Unambiguous."

[129]For example, see American Airlines, 48 LA 705, 717–718 (Seitz, 1967). In Overhead Door Corp., 61 LA 1229, 1232 (1973), Arbitrator Clair V. Duff found that the parties in adopting a provision had acted under "mutual mistake of fact," and, though not using the term "rescission," his remedy was to "excise" the provision from the agreement and to direct the parties "to promptly return to the bargaining table."

[130]For a thorough discussion of mistake as a basis for rescission, see Arbitrator Archibald Cox in United Drill & Tool Corp., 28 LA 677, 687–689 (1957), and Arbitrator Douglas B. Maggs in Glendale Mfg. Co., 28 LA 298, 300–301 (1957). Also see Forrester in 17 LA 592, 594; Townsend in 17 LA 472, 478.

[131]A.D. Julliard & Co., 20 LA 579, 582–583 (Maggs, 1953). Also see Arbitrator Duff in 73 LA 1183, 1185.

Where an employer makes a mistake in the employee's favor, the employer may seek to correct it for the future and he sometimes will seek recoupment. It appears clear that the employer will be permitted to correct mathematical or clerical errors in wage computation where the payment has not yet been made; and there is a probability that the arbitrator will find some right of recoupment in the employer as to those erroneous payments which were made before the error was detected.[132] Where the clerical error concerns an employee's rate (or its basis) and has continued for some time, the employer still may be permitted to correct it for the future if he acts promptly upon discovery of the error, but the arbitrator may be less inclined to permit recoupment.[133]

Where the employer's error is not of a clerical nature but is in the nature of a "mistake of law" or "mistake of judgment" with full knowledge of all the facts, he may or may not be permitted to correct it for the future;[134] but it is unlikely that recoupment will be permitted.[135]

Unjust Enrichment

The principle of unjust enrichment holds that "one shall not unjustly enrich himself at the expense of another."[136] Arbitrator R.H. Marshall elaborated:

> "The general principle of unjust enrichment is that one person should not be permitted to enrich himself unjustly at the expense of another, but the party so enriched should be required to make restitution for property or benefits received, where it is just and equitable, and where such action involves no violation or frustration of the law."[137]

In some arbitration cases the evidence has supported the application of this doctrine.[138]

---

[132]Recoupment permitted in whole or in part by Arbitrator Cantor in 69 LA 794, 799–800; Schurke in 56 LA 1270, 1275; Kesselman in 49 LA 493, 498; Walsh in 49 LA 206, 210; Kates in 48 LA 773, 775 (dictum); Stouffer in 44 LA 397, 401; Williams in 42 LA 1084, 1086–1087 (practice supported it); McDermott in 41 LA 10, 13–14 (practice supported it); Garrett in 36 LA 385, 387; Duff in 33 LA 564, 566–567. Cf., Willingham in 40 LA 442, 444 (no recoupment permitted). Permitting recoupment of overpayment caused by BLS error in consumer price index, see Arbitrator Platt in 69 LA 52, 59, and Roberts in 68 LA 970, 973; not permitting recoupment, see Karasick in 64 LA 862, 864.

[133]See Arbitrator Margolin in 70 LA 779, 783; Dworkin in 45 LA 1015, 1017–1018; Willingham in 40 LA 91, 94; Pigors in 39 LA 640, 642; Coleman in 33 LA 333, 335. In Valley-Todeco, 75 LA 661, 664 (Anderson, 1980), recoupment was *required* under the circumstances involved. But see Arbitrator Drake in 32 LA 453, 458–459.

[134]Compare Eastern Airlines, 48 LA 1005, 1009 (Seidenberg, 1967), with Northern Ohio Tel. Co., 48 LA 773, 775 (Kates, 1966). Also see Arbitrator Lipson in 80 LA 994, 999.

[135]See Eastern Airlines, 48 LA 1005, 1009 (Seidenberg, 1967); Milwaukee Linen Supply Co., 23 LA 392, 394 (Anderson, 1954).

[136]Bouvier's Law Dictionary 3376 (8th Ed.).

[137]Cyclops Corp., 51 LA 613, 616 (1968), also stating that reliance upon the doctrine "must be supported by clear and convincing evidence," which did not exist in that case.

[138]See Arbitrator Eyraud in 72 LA 1178, 1180; Richman in 71 LA 813, 816; Somers in 51 LA 822, 835; Cantor in 48 LA 931, 933. In American Maize Prods. Co., 37 LA 673, 675 (Sembower,

The "unjustly at the expense of another" element is not always present when a person receives an apparent "windfall." Thus, Arbitrator Samuel S. Kates upheld the right of a family to double insurance coverage by reason of separate insurance programs covering both spouses furnished by their separate employers; in the absence of a contractual provision to the contrary, the double family benefit was a legitimate result of the family's double employment.[139] On the other hand, it may well be considered improper for an individual to secure double benefits for himself, as where an employee secured unemployment compensation covering a period for which he also received workers' compensation.[140]

Waiver and Estoppel

Frequently one party to a collective agreement will charge that the other party has waived or is estopped from asserting a right under the agreement.[141] Arbitrators generally do not appear to be concerned with all of the fine legal distinctions between the term "waiver" and the term "estoppel," but they have often applied the underlying principle.[142]

Especially common in arbitration is that species of waiver known in law as "acquiescence." This term denotes a waiver which arises by tacit consent or by failure of a person for an unreasonable length of time to act upon rights of which he has full knowledge.

Arbitrators have frequently held that where one party, with actual or constructive knowledge of his rights, stands by and offers no protest with respect to the conduct of the other, thereby reasonably inducing the latter to believe that his conduct is fully concurred in, the matter will be treated as closed insofar as it relates to past transactions; but repeated violations of an express rule by one party or

---

1961), the employer was required to pay an employee under the "quantum meruit" principle for the value of services performed by the employee where the employer knew of it and did nothing to halt the work.

[139]Hawthorn-Mellody Farms, 52 LA 557, 560–561 (1969). Accord in principle, Arbitrator Williams in 51 LA 589, 592; Nichols in 67–2 ARB ¶8390; Seinsheimer in 66–2 ARB ¶8567. Cf., Bothwell in 68–1 ARB ¶6210; Wallen in 41 LA 1321, 1322. For cases in which a "coordination of benefits" provision was present so as to prevent double benefits, see Arbitrator Shister in 54 LA 335, 337; Klamon in 47 LA 1142, 1149; Uible in 39 LA 136, 138; Graff in 38 LA 245, 248. For cases involving the scope of coverage where both spouses are employed by the same company, see Arbitrator Blistein in 49 LA 612 at 612; Thompson in 32 LA 843, 847.

[140]National Union Elec. Corp., 77 LA 815, 818–819 (Traynor, 1981). Also denying entitlement to double benefits, see Arbitrator Strongin in 73 LA 264, 266; Kenaston in 68 LA 638, 643–644; Williams in 62 LA 480, 481.

[141]For related discussion, see Chapter 5, subtopic entitled "Waiver of Employee Rights or Signature Requirement."

[142]For instances in which the arbitrator did note legal distinctions between the two terms, see Continental Distilling Sales Co., 52 LA 1138, 1141 (Sembower, 1969), where an issue was decided on the basis of estoppel; Fox Mfg. Co., 47 LA 97, 101–102 (Marshall, 1966), where there was an express waiver of certain rights for the future. Also see Arbitrator Gibson in 74 LA 854, 856.

acquiescence on the part of the other ordinarily will not affect application of the rule in future operations.[143]

One arbitrator has held that the failure to enforce a right does not constitute a waiver unless the other party is misled to his prejudice, damage, or injury, or unless other elements of estoppel are present.[144] While many arbitrators do not appear to require such a strong showing, most do adhere to fairly strict minimum standards: Clear evidence will be required;[145] only one with authority to waive provisions of an agreement may do so;[146] the waiver of one right or provision, standing alone, will not be held to constitute the waiver of another.[147]

Sometimes arbitrators decide issues specifically on the basis of estoppel.[148] For instance, where a company gave an oral assurance on a matter during contract negotiations to induce the union to agree on a contract and end a strike, Arbitrator Whitley P. McCoy held that an estoppel had been created against the company since the union had changed its position, suffering detriment, in reliance upon the assurance. Accordingly, the company was held bound by the oral assurance, which limited the number of employees the company could reclassify under a provision of the contract.[149]

Sometimes, too, arbitrators decide issues essentially on the basis of estoppel without so stating specifically and without requiring as clear a showing of the elements of estoppel as might be required by a court of law.[150] In the latter type of cases emphasis is often placed upon equity, with something like a "fair and just result" standard being applied.

An approach similar to the "election" principle of equity courts, limiting a party to the exercise of only one of two inconsistent or

---

[143]See Arbitrator Rule in 76 LA 572, 575; Ruben in 76 LA 71, 75; Richman in 73 LA 405, 409; Dennis in 70 LA 1172, 1174; Howlett in 50 LA 829, 831–832; Nichols in 49 LA 310, 313; Allen in 48 LA 219, 222–223; Myers in 42 LA 269, 272; Emery in 17 LA 90, 91; Maggs in 12 LA 311, 316; Douglas in 10 LA 562, 563; Courshon in 9 LA 484, 490–491; Wolff in 5 LA 333, 336; McCoy in 4 LA 231, 233. Also see Anderson in 47 LA 356, 362–363; Seward in 36 LA 162, 164; Morvant in 24 LA 750, 752. For other cases reflecting these principles, see materials on continuing violations and on negligent delay in filing grievances in Chapter 5, topic entitled "Time Limitations"; Chapter 12, topic entitled "Custom and Practice v. Clear Contract Language." Very strong proof is required to establish amendment of the contract by custom. See Chapter 12, subtopic entitled "Amendment of Contract."

[144]Allis-Chalmers Mfg. Co., 8 LA 945, 947 (Gorder, 1947). Similarly, see Arbitrator Cantor in 76 LA 493, 498–499; Sacks in 68 LA 261, 265–266; Somers in 24 LA 324, 327.

[145]Mosaic Tile Co., 13 LA 949, 950 (Cornsweet, 1950); Super-Cold Corp., 8 LA 187, 188 (Cheney, 1947).

[146]Republic Steel Corp., 5 LA 609, 618 (McCoy, 1946), and McCoy in 2 LA 545, 548. Also see Chapter 5, subtopic entitled "Waiver of Employee Rights or Signature Requirement."

[147]Union Carbide Corp., 46 LA 195, 198 (Cahn, 1966); Stearms Coal & Lumber Co., 1 LA 274, 276 (Dwyer, 1946).

[148]Many cases are cited at p. 350 of the Third Edition of this book. For later cases, see Arbitrator Dunn in 77 LA 438, 442–443; Concepcion in 76 LA 732, 735; Marcus in 73 LA 448, 455; Bell in 69 LA 1003, 1011; Sacks in 68 LA 735, 737.

[149]International Harvester Co., 17 LA 101, 103 (1951). Similarly, see Arbitrator Ruben in 68 LA 1248, 1252; Kates in 48 LA 865, 867; Schedler in 36 LA 15, 17; Forrester in 18 LA 306, 307. But see Roumell in 71 LA 864, 868–869; Barsamian in 71 LA 751, 754; Sembower in 51 LA 582, 588; Keefe in 48 LA 373, 376–377; Koven in 48 LA 164, 166–167; Hon in 46 LA 838, 840–841.

[150]See Arbitrator Beitner in 76 LA 190, 194; Goodman in 69 LA 1186, 1188; Bowles in 67 LA 598, 600; Sales in 47 LA 1078, 1081; Fallon in 45 LA 85, 90; Stouffer in 43 LA 901, 905; Klamon in 21 LA 300, 305; Hays in 20 LA 406, 408; Luskin in 16 LA 237, 238; Miller in 10 LA 736, 746; Rosenfarb in 8 LA 214, 217; Blair in 4 LA 110, 111.

alternate rights, was followed by Arbitrator David A. Wolff in not permitting a party to assume the position of "having his cake and eating it too."[151]

Principles of Damages

In empowering the arbitrator to resolve their dispute, the parties generally are considered to have clothed him with authority to grant adequate monetary relief where he finds that the grievance has merit.[152] In this regard, Arbitrator W. Willard Wirtz emphasized that arbitrators have authority to award money damages for contract violations even though the contract does not specifically provide such remedy. To restrict arbitrators to remedies specifically set forth in the contract would negate arbitration as a method of dispute settlement or would result in cluttering contracts with numerous liquidated damages provisions which would invite more trouble than they could prevent.[153]

Compensatory Damages

Monetary damages in arbitration should "normally correspond to specific monetary losses suffered."[154] Arbitrator Ralph T. Seward explained:

"The ordinary rule at common law and in the developing law of labor relations is that an award of damages should be limited to the amount

---

[151]Chrysler Corp., 6 LA 369, 372 (1947). Also see Arbitrator Kindig in 68 LA 461, 468; Klamon in 50 LA 574, 591; Cahn in 22 LA 270, 272–273. Cf., Gibson in 69 LA 697, 704. In Allegheny Ludlum Steel Corp., 33 LA 669, 674–675 (1959), Arbitrator Seward (1) noted that the doctrine of "election of remedies" has been questioned and (2) drew a distinction between "election" and "mistake" of remedies. As to waiver by acceptance of benefits, see Colonial Baking Co., 32 LA 193, 198–199 (Piercey, 1959).

[152]For related discussion, see Chapter 7, topic entitled "Remedy Power and Its Use." Also see Wolff, "The Power of the Arbitrator to Make Monetary Awards," Proceedings of the 17th Annual Meeting of NAA, 176 (BNA Books, 1964).

[153]International Harvester Co., 9 LA 894, 896 (1947). In accord, see Arbitrator Caraway in 73 LA 1074, 1082–1083; Dworkin in 41 LA 219, 222; Seitz in 37 LA 509, 518; Kuhn in 34 LA 814, 825; Reynard in 27 LA 625, 628; Willcox in 23 LA 21 23; Louisell in 21 LA 254, 259; Emery in 17 LA 721, 722–723. Also see Laskin in 18 LA 925, 926; Wolff in 15 LA 822, 827. Cf., Cohen in 71 LA 679, 683, 685. Regarding monetary awards against public-sector employers, compare the following court cases involving such awards: Waterbury Bd. of Educ. v. Teachers Assn., 97 LRRM 2401 (Conn. S.Ct., 1977), upholding the award where the submission expressly empowered the arbitrator to award damages; Bd. of Comm'rs v. Local 502-M, 95 LRRM 3396 (Mich. Ct. App., 1977), upholding the award even though the agreement was silent on remedies; Boston Teachers Union v. School Comm., 93 LRRM 2205 (Mass. S.Ct., 1976), holding the arbitrator could not award damages for a purpose for which public funds could not be expended, and stating also (dictum) that even as to a proper purpose, an arbitrator cannot award damages in excess of amounts which have been lawfully appropriated for the particular purpose.

[154]Patterson-Sargent Co., 23 LA 21, 23 (Willcox, 1954). Also see Arbitrator Sembower in 39 LA 821, 822–823; Laskin in 18 LA 925, 926; Emery in 17 LA 721, 723. Collective agreements often leave the matter of retroactivity of damages to the arbitrator, but with a limitation on the period of retroactivity. See Major Collective Bargaining Agreements: Arbitration Procedures, 77–78 (U.S. Dept. Labor Bull. No. 1425–6, 1966). Also as to retroactivity of damages, see Arbitrator Bailey in 69 LA 294, 302; Koven in 47 LA 8, 11. Where a grievant was now deceased, damages were awarded to his estate or next of kin. Phelps Dodge Aluminum, 52 LA 375, 382 (Howlett, 1969).

necessary to make the injured 'whole.' Unless the agreement provides that some other rule should be followed, this rule must apply."[155]

Thus, for example, where an employer violates the agreement by utilizing junior employees, damages will be due only to those employees whose seniority would have entitled them to the work had the employer acted in accordance with the agreement.[156] Where no grievant suffered any monetary loss as a result of the employer's violation, no damages were awarded.[157]

Arbitrator Maurice S. Trotta required a showing of injury to justify damages, and where the existence of any such injury was too speculative he refused to award damages.[158] Similarly, other arbitrators generally require a party to prove his claim for damages,[159] and they will deny monetary relief where the existence of any injury is too speculative.[160]

---

[155]International Harvester Co., 15 LA 1 at 1 (1950). An employee is entitled to be made whole regardless of the employer's financial problems (see Arbitrator MacLeod in 53 LA 207, 215–216, and McCormick in 45 LA 453, 455), but being made whole is all that is required (see Arbitrator Gray in 43 LA 126, 128, and Drake in 32 LA 453, 458–459). Nonetheless, where a large sum possibly was involved, Arbitrator Paul D. Jackson was "loath to grant a monetary award without having knowledge" concerning "the approximate amount of money that may be required to be paid should the employer be ordered to make full payment" for the violation. He directed the parties to submit information needed in determining the amount involved, along with "any facts or arguments" the party "may have why the full amount * * * should or should not be paid by the employer." Swanson-Dean Corp., 68 LA 682, 687 (undated), Arbitrator Jackson having stated that "Nothing appears to warrant dilution of the liability of the employer for the breach unless it be extreme and unexpected onerousness of the remedy." In Hillman's, 32 LA 453, 458–459 (Drake, 1959), a new employee was hired at a higher rate than the contractual rate being paid other employees in the same classification; the arbitrator refused to increase the rate of said other employees for the future, but he did award back pay in the amount of the difference between their pay and that of the new employee for the disputed period. In Valley-Todeco, 75 LA 661, 664 (Anderson, 1980), the grievance of an employee protesting unequal pay and asking for a similar higher rate was resolved by ordering the employer to recoup the excess that had erroneously been paid to another employee. As to the remedies in the latter two cases, cf., New Testament, Matthew 20:1–16 (parable).

[156]See Arbitrator Killion in 49 LA 1073, 1076–1077; Ross in 41 LA 1204, 1208–1209, and in 32 LA 300, 304; Schedler in 38 LA 207, 209; Boles in 35 LA 845, 850; Gilden in 21 LA 105, 108; Marshall in 17 LA 709, 710; Whiting in 11 LA 495, 498; Copelof in 4 LA 786, 787. Also see Wollett in 35 LA 783, 787–788; Kates in 32 LA 492, 501. Cf., Wolf in 50 LA 357, 361; Loucks in 36 LA 1067, 1070; Shipman in 36 LA 855, 856. In Columbus Auto Parts Co., 43 LA 546, 553–554 (Klein, 1964), the company asserted that the named grievants did not have sufficient seniority to make them proper claimants for damages, but this assertion came too late since it was first made in the posthearing brief. For related discussion as concerns the federal sector, see Chapter 2, subtopics entitled "Comptroller General's Role" and "The Back Pay Act."

[157]See Arbitrator Christopher in 80 LA 1030, 1032; Martin in 72 LA 684, 691; Harkless in 71 LA 1018, 1021; Grenig in 70 LA 645, 648; Bolte in 68 LA 343, 346. But see Foster in 72 LA 271, 276; Crawford in 52 LA 243, 247.

[158]Permutit Co., 19 LA 599, 600 (1952).

[159]See Arbitrator McKay in 77 LA 23, 28 (stating that since "there is not sufficient evidence to determine who suffered a loss or the extent of the loss suffered," the "arbitrator cannot grant specific relief for lost wages"); Feldman in 76 LA 409, 411–412; Mittleman in 75 LA 1194, 1201; Bickner in 74 LA 931, 934; Ross in 74 LA 633, 640; Albrechta in 69 LA 80, 85; Conway in 68 LA 1102, 1108; Callaghan in 47 LA 698, 703 (stating that it "is not the duty of the arbitrator to research the damages allegedly incurred * * * except insofar as the arbitrator may review the substantiation offered for specific damages demanded by one of the parties"). But where the wrongdoer is in a better position to provide evidence as to damages, the arbitrator might place the burden upon him. See Akers Motor Lines, 51 LA 955, 964 (Dunau, 1968). Also see Arbitrator Feller in 52 LA 229, 232.

[160]See Arbitrator Martin in 77 LA 123, 127 (grievant was reinstated but without back pay since his history of absences due to illness made it uncertain that he would have worked even if he had not been discharged); Ellmann in 76 LA 590, 572; Ross in 74 LA 633, 640; Conway in 68 LA 1102, 1108; Gould in 64 LA 620, 624 (sex discrimination was established but only 50 percent back pay was awarded since it was not certain that grievant's capacity to perform her duties could be developed under proper training); Seidenberg in 53 LA 1288, 1294; Ladar in 43 LA 1126, 1131; Redden in 41 LA 1269, 1282–1283; Morvant in 37 LA 297, 302; Cahn in 36 LA 785, 787; Miller in

However, damages will not be denied merely because the amount is difficult to determine.[161] When difficulty is encountered, the simplest fair method available for determining the amount will be used.[162] One possible solution in this type of situation is for the arbitrator to make a finding as to liability and provide that, in the light of the difficulty of determining the exact amount of damages, the liability may be discharged by a lump-sum settlement if the parties can reach one. This was done, for instance, where a time-consuming and expensive process of review of records covering a five-year period would have been necessary to determine the exact amount due.[163]

Where no other solution is available, the arbitrator "is bound to resort to his own good sense and judgment, and after considering all the pertinent facts and circumstances make a reasonable approximation."[164]

In some instances monetary damages have been denied where such damages were not expressly requested in the grievance,[165] but in other instances no such express request was required.[166] Where an express request for back pay is timely made, the awarding of such

---

35 LA 757, 782; Dworkin in 35 LA 703, 711. In Master Builders' Assn., 48 LA 865, 868 (Kates, 1967), an award was made for past damages but not for "contingent damages." As to the latter, the arbitrator stated that his award would be "without prejudice to any subsequent claim for such damages" if future developments should show additional damages to be warranted. In Kroger Co., 34 LA 686, 688 (Warns, 1960), the grievant suffered no monetary loss from the employer's improper assignment and the arbitrator stated that unlike a jury, he had no authority to assess damages for inconvenience occasioned by encroachment upon the grievant's free weekend. Similarly, see Arbitrator Dean in 72 LA 1120, 1223. Although an injury in the form of loss of insurance benefits was established in Plough, Inc., 80 LA 1005, 1009–1010 (Flannagan, 1983), reimbursement was denied on the basis that the grievant's improper discharge was "a remote and not a proximate cause" of the loss.

[161]Five Star Hardware & Elec. Corp., 44 LA 944, 946 (S. Wolff, 1965); Plumbing, Heating & Piping Employees Council, 39 LA 513, 522 (Ross, 1962), the Arbitrator stating: "The wrongdoer must bear the risk of uncertainty. At the same time the plaintiff is obliged to make a reasonable estimate of damages, supported by the evidence in the case." Also see Niagara Bd. of Educ. v. Teachers Assn., 101 LRRM 2258, 2259 (N.Y. Ct. App., 1979). Cf., Arbitrator Sinclitico in 70 LA 608, 613–614.

[162]Eagle-Pitcher Mining & Smelting Co., 6 LA 544, 549 (Elson, 1947).

[163]Corn Prods. Ref. Co., 7 LA 125, 132–133 (Updegraff, 1947). Similarly, see Arbitrator Feinberg in 16 LA 926, 931–932. In Armco Steel Co., 52 LA 108, 112 (Sembower, 1969), the burden of examining past records was minimized by limiting the period of retroactivity for damages. Where a basis existed for determining the total damages for a violation, the difficulty of determining the entitled individuals was circumvented by directing payment of the damages into a fund "to be used for a mutually agreed upon benefit for all employees of the bargaining unit," and this solution withstood court challenge. Newark Wire Cloth Co. v. Steelworkers, 80 LRRM 2094, 2095 (USDC, 1972). Cf., Boston Teachers Union v. School Comm., 93 LRRM 2205, 2210–2211 (Mass. S.Ct., 1976).

[164]American Mach. & Foundry Co., 15 LA 822, 827–828 (S. Wolff, 1950). A liquidated-damages approach was similarly used by Arbitrator Dworkin in 50 LA 621, 624; McCoy in 36 LA 1042, 1044. Some collective agreements specifically provide for liquidated damages for violation thereof. Discussing such provisions, see Mi-Ka Prods., 76 LA 1203, 1210–1211 (Christopher, 1981). Also see Arbitrator Slavney in 25 LA 424, 426.

[165]See Arbitrator Rothschild in 73 LA 965, 968; Daly in 49 LA 64, 66; Seidenberg in 43 LA 33, 35; Haughton in 35 LA 330, 337. Where a contract violation was found but no damages were requested or awarded, a separate claim for damages was subsequently processed to a second arbitrator but was rejected. John Deere Co., 70 LA 997, 998 (1978), Arbitrator Henry M. Grether stating that the "policy to avoid a multiplicity of law suits and have no more than one trial unless there is some very good reason to have more than one trial is based on the reasoning that it is wasteful to society and harassing to the adversary to have more than one trial."

[166]West Virginia Pulp & Paper Co., 39 LA 163, 166–167 (Stark, 1962); Bethlehem Steel Co., 17 LA 295, 300 (Selekman, 1951), where past practice controlled the result.

damages might be implied in an award which merely states that the grievance is sustained.[167]

Damages Payable to Company or Union

The vast majority of arbitral awards for damages are concerned with indemnifying employees. In some cases, however, it is asserted that the company has suffered damages as a result of union violations of the agreement, or that the union has suffered damages as a result of company violations.

Company claims for damages against the union for illicit work stoppages have not been uncommon. Here, many arbitrators have awarded damages for breach of no-strike clauses where the authority to do so was not expressly denied by the agreement (in some of these decisions the arbitrator itemized the elements of damages).[168] A few arbitrators have ruled, however, that express contractual authority is required to empower the arbitrator to award damages for no-strike violations.[169]

Claims for damages in favor of the union as such might involve, among other possibilities, injury to the union through company violation of union representational rights or union security clauses,[170] or damages resulting from contractual violations by the company in connection with plant removals, discontinuance of a department, and the like.[171]

---

[167]California Metal Trades Assn., 41 LA 1204, 1207 (Ross, 1963). Also see Arbitrator Platt in 11 LA 1175, 1179–1180.

[168]See Arbitrator Williams in 77 LA 488, 490; Eigenbrod in 75 LA 189, 196–197; Eaton in 54 LA 1125, 1129–1130; Kates in 53 LA 869, 872–876; Wyckoff in 53 LA 542, 544–545 (stating that an arbitrator "has the inherent power to award damages for breach of a collective bargaining agreement unless the agreement expressly prohibits such an award"); Jarvis in 52 LA 197, 198, 200; Scheib in 52 LA 74, 78; Vadakin in 51 LA 500, 503–504; McDermott in 50 LA 1018, 1020–1022; Johnson in 50 LA 35, 36; Klein in 49 LA 1043, 1044, 1051–1052; Berkowitz in 42 LA 95, 95–96; Seitz in 37 LA 509, 518–520; Kleinsorge in 33 LA 574, 585; Cahn in 20 LA 476, 476–477; Laskin in 18 LA 925, 926–929; Rains in 7 LA 648, 654–657. Upholding arbitral authority to award damages for a no-strike breach where the submission did not contain any clause denying such authority, see Moran Towing & Transp. Co. v. Longshoremen Local 333, 85 L.C. ¶10,969 (CA 2, 1978). Cases involving claims against unions for failure to make reasonable effort to prevent or terminate unauthorized work stoppages are cited in Chapter 5, subtopic entitled "Use of Grievance Procedure v. Self-Help," where the U.S. Supreme Court's Carbon Fuel decision on the subject is also noted. For cases in which employers were awarded damages for union newsletter statements asking employees not to cooperate in surveys properly being conducted by the employer, see Arbitrator Caraway in 73 LA 1074, 1082–1083; LeBaron in 73 LA 455, 463. Cf., Bailer in 73 LA 1016, 1020.

[169]See Arbitrator Dash in 38 LA 509, 513–515; Crawford in 30 LA 1061, 1065; Hildebrand in 28 LA 769, 774; Copelof in 17 LA 610, 623.

[170]See Arbitrator Mittenthal in 76 LA 125, 132; Singer in 49 LA 991, 995–996; Summers in 48 LA 760, 763; Dash in 37 LA 360, 364.

[171]See Arbitrator Foster in 72 LA 271, 276; Lee in 51 LA 884, 891–892; Duff in 46 LA 4, 9; Dash in 36 LA 1364, 1384–1386; Gray in 34 LA 771, 774–776. Also see Bakery Workers v. Cotton Baking Co., 89 LRRM 2665, 2667 (CA 5, 1976), upholding an arbitrator's award of damages to the union where the union had been monetarily damaged and the job security of all members had been indirectly affected by the employer's improper assignment of work outside the bargaining unit.

The "De Minimis" Rule

In denying grievances, arbitrators sometimes apply the rule of *de minimis non curat lex,* under which trifling or immaterial matters will not be taken into account.[172] Often in applying this principle the arbitrator concludes that the action complained of is such a slight departure from what is generally required by the agreement that the action must be viewed either as a permissible exception or as not constituting an injury at all.[173] The *de minimis* concept has sometimes been applied, for example, in denying grievances protesting the performance by management personnel of small amounts of bargaining unit work where a unit employee was not readily available.

Application of the *de minimis* rule has been rejected where "the amount has been small but the principle large."[174] And in any event, Arbitrator Harold W. Davey explained that no hard and fast mathematical line should be drawn between minimal on the one hand and substantial on the other, but that each case should be decided in terms of its own circumstances.[175]

Punitive Damages

Even though a party is found to have violated the agreement, the arbitrator may be expected to refuse to award any penalty which would in essence be an award of punitive damages, unless, under the circumstances of the case, punitive damages are clearly justified.[176] While noting that some state and federal courts have disagreed as to the power of arbitrators to award punitive damages, Arbitrator Burton B. Turkus added: "Power to award punitive damages is a heady wine, however, which carries with it an equally potent obligation and

---

[172]As did Arbitrator Allen in 73 LA 103, 106–107; Hebert in 47 LA 761, 766–767; Morgan in 47 LA 756, 760; Stouffer in 46 LA 557, 559; Cahn in 45 LA 609, 611–612; Heliker in 43 LA 1159, 1162; Bauder in 64–3 ARB ¶9221; Klein in 41 LA 1045, 1049; Swanson in 27 LA 553, 556; Donnelly in 21 LA 681, 682; Shipman in 17 LA 76, 79; Aaron in 15 LA 168, 172; Cheney in 12 LA 422, 426–427.

[173]For a narrow view as to what constitutes a true *de minimis* situation, see Olin Mathieson Chem. Corp., 47 LA 238, 242 (Hilpert, 1966).

[174]Bethlehem-Sparrows Point Shipyard, 26 LA 483, 490 (Feinberg, 1956). The rule is also said to be inapplicable where a "continuing" activity is involved, Union Carbide Corp., 46 LA 195, 198 (Cahn, 1966), and where the arbitration involves "a test case brought seriously to obtain a ruling on a disputed point of contractual interpretation," Tenneco Oil Co., 44 LA 1121, 1128 (Merrill, 1965).

[175]John Deere Planter Works, 29 LA 328, 331 (1957). Also see Westinghouse Elec. Corp., 43 LA 84, 89–90 (Altieri, 1964), for discussion of the *de minimis* concept and problems of its application.

[176]For many cases illustrating the great reluctance of arbitrators to award damages which the arbitrator considers to be of a punitive nature, see p. 356 of the Third Edition of this book. For some later cases, see Arbitrator Ross in 76 LA 101, 103; Mittelman in 75 LA 1194, 1201; House in 75 LA 628, 632; Lipson in 74 LA 489, 494; Curry in 73 LA 1148, 1156; O'Connell in 71 LA 754, 761; Rimer in 71 LA 82, 86; Roberts in 69 LA 623, 630; Beck in 68 LA 1146, 1152; Conant in 68 LA 663, 668. In A.C. & C. Co., 24 LA 538, 541 (Scheiber, 1955), the arbitrator denied the union's demand that a penalty payment be made by the employer to a charity where no employee had suffered loss from the employer's violation. Similarly refusing to award a penalty payment where no employee had suffered loss due to the employer's violation of the agreement, see Arbitrator Carter in 69 LA 999, 1003; Turkus in 53 LA 1056, 1060.

abiding responsibility to invoke the remedy with great care and extreme caution in the situations where otherwise the ends of justice would be defeated or unconscionably denied."[177] Some arbitrators have felt justified in awarding punitive damages where the contractual violation was knowing and repeated,[178] or where it was willful and flagrant.[179]

The good faith of the offending party has sometimes been emphasized by the arbitrator in refusing to award damages where no person was shown to have suffered loss from the violation of the agreement (the arbitrator sometimes terming it a "technical violation" only).[180]

Interest on Award

The question of interest on the principal sum awarded has sometimes arisen. Arbitrator Sanford H. Kadish refused to order payment of interest on his award of holiday pay since neither the collective agreement nor the submission expressly authorized him to order the payment of interest and "it is not customary in arbitrations for the arbitrator to grant interest on claims which he finds owing."[181] A number of other arbitrators have likewise expressly refused to award interest.[182] Although interest has been awarded in a fair number of

---

[177]Seaboard World Airlines, 53 LA 1056, 1060 (1969). As to court decisions, diverse results have been reached concerning the assessment of punitive damages by arbitrators. For example, see Desert Palace v. Local Joint Executive Bd., 105 LRRM 3053, 3060 (USDC, 1980), holding the arbitrator exceeded his authority in awarding punitive damages where that remedy had not been requested; Baltimore Regional Joint Bd. v. Webster Clothes, 100 LRRM 3225, 3227 (CA 4, 1979), holding an award invalid as punitive rather than compensatory; Local 416 v. Helgesteel Corp., 80 LRRM 2113, 2115–2116 (USDC, 1971), the court stating that an award of punitive damages is not per se improper, and that the question is whether the award draws its essence from the agreement and is reasonable in light of the arbitrator's findings; Wanzer & Sons v. Milk Drivers Union, 61 LRRM 2376, 2381 (USDC, 1966), holding that the arbitrator's remedial power under LMRA § 301 includes punitive awards, but that such power is extraordinary and should be reserved for situations which cannot be pacified by other remedies. Also see Hackett, "Punitive Damages in Arbitration: The Search for a Workable Rule," 63 Cornell L. Rev. 272 (1978).

[178]Mallinckrodt Chem. Works, 50 LA 933, 935–940 (Goldberg, 1968). Also indicating that punitive damages would be justified for repeated violations, see Arbitrator Yarowsky in 48 LA 582, 585; Klein in 46 LA 450, 455; Gill in 37 LA 134, 136.

[179]Five Star Hardware & Elec. Corp., 44 LA 944, 946 (Wolff, 1965). Also see Arbitrator Yaffe in 77 LA 344, 348; Conway in 69 LA 264, 278, 281.

[180]See Arbitrator Moran in 70 LA 1041, 1043; Lubow in 69 LA 847, 852–853; Prewett in 50 LA 344, 347; Larkin in 48 LA 1031, 1034–1035; McDermott in 44 LA 840, 845; Marshall in 36 LA 962, 964–965; Reid in 36 LA 458, 462; Gray in 26 LA 723, 726; Duff in 24 LA 623, 625. Also see Albrechta in 69 LA 80, 85; Seitz in 48 LA 609, 614; Horvitz in 22 LA 390, 392; Shister in 17 LA 254, 256. In some cases it appears that the good faith of the offending party was the reason for not awarding damages notwithstanding any loss suffered. See Arbitrator Grabb in 74 LA 1046, 1048; Raffaele in 71 LA 587, 589; Bailey in 69 LA 294, 302. Also see Capital City Tel. Co. v. CWA, 97 LRRM 2394, 2398 (USDC, 1977), affirmed, 98 LRRM 2438 (CA 8, 1978).

[181]Intermountain Operators League, 26 LA 149, 154 (1956).

[182]See Arbitrator Carter in 79 LA 1285, 1293–1294 (refusing to award interest where the violation was not "willful, capricious and arbitrary"); Dean in 74 LA 422, 432; Sartain in 74 LA 121, 125; Eagle in 72 LA 890, 892; Michelstetter in 72 LA 757, 759; Spencer in 69 LA 674, 677; Finston in 68 LA 1022, 1032; Christopher in 68 LA 192, 197; Willingham in 48 LA 782, 788; Dolson in 45 LA 705, 706; Keefe in 44 LA 530, 540; Crawford in 43 LA 247, 249; Koven in 41 LA 1310, 1313–1314; Di Leone in 41 LA 856, 862; Davis in 39 LA 177, 179. In Westinghouse Elec. Corp., 47 LA 621, 629 (Altrock, 1966), a request for interest on back pay awarded in the reversal of discipline was rejected, the arbitrator adhering to the view that interest should be allowed only where the discipline was "willful, capricious, arbitrary and unconscionable." Also following the latter view, see Arbitrators Dean, Sartain, Michelstetter, and Spencer, cited above in this footnote. Regarding the federal public sector, interest cannot be awarded absent statutory

cases,[183] most cases still make no mention of interest and this indicates the continued validity of Arbitrator Kadish's statement that "it is not customary in arbitrations for the arbitrator to grant interest on claims which he finds owing."

Attorney Fees

Regardless of whether the subject of attorney fees falls technically within the general subject of damages, the Authors deem it preferable to consider the question of awarding attorney fees at this point.[184]

It was pointed out in the preceding subtopic that most awards make no mention of interest. Even less frequently does an arbitration decision mention the matter of attorney fees. Thus, here too, it appears clear that it is not customary practice to award attorney fees against the offending party in arbitration. Among the few decisions mentioning the matter (many but not all being cited here), a request for attorney fees was rejected in some,[185] but was granted in others.[186]

---

authorization. See Portsmouth Naval Shipyard, 7 FLRA No. 9 (1981); Arbitrator Aronin in 80 LA 46, 53.

[183]See Arbitrator Goodman in 81 LA 191, 193; Kossoff in 80 LA 1058, 1059–1060 (stating that never before had he awarded interest but special facts called for it here); Keltner in 80 LA 1, 7; Ellmann in 77 LA 370, 372; Christopher in 76 LA 1203, 1212 (stating that the original claim was for a determined sum and that interest thus was appropriate from the date such liquidated damages first became due); Berman in 75 LA 131, 135; Richman in 74 LA 923, 926–927 (stating that the circumstances were appropriate for awarding interest since certain additional hardship had been suffered by grievant due to the employer's action); Katz in 71 LA 1238, 1243; Beck in 68 LA 1146, 1153 (stating special circumstances justifying an award of interest); Eckhardt in 68 LA 928, 931; Edelman in 64 LA 816, 821–822 (stating that sufficient arbitral precedent exists for an award of interest, "but even more important, there is justification for so doing especially here"); Gould in 64 LA 563, 571; Lennard in 62 LA 276, 279; Hilpert in 47 LA 686, 690, and in 39 LA 897, 906–907; Whiting in 41 LA 567, 567–568. Going only part way, some arbitrators have awarded interest to commence running from the date of the award. See Arbitrator Killion in 52 LA 1082, 1087; Miller in 35 LA 757, 782. Awarding interest because of the employer's dilatory tactics in reinstating an employee pursuant to an earlier award, see Arbitrator Williams in 73 LA 1292, 1300, 1302; Jones in 66 LA 354, 356.

[184]For related discussion, see Chapter 1, topic entitled "Arbitration Costs."

[185]Gentile in 81 LA 132, 140–141; Mitrani in 79 LA 732, 737; Platt in 72 LA 458, 470; Bothwell in 71 LA 396, 409–411; Sergent in 69 LA 1210, 1214–1215; Conant in 68 LA 663, 668–669; Sacks in 68 LA 261, 269–270 (refusing to award attorney fees to the union, absent any provision for it in the agreement, even if the company's violation of the agreement was willful and deliberate); Dworkin in 62 LA 1278, 1281; Gorsuch in 60 LA 1310, 1319. Refusing to order reimbursement for attorney fees expended by a party in court proceedings connected with the grievance, see O'Connell in 71 LA 754, 761; Caraway in 69 LA 541, 547; R.R. Williams in 62 LA 133, 139. But awarding such reimbursement, see R.G. Williams in 77 LA 488, 490–491; Bothwell in 49 LA 760, 767.

[186]See Arbitrator Conway in 69 LA 264, 282; Helfeld in 65 LA 453, 468–469, 471; Gould in 64 LA 620, 625; Lennard in 62 LA 276, 279. The Civil Service Reform Act of 1978 made certain provision for awarding attorney fees to federal employees in connection with the processing of their unjustified personnel action grievance through a negotiated grievance procedure. See 5 U.S.C.A. §§ 5506, 7701(g). For discussion, see Bufe & Ferris, "A Second View of Awarding Attorney's Fees in Federal Sector Arbitration," 38 Arb. J. No. 1, p. 21 (1983); Moore, "Awarding Attorney's Fees in Federal Sector Arbitration," 37 Arb. J. No. 4, p. 38 (1982); Kagel, "Grievance Arbitration in the Federal Service: Still Hardly Final and Binding?" Proceedings of the 34th Annual Meeting of NAA, 178, 193, (BNA Books, 1982). Denying a request for attorney fees in United States Customs Serv., 77 LA 1001, 1003 (1981), Arbitrator Leroy S. Merrifield did not find an award of attorney fees to be "warranted in the interest of justice on the facts" of the case. Attorney fees were awarded by Arbitrator Joseph R. Rocha, Jr., in United States Customs Serv., 77 LA 1113, 1121 (1981); and in further proceedings in 79 LA 284, 289–290, he decided both (1) what was a "reasonable" fee and (2) that the union was entitled to it although it had used its in-house counsel to represent the grievant.

Mitigating Damages—Deduction of Outside Compensation

In awarding back pay to employees in certain types of cases, particularly those involving discharge or discipline, arbitrators commonly specify that the employer's liability shall be reduced by the amount of the grievant's earnings from other employment during the period in question. Indeed, there is general agreement by courts, arbitrators, and the NLRB that outside earnings properly are deducted from back pay.[187] Many arbitrators also have specified the deduction of unemployment compensation received by the grievant for the relevant period;[188] but in some cases the arbitrator has expressly concluded that he could not or should not do so.[189]

In the view of many arbitrators an affirmative duty may rest upon employees, when wronged by the employer, to take reasonable steps to mitigate the damages. Even where the agreement provided that an unjustly discharged employee "shall be * * * paid for all time lost," Arbitrator Lewis E. Solomon explained that a duty to attempt to mitigate damages existed:

> "It is commonly and generally recognized that the purpose of a contract provision calling for payment of 'all time lost,' when disciplinary action or discharge has been found to be without justifiable cause is to compensate and indemnify the injured employee and make him whole for loss of earnings suffered by him as a result of the inappropriate exercise of judgment by the Company. The loss of earnings is usually to be measured by the wages he would have earned for the period they were improperly denied to him, subject, however, to a recognized duty and responsibility reposed in the employee to mitigate, so far as reasonable, the amount of that loss. If, as a result of employee's action or inaction, he

---

[187]For an indication of National Railroad Adjustment Board practice as to outside earnings, see National Railway Labor Conference, 53 LA 555, 563 (Seward, Howlett & Livernash, 1969).

[188]Many cases are cited at p. 358 of the Third Edition of this book. For some of the many later cases, see Arbitrator Lewis in 77 LA 432, 438; Woolf in 76 LA 467, 473; Hunter in 76 LA 399, 403 (he adjusted the unemployment compensation amount upward "by 25% to reflect their non-taxable status," and thus their "true offset value"); Sabo in 76 LA 144, 152; Siegel in 76 LA 54, 56; Perry in 71 LA 1109, 1113; Harter in 69 LA 414, 419; Bowles in 69 LA 351, 355; Lipson in 69 LA 93, 102; Rothschild in 68 LA 217, 221 (ordering deduction of "all welfare or other unemployment or union benefits received"); Marcus in 68 LA 204, 211 (additionally ordering deduction of benefits from other governmental programs). In General Felt Indus., 74 LA 972, 977 (1979), Arbitrator Charles N. Carnes ordered deduction of unemployment compensation but also ordered that "in the event that Grievants are required to repay any amount of unemployment compensation because of their reinstatement, the Company shall reimburse them for such amounts as they may be required to repay." Also providing for the contingency that the state might recapture the benefits, see Arbitrator Roberts in 74 LA 835, 840; Holman in 73 LA 829, 832; Brown in 69 LA 555, 563. In allowing a deduction in favor of the employer, some arbitrators ordered the employer to reimburse the unemployment compensation commission. See Arbitrator Rice in 44 LA 16, 20; Purdom in 43 LA 1106, 1111; Gunderman in 43 LA 907, 911. Permitting deduction of workers' compensation benefits received by grievant as a result of injury while working for another employer after his discharge, see Champion Intl. Corp., 76 LA 942, 945–946 (Nicholas, 1981).

[189]See Arbitrator Aaron in 76 LA 96, 100; Dunn in 74 LA 857, 858; Herring in 73 LA 1057, 1059 (stating that unemployment compensation "shall not be deducted by the Employer, since the Grievant is legally obligated to repay some or all such sums directly to the State as a consequence of this award"); Davis in 70 LA 572, 574; Blackmar in 69 LA 1179, 1182; Williams in 53 LA 867, 868; Warns in 62–3 ARB ¶8840; Wagner in 38 LA 1091, 1092; Miller in 35 LA 757, 782; Seward in 16 LA 376, 377; Courshon in 9 LA 484, 487–488.

has failed to mitigate the loss, then to the degree of such failure he is himself partially responsible."[190]

Back pay may be wholly or partially denied where the employee fails to take advantage of reasonable employment opportunities.[191] But this view has not always been accepted, as where an arbitrator stated that "while it may be proper to deduct from a back pay award sums actually earned by an employee before reinstatement, or sums received indirectly from his employer, as through unemployment compensation, no authority exists in an Arbitrator to penalize an employee financially for failing to have earnings."[192]

Even the arbitrators who recognize a duty to mitigate damages may apply some limitations, such as requiring the employer to introduce affirmative evidence to show the inexcusable failure of the employee to minimize damages,[193] and not requiring the employee to use more than "ordinary diligence" to obtain other work.[194] Furthermore, the employee may not be required to accept unsuitable or lower rated work during the pendency of his appeal,[195] and he may be given credit for the added expense involved in actually getting and working at interim employment.[196]

In one case the grievant's duty to mitigate damages was satisfied by expanding his prior farm operations; in this case the arbitrator also concluded that only the extra income from farm work during the grievant's regular working hours with his employer should be deducted.[197]

---

[190]Love Bros., 45 LA 751, 752, 756 (1965). Also see Arbitrator Serot in 71 LA 897, 900. In Continental Can Co., 39 LA 821, 822–823 (Sembower, 1962), outside earnings and unemployment compensation were deducted where the agreement stated the grievant was to be paid the "amount he would have earned." But see United States Steel Co., 40 LA 1036, 1039–1041 (McDermott, 1963).

[191]Many cases are cited at p. 359 of the Third Edition of this book. For later cases see Arbitrator Beitner in 79 LA 993, 999; Andersen in 75 LA 737, 742 (grievant "made only a minimal effort to obtain other employment"); LeBaron in 73 LA 1171, 1174 (stating that "Grievant's testimony does not reflect reasonable diligence in seeking interim employment"); Allen in 72 LA 184, 189–190; Springfield in 70 LA 788, 793; Rinaldo in 70 LA 428, 430; Draznin in 69 LA 191, 193; White in 68 LA 498, 503. In Permanente Medical Group, 52 LA 217, 221 (1968), Arbitrator Howard S. Block made an "educated guess" as to time reasonably necessary for grievant to find other work.

[192]Shakespeare & Shakespeare Prods. Co., 9 LA 813, 817–818 (Platt, 1948). In Bell Helicopter Textron, 71 LA 799, 801 (1978), Arbitrator Jack Johannes denied back pay for the period during which the grievant was incarcerated and thus unavailable for work; a requirement of pay for the period of incarceration "would be to go beyond making him whole and take on the attributes of a punitive remedy against the Company." Also denying back pay for a period of incarceration, see Arbitrator Fitch in 76 LA 44, 46. Regarding strike periods, see Arbitrator Williams in 73 LA 1292, 1295–1296.

[193]See Arbitrator Modjeska in 77 LA 530, 535; Serot in 71 LA 897, 900; Merrill in 52 LA 121, 127–128; Gilden in 11 LA 600, 605.

[194]Standard Transformer Co., 51 LA 1110, 1113 (Gibson, 1968). Reporting periodically to the unemployment office, answering newspaper job advertisements, and applying directly for jobs, were considered to constitute "reasonable" or "diligent" efforts to mitigate damages in Orlando Transit Co., 71 LA 897, 900–903 (Serot, 1978), where Arbitrator Serot also discussed the significance of grievant's enrolling in school, moving, and spending time working on his house.

[195]See Arbitrator Modjeska in 77 LA 530, 535; Jones in 45 LA 635, 640; Parker in 23 LA 640, 642; Aaron in 10 LA 162, 164. Cf., White in 68 LA 498, 499, 503.

[196]Ingalls Shipbuilding Corp., 37 LA 953, 956 (Murphy, 1961).

[197]American-International Aluminum Corp., 49 LA 728, 730 (Howlett, 1967). Also see Arbitrator Bard in 80 LA 1161, 1173 (income from work outside grievant's regular working hours with his employer not deducted); Williams in 73 LA 1292, 1298–1299 (grievant mitigated damages by expanding his part-time work with another employer); Howlett in 48 LA 283, 288.

When an arbitrator concludes that the grievant's outside compensation is to be deducted in the computation of back pay, the grievant has a duty to reveal the facts in regard thereto. Some arbitrators have ordered him to submit a notarized statement as to his outside earnings;[198] and in one case arbitral relief was conditioned upon the grievant's authorization of the release of information showing the public assistance payments he had received.[199]

Other Avoidable Damages; Delayed Arbitration

In some cases back pay has been denied or reduced where the grievant could have avoided being wronged by the employer by speaking up to explain his situation and actions, but he failed to do so.[200] The concept of avoidable damages was applied also against the employer in one case, where he was ordered to pay all arbitration costs since the need for arbitration might have been obviated had he explained his position to the union.[201]

An employer's liability for back pay may be reduced by reason of delay in the arbitration process caused or contributed to by the employee or union.[202] However, no reduction was ordered by the arbitrator where there was no evidence to show that delay was caused by either employee or union;[203] and another arbitrator apparently would in no case reduce back pay because of delay caused by the company or the union.[204]

---

[198]See Arbitrator Jones in 68 LA 1343, 1346, and in 37 LA 700, 704; Volz in 68 LA 1314, 1318 (additionally requiring grievant to submit copies of his federal income tax returns "and permit the arbitrator in private to compare them with the information included in the notarized statement or affidavit"); Chalfie in 68 LA 129, 142; Buckwalter in 50 LA 177, 181. Also see Sabo in 76 LA 144, 152.

[199]United States Steel Corp., 52 LA 1210, 1212 (Dybeck, 1969), where the agreement called for deduction of "such earnings or other amounts as he would not have received except for such suspension or discharge." In Orlando Transit Co., 71 LA 897, 903 (Serot, 1978), the agreement required deduction of "any unemployment or other compensation from any source"; benefits under the G.I. bill were not deemed "compensation" to be deducted under this provision.

[200]See Arbitrator Daniel in 76 LA 379, 386; Elson in 72 LA 780, 783–784; Naehring in 69 LA 132, 135; Shanker in 68 LA 13, 17–18; Krislov in 61 LA 14, 16; Stouffer in 51 LA 234, 240–241; McCoy in 50 LA 8, 9; Merrill in 24 LA 522, 526; Wardlaw in 8 LA 248, 250. In Checker Motors Corp., 70 LA 805, 808–809 (Allen, 1978), the "failure to raise a vital defense prior to arbitration" led to the denial of back pay for a grievant whose reinstatement was ordered.

[201]Ralph Rogers & Co., 48 LA 40, 43 (Getman, 1966). But see Madison Bus Co., 52 LA 723, 727–728 (Mueller, 1969). In Thorsen Mfg. Co., 55 LA 581, 585 (Koven, 1970), the arbitrator upheld a discharge but he awarded some back pay because the company unreasonably complicated and prolonged the proceedings, leaving the grievant in doubt as to his status for a substantial period. For similar results see Arbitrator Lubow in 77 LA 219, 222.

[202]Yale & Towne Mfg. Co., 39 LA 1156, 1162–1163 (Hill, Horlacher & Seitz, 1962), where the matter is fully discussed. Back pay was also reduced for this reason by Arbitrator Taylor in 72 LA 1248, 1250; Alutto in 71 LA 828, 832; Roberts in 68 LA 1354, 1359 (he ordered the union to pay a portion of the back pay because of its delay in processing the case to arbitration); Mansfield in 68 LA 565, 571; Reid in 54 LA 681, 683; Bothwell in 49 LA 760, 766–767; Solomon in 42 LA 1, 13; Tsukiyama in 38 LA 404, 413. Cf., Stark in 39 LA 163, 166–167.

[203]Acme Fast Freight, 37 LA 163, 166 (Warns, 1961). Also see Arbitrator Stone in 72 LA 981, 987. But in Indian Head, 71 LA 82, 86 (1978), Arbitrator J. Thomas Rimer, Jr., did "not attempt to assess the cause or causes" of the long delay in processing the case through the grievance procedure; in light of the delay, and considering the relatively short service of the grievant, he concluded that an award of back pay "would be clearly punitive."

[204]Gulfport Shipbuilding Corp., 43 LA 1053, 1056 (Ray, 1964).

Judicial Notice and Presumptions

The subjects of judicial notice and presumptions could have been considered in Chapter 8, Evidence. The Authors, however, recognize the view of those who believe that these subjects belong to the general topic of legal or judicial reasoning, and they are accordingly considered here.

Judges take judicial notice of widely known facts of commerce, industry, history, and natural science, and of ordinary meanings of words. Similarly, in arbitration many matters are assumed or accepted without discussion or citation of authority. Thus, it may be said that arbitrators also take judicial notice.[205] Not surprisingly, some arbitrators have spoken in terms of taking "arbitral" notice, as did Arbitrator David C. Altrock in noting the short supply of electricians in the area at the time.[206]

Of special significance is the practice of arbitrators of taking judicial notice of industry practice affecting some disputed matters.[207] Thus, judicial notice has been taken of the "general understanding that tips, unless guaranteed by the employer, cannot and should not be used in making a 'wage adjustment.' "[208] Another arbitrator took judicial notice of the fact that it is not common industrial practice to use the rate received by the highest paid experimental employees as the base rate on new jobs when production begins.[209]

Arbitrators also may use presumptions as aids in deciding issues. Presumptions, which are related to the matter of judicial notice, result in the prima facie assumption of the truth of a matter. Thus, they take the place of evidence on the part of the party in whose favor they operate, and they require the other party to produce evidence or argument to show that that which is presumed is not true.

To illustrate, Arbitrator Mitchell M. Shipman held that in determining the right to benefits under an employee group insurance plan a wife's dependency upon her husband for support is so basic that it will

[205]For instance, see Arbitrator Kaplan in 69 LA 1149, 1151; Katz in 68 LA 249, 253; Roberts in 48 LA 978, 980; Kelliher in 46 LA 707, 708; Kerrison in 46 LA 613, 615; Stouffer in 43 LA 901, 905; Dworkin in 43 LA 507, 509; Wildebush in 41 LA 895, 897; Cayton in 39 LA 159, 160; Rock in 36 LA 65, 70; Lockhart in 20 LA 658, 662–663; Ryder in 20 LA 337, 340; Komaroff in 19 LA 10, 13; Wagner in 6 LA 575, 578, and in 6 LA 292, 294. It should also be recognized in passing that arbitrators sometimes rely upon their own prior knowledge and experience. See Arbitrator Sobel in 70 LA 1073, 1076; Kaplan in 69 LA 1149, 1151; Sembower in 68 LA 593, 595–596. In the latter case Arbitrator John F. Sembower stated: "The Arbitrator is fully aware that no arbitrator should stray beyond the record, but the principle also is universally accepted than no arbitrator or other finder of facts has to ignore all of his prior learning and experience, for indeed it is that which the parties take into account when they compliment him with their mutual selection as arbitrator." In Eder Bros., Inc. v. Teamsters Local 1040, 92 LC ¶55,296 (Conn. S.Ct., 1980), it was held that arbitrators, as experts in the field under dispute, could rely on their own knowledge.
[206]Textron, 48 LA 1373, 1376 (1967). In W-L Molding Co., 72 LA 1065, 1068 (1979), Arbitrator Robert G. Howlett took "arbitral notice that people do pound on vending machines when the product they seek to purchase is not returned * * * or their change is not returned."
[207]See Arbitrator Kerrison in 46 LA 613, 615; Komaroff in 19 LA 10, 13; Maggs in 17 LA 451, 454; Donnelly in 16 LA 914, 915; Platt in 16 LA 317, 319; Cahn in 7 LA 355, 357; Shipman in 7 LA 121, 122. Also see In re Hopkins, 13 LA 716, 717 (N.Y. Sup. Ct., 1949).
[208]Christ Cella's Restaurant, 7 LA 355, 357 (Cahn, 1947).
[209]Pittsburgh Steel Co., 6 LA 575, 578 (Wagner, 1947).

be presumed in the absence of proof to the contrary.[210] Presumptions are used frequently in the interpretation of contract provisions. For instance, parties are presumed to have intended a valid contract,[211] to have intended all words used in an agreement to have effect,[212] and to have intended language to have its commonly accepted meaning.[213]

Presumptions may also be used in "interests" matters. Thus, Arbitrator David L. Cole, in determining the amount of wage increase necessary to offset a rise in living costs, ruled that it was "presumptively proper" to consider only the change in living costs occurring after the parties' last wage negotiation, there being a presumption that all pertinent factors were considered in previous bargaining.[214]

Parol Evidence

Under the parol-evidence rule a written agreement may not be changed or modified by any oral statements or arguments made by the parties in connection with the negotiation of the agreement. A written contract consummating previous oral and written negotiations is deemed, under the rule, to embrace the entire agreement, and, if the writing is clear and unambiguous, parol evidence will not be allowed to vary the contract.[215] This is said to be a rule of substantive law which when applicable defines the limits of a contract.[216]

The parol-evidence rule is very frequently advanced and generally applied in arbitration cases.[217] Sometimes the collective agreement will provide specifically against verbal agreements that conflict with it.[218]

While some might argue that arbitrators should consider any evidence showing the true intention of the parties and that this intention should be given effect whether expressed by the language used or not, the general denial of power to add to, subtract from, or modify the agreement provides special justification for the observance of the parol-evidence rule by arbitrators.

---

[210]Rock Hill Printing & Finishing Co., 21 LA 335, 340 (1953). For other illustrations, see Arbitrator Kabaker in 50 LA 1080, 1082; Gross in 46 LA 882, 884.
[211]See Arbitrator Gorder in 20 LA 880, 889; Horvitz in 9 LA 702, 703; Tischler in 5 LA 282, 283.
[212]John Deere Tractor Co., 5 LA 631, 632 (Updegraff, 1946).
[213]See Arbitrator Anrod in 48 LA 310, 312–313; Summers in 48 LA 137, 142; McCoy in 2 LA 367, 370–371.
[214]New York City Omnibus Corp., 7 LA 794, 802 (1947).
[215]See Wigmore, Evidence, § 2400 (2d Ed.); Cohn v. Dunn, 149 Atl. 851, 70 A.L.R. 740 (Conn., 1930). For full discussion of this rule, see United Drill & Tool Co., 28 LA 677, 679–683 (Cox, 1957).
[216]2 Williston, Contracts, § 631 (1920 Ed.).
[217]Many cases are cited at p. 362 of the Third Edition of this book. For some later cases, see Arbitrator Koven in 79 LA 946, 947–948; Boner in 77 LA 405, 408; Mukamal in 76 LA 1220, 1228; Lumbley in 75 LA 1224, 1226; Foster in 71 LA 86, 89; Lewis in 69 LA 1036, 1040; Finley in 69 LA 175, 176; Weiss in 69 LA 10, 13; Sisk in 68 LA 1006, 1009; Cooley in 68 LA 983, 985–986; Render in 68 LA 57, 63. The rule might be held waived if not advanced at the hearing. See American Can Co., 1 ALAA ¶67,165 (1943).
[218]As in Pillsbury Mills, 14 LA 1045, 1047–1048 (Kelliher, 1950).

There are exceptions to the parol-evidence rule, however. Thus, a collateral agreement not intended to be reduced to writing or an entirely distinct contemporaneous agreement may be held valid.[219] Moreover, an arbitrator may permit the use of parol evidence to show fraud or mutual mistake at the time of negotiations.[220] Then, too, if the contract is ambiguous, evidence of the precontract negotiations is admissible to aid in the interpretation of the ambiguous language.[221]

It should also be remembered that the parties to a contract may amend or add to it by subsequent agreement, as was elaborated by Arbitrator A.R. Marshall:

> "Although the Labor Agreement is the chief instrument that guides the parties in their relationships there frequently arises an occasion when it is thought necessary or desirable to clarify, add to, or change the Agreement in some manner. This is what a side agreement does. They are very commonly used because the parties find them useful in some instances and necessary in other cases."[222]

Furthermore, on the basis of very strong proof the collective agreement may be held to have been amended by subsequent practice based upon mutual intent for a definite modification.[223]

---

[219]See Arbitrator Gootnick in 70 LA 383, 385–386; Merrill in 46 LA 503, 505; Cox in 28 LA 677, 680–681; Spillane in 23 LA 574, 580; Gregory in 8 LA 428, 429. Also see Roberts in 50 LA 413, 416–417; Krimsly in 42 LA 311, 313. A party alleging a contemporaneous oral agreement has the burden of proving it by clear and convincing evidence. See Arbitrator Howlett in 52 LA 252, 255; Dugan in 46 LA 1018, 1020–1021; Tongue in 32 LA 708, 711. Also see Yagoda in 48 LA 1040, 1044. Arbitrators have held the collective agreement to be the controlling document where it conflicts with group insurance policies. See Chapter 9, topic entitled "Relationship of Insurance Policy to Collective Agreement."

[220]International Harvester Co., 17 LA 592, 594 (Forrester, 1951); Terre Haute Water Works Corp., 5 LA 747, 749 (Updegraff, 1946). Also see this Chapter, topics entitled "Remedies for Mistake" and "Waiver and Estoppel."

[221]See Chapter 9, topic entitled "Precontract Negotiations." In Brigham Apparel Corp., 52 LA 430, 431 (1969), Arbitrator Andersen acted on the basis that the parol-evidence "doctrine does not preclude the admissibility of evidence designed to explain an ambiguity or to establish the meaning of terms or provisions which have a particular trade or occupational meaning."

[222]Fox Mfg. Co., 47 LA 97, 101 (1966). Also see Arbitrator Cantor in 70 LA 1225, 1228. Recognizing certain requirements for the binding effect of such subsequent agreements, see Arbitrator Ipavec in 76 LA 76, 81; Richman in 71 LA 813, 815–816.

[223]See Chapter 12, subtopic entitled "Amendment of Contract."

Chapter 11

Precedent Value of Awards

Diverse views exist concerning the use of prior awards as precedents in the arbitration of labor-management controversies. The Authors propose to develop some of these views and to consider the degrees of precedential force actually exerted by arbitration awards. In order to obtain a more accurate and realistic picture of the use of awards, some consideration will be given to the force of legal decisions under the doctrine of stare decisis. A comparison of arbitration awards and legal decisions, it is believed, will lead to helpful conclusions concerning the precise effect of arbitration awards as precedent. It is believed also that the views expressed by individual arbitrators will be especially enlightening.

The reporting of labor arbitration awards has been said to represent a necessary means of making available one of the most hopeful factors in lessening the economic and social cost of industrial disputes.[1] It also has been said that arbitrators are producing a tremendous mass of hard, practical experience in the field of labor relations and that the welfare of the country demands that their expressions of experience be made available to labor and management.[2]

While serving with the Federal Mediation and Conciliation Service as Director of its Office of Arbitration Services, L. Lawrence Schultz recognized the following "values" of published arbitration awards:

"(1) They constitute a key portion of the current news that makes up the collective bargaining arena. (2) They serve as guidelines for the parties in their continuing relationship and provide information for them to use in resolving their grievances prior to arbitration. (3) They fashion the industrial common law of the shop, which is repeatedly referred to by the highest court of the land. (4) They provide arbitrators with an indication

---

[1]Statement of John W. Taylor, "Reporting of Labor Arbitration: Pro and Con," 1 Arb. J. (N.S.) 420 (1946). Publication of awards is strongly favored by unions, management, and arbitrators alike according to statistics in Warren & Bernstein, "A Profile of Labor Arbitration," 16 LA 970, 983 (1951).

[2]Statement of Theodore Kheel, "Reporting of Labor Arbitration: Pro and Con," id. at 424.

414

of where others are going in similar situations. And (5) they furnish a complete or partial response to a question he frequently hears. 'Who is this arbitrator?'"[3]

Accepting that a highly logical reason for reporting awards is to make them available for some type of precedential or guidance use in other cases, we also may observe that publication of awards is an effective way to help insure accountability of arbitrators. No doubt, an arbitrator will take greater care to make his award clear and his reasoning logical if he knows that the award will be subject to public inspection. The old Holmesian adage that the best test of truth is in the open market would appear to be applicable here. If the product of labor arbitration is worthy, it can survive open-market inspection.

While emphasizing the importance of independent thinking by arbitrators, Arbitrator A.R. Marshall recognized that the reasoning used and the principles enunciated by outstanding arbitrators have had a decidedly good effect on the general caliber of arbitration decisions.[4] Arbitrator Carl A. Warns stated that "it is obvious that in arbitration as in other fields, respect must be paid to accumulated wisdom and experience."[5] Reported awards have been said to be "live tools, to be used in shaping and applying the collective bargaining agreement."[6] Arbitrator Arthur Ross once commented that "published awards are not binding on another arbitrator, but the thinking of experienced men is often helpful to him."[7] Arbitrator Raymond Roberts, in turn, stated that prior awards "may be referred to for advice and for statements of the prevailing rule and standards."[8] Numerous other arbitrators have made similar statements.[9] These statements are consistent with the undoubted wisdom of seeking to profit by past experience. Published awards on a matter will, in any event, provide the setting for evaluating related cases.[10]

A highly practical need for the reasoned opinions of prior awards was made clear in the report of an emergency board created under the Railway Labor Act. One conclusion of the board was that the principal cause of the large number of undisposed claims before the First Division of the National Railroad Adjustment Board was that the First Division did not write fully reasoned opinions or encourage such opinions by referees assigned to it. The result was the accumulation of

---

[3]"The Publication of Arbitration Awards," Proceedings of the 28th Annual Meeting of NAA, 208, 209 (BNA Books, 1976). Publication of awards also makes them widely available as university teaching materials.

[4]Day & Zimmerman, 51 LA 215, 219 (1968).

[5]Cochran Foil Co., 26 LA 155, 157 (1956).

[6]Justin, "Arbitration: Precedent Value of Reported Awards," 21 LRRM 8 at 8 (1947).

[7]S.H. Kress & Co., 25 LA 77, 79 (1955). Similarly, see Arbitrator Shanker in 73 LA 1050, 1053; Larkin in 47 LA 513, 517.

[8]National Lead Co., 28 LA 470, 474 (1957).

[9]E.g., Arbitrator Sisk in 69 LA 484, 487; Whyte in 47 LA 1065, 1072; Tsukiyama in 47 LA 1051, 1053; Teele in 46 LA 215, 218; Lugar in 40 LA 343, 348; Thompson in 29 LA 518, 523; Boles in 26 LA 84, 87; Scheiber in 25 LA 379, 381–382; Reid in 25 LA 146, 149; Livengood in 21 LA 456, 460; Wettach in 19 LA 797, 799; Schmidt in 19 LA 432, 434.

[10]See Statement of Arbitrator John Dunlop in Pratt & Whitney Co., 28 LA 668, 672 (1957).

a vast number of awards of no precedential value and of no assistance in the application of rules interpreted by the awards.[11]

A cogent statement regarding use of prior awards is that of Arbitrator Maurice H. Merrill:

> "As to arbitral decisions rendered under other contracts between parties not related to those in the case at hand, usefulness depends upon similarity of the terms and of the situations to which they are to be applied. They must be weighed and appraised, not only in respect to these characteristics, but also with regard to the soundness of the principles upon which they proceed. Certainly, an arbitrator may be aided in formulating his own conclusions by knowledge of how other men have solved similar problems. He ought not to arrogate as his own special virtues the wisdom and justice essential to sound decision. In at least two instances in recent months I have found by investigation that a strong current of arbitral decision had overborne my first impression of the implications of particular language. To yield to this 'common sense of most,' especially as, on examination, the reasoning on which it was based carried plausibility, was neither to evade my responsibility nor to sacrifice my intellectual integrity. Contrariwise, it reduced discriminatory application of similar provisions. It enabled me to make use of the wisdom of others at work in the same field."[12]

Prior awards can be of value to parties engaged in the negotiation of collective bargaining agreements. Knowledge of how specific clauses have been interpreted by arbitrators will help negotiators avoid pitfalls in the use of agreement language. That awards have such value has been recognized, and is one of the important reasons for writing fully reasoned opinions.[13]

The opponents of the precedential use of awards often voice the same type of criticism sometimes directed toward the doctrine of precedent in law; i.e., the binding force of prior decisions ties the present to the past in such a degree as to stultify progress, and the observance of precedent becomes an end in itself, with the result that justice sometimes is forced to give way to the symmetrical majesty of the decisions. These antagonists assert that the arbitrator should search for a rule of reason which will render justice and at the same time permit the parties to continue "living together"; they say that the desirable rule is determined in part by the character of the disputants—by their economic position, their strength or weakness, their importance to the community, the history of their past relationships, and their objectives in taking their present stand. These factors require each case to be decided on its own and explain why two

---

[11]Report to the President by the Emergency Board created July 18, 1947 (Report dated July 30, 1947). In contrast to Division I, Divisions II, III, and IV do prepare fully reasoned opinions. Sometimes arguments before a referee sitting with one of these Divisions will consist largely of debates about the meaning and applicability of particular precedents. See Miller, "The Railroad Adjustment Board," 3 Arb. J. (N.S.) 181 (1948); Garrison, "The National Railroad Adjustment Board: A Unique Administrative Agency," 46 Yale L.J. 567, 581–582 (1937). Also see Daugherty, Whiting & Guthrie, "Arbitration by the National Railroad Adjustment Board," Arbitration Today, 93–127 (BNA Books, 1955).

[12]Merrill, "A Labor Arbitrator Views His Work," 10 Vand. L. Rev. 789, 797–798 (1957).

[13]Crane Carrier Co., 47 LA 339, 341 (Merrill, 1966); Deep Rock Oil Corp., 11 LA 25, 26 (Merrill, 1948).

arbitrators dealing with different parties but similar facts will arrive at seemingly opposing decisions.[14]

Another argument is that arbitration proceedings are private business matters, involving the presentation of confidential data which should be kept secret from competitors. In this regard it may be noted, however, that the private nature of arbitration and the obligation not to publish or comment publicly on the award without the consent of the parties are emphasized by the Code of Professional Responsibility.[15]

It is also said that one of the great advantages of arbitration, namely, its high degree of informality, would be lost should the arbitration tribunal be bound by precedent and legalism. One of the strongest and most bitter statements against giving precedential force to awards was by Leo Cherne:

> "The effects of publishing domestic arbitration awards are inevitable and inevitably undesirable. The fact of publication itself creates the atmosphere of precedent. The arbitrators in each subsequent dispute are submitted to the continuous and frequently unconscious pressure to conform. A bad award—and there are such in both the courtroom and the arbitration tribunal—will have the effect of stimulating other bad ones; a good one, by the weight of precedent, may be applied where the subtleties of fact should urge a different award."[16]

Despite the opposition of such critics, it is now recognized widely that prior awards do have great value. Many employers and unions

---

[14]See views of Levenstein in "Reporting of Labor Arbitration: Pro and Con," 1 Arb. J. (N.S.) 420, 426 (1946).

[15]Sec. II(C), 64 LA 1321–1322. In 1983 the American Arbitration Association announced a new policy regarding permission to publish awards:

"In a recent change in policy, parties in both public and private sector cases administered by the AAA are now sent, along with the arbitrator's award, a letter that states:

"We would like to consider the enclosed case of yours for reporting in a forthcoming issue [of one of AAA's three labor reporting services]. Unless we hear from you to the contrary within one (1) month from the date of this letter of transmittal, we will assume that you have no objection to our doing so.

"In the past, the AAA required written permission to publish from both parties in private sector cases, and no time limit was given in which the parties in either public or private sector cases were expected to respond.

"This change in policy, which became effective September 1, 1983, was implemented to simplify approval procedures and to encourage the parties to make more awards available for publication."

AAA Study Time, Oct. 1983, 10. Regarding earlier AAA policy, see "The Publication of Arbitration Awards," Proceedings of the 28th Annual Meeting of NAA, 208, 210 (BNA Books, 1976). As concerns the Federal Mediation and Conciliation Service, that agency's regulations state that: "The Service encourages the publication of arbitration awards. However, the Service expects arbitrators it has nominated or appointed not to give publicity to awards they issue if objected to by one of the parties." § 1404.15(d) as amended effective Apr. 1982, 29 CFR 1404.15(d). FMCS procedure for determining party objection to publication of awards has varied. By memorandum of January 3, 1978, the FMCS informed its arbitrators that they would no longer be expected to ask parties if they consent to publication, the new procedure being that consent would be inferred by a party's failure to register objection directly to the Service. By Mini Memo No. 82–1 of March 8, 1982, the FMCS informed its arbitrators that under amended regulations they no longer were expected to provide FMCS with a copy of their award, and further informed them that: "It is now your responsiblity to obtain permission from the parties for publication of awards. Publishable awards should be submitted directly to the publishers." FMCS statistics transmitted with the latter Memo indicated that under the prior procedure, objection to publication had been filed for 1081 of the 6967 awards in FMCS fiscal year 1981.

[16]Cherne, "Should Arbitration Awards Be Published?" 1 Arb. J. (N.S.) 75 (1946). For other arguments against use of awards as precedent, see McPherson, "Should Labor Arbitrators Play Follow-the-Leader?" 4 Arb. J. (N.S.) 163 (1949).

acknowledge arbitration awards to be a rapidly expanding body of labor-management rules. Parties in arbitration cases very frequently cite and discuss many prior awards of other parties as well as their own.[17] Indeed, parties sometimes specifically authorize or even direct their arbitrator to consider awards of other arbitrators.[18] Parties thus appreciate the great value of using tested experience, and even where collective agreements expressly provide that no decision is to establish a precedent for other cases, actual practice under such provisions may disclose the parties themselves applying decisions to other disputes involving the same point.[19]

Also from the standpoint of the parties, recognition that "the body of recorded decisional precedent in arbitration proceedings is constantly growing" was one reason for preparation of a dissenting opinion by a partisan member of a tripartite board "to guide those who may have occasion in the future to refer to the decision and award as a precedent."[20]

Of great practical significance is the attitude of arbitrators themselves. An extensive survey of labor arbitration disclosed that 77 percent of the 238 responding arbitrators believed that precedents, even under *other* contracts, should be given "some weight."[21] In this regard, the Code of Professional Responsibility recognizes that arbitrators may exercise independent discretion concerning use of precedents unless the parties have indicated mutual agreement to the contrary.[22]

---

[17]For example, see Arbitrator Howlett in 75 LA 729, 730; Strasshofer in 69 LA 766, 767–768; Kindig in 69 LA 712, 717; Harter in 69 LA 414, 416–418; Sembower in 53 LA 178, 181–183; Klamon in 22 LA 336, 341–345. For many other such instances the reader need merely scan volumes of reported awards.

[18]Burris Mills, 26 LA 250 at 250 (Whittaker, 1956); Southern Bell Tel. & Tel. Co., 25 LA 85, 86 (Alexander, et. al., 1955). One survey indicated that there is considerable support, particularly from the management side, for the proposition that arbitrators should make greater use of precedent in deciding cases. Jones & Smith, "Management and Labor Appraisals and Criticisms of the Arbitration Process: A Report With Comments," 62 Mich. L. Rev. 1115, 1150 (1964). Union acceptance of the precedent concept is illustrated by the fact that precedents are often used in arbitration under the AFL-CIO internal disputes plan. For instance, see Umpire Cole in 43 LA 255, 257, and in 43 LA 249, 252.

[19]Rosenblatt, "The Impartial Machinery of the Coat and Suit Industry," 3 Arb. J. 224, 226 (1939).

[20]Journal Publishing Co., 22 LA 108, 113 (1954).

[21]Warren & Bernstein, "A Profile of Labor Arbitration," 16 LA 970, 982 (1951). For citation of many cases where precedents under *other* contracts did have some persuasive influence on the arbitrator, see this Chapter's topic entitled "Persuasive Prior Awards."

[22]The Code of Professional Responsibility provides in § II(G) that:

"1. An arbitrator must assume full personal responsibility for the decision in each case decided.

"a. The extent, if any, to which an arbitrator properly may rely on precedent, on guidance of other awards, or on independent research is dependent primarily on the policies of the parties on these matters, as expressed in the contract, or other agreement, or at the hearing.

"b. When the mutual desires of the parties are not known or when the parties express differing opinions or policies, the arbitrator may exercise discretion as to these matters, consistent with acceptance of full personal responsibility for the award."

For relevant court cases, see subtopic entitled "Temporary Arbitrators," below in this Chapter. Particularly in expedited arbitration the parties may place some or even severe limitations upon the use of precedents and/or upon the precedential force of the expedited awards themselves. See Chapter 7, topic entitled "Expediting the Arbitration Machinery"; Dresser Indus., 72 LA 138, 141–142 (Laybourne, 1979).

Arbitrators are often unwilling to rely solely upon the parties for making precedents available, and such arbitrators "search out" relevant awards on their own.[23] Where one party has cited precedents, the arbitrator may allow the other party time to consider and answer them.[24] Where neither party has cited precedents, the arbitrator may invite both parties to submit any that are considered relevant.[25]

While it might be expected that persons trained in law would be more inclined to adhere to the doctrine of precedent, it is important to note that many of the arbitrators who give precedential force to prior awards are not lawyers. The Authors, like another observer, have received the "distinct impression that laymen in a judicial position are quite as eager as lawyers in pursuing, and quite as contentious in dissecting, the available precedents * * *."[26]

Accepting, then, that prior awards are of some precedential value and realizing that they do have and will continue to have some force as precedent, the Authors turn to inquire into the quantum of force given them and to the probable course of future development. In seeking an answer it is helpful to consider the force given legal decisions under the doctrine of precedent.

Precedent Value of Legal Decisions

Confusion results when one has in mind the inflexible English rule of stare decisis because even in England the force actually given to prior decisions is not always absolute and inflexible. Therefore, for the purpose of this discussion, the Authors speak of the doctrine of precedent as meaning *the force which is given to prior decisions.*

A basic difference between the Anglo-American systems of law and the civil law systems is the official nonacceptance of the doctrine of precedent by the civil law systems. But Professors Shartel and Wolff pointed out that the difference between the common law and civil law systems on this point is more apparent than real in that our own courts do not follow precedents as slavishly as many of their utterances would suggest, while the civil law courts do not ignore precedents to the extent that their general theories might indicate. Further, they pointed out that in all of the civil law countries the binding force of precedents is recognized definitely in practice in one situation, termed a settled course of decision. Thus, although a single prior decision is not regarded as binding, a settled course of decision on a point is regarded as controlling.[27] As will appear presently, the precedential

---

[23]See Arbitrator Handsaker in 73 LA 1305, 1307; Jedel in 73 LA 581, 584–585; Ferguson in 69 LA 1245, 1246; Rule in 69 LA 1167, 1171; Morgan in 69 LA 919, 921; Rutherford in 69 LA 406, 410; Bowles in 69 LA 351, 352. For earlier cases, see p. 370 of the Third Edition of this book.

[24]Simmons Co., 15 LA 921, 922 (Elson, 1950).

[25]A.D. Julliard & Co., 15 LA 934, 938 (Maggs, 1951).

[26]Garrison, "The National Railroad Adjustment Board: A Unique Administrative Agency," 46 Yale L.J. 567, 583 (1937).

[27]Shartel & Wolff, "Civil Justice in Germany," 42 Mich. L. Rev. 863, 866–867 (1944). Also see Lloyd, Introduction to Jurisprudence, 366–372 (2d Ed., 1965); Bodenheimer, Jurisprudence, 290–291 (Harvard U. Press, 1962).

operation of labor arbitration awards seems to be something of a hybrid of the civil law and common law approaches.

But how does the doctrine of precedent under the common law system operate? As was indicated above, it does not operate as inexorably as many persons assume. Salmond, in his *Jurisprudence,* considered the English doctrine of precedent.[28] He divided decisions into two classes, authoritative and persuasive. These were said to differ in the kind of influence exercised by each upon the future course of the administration of justice.

The authoritative precedent was defined as one which judges must follow whether they approve of it or not; the persuasive precedent, one which judges are under no obligation to follow, but which is to be taken into consideration and given such weight as its intrinsic merit seems to demand.

Salmond specified as authoritative the decisions of the superior courts of justice in England.[29] A great body of decisions were designated as persuasive, including (1) foreign judgments, and more especially those of American courts, (2) decisions of superior courts in other parts of the British Commonwealth of Nations, (3) the judgments of the Privy Council when sitting as the final court of appeal from other members and parts of the Commonwealth, and (4) judicial dicta. Thus, we see that even in England, where the most extreme adherence to the doctrine of precedent is found, a large body of decisions have persuasive force only.[30]

In America, the doctrine is even more flexible than in England. That the degree of control to be allowed a prior decision varies with the particular case has been emphasized by von Moschzisker, who, after referring to the tenet that stare decisis is based on the premise that certainty in law is preferable to reason and correct legal principles, made the following statement:

> "If the rule demanded absolute rigid adherence to precedents (as in the English House of Lords), then there might be good ground for the persistence among the uninformed of the erroneous idea just referred to, but the proper American conception comprehends *stare decisis* as a flexible doctrine, under which the degree of control to be allowed a prior judicial determination depends largely on the nature of the question at issue, the circumstances attending its decision, and, perhaps, somewhat on the attitude of individual participating judges."[31]

Von Moschzisker also spoke of the situation in which the precedent should be departed from:

---

[28]Salmond on Jurisprudence, § 53 (11th Ed. by Glanville Williams, 1957). All additional reference to Salmond by the Authors pertain to said § 53.

[29]Salmond also divided authoritative precedents into two kinds, absolute and conditional. Absolute decisions must be followed without question, however unreasonable or erroneous they may be considered to be. On the other hand, courts possess a certain limited power to disregard decisions having merely conditional authority.

[30]For explanations as to why this should be so, see Cross, Precedent in English Law, 12–14 (Oxford U. Press, 1961).

[31]Moschzisker, "Stare Decisis in Courts of Last Resort," 37 Harv. L. Rev. 409, 414 (1924).

"Therefore, except in the classes of cases which demand strict adherence to precedent, when a court is faced with an ancient decision, rendered under conditions of society radically different from those of today, and when it is sought to have this ancient decision control present-day conditions even though the attending facts in the two controversies be alike, still there is nothing in the doctrine of *stare decisis* to prevent a departure from the earlier decision and (in the absence of a legislative enactment covering the matter) the restatement of the governing rule there laid down, or acted on, to meet the change in the life of the people to serve whose best interests it was originally invoked."[32]

Professor Shartel stated that precedents are not self-effectuating; rather, that they control only to the extent that they are accepted as binding by judges in later cases, and that varying force is attached to different kinds of precedents.[33] An effective summary of the American doctrine of stare decisis is contained in Chamberlain's classic statement:

"A deliberate or solemn decision of a court or judge, made after argument on a question of law fairly arising in a case, and necessary to its determination, is an authority, or binding precedent, in the same court or in other courts of equal or lower rank, in subsequent cases, where 'the very point' is again in controversy; but the degree of authority belonging to such precedent depends, of necessity, on its agreement with the spirit of the times or the judgment of subsequent tribunals upon its correctness as a statement of the existing, or actual law, and the compulsion or exigency of the doctrine is, in the last analysis, moral and intellectual, rather than arbitrary or inflexible."[34]

The essence of the above discussion of the doctrine of precedent at common law supports the foregoing definition of precedent as meaning *the force which is given to prior decisions*. Confusion naturally results when one seeks to limit the doctrine to one of inflexibility, since, in fact, the weight given to any prior decision is a question of degree.

Authoritative Prior Awards

Although prior labor arbitration awards are not binding in exactly the same sense that authoritative legal decisions are, yet they may have a force which can be characterized as authoritative. This is true of arbitration both by permanent umpires and by temporary or ad hoc arbitrators.

Giving authoritative force to prior awards when the same issue subsequently arises (stare decisis) is to be distinguished from refusing

---

[32]Id. at 418.

[33]Shartel, Our Legal System and How It Operates, 418–419 (U. of Mich., 1951). Professor Shartel indicated the several respects in which the variation in weight of precedents is apparent: (1) As regards the place and court in which the precedent is cited—a decision of the supreme court of state X has a different weight when cited in state X than when cited in state Y; (2) as regards the character of the judicial statement—a unanimous opinion will have more weight than a divided opinion; (3) as regards the scope of acceptance of the view—one supported by general authority will be more forceful; (4) as regards age and confirmation in later cases; (5) as regards the subject matter involved in the previous decision. Ibid.

[34]Chamberlain, The Doctrine of Stare Decisis, 19 (1885). Also see Catlett, "The Development of the Doctrine of Stare Decisis and the Extent to Which It Should Be Applied," 21 Wash. L. Rev. 159 (1946).

to permit the merits of the same event or incident to be relitigated (res judicata). Where a new incident gives rise to the same issue that is covered by a prior award, the new incident may be taken to arbitration but it may be controlled by the prior award. The destiny of a party's claim thus may be governed by a prior award which either precludes the claim under res judicata concepts or controls the decision on the claim by stare decisis concepts. In some instances arbitrators likewise have made the prior award the governing factor by application of a third judicial concept, collateral estoppel, which stands somewhere between the concepts of res judicata and stare decisis (collateral estoppel also overlaps somewhat with res judicata and, in a sense, with the authoritative precedent area of stare decisis).[35] However, regardless of whether the arbitrator speaks in terms of res judicata, collateral estoppel, or stare decisis, ordinarily the prior award by some procedure will have been the governing factor in the disposition of the present claim.

Still another situation which may be noted is that in which an arbitrator enforces the prior award of another arbitrator.[36]

Permanent Umpires

The most pronounced situation in which prior arbitration awards have "authoritative" type force is that of arbitration by permanent

---

[35]For example, see Bofors-Lakeway, 72 LA 159, 161–163 (1979), where Arbitrator Maurice Kelman also made reference to res judicata and stare decisis. Stare decisis is treated throughout this Chapter and will not be dealt with in this footnote. "Under res judicata, a final judgment on the merits of an action precludes the parties or their privies from relitigating issues that were *or could have been* raised in that action." Allen v. McCurry, 101 S.Ct. 411, 414 (1980), emphasis added. The "essential elements" of res judicata "are generally stated to be (1) a final judgment on the merits in an earlier suit, (2) an identity of the cause of action in both the earlier and the later suit, and (3) an identity of the parties or their privies in the two suits." Nash County Bd. of Educ. v. Biltmore Co., 1980–81 Trade Cases ¶63,715, p. 77,816 (CA 4, 1981), stating also at p. 77,819 that "collateral estoppel is generally regarded as merely a 'branch' or 'other prong' of res judicata." In one sense collateral estoppel is broader than res judicata in that "[u]nder collateral estoppel once a court has decided an issue of fact or law necessary to its judgment, that decision may preclude litigation of the issue in a suit *on a different cause of action* involving a party to the first case." Allen v. McCurry, 101 S.Ct. 411, 414 (1980), emphasis added, where the Court referred to the "related" doctrines of res judicata and collateral estoppel. Regarding collateral estoppel where the U.S. Government is involved, see United States v. Stauffer Chem. Co., 104 S.Ct. 575 (1984); United States v. Mendoza, 104 U.S. 568 (1984). In another sense collateral estoppel is narrower than res judicata in that collateral estoppel "extends only to questions 'distinctly put in issue and directly determined' in" the prior action. Emich Motors Corp. v. General Motors Corp., 71 S.Ct. 408, 414 (1951). For a detailed analysis of the judicial doctrines of stare decisis, res judicata, and collateral estoppel, see Timken Roller Bearing Co., 32 LA 595, 597–599 (Boehm, 1958). On stare decisis and res judicata, see Block, "Decisional Thinking—West Coast Panel Report," Proceedings of the 33rd Annual Meeting of NAA, 119, 143 (BNA Books, 1981). The issuance of an arbitration award generally bars any subsequent court or arbitration action on the merits of the same event. See Chapter 2, subtopic entitled "De Novo Litigation Following Arbitration"; Todd Shipyards Corp. v. Marine & Shipbuilding Workers, 242 F.Supp. 606 (USDC, 1965); Hi-Torc Motor Corp., 40 LA 929, 930–931 (Kerrison, 1963); Hall v. Sperry Gyroscope Co., 21 LA 758, 762 (N.Y. S.Ct., 1954), where numerous court cases are collected. It was not considered a res judicata situation, however, where the subsequent proceedings involved a different issue (Arbitrator Shanker in 75 LA 1163, 1166–1167; Dennis in 70 LA 581, 582–583; Koven in 52 LA 314, 315), a different party (Johannes in 45 LA 413, 416), or a similar issue but different incident (Brecht in 41 LA 59, 60–61).

[36]As did Arbitrator Williams in 54 LA 428, 429–430; Koven in 41 LA 1310, 1311–1313; Platt in 11 LA 1175, 1179–1180; Singer in 6 LA 463, 464–465. Also see Singer in 49 LA 991, 994–996; May in 43 LA 433, 439–441; Shaughnessy in 39 LA 636, 639. As to an arbitrator's authority to enforce his own award, see view stated by Arbitrator Koven in 43 LA 1060, 1063.

umpires or chairmen. In this regard, Umpire Charles C. Killingsworth offered the following basic thought: "Where a reasonably clear precedent can be found in prior Umpire decisions, the considerations in favor of following that precedent are very strong indeed, in the absence of relevant changes in contract language or a showing that the precedent decision or decisions were erroneous."[37] Umpire Harry Shulman, who served for many years as umpire for the Ford Motor Company and the United Automobile Workers, spoke of precedent in permanent umpire systems as follows:

> "[I]n this system a form of precedent and stare decisis is inevitable and desirable. I am not referring to the use in one enterprise, say United States Steel, of awards made by another arbitrator in another enterprise, say General Motors. * * *
>
> "But the precedent of which I am now speaking refers to the successive decisions within the same enterprise. Even in the absence of arbitration, the parties themselves seek to establish a form of stare decisis or precedent for their own guidance—by statements of policy, instructions, manuals of procedure, and the like. This is but a means of avoiding the pain of rethinking every recurring case from scratch, of securing uniformity of action. * * *
>
> "When the parties submit to arbitration in the system of which I speak, they seek not merely resolution of the particular stalemate, but guidance for the future, at least for similar cases. They could hardly have a high opinion of the arbitrator's mind if it were a constantly changing mind. Adherence to prior decisions, except when departure is adequately explained, is one sign that the determinations are based on reason and are not merely random judgments."[38]

In the full-fashioned hosiery industry it was explained at one point that prior awards had become a part of the "common law" of the industry. "The Impartial Chairman will hesitate, therefore, to write any decision contrary to the precedents already established."[39] In that industry the principles enunciated in the decisions, not the personage of the Impartial Chairman, were said to be all-important; the mere

---

[37]Goodyear Tire & Rubber Co., 36 LA 1023, 1025 (1961). In this instance, however, he could not find a clear guide from prior umpire decisions. The authoritative force of prior umpire decisions is illustrated by Bethlehem Steel Co., 43 LA 228, 232 (Crawford, 1964). For illustrations as to how basic principles established by prior umpire decisions are utilized, see Umpire Strongin in 70 LA 162, 163–164; McCoy in 47 LA 609 at 609; Florey in 46 LA 414, 416. Of course, a prior umpire decision is not an authoritative precedent for a distinguishable case. See Bethlehem Steel Corp., 47 LA 270, 272 (Gill, 1966).

[38]Shulman, "Reason, Contract, and Law in Labor Relations," 68 Harv. L. Rev. 999, 1020 (1955), reprinted in Management Rights and the Arbitration Process, 169, 193–194 (BNA Books, 1956). For more on the important role of precedent in umpireships, see Killingsworth, "Arbitration: Its Uses in Industrial Relations," 21 LA 859, 861–863 (1953); Reilly, "Arbitration's Impact on Bargaining," 16 LA 987, 990–991 (1951); Davey, "The John Deere-UAW Permanent Arbitration System," Critical Issues in Labor Arbitration, 161, 174 (BNA Books, 1957); Wolff, Crane & Cole, "The Chrysler-UAW Umpire System," Proceedings of the 11th Annual Meeting of NAA, 111, 115, 128 (BNA Books, 1958).

[39]Kennedy, Effective Labor Arbitration, 63 (1948). "In fact each decision becomes a part of the National Labor Agreement which provides 'all decisions and rulings of the Impartial Chairman * * * not in conflict with the terms of this Agreement are hereby adopted and shall be binding upon the parties hereto.'" Id. at 62.

fact that the person of the Impartial Chairman changed from time to time did not lead to the voiding of past decisions.[40]

One permanent board of arbitration, Arbitrator Herbert Blumer serving as Chairman, was called upon to render an opinion as to the binding effect of decisions made at grievance meetings or arbitration hearings. After defining "grievance" as referring to a particular complaint and "issue" as referring to the general contractual question that is raised, the arbitrators made the following statement of position:

"(1) A grievance which has been settled in grievance meetings or in arbitration or which has not been appropriately appealed if the proposed settlement has not been accepted, remains settled. This grievance cannot be reinstituted.

"(2) An issue that is settled by the parties in grievance meetings remains settled. Such a settlement, if accepted by both parties, is equivalent to a separate, local agreement. [For full discussion of the precedential effect of grievance settlements, see Chapter 5.]

"(3) Either party may bring an issue to this Board (by the appropriate procedure) even though the party has not appealed the decision on a grievance incorporating the issue. While the given grievance may not be reinstated, another grievance may be processed to the Board in order that the party may secure a final ruling on the issue.

"(4) A grievance even though generally similar to a grievance which has been settled may be processed if it raises an issue which is anyway different from an issue that has been settled.

"(5) An issue which has been ruled on by an umpire prior to the constitution of this Board remains settled unless the ruling is in conflict with the ruling of other umpires entrusted with the same issue. In such a situation, either party is entitled to a ruling from this Board (by following the procedure prescribed in the Agreement) which will dissipate the conflicting arbitration decisions. Further, if the ruling by the umpire is not clear, either party is privileged to process a grievance to this Board so as to secure a clear ruling on the issue. Also, if the ruling of the umpire on an issue appears not to be in line with the rulings of this Board, a grievance dealing with that issue may be processed to this Board. Rulings by this Board on issues have precedence over the rulings made by other umpires. Issues ruled on by this Board shall remain settled and no grievance clearly confined to such issues may be processed to this Board."[41]

Bethlehem Steel Company Umpire Ralph T. Seward stated that "though he does not consider that he is necessarily bound by the decisions of prior umpires, he does believe that a heavy burden of persuasion rests on the party who urges that such prior decisions should be reversed."[42] When this heavy burden is met and a later

---

[40]Full-Fashioned Hosiery Indus., 2 ALAA ¶67,542 (1946). Somewhat similar to national labor-management arrangements as concerns precedential force of decisions, umpire decisions rendered under the AFL-CIO Internal Disputes Plan have been researched for precedential use: "While it is clear that each complaint made under this plan must rise or fall on its own facts and merits it is also clear that there should be some uniformity in the interpretation of" the Plan. United Steelworkers v. Mechanics Educ. Soc., 51 LA 1080, 1084 (Kleeb, 1968). Also see Arbitrator Steuer in 73 LA 64, 67; Kleeb in 71 LA 858, 860.

[41]Tennessee Coal, Iron & R.R., 6 LA 426, 429 (1945). It was decided that the issue presently involved had been ruled on previously, so the grievance was denied. Also see American Steel & Wire Co., 11 LA 945 at 945 (Seward, 1948).

[42]Bethlehem Cornwall Corp., 25 LA 894, 897 (1956). For more of Umpire Seward's views on this, see Bethlehem Steel Co., 20 LA 87, 90–91 (1953). Also see Arbitrator McDermott in 46 LA 774, 775–776; Crawford in 41 LA 587, 590.

umpire is convinced that a prior decision is erroneous, it will be reversed.[43]

Then, too, umpires sometimes reverse themselves, as in the case of Umpire Seward.[44] Finally, Umpire Seward has observed that mere dictum statements of other Bethlehem system umpires "are entitled to respect," but are not binding.[45]

In implementing such views as those noted hereinabove, the awards of many permanent umpires are published for the guidance of both unions and management and to discourage the appeal of cases which do not present issues or involve situations different from those previously considered.

Temporary Arbitrators

Prior awards also may have authoritative force where temporary arbitrators are used. An award interpreting a collective agreement usually becomes a binding part of the agreement and will be applied by arbitrators thereafter.[46]

---

[43]Bethlehem Steel Co., 24 LA 379, 380–381 (recommended decision by Alexander, approved by Seward, 1955). Where there was a much more complete presentation of evidence before a subsequent umpire, he modified a prior umpire ruling. United States Steel Corp., 48 LA 1149, 1158–1159 (McDermott, 1967).

[44]See comments of Permanent Arbitrator David L. Cole in International Harvester Co., 21 LA 214, 215 (1953).

[45]Bethlehem Steel Co., 28 LA 351, 352 (1957).

[46]In the cases that follow (each of which is considered to support the statement by the Authors in the text) many of the arbitrators spoke in terms of adhering to the precedent, but in some instances the arbitrator spoke in terms of collateral estoppel or res judicata. Regardless of the arbitrator's terminology or of the label borrowed from judicial doctrine, the net result in each case was that the disposition of the current grievance was controlled by the prior award. See Arbitrator Seidman in 80 LA 1146, 1148; Brand in 80 LA 1138, 1139–1140; Levak in 78 LA 620, 624; Yaffe in 78 LA 89, 98; Brown in 77 LA 1088, 1096; Ross in 76 LA 197, 200; Madden in 75 LA 798, 800; Johnston in 75 LA 720, 721–722; Fitch in 75 LA 523, 529; Lipson in 73 LA 565, 568–569; Hill in 73 LA 310, 314–315; Kelman in 72 LA 159, 161–163; Sergent in 71 LA 306, 313; Ellmann in 70 LA 240, 244–245; Dobranski in 68 LA 439, 441; Simon in 68 LA 421, 431. For many earlier cases, see p. 377 of the Third Edition of this book. For the opposing view, see Baab in 23 LA 562, 567; Wallen in 9 LA 757, 763 (but Wallen did hold prior awards binding in 43 LA 1041, 1042–1043, and in 16 LA 365, 368). Arbitrator Ryder, in 22 LA 605, 606, would give such awards "serious and weighty consideration though not binding." Similarly, see LeBaron in 75 LA 76, 81. It appears clear from court decisions that an arbitrator is not *required* to follow a prior award construing the same agreement. See Little Six Corp. v. Mine Workers Local 8332, 112 LRRM 2922 (CA 4, 1983), holding it is for the arbitrator to determine the preclusive effect of a prior award; Connecticut Light & Power Co. v. Local 420, 114 LRRM 2770, 2775 (CA 2, 1983); New Orleans S.S. Assn. v. ILA, 105 LRRM 2539, 2548 (CA 5, 1980), stating that the question whether an "award can be given an effect akin to res judicata or stare decisis with regard to future disputes that may arise between the parties" is a proper question for the arbitrator if the parties do not agree otherwise; Riverboat Casino, Inc. v. Executive Bd., 99 LRRM 2374, 2375 (CA 9, 1978); Westinghouse Elevators v. SIU, 99 LRRM 2651, 2653 (CA 1, 1978). Also see Fournelle v. NLRB, 109 LRRM 2441, 2450 n. 22 (D.C. Cir., 1982). In W.R. Grace & Co. v. Rubber Workers Local 759, 103 S.Ct. 2177, 113 LRRM 2641, 2644 (1983), the arbitration clause in the collective agreement limited the authority of arbitrators to the interpretation and application of the "express" provisions of the agreement, and the finality clause specified that the decision of an arbitrator "within his jurisdiction and authority as specified in this Agreement shall be final and binding." Under these provisions an arbitrator concluded that a prior arbitrator had acted outside his jurisdiction and that this deprived the prior award of precedential force under the agreement. As to this the Supreme Court stated:
"[The arbitrator's] initial conclusion that he was not bound by the [prior] decision was based on his interpretation of the bargaining agreement's provisions defining the arbitrator's jurisdiction and his perceived obligation to give a prior award a preclusive

This was emphasized by Arbitrator Whitley P. McCoy, who declared that where a "prior decision involves the interpretation of the identical contract provision, between the same company and union, every principle of common sense, policy, and labor relations demands that it stand until the parties annul it by a newly worded contract provision."[47] Moreover, Arbitrator McCoy expressed the view that where identical contractual provisions are adopted by joint negotiations of a union with a number of competing companies, an award construing the provision should be given great weight in like cases involving any of the companies.[48]

Arbitrator Russell A. Smith urged that a proper regard for the arbitration process and for stability in collective bargaining relations requires acceptance by an arbitrator, even though he is not technically bound, of any interpretation of the parties' contractual relations rendered by a previous arbitrator, if in point and if based on the same agreement.[49]

It seems obvious that the binding force of any award ordinarily should not continue after the provision upon which it is based is materially changed or is eliminated entirely from the parties' agreement.[50] However, if the agreement is renegotiated without materially changing a provision that has been interpreted by arbitration, the parties may be held to have adopted the award as a part of the contract.[51] Indeed, the binding force of an award may even be strength-

---

effect. * * * Because the authority of arbitrators is a subject of collective bargaining, just as is any other contractual provision, the scope of the arbitrator's authority is itself a question of contract interpretation that the parties have delegated to the arbitrator. [The arbitrator's] conclusions that [the prior arbitrator] acted outside his jurisdiction and that this deprived the [prior] award of precedential force under the contract draw their 'essence' from the provisions of the collective bargaining agreement. Regardless of what our view might be of the correctness of [the arbitrator's] contractual interpretation, the Company and the Union bargained for that interpretation. A federal court may not second-guess it."
113 LRRM at 2644. By use of the phrase "*his perceived* obligation to give a prior award a preclusive effect" (emphasis added), the Court does not appear to be expressing any view of its own concerning the precedential force of a prior award. Rather, by the total quoted statement the Court was indicating merely that the arbitrator was authorized to reach conclusions, that his conclusions did draw their essence from the agreement, and that a court accordingly may not substitute its own views and conclusions. Another U.S. Supreme Court decision touching upon the precedential force of prior awards under the same agreement is the *Metropolitan Edison* decision discussed below in this subtopic.

[47]Pan Am. Ref. Corp., 2 ALAA ¶67,937, p. 69,464 (1948).

[48]American-St. Gobain Corp., 39 LA 306 at 306 (1962). Similarly, see Arbitrator Dobranski in 68 LA 439, 441. Arbitrator Bauder considered that prior awards involving identical contractual language between locals of the same union and divisions of the same company should be given "great, but not controlling, weight." Reynolds Mining Corp., 33 LA 25, 28 (1959). But see Arbitrator Rubin in 35 LA 680, 681.

[49]O & S Bearing Co., 12 LA 132, 135 (1949), where the prior award was not followed, however, since it involved a temporary special agreement rather than the agreement before Arbitrator Smith. In general accord with Arbitrator Smith's suggestion, see Arbitrator Duff in 46 LA 132, 137; Hebert in 46 LA 140, 146; Turkus in 38 LA 679, 680.

[50]Bethlehem Steel Co., 41 LA 624, 626 (Porter, 1963). Similarly, see Arbitrator Raymond in 76 LA 932, 934; Dunau in 43 LA 661, 662–664. An award may cease to be binding even before the contract expires if the parties follow a practice inconsistent with the award. Waterfront Employers Assn. of the Pac. Coast, 2 ALAA ¶67,949 (1948).

[51]See Arbitrator Jones 69 LA 27, 28; Stouffer in 50 LA 208, 212; Dworkin in 43 LA 715, 721; Marshall in 64–1 ARB ¶8292; Geissinger in 41 LA 348, 351; Crawford in 37 LA 711, 715; Uible in 33 LA 816, 819; Justin in 22 LA 721, 725–727; Kelliher in 16 LA 816, 818; Wallen in 16 LA 365, 368; McCoy in 16 LA 217, 218–219. Also see Killion in 37 LA 853, 856–857; Kaplan in 18 LA 777, 779–780. Contra, Kamin in 50 LA 1093, 1095–1096.

ened by such renegotiation without change.[52] In this regard, Arbitrator Edgar A. Jones, Jr., explained:

"[T]he arbitration process would hardly survive the erosion of confidence in its effectiveness were second-thought arbitrators freely to set aside first-impression arbitral awards so that awards would lose their acceptability as being final and binding. It is not surprising, therefore, that it is unusual, indeed rare, for a later arbitrator to find the earlier award not final and binding. Even so, however, there do arise circumstances in which the occasion seems compelling to the later arbitrator to disregard or modify the earlier award. After all, it is the integrity and intelligence of each arbitrator that are commissioned by the disputants who jointly select each to make his or her own appraisal and decision. * * *

"But this dilemma for the second arbitrator largely if not wholly disappears once the agreement has expired after issuance of the prior award. For upon its expiration the opportunity exists in negotiations to alter, amend or modify any arbitral interpretation deemed to have warped or otherwise sufficiently mutilated the intent of the earlier draftsmen as to warrant that effort by the disadvantaged party. Of course, such an effort has its costs too and they may militate against undertaking it. But that is a decision for the bargainer to make in terms of its own priorities in the overall bargaining relationship. That the earlier award remains untouched by later negotiations, or even demonstrably unmentioned in them, in no wise signifies that a cost-benefit appraisal has not been made, however crude or casual it may have been.

"So an arbitrator who is summoned to office by the parties in the course of a subsequent term of their agreement, and is importuned by one of them to overturn that earlier award, should feel considerably relieved of any concern for possible error having done violence to the intent of the parties by the earlier arbitrator. That latter's award has now had the ultimate review of subsequent collective bargaining negotiations and has survived the test for whatever reason. * * *"[53]

---

[52]See Arbitrator Seidman in 80 LA 1146, 1147–1148; Jones in 69 LA 27, 28; Johnston in 42 LA 304, 306–307; Justin in 22 LA 721, 725–727 (while he apparently was otherwise inclined to give an award of the same parties only "a 'persuasive' force which compels consideration," still, where the parties did not disturb the award in renegotiating their agreement, he found "no basis or warrant to disturb it"); Wallen in 16 LA 365, 368. Also see Tharp in 73 LA 603, 604–605; Geissinger in 43 LA 1022, 1024.

[53]Todd Shipyards Corp., 69 LA 27, 28 (1977). For a similar statement, see Block, "Decisional Thinking—West Coast Panel Report," Proceedings of the 33rd Annual Meeting of NAA, 119, 143 (BNA Books, 1981). It seems likely that for purposes other than establishing a waiver of statutory rights, an arbitrator properly may hold that an award is still binding under a subsequent agreement on the basis of a less demanding showing than the "clear and unmistakable" showing required by the U.S. Supreme Court for an award to qualify as an "explicit" waiver of NLRA protection. In this regard, in Metropolitan Edison Co. v. NLRB, 103 S.Ct. 1467, 1477–1478, 112 LRRM 3265 (1983), the Court held that:

1) A general no-strike clause did not impose a higher duty upon union officials than upon other employees to prevent illicit work stoppages, and NLRA § 8(a)(3) protected union officials against being disciplined more severely than other employees for like misconduct.

2) This NLRA protection can be waived by the union, but any waiver of the statutory right must be "explicitly stated," or "More succinctly, the waiver must be clear and unmistakable."

3) While two arbitration decisions under the parties' prior agreement had imposed a higher duty on union officials, this did not "establish a pattern of decisions clear enough to convert the union's silence into binding waiver," and this was especially so in light of the collective agreement provision making arbitration decisions binding "for the term of this agreement." (emphasis added by Court)

The employer had argued that "the union's failure to change the relevant contractual language in the face of two prior arbitration decisions constitutes an implicit contractual waiver." To this the

The parties are free in any case to stipulate as to what precedential role a forthcoming award shall play.[54]

While Arbitrator Herbert Blumer declared that "it is only fair and reasonable to expect an arbitrator's decision to apply to subsequent cases of the same nature" and that "the refusal to apply the arbitrator's decision to similar cases leaves unsolved and unsettled the general problem covered by the decision," nevertheless he added that the refusal to apply an award to cases of the same nature is justified where it is shown that any one of the following elements is present: (1) The previous decision clearly was an instance of bad judgment; (2) the decision was made without the benefit of some important and relevant facts or considerations; or (3) new conditions have arisen questioning the reasonableness of the continued application of the decision.[55] Other arbitrators have agreed that an arbitrator is justified in refusing to follow an award considered to be clearly erroneous,[56] or one whose continued application is rendered questionable by changed conditions.[57] Arbitrator Leo Kotin has expressed the view that a party is not ordinarily justified in seeking an award contrary to a prior decision by submitting (in a different case but with the same issue) additional evidence to a subsequent arbitrator;[58] but in several cases the presen-

---

Court replied:

"[W]e do not doubt that prior arbitration decisions may be relevant—both to other arbitrators and to the Board—in interpreting bargaining agreements. But to waive a statutory right the [union official's higher] duty must be established clearly and unmistakably. Where prior arbitration decisions have been inconsistent, sporadic, or ambiguous, there would be little basis for determining that the parties intended to incorporate them in subsequent agreements." 103 S.Ct. at 1477–1478.

The Court stated also that:

"An arbitration decision may be relevant to establishing waiver of this statutory right when the arbitrator has stated that the bargaining agreement itself clearly and unmistakably imposes an explicit duty on union officials to end unlawful work stoppages. Absent such a statement, the arbitration decision would not demonstrate that the union specifically intended to waive the statutory protection otherwise afforded its officials. In this case, however, the two arbitration decisions did not purport to determine the parties' specific intent." Ibid. n. 13.

Cf., Fournelle v. NLRB, 109 LRRM 2441, 2446, 2450 (D.C. Cir., 1982), in which the court pointed to certain distinctions between the facts there and those in the *Metropolitan Edison* case.

[54]For instance, see Arbitrator Beatty in 49 LA 55, 56 (award to govern the disposition of pending like grievances); Smith in 42 LA 517, 523 (award not to bind other parties to master agreement); Anderson in 19 LA 106 at 106 (award to govern future like grievances). Such a stipulation itself required interpretation in Howard P. Foley Co., 73 LA 1205, 1206–1207 (Smith, 1979). Only a small percentage of collective agreements contain any provision as to the precedential effect of awards. See "Basic Patterns in Labor Arbitration Agreements," 34 LA 931, 940 (1960). Sometimes the arbitrator himself will specify that his award is not to have authoritative precedential force. See Arbitrator Barrett in 72 LA 898, 905; Smith in 48 LA 213, 219; Lehoczky in 36 LA 21, 22.

[55]Inland Steel Co., 1 ALAA ¶67,121, p. 67,248 (1944). Arbitrator Clark Kerr would add obvious and substantial errors of fact or law and the lack of fair and full hearing as justification for refusal to apply the prior award, but he would place the burden of proof upon the party alleging any of these grounds. Waterfront Employers Assn. of Pac. Coast, 7 LA 757, 758 (1947).

[56]See Arbitrator Roumell in 68 LA 848, 853; Carter in 52 LA 357, 359; Waldron in 49 LA 314, 319; Hilpert in 32 LA 1013, 1017; Klamon in 19 LA 779, 787; Komaroff in 15 LA 626, 630–631. Also see discussion in Connecticut Light & Power Co. v. Local 420, 114 LRRM 2770, 2775 (CA 2, 1983).

[57]See Braun Baking Co., 43 LA 433, 439–440 (May, 1964); Armstrong Cork Co., 34 LA 890, 894 (Morvant, 1960). In National Broadcasting Co., 71 LA 762, 769 (Gentile, 1978), the parties themselves had provided in their master agreement that an arbitrator shall not consider any issue which had been the subject of a previous arbitration, "except upon a showing of * * * new evidence, change of condition, or circumstances."

[58]Douglas Aircraft Co., 49 LA 744, 748, 752 (1967), where he also indicated that this may be justified where production of the evidence was foreclosed by circumstances beyond the control of the party.

tation of additional evidence or clarification of previously presented evidence has produced a contrary award by the subsequent arbitrator.[59]

An arbitrator understandably may feel less firmly bound by another arbitrator's award if it is not accompanied by a reasoned opinion;[60] and dictum statements of a prior ad hoc arbitrator may carry little or no weight.[61]

Frequently when prior awards are cited as being authoritative, the arbitrator will avoid such effect by distinguishing them.[62] Often the distinction will be clear, but there are cases where the drawing of a distinction can prove to be troublesome. For instance, in one case the company cited an award rendered two years earlier in a case involving the same company but a different union. The arbitrator, James J. Healy, said that the similarity of the two cases made the prior award germane; moreover, the question itself was not one of peculiar relevancy to a particular bargaining unit. But then he stated that, while the prior decision carried weight in appraising the merits of the present case, its mere existence did not foreclose the arbitrator from reaching a different conclusion. Apparently realizing the inconsistency, he qualified the latter statement by saying that there was no adequate opinion in the earlier award and that it was on a slightly different issue. The arbitrator expressed the dilemma in the following words:

> "Placing the Company in the position of having two arbitrators make different rulings on the same question is repugnant to all parties; the very dignity of arbitration is endangered, and, on the surface, it would appear that arbitration is dangerously subjective. Therefore, it is only after sincere and prolonged deliberation that the undersigned makes the following ruling."[63]

It appears that the fact situations of the cases were enough alike that he did not feel entirely free to deviate from the prior award because to do so would make it appear that arbitration is "dangerously subjec-

---

[59]See Arbitrator Rothschild in 78 LA 79, 88; Jones in 53 LA 477, 480; McDermott in 48 LA 1149, 1158–1159; Cayton in 45 LA 889, 891–892; Murphy in 38 LA 1199, 1207.

[60]See General Dynamics Corp., 53 LA 424, 427 (Roberts, 1969); John J. Nissen Baking Co., 48 LA 12, 17 (Fallon, 1966).

[61]See Blaw-Knox Co., 50 LA 1086, 1088 (Meltzer, 1968).

[62]See Arbitrator Stonehouse in 78 LA 339, 341; Petrie in 76 LA 611, 619; Fitch in 74 LA 1055, 1057; Hays in 74 LA 627, 629; Dunsford in 70 LA 1131, 1135; Harrison in 70 LA 584, 586; Dennis in 70 LA 581, 584; Murphy in 70 LA 538, 543; Roberts in 70 LA 278, 283; Ruben in 69 LA 944, 953; Taylor in 69 LA 857, 861; Teple in 69 LA 599, 601; Moore in 68 LA 375, 377. For earlier cases, see p. 380 of the Third Edition of this book.

[63]Brown & Sharpe Mfg. Co., 7 LA 134, 138–139 (1947). For possible courses of action available to a third arbitrator when confronted with the conflicting decisions of two prior arbitrators, see Arbitrator Haemmel in 75 LA 534, 536; Foster in 75 LA 380, 384; Wann in 55 LA 510, 513; Goldberg in 50 LA 933, 935; Rock in 45 LA 43, 44. In Graphic Arts Local 97-B v. Haddon Craftsmen, Inc., 489 F.Supp. 1088, 1096–1098 (USDC, 1981), the court refused to set aside either of two conflicting awards where each drew its essence from the agreement. In Connecticut Light & Power Co. v. Local 420, 114 LRRM 2770, 2775 (CA 2, 1983), the court did set aside one of two conflicting awards even though each drew its essence from the agreement, but the court stressed that special circumstances required its action and it recognized that generally "inconsistency with another award is not enough by itself to justify vacating an award."

tive." He concluded, however, that there was sufficient distinction between the cases to justify a refusal to be bound by the prior award.

Persuasive Prior Awards

While prior awards have authoritative force in some situations, the great mass of awards are considered to have persuasive force only.[64] Nothing is settled by saying that prior awards do or do not have the force of precedent. Rather, it is essential that one recognize that the precedential force of prior awards always is a question of degree. The range is broad, including prior awards that have absolutely no persuasive force, through those with varying degrees of persuasiveness, to those which are binding in future like cases. The dividing line cannot be drawn with finality, just as the line between authoritative force and persuasive force cannot be established absolutely. Confusion is avoided by remembering that it is only a question of degree in each particular case. The following analysis is made with these thoughts in mind.

There are many cases where, in varying degree, the arbitrator was persuaded by prior awards; in some of these cases the arbitrator spoke in terms of finding "support" in prior awards, but in either case the effect is the same—the arbitrator relied upon or otherwise made use of prior awards.[65]

It is easy for an arbitrator to be persuaded by or to rely upon a prior award that is in near agreement with his own views. Moreover, most *careful* awards rely upon principles which will command respect by reason of their logic and the fair result which they yield under the facts. In law we speak of the "reasonably prudent person." Most good awards can be said to incorporate the view of the reasonably prudent person, and it is reasonable to expect other persons, in similar cases, to be persuaded to some extent by the awards and their supporting reasoning. In particular, the considered judgment of any widely

---

[64]Salmond defined the persuasive precedent as one which depends for its influence upon its own merits and upon that alone. Salmond on Jurisprudence § 53 (11th Ed. by Glanville Williams, 1957). He also included judicial dicta with the persuasive precedents. Thus, it might be said that dicta in prior awards differ from decisions in prior awards primarily in regard to the degree of force exerted by each.

[65]For many cases, see pp. 381–382 of the Third Edition and p. 258 of the 1960 Edition of this book. For some of the many later cases from a few LA volumes, see Arbitrator Clarke in 71 LA 1232, 1235; Fisher in 71 LA 1208, 1210; Barone in 71 LA 1034, 1038; Allen in 71 LA 942, 947; Kanner in 71 LA 937, 941; Hon in 71 LA 494, 497; Fogelberg in 71 LA 445, 449; Seward in 71 LA 420, 425; Maroney in 71 LA 164, 169; Cohen in 71 LA 1, 5; Johannes in 70 LA 1269, 1272; Kennedy in 70 LA 1217, 1223; Boyer in 70 LA 1078, 1083; Gundermann in 70 LA 756, 759; Goodman in 70 LA 729, 741; Ross in 70 LA 676, 679; Nigro in 70 LA 574, 575; Davis in 70 LA 572, 573; Beck in 70 LA 494, 496; Welch in 70 LA 426, 427; Herman in 70 LA 304, 308; Ferguson in 70 LA 245, 247–249; Cox in 70 LA 185, 186; Tharp in 70 LA 182, 185; Fitzsimmons in 70 LA 116, 120; Baum in 70 LA 89, 92; Williams in 70 LA 58, 65; Hunter in 69 LA 1080, 1083; Brown in 69 LA 980, 983; Roberts in 69 LA 930, 939; Flannagan in 69 LA 928, 930; Klein in 69 LA 922, 927; Spencer in 69 LA 674, 676; Hatcher in 69 LA 665, 669; Kanzer in 69 LA 609, 611; Teple in 69 LA 599, 603; Abrams in 69 LA 594, 598; Marcus in 69 LA 469, 475; Croft in 69 LA 176, 179; Ward in 69 LA 170, 175. Regarding possible effects of citing precedents in arbitration, cf., Jennings & Martin, "The Role of Prior Arbitration Awards in Arbitral Decisions," 29 Lab. L.J. 95, 100–106 (1978); Harris, "The Use of Precedent in Labor Arbitration," 32 Arb. J. 26 (1977).

known and respected arbitrator cannot be dismissed lightly or ignored.[66]

The attitude of one eminent arbitrator confronted by an award of another eminent arbitrator is possibly typified by the late David A. Wolff (Chrysler Umpire) in considering an award of the late Harry Shulman (Ford Umpire):

> "The Chairman realizes that, despite the great similarity of contract provisions and their apparent common origin and despite the fact of similarity of parties, location and type of business, there are distinctions which exist and must be observed. The parties are not the same parties. Their practices are not identical. Even their application of the considered contract provisions has varied. Further, while Dr. Shulman and the Chairman both act as umpires they were not selected, nor do they act for, the same parties. The parties making the selections undoubtedly had in mind the known general thinking of each at the time of selections and made the selections on an individual basis. On the other hand, points of similarity may not be disregarded. In addition the Chairman has high regard for Dr. Shulman's sincerity, clarity of thought, and reasoning processes. The Chairman does not propose to unthinkingly adopt Dr. Shulman's determination in another case as his own in the instant case. However, to the extent to which he believes it here applicable, he makes use of it with appreciation."[67]

In any event, it would seem that when either party cites an award, the arbitrator cannot disregard it lightly. Good faith and respect for the citing party require the arbitrator at least to consider the contentions of the party.[68] An interesting case illustrating the extreme to which an arbitrator might go in order to consider a prior award relied upon by one of the parties is that in which the hearing was reconvened for that basic purpose.[69] While precedential use of awards occurs primarily in rights arbitration, such use is by no means unknown to interest arbitration as well. Prior awards are considered fairly frequently in interest cases.[70] In some circumstances a prior interest award may have special persuasive significance to other parties "similarly facing the same inquiry."[71]

In all civil law countries, as we have noted, the binding force of precedents is recognized definitely in practice in one situation, which

---

[66]See statement of Arbitrator Spaulding in 25 LA 181, 185; Reynard in 22 LA 880, 882–883; Gorder in 20 LA 880, 888; Fulda in 18 LA 315, 319; Aaron in 8 LA 261, 272; Levy in 6 LA 397, 402. Also see Stix in 47 LA 870, 873.

[67]Chrysler Appeal Bd. Case No. 573 (1948).

[68]Even where the parties agreed that their arbitrator was not bound by precedents, he considered those cited by the parties. Meyer's Bakery of Little Rock, 38 LA 1135, 1140 (Hon, 1962). Also see Arbitrator Sisk in 68 LA 1006, 1009. Sometimes the bulk of an opinion will be devoted to the discussion of precedents cited by the parties and researched by the arbitrator. See Watkins Trucking, Inc., 48 LA 1101, 1102–1104 (Klein, 1967). In Bethlehem Steel Co., 43 LA 79, 83 (1964), Arbitrator Valtin stated that he had extensively reviewed the precedents cited by the parties "because he thinks that it is important to make clear what effect is being given them in deciding the present case."

[69]Boston Daily Newspapers, 6 LA 179, 183–186 (Wallen, 1946). Also see Arbitrator Culley in 69 LA 912, 915. In Warehouse Employees v. Acme Mkts., 105 LRRM 3206 (USDC, 1980), an award was not vacated merely because the arbitrator refused to reopen the hearing to consider an award in another case.

[70]For example, in Patriot News Co., 15 LA 871, 874 (1950), Arbitrator Egan spoke of studying "dozens of arbitration decisions."

[71]Union R.R., 20 LA 219, 224 (Gilden, 1953).

is called a settled course of decision. An analogous situation is found in labor arbitration awards. Where there is a settled course of arbitral decision on a point, the principle stated in the decisions is often very persuasive, or at least highly comforting support for a later ruling.[72] It is unlikely that any such course of decision will be achieved upon faulty reasoning. In this sense, it can be correctly said that "it is not the long line of previous decisions that is determinative," but "the validity of the reasoning behind the principle."[73]

By no means are arbitrators always swayed by cited awards, even awards which are reasonably in point. Arbitrators are alert to distinction between cases.[74] Moreover, when arbitrators cannot agree with the conclusion of cited precedents, they do not hesitate so to state.[75] It is also possible that prior decisions, though sound for their day, will be considered to be out of step with changed times.[76]

When confronted with conflicting prior awards, an arbitrator may reject those which are unconvincing or which fail to set forth with clarity the reasons therefor and he may accept clearly reasoned opinions with the statement that the "reasoning applies with persuasive force to the instant case."[77] Where there are clear lines of arbitral precedent going each way on an issue, the arbitrator will of course use his best judgment as to which line should be applied to the case under consideration.[78]

Sometimes an arbitrator will dismiss cited awards with the statement that he has examined them carefully and has found nothing to alter his thinking on the matter.[79] Then, too, an arbitrator might

---

[72]For many cases, see p. 383 of the Third Edition and p. 260 of the 1960 Edition of this book. For some later cases, see Arbitrator Leeper in 78 LA 8, 14; Rule in 76 LA 572, 575; Goldstein in 76 LA 32, 40; Heinsz in 76 LA 21, 26; Eischen in 75 LA 555, 559; Roumell in 73 LA 1129, 1132; Martin in 72 LA 684, 687–688; Hon in 70 LA 830, 832; Ferguson in 70 LA 245, 249; Sisk in 69 LA 484, 487; Walter in 69 LA 388, 393; Ashe in 68 LA 973, 975; Jewett in 68 LA 188, 191; Johnson in 68 LA 1, 6. In Koehring Div., 46 LA 827, 829 (1966), Arbitrator King stated that parties should take notice as to how given provisions have generally been interpreted by arbitrators, and that if a party desires some other meaning, it should negotiate the other meaning into the contract by clear language.

[73]Bachmann Uxbridge Worsted Corp., 23 LA 596, 602 (Hogan, 1954).

[74]See Arbitrator Petrie in 77 LA 780, 783; Kates in 72 LA 417, 421; Klein in 71 LA 124, 128–129 (distinguishing certain cases cited by one party and following cases cited by the other party); Lewis in 70 LA 1288, 1289; Laybourne in 70 LA 575, 578; Snow in 70 LA 491, 494; Krinsky in 70 LA 290, 294 (distinguishing his own prior decision); Robertson in 70 LA 71, 75; Render in 69 LA 477, 483; Saracino in 68 LA 1359, 1362; Sisk in 68 LA 1006, 1009; Marcus in 68 LA 762, 765. For earlier cases, see p. 384 of the Third Edition of this book. In Glidden-Durkee Div., 52 LA 457, 461–463 (1969), Arbitrator Edgett distinguished precedents cited by a party, and he supplied other precedents to "buttress" his finding.

[75]See Arbitrator Brisco in 77 LA 424, 427; Karlins in 75 LA 148, 152; Beckman in 74 LA 42, 46; Platt in 69 LA 52, 58; Bothwell in 52 LA 1035, 1043; Hilpert in 47 LA 129, 140; Autrey in 45 LA 783, 787; Altieri in 43 LA 602, 604; Crane in 36 LA 635, 639; McCoy in 20 LA 34, 36; Handsaker in 16 LA 964, 966; Whitton in 6 LA 714, 716.

[76]As in Southern Airways, 47 LA 1135, 1141 (Wallen, 1966).

[77]Consolidated Chem. Indus., 6 LA 714, 716–717 (Whitton, 1947). Similarly, Arbitrator Kanner in 70 LA 295, 297–298; Bellman in 52 LA 1218, 1220; Bothwell in 51 LA 1129, 1133; Lennard in 49 LA 76, 77; Teple in 46 LA 1106, 1110; Tsukiyama in 46 LA 849, 851; Yagoda in 46 LA 692, 696; Merrill in 19 LA 854, 855–856.

[78]See Arbitrator Maniscalco in 77 LA 976, 977; Hilgert in 77 LA 953, 959; Jones in 77 LA 807, 813; Stieber in 48 LA 1069, 1073; Beatty in 40 LA 544, 547; Valtin in 35 LA 535, 541. In Omaha Cold Storage Terminal, 48 LA 24, 26, 32 (Doyle, 1967), the Arbitrator decided contra to his view in an earlier case with other parties, now having been persuaded by a later line of cases which he considered to be better reasoned.

[79]See Arbitrator Prasow in 44 LA 691, 694, and in 7 LA 67, 69; Cheney in 8 LA 518, 525. Also see Steiber in 46 LA 967, 970.

acknowledge cited awards but give no indication as to their persuasive force upon him.[80]

Because arbitrators recognize that use of their awards may be sought in similar cases, they sometimes caution against the precedential use of a particular award, especially if there are features peculiar to that case which make the award inappropriate as a guide for any other case.[81]

Finally, in the event of court review an award may be strengthened in the eyes of the court if supported by prior awards.[82]

Precedent and Development of Substantive Principles

The controversy over use of awards as precedents is accompanied by a related and integrated controversy regarding development of substantive principles through arbitration. The Authors offer in the following discussion their own evaluation of these matters.

The Authors are convinced that considerable use of precedents in arbitration is inevitable. They are convinced also that development of substantive principles through arbitration is likewise inevitable—and desirable. Most arbitrators, able though they be, do not possess enough of Solomon's wisdom to justify rule by man instead of rule by principle. Not all cases can best be decided in a vacuum.

The Authors agree that the question is "not *whether* principles are being evolved, but *what* they are and *how far* they should carry."[83]

As to "how far" substantive principles should carry, it is obvious that no principle should be promiscuously applied.[84] In any event, general principles should be applied to cases only after careful thought and thorough consideration.

Precedent, the Siamese twin of substantive principles,[85] is totally out of place in some arbitration cases. In other cases only a little use of precedent is justified. In a sense, each collective bargaining relationship is a world of its own—a world which may be given features of infinite variety under the virtually unlimited right of contract enjoyed by Americans. The phrase "each case must be decided on its own" does have a definite place in arbitration.

Still, issues being arbitrated do frequently have counterparts in reported awards. In arbitration as in other important areas of human activity, growth and refinement through use of tested experience is

---

[80]See Anaconda Wire & Cable Co., 10 LA 20, 24 (Scheiber, 1948); Lebanon Steel Foundry, 6 LA 633, 634 (Brandschain, 1947).

[81]See Arbitrator Kornblum in 45 LA 885, 889; Seitz in 29 LA 322, 324; Ralston in 20 LA 465, 467; Wolff in 19 LA 430, 431; Prasow in 6 LA 323, 326. Also see Raymond in 76 LA 62, 68.

[82]See Bakery Workers Union v. Hall Baking Co., 69 N.E.2d 111, 115 (Mass. Sup. Ct., 1946).

[83]Petshek, "Discussion of Principles Emerging From Grievance Arbitration," 1953 Proceedings of IRRA, 154, 156.

[84]See words of Arbitrator Joseph Shister in Electro Metallurgical Co., 22 LA 684, 686 (1954).

[85]"The appearance of precedent in labor arbitration probably results less from a conscious effort to develop a case law, and more from general recognition of the validity of certain principles for the treatment of similar cases." Holman, "The Back-Pay Issue in Arbitration," I. L. Research, Vol. II, No. 1, pp. 6–8 (1955).

inevitable and desirable. Then, too, from the arbitrator's viewpoint, it is comforting to know that his decision finds support in other awards, or to know at least that it does not vary drastically from what others have decided.

No arbitrator can serve long without becoming aware of the existence of certain more or less generally recognized principles and penetrating propositions. It is questionable whether any arbitrator, and especially the experienced, can always eliminate the influence of what he knows others have done.

It is difficult to determine precisely the extent to which substantive principles are being evolved and applied since, for a variety of reasons, many awards are never published.[86] Frequently where an arbitrator might be inclined to consider precedent, there simply is no reported case similar to that under consideration.[87]

Moreover, many of the awards which are published have little utility as guides for other parties. However, as one spokesman has stated, some decisions, "due to the logic of their problem-solving persuasiveness, are potential candidates for wide application beyond the parties."[88] And, as another observer has begrudgingly admitted, "From the published awards, it is evident that standards have been turned by the lathe of arbitration for a wide range of problems."[89]

The authors readily agree with those who believe that the term "principle" is "abused when it is employed as a synonym for *binding* precedent."[90] However, it should be recognized that regarding the development of principles for widespread application there is not too

---

[86]For factors which various publishers consider in deciding which awards to publish, of those which are available for publication, see "The Publication of Arbitration Awards," Proceedings of the 28th Annual Meeting of NAA, 208, 210–213 (BNA Books, 1976); "How Representative Are Published Decisions?" Proceedings of the 37th Annual Meeting of NAA, 170–193 (BNA Books, 1985). Also see Stewart, "Memo From the Executive Editor," 36 LA vii–viii (1962), where users of LA are also assured that they "can rely on the long experience and mature judgment of BNA's editorial staff to provide full coverage of significant new decisions." Nonetheless, concern has been expressed that the total of all published awards is only a small percentage of those rendered. Jones & Smith, "Management and Labor Appraisals and Criticisms of the Arbitration Process: A Report with Comments," 62 Mich. L. Rev. 1115, 1152 (1964).

[87]See Arbitrator Rule in 76 LA 180, 184; Allen in 76 LA 3, 5; Hannan in 73 LA 162, 163; Hathaway in 73 LA 51, 55; Dworkin in 72 LA 337, 340; Springfield in 70 LA 788, 791; Edes in 70 LA 669, 671; Rose in 70 LA 420, 421; Lucas in 69 LA 394, 398. For earlier cases, see p. 386 of the Third Edition of this book.

[88]Petshek, "Discussion of Principles Emerging From Grievance Arbitration," 1953 Proceedings of IRRA, 154, 157.

[89]Manson, "Substantive Principles Emerging From Grievance Arbitration: Some Observations," 1953 Proceedings of IRRA, 136, 137. A president of the National Academy of Arbitrators stated it as follows:

"The greatest accomplishment [of the arbitration process], in my estimation, has been the development of a quite substantial and functional industrial jurisprudence. To some extent, we have drawn upon and adapted legal doctrines from the larger society; but to a much greater extent, we have evolved doctrines carefully tailored to the particular circumstances of American industrial relations. Our raw material has been millions of hours of testimony and argument from the contesting parties themselves. We have winnowed and sifted, accepted and rejected, and then reconsidered and modified. We have sat at the center of one of the greatest free markets for ideas that our nation, or any nation, has ever seen. From the competition of ideas has gradually developed a substantial body of principles that is generally accepted not only by arbitrators but by labor and management."

Killingsworth, "Twenty-Five Years of Labor Arbitration—And the Future," Proceedings of the 25th Annual Meeting of NAA, 11, 18 (BNA Books, 1973). Compare the statement of another NAA president in Barrett, "The Presidential Address: The Common Law of the Shop," Proceedings of the 26th Annual Meeting of NAA, 95, 97 (BNA Books, 1974).

[90]Manson, id. at 74 (emphasis added).

much concern with the "authoritative" or "binding" force which awards often exert in subsequent cases involving the same parties and the same contract language. Rather, the emphasis falls much more on the "persuasive" or "guiding" force that awards under *other* contracts often exert. Arbitration awards under other contracts *are* important as precedents. A glance through recent volumes of reported arbitration decisions reveals the very frequent citation, discussion, and use of such precedents.

The persuasive or guidance force of prior awards varies widely. Many awards exert little or no force, but some awards are quite useful in other cases, especially where there is a settled course of arbitral decision on a point.

Furthermore, a substantive principle might be revealed through a single well-reasoned decision, which becomes the "leading case" on the point.[91] Then, too, arbitrators sometimes discern substantive principles through a process which might be called "negative inference." For instance, in one case Arbitrator Whitley P. McCoy stated that he had been "unable to find any authority among the thousands of arbitration decisions" for a holding that a certain type of conduct by an employee constitutes a punishable offense.[92] In another case, Arbitrator Edwin R. Teple upheld a company's actions in training employees for duties outside their assigned classification where a study of arbitration decisions revealed no suggested limitation upon the right of management to do so.[93]

In actual practice it is not at all uncommon for an arbitrator to preface the assertion of an established rule or principle with some statement such as "it has become a well-accepted principle," or "it is a general rule that," or "the consensus is," or "the weight of authority is." In doing this arbitrators frequently cite precedents,[94] but just as frequently they cite few or no specific cases to support their assertion that the principle does in fact exist.[95] Possibly the true significance of

---

[91]For example, see Struthers-Wells Corp., 17 LA 483, 485 (Strashower, 1951), recognizing the leading-case status of a decision of Umpire Harry Shulman; Grand Sheet Metal Prods. Co., 17 LA 388, 390 (Kelliher, 1951), noting the leading-case status of a decision by Arbitrator Irving Bernstein.

[92]U.S. Pipe & Foundry Co., 20 LA 513, 516 (1953). A similar approach was taken by Arbitrator Sacks in 68 LA 261, 269; Teple in 45 LA 671, 680; Hebert in 37 LA 42, 49; Howard in 23 LA 440, 446; Cheit in 21 LA 293, 298; Williams in 20 LA 784, 787.

[93]Goodyear Atomic Corp., 45 LA 671, 680 (1965).

[94]For many cases see p. 388 of the Third Edition and p. 264 of the 1960 Edition of this book. For some of the many later cases, see Arbitrator Rule in 76 LA 572, 575; Eischen in 75 LA 555, 559; Schor in 74 LA 578, 579; Barsamian in 74 LA 30, 32; Roumell in 73 LA 1129, 1132; Nathan in 70 LA 1091, 1095; Baum in 70 LA 89, 92; Kaye in 69 LA 1239, 1242; Strasshofer in 69 LA 766, 770; Wren in 69 LA 756, 758; Johnston in 69 LA 604, 607; Milentz in 69 LA 379, 386; Kornblum in 69 LA 344, 349; Mallon in 69 LA 303, 306; Marcus in 68 LA 1099, 1101; Yarowsky in 68 LA 628, 632.

[95]For many cases see p. 388 of the Third Edition and p. 264 of the 1960 Edition of this book. For some of the many later cases, see Arbitrator Denson in 76 LA 685, 690; Carnes in 74 LA 972, 975; Hutchison in 74 LA 437, 439; Rimer in 74 LA 30, 32; Gerhart in 73 LA 556, 561; Bothwell in 72 LA 1214, 1216; Stone in 72 LA 981, 986; Sembower in 72 LA 916, 927; Chalfie in 72 LA 668, 673; Shister in 72 LA 408, 410; Ferguson in 72 LA 164, 167; Kanner in 71 LA 585, 586; Beck in 71 LA 314, 319; Abrams in 70 LA 1174, 1176; Cohen in 70 LA 895, 897; Nigro in 70 LA 574, 575; Denson in 70 LA 514, 517; Murphy in 70 LA 413, 416; Christopher in 70 LA 308, 318; Schroeder in 70 LA 199, 200; Griffin in 69 LA 1123, 1128; Bergeson in 69 LA 759, 762; Curry in 69 LA 375, 377; Chaffin in 69 LA 307, 309; Seidenberg in 68 LA 1054, 1056; Oestreich in 68 LA 767, 769; Morgan

such statements lies in the fact that the arbitrator was willing to accept arbitration awards as a source of fundamental substantive principles.

Finally, it must be emphasized that a great contribution to industrial stability lies in the probability that many disputes are settled by the parties themselves before reaching arbitration because they are aware of prior awards on the issue involved which point out the objective merits of contentions and which are indicative of results likely to be had through arbitration.

---

in 68 LA 708, 712; Roberts in 68 LA 444, 447; Hadlick in 68 LA 114, 123; Cabe in 68 LA 94, 98; Shanker in 68 LA 13, 19. However, if the parties themselves allege existence of established principle, they should be prepared to prove it. See comments of Arbitrator Fisher in 27 LA 812, 814; Hill in 25 LA 587, 591.

Chapter 12

Custom and Past Practice

Unquestionably custom and past practice constitute one of the most significant factors in labor-management arbitration. Evidence of custom and past practice may be introduced for any of the following major purposes: (1) to provide the basis of rules governing matters not included in the written contract; (2) to indicate the proper interpretation of ambiguous contract language; or (3) to support allegations that clear language of the written contract has been amended by mutual action or agreement. In this Chapter use of custom and past practice for each of these purposes will be discussed.[1]

Custom and Practice as Part of the Contract

Under certain circumstances custom and past practice may be held enforceable through arbitration as being in essence a part of the parties' "whole" agreement. Some of the general statements of arbitrators in this regard may be noted:

Arbitrator Dallas L. Jones: "It is generally accepted that certain, but not all, clear and long standing practices can establish conditions of employment as binding as any written provision of the agreement."[2]

Arbitrator Arthur T. Jacobs: "A union-management contract is far more than words on paper. It is also all the oral understandings, interpretations and mutually acceptable habits of action which have grown up around it over the course of time. Stable and peaceful relations between the parties depend upon the development of a mutually satisfactory superstructure of understanding which gives operating significance and practicality to the purely legal wording of the written contract. Peaceful relations depend, further, upon both parties faithfully living up to their

---

[1]For other discussions of custom and practice, see McLaughlin, "Custom and Past Practice in Labor Arbitration," 18 Arb. J. 205 (1963); Mittenthal, "Past Practice and the Administration of Collective Bargaining Agreements," Proceedings of the 14th Annual Meeting of NAA, 30 (BNA Books, 1961); Davis, "Arbitration of Work Rules Disputes," 16 Arb. J. 51 (1961); Aaron, Davis & Bailer, "The Uses of the Past," Arbitration Today, 1–24 (BNA Books, 1955).

[2]Alpena Gen. Hosp., 50 LA 48, 51 (1967).

mutual commitments as embodied not only in the actual contract itself but also in the modes of action which have become an integral part of it."[3]

Arbitrator Marlin M. Volz: "[I]t is well recognized that the contractual relationship between the parties normally consists of more than the written word. Day-to-day practices mutually accepted by the parties may attain the status of contractual rights and duties, particularly where they are not at variance with any written provision negotiated into the contract by the parties and where they are of long standing and were not changed during contract negotiations."[4]

Arbitrator Whitley P. McCoy: "Custom can, under some circumstances, form an implied term of a contract. Where the Company has always done a certain thing, and the matter is so well understood and taken for granted that it may be said that the contract was entered into upon the assumption that that customary action would continue to be taken, such customary action may be an implied term."[5]

Arbitrator Maurice H. Merrill: "In the light of the [arbitration] decisions, * * * it seems to me that the current of opinion has set strongly in favor of the position that existing practices, in respect to major conditions of employment, are to be regarded as included within a collective bargaining contract, negotiated after the practice has become established and not repudiated or limited by it. This also seems to me the reasonable view, since the negotiators work within the frame of existent practice and must be taken to be conscious of it."[6]

Many other arbitrators,[7] and the U.S. Supreme Court,[8] have expressed similar thoughts.

Statement of such general thoughts, however, does not always decide specific cases. The problem remains: Under what circumstances shall custom be binding for the future? Are all types of matters to be treated as "custom" for this purpose? What of the clash between two legitimate objectives: (1) the need for industrial stability, which is served by custom, and (2) the need for managerial freedom of action to operate the business efficiently?

Examination of many reported decisions suggests that there are no unanimously accepted standards for determining precisely under what circumstances unwritten practices and custom will be held binding by arbitrators, or for determining what matters may be the subject of such binding practice. Certainly the result reached in any given case may depend in part upon the thinking of the particular person who has been authorized by the parties to decide the case. However, it may be noted that in some of the cases cited above, and in other cases, certain considerations have been stressed.

---

[3]Coca-Cola Bottling Co., 9 LA 197, 198 (1947).
[4]Metal Specialty Co., 39 LA 1265, 1269 (1962).
[5]Esso Standard Oil Co., 16 LA 73, 74 (1951). In Beaunit Fibers, 49 LA 423, 424 (1967), Arbitrator McCoy emphasized the "under some circumstances" words of limitation.
[6]Phillips Petroleum Co., 24 LA 191, 194–195 (1955).
[7]See Arbitrator Mills in 53 LA 845, 848; Kates in 48 LA 1275, 1276; Koven in 47 LA 353, 355; Schmidt in 44 LA 467, 468; Horlacher in 43 LA 145, 148; E. Jones in 29 LA 372, 375; Prasow in 27 LA 6, 10; Dworkin in 24 LA 614, 618–619; Levinson in 23 LA 277, 280; Gorder in 20 LA 880, 883; Hale in 20 LA 818, 823; Wirtz in 20 LA 276, 280; Updegraff in 20 LA 243, 244; Talbott in 19 LA 628, 629; Marshall in 17 LA 105, 108; Gilden in 17 LA 81, 85; Whiting in 16 LA 115, 117; Hampton in 16 LA 59, 62.
[8]United Steelworkers v. Warrior & Gulf Navigation Co., 80 S.Ct. 1347, 1351–1352 (1960).

First, even assuming that a matter is such that it may otherwise be given "binding practice" effect as an implied term of the agreement, it will not be given that effect unless it is well established—strong proof of its existence will ordinarily be required.[9] Indeed, many arbitrators have recognized that, as stated by Arbitrator Jules J. Justin: "In the absence of a written agreement, 'past practice,' to be binding on both Parties, must be (1) unequivocal; (2) clearly enunciated and acted upon; (3) readily ascertainable over a reasonable period of time as a fixed, and established practice accepted by both Parties."[10] However, the mutual acceptance may be tacit—an implied mutual agreement—arising by inference from the circumstances.[11]

While another factor sometimes considered is whether the activity was instituted by bilateral action or only by the unilateral action of one party,[12] it would seem that the fact of unilateral establishment should not necessarily be given controlling weight.[13]

---

[9]See Arbitrator Beilstein in 77 LA 990, 993; Chapman in 75 LA 337, 341; Caraway in 72 LA 253, 256; Tsukiyama in 47 LA 781, 783; Seitz in 43 LA 322, 325; Gorsuch in 41 LA 105, 108; Davis in 39 LA 97, 99; Justin in 24 LA 753, 754; Updegraff in 20 LA 243, 244. The party alleging the existence of a binding practice has the burden of establishing it. See Arbitrator Duff in 75 LA 1216, 1219; Heinsz in 74 LA 50, 53; Ray in 48 LA 919, 922.

[10]Celanese Corp. of Am., 24 LA 168, 172 (1954). These three requirements (or similar requirements) have been recognized by Arbitrator Sass in 78 LA 766, 768–769; Cohen in 78 LA 241, 242; Griffith in 77 LA 689, 691; Richard in 77 LA 683, 688; Lieberman in 77 LA 545, 551; Curry in 77 LA 217, 218; McKenna in 77 LA 1, 7; McDonald in 76 LA 569, 571–572; Goldstein in 76 LA 403, 408; Shanker in 76 LA 10, 12; Mewhinney in 74 LA 5, 6; Greco in 73 LA 1146, 1147; High in 72 LA 1013, 1014; Gootnick in 72 LA 733, 736; Caraway in 72 LA 253, 256; Strasshofer in 71 LA 1269, 1273; Megley in 70 LA 925, 928; Blackmar in 70 LA 590, 593; Ross in 70 LA 470, 474; Fitzsimmons in 70 LA 116, 121; Simon in 69 LA 687, 692; Grassy in 69 LA 364, 368. For many earlier cases recognizing these or similar requirements, see p. 391 of the Third Edition of this book. In Great Atl. & Pac. Tea Co., 46 LA 372, 374 (1966), Arbitrator Israel Ben Scheiber stated that "Just as the proverbial solitary swallow does not make a spring or summer, so a past practice, to be binding, must be long-continued, well understood, and mutually concurred in by the parties." For other statements of criteria for a binding practice, see Arbitrator Johnson in 75 LA 1226, 1230; Bard in 75 LA 615, 621–622; Chapman in 75 LA 337, 341; Goodman in 72 LA 57, 61–62; Bognanno in 71 LA 544, 549; Leahy in 69 LA 1088, 1092; Hatcher in 69 LA 665, 670; Beckerman in 68 LA 229, 231. In Univac, 54 LA 48, 52 (1969), Arbitrator Marlin M. Volz stated that "Leniency by individual supervisors must be distinguished from mutual agreement or acquiescence by the contracting parties in a consistent course of repetitive action." Also see Arbitrator Kahn in 73 LA 949, 951. Where national policy of a federal agency employer governed a matter, local departure from that policy could not result in a binding practice. Immigration & Naturalization Serv., 77 LA 638, 643 (Weckstein, 1981), where higher management had been unaware of the local departure. Also concerning certain limitations upon the binding quality of past practice in the federal sector, see Arbitrator Wiggins in 74 LA 770, 774–775; Griffin in 70 LA 360, 364–365.

[11]See Arbitrator Levy in 76 LA 620, 623; Wood in 45 LA 881, 884; Jones in 44 LA 698, 700; Schmidt in 44 LA 467, 468; Updegraff in 20 LA 309, 311. Awareness of a practice is to be presumed from its long-established and widespread nature. Bethlehem Steel Co., 33 LA 374, 376 (Valtin, 1959). For a discussion of what a party should do to avoid being bound by a practice commenced by the other party, see Donaldson Co., 20 LA 826, 830–831 (Louisell, 1953).

[12]See Arbitrator Lubic in 71 LA 1031, 1033; McCoy in 49 LA 423, 424; Roberts in 48 LA 1166, 1168; Turkus in 47 LA 75, 78; Dugan in 46 LA 1007, 1008; Howlett in 42 LA 385, 388; Seinsheimer in 36 LA 166, 170; Wirtz in 20 LA 276, 280; Cahn in 17 LA 780, 783. Also see Mittenthal, "Past Practice and the Administration of Collective Bargaining Agreements," Arbitration and Public Policy, 30, 33 (1961).

[13]See Sterling Furniture Mfrs., 46 LA 705, 706 (Hanlon, 1966); Union Asbestos & Rubber Co., 39 LA 72, 75 (Volz, 1962), both holding a practice as to employee benefits to be binding though unilaterally instituted by the employer. In contrast, in some of the decisions cited elsewhere in this Chapter certain methods of operations unilaterally instituted by management, in the exercise of discretion in the performance of management functions, were held not to constitute binding practices. Thus, the critical consideration may be the subject matter of the practice rather than whether it was established by unilateral or bilateral action.

Where a practice is otherwise found to be binding, question may arise as to its scope. In this general regard, it appears reasonable that the underlying circumstances must be considered to give a practice its true dimensions: "A practice is no broader than the circumstances out of which it has arisen, although its scope can always be enlarged in the day-to-day administration of the agreement."[14]

The question remains as to what types of matters should be given "binding practice" status as an implied term of the agreement (assuming the practice is otherwise adequately established under standards such as those noted hereinabove). One arbitrator suggested that an established practice may be unilaterally discontinued if it involves a "gratuity," but that it is binding if it concerns a "working condition."[15] But another arbitrator doubted the validity of this test and suggested that perhaps the best test, though admittedly inexact, is that the usage, to achieve contractual status, must concern a "major condition of employment."[16]

The latter arbitrator cited Professors Archibald Cox and John T. Dunlop, who had urged that: "A collective bargaining agreement should be deemed, unless a contrary intention is manifest, to carry forward for its term the major terms and conditions of employment, not covered by the agreement, which prevailed when the agreement was executed."[17] As noted above, the "major condition of employment" test is inexact. From whose standpoint is something "major"? Where is the line to be drawn? Cox and Dunlop included as "major" such things as "basic wages, seniority, and pensions," but they were apparently willing to exclude such matters as job content, work loads, and incentive systems.[18]

The line between practices which are binding and those which are not may well be drawn on the basis of whether the matter involves methods of operation or direction of the working force, or whether it involves a "benefit" of peculiar personal value to the employees (though also involving the employer's purse).

Arbitrators are often hesitant to permit unwritten past practice or methods of doing things to restrict the exercise of legitimate functions of management. For example, such hesitance was evidenced by Arbitrator Whitley P. McCoy:

"But caution must be exercised in reading into contracts implied terms, lest arbitrators start re-making the contracts which the parties have themselves made. The mere failure of the Company, over a long

---

[14]Mittenthal, "Past Practice and the Administration of Collective Bargaining Agreements," Arbitration and Public Policy, 30, 32–33 (1961). Also see Arbitrator Rollo in 72 LA 1279, 1284; Bode in 69 LA 217, 221.

[15]Fawick Airflex Co., 11 LA 666, 668–669 (Cornsweet, 1948).

[16]Phillips Petroleum Co., 24 LA 191, 194 (Merrill, 1955). Other arbitrators have utilized some type of major-minor test: Mueller in 68 LA 584, 590; Koven in 47 LA 353, 356; Anrod in 45 LA 34, 37–38; Reynard in 25 LA 611, 613; Updegraff in 20 LA 309, 311; Talbott in 19 LA 628, 629. Also see Flagler in 72 LA 479, 485.

[17]Cox & Dunlop, "The Duty to Bargain Collectively During the Term of an Existing Agreement," 63 Harv. L. Rev. 1097, 1116–1117 (1950).

[18]Id. at 1118.

period of time, to exercise a legitimate function of management, is not a surrender of the right to start exercising such right. If a Company had never, in 15 years and under 15 contracts, disciplined an employee for tardiness, could it thereby be contended that the Company could not decide to institute a reasonable system of penalties for tardiness? Mere non-use of a right does not entail a loss of it."[19]

One of the most cogent and provocative statements published regarding the binding force of custom was that of Umpire Harry Shulman, in a case involving operating methods and direction of the working force (assignment of work), wherein he urged that past practice not be "enshrined without carefully thought out and articulated limitations":

"A practice, whether or not fully stated in writing, may be the result of an agreement or mutual understanding. And in some industries there are contractual provisions requiring the continuance of unnamed practices in existence at the execution of the collective agreement. (There are no such provisions in the Ford Agreement or in those of the automobile industry generally.) A practice thus based on mutual agreement may be subject to change only by mutual agreement. Its binding quality is due, however, not to the fact that it is past practice but rather to the agreement in which it is based.

"But there are other practices which are not the result of joint determination at all. They may be mere happenstance, that is, methods that developed without design or deliberation. Or they may be choices by Management in the exercise of managerial discretion as to the convenient methods at the time. In such cases there is no thought of obligation or commitment for the future. Such practices are merely present ways, not prescribed ways, of doing things. The relevant item of significance is not the nature of the particular method but the managerial freedom with respect to it. Being the product of managerial determination in its permitted discretion such practices are, in the absence of contractual provision to the contrary, subject to change in the same discretion. The law and the policy of collective bargaining may well require that the employer inform the Union and that he be ready to discuss the matter with it on request. But there is no requirement of mutual agreement as a condition precedent to a change of practice of this character.

"A contrary holding would place past practice on a par with written agreement and create the anomaly that, while the parties expend great energy and time in negotiating the details of the Agreement, they unknowingly and unintentionally commit themselves to unstated and perhaps more important matters which in the future may be found to have been past practice. The contrary holding would also raise other questions very difficult to answer. For example, what is properly a subject of a practice? Would the long time use of a wheelbarrow become a practice not to be changed by the substitution of four-wheeled buggies drawn by a tractor? Or would the long time use of single drill presses be a practice prohibiting the introduction of multiple drill presses? Such restraints on technological change are alien to the automobile industry. Yet such might be the restraints, if past practice were enshrined without

[19]Esso Standard Oil Co., 16 LA 73, 74 (1951). Citing this case with clear approval, see Arbitrator Mewhinney in 80 LA 267, 269; Abrams in 78 LA 404, 408; Erbs in 77 LA 626, 632; Roberts in 74 LA 537, 542; Babiskin in 74 LA 312, 315; Goodman in 73 LA 207, 212; Cohen in 68 LA 396, 399; Turkus in 52 LA 493, 496; Ray in 43 LA 395, 399. Agreeing that mere nonuse of a right does not entail its loss, see Chandler in 78 LA 537, 540.

carefully thought out and articulated limitations. Again, when is a practice? How frequently and over how long a period must something be done before it is to be called a practice with the consequences claimed? And how is the existence of the past practice to be determined in the light of the very conflicting testimony that is common in such cases? The Union's witnesses remember only the occasions on which the work was done in the manner they urge. Supervision remembers the occasions on which the work was done otherwise. Each remembers details the other does not; each is surprised at the other's perversity; and both forget or omit important circumstances. Rarely is alleged past practice clear, detailed and undisputed; commonly, inquiry into past practice of the type that is not the result of joint determination or agreement produces immersion in a bog of contradictions, fragments, doubts, and one-sided views. All this is not to say that past practice may not be important and even decisive in applying provisions of the Agreement. The discussion is addressed to the different claim that, apart from any basis in the Agreement, a method of operation or assignment employed in the past may not be changed except by mutual agreement."[20]

Statements by numerous other arbitrators reflect lines of thought similar to the underlying viewpoint of the McCoy and Shulman statements quoted hereinabove.[21]

Arbitrators frequently (but not always) have recognized wide authority in management to control methods of operation and to direct the working forces, which authority includes the right without penalty to make changes *if these do not violate some right of the employees under the written contract.* If a given change or the method of putting it into effect does result in the violation of some contractual right of identified employees, then the arbitrator can be expected to award compensation to the employees for the loss sustained, even if he does not take the further step of ordering management to revert to the prior practice.

Numerous cases involving the authority of management to control methods of operation and to direct the working forces are collected in Chapter 13, topics on Control of Quality Standards, Control of Operation Methods (some changes in operation methods may require new rates of pay for jobs affected by the change), Job and Classification Control, Scheduling Work, Determination of Size of Crews, and other such topics. At this point, however, some specific examples may be noted.

---

[20]Ford Motor Co., 19 LA 237, 241–242 (1952). Citing this Shulman statement with clear approval, see Arbitrator Abrams in 80 LA 1267, 1273; Guenther in 79 LA 430, 432; R. Roberts in 78 LA 729, 736; Hannan in 76 LA 254, 256; Shanker in 75 LA 10, 12; Konvitz in 75 LA 548, 550; Goodman in 73 LA 207, 212; Teple in 72 LA 229, 233; Mewhinney in 71 LA 852, 855; Anderson in 70 LA 81, 84; Cohen in 68 LA 396, 400; Updegraff in 54 LA 869, 871; Solomon in 51 LA 1102, 1107; Eyraud in 49 LA 654, 658; Dugan in 46 LA 1007, 1008; Mittenthal in 46 LA 335, 337, and in 39 LA 65, 67; Turkus in 44 LA 1219, 1222; Ray in 43 LA 395, 399; Scheiber in 42 LA 965, 970–971; Donaldson in 37 LA 528, 531. For additional discussion of this subject, see Shulman, "Reason, Contract, and Law in Labor Relations," 68 Harv. L. Rev. 999, 1011–1013 (1955), reprinted in Management Rights and the Arbitration Process, 169, 184–188 (BNA Books, 1956).

[21]See arbitrators cited in the two preceding footnotes, and see Arbitrator Gibson in 77 LA 876, 880; Kiok in 75 LA 16, 18; Leahy in 73 LA 418, 421; Simon in 72 LA 1115, 1123; Volz in 68 LA 51, 53; Cahn in 53 LA 809, 810; T. Roberts in 48 LA 1166, 1168; Turkus in 47 LA 75, 78; Summers in 45 LA 1149, 1151; Updegraff in 45 LA 557, 557–558; Howlett in 42 LA 385, 388. But see Cahn in 51 LA 705, 706.

For instance, in some cases past practice has not operated to prevent management from changing work schedules,[22] reassigning work,[23] determining the number of workers needed on a job,[24] adding or eliminating job duties within reasonable limits,[25] eliminating a job,[26] discontinuing a particular line of business services or activity,[27] not filling a temporary vacancy,[28] discontinuing collateral information on seniority lists,[29] changing the method of using work-progress time cards,[30] using a formal instead of informal method of determining skill and ability of employees,[31] rotating certain employees between two operating units to familiarize them with both operations,[32] changing payday to Friday in order to reduce Friday absenteeism,[33] determining the frequency of holding safety meetings,[34] or from making other changes in methods of operation or in the direction of the working forces.[35] But if past practice *supports* management's actions in such matters, it will provide additional reason for upholding management.[36]

In permitting unilateral change by management, arbitrators sometimes have pointed out that the matter may be subject to negotiations if requested by the union; but, if any such negotiations fail to produce agreement, management may exercise its unilateral judgment in making or continuing the change.[37]

---

[22]See Arbitrator Leahy in 73 LA 418, 421; Volz in 68 LA 51, 53; Solomon in 51 LA 1102, 1110; Hebert in 44 LA 226, 233; Howlett in 42 LA 25, 30; Tsukiyama in 41 LA 1115, 1116–1117; Reid in 27 LA 123, 125; Ryder in 24 LA 496, 499–500; McCoy in 16 LA 73, 74–75. Also see McKay in 77 LA 23, 26–27. Cf., Meyers in 39 LA 93, 95–96.

[23]See Arbitrator O'Connell in 79 LA 272, 275–276; Daniel in 77 LA 393, 395; Goodman in 73 LA 207, 215; Kossoff in 70 LA 855, 859; Shister in 70 LA 110, 113; Cox in 68 LA 864, 866–867; Daugherty in 49 LA 234, 236–237; Kesselman in 45 LA 201, 206; Turkus in 44 LA 1219, 1224; Larkin in 43 LA 1064, 1066; Mittenthal in 39 LA 65, 67–68; Beatty in 35 LA 637, 640; Abernethy in 35 LA 353, 356; Blair in 22 LA 701, 703; Shulman in 19 LA 237, 240–242. Cf., Myers in 23 LA 776, 778–779. Essentially contra, Buchanan in 71 LA 48, 54.

[24]See Arbitrator Mittenthal in 42 LA 1188, 1190–1191; Updegraff in 30 LA 115, 117, and in 18 LA 827, 830–831; Marshall in 29 LA 687, 692–693. Also see Wright in 69 LA 315, 319–320.

[25]See Arbitrator McDaniel in 54 LA 155, 158; Kelliher in 43 LA 1006, 1009–1010; Reynard in 25 LA 611, 613–614; Klamon in 22 LA 336, 342–343, 351; Updegraff in 20 LA 890, 891, and in 18 LA 320, 322–323. Cf., Ellmann in 67 LA 368, 371.

[26]See Arbitrator Warns in 29 LA 324, 326–328, and in 26 LA 155, 160; Warren in 19 LA 283, 286–287.

[27]Detroit Edison Co., 43 LA 193, 209 (Smith, 1964).

[28]Celotex Corp., 43 LA 395, 399–400 (Ray, 1964).

[29]International Harvester Co., 22 LA 191, 192 (Platt, 1954).

[30]W.O. Larson Foundry Co., 42 LA 1286, 1292 (Kates, 1964).

[31]Lockheed Aircraft Corp., 25 LA 748, 751–752 (Williams, 1956). Also see Arbitrator Garrett in 15 LA 840, 841–842.

[32]Mathieson Chem. Corp., 18 LA 620, 624–625 (Smith, 1952). But as to the frequency of shift rotation, see Arbitrator Marshall in 34 LA 345, 349–350.

[33]Glamorgan Pipe & Foundry Co., 46 LA 1007, 1008 (Dugan, 1966).

[34]Ingalls Shipbuilding Corp., 49 LA 654, 657–658 (Eyraud, 1967).

[35]See Arbitrator Keenan in 76 LA 827, 833–834; Morgan in 73 LA 837, 840; Whyte in 72 LA 1047, 1050; Eagle in 70 LA 938, 940; Roberts in 70 LA 278, 281–282; Karlins in 67 LA 103, 107.

[36]See Arbitrator Hauck in 73 LA 990, 991–992; Snyder in 54 LA 1159, 1162; Holly in 39 LA 496, 500; Reynard in 25 LA 611, 613–614; Whiting in 16 LA 115, 117. Also see Berger in 68 LA 510, 513; McKenna in 48 LA 941, 949.

[37]See Arbitrator Seidman in 72 LA 594, 596–597; Sharnoff in 69 LA 1099, 1101; Hepburn in 28 LA 467, 467–468; Williams in 25 LA 748, 751–752; Updegraff in 7 LA 943, 945; Whiting in 7 LA 183, 187. It has been suggested also that even concerning changes which management may not be strictly required to discuss, discussion may be "the better practice." Bethlehem Steel Co., 16 LA 68, 70 (Feinberg, 1950). Also see Chamberlain & Kuhn, Collective Bargaining, 2d Ed., 135–136 (1965); Chamberlain, "Management's Reserved Rights," Management Rights and the Arbitration Process, 118, 145–147 (BNA Books, 1956).

In contrast to the above-indicated freedom of management to make changes in the exercise of basic management functions, arbitrators have often ruled custom to be binding where it involved a "benefit" of peculiar personal value to the employees. These cases generally did not involve methods of operation or control of the working force (except perhaps indirectly). Thus, where the benefit was supported by established custom, management was not permitted to discontinue (or in some cases to change) the following "benefits" or "working conditions": wash-up periods,[38] lunch period arrangements,[39] paid work breaks,[40] free coffee or free meals,[41] utilities at discount or nominal charge,[42] bonuses,[43] various other monetary benefits or allowances,[44] maternity leaves of absence,[45] notice to union before discharge for dishonesty is effected,[46] special rights for senior employees,[47] and a wide variety of other "benefits" or "working conditions."[48] In some cases, however, management has been upheld in discontinuing or reducing customary employee benefits.[49] In some of these cases the company in giving the benefit had emphasized that it

---

[38]See Arbitrator Holly in 51 LA 549, 551; Duff in 45 LA 277, 279; Anrod in 40 LA 1329, 1331–1332; Killingsworth in 35 LA 929, 930–931; Wirtz in 20 LA 276, 280; Davey in 18 LA 276, 278. Cf., Davey in 49 LA 773, 783–784.

[39]See Arbitrator Bognanno in 71 LA 544, 550; Kates in 51 LA 490, 493–494; Teple in 40 LA 13, 17; Klamon in 39 LA 964, 974–975; Murphy in 32 LA 228, 233; Wagner in 30 LA 35, 38; Dworkin in 24 LA 614, 619; McCoy in 3 LA 137, 138. Cf., Kiok in 75 LA 16, 18; Marshall in 54 LA 311, 314; McIntosh in 33 LA 137, 138–139.

[40]See Formica Corp., 44 LA 467, 468 (Schmidt, 1965); Ingalls Iron Works Co., 32 LA 960, 961 (Reid, 1959).

[41]See Arbitrator Grether in 76 LA 446, 450; Heneman in 72 LA 1302, 1307; Christopher in 60 LA 838, 842; Jones in 50 LA 48, 51–52; Wolf in 44 LA 107, 110; Handsaker in 39 LA 1188, 1191; Scheiber in 37 LA 381, 383. Regarding restaurant meals versus TV dinners or box lunches, see Arbitrator Jones in 73 LA 107, 110; Dolson in 62 LA 96, 101–102.

[42]Central Ill. Pub. Serv. Co., 42 LA 1133, 1149–1150 (Willingham, 1964); Phillips Petroleum Co., 24 LA 191, 195 (Merrill, 1955).

[43]See cases cited in Chapter 13, topic entitled "Bonuses," where cases permitting the discontinuance of bonuses are also cited.

[44]See Arbitrator Hauck in 74 LA 459, 467–468 (low rental housing); Potter in 72 LA 534, 536 (right to work on employee's birthday falling on a holiday and thus earn double pay); Flagler in 72 LA 479, 485 (receipt of 25 shares of stock after 25 years of service); Morris in 72 LA 333, 336 (commercial driver's license paid for by employer); LeWinter in 72 LA 102, 107 (paid insurance premiums during layoff); Ross in 70 LA 470, 475 (payment of employee's salary during workers' compensation waiting period); Ruben in 69 LA 944, 955–956 (holiday pay); Burns in 68 LA 855, 858 (paid committee time). For earlier cases involving other benefits, see p. 398 of the Third Edition of this book.

[45]Northland Greyhound Lines, 23 LA 277, 280 (Levinson, 1954).

[46]Coca-Cola Bottling Co., 9 LA 197, 198 (Jacobs, 1947).

[47]International Minerals & Chems. Corp., 36 LA 92, 95 (Sanders, 1960); Fruehauf Trailer Co., 29 LA 372, 375 (Jones, 1957).

[48]See Arbitrator Bowles in 76 LA 1273, 1277–1278 (time off for union executive board meetings); McCrary in 76 LA 333, 335 (assistance in starting car in cold weather); Murphy in 74 LA 475, 481 (use of chewing tobacco); Chandler in 73 LA 174, 177 (employee option as to form of payment for overtime); Martin in 72 LA 1285, 1289–1290 (use of progressive discipline); Lynch in 71 LA 929, 931 (use of personal coffee pots and radios on company premises); Fields in 68 LA 1000, 1005–1006 (holiday on Inauguration Day); Seidenberg in 66 LA 399, 403 (paid leave immediately prior to retirement). For earlier cases involving other benefits, see p. 398 of the Third Edition of this book.

[49]See Arbitrator Atleson in 70 LA 699, 706–707; Cohen in 68 LA 396, 401; Render in 67 LA 493, 496; Teple in 53 LA 405, 409; Roberts in 48 LA 1166, 1168; Stein in 42 LA 765, 766; Hilpert in 38 LA 267, 268–269; Volz in 37 LA 635, 637–638; McDermott in 36 LA 220, 222; Fallon in 34 LA 59, 62; Kleinsorge in 33 LA 157, 161–164; Reid in 32 LA 960 at 960; Schmidt in 30 LA 593, 595–598; Lynch in 26 LA 749, 750–751; Morris in 24 LA 745, 747–748; Louisell in 20 LA 826, 829–831; Giardino in 19 LA 421, 422; Naggi in 10 LA 804, 805.

was to be a gratuity only and not a part of the wage structure, or there was some special justification for discontinuing the benefit.

We have noted that where custom has been enforced, the element of "mutuality" has usually been supplied by implication—that is, there has been "implied mutual agreement." In this regard, existing employee benefits usually affect all or at least sizable groups of employees, and thus are likely to be in the thoughts of union and company negotiators. It may reasonably be assumed that the parties in shaping bargaining demands as to wages and other employee benefits do so with silent recognition of existing unwritten benefits and favorable working conditions. This accepted, such matters may well be called "major" (for those who would apply a "major-minor" test).

It may be less plausible to assume that such bargaining demands are shaped with any comparable silent thought as to existing practices regarding methods of operation and direction of the working force— matters legitimately falling within the fundamental areas of basic management responsibility.

In the final analysis, management in most cases is not really oppressed when it is required to continue customary benefits for the remainder of the contract term. Management itself, either unilaterally or by mutual decision, initially agreed to grant the benefits in most cases. In negotiating the collective bargaining agreement management, because of existing benefits, may very well have been faced with tempered wage demands by the employees. On the other hand, in most instances, it does not oppress the employees to deny continuance of established methods of operation or established practice regarding direction of the working force. Management freedom of action in the latter matters, though sometimes considered unjustified by the workers directly affected (frequently a small number), is essential for efficient and progressive operation of the enterprise, and this serves the long-run interests of all the employees as well as management.[50]

---

[50]Illustrating that good faith changes by management in methods of operation or in the direction of the working force may be upheld notwithstanding express recognition that the change would result in a loss of wages or benefits by some employees, see Arbitrator Konovitz in 75 LA 548, 550; Goodman in 73 LA 207, 215; Teple in 68 LA 1347, 1351–1352; Volz in 54 LA 52, 55–56; Doyle in 52 LA 440, 443, 445 (stating that the "fact that the Company's basic motive is economy is not evidence of bad faith"); Solomon in 51 LA 1102, 1107–1108; Turkus in 44 LA 1219, 1223. However, where Arbitrator Leo Weiss found that the "only reason" for a change in work assignments was to avoid payment of overtime which by 20-year practice had been a "substantial segment" of employee paychecks, he decided against the employer on the basis that "the economic benefit to the employees outweighs the Company's interest in changing its method of operation." Liquid Air, 73 LA 1200, 1203–1205 (1979), where he stated in regard to other past practice cases that "often the result can be explained by a weighing of the gravity of the Company's interest in making the change against the gravity of the employees' interest in retaining the traditional practice." In the latter regard, Arbitrator Marshall J. Seidman denied a grievance in Anheuser-Busch, 72 LA 594, 597 (1979), where he found that the employer's action in lowering the temperature in the beer storage area "was dictated by marketing conditions"; the change did not adversely affect the health or safety of employees, but "it inconvenienced the employees in requiring them to purchase extra clothing and to work in a less desirable environment"; the change "assured their continued employment during a period that usually resulted in layoffs"; and "On the whole it therefore had a beneficial rather than a deleterious effect on their economy."

The above discussion suggests a test of "employee benefits" versus "basic management functions," with which test many reported arbitration awards are compatible.[51] Moreover, some of the awards which appear at first glance to be contrary to this test may conform to it upon closer analysis, the award being based in fact upon some clause of the written contract. The test gives the employees the benefit of the doubt as to certain matters and management is given the benefit of the doubt as to others. From this standpoint, too, the test may be deemed "fair" or "just."

While the above discussion provides some general guides for predicting the extent to which unwritten practice and custom will be enforced by arbitrators, variations will often result from the peculiar facts and circumstances of the individual cases as well as from the thinking of the particular arbitrator making the ruling. It is entirely possible that under very similar circumstances one arbitrator might hold established practice subject to change or discontinuance during the term of the contract only by mutual agreement, but a second arbitrator might hold it subject to unilateral change or discontinuance at any time even without negotiations. Taking an intermediate approach, a third arbitrator might hold the practice subject to unilateral change or discontinuance during the term of the contract, but only after negotiations have failed to produce agreement.[52]

Regulation, Modification, or Termination of Practice as Implied Term of Contract

In a number of cases arbitrators have held a given practice to be binding on management but at the same time have upheld the right of management to regulate and police it against abuse.[53] For example, where management imposed a limitation as to how often employees could take breaks to use the company vending machine, Arbitrator Marlin M. Volz upheld the limitation with the following explanation:

"[I]nherent in every practice is the principle that it is not to be abused and that, if it is, reasonable corrective action may be taken. It can not be

---

[51]In some cases the arbitrator has spoken expressly in terms of this distinction between employee benefits and basic management functions as concerns the binding status of practice. See Arbitrator Mittleman in 79 LA 449, 457–459; Lieberman in 77 LA 545, 551; Ruben in 76 LA 911, 914; Keenan in 76 LA 827, 833–834; Hauck in 74 LA 459, 466–467; Ross in 74 LA 92, 95; Goldberg in 73 LA 892, 895–896; Maniscalco in 73 LA 391, 395; Volz in 54 LA 52, 55–56, and in 39 LA 72, 75; Witney in 51 LA 813, 818–819; Eyraud in 49 LA 654, 657–658; Kates in 48 LA 1275, 1276, and in 44 LA 1217, 1218; Warns in 66–1 ARB ¶8039, p. 3129; Summers in 45 LA 1149, 1151; Kennedy in 45 LA 353, 355; Turkus in 44 LA 1219, 1223–1224; Ray in 43 LA 395, 399–400; Rubin in 42 LA 833, 835–837; Tsukiyama in 41 LA 1115, 1116–1117; Anrod in 40 LA 1329, 1331–1332; Morvant in 39 LA 1020, 1023.

[52]See Ryan Aeronautical Co., 17 LA 395, 398–399 (Komaroff, 1951).

[53]See Arbitrator McCandless in 75 LA 847, 849; Murphy in 74 LA 475, 481; Abrams in 72 LA 470, 475; Ross in 70 LA 470, 475; Edes in 69 LA 779, 782; Miller in 50 LA 974, 976; Kates in 48 LA 1275, 1276, and in 44 LA 1217, 1218; Schmidt in 44 LA 467, 468; Rubin in 42 LA 833, 835–837; Rohman in 40 LA 1217, 1221; Volz in 39 LA 1265, 1269; McIntosh in 33 LA 860, 861–862. Abuse of a practice was one of the factors justifying the termination of the practice by the employer in Kentile Floors, Inc., 55 LA 808, 813 (Cyrol, 1970). Also see Lawson-United Feldspar & Mineral Co., 76 LRRM 1588 (NLRB, 1971).

inferred that the other party has accepted or acquiesced in the excesses constituting the abuse so as to make them binding. The employees, no less than management, are under a duty to act reasonably. Both must cooperate and meet the other halfway in following sound industrial practices which will enable the plant to be operated efficiently for the ultimate benefit of the men as well as the Company."[54]

Also, the mere fact that a given employee-benefit practice is binding does not necessarily mean that the administrative arrangements by which the company has provided the benefit are frozen.[55] Furthermore, in two cases management was permitted to provide substitute parking facilities for employees when the established benefit (parking near work situs) and legitimate management interests came into conflict.[56]

Arbitrators have recognized that an otherwise binding practice may be modified or eliminated where the underlying basis for the practice has changed.[57] The rule was elaborated by Arbitrator Sidney L. Cahn:

"It must be stated as a general proposition that, absent language in a collective bargaining agreement expressly or impliedly to the contrary, once the conditions upon which a past practice has been based are changed or eliminated, the practice may no longer be given effect."[58]

Thus, a 25-year practice of allowing painters 10 minutes overtime to clean their brushes could be unilaterally discontinued by management when it eliminated the congestion problem which had been the underlying reason for the practice.[59]

Even absent any such change in the underlying basis of a practice, an impressive line of arbitral thought holds that a practice which is

---

[54]Metal Specialty Co., 39 LA 1265, 1269 (1962).

[55]Bethlehem Steel Corp., 50 LA 202, 205 (Strongin, 1968), holding that the company could relocate the place of giving medical services by closing a branch dispensary and centralizing all services in one dispensary. For other indications of management control over arrangements in providing employee benefits, see Arbitrator Walker in 55 LA 294, 301–302 (company could reposition vending machines and require employees to use only certain ones); Florey in 48 LA 55, 57 (practice required company to make food service available, but company could decide "how," providing the arrangement be reasonable).

[56]Jervis B. Webb Co., 52 LA 1314, 1315 (Holly, 1969); Beaunit Fibers, 49 LA 423, 424–425 (McCoy, 1967). Exceptions to the requirements of past practice may be justified by special circumstances. See Sterling Brewers, 53 LA 1078, 1087 (Witney, 1969), where the arbitrator refused to give "slavish adherence" to past practice under the circumstances.

[57]See Arbitrator Duff in 76 LA 903, 908; Silver in 75 LA 988, 991; Whyte in 72 LA 1047, 1050; Fitzsimmons in 70 LA 116, 121; Mueller in 68 LA 584, 590; McDermott in 68 LA 547, 553 ("there were changes that affected one of the conditions giving rise to the past practice" and management accordingly could "make changes in the past practice to the extent necessary to meet the changed conditions"); Bloch in 67 LA 989, 992; Kates in 51 LA 490, 493; Crawford in 48 LA 1239, 1242–1243; Kelliher in 48 LA 1000, 1002; Mullin in 47 LA 848, 852–853; Kahn in 42 LA 148, 152; Strong in 41 LA 1038, 1041; Mittenthal in 39 LA 65, 67; Cahn in 34 LA 99, 100. In Saginaw Mining Co., 76 LA 911, 915 (1981), Arbitrator Alan M. Ruben held that a practice of giving Christmas hams could be discontinued during unprofitable years where he found that the practice grew out of and was dependent upon profitable operations. The "maintenance of local working conditions" provisions in steel industry agreements are accompanied by provisions which specifically permit changes by management if the basis for the existence of the local working condition is changed or eliminated. See Arbitrator Seward in 77 LA 372, 374; Sharnoff in 69 LA 1099, 1101; Garrett in 44 LA 317, 320–321, and in 33 LA 394, 396, 399; Blair in 40 LA 239, 240; Valtin in 36 LA 394, 396.

[58]Gulf Oil Co., 34 LA 99, 100 (1959).

[59]Newport News Shipbuilding & Drydock Co., 48 LA 1239, 1242–1243 (Crawford, 1967).

not subject to unilateral termination during the term of the collective
agreement is subject to termination at the end of said term by giving
due notice of intent not to carry the practice over to the next agreement; after being so notified the other party must have the practice
written into the agreement to prevent its discontinuance.[60] Arbitrator
Richard Mittenthal explained:

> "Consider first a practice which is, apart from any basis in the
> agreement, an enforceable condition of employment on the theory that
> the agreement subsumes the continuance of existing conditions. Such a
> practice cannot be unilaterally changed during the life of the agreement.
> For * * * if a practice is not discussed during negotiations most of us are
> likely to infer that the agreement was executed on the assumption that
> the practice would remain in effect.
>
> "That inference is based largely on the parties' acquiescence in the
> practice. If either side should, during the negotiation of a later agree-
> ment, object to the continuance of this practice, it could not be inferred
> from the signing of a new agreement that the parties intended the
> practice to remain in force. Without their acquiescence, the practice
> would no longer be a binding condition of employment. In face of a timely
> repudiation of a practice by one party, the other must have the practice
> written into the agreement if it is to continue to be binding."[61]

Another possible basis for upholding the refusal to continue a
practice is a finding that any binding status of the practice ended

---

[60]See Arbitrator Feldman in 79 LA 1333, 1336; Hauck in 74 LA 459, 467; Lubic in 71 LA
1031, 1033; Rauch in 71 LA 61, 63; Jones in 50 LA 48, 51; Guild in 49 LA 94, 96; Dunau in 43 LA
661, 662–664; Koretz in 40 LA 235, 238; Stutz in 14 LA 951, 952–953; Meltzer, "Ruminations
About Ideology, Law, and Labor Arbitration," Proceedings of the 20th Annual Meeting of NAA,
1, 35–36 (BNA Books, 1967); Mittenthal, "Past Practice and the Administration of Collective
Bargaining Agreements," Proceedings of the 14th Annual Meeting of NAA, 30, 56–57 (BNA
Books, 1961). Also see Singer in 80 LA 950, 956–957; Goodman in 72 LA 57, 62-63; Killingsworth
in 35 LA 929, 931; McKelvey in 35 LA 602, 606. But see Bernstein in 48 LA 641, 643–647. For
NLRB decisions not requiring mutual assent for the discontinuance of a practice after giving due
notice of intent not to carry it over to the next agreement, see City Hosp., 97 LRRM 1125, 1126
(NLRB, 1978), where the union had notice of proposed changes and failed to make a timely
request for bargaining; Lee Deane Prods., Inc., 181 NLRB 1047 (1970), where there was extensive bargaining before management discontinued the practice. In Aeronca, Inc., 105 LRRM 1541,
1544 (NLRB, 1980), the NLRB said that "an employer is not required to forgo needed changes,
but it must first notify and bargain with the Union." On review, the Court of Appeals held that
the NLRB was not warranted in finding that the employer violated the Act when it discontinued
its past practice of giving Christmas turkeys, the court finding that bargaining on the matter had
been waived. Aeronca, Inc. v. NLRB, 107 LRRM 2687 (CA 4, 1981). Also see Torrington Co. v.
Metal Prods. Workers, 362 F.2d 677 (CA 2, 1966). There may or may not be a statutory duty to
bargain on the discontinuance of a practice. For instance, contrast Benchmark Indus., Inc., 116
LRRM 1032 (NLRB, 1984), and Peerless Food Prods., 98 LRRM 1182 (NLRB, 1978), with NLRB
v. Pepsi-Cola Distrib. Co., 107 LRRM 2252 (CA 6, 1981), and Beacon Journal Publishing Co., 164
NLRB 734 (1967). On the question of whether it is an arbitrator's function to decide whether any
statutory duty to bargain has been violated, see Chapter 10, subtopic entitled "The NLRA, the
Arbitrator, and the NLRB." For general discussion of the duty to bargain, see Chapter 13,
subtopics entitled "The Duty to Bargain: Right of Unilateral Action"; "Duration of Limitation on
Unilateral Action: Contract Limitation v. Statutory Duty to Bargain."

[61]Mittenthal, "Past Practice and the Administration of Collective Bargaining Agreements,"
Proceedings of the 14th Annual Meeting of NAA, 30, 56 (BNA Books, 1961). In contrast,
repudiation of a practice which gives meaning to ambiguous language in the written agreement
would not be significant—the effect of this kind of practice can be terminated only by rewriting
the language. Ibid. Similarly, a practice could not be unilaterally terminated where to do so
would defeat rights under a newly adopted contract provision which was premised upon the
practice. Kroger Co., 36 LA 129, 130–131 (Updegraff, 1960).

through the give and take of bargaining.[62] Then, too, the termination of a practice may be based upon its gradual discontinuance over a period of time.[63]

Contract Clauses Regarding Custom

The status of unwritten practice and custom may be dealt with specifically in the written agreement. All binding force of customary practices may be eliminated *if* the contract language is quite strong. Thus, even where a bonus practice was the product of negotiations between company and union and had been paid for several years (but where it was not written into the contract) it could be unilaterally discontinued by the employer since the written contract provided:

> "This contract represents complete collective bargaining and full agreement by the parties in respect to rates of pay, wages, hours of employment or other conditions of employment which shall prevail during the term hereof and any matters or subjects not herein covered have been satisfactorily adjusted, compromised or waived by the parties for the life of this agreement."[64]

But a weaker clause, stating that "this contract expresses the entire agreement between the parties," was held to eliminate automatically only those practices which conflicted with the contract's terms, since practices, the arbitrator said, are not necessarily matters for agreement.[65]

Though a contract provided that it "cancels all previous Agreements, both written and oral, and constitutes the entire Agreement between the parties," an arbitrator declared that the provision "has no magical dissolving effect upon practices or customs which are continued in fact unabated and which span successive contract periods."[66]

---

[62]See Arbitrator Kelliher in 54 LA 647, 648; Roberts in 50 LA 125, 127–128; Gundermann in 39 LA 1270, 1273. Also see Simon in 69 LA 687, 696 (a practice could be terminated by management "in view of the fact that the vehicle upon which past practice was based was done away with by the parties in hard-nosed negotiations at the insistence of the Union"); Stouffer in 45 LA 470, 475. Cf., Cohen in 70 LA 369, 375 (new contract clause did not terminate a practice by inference where the proponent of the clause failed to state in negotiations that a collateral effect would be discontinuance of the practice). On the other hand, the binding effect of a practice may be confirmed as a result of negotiations. See Leeds & Northrup Co. v. NLRB, 67 LRRM 2793 (CA 3, 1968), where the union had reduced its demands because management withdrew its proposal to modify a practice.

[63]See Bethlehem Steel Co., 37 LA 956, 958 (Seward, 1961). But a practice will not be deemed to have been changed or eliminated merely by a single unprotested departure from the practice. Bethlehem Steel Corp., 48 LA 1205, 1208 (Seward, 1967).

[64]Bassick Co., 26 LA 627, 630 (Kheel, 1956). Also see Arbitrator Cabe in 68 LA 94, 98; Autrey in 53 LA 1317, 1319–1320; Dworkin in 44 LA 630, 634; Klein in 42 LA 165, 168; Larkin in 36 LA 160, 162; Edes in 21 LA 398, 400.

[65]American Seating Co., 16 LA 115, 116–117 (Whiting, 1951). Also see Arbitrator Abrams in 72 LA 470, 474–475; Teple in 53 LA 405, 407; Murphy in 32 LA 228, 233. Cf., Lewis in 53 LA 1024, 1027.

[66]Fruehauf Trailer Co., 29 LA 372, 374–375 (Jones, 1957). Also see Arbitrator Kates in 52 LA 1146, 1150; Duff in 50 LA 417, 421. Cf., Giardino in 19 LA 421, 423.

Nor would such a provision negate practices that cast light upon ambiguous contract language.[67]

Some collective agreements contain clauses designed to insure continuance of certain established practices or local working conditions.[68] Of course, under such clauses the question often arises as to when a practice or local working condition exists.[69]

Where a letter of agreement on local practices specifically listed certain practices to be continued, an arbitrator ruled that the omission of other practices from the list did not imply that they could be unilaterally eliminated; rather, the effect of the list was to eliminate need for proof as to the existence of the practices listed. Other usages were not annulled without explicit language supporting their termination.[70] However, where other parties similarly listed certain practices to be continued, another arbitrator upheld the employer's unilateral termination of an unlisted practice.[71]

"A general 'catch-all' provision, designed to freeze general working conditions, cannot be construed to nullify an express provision of the contract."[72] Thus, such a clause was held not to require the employer to continue a customary paid holiday the day before Christmas since the contract specifically listed paid holidays and Christmas Eve was not on the list. The general "custom" clause could not "expand and broaden an already specific provision."[73] Furthermore, such a clause has been construed to refer to such things as employee benefits, and not to restrict basic management functions absent clear indication of such intent.[74]

The agreement may provide that if the employer changes or eliminates established practices, he shall, upon challenge through the grievance procedure, bear the burden to "justify" his action.[75] In one

---

[67]See Edmont Wilson, 54 LA 686, 688 (Nichols, 1970); Kelsey-Hayes Co., 37 LA 375, 376–377 (Gill, 1961).

[68]For a variety of such clauses, see Arbitrator Yaffe in 77 LA 8, 8–9; Silver in 75 LA 988, 991; Mullennix in 72 LA 639, 643; Snow in 68 LA 503, 506; Cahn in 52 LA 176, 177; Lee in 48 LA 206, 209; Prasow in 47 LA 1131, 1133, 1135; Stashower in 40 LA 73, 75. For clauses insuring that existing minimum standards will not be lowered, see Arbitrator Stern in 74 LA 691, 694; Belshaw in 68 LA 75, 76; Keefe in 50 LA 453, 454; Turkus in 35 LA 503, 504. For a Board of Inquiry report as to the history of the steel industry "local working conditions" clause and as to union and employer contentions regarding the effect of the clause upon progress, see Steel Indus., 33 LA 236, 239–240 (Taylor, Perkins & Lehoczky, 1959). In two cases public sector interest arbitrators were reluctant to bind public employers by maintenance of practices clauses which would impair management's efforts to achieve efficient and high quality operations. Oscoda Area Schools, 55 LA 568, 573 (Block, 1970); Arlington Educ. Assn., 54 LA 492, 495–496 (Zack, Fitzgerald & Cohen, 1970).

[69]See Arbitrator Yaffe in 77 LA 8, 10; Stutz in 52 LA 963, 964; Florey in 40 LA 1201, 1202 (where he quotes "guideposts" for resolving the question under the steel industry clause); Valtin in 35 LA 755, 756.

[70]Bakelite Co., 29 LA 555, 558–559 (Updegraff, 1957). Cf., Sargent Indus., 52 LA 1273, 1275–1276 (Lennard, 1969).

[71]Latrobe Die Casting Co., 69 LA 678, 678–679 (Altrock, 1977).

[72]Valley Dolomite Corp., 11 LA 98, 100 (McCoy, 1948). Similarly, see Arbitrator Seward in 45 LA 778, 779; Abersold in 41 LA 193, 199.

[73]Machlett Laboratories, 26 LA 117, 120 (Scheiber, 1956).

[74]Borden Co., 39 LA 1020, 1023 (Morvant, 1962).

[75]Bethlehem Steel Co., cases in 29 LA 418, and in 17 LA 382. Also see Arbitrator Wahl in 74 LA 1169, 1173–1174 (practices made subject to change if not done "in an arbitrary or capricious manner"); Garrett in 71 LA 1188, 1195–1196; Gill in 23 LA 210, 212. A similar result might be reached even without a specific contract clause. John Deere Waterloo Tractor Works, 18 LA 276, 278 (Davey, 1952).

case the agreement provided that past practice should not be considered to control or to prohibit change if the practice contributes to inefficient or uneconomical operations.[76]

Question of Arbitrability

The question of arbitrability in disputes concerning the binding status of custom was not raised in many of the cases cited above. Ordinarily there is little basis for raising the question where the collective agreement contains a broad arbitration clause or where the dispute is taken to arbitration by a joint submission. However, the question of arbitrability of custom disputes has sometimes been raised where the arbitration clause was limited to disputes concerning the interpretation or application of the "agreement." The question was answered in the affirmative in some cases,[77] but not in others.[78]

Role of Custom and Practice in Interpretation of Ambiguous Language

One of the most important standards used by arbitrators in the interpretation of ambiguous contract language is the custom or past practice of the parties. Indeed, use of past practice to give meaning to ambiguous contract language is so common that no citation of arbitral authority is necessary.[79] The general attitude of arbitrators is illustrated by Arbitrator Charles C. Killingsworth, who, in noting that the parties had operated under a provision for nearly three years before requesting an arbitrator to interpret it, stated that he had "a context of practices, usages, and rule-of-thumb interpretations by which the parties themselves" had gradually given substance to the disputed term.[80] Nonetheless, in another case Arbitrator Clyde W. Summers added a note of caution when he stated that "In interpreting a collective agreement probably nothing is more capable of constructive use or susceptible to serious abuse as appeals to custom and practice."[81]

Where practice has established a meaning for language contained in past contracts and continued by the parties in a new agreement, the

---

[76]Mead Corp., 42 LA 643, 646 (Hawley, 1964).

[77]See Arbitrator Morgan in 73 LA 837, 839; Mewhinney in 71 LA 852, 854; Moore in 71 LA 702, 705; Ross in 70 LA 470, 473; Dyke in 63 LA 810, 813–814; Christopher in 60 LA 838, 841; Kates in 51 LA 490, 492–493; Handsaker in 39 LA 1188, 1190–1191; Volz in 39 LA 72, 74–75; Crawford in 34 LA 732, 735; Gilden in 7 LA 614, 620–621. Also see Midwest Glasco v. Local Union 513, 87 LRRM 3065 (USDC, 1974). Cf., Allegheny County v. Prison Employees, 96 LRRM 3396 (Pa. S.Ct., 1977); Firefighters Local 215 v. Milwaukee, 95 LRRM 2684 (Wis. S.Ct., 1977).

[78]See Arbitrator Seinsheimer in 72 LA 863, 865; Alexander in 28 LA 401, 402; Copelof in 7 LA 585, 587. Also see Morgan (dissenting) in 50 LA 417, 422; Brandschain in 3 LA 254, 255–256.

[79]For court decisions upholding the authority of arbitrators to consider past practice in interpreting collective agreements, see Smith Steel Workers v. A.O. Smith Corp., 105 LRRM 2044 (CA 7, 1980); Boise Cascade Corp. v. Local 7001, 100 LRRM 2481 (CA 5, 1979); Auto Workers v. White Motor Corp., 87 LRRM 2707 (CA 8, 1974).

[80]Eastern Stainless Steel Corp., 12 LA 709, 713 (1949).

[81]Standard Bag Corp., 45 LA 1149, 1151 (1965).

language will be presumed to have the meaning given it by that practice.[82] It has been stated:

> "There would have to be very strong and compelling reasons for an arbitrator to change the practice by which a contract provision has been interpreted in a plant over a period of several years and several contracts. There would have to be a clear and unambiguous direction in the language used to effect such a change * * *."[83]

The weight to be accorded past practice as an interpretation guide may vary greatly from case to case. In this regard, the degree of mutuality is an important factor. Unilateral interpretations might not bind the other party.[84] However, continued failure of one party to object to the other party's interpretation is sometimes held to constitute acceptance of such interpretation so as, in effect, to make it mutual.[85]

While arbitrators sometimes refuse to charge a party with knowledge of what is going on in the plant,[86] claims of lack of knowledge often carry relatively little weight. Thus, a party may be "assumed" to

---

[82]See Arbitrator Murphy in 78 LA 819, 822; Richman in 77 LA 1045, 1048; Lipson in 77 LA 203, 206–207; Mueller in 76 LA 1236, 1240; Johannes in 75 LA 106, 109; Allen in 74 LA 13, 15; Kapsch in 72 LA 1104, 1106; Moran in 72 LA 364, 366; Mallon in 71 LA 699, 701; Megley in 70 LA 925, 928; Aaron, Garrett & Seward in 70 LA 442, 454 (although management asserted that a new agreement dealt with "a totally new concept," the Arbitrators held that absent specific declaration by management to the contrary in negotiations, the union was justified in assuming that certain key terms used in the new agreement would carry the meaning given those same terms in previous agreements by unvarying practice of the parties); Gratz in 70 LA 92, 96; Spencer in 69 LA 674, 677. For earlier cases, see p. 406 of the Third Edition of this book. In Genova Pa., Inc., 70 LA 1303, 1305 (Wolf, 1978), precontract practice was given significant weight in resolving an ambiguity in the parties' initial contract.

[83]Webster Tobacco Co., 5 LA 164, 166 (Brandschain, 1946). Also see Arbitrator Krimsly in 54 LA 1146, 1149. However, prior practice may be "an unsafe guide" after contract provisions have been changed. Huebsch Originators, 47 LA 635, 639 (Merrill, 1966). Similarly, see Arbitrator Bothwell in 53 LA 584, 585. Holding past practice to be superseded by the adoption of new contract language that is clear and unambiguous, see Arbitrator Heinsz in 74 LA 1030, 1032; Gratz in 70 LA 92, 97; Simon in 63 LA 400, 403.

[84]See Arbitrator Roumell in 74 LA 569, 570; Roberts in 47 LA 916, 920–921 (verbal protest each time company did the act and grievance was ultimately filed after protests were disregarded); Howlett in 44 LA 954, 956 (union lacked knowledge of company's method of payment, so no showing of mutuality); Altieri in 43 LA 651, 660; Hebert in 27 LA 762, 766–767; Baab in 23 LA 562, 569; Updegraff in 11 LA 825, 826; Potter in 7 LA 81, 84. Also see Sullivan in 54 LA 381, 387.

[85]See Arbitrator Seinsheimer in 76 LA 1253, 1256; Dallas in 76 LA 1261, 1264; Raymond in 76 LA 62, 68; Ashe in 69 LA 763, 766; Shister in 54 LA 335, 338–339; Boothe in 53 LA 941, 944; Marshall in 53 LA 234, 239 (union reluctantly went along with management's action for a time, then negotiated briefly on it without reaching agreement, then failed to pursue the matter for several years thereafter); Teple in 49 LA 220, 223–224, and in 33 LA 46, 51; Tatum in 44 LA 373, 376; Layman in 44 LA 326, 334 (arbitrator spoke of "tacit recognition" of the practice); Allen in 22 LA 289, 291; Kirsh in 4 LA 584, 586; Prasow in 1 LA 313, 316. Cf., Arbitrator Cohen in 71 LA 781, 783; Roberts in 70 LA 475, 480 (stating that "acquiescence in a practice on a few occasions when its application is immaterial to claimed rights of the party hardly suggest[s] assent to be bound by the practice under circumstances where it would prejudice claimed rights"); Jones in 53 LA 13, 16–17 (complex method of pay required considerable period of time for various facets to manifest themselves to the employees); Peck in 47 LA 739, 742 (failure to protest trifling matters could not be the basis of a practice).

[86]See Arbitrator Rezler in 77 LA 256, 264–265; Petrie in 76 LA 611, 618–619; Fitch in 69 LA 565, 568; Cole in 39 LA 1148, 1152; Scheiber in 36 LA 958, 960; Jones in 24 LA 821, 826–827.

know what is transpiring,[87] or it may be held that a party "knew or should have reasonably known" of the asserted practice.[88] Even successor unions sometimes are charged with knowledge of practice under the same contract language as administered by the company and the predecessor union.[89]

Another important factor to be considered in determining the weight to be given to past practice is how well it is established. In this regard, Arbitrator Robert E. Mathews stated that to be given significant weight in contract interpretation, "the practice must be of sufficient generality and duration to imply acceptance of it as an authentic construction of the contract."[90] A "single incident" has been held not to establish a "practice."[91] However, it seems reasonable that fewer instances would be required to establish a "practice" where the situation arises only infrequently than would be required where the situation arises often.[92] Thus, even a single incident which was "fully parallel" to the situation before the arbitrator sufficed where parallel situations would not likely arise often.[93]

Past practice, to be given significant weight, need not be absolutely uniform. Arbitrator Dale Yoder, for instance, held the "predominant pattern of practice" to be controlling even though there had been scattered exceptions to the "clearly established pattern."[94] On the other hand, a practice as to the rate to be paid in one situation could not control a somewhat similar but distinguishable fact situa-

---

[87]Baer Bros., 16 LA 822, 824 (Donnelly, 1951). Similarly, see Arbitrator Kapsch in 72 LA 1104, 1106; Berger in 68 LA 510, 513; Tatum in 44 LA 373, 376, stating that as to prior practice "the knowledge of the employee must be the knowledge of the Union." Also see Levy in 76 LA 620, 622–623.

[88]Owens-Corning Fiberglas Corp., 19 LA 57, 63 (Justin, 1952). Similarly, see Arbitrator Roberts in 76 LA 773, 780; Wolf in 73 LA 188, 190; Rule in 70 LA 436, 439; Jones in 44 LA 698, 700; Porter in 22 LA 608, 609. Also see McDermott in 42 LA 1277, 1280.

[89]Wagner Elec. Corp., 21 LA 524, 527 (Brown, 1953). Also see Arbitrator Jones in 44 LA 698, 700; Anderson in 29 LA 45, 49–50. The successor union's actual knowledge of a practice and its failure to negotiate a change in contract language is still stronger basis for holding it bound by the practice. See National Cash Register Co., 50 LA 1242, 1246 (Wolff, 1968). Similarly, see Arbitrator Updegraff in 20 LA 243, 247. Cf., Moberly in 51 LA 400, 404. Successor employers were held bound by their predecessor's practice in Tri-State Asphalt Corp., 72 LA 102, 105–107 (LeWinter, 1979); Darling & Co., 68 LA 917, 920 (Martin, 1977).

[90]Sheller Mfg. Corp., 10 LA 617, 620 (1948). Also see Arbitrator Daugherty in 45 LA 494, 495; Kesselman in 45 LA 201, 206; Feinberg in 45 LA 26, 29; Hebert in 27 LA 762, 766–767. Erroneous administrative procedure by one department though carried on for 10 years did not bind the company as a practice where no rational basis for the procedure was shown. U.S. Indus. Chems. Co., 47 LA 651, 654 (McGury, 1966). Also see Arbitrator Mewhinney in 76 LA 603, 606 (a mistake by a payroll clerk "does not in itself constitute a binding past practice"), and in 71 LA 449, 452; Harter in 71 LA 504, 508 (isolated mistakes by employer clerks or even officials do not create established practices, but "when an official is responsible for a policy to be followed four or five years * * * his action can not be dismissed as an isolated one that sheds no light on company policy").

[91]Arbitrator Goldsmith in 73 LA 372, 377; Solomon in 49 LA 718, 725; Duff in 43 LA 678, 681; Smith in 22 LA 835, 837. Also see Arbitrator Barone in 71 LA 1034, 1038; Keefe in 70 LA 935, 936; Dybeck in 53 LA 1215, 1216. Two incidents did not suffice in York Bus Co., 24 LA 81, 87 (Loucks, 1955). Also see Arbitrator Doyle in 69 LA 800, 803.

[92]See Arbitrator Roumell in 81 LA 105, 114–115; Cohen in 79 LA 1220, 1224; Mullin in 54 LA 593, 596; Kadish in 34 LA 763, 771; Callaghan in 28 LA 414, 417. Also see Holley in 74 LA 330, 332; Fogelberg in 74 LA 248, 252.

[93]Kennecott Copper Corp., 34 LA 763, 771 (Kadish, 1960).

[94]Curtis Cos., 29 LA 434, 439 (1957). Similarly, see Arbitrator Prasow in 50 LA 645, 657; Rohman in 47 LA 1178, 1181. Also see McDermott in 42 LA 1172, 1179.

tion, the arbitrator stating: "A practice implies the consistent handling of repetitive and like situations. An arbitrator has no more authority to extend a practice beyond its limits than he has to amend or add to the written contract."[95]

It is obvious that past practice provides no guide where evidence regarding its nature and duration is "highly contradictory."[96] Where such conflict exists the arbitrator will be inclined to rely entirely upon other standards of interpretation.

Custom and Practice Versus Clear Contract Language

While custom and past practice are used very frequently to establish the intent of contract provisions which are so ambiguous or so general as to be capable of different interpretations, they ordinarily will not be used to give meaning to a provision which is clear and unambiguous. For instance, note the following statements:

Arbitrator Jules J. Justin: "Plain and unambiguous words are undisputed facts. The conduct of Parties may be used to fix a meaning to words and phrases of uncertain meaning. Prior acts cannot be used to change the explicit terms of a contract. An arbitrator's function is not to rewrite the Parties' contract. His function is limited to finding out what the Parties intended under a particular clause. The intent of the Parties is to be found in the words which they, themselves, employed to express their intent. When the language used is clear and explicit, the arbitrator is constrained to give effect to the thought expressed by the words used."[97]

Arbitrator Hubert Wyckoff: "[Established practice] is a useful means of ascertaining intention in case of ambiguity or indefiniteness; but no matter how well established a practice may be, it is unavailing to modify a clear promise."[98]

Many other arbitrators have expressed similar views.[99]

A related rule is that a party's failure to file grievances or to protest past violations of a clear contract rule does not bar that party, after notice to the violator, from insisting upon compliance with the clear contract requirement in future cases.[100]

---

[95]General Refractories Co., 54 LA 1180, 1182 (Volz, 1970). Also see Arbitrator Barsamian in 75 LA 275, 279; Daniel in 74 LA 326, 329; Gamser in 70 LA 1189, 1193; Chapman in 69 LA 1103, 1107; Klein in 53 LA 266, 269; Leach in 45 LA 1039, 1045.

[96]Reliance Steel Prods. Co., 24 LA 30, 32 (Lehoczky, 1954). Also see Arbitrator Gibson in 70 LA 530, 533; Rimer in 68 LA 1094, 1096; Gould in 48 LA 1161, 1165; McCoy in 47 LA 648, 649 (practice could not be established by mere general statement without reference to names or dates); Merrill in 44 LA 1121, 1127; Reynard in 27 LA 793, 795.

[97]Phelps Dodge Copper Prods. Corp., 16 LA 229, 233 (1951).

[98]Tide Water Oil Co., 17 LA 829, 833 (1952).

[99]For many cases, see p. 409 of the Third Edition and p. 281 of the 1960 Edition of this book. For some later cases, see Arbitrator Reynolds in 80 LA 623, 625; Cohen in 78 LA 804, 806; Witney in 77 LA 1058, 1063; Petrie in 77 LA 780, 784; Stix in 75 LA 1254, 1261; McDermott in 74 LA 1072, 1076; Handsaker in 73 LA 924, 926; Dolnick in 72 LA 993, 995; Heinsz in 72 LA 380, 382; Goodman in 72 LA 57, 62; Peterschmidt in 70 LA 1229, 1231; Sinclitico in 70 LA 608, 613; Bailey in 68 LA 362, 367. But see Arbitrator Eaton in 79 LA 658, 664.

[100]For many cases, see p. 409 of the Third Edition of this book. For some later cases, see Arbitrator Briggs in 80 LA 1217, 1220; McDermott in 74 LA 1072, 1076; Charm in 71 LA 676, 679; Peterschmidt in 70 LA 1229, 1231; Perry in 68 LA 1294, 1300. For discussion of related points, see Chapter 10, topic entitled "Waiver and Estoppel."

The clear language of the contract has been enforced even where the arbitrator believed that, on the basis of equity, past practice should have governed:

> "In the opinion of the Impartial Tribunal the practice would not have grown up in the first place and would not have been tolerated by the parties if the situation did not justify it. The sudden refusal of the union to continue with a practice that has apparently proved satisfactory for many years, thus precipitating the present dispute, may well be severely criticized as an unreasonable stand not necessary to protect any substantial right of the workers. * * * If it were at all possible the decision should be that the position of the workers is in violation of the contract."[101]

Amendment of Contract

While Arbitrator Harry H. Platt emphasized that evidence of past practice "is wholly inadmissible where the contract language is plain and unambiguous,"[102] he also recognized that, on the basis of very strong proof, the clear language of the contract may be amended:

> "While, to be sure, parties to a contract may modify it by a later *agreement,* the existence of which is to be deduced from their course of conduct, the conduct relied upon to show such modification must be unequivocal and the terms of modification must be definite, certain, and intentional."[103]

Arbitrator Hamilton Douglas declared that a party contending that clear language has been modified must "show the assent of the other party and the minds of the parties must be shown to have met on a definite modification."[104] Arbitrator Charles C. Killingsworth required a showing that "both parties * * * have evinced a positive acceptance or endorsement" of the practice.[105] Other arbitrators, too, have required a showing equivalent to mutual agreement to amend the contract.[106]

---

[101]Chicago Assn. of Dress Mfrs., 1 ALAA ¶67,234, p. 67,521 (Hodes, 1945).

[102]Penberthy Injector Co., 15 LA 713, 715 (1950).

[103]Gibson Refrigerator Co., 17 LA 313, 318 (1951), emphasis added. Also see comments of Arbitrator Platt in 22 LA 65, 68. Compare the view of Arbitrator Nathan Lipson in Vlasic Foods, 74 LA 1214, 1217–1218 (1980), where he stated "it to be poor policy to allow a 'practice' to modify a clear contractual undertaking of the parties," but where he did permit use of practice to establish that the parties never intended contractual language to be given its ordinary meaning. Also see Arbitrator Eaton in 79 LA 658, 664.

[104]Merrill-Stevens Dry Dock & Repair Co., 10 LA 562, 563 (1948).

[105]Bethlehem Steel Co., 13 LA 556, 560 (1949). Also see Arbitrator Goodman in 81 LA 191, 193, finding that "the parties by their actions effectively modified the written agreement."

[106]See Arbitrator R.R. Roberts in 78 LA 729, 737, and in 69 LA 623, 626; Rimer in 71 LA 1055, 1057; Felice in 70 LA 887, 890; Daniel in 68 LA 54, 56; Mittenthal in 54 LA 716, 719–720; Daugherty in 48 LA 1355, 1357; Wolff in 47 LA 993, 994; Updegraff in 47 LA 720, 722–723; Koretz in 47 LA 495, 500–501; Traynor in 47 LA 193, 195–196; Volz in 46 LA 1208, 1212–1213; Hebert in 46 LA 140, 151; McCormick in 45 LA 453, 458; Fallon in 45 LA 271, 276–277; Williams in 44 LA 5, 6–7; Anrod in 43 LA 1173, 1176; Yagoda in 42 LA 421, 424–425; R.S. Roberts in 28 LA 470, 474; Hoban in 27 LA 605, 607; Emery in 17 LA 90, 91. But long, unchallenged practice was deemed sufficient by Arbitrator Lennard in 27 LA 376, 383; Gifford in 25 LA 826, 827; Sherbow in 17 LA 524, 526. Also see LeBaron in 74 LA 1191, 1195; Seinsheimer in 49 LA 709, 714–718; Duff in 46 LA 920, 923. The mere fact that an arbitrator adheres to past practice as against literal language of the agreement does not mean that the award does not draw its essence from the agreement. See discussion in Teamsters Local 249 v. Potter-McCune Co., 92 LRRM 2701 (USDC, 1976); Porter Co. v. Saw Workers, 56 LRRM 2534 (CA 3, 1964).

Of course, the parties to a contract may amend it by a subsequent agreement. This result was produced, for instance, by a special "interpretation agreement" of the parties.[107]

Gap-Filling

Arbitrators have sometimes recognized that contract language may cover a matter generally but fail to cover all of its aspects—that is, "gaps" sometimes exist. It has been recognized that established practice may be used, not to set aside contract language, but to fill in the contract's gaps.[108] Similarly, past practice might indicate an exception to the general application of a contract clause.[109]

---

[107]Borg-Warner Corp., 29 LA 629, 633–634 (Marshall, 1957). Also see Arbitrator Marshall in 47 LA 97, 101 (contract amended by subsequent side agreement); Summers in 40 LA 575, 575–576.

[108]See Arbitrator McCoy in 44 LA 246, 250; Roberts in 28 LA 470, 474; Hogan in 25 LA 216, 225; Emery in 17 LA 90, 91; Killingsworth in 17 LA 65, 67. Also see Greer in 71 LA 1136, 1138.

[109]Standard Brands, Inc., 25 LA 851, 853 (Justin, 1955). Also see Arbitrator Roberts in 77 LA 402, 404–405.

Chapter 13

Management Rights

Views Regarding Management Rights

Under the common law, owners of business establishments possess certain freedoms of action, incidental to their legal status, which are commonly called management rights or management prerogatives. The word "right" has been defined by Webster to mean "any power, privilege, or immunity, vested in one by authority, social custom * * * or * * * by the law * * *." Webster has defined the word "prerogative" to mean the "right to exercise a power or privilege in priority to, or to the exclusion of, others * * * for the exercise of which in theory there is no responsibility or accountability as to the fact and the manner of its exercise."

Two management spokesmen, noting that the term "management prerogative" is as distasteful to union representatives as the term "closed shop" is to many management representatives, denied that "management prerogative" refers to a divine right to manage. These spokemen would define the term to refer to "those rights, or that authority, which management must have in order successfully to carry out its function of managing the enterprise."[1]

Management spokesmen generally adhere rigidly to the position that "residual" or "reserved" powers are in management. These spokesmen declare that under the common law an employer, as property owner, may operate his business as he chooses, except where his common law rights have been limited by constitutional legislation or by collective bargaining agreements.[2] Management takes the position that it need not look to the collective agreement to determine what rights it has reserved to itself, but should look to the agreement only to

---

[1]Hill & Hook, Management at the Bargaining Table, 56 (1945). Also see Phelps, "Management's Reserved Rights: an Industry View," Management Rights and the Arbitration Process, 102 (BNA Books, 1956).

[2]See Story, Arbitration as a Part of the Collective Bargaining Agreement, 9 (1948); Hill, "Using Management's Rights in Day-to-Day Labor Relations," American Management Association Personnel Series, No. 82, p. 11 (1944).

determine what rights it has ceded away or agreed to share with employees. Thus, one management spokesman defined "the doctrine of reserved rights" as "the simple and understandable view that management, which must have the right to manage, has reserved its right to manage unless it has limited its right by some specific provision of the labor agreement."[3]

As might be expected, labor spokesmen deny that the rights of management are so broad. For instance, while serving as General Counsel of the United Steelworkers of America, Arthur Goldberg expressed that union's view of the reserved rights concept:

> "This concept is not only distasteful; it is based on extreme over-simplification of history. It overlooks the degree to which collective bargaining modifies workers' rights—the right to cease work, the right to press a point without regard to any set of rules or guides, the right to improvise concepts of fairness on the basis of the necessities of the moment without commitment to the future. How could management obtain employee acceptance of job evaluation without the union's modification of the inherent right of workers to press wage complaints on whatever ground appears suitable at the moment. No—this wresting away process is not all one way by any means."[4]

He also offered the following position as to management's reserved rights:

> "What then are management's reserved rights? These are usually rights reserved in the agreement subject to the substantive clauses of the agreement. Some of these rights relate to subjects excluded from the collective bargaining area by custom, by law, or by express provision. When a contract says that management has the exclusive right to manage the business, it obviously refers to the countless questions which arise and are not covered by wages, hours, and working conditions, such as determination of products, equipment, materials, prices, etc.
>
> "Not only does management have the general right to manage the business, but many agreements provide that management has the exclusive right to direct working forces and usually to lay off, recall, discharge, hire, etc.
>
> "The right to direct, where it involves wages, hours, or working conditions, is a procedural right. It does not imply some right over and above labor's right. It is a recognition of the fact that somebody must be boss; somebody has to run the plant. People can't be wandering around at loose ends, each deciding what to do next. Management decides what the employee is to do. However, this right to direct or to initiate action does not imply a second-class role for the union. The union has the right to pursue its role of representing the interest of the employee with the same stature accorded it as accorded management. To assure order, there is a clear procedural line drawn: the company directs and the union grieves when it objects. To make this desirable division of function workable, it is essential that arbitrators not give greater weight to the directing force than the objecting force."[5]

---

[3]Fairweather, "American and Foreign Grievance Systems," Proceedings of the 21st Annual Meeting of NAA, 1, 15 (BNA Books, 1968).
[4]Goldberg, "Management's Reserved Rights: A Labor View," Management Rights and the Arbitration Process, 118, 122–123 (BNA Books, 1956).
[5]Goldberg, id. at 120–121.

In the past some attempt has been made to draw a line separating matters of interest to the union from those of sole concern to management. Such an attempt was made at the President's Labor-Management Conference in 1945, but with no success. There, management members of the Committee on Management's Right to Manage did agree upon a specific classification of management functions. The labor members, however, were unable to accept any such clear-cut classification. They submitted a separate report explaining their position:

"The extensive exploratory discussions of the committee have brought forth the wide variety of traditions, customs, and practices that have grown out of relationships between unions and management in various industries over a long period of time.

"Because of the complexities of these relationships, the labor members of the committee think it unwise to specify and classify the functions and responsibilities of management. Because of the insistence by management for such specification, the committee was unable to agree upon a joint report. To do so might well restrict the flexibility so necessary to efficient operation.

"It would be extremely unwise to build a fence around the rights and responsibilities of management on the one hand and the unions on the other. The experience of many years shows that with the growth of mutual understanding the responsibilities of one of the parties today may well become the joint responsibility of both parties tomorrow.

"We cannot have one sharply delimited area designated as management prerogatives and another equally sharply defined area of union prerogatives without either side constantly attempting to invade the forbidden territory, thus creating much unnecessary strife."[6]

Objective observers appear to share, in part at least, the views expressed by the labor members of the Committee.[7] "Collective bargaining is too dynamic to permit drawing a statutory line between management's prerogatives and the areas of joint responsibility."[8]

Various conclusions have at different times been reached by objective observers concerning how far unions may desire or be inclined to push into management areas:

"Some unions appear constantly to seek a larger share in the governance of the industry while others believe that they should avoid responsibility for the conduct of the business."[9]

"There is no consciousness of invading managerial prerogatives. By the same token there is no area of management which most [unions] would hesitate to put on 'next year's list' if they felt the interests of the union were involved."[10]

---

[6]The President's National Labor-Management Conference, Nov. 5–30, 1945 (U.S. Dept. of Labor, Div. of Labor Standards, Bull. No. 77, pp. 57–59, 61, 1946).

[7]See Chamberlain, The Union Challenge to Management Control, 156–157 (1948). Another stimulating book is by Ewing, Do It My Way or You're Fired: Employee Rights and the Changing Role of Management Prerogatives (1983).

[8]Cox & Dunlop, "Regulation of Collective Bargaining by the National Labor Relations Board," 63 Harv. L. Rev. 389, 430 (1950).

[9]Cox & Dunlop, id. at 431. In 1980 UAW President Douglas Fraser won election to the board of directors of Chrysler Corporation, becoming "the first U.S. labor leader to participate in management of a company with which his union bargains." LRR (BNA), May 19, 1980.

[10]Chamberlain, The Union Challenge to Management Control, 157 (1948).

"In the daily shop work of job assignments, skill classification, production standards, and maintenance of discipline, union officers show little desire to join in managing and in initiating action; they prefer to retain their freedom to protest management's decisions and to stay out of the cross fire of criticism and avoid the wounding resentments of their own members.

"Unions have not pushed massively and inexorably into vital policy areas. They have pushed when they could and when it was in their clear interest to do so, advancing when management was careless or weak and retreating when management aggressively resisted them. When unions do enlarge their powers, it is almost always in those areas where they have long been established: wages, hours, and conditions of employment."[11]

In any study of arbitration the view taken by arbitrators in regard to management rights is of great interest and importance. Many arbitrators have expressly recognized that the residual powers are in management.[12] No doubt, the likelihood that arbitrators will have occasion to refer to the residual rights doctrine is greatly reduced by the extensive practice of parties expressly to include a management rights clause in their collective agreement. Nonetheless, even where the agreement does contain such a clause, the arbitrator still may recognize the residual rights doctrine.[13]

To illustrate the variations in arbitral statements recognizing the "residual" or "reserved" rights doctrine, we may note the following:

Arbitrator C. Chester Brisco: "It is a well recognized arbitral principle that the Collective Bargaining Agreement imposes limitations on the employer's otherwise unfettered right to manage the enterprise. Except as expressly restricted by the Agreement, the employer retains the right of management. This is known as the Reserved Rights Doctrine; it lies at the foundation of modern arbitration practice."[14]

Arbitrator Lewis E. Solomon: "Collective bargaining agreements, generally, are devised to establish and grant certain rights to employees, which rights they would not otherwise have under common law. It is also

---

[11]Chamberlain & Kuhn, Collective Bargaining, 92 (1965).

[12]For many instances, see p. 416 of the Third Edition and pp. 287–288 of the 1960 Edition of this book. For later instances, see Arbitrator Boyer in 81 LA 338, 341; Nelson in 80 LA 1180, 1183; Gallagher in 79 LA 292, 296; Leeper in 78 LA 8, 11; Mullaly in 77 LA 1224, 1227; Hilgert in 77 LA 953, 957–958; Dean in 77 LA 940, 943; Lennard in 76 LA 114, 116; Johnston in 75 LA 716, 718; Mann in 75 LA 655, 658; Van Pelt in 75 LA 498, 502; Babiskin in 74 LA 312, 314; Herrick in 74 LA 296, 298; R. Ross in 74 LA 92, 95; Hunter in 72 LA 1234, 1236 (stating that where the agreement contains "no reference to managerial prerogatives," it "must be assumed the general labor relations principle of the right of the employer to operate his business enterprise at his discretion applies unless limited or restricted by" the agreement); Goodstein in 72 LA 1127, 1129; Madden in 72 LA 20, 30; Mewhinney in 71 LA 1205, 1208; Brisco in 71 LA 1026, 1028; Bolte in 71 LA 716, 719; Gowan in 71 LA 696, 697–698; M. Ross in 71 LA 632, 634; Roberts in 70 LA 475, 481–482; Oppenheim in 70 LA 326, 329; Finley in 69 LA 175, 176; Teple in 68 LA 1347, 1351–1352; Schuman in 68 LA 1178, 1179; Morgan in 68 LA 708, 712; Beck in 68 LA 386, 389, 391; Volz in 68 LA 51, 52.

[13]As did Arbitrator Eyraud in 77 LA 857, 858, 860; Raymond in 76 LA 932, 934; Ordman in 75 LA 1288, 1291–1292; Roberts in 73 LA 781, 787; Goodman in 73 LA 207, 209–210; Hayes in 72 LA 788, 791, 793; Chalfie in 72 LA 668, 673; Grooms in 70 LA 1196, 1197; Sinclitico in 70 LA 608, 611; Lubow in 68 LA 1379, 1381; Brown in 68 LA 1202, 1205; Hays in 68 LA 989, 991.

[14]Vacaville Unified School Dist., 71 LA 1026, 1028 (1978). Another concise statement is that by Arbitrator Harry J. Dworkin in Cleveland Newspaper Publishers Assn., 51 LA 1174, 1181 (1969), as follows: "It is axiomatic that an employer retains all managerial rights not expressly forbidden by statutory law in the absence of a collective bargaining agreement. When a collective bargaining agreement is entered into, these managerial rights are given up only to the extent evidenced in the agreement."

a normal and well recognized principle in the interpretation of such Agreements that the rights of management are limited and curtailed only to the degree to which it has yielded specified rights. The right of Management to operate its business and control the working force may be specifically reserved in a labor agreement. However, even in the absence of such a specific reservations clause, as is the case here, those rights are inherent and are nevertheless reserved and maintained by it and its decisions with respect to the operations of the business and the direction of the working forces may not be denied, rejected, or curtailed unless the same are in clear violation of the terms of the contract, or may be clearly implied, or are so clearly arbitrary or capricious as to reflect an intent to derogate the relationship."[15]

Arbitrator Raymond R. Roberts: "[T]he underlying premise of collective bargaining agreements is that management retains all rights of a common law employer which are not bargained away or limited by the collective bargaining agreement. The parties commenced their negotiations from a position where management enjoys all rights of a common law employer. That is, it is free to set the conditions of employment in any manner it desires without any limitation, except those imposed by law. The employee's options are to either accept or reject employment upon those terms. In collective bargaining the employees withhold or threaten to withhold acceptance of employment unless the conditions of employment are modified in the respects successfully bargained for. Where the collective bargaining agreement does not modify or limit management's prerogatives, management retains the prerogatives of a common law employer. The significance of the silence of a collective bargaining agreement upon a subject matter is that management retains its common law rights toward that subject matter which it has not bargained away. The Union argument presupposes the Employer must have contract authority to take a particular action. In fact the converse is true, and the Union must show that a particular act of management was contrary to contractual limitations placed upon management or obligations imposed upon management by the contract."[16]

We have noted the management view that management "has reserved its right to manage unless it has limited its right by some *specific* provision of the labor agreement."[17] In many cases arbitrators have in fact spoken in terms of a specific contractual provision (containing either an express or implied limitation) as being necessary in order to limit management's rights. In other cases some arbitrators (at least as to some types of issues, such as subcontracting) have taken the view that limitations upon management rights are not necessarily restricted to those contained in some specific provision of the agreement but may exist as "implied obligations" or "implied limitations" under some general provision of the agreement such as the recognition clause, seniority provisions, or wage provisions.[18]

---

[15]Fairway Foods, 44 LA 161, 164 (1965). Also see Arbitrator Solomon in 55 LA 997, 1001–1002.

[16]Saint Louis Symphony Soc., 70 LA 475, 481–482 (1978). Also see the detailed statement by Arbitrator John Day Larkin in National Lead Co., 43 LA 1025, 1027–1028 (1964), and his reiteration of the general principle in 55 LA 329, 335.

[17]Fairweather, "American and Foreign Grievance Systems," Proceedings of the 21st Annual Meeting of NAA, 1, 15 (BNA Books, 1968), emphasis added.

[18]For example, see topic entitled "Right to Subcontract" in this Chapter. Also see discussion by Arbitrator Seward in Bethlehem Steel Co., 30 LA 678, 682–683 (1958). The term "implied obligations" has sometimes been given a meaning much more restrictive upon management than the term "implied limitations." See discussion in Wiggins, The Arbitration of Industrial Engineering Disputes, 73–74 (BNA Books, 1970).

Also, it has been observed that in practice arbitrators may tend to modify the residual rights theory by imposing a standard of reasonableness as an implied term of the agreement.[19] Certainly, many arbitrators are reluctant to uphold arbitrary, capricious, or bad faith managerial actions which adversely affect bargaining unit employees. Even where the agreement expressly states a right in management, expressly gives it discretion as to a matter, or expressly makes it the "sole judge" of a matter, management's action must not be arbitrary, capricious, or taken in bad faith.[20]

It is also to be remembered that numerous arbitrators have accepted the view that under some circumstances unwritten practices and custom, as to some matters, should be held binding upon both parties as being in essence a part of their "whole" agreement. Thus, past practice is another possible source of limitation upon management rights.[21]

Finally, it may be noted that there has been Court of Appeals recognition and approval of the residual rights doctrine in a LMRA case.[22] The U.S. Supreme Court also has commented relative to management rights, in the *Warrior & Gulf* case, but the significance of the Court's comments is not clear.[23] One able arbitrator suggested that the *Warrior & Gulf* decision "would appear to give full weight to the reserved rights doctrine" but with the additional condition that such rights are likewise subject to the willingness of employees to work under the particular unilaterally imposed conditions.[24] Another able arbitrator suggested that the decision in effect rejects the "pristine" or "original" reserved rights doctrine.[25] As to the NLRB, some of the Board's concepts and policies in regard to the bargaining duty are at odds with the residual rights doctrine applied by many arbitrators and can produce results different from those reached by the arbitrator.

---

[19]See discussion in Robert E. McKee, General Contractor, 39 LA 411, 413–414 (Oppenheim, 1962). Also, again see topic entitled "Right to Subcontract" in this Chapter. In Johnson Bronze Co. v. UAW, 104 LRRM 2378, 2380 (CA 3, 1980), the court stated that an arbitrator had "imposed a reasonableness requirement onto" management's decision and could properly do so.

[20]See Arbitrator Barnhart in 70 LA 664, 666; Grenig in 70 LA 645, 647–648; Kornblum in 70 LA 375, 379; Roberts in 54 LA 896, 900; Sandler in 53 LA 482, 486; Gorsuch in 52 LA 552, 556; Krimsly in 51 LA 49, 53; Merrill in 36 LA 1353, 1355–1356. Where an agreement expressly retained residual rights for management, Arbitrator Ralph C. Hon cautioned that "Management's actions in exercising its reserved powers must not be arbitrary, capricious, or taken in bad faith." Reichhold Chems., 73 LA 636, 640 (1979).

[21]For full discussion, see Chapter 12, topic entitled "Custom and Practice as Part of the Contract."

[22]United States Steel Corp. v. Nichols, 229 F.2d 396, 399–400, 37 LRRM 2420 (CA 6, 1956), cert. denied, 351 U.S. 950. The *Nichols* case view as to residual rights was quoted with approval in Gunther v. San Diego & Ariz. E. Ry., 198 F.Supp. 402 (USDC, 1961), reversed on other grounds, 86 S.Ct. 368 (1965). For arbitral reference to the *Nichols* case, see Arbitrator Young in 55 LA 933, 935–937, 943; Dworkin in 51 LA 1174, 1181; Sembower in 50 LA 1177, 1181; Altieri in 42 LA 559, 560–562; Jones in 37 LA 771, 775–776; Ross in 32 LA 713, 717–718.

[23]United Steelworkers v. Warrior & Gulf Navigation Co., 34 LA 561, 565 (1960).

[24]International Smelting & Ref. Co., 54 LA 657, 660 (Cahn, 1970).

[25]Killingsworth, "Management Rights Revisited," Proceedings of the 22nd Annual Meeting of NAA, 1, 7–10 (BNA Books, 1970).

This will be treated in detail hereinbelow in the subtopic entitled "The Duty to Bargain: Right of Unilateral Action."

Limitations on Management Rights

In recent decades there has been progressive invasion of once unchallenged areas of exclusive managerial decision. Many matters which were once regarded as the "rights" or "prerogatives" of management have ceased to be so characterized. Inroads into management areas have been made by legislation, collective bargaining, and arbitration. Some inroads were noted in the preceding topic. Others will be noted in topics that follow.

Inroads Made by Legislation

Beginning about 1890 and continuing through the years, the enactment of state and federal legislation has restricted, to some extent, the right of management to offer employment upon its own terms. Restrictions are found in laws relating to minimum wages and maximum hours, child labor, health and safety, workers' compensation, unemployment insurance, yellow-dog contracts, fair employment practices, and the like. Such legislation as the Sherman Act, the Clayton Act, the Robinson-Patman Act, and the Securities Exchange Act, each in its own way, has drained the reservoir of management rights. Much of this legislation was enacted largely and directly in the interest of the public. More direct restriction upon management rights came about through the Railway Labor Act of 1926, the National Labor Relations Act of 1935, the Labor-Management Relations Act of 1947, the Labor-Management Reporting and Disclosure Act of 1959, and the Civil Rights Act of 1964. Of course, any discussion of legislation necessarily involves consideration of court and NLRB decisions construing that legislation, as is apparent in the following subtopic.

The Duty to Bargain: Right of Unilateral Action

The labor relations acts, by stimulating collective bargaining, set the stage for overall restriction of management rights through the provisions of collective bargaining agreements. The original National Labor Relations Act placed on employers a legally enforceable or "mandatory" duty to bargain with duly authorized employee representatives on subjects falling within the terms "rates of pay, wages, hours of employment, or other conditions of employment."[26] The same obligation is continued (and made applicable to unions also) in the Act as amended by the Labor-Management Relations Act.

Cases decided by the NLRB or the courts have held that, in addition to wages and hours, the area of mandatory bargaining may cover such subjects as holiday and vacation pay,[27] subcontracting,[28] discharges,[29] work loads and work standards,[30] bonuses,[31] pensions,[32] profit sharing,[33] insurance benefits,[34] change of insurance plan administrator,[35] merit increases,[36] union shop,[37] checkoff of union dues,[38] hiring hall,[39] work schedules,[40] plant rules,[41] rest periods,[42] placing existing practices in the contract,[43] management rights,[44] "zipper" clauses,[45] "most favored nations" clauses giving employer equality in terms negotiated by union with employer's competitors,[46] incentive pay plans,[47] in-plant cafeteria and vending machine food and beverage prices and services,[48] company owned houses,[49] stock

---

[26]For the concept of mandatory, permissible, and unlawful subjects of bargaining, see NLRB v. Wooster Div. of Borg-Warner Corp., 78 S.Ct. 718 (1958). For articles containing discussion of the duty to bargain and unilateral action (in addition to articles cited elsewhere in this subtopic), see Barron, "A Theory of Protected Employer Rights: A Revisionist Analysis of the Supreme Court's Interpretation of the National Labor Relations Act," 59 Tex. L. Rev. 421 (1981); Naylor, "Subcontracting, Plant Closures and Plant Removals: The Duty to Bargain and Its Practical Implications Upon the Employment Relationship," 30 Drake L. Rev. 203 (1981); Heinsz, "The Partial-Closing Conundrum: The Duty of Employers and Unions to Bargain in Good Faith," 1981 Duke L.J. 71 (1981); Modjeska, "Guess Who's Coming to the Bargaining Table?" 39 Ohio St. L.J. 415 (1978); Nelson & Howard, "The Duty to Bargain During the Term of an Existing Agreement," 27 Lab. L.J. 573 (1976); Rabin, "Limitations on Employer Independent Action," 27 Vand. L. Rev. 133 (1974); Note, "Mid-Term Modification of Terms and Conditions of Employment," 1972 Duke L.J. 813 (1972).
[27]Singer Mfg. Co., 6 LRRM 405 (1940), enforced, 8 LRRM 740 (CA 7, 1941); Union Mfg. Co., 21 LRRM 1187 (NLRB, 1948).
[28]Fibreboard Paper Prods. Corp. v. NLRB, 379 U.S. 203, 57 LRRM 2609 (1964). For some limits as to the duty, see Westinghouse Elec. Corp., 58 LRRM 1257 (NLRB, 1965).
[29]NLRB v. Bachelder, 8 LRRM 723 (CA 7, 1941).
[30]Woodside Cotton Mills Co., 6 LRRM 68 (NLRB, 1940).
[31]NLRB v. Niles-Bement-Pond Co., 31 LRRM 2057 (CA 2, 1952).
[32]Inland Steel Co., 21 LRRM 1310 (1948), enforced, 22 LRRM 2506 (CA 7, 1948), cert. denied, 24 LRRM 2019 (1949).
[33]NLRB v. Black-Clawson Co., 33 LRRM 2567 (CA 6, 1954).
[34]NLRB v. W.W. Cross & Co., 24 LRRM 2068 (CA 1, 1949).
[35]Keystone Consol. Indus., 99 LRRM 1036 (NLRB, 1978).
[36]NLRB v. J.H. Allison & Co., 18 LRRM 1369 (1946), enforced, 21 LRRM 2238 (CA 6, 1948), cert. denied, 22 LRRM 2564 (1948).
[37]NLRB v. Andrew Jergens Co., 24 LRRM 2096 (CA 9, 1949). The amended NLRA bans closed shops and restricts other forms of union security.
[38]United States Gypsum Co., 28 LRRM 1015, 29 LRRM 1171 (NLRB, 1951).
[39]NLRB v. Associated Gen. Contractors, 59 LRRM 3013 (CA 5, 1965).
[40]Hallam & Boggs Truck Co., 28 LRRM 1457 (1951), enforced, 30 LRRM 2602 (CA 10, 1952); Wilson & Co., 5 LRRM 560 (1940), enforced, 7 LRRM 575 (CA 8, 1940).
[41]Timken Roller Bearing Co., 18 LRRM 1370 (1946), enforcement denied on other grounds, 20 LRRM 2204 (CA 6, 1947).
[42]National Grinding Wheel Co., 21 LRRM 1095 (NLRB, 1948).
[43]National Carbon Div., Union Carbide & Co., 30 LRRM 1338 (NLRB, 1952), amended without affecting this point, 32 LRRM 1276 (NLRB, 1953).
[44]NLRB v. American Natl. Ins. Co., 343 U.S. 395, 30 LRRM 2147 (1952).
[45]NLRB v. Tomco Communications, Inc., 97 LRRM 2660, 2664 (CA 9, 1978).
[46]Dolly Madison Indus., Inc., 74 LRRM 1230 (NLRB, 1970).
[47]NLRB v. East Tex. Steel Castings Co., 33 LRRM 2793 (CA 5, 1954).
[48]Ford Motor Co. v. NLRB, 99 S.Ct. 1842 (1979), the Court commenting (p. 1850) that the establishment of in-plant food prices is not among those managerial decisions "which lie at the core of entrepreneurial control."
[49]NLRB v. Lehigh Portland Cement Co., 32 LRRM 2463 (CA 4, 1953). Cf., NLRB v. Bemis Bros. Bag Co., 32 LRRM 2535 (CA 5, 1953).

purchase plans,[50] employee discounts,[51] paid coffee break,[52] accumulation of seniority while employee is in a supervisory status,[53] no-strike clauses,[54] production work by supervisors,[55] installation of new machinery,[56] transfer of employees to a new location,[57] and pay to employees while serving on union negotiating committee.[58]

The above enumeration of mandatory bargaining subjects is not exhaustive. Nor is it final. Subjects that have been directly held to fall within or without the area of mandatory bargaining might be held otherwise by future decision. In general, the tendency has been to expand the area. For instance, the NLRB has moved significantly in holding economic decisions of management to be mandatory subjects of bargaining if job security or working conditions are affected.[59] However, the NLRB sometimes has encountered stiff Court of Appeals resistance, particularly as to economic decisions to move or terminate all or part of the business.[60] In this regard, in its *Darlington* decision under the NLRA the U.S. Supreme Court did not reach any question as to whether an employer must bargain on a purely economic decision to terminate the business.[61] In 1981 the Supreme Court did reach such question in its *First National Maintenance* decision, where the Court stated its conclusion to be "that the harm likely to be done to an employer's need to operate freely in deciding whether to shut down part of its business purely for economic reasons outweighs the incremental benefit that might be gained through the union's participation in making the decision," the Court then stating its holding to be "that

---

[50]NLRB v. Richfield Oil Corp., 37 LRRM 2327 (D.C. Cir., 1956).
[51]Central Ill. Pub. Serv. Co., 51 LRRM 1508 (1962), enforced, 54 LRRM 2586 (CA 7, 1963).
[52]Fleming Mfg. Co., 41 LRRM 1115 (NLRB, 1957).
[53]Mobile Oil Co., 147 NLRB 337 (1964).
[54]Shell Oil, 22 LRRM 1153 (NLRB, 1948).
[55]Globe-Union, Inc., 29 LRRM 1198 (NLRB, 1952).
[56]Renton News Record, 49 LRRM 1972 (NLRB, 1962).
[57]Cooper Thermometer Co. v. NLRB, 65 LRRM 2113 (CA 2, 1967).
[58]Axelson, Inc., 97 LRRM 1234 (NLRB, 1978).
[59]See Dixie Ohio Express Co., 167 NLRB 573, 66 LRRM 1092 (1967); NLRB v. Town & Country Mfg. Co., 136 NLRB 1022, 1027 (1962). The NLRB had previously long held that the employer, absent any antiunion motive, was not required to bargain over economic decisions to make technological improvements, to relocate operations, to subcontract, and the like, although there was a duty to bargain about the effects of such decisions on the employees.
[60]NLRB v. International Harvester Co., 104 LRRM 3098 (CA 9, 1980); NLRB v. Acme Indus. Prods., Inc., 76 LRRM 2697 (CA 6, 1971); NLRB v. Drapery Mfg. Co., 74 LRRM 2055 (CA 8, 1970); Morrison Cafeterias, Inc. v. NLRB, 74 LRRM 3048 (CA 8, 1970); NLRB v. Transmarine Navigation Corp., 65 LRRM 2861 (CA 9, 1967); NLRB v. Royal Plating & Polishing Co., 60 LRRM 2033 (CA 3, 1965). However, in these cases the court did recognize a duty to bargain about the effects of the employer's decision upon the employees.
[61]Textile Workers Union v. Darlington Mfg. Co., 85 S.Ct. 994, 998, 58 LRRM 2657 (1965), holding that an employer has the absolute right to terminate his entire business for any reason he chooses, including antiunion bias, but that termination of part of a multienterprise business will violate the NLRA if the employer is motivated by a purpose to "chill" unionism in the remaining parts of the business and if he reasonably can foresee that the partial closing will have that effect. In a case under the Railway Labor Act a union threatened to strike to force a railroad to amend the collective agreement to require mutual consent in order to abolish existing jobs (the railroad had received public utility commission approval to close certain stations which were little used and wasteful); the Supreme Court held that the union's demand was "not unlawful" under the RLA and that the Norris-LaGuardia Act prevented an injunction against the strike. Railroad Telegraphers v. Chicago & Nw. Ry., 80 S.Ct. 761, 767, 45 LRRM 3109 (1960).

the decision itself is *not* part of §8(d)'s 'terms and conditions' * * * over which Congress has mandated bargaining."[62]

Although the Supreme Court stated in *First National Maintenance* that "we of course intimate no view as to other types of management decisions, such as plant relocations, sales, other kinds of subcontracting, automation, etc., which are to be considered on their particular facts,"[63] the Supreme Court did make the following statement of obvious relevance in the judging by the NLRB and the courts of future cases involving the duty to bargain in reference to such other types of purely economic decisions:

> "Management must be free from the constraints of the bargaining process to the extent essential for the running of a profitable business. It also must have some degree of certainty beforehand as to when it may proceed to reach decisions without fear of later evaluations labeling its conduct an unfair labor practice. Congress did not explicitly state what issues of mutual concern to union and management it intended to exclude from mandatory bargaining. Nonetheless, in view of an employer's need for unencumbered decisionmaking, bargaining over management decisions that have a substantial impact on the continued availability of employment should be required only if the benefit, for labor-management relations and the collective bargaining process, outweighs the burden placed on the conduct of the business."[64]

Section 8(d) of the NLRA as amended by the LMRA provides, in part, that "* * * to bargain collectively is the performance of the

---

[62]First Natl. Maintenance Corp. v. NLRB, 101 S.Ct. 2573, 2584, 107 LRRM 2705 (1981), rejecting both the NLRB conclusion that the employer had an obligation to bargain on the economic decision itself, and the Court of Appeals conclusion that the employer presumptively had such obligation.

[63]Ibid., n. 22. For different views of NLRB members as to what is the critical factor in determining whether these other types of management decisions are subject to mandatory bargaining, see United Technologies, 115 LRRM 1281 (NLRB, 1984), where the Board reconsidered its earlier decision against an employer "in light of the Supreme Court's opinion in First National Maintenance" and held that the employer lawfully refused to bargain over its decision to consolidate and transfer bargaining unit work from one facility to another.

[64]101 S.Ct. at 2580–2581. This statement was a part of the Court's preliminary discussion of the duty to bargain on management decisions, after which discussion the Court turned "to the specific issue at hand: an economically-motivated decision to shut down part of a business." In its preliminary discussion the Court also stated that "Congress had no expectation that the elected union representative would become an equal partner in the running of the business enterprise in which the union's members are employed." Id. at 2579. Relevant to the determination of any bargaining obligation, the Court categorized management decisions:
"Some management decisions, such as choice of advertising and promotion, product type and design, and financing arrangements, have only an indirect and attenuated impact on the employment relationship. * * * Other management decisions, such as the order of succession of layoffs and recalls, production quotas, and work rules, are almost exclusively 'an aspect of the relationship' between employer and employee. * * * The present case concerns a third type of management decision, one that had a direct impact on employment, since jobs were inexorably eliminated by the termination, but had as its focus only the economic profitability of [the operations being shut down]." Id. at 2579.
In discussing the specific issue of "an economically-motivated decision to shut down part of a business," the Court stated:
"There is an important difference * * * between permitted bargaining and mandated bargaining. Labeling this type of decision mandatory could afford a union a powerful tool for achieving delay, a power that might be used to thwart management's intentions in a manner unrelated to any feasible solution the union might propose." Id. at 2583.
Finally, while the employer was not required to bargain on the economic decision itself, the Court stated that the union must be given an opportunity to bargain over the effects of the decision, and that "bargaining over the effects of a decision must be conducted in a meaningful manner and at a meaningful time, and the Board may impose sanctions to insure its adequacy." Id. at 2582.

mutual obligation of the employer and the representative of the employees to meet at reasonable times and confer in good faith with respect to wages, hours, and other terms and conditions of employment, or the negotiation of an agreement, or any question arising thereunder and the execution of a written contract incorporating any agreement reached if requested by either party, but such obligation does not compel either party to agree to a proposal or require the making of a concession * * *."[65] In general, the duty is to bargain upon request.[66]

Section 8(d) also provides that there is no duty to bargain about proposals to make changes in the collective agreement that would take effect during its term. But in the *Jacobs* case the NLRB held, and was affirmed by the Court of Appeals, that "those bargainable issues which have never been discussed by the parties, and which are in no way treated in the contract, remain matters which both the union and the employer are obliged to discuss at any time."[67] The Board emphasized, however:

> "In so holding, we emphasize that under this rule, no less than in any other circumstance, the duty to bargain implies only an obligation to *discuss* the matter in question in good faith with a sincere purpose of reaching some agreement. It does not require that either side agree, or make concessions. And if the parties originally desire to avoid later discussion with respect to matters not specifically covered in the terms of an executed contract, they need only so specify in the terms of the contract itself. Nothing in our construction of §8(d) precludes such an agreement, entered into in good faith, from foreclosing future discussion of matters not contained in the agreement."[68]

It thus appeared from the *Jacobs* case that any duty to bargain during the term of the agreement could be avoided by use of general waiver or so-called zipper clauses stating that the right to bargain on matters not covered by the agreement is waived or stating that the collective agreement constitutes the complete agreement of the parties. However, the NLRB developed a doctrine (which has received considerable court support) of narrowly construing such clauses so as to give them very limited effect. For instance, in holding a general waiver or zipper clause insufficient to constitute a waiver of the union's right to demand bargaining on a change in the method of handling operations in the employer's shipping room (the employer had refused to discuss the change but had referred the union to the

---

[65]As to the general nature of the duty to bargain, see NLRB v. Insurance Agents' Intl. Union, 80 S.Ct. 419, 45 LRRM 2704 (1960).

[66]See NLRB v. Columbian Enameling & Stamping Co., 59 S.Ct. 501, 504, 4 LRRM 524 (1939); NLRB v. Sands Mfg. Co., 59 S.Ct. 508, 514, 4 LRRM 530 (1939). Where a union did not object or request bargaining after being notified by management of anticipated changes, the employer did not violate the bargaining duty by making the changes unilaterally. NLRB v. Humble Oil & Ref. Co., 161 NLRB 714 (1966). Similarly, see NLRB v. Island Typographers, 113 LRRM 2207 (CA 2, 1983); United States Contractors, Inc., 108 LRRM 1048 (NLRB, 1981); City Hosp., 97 LRRM 1125 (NLRB, 1978).

[67]In re Jacobs Mfg. Co., 94 NLRB 1214, 1219, 28 LRRM 1162 (1951), affirmed, 196 F.2d 680 (CA 2, 1952).

[68]Ibid.

grievance and arbitration procedure), the Board stated that a "union's statutory right to be notified and consulted concerning any substantial change in employment may be waived by contract, but such waiver must be expressed in clear and unmistakable terms, and will not lightly be inferred"; furthermore, the Board reiterated that even where a waiver clause is stated in sweeping terms, it must appear from an evaluation of the negotiations that the particular matter in issue was fully discussed or consciously explored and that the union consciously yielded or clearly and unmistakably waived its interest in the matter.[69] The NLRB subsequently continued general recognition of these requirements,[70] although not always applying them rigidly;[71] and in at least one type of situation the NLRB moved to "literal" application of zipper clauses.[72]

As previously noted, the duty to bargain in good faith does not mean that agreement must be reached.[73] Where bargaining to an

---

[69]Unit Drop Forge Div., Eaton, Yale & Towne, Inc., 171 NLRB 600, 68 LRRM 1129, 1131 (1968).

[70]In Rockwell Intl. Corp., 109 LRRM 1366, 1367 (NLRB, 1982), the Board rejected the Administrative Law Judge's finding that a zipper clause waived the union's right to bargain over the cost of coffee at the plant, the Board reiterating that: the duty to bargain "continues during the existence of a bargaining agreement concerning any mandatory subject of bargaining which has not been specifically covered in the contract and regarding which the union has not clearly and unmistakably waived its right to bargain," and where "an employer relies on a purported waiver to establish its freedom unilaterally to change terms and conditions of employment not contained in the contract, the matter at issue must have been fully discussed and consciously explored during negotiations and the Union must have consciously yielded or clearly and unmistakably waived its interest in the matter." For other cases illustrating the Board's reluctance to find a waiver even though the agreement contains a zipper clause, and indicating a reviewing court's response in the given case, see Aeronca, Inc., 105 LRRM 1541 (NLRB, 1980), enforcement denied, 107 LRRM 2687 (CA 4, 1981); Pepsi Cola Distrib. Co., 100 LRRM 1626 (NLRB, 1979), enforced, 107 LRRM 2252 (CA 6, 1981); Auto Crane Co., 88 LRRM 1143 (NLRB, 1974), enforcement denied, 92 LRRM 2363 (CA 10, 1976).

[71]In Radioear Corp., 81 LRRM 1402, 1403 (NLRB, 1972), an NLRB majority stated that in some situations the rule of "clear and unequivocal" waiver should not be rigidly applied and rather that a variety of factors may be considered, such as the precise wording of the zipper clause, bargaining history, and past practice. In this case the Board ultimately found a waiver upon considering the particular circumstances along with the existence of a zipper clause. Radioear Corp., 87 LRRM 1330 (NLRB, 1974). Similarly, Columbus & Southern Ohio Elec. Co., 116 LRRM 1148 (NLRB, 1984); Bancroft-Whitney Co., 87 LRRM 1266 (NLRB, 1974).

[72]Shortly after issuing its 1982 *Rockwell* decision, above, the NLRB in *GTE Automatic Electric* "decided to reconsider the issue of whether a wrap-up (or zipper) clause, by itself, constitutes a waiver of the Union's right to bargain during the term of the contract concerning matters not specifically covered by the contract." The zipper clause in that case expressly waived the right to bargain "with respect to any subject or matter referred to, or covered in" the agreement, and also "with respect to any subject or matter not specifically referred to or covered by" the agreement. The Board concluded that the zipper clause waived midterm bargaining over the implementation of a savings and investment plan for nonunion employees "because the implementation of the plan benefiting the nonunion employees does not constitute a unilateral change of existing working conditions and because the bargaining history is completely silent on the matter in issue"; the Board stated that by permitting the employer "to invoke the zipper clause as a shield against the Union's demand for bargaining over a new benefit, and by giving literal effect to the parties' waiver of their bargaining rights, industrial peace and collective-bargaining stability will be promoted." GTE Automatic Elec., 110 LRRM 1193, 1193–1194 (NLRB, 1982), one member dissenting, and the majority cautioning that:

"Our holding does not disturb cases involving (1) a party's waiver or lack of waiver of its right to bargain over specific matters during a contract term because of the negotiating history and surrounding circumstances * * *; (2) a party engaging in deceptive conduct during negotiations, so that there is no conscious or knowing waiver of rights * * *; or (3) an employer unilaterally changing the employees' existing working conditions, then using the zipper clause as a 'sword' to justify its refusal to discuss the unilateral changes made to the status quo * * *." Id. at 1194, n. 3, asterisks indicating omission of Board's citations.

[73]The NLRB is without power to compel a company or a union to agree to any substantive contractual provision of a collective agreement. NLRB v. Burns Intl. Sec. Servs., Inc., 92 S.Ct. 1571, 80 LRRM 2225 (1972); Porter Co. v. NLRB, 90 S.Ct. 821, 73 LRRM 2561 (1970). In

impasse fails to produce agreement on a matter, management is privileged to take unilateral action consistent with its proposals in bargaining.[74] However, unilateral action by an employer on matters "which are in fact under discussion" has been viewed by the Supreme Court as obstructing bargaining as much as "a flat refusal" to bargain and has been held (absent excusing or justifying circumstances) to be a violation of the bargaining duty.[75] Moreover, under NLRB doctrine the employer generally must bargain before changing wages or terms and conditions of employment established by a collective agreement even though the agreement has expired.[76]

Brotherhood of Locomotive Eng'rs. v. Baltimore & Ohio R.R., 83 S.Ct. 691, 694 (1963), the Supreme Court reiterated that the Railway Labor Act "does not undertake governmental regulation of wages, hours, or working conditions."

[74]In NLRB v. Crompton-Highland Mills, Inc., 69 S.Ct. 960, 961, 963, 24 LRRM 2088 (1949), after a bargaining impasse had been reached but before negotiations had been completely terminated, the employer unilaterally granted a wage increase substantially greater than he had proposed in bargaining; the Supreme Court concluded that "under the circumstances" this was an unfair labor practice, but the Court indicated that it would have been proper for the employer to unilaterally grant the increase proposed by him but rejected by the union in bargaining. For other cases recognizing the employer's right to institute proposals after bargaining has failed, see Newspaper Printing Corp. v. NLRB, 111 LRRM 2824, 2828 (CA 6, 1982), where the employer was upheld in changing work assignments after bargaining to impasse, the court expressly stating that "Following good faith bargaining to impasse on a mandatory subject, an employer may unilaterally change terms and conditions of employment"; University of Chicago v. NLRB, 89 LRRM 2113 (CA 7, 1975), upholding unilateral action taken during the term of the agreement after having bargained to impasse; Times Herald Printing Co., 90 LRRM 1626, 1629–1630 (NLRB, 1975); NLRB v. Burns Intl. Sec. Servs., Inc., 92 S.Ct. 1571, 1586, 80 LRRM 2225, 2234 (1972); Television & Radio Artists v. NLRB, 57 LC ¶12,612 (D.C. Cir., 1968); NLRB v. United States Sonics Corp., 312 F.2d 610, 615 (CA 1, 1963). Explaining the necessity for this rule, see Schatzki, "The Employer's Unilateral Act—A per se Violation—Sometimes," 44 Tex. L. Rev. 470, 495–496 (1966); Durbin & Gooch, "Unilateral Action as a Legitimate Economic Weapon: Power Bargaining by the Employer Upon Expiration of the Collective Bargaining Agreement," 37 N.Y.U. L. Rev. 666, 673 (1962). In Allied Chem. & Alkali Workers v. Pittsburgh Plate Glass Co., 92 S.Ct. 383, 402 (1971), the Supreme Court held that benefits for retired workers are only a "permissive" and not a "mandatory" subject of bargaining, and that "a unilateral mid-term modification of a permissive term such as retirees' benefits does not" violate the NLRA duty to bargain.

[75]NLRB v. Katz, 82 S.Ct. 1107, 50 LRRM 2177 (1962). For interpretations giving a limited scope to this decision, see Fairweather, "The 'Fibreboard' Decision and Subcontracting," 19 Arb. J. 76, 77 (1964); Durbin & Gooch, "Unilateral Action as a Legitimate Economic Weapon: Power Bargaining by the Employer Upon Expiration of the Collective Bargaining Agreement," 37 N.Y.U. L. Rev. 666, 699–702 (1962). Business needs may privilege unilateral action, consistent with offers rejected by the union, although no impasse has been reached. Raleigh Water Heating Mfg., Co., 136 NLRB 76 (1962); NLRB v. Bradley Washfountain Co., 192 F.2d 144 (CA 7, 1951).

[76]See observations in NLRB v. Burns Intl. Sec. Servs., Inc., 92 S.Ct. 1571, 1585, 80 LRRM 2225, 2233 (1972). In Clear Pine Mouldings v. NLRB, 105 LRRM 2132, 2137 (CA 9, 1980), the court in upholding an NLRB decision stated that "as long as the bargaining obligation is not extinguished, the Company has a continuing duty to bargain without instituting unilateral benefit changes, even after expiration of the prior agreement." Also see Arbitrator Koven in 78 LA 777, 779–780. Thus, even if a mandatory matter of bargaining is not under discussion and the agreement has expired, unilateral action generally is permitted under NLRB doctrine only after the matter has been placed on the bargaining table and an impasse in bargaining has been reached (or after notice of intended action is given and the other party fails to request bargaining). The rationale offered by Arbitrator David E. Feller is that: "The natural assumption of both parties, when work continues beyond the expiration date of an agreement, is that those provisions of the expired agreement not in issue in the negotiations will continue to govern." He added that the expiration date of a collective agreement, "unlike that of a commercial contract, does not indicate an intention of the parties that the rules contained in the agreement will terminate at that time but merely that, until the specified date, neither party will use its economic power to compel changes in the rules." Feller, "The Law & Arbitration," The Chronicle (NAA, Sept. 1980), 1, 3. However, an employer can make unilateral changes in wages, hours, and working conditions after the expiration of an agreement where the employer has "a reasonably based good faith doubt of the union's majority status." Pride Ref., Inc. v. NLRB, 95 LRRM 2958, 2963 (CA 5, 1977). Accord, Beacon Upholstery Co., 226 NLRB 1360, 1367–1368 (1976). Under the Railway Labor Act the Supreme Court has held that the obligation of both parties in major disputes where the Act's

The significance of collective agreement arbitration clauses (and awards issued thereunder) in relation to the legal duty to bargain has been considered in the courts and by the NLRB. One view is illustrated by the Court of Appeals decision in the *Timken* case. Here the union charged the employer with an illegal refusal to bargain on the subject of subcontracting. The employer claimed the right to subcontract under the management rights clause of the agreement. In holding that the employer's action was not a refusal to bargain the court said that the dispute "was a dispute as to the interpretation of the management clause, and the contract specifically provided that such disputes were to be settled within the grievance procedures and, if they failed, by arbitration." Thus, the court held that the company could lawfully insist on the use of the grievance procedure and ultimately on arbitration to determine whether the management rights clause was broad enough in scope to include subcontracting.[77] Concerning this decision, Professors Archibald Cox and John T. Dunlop explained that it "implies that [the company] could lawfully stand on a favorable arbitration award until the expiration of the contract."[78] Furthermore, they expressed the conclusion that any duty to bargain during the term of the agreement can be channeled into a grievance and arbitration procedure:

> "During the term of a collective bargaining agreement, an offer to follow the contract grievance procedure satisfies any duty to bargain collectively with respect to a matter to which the contract grievance procedure may apply. A refusal either to follow the contract procedure or to discuss the issue at large is a violation of Sections 8(a)(5) and 8(b)(3) [of the National Labor Relations Act]."[79]

---

status quo provisions have been invoked "is to preserve and maintain unchanged those actual, objective working conditions and practices, broadly conceived, which were in effect prior to the time the pending dispute arose and which are involved in or related to that dispute," whether or not those conditions are covered in an existing collective agreement; the Court held that a railroad accordingly was precluded from making certain outlying assignments at places in which there previously had been none. Shore Line R.R. v. Transportation Union, 90 S.Ct. 294, 300–301, 72 LRRM 2838, 2842 (1969), the Court not reaching the duty to bargain issue. In World Airways, 54 LA 101, 105–107 (Roberts, 1969), the arbitrator considered the "Shore Line" decision inapplicable where the employer claimed contractual right for the contested action and the dispute thus involved contract interpretation rather than a major dispute under the RLA. Also see United Transp. Union v. Georgia R.R., 78 LRRM 3073 (CA 5, 1971). As to permitted unilateral action under the RLA after bargaining has been exhausted, see Brotherhood of Locomotive Eng'rs. v. Baltimore & Ohio R.R., 83 S.Ct. 691 (1963) (employer may put its bargaining proposals as to crews into effect); Brotherhood of Ry. & S.S. Clerks v. Florida E. Coast Ry., 86 S.Ct. 1420 (1966) (within limits employer may make unilateral changes beyond its bargaining proposals).

[77]Timken Roller Bearing Co. v. NLRB, 161 F.2d 949, 955 (CA 6, 1947), denying enforcement to 70 NLRB 500 (1946). Also see Square D Co. v. NLRB, 322 F.2d 360 (CA 9, 1964).

[78]Cox & Dunlop, "Regulation of Collective Bargaining by the National Labor Relations Board," 63 Harv. L. Rev. 389, 424 (1950).

[79]Cox & Dunlop, "The Duty to Bargain Collectively During the Term of an Existing Agreement," 63 Harv. L. Rev. 1097, 1101 (1950), italics omitted. Also see Professor Cox serving as arbitrator in National Radion Co., 60 LA 78, 82, 85 (1973). Compare the view of Arbitrator Charles J. Morris in Keebler Co., 75 LA 975, 982–984 (1980). Where the situation does point toward the use of arbitration, the union may have some possibility of obtaining a court injunction to maintain the status quo pending arbitration of its dispute over unilateral changes by management. See Texaco Indep. Union v. Texaco, Inc., 98 LRRM 2128 (USDC, 1978), collecting other cases on the matter.

Under one pre-*Collyer* line of NLRB decisions the duty to bargain could be so channeled,[80] but another pre-*Collyer* line of NLRB decisions held that unilateral action by an employer could justify NLRB action on refusal to bargain charges despite provision in the agreement for arbitration.[81] It has been stated that the "decision in the *Collyer* case * * * might arguably be viewed as a step in the direction of channeling refusal-to-bargain claims during the contract term through the arbitration machinery as claimed breaches of contract."[82] But it is in any event *only* a step in that direction.[83]

We have noted the NLRB's tendency (1) to hold economic decisions of management (not merely the effects of the decision but the making of the decision itself) to be matters of mandatory bargaining if job security or working conditions are affected, and (2) to construe waiver or zipper clauses narrowly, giving them very limited effect. Neither tendency gives weight to general management rights clauses or to the residual rights doctrine adhered to by many arbitrators. We

---

[80]For example, see McDonnell Aircraft Corp., 109 NLRB 930, 935 (1954), where the Board stated that the employer had satisfied the bargaining duty by willingness to arbitrate a grievance over unilateral action. For other cases in this line of decisions, see Bemis Bros. Bag Co., 143 NLRB 1311 (1963); Hercules Motor Corp., 136 NLRB 1648 (1962); National Dairy Prods. Corp., 126 NLRB 434 (1960).

[81]For example, see Unit Drop Forge Div., Eaton, Yale & Towne, Inc., 171 NLRB 600, 68 LRRM 1129 (1968); Cloverleaf Div. of Adams Dairy Co., 147 NLRB 1410 (1964); Beacon Piece Dyeing & Finishing Co., 121 NLRB 953 (1958); John W. Bolton & Sons, Inc., 91 NLRB 989 (1950). For discussion of both lines of cases see Peck, "Accommodation and Conflict Among Tribunals," Southwest Legal Foundation 15th Ann. Inst. on Labor Law 138–142 (1969). In NLRB v. C & C Plywood Corp., 87 S.Ct. 559, 64 LRRM 2065 (1967), the agreement contained a wage scale to be effective upon signing of the agreement, "with wages closed for the term of" the agreement. However, the agreement gave the employer the right "to pay a premium rate over and above the contractual classified wage rate to reward any particular employee for some special fitness, skill, aptitude or the like." Soon after signing the agreement the employer announced that all members of certain crews would be paid a premium if their crews met certain production standards. The NLRB denied that the agreement gave the employer the right to do this and held the unilateral change in contractual pay rates a violation of the bargaining duty. The Court of Appeals reasoned that the agreement "arguably" allowed the employer's act and divested the NLRB of jurisdiction over the union's unfair labor practice charge. The Supreme Court upheld the Board's jurisdiction to interpret the agreement in order to determine whether the employer had violated any duty to bargain. In so holding, the Court noted that the agreement did not contain an arbitration clause. In NLRB v. Huttig Sash & Door Co., 377 F.2d 964, 968–969 (CA 8, 1967), even though the agreement did contain an arbitration clause, the court relied on *C & C Plywood* in upholding NLRB jurisdiction to find a bargaining duty violation in the unilateral reduction of wages. That dual jurisdiction technically does exist in the NLRB (to enforce the statute) and the arbitrator (to interpret and apply the agreement) appears clear. See Chapter 10, subtopic entitled "The NLRA, the Arbitrator, and the NLRB."

[82]Cox, Bok & Gorman, Labor Law Cases and Materials, 659 (9th Ed., 1981).

[83]The aforementioned argument finds some support in cases such as Roy Robinson Chevrolet, 94 LRRM 1474, 1475 (NLRB, 1977), where an NLRB majority in deferring to arbitration prior to issuance of any award stated that "if the arbitrators should decide that the contract terms did give the Employer" the right to take the challenged unilateral action, "then the Employer's conduct would also perforce have been lawful under the Act." However, this support for the argument is obviously weakened by the Board's retention of jurisdiction for use if the arbitrators "reach a result which is repugnant to the Act." Id. at 1477. Illustrating NLRB refusal to defer to awards considered to be repugnant to its bargaining duty doctrine, see Alfred M. Lewis, Inc., 95 LRRM 1216 (NLRB, 1977). The argument is additionally weakened by cases such as Radioear Corp., 87 LRRM 1330 (NLRB, 1974), where the NLRB, after having deferred to arbitration prior to issuance of an award, ultimately refused to defer to the arbitrator's award since he had refused to rule upon the statutory bargaining issue along with his express ruling that the employer's unilateral action had not violated the collective agreement. Upon considering the *Radioear* case *on the merits*, the Board itself found a waiver of bargaining and thus no statutory violation. For discussion of NLRB deferral policy see Chapter 10, subtopic entitled "The NLRA, the Arbitrator, and the NLRB."

have also noted NLRB decisions under which the Board may take jurisdiction in unilateral action cases despite the presence of an arbitration clause (or even after an award has been issued). As General Counsel of the National Labor Relations Board, Arnold Ordman compared the approach taken by many arbitrators with that of the Board and he explained:

> "In evaluating contractual provisions urged as a defense to unfair labor practice charges involving unilateral action, many arbitrators differ from the Board in their approach.
>
> "The Board's evaluation of the circumstances in which the claim of privileged unilateral action is made usually involves considerations other than the interpretation of a single specific contract provision. Frequently, the claim of privilege is predicated, at least in part, on the presence of a generalized management prerogative clause, the absence of any express contractual prohibition of the particular action taken, or the union's failure to obtain a specific prohibition during negotiations. The Board has developed statutory principles for evaluating these general circumstances. For example, the Board with court approval has held that a waiver of statutory rights must be clear and unmistakable; waiver will not be found merely because a contract is silent on a subject protected by the Act, or because the contract contains a general management prerogative clause, or because the union in contract negotiations failed to obtain contractual protection for its statutory rights.
>
> "Many arbitrators, since they are concerned solely with whether there has been a breach of contract, consider it improper for arbitrators to apply the statutory principles developed by the Board or to apply them differently than the Board does. Some arbitrators apply the so-called 'residual rights' theory where management takes unilateral action, holding that management is free to act unless the collective bargaining agreement expressly prohibits the challenged conduct. * * *
> * * *
> "* * * In short, in a unilateral-action case, a reference to an arbitrator for a decision of the contract question may well either be a futile gesture or lead to a result in conflict with the policies of the Act."[84]

In turn, Arbitrator Clyde W. Summers stated that a bargaining duty claim which he had been asked to consider was "one which an arbitrator would tend to view from a perspective quite different from that of the Board," and he explained:

> "The Union's claim here is not substantive but procedural—that the Company took action which it was ultimately entitled to take, but it did so without first notifying and bargaining with the Union. From an arbitrator's perspective, the Company's procedure followed the customary sequence—the Company took an action it believed it was entitled to take, the Union filed a grievance, and the parties then discussed whether the Company could or should take that action. This is the procedure through which almost all cases reach arbitration and is taken so much for granted that the wording of most grievance provisions, like

---

[84]Ordman, "The Arbitrator and the NLRB," Proceedings of the 20th Annual Meeting of NAA, 47, 64–66 (BNA Books, 1967), citations omitted. General Counsel Ordman's conclusion was that "The exercise of Board discretion to defer to arbitration must be determined on a case-by-case basis." Id. at 67. For discussion and cases reflecting the Board's practice as to deferring to arbitration (both before and after an award has been rendered), see Chapter 10, subtopic entitled "The NLRA, the Arbitrator, and the NLRB."

the one here, presuppose that the employer will first act and the union will then grieve. To be sure employers frequently discuss matters with the union before taking action to minimize problems and promote good labor relations, but from perspective of the arbitrator there would normally be no implied obligation on the employer to do so.

"The perspective of the Board is quite different. The Board apparently starts from the base line proposition that an employer can make no changes in wages, hours or working conditions without first bargaining with the union to impasse. This duty to bargain before acting continues substantially unchanged after the parties have made a collective agreement, and even broad management rights clauses and 'zipper' clauses may not be sufficient to relieve the employer of this obligation unless the particular term or condition of employment which the employer seeks to change is specifically described as being within the employers' unilateral control. The Board's perspective is so different that an arbitrator may fail to appreciate the Board's view and sympathetically apply it. Nor will the arbitrator find much helpful guidance in the Board's decisions. The Board does not explain why, after the parties have constructed a grievance procedure to order their relationship, the employer's willingness to bargain through the grievance procedure after taking action is not sufficient to fulfill his statutory obligation to bargain in good faith."[85]

From the standpoint of an arbitrator *who is limited by the common prohibition that the arbitrator not add to, subtract from, or modify the agreement,* the following categories or possibilities appear most likely when action taken by an employer in the management of the enterprise is challenged by an arbitrable grievance:[86]

A. The arbitrator may find that the action is prohibited (1) expressly or impliedly by some specific provision of the agreement, or (2) by an "implied limitation" or "implied obligation" under some general provision of the agreement such as the recognition clause, or (3) by the arbitrary, capricious, or bad-faith character of the action, or (4) by some binding past practice deemed a part of the "whole" agreement.[87]

B. The arbitrator may find that management expressly or impliedly has an affirmative right to take the action under the management rights clause or some other provision in the agreement, or under some past practice.

C. The arbitrator may find that the action is neither expressly nor impliedly covered by any part of the agreement or by any binding practice, but is an action taken in the good faith management of the enterprise.

No doubt many arbitrators, and certainly those who adhere to the residual rights doctrine, would deny the grievance unless the

---

[85]Western Mass. Elec. Co., 65 LA 816, 823–824 (1975), footnotes omitted. Also see discussion in Summers, Wellington & Hyde, Labor Law Cases and Materials, 750, 867–868 (2d Ed., 1982).

[86]For a different method of classifying cases, and from a somewhat different standpoint, see Simkin, Mediation and the Dynamics of Collective Bargaining, 301–305 (BNA Books, 1971).

[87]For discussion, see topic entitled "Views Regarding Management Rights," above.

arbitrator finds that one of the possibilities under category (A) properly applies under the facts.[88]

In contrast to the aforementioned possibilities, the essence of NLRB doctrine is "that the contract does not permit unilateral action *without prior discussion* unless the employer's right to take such action is clearly and unmistakably spelled out in the contract."[89]

The NLRB's views as to required bargaining before management makes economic decisions and the Board's requirement that any waiver be express and specific were criticized by former NLRB Chairman Guy Farmer:

> "A requirement placed on employers to bargain individually and piecemeal over their decisions affecting employment conditions constitutes a none-too-subtle, dramatic shift of bargaining power to unions, in that it requires employer bargaining at the critical time when employer action is essential and delay is costly. Presumably, having been placed in such an advantageous bargaining position, the union will expect some quid pro quo each time management proposes to implement a decision which, by definition, has become negotiable. Depending on the need for promptness, the employer may well find it necessary to give the quid pro quo or to abandon the proposed action, in order to avoid the time-consuming rituals of bargaining as viewed by the Board.
>   * * *
> "Two unfortunate consequences may be foreseen * * *. First, the added strain on the collective bargaining mechanism will cause a deterioration of the labor-management relationship, which may be manifested in more serious disputes and an increase in the incidence of strikes. Second, the bargaining stalemates which will ensue will have a depressing effect on business expansion and, over the long haul, will retard automation, perpetuate uneconomic business operations and blunt competition. They will tend to convert an essentially flexible industrial economy into a crystallized, inefficient and antiquated system."[90]

As to the possibility of narrowing the area of conflict between arbitrators and the NLRB, one arbitrator suggested that the evolution of basic principles which command general acceptance "is more likely

---

[88]In this general regard, many arbitrators have taken the view that their function is to interpret and apply the agreement rather than to enforce affirmative duties under the NLRA, and they have refused to decide whether any statutory duty to bargain has been violated; it is also to be noted, however, that where the NLRB had expressly deferred an NLRA bargaining duty issue to arbitration, many arbitrators have considered and expressed a conclusion on it. See Chapter 10, subtopic entitled "The NLRA, the Arbitrator, and the NLRB."

[89]Mittenthal, "The Role of Law in Arbitration," Proceedings of the 21st Annual Meeting of NAA, 42, 56–57 (BNA Books, 1968). As noted above in this subtopic, the "clear and unmistakable" rule subsequently has not always been applied rigidly by the NLRB. As also noted above in this subtopic, generally under NLRB doctrine the employer also must bargain before changing wages or terms and conditions of employment established by a collective agreement even though the agreement has expired.

[90]Farmer, Management Rights and Union Bargaining Power, 9–10 (1965). For other severe criticisms of NLRB bargaining doctrine from the management point of view, see O'Connell, "Erosion of Management Rights," 1969 Labor Relations Yearbook, 345 (BNA Books, 1970); O'Connell, "The Drive Toward Joint Participation and Co-Determination," 1967 Labor Relations Yearbook, 71 (BNA Books, 1968); Anderson, "The Duty to Bargain During the Term of the Contract," 1967 Labor Relations Yearbook, 242 (BNA Books, 1968). For severe criticism from a neutral source, see Northrup, Compulsory Arbitration, 98–99 (1966). Again, see the U.S. Supreme Court's statements in the *First National Maintenance* decision as noted above in this subtopic.

to be achieved by Board movement toward arbitration concepts than the other way around."[91]

Duration of Limitation on Unilateral Action: Contract Limitation Versus Statutory Duty to Bargain

Where an arbitrator finds that management *is* contractually bound as to a matter, either by the parties' written collective agreement or by virtue of a binding past practice as part of their "whole" agreement, management generally will remain bound at least until the end of the term of the collective agreement.[92] When that point is reached, management of course may make proposals with the thought of altering or terminating the contractual limitation on management's freedom to act. If bargaining reaches an impasse (or if bargaining has been waived by the union), management then will be privileged to put its proposal into effect unilaterally.

On the other hand, where an arbitrator finds that management is *not* contractually bound as to a matter, either by the parties' written collective agreement or by virtue of any binding past practice, management is restricted from acting on the matter only if there is a statutory duty to bargain on it. And if a duty to bargain does in fact exist, management, not being contractually bound, may open the matter for bargaining even before the end of the term of the collective agreement. Furthermore, after bargaining to an impasse (or if bargaining has been waived by the union), management then will be privileged to put its proposal into effect notwithstanding that the term of the collective agreement may not have expired.[93]

It is thus apparent that a statutory bargaining duty limitation on management's freedom to act may be of shorter duration than a contractual limitation on that freedom.[94]

---

[91]Mittenthal, "The Role of Law in Arbitration," Proceedings of the 21st Annual Meeting of NAA, 42, 57–58 (BNA Books, 1968). Were arbitrators to make decisions consistent with "Board law" it "would mean the rejection of a method of contract construction which [arbitrators] have helped to develop over the past 25 years and which the parties have accepted by and large. * * * On the other hand, if arbitrators continue on the present course, the division between the arbitrator and Board is likely to widen." Id. at 57. For general discussion of arbitral adherence to legal doctrine, see Chapter 10, topic entitled "Range of Views as to Application of 'Law.'"

[92]Regarding past practice, see Chapter 12, subtopic entitled "Regulation, Modification, or Termination of Practice as Implied Term of Contract."

[93]For example, as in Pet, Inc., 111 LRRM 1495, 1498 (NLRB, 1982), in which the NLRB deferred to an arbitration award where the arbitrator had determined that "work rules are separate from the collective-bargaining agreement and can be changed (either tightened or relaxed) midterm after the required bargaining as long as the rules as changed do not conflict with the collective-bargaining agreement"; University of Chicago v. NLRB, 89 LRRM 2113, 2117 (CA 7, 1975), in which the court upheld the employer's unilateral transfer of work after bargaining to impasse during the term of the agreement. The NLRB expressly agreed with the latter decision and reached a similar result in Illinois Coil Spring Co., 115 LRRM 1065, 1067 (NLRB, 1984).

[94]In this regard, also see discussion by Arbitrator Gerald B. Chattman in Superior Dairy, 68 LA 976, 980 (1976).

Inroads Through Collective Bargaining

Collective bargaining is said to be "the very mechanism by which organized workers may achieve control and exercise it jointly with management"; and again, "The primary mechanism by which unions may share managerial authority in the corporation is collective bargaining, including both contract negotiations and grievance procedures, supported by the power of the strike."[95]

Restrictions made by collective bargaining agreements upon management rights are not always confined to the area of wages, hours, and conditions of employment. In fact, it is conceivable that such restrictions might invade the entire field of management functions. There is nothing to prevent weaker employers from bargaining, and making concessions, with respect to practically any matter in the area of management functions concerning which stronger unions may wish to have a voice.

Management has been cautioned that the invasion of its rights through collective bargaining may be more far-reaching than appears on the surface, and that its rights often are given away unwittingly:

> *Economist Sumner H. Slichter*: "In actual bargaining, the working rules of trade unions are built up gradually one or two at a time. This leads to an atomistic consideration of their effects, which may cause their effects as a whole to be overlooked."[96]

> *Attorney Robert Abelow*: "Rights are often given away—not taken away. Employers frequently negotiate away their responsibilities by accepting proposals which at the time seem innocuous or not immediately harmful. Being mainly concerned with the immediate problems at hand, employers are prone to make concessions on proposals, the effect of which they do not foresee, or if they do, seem too far off to worry about."[97]

It has similarly been cautioned that where frontal attacks on management rights have not met with success, union negotiators have developed flanking maneuvers which have been more effective. The success of such maneuvers is said to be due to the fact that they are methods of approach which appear on the surface to be reasonable and that their danger to management often is not perceived until too late. These indirect methods of invasion are considered to include (1) mutual-consent clauses, (2) joint committees of labor and management, (3) clauses for the application of strict length-of-service seniority, and (4) unlimited arbitration clauses.[98]

---

[95]Chamberlain, The Union Challenge to Management Control, 105 (1948).

[96]Slichter, Union Policies and Industrial Management, 578 (1941).

[97]Abelow, "The Challenge to Management's Rights," Symposium on Labor Relations Law, 260, 263 (Edited by Ralph Slovenko, 1961).

[98]Hill & Hook, Management at the Bargaining Table, 61 (1945); Dunn, Management Rights in Labor Relations, 111–112 (1946). Also see Abelow, "The Challenge to Management's Rights," Symposium on Labor Relations Law, 260, 263 (Edited by Ralph Slovenko, 1961).

Inroads Through Arbitration

Sometimes belief is expressed that arbitration is a device by which a union may broaden its authority within an industrial enterprise.[99] It is said that management rights may be lost through the use of "wide open" arbitration clauses under which the arbitrator is given authority to decide questions raised by the union concerning any matter, whether within or without the scope of the collective agreement. Moreover, warning is given that management rights also may be lost through "the creation of contract ambiguities due to inept use of the English language, which enable an arbitrator to interpret a clause in a manner not intended by the employer."[100] This spokesman also added, however, that management rights may be protected, too, through the arbitration provisions of an agreement.[101]

When an interest dispute is submitted to arbitration, there is some substitution of the judgment of the arbitrator for that of the parties. "To the extent that his decision finds in favor of the union, whether in whole or in part, he becomes the instrument by which union power has been extended."[102]

In regard to arbitration clauses, management spokesmen have recommended the use of certain "protective" clauses designed to prevent the invasion of management rights through arbitration. For example, the following clause has been suggested:

"The sole and only function of the arbitrator shall be to decide if there was or was not a violation of an express provision or provisions of the agreement, and in the performance of such function he shall apply the law of the state in which the agreement was executed."[103]

Another suggested clause would state:

"Provided, however, that if such a grievance is carried to arbitration, the Arbitrator shall not substitute his judgment for that of Management and shall reverse the decision of Management only if he finds

---

[99]Hill & Hook, ibid.; Dunn, ibid.; Abelow, id. at 266–268. Also, Chamberlain, The Union Challenge to Management Control, 107 (1948). However, it has been reminded that union rights also may be lost through arbitration. Cooper, "Comments," Symposium on Labor Relations Law, 285, 287 (Edited by Ralph Slovenko, 1961).

[100]Story, Arbitration as a Part of the Collective Bargaining Agreement, 4 (1948).

[101]Id. at 1.

[102]Chamberlain, The Union Challenge to Management Control, 107 (1948). For one arbitration board's explanation for the surrender of management rights (and also of the union's right to test its contentions by a show of economic strength) in interest arbitration, see Pan Am. Airways, 5 LA 590, 595 (Cahn, Snyder & Forge, 1946).

[103]Lamfrom, "Comments," Symposium on Labor Relations Law, 283, 284 (Edited by Ralph Slovenko, 1961). For a similar suggestion, see Story, Arbitration as a Part of the Collective Bargaining Agreement, 10 (1948). Also see clause in Van Der Vaart Brick & Bldg. Supply Co., 72 LA 663, 664 (McCrary, 1979). In Worcester Teachers' Assn., 54 LA 796, 806 (1970), Fact-Finder Seidenberg recommended adoption of an arbitration clause prohibiting the arbitrator from adding to, subtracting from, or altering the terms of the agreement, and also providing: "Neither shall the Arbitrator have the power to alter or modify any policy of the School Board or action of the Superintendent of Schools, not clearly inconsistent with the terms of the Agreement."

that it has acted arbitrarily and without reason, or for the purpose of escaping or defeating any of the other articles of this Agreement."[104]

A variety of protective or limitation clauses have been suggested by management representatives as a response to the *Trilogy* and subsequent decisions of the U.S. Supreme Court.[105]

Management Rights Clauses

While management representatives have sometimes disagreed in the past regarding the advisability of having a management rights clause, such provisions now appear to be widely favored by management.[106]

Management rights clauses vary widely in form and content. The clause may provide simply that "all normal prerogatives of management shall be retained by the Company except as specifically limited or abridged by the provisions of this agreement."[107] Clauses with much more detail as to management's rights are illustrated by the following provision stating specific powers to be exercised by management:

"Section 1. It is expressly agreed that all rights which ordinarily vest in and are exercised by employers such as COMPANY, except such as are clearly relinquished herein by COMPANY, are reserved to and shall continue to vest in COMPANY. This shall include, this enumeration being merely by way of illustration and not by way of limitation, the right to:

"(a) Manage the plant and direct the working forces, including the right to hire and to suspend, discipline or discharge employees for proper cause.

"(b) Transfer employees from one department and/or classification to another.

"(c) Lay off or relieve employees from duty because of lack of work or for other legitimate reasons.

"(d) Promote and/or transfer employees to positions and classifications not covered by this agreement, it being understood employees in the bargaining unit cannot be forced to take a position outside the bargaining unit.

"(e) Make such operating changes as are deemed necessary by it for the efficient and economical operation of the plant, including the right to change the normal work-week, the number of hours normally worked during the work-week, the length of the normal workday, the hours of

---

[104]Clifton, "Management Functions," N.Y.U. First Ann. Conf. on Labor, 89, 97 (1948). A similar clause was involved in DeLaval Separator Co., 18 LA 900, 901–903 (Finnegan, 1952).

[105]See survey by Smith & Jones, "The Impact of the Emerging Federal Law of Grievance Arbitration on Judges, Arbitrators, and Parties," 52 Va. L. Rev. 831, 902–907 (1966).

[106]For a collection of views as to use of management rights clauses, see Cummins Diesel Sales Corp., 34 LA 636, 641 (Gorsuch, 1960). Of 1536 agreements analyzed in one study, 931 contained management rights clauses. Characteristics of Major Collective Bargaining Agreements, January 1, 1978 (U.S. Dept. Labor Bull. No. 2065, 1980), 21. As a mandatory subject of bargaining, employers may insist that the agreement contain a management rights clause. NLRB v. American Natl. Ins. Co., 343 U.S. 395, 30 LRRM 2147 (1952).

[107]K & T Steel Corp., 52 LA 497, 500 (Simon, 1969). Also see Arbitrator Gundermann in 53 LA 1305 at 1305, 1307. The clause in Unit Rig & Equip. Co., 78 LA 788, 790 (Sisk, 1982), states: "The Company retains the exclusive right to manage the business. All the rights, powers, functions, and authority of the Company which are not abridged by the specific provisions of this Agreement are retained by the Company."

work, the beginning and ending time of each shift or assignment, and the number of shifts to be operated.

"(f) Transfer persons from positions and classifications not covered by this agreement to positions and/or classifications covered hereby.

"(g) Maintain discipline and efficiency.

"(h) Hire, promote, demote, transfer, discharge or discipline all levels of supervision or other persons not covered by this agreement.

"(i) Determine the type of products to be manufactured, the location of work within the plant, the schedules of production, the schedules of work within work periods, and the methods, processes, and means of manufacture and the conduct of other plant operations."[108]

The simpler clauses were once favored because of their clear-cut statement of the rule that the employer has all the proprietary rights of management except as restricted by the terms of the agreement.[109] However, as one reaction to the 1960 *Trilogy*, many management representatives now prefer a much more extensive and detailed clause to specify as fully as possible the matters over which management retains full discretion.[110] Indeed, one management spokesman urged that the desirability of a strong and detailed management rights clause is now "redoubled" as serving a dual purpose: "One is statutory—protection against the [NLRB] and its duty-to-bargain philosophy—and the other contractual—protection against the invasion of the management area through arbitration."[111]

No doubt, a management rights clause may strengthen the employer's position before an arbitrator.[112] It is also clear that during the term of a collective agreement which contains a broad and detailed management rights clause the employer may not be required to bargain about some changes upon which, in the absence of such clause, he might otherwise be compelled to bargain.[113] Another significant pur-

---

[108]Southern Aircraft Corp. and International Union of United Auto., Aircraft & Agricultural Implement Workers of Am. For some other detailed clauses, see Arbitrator Tilbury in 78 LA 1081, 1084 (county employer); Hardin in 76 LA 278, 280; McCrary in 72 LA 663, 664; Keefe in 71 LA 177, 180 (public school employer); Fitzsimmons in 70 LA 116, 118; Bell in 69 LA 1003, 1004 (university employer); Mallon in 69 LA 303 at 303 (municipal employer); Ipavec in 69 LA 115, 117. Management rights clauses in federal-sector agreements often amount to an incorporation into the agreement of management rights provisions of the Civil Service Reform Act. See Arbitrator Phelan in 78 LA 740 at 740; Heliker in 77 LA 918, 919; Weckstein in 77 LA 638, 639.

[109]See Story, Arbitration as a Part of the Collective Bargaining Agreement, 11 (1948); Dunn, Management Rights in Labor Relations, 109 (1946).

[110]Smith & Jones, "The Impact of the Emerging Federal Law of Grievance Arbitration on Judges, Arbitrators, and Parties," 52 Va. L. Rev. 831, 897–902 (1966), where detailed clauses favored by management representatives are quoted. For an agreement using *both* the simpler "residual rights" clause and the detailed clause, see Almaden Vineyards, 56 LA 425, 426 (Kagel, 1971). Similarly, see Arbitrator Eyraud in 77 LA 857 at 857; Raymond in 76 LA 932, 932–933.

[111]O'Connell, "Erosion of Management Rights," 1969 Labor Relations Yearbook, 345, 350, 353 (BNA Books, 1970).

[112]For example, see Arbitrator Lipson in 76 LA 295, 298–299; Hatcher in 69 LA 665, 670; Abrams in 69 LA 594, 598; Chattman in 68 LA 976, 982; Kates in 46 LA 317, 320. In A. Hoen & Co., 64 LA 197, 199, 204 (1975), the company claimed residual rights but Arbitrator Feldesman gave "some significance" to the union's assertion that "the lack of a management rights clause in the collective agreement is a telling blow" to the company's case.

[113]See Consolidated Foods Corp., 183 NLRB 832 (1970); Cello-Foil Prods., Inc., 72 LRRM 1196 (NLRB, 1969); LeRoy Mach. Co., 56 LRRM 1369 (NLRB, 1964); The Borden Co., 35 LRRM 1133 (NLRB, 1954). As to management's right to insist on a clause insuring it the right to take unilateral action on matters not specifically covered by the agreement, see Long Lake Lumber Co., 182 NLRB 435, 74 LRRM 1116 (1970), holding that insistence on such a clause was not an unlawful refusal to bargain.

pose of such clauses is to aid union officials in explaining to the membership what the agreement does and does not give them.[114]

Impact of Arbitration Upon Management Rights

The extensive use of labor-management arbitration has resulted in the evolution of a continually developing private system of industrial jurisprudence. Included within the growing body of industrial rulings are many involving management rights issues. While legal principles, as well as court and administrative board decisions, loom in the background, relatively wide discretion generally is left to arbitrators in the private sector to deal with the law according to their best judgment.[115] It should be recognized, therefore, that arbitral case law is in itself a separate and distinct institution. It also should be recognized that the industrial jurisprudence of arbitrators will not always be in absolute harmony with the course of decisions under the National Labor Relations Act.[116]

The primary objective of the remainder of this Chapter will be to consider the effective scope of management rights as evidenced and outlined by arbitration awards.

Control of Operation Methods

In general, arbitrators have recognized broad authority in management (absent clear limitations in the agreement) to determine methods of operation.[117] It has been said that unless restricted by contract, management has the right "to determine what is to be produced, when it is to be produced, and how it is to be produced."[118] Again, unless restricted by the agreement management has the right

---

[114]See Phelps, "Management's Reserved Rights: An Industry View," Management Rights and the Arbitration Process, 103, 113–114 (BNA Books, 1956).

[115]For extensive discussion, see the first few topics in Chapter 10, where comment is made also in reference to arbitrators in the public sector.

[116]See this Chapter, subtopic entitled "The Duty to Bargain: Right of Unilateral Action"; Chapter 10, subtopic entitled "The NLRA, the Arbitrator, and the NLRB."

[117]See general statements by Arbitrator O'Connell in 79 LA 272, 276; Fitch in 75 LA 523, 529, 531; Kiok in 75 LA 16, 17; Ross in 74 LA 92, 95; Swain in 69 LA 493, 498–499, 501; A. Roberts in 54 LA 896, 900; Whyte in 54 LA 807, 814; Turkus in 44 LA 1219, 1223; Kamin in 42 LA 173, 175; Markowitz in 41 LA 1087, 1090; Koven in 39 LA 939, 940–941; Raimon in 36 LA 621, 626; Dworkin in 29 LA 787, 792; Kesselman in 28 LA 441, 444–445; R. Roberts in 27 LA 736, 742–743; Klamon in 22 LA 336, 351; McCoy in 6 LA 681, 687. Also see Gallagher in 79 LA 1151, 1154; Taylor in 71 LA 1072, 1076; Heinsz in 70 LA 216, 220; Davey in 40 LA 700, 705–706; Fleming in 30 LA 147, 149. For related discussion see Chapter 12, topic entitled "Custom and Practice as Part of the Contract"; Stein, "Management Rights and Productivity," 32 Arb. J. 270 (1977). Contract clauses requiring management to discuss or give notice of operational changes have been narrowly construed so as not to impose an undue limitation on management. See Arbitrator Kelliher in 43 LA 267, 268–269; Smith in 43 LA 193, 206–207; Uible in 41 LA 510, 512; Jaffee in 40 LA 114, 117–118. Cf., Hall in 68 LA 147, 150–151, imposing a notice requirement where the contract was silent.

[118]Torrington Co., 1 LA 35, 42 (Courshon, 1945). Similarly, see Arbitrator Swain in 69 LA 493, 501; Roberts in 54 LA 896, 900; Bauder in 22 LA 163, 165.

to determine what work shall be done,[119] to determine what kinds of services and business activity to engage in,[120] and to determine the techniques, tools, and equipment by which work in its behalf shall be performed.[121]

Management must have some discretion as to the method of carrying on its operations. It "should not be put in a straight jacket."[122] A primary function of management is to operate on the most efficient basis.[123] "In the operation of any plant, management has a fixed obligation to see that unnecessary costs are dispensed with and that production programs are changed to meet changing production demands. This is an inherent right * * *."[124]

The line of demarcation between "operation methods" and "working conditions" often must be determined. In one case Arbitrator Whitley P. McCoy noted the difficulty which such determination may entail. The agreement of the parties recognized the exclusive right of management to determine methods of operation, but it also restricted the right of management to change working conditions by requiring negotiations with the union before such changes could be made. The employer changed the operations of some employees from a noncontinuous to a continuous basis in the interest of plant efficiency, with the result that the employees were ordered to work through a period previously allowed for washing up. Arbitrator McCoy ruled that the order requiring the employees to work through the wash-up period was proper as an incidental result of the employer's good-faith exercise of the exclusive right to determine methods of operation. He stated the general considerations involved:

> "The distinction between a change in working conditions, which by the terms of the contract must be the subject of negotiation prior to its institution, and a change in methods of operation, which by the terms of the contract is a sole function of management, is not easy to define or even to make clear by example. Abolition or sharp curtailment of an

---

[119]Pacific Mills, 9 LA 236, 238 (McCoy, 1947); Gulf Oil Corp., 3 LA 798, 800 (Carmichael, 1946).

[120]Detroit Edison Co., 43 LA 193, 209 (Smith, 1964), also holding that a past practice of engaging in a particular line of activity of itself provides no contractual assurance that it will be continued. Also see First Natl. Maintenance Corp. v. NLRB, 101 S.Ct. 2573, 2579–2584; 107 LRRM 2705 (1981), discussed above in subtopic entitled "The Duty to Bargain: Right of Unilateral Action."

[121]Corn Prods. Co., 42 LA 173, 175 (Kamin, 1964). Also see Arbitrator Crane in 73 LA 1007, 1011; Simon in 72 LA 1115, 1121–1123; Rohman in 44 LA 682, 686.

[122]Shell Oil Co., 44 LA 1219, 1223 (Turkus, 1965); Thompson Mahogany Co., 5 LA 397, 399 (Brandschain, 1946).

[123]See Arbitrator Hauck in 73 LA 990, 991; Goodman in 73 LA 207, 209; Larrabee in 72 LA 1204, 1209; Swain in 69 LA 493, 501; Cox in 68 LA 864, 866; Larkin in 54 LA 250, 252; Turkus in 44 LA 1219, 1223; Eyraud in 36 LA 1388, 1392; McIntosh in 33 LA 860, 861; Dworkin in 29 LA 787, 792; Marshall in 29 LA 687, 692; Kesselman in 28 LA 441, 445; Ridge in 26 LA 422, 426–427; Myers in 10 LA 261, 265.

[124]Youngstown Sheet & Tube Co., 4 LA 514, 517 (Miller, 1946). Also see Arbitrator Fitch in 75 LA 523, 529; Roumell in 71 LA 822, 827 (stating that the municipal employer in question "could have been charged with incompetency if it had not taken steps to modernize its procedures"); Gross in 20 LA 749, 750; Klamon in 15 LA 782, 789. However, where the agreement expressly prohibited the employer from using spray equipment without written consent of the union, the arbitrator enforced the restriction even though such equipment would have been more efficient for the particular job. Claremont Painting & Decorating Co., 46 LA 894, 895–896 (Kerrison, 1966).

existing practice concerning rest time, wash-up time, paid lunch period, furnishing of shower baths and lockers, matters pertaining to sanitation, safety and health, or such like matter are clearly changes in working conditions. On the other hand, a change from the use of pot heaters to McNeill presses or from noncontinuous to continuous operation is just as clearly a change primarily in methods of operation. The latter changes usually cause, with respect to the individuals affected, some change of their working habits, but they are primarily and essentially changes in methods, not in conditions, and as such are exclusively a management function, subject only to the right of affected employees to resort to the grievance procedure to correct abuses or hardships such as decreased earnings or stretchout. Of course a change that was merely in form one of method, used as a pretext to institute a change of working conditions, would not be justifiable."[125]

The right of management to determine the types of machinery and equipment to be used and to determine the processes of manufacture may be stated specifically in the agreement. This right also might be ruled to be included in a clause reserving the right of general management of the plant to the employer.[126] Even if such right is not specified in the agreement, numerous cases expressly or inferentially recognize that it can be exercised as a residual management power except as it has been restricted by the agreement.[127]

As a corollary it follows that the employer has the right to have the employees operate improved machines and perform changed operation methods in good faith up to the level of their productive capacity.[128] Employees may be inclined to resist technological change, for workers who have spent years in a skilled trade are reluctant to risk its disappearance. "The need of the manufacturer to improve production methods is matched by the concern of the employees that they may be thrown out on the streets."[129]

In this general regard, it has been observed that:

---

[125]Goodyear Tire & Rubber Co. of Ala., 6 LA 681, 687 (1947). Also dealing with the line between "operation methods" and "working conditions," see Arbitrator Gallagher in 79 LA 1151, 1154; Curry in 77 LA 217, 219; Cantor in 75 LA 369, 374–376 (federal agency employer); Kabaker in 55 LA 1306, 1308–1309; Stouffer in 44 LA 1134, 1137–1138; Kovenock in 40 LA 300, 303–304; Koven in 39 LA 939, 940–941; Dworkin in 29 LA 787, 792–793; Marshall in 29 LA 687, 692–693; Kesselman in 28 LA 441, 444; Roberts in 27 LA 736, 742–743; Updegraff in 20 LA 890, 891; Hampton in 15 LA 603, 607–608.

[126]For example, see Associated Shoe Indus. of Se. Mass., 10 LA 535, 537–539 (Myers, 1948). Also see Arbitrator Pritzker in 72 LA 314, 322; Nitka in 70 LA 1140, 1143–1144; Raimon in 36 LA 621, 626; Healy in 11 LA 703; 705–706; Myers in 10 LA 261, 264–265.

[127]See Arbitrator Ross in 74 LA 92, 95–96; Dworkin in 45 LA 897, 902; Cahn in 45 LA 609, 610–611; Markowitz in 41 LA 1087, 1090; Kagel in 40 LA 62, 63; Koven in 39 LA 939, 940–941; Eyraud in 36 LA 1388, 1392; Ross in 35 LA 695, 697–698; Updegraff in 30 LA 115, 117, and in 7 LA 943, 945; Beatty in 26 LA 1, 3; Townsend in 17 LA 472, 475. Even where the agreement expressly imposed some requirement or limitation upon management in regard to automation or technological changes, the provisions were narrowly interpreted to apply only to sweeping and fundamental changes. Los Angeles Herald Examiner, 45 LA 860, 861–862 (Kadish, 1965); Mackay Radio & Tel. Co., 42 LA 612, 617–619 (Koven, 1964).

[128]Associated Shoe Indus. of Se. Mass., 10 LA 535, 539 (Myers, 1948). To similar effect, Arbitrator O'Connell in 79 LA 272, 276; Porter in 52 LA 162, 164; Lehoczky in 45 LA 996, 998; Tatum in 41 LA 1147, 1150; Whiting in 38 LA 644, 646; Stouffer in 34 LA 165, 169; Brecht in 17 LA 268, 270. In San Antonio Air Logistics Center, 73 LA 455, 463 (LeBaron, 1979), the union improperly encouraged employees not to cooperate in an employer survey being conducted to improve production. Similarly, see Arbitrator Caraway in 73 LA 1074, 1079–1081.

[129]Associated Shoe Indus. of Se. Mass., 10 LA 535, 538 (Myers, 1948).

"Whenever a job is abolished, a machine discontinued, or work in a department is discontinued, men lose jobs and their seniority rights to jobs are affected. But this involves no wrong of itself; it is merely one of the forms of injury or damage flowing from an act. The primary question is whether the act was wrongful. If it was not, then no question can properly arise as to damage."[130]

It has been suggested, too, that the exercise of this management function serves to protect the interests of the employees as well as of the employer, for if the employer is permitted to operate new machinery, "his competitive position will be enhanced, improving his chance to win new business and thereby to provide greater employment."[131] Similarly, an Emergency Board under the Railway Labor Act declared that: "An employment stabilization program based upon rules which freeze existing jobs, bar improvement in work methods and block technological progress reaps more damage than benefit."[132] The Board recommended against a union proposal which would freeze existing jobs, but the Board recommended that the parties take steps to minimize the adverse effects upon employees resulting from operational changes by the employer.[133]

Wage Adjustments Following Changes in Operation Methods

Changes in operation methods, which are largely left within the discretion of management, often necessitate adjustments in wage rates. While the employer has wide discretion in determining operation methods, he is closely restricted in the determination of wage rates for new or changed processes.

The right initially to determine the job rate for a new or altered job may be given to management by the agreement. The following clause is illustrative:

"rates on all new or changed operations shall be temporarily established by the employer * * *. If a grievance arises therefrom, the price shall be negotiated * * *. If unable to agree the matter shall be arbitrated in accordance with this contract."[134]

---

[130]Allegheny Ludlum Steel Corp., 20 LA 455, 457 (McCoy, 1953). Also see Arbitrator Kagel in 56 LA 425, 429; Ross in 35 LA 695, 697–698; Fleming in 30 LA 147, 149; Updegraff in 28 LA 135, 136–137; Roberts in 27 LA 736, 742–744; Beatty in 26 LA 1, 3. However, in Premier Albums of N.J., 41 LA 945, 946–947 (Mazur, 1963), it was held that while the employer had the right to introduce new machinery, no worker could be terminated due to the change.

[131]Associated Shoe Indus. of Se. Mass., 10 LA 535, 539 (Myers, 1948).

[132]Southern Pac. Co. v. Railroad Telegraphers, 37 LA 413, 421 (Platt, Wyckoff & Handsaker, 1961).

[133]Id. at 422–424.

[134]Associated Shoe Indus. of Se. Mass., 10 LA 535, 537 (Myers, 1948). Also see Arbitrator Taylor in 80 LA 166, 167; Cerone in 69 LA 168, 169; Seinsheimer in 63 LA 384, 385; Duff in 46 LA 295, 296; Lehoczky, Fisher & Myers in 32 LA 957, 958–959 (here interests arbitrators ordered use of a similar clause); Shipman in 21 LA 387, 389–390; Gilden in 9 LA 931, 937. Absent a specific provision for arbitration of rates of changed jobs, some arbitrators have denied their authority to set the rate. See Arbitrator Erbs in 49 LA 1270, 1274; Gregory in 41 LA 1169, 1174–1176. But a different conclusion was reached by Arbitrator Marshall in 23 LA 228, 233–234. For other cases dealing with the arbitrator's authority to set the rate on changed jobs, see Arbitrator Shister in 47 LA 601, 605–606; Willingham in 41 LA 1076, 1081–1082.

If the agreement does not give the employer the right initially to set the new rate, an arbitrator may require him to bargain before setting a rate. Arbitrator Harry H. Platt, for instance, speaking as chairman of an arbitration board, ruled that, under an agreement recognizing the union "as the sole collective bargaining agency for the employees of the company" and in the light of the continuing legal duty of the employer to bargain during the entire life of the contract, the employer could not unilaterally establish the rate for a new job.[135] However, Arbitrator Arthur M. Ross, speaking as chairman of another arbitration board, ruled that after negotiations had ended in disagreement the employer could install new rates, subject to challenge through the grievance and arbitration procedure, for this "is almost universally the practice in American industry."[136]

Another arbitrator, considering a contract which reserved the direction of the working forces to management and which provided that the company could re-time-study and adjust piece rates after changes in materials, tools, or methods, expressed the view that management had and should have the right initially to determine job duties and job rates for new or altered jobs, because the "exigencies of production do not permit the problems arising from improved production methods to be settled in advance." This arbitrator noted that in some industries these matters are left initially to management determination, subject to the grievance procedure. He did recognize, however, that this "requires the union to have the patience to endure management's determinations until the grievance procedure produces a remedy."[137]

Even where an agreement provided that existing rates should be continued without change, this was held not to preclude management from establishing new piece rates after introducing new equipment which materially changed job duties; Arbitrator Wayne L. Townsend reasoned that the requirement that rates be continued was based upon the assumption that equipment and methods would remain the same and, since that assumption was not borne out by subsequent events, the requirement did not apply.[138]

Many disputes concerning rates for new or changed operating methods have reached arbitration.[139] Arbitrators have recognized

---

[135]Copco Steel & Eng'g. Co., 6 LA 156, 164 (1947). To similar effect, Arbitrator Marshall in 23 LA 228, 233; Carmichael in 14 LA 544, 546; Justin in 13 LA 177, 180. But see Lewis in 49 LA 202, 204 (management's right to create new jobs carries with it the right to set a new rate for the job if job is not same as existing classifications); Sizelove in 24 LA 726, 728; Klamon in 15 LA 782, 791. Also see Gregory in 14 LA 802, 805, where past practice strongly influenced the result reached.

[136]Keasbey & Mattison Co., 36 LA 423, 424 (1960). For illustrations of this course of procedure by contract provision, see Arbitrator Rule in 74 LA 146, 146–147; Waite in 71 LA 141 at 141.

[137]Diemolding Corp., 2 LA 274, 276 (Kharas, 1945). Also see Thor Corp., 16 LA 770, 772–774 (Baab, 1951). But the view has been expressed that to consider a unilateral action of management as a grievance is not a substitute for negotiation prior to the action. General Motors Corp., 7 LA 368, 371 (Griffin, 1947).

[138]A.C.L. Haase Co., 17 LA 472, 477–479 (1951).

[139]In some cases such disputes have been held nonarbitrable. See Arbitrator Teple in 46 LA 1189, 1194; McDermott in 44 LA 774, 777; Warns in 36 LA 329, 330.

certain principles or standards to be considered in determining rates for new or changed operations (these standards are sometimes stated in the agreement). The standards observed by arbitrators should be noted because of their obvious practical importance.[140]

Hourly Rated Employees

The rule generally applied in the case of employees who work for hourly rather than incentive rates is that an increase in hourly rates should accompany any *material* increase in the workload.[141] Where the matter was not specifically covered by the contract, for instance, Arbitrator Whitley P. McCoy ruled that when a change is made in job content, the job should be restudied to determine whether the original workload has been changed sufficiently to necessitate an adjustment in the wage rate. He stated that it does not follow that simply because work has been added to a job there must necessarily be an increase of pay, though presumptively there should be; whether there should be an increase in pay "depends upon whether the workload was too light and the increase does not make it too heavy or whether the workload was proper and the increase is material and makes it too heavy."[142]

A similar ruling was made by Arbitrator A. Howard Myers under a contract containing provision for rate revision following workload changes. Arbitrator Myers ruled that not all changes in workload necessitate a revision of wages.

> "The theoretical issue arises as to whether every change in workload or equipment, irrespective of competitive conditions and original workload, justifies a rate increase. I think that the answer must be in the negative where, as here, the change results in raising an abnormally slow job rate to a still slow rate, with pay that is not inequitable in terms of comparable rates in this plant or in other plants * * *."[143]

However, Arbitrator Clarence M. Updegraff appeared unwilling to give so much weight to the factor of a previously light workload where the agreement provided that consideration should be given to the adjustment of rates when the workload is materially increased. He ruled that such a provision does not permit the employer to discount entirely a material increase in the workload on the ground that the previous workload was too light, but that this is one of the factors

---

[140]For related material, see this Chapter, topic entitled "Production Standards, Time Studies, and Job Evaluation."

[141]For related material, see this Chapter, topic entitled "Determination of Size of Crews."

[142]Goodyear Tire & Rubber Co. of Ala., 6 LA 924, 925 (1947). Similarly, see Arbitrator Waite in 71 LA 141, 142; Marshall in 51 LA 1051, 1054–1055; Shister in 44 LA 992, 995–996; Seinsheimer in 35 LA 113, 116–117. Also see Prasow in 40 LA 966, 969–970; Marshall in 29 LA 687, 692–693; Valtin in 28 LA 530, 531–532. For factors which an arbitrator considered in applying a contractual requirement that employees do "a reasonable day's work," see Arketex Ceramic Corp., 42 LA 125, 130–131 (Seinsheimer, 1964).

[143]Verney Corp., 7 LA 27, 29 (1946). To similar efffect, Aleo Mfg. Co., 19 LA 647, 649–650 (Maggs, 1952). Also see Arbitrator Markowitz in 52 LA 1306, 1309; Seward in 27 LA 906, 907.

which, without having a decisive effect, may be taken into consideration as limiting the increase to be granted.[144]

A slight increase in workload does not call for a higher rate.[145] It
has been held that changing to new machines which produce more but
which require less skill and effort does not constitute such change in
the workload as to require revision of rates.[146] Where, however, a new
machine or operation involves more than a slight increase in duties,
skill, responsibility, or hazards, rate revision may be required.[147] In
one case a wage increase was ordered for operators of a new machine
even though it was easier to operate than any other equipment in the
plant, the Arbitrator stating that the operator "is responsible for
operating a more sophisticated—and expensive—piece of machinery
which at least has the potential for significantly greater profits than
other machines and he should share in the expected increase in productivity * * *."[148]

Incentive Employees

Concerning incentive wage plans, a study by the U.S. Department
of Labor explained:

> "An incentive wage plan is a method of wage payment by which
> workers receive extra pay for extra production. In establishing wage
> incentive plans, consideration must be given to (1) the base rate for the
> job; (2) the amount of work required to earn the base rate; and (3) the
> relationship between extra work above the base and extra pay for the
> extra performance."[149]

---

[144]Continental Can Co., 5 LA 247, 250 (1946).

[145]See Arbitrator Edes in 80 LA 1106, 1108; Strong in 41 LA 1038, 1041; Seinsheimer in 35 LA
113, 116–117; Abernethy in 4 LA 773, 775. Also see Miller in 80 LA 1078, 1081–1082, where the
contract dealt expressly with the matter. As to what might be considered more than slight, see
Arbitrator Kelliher in 13 LA 220, 222; Copelof in 5 LA 115, 118.

[146]Central Screw Co., 11 LA 108, 111 (Edes, 1948); E.F. Houghton & Co., 4 LA 716, 717–718
(Cahn, 1946). Also see Arbitrator Taylor in 80 LA 166, 170–171 (by management's introduction of
computer terminals the employees in question "were merely exposed to a new tool which
permitted them to perform their work easier and more accurately"); Cerone in 69 LA 168, 170;
Wood in 32 LA 216, 220; White in 13 LA 223, 225.

[147]See Arbitrator McIntosh in 54 LA 418, 420; Hertz in 48 LA 577, 578; Rubin in 47 LA 577,
579–580; Roberts in 45 LA 964, 967; Mazur in 41 LA 945, 947; Prasow in 40 LA 565, 568–569;
Lehoczky in 38 LA 584, 585; Dworkin in 37 LA 323, 330; Justin in 28 LA 548, 553; Harbison in 21
LA 609, 611–612; Jaffee in 19 LA 452, 454; Reid in 19 LA 358, 361; Copelof in 16 LA 76, 78–79;
Gilden in 9 LA 931, 937; Blair in 2 LA 572, 576. Also see Seward in 27 LA 906, 907; Donnelly in 23
LA 782, 783–784; Cahn in 17 LA 277, 278–280; Brecht in 17 LA 268, 271–272; Healy in 8 LA 88,
91. In Southwest Steel Corp., 38 LA 344, 345–346 (Duff, 1962), a temporary (one day) increase in
workload required additional pay.

[148]Printing Indus. of Metropolitan Washington, D.C., 71 LA 838, 842 (Ables, 1978), where
the amount of increase was limited, however, in recognition of "the impact of such increase in
wages on the existing relationship between wages and other equipment * * *." Compare Marsh
Stencil Mach. Co., 33 LA 1, 4–5 (Klamon, 1959), where less skill was required on new machines
and hourly rated employees claimed the benefit of increased productivity.

[149]Incentive Wage Provisions; Time Studies and Standards of Production, p. 1 (U.S. Dept. of
Labor, Bureau of Labor Statistics, Bull. No. 908–3, 1948). For an explanation of several different
types of incentives used in industry (productivity incentive, continuity of operation incentive,
quality incentive), see Keystone Steel & Wire Co., 55 LA 41, 50 (McKenna, 1970). In Weatherhead
Co., 55 LA 837, 840 (Fish, 1970), the arbitrator listed reasons which might justify management in
placing a ceiling on incentive production. For cases dealing with union access to incentive system
data and records, see Tappan Co., 49 LA 922, 928 (Dworkin, 1967); Hydril Co., 37 LA 279, 282
(Lehoczky, 1961). For labor, management, and neutral views on arbitration of incentive disputes,
see "Arbitration of Disputes Involving Incentive Problems," Critical Issues in Labor Arbitration,

Another study by the same agency stated that incentive plans basically are either a piecework plan or some type of standard-hour plan.[150] It was noted, however, that "Many agreements do not clearly indicate whether the applicable system is piecework or a form of standard-hour plan."[151]

A standard sometimes applied by arbitrators in reviewing the rates of incentive employees whose workload has been changed is the maintenance of prior earnings.[152] The theory underlying this standard is that incentive employees should be able to earn as much under the new operation as under the old.[153]

Another standard, much less concrete, requires the maintenance of the ratio of earnings to effort expended.[154] Under the "ratio of earnings to effort" standard no change in incentive rates is in order unless there is a change in the amount of incentive effort required per

---

61–97 (BNA Books, 1957). For other general discussions, see Rubin, "The Arbitration of Incentive Issues," Proceedings of the 32nd Annual Meeting of NAA, 92 (BNA Books, 1980); Gomberg, "The Present Status of Arbitration Under Wage Incentive Payment Plans," id. at 116; Unterberger, "The Arbitration of Wage Incentive Cases," 23 Arb. J. 236 (1968); Davis, "Incentive Problems," Management Rights and the Arbitration Process, 50 (BNA Books, 1956); Morrison, "Arbitration of Wage Incentives," 11 Arb. J. (n.s.) 199 (1956); Waite, Seybold & Unterberger, "Problems in the Arbitration of Wage Incentives," Arbitration Today, 25–44 (BNA Books, 1955).

[150]Major Collective Bargaining Agreements: Wage-Incentive, Production Standard, and Time-Study Provisions, 3 (U.S. Dept. of Labor, Bureau of Labor Statistics Bull. No. 1425–18, 1979). "Piecework, the simplest system, pays the individual a set 'price' per unit of output. A minimum or base rate usually is set, and employees producing below or at the base rate receive the minimum; faster workers receive more." Ibid. On the other hand, a standard-hour plan "is usually based on time, rather than money, per unit or output. The standard, often expressed as 100 percent, refers to the amount of work of specified quality which an average experienced employee can produce in an hour, working at normal performance with proper allowances for rest, personal needs, and minor delays. Under most standard-hour plans, employees are credited with additional earnings for production exceeding the standard." Ibid.

[151]Ibid. The study explained also that incentive systems "are best suited to work that is repetitive, readily measurable, and performed at a pace subject to control by the worker or group"; that group incentives are most appropriate where a number of employees work together on a task and an individual's work cannot be separately measured; that the incentive concept always has been somewhat controversial; that some employers reject incentive plans as too difficult and costly to administer, or as creating friction among employees; that some unions claim, among other criticisms, that incentive plans "are divisive, undermine group solidarity, create undesirable competition among employees, and contribute to excessive stress and fatigue"; but that incentive systems can be successful under collective bargaining, as "is evident from the large number of such plans that have continued over many years." Id. at 1, 4.

[152]See Arbitrator Stouffer in 28 LA 259, 264–265; Copelof in 10 LA 933, 940; Keister in 4 LA 386, 389; Dwyer in 4 LA 355, 358. This standard was given a significant role in the award of a steel industry incentive coordinating committee. See Coordinating Comm., Steel Cos., 53 LA 145, 149 (Simkin, Seward, Garrett, 1969). Also see Arbitrator McDermott in 46 LA 660, 664; Markowitz in 41 LA 1087, 1090; Garrett in 26 LA 812, 822; Townsend in 17 LA 472, 479. For discussion of steel industry cases, see Dybeck, "Arbitration of Wage Incentives From the Perspective of the Steel Industry," Proceedings of the 32nd Annual Meeting of NAA, 105 (BNA Books, 1980).

[153]In this regard, there have been a number of cases dealing with management efforts to change from incentive to hourly rates. See Arbitrator Duff in 47 LA 1157, 1159–1160; Lehoczky in 40 LA 875, 878; Horlacher in 38 LA 434, 435–436; Warns in 27 LA 758, 760–761; Davey in 23 LA 490, 493–494; Seward in 17 LA 918, 920–921; McCoy in 13 LA 414, 416–417.

[154]This standard was used by Arbitrator Shipman in 37 LA 669, 670; Lehoczky in 22 LA 450, 452; Scheiber in 10 LA 20, 23–24; Blumer in 8 LA 846, 849; Hampton in 6 LA 579, 582; Whiting in 6 LA 218, 219–220; Dwyer in 4 LA 482, 483. Also see Arbitrator Briggs in 79 LA 889, 893–894. As a preamble to his discussion of incentive issues, Arbitrator Milton Rubin stated: "I should emphasize the basic theme that the so-called incentive issues arise from pay-for-production systems of compensation. The employer and the union have established this relationship of work and pay by negotiation and practice; it is the function of the arbitrator to decide the issues to confirm and continue the accepted ratio." Rubin, "The Arbitration of Incentive Issues," Proceedings of the 32nd Annual Meeting of NAA, 92 at 92 (BNA Books, 1980), where he also stated (p. 93) that the "paucity" of published incentive cases "should not be misunderstood * * * to be the true picture of the number of such issues arbitrated in this country."

unit of incentive production.[155] Application of this standard means that employees receive increased earnings on that part of increased production that is due to increased work effort, and that management receives the benefit from that part of increased production that is due to mechanical improvements as such.[156]

Use of this standard is illustrated by a case in which the employer ordered an increase in the speed at which a machine was to be operated and simultaneously decreased the incentive rate. Although the decreased rate yielded higher earnings than the employees had received before the increase in machine speed, they demanded that the prior incentive rate be reestablished since, even at the higher prior rate, earnings would be increased by a smaller percentage than the increase in effort required to control the machine at the higher speed. The arbitrator found that the increase in machine speed was 19 percent, that the increase in work effort was 16 percent, and that, even if the prior higher rate were used, the increase in earnings would amount only to 11.6 percent. Accordingly, he held the demand of the employees to be reasonable and ordered that the prior rate be reestablished.[157]

Reduction of incentive rates has been allowed where the introduction of new machinery has resulted in increased production without requiring an increase in effort.[158] Moreover, reduction of incentive rates has been ordered where employees controlled production on new machines at a very low level.[159]

It can be expected that no adjustment in incentive rates will be required as long as the change in the workload is slight.[160]

Production Standards, Time Studies, and Job Evaluation

"Whether wages are computed on a time or incentive basis, there is usually some formal or informal determination of the output

---

[155]American Steel & Wire Co., 8 LA 846, 849 (Blumer, 1947).

[156]Carnegie Ill. Steel Corp., 5 LA 712, 720 (Blumer, 1946), where it was also explained that the change in incentive effort is not necessarily the same as the change in work required for the operation. Also see Arbitrator McCoy in 28 LA 129, 131; Shipman in 21 LA 386, 390.

[157]Anaconda Wire & Cable Co., 10 LA 20, 24 (Scheiber, 1948).

[158]Jenkins Bros., 11 LA 432, 435 (Donnelly, 1948); Reliance Mfg. Co., 3 LA 677, 679 (Whiting, 1946). Cf., Arbitrator Shipman in 17 LA 650, 653–654. For the imposition of a time limit (within a "reasonable time") for changing incentive rates in response to changes in production methods, see Worthington Corp., 34 LA 497, 503 (Crawford, 1959), where management waited too long to change the rate (producing lower earnings). Also see Arbitrator Dunn in 70 LA 1154, 1156. But see Seinsheimer in 63 LA 384, 386. For an illustration that the incentive premium can lose its appeal to employees, see Jenkins Bros., 33 LA 275, 277 (Donnelly, 1959).

[159]Associated Shoe Indus. of Se. Mass., 10 LA 535, 538–539 (Myers, 1948); Wolverine Shoe & Tanning Corp., 15 LA 195, 196–197 (Platt, 1950). Concerning the pace at which employees should work when paid on a group incentive basis, see Pittsburgh Plate Glass Co., 36 LA 21, 22 (Lehoczky, Fisher & Myers, 1960).

[160]Schlueter Mfg. Co., 10 LA 295, 296–297 (Hilpert, 1948), where it was ruled, however, that the overall effect of a succession of minor additions to an operation could be considered; Goodyear Tire & Rubber Co. of Ala., 5 LA 30, 35 (McCoy, 1946). Some agreements expressly provide for change in incentive rates when there is a "substantial" change in operations. For cases involving the application of such provisions, see 28 LA 129; 21 LA 387; 21 LA 84; 20 LA 455; 18 LA 375.

expected of employees on each operation. This expected production is commonly called the work load or production standard and represents the amount of work required or expected to be done in a given time by the average, qualified operator under normal conditions * * *."[161]

Where the agreement contains no express provisions on the subject, it has been held in many cases that management has the right to set reasonable production standards and to enforce them through discipline.[162] In other cases this general right of management was expressly or impliedly recognized, but the discipline for failure to meet a production standard did not stand because the standard was unreasonable or because the discipline was unjust for some other reason.[163]

Production standards are commonly determined through time study, but they also may be based on past experience or production records or on "rule of thumb" determination.[164] Management's right

[161]Incentive Wage Provisions; Time Studies and Standards of Production, p. 37 (U.S. Dept. of Labor, Bureau of Labor Statistics Bull. No. 908–3, 1948). A "production standard is the level of production which may be reasonably expected from an average worker, or a group of workers, when working to normal capacity on specified jobs, or job classifications, with due consideration for quality of workmanship, an efficient method of operation, and the continued health and safety of the worker." Major Collective Bargaining Agreements: Wage-Incentive, Production-Standard, and Time-Study Provisions, 22 (U.S. Dept. of Labor, Bureau of Labor Statistics Bull. No. 1425–18, 1979). To be suitable for a production standard: "the work performed must be repetitive and capable of being done uniformly by all workers involved in the task"; the "job content must remain constant from one measuring period to the next"; and the "method of operation and the good produced must be capable of being objectively and accurately measured." Ibid. Of 1438 agreements surveyed, 23 percent contained production-standard provisions and "virtually all" of these "allow union input to the establishment of the standard or a procedure through which an appeal may be made." Ibid.

[162]See Arbitrator Ray in 80 LA 588, 589, 591 (having previously upheld the Company's right "to unilaterally institute production standards," in the present challenge to a standard he stated that the "burden of proving that the standard is unreasonable rests upon the Union" and has not been met); Seinsheimer in 71 LA 263, 265–266; Kasper in 69 LA 71, 73, 75 (the company had "no formal production standards," but grievant had notice "about the numerical rate of production" which the company reasonably expected); Seidenberg in 68 LA 485, 488; C. McCoy in 50 LA 917, 921, and in 50 LA 136, 140; Solomon in 50 LA 888, 894–895; McIntosh in 49 LA 581, 583, and in 37 LA 758, 759–760; Roberts in 46 LA 1196, 1199–2000; Gilden in 44 LA 393, 394–395; Willingham in 43 LA 1155, 1157–1158; Kates in 42 LA 1286, 1291–1292; Altieri in 38 LA 894, 896; Mueller in 36 LA 1442, 1444–1445 (but discharge was reversed on contract procedural grounds); Schmidt in 33 LA 913, 915; Schedler in 32 LA 865, 867; Bradley in 32 LA 317, 321; Williams in 32 LA 122, 124; Prasow in 31 LA 33, 37; Eckhardt in 30 LA 1048, 1049–1050; Neff in 30 LA 264, 266. Cf., Jones in 70 LA 201, 203–204. For cases upholding discharge of incentive employees who consistently failed to produce enough to earn the federal minimum wage, see Arbitrator Roberts in 74 LA 705, 709; Bradley in 54 LA 737, 744. In Wallace-Murray Corp., 55 LA 372, 375–376 (Kabaker, 1970), the arbitrator explained that incentive workers may not be performing satisfactorily even though they may be earning their guaranteed minimum hourly wage, the guarantee being intended merely to protect them against complete loss of earnings due to some outside cause such as a mechanical breakdown. Somewhat akin to the application of production standards, see Arbitrator Heinsz in 70 LA 216 (involving low productivity in issuance of traffic citations where municipal employer had ordered increased citations in effort to reduce traffic fatalities); Taylor in 68 LA 1332 (involving discharge of a TV weather reporter who had a low popularity rating).

[163]See Arbitrator Crane in 79 LA 582, 584; Steele in 77 LA 409, 415; Krimsly in 51 LA 1280, 1283–1284 (production standard was "fraught with statistical distortions"); W.P. McCoy in 42 LA 1162, 1166 (employer may not set production standard on individual employee basis but must set it for the job involved); Teple in 40 LA 866, 872–874; Murphy in 39 LA 130, 133–134; Davis in 38 LA 896, 902 (failure to meet new production standard was due to lack of practice rather than alleged slowdown); Ruckel in 35 LA 584, 586–587 (discipline for failure to make standard must be related to consistency with which employee falls below standard); Maggs in 33 LA 694, 698–700; W.P. McCoy in 33 LA 203, 204–205 (constantly changing standard was unfair and unreliable). Also see Sinicropi in 66 LA 602, 604.

[164]Incentive Wage Provisions; Time Studies and Standards of Production, p. 37 (U.S. Dept. of Labor, Bureau of Labor Statistics Bull. No. 908–3, 1948). Of 1438 agreements surveyed in one

to undertake time studies unilaterally has been emphasized,[165] and the union's right to make independent time studies for grievance purposes has also been recognized.[166]

Arbitrators use time study in reviewing rates after operation changes if the parties do not object.[167] Also, they may order or sustain its use in rate setting where it has been used by the parties for this purpose in the past.[168]

The purpose of time study is to measure the work of an operation. "Each element of the operation is studied and a determination is made of the time required for its performance by a normal experienced operator working with normal effort and without undue fatigue."[169] Concerning the use of time study in incentive rate setting, Arbitrator Paul N. Lehoczky explained:

> "* * * in conjunction with job evaluation (which determines relative base rates) it actually evaluates each incentive job in like terms and makes the ideal of 'equal pay for equal work' possible. When properly carried out, all jobs in the plant pay relatively equally well, and an expenditure of extra effort or skill applied to any job pays off equally well."[170]

We have just noted that "job evaluation" is used in determining relative base rates. As stated by one authority, "Job evaluation attempts to determine the worth of each job in relationship to the worth of all other jobs."[171]

---

study, 263 agreements, "almost all in manufacturing industries, contain provisions for setting production or incentive standards through the use of time studies or related measurement techniques." Major Collective Bargaining Agreements: Wage-Incentive, Production-Standard, and Time-Study Provisions, 31 (U.S. Dept. of Labor, Bureau of Labor Statistics Bull. No. 1425–18, 1979). For other discussion of principles involved and methods utilized in setting production standards, see Arbitrator Dworkin in 51 LA 101, 105; Altrock in 49 LA 320, 323–324; Sembower in 42 LA 298, 300–302; Nichols in 41 LA 953, 956–957; Lehoczky in 40 LA 33, 36–37; Mueller in 36 LA 1442, 1444–1445; Cahn in 32 LA 640, 641, and in 29 LA 828, 832–833; Meltzer in 32 LA 610, 611–612; Bradley in 32 LA 317, 321. For cases recognizing the propriety of using videotape equipment to measure time in establishing production standards, see Arbitrator Kates in 65 LA 1080, 1083–1084; Kabaker in 62 LA 1285, 1287. For detailed treatment of time study, see Barnes, Motion and Time Study (5th Ed., 1963); Mundel, Motion and Time Study (3rd Ed., 1960).

[165]F & M Schaefer Brewing Co., 40 LA 199, 200–201 (Turkus, 1963). Also recognizing the right, see Arbitrator Nicholas in 70 LA 1152, 1153–1154; McDermott in 63 LA 627, 630, 633; Roberts in 46 LA 1196, 1199–2000.

[166]Fafnir Bearing Co. v. NLRB, 62 LRRM 2415 (CA 2, 1966); Armstrong Cork Co., 41 LA 1053, 1056–1058 (Shister, 1963). As to the use of company-paid union time study personnel, see Pittsburgh Plate Glass Co., 34 LA 908, 910–911 (Lehoczky, Fisher & Myers, 1960).

[167]See Simmons Co., 33 LA 725, 727(Ross, 1959); Container Co., 6 LA 218, 220 (Whiting, 1946).

[168]See Timken Roller Bearing Co., 6 LA 979, 983–984 (Lehoczky, 1947); National Malleable & Steel Castings Co., 4 LA 189, 194 (Gilden, 1946). Cf., Arbitrator Hilpert in 10 LA 295, 296.

[169]Ford Motor Co., 12 LA 949, 951 (Shulman, 1949). Similarly, see Timken Roller Bearing Co., 51 LA 101, 105 (Dworkin, 1968).

[170]Timken Roller Bearing Co., 6 LA 979, 983 (1947), also noting that use of time study in setting new rates may be favored over comparison with rates for similar operations since the establishment of new rates on the basis of existing rates tends to perpetuate existing intraplant inequities. But under the concept of "red circle" rates, which may be used for a variety of bona fide reasons, there is at least a temporary departure from the job evaluation objective of relative equality. For explanation and discussion of red circle rates see Arbitrator Nathan in 76 LA 1017, 1021–1022; Sisk in 72 LA 87, 88–89 (stating that a red circle rate "is assigned to an individual employee and as such it is considered a personal rate as distinguished from the established rate set forth in the rate schedules"); Simon in 69 LA 687, 692–693.

[171]Lanham, Job Evaluation, 3 (1955). Job evaluation "involves several major phases such as securing and analyzing facts about jobs, writing up these facts into descriptions of the jobs,

A widely used method of job evaluation is the "point" method, under which, in general:

1. Factors are selected (and defined or described) which are common to the range of jobs to be rated (for example, the factors may be learning time, skill, responsibility, judgment decision, physical demand, working conditions, and the like).
2. Different grades or degrees are specified (and defined or described) for each factor (for example, Grade A, Grade B, and so on), to be used to indicate the extent to which the factor exists in the given job.
3. A point value is assigned to each grade or degree of each factor (for example, Responsibility Factor Grade C may be assigned 45 points).
4. The job evaluator selects the grade or degree of each factor which most nearly describes the requirements for the job as indicated by the facts and evidence.
5. The total point value of the job is then obtained by simple addition.

To illustrate, if it is concluded that Skill Factor Grade A (10 points), Responsibility Factor Grade D (65 points), Judgment Decision Factor Grade B (25 points), and Working Conditions Factor Grade B (20 points) apply to the job, the total point value of the job will be 120 points. A job thus evaluated at 120 points will, by a previously set scale, carry a specified wage rate.[172] When an arbitrator is involved in job evaluation, his task under this system is to determine the applicable grade for each factor on the basis of the evidence and his observations during a plant visit (very important in job evaluation cases). The parties may then determine the total point value of the job and the rate or Labor Grade which that point value calls for under their agreement.

A basic function of job evaluation—determining the true requirements of the job—clearly emerges from the following statement by Arbitrator Paul N. Lehoczky:

> "One of the major blocks to the bilateral settlement of job evaluation disputes is rooted in the fact that the parties concerned do not have a common basis for their discussions. In this case, for example, the grievant is strongly influenced by what he knows he brings to the job while the Company insists that only those characteristics listed in the job's

studying these descriptions and evaluating the jobs according to some rating method, and then pricing the jobs in relation to the evaluation." Id. at 5. For other writings on job evaluation, see Zack & Bloch, Labor Agreement in Negotiation and Arbitration, 208–212 (BNA Books, 1983); Wiggins, The Arbitration of Industrial Engineering Disputes, 91–121 (BNA Books, 1970); Unterberger, "Automation and Job Evaluation Techniques," Proceedings of the 16th Annual Meeting of NAA, 238 (BNA Books, 1963); Unterberger, "Arbitration of Job Evaluation Cases," 17 Arb. J. 219 (1962); Murphy, "Job Classification Arbitrations Under Bethlehem Steel Agreements," 16 Arb. J. 8 (1961); Johnson, Boise & Pratt, Job Evaluation (1946).

[172]For extensive discussion of the point method, see Lanham, Job Evaluation, 73–74 (1955); the Lanham study also discusses several other generally accepted methods. For citation of arbitration cases revealing a variety of job evaluation plans, see Wiggins, The Arbitration of Industrial Engineering Disputes, 103 (BNA Books, 1970). Also see Sherwin Williams Co., 80 LA 649, 651–652 (Wolff, 1983), where the job evaluation plan utilized 11 factors.

description and only to the degree that they are detailed, are of value. In actual application, neither position is wholly correct; many of the grievant's abilities are not required to the degree he thinks they are and conversely, the availability of certain 'extra' ability, over and above what the job description calls for, is frequently essential. The job's description, after all, represents a theoretical analysis of what the job has been planned to require and not necessarily what it actually requires. This statement cuts both ways. Your arbitrator knows of many jobs whose descriptions call for degrees of knowledge and skills which the specific occupant could *never* produce nor will he ever be required to produce them."[173]

Arbitrator Lehoczky also emphasized that it is the job, not the man or machine, that is being evaluated:

"Again, two different jobs performed on the same make and model machine tool by the same operator in the same type of department may still carry different wage rates, all because it is the specific job that is being evaluated and not the man or the machine as such. The same lathe, for example, could be utilized for work which could range in value through perhaps five labor grades, from rough turning through the most intricate precision work. For this basic reason, one cannot accept unsupported examples from other plants as 'evidence' of specific job—or factor—values."[174]

Control of Quality Standards

Management has been held to have the right at all times to exercise control over the standards of quality of its products since "a lowering in the degree of quality under a competitive market may have serious and disastrous results."[175] Thus, it has been ruled that management had the right to determine what work was faulty and whether it should be reworked or scrapped where the determination was made by men well qualified and experienced in all departments and where it was the employer's policy to resolve all doubts in favor of the employees.[176] In another case management was upheld in slowing the pace of processing hides through vats, Arbitrator Thomas L. Hewitt declaring that "the Company has the right to maintain quality within its operation and no incentive pace can be justified which does not produce quality product."[177]

The "competitive market" has been stressed by Arbitrator Clair V. Duff in sustaining the demotion of an employee for faulty work:

[173]Victor Mfg. & Gasket Co., 48 LA 957, 958 (1967).
[174]Id. at 959. Also see McGill Mfg. Co., 67 LA 1094, 1097–1098 (1976), where Arbitrator Donald J. Petersen (1) reiterated the "caveat that the function of job evaluation is to rate the job and not the man," and (2) placed the burden of proof upon the union to show by "tangible and convincing evidence" that management's judgment in job evaluation was incorrect and should be reversed by the arbitrator.
[175]Torrington Co., 1 LA 20, 26 (Courshon, 1945).
[176]Ibid. As to management's right to establish and enforce a quality control program, see Patent Button Co., 43 LA 1208, 1211–1214 (King, 1965).
[177]Howes Leather Co., 71 LA 606, 609 (1978).

"In managing the Plant and directing the working forces Management has the right and the duty to insure the highest quality standards so that its product can be sold in a competitive market with the resultant benefits to the employer and employees, each of whom has a stake in the success of the enterprise. How this quality-control is to be attained is also the responsibility of Management.

"* * * We are aware that most industries are becoming more competitive as their respective sales forces contest for a place in the market. Unless quality standards are maintained and unless a Company is in a position where it can provide a high quality product it cannot successfully exist in a competitive economy. Failure to achieve quality in a product not only reduces the benefit to the ultimate consumer but also places the Company in jeopardy with, at least potentially, a resultant disadvantage to itself and to its employees. In not a few industries the competition in quality of final product is as important as price competition."[178]

The company may have a legitimate concern not only with respect to the sale of its product, but also with regard to its reputation and the safety of persons who use its product. In this connection, the grievance of an employee who was discharged for faulty work was denied by Arbitrator Robert G. Howlett, who stated:

"* * * In such situations the manufacturing concern must be in a position to protect its reputation and the quality of its product. A company's failure to do so would redound to the detriment of all persons connected with the enterprise—owners, management and employees."[179]

He stated further:

"The Company necessarily is concerned with the production of good castings and the safety of persons who use its products. If faulty castings are produced by the * * * Company it will not only lose customers but property may be damaged and persons who come in contact with equipment in which its castings are placed may be injured, or even death may result."[180]

Management has the right to formulate and enforce reasonable rules for protecting the quality of its products.[181] Pursuant to such rules, it may in appropriate circumstances discharge or discipline employees who fail to meet quality standards.[182] Management also has the right to institute an inspection and testing program as declared by Arbitrator Rolf Valtin:

---

[178]American Radiator & Standard Sanitary Corp., 29 LA 167, 170 (1957). Similarly, Arbitrator McCoy sustained the demotion of an employee where management's action was based upon an "honest desire to improve efficiency and the quality of the Company's product." Firestone Tire & Rubber Co., 33 LA 206, 208 (1959).

[179]Valley Steel Casting Co., 22 LA 520, 525 (1954).

[180]Id. at 526. Also see Macomber, Inc. 39 LA 719, 723 (Teple, 1962); Lockheed Aircraft Corp., 31 LA 1036, 1037 (McIntosh, 1958). But in Lockheed Aircraft Corp., 35 LA 684, 685 (Grant, 1960), discharge was commuted to layoff despite serious faulty work, the arbitrator determining that the company must share the responsibility for the failure to inspect the work properly.

[181]Kellogg Co., 55 LA 84, 88 (Shearer, 1970), where management had a rule regulating the length of hair and sideburns to protect its products from hair contamination.

[182]Ibid. Also Patent Button Co., 43 LA 1208, 1214 (King, 1965).

"Management obviously is free to inspect products and to make sure that quality standards are being met. Inspection is a recognized and commonly followed part of practically every manufacturing process. Equally well-established is the rule that the work of any employee—craft or otherwise—is at all times subject to scrutiny and critical examination."[183]

While management has wide freedom to control quality standards, the fairness of penalties imposed for faulty work may be closely scrutinized by arbitrators.[184]

Job and Classification Control

It is difficult to formulate neat or precise categories in the discussion of cases involving the right of management to establish, eliminate, or combine jobs or job classifications, or cases involving its right to transfer duties between jobs or between job classifications. This is likewise true of cases involving the right of management to assign duties and tasks to workers.

This difficulty springs in part from the fact that the words "job" and "classification" at times are used synonymously and at other times are intended to carry different meanings.[185] In addition, different terminology utilized in the decision of cases involving similar issues (the arbitrator's choice of terminology often conforms to that utilized by the parties in presenting the given case), different meanings apparently intended in the use of similar terminology, failure of cases to define clearly the terminology that is used, and other such practices make it virtually impossible to arrange the cases into clearly outlined compartments. The many borderline situations, too, have produced many shadings of arbitral opinion touching upon otherwise basic issues.

For these reasons the Authors urge the reader to keep in mind the close relationship between (and frequent overlapping of) the materials in the subtopics which make up the remainder of this topic.[186]

---

[183]Bethlehem Steel Co., 32 LA 541, 542 (1959). In United States Pipe & Foundry Co., 79 LA 936, 940 (1982), Arbitrator Eva C. Galambos stated that: "Supervision entails quality control. There is no way a foreman could be expected to supervise those who are assigned to his supervision without exerting a control over the quality of their work."

[184]See Arbitrator Lucas in 44 LA 20, 22–23; King in 43 LA 1208, 1212–1214; McKelvey in 38 LA 586, 592–593; Marshall in 36 LA 1303, 1304; Dworkin in 36 LA 491, 495; Grant in 35 LA 684, 685; Duff in 29 LA 167, 169–170; Graff in 27 LA 656, 659–662; Howlett in 22 LA 520, 524–527; Noel in 19 LA 650, 652.

[185]"There is no question that the word 'job' may have a different meaning from the word 'classification.' Two men may have the same classification, for example, 'painter,' but one may have the job of keeping certain rooms painted while the other has the job of keeping certain equipment painted. On the other hand, the two words are sometimes used synonymously. The question is in what sense did the parties use the word [in their agreement]." Fulton-Sylphon Co., 2 LA 116, 117–118 (McCoy, 1946). Also see Arbitrator Talent in 50 LA 1061, 1066–1067; Hebert in 49 LA 445, 450, and in 27 LA 762, 764–765; Livengood in 20 LA 19, 21; McCoy in 1 LA 121, 124.

[186]For other important related material, see Chapter 12, topic entitled "Custom and Practice as Part of the Contract."

Establishing, Eliminating, and Combining Jobs and Classifications

The right of management to establish new jobs or job classifications is sometimes specifically stated in the agreement, along with some provision for union challenge of management's actions via the grievance procedure and arbitration.[187] The right also has been recognized as being vested in management except as restricted by the agreement and it likewise might be included within the scope of a general management rights clause.[188] Moreover, under an agreement stating that rates "for any new classifications will be negotiated," management not only had the right but was held to have an implied duty to establish a new classification when the company introduced a new and substantially different machine.[189]

Where job classifications are specifically set up by the agreement, and especially if the agreement is rigid as to classifications, management may not be permitted unilaterally to establish new classifications,[190] but as noted hereinbelow, many arbitrators have rejected the view that jobs or classifications are frozen by the mere fact that they are included in the agreement.

Arbitrators often have recognized the right of management, unless restricted by the agreement, to eliminate jobs (and where a few duties remain to reallocate them) where improved methods or other production justification exists and management otherwise acts in good faith.[191] Arbitrators likewise have recognized management's right,

---

[187]For example, see Arbitrator Hardin in 76 LA 278, 281; Ceone in 69 LA 168, 169.

[188]See Arbitrator Laybourne in 50 LA 997, 999–1000; Buckwalter in 50 LA 624, 631–632 (but here the contract did restrict the right); Ray in 46 LA 91, 94; Shafer in 45 LA 448, 450; Murphy in 36 LA 1392, 1394; Prasow in 30 LA 444, 448; Platt in 17 LA 697, 700–701; Bowles in 16 LA 955, 957; Reynolds in 8 LA 1041, 1042–1043. Also see Stephens in 66 LA 941, 942, 944; Lewis in 49 LA 202, 204; Autrey in 41 LA 1140, 1143; Stouffer in 40 LA 898, 901–902; Sembower in 25 LA 188, 191; Marshall in 23 LA 228, 233–234; Wallen in 22 LA 831, 833; Gaffey in 18 LA 462, 468; Coffey in 12 LA 676, 679–680. Contra as to job classifications (requiring bargaining before their establishment), Donnelly in 18 LA 90, 92; Griffin 7 LA 368, 371. In some cases the question arises as to what constitutes a "new job." For the answer given in one case, see Allegheny Ludlum Steel Corp., 32 LA 446, 451–452 (Platt & Mittenthal, 1949). Also see Arbitrator Sinicropi in 69 LA 842, 846–847; Bryan in 63 LA 1007, 1010–1011.

[189]Lockheed-Georgia Co., 48 LA 518, 519, 521 (King, 1967).

[190]See Arbitrator Ray in 45 LA 78, 80–81; Gilden in 13 LA 369, 371; Howard in 13 LA 3, 8. Also see Volz in 46 LA 1208, 1212–1213; Autrey in 42 LA 697, 698, 700–702; Willingham in 35 LA 662, 664; McCoy in 2 LA 319, 321. Cf., Davey in 48 LA 339, 341–342, 348; Wolff in 41 LA 1150, 1151–1152.

[191]See Arbitrator Ross in 80 LA 338, 343; Curry in 76 LA 1129, 1131; Barsamian in 74 LA 318, 322; Ferguson in 64 LA 421, 424–425; Kaplan in 61 LA 517, 523; Hilpert in 47 LA 778, 779–780; Bradley in 46 LA 685, 691; Abrahams in 44 LA 359, 361; Volz in 43 LA 353, 355; Marshall in 42 LA 945, 946; Stouffer in 41 LA 927, 931; Seward in 40 LA 850, 851; Seitz in 40 LA 511, 512; McDermott in 40 LA 70, 72; Altrock in 40 LA 65, 66; Raimon in 38 LA 196, 199–200; Di Leone in 37 LA 24, 29; Fleming in 32 LA 836, 837; Warns in 29 LA 324, 326–328; Wettach in 19 LA 797, 799; Sachs in 18 LA 616, 619–620; Gilden in 16 LA 252, 255–256; Klamon in 15 LA 782, 790–791; Copelof in 15 LA 754, 761; Smith in 12 LA 719, 721–722; Pollard in 10 LA 498, 510; Willcox in 10 LA 371, 378; Abernethy in 6 LA 314, 318–319. Also see Abbott in 70 LA 1156, 1157; Gootnick in 69 LA 808, 810; Schatzki in 67 LA 1308, 1309; Seitz in 65 LA 435, 437–438; Sembower in 49 LA 874, 880. Even where a contract contained a job-freezing clause, it was narrowly construed to permit elimination of a job as justified by changes in equipment and method. Anheuser-Busch, 36 LA 1289, 1295, 1300 (Hill, 1961). But see Arbitrator Nichols in 43 LA 1057, 1058–1060. In Borg-Warner Corp., 35 LA 367, 371–372 (Klein, 1960), the employer could not abolish a job and assign

where not restricted by the agreement, to eliminate job classifications (and reallocate the remaining duties) when done in good faith for a justifiable purpose.[192]

In upholding this right of management to eliminate jobs or classifications, Arbitrator Howard S. Block offered the following evaluation:

"The impact of a changing technology upon the work force has posed problems to both management and labor not easy of solution. That this issue has been a persistent and vexing one over the years is indicated by the significant number of arbitration proceedings on this subject dating back to the earliest reported decisions. A review of these decisions reveals that they fall into two fairly distinct categories which seem noteworthy here: (1) One line of cases emphasizes that where a Collective Bargaining agreement sets forth a comprehensive rate structure, the wage rate established for each classification evidences an agreement between the parties as to the wage rate, as well as the classification; these cases then go on to provide that, in general, the terms of this bargained for exchange may not be unilaterally altered. To the extent that some of these decisions regard the classification structure as being unalterably frozen during the life of the Agreement, they do not represent the weight of arbitration authority. (2) A second group of cases holds that the existence in the Agreement of a negotiated rate structure does not guarantee that the classifications will remain unchanged during the term of the Agreement. The reason advanced for this interpretation is that economic necessity in a competitive market makes it essential that management have the degree of flexibility necessary to adapt the work force to changed conditions. Where arbitrators have upheld management's right to eliminate jobs or classifications and reallocate residual job duties, they have stressed that such changes must be made in good faith, based upon factors such as a change in operations, technological improvements, substantially diminished production requirements, established past practice, etc. It is this second line of cases which appears to reflect the present weight of authority on this issue."[193]

In this general regard, the view of an early case that "Combining the duties of classifications recognized in the contract is a different thing from combining the duties or job content of various jobs, or

the duties to another employee where the duties continued to exist in significant proportions and substantially in the original form—the job was abolished in name only. Also see Arbitrator Coyne in 77 LA 266, 269; Bailey in 69 LA 294, 301–302; Leach in 68 LA 492, 498; Schedler in 41 LA 120, 121–122.

[192]See Arbitrator McIntosh in 80 LA 1043, 1045–1046; Loihl in 80 LA 11, 13; Eyraud in 77 LA 857, 859–860; Ross in 77 LA 284, 287; Hutcheson in 62 LA 1132, 1134; Roberts in 54 LA 896, 900; Whyte in 54 LA 807, 814–816; Dworkin in 51 LA 1174, 1180–1181, and in 51 LA 1031, 1038–1039; Block in 48 LA 72, 76, and in 46 LA 1027, 1029–1030; Doyle in 48 LA 24, 25–32; Graff in 46 LA 329, 332–335; Horlacher in 64–1 ARB ¶8287; Leflar in 40 LA 769, 772–774; Murphy in 36 LA 1392, 1394–1395; Bothwell in 34 LA 24, 28–29; Updegraff in 33 LA 169, 171; Bauder in 33 LA 25, 28–29; Fleming in 32 LA 115, 116; Ridge in 26 LA 422, 427; Prasow in 25 LA 44, 49; Ryder in 20 LA 764, 767. Also see Witney in 54 LA 197, 203–204. But see Arbitrator Seidenberg in 51 LA 303, 308–309; Dworkin in 47 LA 396, 404; Gilden in 38 LA 799, 802; Davey in 38 LA 20, 28–31; Beatty in 25 LA 838, 840–841; Reynard in 22 LA 880, 882. For related discussion, see this Chapter, topic entitled "Assigning Work Out of Bargaining Unit."

[193]American Cement Corp., 48 LA 72, 76 (1967). For similar general evaluations and conclusions, see Arbitrator Curry in 76 LA 1129, 1131; Holden in 67 LA 334, 337–338; Ferguson in 64 LA 421, 424–425; Kaplan in 61 LA 517, 521–523; Sembower in 57 LA 869, 872; Doyle in 48 LA 24, 25–32; Leflar in 40 LA 769, 772–774. Also see Vadakin in 72 LA 738, 739–741; Seitz in 65 LA 435, 437.

abolishing those jobs," and that the inclusion of classifications and their wage rates in the agreement has the implied effect of freezing such classifications (though not freezing jobs within a classification) for the life of the agreement,[194] has been expressly rejected in later cases.[195]

Many arbitrators have spoken in terms of combining jobs or job classifications. Again, it often has been held that management has the right, where not restricted by the agreement, to combine jobs or job classifications in determining methods of operation.[196] Arbitrators also have held that management has the right, unless restricted by the agreement, to combine jobs or classifications where there is insufficient work in one (or in each) of them for a normal day's work and where excessive workloads do not result from the combination.[197]

Likewise, in the absence of contractual restriction management has been permitted to abolish two job classifications and establish a new classification following technological change in equipment,[198] or following a change in products.[199]

Interjob and Interclassification Transfer of Duties

Short of eliminating or combining jobs or job classifications, some of the duties of one job or classification are sometimes transferred to

---

[194]Esso Standard Oil Co., 19 LA 569, 571 (McCoy, 1952).

[195]See Arbitrator Dean in 68 LA 236, 239; Doyle in 48 LA 24, 26–31; Leflar in 40 LA 769, 774; Bothwell in 34 LA 24, 28, and in 32 LA 260, 264. Arbitrator Doyle had previously cited and followed the *Esso* case view, and in subsequently rejecting it he explained: "The prevailing rule is based on the premise that a freezing of classifications by implication would unduly restrict and hamper the Company in making decisions that would improve the economy and productivity of the plant. Such a limitation should not be lightly inferred." Omaha Cold Storage Terminal, 48 LA 24, 31 (1967). Also see Arbitrator Nelson in 78 LA 660, 662–663. In Teple, "Contract Provisions Affecting Job Elimination," 17 Case W. Res. L. Rev. 1253, 1264–1267 (1966), cases are cited for the conclusion that neither seniority provisions nor "local working conditions" clauses (technological improvements or the like often establish a change in the underlying basis of the local condition) are likely to bar the elimination of jobs or classifications. This conclusion is supported also by various cases cited in this topic. But a provision requiring maintenance of local working conditions was held violated by elimination of a job for "efficiency alone," there being no "change in the workload, equipment or in any factor that would constitute a basis for eliminating the job." United States Steel Corp., 62 LA 125, 127 (Witt, 1973).

[196]See Arbitrator Cohen in 65 LA 577, 581; Warns in 61 LA 357, 358–359; Marshall in 51 LA 1051, 1055 (right reinforced by general management rights clause); Moskowitz in 44 LA 801, 802; Prasow in 35 LA 63, 66 (seniority rights no bar); Pollock in 34 LA 226, 228–229 (right reinforced by general management rights clause); Regester in 34 LA 209, 212; Quinlan in 33 LA 379, 384–385; Wersing in 23 LA 797, 798–799; Bowles in 16 LA 955, 957–958. Also see Forsythe in 63 LA 179, 182 (merger of classifications in connection with prohibition against sex discrimination); Gorsuch in 40 LA 879, 886–888; Bothwell in 32 LA 260, 263. But see Arbitrator McIntosh in 41 LA 997, 999 (clause freezing classifications was strictly enforced); Crawford in 41 LA 285, 286–287 (where contract provided for craft jobs and training programs, management could not combine jobs in such a way as to virtually eliminate the craft system); Coffey in 39 LA 1058, 1059, 1063–1064.

[197]See Arbitrator Rill in 66 LA 1069, 1071; Florey in 47 LA 1092, 1093; Duff in 40 LA 305, 306; Kesselman in 28 LA 441, 443–445; Somers in 27 LA 466, 467–468; Kelliher in 18 LA 216, 217–218. Also see Crawford in 37 LA 711, 714–715; Hampton in 17 LA 666, 668; Gilden in 16 LA 252, 255–256; Klamon in 15 LA 782, 789–790. Cf., Sembower in 25 LA 188, 190–191.

[198]See Arbitrator Marshall in 43 LA 1118, 1123–1124, and in 43 LA 1137, 1142; Cobb in 37 LA 466, 467–468; Uible in 35 LA 434, 436; Wettach in 19 LA 797, 799. Also see Bothwell in 71 LA 396, 404; Towers in 71 LA 185, 190–191 (where management had the right to merge departments following equipment change); Blair in 36 LA 1097, 1100; Fleming in 32 LA 115, 116–117; Copelof in 15 LA 754, 761.

[199]Square D Co., 46 LA 39, 43 (Larkin, 1966); Hewitt-Robins, Inc., 30 LA 81, 83–86 (Kates, 1958).

another job or classification. The right of management to require workers in the "receiving" job or classification to perform the work is discussed hereinbelow in the subtopic on "Assignment of Duties and Tasks." At this point, however, the matter is considered primarily (but not exclusively) from the standpoint of the effect of the transfer upon workers in the "giving" job or classification.[200]

In a variety of situations the interclassification transfer of work has been upheld where no restriction was found in the agreement (in some instances the employer's right of action was reinforced by a general management rights clause).[201] For example, under a contract giving management the right to manage the works and direct the working force and containing no provision expressly prohibiting unilateral changes in job content, Arbitrator Benjamin Aaron held that management could remove from the oiler's job the relatively minor tasks of lubricating and cleaning cranes and assign these duties to crane men, even though said duties were mentioned in the oiler's job description and not in the craneman's; the union could request reevaluation of the craneman's job if it believed that the added duties justified a higher rate, but it could not prevent management from making the changes in job content.[202]

Under another contract reserving to the company the right to "manage the plant and direct the working force" and stating that "the usual and customary rights of the employer remain unimpaired," Arbitrator Clarence M. Updegraff upheld the transfer of certain unskilled and semiskilled work from one classification to another, and he explained:

> "In part the union relied upon a contention that since the agreement between the parties includes a list of job classifications with the hourly wage rates agreed for the same that none of the duties of any job classification so listed may be essentially changed since this would indirectly at least alter the compensation for work in the designated classification.
>
> "The company asserts the position that in the absence of negotiated job descriptions it is within the usual rights, powers and privileges of management to assign duties to one classification and subsequently when efficiency and economy seem to require the same, to take such job duties from a classification which has been discharging them and assign such duties to another classification.

---

[200]For important related discussion, see this Chapter, topics entitled "Right to Subcontract" and "Assigning Work Out of Bargaining Unit."

[201]See Arbitrator Goodman in 73 LA 207, 210–213; Cox in 68 LA 864, 866–867; Volz in 62 LA 695, 696–697; Doyle in 61 LA 791, 796–797, and in 61 LA 448, 449–550; Jones in 60 LA 423, 425–426; King in 59 LA 340, 344; Daugherty in 49 LA 234, 236–237; Kelliher in 48 LA 1000, 1002–1003; Updegraff in 45 LA 557, 557–558; Smith in 43 LA 193, 206–207; Hebert in 36 LA 186, 192–193; Shister in 35 LA 664, 667; Abernethy in 35 LA 353, 355–357; Beatty in 33 LA 311, 312–313 (operation could be assigned to different craft after the work was simplified by technological improvement); Bauder in 33 LA 308, 310; Aaron in 26 LA 666, 668. But see Dworkin in 43 LA 1188, 1196; Bothwell in 39 LA 833, 844–849. The temporary transfer of work (such as on holidays) merely to effect a savings in labor costs was found improper by Arbitrator Atwood in 55 LA 964, 969; Seinsheimer in 33 LA 14, 18–19; McCoy in 32 LA 848, 849–850. But see Foster in 75 LA 1070, 1073; Marcus in 61 LA 797, 801.

[202]National Supply Co., 26 LA 666, 668 (1956), where Arbitrator Aaron also noted that the transfer in no way impaired job security.

"In this connection it must be observed that innumerable unskilled and semi-skilled duties are commonly found in industrial plants to be within the scopes of duties of several job classifications. It is normally regarded as within the prerogatives of management to transfer unskilled or semi-skilled duties which do not characterize or fall within the scope of characteristically high skilled jobs, to one or another group of skilled, semi-skilled or unskilled workers from time to time as convenience and economy within the plant appeared to make it desirable. This is all within the commonly recognized scope of managerial authority and normally under management clauses is recognized to be proper.
* * *
"* * * There can be no doubt that normally in industry generally, the assignment and reassignment of unskilled and semi-skilled duties such as those here involved would be entirely and exclusively within the discretion of management in the absence of a clear, express agreement otherwise."[203]

Arbitrator Joseph M. Klamon recognized an "inherent right of management to take a job which initially or originally may require a considerable degree of skill and then to establish a production line in which a fairly complex job becomes essentially routine and repetitive."[204] In that case management was permitted to discontinue the assignment of certain work, after it had become simplified, to skilled workers (who claimed a "proprietary interest in the work") and to assign it exclusively to employees in a lower classification. To hold otherwise, he declared, would deny the company the right to operate with the greatest degree of skill and efficiency; he noted that nothing in the contract prevented the company "from using lesser grades of skill on a job if higher grades of skill are wholly unnecessary to perform such jobs."[205]

Where workers in one classification must suffer layoff or other such consequence as a result of management's transfer of substantial work from their classification to another, arbitrators have sometimes deemed such transfer a violation of the workers' seniority rights where the transfer was not justified by emergency or other such reason.[206]

But some arbitrators are unwilling to accept seniority as a guarantee that the job or classification will remain unchanged. For instance, in upholding the right of management to transfer work from one classification to another where not expressly restricted by the agreement, Arbitrator Paul Prasow reasoned:

"Seniority protects and secures an employee's rights in relation to the rights of other employees in his seniority group; it does not protect him in relation to the existence of the job itself. By the use of an objective

[203]Pure Oil Co., 45 LA 557, 558 (1965).
[204]McConnell Aircraft Corp., 21 LA 424, 427–428 (1953).
[205]Ibid. Also see Arbitrator Brisco in 74 LA 1225, 1228–1229; Koven in 39 LA 939, 940–941; Klamon in 33 LA 1, 4–5.
[206]See Arbitrator Dworkin in 34 LA 743, 750–751 (the possibility of future harm sufficed); Livengood in 23 LA 196, 199–202; Gregory in 15 LA 147, 150–151; Ebeling in 14 LA 163, 164–165. Also see Klamon in 32 LA 870, 872–873.

measure, length of service, the rights of one employee are balanced against the other employees' rights.

"The rights inherent in seniority do not themselves guarantee the continued existence of the job, or that it shall be maintained without change in content. Seniority can only stand as a bar to changes in job content if the contract so expressly provides, or if it can be shown that the changes are motivated on the part of management by a desire to evade the seniority clause. * * *

"While it is certainly true that changes in job content of a classification may adversely affect the job opportunities of the employees involved by reducing the amount of work available to them, the problem is still essentially one of jurisdiction, rather than of seniority. It is a well-established principle in industrial arbitration that management has the right, if exercised in good faith, to transfer duties from one classification to another, to change, eliminate or establish new classifications, unless the Agreement specifically restricts this right."[207]

Speaking in terms of the right of management to transfer work from one seniority unit to another, one arbitrator held that management may not do so even though there is no express prohibition in the agreement.[208] But in another case management was permitted to transfer work from one seniority unit to another where there was no specific restriction in the agreement and the transfer was made in good faith in the interest of efficiency.[209]

Assignment of Duties and Tasks

In general management is permitted to exercise much more discretion in assigning individual duties and tasks to workers than it is permitted in assigning workers to regular jobs. While the assignment of workers to regular jobs often requires the observance of contractual "seniority" and "fitness and ability" considerations,[210] collective agreements much less frequently contain direct restrictions upon the right of management to assign duties and tasks to workers. Thus, in the latter regard, arbitrators have held that unless the agreement provides otherwise, employees are not entitled to exercise their

---

[207]Reynolds Metals Co., 25 LA 44, 48–49 (1955). For similar statements or results, see Arbitrator Goodman in 73 LA 207, 215; Hon in 40 LA 259, 262; Holly in 39 LA 496, 499–500; Quinlan in 38 LA 714, 717; Prasow in 35 LA 63, 66; Warns in 33 LA 357, 359–360 (also suggesting that jobs "tailor-made" to the company's requirements are more subject to unilateral change than traditional craft jobs); Bauder in 33 LA 25, 28–29; Updegraff in 29 LA 555, 557; Thompson in 28 LA 374, 376–377; Uible in 25 LA 897, 899; Platt in 17 LA 697, 700–701.

[208]Lukens Steel Co., 15 LA 408, 411–412 (D'Andrade, 1950). In general accord, though applying a "de minimis" exception, United States Steel Corp., 35 LA 832, 835 (Shipman, 1960). Also see Arbitrator LeWinter in 72 LA 742, 746; Sullivan in 63 LA 202, 206–207; Anderson in 44 LA 873, 877; Seitz in 40 LA 742, 749–753; Myers in 23 LA 776, 778–779. Cf., Lubow in 68 LA 1379, 1382.

[209]Douglas & Lomason Co., 23 LA 691, 695 (Bowles, 1954). In general accord, Arbitrator Shister in 70 LA 110, 113; Cahn in 40 LA 865, 865–866; Kelliher in 33 LA 828, 829–830. Also see Abrams in 80 LA 1267, 1274–1275; Dybeck in 66 LA 596, 597; Daugherty in 49 LA 234, 236–237; Crawford in 36 LA 273, 276, 280; Garrett in 35 LA 541, 543; Prasow in 35 LA 63, 66; Springfield & Seward in 25 LA 366, 368.

[210]See Chapter 14, Seniority.

seniority to select the duties or machines which they particularly prefer within their classification.[211]

In one case Arbitrator Clarence M. Updegraff observed (speaking of hourly rated employees) that "it is assumed throughout industry that the employer has the general right to make reasonable changes from time to time in the job duties of every individual. The employer may decrease or increase the duties as long as the total work load remains in reasonable bounds."[212] This broad right of management in the assignment of duties and tasks is evidenced by numerous other arbitration cases (in some of the cases the right was reinforced by a general management rights clause).[213]

Certainly, where jobs are classified by titles (if formally classified at all) but the parties have not negotiated a detailed description of job content, management will be permitted wide authority to assign any work which is of the same general type as, or is reasonably related to, or is incidental to the regular duties of the job.[214] However, a change in job duties by adding work which is not related in such ways to the regular duties may be held improper.[215] Even where an agreement expressly recognized a right of management to reassign duties across classification lines the arbitrator cautioned management that a lim-

---

[211]See Arbitrator Howlett in 42 LA 385, 388; Burris in 41 LA 502, 506; Stashower in 37 LA 591, 593; Bowles in 36 LA 1160, 1162–1163; Beatty in 35 LA 637, 639–640; Montgomery in 26 LA 546, 548; Sanders in 24 LA 160, 162. Also see Stoltenberg in 73 LA 1123, 1126.

[212]St. Joseph Lead Co., 20 LA 890, 891 (1953).

[213]See Arbitrator Talarico in 80 LA 1111, 1114; Bothwell in 71 LA 396, 404; Finley in 69 LA 175, 176; Dean in 68 LA 236, 239; Witney in 54 LA 197, 203–205; Hebert in 50 LA 458, 460; Madden in 49 LA 487, 488–490; Larkin in 47 LA 382, 384; Clayton in 41 LA 925, 926; Dworkin in 39 LA 801, 805–806; Cahn in 36 LA 822, 823–824; Abernethy in 34 LA 278, 283; Ryder in 29 LA 677, 679; Ridge in 26 LA 422, 426–427; Uible in 25 LA 897, 899; Prasow in 25 LA 44, 48–49; Wallen in 22 LA 831, 833; Klamon in 22 LA 336, 351; Marshall in 20 LA 800, 802; Smith in 18 LA 620, 624; Ryan in 17 LA 800, 803. Cf., Dworkin in 29 LA 787, 792. Regarding the duty of employees to do the work assigned to them and to utilize the grievance procedure rather than self-help if they think an assignment is improper, see Chapter 5, topic entitled "Observance of Grievance Procedure."

[214]See Arbitrator Goetz in 70 LA 569, 571; Hebert in 49 LA 445, 450–451; Dybeck in 49 LA 86, 89 ("maintenance of local conditions" provision does not limit the level of work load); Whyte in 49 LA 33, 38; Duff in 48 LA 52, 54; Kelliher in 43 LA 1006, 1009–1010; Oppenheim in 40 LA 257, 259; Donaldson in 37 LA 528, 531; Ryder in 29 LA 677, 679; Thompson in 28 LA 374, 376; Uible in 25 LA 897, 899; Reynard in 25 LA 611, 613; Berkowitz in 25 LA 422, 424; Prasow in 25 LA 44, 48–49; Bowles in 23 LA 691, 695; Blair in 22 LA 701, 703; Hawley in 22 LA 157, 161; Dworet in 20 LA 803, 806; Marshall in 20 LA 800, 802; Shulman in 19 LA 237, 238–242; Gaffey in 18 LA 462, 468; Gilden in 17 LA 408, 409; Lesser in 16 LA 505, 507; Kharas in 2 LA 274, 276–277. In some of these cases the agreement contained a management rights clause; in others it did not. In Federal Aviation Admin., 68 LA 1213, 1216–1217 (1977), Arbitrator Sol M. Yarowsky refused to interpret in a "restrictive and limited fashion" a new provision which prohibited assigning to air traffic controllers duties not having a reasonable relationship to their primary function; he upheld the assignment to controllers of the task of changing and filing tapes, stating that it would be economically wasteful to call a technician to change the tapes, the controllers previously had shared the task with supervisors, and, unlike certain other tasks formerly performed by controllers (such as cutting grass around the tower, keeping time and attendance records, and conducting public tours around the facility), this task was not "far removed from the essential function of traffic controllers."

[215]American Zinc Co., 18 LA 827, 830–831 (Updegraff, 1952). Also see Arbitrator Ellmann in 67 LA 368, 371; Dorsey in 55 LA 1182, 1183; Snyder in 54 LA 1159, 1162–1163. Where an agreement excluded supervisors from the bargaining unit, supervisory duties could not be assigned to unit employees. Arkla Chem. Corp., 54 LA 62, 64–65 (Prewett, 1969). The right to assign workers to tasks outside the plant has sometimes been arbitrated, such assignment being held improper by Arbitrator Stone in 2 LA 552, 553, but held proper by Arbitrator Williams in 53 LA 1308, 1310, and by Anrod (on the basis of practice) in 20 LA 653, 656–657.

itation was necessarily implied under the standard of reasonableness—duties must be compatible with the classification to which
they are transferred.[216] Nonetheless, where the need is sufficiently
strong, employees may be assigned duties or tasks which are foreign to
their regular job.[217]

A significant limitation upon the right of management to assign
work to skilled tradesmen (as opposed to production workers) was
recognized in two decisions by Umpire Harry Shulman—he did not
permit the assignment of work which is of a different trade.[218] Some
years later Umpire Harry H. Platt "reaffirmed" these decisions, but in
doing so he pointed out important exceptions:

> "(a) Umpire Opinions A-223 and A-278 are reaffirmed. It is ruled
> that a skilled tradesman may not be required to do work wholly different
> from and unrelated to the central skill of his trade. If such bald assign-
> ment is attempted because of a shortage of work in his trade or a desire to
> get the other work done, he may refuse it and take a layoff instead.
>
> "(b) In emergencies, the Company may make assignments across
> trade lines.
>
> "(c) In cases where the capabilities of tradesmen overlap, work
> which is within the scope of two or more trades may be assigned to any of
> the trades within whose normal and proper scope it falls. In determining
> whether a task falls within the normal scope of more than one trade, due
> regard must be had for accepted standards in the trades generally and
> for clearly established in-plant assignment practices which are based on
> agreement or mutual understanding or which are characterized by
> acquiescence for a long time, with the consequences that the parties may
> be assumed to have agreed with reference to them and for their continu-
> ance.
>
> "(d) Relatively minor tasks which are complementary to a principal
> job but which do not require a long period of reasonably continuous work
> and which are within the capabilities of the principal tradesman on the
> job and can be performed by him with safety, are incidental work which
> can properly be assigned to the principal tradesman."[219]

Another set of "standards to determine whether management validly
exercised its right to assign * * * challenged work * * * in keeping
with the principle of craft integrity" was offered by Arbitrator Louis C.
Kesselman:

> "1) Skilled tradesmen should not be required to do work wholly
> different from and unrelated to the central skill of their trades;

---

[216]Vickers, Inc., 47 LA 716, 719 (Keefe, 1966). Also see Arbitrator Haber in 69 LA 251, 253.
[217]See Arbitrator Kossoff in 72 LA 909, 913–914; Teple in 45 LA 671, 680 (where all
employees were required to handle emergency equipment); Turkus in 38 LA 904, 906 (where the
task of walking the company watchdog could fall on any employee, except the union steward).
[218]The first case was Ford Motor Co., 3 LA 782, 783 (1946). In the second case, Ford Motor Co.,
19 LA 237, 238–239 (1952), he repeated the restriction but emphasized that it was to be narrowly
applied. In Champion Papers, 49 LA 33, 38 (Whyte, 1967), the multicraft assignment of work to
craft workers was upheld.
[219]Ford Motor Co., 30 LA 46, 55 (1958). The exception stated in Arbitrator Platt's paragraph
(d) was applied by Arbitrator Rezler in 70 LA 485, 490–491; Turkus in 44 LA 1219, 1223–1224;
Updegraff in 44 LA 989, 990–991. In Kaiser Aluminum & Chem. Corp., 44 LA 449, 452 (1965),
Arbitrator Rohman explained: "A modern development coincidental with automation is the
fostering of combination skills. No longer will an individual skilled in that one craft perform
work solely of that craft. True, his primary duties will be confined to that craft but, in addition, he
will also perform the work of other crafts which are incidental to the necessary completion of that
task."

"2) Intent must not be to destroy jobs or deny any other contract rights and the assignment made must be in good faith and be reasonably related to the efficient operation of the plant;

"3) Greater latitude should be given where there is no economic loss to the employees—no layoffs or denial of overtime work opportunities;

"4) Assignments which are occasional and of short duration rather than permanent should be viewed with greater liberality as reasonable exercises of management prerogatives in overlapping areas of work; and

"5) Borderline work assignments which will be made only when members of classifications, for whom work is central rather than peripheral, are not available should be given more leeway than when permanent reassignments of duties are made.

* * *

"Obviously, there is no craft whose work, tools, and skills are absolutely independent of all other crafts. Principles of craft jurisdiction must be applied with common sense and some flexibility. Judgments may be based upon:

1) the type of tools required
2) nature of the materials being worked on
3) character of the training required
4) level of skill involved
5) generally accepted elements of the trade * * *.

"No one of these by itself is necessarily controlling. One can only judge on the basis of all the relevant facts, whether a job requires the special skills of a particular trade."[220]

Regarding the assignment of unskilled work to skilled workers, Arbitrator Edgar L. Warren observed that: "While workers in skilled classifications obviously should not be required to do a large amount of unskilled work, some measure of this is a part of every job. The most practical restraint on the amount of unskilled work that a company will assign to highly skilled workers is the cost involved. Few employers would feel that they could afford to have highly paid hourly employees doing chores which could be performed by unskilled laborers."[221] In another case an added reason was recognized for assigning some associated greasing and lubricating duties to skilled repairmen—they are more likely to spot trouble than other employees with less skill.[222]

In the absence of contractual restrictions on the right of management to assign new duties or reallocate old duties as reasonably required by technological changes, management may be permitted considerable leeway to do so.[223]

---

[220]Tennessee River Pulp & Paper Co., 45 LA 201, 205 (1965). These standards were quoted and followed by Arbitrator Brisco in 74 LA 1225, 1229; Block in 56 LA 353, 356.

[221]Lockheed Aircraft Serv., 21 LA 292, 293 (1953), upholding the assignment of cleanup work to craftsmen for a short time every few weeks despite the fact that their job descriptions did not mention such work. Also see Arbitrator Altrock in 68 LA 994, 996; McDaniel in 54 LA 155, 157–158; Mittenthal in 40 LA 446, 448. But see Willingham in 36 LA 531, 536. In Mosaic Tile Co., 21 LA 278, 282–283 (Young, 1953), cleanup work could not be required of incentive workers, who were distinguished from hourly rated workers on the basis that additional duties do not reduce the earnings of the latter.

[222]United States Steel Corp., 40 LA 414 at 414 (Florey, 1963).

[223]See Arbitrator Shipman in 46 LA 833, 837; Bradley in 46 LA 685, 691; Rohman in 45 LA 758, 761; Oppenheim in 40 LA 923, 926–927; Seward in 26 LA 146, 147; Beatty in 26 LA 1, 2; Updegraff in 20 LA 890, 891. Also see Gorsuch in 53 LA 23, 32; Larson in 29 LA 59, 66–67; Roberts in 27 LA 736, 741–743; Shister in 26 LA 212, 213; Gilden in 23 LA 164, 166–167. But see LeWinter in 72 LA 742, 746; Doyle in 22 LA 785, 788–790; Hampton in 12 LA 631, 634. For related discussion, see this Chapter, topic entitled "Determination of Size of Crews."

Even when there are detailed job descriptions, Arbitrator J. Fred Holly has held that they do not prohibit minor changes in job content, noting that any ban on such changes must be stated in the agreement "in unmistakable language," and that the "purpose of job evaluation and job descriptions is to provide for equitable wage rates, not to provide a control over job content."[224] But the existence of detailed job descriptions, especially if negotiated, may deprive management of the right to make substantial changes in job duties.[225] One arbitrator went a step further, holding that even where there is no written job description management may not make a substantial change in the traditional job content of classified occupations during the life of the contract;[226] however, in subsequently upholding the right of management to eliminate a contract classification and assign its duties to another classification, that arbitrator acted "on the premise that a freezing of classifications by implication would unduly restrict and hamper the Company in making decisions that would improve the economy and productivity of the plant."[227]

Many cases have spoken in terms of job classifications. In one such case, Arbitrator Marion Beatty upheld the right of management to assign an employee small amounts of work outside his classification, observing that work jurisdictional lines can be very crippling to efficient operations and should not be read into an agreement by inference.[228] While recognizing that management may require employees to perform duties outside their classification for temporary periods, Arbitrator Joseph Shister held that management may not require the performance of such duties as a regular and continual part of their jobs.[229]

It is not unusual, of course, to find duties and tasks which may properly fall within two or more separate job classifications. In this regard, Arbitrator Robert S. Thompson expressed the following opinion:

---

[224]United States Steel Corp., 26 LA 325, 326 (1956). Also see Arbitrator Hon in 71 LA 59, 61; Witney in 70 LA 620, 625 (the contested assignment was "reasonably related to the essence of the duties and the fundamental characteristics of" the detailed job description); Cahn in 53 LA 1130, 1131 ("job description cannot be considered as an agreement in and of itself as to how the job will be performed in the future or that it will continue to be performed without change"); Klamon in 27 LA 784, 786–787; Davey in 23 LA 206, 209; Whiting in 5 LA 304, 306–307.

[225]See Arbitrator Block in 45 LA 807, 810–811; Bowles in 26 LA 415, 421; Ryder in 23 LA 829, 832–834. Also see Livengood in 23 LA 520, 521; Donnelly in 20 LA 586, 588.

[226]Nebraska Consol. Mills Co., 22 LA 785, 789–790 (Doyle, 1954). For similar results, see Arbitrator Rubin in 44 LA 1264, 1270–1271, 1273; Stouffer in 44 LA 1134, 1138; Wolff in 18 LA 853, 854 (he reached a different result in 45 LA 234, 238, where there was a special agreement).

[227]Omaha Cold Storage Terminal, 48 LA 24, 31 (Doyle, 1967). For related discussion, see subtopic entitled "Establishing, Eliminating, and Combining Jobs and Classifications," above.

[228]Phillips Petroleum Co., 29 LA 226, 228 (1957). Similarly upholding management's action, see Arbitrator Goldberg in 73 LA 892, 895; Dworkin in 72 LA 816, 818–819; Hon in 71 LA 59, 61; Larkin in 54 LA 250, 252; Solomon in 48 LA 364, 370–372; Morgan in 47 LA 756, 760; Williams in 46 LA 602, 604–605; Hebert in 43 LA 491, 497; Klein in 41 LA 1045, 1049–1050; Beatty in 40 LA 733, 735; Thompson in 28 LA 374, 376–377; Uible in 25 LA 897, 899; Prasow in 25 LA 44, 48–49; Wallen in 22 LA 831, 833. But see Arbitrator Caraway in 54 LA 1080, 1083; Volz in 42 LA 336, 338–339; Teple in 41 LA 815, 818–819; Hale in 32 LA 873, 879–882; Cahn in 32 LA 221, 221–222.

[229]Linde Air Prods. Co., 20 LA 861, 864 (1953). Also see Arbitrator Donnelly in 20 LA 586, 588; Hampton in 17 LA 666, 668; Feinberg in 16 LA 926, 928–930; Simkin in 8 LA 113, 115–116.

"* * * management may assign tasks which involve minor and occasional variation from job descriptions to employees in different classifications when what is required falls within the skills and other factors which are common to the several classifications. The arbitrator believes that this principle is well established except where there are specific contract provisions otherwise."[230]

In reaching this conclusion Arbitrator Thompson spoke at length of the natural overlapping of duties between classifications:

"It is understandable that in the interests of job security, unions press for inviolability of job classifications. Certainly, practices which permitted more or less discriminate transfer of duties from one classification to another, or the assignment of tasks now to one classification and now to another, would lead to anxieties about the kind and amount of work that might be available to particular employees at different times.

"However, the reality is that there is much overlapping in jobs and their classifications. It would take an almost completely rationalized industry to provide for each worker absolutely distinct jobs. In highly specialized production work, operations are split off from general operations, and there may in consequence be an approach to fairly exclusive jobs one from another. However, in maintenance work duties are by the nature of the needs necessarily more general.

"It is reassuring to be able to place things in neat categories. Is aspirin a drug and therefore to be sold only under a physician's prescription? How about the new tranquilizers? Is there a sharp line between intelligence and stupidity, or a gradually changing quality ranging from genius to idiot?"[231]

When work falls within the job descriptions of two or more crafts or classifications, or is by nature a borderline or overlapping duty of two or more crafts or classifications, or if it has been performed by two or more crafts or classifications in the past, management has been permitted considerable leeway in assigning the work and ordinarily has not been limited to assigning it exclusively to one of the crafts or classifications.[232] However, where work of an overlapping nature had

---

[230]Goodyear Tire & Rubber Co., 28 LA 374, 377 (1957).
[231]Id. at 376.
[232]See Arbitrator Bickner in 81 LA 421, 422–424; Porter in 78 LA 239, 240–241; Heneman in 75 LA 1238, 1239–1240; Brisco in 74 LA 1225, 1229; Yatsko in 73 LA 1041, 1042; Frost in 73 LA 1011, 1014; Goodman in 73 LA 207, 211, 215; Gilson in 72 LA 1209, 1213–1214; Kossoff in 71 LA 204, 214; Morgan in 70 LA 1243, 1245; Altrock in 70 LA 644, 645; Fields in 64 LA 1069, 1071–1072; Belstein in 62 LA 762, 763; Block in 56 LA 353, 356; Wren in 51 LA 411, 413; Bothwell in 51 LA 41, 44–45 ("in dealing with the problem of work jurisdiction where there are several crafts in a plant, the arbitrator cannot ignore the language contained in other craft union agreements with the Company, or practice in the past in administering the language"); Eyraud in 50 LA 1001, 1003; Seward in 50 LA 1214, 1216; Block in 50 LA 361, 366; McKenna in 48 LA 941, 948; Anrod in 48 LA 310, 313; Duff in 48 LA 52, 54; Uible in 41 LA 510, 512; Sembower in 40 LA 481, 486–487; Oppenheim in 40 LA 257, 258–259; Strong in 39 LA 1207, 1208–1209; Mittenthal in 39 LA 65, 67–68; Quinlan in 38 LA 714, 717–718; Rubin in 38 LA 538, 541–543; Klein in 38 LA 180, 182; Donaldson in 37 LA 528, 530–531; Duff in 36 LA 376, 379; McCoy in 32 LA 848, 851; Prasow in 30 LA 444, 447–448; Klamon in 22 LA 336, 350–351; Cole in 21 LA 814, 815 (when work falls within the job descriptions of two classifications management has the right to decide which shall do it if there is insufficient work to keep both classifications busy). As to claiming a particular share of work over which there is overlapping craft jurisdiction, see United States Steel Corp., 54 LA 184, 187–188 (Garrett, 1969). In Rayonier, Inc., 36 LA 883, 888 (Christon, 1961), procedures were suggested for harmonious operations where the company had contracts with each of four unions, each contract reserving work within the union's jurisdiction to its members.

long been assigned to one craft, the mere whim or caprice of management was not a reasonable basis for diverting the work to another craft.[233] Furthermore, work which was the "jugular vein" of one craft and not de minimis could not be assigned to another craft.[234]

Management generally has been held to have considerable discretion in unusual situations to make temporary or emergency assignments of tasks across job or classification lines. For instance, Arbitrator James P. Miller ruled that in case of emergency or breakdown it is reasonable for an employer to require maintenance employees with certain occupational titles to assist employees with other occupational titles:

> "Many years of experience have proven to me that a plant maintenance crew is somewhat similar to the crew of a ship or a football team. Each member has a designated position or title and spends most of his team time attending to the duties and tasks associated with his designated position. However, when an emergency arises, they all respond as a crew and assist in getting the ship back on an even keel, weathering the storm, or, as in the case of the football team, advancing the ball to the opposing team's goal line."[235]

What Arbitrator Miller thus said in regard to maintenance employees would appear to apply to plant employees generally. For instance, an employer was upheld in assigning an emergency job which arose on a nonworkday to the only two employees scheduled to work on that day, despite the fact that the work did not fall within the duties of their job classifications. The arbitrator stated that management should have the right to meet unusual situations in this manner unless restricted from doing so by the agreement.[236]

Finally, it should be remembered that while management often has wide authority to assign duties and tasks to employees, they in turn may challenge the fairness of the rate paid for the job after its change.[237] Moreover, employees temporarily performing work which is rated higher than their regular work may be entitled to the higher rate for performing the higher rated work.[238]

---

[233]Dow Chem. Co., 32 LA 587, 592 (Gorsuch, 1964).

[234]Shell Chem. Co., 47 LA 1178, 1180–1181 (Rohman, 1967).

[235]Youngstown Sheet & Tube Co., 4 LA 514, 520 (1946).

[236]Thompson Mahogany Co., 5 LA 397, 399 (Brandschain, 1946). For other cases permitting such temporary and/or emergency assignments, see Arbitrator Weiss in 77 LA 714, 716; Larrabee in 72 LA 1204, 1209; Mikrut in 65 LA 968, 974–975; Belcher in 62 LA 205, 208; Mewhinney in 61 LA 1147, 1149; Valtin in 49 LA 411, 414–415; Stouffer in 49 LA 169, 172; Dworkin in 49 LA 131, 139; Teple in 44 LA 853, 857; Klamon in 43 LA 982, 994, and in 22 LA 336, 351; Autrey in 39 LA 961, 964; Lehoczky, Fisher & Myers in 36 LA 21, 27 ("interests" arbitration); Ross in 34 LA 752, 755; Sembower in 29 LA 704, 706; Williams in 27 LA 790, 792; Reid in 22 LA 358, 361; Hawley in 22 LA 157, 161; Gilden in 19 LA 802, 805; Kelliher in 18 LA 216, 217–218; Hampton in 17 LA 666, 668; Elson in 8 LA 129, 132.

[237]See Arbitrator Draznin in 78 LA 1263, 1265, 1267; Cohen in 65 LA 577, 581; Dworkin in 39 LA 1065, 1073; Cahn in 36 LA 822, 823–824; Klamon in 22 LA 336, 351. For full discussion, see this Chapter, topic entitled "Wage Adjustments Following Changes in Operation Methods."

[238]For example, see Arbitrator Madden in 65 LA 1267, 1270; Styles in 65 LA 773, 775; Lippman in 63 LA 487, 499; Larkin in 35 LA 265, 268; Seward in 32 LA 200, 212–215; Kelliher in 25 LA 64, 65–66; Platt in 16 LA 215, 216; Hepburn in 11 LA 145, 147; Elson in 8 LA 389, 393–394. Cf., Steele in 47 LA 796, 798; Howlett in 35 LA 480, 482–483; McCoy in 8 LA 883, 890–891. In view of the overlap of duties among different classifications, guides (garnered from reported arbitration decisions) have been offered for determining whether an employee is performing work of a higher classification. See Alaska Dept. of Transp., 78 LA 999, 1005–1006 (Tilbury, 1982); Hanna Mining Co., 73 LA 123, 125–126 (Axon, 1979).

Hiring of Employees

Except as restricted by statute or the collective agreement management retains the unqualified right to hire or not to hire. Particularly significant statutory restrictions are (1) those against discrimination on the basis of unionism under the National Labor Relations Act and the Railway Labor Act,[239] (2) the Age Discrimination in Employment Act of 1967,[240] and (3) the Civil Rights Act of 1964 prohibiting discrimination because of race, color, religion, sex, or national origin.[241] Contractual restrictions upon the right to hire exist most often in seniority or union security provisions (discussed hereinbelow).

Arbitral recognition of management's basic right and control in hiring is illustrated by the following lines of cases: Company rules against hiring spouses or other relatives of present employees have been upheld.[242] Management's right to hire includes the right to set preemployment standards and to implement them by requiring applicants to give accurate information as to their work and medical history and concerning their record as law abiding citizens.[243] The employer's right to hire includes the right to hire additional employees even though this may mean less overtime or other reduced opportunities for employees,[244] and has been held to include the right not to hire any new employee to fill a vacancy where the employer had no bids from his employees and there was no contractual requirement for maintaining a certain number of employees within the classification.[245]

Specific restrictions on hiring contained in the seniority provisions of the collective agreement may be to the effect, for example, that

---

[239]For example, see Phelps Dodge Corp. v. NLRB, 61 S.Ct. 845 (1941), upholding the NLRB's power to require an employer to hire applicants who had been rejected because of their union affiliation even though they had obtained substantially equivalent employment elsewhere.

[240]Another statute of interest is the Rehabilitation Act of 1973, under which employers who enter into certain procurement contracts with federal agencies must adopt affirmative action plans for employment and advancement of qualified handicapped individuals. See Volz, "Medical and Health Issues in Labor Arbitration," Proceedings of the 31st Annual Meeting of NAA, 156, 184–186 (BNA Books, 1979). Also see Segal, "Employee Benefit Plans in Arbitration of Health and Medical Issues," id. at 187, 201. Programs or activities receiving federal financial assistance are prohibited by the Act from discriminating (including employment discrimination) against qualified handicapped individuals. See Consolidated Rail Corp. v. Darrone, 104 S.Ct. 1248 (1984).

[241]For example, see Phillips v. Martin Marietta Corp., 91 S.Ct. 496 (1971), holding the Act does not permit one hiring policy for women with pre-school-age children and another for men with such children. In Furnco Constr. Corp. v. Waters, 98 S.Ct. 2943, 2950 (1978), the U.S. Supreme Court stated that the Act prohibits the employer "from having as a goal a work force selected by any proscribed discriminatory practice, but it does not impose a duty to adopt a hiring procedure that maximizes hiring of minority employees." In Texas Dept. of Community Affairs v. Burdine, 101 S.Ct. 1089, 1097 (1981), the Court stated than an employer is not required "to hire the minority or female applicant whenever that person's objective qualifications" are equal to those of a white male applicant.

[242]See Arbitrator Novak in 68 LA 1309, 1314; Block in 55 LA 283, 286; McNaughton in 55 LA 258, 260; Davey in 49 LA 105, 109–110; Beatty in 48 LA 1123, 1124; Kates in 45 LA 641, 643.

[243]E.g., see Arbitrator Koven in 55 LA 581, 585; McNaughton in 55 LA 258, 260; Myers in 54 LA 534, 539–540; Duff in 53 LA 597, 600; Holly in 53 LA 503, 506; Cohen in 52 LA 89, 92; McCoy in 47 LA 752, 754–755; Stouffer in 46 LA 654, 658–659; Altieri in 46 LA 559, 562; Lehoczky in 45 LA 513, 515; Kelliher in 45 LA 335, 336; Sherman in 42 LA 323, 324. Also see Inland Steel Corp., 111 LRRM 1193 (NLRB, 1982).

[244]See Arbitrator McCoy in 45 LA 1165, 1166; Geissinger in 42 LA 1293, 1295–1296; Larson in 38 LA 1152, 1154; Hale in 33 LA 685, 692. Also see Arbitrator Wright in 69 LA 315, 318, 320.

[245]Connecticut Coke Co., 28 LA 360, 361–362 (Stutz & Mottram, dissent by Curry, 1957). For related material, see this Chapter, topics entitled "Vacancies" and "Determination of Size of Crews."

the employer may not hire new employees to fill vacancies until the rehiring list of laid-off employees is exhausted,[246] or that the employer must consider present employees for vacancies before hiring new workers.[247]

Where the contract neither explicitly nor by strong implication restricted the right of management to hire new employees, one arbitration board refused to read a restriction into the contract. That board distinguished between the right to hire and the right to promote under a contract which did not specifically restrict management's right to hire but did require the observance of seniority in the event a promotion was made, the arbitrators stating that this "agreement to promote by seniority does not, as such, exclude either explicitly or implicitly the right of the Company not to promote but to hire."[248] Other arbitrators, however, while not speaking in terms of the right to hire, did find a violation of the seniority provisions requiring preferential consideration of senior employees when the company failed to consider its employees for a vacancy and hired an outsider.[249]

In another situation where the company conceded that its right to hire was qualified by the seniority clause, the company was nevertheless held not required to fill a job opening from present employees when none of them could perform the job without intensive training— it was permitted to hire an already qualified person.[250] In the latter regard, other arbitrators likewise have recognized management's right to hire a new employee where it has no qualified employee for the job,[251] or where other reasonable justification exists for the action.[252]

---

[246]As in San Francisco Chronicle, 21 LA 253 at 253 (Kerr, 1953).

[247]As in Electric Auto-Lite Co., 24 LA 765, 766 (Kahn, 1955).

[248]Travelers Ins. Co., 18 LA 534, 535 (Donnelly & Mottram, dissent by Sviridoff, 1952). Also see Arbitrator Hayes in 66 LA 180, 182; Liebowitz in 62 LA 1275, 1277–1278; Donnelly, Mannino & Mottram in 24 LA 631, 632. For similar results where the contract contained a general management rights clause, see Chrysler Corp., 32 LA 988, 991 (Wolff, 1959), the arbitrator stating that the section on promotions governs the manner in which a vacancy is to be filled *if* it is filled by promotion—it does not restrict management's right to fill the vacancy by a new hire even if a present employee is qualified for the job (past practice also supported this interpretation). Some arbitrators have recognized that employers in the field of education need added leeway for hiring in instructional areas. West Mifflin Area School Dist., 74 LA 627, 628–629 (Hays, 1980); Dyke College, 72 LA 1175, 1177 (Siegel, 1979). In Kansas City Power & Light Co., 52 LA 1087, 1097–1098 (Klamon, 1969), a qualified probationary employee had no standing to protest the hiring of an equally qualified new employee for a vacancy; the contract stated that probationers had no contractual rights prior to becoming regular employees.

[249]See Arbitrator Marshall in 49 LA 69, 70–71; Yarowsky in 48 LA 582, 585 (under the facts it was a technical violation only); Gilden in 27 LA 544, 546–547; Dworkin in 21 LA 589, 595. Also see Beilstein in 75 LA 511, 517–518; Hunter in 72 LA 1234, 1237–1238; Tatum in 41 LA 1027, 1030–1031; Feinberg in 13 LA 991, 999. Cf., Yarowsky in 68 LA 321, 324. Regarding simultaneous v. preferential consideration of federal agency employees in relation to outside applicants to fill vacancies, see Internal Revenue Serv., 71 LA 1018, 1019–1020 (Harkless, 1978). For related material, see Chapter 2, federal-sector subtopics entitled "Management Rights—Prohibited Bargaining Items" and "Management Rights—Permitted Bargaining Items."

[250]Wagner Elec. Corp., 20 LA 768, 775 (Klamon, 1953).

[251]See Arbitrator Bilder in 62 LA 1184, 1186; Hertz in 50 LA 463, 465; Marshall in 49 LA 69, 71; Altrock in 48 LA 629, 633; Daugherty in 47 LA 554, 558–559; Merrill in 36 LA 145, 147–148; Stouffer in 35 LA 397, 399; Seward in 31 LA 267, 268–269. Also see Block in 54 LA 460, 461, 467; Sembower in 53 LA 950, 954–955; Singletary in 44 LA 1193, 1194–1195, and in 41 LA 1033, 1037–1038; Kornblum in 40 LA 403, 407. For a contract giving management broad authority to hire persons needed because of their special training, ability, or experience, see Jefferson City Cabinet Co., 35 LA 117, 123 (Marshall, 1960).

[252]See Otis Elevator Co., 5 LA 173, 174 (Davey, 1944). An employer who had been unable to fill certain jobs due to a tight labor market was upheld in offering a higher than contractual

In one case the employer could fill a vacancy by hiring a new employee where the only employees who were qualified to perform the job were on strike and a posting of the vacancy for bids "would have been an idle gesture."[253]

The employer's discretion in hiring may be restricted by a union security clause to the extent that any such clause is legal under applicable state and federal statutes. Where the union security provision is lawful, arbitrators appear to frown upon hiring practices which accomplish by indirection the condition which the provision was designed to prevent, or which prevent the condition which the provision was intended to accomplish.[254] For instance, one employer was ordered to discharge again an employee previously discharged pursuant to a maintenance-of-membership provision while employed as a production worker and subsequently rehired as an assistant foreman. The arbitrator declared that the rehiring of the worker under these circumstances was a cause of dissention and violated the intent of the maintenance-of-membership provision.[255]

Under contracts providing for union referrals in hiring but containing the requirement that referrals be satisfactory to management, arbitrators have allowed employers considerable discretion in rejecting union-referred candidates.[256] But it has been held that the employer must exercise good faith in reaching his decision.[257] It has also been held that while an employer had discretion in selecting from among those referred by the hiring hall, he could not secure employees through direct hire where the contract did not reserve the right to do so.[258]

---

starting wage rate to new hires who already possessed certain experience or training. Bowmar Instrument Corp., 62 LA 955, 958 (Volz, 1974). For other cases in which management was challenged for hiring at a higher than contractual starting wage rate, see Arbitrator Dennis in 70 LA 1172, 1174; Kallenbach in 60 LA 453, 457–458.

[253]Allied Chem. & Dye Corp., 16 LA 28, 29 (McCoy, 1951). For legal doctrine concerning management's right to hire and retain workers hired during economic strikes, see NLRB v. Fleetwood Trailer Co., 88 S.Ct. 543 (1967); NLRB v. Mackay Radio & Tel. Co., 58 S.Ct. 904 (1938). Also, The Laidlaw Corp., 171 NLRB 1366 (1968). For arbitration decisions, see Arbitrator Merrill in 55 LA 109; Gorsuch in 53 LA 784; Turkus in 42 LA 823; Hill, Horlacher & Seitz in 39 LA 1156; Crane in 36 LA 635; Weinstein in 34 LA 125; Loucks in 33 LA 777.

[254]See Arbitrator Aaron in 10 LA 227, 232–233; Updegraff in 1 LA 331, 333; Fabinski in 1 LA 15, 19–20.

[255]Merrill-Stevens Co., 1 LA 15, 19–20 (Fabinski, 1944).

[256]See Arbitrator Taylor in 74 LA 550, 557–558; Latimer in 52 LA 327, 332; Feinberg in 8 LA 593, 595; Reynolds in 3 LA 367, 369. Also see Hays in 68 LA 989, 991; Bennett in 18 LA 764, 766 (interest dispute); Wyckoff in 5 LA 38, 40 (interest dispute). In Consolidated Papers, 71 LA 595, 598 (1978), Arbitrator Robert J. Mueller reminded that "in the absence of a contractual hiring hall arrangement * * * the matter of determining who to hire into employment is generally recognized as solely a management prerogative." Also regarding management's determination of *who* to hire where there was no hiring hall or other such limitation, see Arbitrator Flannagan in 78 LA 900, 903; Traynor in 71 LA 667, 671–672.

[257]Matson Navigation Co., 29 LA 209, 213 (Cobb, 1957). Also see Arbitrator Schmertz in 43 LA 245, 246.

[258]Union Painting Contractors Assn., 42 LA 902, 908–909 (Seligson, 1964). Also see Arbitrator Platt in 50 LA 239, 245. But see Koven in 65 LA 1019, 1023, where an affirmative action plan was a factor, and see Traynor in 66 LA 403, 408, where the union failed to refer workers through the hiring hall. The use of hiring halls is legal under the NLRA if not used as an instrument of discrimination on the basis of unionism. Local 357, IBT v. NLRB, 81 S.Ct. 835 (1961). By virtue of federal preemption, hiring hall discrimination which violates or arguably

Determination of Size of Crews

Many grievances have involved the right of management to determine the number of employees to be utilized in a given operation.[259] Crew size determinations may be of a more or less permanent nature, as, for example, where a new operation or new equipment is installed or where management eliminates a job to accommodate reduced production needs and market changes; or such determinations may affect a given crew only temporarily, as where the company does not fill a crew member's position during his brief absence.

It has been held that management has the right unilaterally to determine the size of crews necessary for operation of the plant, either under a general management rights clause,[260] or as a matter of management prerogative,[261] so long as no other provision of the agreement is violated by the employer's determination.[262]

Union challenges to management action in determining the size of crews have presented arbitrators with a variety of factors for their consideration, including the following: the union may argue that a contract manning provision limits the company's right of action; it may charge the violation of a clause not specifically related to crew size, such as the recognition clause, seniority or layoff clauses, or clauses concerned with filling vacancies;[263] there may be safety or health considerations, or a question of increased burden on remaining crew members; technological or process changes or changes in operations methods and procedures may result in idle time for employees affected by such changes; or economic and production needs may be a factor.[264] These factors are discussed below.

---

violates the NLRA may not be remedied by a state court award of damages. Farmer v. Carpenters Local 25, 97 S.Ct. 1056 (1977). In General Bldg. Contractors Assn. v. Pennsylvania, 102 S.Ct. 3141 (1982), an employer who had no right to control the union was not liable for its violation of Title VII of the Civil Rights Act by racially discriminatory operation of a hiring hall.

[259]It may be noted, too, that one of the most critical interest disputes of many years involved crew consist for the railroad industry. See Railroads v. Operating Bhds., 41 LA 673 (Aaron, Healy & Seward, 1963).

[260]See Arbitrator B. Wolf in 47 LA 425, 427; King in 46 LA 70, 71; Sembower in 40 LA 720, 726; T. McDermott in 40 LA 67, 70, and in 34 LA 365, 367; Marshall in 28 LA 252, 254; Updegraff in 12 LA 865, 869.

[261]See Arbitrator Bothwell in 71 LA 396, 405; Greene in 61 LA 1253, 1258; Teple in 55 LA 19, 22; Hebert in 46 LA 140, 151; Mittenthal in 42 LA 1188, 1191; Hon in 38 LA 1135, 1139; Marshall in 29 LA 687, 692–693; Miller in 10 LA 736, 745. Also see Arbitrator Richardson in 70 LA 817, 825–826; Updegraff in 30 LA 115, 117. The National War Labor Board recognized this to be a management function. American Smelting & Ref. Co., 21 War Lab. Rep. 163 (1945).

[262]See Arbitrator King in 46 LA 70, 72; Ross in 33 LA 421, 423; Willingham in 6–1 ARB ¶8069. Some arbitrators would require management's action in reducing the size of a crew to "meet the test of reasonableness." Continental Can Co., 35 LA 602, 607 (McKelvey, 1960). Also see Arbitrator Hoffman in 63–1 ARB ¶8199; Reid in 33 LA 442, 445.

[263]See Arbitrator Daugherty in 45 LA 648, 650; Mittenthal in 42 LA 1188, 1190; Hale in 36 LA 919, 921; Stouffer in 36 LA 245, 248; Bauder in 33 LA 25, 27; Dworkin in 29 LA 787, 789; Stutz in 28 LA 360, 361; Feinberg in 19 LA 523, 525; S. Wolff in 19 LA 487, 488. For related material, see this Chapter, topics entitled "Layoff of Employees," "Vacancies," "Control of Operation Methods," "Job and Classification Control"; Chapter 14, Seniority.

[264]In Pittsburgh Plate Glass Co., 33 LA 614, 617–619 (1959), and 36 LA 21, 22–23 (1960). Arbitrators Lehoczky, Fisher, and Myers developed general principles as a guide in determining specific manpower proposals.

Does a Crew in Fact Exist?

The preliminary question may arise as to whether a group of employees actually constitute a "crew." Commenting in regard to the parties' local working conditions clause, Arbitrator Sylvester Garrett noted that the mere fact that a certain number of employees perform a given operation for a number of years does not necessarily establish a local working condition governing crew size; and he continued, "It is the *relationship* between this course of conduct, and some *given set of underlying circumstances* which is important in determining whether there has been a recurring response which has evolved as the normal and accepted reaction in dealing with the problem."[265]

In holding that the employer had acted within its rights under the management rights clause when it eliminated two maintenance employees, Arbitrator Thomas J. McDermott stated that employees are not a "crew" simply because employment has been stable for a long period of time and thus manning requirements have remained the same. He further observed:

> "Most arbitrators hold to the position that a crew for purposes of local working conditions exists where the employees making up the work force have a relationship that is interdependent to each other. This would mean that, when one member is removed or absent, the remaining workers are required to assume an increased amount of work, or there is a significant change in the type of work they are required to perform. In other words, there must be a relationship between the repetitive nature of the work and the interdependence of members to each other."[266]

Arbitrator Clair V. Duff cautioned that "The problem of *crew* sizes must be differentiated from the size of a work force in a particular department or other sub-division of the plant which usually fluctuates in size, depending on many circumstances."[267]

In summary, then, to demonstrate the existence of a "crew" in the absence of a contractual definition thereof, it must be shown that (1) an established course of conduct has existed (2) with respect to the assignment of a specific number of employees (3) who have performed in an interdependent manner (4) a particular type of work (5) under a given set of circumstances (6) for a significant period of time.

The above views have been expressed under agreements containing local working conditions clauses. It has been suggested that an even stronger showing as to the existence of a "crew" would be required in the absence of such local working condition clauses.[268]

---

[265]United States Steel Corp., 33 LA 394, 404 (1959).

[266]Pittsburgh Steel Co., 40 LA 67, 68–69 (1963). Also see Arbitrator Klaus in 66 LA 543, 547; Sherman in 47 LA 317, 319; T. McDermott in 46 LA 733, 734; Duff in 39 LA 151, 153. Cf., Arbitrator Crawford in 40 LA 903, 907–908; Porter in 39 LA 921, 925.

[267]Jones & Laughlin Steel Corp., 39 LA 151, 153 (1962).

[268]See Comments of Arbitrator Harry H. Platt in "The Silent Contract vs. Express Provisions," Proceedings of the 15th Annual Meeting of NAA, 140, 147 (BNA Books, 1962).

The remaining topics discussed below involve established crews.

Limiting Contract Provisions

Of course, a particular crew size may be fixed by a specific contract provision stating the number of employees in the crew with the result that management likely would be denied the right to eliminate a member of that crew. This was the arbitrator's ruling despite the fact that new equipment was installed which, absent the clause specifying the crew size, might have justified the reduction.[269]

Somewhat less specifically, a clause may call for "adequate help,"[270] "adequate manpower,"[271] or a "sufficient number" of employees.[272] Or the contract may require the employer to schedule the "normal number" of employees,[273] the "standard force,"[274] or the "full crew."[275]

Management's right to determine crew size may be restricted by a contract clause requiring joint determination with the union following any significant change in equipment or method of operation.[276] The right of management to reduce the size of a crew may also be limited by a clause, such as is prevalent in the steel industry contracts, which requires maintenance of established local working conditions unless the underlying basis for the condition is changed.[277] However, the mere existence of a local working conditions clause or one calling for "adequate help," etc., does not necessarily freeze the number of employees in a crew, since many factors, discussed hereinbelow, singly or in combination may nevertheless justify a change in the size of the crew. Many of the cases involving such contract clauses also involved changes in operations, technological changes, or questions of employee safety, and the like; and the arbitrator's finding that a

---

[269]Barton Salt Co., 46 LA 503, 505 (Merrill, 1966); Edition Bookbinders of N.Y., 42 LA 1167, 1171 (Altieri, 1964). In both cases the contract was specific as to certain crew complements but not as to others. Also see Arbitrator Chalfie in 68 LA 129, 141 (a layoff which would not have resulted "but for" the introduction of new equipment violated a provision requiring that any reduction in force resulting from automation be accomplished by attrition rather than layoff, and this was so regardless of the need to reduce the work force because of economic problems); Flink in 21 LA 653, 654.

[270]Schlitz Brewing Co., 30 LA 147, 148 (Fleming, 1958); Pabst Brewing Co., 29 LA 617, 621 (Fleming, 1957).

[271]Lone Star Brewing Co., 50 LA 458 (Hebert, 1968); Pearl Brewing Co., 42 LA 145, 147 (Bothwell, 1964).

[272]American Pipe & Constr. Co., 43 LA 1126, 1134 (Ladar, 1964).

[273]Gulf Oil Corp., 42 LA 294, 297 (Rehmus, 1964); Sherwin-Williams Co., 25 LA 879, 881 (Kelliher, 1956).

[274]Keystone Steel & Wire Co., 45 LA 648, 650 (Daugherty, 1965).

[275]Plymouth Oil Co., 36 LA 919, 922 (Hale, 1961); Continental Can Co., 35 LA 602, 603 (McKelvey, 1960).

[276]As in Memphis Publishing Co., 50 LA 186, 190 (Duff, 1967).

[277]See United States Steel Corp., 33 LA 394, 397–404 (Garrett, 1959). Also see Arbitrator Beilstein in 75 LA 229, 232–233; Florey in 43 LA 1048, 1050; Crawford in 40 LA 984, 986; T. McDermott in 39 LA 432, 434. Some contracts are silent as to past practices, while other contracts contain local working conditions clauses. On the question whether there is significant difference in results reached by arbitrators under these two types of contracts, see views by Saul Wallen, Lloyd H. Bailer, and Harry H. Platt, "The Silent Contract vs. Express Provisions," Proceedings of the 15th Annual Meeting of NAA, 117–147 (BNA Books, 1962).

proper crew had or had not been provided was based upon the evidence presented in the given case.

Technological and Process Changes

Arbitrators are in general agreement that where substantial changes in technology or manufacturing processes have been made management has the right to make changes in the size of the crew, unless restricted by the agreement.[278] This is true even where the contract contains a local working conditions clause, for it is reasoned that the changes in technology or processes cause a change in the basis for the existence of such condition.[279] Of course, the changes must be substantial enough to result in a material reduction in the employees' work load in order to justify the reduction in crew size.[280]

Moreover, there must be a "reasonable causal relationship" between the changes and the reduction in the crew, not only in the substance of the change, but also in the span of time between the change in equipment or process and the change in crew size.[281] Thus, where a series of changes was completed and the employer did not act to reduce the crew size until 10 years later, the arbitrator refused to uphold the reduction.[282]

However, even though there was a substantial span of time between the first of several changes and the reduction in crew size, management was upheld where it acted with "reasonable dispatch following the last of several related changes which rounded out the total picture of altered circumstances affecting the jobs in question." The arbitrator stated that the changes "are not properly considered as individual and isolated changes but must be viewed in their cumulative effect."[283]

Changes in Type of Operations, Methods, and Procedures

Substantial changes in the type of operations or in the method of operations[284] have been considered justifying factors in upholding

[278]See Arbitrator Duff in 76 LA 903, 908; Towers in 71 LA 185, 190; Hebert in 50 LA 458, 461; Altieri in 42 LA 1167, 1171; Hawley in 42 LA 479, 482; Hoffman in 63–1 ARB ¶8199; Joseph in 63–1 ARB ¶8092; Hon in 38 LA 1135, 1140; McKelvey in 35 LA 602, 607; Reid in 33 LA 442, 445. Also see Ables in 71 LA 838, 841–842.

[279]See Arbitrator Seward in 77 LA 372, 374; Chapman in 67 LA 759, 762–763 (acquisition of new equipment changed the underlying basis for the "team concept" asserted by the union, and, in any event, the union's "team concept" did not qualify as a "condition" but rather fell within management's right to direct the working force); T. McDermott in 43 LA 770, 772; Duff in 41 LA 432, 434, and in 41 LA 300, 301–302; Garrett in 62–2 ARB ¶8676, and in 34 LA 127, 135; Alexander in 37 LA 318, 320. Also see Seinsheimer in 77 LA 1042, 1045.

[280]See Arbitrator Dybeck in 51 LA 1303, 1306; Platt in 49 LA 1018, 1026; Florey in 43 LA 1048, 1050; May in 43 LA 433, 440; T. McDermott in 39 LA 432, 435. Also see McKenna in 55 LA 41, 53–54.

[281]See United States Steel Corp., 40 LA 984, 987–988 (Crawford, 1963). Also see Kaiser Steel Corp., 44 LA 353, 357–358 (Bernstein, 1965).

[282]United States Steel Corp., 40 LA 984, 987–988 (Crawford, 1963).

[283]United States Steel Corp., 41 LA 468, 479–480 (C. McDermott, 1963). Also see Arbitrator Hebert in 46 LA 140, 148–149; McKelvey in 35 LA 602, 607; Sherman in 34 LA 556, 558.

[284]As to changes in the type of operations, see Arbitrator T. McDermott in 43 LA 770, 772; Hawley in 42 LA 479, 482; Rehmus in 42 LA 294, 297. As to changes in the method of operations, see Arbitrator Gilson in 76 LA 1099, 1104; Fallon in 64–3 ARB ¶9169; Seward in 36 LA 162, 163; Brown in 35 LA 618, 620–621.

management's reduction in the size of crews. Thus, under a contract providing for "the normal number of men * * * required for the then existing conditions," the company was upheld when it eliminated a helper from a crew since a modernization program had made substantial changes in the type of operation and had substantially reduced the quantity of work to be performed by such helper. The work that remained did "not appear * * * to burden unduly" the remaining crew members.[285]

Under a local working conditions clause, an arbitrator held that substantial cumulative changes in warehouse and shipping procedures justified the reduction in crew size; even though instituted over a period of years, the changes were considered to be "part and parcel of the same improvement pattern."[286]

Market Changes

One arbitrator considered market changes an important factor, along with improved and new equipment and procedures, in upholding management's right to reduce the size of crews.[287] Similarly, in the absence of a contractual requirement to maintain crew sizes, where changes occurred in customer's buying habits as well as in methods of operation, which in turn substantially reduced the amount of work available to the employees involved, it was held that the company had the right to reduce the crew size.[288]

Production Needs and Reduced Operations

When operations are reduced in order to adapt to production needs, arbitrators appear to be in general agreement that management may reduce the size of crews so long as such action is not barred by the contract or does not create a safety hazard.[289] Thus, when a certain operation had been discontinued, it was held that management had the right to eliminate a job pertaining to such operation and assign the relatively few remaining duties of the job to another crew member.[290]

Work Load and Idle Time

The union frequently challenges the company's action on the basis that a reduced crew results in an excessive work load for the

---

[285]Gulf Oil Corp., 42 LA 294, 297 (Rehmus, 1964).

[286]United States Steel Corp., 41 LA 56, 58–59 (Altrock, 1963). Also see Cities Serv. Oil Co., 42 LA 479, 482 (Hawley, 1964).

[287]Cities Serv. Oil Co., 42 LA 479, 482 (Hawley, 1964). Regarding fiscal crises as cause for crew reductions by public-sector employers, see Arbitrator Zack in 66 LA 318, 321; Schmertz in 66 LA 261, 265–266.

[288]Mead Corp., 64–3 ARB ¶9169 (Fallon, 1964).

[289]See Arbitrator Mittenthal in 42 LA 1188, 1190–1191; T. McDermott in 40 LA 487, 489; Seward in 37 LA 83, 84, and in 34 LA 584, 585; Valtin in 36 LA 217, 218; Platt in 31 LA 217, 218.

[290]Pittsburgh Steel Co., 40 LA 70, 72 (T. McDermott, 1962). The arbitrator made no finding regarding the question of excessive work load on the remaining crew.

remaining crew members. However, working conditions may be changed significantly by technological or process improvements, by reducing or discontinuing certain operations, or by changes in methods and procedures, and the like. When such factors have resulted in a substantial amount of idle time for the employees in a crew, arbitrators have held that the company could properly reduce the crew and reallocate whatever duties remain to other employees in the crew.[291] In most of such cases the arbitrator has found that the remaining work allocated to the other crew members did not excessively increase their work load.[292]

If there is a finding that the elimination of a job from the crew has increased the work load of the remaining crew members, some adjustment in their rate of pay may be ordered. Under such circumstances, one arbitrator held that there was an "increase in job content" which was justification under the contract for negotiation of an adjustment in wage rate.[293]

In another situation, where the company was not permitted under the contract to operate with a crew member absent but nevertheless required three members of a four-man crew to perform all the tasks of the crew, the arbitrator directed the company to pay each of those three members an additional sum equivalent to one third of the regular wages the fourth crew member earned, as compensation for the additional work duties performed while he was absent.[294]

Use of Supervisors or "General Help"

The fact that the company assigns supervisors or "general help" to perform work which would have been done by the eliminated crew member may be pertinent in determining whether a reduction in the crew was in fact justified. The weight to be accorded such a factor would depend upon the amount and frequency of work performed by personnel outside the crew in question. Thus, where foremen or "general help" have not given inordinate assistance to those remaining in the reduced crew, arbitrators have held that such factor would not be determinative of the decision in the case.[295] However, where the union proved that foremen were persistently performing the work that would have been done by the eliminated crew member, the

---

[291]Pittsburgh Steel Co., 40 LA 70, 72 (T. McDermott, 1962); Reynolds Mining Co., 33 LA 25, 28 (Bauder, 1959). Also see Foster Wheeler Corp., 64–1 ARB ¶8103 (Shister, 1963).

[292]See Arbitrator Hebert in 50 LA 458, 461; T. McDermott in 46 LA 733, 734, and in 34 LA 365, 367; Bothwell in 42 LA 145, 147–148; Rehmus in 42 LA 294, 297; Fallon in 64–3 ARB ¶9169; Marshall in 29 LA 687, 692. One arbitrator found that in fact the work load of the remaining crew was less than it had been before the crew was reduced by reason of reduced operations and improved methods. Midwest Carbide Corp., 35 LA 618, 621 (Brown, 1960).

[293]Mobil Oil Co., 61–4 ARB ¶8069 (Willingham, 1961).

[294]Southwest Steel Corp., 38 LA 344, 346–347 (Duff, 1962). Similarly, Pittsburgh Steel Co., 66–1 ARB ¶8286 (T. McDermott, 1966).

[295]See Arbitrator Kadish in 41 LA 381, 384; Valtin in 35 LA 289, 292–293; Updegraff in 30 LA 115, 116.

arbitrator considered that the company by such action tacitly recognized that the crew was short-handed.[296]

Safety or Health Hazard

Management's right to determine the size of work crews has frequently been challenged on the ground that a reduction in the size of the crew has resulted in a safety or health hazard to the remaining employees. This argument has been advanced in the wake of technological changes,[297] introduction of safety equipment and procedures,[298] changes in operations and methods,[299] changes in production needs and reduced operations,[300] introduction of new production procedures,[301] and the like. However, by far the preponderance of cases involving such changes have held either that there was no sufficient showing of a safety hazard or that there was no increase in the normal and inherent hazard of the job.[302]

It should be observed that in many jobs there are certain normal and inherent risks which cannot be avoided if the jobs are to be performed at all. Thus, in crew safety cases it must be determined (1) whether a safety hazard actually exists, and (2) if so, whether it is an abnormal safety hazard. Of course, such determinations must be made on the basis of the facts in each case.

A crew safety dispute may include the question whether an additional employee would eliminate the alleged safety hazard, or the question of possible increased hazard to an employee left working alone when all the other crew members are eliminated. In a case involving the former issue, Arbitrator Clair V. Duff required the return of an employee to the crew when he found that a genuine safety hazard existed despite the installation of electronic safety devices and other automatic equipment. He held the innovations were not adequate to "insure an equivalent amount of protection which would be furnished if a vigilant employee was also on duty."[303] On the other

---

[296]United States Steel Corp., 61–2 ARB ¶8527 (Garrett, 1961). Also see Keystone Steel & Wire Co., 45 LA 648, 650–651 (Daugherty, 1965).

[297]See Arbitrator Seward in 77 LA 372, 374; Gershenfeld in 74 LA 820, 822; Bothwell in 42 LA 145, 147–148; Duff in 41 LA 432, 434–435, and in 41 LA 300, 301–302; Howlett in 41 LA 230, 236; Garrett in 34 LA 127, 135–136; Reid in 34 LA 442, 445.

[298]See Arbitrator Duff in 76 LA 903, 907, and in 43 LA 583, 587; Lehoczky in 43 LA 427, 429; Sembower in 39 LA 341, 346–347; Murphy in 37 LA 501, 503.

[299]See Arbitrator Murphy in 78 LA 1229, 1233; Gilson in 76 LA 1099, 1104; Lehoczky in 43 LA 427, 429; Duff in 41 LA 432, 434–435; Howlett in 41 LA 230, 236; Reid in 33 LA 442, 445.

[300]See Arbitrator Sharnoff in 69 LA 162 at 162; Mittenthal in 42 LA 1188, 1191; Seward in 37 LA 83, 84; Valtin in 36 LA 217, 218; Platt in 31 LA 217, 218–219.

[301]United States Steel Corp., 41 LA 300, 301–302 (Duff, 1963).

[302]See cases cited in notes 297–301 above. In only two of these cases was an increased hazard found (Arbitrator Sharnoff in 69 LA 162, 163, and Duff in 43 LA 583, 587). Also see Arbitrator Ladar in 43 LA 1126, 1134–1135.

[303]Jones & Laughlin Steel Corp., 43 LA 583, 587 (1964). Also see Arbitrator Ladar in 43 LA 1126, 1134–1135. In United States Steel Corp., 54 LA 317, 320 (Garrett, 1969), an apprentice could not be substituted for one of the two regular men on a crew, the practice being to use two journeymen for safety reasons and there being no change in conditions to affect the need for two journeymen. Similarly, see Arbitrator Sharnoff in 69 LA 162, 163–164, finding that the hazard involved in the operation left "little or no margin for error."

hand, conditions may be such that the presence of an additional experienced employee would still not eliminate the alleged hazard.[304]

In instances where the company has reduced a crew leaving only one employee, arbitrators appear to be in general agreement that working alone is not a "hazard per se."[305] Moreover, where an employee had instructions to request additional help if he felt that it was necessary, the arbitrator found it significant that no such requests had been made.[306] Nor is it felt that such instructions place an "unreasonable psychological or physical burden" on the employee.[307]

Two other aspects of crew size issues, discussed elsewhere in this book, may be noted briefly here. These relate to (1) the obligation of management to provide reasonably safe working conditions; and (2) the obligation of an employee to stay on the job unless a real safety or health hazard exists, and, conversely, the employee's right to be relieved of duty pending correction of abnormally hazardous conditions.[308]

Vacancies

It is generally recognized that in the absence of a contract provision limiting management's rights in regard to filling vacancies, as, for example, a clear requirement to maintain a certain number of employees on a particular job, it is management's right to determine whether a vacancy exists and whether and when it shall be filled.[309]

Moreover, contractual provisions dealing with posting of vacancies but not specifically requiring management to fill vacancies have been narrowly construed. Thus, a contractual provision for posting of

---

[304]Bethlehem Steel Co., 36 LA 217, 219 (Valtin, 1961). Also see Arbitrator B. Wolf in 47 LA 425, 429; Duff in 41 LA 432, 434–435. In Newport Steel Corp., 78 LA 1229, 1234 (1982), Arbitrator John J. Murphy concluded that (1) obstruction of the engineer's line of vision was "an inherent safety risk which cannot be avoided if locomotive engines are to be used" for certain purposes in the employer's operations, and (2) the risk could "be managed by steps other than adding an additional person on the crew operating each locomotive engine." Conditioned upon use of alternative measures, including installation and maintenance of equipment for direct radio communication between crew members, use of an additional crew member was not required. Also see Arbitrators Reel and Strongin in 66 LA 77, 79. In Lever Bros. Co., 64 LA 503, 507 (1975), Arbitrator Stanley M. Block concluded that adding another crew member would not substantially reduce possible risks, and he stated that "it is not reasonable to ask a Company to increase their operating costs, and ultimately the price of their products to the public, in order to achieve a *minimal hypothetical* reduction in *possible* risk to a few employees."

[305]Pickands-Mather Co., 43 LA 427, 429 (Lehoczky, 1964). Also see Arbitrator Gershenfeld in 74 LA 820, 824; Mittenthal in 42 LA 1188, 1192; Duff in 41 LA 300, 301–302; Valtin in 36 LA 217, 219.

[306]Pearl Brewing Co., 42 LA 145, 148 (Bothwell, 1964).

[307]Brooklyn Union Gas Co., 47 LA 425, 428 (B. Wolf, 1966).

[308]For discussion on these points, see Chapter 5, subtopic entitled "Use of Grievance Procedure v. Self-Help," and Chapter 16, Safety and Health.

[309]See Arbitrator Hearne in 80 LA 1115, 1118; Bowles in 75 LA 1097, 1101; Grooms in 70 LA 1196, 1197; Tharp in 70 LA 182, 184; Abrams in 69 LA 594, 597; Roberts in 54 LA 896, 900–901; Kesselman in 52 LA 894, 897–898; Larkin in 44 LA 580, 584; Solomon in 44 LA 161, 164–168; Hardy in 43 LA 1276, 1287; Seinsheimer in 40 LA 819, 821; Murphy in 39 LA 1074, 1077; Crawford in 36 LA 825, 827; Dworkin in 35 LA 649, 653; Fleming in 32 LA 115, 116; Donnelly in 29 LA 162, 166; Livengood in 28 LA 844, 847; Seligson in 25 LA 360, 364; Kelliher in 22 LA 576, 577; Dworet in 22 LA 71, 74. But see Davey in 29 LA 13, 16–17, where the contract made it mandatory to fill vacancies. For related discussion, see this Chapter, topic entitled "Determination of Size of Crews."

"permanent vacancies" was held to apply only if management decides that a vacancy exists; in this instance the company had decided that there was no need to replace a promoted employee, so no vacancy existed.[310] Under another contract requiring posting and giving preference to senior employees in their given classification, it was held that neither the posting nor the seniority or classification provisions of the contract contained any implied restriction on management's right to determine if a vacancy existed and, if so, whether to fill it.[311] It has been held also that where insufficient work existed to justify filling the job of an employee who had retired, management was not required to post the job and could assign the excess duties occasioned by the retirement to another employee (subject only to the possibility that the job of the latter employee may need to be reevaluated).[312]

Even where a job has been posted for bid, this does not necessarily guarantee that a vacancy exists and will be filled.[313] In one case management was upheld in permitting a successful bidder to withdraw his bid and return to his original job even though the latter had in turn been posted for bid.[314]

The filling of temporary vacancies also has been arbitrated. It is well established that management has the right, unless clearly restricted by the agreement, to decide whether or not to fill temporary vacancies occasioned by absences due to illness, vacations, and the like.[315] Contract provisions stating that temporary vacancies "will" or "shall" be filled by a stated procedure have been construed merely to specify the procedure to be used *if* management decides to fill a vacancy.[316]

---

[310]Sherwin Williams Co., 49 LA 74, 75 (Ray, 1967). Similarly, see Arbitrator Hutcheson in 62 LA 1132, 1134; Block in 46 LA 1027, 1029–1030; Seinsheimer in 40 LA 819, 821. In Philips ECG, 79 LA 123, 126–127 (1982), the agreement provided that "All vacancies in jobs covered by the agreement will be posted by the Company," but Arbitrator Joseph Shister stated that all that this "dictates is the posting and filling *procedure, if* the attending facts and circumstances warrant the posting and filling of the vacancy"; in holding that the employer had a right not to post a job that was vacated by the incumbent's retirement and to transfer the remaining duties to other classifications in an effort to make operations more efficient, Arbitrator Shister cautioned that there "must be—as there was here—a compelling reasonable and good faith basis for the Company's abstention from filling a vacancy."
[311]Fairway Foods, 44 LA 161, 164–168 (Solomon, 1965). The mere fact that a job classification has been dormant for a lengthy period does not mean that it has been abolished. See Ohio Chem. & Surgical Equip. Co., 40 LA 481, 485 (Sembower, 1963).
[312]Link-Belt Co., 36 LA 825, 827 (Crawford, 1961). Similarly, see Arbitrator Roberts in 54 LA 896, 900–901.
[313]See Arbitrator Shieber in 61 LA 261, 267; Kesselman in 52 LA 894, 897–898; Layman in 43 LA 951, 956. Also see Sembower in 71 LA 498, 503.
[314]R.C. Can Co., 52 LA 894, 897–898 (Kesselman, 1969), where a prior agreement existed, however, which would produce a different result if a successful bidder already has commenced work on his new job.
[315]See Arbitrator Tharp in 64 LA 259, 260; Teple in 55 LA 19, 22; Ray in 43 LA 395, 399–400; Roberts in 41 LA 492, 496; Larson in 38 LA 1152, 1154; Stouffer in 36 LA 245, 249–250; Seligson in 36 LA 266, 267–268; Abernethy in 29 LA 467, 468; Hebert in 28 LA 538, 541–542; Marshall in 28 LA 252, 254; Hawley in 22 LA 157, 159; Klamon in 16 LA 352, 356. In Minnesota Mining & Mfg. Co., 73 LA 378, 380 (1979), management was upheld in filling a temporary vacancy by overtime rather than by recalling an employee from layoff; Arbitrator James L. Stern pointed out that the utilized procedure was not specifically prohibited by the agreement, that the union had failed to establish its allegation of employer purpose to avoid holiday pay, and that "[s]table employment and the avoidance of temporary callbacks is usually regarded as a sound practice." The fact that management may have elected to fill temporary vacancies in the past does not bind it to do so in the future. See Arbitrator Ray in 43 LA 395, 399–400; Roberts in 41 LA 492, 496.
[316]See Arbitrator Hebert in 28 LA 538, 541; Roberts in 25 LA 885, 888; Hawley in 22 LA 157,

Scheduling Work

Collective agreements may deal expressly with the scheduling of work. For example, the agreement may fix or in some respect regulate shifts,[317] or expressly fix the workweek,[318] or expressly provide that scheduling is an exclusive function of management,[319] or in some respect expressly limit the employer's right to schedule work.[320] Another possibility is that the agreement may impliedly restrict management's rights in the scheduling of work, as where certain contract language was construed to prevent management from instituting seven-day continuous shift operations.[321]

Many arbitrators have recognized that except as restricted by the agreement the right to schedule work remains in management.[322] Much of the material in the remainder of this topic deals with the application of this rule, giving some indication as to the scope of management's rights—and limitations thereon—in this area.

In proper circumstances management has been permitted to suspend operations temporarily, eliminate double-time work, change the number of shifts, change the number of days to be worked, and the like. Thus, where nothing in the agreement clearly guaranteed any particular amount of work each week and the agreement did not otherwise restrict management's right to suspend operations, management could determine whether work should go forward and its decision to close down on a given day was upheld since it acted for a valid reason and not arbitrarily.[323] The elimination of Sunday (double-time) work was upheld even though such work had been regularly scheduled for many years, the arbitrator stating that "While the agreement contains no 'management rights' clause, the scheduling of work is a normal and customary function of management which would

---

159. The posting of schedules and scheduling of employees does not guarantee the number of employees who are to work and require replacements for sick employees. Standard Oil Co., 36 LA 245, 249–250 (Stouffer, 1960).

[317]For example, see Curtiss-Wright Corp., 36 LA 629, 629–630 (Crawford, 1960).

[318]For example, see Norfolk Naval Shipyard, 54 LA 588, 589 (Cushman, 1970).

[319]For example, see Celanese Corp. of Am., 30 LA 797, 798 (Jaffee, 1958).

[320]For example, see Ambridge Borough, 73 LA 810, 812 (Dean, 1979); Taylor Stone Co., 29 LA 236, 237 (Dworkin, 1957).

[321]Morse Chain Co., 43 LA 557, 560–561 (Cahn, 1964).

[322]See Arbitrator Mewhinney in 77 LA 1156, 1158–1159; McKay in 77 LA 23, 26–27; Eischen in 75 LA 555, 558; Konvitz in 75 LA 548, 550; Kiok in 75 LA 16, 18; Roberts in 73 LA 781, 787; Leahy in 73 LA 418, 420–421; Gibson in 70 LA 530, 532; Volz in 68 LA 51, 52–53; Solomon in 51 LA 1102, 1107–1108; Kabaker in 48 LA 1365, 1367; Howlett in 42 LA 25, 28–31; Stark in 35 LA 788, 790–792; Hill in 33 LA 320, 322; Shister in 32 LA 77, 80; Kelliher in 29 LA 615, 617; Dworkin in 29 LA 236, 239; Duff in 28 LA 37, 40; Warns in 24 LA 619, 622; Davey in 22 LA 657, 660; Uible in 19 LA 213, 214–215; Rule in 16 LA 328, 330; McCoy in 16 LA 73, 75; Schedler in 13 LA 192, 199; McCreary in 9 LA 834, 839–840; Whiting in 3 LA 482, 485; Korey in 1 LA 430, 432–433. Also see Arbitrator Davidson in 42 LA 51, 53; Scheiber in 40 LA 152, 159; Swauger in 37 LA 883, 886; Willcox in 36 LA 1117, 1119–1120; Coffey in 20 LA 432, 433; Klamon in 15 LA 733, 739; Tischler in 13 LA 396, 398.

[323]See Arbitrator Kabaker in 48 LA 1365, 1367–1368 (closing on the day before Christmas and the day before New Year's because of reduced orders); Solomon in 45 LA 388, 396–398 (closing to give holiday to nonunit employees though this meant unit employees did not work); Davidson in 42 LA 51, 53; Kabaker in 41 LA 970, 972–974 (shortage of materials justified sending certain employees home); Klamon in 36 LA 1031, 1034; Stark in 35 LA 788, 790–792.

not ordinarily be deemed limited or waived except by some express provision of the agreement."[324]

Moreover, where the contract contained no express limitation on work scheduling it was held that management could change from a schedule of two six-hour shifts six days a week to a schedule of one eight-hour shift five days a week; the arbitrator held that the change was not barred either by the contract's reference to six-hour shifts (which he said did not crystallize the workweek but merely provided the framework for overtime computation) or by the provision on preservation of "present practices and policies."[325] Management's right to change from a five-day work schedule to a six-day schedule has similarly been upheld.[326] In upholding such changes arbitrators have spoken of management's right "to schedule the work with a view to optimum efficiency,"[327] and have expressed the view that limitations on the right "ought not be lightly inferred."[328]

The mere fact that a work schedule has been traditionally on a workweek basis of five consecutive days has been held not to establish a vested interest in employees in the continuation of the schedule.[329] Thus, where nothing in the agreement prohibited management's action and where there was a general management rights clause management was within its rights in establishing staggered work schedules,[330] in changing from fixed to rotating shifts,[331] or in adding

---

[324]New Jersey Brewers' Assn., 33 LA 320, 322 (Hill, 1959).

[325]Kimberly-Clark Corp., 42 LA 982, 986–988 (Sembower, 1964), where the change was discussed with the union prior to being instituted. For a case similarly permitting management to change from a six-day work schedule to a five-day schedule, see St. Regis Paper Co., 51 LA 1102, 1107–1108 (Solomon, 1968), where there was no express restriction and the contract contained a general management rights clause; the arbitrator distinguished several other cases in which past actions of the parties made out a joint understanding as to scheduling. A "maintenance of standards" clause was held not to prevent management from changing from a 48-hour workweek to a 40-hour workweek in Borden Co., 39 LA 1020, 1023–1024 (Morvant, 1962). Long-established differences in a company's summer and winter schedules did constitute a binding "local working condition" under the agreement in Bethlehem Cornwall Corp., 31 LA 793, 795–796 (Valtin, 1958). Also see Arbitrator Maloney in 72 LA 410, 413.

[326]Goodyear Tire & Rubber Co., 32 LA 77, 80 (Shister, 1958); Screw Mach. Prods. Co., 3 War Lab. Rep. 553, 556 (1942), where the decision was signed by the public, labor, and management members of the panel. In Belcor, Inc., 77 LA 23, 26–27 (McKay, 1981), a work schedule change from five days on and two days off to seven days on and three or four days off in order to distribute the burden of working weekends was upheld.

[327]Kimberly-Clark Corp., 42 LA 982, 986 (Sembower, 1964).

[328]St. Regis Paper Co., 51 LA 1102, 1107 (Solomon, 1968).

[329]Calumet & Hecla, 42 LA 25, 28–31 (Howlett, 1963), where the employer changed from scheduling Monday through Friday and began scheduling employees for five days during the week as required by operational needs; Columbia Steel Co., 7 LA 881, 883 (Blumer, 1947). Also see Arbitrator Mewhinney in 77 LA 1156, 1158–1159 (upholding a schedule change which no longer assured some employees of having two consecutive days off).

[330]Ingram-Richardson Mfg. Co. of Ind., 3 LA 482, 485 (Whiting, 1946). For other cases construing the contract as not requiring the workweek to be composed of five consecutive days and thus permitting "staggered" or "split" work schedules, see Arbitrator Koven in 49 LA 1000, 1002–1004; Hayes in 47 LA 449, 452; Schedler in 13 LA 192, 199; Blumer in 7 LA 881, 883. Also see Jaffee in 30 LA 797, 799–803; Abrahams in 15 LA 142, 146–147.

[331]Morris P. Kirk & Son, 27 LA 6, 10 (Prasow, 1956); General Cable Corp., 15 LA 910, 912 (Kaplan, 1950), where there was no management rights clause. Also see Arbitrator Tilbury in 78 LA 1081, 1091. For a case dealing with arbitrability where the agreement contained no provision relating expressly to management's action in changing from fixed to rotating shifts, see Iowa Beef Processors v. Meat Cutters, 105 LRRM 2149, 2152 (CA 8, 1980). In Carnation Co., 34 LA 345, 349–350 (Marshall, 1960), management was bound by past practice as to the frequency of shift rotation.

an extra shift to permit seven-day operations.[332] However, while recognizing management's right to establish work schedules except as restricted by the agreement, Arbitrator Joseph D. Lohman held that management was not privileged to schedule shifts in such a way as to deprive employees of certain rest periods to which they were entitled under the contract.[333] Nor could a company change from fixed to rotating shifts where the change would impair the contractual right of senior employees to their preferred shift and "days off."[334]

One arbitrator was asked to decide whether, in the absence of a contractual provision, an employer had the right to reschedule hours of work for operations at night and, if so, on what basis of compensation. The arbitrator ruled that there was no question as to the company's right to assign employees to night work, but that it must pay a night-work differential that had been paid in the past.[335] Another arbitrator upheld management's right to schedule Sunday work where not prohibited by the agreement; the reasonableness of management's action was tested from the point of view of the needs of the business rather than the convenience of the employees.[336]

It has been held that, where an agreement is silent as to the workweek insofar as its commencement and end are concerned, the employer may change the day on which the workweek begins if the change is not made arbitrarily.[337] Similarly, where the contract con-

---

[332]Minnesota Mining & Mfg. Co., 15 LA 46, 49 (Kelliher, 1950). For other cases permitting the adding of shifts, see Arbitrator Roberts in 73 LA 781, 785 (stating that "the Arbitrator cannot find a limitation upon the Company's right to establish new, different, or additional shifts from time to time as its requirements dictate"); Seidenberg in 68 LA 1054, 1056 (pointing out that the employer established the new shift for bona fide business reasons, Arbitrator Seidenberg stated that the "weight of arbitral authority is that the institution, or modification of existing shifts, absent a specific contractual prohibition against it, is an appropriate exercise of managerial judgment"); Volz in 58 LA 51, 53; McCoy in 34 LA 34, 36. Where an agreement established three specific "regular" shifts and contained a general management rights clause, operational requirements were held to justify management's establishment of an "oddball" shift for one employee different from the shifts specified in the agreement. Scott Paper Co., 48 LA 591, 593 (Williams, 1967).

[333]Wilson & Co., 1 LA 342, 347 (1946). Also see Bakelite Co., 29 LA 555, 559 (Updegraff, 1957), involving a change in scheduled lunch periods.

[334]Reynolds Metals Co., 35 LA 800, 802–803 (Ross, 1961). Other contractual rights of employees have likewise been protected against invasion by managerial scheduling actions. See Arbitrator McNaughton in 50 LA 304, 306; Howard in 45 LA 72, 74.

[335]Everett Dyers & Cleaners, 11 LA 462, 466 (Myers, 1948). In FMC Corp., 50 LA 261, 263 (Koven, 1968), management could change an employee from an evening schedule to a daytime schedule where the change was for sound business reasons and where management had changed schedules in the past.

[336]Drake Bakeries, 38 LA 751, 753–754 (Wolf, 1962). Also see Arbitrator Summers in 39 LA 374, 378. For related discussion, see Chapter 17, topic entitled "Accommodation of Employees' Religious Beliefs." The Vietnam Era Veterans' Readjustment Assistance Act does not require employers to make work schedule accommodations for employee-reservists not made for other employees. Monroe v. Standard Oil Co., 101 S.Ct. 2510, 103 LRRM 2317 (1981). Also see Arbitrator Kramer in 78 LA 877, 880 (contract provision giving employees the right to two out of five weekends off was not violated by employer's action in scheduling an employee's weekends off to coincide with her reservist obligations).

[337]Schulze's Bakery, 5 LA 255, 257 (Wardlaw, 1946), where the Arbitrator pointed out also that the change was made in conformance with industry practice in the area. Also see Arbitrator Colbert in 75 LA 653, 654–655 (employer could utilize a Wednesday through Wednesday schedule even though the agreement specified a Monday through Sunday workweek for overtime payment purposes); Rezler in 65 LA 636, 637; Valtin in 33 LA 324, 326. A provision requiring union consent for changing the day on which the workweek begins was strictly enforced in Redi-Gas Serv., 48 LA 197, 198 (Olson, 1967).

tained no express restriction on the employer's right to determine the starting time for work shifts, the employer has been permitted unilaterally to change the starting and stopping time.[338] Even where the agreement specified the shift starting times, essential preshift "start-up" work has justified management in requiring certain employees to report early for the work.[339]

Under agreements which expressly state what is a "normal" or "regular" workweek management often has been permitted considerable leeway in making adjustments in the workweek as needed for efficient operations.[340] For example, although an agreement specified a "normal" workweek of Monday through Friday, special production needs justified the scheduling of one employee to a Tuesday through Saturday workweek.[341] Although another agreement provided for a "regular" workweek of five days, management could schedule a four-day workweek during a period of reduced production. The arbitrator stated that the provision for a "regular" workweek was designed to regularize employment and furnish norms from which overtime premiums may be calculated—it cannot be regarded as a guarantee of employment for all or any group of employees for any specific number of hours per day or days per week.[342]

However, even where the agreement specifically provided that there was no work guarantee and expressly reserved the right to management to adjust work schedules to meet operating requirements, it was held that the contractual provision establishing "normal" workday, workweek, and shift hours was violated when the schedule was modified during Christmas and New Year's weeks; the employer was held not to have a right to change the schedule arbitrarily, the arbitrator stating that the employee "adjusts his life" to the "normal routine" and that the employer had not demonstrated satisfactorily that a change from the normal work schedule was necessary.[343]

---

[338]See Arbitrator Howlett in 44 LA 954, 955; Schedler in 42 LA 345, 346–348; Tsukiyama in 41 LA 1115, 1116–1117; Mittenthal in 41 LA 1050, 1052–1053; Warns in 36 LA 1035, 1036–1037 (contractual requirement to "consult" with union as to change in starting time did not require union consent for a change); Hepburn in 28 LA 467, 467–468; Reid in 27 LA 123, 125. Also see Aisenberg in 68 LA 898, 900; Kates in 50 LA 741, 743; Hayes in 46 LA 129, 131–132. The agreement itself may be construed to give management the unilateral right to make the change (see Arbitrator McIntosh in 49 LA 661, 663, and in 49 LA 659, 660–661), or it may be construed to deny such right (see Arbitrator Meyers in 39 LA 93, 96; Koven in 38 LA 803, 807–808).

[339]Fitchburg Paper Co., 47 LA 349, 351–352 (Wallen, 1966); American Brake Shoe Co., 33 LA 344, 347–348 (Gilden, 1959). Also see Arbitrator Klamon in 21 LA 91, 97. But see Myers in 24 LA 565, 566.

[340]See Arbitrator Robins in 70 LA 1144, 1147; Gibson in 70 LA 530, 532–533; Daugherty in 50 LA 1211, 1213 (shut down for one day on three separate occasions); Cayton in 48 LA 570, 572; Hebert in 44 LA 226, 229–230, 233; Summers in 39 LA 374, 377 (although contract spoke of normal Monday through Friday workweek management could use seven-day continuous shift schedules for certain operations); Gamser in 33 LA 610, 613; Boles in 30 LA 465, 469–470; Kelliher in 29 LA 615, 617; Ryder in 24 LA 496, 500. Also see Howell in 71 LA 1256, 1259.

[341]Universal Foods Corp., 44 LA 226, 229–230, 233 (Hebert, 1965).

[342]Triangle Conduit & Cable Co., 33 LA 610, 613 (Gamser, 1959), the arbitrator stating that the layoff provisions were not violated. Very clear language is required for a guaranteed wage. New York Herald Tribune, 36 LA 753, 761 (Cole, 1960). Of similar substance, see Arbitrator Traynor in 80 LA 553, 557–558; Whyte in 78 LA 880, 883; Eischen in 75 LA 555, 558; Bolte in 71 LA 716, 718–719. Cf., Abrams in 81 LA 502, 507–509.

[343]Aro, Inc., 34 LA 254, 259 (Tatum, 1960). For other cases in which deviation from the

In the absence of a specific contract provision regarding the right of management to reduce the workweek in lieu of making layoffs, arbitrators have gone both ways on the issue.[344] Thus, one arbitration board held that management had the right to reduce hours of work in the absence of anything in the agreement restricting such right. There the contract defined the normal workweek as five days of eight hours each and set forth the procedure for layoffs in case of reduction in work. Speaking through its Chairman, Herbert Blumer, the board held that the employer was not prohibited from reducing hours per day to seven in lieu of making layoffs, declaring that the clauses defining the normal workday and normal workweek were standard clauses serving ostensibly as a basis for the calculation of overtime, that the working of the hours specified was not made mandatory, and that the agreement said nothing in regard to the necessity of making layoffs in lieu of reducing hours of work.[345]

A different result was reached by another arbitration board, which held that an employer who reduced the workweek of some employees from five to four days was required to apply the "layoff" provisions of the agreement in doing so. The agreement provided for a basic workweek of five days and made seniority govern in case of layoff.[346] In another case a provision defining the "basic working week" as 40 hours was similarly held violated by a reduction of the workweek for the purpose of sharing the work, the arbitrator stating that seniority must be honored by the use of layoffs; but he cautioned that the aforementioned provision did not guarantee individual

---

"normal" or "regular" schedule was held improper, see Arbitrator Roberts in 42 LA 589, 593; Crawford in 36 LA 687, 689–690 (employer could not expand workweek to continuous shift where contract spoke of "normal" workweek of 40 hours); Carmichael in 28 LA 20, 33; Reynard in 27 LA 625, 627; Donnelly, Mottram & Curry in 17 LA 463, 465–466. Also see Yagoda in 65 LA 582, 587–588.

[344]Some arbitrators have emphasized their conclusion that each case on this issue must turn on its own facts and contractual provisions. See Arbitrator Briggs in 80 LA 472, 477; Feldesman in 64 LA 197, 199; Stouffer in 37 LA 877, 882; Boles in 35 LA 845, 848; Kates in 32 LA 492, 496.

[345]Geuder, Paeschke & Frey Co., 12 LA 1163, 1164–1165 (1949). Also permitting a reduction in the workweek in lieu of layoffs, see Arbitrator Briggs in 80 LA 472, 476–478 (stating certain limitations on the right); Miller in 77 LA 474, 477 (stating that "no language limits the Company's freedom to decide on a reduction in the workweek instead of a layoff," and, rather, two provisions in the agreement "reinforce one another and provide that absolute right"); Grooms in 66 LA 118, 127; Murphy in 52 LA 852, 855–857; Stouffer in 37 LA 877, 881–883; Cahn in 32 LA 746, 748; Witney in 30 LA 938, 947; Prasow in 25 LA 794, 797–799; Ebeling in 24 LA 874, 876–877; Slavney in 22 LA 473, 475; Piper in 18 LA 801, 807; Dash in 18 LA 625, 627.

[346]United Smelting & Aluminum Co., 13 LA 684, 685–686 (Donnelly & Sviridoff, Mottram dissenting, 1949). Also disallowing a reduction in the workweek in lieu of layoffs, see Arbitrator Dunn in 77 LA 901, 903–904; McDonald in 76 LA 811, 815; Cole in 76 LA 368, 372; McKenna in 74 LA 1254, 1260; Cohen in 70 LA 895, 898 (the agreement provided that its terms "in all instances shall be subject to and subservient to local budgetary requirements," but the Arbitrator rejected the County's contention that this permitted reduction in workweek in lieu of layoff by seniority where a budget deficit existed); Sembower in 68 LA 1072, 1075; Feldesman in 64 LA 197, 199, 203–204; Hertz in 55 LA 859, 861; Hughes in 40 LA 460, 464; Williams in 40 LA 456, 459–460; Boles in 35 LA 845, 848–849; Kates in 32 LA 492, 500–501; Larkin in 25 LA 308, 312; Ryder in 25 LA 83, 84; Donnelly in 24 LA 846, 848; Cole in 24 LA 311, 313; Davey in 24 LA 88, 91–92; Selekman in 14 LA 1031, 1039. In one such case the arbitrator rejected the employer's contention that "layoffs believed at their inception to be but of brief duration are not layoffs but are matters of scheduling work." Bethlehem Steel Co., 5 LA 578, 588 (Brandschain, 1946). In Wilshire Mfg. Jewelers, 49 LA 1079, 1082 (Jones, 1967), a contractual provision on work sharing was construed to *require* management to reduce hours of employees instead of laying off or discharging some of the employees for lack of work.

employees 40 hours of work and would not limit management's right to reduce the workweek as necessary for plant efficiency or product quality.[347]

Management may be denied the right to make temporary changes in the work schedule where the purpose of doing so is to avoid overtime payments. Even under a contract providing that nothing therein should "be interpreted as interfering in any way with the Company's right to alter, rearrange or change, extend, limit or curtail its operations *·* * whatever may be the effect upon employment, when, in its sole judgment and discretion, it may deem it advisable to do all or any of said things," it was held that the employer could not change the work schedule for one week where the sole purpose in doing so was to avoid contractual overtime payments.[348] Some arbitrators, however, have held otherwise where the change is made prior to the commencement of the workweek[349] or is made with a full week's notice.[350] Such cases were regarded as not analogous to changes made on short notice.

In the absence of limiting contract language, other arbitrators have permitted management to change work schedules to avoid the payment of overtime, holding that the company is not obligated to provide overtime work.[351]

Finally, it may be noted that the "right" of management to schedule work has been held to carry with it the "duty" to do so; in that case Arbitrator Charles G. Hampton ruled that an employer who abdicates such right by permitting employees to determine their own overtime schedules must be held partly responsible for trouble caused by such schedules.[352]

Emergency Changes in Work Schedule

Arbitrators appear to be generally inclined to allow management a great deal of flexibility, where it is possible to do so under the agreement, in making unscheduled and emergency changes in the work schedule if made in good faith and for reasonable cause.[353] Even where the agreement in some respect limits management's right or imposes some obligation upon management in regard to making changes in the work schedule, the limitation or obligation may be held

---

[347]Motch & Merryweather Mach. Co., 32 LA 492, 497–498, 500–501 (Kates, 1959).

[348]Kennecott Copper Corp., 6 LA 820, 822 (Kleinsorge, 1947). For other awards denying management the right in question, see Arbitrator Hale in 39 LA 310, 314–315; Maggs in 35 LA 249, 254; Beatty in 21 LA 416, 419; Platt in 17 LA 313, 315; Gilden in 12 LA 624, 627; Blumer in 5 LA 402, 406; Trotta in 5 LA 69, 71.

[349]National Zinc Co., 4 LA 768, 772 (Wardlaw, 1946). Also see Arbitrator Autrey in 44 LA 961, 964; Hale in 39 LA 310, 315.

[350]Wilson & Co., 7 LA 601, 602 (Lohman, 1947).

[351]See Arbitrator Stutz & Williams, Curry dissenting, in 27 LA 92, 93; Wolff in 21 LA 210, 214; Uible in 19 LA 213, 214–215. Also see Brown in 68 LA 1202, 1205–1206; Jones in 62 LA 769, 771; Dworkin in 36 LA 233, 238; Rohman in 34 LA 781, 784; Warns in 24 LA 619, 622; Coffey in 20 LA 432, 433; Sturges in 16 LA 517, 525. For related discussion, see subtopic entitled "Equalization of Overtime" below.

[352]Fulton Glass Co., 10 LA 75, 78 (1948).

[353]See Arbitrator Bolte in 71 LA 716, 719; MacLafferty in 70 LA 982, 983–894; Leahy in 69 LA 1088, 1092–1093; Ipavec in 63 LA 73, 75–76; Eriksen in 62 LA 1221, 1226; Cole in 36 LA 753, 757–758; Reid in 31 LA 93, 95; Thompson in 28 LA 494, 503; Graff in 26 LA 43, 46–47; Platt in 17 LA 313, 315, and in 7 LA 485, 489; Reynolds in 13 LA 326, 327–328; Stein in 10 LA 579, 581.

inapplicable if there is an emergency, an act of God, or a condition beyond the company's control.[354] For some general definitions of such terms the reader is directed to the topic in this Chapter entitled "Emergencies, Acts of God, and Conditions Beyond the Control of Management."

The right to make some unscheduled changes in the work schedule is implicit in the agreement itself if the agreement contains a provision for reporting pay, as a great number of agreements do. The import is that management has the right to make such changes but the right is accompanied by an obligation to make the contractually specified payment to employees.[355] Moreover, many reporting pay clauses state express exceptions even as to the obligation to pay if the employees are not used because of an emergency or condition beyond the control of management. Thus, in the bulk of the cases the right to make the unscheduled change in work has not been questioned, the dispute centering rather on the company's obligation for reporting pay where employees reported for work but were not used.

Turning next to the consideration of specific cases, we note one arbitrator's ruling that a clause giving management the exclusive right to schedule working hours permits it to make temporary changes in the work schedule without consulting the union. In that case the arbitrator held that the employer was not obligated to pay employees for a half-hour waiting period on a day when they were scheduled to work at 10 a.m. but were unable to begin work until 10:30 a.m. The call-in pay clause was held not to cover the situation because the employees actually worked and received pay for more hours than were guaranteed by the clause. In sustaining the right of the employer to make temporary changes in the work schedule, Arbitrator R.W. Fleming said:

> "This is the usual 'management prerogative' type of clause [speaking of the clause giving the employer the right to schedule working hours]. Experience shows that this clause is inserted in the contract at the instance of management to make clear that it has freedom to do certain things without having to consult with the union. So, in this case, the Company retained the exclusive right to schedule working hours, without consultation with the union. In the opinion of the arbiter the clause cannot fairly be read to mean in addition that the Company, once it has set the working hours, must pay for hours not worked unless failure to work was for reasons beyond the Company's control."[356]

---

[354]See Arbitrator Gershenfeld in 74 LA 191, 194; Koven in 51 LA 1151, 1153 (provision requiring notice of layoff applies to normal layoff situations, not to abnormal situation of suspension of operations due to strike); Moran in 51 LA 1069, 1071 (riot justified shutdown though riot was not one of the express contractual exceptions to notice of layoff requirement); Cantor in 51 LA 720, 721 (contract stated no exception to reporting pay but one was implied for civil disorders); Madden in 51 LA 692, 695–696 ("act of God" was only express exception to reporting pay provision but civil disorders justified shutdown); Prasow in 25 LA 794, 797–799; Cornsweet in 16 LA 277, 279. But see Albrechta in 69 LA 80, 83; Emerson in 32 LA 112, 114 (provision for notice of schedule change stated no exception for strike and none would be implied). In Airborne Freight Corp., 74 LA 1037, 1040 (1980), the agreement expressly guaranteed 40 hours of work "for the scheduled work week," and Arbitrator Darrow refused to imply any exception based upon acts of God or conditions beyond the control of management. Cf., Arbitrator Lubow in 69 LA 847, 851.

[355]For a similar conclusion, see Bethlehem Steel Co., 33 LA 285, 291 (Stark, 1959).

[356]Libby, McNeill & Libby, 11 LA 872, 874 (1948).

Under an agreement containing a minimum pay guarantee of four hours for employees who report to work and are not put to work and also for employees who, after having been put to work, are laid off before completing four hours of work, but providing that the guarantee should not apply in case of strike, breakdown of equipment, or act of God, Arbitrator Joseph Brandschain ruled that the employer's decision to send employees home when the machine to which they were assigned broke down, rather than to provide them with other work, represented the exercise of a management prerogative which the union was not entitled to challenge in the absence of a contractual requirement that the employer provide alternative work. As to the wisdom of the employer's decision, he said:

> "However, in most instances, it might be much wiser from both the point of view of economy of operation and employee morale if a determined effort were made to find other work in these situations, particularly if it is true that preceding foremen used to concern themselves more with this problem. As the union points out, the men suffer the inconvenience and expense of coming to work, packing lunch, and paying for transportation so that management should make every effort to find work for the men to do wherever possible. Still, this is entirely a matter of management policy and not something that management would have to do because of any contract obligation."[357]

Many times unscheduled changes in work have been made as a direct or indirect result of weather conditions. For instance, under an agreement giving management exclusive authority to schedule production and determine shifts,[358] and under an agreement giving it the right to direct and assign the working force,[359] management was not required to pay employees for scheduled hours not worked when, because of severe weather, employees were dismissed early to permit them to reach their homes safely—despite the fact that sufficient work was available. In other cases, too, weather conditions have been found to present an emergency, an act of God, or a condition beyond the control of management so as to justify unscheduled changes in work or (where it was the issue) to relieve management of any reporting pay or other such obligation.[360] But a different fact situation may result in a different conclusion.[361]

---

[357]Bethlehem Steel Co., 4 LA 450, 454–455 (1946). For a similar ruling, see Terre Haute Water Works Corp., 5 LA 747, 749 (Updegraff, 1946).

[358]Sealed Power Corp., 7 LA 485, 489 (Platt, 1947).

[359]Pan Am. Airways, 13 LA 326, 327–328 (Reynolds, 1949).

[360]For example, see Arbitrator Gershenfeld in 74 LA 191, 194; Yarowsky in 74 LA 55, 57 (the agreement contained an express guarantee of 40 hours, but "when the plant cannot be operated for a limited time because of conditions beyond the control of the employer, performance of the contract according to its strict terms is excused"); Shister in 71 LA 283, 285 (insufficient gas for production due to extremely cold weather); Grabb in 70 LA 656, 660 (the weather "kept 30% of the employees at home" and the union "did not seriously nor effectively question that the assembly line could not function with 30% of the employees absent"); McLeod in 63 LA 213, 215; Stouffer in 46 LA 1123, 1125–1129 (in snowstorm it sufficed that impossibility of orderly and efficient operations could be reasonably anticipated); Cabe in 38 LA 655, 657 (plant too cold because gas company could not supply enough fuel); Platt in 36 LA 991, 993; Stark in 33 LA 285, 291; Stein in 10 LA 579, 581.

[361]For example, see Arbitrator Gibson in 70 LA 530, 533–534; Jaffee in 52 LA 1023, 1025 (fuel shortage was fault of employer); Krimsly in 51 LA 246, 249 (no imminent danger to employees or equipment); Brandschain in 37 LA 1001, 1003.

One arbitrator held that "The decision as to the suitability of weather conditions for certain types of work must be made by Management; this decision should be made on the basis of its best judgment in the light of the immediate circumstances and must be respected provided there is no abuse by Management of its authority."[362] Nonetheless, weather conditions were held not to constitute an emergency so as to relieve management of a reporting pay obligation where the employer's fears of much absenteeism (and thus of inefficient operations) due to a snowstorm proved to be unfounded, the arbitrator determining that the storm was not severe enough to create an emergency.[363]

A power failure was held not to be beyond the control of management where the company had known of the potential danger and did not take steps to correct it.[364] Machine or equipment breakdowns have similarly been held not to be beyond the control of management in some cases,[365] but have been held otherwise under the circumstances of other cases.[366]

Under an agreement providing for notice when employees are laid off due to a reduction in force except in emergencies, it was held that a strike by some of the employees was an emergency.[367] It has also been held that an emergency existed when a deliberate slowdown by the employees resulted in an accumulation of stock in one department making continued production impossible.[368] Under a contract not

[362]Bethlehem Steel Co., 27 LA 482, 485 (Feinberg, 1956), quoting Umpire Stowe in a previous case between the parties.

[363]Westinghouse Elec. Corp., 51 LA 298, 300–301 (Altrock, 1968). Also see Arbitrator Dobranski in 71 LA 1106, 1108. For cases in which excessive absenteeism (making operations impracticable) was held not to be a condition beyond management's control under the facts, see Arbitrator Alexander in 51 LA 1089, 1092; Leach in 43 LA 888, 890–891. But in Dresser Indus., 71 LA 1007, 1009 (Kreimer, 1978), there was an "unanticipated shortage of available manpower" when employees "necessary to effectuate production" failed to report for work, and this constituted a condition beyond the control of management.

[364]Chrysler Corp., 21 LA 573, 579 (D. Wolff, 1953). Similarly, see Arbitrator Porter in 54 LA 1218, 1219. In other cases, however, power failures have been found to be beyond management's control. See Arbitrator Geissinger in 55 LA 522, 525; Strasshofer in 51 LA 850, 852 (trouble could not be anticipated); Altieri in 41 LA 47, 51. In General Elec. Co., 70 LA 330, 331 (1978), a shortage of natural gas making production impossible was held to constitute a "power failure" within the meaning of the agreement notwithstanding the union's contention that the parties had never considered gas to be power, Arbitrator David C. Altrock stating that: "The fact that the Union, at least, was not thinking about gas when the contract was negotiated is of interest, but many things happen to us that cannot be foreseen; otherwise, life would be a total bore." Also see Arbitrator Wagner in 68 LA 986, 988. Regarding management's obligation where it detained employees longer than was reasonably necessary to investigate a power outage, see La Favorite Rubber Mfg. Co., 74 LA 513, 514 (Brent, 1980).

[365]See Arbitrator Sullivan in 51 LA 1183, 1194 (trouble was foreseeable); Luckerath in 51 LA 873, 875 (failure to make reasonable inspection). Also see Arbitrator Powers in 52 LA 1270, 1272.

[366]See Arbitrator Klein in 44 LA 748, 751–752; Koven in 37 LA 811, 818; Anderson in 36 LA 654, 657.

[367]American Airlines, 27 LA 448, 450 (S. Wolff, 1956); Owens-Corning Fiberglas Corp., 23 LA 603, 605–606 (Uible, 1954). Strikes were held to create emergencies or conditions beyond management's control by Arbitrator Hebert in 51 LA 312, 319–320 (strike threat); Gorsuch in 49 LA 194, 195–196 (unforeseen strike at supplier plant); Seitz in 33 LA 502, 506. A plant shutdown when some of the company's employees struck did not violate the no-lockout provision in the agreement of other employees. Bell Aerosystems Co., 54 LA 745, 749 (Seitz, 1970). Cf., Arbitrator Wyckoff in 51 LA 603, 605–606. A consumer boycott of meat confronted the employer with a severe drop in sales and qualified as an "emergency" permitting a work schedule change in Thriftimart, 61 LA 992, 994 (Irwin, 1973).

[368]Lone Star Steel Co., 28 LA 465, 466 (McCoy, 1957). Where a slowdown by some employees made operations impossible a no-lockout clause was not violated when innocent employees were

providing for emergencies but stating that employees shall be given one week's advance notice in case of "arbitrary layoff," the employer was not required to give advance notice of layoff when a shipment of materials failed to arrive on time, the arbitrator stating that the situation was an emergency.[369]

Bomb threats and actual or threatened riots or civil disturbances have been deemed conditions beyond the control of management, thus employers have not been required to pay reporting pay or otherwise to compensate employees for time lost when management cancelled scheduled work in view of the circumstances.[370] However, if under the facts the employees reasonably can be viewed as having been held on standby under the employer's control while a bomb search was conducted, they likely will be held entitled to pay for the time involved.[371] In the so-called National Day of Mourning cases involving claims for reporting pay or other restitution for time lost when management cancelled work on the proclaimed day of mourning following political assassinations, the claims have been sustained in some cases but denied in others—some of the denial awards stressed that the agreement's reference to a five-day or 40-hour workweek did not constitute either an express or an implied guarantee of work whereas some of the sustaining awards stressed that the decision to close was not a matter or condition beyond the control of management.[372]

It is to be noted that even where a change in the work schedule is fully justified, the question still may be presented as to whether the agreement or the circumstances impose a duty upon the employer to notify the employees of the change, or at least to make a reasonable

sent home. United States Steel Corp., 42 LA 97, 100–101 (Garrett, 1963). For cases involving the shutdown of operations (with consequent reporting pay claims) when some employees began drinking prematurely before a holiday, see Arbitrator King in 66 LA 1122, 1124; Emery in 60 LA 544, 546.

[369]Lavoris Co., 16 LA 173, 175 (Lockhart, 1951). For other cases in which cancellation of operations was justified because of unexpected shortage or materials, parts or merchandise, see Arbitrator Sabo in 77 LA 611, 617; Seifer in 70 LA 417, 419; Krinsky in 61 LA 274, 278; Kabaker in 41 LA 970, 972–974. Cf., Millious in 74 LA 844, 846. An interest arbitrator recommended that the new agreement provide that no notice be required in emergencies. National Airlines, 16 LA 532, 534 (Payne, 1951).

[370]See Arbitrator Erbs in 62 LA 463, 465; Strongin in 58 LA 355, 356; Sartain in 55 LA 1119, 1120; Updegraff in 54 LA 696, 697; Duff in 54 LA 408, 411; Feller in 52 LA 736, 740; Moran in 51 LA 1069, 1071; Cantor in 51 LA 720, 721; Madden in 51 LA 692, 695–696. Also see Plumbers Local 198 v. Nichols Constr. Corp., 502 F.Supp. 465 (USDC, 1980). In Pennsylvania St. Univ., 67 LA 33, 35 (Stonehouse, 1976), the campus was closed for one day in order to avoid potential hazards arising from a rock concert being held in the vicinity, and it was held that the rock concert constituted an "unforeseen circumstance" within the meaning of that term in the agreement as an exception to the required two-week notice of layoff.

[371]See Arbitrator Warns in 72 LA 1232, 1234; Ross in 70 LA 676, 679; Nitka in 69 LA 511, 513.

[372]Claims were sustained by Arbitrator McCoy in 43 LA 1035, 1038–1039; Suagee in 42 LA 1181, 1183–1184; Kabaker in 42 LA 705, 708; Kornblum in 42 LA 692, 694. Claims were denied by Arbitrator Wolff in 50 LA 921, 926; Altieri in 43 LA 602, 603–604 (employer was justified in closing restaurant business since there would be few customers); Bauder in 42 LA 1272, 1274–1275; Davey in 42 LA 1071, 1072; Prasow in 42 LA 1067, 1070–1071 (arbitrator did recommend that employees receive part pay); Kesselman in 42 LA 884, 890 (employees were not guaranteed a 40-hour workweek, but he did award reporting pay to those employees who did not get word of shutdown and reported for work). In one case it was the union that instituted the day of mourning and it was held to violate the no-strike clause. American Radiator & Standard Sanitary Corp., 43 LA 644, 648 (Koven, 1964).

effort to give notice; and if such duty does exist, the question may remain as to whether the effort to give notice was a reasonable one in reference to those employees who did not actually receive word of the change and who accordingly reported for work.[373] In one case after recognizing that a severe snowstorm can be regarded as an act of God and that "management has the right to decide when to operate or not operate the plant, in the light of weather conditions and the general capability of employees to get to work," Arbitrator Leroy S. Merrifield stated:

> "However, when management makes the decision not to operate the plant on a certain shift, its contractual exemption from reporting pay must be construed in a reasonable way—subject to a rule of reason. If management holds off its decision whether to operate a shift or not until a time that is so close to the actual shift starting time that all employees cannot be expected to get the word before they leave home, it is only fair that those relatively few employees in the circumstances of this case who reported for work in good faith believing that they were required to do so, should receive the reporting pay called for in the collective agreement."[374]

Many cases have considered the adequacy of radio announcements as a method of giving notice. Management's effort to notify employees of schedule changes by radio announcements was deemed adequate under the circumstances of some cases,[375] but not adequate in other cases.[376]

Emergencies, Acts of God, and Conditions Beyond the Control of Management

Management's freedom to act may possibly be expanded and managerial obligations may possibly be narrowed if an emergency, an

---

[373]For some cases dealing with these aspects, see Arbitrator Dean in 71 LA 551, 554; MacLafferty in 70 LA 982, 984; Grabb in 70 LA 656, 660 (under the facts, notice on the day in question was not possible and notice on the prior evening would have been "imprudent" since there are "simply too many winter storm watches which do not develop into crippling storms such as the one in question"); Gibson in 70 LA 530, 533–534; Stieber in 67 LA 1029, 1031; Heilbrun in 55 LA 685, 689; Young in 55 LA 396, 402; Duff in 54 LA 408, 410; Larkin in 52 LA 705, 707; Roberts in 51 LA 276, 278; Klein in 44 LA 748, 752; Davis in 43 LA 300, 302; Altieri in 41 LA 47, 51.

[374]Environmental Elements Corp., 72 LA 1059, 1061 (1979), where he added that each case of this type "must be judged on the basis of the particular circumstances." This also appears true of cases in which employees arrive at the plant and find it closed at their regular starting time, they leave promptly assuming that operations have been cancelled, the plant is opened shortly thereafter, and the employees then request reporting pay. See Fruehauf Corp., 73 LA 627 (Thompson, 1979); Wisconsin Wood Prods. Co., 1 LA 435 (Updegraff, 1946).

[375]See Arbitrator Volz in 49 LA 929, 931–932 (employees knew that this method would be used); Yagoda in 49 LA 856, 861–863; Warns in 38 LA 1064, 1067–1068 (there were many employees to be notified and this method had been used previously). In Kiowa Corp., 72 LA 96, 101 (McKenna, 1979), the company was upheld in using the radio to call employees back to work following the end of a strike.

[376]See Arbitrator Dobranski in 71 LA 1106, 1108; Dean in 71 LA 551, 554; Luckerath in 51 LA 873, 874–875 (normal method was telephone or visit to employee's home); Altrock in 51 LA 298, 302 (radio announcement two hours before shift start); Wildebush in 43 LA 919, 932 (radio would not suffice where other methods were specified by the contract); Hoban in 40 LA 1157, 1160–1161.

act of God, or a condition beyond the control of management is involved. The collective agreement may expressly state an exception for emergencies, acts of God, or conditions beyond the control of management, or an arbitrator may hold such exception to be inherently and necessarily implied.

Unquestionably, each case must be decided largely on the basis of its own facts and circumstances insofar as determining whether an emergency, an act of God, or a condition beyond the control of management is actually involved. Emphasizing this concerning emergencies, one arbitrator refused to generalize as to what constitutes an emergency, considering it not to be within the arbitrator's province to provide a workable definition of the term "emergency" for future use.[377] Nonetheless, some arbitrators have offered definitions or guides which may be found useful in other cases and which are noted in the present topic with this possibility in mind.

One arbitrator defined the term "emergency" as "an unforeseen combination of circumstances which calls for immediate action," and he added that it is not an emergency where the situation permits the exercise of discretion.[378] In determining whether a breakdown of equipment constituted an emergency and, if so, whether it was such an emergency as would justify a departure from contractual procedures for distribution of overtime, Arbitrator Louis C. Kesselman expressed the following views:

> "Does Management have the power to meet emergencies in an exceptional manner?
> "Common sense and the entire pattern of American industrial experience make it necessary to acknowledge that emergencies do develop as a result of factors beyond the control of even the best of Managements and that a Company should not be penalized for taking steps to cope with such unforeseen developments even if it necessitates failure to observe all provisions of the contract. However, there are limits and standards which must be observed:
> 1) Management must not be directly responsible for the emergency
> 2) The emergency must involve a situation which threatens to impair operations materially
> 3) The emergency must be of limited time duration
> 4) Any violation or suspension of contractual agreements must be unavoidable and limited only to the duration of the emergency
> * * *
> "The breakdown of one of the production lines in the acid plant on June 12 did pose what could broadly be called an emergency because it

---

[377]Coleman Co., 49 LA 431, 432 (Lazar, 1967).

[378]Canadian Porcelain Co., 41 LA 417, 418 (Hanrahan, 1963). For other statements or guides as to what is an emergency, see Arbitrator Westbrook in 80 LA 297, 301; Dean in 73 LA 810, 813; Seifer in 70 LA 417, 419 (stating that "emergency" is acceptably defined as "a sudden, generally unexpected occurrence or set of circumstances demanding immediate action"); Siegel in 68 LA 418, 420; Suagee in 42 LA 1181, 1183; Killion in 40 LA 513, 521; Koven in 37 LA 811, 817–818. Where an *employee* relies upon an alleged emergency, the number of employees affected sometimes may be a relevant consideration. For example, see Social Sec. Admin., 74 LA 1117, 1120–1121 (Garman, 1980), construing Federal Personnel Manual provisions; Social Sec. Admin., 72 LA 951, 954–956 (Hildebrand, 1979), where the agreement required consideration of the individual employee's situation.

created a situation which called for quick action. However, the Arbitrator feels that a distinction must be made between: 1) those emergencies which can and should be met within the provisions of the Agreement because the dangers to production etc. are minimal, and 2) those which are so exceptional and so dangerous to the operations of a plant that measures going beyond the Agreement must be taken to cope with the problems."[379]

An "act of God" was defined by Arbitrator Harry H. Platt as "an act, event or occurrence which is due exclusively to an extraordinary natural force free of human interference and which could not have been prevented by the exercise of reasonable care and foresight."[380]

A "condition beyond the control of management" was briefly defined as "a condition which could not be reasonably expected and prepared for by the Company."[381] A more detailed definition was given by Arbitrator David A. Wolff:

"Considered in context 'cause beyond the control of the management' cannot mean all causes over which, regardless of reason, the Company exercises no control. Rather, and at most, it must mean either a cause not falling within the general area of the Company's responsibilities or, if falling within this area, a cause which could not be anticipated or, if anticipated, could not have been guarded against at all or except by unreasonably burdensome or unrealistic measures. However, if a cause does fall within this area and could have been anticipated and reasonably guarded against, failure to provide such necessary safeguards, either unintentionally or as a calculated risk, would not place the cause beyond the control of the management."[382]

Overtime

Although numerous overtime issues have reached arbitration, those which appear to have been arbitrated most frequently concern (1) management's right to require employees to work overtime, (2) management's contractual obligation to equalize overtime opportunities among the employees, and (3) the determination of a proper remedy where management has violated an employee's contractual right to overtime. The present topic discusses these three basic issues.

---

[379]Virginia-Carolina Chem. Co., 42 LA 237, 240 (1964). In NCR-Worldwide Serv. Parts Center, 74 LA 224, 234–235 (1980), Arbitrator Ferrin Y. Mathews concluded that "while an emergency may have existed overall," its impact did not reach the "particular situation" involved in the grievance and thus the emergency could not justify the course of action being challenged by the grievance.

[380]United States Steel Co., 36 LA 991, 993 (1961). The Platt definition was applied in Bethlehem Steel Corp., 71 LA 817, 819 (Sharnoff, 1978), where the union unsuccessfully contended that the 1977 "Johnstown flood" could have been prevented by the exercise of reasonable care and foresight by the Johnstown community and thus should not be classified as an act of God. In National Homes Corp., 71 LA 1106, 1108 (1978), Arbitrator Bernard Dobranski offered a definition of the term "natural calamity" used in the agreement involved there.

[381]Gould Natl. Batteries, 42 LA 609, 611 (Linn, 1964). Also see Arbitrator Andrews in 71 LA 519, 524. For distinctions between the terms "act of God" and "condition beyond the control of management," see Arbitrator Thomas J. McDermott in Miller Printing Mach. Co., 64 LA 141, 145 (1975). Also see Arbitrator Robins in 72 LA 845, 847.

[382]Chrysler Corp., 21 LA 573, 579 (1953).

Right to Require Overtime

Although the right of management to require employees to work overtime has been stated variously, the essence of most decisions is that where the agreement is silent on the subject management has the right to make reasonable demands for overtime work from employees.[383] The thinking of many arbitrators in this regard appears to be that management may require overtime work in the absence of contract prohibition provided that it is of "reasonable duration, commensurate with employee health, safety and endurance, and the direction is issued under reasonable circumstances."[384] Another qualification is that management must be willing to accept reasonable excuses advanced by the employee.[385] Several arbitrators have suggested that reasonable notice must be given,[386] but the adequacy of notice may be viewed merely as one of the relevant considerations in determining the adequacy of any excuse offered for not working overtime.

Even apart from the frequent recognition of the right to require overtime work as an inherent or residual right of management, arbitrators have often found implied contractual support for or confirmation of the right in provisions recognizing management's right to direct the working forces, in scheduling provisions, in provisions for

---

[383]See Arbitrator Chandler in 78 LA 537, 540; Erbs in 77 LA 626, 632; Robins in 73 LA 1048, 1049; Gibson in 55 LA 1185, 1186–1187; Witney in 54 LA 773, 779; Volz in 53 LA 703, 705–706; Geissinger in 50 LA 1181, 1184–1185; Bothwell in 49 LA 1172, 1175–1176; Epstein in 49 LA 429, 431; Howlett in 67–1 ARB ¶8115; Dammers in 48 LA 1327, 1329–1330; Kabaker in 48 LA 925, 928; Cayton in 48 LA 570, 571–572; Dworkin in 46 LA 15, 20–21; Anrod in 45 LA 738, 740–741; Helfeld in 41 LA 834, 837–842; Barrett in 39 LA 299, 302; Brecht in 39 LA 292, 298; Bradley in 35 LA 306, 310; Hoel in 32 LA 88, 92; Kharas in 25 LA 755, 757; Fleming in 24 LA 526, 528; Douglas in 21 LA 513, 515; Reeves in 20 LA 564, 566; Gilden in 14 LA 146, 149; Seward in 12 LA 810, 811; Kelliher in 12 LA 779, 783; Wolff in 10 LA 98, 100; Platt in 9 LA 735, 740. Also see County of Cambria, Pa., 70 LA 626, 628 (1978), where in upholding mandatory overtime Arbitrator Clair V. Duff suggested that public-sector employees have a particularly strong obligation to work overtime in emergency situations of the type involved there, but where he expressed no view as to "whether an employee may refuse overtime under non-emergency situations."

[384]Texas Co., 14 LA 146, 149 (Gilden, 1949). Similarly, see Arbitrator Gibson in 55 LA 1185, 1186–1187; Bothwell in 49 LA 1172, 1175; Kabaker in 48 LA 925, 928; Dworkin in 46 LA 15, 20; Anrod in 45 LA 738, 740.

[385]American Body & Equip. Co., 49 LA 1172, 1175–1176 (Bothwell, 1967). Similarly, see Arbitrator Richman in 69 LA 751, 756; Harter in 69 LA 414, 418; Gibson in 55 LA 1185, 1187; Volz in 53 LA 703, 705–706; Howlett in 67–1 ARB ¶8115; Geissinger in 50 LA 181, 184–185; Anrod in 45 LA 738, 741; Barrett in 39 LA 299, 302; Brecht in 39 LA 292, 298; Bradley in 35 LA 306, 312–313; Kharas in 25 LA 755, 758; Fleming in 24 LA 526, 528; Douglas in 21 LA 513, 515. Even with a reasonable excuse, an employee who is unable to work any overtime for a prolonged period (as distinguished from refusing a particular overtime assignment), may risk involuntary leave of absence. See discussion of cases in Iowa Gen. Tire, 75 LA 324, 327–330 (Roumell, 1980). Also see Arbitrator Weiss in 80 LA 945, 949. In Fruehauf Corp., 46 LA 15, 21 (Dworkin, 1966), flimsy excuses of personal inconvenience did not suffice to justify the refusal to work overtime. In Westinghouse Elec. Corp., 47 LA 621, 628 (1966), Arbitrator Altrock stated that "in an atmosphere of concerted action, individual excuses should be subjected to particular scrutiny." Accord, Arbitrator Edes in 51 LA 472, 476; Keefe in 48 LA 1077, 1081. For the NLRB's view that a concerted refusal to work overtime is a strike, see IUE Local 942, 87 LRRM 1272 (NLRB, 1974); Meat Cutters Local P-575, 76 LRRM 1273 (NLRB, 1971). Often under the facts such refusal to work overtime will be unprotected conduct under the NLRA as a partial strike or as a breach of a no-strike clause. See NLRB v. GAIU Local 13-B, 110 LRRM 2984, 2987 (CA 2, 1982); Excavation-Construction Co. v. NLRB, 108 LRRM 2561, 2564–2565 (CA 4, 1981); Poppin Fresh Pies, Inc., 107 LRRM 1201 (NLRB, 1981). Also see discussion of NLRA doctrine by Arbitrator Kossoff in 76 LA 300, 305–306; Roumell in 75 LA 83, 94–95.

[386]See Arbitrator Volz in 53 LA 703, 705; Howlett in 67–1 ARB ¶8115; Anrod in 45 LA 738, 741; Helfeld in 41 LA 834, 842; Brecht in 39 LA 292, 298.

the distribution of overtime, and the like.[387] In contrast, arbitrators have been reluctant to find any implied contractual prohibition of the right. It has been held, for instance, that the fact that an agreement specifies a "normal" workday as one of a certain number of hours or a "normal" workweek as one of a certain number of days does not prohibit management from requiring employees to work overtime since the word "normal" implies occasional resort to "abnormal."[388] This is said to be especially so where the agreement provides for time and one half for hours over a certain number a week, since the latter provision "clearly recognizes an obligation on the company to pay for overtime, and surely by implication, that workers are obliged to work reasonably necessary overtime unless specifically excused."[389] Also, there was no implied prohibition of management's right to require overtime in a contract provision stating that "employees refusing overtime will be charged with such overtime for purposes of equalization," the provision being deemed merely to provide a guide for management in administering overtime and not to give employees the right to refuse overtime.[390]

Furthermore, the fact that the employer has been lenient in exercising the right to require overtime work or the fact that overtime has been voluntary in the past has not affected management's right to require overtime where the volunteer approach fails to supply sufficient workers for needed overtime work.[391]

An agreement may specifically or by implication provide that the employee has an option as to overtime work and that he may ask to be excused from it.[392] Under such a provision it has been held that the employee must ask to be excused if he does not intend to work overtime.[393] Where employees did properly exercise their option not to

---

[387]See Arbitrator Cohen in 55 LA 31, 32; Turkus in 52 LA 493, 496; Keefe in 48 LA 1077, 1081; Cayton in 48 LA 570, 572; Dworkin in 46 LA 15, 21; Anrod in 45 LA 738, 740; Roberts in 41 LA 868, 869; Oppenheim in 40 LA 407, 409–410; Strong in 39 LA 1080, 1082; Bradley in 35 LA 306, 311. Also see Newspaper Guild v. BNA, 97 LRRM 3068 (USDC, 1978).

[388]Carnegie-Illinois Steel Corp., 12 LA 810, 811 (Seward, 1949). Accord, Arbitrator Volz in 51 LA 261, 263; Cayton in 48 LA 570, 572; Dworkin in 46 LA 15, 20–21; Cahn in 29 LA 708, 709–710. Cf., Daly in 69 LA 1133, 1138. However, management could not require overtime where an agreement definitely established the length of the workweek by providing that the "eight (8) hour day and forty (40) hour week * * * shall be in effect without revision, during the term of this contract." Connecticut River Mills, 6 LA 1017, 1019 (Wallen, 1947). To similar effect, Baker & Taylor Co., 1 ALAA ¶67,318 (1944). In Midcon Fabricators, 68 LA 1264, 1272 (Dugan, 1977), it was held unreasonable to require an employee to work one hour overtime on a regular daily basis, especially since "such a regular 9 hour work day schedule is in derogation of" a contract provision "calling for" an 8-hour day. Also see Arbitrator Christopher in 79 LA 399, 402–403.

[389]Nebraska Consol. Mills Co., 13 LA 211, 214 (Copelof, 1949). Accord, Arbitrator Erbs in 77 LA 626, 631; Anrod in 45 LA 738, 740–741; Bradley in 35 LA 306, 311; Klamon in 21 LA 91, 94. Contra, Maggs in 17 LA 606, 608–609; Lehoczky in 1 LA 468, 470.

[390]Roberts Brass Mfg. Co., 53 LA 703, 705 (Volz, 1969). Similarly, see Arbitrator Geissinger in 50 LA 181, 183–184; Anrod in 45 LA 738, 741.

[391]See Arbitrator Erbs in 77 LA 626, 632; Bell in 65 LA 313, 316; Volz in 53 LA 703, 706; Turkus in 52 LA 493, 496; Carpenter in 51 LA 287, 288; Bothwell in 49 LA 1172, 1176; Keefe in 48 LA 1077, 1081; Kabaker in 48 LA 925, 928; Cayton in 48 LA 570, 571–572; Dworkin in 46 LA 15, 21; Anrod in 45 LA 738,742; Strong in 39 LA 1080, 1082. But past practice was held controlling by Arbitrator Rock in 29 LA 482, 484–485; McCoy in 9 LA 374, 374–375.

[392]Lear, Inc., 28 LA 242, 245–246 (Bradley, 1957); West Penn Power Co., 27 LA 458, 462 (Begley, 1956).

[393]Lear, Inc., 28 LA 242, 245–246 (Bradley, 1957).

work overtime, management could not force them to do so by calling the work a work assignment which must be protested under the grievance procedure.[394]

Sometimes the agreement will contain a provision specifically giving management the right to require overtime work of employees.[395] Even so, the right of the employer to punish for refusal to work overtime may be held to depend upon the facts of the case. There may be extenuating circumstances. Thus, Umpire Harry Shulman stated that, while "an employee's refusal to work overtime may be a breach of duty for which he may properly be disciplined, his refusal may be justified and, if justified, is not ground for disciplinary penalty."[396]

Equalization of Overtime

By no means are employees always compelled to work overtime. To the contrary, many employees "prize the opportunity" to work overtime:

> "Many employees prize the opportunity to add to their income by working overtime. Indeed the possibility of earning such extra income has come to be regarded as a vital ingredient of the whole employment package and is often featured as such in company recruitment advertisements. Hence the demand for equitable distribution of overtime work assignments."[397]

However, it has been recognized that where the agreement does not contain any provision guaranteeing overtime to employees, management has the right to determine whether work shall be performed on an overtime basis.[398] It also has been recognized that except as restricted by the agreement, the allocation of overtime (where overtime is to be worked) is an exclusive right of management.[399]

Many agreements do deal with the allocation of overtime. Some leave management little or no discretion in the matter. For example, where the agreement provided that "overtime shall be distributed

---

[394]West Penn Power Co., 27 LA 458, 463 (Begley, 1956).

[395]See Arbitrator Roumell in 75 LA 324, 326; Copelof in 13 LA 269, 272; Shulman in 11 LA 1158, 1160; Updegraff in 11 LA 561, 565; Klamon in 2 LA 201, 202.

[396]Ford Motor Co., 11 LA 1158, 1160 (1948). Also see Arbitrator Ekstrom in 74 LA 967, 969. In the "Ford Motor" case, it was found that the employee's refusal was justified since the order for overtime work was made shortly before quitting time, and the reason for the refusal was that the employee would miss his usual ride and the use of public transportation would require additional time far out of proportion to the overtime he was asked to work. In Cyclops Corp., 78 LA 1067, 1069 (1982), Arbitrator Marlatt stated that "for transportation problems to justify a refusal to work [overtime], there would have to be evidence that the employee would be exposed to some genuine hardship or danger."

[397]American Enka Corp., 52 LA 882, 884 (Pigors, 1969).

[398]Continental Can Co., 53 LA 809, 810 (Cahn, 1969). Similarly, see Arbitrator Daniel in 77 LA 394, 395; Bailey in 70 LA 1251, 1254–1255; Zack in 56 LA 751, 752; McDermott in 53 LA 741, 746; Klamon in 46 LA 459, 471; Lanna in 45 LA 451, 453; Emerson in 61–3 ARB ¶8812. In Liquid Air, 73 LA 1200, 1203–1205 (Weiss, 1979), certain overtime by 20-year practice had been a "substantial segment" of employee paychecks and was held not subject to unilateral discontinuance by the employer. Similarly, see Arbitrator Crane in 79 LA 415, 416; King in 66 LA 1065, 1066. For related discussion, see this Chapter, topic entitled "Scheduling Work"; Chapter 12, topic entitled "Custom and Practice as Part of the Contract."

[399]Graham Bros., 16 LA 83, 85 (Cheney, 1951), citing a War Labor Board case. Also see Arbitrator Cushman in 71 LA 412, 419; Comey in 69 LA 1093, 1096; Morris in 51 LA 1146, 1147–1148; Hilpert in 46 LA 641, 643; Marshall in 20 LA 212, 216.

proportionately among all qualified employees" within a given work group, it was held that day-to-day equalization of overtime was called for.[400] More often the agreement will contain a modified equalization provision calling for equalization of overtime among the employees within the specified equalization unit or group "as far as practicable," or "as equally as possible," or the like. Such provisions have generally been held to allow management reasonable flexibility to permit efficient operations—they have been construed to permit equalization over a reasonable period of time.[401] In the latter regard, it has been stated that under an "as equally as possible" provision "no employee has a pre-emptory right to overtime on any particular day that it is available."[402] Under a similar provision, Arbitrator Vernon L. Stouffer said:

> "The decision as to what is as 'equitable a basis as possible' rests with Management, subject to the Union's right to grieve that it was equitably possible for the Company to have given the assignment to employees other than those selected. In so doing the Union has the burden of proving that the Company deliberately or unreasonably bypassed the employee with the lower amount of overtime."[403]

But Arbitrator Morris L. Myers held that "the burden falls on the employer to justify its action" where an employee who already has more overtime than other employees is afforded the next overtime opportunity.[404]

Regardless of where the ultimate burden of proof is held to fall, it is clear that management must remain alert to the underlying objective of equalization provisions. Thus, Arbitrator John F. Sembower cautioned that, while recognizing the need for flexibility, also to be taken into account is "the rule that the general aim of the agreement is for overtime to be equalized, albeit qualified by the Company's doing so with some latitude, and that this imposes a duty upon the Company to meet an appropriate test of diligence under the particular circumstances of each instance."[405]

---

[400]Mason & Hanger-Silas Mason Co., 36 LA 425, 434–435 (Hale, 1961). Also requiring daily equalization or otherwise leaving little flexibility in the distribution of overtime, see Arbitrator Listerhill in 66–3 ARB ¶8950; Sullivan in 33 LA 335, 338–339; Doyle in 28 LA 100, 101–102.

[401]See Arbitrator Bothwell in 54 LA 613, 617–618; Stouffer in 49 LA 933, 939; Kelliher in 49 LA 886, 888; Ray in 49 LA 360, 362–364; Shister in 48 LA 848, 851; Tsukiyama in 47 LA 781, 784–785; Guild in 46 LA 385, 386; Cugna in 68–1 ARB ¶8266; Hardy in 68–1 ARB ¶8091 (past practice refuted the union's contention for day-to-day equalization); Seinsheimer in 64–1 ARB ¶8303; Cahn in 42 LA 830, 831; McCoy in 40 LA 526, 529; Williams in 39 LA 929, 930. Also see Jason in 73 LA 56, 58–59. But see Arbitrator Sullivan in 33 LA 335, 338–339.

[402]Sundstrand Corp., 66–2 ARB ¶8700 (Kelliher, 1966). Accord, Duquesne Light Co., 48 LA 848, 851 (Shister, 1967). Also see Arbitrator Kelliher in 49 LA 886, 888.

[403]McCall Corp., 49 LA 933, 939 (1967). Accord, Standard Ultramarine & Color Co., 64–1 ARB ¶8303 (Seinsheimer, 1963).

[404]Vendorlator Mfg. Co., 53 LA 494, 497 (1969), where the agreement provided that "every effort will be made to distribute overtime equally." Accord, see Arbitrator Bergeson in 69 LA 759, 761.

[405]Pittsburgh Plate Glass Co., 32 LA 622, 624 (1958). Also see Arbitrator Belshaw in 73 LA 1087, 1089, 1091; Jason in 73 LA 56, 59. For some guidelines that have been offered for the equalization of overtime, see Arbitrator Stouffer in 49 LA 933, 939–941; Cahn in 35 LA 526, 529. As to the scope of management's obligation to notify employees of available overtime, see

Arbitrators have recognized various considerations which may be relevant in judging whether management has administered the overtime equalization provision in a reasonable manner. Among others, these include such factors as ability to do the required work,[406] safety and plant protection,[407] and reasonably assured availability.[408] Arbitrators have disagreed as to whether the cost factor is a relevant consideration.[409]

Remedy for Violation of Right to Overtime

Unquestionably the most frequently utilized remedy where an employee's contractual right to overtime work has been violated is a monetary award (generally at the overtime rate) for the overtime in question.[410] In some cases, however, the arbitrator has considered make-up overtime within a reasonable time to be the appropriate remedy.[411]

In using the make-up overtime remedy one arbitrator stated that in the absence of specific contract language, a monetary award for violation of overtime rights must be based upon a "clearly established past practice or upon a showing that the grievant-claimant actually did suffer damages rather than temporary postponement of an over-

---

Arbitrator Boals in 74 LA 110, 114–115; Fields in 67 LA 778, 779; Sembower in 55 LA 474, 476–477; Markowitz in 55 LA 384, 385; Geissinger in 55 LA 353, 356. On the other hand, as concerns mandatory overtime and the individual's right of privacy, the question has arisen whether the union may contractually obligate employees to answer their home telephone for possible calls from the employer. See Tennessee River Pulp & Paper Co., 60 LA 627, 632–633 (Murphy, 1973), giving an affirmative answer under the facts. Also see Arbitrator Gallagher in 79 LA 1151, 1154.

[406]See Arbitrator Clark in 77 LA 128, 132–133; Koven in 55 LA 1048, 1052; Merrill in 51 LA 1086, 1089. Also see Cushman in 71 LA 412, 419. But management cannot insist that ability, if adequate, be as great as that of the employee who normally performs the work. Paragon Bridge & Steel Co., 48 LA 995, 1000 (Gross, 1967).

[407]Airco Alloys & Carbide Co., 51 LA 156, 160–161 (Kesselman, 1968).

[408]See Arbitrator Marcus in 71 LA 1062, 1064; Waldron in 56 LA 848, 851; France in 54 LA 950, 953. Cf., Roberts in 69 LA 623, 627; Lehoczky in 52 LA 1098, 1100.

[409]Holding it a relevant factor, Arbitrator Guild in 46 LA 385, 386; Bladek in 68–1 ARB ¶8148; Livengood in 22 LA 144, 147. Holding it not relevant, Arbitrator Jedel in 68 LA 1183, 1190; Levin in 54 LA 387, 392; Pigors in 52 LA 882, 885; Merrill in 51 LA 1086, 1088; Gilden in 16 LA 811, 816.

[410]Numerous cases are cited at p. 499 of the Third Edition of this book. For some later cases, see Arbitrator Yancy in 78 LA 1157, 1160; Tamoush in 78 LA 299, 302; Ross in 77 LA 884, 888; Modjeska in 77 LA 853, 854; Herrick in 77 LA 619, 622; Epstein in 77 LA 464, 467; Boals in 74 LA 110, 115; Belshaw in 73 LA 1087, 1091–1092; Cantor in 70 LA 1225, 1229; Siegel in 70 LA 430, 432; Jedel in 68 LA 1183, 1191; Fields in 67 LA 778, 780; King in 66 LA 1065, 1067. One arbitrator emphasized that a monetary award is the only proper remedy if the alternative remedy of make-up overtime would unjustly and adversely affect either the grievant or any other employee. Giant Tiger Super Stores Co., 43 LA 1243, 1246 (Kates, 1965). For a case involving the determination of compensation for an incentive employee's loss of an overtime opportunity, see Joy Mfg. Co., 77 LA 683, 687–689 (Richard, 1981).

[411]See Arbitrator Shanker in 76 LA 10, 13–14 (stating that in the absence of "special circumstances" justifying a monetary award, make-up overtime is the more equitable remedy since, without penalizing the employer, the employee "is made whole, and it should not make that much difference whether the overtime to which he is entitled is worked on an earlier rather than a later date"); Bergeson in 69 LA 759, 762–763; Bothwell in 54 LA 613, 617; Edes in 53 LA 616, 619; Stouffer in 49 LA 933, 939–941; Updegraff in 33 LA 365, 366; Shister in 27 LA 634, 636; Justin in 24 LA 168, 172–173; McCoy in 5 LA 30, 32. In Giant Tiger Super Stores Co., 43 LA 1243, 1246 (Kates, 1965), the award was 50 percent back pay and 50 percent make-up overtime. An apportionment was also made in Bridgeport Brass Co., 19 LA 690, 693 (Donnelly, 1952). In Public Works Dept., 78 LA 1172, 1176 (Chandler, 1982), the sole remedy used was a cease and desist order.

time work opportunity."[412] In contrast, another arbitrator declared that the only proper remedy for violation of overtime rights is a monetary award:

> "Offering an employee an opportunity to make up improperly lost hours at a later date is not an adequate remedy. He is entitled to work those hours at the time they are available, to know when he may expect his turn, and not be expected to work at some time more convenient to the employer, or at the personal whim of a foreman.
>
> * * *
>
> "The one sure way of putting an end to foremen's inadvertent errors, or their favoritism in making overtime assignments under the round-robin system, is to hold the Company liable for these breaches of contract by awarding pay to the employee who failed to get his proper assignment."[413]

The latter arbitrator's view was expressed in a case in which the improper overtime assignment had been made to an employee within the overtime equalization unit. But some arbitrators would make a distinction in this regard, considering make-up overtime to be the preferred remedy where the improper assignment of overtime was made within the equalization unit or other group entitled to the overtime but viewing a monetary award as essential where the improper assignment was made to employees outside such unit or group. It is reasoned that if the overtime was assigned within the entitled unit or group, it is possible to make it up since the employee who received the improperly assigned overtime is charged with it and will receive that much less future overtime within the unit or group; however, if the improper assignment of overtime was made to employees outside the unit or group, it is impossible to make it up since it can never be recovered and the only logical remedy is a monetary award.[414]

Right to Subcontract

The right of management to subcontract, in the absence of specific contract restriction, has been the subject of numerous arbitration

---

[412]A.O. Smith Corp., 33 LA 365, 366 (Updegraff, 1959). Also indicating that past practice may be a factor in selecting the remedy, see Arbitrator Bothwell in 54 LA 613, 617, and Stouffer in 49 LA 933, 940; but refusing to consider past practice as a relevant factor, see Arbitrator Abernethy in 41 LA 1065, 1069–1070, and Edes in 37 LA 888, 891.

[413]John Deere Dubuque Tractor Works, 35 LA 495, 498 (Larkin, 1960). Also see Arbitrator Tamoush in 78 LA 299, 302. Some arbitrators have indicated that they would issue a monetary award if management's action was deliberate but that the make-up overtime remedy might be appropriate (if other considerations permit it) if inadvertent error produced the violation. See Arbitrator Chalfie in 52 LA 33, 36; Stouffer in 49 LA 933, 939; Kates in 43 LA 1243, 1246; Hebert in 34 LA 643, 651–652. Even where the contract specified use of the make-up remedy, a monetary award was used where the violation was deliberate. See Arbitrator Chalfie in 52 LA 33, 36; Hon in 39 LA 216, 220.

[414]For arbitrators approving this distinction, see Arbitrator Bothwell in 54 LA 613, 617–618; Edes in 53 LA 616, 619; Cahn in 52 LA 1144, 1145; Shister in 48 LA 848, 853; Hebert in 42 LA 525, 531–532; Dworkin in 41 LA 219, 223; Brecht in 41 LA 59, 62–63; Kelliher in 26 LA 540, 541. In one case where the erroneous assignment was within the entitled group the arbitrator awarded make-up overtime but specified that it must be upon work which would not otherwise have been performed at overtime rates. Morton Salt Co., 42 LA 525, 531 (Hebert, 1964). Similarly, see Arbitrator Crawford in 38 LA 70, 73–74.

cases.[415] The basic and difficult problem is that of maintaining a proper balance between the employer's legitimate interest in efficient operation and effectuating economies on the one hand and the union's legitimate interest in protecting the job security of its members and the stability of the bargaining unit on the other.[416]

In earlier cases, arbitrators generally held that management has the right, if exercised in good faith, to subcontract work to independent contractors (the work thus to be done by nonemployees of the employer) unless the agreement specifically restricts the right.[417] This view is also stated in some of the later cases.[418] The basic reasoning is indicated by the following statement:

> "It is true, of course, that job security, and an opportunity to perform available work, is of concern to a union and that the letting of work to outsiders by an employer may in some instances be said to be a derogation of the basic purposes of their collective bargaining agreement. Nevertheless, it is also true that where the subject has assumed importance in the relations between the parties a provision is generally inserted in the agreement defining their respective rights. It has almost been universally recognized that in the absence of such a provision an employer may, under his customary right to conduct his business efficiently, let work to outside contractors if such letting is done in good faith and without deliberate intent to injure his employees."[419]

Most of the later cases have somewhat modified the above view. Where the agreement does not deal specifically with subcontracting, most of the more recent cases fall into either of two categories: (1) The essence of some cases appears to be that the recognition, seniority, wage, and other such clauses of the agreement limit management's

---

[415]The arbitrability of subcontracting disputes has also been the subject of arbitration decisions, many of which are collected in Celanese Corp. of Am., 33 LA 925, 936–948 (Dash, 1959). For some later instances, see Arbitrator Dybeck in 77 LA 190, 194; Madden in 72 LA 20, 27. For Supreme Court doctrine as to arbitrability, see United Steelworkers v. Warrior & Gulf Navigation Co., 80 S.Ct. 1347 (1960). For a general discussion of arbitrability, see Chapter 6. Many arbitration cases involve the interpretation and application of contract provisions expressly dealing with subcontracting. Arbitrators have also treated the question of whether clauses denying management the right to assign work of unit employees to employees outside the unit prohibit the subcontracting of such work to persons not in the employ of the company at all. See Arbitrator Gibson in 76 LA 286, 290–291; Fitzsimmons in 70 LA 116, 120; Witney in 51 LA 363, 371; Klamon in 27 LA 57, 73; Aaron in 26 LA 870, 873; Porter in 22 LA 608, 608–609; Cahn in 19 LA 882, 883; McCoy in 12 LA 707, 709. Also see Harrison in 78 LA 35, 38 (contractual prohibition against supervisors performing unit work did not apply where the supervisor actually performed the contested work as an independent contractor). For an extensive discussion of subcontracting disputes, see Sinicropi, "Revisiting an Old Battle Ground: The Subcontracting Dispute," Proceedings of the 32nd Annual Meeting of NAA, 125 (BNA Books, 1980), citing several other articles on the subject.

[416]See Arbitrator Hon in 52 LA 190, 192; Hebert in 43 LA 307, 313; Larson in 27 LA 233, 235; Lennard in 25 LA 118, 120; Aaron in 16 LA 644, 648.

[417]See Arbitrator Feinberg in 13 LA 991, 1001; McCoy in 12 LA 707, 709; Kelliher in 11 LA 197, 199; Healy in 10 LA 842, 843; Hill in 10 LA 396, 405–406; Copelof in 8 LA 990, 992.

[418]See Arbitrator Bladek in 52 LA 670, 672; Stouffer in 49 LA 471, 473; Klamon in 46 LA 459, 468–470; Warns in 30 LA 493, 495–496; Dworkin in 27 LA 704, 709; Marshall in 26 LA 74, 78. In Singer Co., 71 LA 204, 208–211 (1978), Arbitrator Sinclair Kossoff surveyed court decisions on subcontracting as an alleged violation of the agreement (as distinguished from any possible violation of a statutory duty to bargain) where the agreement does not expressly prohibit subcontracting, and he concluded (p. 208) that: "Most courts who have considered the issue have held that where a contract contains no express prohibition of subcontracting there is no violation where an employer replaces employees covered by the contract by giving out the work to an independent contractor."

[419]National Sugar Ref. Co., 13 LA 991, 1001 (Feinberg, 1949).

right to subcontract, and certain standards of reasonableness and good faith are applied in determining whether these clauses have been violated.[420] (2) The essence of other cases is that management can subcontract if it does so reasonably and in good faith.[421]

It appears obvious, however, that the end result ordinarily would be the same regardless of which of these approaches is taken—that is, the right to subcontract depends upon "reasonableness" and "good faith."[422] To illustrate, one arbitrator emphasized that the recognition, seniority, and wage clauses restrict subcontracting:

> "After a thoughtful consideration of this question the Arbitrator concludes that the Recognition Clause when considered together with the Wage Clause, the Seniority Clauses, and other clauses establishing standards for covered jobs and employees limits the Company's right to subcontract during the term of the Contract. The Contract sets forth standards of wages and working conditions applicable to those employees and those jobs covered by the Recognition Clause. When the contract was signed the employees in the mending room were on the covered jobs, and the Contract contemplated that work normally performed by them would continue to be so performed as long as the work was available. To allow the Company, after signing an agreement covering standards of wages and conditions for mending room jobs and employees, to lay off the employees and transfer the work to employees not covered by the agreed standards would subvert the Contract and destroy the meaning of the collective bargaining relation."[423]

But in this same case, the arbitrator stated some "conditions crucial to the decision" that subcontracting violated the recognition, wage, and seniority clauses of the contract, which "conditions" are similar to some of the standards (outlined below) for determining reasonableness and good faith used by other arbitrators, including those who do not rely upon such clauses.

---

[420]For cases holding that such clauses do limit management but listing standards pointing to the test of good faith and reasonableness, see Arbitrator Mittenthal in 79 LA 1273, 1277–1278; Ross in 73 LA 1036, 1039; Lipson in 71 LA 120, 123–124; Dolnick in 54 LA 1251, 1255; Somers in 49 LA 585, 587–588; Williams in 36 LA 714, 716; Larson in 27 LA 233, 235; Lennard in 25 LA 118, 120; Hogan in 21 LA 713, 724–725. For cases not listing standards but recognizing a general test of reasonableness and good faith, see Arbitrator King in 52 LA 588, 592; Kadish in 40 LA 737, 740; Hill in 30 LA 379, 380; Hebert in 27 LA 413, 419; Aaron in 26 LA 870, 873; Reid in 22 LA 124, 128; Garrett in 17 LA 790, 792–794. For instances in which the arbitrator found a strict limitation in such clauses, see Cocalis in 72 LA 619, 620–621; Gundermann in 42 LA 1121, 1122.

[421]For holdings that the recognition, seniority, wage, and other such clauses do not restrict management's right to subcontract and basing the award upon factors pointing to the reasonableness and good faith test, see Arbitrator Ipavec in 78 LA 262, 267; Madden in 72 LA 20, 28–30; Gould in 51 LA 752, 757; Emery in 51 LA 575, 577; Shister in 49 LA 805, 809; Abrahams in 47 LA 325, 327; Murphy in 43 LA 554, 557; Kates in 40 LA 444, 447; Smith in 39 LA 1213, 1218; Larkin in 38 LA 718, 721–722; McDermott in 36 LA 1147, 1151–1152; Teple in 34 LA 215, 220; Wolff in 29 LA 594, 594–595; Wallen in 28 LA 491, 493–494; Kornblum in 28 LA 270, 273; Gray in 26 LA 723, 725; Kelliher in 24 LA 158, 159–160; Kagel in 24 LA 33, 34–37; Coffey in 20 LA 432, 433–434; Maggs in 19 LA 503, 506; Grant in 19 LA 219, 220.

[422]For court approval of arbitral use of a "reasonableness" or "balancing" test in determining the permissibility of subcontracting where the contract is silent or ambiguous on the right to subcontract, see Sears, Roebuck & Co. v. Teamsters Local 243, 110 LRRM 3175 (CA 6, 1982), in which case, however, the court found that an arbitrator had improperly used such a test to overrule subcontracting where the employer had a clear right under an express contract provision.

[423]A.D. Juilliard Co., 21 LA 713, 724 (Hogan, 1953).

In the final analysis, the thinking of many arbitrators is probably reflected in the statement that:

> "In the absence of contractual language relating to contracting out of work, the general arbitration rule is that management has the right to contract out work as long as the action is performed in good faith, it represents a reasonable business decision, it does not result in subversion of the labor agreement, and it does not have the effect of seriously weakening the bargaining unit or important parts of it. This general right to contract out may be expanded or restricted by specific contractual language."[424]

Standards for Evaluating Propriety of Subcontracting

It should be emphasized that the standards used by arbitrators in evaluating subcontracting cases are merely guides and are not necessarily conclusive. True, sometimes one factor has been considered decisive of the case. More frequently, however, several factors have been considered and applied in combination. This often means that a weighing process is involved—where some considerations support the subcontracting but others do not, the arbitrator must weigh the counterworking considerations in deciding whether the subcontracting should be upheld.[425] The standards most frequently used are:

1. *Past practice.* Whether the company has subcontracted work in the past.[426]

2. *Justification.* Whether subcontracting is done for reasons such as economy,[427] maintenance of secondary sources for

---

[424]Shenango Valley Water Co., 53 LA 741, 744–745 (McDermott, 1969). For other arbitrators expressly approving this statement, see Davies in 78 LA 702, 704; Light in 78 LA 144, 147; Nolan in 76 LA 1049, 1052; Chapman in 74 LA 616, 619; Doyle in 73 LA 947, 949; Handsaker in 71 LA 9, 15. Also see similar rule of reason statements by Arbitrator Gross in 75 LA 665, 666–667; Ipavec in 74 LA 659, 662; Ross in 73 LA 1036, 1039; Atleson in 72 LA 800, 803; Hunter in 68 LA 316, 320; Gould in 51 LA 752, 757; Valtin in 48 LA 797, 801; Kesselman in 46 LA 1166, 1169; Dworkin in 44 LA 762, 766; Kadish in 40 LA 737, 740. For arbitrators emphasizing that each subcontracting case must be decided on its own, see Seidenberg in 53 LA 819, 823; Somers in 49 LA 585, 587; Kates in 46 LA 444, 447. It may be noted in passing that if subcontracting is found to have been proper, the union might be found to have violated the no-strike clause by refusing to handle subcontracted material. See Arbitrator McDermott in 53 LA 470, 475; Kagel in 24 LA 33, 37–38.

[425]For example, see Arbitrator Seidenberg in 53 LA 819, 823–824; Seinsheimer in 51 LA 842, 846–848; Shister in 49 LA 805, 806–808; Valtin in 48 LA 797, 801. Where the contract states standards to be considered, the arbitrator may feel limited thereto. See Arbitrator Beatty in 48 LA 1025, 1026–1027; Gibson in 45 LA 331, 332.

[426]Many cases are cited at p. 504 of the Third Edition of this book. For some of the later cases in which past practice was one of the factors considered, see Arbitrator Boals in 78 LA 710, 715; Light in 78 LA 144, 147; Harrison in 78 LA 35, 38; Cyrol in 77 LA 1096, 1101; Sherman in 76 LA 670, 673; Turkus in 73 LA 29, 31; Atleson in 72 LA 800, 803, 804; Seidman in 64 LA 101, 102. Subcontracting was permitted as to perishables, largely on the basis of long past practice, even where the contract expressly prohibited subcontracting without negotiations. Safeway Stores, 51 LA 1093, 1094–1095 (Koven, 1969). For another past practice exception to an express contract limitation, see Arbitrator Keefe in 69 LA 7, 10. For full discussion of custom and practice generally, see Chapter 12, Custom and Past Practice.

[427]For cases in which economy was considered along with other factors in upholding subcontracting, see Arbitrator Van Pelt in 78 LA 57, 59; Vause in 76 LA 1174, 1178; Chapman in 74 LA 616, 620; Handsaker in 71 LA 9, 17 (stating that the employer, as a public body, "has an obligation to operate as efficiently as possible in the interest of the taxpayer"); Stix in 69 LA 1057, 1066, 1071 (in upholding the subcontracting he stated that it related to "an important element of cost bearing on the Company's ability to be competitive on a particular job which was up for bids"); Seidenberg in 53 LA 819, 824; Gould in 51 LA 752, 758; Hebert in 51 LA 660, 664–665;

production and manpower aid,[428] augmenting the regular work force,[429] plant security measures,[430] or other sound business reasons.[431]

3. *Effect on the union or bargaining unit.* Whether subcontracting is being used as a method of discriminating against the union and/or whether it substantially prejudices the status and integrity of the bargaining unit.[432]

4. *Effect on unit employees.* Whether members of the bargaining unit are discriminated against,[433] displaced,[434] deprived of jobs previously available to them,[435] or are laid off[436] by reason of the subcontract. Subcontracting may be justified by other considerations even where layoffs will result.[437] Moreover, arbitrators have considered whether layoffs could be anticipated, saying that subcontracting is to be judged by foresight rather than hindsight.[438] Another factor in judging subcontracting is whether unit employees lose regular or overtime earnings,[439] but loss of overtime often has not been

---

Somers in 49 LA 585, 587–588; Smith in 39 LA 1213, 1219–1220; McDermott in 36 LA 1147, 1152; Wallen in 28 LA 491, 492–493; Kornblum in 28 LA 270, 273; Wolff in 27 LA 174, 178; Aaron in 26 LA 870, 873; Reid in 22 LA 124, 126; Williams in 21 LA 330, 334. For cases in which the economy factor was outweighed by other considerations, see Arbitrator Volz in 51 LA 997, 1001; Seinsheimer in 51 LA 842, 846; Valtin in 48 LA 797, 801; McCoy in 27 LA 671, 674; Aaron in 16 LA 644, 648–650. Some arbitrators have stressed that economy in the form of lower labor costs gives little or no support to management's action. See Nolan in 76 LA 1049, 1053–1054; Gibson in 76 LA 286, 291; Volz in 51 LA 997, 1001; Gould in 51 LA 752, 758; Warns in 41 LA 905, 907; Smith in 39 LA 1213, 1219.

[428]Dalmo Victor Co., 24 LA 33, 37 (Kagel, 1954). Also see Arbitrator Kadish in 40 LA 737, 741.

[429]Phillips Pipe Line Co., 20 LA 432, 433 (Coffey, 1953); Carborundum Co., 20 LA 60, 61 (Cummins, 1952).

[430]See Arbitrator Kossoff in 71 LA 204, 213–214; Ludolf in 63 LA 798, 800; Chattman in 68 LA 976, 981; Kelly in 22 LA 266, 270. Cf., Horovitz in 22 LA 390, 391.

[431]See Arbitrator Doyle in 73 LA 947, 949 (reason was to improve product quality); Madden in 72 LA 20, 28–29; Roumell in 71 LA 822, 827; Hunter in 68 LA 316, 321; Shister in 49 LA 805, 806–807; Kesselman in 46 LA 1166, 1169–1170; Kadish in 40 LA 737, 741; Smith in 39 LA 1213, 1219; Larkin in 38 LA 718, 722; Seward in 30 LA 678, 683; Hill in 10 LA 396, 405.

[432]For many cases see p. 505 of the Third Edition of this book. For some later cases see Arbitrator Madden in 78 LA 1124, 1127; Boals in 78 LA 710, 715–716; Davies in 78 LA 702, 705; Vause in 76 LA 1174, 1178; Gross in 75 LA 665, 667; Chapman in 74 LA 616, 620; Ross in 73 LA 1036, 1039; Kossoff in 71 LA 204, 213; Chattman in 68 LA 976, 982; Sembower in 61 LA 333, 339.

[433]See Arbitrator Slade in 54 LA 1135, 1139; Bladek in 52 LA 670, 672; Hebert in 27 LA 413, 420; Williams in 21 LA 330, 334; Holly in 19 LA 815, 818.

[434]See Arbitrator Garrett in 78 LA 1183, 1189; Chapman in 74 LA 616, 620; Seinsheimer in 51 LA 842, 847; Turkus in 51 LA 600, 601; Wolff in 50 LA 69, 72–73; Somers in 49 LA 585, 588 (there was displacement but it was de minimis); Valtin in 48 LA 797, 801–802; Gray in 26 LA 723, 725–726; Blair in 23 LA 171, 173–174.

[435]See Arbitrator Roumell in 71 LA 822, 826; Fitzsimmons in 70 LA 116, 121; Seward in 30 LA 678, 679, 683; Lennard in 25 LA 118, 121.

[436]See Arbitrator Handsaker in 71 LA 9, 16; Dolnick in 54 LA 1251, 1256; Abrahams in 47 LA 325, 326–327; Kesselman in 46 LA 1166, 1170; Kornblum in 28 LA 270, 273; Haughton in 28 LA 158, 162; Klamon in 27 LA 57, 70–71; Aaron in 26 LA 870, 874; Jones in 24 LA 821, 827; Kelliher in 24 LA 158, 160; Gilden in 22 LA 68, 70.

[437]See Olympia Brewing Co., 72 LA 20, 29–30 (Madden, 1978); Dutch Maid Bakery, 52 LA 588, 592–593 (King, 1969).

[438]Marquette Mfg. Co., 51 LA 230, 234 (Mullin, 1968); Columbus Auto Parts Co., 36 LA 1079, 1081 (Alexander, 1961).

[439]See Arbitrator Seinsheimer in 51 LA 842, 847; Wolff in 50 LA 69, 72; Kesselman in 46 LA 1166, 1170; Reid in 22 LA 124, 126–127.

a weighty factor where the agreement did not contain any overtime guarantee.[440]

5. *Type of work involved.* Whether it is work which is normally done by unit employees,[441] or work which is frequently the subject of subcontracting in the particular industry,[442] or work which is of a "marginal" or "incidental" nature.[443]

6. *Availability of properly qualified employees.* Whether the skills possessed by available members of the bargaining unit are sufficient to perform the work.[444]

7. *Availability of equipment and facilities.* Whether necessary equipment and facilities are presently available or can be economically purchased.[445]

8. *Regularity of subcontracting.* Whether the particular work is frequently or only intermittently subcontracted.[446] In one case the arbitrator pointed out that the subcontracting had not been so regular in amount or type of work that additional places could have been made available to permanent employees within the bargaining unit.[447]

---

[440]See Arbitrator Atleson in 72 LA 800, 803; Ipavec in 70 LA 891, 895 (under contract permitting subcontracting if employer does not have "available" employees, employer could subcontract where employees could be available only through overtime work); Petrie in 68 LA 7, 12; Cahn in 53 LA 809, 810; McDermott in 53 LA 741, 746; Larkin in 52 LA 1028, 1030; Turkus in 51 LA 600, 601; Klamon in 46 LA 459, 471; Lanna in 45 LA 451, 453; Hebert in 27 LA 413, 419; Coffey in 20 LA 432, 433. But see King in 66 LA 1065, 1066 (by virtue of years of past practice the overtime work in question had become an implied term of the contract); Carmichael in 64 LA 1244, 1247 (awarding employees overtime compensation for improperly subcontracted work "inasmuch as they were fully occupied and would have had to do the disputed work on overtime"); Larson in 21 LA 267, 270.

[441]See Arbitrator Ipavec in 78 LA 262, 266–267; Vause in 76 LA 1174, 1178; Amis in 52 LA 901, 903; Shister in 52 LA 40, 43–44; Seinsheimer in 51 LA 842, 847; Murphy in 43 LA 554, 556; Hebert in 43 LA 307, 313–314; Hogan in 21 LA 713, 725. Even where this factor is in the union's favor, it may be outweighed by other considerations in the company's favor. See Arbitrator Seidenberg in 53 LA 819, 823; Shister in 49 LA 805, 807.

[442]See Arbitrator Seidenberg in 53 LA 819, 824; Wolff in 50 LA 69, 72; Valtin in 48 LA 797, 802; Seward in 30 LA 678, 683; Maggs in 19 LA 503, 506.

[443]See Arbitrator Dolnick in 54 LA 1251, 1256; Seidenberg in 53 LA 819, 824; Wallen in 28 LA 491, 494; Kornblum in 28 LA 270, 273. Also see Handsaker in 71 LA 9, 17.

[444]See Arbitrator Wren in 79 LA 535, 538; Boals in 78 LA 710, 715; Sinicropi in 75 LA 742, 746; LeWinter in 75 LA 485, 492; Talent in 52 LA 93, 96 (same result was possible by using methods within employee skills); Geissinger in 52 LA 37, 39 (volume of orders exceeded capacity of company workforce); Wagner in 51 LA 435, 439; Mullin in 51 LA 230, 233; Murphy in 43 LA 554, 556; Warns in 41 LA 905, 907; Duff in 29 LA 609, 612–613; Shister in 28 LA 461, 463 (all employees were working); Larson in 27 LA 233, 235; Wolff in 27 LA 174, 178 (shortage of trained personnel); Klamon in 27 LA 57, 70; Lennard in 25 LA 118, 121; Hogan in 21 LA 713, 725.

[445]See Arbitrator Beckman in 76 LA 336, 339; Simon in 72 LA 1115, 1124–1126; Roumell in 71 LA 822, 827–828; Shister in 49 LA 805, 807; Murphy in 43 LA 554, 556; Warns in 41 LA 905, 907; Seward in 30 LA 678, 683; Wallen in 28 LA 491, 492; Wolff in 27 LA 174, 178; Haughton in 26 LA 438, 454; Lennard in 25 LA 118, 121; Blair in 23 LA 171, 174; Hogan in 21 LA 713, 725; Holly in 19 LA 815, 818; Grant in 19 LA 219, 220.

[446]See Arbitrator Hebert in 27 LA 413, 419 (first time the job had been necessary); Larson in 27 LA 233, 236; Lennard in 25 LA 118, 121 (subcontracted work was to be done continuously, not intermittently).

[447]Temco Aircraft Corp., 27 LA 233, 236 (Larson, 1956).

9. *Duration of subcontracted work.* Whether the work is sub-contracted for a temporary or limited period,[448] or for a permanent or indefinite period.[449] Even where it is permanent, however, the harm may be outweighed by the justifications for the subcontracting.[450]

10. *Unusual circumstances involved.* Whether the action is necessitated by an emergency, some urgent need, or a time limit for getting the work done.[451] Also, the subcontracting may be justified because a "special job" is involved,[452] or because it is necessitated by a strike or other such situation.[453]

11. *History of negotiations on the right to subcontract.* Whether management's right to subcontract has been the subject of contract negotiations.[454] Arbitrators have pointed to the union's unsuccessful attempt to negotiate a restriction on subcontracting.[455] However, it has been emphasized that while this factor may support a claim to considerable latitude in subcontracting it cannot imply that there is no restriction at all, for parties may try to solidify or expand existing rights through bargaining.[456]

Another possible standard bears comment. In some cases, an ostensible standard for disapproving subcontracting is the fact of performance of the work on the company's premises. However, review of such cases indicates that the arbitrator was primarily concerned about employee layoff, displacement, or the like, thus the "premises" standard may be of minimal significance.[457]

---

[448]See Arbitrator Boals in 78 LA 710, 715 (the "work was of a 'one-shot' nature"); Vause in 76 LA 1174, 1178; Sinicropi in 75 LA 742, 746; Roumell in 71 LA 822, 828; Emery in 51 LA 575, 577; Kesselman in 46 LA 1166, 1170; Kadish in 40 LA 737, 741 (subcontracting was episodic and temporary); Larson in 27 LA 233, 235; Maggs in 16 LA 829, 831.

[449]See Arbitrator Seinsheimer in 51 LA 842, 847–848; Valtin in 48 LA 797, 801; Kates in 46 LA 444, 447–448; Lennard in 25 LA 118, 121.

[450]See Arbitrator Kossoff in 71 LA 204, 211–214; Chattman in 68 LA 976, 981–982; Ludolf in 63 LA 798, 800; Seidenberg in 53 LA 819, 823–824.

[451]See Arbitrator O'Reilly in 78 LA 1221, 1225; Ipavec in 74 LA 659, 662–663; Estes in 74 LA 269, 272; Gibson in 73 LA 734, 737; Nichols in 53 LA 670, 675; King in 52 LA 588, 593; Wagner in 51 LA 435, 439; Murphy in 43 LA 554, 556; Smith in 39 LA 1213, 1220; Sembower in 36 LA 1173, 1176; Duff in 29 LA 609, 612; Lennard in 25 LA 118, 121; Kelly in 22 LA 266, 270.

[452]See Texas Gas Transmission Corp., 27 LA 413, 419 (Hebert, 1956).

[453]See Arbitrator Updegraff in 36 LA 510, 512; Uible in 23 LA 603, 605–606; Maggs in 16 LA 829, 831.

[454]Bargaining history may, for instance, indicate the intended limits of permissible subcontracting. As in Great Atl. & Pac. Tea Co., 54 LA 1189, 1191–1192 (Britton, 1970). As to failure to object when put on notice of management's subcontracting intentions, see Continental Oil Co., 52 LA 532, 537 (Abernethy, 1969).

[455]See Arbitrator Light in 78 LA 144, 147; Van Pelt in 78 LA 57, 59; McDermott in 53 LA 741, 746; Bladek in 52 LA 670, 672; Wolff in 50 LA 69, 70–71; Guse in 45 LA 184, 188–189; Wolff in 27 LA 174, 177–179; Klamon in 27 LA 57, 71–74; Haughton in 26 LA 438, 453–454; Kates in 25 LA 281, 289.

[456]Allis-Chalmers Mfg. Co., 39 LA 1213, 1218 (Smith, 1962).

[457]For cases mentioning the "premises" aspect, see Arbitrator Warns in 41 LA 905, 907; Gray in 26 LA 723, 725–726; Stutz in 24 LA 882, 884; Jones in 24 LA 821, 827–828; Larson in 21 LA 267, 269–273. Also see Howell in 72 LA 421, 430.

Although the test of reasonableness and good faith may appear nebulous and uncertain, nevertheless we have observed the emergence of a set of standards or guides by which the arbitrator may determine whether, under all the circumstances of the case, the action of management in subcontracting was reasonable and in good faith. Indeed, the use of flexible guides has an important and time-honored counterpart in the development and use by courts of general guides under the law of agency for determining whether a given relationship is that of "independent contractor."[458] Although the latter guides do not produce automatic results, they are nonetheless very useful. Likewise it does not suffice to say that each subcontracting case must be decided on the basis of its own facts; there must be guides or standards against which to measure those facts, and reported arbitration decisions have provided guides of great utility.

Notice of Intent to Subcontract; Duty to Bargain

The collective agreement may require notice of intent to subcontract.[459] Where the contract was silent as to subcontracting, one arbitrator emphasized that prior notification of planned subcontracting generally should be given,[460] while another arbitrator held that no notice was required.[461]

Notice requirements may be strictly construed. Thus, under a contract stating that when work is contracted out the company will promptly notify the union "of the reason for contracting it out," advance notice of intent to subcontract was not required.[462] In another case the parties had a mutual understanding that under their collective agreement the company would give notice and discuss its subcontracting plans with the union before entering into subcontracting arrangements. When this understanding was violated an arbitrator devised a special remedy designed to return the parties as nearly as possible to the status quo ante and to deter future violations of the notice and discussion requirement.[463]

Apart from any contractual requirement for notice and discussion, the U.S. Supreme Court's *Fibreboard* decision holds that in

---

[458]See, Restatement of Law of Agency, § 220. In some arbitration cases an issue has been whether the relationship involved was in fact that of independent contractor. See Arbitrator Bogue in 76 LA 883, 887–888; Parkinson in 76 LA 391, 395; Cox in 72 LA 431, 434; Petrie in 68 LA 7, 10, 13; Cantor in 67 LA 88, 91; White in 57 LA 193, 195; Seidenberg in 51 LA 271, 275; Sembower in 29 LA 67, 72–73; Vokoun in 26 LA 79, 82–83; Wolff in 14 LA 31, 34.

[459]See Arbitrator Malkin in 70 LA 1182, 1184; High in 70 LA 322, 324–325; Fitzsimmons in 70 LA 116, 120; Duff in 54 LA 1207, 1209; Strongin in 53 LA 993, 996 (failure to give notice did not prejudice union in this instance); Graff in 46 LA 724, 727–729. Contractual notice requirement was not violated by failure to give notice in an emergency. Schlitz Brewing Co., 51 LA 41, 46 (Bothwell, 1968). Cf., Arbitrator Jacobs in 61 LA 1008, 1013–1014.

[460]Pittsburgh Brewing Co., 53 LA 470, 477 (McDermott, 1969). Also see Arbitrator Boals in 78 LA 710, 716; Lipson in 71 LA 120, 124.

[461]Haveg Indus., 52 LA 1146, 1151 (Kates, 1969).

[462]Electric Autolite Co., 35 LA 415, 420 (Willcox, 1960), the arbitrator emphasizing that the contract used the word "when" rather than "before."

[463]Milprint, Inc., 51 LA 748, 750–751 (Somers, 1968). Also see Arbitrator High in 70 LA 322, 324–325.

certain circumstances the employer has a duty to bargain about sub-contracting under the National Labor Relations Act.[464] In this decision the Court said:

"We are * * * not expanding the scope of mandatory bargaining to hold, as we do now, that the type of 'contracting out' involved in this case—the replacement of employees in the existing bargaining unit with those of an independent contractor to do the same work under similar conditions of employment—is a statutory subject of collective bargaining under §8(d). Our decision need not and does not encompass other forms of 'contracting out' or 'subcontracting' which arise daily in our complex economy."[465]

In evaluating the scope of *Fibreboard,* one arbitrator spoke of the Supreme Court's "cautious approach toward recognizing unilateral subcontracting as a mandatory subject for bargaining";[466] another reminded that the Court "limited the decision to the facts in the case";[467] and a third arbitrator concluded that the decision does not apply where the agreement contains a subcontracting clause.[468]

In a case in which Arbitrator Arvid Anderson concluded that there was a legal duty to bargain, he also concluded (1) that he had authority to decide whether the employer fulfilled the duty to bargain, and (2) that the employer did fulfill its duty to bargain by giving advance notice of its plan to subcontract and by giving the union an advance opportunity to examine the proposed specifications for the work to be subcontracted—the union did not request bargaining and

[464]Fibreboard Paper Prods. Corp., v. NLRB, 85 S.Ct. 398, 57 LRRM 2609 (1964).

[465]85 S.Ct. at 405. In Westinghouse Elec. Corp., 150 NLRB 1574, 58 LRRM 1257 (1965), the NLRB held that the company did not violate the NLRA by failing to consult the union about each of thousands of annual subcontracting decisions where the subcontracting was motivated solely by economic considerations; it comported with traditional methods by which the company conducted its operations; it did not vary significantly in kind or degree from subcontracting of work under established practice; it had no demonstrable adverse effect on employees in the bargaining unit; and the union had an opportunity to bargain about subcontracting practices at general negotiating meetings. But the Board said that bargaining would be required if the subcontracting involved a departure from previously established operating practices, effected a change in conditions of employment, or resulted in a significant impairment of job tenure, employment security, or reasonably anticipated work opportunities for those in the bargaining unit. In Union Carbide Corp., 72 LRRM 1150 (NLRB, 1969), the Board considered the elimination of job classifications to be merely one factor to be considered, and this factor in this instance was outweighed by other considerations. In Hayes-Albion Corp., 77 LRRM 1052 (NLRB, 1971), the layoff of one employee was similarly just one of several factors to be considered, and it was outweighed by other considerations. The NLRB's *Westinghouse* standards were accepted and applied by the Court in Equitable Gas Co. v. NLRB, 106 LRRM 2201 (CA 3, 1981), where, however, the Court upon applying the standards rejected the Board's finding that there was a duty to bargain over the subcontracting in question. In instances where a duty to bargain does exist, the following statement becomes relevant as concerns the scope of the employer's obligation: "[U]nless transfers are specifically prohibited by the bargaining agreement, an employer is free to transfer work out of the bargaining unit if: (1) the employer complies with [*Fibreboard*] by bargaining in good faith to impasse; and (2) the employer is not motivated by anti-union animus * * *." University of Chicago v. NLRB, 89 LRRM 2113, 2117 (CA 7, 1975), quoted with approval in Newspaper Printing Corp. v. NLRB, 111 LRRM 2824, 2830 (CA 6, 1982).

[466]Hess Oil & Chem. Co., 51 LA 752, 759 (Gould, 1968).

[467]Peet Packing Co., 55 LA 1288, 1296 (Howlett, 1971). Also see Arbitrator Boals in 78 LA 710, 716.

[468]Hughes Aircraft Co., 45 LA 184, 189–190 (Guse, 1965). For other cases in which the arbitrator commented as to the *Fibreboard* decision or considered its applicability to the dispute before him, see Arbitrator Murphy in 79 LA 843, 847; Ross in 73 LA 1036, 1040; Chattman in 68 LA 976, 979–980; Witney in 54 LA 886, 894–895; McDermott in 53 LA 470, 474, 477; Volz in 48 LA 409, 411; Gundermann in 45 LA 177, 181; Guild in 45 LA 174, 175–176.

Arbitrator Anderson considered that it had failed to take advantage of the opportunity to discuss the proposed project.[469]

Arbitral Remedies Where Subcontracting Violated the Agreement

In some cases the arbitrator is asked only to rule on the permissibility of subcontracting, in which case he merely states whether past or contemplated subcontracting is sanctioned by the agreement.[470]

Where the arbitrator is called upon to remedy improper subcontracting he may select one or more forms of relief as justified by the particular case. He may make a monetary award of damages for lost work. Where he does so, the award may simply call for the grievants to be made whole or it may expressly indicate whether payment is to be made at the straight time rate or at the overtime rate.[471] The proper measure of damages has been said to be what the grievants would have earned rather than any larger amount that the independent contractor's employees were paid for the work,[472] and no damages were awarded where no monetary loss had been suffered.[473]

Awards have sometimes spoken in terms of the employer being required to cease and desist from the improper subcontracting,[474] in terms of the employer being required to cancel improper sub-

---

[469]Milprint, Inc., 44 LA 678, 681–682 (1965). Also see Arbitrator Chattman in 68 LA 976, 979–980. For extensive discussion of the duty to bargain, see this Chapter, subtopics entitled "The Duty to Bargain: Right of Unilateral Action"; "Duration of Limitation on Unilateral Action: Contract Limitation v. Statutory Duty to Bargain." Included there is some reference to the Supreme Court's *First National Maintenance Corp.* decision, in which the Court commented regarding *Fibreboard* (107 LRRM at 2710), and which sometimes may be relevant in determining the existence of a duty to bargain on subcontracting. In the latter regard, compare the different views expressed in the three opinions by NLRB members in United Technologies, 115 LRRM 1281 (NLRB, 1984), and in the two opinions in Marriott Corp., 111 LRRM 1354 (NLRB, 1982). Many arbitrators have taken the view that it is not their function to decide whether any statutory duty to bargain has been violated, but in fact many arbitrators have considered and expressed a conclusion on some bargaining duty issue where the NLRB had expressly deferred it to arbitration. For cases, see Chapter 10, subtopic entitled "The NLRA, the Arbitrator, and the NLRB."

[470]For example, see Arbitrator Gross in 75 LA 665, 668 (the grievant had left the Company and the Union sought "a ruling only on the Company's right to subcontract under the circumstances of this case"); Seinsheimer in 51 LA 842, 849; Valtin in 48 LA 797, 802.

[471]For cases reflecting these possibilities, see Arbitrator Smith in 80 LA 864, 871–872; Gibson in 78 LA 1252, 1257; Nolan in 76 LA 1049, 1054; Cocalis in 72 LA 619, 622; Daniel in 68 LA 54, 57; Sembower in 61 LA 333, 341; Duff in 54 LA 1207, 1210; Bothwell in 53 LA 627, 631; Kesselman in 53 LA 270, 273; Yaffe in 52 LA 1013, 1018–1019; Crawford in 52 LA 243, 247; Witney in 51 LA 363, 382; Kates in 46 LA 444, 449; Gundermann in 45 LA 177, 183; Dworkin in 44 LA 762, 768; Anderson in 43 LA 65, 74; Prasow in 38 LA 347, 350 (pay was awarded for one half of the hours involved).

[472]Bethlehem Steel Co., 37 LA 499, 500 (Seward, 1961). In Kaiser Found. Hosps., 61 LA 1008, 1010, 1014 (Jacobs, 1973), the employer was ordered to pay damages to employees equal to the actual sum paid to the subcontractor. Also see Arbitrator Herrick in 80 LA 1358, 1363.

[473]Chamberlain Mfg. Corp., 54 LA 1135, 1139 (Slade, 1970). For related discussion see this Chapter, below, subtopic entitled "Arbitral Remedies for Improper Assignment of Bargaining Unit Work to Outsiders"; Chapter 10, topic entitled "Principles of Damages."

[474]See Arbitrator Beck in 76 LA 535, 540; Gibson in 76 LA 286, 292; Siegel in 76 LA 225, 228; Wren in 71 LA 267, 271; Yaffe in 52 LA 1013, 1019; Volz in 51 LA 997, 1001; Keefe in 49 LA 544, 551. But see Bernstein in 42 LA 931, 935.

contracts,[475] and/or in terms of an obligation (sometimes qualified) of the employer to give the work to his employees.[476] There also have been instances in which seniority adjustments have been ordered by the award.[477]

Assigning Work Out of Bargaining Unit

Arbitrators have ruled both ways on the question of whether, in the absence of contract provisions to the contrary, management has the right to assign bargaining unit work to employees outside the unit. Many of the decisions have involved the assignment of such work to supervisory employees; others involve professional, clerical, or other salaried workers, or nonunit production or maintenance employees. The cases in which such action has been permitted occasionally, but not always, conflict with those in which the right has been denied. We will consider herein the factors that have been significant in the thinking of arbitrators.

In holding that management has such right, some arbitrators have emphasized the absence of a specific restriction in the contract. For example, in one case Arbitrator Robert K. Burns stated:

> "A careful examination of the contract fails to reveal any provision that specifically prohibits the Company from making a bona fide transfer, allocation or assignment of work out of the bargaining unit—which is the issue posed in this particular case. In the absence of a specific prohibition or limitation to the contrary it must be assumed that these are reserved and retained powers of management * * *."[478]

Where there likewise was no specific contract restriction and management acted in good faith in assigning the work to nonunit employees, other arbitrators have emphasized in varying degrees certain considerations or justifying circumstances in upholding man-

---

[475]See Arbitrator Gibson in 76 LA 286, 292; Somers in 51 LA 748, 752; Anderson in 43 LA 65, 74; Tsukiyama in 39 LA 676, 684–685; Marshall in 30 LA 449, 455 (company was allowed a reasonable time to comply). In Mullite Refractories, 13 LA 690, 691 (Donnelly, 1949), it was stated that: "The Board recognizes that many circumstances might make it impossible for the Company to recover the work but the Board also recognizes the obligation of an attempt to do so as resting with the Company."

[476]See Arbitrator Ross in 73 LA 1036, 1040; Somers in 51 LA 748, 751–752; Keefe in 49 LA 544, 551; McGury in 43 LA 682, 684; Anderson in 43 LA 65, 74–75; Tsukiyama in 39 LA 676, 684–685 (company not required to reinstate uneconomical operation). In Buhr Mach. Tool Corp., 61 LA 333, 341–342 (Sembower, 1973), where serious erosion of the bargaining unit had resulted from subcontracting in violation of the agreement, there was an extensive monetary award and also an order requiring the employer to return the unit to its former size by a vigorous program of "hiring new employees [with the aid of help-wanted advertisements and other steps expressly outlined by the Arbitrator], reinstating former employees and/or recalling any employees who may be on layoff status."

[477]See Warrior & Gulf Navigation Co., 36 LA 695, 705–706 (Holly, 1961).

[478]Stewart-Warner Corp., 22 LA 547, 551 (1954). For other cases in which the arbitrator stressed the absence of any clear contractual prohibition (in some of the cases the arbitrator also relied upon a management rights clause), see Arbitrator Abrams in 69 LA 594, 598; Lucas in 69 LA 394, 398; Kates in 54 LA 692, 696; Klamon in 42 LA 1025, 1040–1041; Yagoda in 42 LA 31, 39; Larkin in 38 LA 718, 722; Hampton in 16 LA 59, 65; Lane in 13 LA 135, 136; Cheney in 7 LA 412, 413–414. Also see Doyle in 52 LA 440, 443–445; Roberts in 44 LA 1109, 1113–1114.

agement's action. Included among such considerations or circumstances are the following fact situations:

1. The quantity of work or the effect on the bargaining unit is minor or de minimis in nature.[479]
2. The work is supervisory or managerial in nature.[480]
3. The work assignment is a temporary one for a special purpose or need.[481]
4. The work is not covered by the contract.[482]
5. The work is experimental.[483]
6. Under past practice the work has not been performed exclusively by bargaining unit employees.[484]
7. There is a change in the character of the work.[485]
8. Automation or a technological change is involved.[486] Removal of accounting, payroll, billing, time keeping, and other clerical work from the bargaining unit upon establishment of centralized electronic data processing programs has been upheld in numerous cases.[487] In one such case the arbitrator stated that "utilization of computer technology and centralization of data processing have become very com-

---

[479]See Arbitrator Chandler in 72 LA 905, 908; Abrams in 69 LA 594, 598; Lucas in 69 LA 394, 398; Altrock in 49 LA 1083, 1085–1086; Drake in 49 LA 243, 246; Graff in 48 LA 1065, 1068–1069; Block in 48 LA 746, 750; Morgan in 47 LA 756, 760–761; Murphy in 46 LA 798, 801; Wood in 45 LA 881, 884–885; Tatum in 45 LA 797, 800; Larkin in 43 LA 1064, 1065–1066; Marshall in 30 LA 710, 713; Mann in 28 LA 728, 731; Donnelly in 21 LA 681, 682; Shipman in 17 LA 76, 79; Gilden in 16 LA 252, 258; Blumer in 5 LA 237, 240. Cf., Daniel in 78 LA 1268, 1270–1271.

[480]See Arbitrator Mullaly in 77 LA 1224, 1227; Beck in 76 LA 535, 537, 539; Calhoon in 50 LA 107, 109; Hardy in 43 LA 1276, 1287; Klein in 40 LA 1032, 1034–1035; Bothwell in 34 LA 24, 30; Ridge in 26 LA 422, 427; Healy in 23 LA 504, 510–511; Wolff in 23 LA 247, 251; Shipman in 17 LA 76, 78; Kerr in 13 LA 390, 390–391; Uible in 12 LA 893, 895–896. In Daniel Scharlin & Assocs., 69 LA 394, 398–399 (Lucas, 1977), the "confidential" nature of the work was a significant factor in the decision for the employer.

[481]See Arbitrator Fulda in 13 LA 456, 459; Kerr in 13 LA 390, 390–391; D'Andrade in 12 LA 584, 585.

[482]See Arbitrator Fitzsimmons in 80 LA 478, 483; Neill in 72 LA 643, 648; Kates in 54 LA 692, 695–696; Rohman in 36 LA 938, 940; Klamon in 36 LA 732, 738–739, and in 19 LA 264, 267; Jones in 30 LA 358, 364; Barrett in 26 LA 853, 854; Hildebrand in 16 LA 950, 953–954.

[483]See Arbitrator Dybeck in 52 LA 880, 882; Coffey in 42 LA 601, 603; Duff in 39 LA 190, 192; Sturges in 18 LA 219, 225–227. For some definitions and views as to what constitutes "experimental" work in this regard, see Addison Prods. Co., 74 LA 1145, 1149, 1153–1154 (Stephens, 1980).

[484]See Arbitrator Guenther in 79 LA 430, 433; Beck in 76 LA 535, 539; Feldman in 75 LA 963, 966; Neill in 72 LA 643, 649; Abrams in 69 LA 594, 598; Murphy in 46 LA 798, 800; Begley in 46 LA 782, 789; Wood in 45 LA 881, 884; Lugar & Furbee in 43 LA 369, 377–378 (past practice also determined the amount of unit work which could be performed by supervisors); Singletary in 33 LA 94, 97; Feinberg in 14 LA 159, 161. Also see Howlett in 55 LA 1288, 1298.

[485]See Arbitrator Neill in 72 LA 643, 649; Kates in 54 LA 692, 695–696; Stutz in 30 LA 282, 288; Reynard in 24 LA 369, 374.

[486]See Arbitrator Ross in 80 LA 338, 342–343; Block in 48 LA 746, 750; Cahn in 66–2 ARB ¶8430; Roberts in 27 LA 736, 743. Regarding technological change, also see Garrett in 75 LA 750, 760–761. In Hamm Brewing Co., 28 LA 46, 49 (Lockhart, 1956), the new machine did not change the job, but only made it more efficient.

[487]See Arbitrator Dworkin in 50 LA 322, 334–337, and in 44 LA 201, 208–210; Altrock in 45 LA 555, 556; Seitz in 43 LA 5, 8; Ross in 42 LA 353, 356–358; Altieri in 41 LA 506, 509; Garrett in 37 LA 302, 305; Feinberg in 35 LA 72, 73; Pigors in 28 LA 791, 796–797. Cf., Leach in 68 LA 492, 498; Platt in 41 LA 124, 126–129; Gilden in 62–3 ARB ¶8944; Anderson in 39 LA 24, 27. Centralization of design engineering work was upheld in United States Steel Corp., 44 LA 1224, 1228 (Florey, 1965), as was centralization of reproduction and stationery operations in Phillips Chem. Co., 39 LA 82, 84–85 (Larson, 1962). For other cases involving work claims in connection with centralized control systems, see Arbitrator Ipavec in 78 LA 262, 266–267; Cox in 73 LA 945, 947; Rule in 69 LA 136, 140.

mon in American business practice" and that "the Company would be at a competitive disadvantage if it could not make use of these possibilities."[488]

9. An emergency is involved.[489]

10. Some other special situation or need is involved.[490]

Other arbitrators have ruled against the right of management to assign work out of the bargaining unit, even in some cases in which there might have been justification, on the basis that it is not included within the various types of general management rights clauses.[491] Similarly, arbitrators have so ruled on the basis that the recognition,[492] seniority,[493] or job security clause[494] is violated by such action; or that the job, being listed in the contract, is a part of the contract, the action thus violating the contract.[495]

The reasoning underlying this view was elaborated by Arbitrator Saul Wallen, who rejected the management rights clause and applied the seniority provisions of the contract:

"Job security is an inherent element of the labor contract, a part of its very being. If wages is the heart of the labor agreement, job security may be considered its soul. Those eligible to share in the degree of job security the contract affords are those to whom the contract applies. * * *

"The transfer of work customarily performed by employees in the bargaining unit must therefore be regarded as an attack on the job security of the employees whom the agreement covers and therefore on one of the contract's basic purposes."[496]

However, some arbitrators have agreed that the recognition, seniority, and other such clauses do evidence an intention to restrict the performance of unit work to unit employees, but at the same time they have considered that it is not an absolute restriction. Thus, some

---

[488]Safeway Stores, 42 LA 353, 358 (Ross, 1964). Computer monitoring and control of production machines near the production situs may be a significantly different matter. See Arbitrator Seward in Bethlehem Steel Co., 46 LA 730, 732 (1966), and Valtin in Alan Wood Steel Co., 35 LA 157, 159 (1960), both upholding the union. Cf., Killingsworth in Goodyear Tire & Rubber Co., 35 LA 917, 918–919 (1961), in which past practice and de minimis were factors in favor of the company.

[489]See National Cash Register Co., 46 LA 782, 789 (Begley, 1966); Intermountain Chem. Co., 26 LA 58, 61 (Kadish, 1956). Also see Arbitrator McCoy in 19 LA 372, 374.

[490]See Arbitrator Nelson in 80 LA 1180, 1184 (economic necessity); Updegraff in 48 LA 400, 401–402 (unit employees were absent); Merrill in 27 LA 748, 754 (need for supervisor's presence); Aaron in 27 LA 332, 334–335 (plant security problem); Aaron in 25 LA 263, 266 (safety problem); Klamon in 20 LA 690, 703 (minor preparations for reopening plant after shutdown due to strike).

[491]See Arbitrator Hon in 46 LA 769, 772; Selekman in 17 LA 295, 299; Copelof in 12 LA 1074, 1080; Coffey in 10 LA 254, 256–257; Wallen in 8 LA 720, 722–723.

[492]See Arbitrator Belcher in 74 LA 69, 75; Peck in 51 LA 1221, 1223; Porter in 48 LA 305, 309; Howlett in 33 LA 188, 193; Lockhart in 28 LA 46, 48–49; Kelliher in 27 LA 631, 633; Feinberg in 21 LA 283, 284; Boyce in 20 LA 681, 683–684; Komaroff in 13 LA 545, 550.

[493]See Arbitrator Belcher in 74 LA 69, 75; Jaffee in 50 LA 613, 614; Kelliher in 27 LA 631, 633; McCoy in 19 LA 372, 374; Gilden in 18 LA 346, 351; Killingsworth in 16 LA 111, 113; Copelof in 12 LA 1074, 1080; Wallen in 8 LA 720, 722–723.

[494]See Hamm Brewing Co., 28 LA 46, 48–49 (Lockhart, 1956). Also see Arbitrator Dykstra in 40 LA 466, 468–469.

[495]See Arbitrator Hon in 46 LA 769, 772; Oppenheim in 41 LA 1348, 1350; Reynard in 22 LA 880, 882; Shipman in 21 LA 35, 40–41; Lehoczky in 20 LA 603, 604. In some cases the work was supervisory in nature, but this did not privilege the assignment. See Arbitrator Levy in 19 LA 761, 763; Selekman in 17 LA 295, 300; Pollard in 10 LA 498, 502.

[496]New Britain Mach. Co., 8 LA 720, 722 (1947).

of these arbitrators have recognized that the assignment of such work outside the bargaining unit may be proper where there is "good cause,"[497] where it is de minimis,[498] where the work is supervisory in nature,[499] or where there is an emergency or some other justification.[500]

Another view as to the proper approach for judging the assignment of bargaining unit work to persons outside the unit was offered in a decision by Arbitrator Russell A. Smith. In that case the agreement recognized management's right "to manage its plants and offices and direct its affairs and working forces." Arbitrator Smith stated that "This 'right' which obviously exists even though the Agreement does not so provide, must be balanced against the interests and rights which the union and bargaining unit employees have under the [recognition, seniority, and wage clauses of the] Agreement." He explained:

> "In the opinion of the Umpire, this is not a case of 'absolutes' one way or the other. Rather, it is a case of an appropriate balancing of the legitimate interests of management, the bargaining unit employees, and their union representative. The managerial interest in efficient allocation of work should not have to stop at the boundaries of a defined bargaining unit. On the other hand, the decision to allocate work to employees outside the bargaining unit should be one made in the honest exercise of business judgment, and not arbitrarily, capriciously, or in bad faith."[501]

Other arbitrators, too, have used a similar "balancing of interests" approach.[502]

Sometimes the agreement will specifically prohibit management from assigning work of unit employees to nonunit employees. Where such prohibition exists, absent some justifying circumstance, arbitrators generally hold that such action is not permitted under the contract.[503] However, arbitrators sometimes have construed the prohibitory clause narrowly to apply only to the category of nonunit employees specifically stated in the clause or to apply only to assign-

---

[497]Cotton Bros. Baking Co., 51 LA 220, 223–224 (Hebert, 1968); Great Lakes Pipe Line Co., 27 LA 748, 753 (Merrill, 1956).

[498]See Arbitrator Roberts in 52 LA 1183, 1186; Crawford in 41 LA 883, 883–884; McCoy in 19 LA 372, 374.

[499]Crown Zellerbach Corp., 52 LA 1183, 1186 (Roberts, 1969); Kroger Co., 33 LA 188, 193 (Howlett, 1959). Also see Arbitrator Duff in 46 LA 920, 924 (quality testing purposes).

[500]See Arbitrator Peck in 51 LA 1221, 1223; Oppenheim in 41 LA 1348, 1350; McCoy in 19 LA 372, 374.

[501]Chrysler Corp., 36 LA 1018, 1022 (1961).

[502]See Arbitrator Matthews in 73 LA 751, 755 (the work transfer was a "reasonable and necessary response to changing technology" and was done "without animus towards the Union"); Keefe in 71 LA 177, 180–181 (school employer was motivated by economy and efficiency, not by prejudice toward the bargaining unit); Gibson in 46 LA 978, 981–982; Ross in 42 LA 353, 357. Also see Garrett in 75 LA 750, 760–761 (discerning "common basic principles reflected in" the opinions of other arbitrators who had served the same parties in this type of case).

[503]See Arbitrator Cantor in 72 LA 624, 626; Thomson in 70 LA 959, 963; Bolte in 68 LA 343, 346; Knudson in 64 LA 938, 940; Fisfis in 62 LA 743, 748; McDermott in 55 LA 160, 169–170; Solomon in 49 LA 474, 478–479; Rubin in 48 LA 657, 662; Gamser in 28 LA 70, 71–72; Klamon in 27 LA 692, 696; Emery in 26 LA 397, 398–399; Cole in 24 LA 332, 333; Ralston in 17 LA 669, 670; Hawley in 17 LA 516, 520; Gilden in 16 LA 162, 165; Wardlaw in 10 LA 143, 147.

ments at certain locations, and the like.[504] Also, the disputed work may be held in fact not to be bargaining unit work or not to be exclusively so within the meaning of the restrictive clause.[505]

Where the prohibitory clause is otherwise applicable some arbitrators still may permit the assignment of work out of the unit if there is some justifying circumstance, if the work is supervisory in nature, or if the work is de minimis in amount.[506] But other arbitrators may adhere strictly to the letter of the contract and refuse to permit such action.[507]

Arbitral Remedies for Improper Assignment of Bargaining Unit Work to Outsiders

In some cases the arbitrator is asked to decide only whether the agreement was violated by the assignment of bargaining unit work to persons outside the unit.[508] Where the arbitrator is called upon also to

---

[504]See Arbitrator Weatherill in 55 LA 1157, 1158–1159 (the clause expressly restricted the performance of unit work by supervisors or salaried employees but no restriction was stated as to such work by any other category of nonunit employees); Wolff in 54 LA 517, 521; Lewis in 50 LA 1165, 1169–1170 (the clause did not apply to other locations); Woodruff in 43 LA 1264, 1265, 1268. Also see Daniel in 79 LA 30, 33; Murphy in 70 LA 538, 541.

[505]See Arbitrator Archer in 79 LA 584, 587; Allen in 74 LA 13, 15; Weisenfeld in 73 LA 529, 531; Kelliher in 70 LA 777, 779; Murphy in 70 LA 538, 540; Anderson in 70 LA 81, 84–85 (operation of new equipment was properly assigned to employees outside the bargaining unit who historically had performed the function now accomplished by use of the new equipment, and unit employees by performing that function more recently on a temporary and de minimis basis did not establish a binding practice in their behalf); Hitchcock in 69 LA 826, 828 (occasional counting of parts by nonunit auditors to verify inventory counts made by unit employees constituted a work element of both jobs); Cohen in 68 LA 479, 480; Garrett in 54 LA 118, 121–123; Dworkin in 46 LA 1065, 1070 (the clause did not apply to radically different work although the end result remained essentially the same); Schedler in 28 LA 349, 350; Luskin in 28 LA 288, 293. In several of the foregoing cases supervisors in the past had also performed the work and the arbitrator concluded that the bargaining unit did not have exclusive right to it. In Kansas City Power & Light Co., 71 LA 381, 386–387 (Elkouri, 1978), the parties in 1971 had negotiated a job description for computer programmers and the collective agreement specifically prohibited the assignment of bargaining unit work to supervisors or employees outside the unit. The Arbitrator concluded that "it would be equally untenable" to hold either, at one extreme, that the programmers were restricted to the programming they were doing on the machines that were in use when the job description was negotiated, or, at the other extreme, that the programmers had the exclusive right to *all* computer programming notwithstanding significant changes that had evolved in data processing technology since the job description was negotiated. The Arbitrator further concluded that "in the absence of job description language pertaining expressly and unequivocally to the particular piece of work being examined, the question whether the given work should be deemed included under the job description and, if so, whether the work is the exclusive domain of" the bargaining unit employees, must be determined by considering various relevant factors (some of which were outlined by the Arbitrator).

[506]See Arbitrator Ipavec in 76 LA 889, 893 (reclaiming supervisory duties); Ward in 75 LA 941, 943 (confidential material was involved); Epstein in 73 LA 594, 598–599; Solomon in 55 LA 997, 1002–1005; Duff in 53 LA 958, 959–960 (de minimis); Meiners in 50 LA 553, 555 (supervisors did work of unit employees who refused to cross picket line); Lucas in 48 LA 1180, 1183–1184; Yagoda in 48 LA 124, 132; Gross in 46 LA 1030, 1034 (supervisors did the work during vacation shutdown, as in the past); Guse in 44 LA 727, 730; Casselman in 44 LA 361, 371–372; Hebert in 40 LA 806, 809–810; P. Davis in 39 LA 224, 229; Ray in 36 LA 1141, 1146–1147; Hale in 36 LA 578, 584; Teple in 36 LA 416, 419; Killingsworth in 35 LA 917, 919; Clements in 30 LA 43, 45; Crawford in 26 LA 399, 400 (de minimis); Fulda in 24 LA 696, 699; Warren in 19 LA 283, 286–287; Ralston in 16 LA 321, 323–324; Gilden in 1 LA 417, 419.

[507]See Arbitrator Amis in 76 LA 963, 965; Helburn in 70 LA 518, 522; Seinsheimer in 44 LA 188, 191–192; Hawley in 28 LA 321, 323; S. Davis in 27 LA 144, 147; Kelliher in 21 LA 657, 658; Jaffee in 19 LA 467, 469–471; Handsaker in 18 LA 476, 477–478; King in 18 LA 156, 158–160. The language of the prohibitory clause may imply that there is to be no de minimis exception. See Arbitrator Williams in 52 LA 49, 50; Tatum in 34 LA 904, 907.

[508]As in Smith's Food King, 76 LA 601 at 601, 603 (Steinberg, 1981).

remedy the improper assignment of bargaining unit work to outsiders, a frequently utilized remedy is a monetary award of damages to unit employees for lost work.[509] In some cases the arbitrator has ordered the employer to cease and desist from the improper assignment,[510] or has ordered the employer to assign the work to employees in the bargaining unit.[511] Of course, the circumstances of the particular case may justify yet other remedies, possibly to be used in combination with one or more of the foregoing remedies.[512]

Plant Removals

In connection with the foregoing discussion of the assignment of work out of the bargaining unit, the related subject of partial or complete plant removal is noted here. Without discussing the reported arbitration cases that deal with plant removals, the Authors merely note that many of the cases have involved collective agreements containing express clauses on the subject (these express clauses may vary widely, ranging from absolute prohibition of removals to a mere requirement that advance notice be given).[513] However, there are many other cases in which a removal was challenged even though the agreement did not contain any express restriction on plant removals.[514]

---

[509]See Arbitrator Archer in 79 LA 584, 587; Mann in 79 LA 336, 340; Stix in 78 LA 324, 327; Duff in 76 LA 665, 666; Darrow in 76 LA 14, 18; Mathews in 74 LA 224, 235–236; Thomson in 73 LA 480, 482; Cantor in 72 LA 624, 626; Aisenberg in 71 LA 637, 647; Bothwell in 71 LA 396, 411. However, where no employee suffered damage as a result of the improper assignment, no damages were awarded by Arbitrator Daniel in 78 LA 1268, 1272; Beck in 76 LA 535, 540; Hazell in 71 LA 1263, 1266; Wren in 71 LA 267, 271; Bolte in 68 LA 343, 346. In Celanese Fibers Co., 72 LA 271, 275 (Foster, 1979), damages were awarded to the union since "the company's behavior * * * lacked even a colorable excuse." For related discussion see this Chapter, above, subtopic entitled "Arbitral Remedies Where Subcontracting Violated the Agreement"; Chapter 10, topic entitled "Principles of Damages."

[510]See Arbitrator Mann in 79 LA 336, 340; Beck in 76 LA 535, 540; May in 75 LA 540, 543.

[511]See Arbitrator Sergent in 77 LA 594, 599 (if the work is to be performed, it shall be assigned to the bargaining unit); Bothwell in 71 LA 396, 411; Wren in 71 LA 267, 271. This remedy was denied where granting it would have sacrificed efficiency without benefiting the bargaining unit. Label Processing Corp., 77 LA 352, 358 (Neufeld, 1981).

[512]For example, where employees had been downgraded in connection with the improper assignment of bargaining unit work to persons outside the unit, Arbitrator Bennett S. Aisenberg ordered that the downgraded employees be reinstated to their former positions with back pay. Board of Water Works of Pueblo, Colo., 71 LA 637, 647 (1978).

[513]See Arbitrator Seibel in 78 LA 825, 831–834; Boner in 69 LA 1074, 1076; Cole in 61 LA 745, 749; Kenaston in 60 LA 56, 58–59; Platt in 55 LA 170, 178–179; Reid in 53 LA 1219, 1220, and in 45 LA 1104, 1108; Keefe in 48 LA 373, 378; Scheiber in 44 LA 979, 988; Dash in 36 LA 1364, 1384–1386; Wolff in 36 LA 1074, 1076–1077; Gray in 34 LA 771, 774–776; Kheel in 25 LA 804, 806–807; Brower in 8 LA 1001, 1004–1005.

[514]See Arbitrator Wren in 80 LA 1355, 1357–1358; Wolff in 78 LA 772, 775–776; Kramer in 74 LA 407, 410–412; Hardy in 71 LA 873, 874; Lipson in 71 LA 120, 123–124; Kronish in 66 LA 800, 802; Perry in 65 LA 1028, 1034; Blum in 65 LA 858, 860; Shister in 62 LA 194, 196; Sembower in 60 LA 1094, 1099–1100; Lande in 58 LA 653, 657–662; Murphy in 40 LA 1073, 1078–1079; Howlett in 39 LA 449, 458–459; McIntosh in 38 LA 621, 622–623; Kelliher in 38 LA 619, 620; McGoldrick in 28 LA 514, 517–518. For cases involving the applicability to plant removals of contractual clauses restricting subcontracting, see Arbitrator Ellmann in 78 LA 1131, 1137; Edes in 65 LA 1299, 1302–1304; Rubin in 42 LA 107, 110–111; Klamon in 37 LA 834, 842–843. The agreement did not contain an express provision on plant removal in Illinois Coil Spring Co., 111 LRRM 1486, 1490 (NLRB, 1982), but under the facts the NLRB held that the employer, "even though it bargained with the Union about its [economic] decision to relocate and is willing to bargain about the effects of its decision, by deciding, without the consent of the Union, to transfer its assembly operations and to lay off unit employees at its Milwaukee facility during the term of its collective-bargaining agreement in order to obtain relief from the labor costs imposed by that agreement, acted in

Plant Rules

It is well established in arbitration that management has the fundamental right unilaterally to establish reasonable plant rules not inconsistent with law or the collective agreement.[515] Thus, when the agreement is silent upon the subject, management has the right to formulate and enforce plant rules as an ordinary and proper means of maintaining discipline and efficiency and of directing the conduct of the working force.[516] Management also may establish and enforce plant rules to insure the health and safety of employees or others.[517]

This unilateral right of management to establish plant rules also exists under the various types of management rights clauses.[518] Even

---

derogation of its bargaining obligation under Section 8(d), and hence violated Section 8(a)(1), (3), and (5) of the Act." However, the NLRB overruled this decision and the line of NLRB decisions upon which it was based in Illinois Coil Spring Co., 115 LRRM 1065, 1067 (NLRB, 1984), where the Board stated that although the parties no doubt could draft a work-preservation clause, it "is not for the Board * * * to create an implied work-preservation clause in every American labor agreement based on wage and benefits or recognition provisions"; the Board concluded that "neither wage and benefits provisions nor the recognition clause * * * preserves bargaining unit work at the Milwaukee facility for the duration of the contract," and that "no other term contained in the contract restricts Respondent's decision-making regarding relocation." There may or may not be a duty to bargain on a given management decision to transfer bargaining unit work from one location to another. See United Technologies, 115 LRRM 1281 (NLRB, 1984); subtopic entitled "The Duty to Bargain: Right of Unilateral Action," above.

[515]See Arbitrator Lane in 81 LA 409, 412–413; Christopher in 80 LA 1104, 1105; Babiskin in 74 LA 312, 314; Markowitz in 74 LA 58, 62; Gundermann in 73 LA 357, 361; Barrett in 73 LA 352, 356; Ables in 71 LA 963, 967; Blue in 71 LA 744, 748; Doering in 70 LA 667, 669; Duff in 69 LA 77, 79; Bloch in 68 LA 31, 34; H. Dworkin in 60 LA 778, 782, and in 46 LA 1098, 1103; Robertson in 55 LA 306, 312; Whyte in 54 LA 942, 945–946; Williams in 54 LA 129, 130; Gordinier in 52 LA 731, 733; Teele in 50 LA 112, 114; Turkus in 48 LA 1337 at 1337; Caraway in 47 LA 372, 373–374; Kesselman in 46 LA 65, 68; McCoy in 44 LA 733, 734; Daugherty in 40 LA 670, 671; Volz in 39 LA 1265, 1268; Kates in 34 LA 581, 583; Updegraff in 11 LA 689, 690; Whiting in 7 LA 150, 153. In Industrial Finishing Co., 40 LA 670, 671 (1963), Arbitrator Carroll R. Daugherty stated that:
"A union sometimes implies that a company's rules have little or no force or effect because same were not agreed to by the union. It is a settled rule of arbitration that a company has the right unilaterally to issue and enforce rules that (1) do not conflict with any provision of the parties' agreement or of law and (2) are reasonably related to the safe, orderly, and efficient operation of the company's business."
But in Keebler Co., 75 LA 975, 982–984 (1980), Arbitrator Charles J. Morris held (1) that the recognition clause in the collective agreement "should be equated to the statutory duty to bargain," (2) that the particular plant rules at issue in the case were mandatory subjects of bargaining under the NLRA, and (3) that the employer's unilateral action in respect to the rules "would constitute a violation of the duty to bargain" under the NLRA and "did constitute a violation of [the recognition clause] of the collective bargaining agreement for the same reason." Also see Arbitrator Richman in 79 LA 900, 904. Regarding the nature of the recognition clause, cf., Illinois Coil Spring Co., 115 LRRM 1065 (NLRB, 1984), discussed above in the preceding subtopic; Newspaper Printing Corp. v. NLRB, 111 LRRM 2824 (CA 6, 1982). For general discussion of plant rules and their enforcement, see Daykin, "Arbitration of Work Rules Disputes," 18 Arb. J. 36 (1963); Stessin, "Management Prerogatives and Plant Rule Violations," 14 Arb. J. 3 (1959).

[516]Federal Mach. & Welder Co., 5 LA 60, 69 (Whiting, 1946). In accord, in addition to some of the cases cited in note 515 above, see Arbitrator Mittleman in 79 LA 433, 435; Keenan in 76 LA 827, 832; Dunne in 55 LA 99, 100; Solomon in 53 LA 878, 883; Platt in 47 LA 1127, 1129; Kotin in 46 LA 481, 484–486; Leflar in 44 LA 104, 105; Kates in 43 LA 1162, 1164; Stouffer in 43 LA 465, 466; Hebert in 39 LA 419, 425; Dworkin in 39 LA 404, 409; Roberts in 37 LA 1064, 1067; Gorsuch in 34 LA 636, 641–642; Friedman in 28 LA 328, 329; Lynch in 27 LA 653, 655–656; Keller in 26 LA 401, 403.

[517]See Arbitrator Clarke in 78 LA 865, 869–870; Gibson in 71 LA 457, 459–460; Conant in 68 LA 912, 915; Hnatiuk in 50 LA 985, 986; Jenkins in 48 LA 1094, 1096; Sembower in 38 LA 443, 450; Logan in 30 LA 252, 253; Yeager in 29 LA 487, 489. For additional cases and related discussion, see Chapter 16, topic entitled "Management Rights and Obligations in Safety and Health Matters."

[518]See Arbitrator J. Dworkin in 70 LA 1299, 1301; Roberts in 70 LA 278, 281; Erbs in 55 LA 197, 208; Bradley in 47 LA 691, 697; Dahl in 46 LA 356, 357; Wallen in 32 LA 1025, 1027; Stouffer

where an agreement required management to discuss plant rules with the union before being put into effect, Arbitrator Harold M. Gilden observed: "The purpose of the discussion is to ascertain whether the rule itself contains any loopholes, or whether its enforcement will give rise to unexpected problems. After a discussion, the company, at its option, may put the rule into effect, even though union approval is not obtained."[519]

Under an agreement which vested in management the right "to establish reasonable rules for the management of the plant and to maintain discipline among its employees," Arbitrator Maurice H. Merrill held that rules so established must be considered a part of the agreement and that a clause prohibiting the arbitrator from adding to the terms of the agreement did not preclude him from considering established plant rules in determining whether an employee had been properly disciplined. In this case Arbitrator Merrill stated:

> "As a practical matter, it is not possible to embody in a collective bargaining contract a complete code of plant rules. Such a code would make the contract too long and cumbersome. It would introduce into collective bargaining new sources of delay and dispute. It would prevent the necessary adjustments and modifications of rules between periods of negotiation."[520]

After plant rules are promulgated, they may be challenged through the grievance procedure (including arbitration) on the ground that they violate the agreement or that they are unfair, arbitrary, or discriminatory.[521] This right to challenge applies also where the agreement expressly gives management the right to establish plant rules.[522] Indeed, in many of the more recent plant rule cases management's general right to promulgate plant rules unilaterally was not challenged, such right being stated expressly in the agreement; the challenge rather was to the content or particular application of some given rule.[523]

---

in 26 LA 638, 640; Shister in 20 LA 448, 450–451; Baab in 16 LA 118, 120; McCoy in 12 LA 73, 74–75; Gilden in 9 LA 931, 934; Healy in 6 LA 430, 432.

[519]Borg-Warner Corp., 16 LA 446, 453 (1951). Similarly, see Arbitrator Sergent in 76 LA 249, 251; McDermott in 48 LA 1149, 1157; Karlins in 44 LA 609, 612. Cf., Traynor in 46 LA 53, 58–59. A plant rule promulgated without giving the union prior notice and opportunity for discussion as required by the agreement was not an acceptable basis for disciplinary action in Capital Area Transit Auth., 69 LA 811, 815 (Ellmann, 1977).

[520]American Zinc Co. of Ill., 20 LA 527, 530 (1953).

[521]See Arbitrator Whyte in 77 LA 807, 814; Fleischli in 69 LA 970, 974; Roberts in 69 LA 930, 935–936 (stating that an implied limitation upon the Company's express contractual right to establish plant rules is that they must not be unreasonable, he rejected management's contention that the only implied limitation is that rules must not be "arbitrary, capricious, or discriminatory"); Towers in 67 LA 173, 178; Dolson in 51 LA 281, 283; Dyke in 48 LA 681, 687; Platt in 47 LA 1127, 1129–1130; Whyte in 47 LA 1065, 1069; Kotin in 46 LA 481, 483–484; Leflar in 44 LA 104, 105; Thompson in 30 LA 231, 235; Crawford in 29 LA 731, 733; Crane in 27 LA 717, 720–722; Smith in 27 LA 99, 104–105; Donaldson in 13 LA 943, 945; Courshon in 2 LA 509, 514.

[522]See Arbitrator Curry in 69 LA 375, 377; Holly in 69 LA 231, 234; Whyte in 68 LA 957, 961–962; Klein in 48 LA 243, 248.

[523]For example, see Arbitrator Mulhall in 79 LA 543, 546; Harr in 78 LA 883, 885; Taylor in 77 LA 249, 255; Berns in 75 LA 397, 399; Buchanan in 74 LA 983, 985; Eischen in 74 LA 412, 416; Murphy in 73 LA 850, 853–854; Roberts in 73 LA 34, 37–38; Feldman in 72 LA 297, 299–301. For instances in which the union unsuccessfully attempted to impose a bargaining obligation even though the agreement expressly authorized management to make plant rules, see Arbitrator Strasshofer in 77 LA 1287, 1289; Heinsz in 76 LA 935, 937.

Rules promulgated unilaterally by the employer have been held subject to challenge when established—the union need not delay its challenge until employees have been disciplined for violation of the rules.[524]

The test of reasonableness of a plant rule "is whether or not the rule is reasonably related to a legitimate objective of management."[525] Of course, the plant rule should be stated clearly to enable employees to appreciate its import.[526] Moreover, plant rules must be reasonable not only in their content but also in their application.[527] Thus, a rule requiring the wearing of safety glasses in the plant could not be applied during lunch periods where the risk of injury was remote.[528]

Management should be permitted to change plant rules, if not restricted by the agreement, to meet changed circumstances.[529] However, it has been emphasized that "Sound industrial relations policy dictates that abrupt changes in rules should be accompanied by a

---

[524]Linde Co., 34 LA 1, 5–6 (1959), Arbitrator Milton H. Schmidt declaring that "Employees should not be forced to run the risk of disciplinary penalty by refusing obedience in order to determine whether a regulation is a proper exercise of management's prerogatives." Accord, Arbitrator Hays in 71 LA 1064, 1066; Fleischli in 69 LA 970, 974; Bloch in 68 LA 31, 33. But in Pacific Sw. Airlines, 70 LA 833, 834–835 (1978), Arbitrator Edgar A. Jones, Jr., rejected the union's request for a ruling as to the reasonableness of a new absenteeism plan unilaterally adopted by management. Being unwilling to rule "in the abstract and without evidence of specific applications," he explained that "the reasonableness or unreasonableness of a promulgated absenteeism policy—or most any kind of detailed written policy, for that matter—cannot realistically be determined until those charged with its implementation have had a chance to translate its abstract expressions into specific applications." Also see Aluminum Co. of Am. v. UAW, 105 LRRM 2390 (CA 9, 1980), where the court held a similar grievance request to be nonarbitrable.

[525]Robertshaw Controls Co., 55 LA 283, 286 (Block, 1970). Similarly, see Arbitrator Schuster in 77 LA 1052, 1055; Hilgert in 77 LA 953, 958–959; Kerkman in 72 LA 1250, 1253; Weiss in 72 LA 133, 135.

[526]See Arbitrator Strasshofer in 77 LA 1287, 1290 ("a reasonable rule must be one which the employees can understand and comply with"); Gibson in 71 LA 457, 459; Sherman in 65 LA 394, 398–399; Trotter in 60 LA 960, 964.

[527]See Arbitrator Eischen in 74 LA 412, 416; Markowitz in 74 LA 58, 64; Roberts in 73 LA 34, 43–45; Cohen in 71 LA 1, 6; Blue in 70 LA 744, 749; Curry in 69 LA 375, 378; Eckhardt in 68 LA 1273, 1277–1278. In upholding an employer's unilaterally established absenteeism policy, Arbitrator James C. Duff stated:

"If a plan is fair on its face and its operation in the concrete cases at hand produces just results, and other common tests of reasonableness are satisfied, a plan ought not to be declared invalid based on the mere existence of some remote probability that it could operate perversely in the indefinite future under hypothetical circumstances which have not as yet materialized."

Robertshaw Controls Co., 69 LA 77, 79 (1977), quoted with approval by Arbitrator Taylor in 77 LA 249, 256.

[528]Bauer Bros. Co., 48 LA 461, 463 (Kates, 1967). It has been held that management's right to supervise employees does not extend to their personal lives after they leave the plant. Pioneer Gen-E-Motors Corp., 3 LA 486, 488 (Blair, 1946). For related material, see Chapter 15, topic entitled "Conduct Away From Plant." However, it also has been held that the employees' personal lives may be governed by plant rules where the conduct or situation in question affects plant operations. See Arbitrator Teple in 43 LA 338, 340; Gorsuch in 34 LA 636, 641–642; Platt in 28 LA 583, 585–586; Willingham in 28 LA 411, 413–414; Friedman in 28 LA 328, 330; Kates in 27 LA 540, 542; Keller in 26 LA 401, 402–404; Holden in 24 LA 810, 812–813; Cole in 21 LA 709, 710.

[529]See Florence Stove Co., 19 LA 650, 651 (Noel, 1952). Similarly, see Arbitrator Lane in 81 LA 409, 412–413; Larkin in 79 LA 835, 837, and in 50 LA 109, 111; Harr in 78 LA 883, 885; Kerkman in 72 LA 1250, 1253; Roberts in 70 LA 278, 281 (stating that among "the rights contemplated in management's prerogative to direct the working force is management's right to promulgate reasonable rules and regulations governing the conduct of employees," and that the right "to promulgate such reasonable rules and regulations includes the right to modify, amend, and change those rules and regulations from time to time to respond to changing conditions and requirements of the business"); Curry in 69 LA 375, 377.

gradual educational process."[530] Moreover, new or changed plant rules which curtail employee privileges supported by long established past practice may be subject to challenge.[531]

Upon demand, management must bargain with respect to such rules as affect conditions of employment, and the filing of a grievance challenging a rule might be construed by an arbitrator "as a demand to negotiate on the subject."[532] Even where the agreement gave management a general right to make and modify rules "for purposes of discipline and efficiency," it was held that "after they have once become a subject of mutual agreements, very specific bargaining and agreement are required to make their modification again exclusively a matter of company decisions and announcements."[533]

Posting of Rules

The decision as to whether plant rules are to be posted is a part of the managerial function, and the posting of rules ordinarily is not a condition precedent to management's right to discipline employees for their violation.[534] However, except where the nature of the prohibited activity is such that employees should know it is improper,[535] rules must be communicated to employees in some manner.[536]

Thus, in the absence of posted rules management's freedom of action may be more restricted than it would be if they were posted,[537] and management is under a somewhat greater responsibility to show

---

[530]Joy Mfg. Co., 6 LA 430, 434 (Healy, 1946). Also see Arbitrator Turkus in 48 LA 1337, 1338; Smith in 27 LA 99, 105.

[531]See Standard Oil Co. (Ind.), 11 LA 689, 690 (Updegraff, 1948). Also see Arbitrator Dolson in 51 LA 281, 283; Kreimer in 43 LA 337, 338; McCoy in 4 LA 775, 777–779. For related discussion, see Chapter 12, topic entitled "Custom and Practice as Part of the Contract."

[532]Federal Mach. & Welder Co., 5 LA 60, 68–69 (Whiting, 1946). In Pet, Inc., 111 LRRM 1495, 1498 (NLRB, 1982), the NLRB deferred to an arbitration award where the arbitrator had determined that "work rules are separate from the collective-bargaining agreement and can be changed (either tightened or relaxed) midterm after the required bargaining as long as the rules as changed do not conflict with the collective-bargaining agreement." Also see Arbitrator Heinsz in 76 LA 935, 937; Gilden in 3 LA 423, 433–434. For related discussion, see this Chapter, subtopics entitled "The Duty to Bargain: Right of Unilateral Action"; "Duration of Limitation on Unilateral Action: Contract Limitation v. Statutory Duty to Bargain."

[533]Ampco Metal, 3 LA 374, 378–379 (Updegraff, 1946). Also see Arbitrator Ellmann in 72 LA 804, 807; Gundermann in 66 LA 1256, 1260–1261; Goodman in 59 LA 697, 698–699; Sembower in 47 LA 20, 25; Hampton in 5 LA 391, 396. Even as to negotiated rules, however, where the term of the agreement has expired management may put its proposals into effect unilaterally after having bargained on them to an impasse. Again, see the subtopics cited in note 532 above.

[534]Bethlehem Steel Co., 7 LA 334, 335 (Killingsworth, 1946); Watt Car & Wheel Co., 4 LA 67, 69 (Blair, 1946). Also see Arbitrator Cowan in 59 LA 1226, 1230; Teple in 50 LA 501, 504 (plant rules need not be in writing); Lovell in 48 LA 498, 501–502; Murphy in 44 LA 459, 461 (there is no one way of either establishing or publicizing a rule); Merrill in 37 LA 862, 864; Schmidt in 35 LA 293, 296.

[535]See Arbitrator Harkless in 69 LA 613, 614; Bradley in 28 LA 874, 877–878; Beatty in 26 LA 641, 642. Also see Dworkin in 70 LA 1299, 1301. Cf., Jenkins in 52 LA 1266, 1269; Harkins in 18 LA 336, 339.

[536]See Arbitrator Mullins in 54 LA 498, 500; Teple in 50 LA 501, 504; Keefe in 48 LA 910, 914; Kates in 47 LA 441, 442–443 (an employer "takes an unnecessary risk of enforcement in failing to put all its shop rules in written form"); Murphy in 44 LA 459, 461; Klein in 43 LA 1268, 1273; Davis in 28 LA 83, 87; Healy in 14 LA 787, 790. Also see Dyke in 69 LA 630, 636, 639.

[537]See Arbitrator Keefe in 48 LA 910, 914; Davis in 28 LA 83, 87; Healy in 14 LA 787, 790.

the absence of discrimination in the discipline of an employee.[538] Especially when management chooses to apply a rule rigidly to the point of meeting its violation with discharge, there should be no doubt in the minds of employees as to the existence and nature of the rule.[539]

Seniority

Management's right of action is very often restricted by requirements of seniority recognition. Chapter 14 is devoted to discussion of seniority concepts and to an examination of the standards utilized by arbitrators in evaluating management actions in the setting of seniority requirements.

Layoff of Employees

In the absence of contractual restriction, it is the right of management to determine the number of employees to be used at any given time and to lay off employees in excess of that number, giving any required recognition to seniority.[540] Recognition of seniority is the most significant type of restriction placed by many agreements upon the layoff right.[541] Clauses requiring advance notice for layoff in order to permit employees to plan ahead are not uncommon, but such a notice requirement ordinarily is not severe from the employer's point of view since he also prefers to plan ahead.[542]

The meaning of the term "layoff," and allegations that employees have been laid off in fact even if not in name or form, are frequent

---

[538]Bethlehem Steel Co., 7 LA 334, 335 (Killingsworth, 1946); Watt Car & Wheel Co., 4 LA 67, 69 (Blair, 1946).

[539]Joy Mfg. Co., 6 LA 430, 434 (Healy, 1946). Also see Arbitrator Krislov in 68 LA 72, 74; Teple in 44 LA 820, 822–823. Cf., Lovell in 48 LA 498, 501–502.

[540]See Arbitrator Ellmann in 73 LA 1083, 1086–1087; Blair in 55 LA 312, 324; Murphy in 46 LA 289, 291; Feinberg in 19 LA 523, 525, and in 10 LA 883, 885; Wolff in 19 LA 487, 488. Also see Turkus in 74 LA 1209, 1212–1214; Edes in 64 LA 256, 258; Hebert in 47 LA 941, 946–947; McCoy in 39 LA 268, 269; Reid in 36 LA 458, 462; Nagle in 24 LA 770, 774. Where the contract listed four reasons for layoffs, management could lay off only for those reasons. City of Milwaukee, 55 LA 926, 931–932 (Sembower, 1970). For discussion of the rights of laid-off employees, see Arbitrator Florey in 78 LA 34, 35; Dean in 74 LA 422, 427–428; Joseph in 59 LA 1193, 1197; McCoy in 39 LA 268, 269; Brown in 35 LA 560, 563–564; Whelan in 25 LA 443, 449–451.

[541]Illustrating the strict application of such restriction, Wayne Pump Co., 35 LA 623, 625 (Horlacher, 1960). For the application of a clause providing for layoff by seniority but authorizing exceptions for special skills, see Trane Co., 44 LA 212, 216 (Markowitz, 1965). For the application of a still less strict requirement of seniority recognition, see American Fedn. of Govt. Employees, 76 LA 473, 478 (Oldham, 1981), where the agreement required seniority recognition in layoff and recall "except where such reduction and recall would cause injury to AFGE operations."

[542]For related discussion, see this Chapter, topic entitled "Emergency Changes in Work Schedule." For a clause interpreted to permit very few exceptions to the notice requirement, see Mobil Chem. Co., 50 LA 80, 81–82 (Kesselman, 1968). In Oregon Steel Mills, 66 LA 79, 81 (1976), the agreement required "a 30-day prior notice before" layoff, and Arbitrator Arthur J. Hedges stressed that the notice must be clear and specific: "It means that the employee is entitled to be put on notice of the date that he is to be laid off 30 days before that date. It does not mean that he is merely entitled to be put on notice that at some indefinite date in the future, more than thirty days following the notice he will be laid off."

issues in arbitration.[543] Arbitrators have ruled that the term "layoff" must be interpreted to include any suspension from employment arising out of a reduction in the work force, and that the scheduling of employees not to work or the use of the term "not scheduled" by management does not make the occurrence any the less a "layoff."[544] One arbitrator defined "layoff," in the context of a particular clause, as an "actual severance from the Company's payroll, and a break in continuous service."[545]

Downgrading is often tied to layoffs. It has been held that downgrading "is such an intimate concomitant of layoff" that layoff seniority provisions must be applied in downgrading.[546] Some contracts contain provisions permitting employees to accept layoff in lieu of downgrading.[547] Where the contract was silent regarding the right of employees to choose layoff rather than downgrading, one arbitrator held that they are deemed to have such right if downgrading involves a significant reduction in pay.[548]

Numerous cases have arisen involving the observance of seniority in temporary layoffs. Contracts sometimes expressly allow management to disregard seniority in making temporary layoffs.[549] Such agreements generally indicate the maximum period that may be considered temporary, such period varying in different contracts from a specified number of hours up to as many as 30 days.[550]

---

[543]See Arbitrator Ordman in 74 LA 719, 721–722; Dean in 74 LA 422, 427–428 (in drawing a distinction between "permanent layoff" and "immediate discharge," he stated that a "layoff is essentially a preservation of some benefits of employment notwithstanding the employee's separation from active employment"); Leahy in 73 LA 882, 884–885; Bothwell in 73 LA 833, 836 (dealing with the "question whether an unrecalled employee at the conclusion of a strike becomes a laid off employee"); Ipavec in 72 LA 1160, 1164 (stating that the term "permanent layoff" connotes a layoff "which is considered lasting or intended to last indefinitely * * * and * * * for a relatively long period of time"); Boner in 69 LA 1075, 1077; King in 69 LA 1017, 1022; Flagler in 68 LA 1167, 1169 (collecting several definitions of "layoff"); Gibson in 68 LA 925, 927; Cole in 68 LA 36, 39–40; Mueller in 65 LA 1, 3, 5 (shutdown as a layoff); Block in 57 LA 742, 750–751; Cohen in 55 LA 981, 985–986; Moran in 51 LA 1069, 1071; Murphy in 46 LA 289, 292–293; Boles in 45 LA 502, 505, 508; Teple in 40 LA 1067, 1069; Prasow in 27 LA 40, 45; Campbell in 26 LA 924, 929–930; Platt in 23 LA 137, 141; McCormick in 22 LA 695, 696–698; Marshall in 22 LA 181, 183; Emery in 19 LA 231, 232–233; Piper in 18 LA 801, 808; Feinberg in 16 LA 71, 72. In Radio Station WFDF, 79 LA 424, 426–427 (1982), Arbitrator Erwin B. Ellmann found that the grievant had not been laid off but rather had been terminated (and thus was entitled to contractual severance pay), since there was no "reasonable expectancy of employment in the near future."

[544]See Arbitrator Chapman in 75 LA 337, 340–341; Feinberg in 14 LA 191, 195; Donnelly in 13 LA 684, 686; Brandschain in 5 LA 578, 587. Cf., Williams in 48 LA 767, 768.

[545]Bethlehem Steel Co., 16 LA 71, 72 (Feinberg, 1950). Also see Arbitrator Campbell in 26 LA 924, 929.

[546]Kenworth Motor Truck Corp., 8 LA 867, 869 (Seering, 1947). A similar result was reached in Ford Motor Co., Opinions of the Umpire, Opinion A-30 (1943). But this result was not reached where downgrading was not tied to layoffs. Lockheed Aircraft Corp., 10 LA 222, 226 (Aaron, 1948). Also see Arbitrator Strongin in 77 LA 396 at 396; Eisler in 76 LA 516, 520; Mathews in 1 LA 298, 300–301.

[547]As in Tappan Co., 40 LA 149, 150 (Dworkin, 1962); Carbide & Carbon Chems. Co., 20 LA 205, 206 (Shister, 1953).

[548]Caterpillar Tractor Co., 23 LA 313, 315–316 (Fleming, 1954). Also see Arbitrator McCoy in 47 LA 164, 169–170; Shipman in 15 LA 698, 703. Cf., Garrett in 31 LA 988, 991–992.

[549]As in 76 LA 773, 774; 70 LA 417 at 417; 65 LA 471, 473; 38 LA 1, 4; 28 LA 494, 497; 24 LA 88, 89; 15 LA 910, 913; 8 LA 792, 794; 1 LA 544, 545. In Barler Metal Prods., 38 LA 1, 4–5 (Sembower, 1962), it was held that the "temporary" character of a layoff is determined in advance rather than retrospectively.

[550]See cases cited in note 549 above. No specific period was stated in 43 LA 1092, 1093–1094; 18 LA 785, 786; 12 LA 826, 828. Even where the contract fixes a maximum period, a series of temporary layoffs without observing seniority has sometimes been permitted. See Anaconda

In cases where the agreement contains no specific exception from the requirement of observing seniority in making "temporary" or "emergency" layoffs, arbitrators have ruled both ways as to the right of management to disregard seniority in making such layoffs.[551] Some of these cases can be reconciled on the basis of differing contract language, including contractual requirement for notice of layoff, or by distinguishing between "temporary" and "emergency" layoffs.[552]

Issues concerning "temporary" or "emergency" layoffs may be approached, as has been done by Arbitrator Russell A. Smith, "in the light of the well known fact that the common purpose of seniority layoff provisions is to give protection as between classes of employees on the assumption that some of them may properly be suspended under conditions of lack of work, and not to guarantee work." He construed the contract in question as being broadly applicable to temporary as well as permanent suspensions of work (those where there is no immediate prospective need of the services involved), but not as requiring the employer to follow seniority "when the emergency is such that, due to time limitations, it would be either impossible or unreasonably burdensome to give effect to these rules."[553]

The question sometimes arises regarding management's right to reduce the workweek of all its employees in lieu of laying off junior employees. In the absence of a specific contract provision covering this issue, arbitrators have ruled both ways.[554]

Bumping

Layoff often gives rise to "bumping" issues. Arbitrators have emphasized that, absent any contract provision permitting it, senior

---

Aluminum Co., 43 LA 775, 777–779 (Volz, 1964); Alliance Mfg. Co., 37 LA 177, 180 (Kates, 1961). Cf., Arbitrator Solomon in 65 LA 471, 476. An interesting situation was presented under a contract which required observance of seniority only in case of layoffs for "indefinite" periods. There the employer was permitted to provide one week's work for all employees and then to lay off all employees for one week, rather than to lay off junior employees indefinitely, the arbitration board ruling that the layoffs were for definite, temporary periods. Whitlock Mfg. Co., 13 LA 253, 254 (Stutz, Mottram & Curry, 1949).

[551]Cases requiring observance of seniority: Arbitrator Kossoff in 66 LA 522, 529–531; Edes in 64 LA 256, 258; LeVerde in 63 LA 409, 412; Tatum in 40 LA 1115, 1118–1120; Killion in 40 LA 513, 520–521; Murphy in 38 LA 1199, 1202; Lugar in 35 LA 299, 303; Duff in 30 LA 441, 443; Howlett in 29 LA 724, 726–727; Platt in 23 LA 137, 141; Thompson in 23 LA 89, 92; McCormick in 22 LA 695, 698; Marshall in 22 LA 181, 184; Stutz in 21 LA 400, 401, and in 10 LA 88, 91; Spaulding in 19 LA 159, 163–164; Feinberg in 14 LA 413, 416; Gorder in 13 LA 529, 531; Uible in 12 LA 893, 895; Brandschain in 5 LA 578, 587–588; Whiting in 5 LA 24, 25; Gilden in 1 LA 530, 537. Cases not requiring the observance of seniority: Arbitrator Nicholas in 73 LA 573, 577; Caraway in 52 LA 368, 372 (past practice supported employer); Klamon in 37 LA 778, 784; Abernethy in 32 LA 345, 350–351; Hebert in 23 LA 497, 500; Garrett in 21 LA 71, 74–75; Prasow in 20 LA 345, 347–348; Marshall in 20 LA 297, 299; Morgan in 18 LA 517, 518; Horton in 18 LA 285, 289; Lockhart in 16 LA 173, 175; Bauder in 14 LA 681, 685; Feinberg in 14 LA 191, 196; Stein in 10 LA 579, 581; Dwyer in 8 LA 506, 509; Elson in 8 LA 129, 134. Also see Howlett in 24 LA 232, 237–238; Healy in 15 LA 192, 194. Observance of seniority in emergency recalls was not required by Arbitrator Platt in 14 LA 970, 976, and in 14 LA 552, 562. Also see Turkus in 48 LA 179, 181. Cf., Dworkin in 22 LA 875, 880.

[552]In at least one instance, however, opposite results were reached within the same month by two different arbitrators applying the same contractual provision to similar fact situations. See International Harvester Co., 9 LA 399, 401 (Hays, 1947), and in 8 LA 129, 134 (Elson, 1947).

[553]Dow Chem. Co., 12 LA 763, 767 (1949). Also see Arbitrator Zimring in 73 LA 1127, 1128–1129; Roberts in 48 LA 1199, 1201.

[554]This is discussed and cases are cited above in topic entitled "Scheduling Work."

employees have no right to bump junior employees merely because the senior employee wants the job of the junior employee—no layoff being involved.[555] However, it has also been emphasized that, in the absence of any contract prohibition, "it is almost universally recognized that senior employees, under a plant-wide seniority system, have the right to bump junior employees from their jobs in order to avoid their own layoff, provided they can perform the work of the juniors."[556] The right to bump in short-term temporary layoff situations may be considerably more limited.[557]

While it is generally accepted that an employee facing layoff may exercise his bumping right laterally or downward, i.e., to a job equal to his own or a lower classification, arbitrators have ruled both ways on the issue of "upward" bumping. Where arbitrators have denied the right of an employee to bump into a higher-rated classification, they have based their decisions upon one or more of the following reasons:

1. A layoff may not be used as a means of achieving a promotion. The rationale of these cases seems to be that a promotion can be sought only when a vacancy exists; promotions must be governed by the promotion clause of the collective agreement; and since upward bumping would result in a promotion in violation of the promotion requirements of the contract, it cannot be permitted.[558]
2. A showing was made that past practice prohibits upward bumping, or there was no showing of past practice allowing it.[559]
3. The history of contract negotiations indicates an intent to preclude upward bumping.[560]
4. While the contract would permit upward bumping, it does not require that it be permitted, and in the absence of a showing of

---

[555]See Arbitrator Nolan in 74 LA 1218, 1220; Volz in 48 LA 579, 581–582; Turkus in 39 LA 670, 671; Williams in 39 LA 494, 495. Also see Krinsky in 54 LA 824, 827–828; Carmichael in 64–1 ARB ¶8255. The purpose of "bumping" is explained and it is distinguished from "transfer" in Borden Ice Cream Co., 37 LA 140, 141–142 (Markowitz, 1961).

[556]Darin & Armstrong, 13 LA 843, 847 (Platt, 1950). Also see Arbitrator Hellman in 67 LA 14, 21–22; Altieri in 43 LA 499, 504; Kornblum in 42 LA 403, 404, 407; Markowitz in 37 LA 140, 141; Larson in 26 LA 532, 535–536; Parker in 22 LA 883, 885; Cornsweet in 14 LA 494, 498; Healy in 11 LA 827, 831. The present ability requirement is obviously important. See Arbitrator Modjeska in 71 LA 789, 790; Kamin in 50 LA 1093, 1099; Geissinger in 41 LA 348, 351–352; Klamon in 35 LA 128, 132. Although the senior employee is not entitled to training, a reasonable trial period to demonstrate his present ability has sometimes been required in bumping situations. See Arbitrator Prasow in 24 LA 437, 442; McKelvy in 22 LA 167, 170; Kelliher in 22 LA 53, 55; Randle in 17 LA 486, 487. Also see Craver in 74 LA 89, 91. Cf., Rotenberg in 78 LA 706, 710; Tatum in 24 LA 517, 518; McCoy in 23 LA 779, 781. Employees *already* on layoff were denied bumping rights by Arbitrator Bourne in 65 LA 617, 620; McCoy in 39 LA 268, 269. Cf., Roberts in 76 LA 773, 776, 781.

[557]See Arbitrator Kates in 42 LA 669, 671; Blair in 30 LA 962, 963; Fuchs in 15 LA 172, 179. Cf., Seibel in 22 LA 306, 310.

[558]See Arbitrator McDonald in 76 LA 899, 902–903; Brown in 71 LA 295, 300; McSwain in 38 LA 430, 433–434; Larson in 26 LA 532, 536; Hall in 25 LA 417, 420–421; Seward in 24 LA 261, 266–267, and in 15 LA 891, 892; Rosenfarb in 23 LA 789, 795–796; Horvitz in 22 LA 736, 737; Abernethy in 14 LA 938, 941. Also see Pieroni in 72 LA 719, 723; Shulman in 3 LA 863, 865.

[559]See Arbitrator Seward in 30 LA 815, 819; Hebert in 30 LA 1, 8; Warns in 23 LA 220, 222. In Empire-Reeves Steel Corp., 44 LA 653, 657 (Nichols, 1965), past practice permitted upward bumping but only on a limited basis—this controlled the decision.

[560]See Bethlehem Steel Co., 24 LA 261, 266–267 (Seward, 1955).

practice by the parties, the arbitrator cannot sustain a claim to upward bumping.[561]

Some of the arbitrators who have permitted upward bumping have done so upon the basis of one or more of the following reasons:

1. The contract does not specifically prohibit it.[562]
2. The layoff provisions of the agreement are broad.[563]
3. Upward bumping does not conflict with the promotion provisions of the agreement.[564]
4. Past practice of the parties either supports or does not prohibit upward bumping.[565]

In regard to exercising the bumping right, it has been held that senior employees have an obligation to notify management of their desire to exercise bumping privileges,[566] whereupon management has a duty to disclose the jobs that may be bumped into and to inform junior employees of their layoff under the seniority provisions of the agreement.[567] In recalls, management has been held to have the duty of taking the initiative in ascertaining from employees whether they are available for jobs to which their seniority entitles them.[568]

Promotion and/or Transfer of Employees

The term "promotion" usually connotes an upward movement to a better job or a higher rating in the same job. However, it is to be noted that some parties or arbitrators have used the term less specifically, with the result that there has been some overlapping and intermingling of the terms "promotion" and "transfer." The mixed nature of some employee job movements should also be kept in mind: promotions often involve transfers, transfers may involve promotions, but

---

[561]See Bethlehem Steel Co., 30 LA 815, 819 (Seward, 1958). Where a contract was "highly permissive" as to upward bumping, the arbitrator said that criteria of "productivity, tensions and morale" should be applied in determining whether to permit it in any particular layoff. C.E. Howard Corp., 38 LA 128, 129–130 (Pollard, 1961).

[562]See Arbitrator Jacobowski in 62 LA 192, 194; Burris in 30 LA 886, 892; Marshall in 29 LA 629, 633–634; Cole in 21 LA 214, 216; Low in 20 LA 394, 396. Cf., Seward in 15 LA 891, 892. In Bethlehem Steel Co., 16 LA 478, 483 (1951), Arbitrator Shipman recognized that downward bumping is the general rule, but he held that there should be some exceptions. In Air Reduction Sales Co., 34 LA 294, 296 (Hawley, 1960), the arbitrator said that to deny upward bumping in layoff would seriously restrict departmental seniority rights and might lead to substitution of classification seniority for the broader departmental seniority specified by the contract.

[563]See Arbitrator Volz in 44 LA 694, 697; Burris in 30 LA 886, 892; Low in 20 LA 394, 396; Seward in 14 LA 502, 503–504.

[564]See Aetna Paper Co., 29 LA 439, 441–442 (Warns, 1957). Also see Arbitrator Ebeling in 12 LA 738, 740.

[565]See International Harvester Co., 21 LA 214, 216 (Cole, 1953). Also see Arbitrator Jacobowski in 62 LA 192, 194; Volz in 44 LA 694, 697.

[566]See Union Elec. Steel Corp., 13 LA 464, 467 (Blair, 1949); General Am. Transp. Corp., 15 LA 672, 676 (Brandschain, 1950). Also see Arbitrator Millious in 74 LA 844, 847; McDermott in 65 LA 1031, 1034; Stein in 43 LA 178, 180–181. But see Arbitrator Warns in 34 LA 297, 300; Howlett in 33 LA 524, 527–528 (involving union representatives with superseniority).

[567]Union Elec. Steel Corp., 13 LA 464, 467 (Blair, 1949). Also see Arbitrator Stein in 43 LA 178, 180–181; Bradley in 37 LA 9, 11–13. Some arbitrators require the employee to specify the job into which he desires to bump. See Arbitrator Prasow in 27 LA 40, 48; Gilden in 6 LA 803, 813.

[568]The Thor Corp., 13 LA 319, 323 (Baab, 1949).

not all promotions involve transfers, and certainly not all transfers involve promotions.

In concluding that the term "promotion" generally indicates movement to a higher job classification, one arbitrator referred to industrial practice, the practice of the particular parties, and the following definitions contained in a dictionary of labor terms:[569]

> "PROMOTION. Transfer of an employee to a higher job classification."
> "TRANSFER. Shift of an employee from one job to another within a Company. A lateral transfer is a change in an employee's job within a department, to another machine or to very similar duties."

Also pointing out that the term "promotion" refers to upward movement, another arbitrator stated that the term generally appears "in a context of collective bargaining agreements connoting an upward movement to a higher occupational classification requiring superior skills or greater effort and to which, for such reasons, a higher minimum wage scale is attached." He also noted that the term is "never associated with an outward or lateral movement of employees, to the operation of different machines, or the performances of different work drawing identical wage rates."[570] It has also been held that a lateral or downward movement could not be considered a promotion "even though such a movement may lead to higher pay, a job more to the liking of the worker, and a higher ultimate maximum pay."[571]

However, where an agreement provided that "Promotions to all vacancies" will be made on the basis of seniority and ability, an arbitrator followed the view that movement to a job with clearly better working conditions or from which advancement opportunities are or may be better, may be viewed as a "promotion" even though the job does not pay more.[572] Moreover, if the agreement provides for recognition of seniority in the filling of vacancies but does not use language which is reasonably clear in linking or limiting job vacancies and bidding procedures to promotion or advancement, the arbitrator may

---

[569]Pittsburgh Plate Glass Co., 30 LA 981, 982 (Kelliher, 1958), referring to the CCH Dictionary of Labor Terms. In another case that arbitrator found that the terms "promotion" and "transfer" had been defined by the contract. United States Steel Co., 21 LA 707, 708 (Kelliher, 1953).

[570]Bunker Hill & Sullivan Mining & Concentrating Co., 8 LA 1010, 1011 (Cheney, 1947), where he also stated that permitting an employee to select his job, machine, or place of work "would in effect be confiding the management of the business, and the direction of the working forces to employees to no small degree."

[571]Rochester Tel. Co., 26 LA 231, 234–235, 238 (Thompson, 1956), in which past practice was a factor in the decision. For other cases considering that lateral or downward movements are not promotions, see Arbitrator Lumbley in 77 LA 831, 836 (there was no upward movement requiring superior skills or greater effort for the work assignment in question, nor was a promotion indicated merely by the higher wage paid for the inconvenience of working at that location); Mullin in 54 LA 593, 595–596 (the contract expressly spoke of right to bid on "higher rated" jobs); Kates in 40 LA 1212, 1214–1215 (the contract provided that employees shall be "promoted" to fill vacancies and the arbitrator said that "in the absence of extraordinary conditions surrounding the opening for which a lateral or downward bid is made, such a bid * * * generally does not involve a 'promotion'"); Seward in 30 LA 550, 551; Reid in 26 LA 849, 852, and in 23 LA 159, 162; Kelliher in 23 LA 105, 107; Selekman in 12 LA 588, 591.

[572]Indiana Chair Co., 34 LA 856, 857–858 (Russell, 1960). Also see Arbitrator Marshall in 36 LA 570, 572; Hawley in 33 LA 719, 721; Pfaus in 24 LA 723, 724; Klamon in 18 LA 701, 711–712. Past practice supported the claimed right to lateral movement in Picker X-Ray Corp., 42 LA 179, 181–182 (Nichols, 1964). Seniority may not be disregarded by calling a promotion a merit increase. Bestwall Gypsum Co., 43 LA 475, 481 (Marshall, 1964).

hold that employees are entitled to exercise their seniority for lateral or downward movement.[573]

Management's general right to control promotions, except as limited by the collective agreement, was elaborated by Arbitrator Whitley P. McCoy as follows:

> "When there is no contract provision at all limiting the Company's rights in selecting men for promotion, the Company's rights, of course, are unlimited. If the only contract restriction is one against discrimination for Union activity, then that is the only restriction. In other words, absent a contract right in favor of the employees, or a contract restriction on a company, the latter may ignore not only seniority but also even skill, ability, and physical fitness. The employees must obtain benefits at the bargaining table, not from arbitrators. Arbitrators are bound by the contract under which they are arbitrating."[574]

The right of management to promote employees, however, is frequently qualified by the seniority provisions. The general problems encountered in the operation of "seniority" and "fitness and ability" clauses discussed in Chapter 14 apply here. There are, in addition, some other considerations which should be noted.

Temporary assignments to better jobs, such as may be made while incumbents are on vacation, may be held not to be "promotions" and thus not to require the application of contract seniority provisions governing promotions.[575] To require the recognition of seniority in such cases, it has been said, would impose a handicap and serious detriment to management in its direction of the working force.[576] Moreover, it has been held that management may compel designated employees to accept temporary promotion against their will.[577]

---

[573]For such holdings, see Arbitrator Ferguson in 77 LA 421, 423–424; Hayes in 55 LA 270, 272–274 (but employee must have a reasonable motive rather than "whim or fancy" for the move); King in 55 LA 89, 91; Altrock in 47 LA 952, 954–955 (fact that senior employee was needed more in present job could not defeat his right to fill vacancy by transfer); Crawford in 44 LA 10, 11–12; Marshall in 41 LA 329, 331; McIntosh in 40 LA 1305, 1307–1308; Slavney in 38 LA 371, 373; Cahn in 36 LA 785, 785–786. But see Arbitrator Doyle in 52 LA 733, 735–736 (contract construed to permit company to fill vacancies by lateral transfer but not to require it—clear language would be required to give employees a right of lateral transfer by seniority); McPherson in 48 LA 573, 575–576 (an express provision would be required to give employees an unqualified right to exercise seniority for downward movement); Gill in 44 LA 457, 458 (absent a local practice permitting it, employee could not exercise seniority for lateral or downward movement); Woodruff in 44 LA 7, 8–9; Pfaus in 24 LA 723, 723–724. In Tenn-Tex Alloy & Chem. Corp., 43 LA 152, 157–159 (Hebert, 1964), the term "any open job" was narrowed in scope by past practice.

[574]New Britain Mach. Co., 45 LA 993, 995–996 (1965). Also see Arbitrator Schuman in 68 LA 1178, 1179; Jones in 50 LA 455, 457–458; Kates in 46 LA 562, 565; Klein in 42 LA 165, 167–168; Bailer in 20 LA 835, 836; Beneduce in 17 LA 568, 569. Cf., Weiss in 75 LA 1298, 1299; Denson in 73 LA 90, 95. In Sun Oil Co., 52 LA 463, 468–469 (Abernethy, 1969), management could select a junior employee for temporary promotion to a supervisory job expressly excluded from the agreement. Also see Arbitrator High in 68 LA 837, 838.

[575]See Arbitrator Prasow in 24 LA 421, 423, and in 17 LA 644, 646–647; D'Andrade in 18 LA 932, 933, and in 12 LA 584, 585; Lohman in 5 LA 695, 696. Also see Chandler in 72 LA 340, 344–346; Collins in 70 LA 1048, 1050; Cayton in 45 LA 889, 890–891; Oppenheim in 44 LA 274, 279–280; Hebert in 33 LA 348, 350–351; Grant in 20 LA 202, 204. But see Seward in 47 LA 549, 551; Copelof in 20 LA 385, 393. For cases concerned with the application of "fitness and ability" requirements of seniority provisions in temporary promotions, see Arbitrator Daugherty in 38 LA 108, 110–111; Emery in 28 LA 733, 734–735; Warren in 21 LA 228, 231.

[576]Wilson & Co., 5 LA 695, 696 (Lohman, 1946).

[577]See Arbitrator Justin in 27 LA 877, 879–880; Ryder in 24 LA 132, 135–136; Howard in 18 LA 798, 801. Also see Cahn in 16 LA 767, 769. But see McCoy in 20 LA 281, 282; Blair in 8 LA 317,

However, management has not been permitted unilaterally to change qualifications customarily required for a job if the change would impair the right of senior employees to be promoted in accordance with the contract's promotion clause.[578] Also, management may not hold a successful bidder on his old job beyond a reasonable time to train his replacement.[579]

The general rule regarding the right of management to transfer employees was stated by Arbitrator David A. Wolff as follows: "Unless restricted by agreement, law, custom, practice, or estoppel, management has the right to effect transfers as a necessary element in the operation of its business."[580] Arbitrator Wolff also considered the right to transfer to be included within the right to direct the working force.[581]

Some agreements explicitly recognize management's right to transfer. While such agreements sometimes make the transfer right subject to other terms of the agreement, it appears that arbitrators generally require any restriction upon the right to be clearly stated.[582] However, management's right to transfer will be restricted to the extent that a limitation is necessary to preserve contractual rights of employees.[583] Thus, for instance, an employer could not require employees to transfer to service outside the unit covered by the collective agreement, for they otherwise might be stripped of rights under the agreement and be required to work under conditions over which they have no control.[584]

A transfer may be effected when the employer requires employees to rotate among jobs within their classification,[585] or to move from one

---

323. In Bethlehem Steel Co., 37 LA 1099, 1102–1103 (Valtin, 1962), the arbitrator concluded that employees could be required to accept temporary promotion but not permanent promotion. For cases holding that management could require senior employees to accept permanent promotion, see Arbitrator May in 75 LA 346, 352–353; Seinsheimer in 43 LA 1011, 1015–1017; Kelliher in 23 LA 105, 108–109. In Ethan Allen, 78 LA 343, 346 (1982), the agreement provided that employees "desiring consideration for a vacancy shall sign their names" at a specified place, and Arbitrator Hirschel Kasper stated that "the right to bid for a vacancy necessarily entails the right to not bid, unless * * * there is language to limit the exercise of that contractual right."

[578]See Arbitrator Howlett in 26 LA 885, 890–891; Stutz in 26 LA 289, 291; Frohlich in 14 LA 12, 16. Also see Gilden in 20 LA 142, 146–147.

[579]Columbus Bolt & Forging Co., 35 LA 215, 220 (Stouffer, 1960).

[580]Chrysler Corp., 6 LA 276, 281 (1947). Also see Arbitrator Newmark in 77 LA 49, 55; Van Pelt in 75 LA 498, 503; Beck in 68 LA 386, 389–390; Howlett in 52 LA 252, 254–255; Gibson in 49 LA 1115, 1117; Klein in 46 LA 450, 454–455; Gorsuch in 40 LA 879, 888; Murphy in 39 LA 1074, 1078–1079; Teple in 35 LA 162, 167; Doyle in 34 LA 179, 180; Sembower in 30 LA 290, 292; Seward in 28 LA 437, 438; Reid in 23 LA 159, 162; Kelliher in 23 LA 105, 107; Feinberg in 14 LA 83, 86; Hepburn in 9 LA 442, 443.

[581]Chrysler Corp., 6 LA 276, 281 (1947). Also see Arbitrator Foster in 81 LA 382, 383; Stockton in 33 LA 219, 223; Donnelly in 24 LA 399, 400; Kelliher in 23 LA 105, 107.

[582]See Arbitrator Eisler in 76 LA 516, 519; Larney in 74 LA 909, 910, 915; Williams in 45 LA 206, 209–210; Fallon in 44 LA 111, 113–114; Dunlop in 42 LA 911, 915; Morvant in 36 LA 1433, 1437; Wettach in 25 LA 629, 634; Singletary in 23 LA 456, 459; Copelof in 23 LA 67, 75; Uible in 11 LA 139, 142–143; Wagner in 8 LA 26, 29.

[583]See Arbitrator Lugar in 48 LA 463, 470–475; Hughes in 42 LA 809, 814; Stouffer in 40 LA 961, 964–965. In Sohio Chem. Co., 44 LA 624, 628 (Witney, 1965), permitting two employees to trade positions was held to violate the intent, if not the letter, of contractual provisions for job bidding; the arbitrator added that the employer could not have ordered the trade. Also see Arbitrator Brooks in 76 LA 1062, 1065–1066.

[584]Corte Constr. Co., 48 LA 463, 470–475 (Lugar, 1967), citing other cases in support of Arbitrator Lugar's conclusions. Also see Arbitrator Fields in 68 LA 448, 453.

[585]Simmons Co., 25 LA 194, 198 (Elson, 1955). Cf., Arbitrator Talent in 50 LA 1061, 1066.

shift to another,[586] or to move from one job to another in a different classification in the same job class,[587] or when the employee is moved to a new machine on the same job,[588] or to a new location for the same job.[589]

In the absence of a contract provision to the contrary, it has been held that the employer's right to transfer workers is not conditioned upon the willingness of the workers to be transferred,[590] and that the employer has the right to determine whether a transfer is temporary or permanent.[591] Moreover, management has been held to have the right and duty to transfer an employee if his presence in a given occupation creates some undue hazard for himself or others.[592] Various other justifications have similarly been accepted by arbitrators in upholding transfers required by management.[593] However, the right to transfer as a form of discipline appears to be definitely limited.[594]

Demotion of Employees

The collective agreement may specifically recognize the right of demotion as belonging to management. Also the right may be held to be included with a general management rights clause, as, for example, one giving management the right to select, assign, and direct the working force and to promote and transfer employees.[595] Then, too, the right may be held to remain in management, except as restricted by the agreement, as a residual power.[596] In many cases the arbitrator

---

[586]Midland Rubber Co., 18 LA 590, 593 (Cheney, 1952). Also see Arbitrator Graff in 69–2 ARB ¶8610. Employees have no right to exercise their seniority for shift preference unless the right clearly exists under a contract provision or past practice. See Arbitrator Newmark in 77 LA 49, 54–55; Van Pelt in 75 LA 498, 502, 504; Pointer in 49 LA 527, 529; Doyle in 44 LA 718, 719; Updegraff in 38 LA 103, 104; Sanders in 36 LA 92, 94–95 (past practice was shown); Platt in 19 LA 199, 200.

[587]Bethlehem Steel Co., 28 LA 437, 437–438 (Seward, 1957).

[588]Gisholt Mach. Co., 23 LA 105, 107 (Kelliher, 1954). Also see Arbitrator Stashower in 37 LA 591, 593.

[589]Phillips Petroleum Co., 34 LA 179, 180 (Doyle, 1960).

[590]See Arbitrator Beck in 68 LA 386, 389–390; Murphy in 39 LA 1074, 1078–1079; Teple in 35 LA 162, 167; Seward in 28 LA 437, 438; Donnelly in 24 LA 399, 400. Also see Goldsmith in 73 LA 372, 375–376; Kahn in 44 LA 1196, 1201.

[591]Jones & Laughlin Steel Corp., 23 LA 33, 36 (Cahn, 1954). For some possible tests for distinguishing between permanent and temporary transfer, see Continental Can Co., 37 LA 386, 388–389 (Sembower, 1961).

[592]International Shoe Co., 14 LA 253, 255 (Wallen, 1950). Similarly upholding management, see Arbitrator Strongin in 64 LA 380, 381; Guse in 50 LA 476, 487; Teple in 49 LA 649, 651; Siegel in 35 LA 103, 105, 109. Cf., Coles in 48 LA 533, 538–539.

[593]See Arbitrator Flagler in 79 LA 203, 207; Weisberger in 69 LA 1138, 1142 (personality clash); Teple in 49 LA 346, 350–351 (personality clash between employee and foreman); Williams in 45 LA 229, 233 (incompetence); Holly in 40 LA 1025, 1027 (need for more direct supervision of indifferent employees). But the justification for involuntary transfer was not accepted by Arbitrator Talarico in 76 LA 562, 565; Wissner in 38 LA 838, 846–847.

[594]See Arbitrator Belcher in 53 LA 410, 413; Johnson in 49 LA 1061, 1062; Kelliher in 47 LA 1162, 1163–1164; Stutz in 30 LA 505, 506; Montgomery in 26 LA 546, 549; Stashower in 16 LA 922, 926. Similarly, see statement and recommendation of Fact-Finder Sembower in Area Educ. Agency 12, 72 LA 916, 927 (1979). Cf., Arbitrator Foster in 81 LA 382, 383.

[595]Drug Prods. Co., 10 LA 804, 805 (Naggi, 1948). Similarly, see Arbitrator Jaffe in 78 LA 1160, 1163; Bridgewater in 71 LA 479, 480, 487; Whyte in 51 LA 192, 195; Duff in 66–3 ARB ¶9060; France in 43 LA 934 at 934, 938.

[596]See E.I. DuPont de Nemours & Co., 17 LA 580, 585 (Cornsweet, 1951). Also see Arbitrator Leeper in 71 LA 659, 666; Whyte in 51 LA 192, 195; Whiting in 7 LA 150, 152.

does not expressly state any particular source of the right to demote, the arbitrator merely upholding management if it has acted on some reasonable basis in making a demotion.[597] The right to demote, however, has been held to be subject to the limitation that it may not be exercised in an arbitrary, capricious, or discriminatory manner.[598]

The right to demote has sometimes been found to have been contracted away. Such was the case, for instance, under a clause providing that wage rates fixed by the contract should be continued during the term of the contract, since the contractual wage rates were established on the basis of specific individuals.[599] A clause requiring promotions to be made on the basis of ability and seniority was interpreted to require the same for demotions, the arbitrator stating that otherwise the promotion clause would be meaningless as employees could be demoted immediately after promotion.[600] Management was also denied the right to demote under an agreement which was silent with respect to demotion and which provided permanent job status for employees surviving a trial period on the job, the employer being held required to lay off employees in slack periods rather than to demote.[601]

In considering an agreement that was silent on the matter of demotion for lack of qualifications, Umpire Harry Shulman stated that it may be assumed that, in the interest of achieving optimum performance, management may make periodic or sporadic appraisals of its employees and demote those whose performance falls below standard. Elaborating, he said:

> "We may assume further that the obligation to perform satisfactorily is a continuous condition of the maintenance of the better job and that an employee's performance, though once adequate, may fall below standard and merit demotion, either because his own performance has deteriorated or, though it has not deteriorated, because the standard in his occupation has been raised by the greater ability of those around him. Such a demotion would be an instance of the Company's continuing interest in the satisfactory performance of each of its jobs."[602]

---

[597]For example, see Arbitrator Falcone in 76 LA 1161, 1163–1164; Seinsheimer in 55 LA 1025, 1027–1029; Gorsuch in 48 LA 429, 437; King in 45 LA 793, 796.

[598]See Arbitrator Goodman in 73 LA 497, 504; Leeper in 71 LA 659, 666; Roberts in 55 LA 261, 268–270; Whyte in 51 LA 192, 195; Malkin in 49 LA 663, 665; Hawley in 26 LA 245, 248; Hale in 24 LA 470, 483; Shister in 19 LA 671, 673.

[599]National Vulcanized Fibre Co., 3 LA 259, 263 (Kaplan, 1946). Also see Arbitrator Aaron in 9 LA 419, 421.

[600]Raytheon Mfg. Co., 15 LA 291, 295 (Healy, 1950). Also see Arbitrator McIntosh in 67 LA 1315, 1316; Roberts in 55 LA 261, 267–270; Hale in 24 LA 470, 483. Cf., Shister in 19 LA 671, 673.

[601]Merrill-Stevens Dry Dock & Repair Co., 10 LA 88, 90 (McCoy, 1948). Similarly, see Armstrong Bros. Tool Co., 65 LA 258, 260 (1975), where Arbitrator Carroll R. Daugherty stated that "however unreasonable in general it might seem to deny to management its traditional right to demote or permanently transfer an employee for proper cause, the Arbitrator is compelled to hold that under the language of this particular Agreement, agreed to by both Parties, this particular Company's management did not possess said right * * * ."

[602]Ford Motor Co., Opinions of the Umpire, Opinion A-30 (1943). In Wheatland Tube Co., 66 LA 247, 248 (1976), Arbitrator Marvin J. Feldman stated the general proposition as follows: "The Company must maintain its competitive place in the market. If the Company was forced to keep incompetent personnel, there would be no jobs for anyone. Management is charged with the efficient operation of the facility. One of the elements of maintaining that efficiency is to remove inefficient personnel." Also permitting demotion for incompetence or lack of qualifications: Arbitrator Goodman in 73 LA 497, 505–506; Seinsheimer in 55 LA 1025, 1028–1029; McKenna in 54 LA 998, 1007 (mere fact that contract expressly authorizes employee's return to his former job

In downgrading for lack of qualifications shortly after an employee begins performing a different job, management may be required to show by substantial proof that the employee is not qualified and cannot qualify for the job within a reasonable time.[603] Where an employee has occupied a job for a long period of time, it has been held that management must show that the employee is no longer able or willing to perform his job duties.[604] However, it has been held that the mere fact that an employee has been retained in a job for a number of years does not necessarily warrant a finding by the arbitrator that he was qualified for it.[605]

A lack of qualifications has been found by the arbitrator, and demotion therefore considered justified, for example, where a truck driver's operator's license was revoked,[606] where the employee was unable to perform the job duties satisfactorily,[607] where the employee was physically or psychologically unable to perform the job duties or was unable to perform them safely,[608] and where a leadman displayed

---

if he is found unqualified at end of trial period does not guarantee that he will be retained in the new job once he passes the trial period); Whyte in 51 LA 192, 195; McDermott in 48 LA 1108, 1111–1112; Gorsuch in 48 LA 429, 437; Duff in 66–3 ARB ¶9060; Block in 47 LA 1001, 1009; King in 45 LA 793, 796; McCoy in 44 LA 1180, 1181; Stouffer in 38 LA 882, 886–887; Uible in 9 LA 77, 80; Abernethy in 7 LA 202, 225. Also see May in 74 LA 906, 909; Harter in 74 LA 896, 901 (stating that "outlasting" the probationary period "does not mean that an employee has a job for life regardless whether he is competent," and upholding the discharge of an employee who had refused the employer's offer of a less demanding job); Platt in 47 LA 1015, 1017; Pollard in 10 LA 498, 508 (demotion for incompetence permitted under contract permitting demotion for "cause"). As between demotion or discharge of unqualified employees, an arbitrator may consider demotion to be the solution that gives fair consideration to the legitimate interests of both management and the employee. See Arbitrator Sembower in 53 LA 357, 360; Tsukiyama in 48 LA 218, 222–223; Dworkin in 40 LA 1054, 1060, all involving formerly qualified employees whose abilities have deteriorated. For a like view where the employee does not perform satisfactorily after promotion, see Arbitrator Klein in 73 LA 20, 27–28; Kamin in 46 LA 539, 543–544; Schedler in 34 LA 860, 863. Cf., Griffin in 77 LA 60, 65–66. For the related discussion of failure to meet production standards, see topic entitled "Production Standards, Time Studies, and Job Evaluation" above. For other related discussion, see topic entitled "Disqualifying Employees for Physical or Mental Reasons" below.

[603]United Aircraft Prods. Inc., 10 LA 143, 146 (Wardlaw, 1948). Similarly, see Arbitrator Roberts in 55 LA 261, 269–270; Nicholas in 51 LA 1300, 1302–1303; Howlett in 35 LA 545, 548. Also see Shister in 38 LA 861, 864–865. Cf., Kubie in 79 LA 1006, 1010–1011; Bridgewater in 71 LA 479, 487–488 (stating that "the Union did not sustain its burden of proving that the Grievant did not, in fact, receive a full break-in," or "its burden of proving that the removal [of Grievant from the] classification for inability was inappropriate").

[604]Dewey & Almy Chem. Co., 25 LA 316, 322 (Somers, 1955). Also see Arbitrator Leeper in 71 LA 659, 666; Moberly in 55 LA 69, 73; McDermott in 48 LA 67, 68–69; Hale in 24 LA 470, 484; Komaroff in 17 LA 784, 789. For cases dealing with the necessity for warning the employee that his work is poor, see Arbitrator Leeper in 71 LA 659, 666; McKenna in 54 LA 998, 1008–1009; Burris in 25 LA 32, 36; Kelliher in 18 LA 447, 449; Komaroff in 17 LA 784, 789.

[605]E.I. DuPont de Nemours & Co., 17 LA 580, 586–587 (Cornsweet, 1951). Similarly, see Arbitrator Simon in 53 LA 1181, 1192. Also see Keeler in 36 LA 970, 973–974; Duff in 29 LA 167, 170.

[606]Virginia-Carolina Chem. Corp., 18 LA 892, 895 (Hepburn, 1952). In J.A. McMahon Co., 44 LA 1274, 1277–1279 (Dworkin, 1964), an employee's physical condition made him uninsurable and this was a "legitimate" reason for placing him on layoff status under the contract.

[607]See Arbitrator Clarke in 71 LA 1232, 1235; Block in 49 LA 1144, 1147; Malkin in 49 LA 663, 665; France in 43 LA 934, 938; Willingham in 41 LA 40, 46 (employee could not do all elements of job due to fear of heights); Duff in 29 LA 167, 170; Wolff in 27 LA 682, 684; Hawley in 26 LA 245, 248; Morris in 24 LA 745, 746; Cornsweet in 17 LA 580, 586–587. Also see Falcone in 76 LA 1161, 1163–1164.

[608]See Arbitrator Strongin in 80 LA 28 at 28 (stating that management "is not required to keep on the job an employee who cannot perform 100 percent of it"); Jaffe in 78 LA 1160, 1163; Simon in 53 LA 1181, 1192; Killingsworth in 47 LA 146, 150; Murphy in 44 LA 1252, 1263; Porter in 42 LA 137, 138; Autrey in 41 LA 519, 523; Tripp in 41 LA 112, 116–117; Ryder in 38 LA 105, 107; Keeler in 36 LA 970, 973–974; Copelof in 7 LA 560, 563–564. Also see Davey in 55 LA 1206, 1214

racial prejudice in a plant employing many blacks.[609] In the latter instance, the arbitrator said that the employee's prejudice "made it clear that he could no longer do an effective job as leadman." One arbitrator, however, refused to permit the company to demote an employee for lack of qualifications where the company was aware of the employee's shortcomings at the time of his promotion but promoted him in spite of them. The promotion was not made on a trial basis, and the employee's work was no worse after the promotion than it had been before.[610]

Some arbitrators have held that management may not use demotion as a form of discipline unless the agreement specifically so provides, since such action would violate the contract seniority rights of the employees.[611] It was held in one case, for instance, that management did not have the right to use temporary demotion as a means of discipline for negligence in job performance (as opposed to lack of ability to perform the job), where such discipline was not provided for specifically by the agreement and where the demoted employee's position was temporarily filled by a junior employee in contravention of the seniority clause. The arbitrator said:

> "The company's right to discipline flows from the general managerial prerogative recognized in the management clause. In accordance with established legal construction, the exercise of such general prerogatives is limited by the specific clauses in the labor agreement. Thus, management in exercising its general prerogatives lacks the contractual right to abridge designated contractual privileges of the employees covered by the agreement unless specific provision is made for [such] * * * ."[612]

Management has also been denied the right to discipline an employee by demotion where the contract gave the employer the right to discipline employees by various specified means which did not include demotion, on the theory of "expressio unius est exclusio

---

(demotion upheld though failure to take required training course was due to employee's nervous condition). Cf., Arbitrator Horlacher in 39 LA 107, 110–113 (demotion based primarily upon workmen's compensation medical reports and award). In Simoniz Co., 54 LA 172, 174–175 (Talent, 1969), an employee claimed (unsuccessfully) a contractual right to demotion on the basis of his alleged physical condition.

[609]North Am. Aviation, 20 LA 789, 794 (Komaroff, 1953). In Pacific Gas & Elec. Co., 48 LA 264, 266 (Koven, 1966), a service man who made improper advances to a female customer could be demoted from his public-contact job.

[610]Bethlehem Steel Co., 18 LA 368, 369 (Feinberg, 1951). Also see Arbitrator Emery in 37 LA 973, 975. For cases dealing with how long a period management may be permitted to determine the fitness of an employee who has been promoted, see Arbitrator Owen in 49 LA 669, 672; Burns in 48 LA 270, 272.

[611]See Arbitrator Moberly in 55 LA 69, 72–73; McDermott in 48 LA 1108, 1111 (also noting the view that disciplinary demotion may be viewed as an indeterminate sentence which has no terminal point and may go far beyond the extent of the penalty warranted by the infraction committed); Kelliher in 48 LA 454, 456; Kesselman in 47 LA 154, 157–158; Rosen in 47 LA 67, 73; Dworkin in 46 LA 1098, 1105; Blumer in 6 LA 379, 382. Also see Reid in 33 LA 108, 110; Hawley in 26 LA 245, 247–248. Cf., Whyte in 74 LA 565, 567–568; Talent in 74 LA 80, 86–87; Altieri in 39 LA 1143, 1147. Arbitrators have reached different conclusions as to whether disciplinary demotion is permitted under a clause giving the right to "demote" for "cause." See Arbitrator Crawford in Lukens Steel Co., 42 LA 252, 254 (1963), not permitting it; Updegraff in Macomber, Inc., 37 LA 1061, 1063–1064 (1961), permitting it.

[612]American Steel & Wire Co., 6 LA 379, 382 (Blumer, 1946).

alterius."[613] Management likewise has not been upheld in demoting an employee for occasional carelessness or failure to obey instructions, the arbitrator distinguishing between a lack of ability and temporary poor performance, but recognizing that some form of discipline should be imposed in such a case.[614]

On the other hand, management has been held justified in using demotion as a form of discipline where the employee's refusal to obey a work order was typical of his uncooperative attitude and the contract did not set out any particular methods of discipline,[615] and where demotion of the employee was deemed necessary as a safety measure.[616] Furthermore, Arbitrator J.D. O'Shea expressed the view that demotion *for a fixed period* should be available to management as a disciplinary measure whenever the employee would be subject to disciplinary suspension:

> "Although I am aware that some arbitrators have expressed the opinion that demotion is an inappropriate disciplinary response, I cannot accept this view. If an employer can suspend an employee for disciplinary reasons, it logically follows that the employer has the right to suspend such an employee from his regular job and place him in a lower rated job for disciplinary reasons. Indeed, * * * the collective agreement in this matter specifically provides that the employer may relieve an employee from duty 'for other legitimate reasons.' However that may be, a disciplinary demotion, like a suspension, should be for a definite period of time if it is to be corrective discipline rather than mere punishment."[617]

Finally, it has been emphasized that if demotion is used as discipline, the contract's procedural requirements for discipline must be met.[618]

Discharge and Discipline

The right of management to discipline or discharge employees has been dealt with extensively by arbitrators and is a subject to which a

---

[613]See Reynolds Alloys Co., 2 LA 554, 555 (McCoy, 1943). Also see Arbitrator Kelliher in 48 LA 454, 456; Dworkin in 46 LA 1098, 1105; McCoy in 14 LA 882, 883. Also see Chapter 9, topic entitled "To Express One Thing Is to Exclude Another."

[614]Republic Steel Corp., 25 LA 733, 735 (Platt, 1955). Similarly, see Arbitrator Keefe in 70 LA 195, 197–198 (quoting a textbook discussion of distinctions between "careless work" and "incompetence"); Moberly in 55 LA 69, 73; Valtin in 28 LA 330, 332. In Greater Cleveland Transit Auth., 71 LA 27, 28 (Young, 1978), applicable Merit System Rules permitted discharge or discipline for acts of "misfeasance, malfeasance, or nonfeasance," but also expressly permitted disciplinary demotion rather than discharge where the offending employee "is considered worthy of a trial in a lower grade."

[615]Lewers & Cooke, 30 LA 542, 545 (Cobb, 1958). Also permitting demotion as discipline, see Arbitrator Yagoda in 46 LA 1034, 1038–1039; Altieri in 39 LA 1143, 1147; Lehoczky in 8 LA 923, 924 (the arbitrator did not speak of "discipline" but the demotion was clearly disciplinary).

[616]See Arbitrator Mann in 68 LA 46, 50–51; Strongin in 64 LA 380, 381; Steele in 61 LA 765, 768; Somers in 61 LA 617, 621 (permitting temporary demotion, possibly to become permanent); Yeager in 29 LA 487, 488–489; Donnelly & Mottram in 18 LA 457, 458–459 (Curry dissenting). Also see O'Shea in 68 LA 613, 617–618; Tongue in 36 LA 1038, 1041; Morgan in 17 LA 328, 329.

[617]Libby, McNeill & Libby of Can., 74 LA 991, 998 (1980).

[618]Alexander's Mkts., 51 LA 165, 168, 170 (Levin, 1968). Also see Arbitrator Whyte in 74 LA 565, 568.

separate chapter is devoted in this book. For discussion of discharge and discipline the reader is directed to Chapter 15.

For discussion of nondisciplinary termination of employees the reader is directed to the present Chapter, topics entitled "Compulsory Retirement" and "Disqualifying Employees for Physical or Mental Reasons."

Merit Increases

Merit rating is concerned not with the what an employee does but with how he does it. Thus, it may be immaterial that some employees receive a higher rate than others doing the same work.[619] Furthermore, in determining eligibility for merit increases, there is no presumption of progress or improvement due solely to passage of time.[620]

The collective agreement may make specific provision for merit increases.[621] In this regard, Arbitrator Dudley E. Whiting observed:

"It is well established that merit increases are an appropriate subject for collective bargaining, and bargaining thereon frequently results in contractual provisions establishing objective standards for merit increases or fixing a regular review period or making such increases subject to review or negotiation by the union, or other types of such provisions."[622]

Where a collective agreement specified minimum wage rates for classifications and provided for a ten-cent-per-hour premium over the rates shown "for an employee in any of such classifications who achieves and applies a high degree of proficiency in all phases of his work, as determined by the Employer," Arbitrator Gerald G. Somers held that this specific provision for rewarding meritorious service implied that it was the only means of giving individual merit increases without negotiations.[623] Arbitrator Somers also expressed the view that, absent a clause expressly giving management such

---

[619]Bethlehem Steel Co., 21 LA 614, 616 (Feinberg, 1953); International Harvester Co., 14 LA 77, 79 (Seward, 1948). For arguments against permitting merit increases, see American Bakeries Co., 68 LA 414, 417 (Schatzki, 1977). On the question whether merit increases may terminate when the employee transfers to a different job, see Whittaker Corp., 63 LA 193, 196 (Rybolt, 1974), where past practice controlled the result.

[620]Ralph C. Coxhead Corp., 21 LA 480, 483 (Cahn, 1953). In Koehring Co., 65 LA 638, 640 (1975), Arbitrator Thomas Joseph Coyne stressed that "A 'merit' pay raise means just that. It is something awarded a person for meritorious service. It is not a right to which one is entitled by virtue of his presence on the payroll." In contrast, in considering a "longevity related" compensation system in Morris Bean & Co., 69 LA 615, 620 (1977), Arbitrator Alan Miles Ruben stated: "The Company argues that longevity related compensation systems intrinsically presuppose that an employee will continue regularly working at his job increasing in skill and experience over time and thereby becoming more valuable to his employer. This view is reinforced where * * * the parties provide that employees must work a specified percentage of the available working time in order to qualify for the periodic wage increases." Also see Arbitrator Cox in 64 LA 547, 548. Cf., Solomon in 57 LA 503, 509.

[621]As did the agreement involved in Davis Co., 41 LA 932, 933 (Holly, 1963), where the arbitrator emphasized that the word "merit" implies increases, not decreases, in pay under a clause authorizing management to fix wages of individual employees "on a basis of merit."

[622]Sommers & Adams Co., 6 LA 283, 285 (1947).

[623]J. Gruman Steel Co., 54 LA 521, 522, 524–525 (1970). Also see Valve Corp. of Am., 48 LA 869, 871–872 (Johnson, 1967).

right, management cannot unilaterally give individual increases under any agreement which contains a wage schedule.[624]

However, in another case Arbitrator Thomas J. McDermott rejected a union contention that merit increases were no longer a matter of unilateral determination by management (as they had been by past practice) after minimum and maximum salary ranges were written into the collective agreement. Arbitrator McDermott explained:

> "It should be noted that the subject of merit increases has long been an appropriate subject for collective bargaining. Therefore, a Union is within its rights when it seeks to negotiate contractual provisions that will eliminate an existing merit wage increase program, modify it, or that will establish contractual procedures for the operation of any such program. However, if the Union fails to negotiate such contractual provisions, it is not within the power of an arbitrator, absent mutual permission of the parties, either to abolish an existing merit increase system or to write procedures into the contract as to how such system will be administered.
>
> * * *
>
> "* * * [W]hat the Union negotiated into the 1968 contract was a set of rate ranges to apply to salaried workers in the bargaining unit. Nothing was agreed to that relates to how individual employees would move from the bottom job rate in his class to the upper limit. In the absence of any such contractual language, and in view of the past practice that has prevailed at this plant, this determination still remains a function of management. In such circumstances the conclusions of management with respect to the granting of specific merit increases are not generally subject to successful challenge in arbitration unless it can be shown in individual cases that management acted unfairly, arbitrarily, discriminatorily, or completely unreasonable. This has long been the generally-held principle in arbitration. Thus, the negotiation of the rate ranges did not, as the Union contends, eliminate the merit increase system. The very presence of a rate range requires either that the maximum rate be achieved through a prescribed procedure, usually referred to as automatic progression, or in the absence of joint agreement on such procedure, the movement from bottom to top remains subject to the evaluation of management.
>
> "* * * There is no right in the existing agreement for the Union to insist that the Company negotiate individual merit increase cases. The most that can be required is that, given the requirement in Paragraph 2 of the intent to establish a harmonious relationship, the Company has the obligation to discuss cases with the Union and to explain the Company position. It does not have to secure Union agreement, and it retains the right to make the final determination. As long as that determination

---

[624]J. Gruman Steel Co., 54 LA 521, 525 (1970). Similarly, see Arbitrator Ruben in 69 LA 615, 621; Lee in 42 LA 426, 428–429. Even where a unilateral right of management to give merit increases on an individual basis is conceded, this does not include the right to give a blanket increase to a group of employees. Atlanta Newspapers, 43 LA 758, 759–760 (King, 1964). As to group increases, also see Arbitrator Carson in 73 LA 599, 602; Caraway in 65 LA 178, 181; Thomson in 62 LA 1036, 1039–1040. In NLRB v. C & C Plywood, 87 S.Ct. 559 (1967), the contract expressly recognized management's right to give individual merit increases but this did not include the right to give group increases. The case concerned the duty to bargain under the NLRA. For further discussion, see subtopic entitled "The Duty to Bargain: Right of Unilateral Action" above.

was not arbitrary, unfair, discriminatory or very unreasonable it is not subject to being overruled."[625]

Many other arbitrators have similarly recognized that where the collective agreement contains no provision regarding the granting of merit increases or where it makes provision for merit increases without stating by whom the initial determination is to be made, the determination of when individual employees should be given merit increases still remains the function of management.[626]

Where management has the right to make this determination (regardless of the source of the right), it appears clear that its conclusions in regard to merit increases are not generally subject to successful challenge in arbitration unless unfair, arbitrary, or discriminatory,[627] or unless the decision is based upon a misconception of existing facts or insufficient evidence.[628] In this general connection, Arbitrator I. Robert Feinberg stated:

"[M]erit is difficult to prove and the parties themselves, through daily observation of the employee, have usually gained greater knowledge of the employee's abilities and efficiency than the Umpire can ever have. In the absence of detailed proof, a third party is generally not in a position to determine whether an employee has demonstrated increased efficiency or whether the quality of his work has improved. It is recognized that that determination can best be made by the employee's supervisor, who is closest to the employee in these matters."[629]

Under certain circumstances management may be required to review employee merit ratings at reasonable intervals. This was the

---

[625]H.K. Porter Co., 55 LA 593, 595–596 (1970). In Means Stamping Co., 46 LA 324, 326 (Cole, 1966), the contract stated maximum and minimum rates for classifications and it was held that management could not give merit increases which would result in rates above the specified maximum.

[626]See Arbitrator Seidenberg in 41 LA 314, 315; Wood in 40 LA 143, 145–146; Feinberg in 21 LA 614, 616; Beneduce in 17 LA 568, 569–570; Luskin in 15 LA 180, 181–182; Townsend in 15 LA 4, 12; Updegraff in 10 LA 678, 680; Abernethy in 7 LA 202, 217; Whiting in 6 LA 283, 285; Gorder in 3 LA 1, 3. Also see Light in 75 LA 135, 137; Deitsch in 74 LA 1090, 1093, 1095; Fish in 70 LA 403, 408; Kates in 45 LA 153, 155–156; Porter in 40 LA 411, 413; Cahn in 14 LA 96, 102. This right may be held to be included within a general management rights clause (see Arbitrator Erbs in 73 LA 181, 194, and Platt in 9 LA 91, 94–95), or it may be given specifically to management by the agreement (see Arbitrator Seward in 26 LA 824, 826, and Bernstein in 14 LA 139, 142).

[627]See Arbitrator Erbs in 73 LA 181, 184; Denson in 70 LA 514, 517–518; Kaye in 69 LA 1239, 1242; Marshall in 64 LA 663, 667–668; Allen in 60 LA 852, 856–857; Cayton in 50 LA 296, 298; Kates in 48 LA 606, 608; Altrock in 47 LA 126, 128; Stouffer in 40 LA 452, 454–456; Wood in 40 LA 143, 146; McIntosh in 39 LA 799, 800; Feinberg in 21 LA 614, 616; Cahn in 21 LA 480, 482–483 (who considered criteria used by management in evaluating eligibility for merit increases); Bernstein in 14 LA 139, 143; Updegraff in 10 LA 678, 680; Platt in 9 LA 91, 95–96; Abernethy in 7 LA 202, 217.

[628]Bethlehem Steel Co., 21 LA 614, 616 (Feinberg, 1953); Atlas Imperial Diesel Engine Co., 3 LA 1, 4 (Gorder, 1946). In Dahlstrom Mfg. Corp., 39 LA 90, 92 (Duff, 1961), the contract expressly required management to state its reason for refusing a merit increase; the arbitrator said that this "strongly implies that Management's reason must not be arbitrary, capricious or discriminatory. When challenged in Arbitration, the Company should show that its reason is based on evidence and standards that are reasonable, demonstrable and objective." Also see Arbitrator Marshall in 64 LA 663, 668.

[629]Bethlehem Steel Co., 21 LA 614, 616 (1953). Similar language was used by Arbitrator Denson in 70 LA 514, 517–518; Duff in 39 LA 90, 92 ("Management's discretion must be heavily relied upon because no other rule is practicable"); Cahn in 21 LA 480, 483; Warren in 16 LA 508, 509; Bernstein in 14 LA 139, 143.

result under an agreement which, in providing for merit increases, gave management the right to make initial determinations but required management to be "fair,"[630] and it was also the result under another agreement which permitted the company to determine merit increases subject only to the restriction that the determination not be [. . .]ricious.[631] Of course, as noted above, the contract may [. . .]vide for periodic review of each employee's rate and

Bonuses

[. . .] have ruled both ways on the question of the right of [. . .] the absence of contractual limitation, unilaterally to [. . .]r bonus practices.[633]

[. . .]re the facts indicated that the bonus had become an [. . .]he wage structure, thus constituting a deferred wage [. . .]ators have held that management may not uni- [. . .]te or alter bonus plans, despite the fact that bonuses [. . .]ed in the contract.[634] The presence of several or all of [. . .]s of evidence would tend to indicate that a bonus has [. . .]al part of wages: long usage; treatment by the com- [. . .]yments as relevant considerations during contract [. . .]age calculations (such as vacation pay), or in hiring; [. . .]pany to make it clear that the bonus was a gift or [. . .]y and predictability of the amount of the bonus; [. . .] to work performed by the employee; payment of the [. . .]y as to create an expectation by the employees at the

[. . .] hand, in cases where the facts indicated that the [. . .]ity given at the discretion of management and not [. . .]es, management was permitted unilaterally to alter [. . .] bonus plan in the absence of contractual

[handwritten marginal note, right side: "can it be modified"]

[handwritten card, left side: "Changing Past Practice — Chapter 12   437-456; Dating Past Prac.   360; Mgmt Rights – Plant Rules   553; Abstention   692; No providing pract.   817; Burg Huot   843"]

[630]International Harvester Co., 13 LA 809, 812 (Seward, 1949).

[631]Bethlehem Steel Co., 26 LA 824, 826 (Seward, 1956).

[632]As in Domore Office Furniture, 58 LA 817, 818 (Ray, 1972); Pacific Airmotive Corp., 16 LA 508, 508–509 (Warren, 1951). For related discussion, see Chapter 14, subtopic entitled "Merit Rating Plans."

[633]For important related materials, see Chapter 12, topic entitled "Custom and Practice as Part of the Contract."

[634]See Arbitrator Lee in 69 LA 1250, 1254; Gundermann in 65 LA 810, 815; Fitzsimmons in 64 LA 571, 575; Kerrison in 62 LA 637, 639; Anrod in 45 LA 34, 37–38; Seitz in 43 LA 892, 894–896; Horlacher in 43 LA 145, 149–151; Ellmann in 42 LA 415, 416; Berkowitz in 41 LA 182, 184; Crawford in 36 LA 1335, 1340, and in 34 LA 732, 739–740; Dash in 22 LA 808, 818–819; Justin in 17 LA 505, 509–510; Prasow in 5 LA 564, 571; Courshon in 2 LA 509, 514; McCoy in 2 LA 483, 490. Also see Stutz in 29 LA 400, 404; Sullivan in 25 LA 165, 170; Lehoczky in 15 LA 618, 622, all involving contract clauses providing for payment of bonuses to employees.

[635]See cases cited in note 634 above. Maintenance of benefits clauses have had some weight in some cases (see Arbitrator Emery in 65-2 ARB ¶8464; Ellmann in 42 LA 415, 416; Berkowitz in 41 LA 182, 184), but not in others (see Duff in 62 LA 209, 211; Stein in 42 LA 765, 766; Singer in 33 LA 139, 140; Klamon in 32 LA 395, 399–400), depending upon other supporting evidence.

gift—no neg. required [handwritten margin note, rotated]

restriction.[636] The presence of several or all of the following types of evidence would tend to indicate that the bonus is a gift: annual consideration and vote by the board of directors as to whether, when, and how much to pay; distribution of bonus checks separately from paychecks; variation in amount or nature of the bonus; payment to all employees without having previously announced a bonus plan; statements posted by the company that bonus payments are discretionary and union acquiescence in some way to such statements.[637]

The development of the concept of the compulsory bargaining obligation, treated earlier in this Chapter, has a bearing on what individual arbitrators will do with respect to this type of matter.

Compulsory Retirement

In the earlier cases on compulsory retirement due to age, arbitrators often stated that is was a general principle that in the absence of specific contractual restriction management has the right unilaterally to establish compulsory retirement plans (in some of these cases the arbitrator expressly denied that compulsory retirement would violate the seniority or discharge provisions of the agreement).[638] However, in upholding compulsory retirement these arbitrators and others (who did not state such general principle) usually emphasized the fact that the plan under consideration was of long standing; that it had been established and administered without objection from the union; and that it had been administered without arbitrariness, discrimination, or caprice.[639] On the other hand, where

---

[636]See Arbitrator Williams in 79 LA 334, 336; Render in 67 LA 493, 496; Duff in 62 LA 209, 211–212; Larkin in 55 LA 329, 335–336; Eaton in 51 LA 533, 536–537; Small in 46 LA 1077, 1078; Singer in 46 LA 472, 472–473, and in 33 LA 139, 140; Stein in 42 LA 765, 766; Russell in 42 LA 417, 419–420; Kelliher in 42 LA 331, 332–333; McIntosh in 38 LA 216, 217; Duff in 34 LA 586, 592, and in 32 LA 388, 392–393; Klamon in 32 LA 395, 399–401; Kheel in 26 LA 627, 628–630; Kharas in 25 LA 853, 855–856; Delehanty in 24 LA 500, 506; Cheney in 8 LA 518, 526; Cahn in 6 LA 654. Under particular contract clauses providing for a bonus, a bonus may nevertheless be considered a gratuity. See Cheney in 10 LA 341, 344; Epstein in 3 LA 412, 418. In T & M Rubber Specialties Co., 54 LA 292, 296–298 (Sembower, 1970), the arbitrator concluded that the bonus was not a gratuity but that he could not make an award in favor of the employees since the amount for payment as bonuses had been determined by the board of directors in the past depending on "success of year"; he directed the parties to bargain on the matter.

[637]See cases cited in note 636 above.

[638]See Arbitrator Prasow in 27 LA 153, 156; Shister in 25 LA 50, 52–53; Reynolds in 13 LA 326, 328–329; Gregory in 9 LA 560, 561; Gorsuch in 9 LA 124, 126; Ridge in 7 LA 773, 778; Kirsh in 4 LA 601, 603–604.

[639]Again, see the cases cited in note 638 above. For cases in which the arbitrator emphasized these facts while not stating the aforementioned principle, see Arbitrator Ferguson in 70 LA 245, 249–250; Caraway in 66 LA 1207, 1210–1211; Prasow in 50 LA 645, 657; Gilden in 46 LA 302, 305, and in 22 LA 732, 735–736; Schedler in 29 LA 541, 543–545, and in 27 LA 669, 671; Shipman in 23 LA 214, 216–217; McConnell in 17 LA 587, 589; Lehoczky in 14 LA 490, 491–492. In United States Steel Corp. v. Nichols, 229 F.2d 396, 399–400, 37 LRRM 2420 (CA 6, 1956), cert. denied, 351 U.S. 950, the company had a reasonable and nondiscriminatory policy of compulsory retirement going back some years. Then the parties bargained on the question of dealing expressly with the subject in the collective agreement. The court held that their failure to reach agreement did not deprive management of the right to compel an employee to retire under its policy and that the employer did not violate the collective agreement in doing so (the employee had alleged violation of the "proper cause" for discharge provision). For related discussion, see this Chapter, subtopic entitled "The Duty to Bargain: Right of Unilateral Action." The *Nichols* case was discussed by Arbitrator Ferguson in 70 LA 245, 248; Caraway in 66 LA 1207, 1210; Young in 55 LA 933, 935–937, 943; Sembower in 50 LA 1177, 1181; Altieri in 42 LA 559, 560–562; Teple in 39 LA 1003, 1007–1008; Jones in 37 LA 771, 775–776; Ross in 32 LA 713, 717–718.

the collective agreement was likewise silent as to compulsory retirement but where there was no established policy of compulsory retirement which had been accepted in practice by both parties, many arbitrators have held that compulsory retirement violated the seniority, discharge, or discrimination provisions of the agreement.[640]

The previous existence of an established plan of compulsory retirement became even more significant upon enactment of the Age Discrimination in Employment Act of 1967 (ADEA). Although there were differing views concerning the matter, under the view that was ultimately upheld by the U.S. Supreme Court in 1977, the Act was construed as still permitting compulsory retirement of persons covered by the Act (ages 40 through 64) *provided* the employer acted pursuant to a bona fide retirement plan which was in existence before passage of the Act.[641]

However, Congress by 1978 amendments to the ADEA both (1) expanded the range of protected ages to 40 through 69,[642] and (2) expressly provided that "no * * * plan shall require or permit the involuntary retirement of any individual * * * because of the age of such individual."[643] The ADEA does continue to permit age discrimi-

---

[640]See Arbitrator Chiesa in 73 LA 59, 62–63 (the union did not have and could not be charged with knowledge of the employer's policy of compulsory retirement); Kelliher in 61 LA 387, 388; Anrod in 56 LA 251, 253–255; Young in 55 LA 933, 942–943; Gorsuch in 51 LA 909, 913–915; Moore in 51 LA 46, 48–49; Sembower in 50 LA 1177, 1180–1182 (contract was not silent but was ambiguous as to compulsory retirement); Block in 49 LA 224, 227–228; Larkin in 47 LA 513, 516–518 (past practice of compulsory retirement not adequately shown, but even if shown the arbitrator stated it would violate seniority provisions of contract); Altieri in 42 LA 559, 561–562; Scheiber in 42 LA 483, 489–490 (most recent practice was not to compel retirement); Teple in 39 LA 1003, 1007–1010; Jones in 37 LA 771, 775–777; Granoff in 37 LA 350, 355; Schedler in 33 LA 84, 87–88; Hepburn in 32 LA 1022, 1025; Ross in 32 LA 713, 717–719, and in 25 LA 77, 79–82; Justin in 9 LA 921, 924–926. Notwithstanding the significance which many arbitration cases have placed upon the existence or absence of a long-standing and applied compulsory retirement policy in determining whether to uphold compulsory retirement, some cases have upheld management's unilateral institution of compulsory retirement (where the agreement did not expressly restrict the right) even though there was no established practice for it. In particular see the comments and holding of Arbitrator Beatty in Packaging Corp. of Am., 40 LA 544, 546–547 (1963). Also see Arbitrator Rice in 50 LA 597, 600; Bell in 45 LA 500, 500–502.

[641]United Air Lines v. McMann, 98 S.Ct. 444, 446, 450, 16 FEP Cases 146 (1977), the Court relying upon ADEA § 4(f)(2), and the Court stating that it found "nothing to indicate Congress intended wholesale invalidation of retirement plans instituted in good faith before" passage of the Act.

[642]29 U.S.C.A. § 631, which, however, also states an exception applicable to executives and tenured college professors, who are not protected beyond age 64. The ADEA protects federal employees in general even at age 70 and above (see 29 U.S.C.A. §§ 631, 633a), but some must retire at a stated age, as in the case of air traffic controllers at age 56 or firefighters and law enforcement officers at age 55 (see 5 U.S.C.A. § 8335). The Foreign Service Act of 1946 requires persons covered by the Foreign Service retirement system to retire at age 60, a requirement upheld as to constitutionality in Vance v. Bradley, 99 S.Ct. 939 (1979). Employees of state and local governments are covered by the ADEA and the U.S. Supreme Court upheld the constitutionality of that coverage in EEOC v. Wyoming, 31 FEP Cases 74 (1983).

[643]29 U.S.C.A. § 623(f)(2), the amended ADEA § 4(f)(2). Congress did specify a grace period within which compulsory retirement because of age would not be covered by the express prohibition in certain circumstances, the grace period to end by January 1, 1980. The January 1, 1980 termination of grace period came "three months too late to help Grievant escape his mandatory retirement at age sixty-five" in Reynolds Metals Co., 74 LA 1121, 1123 (Welch, 1980). Sometimes protection beyond that accorded by the ADEA will be available from another source. For example, in MaGee-Women's Hosp., 62 LA 987, 990 (Joseph, 1974), a contractual prohibition against discrimination "on account of * * * age" was held equally applicable to all employees and not merely a parallel protection of employees covered by the ADEA; thus, the employer could not involuntarily retire an employee who was too old to be protected by the Act. In Pepsi-Cola Gen. Bottlers, 80 LA 752, 756 (Lieberman, 1983), it was concluded that the agreement's non-

nation "where age is a bona fide occupational qualification [BFOQ] reasonably necessary to the normal operation of the particular business."[644]

The "major short-term impact of the [1978 ADEA] amendments was to force employers to raise their mandatory retirement age limits."[645] In this regard, a 1980 study indicated that most companies were requiring their employees to retire at age 70.[646] A likely additional impact is that arbitrators will be called upon less frequently to review compulsory retirements.

Disqualifying Employees for Physical or Mental Reasons

The material contained in the present topic constitutes only a portion of the Authors' treatment of the subject. For other portions the reader is directed to Chapter 8, topic entitled "Medical Evidence," and to Chapter 16, topic entitled "Physical or Mental Condition as a Safety Hazard."

There are a great many reported arbitration decisions concerning managerial action in disqualifying employees for physical or mental reasons. While the disqualification often is in the form of termination, it also may be effected by layoff, leave of absence, or a refusal to permit the employee to return to work following an accident or medical leave.

There are many cases upholding management's right to terminate employees whose physical condition renders them unable or unfit

---

discrimination clause was intended merely to make the agreement conform to federal law and did not bar compulsory retirement at age 70, but compulsory retirement nonetheless was barred by a pension plan which was made a part of the agreement and contemplated voluntary retirement only. Also, state law may protect against compulsory retirement because of age and place no age limit on the protection. For example, see Alta Bates Hosp., 74 LA 278, 279–280 (Barsamian, 1980). In any event, an involuntarily retired employee may be required at least to "commence" proceedings under state law before going to federal court under the ADEA. See Curto v. Sears, Roebuck & Co., 30 FEP Cases 1196, 1200–1203 (USDC, 1982); Oscar Mayer & Co. v. Evans, 99 S.Ct. 2066, 19 FEP Cases 1167 (1979).

[644]29 U.S.C.A. § 623(f)(1). For example, in Murane v. American Airlines, 482 F.Supp. 135, 21 FEP Cases 284, 291–293 (USDC, 1979), the court upheld the Company's policy of hiring persons under the age of 40 as flight officers since: long training and experience is required for ultimate promotion of a flight officer to copilot and then to captain; FAA regulations require airlines to retire captains at age 60; the captain is in command of the aircraft and is primarily responsible for the safety of passengers and crew; the safest captain is one who is age 55 to 59 and has been flying for the airline as a captain for 10 to 15 years; unless hired under the age of 40 the captain could not acquire the essential experience before being required to retire at age 60. The Federal Aviation Agency's "age 60 rule" was upheld in O'Donnell v. Shaffer, 491 F.2d 59, 9 FEP Cases 1299 (D.C. Cir., 1974). In Trans World Airlines v. Thurston, 105 S.Ct. 613, 621–623 (1985), the ADEA was violated by a policy which made it more difficult for captains who had been disqualified as captain under the age 60 rule to transfer to flight engineer (and thus avoid involuntary retirement) than it was for captains disqualified for other reasons; age was not a BFOQ for the flight engineer position and the transfer policy discriminated on the basis of age. A Massachusetts statute requiring retirement of state police officers at age 50 was upheld as to constitutionality in Massachusetts Bd. of Retirement v. Murgia, 96 S.Ct. 2562, 12 FEP Cases 1569 (1976). In Orzel v. City of Wauwatosa Fire Dept., 30 FEP Cases 1070, 1074 (CA 7, 1983), the court held that "the fact that Congress has determined that age 55 is an appropriate retirement age for one group of firefighters [U.S. Government firefighters] does not automatically establish that the same retirement age is a valid BFOQ, under Section 623(f) of the ADEA, for a wholly different group of employees, operating under different working conditions and performing significantly different job functions."

[645]"Impact of Raising Mandatory Retirement," Labor Relations Yearbook-1981, 35, 36 (BNA Books, 1982), summarizing a report by the House Aging Committee, U.S. Congress.

[646]103 LRR 238 (1980), reporting the results of a study by Hewitt Associates.

to perform their job,[647] and there are cases upholding termination of employees because of mental unfitness (psychiatric problems or mental illness) for work.[648] There are many other cases which have upheld termination because the employee's physical or mental condition rendered his continued employment unduly hazardous to himself or to others.[649]

On the other hand, there are many cases in which the arbitrator required management to return an employee to work where the evidence indicated that the employee was not so affected or disabled as to be unable to perform his job satisfactorily or safely.[650] A similar result has been reached where the employee's condition had existed for a long period of time, during which the employee had performed satisfactorily and safely.[651] In one case management could not terminate an employee who was physically handicapped when hired 17 years earlier, whose condition was not deteriorating, and who, though a slow worker, had not received any complaint from supervision as to his work.[652]

Significance of Workers' Compensation Disabilities and Costs

The mere fact that an employee has previously been awarded workers' compensation for permanent partial disability (or has

---

[647]For example, see Arbitrator Stevens in 80 LA 846, 850; Thomson in 78 LA 1038, 1044; Welch in 70 LA 426, 427–428; Stashower in 68 LA 69, 71–72; Doyle in 60 LA 933, 936–937; Holly in 51 LA 579, 581; Blair in 44 LA 635, 639–640; Duff in 43 LA 678, 680–682; Epstein in 43 LA 640, 643; Seinsheimer in 43 LA 613, 615; Autrey in 41 LA 796, 799–800; Updegraff in 39 LA 53, 57–58 (employer could terminate four employees, all 65 or older, whose work was too heavy for them to keep up in view of physical disabilities that had developed with advanced age). Also see Garrett in 70 LA 171, 173, and Kerrison in 45 LA 724, 726, in both of which cases the employer could refuse to permit return to work. But under the facts of some cases the arbitrator considered transfer or demotion, rather than termination, to be warranted. See Arbitrator Roberts in 49 LA 121, 126; Keefe in 45 LA 986, 989–990. For related discussion, see this Chapter, topic entitled "Demotion of Employees"; Volz, "Medical and Health Issues in Labor Arbitration," Proceedings of the 31st Annual Meeting of NAA, 156 (BNA Books, 1979).

[648]See Arbitrator Roomkin in 76 LA 167, 169–170; Duff in 75 LA 12, 14; Rentfro in 59 LA 726, 729; Turkus in 66–1 ARB ¶8011. Also see Thompson in 76 LA 509, 512–513; Hazelwood in 56 LA 832, 834; Rock in 46 LA 545, 548–549 (upholding refusal to recall). Cf., Mullin in 72 LA 1073, 1075. For cases in which mental illness was asserted as a mitigating factor in discharge for misconduct, see Arbitrator O'Shea in 73 LA 1256, 1259; Goetz in 73 LA 1230, 1233–1234; Sugerman in 49 LA 564, 568; Coffey in 39 LA 604, 606. For general discussions of these and related aspects, see Greenbaum, "The 'Disciplinatrator,' the 'Arbichiatrist,' and the 'Social Psychotrator'—An Inquiry Into How Arbitrators Deal With a Grievant's Personal Problems and the Extent to Which They Affect the Award," 37 Arb. J. No. 4, p. 51 (1982); Cramer, "Arbitration and Mental Illness: The Issues, the Rationale, and the Remedies," 35 Arb. J. No. 3, p. 10 (1980).

[649]See Chapter 16, topic entitled "Physical or Mental Condition as a Safety Hazard."

[650]For physical condition cases, see Arbitrator Leahy in 78 LA 386, 388; McDermott in 48 LA 1271, 1274 (obese employee); Kevin in 45 LA 217, 221; Cobb in 43 LA 599, 600–601; Cahn in 42 LA 1042, 1044 (loss of one eye); Kabaker in 42 LA 513, 517; Berkowitz in 42 LA 374, 376; Scheiber in 41 LA 278, 284; Valtin in 39 LA 918, 920–921; Ross in 24 LA 857, 861–862 (further employment conditioned on employee's taking treatment for his ailment); Williams in 20 LA 784, 787 (no showing that prior ailment was likely to recur); Pollard in 18 LA 889, 892. Also see McNaughton in 50 LA 1277, 1279. For mental condition cases, see Arbitrator Roumell in 76 LA 355, 363; Mallon in 69 LA 303, 306; Rentfro in 59 LA 722, 725; Stouffer in 43 LA 959, 963; Davis in 43 LA 568, 569; Guthrie in 38 LA 297, 299. Management's action may be especially vulnerable if taken without or in complete disregard of professional medical opinion. See Arbitrator Keefe in 50 LA 965, 968; Dybeck in 48 LA 1085, 1087–1088; McDermott in 37 LA 736, 737.

[651]See Arbitrator Christopher in 68 LA 192, 196; Dworkin in 46 LA 719, 723–724; Teple in 42 LA 818, 821–822; Lande in 40 LA 799, 804–805. Also see Rothschild in 68 LA 217, 220.

[652]American Optical Co., 42 LA 818, 821–822 (Teple, 1964).

received compensation under a settlement of his claim) does not per se establish his inability or unfitness for employment so as to justify management's refusal to use him.[653] In one case an employee had asserted and affirmed in a settlement agreement that "my injuries are serious, disabling and permanent in nature," and that such "permanent disability does seriously affect my ability to perform the type of work for which I am otherwise qualified." The arbitrator declared that this was not conclusive as to the employee's physical status three months later and that the employer improperly refused to permit his return to work where the employer offered no other evidence to establish the employee's inability to work and where the employee's physician certified to his physical capacity to perform the job.[654]

Moreover, where it was found that an employee was otherwise able and fit to perform his job, some arbitrators have not permitted the employer to deny the right to continued employment merely because it could impose workers' compensation liability on the employer in the future or could increase his insurance rates.[655] However, other arbitrators have indicated that these potential liabilities are relevant though not conclusive considerations in reference to the right to continued employment.[656]

Excessive Absences Due to Illness

All reasonable management readily excuses occasional absences due to illness. However, management may properly seek to guard against false claims of illness.[657] Moreover, it may feel impelled to terminate employees whose genuinely poor condition of health requires excessive absences.

The right to terminate employees for excessive absences, even where they are due to illness, is generally recognized by arbitrators (as elaborated below, however, no simple rule exists for determining

---

[653]See Arbitrator Williams in 78 LA 1205, 1214–1215; Christopher in 68 LA 192, 195 (compensation agency's finding of 69 percent permanent disability was not proof of actual inability to perform work); Stashower in 68 LA 69, 71; Teple in 53 LA 334, 337; Ray in 52 LA 55, 56; Somers in 51 LA 137, 140 (arbitrator should take notice of agency's 33 percent disability finding but it is not conclusive as to right to return to work); Allen in 50 LA 1152, 1155 (10 percent disability); Emery in 49 LA 403, 404–405 (50 percent disability); Roberts in 47 LA 812, 815, and in 37 LA 729, 731–732; Kiroff in 42 LA 1051, 1055–1056 (50 percent disability); Sembower in 42 LA 734, 736–737, 739; Blumrosen in 42 LA 392, 398–399; Volz in 39 LA 138, 141–142 (35 percent disability); Jaffee in 36 LA 797, 803 and in 19 LA 189, 191; Cayton in 34 LA 149, 152. But see Epstein in 43 LA 640, 643; Crawford in 39 LA 600, 602–603; Stouffer in 34 LA 204, 206–207.

[654]Goodyear Tire & Rubber Co., 52 LA 55, 56 (Ray, 1968).

[655]See Arbitrator Kevin in 45 LA 217, 221; Kabaker in 42 LA 513, 517; Berkowitz in 42 LA 374, 376.

[656]See Arbitrator Creo in 78 LA 437, 443; Rollo in 72 LA 1279, 1285; Doyle in 60 LA 933, 938; Davis in 58 LA 1120, 1122; Somers in 51 LA 137, 143; Seinsheimer in 50 LA 1171, 1176 (management has right "to protect itself"); Stouffer in 34 LA 204, 208. Also see Dallas in 76 LA 263, 266–267; Parkinson in 74 LA 814, 819; Kossoff in 67 LA 1230, 1235.

[657]For discussion of the steps available to management for this purpose, see Chapter 17, subtopic entitled "Sick Leave."

whether absences are in fact "excessive").[658] In this regard, Arbitrator Edwin R. Teple explained:

"At some point the employer must be able to terminate the services of an employee who is unable to work more than part time, for whatever reason. Efficiency and the ability to compete can hardly be maintained if employees cannot be depended upon to report for work with reasonable regularity. Other arbitrators have so found, and this Arbitrator has upheld terminations in several appropriate cases involving frequent and extended absences due to illness."[659]

In another statement, Arbitrator Marlin M. Volz explained that:

"Illness, injury, or other incapacitation by forces beyond the control of the employee are mitigating circumstances, excuse reasonable periods of absence, and are important factors in determining whether absences are excessive. However, if an employee has demonstrated over a long period of time an inability due to chronic bad health or proneness to injury to maintain an acceptable attendance record, an employer is justified in terminating the relationship, particularly where it has sought through counselling and warnings to obtain an improvement in attendance."[660]

Examination of the cases cited in this subtopic makes it readily apparent that there is no fixed or generally accepted rule as to when the "excessive" absence point is reached—the particular facts and circumstances of the given case often will be considered along with the number of absences, the amount of time involved, and the prospects as to future absences.[661] Moreover, an arbitrator may require consider-

---

[658]See Arbitrator Wolk in 80 LA 7, 10–11; Weizenbaum in 79 LA 128, 132; O. Richardson in 78 LA 673, 680–682 (upholding discharge following progressive discipline for excessive absences, some of which were due to illness); Thompson in 76 LA 509, 513; Tsukiyama in 74 LA 531, 532 (stating that "an excessive absentee record covering an extended period of employment, even though attributable to genuine and medically verified illnesses or for other non-fault reasons, provide a sufficient basis to terminate the employment relation"); Welch in 70 LA 426, 427; Hoffman in 70 LA 422, 425; Griffin in 69 LA 1123, 1128; Sisk in 69 LA 484, 492–493 (holding also at 490–491 that the employee was not subject to progressive discipline); Chattman in 69 LA 18, 20–23; Stouffer in 65 LA 482, 486–487; Oberdank in 65 LA 357, 358–359; R. Richardson in 65 LA 47, 58 (upholding discharge for excessive absences caused by short-term illnesses over a six-year period, where the employee did not cooperate or improve his attendance after warning); Shieber in 62 LA 1119, 1121–1122; Simon in 59 LA 1078, 1082–1083; Teple in 48 LA 615, 618; Anderson in 46 LA 436, 439–440 (but the employee could not be denied insurance or pension benefits, there being no misconduct); Klamon in 43 LA 703, 714; Duff in 43 LA 678, 680–682 (the contract provided that employees "shall not lose their seniority rights" when off due to illness, but the arbitrator said that this did not require that sick leave be extended beyond a reasonable time); Solomon in 41 LA 1257, 1267–1268; McCoy in 39 LA 187, 188 (citing many earlier cases). In one case Arbitrator Sylvester Garrett purported to deny that there is a "right" to terminate an employee for excessive absences due to illness, but nonetheless in substance he did recognize it as an ultimate right (the contract expressly requiring corrective discipline) by his refusal to bar management "from seeking to apply discipline to combat serious, repetitive absenteeism by individual employees, even though absences on sick leave or approved leave without pay may be involved." United States Postal Serv., 73 LA 1174, 1181 (1979).

[659]Cleveland Trencher Co., 48 LA 615, 618 (1967). Also see statement by Arbitrator McCoy in 9 LA 143, 145.

[660]Louisville Water Co., 77 LA 1049, 1052 (1981), where, however, reinstatement was ordered (but without back pay) because the employee "may well have been lulled into a false sense of job security."

[661]Ordinarily neither the number of absences nor any other single factor will be conclusive in determining whether an employee's absenteeism may reasonably be deemed "excessive" where illness is involved. For instance, see Arbitrator MacLean in 79 LA 742, 744, 746; Kelliher in 78 LA 1163, 1165 (discharge under an absenteeism policy that applied automatic penalties was

able tolerance on the part of management where the equities in favor of the employee are strong.[662]

In one case the arbitrator recognized the general right of management to terminate employees for excessive absences due to illness, but he stated that the right "cannot be exercised capriciously or with disregard for the employee's seniority and stake in maturing fringe benefits." He also noted a distinction between "intermittent" absences and "extended" absences, pointing out that an extended absence imposes a lesser burden upon management in that it permits "continuous coverage of the vacancy without taxing the employer with constant uncertainty over the filling of the opening."[663]

Finally, it may be noted that grievances challenging management's adoption of absentee control plans and/or challenging the application of such plans in specific instances have frequently reached arbitration.[664]

Right to Require Physical Examination

Management's good faith right to require job applicants to submit to a physical examination is so basic that it has rarely been an issue in

---

overruled because management had not considered excusing occasional absences due to illness and had not considered the potential for regular attendance in the future, but he did state that "the Grievant must be warned that if he accepts reinstatement he can be terminated even for justifiable illnesses if they become excessive"); Winograd in 75 LA 430, 437–439; Shieber in 62 LA 1119, 1122 (stating that "in order to sustain the discharge of an employee for excessive absences due to illness or injury," it must be shown both "that the employee has a high rate of absences" and "that the employee will probably be unable to return to work as a dependable employee in the future"); Erbs in 58 LA 881, 885–886.

[662]For example, see Arbitrator Michelstetter in 78 LA 71, 73; Winograd in 75 LA 430, 438; Markowitz in 72 LA 541, 543; Gilden in 44 LA 280, 282–283.

[663]Great Atl. & Pac. Tea Co., 48 LA 910, 912–913 (Keefe, 1967). Also recognizing the latter distinction, Arbitrator Winograd in 75 LA 430, 438; Chattman in 69 LA 18, 23; Wolff in 67 LA 203, 209; Hale in 35 LA 469, 477; Soule in 14 LA 153, 155.

[664]See Arbitrator Kerrison in 80 LA 22, 25; Seibel in 79 LA 916, 920 (upholding management's absenteeism plan involving use of progressive discipline, and in doing so he recognized that "discharge on a non-disciplinary basis may be appropriate, even for absences due to legitimate illness"); de Grasse in 79 LA 679, 680–681; Mittleman in 79 LA 433, 435–436; Byars in 79 LA 89, 94–95; Sanders in 78 LA 15, 16; Nigro in 77 LA 889, 893 (stating that "the Company has the management right unilaterally to adopt an absenteeism policy," but the collective agreement "grants the employees certain rights with which the absenteeism policy cannot conflict"); Deitsch in 77 LA 585, 590–593 (stating that "Termination of an employee whose poor health precludes regular work attendance is understandable, reasonable, and justifiable, given the need of an enterprise to efficiently accomplish its objectives," but that management's new policy on absenteeism was subject to challenge, being neither clear nor consistently administered); Richardson in 77 LA 505, 512–516; Taylor in 77 LA 249, 255–256 (management's "no fault" point system for controlling absenteeism was upheld, Arbitrator Taylor stating that he "cannot set aside what appears to be a reasonable work rule on the grounds that it might be unreasonably applied in the future," and that when "the unfortunate accumulator of assigned points is discharged or some other discipline is imposed, the justice of such a penalty can only be determined on the merits of that particular case"); Keenan in 76 LA 827, 832; Abrams in 74 LA 847, 850–853 (stating that "Merely because the Company has followed its own unilaterally established disciplinary system does not necessarily mean that a resulting discharge was for 'just cause'"); Bowers in 74 LA 681, 683, 687; Nitka in 74 LA 202, 205; Hardbeck in 73 LA 684, 687; Ellmann in 72 LA 804, 807 (holding that management violated past practice by changing its absenteeism plan); Weiss in 72 LA 133, 135; Blue in 71 LA 744, 749; Imundo in 71 LA 195, 196, 199; Cohen in 71 LA 1, 5–6; Jones in 70 LA 833, 834–836; Duff in 69 LA 77, 79–80; McIntosh in 66 LA 674, 676. For related discussion, see Scott & Taylor, "An Analysis of Absenteeism Cases Taken to Arbitration: 1975–1981," 38 Arb. J. No. 3, p. 61 (1983).

arbitration.[665] The utility of physical examinations obviously is not ended once the applicant has been hired and has commenced service with the employer—situations arise to warrant physical examinations during the employment relationship.

It is clear from reported arbitration decisions that management has the right, unless restricted by the agreement, to require employees to have physical examinations where the right is reasonably exercised under proper circumstances, such as where an employee desires to return to work following an accident or sick leave, or following extended layoff, or where an employee has bid on a job requiring greater physical effort.[666] However, it has been emphasized that "this right is not an absolute one exercisable at the whim" of management, and that it "cannot be arbitrarily insisted upon without reasonable grounds."[667]

Selection and Control of Supervisors

Arbitrators have generally recognized it to be the function and responsibility of management to run the business and to produce profits. It is generally accepted as an incident to management's right to control operations that management must be permitted to select

---

[665]In Conveyor Co., 38 LA 1141, 1143 (Roberts, 1962), the arbitrator emphasized the "inherent right" to require a physical examination of job applicants, but in that case there was strong evidence that the contract was intended to prohibit exercise of the right.

[666]See Arbitrator Rothschild in 78 LA 784, 786–787; Moore in 78 LA 617, 619–620 (dealing also with the scope of permitted use of information obtained in the course of the examination); Roberts in 76 LA 103, 107–108 (stating that the "Company's requirement that the examination be administered by the Company physician rather than another is not unreasonable"); Kossoff in 67 LA 1230, 1235–1236; Duff in 52 LA 985, 986–987; Kelliher in 50 LA 351, 352; Johnson in 48 LA 1357, 1358; Keefe in 47 LA 1, 6; McIntosh in 46 LA 530, 532; Bothwell in 45 LA 39, 42; Klein in 43 LA 217, 223–224 (in view of safety considerations, diabetic could be required to submit to weekly medical examination at his own expense); Phelps in 42 LA 161, 164; Sembower in 40 LA 37, 42–43; Klamon in 37 LA 960, 966; Donnelly in 37 LA 456, 458; Stouffer in 32 LA 686, 689; Boles in 31 LA 824, 826; Bothwell in 27 LA 404, 406 (could require physical examination in recall); Stashower in 12 LA 896, 897–898. Also see Whitney in 53 LA 1078, 1086 (under past practice employees had returned to work on basis of their own doctor's certifications, but this did not make demand for physical examination by company-designated doctor improper where justified by the circumstances). The fact that the contract states certain ailments or situations for which a physical examination may be required does not deprive management of the right to require one in other proper circumstances. See Arbitrator Block in 50 LA 58, 62; Solomon in 42 LA 1, 8–11. Cf., Klein in 42 LA 1151, 1156–1158. In Western Airlines, 74 LA 923, 925–926 (Richman, 1980), an employee who agreed to release his medical records for examination only by the company physician could not be required to release them for examination by other company personnel as a precondition for returning to work after medical leave of absence.

[667]Conchemco, Inc., 55 LA 54, 57 (Ray, 1970), where reasonable grounds were not found. Also not finding reasonable grounds, Arbitrator Koven in 65 LA 261, 264; France in 61 LA 121, 123–124; Cahn in 50 LA 833, 835; Dworet in 37 LA 378, 379 (could not require all employees absent two weeks for whatever reason to submit to physical examination); Daugherty in 36 LA 104, 105–106 (reasonable grounds did not exist for requiring psychiatric examination). An employer's use of physical examinations ordinarily would not violate Title VII of the Civil Rights Act. See, for instance, Warren v. Veterans Hosp., 382 F.Supp. 303, 10 FEP Cases 1169, 1172 (USDC, 1974). However, in some cases a violation has been indicated, such as where the physical examination was purposely utilized to further the employer's discriminatory practices. See EEOC Decision No. 71–1332, 3 FEP Cases 489 (1971); EEOC Decision No. 70134, 2 FEP Cases 237 (1969).

and control supervisory personnel without union interference.[668] In the words of Arbitrator Dudley E. Whiting:

"It is a fundamental principle of American industry that the selection and retention of foremen or other supervisory personnel is the sole prerogative of management * * * . There is no doubt that the union may not, as a matter of right, demand the dismissal or demotion of a foreman and that such a demand is not a proper subject matter for a grievance."[669]

Thus, Arbitrator Whitley P. McCoy held that unless the agreement expressly permits, or the employer waives the jurisdiction issue and submits the dispute on the merits, a demand by the union for discipline or discharge of a supervisory employee ordinarily is not arbitrable, and that even where the arbitrator can exercise jurisdiction in such disputes, he should do so sparingly and only on very clear

---

[668]For cases illustrating management's broad control and discretion as to supervisory personnel, see Arbitrator Weston in 78 LA 39, 41–42; Hannan in 75 LA 1042, 1044; Axon in 75 LA 2, 6; Foster in 69 LA 67, 70–71 (in concluding that the collective agreement promotion provisions did "not cover the staffing of supervisory positions which are outside the bargaining unit," he stated that "Since contractual control over out-of-unit promotions is rare in the realm of labor relations," he "must insist on explicit evidence" that the federal agency employer had knowingly agreed to such control); Bothwell in 51 LA 1113, 1115 (can pay management personnel on any basis employer desires); Williams in 51 LA 296, 297–298; Sembower in 51 LA 197, 199–200 (employer has right to determine how many persons are to be made supervisors); Shister in 44 LA 992, 993; Seidenberg in 44 LA 145, 147–148 (selection of supervisors is not governed by seniority or other contract provisions); Oppenheim in 43 LA 9, 11; Hawley in 42 LA 79, 82 (need not consider seniority in filling temporary vacancy in foreman position); Williams in 27 LA 432, 436–437 ("Supervisors hold their positions at the will of the company except where the company has specifically yielded its power"); Whiting in 11 LA 1023, 1031. The NLRA expressly excludes supervisors from the definition of "employee" and also bars the states from compelling employers to accord bargaining rights to supervisors. See Beasley v. Food Fair of N.C., 94 S.Ct. 2023, 86 LRRM 2196 (1974). Also See Arbitrator Goodman in 73 LA 497, 502–503 (quoting the NLRA § 2(11) definition of "supervisor"); Fields in 68 LA 448, 453; Updegraff in 49 LA 1154, 1155; Purdom in 38 LA 301, 305–306. Thus, supervisors are subject to management's unilateral right of control except as management voluntarily limits that right by contract. By decisional law "managerial employees" and certain "confidential" employees are likewise excluded from NLRA coverage. Regarding managerial employees, see NLRB v. Yeshiva Univ., 100 S.Ct. 856, 103 LRRM 2526 (1980); NLRB v. Bell Aerospace Co. Div. of Textron, Inc., 94 S.Ct. 1757, 85 LRRM 2945 (1974), holding that excluded "managerial employees" include not merely those in positions susceptible to conflicts of interest in labor relations but also those who formulate and effectuate management policies. Under the facts in Curtis Noll Corp., 89 LRRM 1417 (NLRB, 1975), certain management trainees were held to be managerial employees not protected by the Act even though as trainees they perform solely nondiscretionary rank-and-file work. Regarding "confidential" employees, see NLRB v. Hendricks County Rural Elec. Membership Corp., 102 S.Ct. 216, 108 LRRM 3105 (1981), upholding the NLRB's practice of excluding from bargaining units only those "confidential" employees who assist and act in a confidential capacity to persons engaged in the formulation and effectuation of management policies in the field of labor relations. As concerns the Railway Labor Act, that statute does not expressly exclude supervisors from its coverage, and, pointing somewhat in the other direction, its rather indefinite definition of the term "employee" refers at one point to "employee or subordinate official" as falling within the term. See RLA § 1, Fifth; 45 U.S.C.A. § 151, Fifth. In Lum v. China Airlines, 413 F.Supp. 613 (USDC, 1976), the court pointed out that persons may be covered by the RLA although they have some supervisory duties. In Frontier Airlines, 8 NMB No. 99 (1981), noted by the National Mediation Board in its 47th Annual Report (p. 22, 1981), certain foremen who had authority to discipline and evaluate employees, to handle and resolve grievances, and to participate in budgetary matters and commit carrier resources, were held to be "management officials" not covered by the RLA. Considering the Act's full definition of "employee" along with cases such as those just noted, it is apparent that the level of a person's authority and the extent to which the person is subject to supervision and direction in the rendition of services are basic factors in determining whether the person is an employee or subordinate official, covered by the RLA, or is a management official subject to unilateral control by the carrier.

[669]King Powder Co., 1 LA 215, 216 (Whiting, 1944). This also was the view of the War Labor Board. Stanoland Oil & Gas, 20 War Lab. Rep. 211 (1944).

grounds.[670] Many other arbitrators have taken positions in general agreement with this view, either by holding the union's demand to be nonarbitrable,[671] or by holding that the arbitrator has no authority to order management to punish supervisory personnel.[672]

However, while recognizing management's control over supervisors as a general right, Arbitrator McCoy explained in another case that "in very extreme cases, where a foreman's conduct is beyond the limits of lawfulness or decency, making for an intolerable condition which management itself could not with decency condone, it may become arbitrable," or where there is "a menace to the life and health of the employees while at their work" an arbitrable issue may be presented.[673] In still another case Arbitrator McCoy required an employer to remove from the department a foreman who, on many occasions, had used profanity in the presence of women employees and had addressed obscene remarks to them. In requiring the removal, he said that "management has, by contract (seniority clauses, etc.), given the employees rights to their jobs under decent working conditions."[674]

Furthermore, even where management may not be required to discipline supervisors, it will be required to compensate employees injured by their wrongful acts.[675] Umpire Harry Shulman, for instance, ruled that "to the extent that a foreman or other representative of managerial authority takes action detrimental to an employee and in violation of the parties' contract, the grievance procedure is properly invoked to provide appropriate redress." He added, however, that "what is called for is protection of the employees within their contractual rights as distinguished from mere punishment of the Company's supervisory or other managerial representatives," and

---

[670]Electro Metallurgical Co., 19 LA 8, 8–10 (1952). For one arbitrator's cautious approach to the imposition of sanctions, even where an express contractual directive regarding the conduct of supervisors had been violated, see United States Customs Serv., 78 LA 945, 951 (Pastore, 1982).

[671]See Arbitrator Archer in 67 LA 284, 287; Sisk in 67 LA 271, 277–278; Solomon in 53 LA 878, 884–886; Sembower in 49 LA 752, 757–760; Brecht in 27 LA 806, 810; Cornsweet in 13 LA 949, 950; Selekman in 5 LA 684, 686; Smith in 1 LA 75, 78–79. Also see Doyle in 72 LA 1033, 1034; Coffey in 45 LA 707, 710–712. In San Juan Star, 43 LA 445, 445–446 (Helfeld, 1964), the employer did agree to arbitrate the alleged misconduct of two supervisors and the submission agreement specified that they would be discharged if the charges were established (they were not established).

[672]See Arbitrator Bailey in 68 LA 893, 897; Schoenfeld in 67 LA 785, 788; Geissinger in 50 LA 221, 225–226; Hilpert in 47 LA 686, 690–691; Klamon in 15 LA 32, 35 (only in "very rare and unusual circumstances" should the demand be sustained); Copelof in 10 LA 237, 240; Shulman in 1 ALAA ¶67,011; Whiting in 1 LA 215, 216. Cf., Arbitrator Elson in 39 LA 870, 874–875, where the arbitrator ordered the company to "formalize" the reprimand which the company itself had given a supervisor for violating the agreement.

[673]Goodyear Tire & Rubber Co. of Ala., 5 LA 30, 34 (1946).

[674]Continental Can Co., 1 LA 65, 68 (1945). For other cases involving alleged abusive language by foremen, see Arbitrator Florey in 50 LA 976, 977–978; McNaughton in 40 LA 125, 127; Brecht in 27 LA 806, 809–811. In Veterans Admin., 75 LA 733, 735 (1980), a regulation requiring "employees to live up to common standards of acceptable work behavior" was held by Arbitrator J.D. Hyman to "apply with perhaps special force to supervisory employees in their dealing with subordinates," and since the evidence established "a pattern of harassment of the Grievant by his supervisor," Arbitrator Hyman "directed" the federal agency employer "to admonish the [supervisor] to exert special efforts to avoid any repetition of similar behavior in the future."

[675]Profile Cotton Mills, 2 LA 537, 538–539 (McCoy, 1942). Also see Arbitrator Brecht in 27 LA 806, 810–811; Cornsweet in 13 LA 949, 950; Whiting in 1 LA 215, 216; Smith in 1 LA 75, 78.

that, while punishment of a supervisor may be the only feasible way to stop improper treatment of employees, the Umpire can direct that such improper conduct be stopped, but "how the result is to be achieved is * * * a matter normally left to the Company."[676] In another case Arbitrator John F. Sembower held a grievance demanding the removal of a foreman not to be arbitrable but he gave the union 10 days to submit an amended grievance requesting an arbitrable type of relief.[677]

Accompanying the right of management to control supervisors is the function and responsibility to inform them fully as to their rights, authorities, and duties. It has been held that management must compensate employees for any loss suffered as a result of its failure to instruct and train its foremen fully.[678]

Management's right to discipline or discharge supervisors may be limited by contract.[679] In one case Arbitrator David Goodman summarized management's broad right of control over supervisors under the NLRA, but he also pointed out that an employer voluntarily may become committed to contractual limitations upon that right of control; he concluded that in the instant case, "by choosing to include * * * supervisory personnel in the bargaining unit, and by failing to provide in any manner that they be afforded less protection, the Company * * * waived its right to treat these employees differently."[680]

Where bargaining unit employees acquire rights under the contract and later become supervisors, their discharge presents an arbitrable issue insofar as the union claims a right under the collective agreement for the individual to return to the bargaining unit (the claimed right has been upheld in some cases but denied in other cases).[681]

---

[676]Ford Motor Co., 1 ALAA ¶67,011, p. 67,012 (1945). Also see Arbitrator Bailey in 68 LA 893, 897; Jensen in 38 LA 781, 784 (union is entitled to assurances against future misconduct by supervisor but no right to a public apology from him); Dworet in 35 LA 381, 383.

[677]Reserve Mining Co., 49 LA 752, 757–760 (1967), stating that any amended grievance would be returned to a lower step of the grievance procedure for de novo proceedings from that point.

[678]Standard Oil Co. (Ind.), 11 LA 689, 691 (Updegraff, 1948).

[679]Even the captain of a ship was protected by a "just cause" requirement where he was covered by the collective agreement. Cargo & Tankship Management Corp., 38 LA 602, 612 (Gellhorn, 1962). By the agreement management may accept other limitations upon its rights as to supervisors. For example, see Southwest Airmotive Co., 41 LA 353, 358 (Elliott, 1963). Where employees are temporarily transferred to supervisory positions, they may remain covered by the agreement for various purposes. See Bethlehem Steel Co., 39 LA 1101, 1103–1104 (Seward, 1963).

[680]Safeway Stores, 73 LA 497, 502–503 (1979). For NLRA limitation upon a *union's* right to discipline supervisor-members whom the employer has permitted to join, see American Broadcasting Cos. v. Writers Guild, 98 S.Ct. 2423, 98 LRRM 2705 (1978), a critical consideration being whether discipline imposed by the union may adversely affect the supervisor's performance of his collective-bargaining grievance-adjustment tasks and thereby unlawfully coerce or restrain the employer. For the application of contracts which require supervisors to be union members but which limit the union's right to discipline them, see Arbitrator Smith in 43 LA 1073, 1075–1083; Rohman in 40 LA 619, 621–624. Also see Gentile in 79 LA 654, 658.

[681]See Arbitrator Kanner in 70 LA 295, 300; Coyle in 68 LA 177, 180, 183; Kelliher in 61 LA 1138, 1141–1142; Davey in 60 LA 572, 575; Fleischli in 59 LA 101, 104–106; Epstein in 58 LA 374, 378, 381; Peters in 57 LA 645, 651, 656; Somers in 57 LA 58, 60–61; Schurke in 56 LA 712, 720; Elliott in 54 LA 965, 972–973, 981; Keefe in 50 LA 1052, 1056; Gibson in 48 LA 1234, 1236–1239; Marshall in 40 LA 193, 198; Merrill in 29 LA 334, 336; Baab in 28 LA 641, 642–643; Williams in 27 LA 432, 436–437; Duff in 26 LA 919, 920–921; Anrod in 25 LA 452, 455; Emery in 16 LA 48, 50. In J.L. Clark Mfg. Co., 68 LA 448, 452–453 (1977), it was held that the "privilege of the Employer

Awards vary on the question of whether management has a right, in the absence of a specific contractual provision on the matter, to place former bargaining unit employees back into the unit on the basis of seniority accumulated during work in the unit or with accumulated seniority for time spent in supervisory service. For discussion and cases on this issue, see Chapter 14, subtopic entitled "Service Outside the Seniority Unit."

---

to select an employee [for supervisory service outside the bargaining unit] without regard to seniority or other qualifications does not imply acceptance is mandatory," Arbitrator Ogden W. Fields declaring that the "authority to compel an employee to work outside the unit in a supervisory capacity has such serious potential consequences that it may not be implied * * *." Also see Arbitrator Wren in 75 LA 224, 227–228 (employee could not be required to accept a responsibility similar to that exercised by the foreman as "a member of the management team").

Chapter 14

Seniority

One of the most severe limitations upon the exercise of managerial discretion is the requirement of seniority recognition. Indeed, the effect of seniority recognition is dramatic from the standpoint of employer, union, and employee alike since "every seniority provision reduces, to a greater or lesser degree, the employer's control over the work force and compels the union to participate to a corresponding degree in the administration of the system of employment preferences which pits the interests of each worker against those of all the others."[1]

In the absence of a definition of the term in the collective agreement, seniority "is commonly understood to mean the length of service with the employer or in some division of the enterprise."[2] Seniority "means that men retain their jobs according to their length of service with their employer and that men are promoted to better jobs on the same basis."[3] "It is generally recognized that the chief purpose of a seniority plan is to provide maximum security to workers with the longest continuous service."[4]

---

[1]Aaron, "Reflections on the Legal Nature and Enforceability of Seniority Rights," 75 Harv. L. Rev. 1532, 1534–1535 (1962).

[2]Curtiss-Wright Corp., 11 LA 139, 142 (Uible, 1948). Also see Arbitrator Carter in 79 LA 1081, 1083; Dworkin in 24 LA 73, 76; Williams in 23 LA 366, 367.

[3]Lapp, How to Handle Problems of Seniority, 1 (1946). Also see Arbitrator Dworkin in 24 LA 73, 76.

[4]Darin & Armstrong, 13 LA 843, 845 (Platt, 1950). Also see Arbitrator Williams in 23 LA 366, 367; Reid in 22 LA 379, 381; Cole in 21 LA 231, 232. "In the broadest sense, the set of rights that make up 'seniority' may be separated into two distinct categories: (1) the rights of an employee relative to other employees in competitive situations, as in layoffs, promotions, transfers, and choice of shifts or vacation periods, and (2) the rights of the employee to benefits, usually financial, that increase automatically with length of service." Major Collective Bargaining Agreements: Administration of Seniority, 1 (U.S. Dept. Labor Bull. No. 1425–14, 1972). For U.S. Supeme Court discussion of seniority and seniority systems, see American Tobacco Co. v. Patterson, 102 S.Ct. 1534, 1541, 28 FEP Cases 713 (1982), stating that "Seniority provisions are of 'overriding importance' in collective bargaining"; California Brewers Assn. v. Bryant, 100 S.Ct. 814, 819–821, 22 FEP Cases 1 (1980); Franks v. Bowman Transp. Co., 96 S.Ct. 1251, 1265, 12 FEP Cases 549 (1976), speaking of competitive status seniority and recognizing that "Seniority systems and the entitlements conferred by credits earned thereunder are of vast and increasing importance in the economic employment system of this Nation."

It should be kept in mind that "seniority is a relationship between employees in the same seniority unit, rather than a relationship between jobs."[5] As stated by Arbitrator Paul Prasow:

"Seniority protects and secures an employee's rights in relation to the rights of other employees in his seniority group; it does not protect him in relation to the existence of the job itself. By the use of an objective measure, length of service, the rights of one employee are balanced against other employees' rights."[6]

Because of the interrelationship between employees with respect to seniority rights, one court permitted intervention by employees in an arbitration involving seniority rights of other employees in the same seniority unit, the court saying that in such a controversy "for every person whose seniority is advanced, someone will be adversely affected by such advancement."[7]

Seniority issues in arbitration arise out of the attempt by the parties to promote their respective interests. In this regard, Arbitrator Walter Gellhorn balanced the interests of management against those of the employees and analyzed the "costs" of seniority to both management and employees:

"To be sure, the full utilization of seniors cannot be achieved without costs. When seniors 'get the breaks,' the more ambitious and capable of the junior men may feel frustrated. Moreover, a management that likes to see a clear line of promotability from within the work force does not welcome the inflexibility that sometimes comes from giving preference to older, perhaps less adaptable workers. But these costs were measured when the contract was made. The parties presumably concluded that the price was worth paying. From the standpoint of the men, they must have concluded that the deferment of youthful hope was offset by the assurance of fair opportunity for veteran employees. From the standpoint of management, they must have concluded that an occasional personal rigidity was offset by the enhanced loyalty and stability that are encouraged by an effective seniority clause."[8]

Arbitrator Carl R. Schedler added the union as an interested party, aside from its representation of the employees:

---

[5]Axelson Mfg. Co., 30 LA 444, 448 (Prasow, 1958).

[6]Ibid. Also see statement by Arbitrator Carter in 79 LA 1081, 1083; Cahn in 54 LA 350, 352; Abrahams in 47 LA 325, 326–327.

[7]In re Iroquois Beverage Corp., 28 LA 906, 907 (N.Y. Sup. Ct., 1955). In Belanger v. Matteson, 91 LRRM 2003 (R.I. S.Ct., 1975), a union was held to have breached its duty of fair representation when it argued for the application of strict seniority in the arbitration of grievances of senior employees who had been denied promotion under a clause making seniority controlling only if the qualifications of competing employees are equal—the union had failed to give proper consideration to the qualifications of junior applicants. A court panel's like finding under similar facts was not endorsed by a majority of the full court on rehearing in Smith v. Hussmann Refrigerator Co., 103 LRRM 2321 (CA 8, 1980), but a majority did find a breach of the duty of fair representation in some other respects, as by failure to notify certain affected employees of an arbitration hearing or to invite them to attend, or by agreeing to resubmit an arbitration award for clarification without notifying employees to whom the award was favorable. For an analysis of the Hussmann decision, in which a divided court had produced four opinions, see DeHaven, "Fair Representation in the Arbitration of Grievances—The Eighth Circuit Adds Another Straw," 47 Tenn. L. Rev. 631 (1980).

[8]Universal Atlas Cement Co., 17 LA 755, 757 (1951). Also see Arbitrator Cantor in 80 LA 257, 262, reminding that management, too, benefits from seniority recognition.

"Traditionally, a union considers seniority both as a useful organizing tool and as a basic objective in collective bargaining negotiations. It is, therefore, utilized in invoking what is often considered a latent, if unexpressed, need of workers; and, it is also employed to demonstrate the value of concerted activities as opposed to the results workers can expect from trying to 'go it alone' in dealing with management."[9]

In the latter regard, Arbitrator Edgar A. Jones, Jr., underscored a special concern of workers:

"A major reason why unorganized workers decide to elect a union as their representative is to insulate their job tenure from the adverse effects of the preferential treatment of favored workers in cases of workforce reduction and work opportunities or the retaliatory decisions of supervisors whom they might offend.

"The seniority system has obvious imperfections when compared to an ideally efficient method for determining whom to retain or dismiss in a workforce reduction. To the extent that it is enforced, however, seniority does militate against personal retaliation or preference. * * *"[10]

In an arbitration situation involving not only contract interpretation but some "interest" aspects also, Arbitrator Marion Beatty further analyzed the struggle in relation to the application of seniority in the extreme situation. He first considered the objectives of the parties: the union struggling for greater security in tenure for certain workers and the company trying to avoid a "burdensome seniority system carried to the extreme of shuffling men in the course of one day's work." The objectives of both parties, he felt, were proper. Arbitrator Beatty noted that the company was offering the union a job-standing list which would provide for promotion, reduction in force, and overtime in accordance with strict seniority, but not for such short periods as one day's work. In refusing to award the seniority arrangement requested by the union, he stated:

"I must agree with the company that carrying seniority to the extreme requested by the union would make for a wasteful, cumbersome and uneconomical method of operation. It has in it an element of 'made work' (the few minutes or hours that would be necessary in making the shifts in personnel). It can hardly be denied anymore that made work is economically unsound. If carried to the extreme it would make for much work and little production. Efficiency of operations is something to be desired in every business, it enures to the benefit of all including the public, and an enterprise that cannot operate as efficiently as its competition will suffer the consequences."[11]

Source of Seniority "Rights"

Even prior to the advent of collective agreements employers generally gave job preference to their older employees, not as any binding

---

[9]Schedler, "Arbitration of Seniority Questions," 28 LA 954 at 954 (1957).
[10]Overly Mfg. Co. of Cal., 68 LA 1343, 1345–1346 (1977).
[11]Standard Oil Co. (Ind.), 24 LA 424, 426–427 (1954).

obligation but as a matter of equity, so long as they could do the required work.[12] However, seniority benefits exist as "rights" only to the extent made so by contract.[13] As stated by Arbitrator Joseph Brandschain:

> " * * * whatever seniority rights employees have exist only by virtue of the collective bargaining agreement that is in existence between the union and the employer. Such seniority rights depend wholly upon the contract. They arise out of the contract. Before a collective bargaining contract is in existence, there are no seniority rights.
>
> "Therefore, until we have a contract, the employer has the right, which he has always exercised, to shift workers around and promote and demote them. The very purpose of collective bargaining was to constrict such rights of management and, reciprocally, to gain for the workers job-security rights based upon seniority and to insure such rights contractually. Thus, we start with the situation, before the existence of a contract, where the employer has all rights in connection with promotions and transfers and need pay no heed to seniority of the workers, and the workers have no rights to promotions or transfers because of length of service.
>
> "How does this situation change when a collective bargaining agreement is in existence? It changes to the extent that these rights are given up by the employer and given to the workers under the terms of the contract. Therefore, whatever the employer has yielded in his absolute time-established rights of hiring, firing, promoting, and demoting and whatever the workers have gained in the way of seniority rights with respect to these matters must be measured entirely by the contract."[14]

Thus, an employee who was laid off prior to the effective date of the first contract between the employer and the union was not entitled to any seniority rights or any other rights provided by the contract, which affected only employees of the company who were in its employ on or after the effective date of the contract.[15]

Seniority rights do not necessarily remain static; they may be modified in subsequent agreements, with the current agreement governing. For instance, in ruling that the seniority rights of a returning veteran (who did not qualify for reemployment rights under federal legislation) were governed by the contract in effect at the time of his

---

[12]Lapp, How to Handle Problems of Seniority, 2–3 (1946).

[13]See Arbitrator Roberts in 80 LA 1016, 1018; Howell in 79 LA 265, 267; Tilbury in 78 LA 1081, 1086; Rotenberg in 78 LA 706, 709; Talent in 75 LA 689, 694; Lipson in 75 LA 297, 301; Lubow in 68 LA 1379, 1381; Teple in 68 LA 1347, 1352; Geissinger in 54 LA 828, 829; Cahn in 54 LA 350, 352, and in 30 LA 221, 222; Killion in 49 LA 1073, 1076; Volz in 48 LA 743, 744; Roberts in 48 LA 621, 624; Williams in 48 LA 184, 185; McCoy in 45 LA 993, 995–996; Buckwalter in 44 LA 301, 303; Scheiber in 37 LA 330, 332; Mitchell in 37 LA 240, 244; Luskin in 35 LA 378, 380; Kabaker in 35 LA 74, 76; Boehm in 32 LA 595, 600–601; Dworkin in 24 LA 73, 76; Shipman in 21 LA 604, 607. Also see Larson in 54 LA 555, 558; Oppenheim in 46 LA 860, 864; Smith in 42 LA 517, 524. For court recognition of this rule, see Aeronautical Indus. Lodge v. Campbell, 69 S.Ct. 1287 (1949); Trailmobile v. Whirls, 67 S.Ct. 982 (1947). Of course, seniority benefits sometimes may exist by virtue of statute, as in the case of veterans' employment rights under federal legislation. Regarding the latter, see Chapter 10, subtopic entitled "Some Specific Statutes."

[14]Alan Wood Steel Co., 4 LA 52, 54 (1946). Also see Arbitrator Rubin in 43 LA 347, 348; McIntosh in 35 LA 682, 683; Uible in 11 LA 139, 143.

[15]Acme Galvanizing Co., 19 LA 575, 577 (Gooding, 1952). Also see Arbitrator Talent in 75 LA 689, 694–695; Roumell in 71 LA 864, 867–869; Klamon in 52 LA 1087, 1097–1098. Cf., Morgan in 79 LA 142, 146–147, and Purcell in 62 LA 1059, 1060, in both of which cases employees with contractual seniority suffered layoff while apprentices worked.

return, rather than the contract in effect at the time he entered the armed forces, Arbitrator Harry Shulman stated:

> "Seniority rights under a collective agreement are entirely the products of the Agreement. Their characteristics and their effects are determined solely by the Agreement. In the absence of special provisions to the contrary, the collective Agreement creates rights and binds parties only for the term of the Agreement. Nothing in * * * [any of the parties'] Agreements indicates a purpose to single out seniority rights for individual employees and give them a vested effectiveness beyond the period of the Agreement and beyond the power of the parties to modify by later Agreements. Modification of prior seniority provisions in subsequent Agreements is a fairly common feature of collective bargaining. And while it is true that such modifications commonly result in the increase of seniority rights of some employees, they also necessarily result in some decrease or change in the seniority rights of other employees."[16]

Collective agreements generally provide for the recognition of seniority in several, and often many, aspects of the employment relationship. Among these are promotions, layoffs, rehiring, shift preference, transfers, vacations, days off, and overtime work. Indeed, consideration of seniority looms so importantly that it has been said that "one of the principle purposes for entering into a collective bargaining agreement is usually to secure for the employees the prized right of seniority in case of layoff and promotion."[17]

Contractual Seniority Rights, the Civil Rights Act, and Arbitration

In considering the materials in this subtopic on seniority systems and the Civil Rights Act it should be helpful to keep in mind some possible categories of discrimination:

(1) Discrimination independent of the working of a seniority system. This category is referred to in this subtopic as "independent discrimination," which in some situations can violate the Civil Rights Act even without discriminatory intent. Examples of independent discrimination are the direct refusal to employ minorities or to permit them to hold certain jobs. Other examples are discrimination resulting from the use of tests or from the requirement of occupational qualifications that do not qualify as bona fide occupational qualifications.

---

[16]Ford Motor Co., 23 LA 296, 297 (1954). Also see Arbitrator Kotch in 77 LA 295, 298. For U.S. Supreme Court recognition that seniority rights provided for in a collective agreement may be modified by agreement of the union and the employer acting in good faith, see Ford Motor Co. v. Huffman, 345 U.S. 330 (1953). For many other court cases, see Cooper v. General Motors Corp., 107 LRRM 3161, 3163 (CA 5, 1981); annotation, 90 ALR2d 1003, 1004–1006. Noting various respects in which seniority rights may be neither absolute nor permanent, Kramer, "Seniority and Ability," Management Rights and the Arbitration Process, 41, 41–42 (BNA Books, 1956). Of course, company and union representatives must have been duly authorized in order to validly alter seniority rights. Toledo Edison Co., 79 LA 895, 900 (Kates, 1982).

[17]Cournoyer v. American Television Co., 28 LA 483, 485 (Minn. Sup. Ct., 1957).

(2) Discrimination resulting from the operation of a bona fide seniority system. To qualify as a "bona fide" seniority system under the Civil Rights Act, the system must be established and administered without discriminatory intent. An example of discrimination resulting from the operation of a bona fide seniority system is provided by the case in which an employee had insufficient seniority to avoid working on Saturdays and thus not violate his religious beliefs. In this case the U.S. Supreme Court held that "absent a discriminatory purpose, the operation of a seniority system cannot be an unlawful employment practice even if the system has some discriminatory consequences."[18]

(3) Discrimination intended to be achieved by a seniority system, the system being established or administered with an intent to discriminate against minorities. Such a system would not qualify as "bona fide" under the Civil Rights Act.

(4) Discrimination which is perpetuated by a bona fide seniority system. For instance, a seniority system established and administered without discriminatory intent, but which provides for consideration of seniority in promotions will perpetuate the effects of prior independent discrimination; thus, a female discriminatorily hired one month later than a male may lose a promotion to the male because of his one month greater seniority.

The U.S. Supreme Court has declared that the "unmistakable purpose" of § 703(h) of the Civil Rights Act of 1964 "was to make clear that the routine application of a bona fide seniority system would not be unlawful under Title VII."[19] Section 703(h) provides:

"Notwithstanding any other provision of this subchapter [Title VII], it shall not be an unlawful employment practice for an employer to apply different standards of compensation, or different terms, conditions, or privileges of employment pursuant to a bona fide seniority or merit system * * * provided that such differences are not the result of an intention to discriminate because of race, color, religion, sex, or national origin. * * * "

While § 703(h) provides the above-noted immunity for the "operation" or "routine application" of a bona fide seniority system, that section does not prevent *unlawful* independent discrimination from having some impact upon the bona fide seniority system itself. In the latter regard, it is clear that where unlawful discrimination against a person has occurred *after* the July 2, 1965 effective date of Title VII, the courts upon a timely charge may remedy it by relief adequate to

---

[18]Trans World Airlines v. Hardison, 97 S.Ct. 2264, 2275, 14 FEP Cases 1697 (1977). Compare the Court's statement on bona fide seniority systems and age discrimination under the ADEA, in Trans World Airlines v. Thurston, 105 S.Ct. 613, 623 (1985). For extensive discussion of the Civil Rights Act and bona fide seniority systems, see Schlei & Grossman, Employment Discrimination Law, 2d Ed., 26–57 (BNA Books, 1983).
[19]Trans World Airlines v. Hardison, 97 S.Ct. at 2275.

achieve the "make-whole" purposes of the Act, and that such relief may include an award of retroactive or "constructive" seniority which may date back to the initial discrimination; thus, the person may get the place on the seniority list which would have resulted had the discrimination never occurred.[20] To the extent that a victim does receive such "constructive" seniority, the post-Act discrimination, having thus been remedied, will not be perpetuated even by a bona fide seniority system.

On the other hand, as concerns discrimination occurring prior to the effective date of Title VII, often referred to in Supreme Court decisions as "pre-Act" discrimination, the Supreme Court has held that persons "who suffered only pre-Act discrimination are not entitled to relief, and no person may be given retroactive seniority to a date earlier than the effective date of the Act."[21] The Court held also "that an otherwise neutral, legitimate seniority system does not become unlawful under Title VII simply because it may perpetuate pre-Act discrimination," for "Congress did not intend to make it illegal for employees with vested seniority rights to continue to exercise those rights, even at the expense of pre-Act discriminatees."[22] The Court explained that this immunity given to bona fide seniority systems is an exception. Generally under Title VII prima facie violations may be established by policies or practices that are neutral on their face and in their intent, but whose effect nonetheless is to discriminate against a particular group; one kind of practice "fair in form, but discriminatory in operation" is that which perpetuates the effects of prior discrimination.[23] That is, the innocent perpetuation of prior discrimination by good faith business policies or practices can be illegal. But an exception is that a bona fide seniority system that perpetuates the effects of pre-Act discrimination may lawfully do so by virtue of the § 703(h) immunity.[24]

---

[20]International Bhd. of Teamsters v. United States (T.I.M.E.-DC, Inc.), 97 S.Ct. 1843, 14 FEP Cases 1514 (1977); Franks v. Bowman Transp. Co., 96 S.Ct. 1251, 12 FEP Cases 549 (1976). In *Franks* the Supreme Court held that the § 703(h) exemption of bona fide seniority systems was not intended to "restrict relief otherwise appropriate once an illegal discriminatory practice occurring after the effective date of the Act is proved," and the Court stated that a remedy "slotting the victim in that position in the seniority system that would have been his" had there been no discrimination "ordinarily * * * will be necessary to achieve the 'make-whole' purposes of the Act." 96 S.Ct. at 1263, 1265. Subsequently in *Teamsters* the Court stated that "after the victims have been identified and their rightful place determined, the District Court will * * * be faced with the delicate task of adjusting the remedial interests of discriminatees and the legitimate expectations of other employees innocent of any wrongdoing." 97 S.Ct. at 1873. The Court explained further that "when immediate implementation of an equitable remedy threatens to impinge upon the expectations of innocent parties, the courts must 'look to the practical realities and necessities inescapably involved in reconciling competing interests,' in order to determine the 'special blend of what is necessary, what is fair, and what is workable.'" Id. at 1875.

[21]International Bhd. of Teamsters v. United States (T.I.M.E.-DC, Inc.), 97 S.Ct. 1843, 1865, 14 FEP Cases 1514 (1976).

[22]97 S.Ct. at 1864.

[23]Id. at 1861.

[24]Id. at 1862. Furthermore, post-Act discrimination not timely charged is the legal equivalent of pre-Act discrimination; thus, its effects also may be lawfully perpetuated by a bona fide seniority system. United Air Lines v. Evans, 97 S.Ct. 1885, 14 FEP Cases 1510 (1977). In the latter regard, the requirement for filing a timely charge is subject to waiver, estoppel, and equitable tolling. Zipes v. Trans World Airlines, 102 S.Ct. 1127, 28 FEP Cases 1 (1982). The

To recapitulate, as construed by the Supreme Court § 703(h) immunizes (1) the perpetuation of pre-Act discrimination by a bona fide seniority system, and (2) post-Act discrimination resulting from the operation of a bona fide seniority system. But (3) other discrimination may be illegal, and where it is, § 703(h) does *not* limit a court's authority to remedy the discrimination by adequate relief which may include an award of "constructive" seniority to "slot" the victim into his or her rightful place *ahead of* other employees on the seniority list of even a bona fide seniority system.[25]

We have noted the possibility of remedying illegal post-Act discrimination through court action. Sometimes another possibility is through arbitration, there in fact having been many arbitration cases in which grievants alleged that they were discriminated against because of their race, sex, religion, or the like. Many such cases are included in the Chapter 10 subtopic entitled "Title VII of the Civil Rights Act." There it is noted that many but not all arbitrators subsequent to the Supreme Court's *Gardner-Denver* decision have considered Title VII doctrine in dealing with the discrimination issue. It is also noted there that a factor in some of the cases was the existence of a collective agreement clause expressly stating that the parties would comply with antidiscrimination law, or a clause expressly voiding any part of the agreement to the extent that it conflicts with federal or state law, or a clause simply prohibiting discrimination on the basis of race, sex, religion, and the like. In the present subtopic, however, we note only arbitration cases in which grievants alleged a violation of their contractual seniority rights by the employer in favoring rather than discriminating against other persons as members of a minority group. That is, these are so-called "reverse discrimination" cases. In such cases the employer may or may not have acted with the thought of legal compulsion; but regardless of motivation, a clash with collective agreement rights may result.

It is apparent that bona fide seniority systems on the whole have very strong standing even vis-à-vis Title VII of the Civil Rights Act. It

Supreme Court has held that § 703(h) protects a seniority system equally regardless of whether the seniority system itself was adopted before or after the effective date of the Act. American Tobacco Co. v. Patterson, 102 S.Ct. 1534, 1541, 28 FEP Cases 713 (1982). The Supreme Court dealt with the question of what is a "seniority system" in California Brewers Assn. v. Bryant, 100 S.Ct. 814, 819–821, 22 FEP Cases 1 (1980), indicating that, within limits, significant freedom must be afforded employers and unions to create "differing" seniority systems. Also to be noted is Pullman-Standard v. Swint, 102 S.Ct. 1781, 1784, 1789–1790, 28 FEP Cases 1073 (1982), where the Supreme Court stated that under § 703(h) "a showing of disparate impact is insufficient to invalidate a seniority system"; and reiterating that "absent a discriminatory purpose, the operation of a seniority system cannot be an unlawful employment practice even if the system has some discriminatory consequences," the Court held that "any challenge to a seniority system under Title VII will require a trial on the issue of discriminatory intent," which is "a pure question of fact."

[25]What the situation amounts to is that the operation of a bona fide seniority system cannot be the basis of a charge of illegal discrimination; but the seniority system itself can be affected or compromised to the limited extent that constructive seniority is awarded by a court to remedy illegal discrimination which resulted totally apart from the operation of the seniority system. Stated more concisely, a bona fide seniority system cannot be penalized or compromised as a result of something it did do, but it can be compromised to some extent as a result of something which it did not do.

is also apparent that where illegal post-Act discrimination does occur, the operation of a bona fide seniority system may be reconciled with rights under the Act by an award of "constructive" seniority or other relief from a court. In some cases an arbitrator also may be able fully or partially to reconcile the operation of a collective agreement seniority system with rights under the Act; but in order for the arbitrator to do so by an award enforceable under federal law the award must draw its essence from the collective agreement, and must not order the performance of an unlawful act or one which would violate a strong public policy. No doubt a strong possibility for achieving this would exist, for example, where the collective agreement contains a clause expressly voiding any part of the agreement found to conflict with the Act. And even absent an express provision of this sort, the interpretative process, sometimes aided by bargaining history or past practice, may produce an enforceable award achieving in whole or in part the needed reconciliation of collective agreement and statute. On the other hand, in some cases an arbitrator will find no basis within the arbitrator's authority for achieving the needed reconciliation, and will issue an award based upon the arbitrator's understanding of the collective agreement alone. Here again, to be enforceable the award must draw its essence from the agreement, and must not order the performance of an unlawful act or one which would violate a strong public policy.

Turning now to the cases, we may note first that where an arbitrator finds under the evidence that the employer *with the agreement or approval of the union* has entered into a conciliation agreement or affirmative action plan in behalf of some minority group, the arbitrator likely will honor the conciliation agreement or affirmative action plan as against the collective agreement where they conflict.[26]

---

[26]See Hayes Intl. Corp., 79 LA 999, 1002, 1004–1006 (Valtin, 1982), finding that the conciliation agreement in question had been forced upon the employer "by the government" and that the union through its officers "extended a cooperative hand and thereby gave its approval for the use of the program"; Flint Bd. of Educ., 77 LA 244, 246–248 (Daniel, 1981), stating that the "union by various actions * * * did enter into an agreement with the employer to permit application of affirmative action concepts in the selection of candidates" for apprenticeship, and that "implicit in this is the agreement to accept modification of strict seniority." Also see Arbitrator Lehleitner in 79 LA 1138, 1145; Taylor in 68 LA 155, 159. In United Steelworkers v. Weber, 99 S.Ct. 2721, 20 FEP Cases 1 (1979), only 1.83 percent of the skilled craft workers in the plant were black even though the work force in the local community was approximately 39 percent black. This imbalance resulted because the employer lawfully had previously hired trained outsiders with prior craft experience; the Supreme Court took judicial notice that blacks long had been excluded from craft unions, thus few had craft experience. The employer and the union voluntarily adopted an affirmative action plan for on-the-job craft training, reserving half of the training slots for blacks. Although some blacks accepted for training had less seniority than whites who were excluded, the Supreme Court upheld the plan when challenged under Title VII. The Court pointed out that the plan's purposes mirrored those of the Act, the plan did not unnecessarily trammel the interests of white employees (none was discharged and half of the trainees would be white), and the plan was a temporary measure to eliminate a manifest racial imbalance in traditionally segregated job categories. The Court emphasized that its decision dealt only with private, voluntary plans, and was not concerned "with what Title VII requires or with what a court might order to remedy a past proven violation of the Act." In the latter regard, we have noted above how courts may provide relief for victims of illegal discrimination. Now we should note also that in Firefighters Local Union No. 1784 v. Stotts, 104 S.Ct. 2576, 2588–2590, 34 FEP Cases 1702 (1984), a decision dealing directly with court authority rather than with what private parties may do independently of a court order, the U.S. Supreme Court held that bona fide seniority systems may not be altered by a court for the benefit of persons who themselves were not the victims of illegal discrimination. Stating that the legislative history of Title VII "made

On the other hand, where the employer enters into a conciliation agreement or affirmative action plan *without* obtaining the union's consent, an arbitrator may or may not give priority to the collective agreement where they conflict. At least we know that in cases decided prior to the U.S. Supreme Court's 1983 *W.R. Grace* decision, arbitrators often gave priority to the collective agreement seniority provisions in that situation, but in other instances the arbitrator did not do so.[27] The Authors do not undertake to reach any conclusion regarding the extent to which any of these cases conflict, if at all, with any other of the cases. Certainly, the mere fact that some of the cases gave priority to the collective agreement while other of the cases gave priority to the conciliation agreement or affirmative action plan, does not necessarily mean that the decisions are in conflict. Furthermore, even where two arbitration decisions reach different conclusions on the same issue under the same agreement, both decisions may be valid provided that each draws its essence from the agreement.[28]

In the *W.R. Grace* case the employer without union agreement or approval entered into an EEOC conciliation agreement containing seniority provisions which conflicted with those of the collective agreement. The employer then obtained a federal district court order which declared that the conciliation agreement took precedence over the collective agreement. While this order was still in effect the employer laid off some male employees contrary to their seniority rights under the collective agreement, the employer adhering instead to the EEOC conciliation agreement. Although the male employees were reinstated after reversal of the District Court's order which had given priority to the EEOC agreement, their grievances for back pay remained and proceeded to arbitration. The first grievance to reach arbitration was heard and denied by Arbitrator Anthony J. Sabella,

---

clear that a court was not authorized to give preferential treatment to non-victims," the Court quoted that legislative history's statement that "[u]nder title VII, not even a Court, much less the Commission, could order racial quotas or the hiring, reinstatement, admission to membership or payment of back pay for anyone who is not discriminated against in violation of this title." The Supreme Court concluded that the District Court by an affirmative action consent decree improperly had required white employees to be laid off or demoted when an otherwise applicable and bona fide seniority system would have called for the layoff of black employees who had less seniority and who had not been victims of illegal discrimination.

[27]For cases in which the arbitrator gave priority to the collective agreement, see Arbitrator Kahn in 78 LA 486, 492; Bothwell in 77 LA 553, 558, 561; Sergent in 74 LA 369, 372–373; Daniel in 73 LA 717, 722; Goodstein in 72 LA 892, 896 (holding that the collective agreement was controlling over affirmative action plan, but that selection of a qualified minority member did not violate an unqualified grievant's rights under the seniority and ability clause of the agreement); Gregory in 69 LA 1051, 1056–1057. Also see Ross in 76 LA 101, 103; Edelman in 64 LA 816, 819–821. For cases in which the arbitrator gave priority to the conciliation agreement or affirmative action plan, see Arbitrator Taylor in 69 LA 857, 861; Dunn in 64 LA 310, 312, 314; Strongin in 63 LA 63, 64–65. Also see Koven in 71 LA 290, 294–295; Foster in 62 LA 849, 852–854; Marcus in 60 LA 495, 499–500. For the various and sometimes diverse actions of arbitrators where a court consent decree had been entered against the employer or against both the employer and the union, see Arbitrator Sharnoff in 75 LA 353; Garrett in 70 LA 1235, 1241–1242; Das in 66 LA 663; Platt in 64 LA 316; Jones in 61 LA 942; Murphy in 61 LA 844. For additional discussion of arbitrators and Title VII, see Chapter 10, subtopic entitled "Title VII of the Civil Rights Act."

[28]For example, see Graphic Arts Local 97-B v. Haddon Craftsmen, Inc., 489 F.Supp. 1088, 1096–1098 (USDC, 1981), where the court refused to set aside either of two conflicting awards where each drew its essence from the agreement.

who, as stated by the Supreme Court, "concluded that although the grievant was entitled to an award under the collective bargaining agreement, it would be inequitable to penalize the Company for conduct that complied with an outstanding court order." The next grievance to reach arbitration was heard and sustained by Arbitrator Gerald A. Barrett, who strictly applied the seniority provisions of the collective agreement, found a violation, and awarded back pay. The Sabella award was not taken to court. The Barrett award was. The District Court concluded that public policy prevented enforcement of the Barrett award. The Court of Appeals disagreed. The Supreme Court in turn held unanimously that the Court of Appeals properly enforced Arbitrator Barrett's award of back pay.[29] The Supreme Court made several salient points in its decision, some of which will be noted here in view of their obvious importance for guidance in future cases.

(1) Regarding modification of the collective agreement by the conciliation agreement, the Court of Appeals had held that because the seniority system was not motivated by a discriminatory purpose, it was lawful and could not be modified without the union's consent. The Supreme Court agreed and explained:

"In this case, although the Company and the Commission [EEOC] agreed to nullify the collective bargaining agreement's seniority provisions, the conciliation process did not include the Union. Absent a judicial determination, the Commission, not to mention the Company, cannot alter the collective bargaining agreement without the Union's consent. * * * Permitting such a result would undermine the federal labor policy that parties to a collective bargaining agreement must have reasonable assurance that their contract will be honored."[30]

(2) The Supreme Court stated that the Court of Appeals "was correct" in enforcing the award, which drew its essence from the collective agreement, for under "well established standards for the review of labor arbitration awards, a federal court may not overrule an arbitrator's decision simply because the court believes its own interpretation of the contract would be the better one"; unless the arbitrator's decision does not draw its essence from the collective agreement, "a court is bound to enforce the award and is not entitled to review the merits" of the dispute, "even when the basis for the arbitrator's decision may be ambiguous."[31]

---

[29]W.R. Grace & Co. v. Rubber Workers Local 759, 103 S.Ct. 2177, 113 LRRM 2641 (1983).

[30]113 LRRM at 2647, where the Court also explained in detail why it believed that enforcement of the arbitration award in this case should encourage rather than discourage participation by both the employer and the union in "conciliation and true voluntary compliance with federal employment discrimination law."

[31]113 LRRM at 2644, the Court citing its 1960 *Enterprise Wheel* decision. The Court explained that the award drew its essence from the collective agreement in that Arbitrator Barrett (1) interpreted provisions of the agreement as not requiring him to follow the prior award on the same issue; (2) interpreted the agreement as providing "no good faith defense to claims of violation of the seniority provisions"; and (3) "In effect * * * interpreted the collective bargaining agreement to allocate to the Company the losses caused by the Company's decision to follow the District Court order that proved to be erroneous." Id. at 2644–2645, where the Court also stated that "although conceivably we could reach a different result were we to interpret the contract ourselves, we cannot say that the award does not draw its essence from the collective bargaining agreement." For related discussion concerning the refusal to follow the prior award, see Chapter 11, topic entitled "Authoritative Prior Awards," where the *Grace* decision is included under the subtopic entitled "Temporary Arbitrators."

(3) Regarding the District Court's refusal to enforce the arbitration award on public policy grounds, the Supreme Court agreed that a court may not enforce a collective agreement that is contrary to public policy. However, the Supreme Court noted the limitation that such a public policy "must be well defined and dominant, and is to be ascertained 'by reference to the laws and legal precedents and not from general considerations of supposed public interests.'" Regarding obedience to court orders, the Supreme Court stated:

> "It is beyond question that obedience to judicial orders is an important public policy. An injunction issued by a court acting within its jurisdiction must be obeyed until the injunction is vacated or withdrawn. * * * A contract provision the performance of which has been enjoined is unenforceable. * * * Here, however, enforcement of the collective bargaining agreement as interpreted by [Arbitrator] Barrett does not compromise this public policy. * * *
> "Even assuming that the District Court's order was a mandatory injunction, nothing in the collective bargaining agreement as interpreted by Barrett required the Company to violate that order. Barrett's award neither mandated layoffs nor required that layoffs be conducted according to the collective bargaining agreement. The award simply held, retrospectively, that the employees were entitled to damages for the prior breach of the seniority provisions."[32]

It must be stressed that by no means does the *Grace* decision answer all of the important questions in this complex area. The Supreme Court expressly cautioned, for instance, that it was not deciding "whether some public policy would be violated by an arbitral award for a breach of seniority provisions ultimately found to be illegal," and neither was the Court deciding "whether such an award could be enforced in the face of a valid judicial alteration of seniority

---

[32]113 LRRM at 2645–2646, where the Court continued:
"In this case, the Company actually complied with the District Court's order, and nothing we say here causes us to believe that it would disobey the order if presented with the same dilemma in the future. Enforcement of Barrett's award will not create intolerable incentives to disobey court orders. Courts have sufficient contempt powers to protect their injunctions, even if the injunctions are issued erroneously. * * * In addition to contempt sanctions, the Company was faced with possible Title VII liability if it departed from the conciliation agreement in conducting its layoffs. * * *
"Nor is placing the Company in this position with respect to the court order so unfair as to violate public policy. Obeying injunctions often is a costly affair. Because of the Company's alleged prior discrimination against women, some readjustments and consequent losses were bound to occur. The issue is whether the Company or the Union members should bear the burden of those losses. As interpreted by Barrett, the collective bargaining agreement placed this unavoidable burden on the Company. By entering into the conflicting conciliation agreement, by seeking a court order to excuse it from performing the collective bargaining agreement, and by subsequently acting on its mistaken interpretation of its contractual obligations, the Company attempted to shift the loss to its male employees, who shared no responsibility for the sex discrimination. The Company voluntarily assumed its obligations under the collective bargaining agreement and the arbitrators' interpretations of it. No public policy is violated by holding the Company to those obligations, which bar the Company's attempted reallocation of the burden."
The Court also stated that "while it may have been economic misfortune for the Company to postpone or forgo its layoff plans," it could have avoided liability under either agreement by doing so; that prior to conducting the layoffs, the Company could have requested a stay from the District Court to permit it to follow the collective agreement pending review by a higher court; that compensatory damages for breach of contract may be available even when specific performance of the contract would violate public policy; and that increased cost of performance does not constitute "impossibility" serving as a defense to breach of contract claims. Id. at 2646, ns. 12–13.

provisions * * * to provide relief to discriminatees under Title VII or other law."[33]

Also to be stressed is the possibility that under the *Grace* facts a denial award in the Company's favor could be issued that would be valid as drawing its essence from the collective agreement.[34] The Supreme Court itself appears to have identified two different possible bases upon which an arbitrator could have given priority to the conciliation agreement over the collective agreement, namely, the "legality" clause and impossibility of performance.[35]

The *Grace* decision is a fine decision for arbitration. The Supreme Court again sends a message to the lower courts. The Court forcefully reaffirms that the parties have selected the *arbitrator* to interpret their agreement. It is the *arbitrator's* interpretation that they bargained for. The courts must honor the award if its essence is drawn from the agreement even though a court could reach and may prefer a different interpretation; provided, however, that the award must not order the performance of an unlawful act or one which would violate a strong public policy. In this regard, too, the Authors suggest that neither the parties nor arbitrators should be discouraged by the fact that different arbitrators sometimes reach conflicting conclusions on the same issue under the same agreement. This does not happen too

---

[33]113 LRRM at 2645 n.9. Thus, the Barrett award possibly would not have been enforceable if the collective agreement seniority system in fact had been invalid as the District Court erroneously believed when it ordered priority for the conciliation agreement. Likewise, *if* the District Court had identified victims of sex discrimination and had determined their "rightful place," and then had awarded constructive seniority after having performed the "delicate task" of adjusting their remedial interests and the legitimate expectations of male employees, and *if* Arbitrator Barrett had refused *then* to credit that constructive seniority, the Barrett award may not have been enforceable.

[34]It is possible, too, that the Sabella award would have been upheld had the Union taken it to court. The validity of that award was not directly litigated and the Supreme Court stated that its validity was not relevant to the issue before the Court, which concerned "Only the enforceability of the Barrett award." 113 LRRM at 2644.

[35]First, in upholding the Barrett award, the Supreme Court stated: "although conceivably we could reach a different result were we to interpret the contract ourselves, we cannot say that the award does not draw its essence from the collective bargaining agreement." In stating that the Court itself conceivably could reach a different result from Barrett, the Court pointed to the "legality" clause in the collective agreement. 113 LRRM at 2645. The clause states:

"In the event that any provision of this Agreement is found to be in conflict with any State or Federal Laws now existing or hereinafter enacted, it is agreed that such laws shall supersede the conflicting provisions without affecting the remainder of these provisions."

This "legality" clause is equally a part of the collective agreement, and it is equally subject to interpretation by the arbitrator. Although Arbitrator Barrett obviously did not interpret the clause as requiring priority for the conciliation agreement, different interpretations of the clause may reasonably be reached. The clause could be given an interpretation with controlling weight in the Company's favor. A second possibility for an award in the Company's favor within the essence of the collective agreement, is to utilize impossibility of performance as a defense to the breach of the collective agreement seniority provisions. In this regard, in a footnote the Supreme Court stated:

"Although Barrett could have considered the District Court order to cause impossibility of performance and thus to be a defense to the Company's breach, he did not do so. Impossibility is a doctrine of contract interpretation. * * * For the reasons stated in the text [i.e., because of the limitations on court review of arbitration awards], we cannot revise Barrett's implicit rejection of the impossibility defense. Even if we were to review the issue *de novo*, moreover, it is far from clear that the defense is available to the Company, whose own actions created the condition of impossibility." 113 LRRM at 2645 n. 10.

The Court appears to be saying here that an arbitrator could utilize the impossibility defense to hold for the Company, although a court, as distinguished from an arbitrator, may be more limited in doing so under the facts. In any event, the Supreme Court hardly was rejecting the defense for Arbitrator Barrett's use had he been disposed to apply it.

often. When it does happen, it is a small price to pay in exchange for the benefits of independent arbitration, circumscribed only to the extent that such arbitration truly exceeds the limits of adaptability with our basic legal system.

Seniority Units

Seniority rights relate to a specific group or unit. Seniority units are defined by the collective agreement either specifically or by interpretation. Among other possibilities, a seniority unit may be plantwide,[36] multiplant,[37] departmental,[38] or based upon the bargaining unit,[39] or upon an occupational group or classification,[40] or upon a combination of the foregoing.[41] Then, too, some agreements specify recognition of industry seniority for some purposes.[42]

The seniority unit is basic in the computation of length of service and in the assertion and determination of seniority rights. For example, where a contract called for promotions on the basis of departmental seniority, provided the senior employee was qualified, the employer was not required to make promotions on the basis of plantwide seniority where all bidders for the job were from outside the department in which the vacancy existed.[43] In another case, where several bargaining units in the plant each had separate agreements with the employer, employees laid off from one unit were not permitted to exercise their seniority to bump employees in another unit; Arbitrator Mitchell M. Shipman stated that since the contracts did not expressly provide otherwise, there was a presumption that layoffs and promotions "are to be made on an intra-bargaining unit basis, with the employee's seniority or length of service computed on his service within his bargaining unit and applied only among employees therein."[44]

Although seniority often is both acquired and exercised in one unit, the contract may provide (or be so interpreted) that seniority is acquired in one unit and exercised in another. For example, a contract provision stating simply that the employer shall operate "on a departmental and plantwide seniority basis" was construed (in the light of past practice and the history of contract negotiations) to mean that seniority was to be exercised on a departmental basis, but measured by length of service in the plant.[45]

---

[36]See, for example, 30 LA 406; 29 LA 83.
[37]See 11 LA 207. Cf., 25 LA 37.
[38]See 63 LA 202; 27 LA 685; 25 LA 826.
[39]See 57 LA 366; 21 LA 604.
[40]See 76 LA 635; 52 LA 372; 24 LA 424.
[41]See 30 LA 326; 30 LA 267.
[42]As in Rueter Worth Dairy Co., 45 LA 111, 114 (Elson, 1965).
[43]Charles Bruning Co., 25 LA 826, 827–829 (Gifford, 1955). Also see Arbitrator Randle in 17 LA 486, 488.
[44]Tide Water Assoc'd Oil Co., 21 LA 604, 607 (1953). Also see Arbitrator Cahn in 54 LA 350, 352; Shipman in 46 LA 1053, 1056.
[45]McFeely Brick Co., 22 LA 379, 382 (Reid, 1954). Also see Arbitrator Brown in 74 LA 594, 599–600; Kates in 25 LA 338, 340–341.

Similarly, seniority rights may be based upon different units with respect to the various aspects of the employment relationship. For instance, a contract may provide that departmental seniority shall govern with respect to layoff and recall, while providing for plant seniority to be exercised in bumping.[46]

Seniority Standing and Determining Length of Service

Ordinarily, seniority is based upon length of service, although the collective agreement may provide for exceptions such as "super-seniority" for union officers and stewards,[47] denial of seniority for probationary employees,[48] loss of seniority in whole or in part under specified circumstances,[49] and the like.[50] Since seniority, length of service, and their concomitant rights are creatures of contract, it is necessary always to look first to the contract in determining length of service and the seniority standing of employees.

Seniority Standing

The seniority standing of an employee is his position on the "preference" or seniority list in relation to other employees in his seniority unit. An employee's seniority standing may be a problem where, among other situations, another employee in the same seniority unit began to work on the same day but at a different hour, or had the same hiring date but began to work on a different day. Arbitrators seem to be reluctant to draw too fine a line in such situations. For example, in interpreting a collective agreement providing that an employee's continuous length of service should be computed from the date he first began to work, an arbitrator held that the seniority standing of two employees who commenced work on the same day, though on different shifts, was the same. He stated that "The legal as well as the popular meaning of the word 'date' imports the day, month and year without reference to the hour."[51] Another arbitrator further observed that it would be impractical and inconsistent with existing industrial practice to ascertain length of service in units of less than one day.[52]

The contract may be explicit as to the order of seniority. For instance, it may provide not only that seniority is to be computed from

---

[46]Harsco Corp., 30 LA 326, 327–328 (Koretz, 1957). Also see Arbitrator Shipman in 46 LA 1053, 1056; McCoy in 35 LA 692, 694–695; Logan in 29 LA 279, 281.

[47]For discussion of superseniority, see Chapter 5, subtopic entitled "Superseniority."

[48]For example, see Borden Chem. Co., 32 LA 697, 700 (Prasow, 1959).

[49]See topic entitled "Loss of Seniority," below.

[50]For recognition of a potentially broad leeway in the parties to specify seniority or preference rights on bases other than length of service, see United States Borax & Chem. Corp., 41 LA 1200, 1202 (Leonard, 1963).

[51]Bethlehem Steel Co., 26 LA 567 at 567 (Seward, 1956).

[52]Standard Oil Co. of Ind., 3 LA 758, 759 (Whiting, 1946). Cf., Arbitrator Lyons in 42 LA 961, 963–964.

the first day worked, but also that new employees are to be registered numerically as they check in on the first day worked with their seniority standing to be in the same order as their names appear on the register. Under such a provision, where two employees were hired on the same day, it was held that (barring any discrimination in the assignment of shifts) the one who "clocked in" on the first shift had more seniority than the other who commenced work on the same day but on the second shift.[53]

Under another contract defining seniority as continuous length of service, but containing no clause specifying a starting point from which length of service should be computed, it was held that where one employee started to work a day before another, the former had the greater seniority since he had the longer service record, even though both were hired on the same day.[54]

Where the seniority of employees was found to be equal, management was upheld in breaking the "tie" by considering the ability of the employees.[55]

Seniority Lists

In the absence of a contract provision requiring the posting of seniority lists, the employer may be held to be under an implied obligation to make proper and reasonable disclosure, upon demand by an aggrieved employee or his union, of the seniority standing of the aggrieved and that of other employees in his seniority unit. In this regard, Arbitrator Ralph T. Seward stated:

"An employee—and the union as his representative—clearly has a right to be informed of the seniority date and length of continuous service credited to him on the Company's records. By the same token, since most seniority issues involve a comparison of the relative rights of two or more employees, the employee—and the union as his representative— has a right to know the seniority dates and length of continuous service credited to the other employees in the seniority unit applicable to him at any given time. The only accurate source of such information is obviously the Company. It has the records. It is initiating the various transfers, promotions, demotions, 'bumps,' layoffs, recalls, etc. which are daily causing changes in those records. The information practically obtainable from the employees themselves could never be as accurate, up-to-date or complete as that which the Company can make available. Indeed, some employees might have an interest in concealing information as to their own seniority standing in an effort to protect themselves from being 'bumped.'"[56]

---

[53]Robertshaw-Fulton Controls Co., 22 LA 273, 274 (Williams, 1954). Also see Arbitrator Williams in 74 LA 301, 302–303.

[54]National Biscuit Award, 4 ALAA ¶68,530.1 (Donnelly, 1950).

[55]See Arbitrator Howlett in 50 LA 507, 516; Kahn in 38 LA 1058, 1060–1061; Scheiber in 37 LA 330, 334. In McCall Corp., 49 LA 183, 186 (McIntosh, 1967), the contract specified that ties should be resolved by a joint committee of the parties; the arbitrator specified a "toss of a coin" if the committee should disagree.

[56]Bethlehem Steel Co., 24 LA 699, 702 (1955). Also see Arbitrator Dworkin in 33 LA 60, 66; Platt in 18 LA 907, 909.

The collective agreement may specifically provide for the posting of seniority lists.[57] It may also make provision for challenging the seniority list, often with some stated time limit, and failure of an employee to make a timely protest concerning a seniority date may be deemed a waiver of his right to challenge.[58] Even without a fixed time limit, a waiver may be based upon a failure to protest within a reasonable time after the employee knows or should know that his date is incorrect.[59] However, some arbitrators have been disinclined to cut off an employee's right to challenge an erroneous seniority date.[60] Moreover, even though an employee does not challenge his posted seniority date for several years, an employer may be estopped from refusing to change an admittedly incorrect date where he has consistently treated the employee in accordance with the correct date and not the posted one.[61]

Service Outside the Seniority Unit

The length of service credited to an employee and his seniority standing may be affected by service outside the seniority unit. He may lose or retain previously earned seniority or continue to accumulate seniority, depending upon the wording of the collective agreement and how it is interpreted. Special provision may be made that an employee transferred out of the seniority unit to an exempt job continues to accumulate seniority[62] or retains seniority already earned.[63] In cases where there is no specific contract provision governing the seniority rights of employees transferred out of the seniority unit, awards vary. For example, it has been variously held that in such a situation the employee (1) retained seniority previously earned;[64] (2) could not con-

---

[57]As in Pickett Cotton Mills, 17 LA 405 at 405 (Soule, 1951).

[58]See Arbitrator Kates in 63 LA 750, 751; Shanker in 53 LA 216, 220–221 (also dealing with management's right to correct the list); Merrill in 41 LA 438, 440–441; Wolff in 37 LA 741, 744; Cahn in 30 LA 432, 433–434; Platt in 24 LA 286, 287; Soule in 17 LA 405, 405–406. Employees may challenge incorrect lists at once, not being required to wait until the employee has been adversely treated by the actual application of an erroneous list. Long Beach Oil Dev. Co., 41 LA 583, 586 (Block, 1963).

[59]See Arbitrator Smith in 81 LA 278, 282; Kubie in 67 LA 456, 460; Duff in 32 LA 568, 570. Under the circumstances in General Plywood Corp., 36 LA 633, 634 (Porter, 1961), the employee could not reasonably be charged with knowledge of the error. Also see Arbitrator Aisenberg in 77 LA 880, 882–883.

[60]See Arbitrator Hannan in 78 LA 1328, 1330; Hebert in 51 LA 778, 784; Gross in 41 LA 524, 526–528; Schedler in 41 LA 6, 7. Also see Blackmar in 75 LA 696, 697–698; Stouffer in 37 LA 231, 233.

[61]Republic Steel Corp., 25 LA 434, 435 (Platt, 1955).

[62]As in 79 LA 1022, 1026–1027 (certain employees could continue to accumulate seniority for some purposes); 55 LA 875; 35 LA 932; 29 LA 220; 27 LA 229; 25 LA 452; 24 LA 60; 23 LA 400.

[63]As in 80 LA 490, 494–495 (the contract provided that an employee transferred to a salaried position "shall cease to accumulate seniority," but it did not state that the employee would lose any seniority already earned); 77 LA 1171, 1178–1179; 68 LA 177, 179, 182; 55 LA 1011; 52 LA 383; 41 LA 1200; 37 LA 240; 30 LA 221; 26 LA 195 (could retain seniority up to one year); 26 LA 67.

[64]See Arbitrator Di Leone in 75 LA 1077, 1079–1080 (nor would seniority be lost by virtue of a provision, calling for loss of seniority upon promotion to supervisor, adopted *after* the individual left the bargaining unit for a supervisory position); Taylor in 70 LA 1246, 1249; Marshall in 54 LA 1093, 1095; Elliott in 54 LA 965, 972–973, 981; Leach in 45 LA 1039, 1044–1045; Block in 43 LA 97, 100–101; McDermott in 41 LA 1228, 1230–1231; Feinberg in 40 LA 495, 498–499; Schmidt in 36 LA 1245, 1249; Kates in 36 LA 857, 858; Begley in 32 LA 892, 893; Baab in 28 LA 641, 645; Howard in 23 LA 440, 446; Ryder in 22 LA 769, 771–773; Myers in 22 LA 704, 705–706; Cahn in 22 LA 492, 495; Healy in 14 LA 916, 918; Lohman in 14 LA 537, 540.

tinue to accumulate seniority while outside the unit;[65] (3) continued
to accumulate seniority during temporary promotion out of the unit;[66]
(4) continued to accumulate seniority while working outside the unit
for an extended period;[67] and (5) forfeited all his seniority because he
had in effect voluntarily quit.[68] In some of the cases cited in the above
categories the result was influenced by past practice.

Many arbitrators agree that an individual generally cannot be
credited with seniority for any service performed prior to his entry into
the bargaining unit.[69] For example, individuals who had been promoted to supervisory jobs prior to the date of the first contract with the
union were held to have no seniority when demoted into the bargaining unit.[70] However, seniority credit for preunit service has been
upheld where the agreement referred to seniority in terms of "length
of continuous service with the company," or the like.[71]

Extension of Seniority Rights to Different Plant or Successor Employer

Where employees acquire seniority rights under a collective
agreement by performing service at a given plant for a given employer
and the plant is relocated or closed down, the employees may assert a
right to extend or transfer their seniority to another plant of their
employer. Likewise, where the business is sold or absorbed by merger,
they may assert a right to continue their seniority in the employ of the
successor employer.

Closing or Relocation of Plant

While the collective agreement or some special agreement may
expressly provide for the transfer of seniority rights to other loca-

---

[65]See Arbitrator Kanner in 79 LA 48, 49–50, 53–54; Block in 43 LA 97, 100–101; Schmidt in
36 LA 1245, 1249; Cahn in 29 LA 828, 830, and in 22 LA 13, 17; Marshall in 17 LA 105, 108.

[66]See Arbitrator Caraway in 53 LA 1143, 1145–1146; Volz in 48 LA 743, 744–746; Teple in
45 LA 671, 674; Haughton in 28 LA 315, 317. Also see Hotchkiss in 4 LA 21, 24.

[67]See Arbitrator McDermott in 42 LA 1172, 1177–1179; Mishne in 36 LA 691, 694; Garrett
in 28 LA 740, 743, and in 15 LA 834, 836; Byrnes in 25 LA 595, 596–597; Shipman in 21 LA 682,
685; Fulda in 18 LA 315, 317; Roberts in 14 LA 482, 486; Gregory in 8 LA 51, 52; Reynolds in 3 LA
748, 752. Also see Anrod in 34 LA 285, 290; Smith in 23 LA 338, 340. Cf., Garrett in 48 LA 872,
883.

[68]See Arbitrator Shister in 40 LA 531, 532; Kotin in 27 LA 30, 35; Platt in 26 LA 898,
899–901. Also see Gorsuch in 44 LA 802, 806–807, and in 40 LA 388, 391–392; Marshall in 17 LA
105, 108. Acceptance of a supervisory position at another of the company's plants, which had a
different bargaining unit, resulted in loss of all seniority in The Colo. Fuel & Iron Corp., 47 LA
1131, 1135 (Prasow, 1966).

[69]See Arbitrator Briggs in 80 LA 332, 336; Kanner in 79 LA 48, 55–56; Hannan in 78 LA
1328, 1331; Block in 41 LA 583, 587; Singletary in 41 LA 215, 218–219; Hebert in 37 LA 200, 205;
Loucks in 36 LA 1067, 1069; Schmidt in 33 LA 150, 152; Smith in 32 LA 274, 277; Cahn in 30 LA
221, 223, and in 29 LA 828, 830; McKelvey in 27 LA 229, 231–232; Tatum in 24 LA 517, 521.

[70]United States Radium Corp., 36 LA 1067, 1069 (Loucks, 1961).

[71]See Arbitrator Sisk in 80 LA 625, 627–628; Alexander in 38 LA 741, 744; Cobb in 38 LA
188, 190–192; Anrod in 34 LA 285, 290; Guild in 26 LA 256, 258. But see Kanner in 79 LA 48,
55–56; Shipman in 21 LA 682, 685. In Jenison Pub. School Dist., 81 LA 105, 116 (Roumell, 1983),
seniority credit for preunit service was upheld on the basis of past practice. For a case concerning
seniority credit for employees who worked during a strike which occurred following expiration of
the collective agreement, see Flint Osteopathic Hosp., 81 LA 427, 430–431 (Borland, 1983), also
discussing cases concerning the accrual of seniority by employees while on strike.

tions,[72] in the absence of such express provision numerous arbitrators have construed the collective agreement before them as giving seniority rights to be exercised only at the plant location where service was performed which earned the rights, the seniority rights thus not surviving the closing or removal of the plant.[73]

In the widely repudiated and ultimately overruled court case of *Zdanok v. Glidden* it was held that seniority rights survived the expiration of a collective agreement and a relocation of the plant.[74] In overruling its *Glidden* decision the U.S. Court of Appeals, Second Circuit, explained:

> "We are persuaded that the reasoning of the majority opinion in the Glidden case was erroneous and that erroneous reasoning led to an incorrect result. For example, the basic proposition of the opinion, that seniority is a vested right, finds no support in authority, in logic or in the socio-economic setting of labor-management relations. Seniority is wholly a creation of the collective agreement and does not exist apart from that agreement. The incidents of seniority can be freely altered or amended by modification of the collective agreement. Ford Motor Co. v. Huffman, 345 U.S. 330, 73 S.Ct. 681, 97 L.Ed. 1048 (1953). In giving seniority a conceptual status apart from the provisions of the collective agreement and the intentions of the parties the Glidden opinion seriously misconceived the nature of the employment relationship and dealt 'a blow to labor-management relations.'"[75]

Merger or Sale of Company

In its 1964 *John Wiley & Sons v. Livingston* decision the U.S. Supreme Court upheld the arbitrability of grievances concerning the survival of the seniority and other rights of employees following their employer's disappearance by merger and expiration of their collective agreement, the Court emphasizing that there was a "substantial continuity of identity in the business enterprise" before and after the merger.[76]

After *Wiley* the question remained as to whether not only the arbitration clause, but also other provisions of the predecessor's agree-

---

[72]See C.K. Williams Co., 12 LA 987, 988 (Kerr, 1949). Also see Arbitrator Cole in 61 LA 745, 749 (contract specified preferential hiring rights at new location).

[73]See Arbitrator McCoy in 46 LA 1063, 1065; Kagel in 45 LA 551, 552–554; Scheiber in 44 LA 979, 984–986; Casselman in 44 LA 361, 369; Turkus in 43 LA 798, 803–804; Davey in 43 LA 453, 459; Howlett in 39 LA 449, 454–456; Kelliher in 38 LA 619, 620; Duff in 37 LA 928, 932. Also see Klein in 80 LA 212, 218; Malinowski in 48 LA 1257, 1260–1261 (economic closing of plant does not violate contract seniority or recognition clauses); Lawson in 39 LA 82, 84–85. Cf., Leahy in 73 LA 882, 885; Smith in 42 LA 517, 523–524.

[74]288 F.2d 99, 47 LRRM 2865 (CA 2, 1961).

[75]Local 1251, UAW v. Robertshaw Controls Co., 405 F.2d 29, 33, 68 LRRM 2671 (CA 2, 1968), in which the court cited several articles which had been written in criticism of the *Glidden* decision. Also rejecting the contention that seniority rights are "vested rights" which cannot be cut off or defeated by a relocation of the plant, Charland v. Norge Div., Borg-Warner Corp., 70 LRRM 2705 (CA 6, 1969); Oddie v. Ross Gear & Tool Co., 50 LRRM 2763 (CA 6, 1962). In Cooper v. General Motors Corp., 107 LRRM 3161, 3163 (CA 5, 1981), the court cited *Robertshaw Controls* with approval and reiterated its own prior statement that "collective bargaining agreements do not create a permanent status, give an indefinite tenure, or extend rights created and arising under the contract, beyond its life, when it has been terminated in accordance with its provisions."

[76]84 S.Ct. 909, 55 LRRM 2769 (1964). For the arbitrator's ultimate ruling as to the extent to which the predecessor's contract was binding on the successor in *Wiley*, and, in particular, the extent to which seniority rights of the predecessor's employees survived the merger, see Interscience Encyclopedia, 55 LA 210, 218–221, 225 (Roberts, 1970).

ment, must be honored by the successor employer under the National Labor Relations Act. In its 1972 *Burns International Security Services* decision, the Supreme Court, while cautioning that its resolution of the issues "turns to a great extent on the precise facts involved here," held that a successor employer was required to bargain with the union that had represented its predecessor's employees but that the NLRB had improperly ordered the successor to honor the predecessor's collective agreement.[77] In holding that the successor was not bound by the predecessor's agreement, the Supreme Court stated:

> "In many cases, of course, successor employers will find it advantageous not only to recognize and bargain with the union but also to observe the pre-existing contract rather than to face uncertainty and turmoil. Also, in a variety of circumstances involving a merger, stock acquisition, reorganization, or assets purchase, the Board might properly find as a matter of fact that the successor had assumed the obligations under the old contract. * * * Such a duty does not, however, ensue as a matter of law from the mere fact that an employer is doing the same work in the same place with the same employees as his predecessor, as the Board had recognized until its decision in the instant case."[78]

In *Burns* the Supreme Court distinguished its *Wiley* decision on the basis that *Wiley* "arose in the context of a § 301 suit to compel arbitration" whereas *Burns* arose "in the context of an unfair labor practice proceeding" before the NLRB.[79] However, this distinction was expressly discounted or rejected by the Supreme Court in its 1974 *Howard Johnson* decision, in which the Court held that where there was "no substantial continuity of identity in the work force hired by [the buyer] with that of the [seller], and no express or implied assumption of the agreement to arbitrate," the buyer was not required "to arbitrate the extent of its obligations to" the former employees of the seller; although *Howard Johnson,* like *Wiley,* arose in the context of a § 301 suit to compel arbitration, the Supreme Court believed that "the fundamental policies outlined in *Burns,*" rather than *Wiley,* controlled the disposition of the case.[80]

Thus, it is apparent that even as to the arbitration clause itself, the scope of *Wiley* has been limited.[81] In the latter regard, Professor Robert A. Gorman stated that:

---

[77]NLRB v. Burns Intl. Sec. Servs., Inc., 92 S.Ct. 1571, 80 LRRM 2225 (1972).

[78]Id. at 1584. In Golden State Bottling Co. v. NLRB, 94 S.Ct. 414, 425, 84 LRRM 2839 (1973), the Supreme Court held that a successor purchasing a business with knowledge that the seller had unlawfully discharged an employee could be required by the NLRB to reinstate him with back pay, but the Court cautioned that "We in no way qualify the *Burns*' holdings."

[79]92 S.Ct. at 1581.

[80]Howard Johnson Co. v. Detroit Local Joint Executive Bd., 94 S.Ct. 2236, 2240, 2244, 86 LRRM 2449 (1974). Although the Court discounted or rejected the aforementioned distinction, the Court stated that: "We find it unnecessary, however, to decide in the circumstances of this case whether there is any irreconcilable conflict between *Wiley* and *Burns.*"

[81]In *Howard Johnson* the Supreme Court distinguished *Wiley* on the basis that: (1) *Wiley* involved a merger rather than only a sale of assets, and while "ordinarily there is no basis for distinguishing among mergers, consolidations, or purchases of assets in the analysis of successorship problems," the existence in *Wiley* of a state statute making the surviving corporation in a merger liable for the obligations of the disappearing corporation, and the lack of any remedy against the former employer in *Wiley,* provided the basis in *Wiley* for distinguishing the different

"It is clear that the Court has cut back on its broad pronouncements in *Wiley,* in the interest of unfettered transfer and development of capital and human resources in business transfers. In *Howard Johnson,* it ignored the 'successors and assigns' provision in the [seller's] labor contract as a possible base for arbitral relief against the successor Howard Johnson; it emphasized the technical form which the transfer of assets took; and it gave no weight to the fact that the [seller's] employees retained by Howard Johnson continued to use the same skills performing the same jobs under the same working conditions as before."[82]

Some types of successorship or "successorship related" issues that in some manner have reached arbitration since the 1974 *Howard Johnson* decision, are those dealing with (1) the successor's obligations under the predecessor's collective agreement, often including those concerning seniority or benefits based upon seniority;[83] (2) the predecessor's obligation to require its successor to assume the prede-

---

types of successorship transactions; (2) "Even more important, in *Wiley* the surviving corporation hired *all* of the employees of the disappearing corporation," whereas in *Howard Johnson* the buyer "hired only nine of the 53 former" employees of the seller—the "continuity of identity in the business enterprise necessarily includes * * * a substantial continuity in the identity of the work force across the change in ownership." 94 S.Ct. at 2240–2244. The Court also reiterated that in successor employer cases "the employees of the terminating employer have no legal right to continued employment with the new employer," provided, of course, that the successor does not "discriminate in hiring or retention of employees on the basis of union membership or activity." Id. at 2243–2244. Also see Vantage Petroleum Corp., 103 LRRM 1408 (NLRB, 1980).

[82]Gorman, Basic Text on Labor Law, 583 (1976). For other discussions of the *Wiley, Burns,* and *Howard Johnson* decisions, see Krupman & Kaplan, "The Stock Purchaser After *Burns*: Must He Buy the Union Contract?" 31 Lab. L.J. 328 (1980); Henry, "Is There Arbitration After *Burns*?: The Resurrection of *John Wiley & Sons,*" 31 Vand. L. Rev. 249 (1978); Severson & Willcoxon, "Successorship Under *Howard Johnson*: Short Order Justice for Employees," 64 Cal. L. Rev. 795 (1976); Barksdale, "Successor Liability Under the National Labor Relations Act and Title VII," 54 Tex. L. Rev. 707 (1976).

[83]For a case holding that the successor did *not* have obligations under the predecessor's agreement, see Kroger Co., 78 LA 569, 578–591 (Howlett, 1981), extensively discussing court and arbitration decisions. In concluding that the successor in this case was not bound by the predecessor's collective agreement notwithstanding its successors and assigns clause, Arbitrator Howlett stressed that before the property was transferred to it, the successor had made clear that it refused to be bound by the predecessor's agreement and that the predecessor's employees would not necessarily be hired by seniority; although over 50 percent of those employees were hired by the successor, Arbitrator Howlett declared that the fact that it did hire them, to their benefit, "should not—and does not—obligate the [successor] to adopt a contract which it could have avoided simply by refusing to hire (or refusing to hire a majority of)" the predecessor's employees. In Schneier's Finer Foods, 72 LA 881, 886–888 (Belkin, 1979), it was held that a successor *did* have obligations under the predecessor's agreement, Arbitrator Belkin concluding that the successor could not avoid assuming the predecessor's obligations merely by inserting a disclaimer in the purchase agreement. He stated that "Once a successor employer agrees to hire a majority of its predecessor's employees, as did [the successor here], my reading of Wiley, Burns and Howard Johnson is that the obligation, if any, under the predecessor's agreement should be evaluated in relation to the following factors: continuity of operations; location of the work place; nature of the work itself; and the viability of the predecessor employer." He added that other factors "which must be considered include the wording of the 'successors and assigns' clause of the predecessor's contract (if any): whether or not the successor assented to be bound (expressly or impliedly); and the effect of imposing any portion of the predecessor's labor agreement on the labor policies of the successor." For other cases holding that the successor had obligations under the predecessor's agreement, see Arbitrator LeWinter in 72 LA 102, 102–105; Katz in 71 LA 1238, 1241–1242; Turkus in 71 LA 366, 372–374; Helfeld in 68 LA 633, 636–638. For cases arbitrated in the interim between *Burns* and *Howard Johnson,* see Arbitrator Harter in 62 LA 660, 666–667; Hogan in 61 LA 739, 744. For pre-*Burns* cases dealing with the successor's obligations under the predecessor's agreement, see pp. 563–564 of the Third Edition of this book, where it is indicated that in some cases arbitrators held the successor bound by the predecessor's agreement, including an obligation to recognize the seniority rights of the predecessor's employees under that agreement, but that in other cases the arbitrator held otherwise and did not recognize a right of employees to seniority credit in the employ of a successor employer for service performed with the predecessor.

cessor's collective agreement as a condition of the transfer of the business;[84] (3) the obligation of a predecessor or successor for severance pay to employees of the predecessor who were employed by the successor.[85]

Merger of Seniority Lists

Merger of separate companies or consolidation of plants or departments with separate seniority lists may raise the problem of determining precisely how to combine such lists to make a composite list of employees of both operations. An extensive study of this problem and of published and unpublished cases and other experiences reflecting methods and criteria used in the merger of seniority lists was made by Professor Thomas Kennedy, who reported his findings, including those as to the advantages and disadvantages of each method, to the National Academy of Arbitrators.[86] The reader is directed to that excellent report for its in-depth consideration of methods of merging seniority lists. The present topic will merely note the methods, identified and analyzed by Professor Kennedy, of making a composite seniority list for purposes of layoff, rehire, promotion, transfer, and the like.[87] Said methods are:

---

[84]Holding that the predecessor was *not* obligated to do so, Arbitrator Gallagher in 79 LA 253, 258, 260 (a general successor clause providing that terms of the agreement shall bind all sublessees, assignees, purchasers, or other successors did not clearly and unambiguously oblige the predecessor to obtain an assumption of the agreement by the successor); Howlett in 78 LA 569, 577, 589–590; Joseph in 59 LA 1193, 1198–1199 (case decided in interim between *Burns* and *Howard Johnson*). Also see Gallagher in 79 LA 292, 295–296, 298. Holding that the predecessor *was* obligated to require its successor to assume the collective agreement, Arbitrator Levine in 81 LA 22, 28, 30–31 (itemizing the damages in detail); Gallagher in 80 LA 658, 660, 663 (concluding that "clear and unambiguous" language imposed the obligation); Ross in 76 LA 576, 577, 579 (predecessor's collective agreement expressly imposed the obligation); Simons in 74 LA 129, 131 (predecessor's collective agreement expressly imposed the obligation); Belkin in 72 LA 881, 885 (collective agreement provided that it shall "bind the successors of the respective parties," and this was held violated by predecessor's failure to require successor to accept the agreement); Connolly in 67 LA 239, 248 (collective agreement prohibited use of "any sale, transfer, lease, assignment, receivership, or bankruptcy to evade the terms of this Agreement"). In IAM Local Lodge 1266 v. Panoramic Corp., 109 LRRM 2169 (CA 7, 1981), the sale of corporate assets was enjoined pending arbitration of the union's claim that the collective agreement obligated the employer to secure from any purchaser an assumption of the agreement as a condition of the sale.
[85]Holding the predecessor not obligated for severance pay, Arbitrator Boyer in 81 LA 438, 443; Gamser in 70 LA 1193, 1195. Holding that the predecessor was obligated for severance pay, Arbitrator Epstein in 81 LA 514, 518; Madden in 68 LA 1037, 1040; Dash in 61 LA 1032, 1041–1042. Holding the successor not obligated for severance pay, Arbitrator Marlatt in 63 LA 1300, 1305–1307.
[86]Kennedy, "Merging Seniority Lists," Proceedings of the 16th Annual Meeting of NAA, 1 (BNA Books, 1963).
[87]Professor Kennedy noted that seniority rights may be divided into two distinct types. One type, termed "benefit seniority," is concerned with benefits such as vacations or retirement pay and usually depends solely on length of service. The other type, termed "competitive-status seniority," is concerned with such matters as layoff or promotion and is not necessarily based solely on length of service. Where the distinction between the two types of seniority is applied, it is necessary to have a seniority list for benefits and another for competitive status; this can result in discrepancies between the two types of rights. Id. at 2, 29. Also see Arbitrator Spelfogel in 53 LA 1253, 1258–1259; Duff in 48 LA 600, 603–606 (employees of an acquired company were permitted to keep all their benefit seniority but only one half of their competitive-status seniority—a separate list for each type of seniority was specified by the arbitrator); Anderson in 44 LA 311, 314.

1. *The surviving-group principle.* Here when one company purchases or acquires another company, the employees of the purchasing or acquiring company receive seniority preference over the employees of the purchased or acquired company. The seniority lists are merged by adding the names of the employees of the acquired company to the bottom of the list of the acquiring company.[88]

2. *The length-of-service principle.* Here a combined seniority list is prepared by placing employees on the new list in the order of their length of service regardless of which company or plant the employee worked for prior to the merger or consolidation. All employees are thus treated as if they had always been employed by the same company or plant.[89]

3. *The follow-the-work principle.* Here when companies merge or when plants or departments within a company are consolidated, the employees are given the opportunity to follow their work (if it still can be adequately identified) with the seniority rights to such work protected by continuation of the separate seniority lists. If the work becomes merged or its identity is otherwise lost, the seniority lists may be integrated into a single list on a ratio basis representing the amount of work brought to the consolidation by each group of employees.[90]

4. *The absolute-rank principle.* Here employees are placed on the merged seniority list on the basis of the rank they held on their respective prior lists. Thus, the two employees who were first on the two original lists are given the first two places on the merged list (the employee with the longer service gets the first place and the other employee gets the second); the two employees who were second on the two original lists are given the third and fourth places on the merged list; and so on. The ratio-rank principle, noted below, is much more popular than the absolute-rank principle since the ratio-rank method gives due consideration to the rank factor without producing the serious

---

[88]For instances in which this method, sometimes called "endtailing," was used either exclusively or in combination with another method, see Arbitrator Render in 69 LA 477, 482 (where he found this method required by contract); Spelfogel in 53 LA 1253, 1258–1259; Platt in 36 LA 981, 988–989, where group A list was placed near bottom of group B list, group A list being integrated only with group B employees who were on layoff. Also see union position and comments of Arbitrator Harkless in 71 LA 476, 478–479.

[89]For instances in which this method was used either exclusively or in combination with another method, see Arbitrator Spelfogel in 53 LA 1253, 1258–1259; Rohman in 51 LA 717, 718–719; Wagner in 46 LA 589, 598; Kerrison in 45 LA 1018, 1019, 1021; Anderson in 44 LA 311, 315–316; Kahn in 40 LA 680, 685–686; Di Leone in 31 LA 976, 979 (lists "dovetailed" by length of service); Somers in 24 LA 793, 801–803.

[90]This was done in Sonotone Corp., 42 LA 359, 364 (Wolf, 1964), where a group of employees who only brought 70 percent as much work to the consolidation as another group did were credited with 70 percent of their length of prior service and the resultant figure determined their place on a merged (length of service variety) seniority list. Also see Arbitrator Duff in 48 LA 600, 604–606.

distortions which can occur under the absolute-rank method, as where the groups to be merged are of different size.[91]

5. *The ratio-rank principle*. Here integration of seniority lists may be accomplished by establishing a ratio from the number of employees in each of the groups to be merged and assigning the places on the new seniority list according to this ratio. Thus, if seniority list A has 200 employees and seniority list B has only 100 employees, the ratio is two to one. Therefore, of the first three places on the new seniority list, two are allocated to the first two employees on the A list and one is allocated to the first employee on the B list (as among the three employees, length of service may be used to determine which employee gets each of the first three places); then places 4, 5, and 6 on the new list are allocated to the third and fourth employees on the A list and to the second employee on the B list; and so on, until all the A and B employees are placed on the new list.[92]

In determining which method or combination of methods should be used in the given case (or in determining whether a method agreed to by the parties is fair and should be approved), an arbitrator will of course give intensive consideration to the facts and circumstances of the particular case. Any one of the above methods, particularly the length-of-service method, may possibly be selected for exclusive use in a case.[93] However, it is not unusual for methods to be used in combination.[94] For instance, in merging two pilot seniority lists following the merger of airlines, one-third weight was given to the ratio-rank principle and two-thirds weight to the length-of-service principle; the arbitrator thus considered (1) length of service, and (2) the ratio of pilots in one airline to pilots in the other, but with length of service having greater weight.[95]

Loss of Seniority

Some situations in which seniority rights may be lost in whole or in part have been noted in the preceding topics. It may also be noted that contractual provisions for loss of seniority in designated situations are not uncommon. For example, the agreement may call for loss

---

[91]In Moore Bus. Forms, 24 LA 793, 801–803 (Somers, 1955), the "rank" factor was used in combination with length of service, equal weight being given to (1) overall length of service, and (2) the employees' relative positions on the separate plant lists.

[92]This method was used, or approved, in combination with other methods by Arbitrator Platt in Delta Air Lines, 72 LA 458, 466–469 (1979); Cole in Pan Am. World Airways, 19 LA 14, 20–22 (1952).

[93]For example, see City of Green Bay, 44 LA 311, 315–316 (Anderson, 1965). Length of service is given at least some weight in most cases.

[94]For example, see Arbitrator Wolf in 42 LA 359, 364; Platt in 36 LA 981, 988–989; Somers in 24 LA 793, 801–803; Cole in 19 LA 14, 20–22.

[95]Pan Am. World Airways, 19 LA 14, 20–22 (Cole, 1952).

of seniority in the event of unexcused absence for a specified period,[96] or in the event the employee resigns.[97]

In some instances the agreement will expressly indicate that loss of seniority due to unexcused absences shall also constitute a termination of the employment relationship.[98] Termination of the employee without such express provision has been upheld in some cases as a concomitant of the loss of seniority,[99] but not always.[100]

Seniority Provisions

There are two basic types of seniority provisions. The more rigid type requires the recognition of strict seniority—that is, the employer must give preference to the employee with the longest continuous service without regard to any other considerations.[101] The principal thesis underlying this approach is that, as between a junior man of superior qualities and a senior man of lower qualities, the social claim of the latter should override both the needs of the business and the interest of the public in its efficient operation.[102] The more usual provision, however, is written so as to serve the basic aims of seniority, while recognizing other factors, which basically involve the "fitness and ability" of the employee, in determining preference in employment.[103] Such factors may include skill, ability, aptitude, competence, efficiency, training, physical fitness, judgment, experience, initiative, leadership, and the like.

In regard to this "modified seniority," Arbitrator Harry H. Platt stated:

---

[96]See Arbitrator Devino in 79 LA 1012, 1013; Bickner in 76 LA 1258, 1260; Roumell in 72 LA 1262, 1263; Dworkin in 55 LA 709, 715; Rohman in 49 LA 613, 614–615; Autrey in 43 LA 1066, 1069–1070.

[97]See Arbitrator Kanner in 79 LA 48, 52; Teple in 49 LA 950, 952; R. Seitz in 49 LA 490, 492–493. In Reden Corp., 50 LA 413, 416–417 (Roberts, 1968), the arbitrator enforced a strike settlement agreement under which the accumulation of seniority by strikers was tolled during the period of the strike.

[98]See Arbitrator Devino in 79 LA 1012, 1013; Bickner in 76 LA 1258, 1260; Rohman in 49 LA 613, 614; Larkin in 49 LA 283 at 283.

[99]See Arbitrator Doering in 74 LA 1185, 1187; Daly in 72 LA 613, 615–616; Traynor in 70 LA 963, 966; Cox in 70 LA 185, 186; Dugan in 60 LA 793, 794–795; Shister in 59 LA 869, 871; Stouffer in 47 LA 443, 446–448; Klein in 42 LA 1151, 1161–1162, and in 39 LA 414, 415–416; P. Seitz in 38 LA 278, 279–282. Also see Beilstein in 78 LA 1065, 1067; Barron in 72 LA 1217, 1218, 1220. For related discussion, see Chapter 15, topic entitled "Employer Action Pending Court Hearing on Conduct of Employee," where cases are cited permitting or not permitting discharge of employees for absence from work due to jail confinement.

[100]See Cooper Indus., 78 LA 850, 855–856 (Aisenberg, 1982); Quick Mfg., 43 LA 54, 60–61 (Teple, 1964). Also see Arbitrator Walsh in 49 LA 206, 209.

[101]See strict seniority provision before Arbitrator Jones in 68 LA 1343, 1345; Williams in 65 LA 1265, 1266; Mittenthal in 27 LA 203, 204. In Branch Motor Express Co., 39 LA 795 at 795 (Crawford, 1962), the agreement specified strict seniority except where special training or experience is required, the exception to become effective only by special agreement of the parties.

[102]See Clifton, "Management Functions," N.Y.U. First Ann. Conf. on Labor, 89, 97 (1948).

[103]See Darin & Armstrong, 13 LA 843, 845 (Platt, 1950). Some contracts provide for strict seniority for layoffs while calling for consideration of seniority and ability for promotions, as in J. Weingarten, 42 LA 619, 622 (Rohman, 1964). In New Britain Mach. Co., 45 LA 993, 994–995 (McCoy, 1965), the contract merely stated that the employer "will give consideration to seniority"; the arbitrator said this only required good faith consideration of seniority and did not prevent consideration also of ability or physical fitness, or of the employer's own interest in efficient and profitable operations.

"Generally speaking, such modified seniority is acceptable to most unions and employers because it acknowledges the fact that wide difference in ability and capacity to perform the work required exists between employees in a plant and that such differences are a logical and legitimate consideration in determining preference in employment, especially in making promotions and demotions as well as in the reduction of forces."[104]

Modified Seniority Clauses

Modified seniority clauses fall into one of three basic categories: (1) In one category are those clauses which provide in essence that the senior employee shall be given preference if he possesses fitness and ability equal to that of junior employees.[105] This type of clause might be termed a *"relative ability"* clause, since here comparisons between qualifications of employees bidding for the job are necessary and proper[106] and seniority becomes a determining factor only if the qualifications of the bidders are equal.[107]

The wording of these "relative ability" clauses varies. The contract may provide that seniority shall govern unless there is a marked difference in ability, or unless a junior employee has greater ability. Some clauses provide that seniority shall govern if ability (or other qualifying factors such as physical fitness, competence, etc.) is *relatively equal,* or *substantially equal,* or simply *equal.* Even in the latter regard, however, it has been held that the term "equal" does not mean exact equality, but only substantial equality.[108] Nor does "relatively" equal ability mean "exactly" equal ability.[109] Thus, whether the term used is "equal" or "relatively equal" or "substantially equal," it would appear that only an approximate or near equality of competing employees, rather than an exact equality, should be necessary in order to bring the seniority factor into play.[110] Where the junior employee is

---

[104]Darin & Armstrong, 13 LA 843, 845–846 (1950). Also see comment of Arbitrator Frey in Atlas Powder Co., 30 LA 674, 676 (1958).

[105]For examples of this type of clause, see 76 LA 978, 979; 72 LA 524, 525; 66 LA 342, 344; 56 LA 1206, 1207; 56 LA 399, 401; 56 LA 6, 7; 55 LA 104, 105; 46 LA 1005, 1006; 46 LA 23, 24; 45 LA 444 at 444; 30 LA 674, 675; 29 LA 262, 265; 25 LA 480, 481; 23 LA 322, 323; 21 LA 565, 566.

[106]Alabama Power Co., 18 LA 24, 25 (McCoy, 1952). Relative ability is to be determined in reference to the particular job in question, not in reference to overall ability. New Jersey Tel. Co., 47 LA 495, 500 (Koretz, 1966); Yuba Heat Transfer Corp., 38 LA 471, 474–475 (Autrey, 1962).

[107]See Arbitrator Smith in 76 LA 978, 982–983; Merrifield in 68 LA 1019, 1021; Ross in 34 LA 271, 273; Frey in 30 LA 674, 677; Brecht in 21 LA 565, 568; McCoy in 18 LA 24, 25.

[108]See Poloron Prods. of Pa., 23 LA 789, 792 (Rosenfarb, 1955); Combustion Eng'g. Co., 20 LA 416, 419 (McCoy, 1953). Also see Arbitrator Armstrong in 79 LA 441, 448; Kelliher in 76 LA 852, 853; Ross in 34 LA 271, 273; Howlett in 26 LA 885, 889. Cf., Gregory in 9 LA 432, 435.

[109]See Bethlehem Steel Co., 23 LA 532, 534 (Seward, 1954).

[110]See Republic Steel Corp., 1 LA 244, 247 (Platt, 1945). Also see Arbitrator Armstrong in 79 LA 441, 448; Atleson in 75 LA 1024, 1027, 1033; Roumell in 72 LA 1061, 1064; Volz in 47 LA 263, 265 (junior employee "need not be head-and-shoulders better, but his greater ability should be clearly discernible to outweigh the factor of seniority"); Luskin in 46 LA 23, 26–27 (junior employee loses unless there is a definite, distinct, substantial, and significant difference as to ability in his favor); Ross in 34 LA 271, 273 ("if the junior employee is preferred, he should he 'head and shoulders' above the senior"). But see Ipavec in 72 LA 524, 527 (stating that "only where the margin is diminutive shall seniority determine").

substantially superior in ability, however, he may be given preference over a senior employee.[111]

(2) The second basic type of modified seniority clause provides in general that the senior employee will be given preference if he possesses sufficient ability to perform the job.[112] Minimum qualifications are enough under these *"sufficient ability"* clauses.[113] This type of clause may state that preference will be given to the senior qualified bidder, or to the senior employee provided he is qualified or has the "necessary" ability for the job, and the like. Under this type of provision, "it is necessary to determine only whether the employee with greater seniority can in fact do the job."[114] Comparisons between applicants are unnecessary and improper, and "the job must be given to the senior bidder if he is competent, regardless of how much more competent some other bidder may be."[115] Thus, the senior qualified employee will be entitled to preference even though a junior employee possesses greater skill and ability.[116]

(3) The third basic type of modified seniority provision, which may be called a *"hybrid"* clause, requires consideration and comparison in the first instance of *both* seniority and relative ability.[117] The "hybrid" clause ordinarily is worded in such general terms as "seniority and qualifications shall govern," or "due consideration shall be given to length of service, aptitude, and ability," and the like, without indicating the relative weight to be accorded these factors.[118] Arbitrators, however, require that fair and reasonable consideration be given to both seniority and relative ability, although the weight that may be accorded to each varies from case to case.

---

[111]See Arbitrator Rezler in 72 LA 941, 949; Dworkin in 49 LA 390, 395; Volz in 47 LA 263, 265; Luskin in 46 LA 23, 28; Seward in 29 LA 710, 712; Frey in 19 LA 883, 888; Roberts in 19 LA 270, 278–279.

[112]For examples of this type of clause, see 79 LA 106, 107; 62 LA 84, 86; 61 LA 1021 at 1021; 56 LA 920, 921; 56 LA 40, 41; 55 LA 813, 814; 52 LA 247, 248; 46 LA 238, 239; 29 LA 29, 31; 27 LA 353, 356; 25 LA 479, 480.

[113]Central Franklin Process Co., 19 LA 32, 34 (Marshall, 1952). Also see Arbitrator Schwartz in 79 LA 1147, 1150–1151; Harrison in 79 LA 106, 108–109. In Kingsberry Homes Corp., 53 LA 1345, 1347 (Rauch, 1969), the arbitrator stated that the term "if qualified" must be construed "to mean that the senior employee must have a background of such training, experience, or demonstrated aptitude and physical makeup, as to give a reasonable person cause to believe that this person can be expected to perform the job competently within a reasonable time."

[114]See Arbitrator Garman in 71 LA 850, 852; Nicolau in 68 LA 271, 276; Platt in 1 LA 244, 247. Also see Duncan in 40 LA 364, 366.

[115]Alabama Power Co., 18 LA 24, 25 (McCoy, 1952). Similarly, see Arbitrator Fogel in 80 LA 1328, 1331; Schwartz in 79 LA 1147, 1150–1151; Harrison in 79 LA 106, 108–109; Kates in 78 LA 383, 385; Brown in 72 LA 1167, 1170; Volz in 49 LA 918, 920.

[116]Central Franklin Process Co., 19 LA 32, 34 (Marshall, 1952). Similarly, see Arbitrator Harrison in 79 LA 106, 108–109; Block in 43 LA 1248, 1251–1252.

[117]See Arbitrator Rifkin in 78 LA 64, 65–67; Cyrol in 72 LA 752, 757; Edes in 64 LA 1104, 1109; Cahn in 62 LA 333, 334, 337; Turkus in 61 LA 768, 769; Dolson in 50 LA 990, 991, 994; Alexander in 50 LA 397, 399–400; Knowlton in 38 LA 374, 374–375; Davis in 30 LA 862, 870; Cole in 21 LA 183, 185; Cornsweet in 16 LA 280, 283, 285; Frolich in 14 LA 12, 15; Wolff in 11 LA 1190, 1192; Feinberg in 11 LA 743, 744–745. Also see McCoy in 48 LA 983, 988–989; Beatty in 45 LA 267, 268.

[118]In Reliance Universal, 50 LA 397, 399–400 (Alexander, 1968), the arbitrator held that where the contract listed seniority, ability, and experience as factors to be considered in promotions, the importance of any factor was not to be determined by the order in which it was listed. Accord, Arbitrator Dolson in 50 LA 990, 992. Cf., Fogelberg in 71 LA 116, 119.

It seems clear that under "hybrid" clauses the relative claims of seniority and of ability must be determined by comparing and weighing against each other the relative difference in seniority of competing employees and the relative difference in their abilities. Thus, in comparing two or more qualified employees, both seniority and ability must be considered, and where the difference in length of service is relatively insignificant and there is a relatively significant difference in ability, then the ability factor should be given greater weight; but where there is a relatively substantial difference in seniority and relatively little difference in abilities, then length of service should be given greater weight. To illustrate, Arbitrator I. Robert Feinberg, giving effect to both factors under a "hybrid" clause, held that a much better qualified junior employee should be given preference over a senior employee who could perform the job, since there was relatively little difference in length of service, thus making relative ability the determinative factor.[119] Conversely, a senior employee whose qualifications were only slightly less but whose seniority was much greater than that of a junior employee has been given preference over the better qualified junior employee, the seniority factor determining the issue.[120]

Determination of Fitness and Ability

Provisions for modified seniority, designed on the one hand to give recognition to the right and responsibility of management to manage the enterprise and on the other hand to protect senior employees, involve some of the most troublesome questions confronting arbitrators. Unions tend to overemphasize seniority and forget merit and ability, while management tends to overemphasize supervision's personal judgment of merit and ability and forget seniority.[121]

Arbitrators have frequently held that, where the agreement makes "fitness and ability" a factor to be considered along with seniority under one of the modified seniority clauses but is silent as to how and by whom the determination of qualifications is to be made, management is entitled to make the initial determination, subject to challenge by the union on the ground that management's decision was unreasonable under the facts, or capricious, arbitrary, or discriminatory.[122] This right to determine ability may be held by management

---

[119]Callite Tungsten Corp., 11 LA 743, 744–745 (1948).

[120]See International Harvester Co., 21 LA 183, 185 (Cole, 1953), and in 11 LA 1190, 1192 (Wolff, 1948). Also see Arbitrator Rifkin in 78 LA 64, 66–67; Cahn in 62 LA 333, 337–338; Turkus in 61 LA 768, 769–770 (nine months difference in seniority "outweighed the imperceptibly slight and subtle differential in qualifications"); Elliot in 41 LA 353, 359; Ross in 34 LA 472, 475.

[121]Ford Motor Co., 2 LA 374, 375 (Shulman, 1945).

[122]For cases where the arbitrator stated these or similar grounds for arbitral review, see Arbitrator Harrison in 79 LA 106, 108; Watkins in 77 LA 313, 320; Tillem in 75 LA 910, 911; Rybolt in 73 LA 937, 940–941; Rezler in 72 LA 941, 945 (management is entitled to make the initial determination and the union may challenge its "appropriateness"); Ipavec in 72 LA 524,

either as a residual management right or as a necessary adjunct to the right to manage the plant and direct the working forces.[123]

A collective agreement containing a modified seniority clause may specifically provide that the employer shall be the judge of the qualifying factors, sometimes also providing for challenge of management's decision by the union through the grievance procedure.[124] Here, too, arbitrators may hold that management's determination is subject to challenge on the basis that management's action was unreasonable, capricious, arbitrary, or discriminatory.[125] Furthermore, even where the contract makes the employer the sole judge, arbitrators have held that management's action must not be capricious, arbitrary, or discriminatory, and, some arbitrators have added, must not be unreasonable.[126]

Review of Management's Determination: Evidence and Burden of Proof

In many cases involving issues of seniority and ability, the arbitrator in reviewing management's determination does not speak

---

528; Howell in 72 LA 434, 437; Johannes in 56 LA 40, 42–43; Stouffer in 56 LA 6, 10, and in 52 LA 889, 894; Cahn in 52 LA 247, 252 (union need not show that company action was arbitrary, capricious, or in bad faith, it sufficing to show that company made an incorrect factual determination); Anderson in 49 LA 589, 594; Dworkin in 49 LA 390, 394; Oppenheim in 46 LA 860, 863; Klein in 46 LA 203, 208; Kates in 45 LA 743, 747; Schmidt in 44 LA 283, 285; Koven in 42 LA 1093, 1096; Seligson in 41 LA 528, 532; Rohman in 38 LA 132, 143; Hale in 37 LA 801, 805; Maggs in 37 LA 29, 34; Ross in 34 LA 271, 275 (review not limited to arbitrary or capricious action—company decision may be made in good faith but still be unreasonable); Reid in 29 LA 394, 396; Lockhart in 16 LA 525, 529. In some cases arbitrators have spoken in terms of management's decision being subject to challenge on the ground that it is "clearly wrong," or the like. See Arbitrator Beatty in 40 LA 697, 699–700; Caraway in 35 LA 866, 869; Prasow in 27 LA 40, 49; Marshall in 6 LA 838, 841. In still other cases, particularly earlier cases, the arbitrator limited review of management's decision to the narrower ground of arbitratry, capricious, bad faith, or discriminatory action. See Arbitrator Ray in 46 LA 91, 94; Kelliher in 23 LA 105, 109; Carmody in 23 LA 38, 39; Parker in 22 LA 258, 260; Murphy in 18 LA 757, 758–759; Hawley in 17 LA 516, 518–519; Reynolds in 10 LA 624, 626; Ingle in 9 LA 515, 517; Greene in 7 LA 526, 527.

[123]See Arbitrator Stouffer in 52 LA 889, 894; Beatty in 40 LA 697, 699–700; Rohman in 38 LA 132, 143; Hale in 37 LA 801, 805; Britton in 34 LA 788, 792; Dworkin in 29 LA 29, 36; Williams in 25 LA 748, 751; Reid in 23 LA 322, 326; Baab in 20 LA 137, 141; Kerr in 14 LA 163, 167; Reynolds in 10 LA 624, 626.

[124]For example, see 77 LA 391, 392; 70 LA 729, 730; 55 LA 813, 816; 53 LA 549 at 549; 30 LA 803, 804; 26 LA 773, 774; 19 LA 402, 403.

[125]See North Country Dodge, 77 LA 391, 392–393 (Craver, 1981); Mountain States Tel. & Tel. Co., 70 LA 729, 741 (Goodman, 1978). Also see Truck Terminal Employees v. Sears Co., 92 LRRM 2980, 2982 (CA 8, 1976). In Inmont Corp., 76 LA 1127, 1129 (1981), the agreement provided for recall from layoff on the basis of seniority, but provided also that employees recalled must be able to "perform the available work in the opinion of the Employer under normal direction"; Arbitrator James E. Westbrook concluded that the "use of the words 'in the opinion of the Employer' rather clearly indicates the vesting of a larger measure of discretion in the Company than in the typical collective bargaining agreement," that it "was reasonable to imply a good faith limitation on this discretion from * * * the recognition clause," but that a "good faith test would not impose a reasonableness limitation on the company's discretion." Also see Arbitrator Bothwell in 76 LA 1230, 1231; Foster in 76 LA 626, 632 (recognizing only an "arbitrariness or capriciousness" limitation upon management's contractual right "to consider and determine the qualifications and abilities" of employees on layoff).

[126]See Arbitrator Raymond in 72 LA 693, 695; Rule in 64 LA 266, 270; Shieber in 61 LA 261, 264; Koven in 53 LA 549 at 549; Peterschmidt in 52 LA 476, 479; Lugar in 45 LA 307, 313–314; Warns in 36 LA 380, 381, 384; Meltzer in 30 LA 803, 807; Disman in 26 LA 773, 778–779; Ralston in 19 LA 402, 405; McCoy in 18 LA 24, 27; Wardlaw in 6 LA 786, 788. Cf., Carmichael in 3 LA 313, 317.

in terms of burden of proof but simply considers all the evidence and arguments of both parties and decides from a consideration thereof whether the company's determination should be upheld.[127] On the other hand, in some cases the arbitrator does speak specifically in terms of burden of proof, placing the onus on one party or the other.[128]

There appear to be several basic approaches as to which party should have the burden of proof in cases involving managerial action taken under "relative ability" clauses.[129] In some cases such clauses have been construed to place a relatively light limitation upon the employer and, in effect, to place the burden of proof on the employee. Under this approach, when the union challenges management's determination it must sustain the burden of proving discrimination, caprice, arbitrariness, or bad faith on the part of the employer or proving that the employer's evaluation of abilities was clearly wrong.[130]

In some other cases such clauses have been construed to place a relatively severe limitation upon the employer and, in effect, to place the burden of proof on him. Under this approach the employer must be prepared, when bypassing senior employees, to show, by specific and understandable evidence which relates to capacity for the job in question, that the junior employee is the abler.[131] In still other "relative ability" cases, an even heavier burden is, in effect, placed on the

---

[127]See, for instance, Arbitrator Rezler in 72 LA 941, 949; Johannes in 56 LA 40, 42–43; Larson in 55 LA 813, 816–817; Alexander in 50 LA 397, 399–400; Marshall in 43 LA 475, 483–484; Boles in 30 LA 365, 367–374; Ross in 29 LA 262, 265–267; Prasow in 27 LA 40, 49.

[128]See, for instance, Arbitrator Armstrong in 79 LA 441, 447; Nolan in 74 LA 1218, 1220; Carmichael in 74 LA 1023, 1024; Reid in 68 LA 607, 608; Coburn in 56 LA 733, 737; Stouffer in 56 LA 6, 10; Keeler in 45 LA 444, 446. The contract itself may place the burden of proof on one of the parties. For example, see Inland Steel Co., 16 LA 280, 283 (Cornsweet, 1951).

[129]See discussion of "relative ability" clauses supra, topic entitled "Modified Seniority Clauses." There are various shadings of opinion within the basic approaches regarding the burden and quantum of proof. In this connection, see Howard, "The Role of the Arbitrator in the Determination of Ability," 12 Arb. J. 14–27 (1957). In Truck Terminal Employees v. Sears Co., 92 LRRM 2980, 2982 (CA 8, 1976), the arbitrator's authority to specify the standard of proof to be required under a relative ability clause was upheld where neither the contract language nor the bargaining history expressly prohibited the arbitrator from doing so.

[130]See Arbitrator Hogler in 77 LA 1229, 1234, 1236; Nolan in 74 LA 1218, 1220–1221; Reid in 68 LA 607, 608; Coburn in 56 LA 733, 737; Stouffer in 56 LA 6, 10; Ray in 46 LA 91, 94; Ingle in 9 LA 515, 517; Marshall in 6 LA 838, 841. Also see Carmichael in 74 LA 1023, 1024; Sinicropi in 68 LA 279, 286; Tsukiyama in 55 LA 477, 481; Flannagan in 42 LA 1301, 1306; Dworkin in 39 LA 735, 740; Doyle in 19 LA 47, 49. In some cases, while the arbitrator did not speak in terms of burden of proof, he noted that there was no evidence that the company had acted arbitrarily or in bad faith. For example, see Arbitrator Marshall in 43 LA 475, 484; Disman in 26 LA 773, 779; Jones in 25 LA 600, 604; Brecht in 21 LA 565, 568–569; Wolff in 17 LA 898, 903–904; Hawley in 17 LA 516, 519; Prasow in 17 LA 205, 211–212; Levinson in 16 LA 790, 792; Reynolds in 10 LA 624, 626. Also see Tilbury in 78 LA 1081, 1091–1092.

[131]For cases in which the arbitrator required this or a similar showing by the employer, or in which the burden of proof was otherwise clearly placed on management, see Arbitrator Kahn in 73 LA 508, 512; Roumell in 72 LA 1061, 1064; Howell in 72 LA 434, 437 (stating that when challenged the employer must show, and had done so here, that "standards for comparison of applicants' qualifications were established in good faith," that they "were applied fairly and impartially," and that the "decision that junior applicant was substantially better qualified was not clearly unreasonable"); Tive in 55 LA 325, 328; Beeson in 54 LA 298, 301; Sullivan in 54 LA 264, 268–269; Jones in 49 LA 275, 277; Williams in 48 LA 530, 531–532; Oppenheim in 46 LA 860, 862–863; Luskin in 46 LA 23, 26–27; Schmidt in 44 LA 283, 285; Hawley in 42 LA 276, 279; Autrey in 38 LA 471, 475–476; Teple in 36 LA 343, 348; Garrett in 22 LA 188, 190; Waite in 19 LA 1, 4; Blair in 16 LA 382, 383; Platt in 13 LA 843, 846; Whitton in 13 LA 666, 668; Brandschain in 5 LA 578, 582; Shulman in 2 LA 374, 375–376.

employer, and he is required when challenged not only to show greater ability in the junior employee to whom he has given preference, but also to show the absence of discrimination and arbitrariness and the presence of good faith.[132]

In cases involving "sufficient ability" clauses,[133] arbitrators have placed the burden on the employer to show that the bypassed senior employee is not competent for the job, and the fact that a junior employee is more competent than the senior employee is irrelevant.[134] Apart from this required showing by the employer under such clauses, if the union specifically alleges discrimination or abuse of discretion, it may be required to prove such allegations by clear evidence.[135]

When a "hybrid" clause is involved,[136] arbitrators appear to place the burden on the employer to show why the ability factor was given greater weight than the seniority factor in bypassing the senior employee.[137]

If "strict" seniority is involved, that is, if the agreement requires the observance of seniority but contains no fitness and ability qualifications, the burden is clearly on the employer to justify a failure to give preference to the senior employee. For example, under a strict seniority clause, an employer passing over a senior but handicapped employee would have the burden of proving that the senior employee is not qualified for the work or that the performance of the work would have injurious effects on him.[138]

Finally, it should be emphasized that the approach taken by any arbitrator as to which party has the burden of proof will depend in great measure upon the terms of the contract and the facts of the case—in one case under one contract in one set of circumstances an arbitrator may decide the issue simply by examining the facts without referring to burden of proof, while in another case under another contract in another set of circumstances the same arbitrator may place the burden of proof on one party or the other.[139] This is by no means a

---

[132]See Atlas Powder Co., 30 LA 674, 677 (Frey, 1958); Illinois Bell Tel. Co., 14 LA 1021, 1026 (Kelliher, 1950). Also see Arbitrator Rule in 69 LA 290, 293; Reid in 29 LA 394, 397; Klamon in 24 LA 869, 873.

[133]See discussion on "sufficient ability" clauses supra, topic entitled "Modified Seniority Clauses."

[134]Pittsburgh Plate Glass Co., 8 LA 317, 329 (Blair, 1947). Similarly, see Arbitrator Kelliher in 80 LA 289, 292; Amis in 55 LA 432, 434; Altieri in 43 LA 499, 506; Dykstra in 38 LA 906, 908; Hale in 37 LA 801, 806, and in 25 LA 130, 142; Galenson in 25 LA 681, 684; Shister in 25 LA 618, 623; Ross in 23 LA 556, 558; McKelvey in 22 LA 167, 170; Pollard in 16 LA 586, 587. Cf., Lumbley in 76 LA 540, 542–544; Ergs in 68 LA 379, 385; Dworkin in 39 LA 609, 612–613; Cahn in 29 LA 597, 598.

[135]See Arbitrator Shister in 24 LA 703, 705; Carmody in 23 LA 28, 29; Greene in 7 LA 526, 527. Also see Arbitrator Watkins in 77 LA 313, 318–320.

[136]See discussion on "hybrid" clauses above, topic entitled "Modified Seniority Clauses."

[137]Elkhart Community Schools, 78 LA 64, 66 (Rifkin, 1981); Southwestern Bell Tel. Co., 30 LA 862, 871 (Davis, 1958). Also, in International Harvester Co., 21 LA 183, 185 (Cole, 1953), and 11 LA 1190, 1192 (Wolff, 1948), the employer was held not to have given sufficient weight to the much greater seniority of the senior employee. Also see Arbitrator Cahn in 62 LA 333, 337; Sembower in 43 LA 165, 169–170. Cf., Alexander in 50 LA 397, 399–400. In Callite Tungsten Corp., 11 LA 743, 744 (Feinberg, 1948), the employer was upheld where there was little difference in seniority and much difference in ability. Also see Arbitrator Cyrol in 72 LA 752, 757.

[138]Chrysler Corp., 5 LA 333, 336 (Wolff, 1946). Cf., Arbitrator Reid in 68 LA 607, 607–608.

[139]See, for example, Arbitrator Klamon in 24 LA 869, 873, and in 19 LA 639, 646; Platt in 20 LA 460, 462, and in 13 LA 843, 846; D. Wolff in 11 LA 1190, 1192, and in 5 LA 333, 336.

criticism of the arbitrators. Rather, it serves emphatically to bring the problem into focus and to make clear the basic observation that, as a practical matter, whether or not the arbitrator speaks in terms of burden of proof, in most cases when management's determination is challenged both parties are expected to produce whatever evidence they can in support of their respective contentions; and they ordinarily do so. The arbitrator in turn considers all the evidence and decides whether management's determination should be upheld as being reasonably supported by the evidence and as not having been influenced by improper elements such as arbitrariness, caprice, or discrimination.

Factors Considered in Determining Fitness and Ability

The determination of ability is by no means susceptible to any set formula applicable to any and all circumstances. The precise factors or criteria applicable in one set of circumstances involving one contract may not be proper or sufficient in another situation under another contract. Nevertheless, reported arbitration awards show that in the absence of contract provision for the method to be used or the factors to be considered in determining ability, management has been permitted or required to use a variety of methods and to consider a number of factors, including, in proper circumstances: use of written, oral, performance or aptitude tests; trial period on the job; reliance upon a merit rating plan or upon the opinion of supervision; consideration of production records, attendance or disciplinary records, education, experience, physical fitness, and the like. It has been held that management is entitled to use any method to determine ability so long as the method used is fair and nondiscriminatory.[140]

Technical qualifications for the job in question or a related job are clearly pertinent to management's consideration of an employee's "fitness and ability" for that job. Some of the factors discussed herein, such as the use of tests, technical training, and experience, point to the technical requirements of the job. However, arbitrators generally have permitted or required management to consider other factors as well in determining employees' qualifications. For example, Arbitrator Jerome A. Levinson approved the use of other factors:

" * * * To limit consideration to the one factor of technical knowledge of the job, would appear to be unduly restrictive. * * * [T]he Company could properly consider additional factors in deciding who was qualified for the particular job. * * *

"The criteria used by the Company [education, ability to express himself, alertness, attendance record, flexibility and ability to learn new

---

[140]See Arbitrator Dworkin in 53 LA 746, 755; Anderson in 49 LA 589, 592; Beatty in 45 LA 267, 268; Graff in 35 LA 169, 172; McCoy in 33 LA 951, 952; Williams in 25 LA 748, 751; Bailer in 19 LA 257, 260; Blair in 8 LA 278, 280. Also see Howell in 72 LA 434, 437.

duties] do not appear unreasonable or arbitrary, as related to the job
* * * in this case. They seem to be appropriate and relevant factors for
qualification of a man for the duties and responsibilities of this
job * * * ."[141]

Arbitrator Pearce Davis imposed a duty upon management to
consider other matters in addition to technical knowledge, stating:

> "In its assessment of comparative abilities, the Company has the
> right and the duty to prepare, record, and examine *tangible* and *objective*
> (in so far as possible) evidence concerning such matters as, for example:
> innate capacity; prior job experience and performance; attendance,
> health and related factors; tests, if available, such as those to indicate
> the likelihood of successful performance in the new position."[142]

In any event, the factors considered must relate directly to the
question of what the job requires and the employee's ability to meet
those requirements. Obviously, the factors used must be consistent
with the collective agreement. It is clear that the more objective
factors have greater acceptability, and the more of such factors properly considered by management in a given situation, the stronger is
the case for the decision reached by it.

The factors most commonly utilized are discussed in detail below.
No particular significance is attached to the order in which they
appear, and note should also be taken of the possibility that factors
other than those considered here may also be pertinent to any given
case.[143]

Use of Tests

Even in the absence of specific contract provision, management
has been held entitled to give reasonable and appropriate written,[144]

---

[141]John Deere Tractor Co., 16 LA 790, 792 (1951).

[142]Southwestern Bell Tel. Co., 30 LA 862, 871 (1958). Also see Arbitrator Justin in 20 LA
468, 474–475.

[143]For example, in addition to other factors used, the necessity of personal interviews with
job applicants has been considered. See South Cent. Bell Tel. Co., 52 LA 1104, 1111–1112 (Platt,
1969); Semling-Menke Co., 46 LA 523, 525 (Graff, 1966). In California State Univ., 71 LA 647,
652 (Staudohar, 1978), the following factors indicated merit in connection with promotion to full
professor: "teaching effectiveness, academic honors and awards, publications, professional
activities, and service to the campus and community."

[144]See Arbitrator Mann in 75 LA 655, 658–659; Howell in 72 LA 434, 436; Strongin in 56 LA
503, 505; Freund in 55 LA 79, 83; Block in 54 LA 460, 466; Anderson in 49 LA 589, 592; Gorsuch
in 46 LA 1116, 1121–1123; Florey in 46 LA 414, 416; Gibson in 45 LA 1003, 1005–1006; Kates in
45 LA 21, 25; Bradley in 38 LA 63, 67; Roberts in 37 LA 49, 52; McCoy in 33 LA 951, 952; Seward
in 29 LA 710, 711–712. But see Yarowsky in 62 LA 554, 555–558. Regarding the right of
management to use written tests as an aid in training and instructing employees, see Union
Camp Corp., 73 LA 67, 70–71 (Heinsz, 1979).

oral,[145] performance,[146] and aptitude tests[147] as an aid in determining the ability of competing employees. Moreover, recognizing the company's authority to institute and utilize tests, an arbitrator held that "the company is vested with continuing authority to change its testing methods and procedures in accordance with the exercise of sound judgment."[148] Many arbitrators look with favor upon the use of proper tests in appropriate situations. For example, Arbitrator Harry J. Dworkin noted: "The employment of tests, fairly and objectively administered, would appear to be desirable, and in the interests of the employees, the company, and the union. A sound testing procedure should serve to allay any suspicion among competing employees as to favoritism or discrimination in awarding jobs."[149] Arbitrator David L. Cole declared that use of tests constitutes an "effort to apply some objective measure of qualifications, rather than to leave the determination to the general judgment and subjective reactions of supervision."[150] Arbitrator B. Meredith Reid stated: "In the absence of proof of bias, prejudice, discrimination or injustice, the reasonable exercise of judgment as to ability is helped rather than hindered by the tests in question"—but he cautioned that this approval of the tests was not "open approval for tests of any kind under any circumstances."[151]

---

[145]See Arbitrator Fogelberg in 71 LA 116, 118; Mathews in 70 LA 4, 12, 14–15; Johnson in 68 LA 1, 4–6; Bailer in 19 LA 653, 655. However, oral testing as applied to mechanical skills might not, standing alone, provide a reliable guide since an employee may have skill in performing a mechanical job but lack the ability to communicate the knowledge when questioned orally, and vice versa. Collins Radio Co., 39 LA 436, 440 (Rohman, 1962).

[146]See Arbitrator Herman in 74 LA 811, 813–814; Marcus in 72 LA 1307, 1310; Fogelberg in 71 LA 116, 118; McDaniel in 53 LA 777, 779–780; Bradley in 38 LA 63, 67–68; Singletary in 29 LA 246, 248–249; Bailer in 19 LA 257, 260.

[147]See Arbitrator Fogel in 80 LA 1328, 1332–1333; Erbs in 76 LA 432, 436; Karlins in 75 LA 148 at 148; Morgan in 68 LA 708, 711–712 (the union contended that the company was "bound by past practice since they had not used mechanical aptitude tests up until the time which gave rise to the grievances," but Arbitrator Morgan disagreed, stating that the company previously had been "determining ability and the institution of the test is simply another method of measuring ability"); Wagner in 67 LA 678, 682; Kabaker in 64 LA 307, 310; Simon in 50 LA 1227, 1231–1232; Uible in 49 LA 735, 737; Bennett in 49 LA 465, 467; Wolff in 47 LA 552, 553; Wagner in 46 LA 81, 91 (citing many cases at 87–90); Dworkin in 43 LA 817, 822; Handsaker in 42 LA 349, 351–352; Frey in 30 LA 674, 677. Management has been held entitled to use aptitude tests to select applicants for training for newly created jobs (Arbitrator Fitch in 64 LA 462, 465–466; Wagner in 46 LA 81, 85; Porter in 44 LA 967, 969), even where the contract provides that the senior employee shall be given a trial period on the job (Nichols in 43 LA 779, 783). For cases discussing the propriety of aptitude tests for specific jobs, see Tatum in 41 LA 1027, 1031–1032; Graff in 35 LA 169, 171–174; Schmidt in 31 LA 1002, 1005. As for the use of written tests as an aid to demonstrate the aptitude of employees for other jobs in the line of progression, see Strongin in 56 LA 503, 505–506; Koretz in 47 LA 495, 500; McCoy in 34 LA 37, 38. On the question whether an employee should be permitted to take an aptitude test again after having previously failed it, see Dayton-Walther Corp., 65 LA 529, 532 (Laybourne, 1975).

[148]Celotex Corp., 53 LA 746, 756 (Dworkin, 1969). Also see Arbitrator Gibson in 79 LA 1255, 1259 (employer could change test where its continued use would result in a violation of Civil Rights Act by company and union). But also as to making changes, see Hilgert in 79 LA 868, 875–876; Simon in 61 LA 421, 426–428. In Bethlehem Steel Corp., 48 LA 1205, 1208–1209 (Seward, 1967), a "local working conditions" clause precluded management from adding a second entirely different test in addition to the one which could be used under past practice, but management was not precluded from revising the original test.

[149]Mead Containers, 35 LA 349, 352 (1960). Also see Dworkin in 53 LA 746, 755.

[150]International Harvester Co., 21 LA 183, 184 (1953). Also see Arbitrator Lehoczky in 66–2 ARB ¶8652; Sembower in 27 LA 353, 357 (approving the use of tests but finding the administration of them improper); Marshall in 25 LA 480, 484–485.

[151]Stauffer Chem. Co., 23 LA 322, 326 (1954).

Arbitrators generally hold that tests used in determining ability must be (1) specifically related to the requirements of the job, (2) fair and reasonable, (3) administered in good faith and without discrimination, and (4) properly evaluated. In some awards, the arbitrator may find it necessary to discuss all of the above requirements, or the arbitrator will expressly affirm that all four of the requirements have been met.[152] In others, he may discuss one or more, the implication being that the rest of the requirements have been met.

(1) With respect to the first requirement, it has been held that the test must be related to the skill and knowledge required in the job.[153] For example, a written test given to ascertain clerical and arith-

---

[152]One arbitrator thoroughly examined the testing procedure and the application of its results, noting that management employed a specialist to design and evaluate the tests, that the tests were related to the skills and qualifications required in the job, that a trained administrator and test examiners gave the tests, and that as an extra precaution against error it was standard procedure to offer each employee an opportunity to take the tests twice. Glass Containers Mfrs. Inst., 47 LA 217, 223 (Dworkin, undated). For some instances in which the arbitrator expressly affirmed that all four general requirements had been met, see Arbitrator Hilgert in 79 LA 868, 877, and Marcus in 72 LA 1307, 1310, in both of which cases the arbitrator also briefly discussed some of the requirements.

[153]See Arbitrator Fogel in 80 LA 1328, 1336; Ruben in 77 LA 785, 791; Garrett in 70 LA 1235, 1242 (tests not prepared on basis of the specific requirements of any given trade or craft job were not "job related" within meaning of the agreement, which covered many separate trade or craft jobs with widely different skills and ability); Witney in 64 LA 1093, 1096; Williams in 62 LA 1061, 1073–1074; Larkin in 52 LA 633, 638 (citing other cases on the point that a general aptitude test having no relation to the job in question may not be used as a proper guide for denying a senior employee a promotion); Barnhart in 49 LA 1068, 1073; Gorsuch in 46 LA 1116, 1123; Wagner in 46 LA 81, 91; Dworkin in 35 LA 349, 353; McCoy in 34 LA 37, 38–39. In Griggs v. Duke Power Co., 91 S.Ct. 849, 856, 3 FEP Cases 175 (1971), the Supreme Court stated: "Nothing in the [Civil Rights] Act precludes the use of testing or measuring procedures" so long as the tests used "measure the person for the job and not the person in the abstract." In Albemarle Paper Co. v. Moody, 95 S.Ct. 2362, 2375, 10 FEP Cases 1181 (1975), the Supreme Court reiterated its *Griggs* holding that the Civil Rights Act does forbid the use of employment tests that are discriminatory in effect unless the employer meets the burden of showing that any given requirement has a manifest relation to the employment in question, and then the Court added (citations omitted):

"This burden arises, of course, only after the complaining party or class has made out a prima facie case of discrimination, *i.e.* has shown that the tests in question select applicants for hire or promotion in a racial pattern significantly different from that of the pool of applicants. If an employer does then meet the burden of proving that its tests are 'job related,' it remains open to the complaining party to show that other tests or selection devices, without a similarly undesirable racial effect, would also serve the employer's legitimate interest in 'efficient and trustworthy workmanship.' Such a showing would be evidence that the employer was using its tests merely as a 'pretext' for discrimination."

For some other Supreme Court decisions relating to testing and civil rights, see Connecticut v. Teal, 102 S.Ct. 2525, 29 FEP Cases 1 (1982); County of Los Angeles v. Davis, 99 S.Ct. 1379, 19 FEP Cases 282 (1979), recognizing liability under Title VII for discrimination suffered by employees barred from promotion through use of a non-job-related test even if it was not intended to discriminate and although the "bottom line" result of the promotional process was an appropriate racial balance—the Court pointed to a provision of Title VII whose principal focus is the protection of the individual employee rather than protection of the minority group as a whole; Washington v. Davis, 96 S.Ct. 2040, 12 FEP Cases 1415 (1976). In 1979 the EEOC, OPM, and certain other enforcement agencies for equal employment opportunity issued Uniform Guidelines on Employee Selection Procedures, applicable to most public and private employers. 29 C.F.R. § 1607. Extensive discussion of the uniform guidelines is provided by Schlei & Grossman, Employment Discrimination Law, 2d Ed., 92–97 (BNA Books, 1983); Miner & Miner, Uniform Guidelines on Employee Selection Procedures (BNA Books, 1980); Zimmer, "Basing Employment Decisions on Tests: Compliance With the New Uniform Guidelines," 10 Seton Hall L. Rev. 769 (1980); Guardians Assn. v. Civil Serv. Comm'n, 23 FEP Cases 909 (CA 2, 1980); Miner & Miner, Employee Selection Within the Law (BNA Books, 1979). For some arbitral note or discussion of legal rules regarding testing and civil rights, see Arbitrator Gibson in 79 LA 1255, 1258; Karlins in 75 LA 148, 152; Matthews in 70 LA 4, 16–17; Williams in 62 LA 1061, 1070–1072, 1076. For related discussion, see Chapter 10, subtopic entitled "Title VII of the Civil Rights Act."

metical ability required on the job is a proper aid in determining ability,[154] as is a test requiring performance of duties identical with those actually performed on the job.[155] It has also been held that the employer may not change the requirements of the job through the test,[156] and that he may not include general abstract questions not based upon the type of problems which would actually arise on the job.[157]

(2) A test will probably be considered fair and reasonable if, among other possible characteristics, it covers all relevant factors,[158] the questions are not unduly difficult,[159] and it is given under proper (though not necessarily ideal) conditions.[160] Frequently, the arbitrator will simply state or imply that the test in question has been examined and found to be fair and reasonable.[161]

(3) The test must be fairly administered and graded and uniformly applied.[162] Not only must the test be given to all applicants for the job,[163] but the company may not give the junior employee an unfair advantage by temporarily assigning him to the job shortly before the test is to be given, thus enabling him to learn the practical operation of the machine which is part of the test.[164] A test may be considered questionable if it is so "critical" that it goes beyond determining the type and amount of ability required for the job and selects only the exact number of applicants needed to fill the vacancies.[165] Moreover, where the test is not adopted for uniform application but is devised and given after the promotion has been made or the vacancy filled, in an admitted effort to "reinforce" the company's position, it is entitled to little if any weight since there is too much chance of the test being slanted.[166] In some cases, arbitrators would add the further

---

[154]See United States Steel Corp., 46 LA 414, 416 (Florey, 1966); Wallingford Steel Co., 29 LA 597, 599 (Cahn, 1957).

[155]See Arbitrator McDaniel in 53 LA 777, 779–780; Bradley in 38 LA 63, 67–68; Bailer in 19 LA 257, 260.

[156]See Kuhlman Elec. Co., 26 LA 885, 890–891 (Howlett, 1956).

[157]See Arbitrator Ruben in 77 LA 785, 791; Kates in 56 LA 328, 331; Larkin in 52 LA 633, 638; McCoy in 34 LA 37, 38–39.

[158]See Bendix Aviation Corp., 19 LA 257, 260 (Bailer, 1952).

[159]See Hammarlund Mfg. Co., 19 LA 653, 655 (Bailer, 1952). Where a test was passed by most of the employees who took it, Arbitrator Harry L. Johnson stated that this "would certainly negate the claim that the test is unfair." I-T-E Imperial Corp., 68 LA 1, 6 (1976).

[160]See Hammarlund Mfg. Co., 19 LA 653, 655 (Bailer, 1952), where the fact that conditions under which the test was given were not ideal was not sufficient to make the test unfair or unreasonable.

[161]See Arbitrator Fogelberg in 71 LA 116, 118; Uible in 49 LA 735, 737; Gorsuch in 46 LA 1116, 1123; Cahn in 29 LA 597, 599; Ross in 29 LA 262, 265; Reid in 23 LA 322, 325; Lehoczky in 18 LA 413, 414. In Patterson Steel Co., 66–3 ARB ¶8949 (1966), Arbitrator Charles H. Logan found the test "ill conceived, inexcusably unfair, and flagrantly discriminatory" where it dealt with matters far more complex than would ever be encountered on the job.

[162]See South Cent. Bell Tel. Co., 52 LA 1104, 1109 (Platt, 1969). Similarly, see Arbitrator Lucas in 63 LA 1169, 1179–1180; Williams in 62 LA 1061, 1075.

[163]See Bethlehem Steel Co., 29 LA 710, 711 (Seward, 1957); Bendix Aviation Corp., 19 LA 257, 260 (Bailer, 1952). Also see Arbitrator Johnson in 68 LA 1, 7; Roberts in 37 LA 49, 52; Cahn in 29 LA 597, 599; Ross in 29 LA 262, 265; Shister in 24 LA 703, 705; Reid in 23 LA 322, 325. Cf., McKone in 66 LA 1329, 1331.

[164]See Joseph T. Ryerson & Son, 56 LA 1206, 1209 (Caraway, 1971).

[165]See Ball Bros. Co., 27 LA 353, 357 (Sembower, 1956).

[166]International Nickel Co., 36 LA 343, 349–350 (Teple, 1960). Under the relative ability clause, management was nonetheless upheld in selecting the junior employee since he had greater experience on the job and thus was better qualified.

requirement that the test results must be made available to the union or to the examinees, or they indicated with approval that test results were made available.[167]

(4) The test must be properly evaluated in the light of the contract provisions relating to seniority and job requirements, and it must not be used in a manner inconsistent with the contract.[168] In this regard, where a contract contains a "sufficient ability" clause a test may not be used to determine "relative" ability.[169]

It must be kept in mind that arbitrators usually take the view that while the test may be used as an aid in judging ability or as a "verification" of ability, the employer may not base his determination of ability solely upon the results of a test but must consider other factors and other evidence.[170]

It has been held that employees are obligated to take required tests even though there is no provision in the agreement therefor.[171] Many arbitrators have ruled that management not only can require bidders to take tests designed to determine ability for the job but also that it is justified in disqualifying any who refuse to take the tests.[172] Thus, it has been emphasized:

"* * * [T]he arbitrator wishes to make it emphatically clear that the Company has the right to require job bidders to take written tests, as

---

[167]See Arbitrator Marcus in 72 LA 1307, 1310; Simon in 50 LA 1227, 1233; Bennett in 49 LA 465, 468; Wolff in 47 LA 552, 553; Wagner in 46 LA 81, 91; McCoy in 34 LA 37, 39. Also see Graff in 35 LA 169, 174. Contract language and its bargaining history led the arbitrator to conclude that management was not required to supply information regarding the point scores of successful applicants for promotions to any other applicants in Social Security Admin., 69 LA 1012, 1016–1017 (Ford, 1977). One arbitrator would require that the union "be a party to the giving of the tests, the evaluation of the results, and probably the selection of the tests to be given." Central Soya Co., 41 LA 1027, 1031–1032 (Tatum, 1963). Also see Marshall in 36 LA 570, 573. In Detroit Edison Co. v. NLRB, 99 S.Ct. 1123, 100 LRRM 2728 (1979), the U.S. Supreme Court held (1) that the NLRB had improperly ordered the employer to supply to the union rather than only to a neutral as offered by the employer, the actual questions and answer sheets involved in the employer's psychological aptitude test, and (2) that the employer was not required to disclose to the union, without a written consent from individual employees, the test scores linked with the employee names; the Court underscored the employer's strong interest in test secrecy and in confidentiality of scores, and noted the absence of a showing that the employer's interest was fabricated to frustrate the union in the discharge of its responsibilities.

[168]See Allegheny Ludlum Steel Corp., 66–3 ARB ¶9071 (Crawford, 1966); American Smelting and Ref. Co., 29 LA 262, 265 (Ross, 1957).

[169]See Arbitrator Alexander in 46 LA 801, 805; Kates in 45 LA 21, 25; Di Leone in 41 LA 856, 860; Sembower in 27 LA 353, 357.

[170]See Arbitrator Caraway in 56 LA 1206, 1209; Block in 54 LA 460, 466; Volz in 49 LA 918, 921; Anderson in 49 LA 589, 593–594; Bennett in 49 LA 465, 467; Wolff in 47 LA 552, 553; Strong in 66–1 ARB ¶8306; Beatty in 45 LA 267, 268–269; Kates in 45 LA 21, 25; Gill in 34 LA 71, 75; Frey in 30 LA 674, 677; Seward in 29 LA 710, 712; Cahn in 29 LA 597, 599; Dworkin in 29 LA 29, 36; Howlett in 26 LA 885, 890–892; Reid in 23 LA 322, 325; Lehoczky in 18 LA 413, 414. But for some situations in which a test was permitted as the sole factor, see Arbitrator Hilgert in 79 LA 868, 875, 877; Erbs in 76 LA 432, 434, 436; Karlins in 75 LA 148, 151–152. Arbitrator Harry H. Platt stated that "a determination of how much weight should be given test results, along with other relevant factors, is a matter of judgment," and "when such judgment is exercised honestly and upon due consideration, it is not arbitrary action" even though there may be "room for two opinions." South Cent. Bell Tel. Co., 52 LA 1104, 1110–1111 (1969).

[171]Equitable Gas Co., 46 LA 81, 91 (Wagner, 1965).

[172]See Arbitrator Morgan in 68 LA 708, 710, 712; Dworkin in 53 LA 746, 757, and in 35 LA 349, 353; Johnson in 51 LA 99, 99–100; Anderson in 66–3 ARB ¶8933; McIntosh in 44 LA 720, 721–722; McCoy in 64–3 ARB ¶9258 (holding that employees' refusal meant that they "voluntarily passed up the opportunity to get the job"); Roberts in 37 LA 49, 52–53; Graff in 35 LA 169, 174; Seward in 29 LA 710, 711–712. In some of these cases, the arbitrator found on the evidence that the grievant was not qualified for the job. Cf., American Meter Co., 41 LA 856, 861–862 (Di Leone, 1963).

well as other job related tests, to determine their qualifications, subject to disqualification if they refuse. The bidder cannot reserve to himself the right to determine which tests he will take and which ones he will refuse. He must comply with this requirement. If the test is not a reasonable one, or is not fairly administered, or if unwarranted conclusions are drawn from the results, the appropriate remedy is through the grievance procedure."[173]

In two instances, the arbitrator apparently considered the equities of the case and held that although the company could disqualify a bidder when he refused to take the test on the erroneous advice of the union, he should be given another opportunity to take the test.[174]

Experience

Experience is distinguishable from both seniority and productivity. It is the extent to which an employee has engaged in a particular job, type of work, or occupation. While the term ability does not necessarily imply prior experience on the particular job, experience is ordinarily considered a tangible, objective factor to be taken into consideration in determining fitness and ability.[175] Indeed, management has sometimes been reprimanded by the arbitrator for failing to take into consideration the experience of a senior employee who has been bypassed.[176]

Various views have been expressed concerning the place of experience in determining fitness and ability. Arbitrator Edwin R. Teple stated: "Experience usually is, and should be, one of the most important factors in determining ability."[177] Arbitrator Robert G. Howlett noted that "Other things being equal, the man who has had some experience on a job can become a competent employee in the classification faster than the man who has had no such experience."[178] Arbitrator Otto J. Baab expressed the opinion that it is "reasonable to adopt the criterion of actual experience to determine skill and ability,"[179] but Arbitrator Paul N. Lehoczky stated that "experience is not the sole criterion in forming a judgment of ability."[180] Arbitrator

---

[173]Vulcan Materials Co., 54 LA 460, 466 (Block, 1970), citations omitted. The arbitrator also considered the fact that the grievants had inadequacies in their ability to perform the job in question. Id. at 466–467.

[174]Celotex Corp., 53 LA 746, 757 (Dworkin, 1969); Standard Oil Co. (Ind.), 11 LA 810, 811 (Updegraff, 1948).

[175]See Arbitrator Jenkins in 74 LA 1077, 1084; Heinsz in 74 LA 902, 906; Williams in 48 LA 430, 431–432 (cautioning, however, that experience must not be accorded such "overriding value" as to negate the seniority provision of the parties' agreement); Prasow in 24 LA 437, 441; Baab in 14 LA 512, 515. Also see Arbitrator Dunau in 39 LA 270, 275.

[176]See Arbitrator Stoltenberg in 74 LA 266, 268; Owen in 54 LA 434, 435–436; Kates in 45 LA 743, 749; Cole in 21 LA 214, 217–218. Concerning the obligation of bidders to offer information concerning their experience, and of the employer to seek information concerning the experience of competing bidders, compare the views stated by Arbitrator Witt in 74 LA 788, 792, and by Arbitrator Goodman in 70 LA 729, 742.

[177]International Nickel Co., 36 LA 343, 349 (1960).

[178]Kuhlman Elec. Co., 26 LA 885, 891 (1956). Also see Arbitrator Rezler in 72 LA 941, 947; Alexander in 50 LA 397, 400.

[179]Thor Corp., 14 LA 512, 515 (1950).

[180]Seagrave Corp., 16 LA 410, 412 (1951). Also see Arbitrator Williams in 48 LA 530, 531–532; Kates in 40 LA 590, 597.

Livingston Smith asserted that "experience [is not] in itself a factor in determining fitness and ability save and except to the extent that experience may tend to increase one's skill and ability."[181]

In any event, arbitrators generally give some consideration to experience where it is relevant to the job requirements. It may be one of several factors used, or a major factor, or the sole or determining factor. Work experience on the job in question or on a related job could demonstrate an employee's ability to perform the job,[182] with greater weight being accorded to experience on the particular job than on a related job.[183] The weight which the arbitrator gives to experience may depend in large measure upon the emphasis placed on this factor by the parties and upon the evidence, or lack of evidence, concerning other factors relevant to the determination of fitness and ability.[184] Also, the contract language and the fact situation presented to the arbitrator are of prime importance.

Naturally, if experience is not important to the job, little or no weight will be attached to this factor.[185] On the other hand, experience in the work may be a basic requirement for the job, thereby justifying management in giving preference to an experienced junior employee over a senior who lacks experience.[186] Moreover, the employer may be upheld in giving preference to the junior employee where he has had substantially greater experience than the senior,[187] or where the experience of the junior employee is identical with or is more closely related to the work involved than the experience of the senior employee,[188] or where the job requires extensive training and

---

[181]Tin Processing Corp., 17 LA 193, 198 (1951). In Iroquois Gas Corp., 39 LA 161, 162–163 (O'Rourke, 1962), present ability to perform the particular job was a factor in favor of the junior employee where the senior employee admitted that he knew nothing about the particular job.

[182]See Arbitrator Kelliher in 80 LA 289, 292; Johannes in 56 LA 40, 42–43; Stouffer in 56 LA 6, 9–10; Tsukiyama in 55 LA 477, 479–480; Block in 51 LA 896, 898–899; Sembower in 50 LA 445, 449; Alexander in 50 LA 397, 400; Griffin in 29 LA 870, 874; Prasow in 24 LA 437, 441. Management properly may consider related work experience *off* the job, i.e., training courses taken off the job and work experience in a like occupation for another employer. See Arbitrator Sembower in 50 LA 445, 449; Cantor in 48 LA 777, 778; Warns in 36 LA 380, 382.

[183]See Arbitrator Rezler in 72 LA 941, 947; Coburn in 56 LA 733, 737; Tsukiyama in 55 LA 477, 479–480 (holding that the junior employee's experience and knowledge which were relevant and related to the job constituted the "material difference" required by contract in the qualifications of applicants, justifying his promotion over the senior employee who lacked such experience and knowledge); Warns in 21 LA 392, 397; Roberts in 19 LA 270, 279.

[184]For various treatments of experience, see Arbitrator Larson in 55 LA 813, 816; Alexander in 50 LA 397, 400; McDermott in 49 LA 1160, 1171; Singletary in 44 LA 1193, 1195; Altieri in 43 LA 499, 504–505; Dunau in 39 LA 270, 273–275; Boles in 28 LA 72, 75–76; Howlett in 26 LA 885, 891; Lehoczky in 16 LA 410, 412.

[185]See Arbitrator Raffaele in 71 LA 587, 589; Goodman in 70 LA 729, 742–743; Larkin in 56 LA 399, 402–403; Schmidt in 31 LA 1002, 1005–1006; Boles in 28 LA 72, 75–76.

[186]See Arbitrator Coburn in 56 LA 733, 737; Sembower in 50 LA 445, 449–450; Cahn in 18 LA 536, 538. For some kinds of jobs, such as those requiring qualities of leadership, actual experience is given special weight. See Arbitrator Wolff in 54 LA 447, 447–448; Sembower in 50 LA 445, 449–450.

[187]See Arbitrator Merrifield in 68 LA 1019, 1021; Stouffer in 56 LA 6, 9–10; Roberts in 47 LA 823, 826–827; Luskin in 46 LA 23, 27–28; Maggs in 37 LA 29, 35; Brecht in 21 LA 565, 568–569; Gilden in 15 LA 636, 638; Platt in 12 LA 6, 7. The fact that the junior employee's experience is more recent as well as more substantial is entitled to weight. See Arbitrator Bradley in 38 LA 63, 68–69; Teple in 36 LA 343, 349.

[188]See Arbitrator Ipavec in 75 LA 400, 404–405; Kennedy in 50 LA 1249, 1252; Dolson in 50 LA 990, 994–995; Stouffer in 50 LA 283, 286–287; Murphy in 34 LA 356, 358–359; Warns in 34 LA 46, 49, and in 21 LA 392, 397; Fleming in 30 LA 237, 239–241; Brecht in 21 LA 565, 568–569.

experience which the junior employee has had and the senior lacks.[189]

Other factors being equal, arbitrators have sometimes held that the senior employee should be given a trial or break-in period on the basis of his having had some experience,[190] even though the junior employee selected by the company had somewhat more experience.[191] In this connection, it should be noted that some arbitrators have distinguished temporary from permanent promotions in judging fitness and ability, and when temporary, the tendency is to emphasize present fitness and ability and hence to give greater weight to experience.[192]

Trial or Break-in Period on the Job Versus Training

Agreements sometimes provide for a trial or break-in period on the job to determine ability, and questions in connection with the interpretation and application of such provisions are frequently arbitrated.[193] In the absence of contractual provision, the question arises as to whether management must give the senior employee a trial.[194] Obviously, ability to perform the job, or the lack of it, may be demonstrated by a trial or break-in period on the job. As stated by Arbitrator Carl A. Warns, "The best evidence as to whether an employee can do a job is to give him a fair trial on it."[195] Arbitrator Vernon L. Stouffer stated that "The purpose of a trial period is to afford an employee the opportunity to demonstrate that he has the ability for the job in question or can with some familiarization therewith achieve the necessary skills within a reasonable period of time to perform the job in an acceptable manner."[196]

There appears to be a close relationship between the use of tests or other criteria and a trial period on the job—some arbitrators have expressed the view that the employer should grant the senior employee a trial period on the job, but not training, to demonstrate his

---

In Lockheed-Georgia Co., 49 LA 603, 605 (Di Leone, 1967), management's reliance upon experience was not upheld since the experience of the junior employee was found to bear little resemblance to the job requirements, and the junior and senior employees were found to be otherwise substantially equal in ability.

[189]See Arbitrator Gill in 48 LA 190, 191–192; Oppenheim in 46 LA 860, 863; Jones in 25 LA 600, 604; Prasow in 24 LA 437, 441–442.

[190]See Arbitrator Klamon in 30 LA 279, 282; Randle in 17 LA 486, 487; Copelof in 16 LA 359, 365 (contractual provision for a trial period); McCoy in 12 LA 682, 685.

[191]See Arbitrator Williams in 48 LA 530, 532 (contractual provision for a training period); Rosenfarb in 23 LA 789, 793–794, and Smith in 17 LA 193, 198 (contractual provision for a trial period); Lehoczky in 16 LA 410, 412.

[192]See Arbitrator Emery in 28 LA 733, 735; Marshall in 23 LA 623, 628; Warren in 21 LA 228, 231. Also see Leach in 79 LA 878, 883.

[193]See, for example, 66 LA 1310, 1313; 54 LA 683, 684; 53 LA 1282, 1283; 45 LA 267 at 267; 29 LA 29, 31; 25 LA 661, 662; 24 LA 461, 463; 16 LA 525, 526; 16 LA 359, 361; 9 LA 956, 960; 2 LA 655, 657.

[194]Past practice may be involved. See Arbitrator Kallenbach in 64 LA 271, 275; Fox in 62 LA 84, 89; Flannagan in 56 LA 920, 922, 923–924; Randle in 17 LA 486, 487; Aaron in 15 LA 162, 167; Whitton in 13 LA 666, 670.

[195]Dayton Power & Light Co., 28 LA 624, 626 (1957). Similarly, see I-T-E Imperial Corp., 55 LA 1284, 1287 (White, 1970).

[196]American Welding & Mfg. Co., 52 LA 889, 893 (1969). For discussion of various aspects of trial periods, see Howard, "Seniority Rights and Trial Periods," 15 Arb. J. 51 (1960).

ability if the test results[197] or other criteria used have been inconclusive in determining the ability of the senior bidder.[198]

Thus, arbitrators generally are inclined to the view that if there is a reasonable doubt as to the ability of the senior employee and if the trial would cause no serious inconvenience, it should be granted, but that a trial should not be required in all cases.[199] There is a similar general agreement that the trial period should be a short one,[200] but it also has been held that the trial must be adequate.[201]

From the standpoint of the company also the trial period must be adequate, but the company does not have an unlimited or extended period to determine the fitness of an employee.[202] While most cases involve trial periods of less than 30 days, because of the circumstances some involve greater periods. For example, it has been held that a 9-month trial period ordinarily is too long but was not too long where the employee for 7 months of that time was taking a training course which management expected would improve his performance,[203] that the employer is entitled to a reasonable trial period but that 11 months was not reasonable where the employee had received an automatic pay increase 6 months after his promotion,[204] and that management

[197]See Arbitrator Ruben in 77 LA 785, 791–792; Thompson in 33 LA 213, 217–218; Shister in 25 LA 369, 372. Also see Arbitrator Dworkin in 39 LA 735, 739, and in 29 LA 29, 37, where the contract provision for a trial period was considered as protecting the employer's interests. Some awards appear to have treated a trial on the job as something in the nature of a performance test. See Arbitrator White in 55 LA 1284, 1287; Murphy in 18 LA 757, 760. In Judson Steel Corp., 76 LA 825, 827 (1981), Arbitrator J.J. Griffin held that the senior bidder was not entitled to a trial period even though he passed a qualification test, since the test was only one factor in determining qualifications and the employer could reasonably make "a decision on qualifications based on any other information available to it." Also see Arbitrator Bilder in 62 LA 1184, 1188, construing a trial period clause.

[198]See Arbitrator White in 55 LA 1284, 1287–1288; Elliot in 41 LA 353, 359; Rohman in 39 LA 436, 441; McKelvey in 22 LA 167, 170. The same approach has been taken in cases which involved contract provisions for a trial period on the job. See Kates in 56 LA 328, 331; Lazarus in 28 LA 823, 828; Cole in 21 LA 231, 234. In City of Traverse City, 72 LA 1061, 1065 (1979), the agreement specified a six-month probationary period in any promotion, and Arbitrator George T. Roumell, Jr., spoke of it as a "trial period" which should have been given the senior bidder since there was "really little question that [he] can do the work."

[199]See Arbitrator Cantor in 80 LA 257, 263–264; Nathanson in 75 LA 1001, 1005; White in 55 LA 1284, 1288; Elkouri in 46 LA 238, 242; Reid in 29 LA 743, 746–747; Shister in 25 LA 369, 372; Prasow in 24 LA 437, 442; McKelvey in 22 LA 167, 170; Shulman in 2 LA 374, 376. Cf., Arbitrator Updegraff in 29 LA 50, 52; Murphy in 18 LA 757, 760. In some cases involving a bumping situation, arbitrators have held that the senior employee is required to have the "present ability" to perform the work and that he is not entitled to a trial or break-in period or a training period (some arbitrators citing the specific language of the bumping clause as requiring present ability, others emphasizing the absence of a provision for a trial, break-in, or training period). See Arbitrator Chapman in 76 LA 428, 432; Volz in 44 LA 694, 697; Nichols in 44 LA 653, 656–657; Cahn in 44 LA 24, 24–25; Dworkin in 39 LA 609, 612–613 (citing many cases); McCoy in 23 LA 779, 781; Updegraff in 16 LA 909, 911–912. Cf., Rohman in 39 LA 436, 441, where the senior had previous experience on the work.

[200]See Arbitrator Williams in 53 LA 160, 162; Prasow in 24 LA 437, 442; Seward in 23 LA 532, 533–534; Kerr in 11 LA 567, 568. In American Oil Co., 53 LA 160, 162 (Williams, 1969), it was held that the "sufficient" ability clause "does not contemplate that the senior employee's fitness and ability be sufficient to perform the job at peak efficiency from the first hour on it, but contemplates a reasonable familiarization (but no training) period on the new job."

[201]See Arbitrator Roberts in 55 LA 261, 269–270; Jones in 53 LA 101, 111 (inadequate supervisory assistance and alleged racial bias); Kates in 44 LA 389, 392; McKelvey in 22 LA 167, 170–171; Copelof in 17 LA 324, 326. Also see Coven in 71 LA 333, 337.

[202]Smith Scott Co., 48 LA 270, 272 (Burns, 1966).

[203]Koppers Co., 49 LA 663, 665 (Malkin, 1967), upholding management's removal of the employee since he failed to qualify.

[204]Smith Scott Co., 48 LA 270, 272 (Burns, 1966), noting also that new hires were given a short qualifying period of a week or two.

could remove a senior employee after a 5-month trial period where he had four separate opportunities for merit increases but received only one and had consistently been warned about his work and given low ratings during the trial period.[205]

The contract may specify the amount of time for the trial or it may require only "a reasonable qualifying period." In a case involving the latter language, the arbitrator said that no particular number of hours or days must be provided and that "All that is required under this contract is that a long enough period be allowed to demonstrate to management, viewing the employee's performance impartially and reasonably and in good faith, that he can or cannot fulfill the requirements of the job."[206]

If the senior employee is obviously unfit or unqualified, as in a situation where the job in question requires a high degree of skill which can be acquired only after a long period of training and there is no evidence that the senior employee has these skills or related skills, then management is not required to give him a trial period and may give preference to the junior employee or new hire who already possesses such skills.[207] The same holds true if there is a contract provision for a trial period.[208] Also, no trial on the job is required where the contract makes seniority controlling only if ability is substantially equal and past service of competing applicants shows the junior to possess qualifications considerably superior to those of the senior applicant.[209] Moreover, it has been held that if management has granted a trial as required by the agreement, it need not continue the trial for the full period specified but may cancel it when the candidate demonstrates his inability to perform the job. As stated by one arbitrator, "When it becomes obvious that an employee is not going to be able to acquire the necessary skills to qualify for the job or by his attitude makes it clear that he is not going to become proficient and fails to exhibit any progress, then the employer is not obligated to continue the trial period."[210]

---

[205]Shenango Furnace Co., 46 LA 203, 209–210 (Klein, 1966), noting that the "lengthy trial period tends to negate the probability of any bad faith or prejudice" on management's part.

[206]Decor Corp., 44 LA 389, 392 (Kates, 1965). In Seeger Refrigerator Co., 16 LA 525, 531 (Lockhart, 1951), interpreting similar language, a minimum of three months was considered necessary because of the circumstances of the case and the nature of the work.

[207]See Arbitrator Sherman in 74 LA 962, 963; Hales in 73 LA 1290, 1291; Grant in 64 LA 639, 641; Block in 54 LA 460, 466–467 (no "reasonable expectation of success on the job"); Marshall in 53 LA 1282, 1287; Kennedy in 50 LA 1249, 1252 (lack of qualification shown by employee's past employment record); Kates in 45 LA 21, 25; Wyckoff in 39 LA 538, 541; Miller in 39 LA 336, 340; Dykstra in 38 LA 906, 909 (unsatisfactory work in jobs requiring less skill than job in question); McKelvey in 22 LA 167, 170. Also see Arbitrator Watkins in 77 LA 313, 316, 319; Cahn in 52 LA 247, 249–251; Kornblum in 40 LA 403, 407; Coffey in 39 LA 1117, 1118–1119; Murphy in 34 LA 356, 359; Shister in 25 LA 369, 372; Prasow in 24 LA 437, 442.

[208]See Arbitrator Larkin in 48 LA 1031, 1035; Daugherty in 47 LA 554, 557, 558–559; Singletary in 44 LA 1193, 1195; Dworkin in 39 LA 735, 739, and in 35 LA 391, 396; Merrill in 36 LA 145, 148; Lazarus in 28 LA 823, 828; Platt in 24 LA 79, 80; Cole in 21 LA 231, 234.

[209]Semling-Menke Co., 46 LA 523, 526–527 (Graff, 1966).

[210]American Welding & Mfg. Co., 52 LA 889, 893 (Stouffer, 1969). Also see Arbitrator Cohen in 71 LA 1171, 1176 (agreeing that the specified trial period need not be exhausted where it becomes apparent that the employee is unqualified for the job, but stating that "such an exception * * * becomes operative only where the Grievant is given a reasonable time or adequate help or directions to qualify for the job," which was not done in the present case); Lynch

In one case Arbitrator Marlin M. Volz pointed out that "a significant difference is recognized between a trial and a training period," and he stated his view as follows:

"The purpose of a trial period is to determine whether an employee who possesses the basic qualifications can satisfactorily do a job which she does not regularly perform. It is assumed that she will not have to be trained in all aspects of the job; for a trial period is not a training period, but simply an opportunity to demonstrate ability to do the job. A trial period, in effect, is a lengthened familiarization or orientation period in which the employee is acquainted with the nature and techniques of the job. It presupposes that the employee will be given instruction and assistance and that she will not simply be turned loose to 'sink or swim.' But, it also assumes that she brings with her to the trial period by virtue of prior experience or education considerable knowledge, background, and skill for performing the duties of the new position. She still needs instruction in the peculiar requirements, procedures, equipment, and techniques of the job; but an intensive on-the-job training program, such as would be appropriate for a novice, is not contemplated."[211]

While circumstances of a given case may require that an employer provide a trial or break-in period on the job, he ordinarily would be under no obligation, unless the contract provides otherwise, to provide training for a senior employee to enable him to achieve the fitness and ability called for by the contract.[212] If a senior employee would require such extensive training (in order to qualify for a job) as to make it unreasonable under the contract to expect the employer to provide such training, the employer is justified in giving preference to a junior employee who is already fully qualified.[213]

Where the contract recognizes seniority as a factor, management may not afford training opportunities to junior employees while arbitrarily denying them to senior employees, then promote or retain

---

in 65 LA 869, 874–875; Kornblum in 36 LA 1266, 1269. In the latter case Arbitrator Kornblum quoted from Howard, "Seniority Rights and Trial Periods," 55 Arb. J. 51, 59 (1961), recognizing the "right of management to cancel the trial wherever the job candidate demonstrates his incompetence." Cf., Arbitrator Gruenberg in 63 LA 758, 763–764.

[211]Reynolds Metals Co., 66 LA 1276, 1280 (1976).

[212]See Arbitrator Wagner in 67 LA 678, 682; Rentfro in 66 LA 1299, 1301–1302; Volz in 66 LA 1276, 1280; Krimsly in 51 LA 49, 51–52 (some instruction but no training should be given on new machine); Prasow in 47 LA 726, 734; Oppenheim in 46 LA 860, 863; Volz in 44 LA 694, 697; Roberts in 37 LA 49, 53; Kornblum in 36 LA 1266, 1270; Merrill in 36 LA 145, 148; Emery in 28 LA 733, 735; Klamon in 20 LA 768, 774; Lehoczky in 16 LA 410, 412; Greene in 7 LA 526, 527. Also see Wiggins in 80 LA 1367, 1372; Ipavec in 80 LA 118, 120. Cf., Williams in 65 LA 1265, 1267. The agreement may provide for training as in 74 LA 581, 583–584; 55 LA 432, 433; 49 LA 953, 954; 48 LA 530, 532. In New York Elec. & Gas Corp., 69 LA 865, 869 (Foltman, 1977), it was held under a "relative ability" clause that the employer properly awarded a vacancy to an employee whose qualifications were superior to those of the senior bidder, the contractual provision for training being construed to apply only "after a job award has been made in light of particular individual deficiencies or gaps." For some cases concerning the allegedly premature termination of training, see Arbitrator Fox in 75 LA 1101, 1105; Powell in 66 LA 1198, 1201; Leonard in 65 LA 1070, 1073; Ferguson in 63 LA 924, 927.

[213]See Arbitrator Teple in 36 LA 343, 351; Murphy in 30 LA 598, 599; McKelvey in 22 LA 167, 170; Updegraff in 16 LA 909, 911–912. The need for training would seem to indicate a lack of skill and ability. Poloron Prods. Co. of Pa., 23 LA 789, 792 (Rosenfarb, 1955). Also see Glidden Co., 34 LA 265, 268 (Griffin, 1960).

a junior applicant on the basis of such training.[214] Such action not only may constitute discrimination, but also the seniority clause "might be either nullified or circumvented should the Company provide special and preferential training opportunities for low seniority employees."[215] In two cases, the arbitrators held that training and experience received by junior employees in violation of the contract could not be credited to the juniors in considering relative ability, the contract in one case expressly providing that management would assist senior employees to become qualified for promotion by assigning them to temporary vacancies for training purposes,[216] and the contract in the other expressly precluding temporary assignments exceeding 30 days.[217]

This is not to say that management may not select employees for training under any circumstances. It has been held that management could give training to junior employees where the senior employee was on sick leave,[218] and that management is not required to make special arrangements for senior employees to take part of a training course and not the rest.[219] Furthermore, in the absence of a contract provision dealing with training, it has been held that management should not be denied a reasonable freedom of discretion in selecting employees for training, particularly in connection with new types of activities, but such selection must not be arbitrary or discriminatory or in conflict with the seniority provisions of the contract.[220]

Where the employer has a policy of providing training for employees desiring to take it, he may not automatically disqualify employees who have not taken such training.[221] That is, the employer may not rely on training so provided as a "conclusive determinant of relative ability" but must affirmatively show that the employees selected are actually better qualified.[222] In one case, the junior employee who took

[214]See Arbitrator Rothschild in 79 LA 1193, 1196; Mullin in 79 LA 158, 162–163; Kerrison in 29 LA 747, 749; Williams in 28 LA 56, 59; Rosenfarb in 23 LA 789, 793; Waite in 19 LA 1, 4; McCoy in 18 LA 834, 835. Also see Arbitrator Leach in 80 LA 448, 452–453; Williams in 54 LA 683, 686; Luskin in 46 LA 23, 27; Reynolds in 25 LA 60, 63. Cf., Block in 54 LA 1247, 1250–1251 (involving a past practice of training employees in one of two areas but not in both); Emery in 28 LA 733, 736. Regarding the right of minority group members to equal access to training which could lead to future promotion, see discussion in Safeway Stores, 75 LA 387, 392–393 (Allen, 1980).

[215]Sandvik Steel, Inc., 29 LA 747, 749 (Kerrison, 1957). Also see Arbitrator Rothschild in 79 LA 1193, 1196; Williams in 54 LA 683, 686; Luskin in 46 LA 23, 27; Rosenfarb in 23 LA 789, 793.

[216]United States Steel Corp., 36 LA 1082, 1087–1088 (Crawford, 1961).

[217]Kroger Co., 34 LA 414, 418 (Emerson, 1959).

[218]United States Plywood Corp., 49 LA 726, 728 (Amis, 1967). Also see Arbitrator High in 63 LA 341, 344.

[219]Bethlehem Steel Corp., 48 LA 1, 2 (Gill, 1966), where the seniors resisted taking the entire course because it would have required them to work temporarily in a lower classification.

[220]See Purolator Prods., 25 LA 60, 63 (Reynolds, 1955). Also see Arbitrator Rezler in 72 LA 941, 947. In Vulcan Materials Co., 49 LA 577, 579–580 (Duff, 1967), it was held that tests used for selecting trainees must be appropriate to ascertain the aptitude of bidders to become trainees. In John Strange Paper Co., 43 LA 1184, 1187 (Larkin, 1965), management was permitted to use a test for screening employees to be given a period of on-the-job training (even though for several years it had given each senior employee a chance at such training) so long as the system of selection was fair, uniform, and nondiscriminatory.

[221]United States Steel Corp., 22 LA 188, 190 (Garrett, 1953). Similarly, Whirlpool Corp., 49 LA 529, 533–534 (Sembower, 1967).

[222]United States Steel Corp., 22 LA 188, 190 (Garrett, 1953).

the training was better qualified as a result of the training and experience than the senior employees who refused such training, and he therefore was entitled under the relative ability clause to the promotion.[223] Moreover, the fact that the employee did not take advantage of training offered by the company has been considered a factor against him when he was disqualified at the end of a trial period.[224]

Opinion of Supervision

While the opinion of supervisors regarding the ability of employees is considered important and is entitled at least to some consideration, such opinion without factual support will not be deemed conclusive.[225] However, when supervisory opinion is substantiated by objective, tangible evidence, it may be the basis for management's determination as to the relative ability of employees.[226] Such objective evidence may include factors discussed elsewhere in this topic, such as test results, production records, periodic merit ratings, and other documentary material, as well as evidence of prior experience and results of trial periods.

The importance of supervisory opinion was noted by Arbitrator Arthur M. Ross as follows:

> "Considerable weight should be given to bona fide conclusions of supervisors when supported by factual evidence. In the first place, a supervisor is responsible for the efficient performance of his unit and has a legitimate concern that the employees be properly assigned to achieve this objective. In the second place, he has a deeper and more intimate acquaintance with the men under his charge than an arbitrator is able to acquire in a brief hearing."[227]

---

[223]Patapsco & Back Rivers R.R., 43 LA 51, 53–54 (Seitz, 1964). Similarly, see Arbitrator Rimer in 69 LA 311, 314; Bernstein in 42 LA 1109, 1113, involving layoff of senior employees who lacked the training which the junior employees had.

[224]See American Oil Co., 50 LA 1227, 1233 (Simon, 1968); National Lead Co., 48 LA 405, 408 (Wissner, undated).

[225]See Arbitrator Boetticher in 80 LA 361, 363; Roumell in 72 LA 1061, 1064; Brown in 72 LA 727, 732; White in 55 LA 1284, 1288; Roberts in 55 LA 261, 269; Platt in 20 LA 460, 462; Hays in 12 LA 317, 322.

[226]See Arbitrator Hunter in 75 LA 181, 189; Ipavec in 72 LA 524, 528 (in upholding the employer's transfer of a senior teacher while retaining a junior teacher under a "relative ability" clause, Arbitrator Ipavec stated that the school Principal "was adequately able * * * to substantiate the reasons for his decision * * * using objective factors," and that "Unless there is a showing that the evaluation was arbitrary or unreasonable, the assessment of skill made by a supervisor or administrator in a position to make such a determination should be given considerable weight and should not be reversed by the arbitrator"); Beeson in 54 LA 298, 301–302; Stouffer in 52 LA 889, 893; Klein in 46 LA 203, 210; Larkin in 45 LA 129, 130–131 (supervisory opinion given great weight in this case which involved job of group leader); Feinberg in 64–3 ARB ¶9087; Tsukiyama in 40 LA 1225, 1227; Wyckoff in 39 LA 538, 541; Waite in 19 LA 1, 4. Also see Arbitrator Ralston in 19 LA 402, 405; Grant in 11 LA 312, 315. For cases illustrating the important role of supervisory opinion concerning employee qualifications for promotion in the federal sector, see Arbitrator Tillem in 75 LA 910, 911; Belcher in 71 LA 359, 365; Koven in 70 LA 859, 865; Sinicropi in 68 LA 279, 286–287, 289 (but he stressed that "supervisory opinions without factual support will not be deemed conclusive by this arbitrator").

[227]Pacific Gas & Elec. Co., 23 LA 556, 558 (1954), cited with approval by Arbitrator Tsukiyama in 55 LA 477, 480 (who emphasized the importance of "first line supervisorial participation" in the selection process); Stouffer in 52 LA 889, 893. Also see Arbitrator Hunter in 75 LA 171, 189; Burns in 41 LA 148, 151–152, 154; Burris in 25 LA 32, 36; Cole in 21 LA 214, 218. Arbitrator Ross reaffirmed the above view in San Francisco News–Call Bulletin, 34 LA 271, 273–274 (1960), stating further: "But it does not follow that a clearly mistaken decision should be left undisturbed merely because it has not been shown to be arbitrary, discriminatory, etc."

Arbitrator Harry Shulman emphasized the necessity for supporting evidence:

"A supervisor's testimony that he honestly believes one employee to be superior to another with respect to the promotion is certainly a factor to be considered. It is not, however, either conclusive or sufficient. The supervisor must be prepared to state the basis for his belief and to support it, not by repeated assertions but by specific and understandable evidence * * * ."[228]

Supervisory opinion has been given controlling weight where management's decision to bypass the senior employee was based upon a composite of the opinions of several supervisors who observed or supervised his work, the opinions being formed on the basis of a variety of incidents in the senior's employment record.[229] In another case, the arbitrator stated that the opinion of management was "what actually controlled his decision" where company officers (president, vice president, etc.) were in almost daily contact over many years with the employees, and thus knew them well and knew the processes and machines well.[230]

Supervisory opinion has been given great if not controlling weight where several levels of supervision, familiar with the work performance of the bidders and with the requirements of the job being bid upon, reached a unanimous decision,[231] and where supervisory opinion was later supported by evidence of an employee's inadequate performance during a trial period.[232] Little if any weight has been accorded supervisory opinion where the company relied upon such opinion concerning one of the bidders while not consulting supervisors of another bidder at all,[233] and where the supervisors consulted had little or no opportunity to observe the men they were rating and were not familiar with the requirements of the job being bid upon.[234]

---

[228]Ford Motor Co., 2 LA 374, 376 (1945), cited with approval by Arbitrator Roumell in 72 LA 1061, 1064; Roberts in 55 LA 261, 269; Kates in 45 LA 743, 748.

[229]See Northwestern Bell Tel. Co., 19 LA 47, 50–51 (Doyle, 1952). Also see Eagle-Picher Mining & Smelting Co., 17 LA 205, 211 (Prasow, 1951).

[230]See Pittsburgh Standard Conduit Co., 32 LA 481, 482–483 (Lehoczky, 1959), where the finding was based upon other factors also, including the use of a test.

[231]See Arbitrator Tsukiyama in 55 LA 477, 480; Wolff in 54 LA 447, 448; Beeson in 54 LA 298, 301–302; Larkin in 45 LA 129, 130–131.

[232]See Arbitrator Stouffer in 52 LA 889, 893; Klein in 46 LA 203, 210; Feinberg in 64–3 ARB ¶9087.

[233]See Northwest Airlines, 46 LA 238, 241–242 (Elkouri, 1966); International Nickel Co., 45 LA 743, 748 (Kates, 1965).

[234]See Arbitrator Nathanson in 75 LA 1001, 1004–1005; Amis in 55 LA 432, 434; Alexander in 46 LA 801, 805. In Rainier Port Cold Storage, 79 LA 441, 448 (Armstrong, 1982), a significant factor in the arbitrator's finding that the grievant's layoff was arbitrary and capricious was the fact that officials who made the decision to lay him off instead of a junior employee failed to consult the foreman who was best qualified to give supervisory opinion regarding grievant's ability. In choosing between two nurses bidding to fill a vacancy in Marshalltown Area Community Hosp., 76 LA 978, 984–985 (1981), the promoting supervisor "talked to other hospital personnel to obtain additional information about each of the applicants," and talked with four surgeons "to obtain their input regarding the applicants"; Arbitrator Clifford E. Smith found that this process produced no substantive information concerning the knowledge, skills, or abilities of either candidate, and in concluding that the senior applicant should have been awarded the vacancy, he declared that "the selection procedure could be judged more of a popularity contest than a logical attempt to identify applicants' abilities and qualifications."

Merit Rating Plans

Merit rating plans (or performance reviews) involve essentially a documentation, usually periodically made, of supervisory opinion concerning various aspects of the "fitness and ability" of the employees. A merit rating plan may include such factors as quantity and quality of work, knowledge of the job, ability to learn, initiative, acceptance of responsibility, ability to direct others, safety habits and accident record, attitude toward fellow employees and management, attendance, and personal characteristics such as moral character, physical condition, and appearance.[235] Other factors may include the quality of pertinent experience and training, special conditions of the job, and achievements which have earned incentive awards or other special recognition.[236]

Arbitrators look upon merit rating plans as an aid in judging fitness and ability. However, while considering performance ratings an important aid, Arbitrator Ralph Roger Williams cautioned against placing exclusive reliance upon them in determining fitness and ability, stating:

> "The word 'fitness' is not synonymous with 'merit'; it means the quality of being suitable to the performance of the regular duties of the job, and includes the employee's habits, industry, energy, ambition, tact, disposition, discretion, knowledge of the duties of the job, physical strength, and related attributes. It means suitability. The word 'ability' means the possession of those qualities of mind, physical strength, and related job attainments which are sufficient, under the usual conditions of the job, to satisfactorily perform the basic and usual duties and tasks of the job. The Company placed too much weight on its past evaluations of the Grievant's job performance. While these performance ratings are important and serve to assist in the employer's evaluation of an employee, they are not all-inclusive."[237]

---

[235]See Western Automatic Mach. Screw Co., 9 LA 606, 608 (Lehoczky, 1948). For other discussion of merit rating plans, see Holley, "Performance Ratings in Arbitration," 32 Arb. J. 8 (1977). In Electrical Distribs., 64 LA 608, 609 (Burr, 1974), a joint union-management committee for evaluation of job performance had difficulty making an evaluation and could not agree on criteria by which to do so. A survey of collective agreements in the federal sector revealed that most contained merit promotion plans; about one fourth of the agreements surveyed specified criteria to be used in rating employees for merit promotion purposes, very few specified consideration of seniority as a factor, and none provided "for union participation in the actual decision, itself." A Survey of Merit Promotion Provisions in Federal Post Civil Service Reform Act Agreements, 1, 11, 32–33 (OPM, 1980). For related discussion see Ferris, "Remedies in Federal Sector Promotion Grievances," 34 Arb. J. 37 (1979). In U.S. Dept. of Health & Human Servs., 81 LA 980, 981–982 (1983), Arbitrator H. Raymond Cluster observed that the Civil Service Reform Act of 1978 mandates the establishment of performance appraisal systems and that the Office of Personnel Management had issued regulations requiring individual federal agencies to establish their system by October 1, 1981; he outlined the features of the performance appraisal system involved in the grievance before him.

[236]See United States Dept. of the Interior, 53 LA 657, 659 (Koven, 1969). For yet other factors, see San Antonio Air Logistics Center, 74 LA 486, 487 (Coffey, 1979). Many of the factors noted above are discussed as separate criteria in other subtopics of this Chapter. For an illustration that management may be more restricted in evaluating employee performance where factors are specified in the collective agreement, see Internal Revenue Serv., 64 LA 486, 495–497 (McBrearty, 1975).

[237]American Oil Co., 53 LA 160, 161 (1969), involving a "sufficient ability" clause. Compare, United States Customs Serv., 72 LA 700, 701 (1979), upholding the federal agency employer's denial of grievant's transfer request where his present and previous supervisors had denied him in-grade increases on the ground that he had not performed his duties at an "acceptable level of

Merit or performance ratings have been a factor (along with others) accepted and considered by the arbitrator in upholding management's determination of ability under a "relative ability" clause[238] and under a "sufficient ability" clause.[239] However, one employee evaluation system was considered by the arbitrator to be suspect in that "well meaning as it was intended to be, [it] tended to match the traits of each bidder against the others," thus resulting in a comparison of bidders which was not permitted under the "sufficient ability" clause.[240]

An arbitrator's acceptance or rejection of a merit rating plan as a criterion for measuring ability depends upon whether the factors used in the plan and the weights attached to them are consistent with the collective agreement and the requirements of the job in question.[241] Thus, under a contract providing that seniority should govern where "ability, skill, and efficiency" are substantially equal, management's institution of a performance review plan was upheld since the plan did no more than document on a regular basis supervisory opinion concerning the ability, skill, and efficiency of employees; the arbitrator stated that management could use any method, written or unwritten, to determine the relative ability of employees "so long as that method is not unfair, arbitrary, or based on improper or irrelevant premises."[242] Under another "relative ability" provision, the arbitrator held that some of the factors in the merit rating plan used by the company had no bearing upon an employee's "ability to do the work,"

---

competency," Arbitrator Walter A. Maggiolo reasoning that the employer could reasonably "assume that if the grievant was unable to perform his present GS-12 duties at an acceptable level in his present position, he would not be able to perform GS-12 duties in any branch to which he might be assigned."

[238]See Arbitrator Volz in 47 LA 263, 265; Tsukiyama in 40 LA 1225, 1227–1228; Grant in 11 LA 312, 315; Gilden in 4 LA 657, 666–667.

[239]Jeffrey Mfg. Co., 29 LA 300, 302 (Seinsheimer, 1957).

[240]Ohio Edison Co., 46 LA 801, 805 (Alexander, 1966).

[241]See Arbitrator Hogan in 27 LA 816, 819 (improper weight given to certain factors); Hawley in 17 LA 516, 519; Grant in 11 LA 312, 315.

[242]Lockheed Aircraft Corp., 25 LA 748, 750–751 (Williams, 1956), where the union agreed that the company could determine relative ability of employees but objected to the regular documentation of such determination. Accord, Lockheed Aircraft Serv. Co., 40 LA 1225, 1227–1228 (Tsukiyama, 1963). For a statement of management's residual rights as concerns performance evaluation, see Department of Health, Educ. & Welfare, 72 LA 788, 791–793 (Hayes, 1979). In Acme Steel Co., 9 LA 432, 436–437 (1947), Arbitrator Charles O. Gregory stated that a merit rating plan is preferable to placing "the judgment in the hands of the foremen on an ad hoc basis, with no systematic check on their whims and fancies from top management." For an illustration of capricious evaluations by an employee's immediate supervisor, see Federal Aviation Admin., 64 LA 289, 291 (Amis, 1975). But actions of top management also may trigger improper ratings. In San Antonio Air Logistics Center, 74 LA 486, 488–489 (1979), a federal agency employer reviewed overall ratings within the employer's center and, concluding that they were too high, directed supervisors to "bring them into line if they could"; pursuant to this the grievant's supervisor rated her lower than before even though her performance had not dropped, leading Arbitrator A. Langley Coffey (1) to conclude that she "did not receive a fair and just supervisory appraisal based on her job performance," and (2) to order that a new supervisory appraisal be made for the period in question. Another illustration is provided by Wisconsin Dept. of Indus., 64 LA 663, 667–668 (1975), where Arbitrator Philip G. Marshall found that a management official had made "little or no use" of the customary evaluation criteria (based upon which the grievant's immediate superior considered him to be deserving of a merit increase), and had withheld merit increases "not so much for failure of an individual to perform 'meritorious service' as for a disciplinary device or a substitute for the exercise of appropriate managerial action." Also see Arbitrator Mussmann in 72 LA 666, 668; Kindig in 59 LA 1007, 1014.

and when these were discounted the employees involved were found to have the requisite ability.[243]

Other aspects of merit rating which have reached arbitration concern (1) management's right to place and retain evaluation reports in the employee's personnel file for future use, and/or (2) the right of the employee and union to be apprised of their use and to see such reports before any affirmative action is taken adversely affecting the employee.[244]

Educational Background

Technical training acquired through attendance at trade schools, or at training programs sponsored by company or union, and the like, obviously is highly pertinent to the determination of fitness and ability if such training relates to the requirements of the job in question. Thus, where a job by nature required at least one course in accounting which the grievant had not taken, the company was held justified in selecting a qualified new hire.[245] However, where the junior employee's technical training was not related to the job requirements, the employer was held to have violated the seniority provisions by awarding the job to him since the senior employee otherwise possessed substantially equal ability.[246] The same result was reached in another case even though the junior employee's technical training had potential value for jobs higher in the line of progression, the arbitrator

---

[243]Western Automatic Mach. Screw Co., 9 LA 606, 608–609 (Lehoczky, 1948). Similarly, American Oil Co., 53 LA 160, 162 (Williams, 1969), under a "sufficient ability" clause. In Merrill Stevens Dry Dock & Repair Co., 17 LA 516, 518–519 (Hawley, 1951), most of the factors were accepted but the company was "urged" to remove imprecise factors from its merit rating plan. Of course, even where a given factor is accepted, an arbitrator can be expected to require that its actual application be substantiated in a specific and understandable manner. National Lab. Relations Bd., 68 LA 279, 289 (Sinicropi, 1977).

[244]See Arbitrator Hannan in 76 LA 68, 71 (ordering removal of derogatory material placed in employee's file without her having opportunity to review it as required by agreement); Mittleman in 75 LA 1194, 1200–1201 (dealing with alleged injury due to retention of erroneous appraisal of qualifications in grievant's file, and construing the Privacy Act of 1974 in connection with the claim); Atwood in 70 LA 967, 968–969 (construing the Privacy Act of 1974 and concluding that it does not prohibit the making of records but rather that Congress was concerned with access by individuals to and the improper disclosure of information pertaining to themselves and maintained by federal agencies); Bell in 69 LA 682, 686–687; Peterschmidt in 69 LA 34, 38–39; Gilden in 48 LA 421, 424–425; Leach in 48 LA 299, 304 (where the employee feared that the report was a disciplinary device in the nature of a warning); Gusweiler in 44 LA 200, 201 (upholding management's right to make an efficiency survey, but finding improper the forms used); Morvant in 42 LA 41, 45–47. Also see Mobilization for Youth, 49 LA 1124, 1126–1127 (Wolff, 1967), where a report was orally imparted to supervision, was neither discussed with the employee nor made a part of her personnel record, yet was used to bar advancement. For a court decision upholding an arbitrator's power to order the removal of an unfair performance evaluation from the employee's file, see Unit B, Kittery Teachers Assn. v. Kittery School Comm., 413 A.2d 534 (Me. S.Ct., 1980).

[245]Roosevelt Univ., 56 LA 604, 607 (Larkin, 1971). Also see Arbitrator Sobel in 70 LA 1073, 1076 (employer's requirement of one year training for job of computer operator held "entirely reasonable"); Young in 69 LA 156, 157; Smith in 51 LA 264, 266.

[246]Pennsylvania Power & Light Co., 57 LA 146, 148–149 (Howard, 1971). As to the need of supervisory testimony to correlate technical training with the job requirements, see Laupahoehoe Sugar Co., 38 LA 404, 412–413 (Tsukiyama, 1961).

emphasizing that an employee's qualifications "must be measured a job at a time."[247]

An employee's formal educational background, that is, high school and college education as opposed to technical training, may be a factor in the assessment of fitness and ability if it is pertinent to the job requirements.[248] Where the contract does not specify a formal educational requirement for given jobs, arbitrators appear to have taken several (not necessarily inconsistent) approaches to the question of whether the employer may consider this factor in determining ability. Thus, it has been variously held that (1) management could require a high school education where the job was complex and carried with it automatic progressions through several classifications involving additional responsibilities;[249] (2) the formal educational background of the employee may be considered along with other factors;[250] (3) the employer may not automatically disqualify an employee for want of a formal education but may consider formal education in evaluating the employee's training and experience;[251] (4) the employer violated the contract by denying a promotion to senior employees solely on the basis that they lacked high school education or its equivalent.[252]

In the latter regard, it has been held that the lack of such formal education alone may not be deemed conclusive evidence of a lack of ability, Arbitrator Edward E. McDaniel stating that while the company may establish minimum qualifications for a job, it may not create "exclusionary 'barriers'" which prevent employees from competing for

---

[247]Georgia Kraft Co., 47 LA 829, 830 (Williams, 1966). Also see Realist, Inc., 45 LA 444, 446 (Keeler, 1965). Progression was not automatic in these cases.

[248]In Griggs v. Duke Power Co., 91 S.Ct. 849 (1971), it was held that the employer violated Title VII of the Civil Rights Act of 1964 by requiring a high school education or the passing of a standardized general intelligence test as a condition of employment in or transfer to jobs where it was not shown that such requirements were job-related and where the requirements operated to discriminate against blacks.

[249]Philip Carey Mfg. Co., 30 LA 659, 661 (Warns, 1958). A different result obtained in West Virginia Pulp & Paper Co., 16 LA 359, 365 (Copelof, 1951), where progression was not automatic. For other cases upholding the requirement of a high school education, see Arbitrator Griffin in 74 LA 1248, 1253 (concluding that employer did not violate either the collective agreement or the Civil Rights Act by adding the requirement of a high school education or its equivalent for vacancies in the shipping department, there being need to reduce errors and the employer's evidence indicating that high school graduates in that department perform better than their nongraduate counterparts); Kates in 46 LA 1153, 1156–1157; Seibel in 22 LA 446, 449–450.

[250]See Arbitrator Volz in 47 LA 263, 265; Handsaker in 42 LA 349, 351; O'Rourke in 39 LA 161, 163; Howlett in 26 LA 885, 890. Also see Arbitrator Goodstein in 72 LA 892, 897; Rezler in 72 LA 941, 949; Ables in 67 LA 453, 454, 456; Cantor in 48 LA 777, 778; Baab in 20 LA 137, 142. In Lockheed-Georgia Co., 49 LA 603, 605 (Di Leone, 1967), it was found that the superior education of the senior bidder balanced the experience of the junior so that their overall abilities were substantially equal, entitling the former to the promotion under the "relative ability" clause.

[251]See Union Oil Co., 17 LA 62, 64–65 (Wyckoff, 1951). Similarly, United States Steel Corp., 55 LA 659, 662 (McDaniel, 1970). Also see Arbitrator Brown in 44 LA 92, 94.

[252]See Bridgeport Gas Co., 26 LA 289, 291 (Stutz, 1956). Also see Arbitrator Brown in 72 LA 1167, 1170–1171 (although the employer reasonably required a tenth grade education or its approved equivalent for a job, the "approved equivalent" alternative was applied too rigidly in denying the job to the senior bidder who would have completed the tenth grade equivalent course in time for an award of the job had the course instructors not extended it on their own for another three months); Dworet in 38 LA 91, 92. In a case where the "really serious issue" was the senior employee's age, the arbitrator disposed of the education factor by finding that the "lack of a formal high school education should not constitute a bar to his being considered" for the job. See CIBA Pharmaceutical Co., 41 LA 14, 17 (Berkowitz, 1963).

a given vacancy. He stated further: "Though a high school diploma (or equivalent certificate) is some evidence of basic ability to perform a given job, the lack of such 'credentials' cannot, in itself, be deemed to establish, conclusively, the opposite."[253]

The question of ability to read and write in English has arisen in several cases. Where such ability was necessary to the proper performance of the job, management has been held justified in disqualifying the employee who lacks such ability, as in the case in which the senior bidders could not read and write well enough in English to interpret the repair manual and parts list and to make requisitions, all necessary functions of the job.[254] However, in another case communication difficulties were not considered sufficient to outweigh the job applicant's meritorious service and his ability to do the basic work of the job; even though he had a heavy foreign accent and could read English only slowly, he could read blueprints and had effectively communicated with a new man he had trained on the job.[255]

Production Records

An employee's production record is objective evidence of productivity or output and may be relied upon in whole or in part (depending upon the circumstances) in determining fitness and ability.[256] One arbitrator asserted that ability "is most assuredly tied up with productivity" and that productivity must be measured in terms of both quality and quantity of work.[257] Another stated that "output reflects not only effort, but know-how, skill and general capability, and is generally regarded as a proper item to be considered in measuring ability."[258]

---

[253]United States Steel Corp., 55 LA 659, 662 (1970). Also see Arbitrator Keeler in 45 LA 444, 447; Brown in 44 LA 92, 95; Gill in 37 LA 14, 14–15 (where the company's concern that the removal of the educational requirement would burden it unreasonably with the giving of trial periods to unqualified employees was considered unfounded due to its testing program). In United States Steel Corp., 42 LA 245, 247 (Altrock, 1964), only minimal weight was given to the fact that the junior employee's schooling was from an "accredited" school, while the senior employee's was not, and since other factors indicated that they were relatively equal in ability, the senior was entitled to the job. Cf., Arbitrator Sinicropi in 75 LA 420, 421, 426–427.

[254]Vulcan Materials Co., 54 LA 460, 466 (Block, 1970). Similarly, see Arbitrator Goodstein in 51 LA 31, 34; Phelps in 32 LA 289, 292–293. In Texas Utils. Generating Co., 71 LA 1205, 1207–1208 (1979), Arbitrator Mewhinney concluded from the evidence "that the Grievant, a high school graduate, was given a high school diploma * * * without having acquired the minimum verbal and quantitative skills necessary in order to function satisfactorily in an industrial environment."

[255]Lanson & Sessions Co., 50 LA 959, 960–961 (Dahl, 1968). Also see Gallmeyer & Livingston Co., 20 LA 899, 901–903 (Ryder, 1953).

[256]Regarding the type of data necessary in presenting production records as evidence of fitness and ability, see Jonco Aircraft Corp., 22 LA 819, 823 (Merrill, 1954). The term "work records" may or may not be broader than "production records." For cases in which the "work records" or "production records" of competing employees were a factor, see Arbitrator Byars in 79 LA 1251, 1255; Craver in 77 LA 391, 393; McDermott in 49 LA 1160, 1170–1172; Cantor in 48 LA 777, 781; Daugherty in 47 LA 554, 558–559; Hayes in 31 LA 338, 340–341; Brecht in 21 LA 565, 568; Prasow in 17 LA 205, 211. For a statement regarding the significance of "performance records," see James N. Travirca, Gen. Contracting Co., 56 LA 1083, 1084 (Logan, 1971).

[257]Universal Mfg. Co., 13 LA 238, 241 (Spencer, 1949).

[258]Worth Steel Co., 12 LA 931, 934 (Bell, 1949).

Production records may be the sole factor considered where there is a substantial difference in the productivity of competing employees. Thus, management's determination of relative ability based solely upon productivity was upheld where the grievant's production was considerably below that of other workers,[259] and in another case where there was a 17 percent difference between the senior and junior employee's production earnings.[260] Management's reliance in part upon production records has likewise been upheld where the employee consistently failed to make the minimum wage under an incentive system or where the employee's production record was consistently below the standard.[261]

On the other hand, in situations where there is only a minor difference in productivity of employees, automatic reliance upon productivity alone for the determination of relative ability probably would not be upheld.[262] Moreover, management may not base its determination of ability upon its speculations as to the relative *future* productivity of competing employees.[263]

Attendance Records

Under the various types of seniority clauses, attendance records may be considered at least as one of the factors used in determining fitness and ability, and in some instances may be the sole or controlling factor. In a number of cases an employee's attendance record has been considered as a relevant factor and as tangible and objective evidence in assessing ability and qualifications.[264] An employee's poor attendance record has been the sole or controlling factor where the job involved was critical to operations or otherwise required a high degree of responsibility.[265] Thus, under a contract containing a "relative ability" clause, the promotion of a junior over a senior employee on the basis of their attendance records was upheld where the records showed a "striking" difference in favor of the junior and the job required a high

---

[259]Byer-Rolnick Corp., 45 LA 868, 872 (Ray, 1965); Universal Mfg. Co., 13 LA 238, 241 (Spencer, 1949). Also see Arbitrator Beilstein in 68 LA 1282, 1284.

[260]Worth Steel Co., 12 LA 931, 934 (Bell, 1949).

[261]See Arbitrator Craver in 77 LA 391, 393; Kesselman in 52 LA 568, 570; Hazelwood in 51 LA 382, 383–384; Abernethy in 23 LA 379, 383; Klamon in 19 LA 639, 646; McCoy in 11 LA 419, 425–426. Also see Hawley in 33 LA 719, 721.

[262]United States Steel Corp., 22 LA 80, 81 (Garrett, 1953).

[263]Wurlitzer Co., 41 LA 792, 795 (Duff, 1963).

[264]See Arbitrator Rezler in 72 LA 941, 946–948; White in 55 LA 1284, 1287 (where the arbitrator exercised an "equitable power" in taking into consideration the attendance factor); Amis in 49 LA 726, 728; Elkouri in 46 LA 238, 241 (but promotion may not be denied as punishment for tardiness); Schmidt in 44 LA 283, 285; Davis in 30 LA 862, 871. Cf., Arbitrator Duncan in 40 LA 364, 366; Edes in 11 LA 108, 109 (where the parties agreed at the hearing that "ability and skill" does not encompass absenteeism). In Lockheed Aircraft Serv. Co., 40 LA 1225, 1228 (Tsukiyama, 1963), the company was upheld in its determination that the junior employee's superior qualities of leadership (a requirement of the job) outweighed the much better attendance record of the senior employee.

[265]See Arbitrator Kates in 52 LA 1074, 1077–1078; McCoy in 51 LA 857, 858–859 (stating, however, that ordinarily management cannot deny promotions solely on the basis of a poor attendance record); Turkus in 43 LA 946, 950; Blair in 16 LA 382, 383, and in 8 LA 877, 879. Also see Petersen in 75 LA 1282, 1285.

degree of responsibility.[266] In that case, Arbitrator Jacob J. Blair stated:

> "It is well established as a principle that Management has the right to expect and require regular attendance on the job. While it is true that Management has in this instance been extremely negligent in enforcing this right, its negligence does not bar it from applying the right in the case of a promotion. * * *
>
> "The action of Management in invoking this right at this time is not arbitrary. True, Management could not discipline * * * [grievant] by layoffs or dismissals for an action which they have condoned over a period of time without prior notice or warning. But the right to discipline and the right of Management to choose between candidates for promotion are distinguishable. * * * Management has the right to invoke the attendance records of two employees contending for a promotion because to do otherwise would condone and even approve a record of irregular attendance at work."[267]

It has also been held that the employer may consider the employee's attendance record in determining whether he is "qualified," even though his numerous absences were due to illness.[268]

However, some arbitrators have held that an employee's attendance record is not a factor to be used in determining the ability or qualifications of an employee. They reason that nothing in the contract permits management to use this factor to pass over a senior employee who otherwise meets the contractual requirements, and, further, that if an employee is guilty of absenteeism, it is a matter of discipline and should have been dealt with at the time the offenses occurred.[269]

In cases involving excused absences for the conduct of union business, it has been held that such absences should not operate as a bar to giving the senior man preference; but the arbitrator appears to have based his decision on past practice,[270] or to have conditioned his award upon the satisfactory performance of the job during a trial period,[271] or upon regular attendance by the employee,[272] reserving explicitly or in effect the right of management to take corrective steps should the employee not perform in an acceptable manner.

Disciplinary Record

If an employee's disciplinary record contains offenses which reflect upon his fitness and ability for a given job, such record may be

---

[266]Rogers Bros. Corp., 16 LA 382, 383 (Blair, 1951). Accord, Metal Forge Co., 51 LA 857, 858–859 (McCoy, 1968).

[267]Rogers Bros. Corp., 16 LA 382, 383 (Blair, 1951). Accord, Emhart Mfg. Co., 43 LA 946, 950 (Turkus, 1964), under a "sufficient ability" clause.

[268]See Arbitrator Bailer in 20 LA 835, 836; Levinson in 16 LA 790, 792; McCoy in 11 LA 419, 425–426. Cf., Kelliher in 9 LA 444, 447.

[269]See Arbitrator Kahn in 71 LA 80, 82; Morgan in 69 LA 234, 238; Kallenbach in 64 LA 271, 275; Duncan in 40 LA 364, 366; Dworkin in 34 LA 852, 854–855; Kelliher in 24 LA 599, 600. Also see Kanzer in 81 LA 51, 54–55; Storey in 78 LA 192, 195–197; Freund in 67 LA 901, 914.

[270]See American Lava Corp., 42 LA 117, 120 (Hon, 1964); Douglas Aircraft Co., 23 LA 786, 788 (Warren, 1955).

[271]See Marlin-Rockwell Corp., 17 LA 254, 256 (Shister, 1951).

[272]See Goodyear Decatur Mills, 12 LA 682, 685 (McCoy, 1949).

given some consideration. For example, it has been held that an employee's disciplinary record could be considered since his offenses demonstrated that he lacked maturity, reliability and a sense of responsibility and hence the ability, merit, and capacity required by the contract.[273] Even where the employee had not been disciplined for his offenses in the past, one arbitrator distinguished between the right of management to discipline at a later date and the obligation of management to promote, stating:

> "When the requirements of the job * * * clearly call for maturity, reliability and a sense of responsibility in addition to technical skill or expertness, it would be less than logical to deny or preclude any consideration at all to offenses directly related thereto simply because such offenses through laxity or forbearance lost vitality as a basis for subsequent disciplinary action."[274]

However, other arbitrators have held that if alleged offenses are not made the subject of discipline at the time they are committed, management may not be permitted to rely upon them later in assessing employee abilities and qualifications.[275] Furthermore, a single offense for which the worker has been disciplined may not be sufficient to compel the conclusion that he is incompetent.[276]

The collective agreement may provide specifically or in effect that the personnel records of the employees be considered by management in determining ability. Under such an agreement, personnel records showing that four written reprimands were issued to the senior employee in connection with his work were considered by the arbitrator to justify management's decision to promote the junior employee.[277]

Employee's Physical and Psychological Fitness

Many contracts specifically include physical fitness as a requirement for job preference.[278] However, even where the contract does not contain the physical ability requirement, it has been said that the

---

[273]Dewey & Almy Chem. Co., 25 LA 316, 318–319 (Somers, 1955). Also see Arbitrator Kelliher in 76 LA 852, 853; Rezler in 72 LA 941, 946–948; Stouffer in 50 LA 17, 20; Turkus in 43 LA 946, 949; Klamon in 19 LA 639, 646–647.

[274]Emhart Mfg. Co., 43 LA 946, 949 (Turkus, 1964). Also see Arbitrator Mann in 68 LA 357, 361.

[275]See Arbitrator Rothschild in 73 LA 965, 967; Carlson in 54 LA 151, 155; Kelliher in 24 LA 599, 600; Killingsworth in 19 LA 186, 188.

[276]See Copco Steel & Eng'g. Co., 13 LA 586, 591 (Platt, 1949). Also see Thompson Bros. Boat Mfg. Co., 55 LA 69, 73 (Moberly, 1970), stating that "inability does *not* mean temporary misconduct or improper work attitudes which more properly should be treated by corrective action."

[277]Inland Steel Co., 16 LA 280, 284 (Cornsweet, 1951).

[278]See, for example, 61 LA 621, 624; 51 LA 1143, 1144; 30 LA 237, 238; 23 LA 556, 557; 17 LA 486, 487.

term "ability" includes physical (and mental) ability.[279] Health records showing an employee's physical condition have been considered as "tangible and objective" evidence of his fitness and ability;[280] but "old" records as to an employee's physical condition ordinarily may not be relied upon, arbitrators favoring more recent medical evidence concerning such matters.[281]

In the absence of a contract prohibition, management has been held entitled to require employees to take physical examinations, but the right must be exercised properly and not arbitrarily, capriciously, or unreasonably.[282] Management could require such examinations to determine the physical fitness or ability of the employee to perform the work, for instance, before reinstatement or promotion of an ailing employee in a job requiring weight-lifting activities,[283] or before transfer or promotion of an employee to a job demanding greater physical effort,[284] or where there is serious doubt as to the employee's ability to perform the work safely because of some physical condition or characteristic.[285]

It would seem to be a corollary to this right that it is the duty of the employer to protect the health of his employees despite their willingness to perform heavier duties. In this regard, Arbitrator Joseph M. Klamon stated:

> " * * * Indeed, the Company might incur a legal liability for failure to exercise due care and reasonable judgment to protect the health of operating employees. The ability to perform a job cannot be disassociated from the health hazards involved to male as well as female employees and action the Company takes in this regard is definitely within the inherent rights of Management to operate the plant safely and efficiently."[286]

When the question of physical fitness for a particular job arises, the primary emphasis may be placed on the physical disability of the bypassed employee to fill the job, another employee's greater physical

---

[279]See Arbitrator Simon in 53 LA 1181, 1193; Siciliano in 37 LA 1047, 1050; Jenson in 32 LA 772, 774; Stashower in 12 LA 896, 897. The terms "fitness" and "qualified" also include physical and mental fitness or ability. See Arbitrator Williams in 49 LA 952, 955; Dworkin in 35 LA 391, 394; Tatum in 34 LA 67, 70. Cf., Cahn in 34 LA 426, 427, involving past practice.

[280]See Southwestern Bell Tel. Co., 30 LA 862, 871 (Davis, 1958). Also see Allegheny Ludlum Steel Corp., 42 LA 343, 344 (Shipman, 1963).

[281]See National Lead Co., 42 LA 176, 178 (Seidenberg, 1964); North Shore Gas Co., 40 LA 37, 44 (Sembower, 1963).

[282]See Arbitrator Bothwell in 45 LA 39, 42; Brown in 44 LA 92, 95; Phelps in 42 LA 161, 164; Sembower in 40 LA 37, 42–43. For related discussion, see Chapter 13, subtopic entitled "Right to Require Physical Examination."

[283]See Southern Conn. Gas Co., 48 LA 1357, 1358 (Johnson, 1967); Fulton Glass Co., 31 LA 824, 826 (Boles, 1958). Also see Arbitrator Bothwell in 27 LA 404, 406, involving recall.

[284]See Arbitrator Morgan in 68 LA 708, 709, 712; Jenson in 32 LA 772, 774–776; Stashower in 12 LA 896, 897–898.

[285]See Arbitrator McIntosh in 46 LA 530, 532; Brown in 44 LA 92, 95; Klein in 43 LA 217, 224 (periodic examinations upheld); Phelps in 42 LA 161, 164; Klamon in 37 LA 960, 966.

[286]Mengel Co., 18 LA 392, 399 (1952). Also see Arbitrator Johnson in 48 LA 1357, 1358, where the company in requiring a physical examination argued that "it had a responsibility to all employees to give them jobs which would not prove harmful to them"; Kiroff in 42 LA 1051, 1056, where the company's refusal to reinstate an employee was not justified by a mere "feeling" that he might hurt himself.

ability for it being secondary.[287] Thus, it has been held that if certain work contributes to or would cause a recurrence of an employee's ill health, he cannot justifiably claim physical fitness for that work.[288] Similarly, a physical defect or limitation which impairs an employee's physical fitness for a particular job has been held to render him deficient in the requisite physical fitness.[289] A like result was reached where the employee's physical condition constituted a hazard to himself, to other employees, or to the plant and equipment.[290] However, neither the fact that the senior man weighed less than the junior[291] nor the fact that the senior man was older[292] has been considered proof that he was less able to fulfill the physical requirements of the job. Furthermore, even under a "relative ability" clause which expressly included physical fitness as a factor, a senior employee suffering from hypertension was held entitled to fill a vacancy for which he was physically fit, Arbitrator Jay W. Murphy stating that "the junior man might have been a superior physical specimen in every sense of the word to [grievant], but there was no showing that such outstanding physical fitness was required for the job" in question.[293]

Obesity has sometimes been advanced as a reason for refusal to reinstate an employee following layoff or medical leave, or for refusal to promote a senior employee. Where excess weight or attending physical problems affected the employee's physical fitness for the

---

[287]See Arbitrator May in 55 LA 975, 980–981, where the employee suffered incapacitating injuries in an automobile accident after being promoted; Marshall in 53 LA 1282, 1287, where the company was not required to give a trial period to an employee who lacked the necessary physical coordination and dexterity; Altrock in 51 LA 1143, 1144, stating that physical ability means present, not prospective, ability; Brandschain in 5 LA 579, 581. In Simoniz Co., 54 LA 172, 174–175 (Talent, 1969), the company was upheld in denying an employee's request for demotion to his old job on the ground of physical inability to perform his new job, the arbitrator stating that under the agreement such a request "would be left to management's prerogative to decide."

[288]See Arbitrator Kerrison in 45 LA 724, 726; Singletary in 42 LA 775, 780–781; Dworkin in 35 LA 391, 395; Bailer in 20 LA 835, 836; Spencer in 13 LA 238, 241. Cf., Trotta in 23 LA 800, 803, where there was no conclusive evidence that the new job would aggravate grievant's condition.

[289]See Arbitrator Blackmar in 79 LA 419, 420, 422; Kleinsorge in 76 LA 202, 204; Laybourne in 72 LA 367, 369; Jaffee in 51 LA 27, 28 (speech impediment justified rejection for group leader job); Murphy in 44 LA 1252, 1263 (epileptic not qualified for hazardous work); Willingham in 42 LA 376, 385; Tatum in 34 LA 67, 70–71; Updegraff in 27 LA 680, 682. It has been emphasized that each case must be decided on its own facts. See Arbitrator Altrock in 51 LA 152, 155–156. For a summary of "the fundamental requirements for the successful incorporation of disabled people into a company's work force," see J.R. Simplot Co., 53 LA 1181, 1188–1189 (Simon, 1969), emphasizing that handicapped workers must be properly placed and stating: "The same standards should be used in evaluating a handicapped person's ability and/or qualifications as related to the job under consideration." The company was held justified in demoting a partially blind employee from a job operating mobile equipment when it became aware of his visual problems. Id. at 1192. For similar statements regarding handicapped persons, see Glass Containers Mfrs. Inst., 66–3 ARB ¶8999 (Dworkin, 1966). Under the Rehabilitation Act of 1973 employers who enter into certain procurement contracts with the federal government must adopt affirmative action plans for employment and advancement of qualified handicapped individuals. 29 U.S.C.A. §§ 790, 793. Also, programs or activities receiving federal financial assistance are prohibited by the Act from discriminating (including employment discrimination) against qualified handicapped individuals. See Consolidated Rail Corp. v. Darrone, 104 S.Ct. 1248 (1984).

[290]Allegheny Ludlum Steel Corp., 42 LA 343, 344–345 (Shipman, 1963). Similarly, see Arbitrator Seinsheimer in 77 LA 773, 775. For related discussions, see Chapter 16, Safety and Health.

[291]See Seagrave Corp., 16 LA 410, 412 (Lehoczky, 1951).

[292]See Combustion Eng'g. Co., 20 LA 416, 419 (McCoy, 1953).

[293]Hercules Inc., 61 LA 621, 626 (1973).

work, arbitrators have upheld management in denying him that work.[294] However, where obesity has not adversely affected the employee's job performance in the past, management has not been permitted to deny him the work.[295]

In jobs where psychological requirements are important, an employee's fitness in this regard may also be examined. Thus, with respect to a job entailing "psychological strain and stress," Arbitrator Mitchell M. Shipman stated:

> " * * * And, however intangible these psychological requirements may be, they are not to be minimized. * * * Indeed, just as the Umpire must be convinced that [grievant] does have the requisite experience and ability to do the job, so must he be equally convinced that the psychological requirements thereof can also be fully met by him."[296]

An employee's temperament may be such as to disqualify him for a responsible job, as where an employee's nervousness and excitability in moments of emergency were considered grounds for rejecting his bid.[297] Furthermore, management's refusal to recall an employee in accordance with seniority was upheld where his mental condition was such that he could not perform even the simplest duties without an abnormal amount of supervision.[298]

Sex as a Factor

In cases involving questions of discrimination on the basis of sex, arbitrators have held that management is obligated to determine fitness and ability in relation to the particular job based upon the capabilities of the individual employee and not upon stereotyped ideas of employees' capabilities as a group.[299] It follows that management may not refuse consideration of an employee solely on the basis of sex. Thus, it has been held that the employer discriminated on the basis of sex when he denied contested work to the senior female employee who was found to be qualified for the work physically and on the basis of training, experience, or technical knowledge.[300]

---

[294]See Arbitrator Block in 48 LA 2, 9 (accompanying factors of dizziness, hand tremors, and marked nervousness posed a safety threat); Kates in 43 LA 61, 64; Siciliano in 37 LA 1047, 1050. In Keeney Mfg. Co., 37 LA 456, 458 (Donnelly, 1961), conflict of opinion between the company's doctor and grievant's doctor resulted in a ruling requiring an examination by a neutral doctor.

[295]See Arbitrator Cohen in 79 LA 1100, 1103; Block in 48 LA 2, 9–10; Dworkin in 46 LA 719, 724; Shulman in 8 LA 1015, 1016–1017.

[296]Bethlehem Steel Co., 18 LA 683, 684–685 (1952). Management failed to prove to Arbitrator Shipman's satisfaction that the senior employee had exhibited anxiety and fear in connection with his work. In Titanium Metals Corp., 49 LA 1144, 1146 (Block, 1967), an employee's fear of heights justified disqualifying him from a job requiring high crane duties after completing a trial period.

[297]See Pacific Gas & Elec. Co., 23 LA 556, 558–559 (Ross, 1954). Cf., Arbitrator Lockhart in 16 LA 525, 528–531.

[298]See White Motor Co., 28 LA 823, 828–829 (Lazarus, 1957).

[299]See, for example, Arbitrator Allman in 55 LA 756, 760; Sembower in 55 LA 193, 195; Mueller in 51 LA 785, 790; Ellman in 48 LA 231, 234, 236–237; Williams in 47 LA 896, 898. Also see Arbitrator Goldstein in 76 LA 32, 36, 42–43.

[300]See Arbitrator Duff in 79 LA 324, 326–327; Dworkin in 57 LA 997, 999; Dolson in 57 LA 549, 552–553; Seitz in 55 LA 895, 896–897; Turkus in 54 LA 165, 166; Mueller in 51 LA 785, 789–792; Forsythe in 48 LA 17, 19; Petree in 42 LA 433, 439; Crawford in 36 LA 1082, 1087–1088. In Gross Distrib. Co., 55 LA 756, 759–761 (Allman, 1970), it was found that the company violated the contract when it retained a junior male employee without attempting to determine the senior female employee's physical ability to do the work in question.

Of course, discrimination in favor of female employees has like-wise been held improper, as where preferential work locations were assigned to junior female employees instead of to senior males,[301] where management gave preferential treatment by not assigning the heavy duties of a female employee's job to the female employee,[302] and where a junior female employee was recalled from layoff instead of the senior male for work as a cafeteria helper.[303]

However, management has been upheld in giving preference to junior male employees over senior females where there was adequate justification in the requirements or circumstances of the job or in the qualifications of the individual involved. Such justification has been found in the physical requirements of the job (e.g., heavy weight lifting, physical prowess, overtime hours),[304] in standards of morality or propriety,[305] and in the lack of training, experience, or technical knowledge of the female employee.[306] In such cases, it is the justifying factor and not the sex of the individual which disqualifies the employee.

In some instances where there has been doubt concerning the physical ability of the employee to do the work arbitrators have ordered a trial period.[307]

In many of the cases cited in this subtopic, the arbitrator made reference to Title VII of the Civil Rights Act of 1964 or to state

---

[301]Cincinnati Reds, 56 LA 748, 750 (Kates, 1971).

[302]Sterling Faucet Co., 54 LA 340, 342–343 (Duff, 1970). Cf., Arbitrator Bernhardt in 79 LA 170, 172.

[303]Allied Chem. Corp., 35 LA 268, 270 (Valtin, 1960), finding the two employees relatively equal in ability and rejecting "the notion that the male animal suffers from natural handicaps to perform kitchen duties." Also see Arbitrator Ross in 76 LA 101, 102; Gershenfeld in 49 LA 140, 144.

[304]See Arbitrator Sembower in 55 LA 193, 195, and in 43 LA 165, 169; Altrock in 52 LA 942, 944–945; Davis in 52 LA 112, 114–115; Kates in 51 LA 418, 420; Dworkin in 50 LA 669, 671–672; Seinsheimer in 49 LA 709, 714–718 (an employee must be able to do *all* the job); Teple in 48 LA 819, 823–824; Shister in 48 LA 101, 106; Steele in 46 LA 931, 934–935; Layman in 45 LA 417, 423; Goodman in 40 LA 920, 923; Roberts in 39 LA 1094, 1097, and in 35 LA 657, 661; Reid in 36 LA 458, 462 (grievance sustained in theory but denied in fact since there was no work the female employees could perform); Hebert in 34 LA 41, 45. Also see Stonehouse in 78 LA 1070, 1071. In Sperry-Rand Corp., 46 LA 961, 964–965 (Seitz, 1966), it was held that the company could require female employees to take physical examinations although males were not required to do so, since the jobs in question required physical exertion which "may well be beyond the capacity of some women or dangerous to some." For an illustration of the problems that may be created by totally eliminating sex distinctions in the filling of jobs, see Eagle Mfg. Co., 51 LA 970, 972–973, 983 (Lugar, 1968). Also see Arbitrator Dolnick in 59 LA 596, 598.

[305]See Arbitrator France in 70 LA 760, 761; Duff in 70 LA 567, 569 (school employer could bypass male physical education instructor and select female instructor where the physical education program required the instructor to be physically present in the girls' locker room to observe emotional and other problems of students while changing clothes); Shister in 70 LA 110, 112; Gross in 54 LA 303, 305–306 (female properly was denied job of janitress in men's room); Marshall in 52 LA 624, 631–632 (female teacher properly was denied position with bureau of prisons); Shafer in 45 LA 448, 449–450 (male properly was denied job of janitress in women's restroom). Also see Gentile in 75 LA 63, 66; Lee in 68 LA 1363, 1365. Cf., Bernstein in 54 LA 1142, 1144–1146; Crawford in 36 LA 1082, 1083.

[306]See Arbitrator Jones in 57 LA 929, 930; Rauch in 53 LA 1345, 1346–1348 (although the female employee probably had the physical strength and stamina for the job); Merrill in 47 LA 836, 840; Hawley in 43 LA 289, 293–294 (to rearrange duties so that female employee could handle the job would result in discrimination in favor of female employees against male employees).

[307]See Arbitrator White in 55 LA 1284, 1286–1288; Gershenfeld in 49 LA 140, 144 (male employees given trial period on "delicate" work); Ellman in 48 LA 231, 236; Elkouri in 46 LA 238, 242; Sembower in 43 LA 165, 170. In Paterson Parchment Co., 47 LA 260, 262 (Buckwalter, 1966), a training period was ordered where the contract provided for such in bumping.

antidiscrimination laws; and in some of the earlier of those cases, the arbitrator referred to state protective laws for women (the dearth of recent arbitration decisions making any reference to the latter laws suggests that they no longer constitute a significant factor in arbitration). Title VII of the Civil Rights Act prohibits discrimination in employment based on sex, in addition to the usual grounds of race, color, religion, and national origin. However, the Act provides that "it shall not be an unlawful employment practice for an employer to hire and employ employees * * * on the basis of * * * religion, sex, or national origin in those certain instances where religion, sex, or national origin is a bona fide occupational qualification [BFOQ] reasonably necessary to the normal operation of that particular business or enterprise * * * ."[308]

Prior to the Civil Rights Act, some arbitrators felt bound by the particular agreement and/or the parties' past practice, and separate classifications and separate seniority lists for male and female employees were upheld.[309] In at least one case arising after the Act, where separate lines of progression were maintained in such a way as to provide male employees with experience on higher-rated jobs by means of temporary assignments, the arbitrator directed. the employer and the union (which had countenanced the practice) to negotiate integration of the lines.[310]

Subsequent to the Act, many parties incorporated antidiscrimination language into their agreements. In finding a violation of such a contract, Arbitrator Harry J. Dworkin emphasized that

---

[308]Sec. 703(e). Another statute which may have relevance in this area is the Equal Pay Act of 1963, which amended the Fair Labor Standards Act. For related discussion, see this Chapter's subtopic entitled "Contractual Seniority Rights, the Civil Rights Act, and Arbitration"; Chapter 10, subtopic entitled "Title VII of the Civil Rights Act." For some relevant U.S. Supreme Court decisions, see Arizona Governing Comm. v. Norris, 103 S.Ct. 3492, 32 FEP Cases 233 (1983), holding that paying a woman lower monthly retirement benefits than a man who made the same contributions violates Title VII (just as does requiring a woman to pay larger contributions to obtain the same benefits), and use of sex-segregated mortality tables to calculate retirement benefits violates Title VII whether or not the tables reflect an accurate prediction of longevity of women as a class; Personnel Adm'r of Mass. v. Feeney, 99 S.Ct. 2282, 19 FEP Cases 1377 (1979), holding that a statute requiring veterans to be ranked above all other candidates for state civil service positions does not deny equal protection to women; Dothard v. Rawlinson, 97 S.Ct. 2720, 15 FEP Cases 10 (1977), holding that height and weight qualifications for employment which had a disproportionate impact on women applicants were impermissible under Title VII as being based on stereotyped characterizations of the sexes and not bona fide occupational qualifications (but the refusal to employ female guards for some positions in certain maximum security male penitentiaries was upheld); Corning Glass Works v. Brennan, 94 S.Ct. 2223, 21 WH Cases 767 (1974), finding that an illegal discrimination had been improperly perpetuated by retention of a "red circle" rate for males who had been paid a higher rate on the night shift than was paid females on the day shift at a time when state law prohibited the employment of women at night; Phillips v. Martin Marietta Corp., 91 S.Ct. 496, 3 FEP Cases 40 (1971), holding that Title VII does not permit one hiring policy for women with pre-school-age children and another policy for men with such children, unless it is established to be a BFOQ reasonably necessary to the normal operation of the particular business or enterprise. For related discussion, see Schlei & Grossman, Employment Discrimination Law, 2d Ed., Ch. 12 (BNA Books, 1983); Wrong, "Arbitrators, the Law, and Women's Job Bids," 33 Lab. L.J. 798 (1982); Rosenberg, "Sex Discrimination and the Labor Arbitration Process," 30 Lab. L.J. 102 (1979).

[309]See Arbitrator Dworkin in 43 LA 715, 720–721; Eckhardt in 43 LA 460, 462–463; Hawley in 43 LA 391, 394 (employer's procedure had also been upheld in three prior awards under the contract); Marshall in 42 LA 224, 227–228; Talent in 42 LA 182, 184; Goodman in 40 LA 920, 923.

[310]South Pittsburgh Water Co., 56 LA 1242, 1244–1245 (Altrock, 1971).

"Male and female employees have equal claim to any work opportunity, subject only to their being eligible and qualified."[311] Another
such contract contained a clause obligating the parties to "fully comply with applicable laws and regulations regarding discrimination,"
and it was held that the clause was violated by a scheduling plan
adopted without intent to discriminate but which did have the "disparate impact" of female employees being laid off while males were
hired. In this case Arbitrator Howard V. Finston pointed to U.S.
Supreme Court decisions recognizing that the Civil Rights Act may be
violated if the practice producing the unintentional disparate impact
cannot be justified by business necessity; the employer here attempted
but failed to establish business necessity, and the employer also failed
to establish its BFOQ claim.[312]

Personal Characteristics of Employee

Personal characteristics of an employee may be considered if they
relate directly to his ability to meet the job requirements. For example, it has been held that management may take into consideration the
fact that an employee had been guilty in the past of certain
"injudicious conduct and conversation" evincing his interest in the
cult of nudism, particularly since the job involved not only technical
knowledge but also public relations, the arbitrator stating:

> " * * * [Grievant's] interest in nudism so expressed itself as to
> create in management's mind a reasonable doubt as to this employee's
> discretion and customer-acceptance on the service job for which he bid. It
> should be made clear that such reaction has no necessary relation to the
> employee's beliefs or personal ideas. It relates directly to the question of
> what the job requires and a worker's ability to meet these requirements.
> A decision as to this is management's right and prerogative."[313]

An employee's attitude may be in issue and may be important,
depending upon the nature of the job. It has been held that, in determining whether an employee is qualified for a job, supervision may
evaluate the employee's attitude which may include "conscientious
application, care for materials, concern for others in a group and

---

[311]Glass Containers Corp., 57 LA 997, 999 (1971).

[312]A.J. Bayless Mkts., 79 LA 703, 715–717 (1982), where Arbitrator Finston also noted that
under § 703(h) of the Act discriminatory intent is required in order for discrimination produced
by operation of bona fide seniority systems to become illegal, but he inferred that the present
dispute did not involve the seniority system. For a summary statement concerning employment
practices which have disparate impact, see Teamsters v. United States (T.I.M.E.—DC, Inc.), 97
S.Ct. 1843, 1854 n. 15, 14 FEP Cases 1514 (1977).

[313]Gisholt Mach. Co., 20 LA 137, 141 (Baab, 1953). Also see Arbitrator Amis in 49 LA 726,
728 (involving in part the "personal conduct" of an employee); Murphy in 18 LA 757, 760
(involving a "special class of clients"); Pollard in 16 LA 586, 587–588 (the company failing to
prove inability to perform the "human relations" part of a job). In Eagle-Picher Mining &
Smelting Co., 8 LA 108, 111 (Potter, 1947), the filing of a suit by an employee against his
employer was held not to affect his qualifications, the word "qualifications" being said to relate to
physical fitness and ability rather than to "moral" qualifications.

response to instruction."[314] In another case, the employee's attitude toward the job and spirit of cooperation were said to be included in the word "qualifications" as used in the seniority provisions; and the senior employee's uncooperative attitude could properly be considered in denying him a promotion to a better job.[315] Again, management was upheld in giving preference to a junior employee over the senior where the senior had the experience and aptitude for the job but lacked the important requisite of a mature and dedicated attitude,[316] and where the senior employee was found to be "lacking in interest, effort and basic * * * knowledge" of the job.[317]

However, one arbitrator held that an employee's alleged "surly and uncooperative" attitude could justify denying a promotion only if it were shown that efforts had been made, without success, to correct such attitude, and that his attitude detracted seriously from the employee's ability to perform the job.[318]

Special requirements of the job may call for particular attributes (other than technical knowledge) in the employee filling it, justifying consideration by the employer of the employee's ability to meet those requirements. For example, the job may require qualities of leadership,[319] initiative,[320] responsibility for independent judgment or

---

[314]Swan Rubber Co., 52 LA 59, 61 (Maxwell, 1969), holding that the company did not discriminate against an employee when it disqualified him, on the basis of attitude, for a job vacancy to which he had been assigned for training. For other cases in which an employee's negative attitude was a factor against the employee, see Arbitrator Axon in 75 LA 2, 6; Rauch in 69 LA 803, 805; Stouffer in 52 LA 889, 893–894 (the employee displayed an attitude of unwillingness to learn, rejecting instruction). In Dewey & Almy Chem. Co., 25 LA 316, 318–319 (Somers, 1955), the arbitrator stated: "A promotion represents a public recognition of an employee's ability, merit and capacity to do a higher-paid job. It would be destructive of morale to give such recognition to an employee who has shown lack of concern for his work and for his fellow employees."

[315]Norwich Pharmacal Co., 30 LA 740, 742–743 (Willcox, 1958). Similarly, Arbitrator Koven in 42 LA 1093, 1096; Seligson in 41 LA 528, 534 (holding that management could place strong weight on the factors of cooperation and ability to get along with others).

[316]Leach Co., 51 LA 382, 383 (Hazelwood, 1968). Also see Arbitrator Dallas in 80 LA 708, 712 (at the job interview the unsuccessful senior applicant had an "indifferent, hostile, and lackadaisical" attitude toward the job); Daniel in 78 LA 1114, 1119 (finding that the grievant was seeking the "position simply to transfer out of his current assignment," where he was having difficulty "in getting along with his superior"); Hunter in 75 LA 181, 188; Herman in 74 LA 811, 814 (the grievant "had not displayed the responsibility on the job which the Company had the right to expect"); Babiskin in 73 LA 1215, 1217 (a factor against grievant was his unwillingness to "pull his share of the load").

[317]United States Steel Corp., 51 LA 264, 266 (Smith, 1968).

[318]Bethlehem Steel Co., 19 LA 186, 188 (Killingsworth, 1952). In Pittsburgh Annealing Box Co., 74 LA 266, 268 (1980), the grievant had been reprimanded for spending time away from his work area and for talking too much, but Arbitrator Carl F. Stoltenberg stated that if these offenses occurred in such a manner as to impair job performance, "they should have been dealt with when they occurred," and that "Since they were not matters of discipline, beyond an occasional verbal warning, they cannot now be relied upon as evidence of" lack of ability to perform the work). Also see Arbitrator Rule in 69 LA 290, 293. In San Diego County Dist. Council of Carpenters, 76 LA 513, 515–516 (1981), Arbitrator Walter N. Kaufman drew a distinction between considering attitude as a factor in promotion, where the employee is being rewarded, and in layoff; attitude could not be a factor in layoff where the grievants had never been disciplined or otherwise put on notice that their attitude problems might cost them their jobs.

[319]See Arbitrator Rule in 76 LA 1010, 1012–1013; Gentile in 74 LA 181, 184; Wolff in 54 LA 447, 448; Beeson in 54 LA 298, 302; Cantor in 48 LA 777, 780; Larkin in 45 LA 129, 130–131; Seligson in 41 LA 528, 534.

[320]See Arbitrator Beeson in 54 LA 298, 302; Block in 51 LA 896, 898–899; Cantor in 48 LA 777, 780; Graff in 46 LA 523, 527; Klamon in 19 LA 639, 647. In Penn Controls, 45 LA 129, 130–131 (Larkin, 1965), where the job of leadman required qualities of leadership and initiative, the senior employee had demonstrated initiative in developing his own business outside of work; but it was held that "the Company has every right first to look to the factors of initiative,

self-reliance,[321] the ability to get along with others;[322] or it may involve dealing with a "special class" of customers,[323] or require that the employee be physically available for emergency work.[324]

Age as a Factor

The conflict between the interests of management and the interests of the employees over the use of age as a factor in denying employment opportunities is evident from the following statement by Arbitrator Edward E. McDaniel:

> " * * * It is not unreasonable that management should hesitate to invest great amounts of time and money in an apprentice, who because of age will be unable to offer many years of service as a new craftsman. Some 'rules of reason' then properly should be followed. But clearly to favor youth above 'seniority' is to do violence to benefits traditionally provided longer service employees. And, it surely is unreasonable, we believe, to assume that all persons above a given calendar age are lacking in basic ability or physical fitness for a particular job, and that persons below such age level do possess such qualifications. Such an arbitrary classification, at the very least, fails to give due weight to the fact that people 'age' at radically different rates, both physically and mentally. Moreover, it appears that, historically, seniority and age have been correlative concepts, generally, to determine employee rights under the * * * Agreement.
> " * * * The point is that * * * age, per se, reasonably may not be established as a proper basis for barring further consideration of other relevant qualifying factors in the selection of employees to fill apprenticeship or other vacancies * * * ."[325]

Thus, Arbitrator McDaniel held that age may not be used as an automatic bar to consideration of an employee's basic ability for a job.

It has also been held that age may not be viewed as necessarily a negative element without a showing that the applicant's age had adversely affected his physical or mental ability in such a way as to render him incapable of meeting the job requirements—but in such event it would be ability and not age per se which constitutes the bar.[326] Such was the ruling in an early case where the job required

---

efficiency and leadership qualities displayed on the jobs within the plant," and the junior employee was "ahead of" the senior in this respect.

[321]See Arbitrator Modjeska in 76 LA 142, 144; Wolff in 54 LA 447, 448; Beeson in 54 LA 298, 302; Schmidt in 44 LA 283, 285–286; Klamon in 19 LA 639, 647.

[322]See Arbitrator Block in 51 LA 896, 898–899; Amis in 49 LA 726, 728; McCoy in 45 LA 1028, 1030 (the senior employee was argumentative and the job required a person with an "equable, tactful disposition"); Koven in 42 LA 1093, 1096; Schmidt in 44 LA 283, 285–286; Seligson in 41 LA 528, 534.

[323]See Coca-Cola Bottling Co., 18 LA 757, 759–760 (Murphy, 1952).

[324]See Alabama Power Co., 19 LA 393, 396 (Hawley, 1952), where the grievant lived some distance from town and had no telephone.

[325]United States Steel Corp., 55 LA 659, 662–663 (1970).

[326]See United States Steel Corp., 57 LA 237, 251–252 (Clare B. McDermott, 1971), referring to the McDaniel award in 55 LA 659; Scott Paper Co., 49 LA 45, 46–47 (Hogan, undated), stating that "Age may or may not affect ability critically, depending on the man and the job." None of the above cases made reference to the Age Discrimination in Employment Act. In William Volker & Co., 60 LA 349, 352–353 (1973), an otherwise qualified bidder for a truck driver vacancy was disqualified by the employer because he was under the age of 21, making insurance coverage available only at a higher premium rate. In sustaining the grievance, Arbitrator Howard S.

close attention continuously and a great deal of visual inspection, the arbitrator upholding the employer's determination that a 73-year-old employee did not have the necessary qualifications.[327]

In one case where the agreement prohibited age discrimination, the union contended that such discrimination "must be presumed" because "on this and previous occasions, the job in question was awarded to persons junior to the grievant." However, the arbitrator stated that the union had "the burden of proving that the grievant was the victim of age discrimination," and that the union "did not meet its burden of making a prima facie case."[328]

Under the Age Discrimination in Employment Act of 1967 as amended in 1978, which in general protects "individuals who are at least 40 years of age but less than 70 years of age," it is unlawful for an employer

"(1) to fail or refuse to hire or to discharge any individual or otherwise discriminate against any individual with respect to his compensation, terms, conditions, or privileges of employment, because of such individual's age; (2) to limit, segregate, or classify his employees in any way which would deprive or tend to deprive any individual of employment opportunities or otherwise adversely affect his status as an employee, because of such individual's age; or (3) to reduce the wage rate of any employee in order to comply with this Act."[329]

Some discussion of the coverage and scope of the ADEA is provided in Chapter 13, topic entitled "Compulsory Retirement," and the reader should examine that material along with the present subtopic.

In a case making reference to the ADEA, the arbitrator upheld the company's maximum age limit of 32 for entering a training program, stating:

"There was no illegal application of age limits which resulted in the grievant's rejection. Federal protection against age discrimination does not extend to persons under the age of 40. Furthermore, an age maximum for entry into a training program of extended duration is a reasonable qualification and is so recognize in the administration of apprenticeship programs generally."[330]

Even prior to the Act, in the absence of any age limitation in the contract and in the absence of any showing that the age of the employee detracted from his ability to perform the job, arbitrators appeared reluctant to permit management to rely upon the age factor

---

Block considered the increased cost of insurance to be unrelated to the job's requirements, and he stated that while the Grievant "falls into a broad statistical category (those under 21) that may involve a higher risk," this factor, "*in itself*, does not prove the Grievant less qualified because it relies upon a sweeping generalization, rather than on an evaluation of his qualifications."

[327]Emmons Looms Harness Co., 11 LA 409, 411 (Meyers, 1948).

[328]Charleston Naval Shipyard, 80 LA 708, 712 (Dallas, 1983). Also see Arbitrator Purdom in 53 LA 1157, 1159–1160. In International Trade Comm'n, 78 LA 1, 3–4 (Jones, 1981), the "evidence as a whole" negated the charge of age discrimination. For extensive discussion of what is required in order to establish a violation of the Age Discrimination in Employment Act, see Player, "Proof of Disparate Treatment Under the Age Discrimination in Employment Act: Variations on a Title VII Theme," 17 Ga. L. Rev. 621 (1983).

[329]29 U.S.C.A. §§ 623, 631.

[330]Aro, Inc., 52 LA 372, 375 (Kesselman, 1969).

as justification for passing over a senior in favor of a junior employee, provided the senior met the job requirements. Thus, arbitrators held that the company could not deny an employee consideration for a job solely because of age,[331] and that the company was arbitrary in barring an employee from an apprenticeship or a training vacancy solely because of age.[332] In some other cases, it was held that under the circumstances of the given case the company could set a *reasonable* age limit for apprenticeships or for a training program.[333]

[331]See Arbitrator Berkowitz in 41 LA 14, 18 (a 56-year-old employee should be given a physical examination to determine if he is fit for the job); Anrod in 31 LA 994, 999–1000 (age limit of 30 was arbitrary and unreasonable as was barring a 34-year-old employee solely because of age); Gilden in 20 LA 142, 147 (35-year age limit was not justified for the job in question—the real test is physical ability and qualifications).

[332]See Arbitrator Ross in 28 LA 557, 558–559 (48-year-old employee was entitled to the job if equal in ability); Thompson in 28 LA 374, 378–379 (absolute limit excluding employees over 40 from bidding was arbitrary and unreasonable); Kaplan in 19 LA 508, 512–514 (company's denial of 38-year-old senior's bid on ground that he was too old was improper). Also see Arbitrator Edes in 11 LA 108, 109, where the senior employee was younger.

[333]See Arbitrator Thomas J. McDermott in 47 LA 89, 90–91 (age limit of 35 upheld); Wyckoff in 34 LA 756, 759–760 (airline could set an age limit of 60 for training on new and faster aircraft); Kallenbach in 25 LA 716, 721 (age limit of 35 was not unreasonable). Also see Tsukiyama in 37 LA 553, 558–561. While agreeing that a proper age limit would not be unreasonable, Arbitrator Kates found that 30 was too low (46 LA 1153, 1157), and Arbitrator Brown found that 50 was too low (44 LA 92, 95). In Ozark Smelting & Mining Div., 46 LA 697, 698–699 (Schedler, 1966), where the contract stated that a "beginning trainee shall not be over 40," the age limit was liberally construed to mean that an employee is not "over 40" until the day before his 41st birthday, the arbitrator noting conflicting court decisions on the general subject of age.

Chapter 15

Discharge and Discipline

A significant percentage of cases that reach arbitration involve discharge or disciplinary penalties assessed by management. The present Chapter considers many of the concepts and standards that have been applied by arbitrators in cases of this nature.[1]

Scope of Management Right

In the absence of a collective bargaining agreement arbitrators have recognized the legal principle that the only restriction on management's right to discharge and discipline employees not hired for a definite term is that contained in federal and state labor relations acts

---

[1]For related matter, see Chapter 13, topic entitled "Plant Rules." For books on discharge and discipline, see Redeker, Discipline: Policies and Procedures (BNA Books, 1983); Ewing, Do It My Way or You're Fired: Employee Rights and the Changing Role of Management Prerogatives (1983); Coulson, The Termination Handbook (1981); Lazar, Due Process in Disciplinary Hearings: Decisions of the National Railroad Adjustment Board (UCLA Inst. of Indus. Rel., 1980); Zack & Bloch, The Arbitration of Discipline Cases: Concepts and Questions (AAA, 1979); Stessin, Employee Discipline (BNA Books, 1960). For other discussions, see Knight, "The Impact of Arbitration on the Administration of Disciplinary Policies," 39 Arb. J. No. 1, p. 43 (1984); Nelson, "Insubordination: Arbitral 'Law' in the Reconciliation of Conflicting Employer/Employee Interests," 35 Lab. L.J. 112 (1984); Malinowski, "An Empirical Analysis of Discharge Cases and the Work History of Employees Reinstated by Labor Arbitrators," 36 Arb. J. No. 1, p. 31 (1981); Saxon (management) & Miller (union), "The Discipline and Discharge Case: What Arbitrators are Doing Wrong," Proceedings of the 32nd Annual Meeting of NAA, 63, 75 (BNA Books, 1980); Fallon, "Comment," id. at 82; Osterman, "The Discipline of Public Employees: The New York State Experience," 34 Arb. J. 25 (1979); Jennings & Wolters, "Discharge Cases Reconsidered," 31 Arb. J. 164 (1976); Graham, "Arbitration of Insubordination Disputes in the Public Sector," 31 Arb. J. 191 (1976); Jones, "Ramifications of Back-Pay Awards in Discharge Cases," Proceedings of the 22nd Annual Meeting of NAA, 163 (BNA Books, 1970); Fisher, "Ramifications of Back Pay in Suspension and Discharge Cases," id. at 175; Kadish, "The Criminal Law and Industrial Discipline as Sanctioning Systems: Some Comparative Observations," Proceedings of the 17th Annual Meeting of NAA, 125 (BNA Books, 1964); Teele, "But No Back Pay Is Awarded . . .," 19 Arb. J. 103 (1964); Davey, "The Arbitrator Speaks on Discharge and Discipline," 17 Arb. J. 97 (1962); Holly, "The Arbitration of Discharge Cases: A Case Study," Critical Issues in Labor Arbitration, 1 (BNA Books, 1957); Ross, "The Arbitration of Discharge Cases: What Happens After Reinstatement," id. at 21; Myers, "Concepts of Industrial Discipline," Management Rights and the Arbitration Process, 59 (BNA Books, 1956).

or other laws dealing with discrimination.[2] Where there was no collective agreement in one case, Arbitrator Ralph Roger Williams explained:

> "The employer-employee relationship is always a contractual relationship, whether a labor-management contract exists between the employer and the employee's union or not. But the employment contract between the Grievants and the Company was not for an express period of time; and where no definite term of employment exists, an employer may lawfully discharge an employee whenever and for whatever cause he chooses. The cause need not be 'just' or 'proper.' "[3]

The same result might be reached where a collective agreement exists but contains no express limitation on the employer's right to discharge and discipline employees.[4] Where an agreement expressly recognized the right to discharge and contained no express limitation upon that right, an arbitrator was unwilling to read a "just cause" limitation into the agreement.[5]

---

[2]See Arbitrator Williams in 50 LA 547, 548; Bell in 45 LA 500, 501; Updegraff in 39 LA 53, 57; Potter in 8 LA 634, 637–638; Whiting in 4 LA 399, 403; Babb in 4 LA 56, 64. Also see Wettach in 25 LA 772, 773; Merrill in 19 LA 417, 419; Coffey in 17 LA 125, 129; McCoy in 8 LA 66, 67. Cf., Blumrosen in 41 LA 76, 78–82. As to statutory restrictions on management, see Levy, "The Role of Law in the United States and England in Protecting the Worker From Discharge and Discrimination," 18 Intl. & Comp. L.Q. 558 (1969). Recognizing that the initiation of discipline is within the province of management, arbitrators have disclaimed the existence of arbitral authority to order the discharge or discipline of an employee. See Arbitrator Keefe in 73 LA 1237, 1240; Hilpert in 39 LA 897, 906; Dash in 38 LA 509, 515. Cf., McCoy in 2 LA 537, 538–539.

[3]Burris Chem., 50 LA 547, 548 (1968). This common law principle of "employment-at-will" under which employees may be discharged for any reason, has been qualified in some jurisdictions by court recognition of exceptions which primarily involve instances (1) where public policy appears to have been violated, or (2) where an implied contractual limitation is found to exist. See special report, The Employment-At-Will Issue (BNA Books, 1982). Another study of the recent cases stated that:

> "Although a great many theories have been advanced to restrict the employer's right of termination of the employee for an indefinite term, and although suits arising out of such circumstances have met with greater success than in the past, it should be noted that in the larger number of cases in which courts have actually decided the merits of wrongful termination cases, the employer's right of discharge has been upheld, either because the court refused to recognize the employee's cause of action or because the employee failed to prove his case."

DiSabatino, "Modern Status of Rule that Employer May Discharge At-Will Employee for Any Reason," 12 ALR4th 544, 551 (1982), adding, however, that this is "a developing area of the law in which the courts have indicated an increasing receptiveness to recognizing a variety of exceptions to the rule of terminability, where public policy is deemed to compel such exceptions." For other discussions, see Foster, "Employment at Will: When Must an Employer Have Good Cause for Discharging an Employee?" 48 Mo. L. Rev. 113 (1983); Boeye, "Employment at Will: An Analysis and Critique of the Judicial Role," 68 Iowa L. Rev. 787 (1983); Hill, "Arbitration as a Means of Protecting Employees From Unjust Dismissal: A Statutory Proposal," 3 N. Ill. U.L. Rev. 111 (1983); symposium, "Individual Rights in the Workplace: The Employment-At-Will Issue," 16 U. Mich. J.L. Ref. 199–464 (1983); articles by Hepple, Littrell, St. Antoine, and Epstein, "Arbitration of Job Security and Other Employment-Related Issues for the Unorganized Worker," Proceedings of the 34th Annual Meeting of NAA, 18–67 (BNA Books, 1982); Hermann & Sor, "Property Rights in One's Job: The Case for Limiting Employment-At-Will," 24 Ariz. L. Rev. 763 (1982); Peck, "Unjust Discharges From Employment: A Necessary Change in the Law," 40 Ohio St. L.J. 1 (1979).

[4]See Bohlinger v. National Cash Register Co., 18 LA 595 (N.Y. Sup. Ct., 1952), and cases cited therein. Also see Arbitrator Eaton in 76 LA 172, 174; Jones in 58 LA 489, 491.

[5]Hillyer Deutsch Edwards, 19 LA 663, 664 (Emery, 1952). Also see Arbitrator Zechar in 81 LA 432, 438; Berkowitz in 36 LA 331, 332; Warren in 24 LA 680, 683–684; Krivonos in 22 LA 756, 759–760. Cf., Jones in 46 LA 831, 832; Warren in 19 LA 615, 619–621. For a contract limiting challenges of discharge action to "bad faith" discharges, see Arbitrator Somers in 45 LA 655, 656. In Reynolds Elec. & Eng'g., 72 LA 1012, 1013 (Jones, 1979), a discharge grievance was held not to be arbitrable since the agreement gave management "the absolute right to * * * dis-

However, many arbitrators would imply a just cause limitation in any collective agreement.[6] For instance, Arbitrator Walter E. Boles held that "a 'just cause' basis for consideration of disciplinary action is, absent a clear proviso to the contrary, implied in a modern collective bargaining agreement."[7] The reasoning is: "If the Company can discharge without cause, it can lay off without cause. It can recall, transfer, or promote in violation of the seniority provisions simply by invoking its claimed right to discharge. Thus, to interpret the Agreement in accord with the claim of the Company would reduce to a nullity the fundamental provision of a labor-management agreement—the security of a worker in his job."[8] Moreover, at least one arbitrator has held that management does not have an unrestricted right to discharge at its own discretion even where no bargaining relationship exists, since "the fair and generally accepted understanding of employer-employee relations is that there are obligations on the part of both parties" and that an "obligation on the employer is that an employee shall not be dismissed without cause."[9]

Most collective agreements do, in fact, require "cause" or "just cause" for discharge or discipline. The general significance of these terms was discussed by Arbitrator Joseph D. McGoldrick:

"* * * [I]t is common to include the right to suspend and discharge for 'just cause,' 'justifiable cause,' 'proper cause,' 'obvious cause,' or quite commonly simply for 'cause.' There is no significant difference between these various phrases. These exclude discharge for mere whim or caprice. They are, obviously, intended to include those things for which employees have traditionally been fired. They include the traditional causes of discharge in the particular trade or industry, the practices which develop in the day-to-day relations of management and labor and most recently they include the decisions of courts and arbitrators. They

---

charge * * * employees at its discretion." In the case of In The Round Dinner Playhouse, 55 LA 118, 128 (Kamin, 1970), the arbitrator took "arbitral notice" that any requirement of "just cause" for termination "is virtually unknown in the theatrical world." In Boscobel Bd. of Educ., 55 LA 58, 60–61 (Wilberg, 1970), the "interests" arbitrator recommended a discharge and discipline clause less restrictive upon management than the usual "just cause" clause.

[6]See Arbitrator Newmark in 79 LA 1225, 1233–1234; Deitsch in 78 LA 928, 935–936; Keenan in 75 LA 154, 158–159; Roumell in 75 LA 83, 88; Oppenheim in 52 LA 1164, 1166–1167; Eaton in 51 LA 331, 331–333; Volz in 50 LA 1217, 1219; Jones in 48 LA 240, 241–242; Tsukiyama in 42 LA 490, 493; Eiger in 38 LA 778, 780; Ryder in 36 LA 552, 556; Ross in 36 LA 503, 505; Boles in 25 LA 295, 300–301; Maggs in 22 LA 761, 763; Donnelly in 13 LA 747, 749. Also see Dahl in 46 LA 356, 357; Fallon in 45 LA 532, 533–534; Hebert in 25 LA 439, 440–441. Also, a general "just cause" limitation may be found to be implied from some particular provision in the agreement. See Arbitrator O'Grady in 79 LA 1045, 1049; Harkless in 70 LA 600, 602; Seidenberg in 52 LA 547, 551–552; Sherman in 48 LA 1209, 1212; Merrill in 46 LA 1044, 1046–1047; Morvant in 24 LA 453, 455–456.

[7]Cameron Iron Works, 25 LA 295, 301 (1955).

[8]Atwater Mfg. Co., 13 LA 747, 749 (Donnelly, 1949), quoting at length from a similar view expressed by Arbitrator Wallen in another case. Id. at 750–751.

[9]Daily World Publishing Co., 3 LA 815, 817 (Rogers, 1946). During negotiations but prior to adoption of their first agreement, the parties agreed to arbitrate the dispute in question. In Government Servs., Inc., 40 LA 84, 85 (Schedler, 1963), there was no collective agreement, but in agreeing to arbitrate a discharge the employer was deemed to have accepted a "just cause" standard for the arbitral review. As to the latter point, see Arbitrator Seidenberg in 52 LA 547, 551–552; McIntosh in 43 LA 76, 77–78. Public employees often have statutory protection. Federal employees, for instance, may be removed "only for such cause as will promote the efficiency of the service." 5 U.S.C.A. § 7513(a). Also see Arbitrator Lubic in 80 LA 725, 728; Edes in 77 LA 19, 20. For a summary of the elaborate remedial system available to insure fair and due process treatment of federal employees, see Bush v. Lucas, 103 S.Ct. 2404, 2415–2416 (1983).

represent a growing body of 'common law' that may be regarded either as the latest development of the law of 'master and servant' or, perhaps, more properly as part of a new body of common law of 'Management and labor under collective bargaining agreements.' They constitute the duties owed by employees to management and, in their correlative aspect, are part of the rights of management. They include such duties as honesty, punctuality, sobriety, or, conversely, the right to discharge for theft, repeated absence or lateness, destruction of company property, brawling and the like. Where they are not expressed in posted rules, they may very well be implied, provided they are applied in a uniform, non-discriminatory manner."[10]

Some agreements enumerate specific grounds for discharge or discipline.[11] It has been ruled that the fact that an agreement specifies certain types of misconduct for which employees may be discharged does not mean that causes not expressly stated may not be used where the grounds enumerated are merely illustrative and not exclusive.[12] Similarly, the listing of certain offenses in written plant rules does not necessarily exclude other offenses as grounds for punishment.[13]

Arbitrators have held that a contract giving the right to discharge for cause and making no reference to other forms of discipline does not deprive management of the right to impose forms of discipline less severe than discharge.[14] Discharge may be too severe a penalty for the offense under the circumstances of the case.

---

[10]Worthington Corp., 24 LA 1, 6–7 (1955). Agreeing that there is no significant difference between these terms, Arbitrator Katz in 74 LA 176, 179; Shanker in 73 LA 1050, 1055; Buckwalter in 44 LA 1208, 1211; Harris in 29 LA 567, 571. For other statements defining "cause" or "just cause," see Arbitrator Axon in 77 LA 820, 826 (the "just cause test mandates that the punishment assessed be reasonable in light of all the circumstances"); Belshaw in 75 LA 899, 900 (equating the term "just cause" with "the now-common expression, 'fair shake' "); Gradwohl in 74 LA 1008, 1011 ("proper cause" means that management "must have a reasonable basis for its actions and follow fair procedures"); Weiss in 68 LA 1284, 1286; Hon in 44 LA 574, 576; Parker in 21 LA 671, 672; Barrett in 19 LA 489, 493. As to the purposes of industrial discipline, see Arbitrator Meiners in 73 LA 918, 920; Yagoda in 46 LA 1034, 1039; Howlett in 33 LA 40, 41.

[11]In Meat Cutters v. Neuhoff Bros. Packers, 83 LRRM 2652, 2654 (CA 5, 1973), the agreement authorized discharge for "proper cause" but did not specify individual grounds for discharge; in these circumstances, what constitutes "proper cause" was held to be a question for the arbitrator and not for the court. Courts often have held otherwise, however, where the collective agreement expressly states specific causes for discharge. See subtopic entitled "Authority of Arbitrator to Modify Penalties," below.

[12]See Arbitrator Wyckoff in 44 LA 552, 553; Altieri in 43 LA 689, 693–694; Updegraff in 9 LA 397, 398; Carmichael in 7 LA 752, 755. Also see Ross in 71 LA 710, 716; Lewis in 70 LA 544, 547; Dworkin in 48 LA 457, 462–463. But the listing of some grounds was held to exclude others in Pacific Press, 26 LA 339, 344 (Hildebrand, 1956). Also see Arbitrator Handsaker in 15 LA 616, 618. In Chicago Pneumatic Tool Co., 38 LA 891, 892 (Duff, 1961), the contract specified the right to discharge "for proper cause as agreed to by the parties," but this did not require management to obtain union agreement as to all causes. For a case involving a clause providing that no employee could be discharged "without the consent of the union," see Crawford Clothes, 19 LA 475, 476–479 (Kramer, 1952).

[13]See Arbitrator Traynor in 77 LA 815, 818; Gentile in 72 LA 110, 112; Harkless in 69 LA 613, 614; Krislov in 68 LA 72, 74; Rybolt in 64 LA 721, 725–726 (failure to list an offense did not prevent discipline but did limit the scope of permitted penalty); Mullennix in 48 LA 147, 151; Karlins in 44 LA 609, 612. Also see Neas in 78 LA 985, 994; Mueller in 70 LA 587, 589; Casselman in 68 LA 702, 705.

[14]See Arbitrator Lennard in 76 LA 114, 115–117; Ross in 71 LA 632, 637; Solomon in 50 LA 888, 896; Sembower in 43 LA 1197, 1199–1202; Sears in 41 LA 33, 37–38; Strong in 39 LA 859, 860–861; Ross in 36 LA 503, 504; Kleinsorge in 23 LA 711, 713–714; Cornsweet in 17 LA 580, 585; Copelof in 3 LA 122, 125. But in some situations a different result has been reached. See Arbitrator Abernethy in 50 LA 760, 763–766; Sembower in 39 LA 1231, 1235; Copelof in 18 LA 34, 38; Sugarman in 14 LA 16, 23–24.

Asserting that discharge "inevitably casts a shadow on a worker's character and reputation," an arbitrator would not permit discharge for lack of work where the agreement required just cause for discharge, the arbitrator stating that layoff is the proper action in case of lack of work.[15] Other arbitrators, too, have held that "discharge" is limited to termination due to fault of the employee.[16]

Probationary Employees

It has been held that where, by the agreement, new employees are not to have seniority rights until completion of a probationary period, and where the agreement is otherwise silent as to management rights with respect to new employees, they may be discharged for any reason except discrimination.[17] Under a somewhat more strict limitation placed by an arbitrator upon the right of management to discharge probationary employees, management's action in doing so would "not be set aside unless it was arbitrary, capricious, or discriminatory"; thus, "the question in such a case goes to the good faith of the Company, not to the merits of its conclusion."[18] In some cases a still greater limitation has been placed upon the right of management to discharge probationary employees.[19]

Where an agreement contained a "just cause" requirement for discharge and made no reference to any probationary period for new employees, the requirement was applied fully to new employees.[20] In another instance where an agreement was entirely silent as to management rights with respect to new employees, another arbitrator likewise would not read a probationary period into the agreement but he nonetheless would give management wider latitude in determining just cause for discharge of new employees than allowed in case of employees who have served at least for a short period of time.[21]

---

[15]American Republics Corp., 18 LA 248, 253 (Hale, 1952).

[16]See Arbitrator Howlett in 28 LA 633, 637; Hogan in 23 LA 596, 602; Kelly in 22 LA 266, 268. Also see Ipavec in 68 LA 513, 516. In Revere Copper & Brass, 45 LA 254, 255 (McCoy, 1965), the term "non-disciplinary discharge" was suggested for termination not due to fault.

[17]Joy Mfg. Co., 6 LA 430, 436 (Healy, 1946); Flintkote Co., 3 LA 770, 771 (Cole, 1946). Also see Stone, Labor-Management Contracts at Work, 261 (1961); Arbitrator Miller in 42 LA 187, 188–189; Kerr in 6 LA 98, 102 ("interests" arbitration).

[18]Ex-Cell-O Corp., 21 LA 659, 665 (Smith, 1953). To similar effect, Arbitrator Seibel in 77 LA 1276, 1281; Burns in 48 LA 143, 145; Buckwalter in 44 LA 301, 304; Sembower in 40 LA 757, 762–763; Ross in 38 LA 350, 351–352; Komaroff in 19 LA 565, 569. Also see Cornsweet in 9 LA 625, 630–631.

[19]See Arbitrator Hayes in 70 LA 395, 397 (applying a "test of fairness and reasonableness"); Donaldson in 34 LA 633, 635 (pointing out that the contract did not reserve to management the unrestricted right to discharge probationary employees and that it did specify accumulation of seniority from the date of hire, he required just cause for their discharge); Stutz in 28 LA 456, 458 (although employees had no seniority rights until after a probationary period, just cause was required for discharge of probationary employees). Regarding termination of probationary employees in federal employment, see Arbitrator Gentile in 81 LA 325, 327–330; Bailey in 81 LA 286, 287–288 (relying upon a U.S. Court of Appeals decision in holding that the federal-agency employer was not required to show just cause for the discharge of grievant as a probationary employee); Krislov in 68 LA 90, 92, 94 (where Arbitrator Krislov agreed with management's view that the Federal Personnel Manual yardstick for measuring "cause" differs depending upon whether a probationary employee is involved). Cf., Dworkin in 80 LA 250, 253, 255–257.

[20]Osborn & Ulland, 68 LA 1146, 1150 (Beck, 1977); Mac Coal Co., 52 LA 1125, 1127 (Krimsly, 1969).

[21]Park Sherman Co., 2 LA 199, 200 (Lapp, 1946).

Of course the collective agreement may deal expressly with the discharge of probationary employees, for example, by requiring "cause"[22] or not requiring it.[23] In the latter situation, problems may arise concerning the exact limits of the probationary period.[24]

Discharge Versus Resignation

When an employee voluntarily resigns, concepts associated with discharge are not generally applicable. Thus, where the employee evidenced clear intent to resign arbitrators have refused to treat the matter as discharge.[25] Moreover, where the facts and circumstances are such as to lead management reasonably to conclude that intent to resign exists, the matter may be treated as resignation even though the individual never actually states any intent to resign.[26]

However, if intent to resign is not adequately evidenced or if a statement of intent to resign is involuntary or coerced, an alleged resignation will be treated as discharge for purposes of arbitral review.[27] A similar result has sometimes been reached where a resig-

---

[22]In Ford Motor Co., 48 LA 1213, 1214–1215 (Platt, 1967), the agreement required cause for discharge after the first 30 days of the three-month period required for an employee to acquire seniority; the arbitrator held the "cause" required after 30 days to be no different from the "cause" required for discharge of employees after expiration of the aforementioned three-month period. The arbitrator noted that under previous agreements probationary employees had been subject to discharge for any reason other than discrimination. The "discrimination" exception had been construed to include reasons of race, union activity, personal feeling, or sex. Ford Motor Co., 6 LA 853, 854 (Shulman, 1946).

[23]As in A.S. Abell Co., 49 LA 264, 265–266 (Kennedy, 1967), where it was held, however, that to be free of the "cause" requirement the discharge ordinarily must be effected and communicated to the employee within the probationary period. In accord on both points, Arbitrator Smith in 78 LA 1077, 1079. In Pan American World Airways, 50 LA 722, 724 (Galenson, 1968), the contract gave management the right to discharge probationary employees "at its option," but this did not necessarily mean that the union could be totally disregarded in the matter.

[24]For example, see Arbitrator Ipavec in 69 LA 550, 554 (employee could not be terminated without just cause after having been granted a leave of absence which would extend beyond the probationary period); Erbs in 69 LA 211, 213; Platt in 48 LA 1213, 1216; Merrill in 47 LA 339, 340–341 (probationary period not extended by strike); Buckwalter in 44 LA 301, 303 (period was 30 working days rather than 30 calendar days where contract was not specific on the question).

[25]See Arbitrator Brown in 59 LA 871, 873; Turkus in 57 LA 1200, 1206–1208; Hardy in 48 LA 1036, 1040; Russell in 41 LA 913, 917; Doyle in 29 LA 242, 245; Kelliher in 20 LA 618, 619–621; Anderson in 20 LA 715, 717–718; Donnelly in 20 LA 47, 49; Stein in 17 LA 256, 257; Cahn in 16 LA 890, 891.

[26]See Arbitrator High in 53 LA 1103, 1107; Stouffer in 50 LA 46, 48 (employee did tell other employees she was quitting); Scheib in 49 LA 540, 544; Davis in 48 LA 227, 228; Duff in 47 LA 115, 118–119; Davey in 45 LA 599, 603; Kelliher in 30 LA 224, 225; Jaffee in 26 LA 786, 788; Donnelly in 25 LA 608, 610–611; Lewis in 18 LA 808, 809–810; Crawford in 15 LA 282, 290. Cf., Croft in 69 LA 176, 179–180; Gilden in 18 LA 576, 580; Kelliher in 15 LA 300, 303–304; Platt in 14 LA 462, 465–466.

[27]See Arbitrator House in 79 LA 1157, 1163; Mayer in 78 LA 1012, 1015; Cohen in 73 LA 544, 546; Blackmar in 70 LA 434, 435; Cox in 68 LA 962, 965 (concluding that "because of the limitation on the employee's right to representation, and the limited time grievant had to reflect prior to making his decision to resign," it was not "an effective voluntary quit"); Rose in 55 LA 604, 607; Kates in 51 LA 1098, 1102; McNaughton in 51 LA 869, 871; Dolnik in 48 LA 273, 276; McDermott in 46 LA 985, 988; Cahn in 45 LA 1153, 1154; McIntosh in 43 LA 76, 78; Crawford in 42 LA 849 at 849; Kesselman in 29 LA 128, 131–132; Miller in 27 LA 11, 15–18; Klamon in 26 LA 48, 51–52; Browser in 20 LA 868, 870; Killingsworth in 16 LA 683, 684–685; Whiting in 16 LA 170, 172–173; Shipman in 15 LA 698, 702–703; Handsaker in 15 LA 616, 617; Healy in 6 LA 557, 559–560.

nation was made under severe emotional stress[28] or was based upon a mistake concerning material facts.[29]

Also, Arbitrator Maurice H. Merrill observed that:

"The overwhelming weight of authority holds that there is no voluntary quit by reason of an employee's refusal to perform work to which he is assigned. Unless some affirmation of an intent to quit the job is manifested by the employee, the employer's subsequent refusal to let the employee continue his status constitutes a discharge rather than a resignation."[30]

Moreover, the mere fact that the employee is told to do the work or be deemed to have quit does not appear materially to strengthen management's claim that there was in fact a resignation.[31]

On the other hand, there have been situations in which arbitrators have considered that no intent is required to make a termination a "quit."[32] This was so, for instance, where an employee was terminated under a union security clause.[33]

Sometimes in situations in which an employee has in fact submitted his resignation, he has subsequently attempted to withdraw it. The attempted withdrawal has been upheld in some cases[34] but not in others.[35]

Conduct Away From Plant

The right of management to discharge an employee for conduct away from the plant depends upon the effect of that conduct upon plant

---

[28]See Arbitrator Kaufman in 74 LA 980, 981, 983; Sherman in 70 LA 497, 499–500; Duff in 57 LA 446, 448; Amis in 51 LA 206, 208; Yagoda in 45 LA 590, 593. But see Dworkin in 79 LA 1028, 1034 (stating that "although Grievant quit his job in a state of mind that approached frenzy, he was aware of what he was doing"); Hon in 71 LA 494, 497–498 (concluding that grievant was rational at the time of quitting); Welch in 59 LA 64, 68; Ray in 42 LA 1106, 1108. In Weyerhaeuser Co., 42 LA 845, 848 (Tongue, 1964), there was no "quit" when an employee walked off the job to control his anger and not strike his supervisor.

[29]Honeywell, Inc., 51 LA 1061, 1062 (Elson, 1968). In The Tuttle Press Co., 49 LA 490, 492–493 (Seitz, 1967), a resignation was deemed involuntary where it was prompted by the employee's mistaken belief that he had cancer (this was not a discharge or discipline case).

[30]Oklahoma Furniture Mfg. Co., 24 LA 522, 523 (1955), citing numerous cases. For later cases in accord, see Arbitrator Raymond in 76 LA 62, 68; Quinlan in 53 LA 521, 524; King in 49 LA 27, 31; Block in 48 LA 1027, 1030; Bellman in 47 LA 899, 901; Tatum in 46 LA 583, 588; Lee in 46 LA 297, 300–301; Witney in 45 LA 97, 98–99, and in 41 LA 386, 389. For related discussion, see Chapter 5, topic entitled "Observance of Grievance Procedure."

[31]See Arbitrator Keefe in 74 LA 612, 614; Beck in 68 LA 386, 387; King in 49 LA 27, 31; Bellman in 47 LA 899, 901; Lee in 46 LA 297, 300–301; Witney in 45 LA 97, 98–99.

[32]See Arbitrator Rehmus in 68 LA 1195, 1198; Bailer in 48 LA 157, 159–160; Hebert in 45 LA 621, 628–629; Willingham in 36 LA 852, 854–855.

[33]New York Times, 48 LA 157, 159–160 (Bailer, 1967). Cf., Arbitrator Martin in 72 LA 684, 687–688.

[34]See Arbitrator Daniel in 76 LA 379, 383; Di Leone in 47 LA 332, 336 (notice to quit in the future is not necessarily irrevocable); Tatum in 45 LA 1030, 1033 (employee's tender of resignation is an offer which can be withdrawn prior to its acceptance); Seitz in 41 LA 918, 920–921; Hebert in 38 LA 84, 88–89; Sembower in 34 LA 360, 364–365; Gray in 22 LA 238, 238–239. Also see Bell in 53 LA 1100, 1103 (employee punched out but changed his mind within an hour).

[35]See Arbitrator Winograd in 79 LA 176, 178; Kabaker in 50 LA 637, 640 (employee signed "quit form" and company accepted it); Roberts in 47 LA 454, 457 (employee could not withdraw written resignation which had been processed by the company); Marshall in 40 LA 469, 472 (employer had right to choose whether to accept or reject retraction of resignation); Morvant in 38 LA 425, 429 (resignation is effective even without acceptance and employer is not required to permit withdrawal); Dworkin in 29 LA 700, 703–704; Babcock in 7 LA 330, 333; Kaplan in 3 LA 239, 241.

operations.[36] In this regard, Arbitrator Louis C. Kesselman explained in one case:

> "The Arbitrator finds no basis in the contract or in American industrial practice to justify a discharge for misconduct away from the place of work unless:
> "1) behavior harms Company's reputation or product * * *
> "2) behavior renders employee unable to perform his duties or appear at work, in which case the discharge would be based upon inefficiency or excessive absenteeism * * *
> "3) behavior leads to refusal, reluctance or inability of other employees to work with him * * *."[37]

Arbitrator D. Emmett Ferguson also spoke of the extent to which management may consider conduct away from the plant as the basis for discharge:

> "While it is true that the employer does not [by virtue of the employment relationship] become the guardian of the employee's every personal action and does not exercise parental control, it is equally true that in those areas having to do with the employer's business, the employer has the right to terminate the relationship if the employee's wrongful actions injuriously affect the business.
> "The connection between the facts which occur and the extent to which the business is affected must be reasonable and discernible. They must be such as could logically be expected to cause some result in the employer's affairs. Each case must be measured on its own merits."[38]

Another arbitrator also stressed that the effect of the employee's outside activity on the employer's business must be reasonably discernible, mere speculation as to adverse effect upon the business not sufficing.[39]

---

[36]For a general discussion of this subject, see Sussman, "Work Discipline Versus Private Life: An Analysis of Arbitration Cases," 10 I.L.R. Research 3 (1964). For related material, see Chapter 13, topic entitled "Plant Rules."

[37]W.E. Caldwell Co., 28 LA 434, 436–437 (1957). For other general statements, see Arbitrator Keefe in 78 LA 806, 808 (quoting another source); Dunn in 74 LA 33, 35 (commenting in regard to public-sector employees); McMahon in 50 LA 632, 633; Livengood in 45 LA 495, 497. In Eastern Air Lines, 45 LA 932, 936–939 (Ables, 1965), the arbitrator suggested guidelines and procedures for the parties to utilize in disputes involving off-duty misconduct. Somewhat different or additional considerations may be involved in regard to off-duty conduct of public employees. See state-sector decisions by Arbitrator Madden in 80 LA 639, 642; Roumell in 80 LA 516, 519; Siegel in 76 LA 729, 731; Dunn in 74 LA 33, 35. See federal-sector decisions by Arbitrator Lubic in 80 LA 725, 728–729; Edes in 77 LA 19, 21–23; Krimsly in 72 LA 522, 523–524.

[38]Inland Container Corp., 28 LA 312, 314 (1957).

[39]Allied Supermarkets, Inc., 41 LA 713, 714–715 (Mittenthal, 1963), reversing discharge for second instance of "unwed motherhood." A similar result was reached in Movielab, 50 LA 632, 633 (McMahon, 1968), where the employer introduced no evidence to show adverse effect upon the business as a result of the employee's being convicted (but placed on probation) on narcotics charges. Also see Arbitrator Krimsly in 72 LA 522, 524; Shearer in 56 LA 469, 473. But see Milentz in 69 LA 379, 387; Kerrison in 64 LA 826, 828 (stating that "the seriousness of the drug problem generally and the need for a company to strive to prevent drug abuse amongst its employees does warrant a finding that a company has the right to act immediately to protect its own interests and the interests of its employees from the possibility that an individual charged with possession of drugs for the purpose of sale for profit will engage in such activity on company property and with fellow employees"). In Armco Steel Corp., 43 LA 977, 981 (Kates, 1964), the effect of the employee's morals conviction upon the business was uncertain and the employee had long years of service. Conditional reinstatement was ordered, the employer to be permitted to discharge the employee if adverse effect within the plant or adverse outside reactions against the employer should develop as a result of the conviction.

In many cases discharge for conduct away from the plant was held improper because the requirement of adverse effect of the conduct upon the business was not met.[40] However, in many other cases the employee's conduct away from the plant was found to be related to his employment or was found to have an actual or reasonably foreseeable adverse effect upon the business, thus discharge (or in some instances a lesser penalty) was found to be justified.[41]

Off-Duty Misconduct on Company Premises

It appears clear that off-duty employees have a general obligation to observe plant rules while on company premises and that they may be subject to discipline for their misconduct even though the misconduct (which often will adversely affect employee morale, discipline, or other legitimate company interests) occurs while they are off duty and in a nonworking area of the plant such as the company cafeteria or parking lot.[42]

Employer Action Pending Court Hearing on Conduct of Employee

Where an employee, while on the job, engages in conduct which leads to his arrest, management has been permitted to take action against the employee without waiting for court determination of guilt.

---

[40]In addition to cases in preceding footnote, see Arbitrator Welch in 78 LA 1311, 1313 (selling marijuana); Kaufman in 77 LA 867, 871 (homosexual conduct); Noble in 73 LA 1042, 1044 (vehicle damage); Hunter in 71 LA 1004, 1006 (firing gun); Rimer in 71 LA 82, 85 (possession of marijuana); Goldstein in 68 LA 346, 350 (fighting); Wagner in 68 LA 254, 256 ("affair" with fellow employee); Duff in 46 LA 307, 309 ("romantic exploits at hotel" had no bearing on job as truck driver); Young in 44 LA 133, 140 (taking bankruptcy); Duff in 43 LA 242, 244 (contributing to delinquency of minor); Altrock in 41 LA 460, 463–464 (morals offense); Wyckoff in 37 LA 1040, 1043 (narcotics conviction); Hill in 35 LA 315, 322–323 (invoking Fifth Amendment in Congressional investigation); Brecht in 29 LA 451, 456–459; Kesselman in 28 LA 434, 437 (intoxication); Platt in 23 LA 808, 810–812; Marks in 20 LA 175, 177; Abrahams in 15 LA 42, 45.

[41]See Arbitrator Keefe in 78 LA 806, 809 (verbal abuse of plant manager at company picnic); Boyer in 76 LA 1187, 1191; Simons in 76 LA 387, 389–390 (possession and sale of cocaine); Tanaka in 76 LA 347, 350 (theft); Doyle in 74 LA 1293, 1296 (burglary); Cantor in 74 LA 1084, 1090 (threatening foreman); Gunderman in 70 LA 756, 759 (vandalizing supervisor's home); Benewitz in 69 LA 876, 879 (shooting incident); Sembower in 69 LA 507, 509 (parking in "no-parking zone" near plant); Milentz in 69 LA 379, 387 (possession of heroin); Harkless in 68 LA 1245, 1247 (shoplifting); Gentile in 60 LA 172, 177–178 (possession of stolen property); Florey in 57 LA 725, 730; Johannes in 56 LA 1221, 1226–1227 (incest); Sembower in 53 LA 203, 205–206 (indecent practices of nude photography); Teple in 51 LA 177, 180–181; Wolf in 49 LA 941, 943; Chalfie in 49 LA 117, 120–121 (intoxication); Duff in 47 LA 62, 66 (KKK Acting Grand Dragon); Hughes in 46 LA 857, 859–860 (knife assault); Larkin in 46 LA 346, 348–349 (fight); Ables in 45 LA 932, 936–939; Livengood in 45 LA 495, 497 (bootlegging); Mullin in 45 LA 283, 290–291; Duff in 64–2 ARB ¶8748 (sexual perversion); Granoff in 39 LA 1025, 1028–1029 (employee with sordid private life, whose work required him to enter customers' homes); Volz in 39 LA 245, 248–249; Duncan in 38 LA 1003, 1005 (widespread publicity from bootlegging arrest and grand larceny conviction, reflecting adversely on co-workers and employer); Duff in 38 LA 891, 893 (drug addiction); Roberts in 37 LA 906, 908–909; Ferguson in 28 LA 312, 314; Blair in 27 LA 557, 560–562; Kharas in 26 LA 480, 482–483; Holden in 24 LA 810, 812–813; Granoff in 24 LA 603, 605–606; Cole in 21 LA 327, 328–329; McCoy in 8 LA 647, 652–653; Larkin in 6 LA 58, 59–61.

[42]See Arbitrator Cushman in 65 LA 1233, 1236; Smith in 65 LA 1177, 1182; Gratz in 63 LA 36, 42–44; Doyle in 50 LA 766, 767–768; Willingham in 50 LA 403, 407; Larkin in 49 LA 1253, 1257; Dworkin in 49 LA 370, 374–375; Block in 48 LA 1099, 1100–1101; Merrill in 45 LA 817, 818, 821 (altercation at union meeting on company premises). Cf., Coombs in 64 LA 528, 530; Duff in 48 LA 695, 696–697.

In one case the discharge of the employee, effected prior to court trial on the charges, was upheld since the employer established to the arbitrator's satisfaction that the employee was guilty of conduct justifying the discharge.[43] In a number of cases management has been permitted to suspend the employee pending court determination of guilt,[44] but in some cases the arbitrator limited the period of permitted suspension.[45] In one of the latter cases the arbitrator stated that the employer can make his own investigation and if he finds evidence of the employee's guilt, he can assess discipline against the employee (including discharge if the evidence and offense justify it); but if the employer does not do this, he should not continue the suspension for an unreasonable period of time pending court trial.[46]

In cases where an employee is charged with a crime allegedly committed away from company premises, the type of situation in which management may have a right to suspend the employee pending court determination of guilt was summarized by Arbitrator Robert L. Howard:

> "But whether we consider this type of action [i.e., suspension pending court determination of guilt] as disciplinary or not, and notwithstanding the presumption of innocence in a criminal proceeding, the employer must have the right to protect his business from the adverse effects flowing from public accusation and arrest for serious crime, supported by a judicial finding of probable cause in a preliminary hearing, when the nature of the charge with its attendant publicity reasonably gives rise to legitimate fear for the safety of other employees or of property, or of substantial adverse effects upon the business."[47]

Arbitrator Howard concluded that in the case before him the violent nature of the criminal offense with which the employee was charged (first degree burglary and assault with intent to rape) could reasonably create feelings of danger and fear among fellow employees and supervisors, so as to interfere with the proper operation of the business and justify the suspension pending court determination of guilt.[48]

---

[43]Continental Paper Co., 16 LA 727, 728–729 (Lewis, 1951). Also see Arbitrator Maggs in 16 LA 829, 833–835. If the employer does not otherwise have "cause" for the discharge, there should be no discharge merely because the employee was charged with a crime. Yellow Cab Co., 55 LA 590, 592 (Helbling, 1970), where the employee's on-duty assault of a passenger was done in self-defense. In Philadelphia Transp. Co., 49 LA 606 at 606 (Gershenfeld, 1967), completion of the arbitration of a discharge for on-duty misconduct was delayed pending conclusion of court proceedings so as not to prejudice the employee in the criminal action. Also see statement of Arbitrator Turkus in 68 LA 741, 743; discussion by Roberts, "Judicial Review of 'Misconduct' Cases," Proceedings of the 25th Annual Meeting of NAA, 150, 163–164 (BNA Books, 1973).

[44]See Arbitrator Babiskin in 74 LA 299, 301; Kaufman in 69 LA 776, 778; Russell in 34 LA 342, 345; Seitz in 29 LA 442, 445–447; Ryder in 26 LA 570, 571–572. Cf., Turkus in 71 LA 1113, 1116–1118.

[45]See Arbitrator Autrey in 54 LA 541, 544–546; Berkowitz in 43 LA 511, 512–514; Oppenheim in 41 LA 1091, 1093–1094; Dash in 22 LA 851, 859–860.

[46]Plough, Inc., 54 LA 541, 544–546 (Autrey, 1970).

[47]Pearl Brewing Co., 48 LA 379, 390 (1967), where Arbitrator Howard reached his conclusions after studying numerous arbitration decisions.

[48]For other cases upholding suspension pending court decision, see Arbitrator Chandler in 80 LA 205, 211 (upholding the "indeterminate suspension" of grievant only "insofar as it does not become one of 'unreasonable' length"); Phelan in 78 LA 597, 602–603; Seinsheimer in 75 LA 363, 365–366; Rayl in 68 LA 183, 186–187 (suspension was proper only from the time when charges

In some cases the question before the arbitrator has concerned the employer's action in discharging or disciplining an employee for absence from work due to jail confinement. Various factors may be relevant in such cases, and although management often has been upheld, by no means has this always been the result.[49]

Types of Penalties

The type of penalty assessed for wrongdoing usually is either temporary suspension or discharge.[50] Temporary suspension or "disciplinary layoff," as it is sometimes called,[51] results in loss of pay (and sometimes seniority) for the period of suspension, and mars the employee's record. When an arbitrator reinstates a discharged employee without back pay the end result is not unlike suspension.

Warnings are, in a sense, a lesser type of discipline,[52] and as noted elsewhere in this Chapter they are an important factor in evaluating discipline for subsequent offenses.

The right of management to use types of penalties other than those noted above appears to be definitely limited.[53] This is true, for instance, in regard to use of demotion or downgrading for purposes of discipline.[54] This is likewise true of transfer,[55] withholding monetary benefits (without actual suspension),[56] requiring employees to pre-

---

were filed until they were dismissed); Johannes in 56 LA 1221, 1226–1227; Lennard in 50 LA 274, 277; Johnson in 48 LA 186, 187; Stouffer in 46 LA 124, 126–127; Livengood in 45 LA 498, 499–500, and in 45 LA 495, 497–498. For cases in which the suspension was held improper, see Arbitrator Giles in 66 LA 187, 188–189; Stonehouse in 66 LA 185, 187; Strong in 39 LA 859, 862. Also see Ellmann in 73 LA 464, 475, 477.

[49]For a collection of cases permitting or not permitting discharge or discipline of employees for absences due to jail confinement, see Capitol Mfg. Co., 48 LA 243, 248–249 (Klein, 1967). For some later cases, see Arbitrator McKay in 79 LA 6, 9–10 (discussing factors considered by other arbitrators in such cases); Kramer in 75 LA 967, 968; Leeper in 73 LA 100, 103; Roumell in 72 LA 1262, 1265 (stating that his study of prior decisions indicated that the "reason a discharge is proper in such cases is not because of the crime the employee has committed but rather it is simply that through the employee's own actions, he has made it impossible to fulfill his obligation to report to work"; but reversing the discharge in the present case, Arbitrator Roumell stated that by refusing to sign a Work Release Program contract, it was "the Company and not the employee who * * * made it impossible for him to work"); Daly in 72 LA 613, 615–616; Sharnoff in 72 LA 210, 211; Foster in 71 LA 1095, 1098.

[50]Indefinite suspension has been deemed equivalent to discharge. See Arbitrator Kramer in 70 LA 869, 875; Brecht in 29 LA 451, 455; Barrett in 27 LA 523, 527.

[51]See Koppers Co., 11 LA 334, 335 (McCoy, 1948).

[52]See Federal Labor Union v. American Can Co., 21 LA 518 (N.J. Super. Ct., 1953). Also see Arbitrator Beck in 71 LA 314, 320; Roberts in 37 LA 1064, 1068; Louisell in 20 LA 826, 831; Sanders in 20 LA 36, 38. Cf., Teple in 48 LA 1345, 1349. In Columbus Bd. of Educ., 73 LA 382, 384 (1979), a school official, having noticed that a female employee was wearing pants, spoke to her privately and asked if she understood the dress code requirements; concluding that this did not constitute discipline, Arbitrator Samuel S. Perry explained that the official "did not tell her that her behavior was improper and did not threaten or predict a penalty for any alleged violation."

[53]In some cases, however, arbitrators themselves have utilized various other penalties or remedies in upsetting managerial actions in discharge and discipline cases. See this Chapter, topic entitled "Arbitral Remedies in Discharge and Discipline Cases."

[54]See discussion in Chapter 13, topic entitled "Demotion of Employees."

[55]See Chapter 13, topic entitled "Promotion and/or Transfer of Employees."

[56]See Arbitrator Klein in 80 LA 748, 751; Westbrook in 80 LA 297, 301; Davidson in 75 LA 706, 710; Johannes in 70 LA 1138, 1140; Dworkin in 36 LA 517, 521–522; Ralston in 18 LA 544, 550; Fearing in 9 LA 505, 508. Cf., Scheiber in 55 LA 1309, 1312. As to the denial of overtime work as punishment, compare the view of Arbitrator Belkin in 53 LA 414, 415–417, with that of Arbitrator Markowitz in 55 LA 384, 386.

sent a medical certificate before returning to work after allegedly being sick,[57] and forcing public apologies.[58]

Burden and Quantum of Proof

There are two areas of proof in the arbitration of discharge and discipline cases. The first involves proof of wrongdoing; the second, assuming that guilt of wrongdoing is established and that the arbitrator is empowered to modify penalties, concerns the question of whether the punishment assessed by management should be upheld or modified.[59] The latter is treated below in the topic entitled "Review of Penalties Imposed by Management." The present topic deals with proof of wrongdoing.

Discharge is recognized to be the extreme industrial penalty since the employee's job, seniority and other contractual benefits, and reputation are at stake.[60] Because of the seriousness of this penalty, the burden generally is held to be on the employer to prove guilt of wrongdoing, and probably always so where the agreement requires "just cause" for discharge.[61] There are also other possible reasons for imposing this burden of proof upon the employer.[62]

---

[57]See Continental Moss-Gordin Gin Co., 46 LA 1071, 1073 (Williams, 1966).

[58]See Reynolds Metals Co., 22 LA 528, 534 (Klamon, 1954). But see Arbitrator Rauch in 20 LA 823, 826; Kramer in 19 LA 475, 481–482.

[59]See Arbitrator Kanzer in 80 LA 875, 878; Heinsz in 80 LA 503, 506; Tanaka in 74 LA 236, 239; Larkin in 49 LA 882, 886; Lovell in 48 LA 498, 500; Frey in 48 LA 319, 319–320; Doyle in 44 LA 522, 526; Levy in 28 LA 65, 67; Reynard in 27 LA 400, 404; Donnelly in 26 LA 913, 913–914; Howlett in 22 LA 520, 524; Livengood in 20 LA 451, 455; Stutz in 17 LA 701, 702.

[60]For examples of arbitral reference to discharge as being industrial capital punishment, see Arbitrator Singer in 80 LA 829, 835 (discharge "is the capital industrial penalty, therefore, the burden of proof has rested with the Company"); Grohsmeyer in 80 LA 717, 720 ("discharge is industrial capital punishment"); Milentz in 80 LA 713, 716 (discharge "is considered to be the capital punishment of the industrial society"). One arbitrator suggested that "a more accurate equivalent" to discharge is "permanent exile." Schroeder, "Discharge: Is It Industrial Capital Punishment?" 37 Arb. J. No. 4, p. 65 (1982). On the other hand, another arbitrator suggested that for a young person, discharge "may ultimately bring more benefits than losses." Factory Servs., 70 LA 1088, 1089–1090 (Fitch, 1978).

[61]Included among the many arbitrators who have held that the burden is upon management to prove wrongdoing are Mikrut in 79 LA 852, 855; Sabo in 78 LA 978, 982; Tucker in 78 LA 749, 752; Ordman in 77 LA 978, 984; Thompson in 77 LA 210, 213; O'Connell in 75 LA 1062, 1067; Jedel in 74 LA 737, 741; Hardy in 74 LA 726, 728; Curry in 73 LA 1148, 1155; Dolnik in 73 LA 297, 300; Cutler in 72 LA 1313, 1316; Feldman in 72 LA 1144, 1149; Rose in 72 LA 774, 775; Ross in 71 LA 710, 714; Keltner in 70 LA 1028, 1036; Mullaly in 69 LA 64, 67. For earlier cases see p. 621 of the Third Edition of this book. But the employee has the burden of proving the validity of the defense or excuse which he asserts in justification of his conduct. See Mississippi Lime Co., 29 LA 559, 561 (Updegraff, 1957). Also see Arbitrator Dunne in 51 LA 174, 177; Jaffee in 27 LA 562, 564–565.

[62]"The most frequently advanced reason for imposing the burden of proving 'just cause' upon the employer is the sociological argument that the employer can exact no greater penalty than discharge, or 'economic capital punishment,' and has the social obligation of justifying this action." Hussman Refrigerator Co., 68 LA 565, 569–570 (1977), where Arbitrator Frank C. Mansfield summarized various other "rationales" utilized by arbitrators "to justify the imposition of burden of proof in the strict sense upon the employer" to establish that a punishable offense was committed by the employee. Also see discussion by Smith, "The Search for Truth— The Whole Truth," Proceedings of the 31st Annual Meeting of NAA, 40, 50–53 (BNA Books, 1979). Arbitrator Raymond R. Roberts reminded also that in addition to cases involving "fault, wrongdoing, or culpability by an offending employee, there is another class of reasons for severing the employment relationship of an employee recognized under concepts of good and just cause, which are not disciplinary at all and where termination is predicated not upon fault,

However, the quantum of required proof in this area is unsettled. In some cases proof beyond a reasonable doubt has been required.[63] But in other cases a lesser degree of proof has been required, such as a preponderance of the evidence,[64] or "clear and convincing" evidence,[65] or evidence "sufficient to convince a reasonable mind of guilt."[66]

An arbitrator may require a high degree of proof in one discharge case and at the same time recognize that a lesser degree may be required in others.[67] Similarly, where the proof was not strong enough to support discharge, some arbitrators have nonetheless found it strong enough to justify a lesser penalty.[68]

Concerning the quantum of required proof, Arbitrator Russell A. Smith observed that: "In general, arbitrators probably have used the 'preponderance of the evidence' rule or some similar standard in deciding fact issues before them, including issues presented by ordinary discipline and discharge cases."[69] But Arbitrator Smith also noted that a higher degree of proof frequently is required where the alleged misconduct is "of a kind recognized and punished by the criminal law," and he concluded:

> "[I]t seems reasonable and proper to hold that alleged misconduct of a kind which carries the stigma of general social disapproval as well as disapproval under accepted canons of plant discipline should be clearly and convincingly established by the evidence. Reasonable doubts raised by the proofs should be resolved in favor of the accused. This may mean that the employer will at times be required, for want of sufficient proof,

---

wrongdoing, or culpability upon the part of the employee, but because something arises which so impairs the employment relationship as to render it impossible or highly impractical for the employer to continue that employment relationship"; and, "as in the case of disciplinary actions, the burden of proof rests upon the Company to justify its action of termination for non-disciplinary reasons." Sears Mfg. Co., 70 LA 719, 722–723 (1978). Also see Arbitrator Roberts in 74 LA 705, 708–709.

[63]See Arbitrator Hardy in 71 LA 883, 884; Murphy in 59 LA 283, 286; Cahn in 48 LA 132, 135; Roberts in 46 LA 486, 489; Warns in 24 LA 804, 806; Parker in 21 LA 671, 672–673; Wagner in 7 LA 147, 149. Other instances are cited hereinbelow.

[64]See Arbitrator Spencer in 74 LA 25, 29; Gibson in 73 LA 868, 871; Erbs in 52 LA 959, 962; McIntosh in 49 LA 39, 39–40; Wildebush in 44 LA 1143, 1148; Levy in 28 LA 65, 67; Hale in 27 LA 486, 491; Pollack in 24 LA 401, 405; Osborne in 21 LA 471, 472; Platt in 1 LA 254, 262–263. In State Univ. of N.Y., 74 LA 299, 300 (Babiskin, 1980), the collective agreement expressly placed the burden of proof on the employer in all disciplinary proceedings and specified that: "Such burden of proof, even in serious matters which might constitute a crime shall be preponderance of the evidence on the record and shall in no case be proof beyond a reasonable doubt." By statute a federal agency's action in disciplinary matters may be sustained upon review by the Merit Systems Protection Board only if the agency's decision "is supported by a preponderance of the evidence." 5 U.S.C.A. § 7701(c)(1)(B). Where a discharge for illegal sexual activity with a minor child was taken to arbitration rather than to the MSPB, Arbitrator Lubic cited the latter statute when he also utilized the "preponderance of evidence test." Social Sec. Admin., 80 LA 725, 728 (1983).

[65]See Arbitrator McDonald in 80 LA 596, 599; Roberts in 74 LA 835, 838; Mewhinney in 73 LA 1066, 1068; Richman in 73 LA 531, 533 (stating that "the standard to be applied in a case such as this [possession and use of marijuana while on the job] should be the clear and convincing evidence standard: Less than beyond a reasonable doubt but more than the ordinary prima facie case and preponderance test"); Rose in 72 LA 774, 775; Siegel in 71 LA 1041, 1043; Dworkin in 27 LA 148, 150; Aaron in 8 LA 261, 268.

[66]Stockham Pipe Fittings Co., 1 ALAA ¶67,460 (1946). Also see Arbitrator Kesselman in 49 LA 692, 695, 697.

[67]See Arbitrator Roberts in 46 LA 486, 489; Graff in 38 LA 1157, 1159; Babb in 29 LA 272, 277; Jones in 28 LA 879, 882–883; Hale in 27 LA 486, 491; Wagner in 7 LA 147, 149–150.

[68]See Arbitrator Hon in 48 LA 891, 893; Sembower in 47 LA 890, 896; Davis in 45 LA 844, 845–847; Rohman in 44 LA 417, 421.

[69]Kroger Co., 25 LA 906, 908 (1955).

to withhold or rescind disciplinary action which in fact is fully deserved, but this kind of result is inherent in any civilized system of justice."[70]

In fact, arbitrators have often recognized that proof beyond a reasonable doubt should be required where the alleged offense involves an element of moral turpitude or criminal intent.[71] Moreover, where the offense is of this type management may be required to prove, by a high degree of proof, both the commission of the act and the existence of criminal intent.[72] When, however, the alleged offense is not one that is recognized by the criminal law or does not otherwise involve moral turpitude, Arbitrator Benjamin Aaron urged vigorously that proof beyond a reasonable doubt should not be required by arbitrators.[73]

In many cases the arbitrator may be able to proceed most realistically along the lines followed by Arbitrators Alexander, Schedler, and Whiting in reviewing discharges for strike misconduct:

> "The Arbitration Agreement provides that the Arbitrator shall determine whether there was reasonable cause for the discharge. It does not seem to us that in the making of such determination, we should be bound by a doctrine of the criminal law as to proof beyond a reasonable doubt. We think that the issue we have to decide in any particular case is: Is the employee guilty, and if so, is the act that he committed serious enough to justify discharge?"[74]

Proof in Group Discipline Cases

In a "slowdown" case the evidence was not specific as to the work performance of each individual but the employer was upheld in disciplining all crew members who were on the crew for the full period of the slowdown, the arbitrator stating that "While not every situation would or should lend itself to implicating several employees in slowdown activities, such implications seem justified where [as in the

---

[70]Ibid. In Armour-Dial, 76 LA 96, 99 (1981), Arbitrator Benjamin Aaron stated: "I agree with the Union that a discharge for theft has such catastrophic economic and social consequences to the accused that it should not be sustained unless supported by the overwhelming weight of evidence. Proof beyond any reasonable doubt, even in cases of this type, may sometimes be too strict a standard to impose on an employer; but the accused must always be given the benefit of substantial doubts." Arbitrator Janet Maleson Spencer in such a case stated the requirement to be that "the arbitrator must be completely convinced that the employee was guilty." Columbia Presbyterian Hosp., 79 LA 24, 27 (1982). In American Air Filter Co., 64 LA 404, 406–407 (1975), Arbitrator Elmer E. Hilpert suggested that regardless of which "verbal formulas for the requisite degree of proof" arbitrators may profess to require, the fact is that "most of us—consciously or unconsciously—require the highest degree of proof in discharge cases where the involved employee action * * * also constitutes a crime." Also see statements by Arbitrator C. Chester Brisco in Todd Pac. Shipyards Corp., 72 LA 1022, 1024 (1979); Getman, "What Price Employment? Arbitration, the Constitution, and Personal Freedom," Proceedings of the 29th Annual Meeting of NAA, 61, 96 (BNA Books, 1976).

[71]For many cases see p. 623 of the Third Edition of this book. For later cases see Arbitrator Wilmoth in 80 LA 546, 547; Tucker in 78 LA 749, 752; McKay in 77 LA 648, 655; Johannes in 75 LA 597, 602; Keenan in 75 LA 154, 165; Ray in 73 LA 304, 309; Fields in 72 LA 281, 284–285; Herman in 70 LA 304, 306. Contra, see Arbitrator Katz in 78 LA 1153, 1155; Griffin in 69 LA 965, 966; Purdom in 56 LA 75, 79–82; Block in 49 LA 810, 814; Black in 43 LA 113 at 113.

[72]See Arbitrator Schor in 70 LA 1097, 1098–1099; Herman in 70 LA 304, 306; Morrissey in 44 LA 257, 259; King in 43 LA 940, 945–946; Holly in 27 LA 463, 465; Somers in 24 LA 728, 729–730.

[73]Aaron, "Some Procedural Problems in Arbitration," 10 Vand. L. Rev. 733, 740–742 (1957).

[74]Southern Bell Tel. & Tel. Co., 25 LA 85, 87 (1955). Also see Arbitrator Tanaka in 74 LA 236, 238; Kates in 50 LA 103, 106; Granoff in 17 LA 258, 264.

present case] the group involved is small and the focus of delay represents a team effort."[75] Likewise, group discipline of the six members of a boning crew was upheld where each individual denied any responsibility for the bad work which the crew had done but where each individual also refused to testify against any other member of the crew.[76]

On the other hand, some arbitrators have indicated rather clearly that they consider group discipline to be improper in the absence of evidence establishing the guilt of all.[77]

Still another arbitrator considered an intermediate approach to be justified under the circumstances in his case. He rejected the employer's "theory of collective responsibility" for imposing discipline upon several entire crews since (1) not all jobs on the crews contributed equally to production, (2) the makeup of the crews varied from day to day, and (3) the employer's own evidence absolved some of the crew members. However, he also rejected the union's contention that management must produce specific evidence linking each employee to the slowdown in question, and he held that management could meet its initial burden of proof by evidence showing a grievant's presence on a crew with consistent reduction in production rate during the slowdown period.[78]

Review of Penalties Imposed by Management

Several views have been expressed by arbitrators regarding the nature of their function in reviewing disciplinary penalties imposed by management.

The view that the determination of the penalty for misconduct is properly a function of management and that an arbitrator should

---

[75]Kennecott Copper Corp., 41 LA 1339, 1344 (Dykstra, 1963). Similarly, see Arbitrator Flannagan in 78 LA 612, 616. In Elmira School Dist., 54 LA 569, 570–571 (Markowitz, 1970), the arbitrator applied the New York "Taylor Law" under which public employees absent during a strike were presumed to be strikers and had the "burden of proof" of rebutting the presumption by showing that the absence was not related to the strike. For a similar result apart from statute, see Lone Star Steel Co., 48 LA 949, 951 (Jenkins, 1967). Cf., Arbitrator Welch in 74 LA 877, 880–881.

[76]Marhoefer Packing Co., 54 LA 649, 652–653 (Sembower, 1970). In Koppers Co., 76 LA 175, 177 (1981), Arbitrator Lewis R. Amis stated: "It may be assumed that not all the grievants were directly involved" in the equipment sabotage. "On the other hand, by their silence those members [of the crew] not directly involved are guilty of conspiring to obstruct the Company's investigation of the matter, and they, too, deserve a penalty." Cf., Arbitrator Sass in 78 LA 766, 770–771; Kossoff in 72 LA 909, 912 (citing other cases supporting his conclusion that an employee may not be disciplined where the employer has shown neither that the employee was an actual participant in the misconduct nor that the employee knew the identity of the actual participants). In Babcock & Wilcox Co., 59 LA 72, 75–76 (Nicholas, 1972), the work "gang" located nearest to firecracker incidents in the plant could be suspended without pay in view of safety considerations, but more than mere circumstantial evidence would be required in order to place a disciplinary action against an employee's work record. Group discipline for failure to meet production standards was held not to be guilt by association and was upheld by Arbitrator Solomon in 50 LA 888, 897, McIntosh in 49 LA 581, 583–584.

[77]See Arbitrator Williams in 48 LA 211, 213; Gross in 45 LA 53, 55–57; Marshall in 36 LA 1302, 1303.

[78]United States Steel Corp., 49 LA 1236, 1239–1240 (McDermott, 1968), where the decision was made to discipline some individuals but not others.

hesitate to substitute his judgment and discretion for that of management was elaborated by Arbitrator Whitley P. McCoy:

"Where an employee has violated a rule or engaged in conduct meriting disciplinary action, it is primarily the function of management to decide upon the proper penalty. If management acts in good faith upon a fair investigation and fixes a penalty not inconsistent with that imposed in other like cases, an arbitrator should not disturb it. The mere fact that management has imposed a somewhat different penalty or a somewhat more severe penalty than the arbitrator would have, if he had had the decision to make originally, is no justification for changing it. The minds of equally reasonable men differ. A consideration which would weigh heavily with one man will seem of less importance to another. A circumstance which highly aggravates an offense in one man's eyes may be only slight aggravation to another. If an arbitrator could substitute his judgment and discretion for the judgment and discretion honestly exercised by management, then the functions of management would have been abdicated, and unions would take every case to arbitration. The result would be as intolerable to employees as to management. The only circumstances under which a penalty imposed by management can be rightfully set aside by an arbitrator are those where discrimination, unfairness, or capricious and arbitrary action are proved—in other words, where there has been abuse of discretion."[79]

Under an agreement requiring just cause, Arbitrator Wilber C. Bothwell held that "the arbitrator should not substitute his judgment for that of management unless he finds that the penalty is excessive, unreasonable, or that management has abused its discretion."[80] Views of similar import have been expressed by many other arbitrators (the "unreasonable, capricious or arbitrary action" standard of review often being stated).[81]

A less restricted role of the arbitrator in reviewing discipline assessed under agreements requiring cause is apparent under the following view expressed by Arbitrator Harry H. Platt:

"It is ordinarily the function of an Arbitrator in interpreting a contract provision which requires 'sufficient cause' as a condition precedent to discharge not only to determine whether the employee involved

---

[79]Stockham Pipe Fittings Co., 1 LA 160, 162 (1945), where the submission specifically empowered the arbitrator to determine "what disposition" should be made of the dispute. For some of the many arbitrators expressly approving the McCoy statement, see Arbitrator Nelson in 81 LA 318, 324; Madden in 80 LA 1298, 1301; Nicholas in 80 LA 891, 892; Larkin in 79 LA 422, 424; Neas in 78 LA 985, 998; Sabo in 78 LA 978, 983–984; Talent in 78 LA 859, 863–864 (observing that the McCoy view "has been followed by a substantial and respectable segment of the arbitral community"); Tucker in 78 LA 749, 753. Also see statements of similar import by Arbitrator LeWinter in 74 LA 37, 41–42; Sisk in 69 LA 484, 487; Beatty in 41 LA 142, 144 ("an arbitration clause is not an abdication by management of its duties in regard to discipline and discharge and does not grant to the arbitrator authority to redetermine the whole matter by his own standards as if he were making the original decision"); Stouffer in 26 LA 395, 397; Kadish in 25 LA 568, 571; Gilden in 21 LA 105, 107; Reid in 19 LA 724, 727; Prasow in 13 LA 28, 30.

[80]Franz Food Prods., 28 LA 543, 548 (1957).

[81]See Arbitrator D. Lewis in 81 LA 306, 311; Jackson in 78 LA 394, 398; Maniscalco in 77 LA 146, 152; Tanaka in 74 LA 236, 241; Roberts in 73 LA 1133, 1140; Guenther in 73 LA 551, 554; Doyle in 72 LA 1033, 1035; Boyer in 70 LA 1078, 1084; J. Lewis in 70 LA 544, 547–548; Hadlick in 68 LA 114, 123; Talent in 55 LA 1094, 1098; King in 54 LA 1110, 1113; Dunlop in 52 LA 752, 755; Nathanson in 51 LA 120, 125; Doyle in 50 LA 1157, 1159; Whyte in 47 LA 1065, 1071–1072; Larkin in 47 LA 903, 906; Gibson in 46 LA 633, 636; Altrock in 44 LA 1202, 1204; Meltzer in 28 LA 303, 308; Hale in 27 LA 486, 493; Reynard in 27 LA 400, 404; Dworkin in 23 LA 696, 701; Anrod in 20 LA 653, 658; Luskin in 19 LA 5, 7; Donaldson in 13 LA 943, 945.

is guilty of wrong-doing and, if so, to confirm the employer's right to discipline where its exercise is essential to the objective of efficiency, but also to safeguard the interests of the discharged employee by making reasonably sure that the causes for discharge were just and equitable and such as would appeal to reasonable and fair-minded persons as warranting discharge. To be sure, no standards exist to aid an arbitrator in finding a conclusive answer to such a question and, therefore, perhaps the best he can do is to decide what reasonable man, mindful of the habits and customs of industrial life and of the standards of justice and fair dealing prevalent in the community, ought to have done under similar circumstances and in that light to decide whether the conduct of the discharged employee was defensible and the disciplinary penalty just."[82]

Here again, views of similar import have also been expressed by arbitrators in other cases.[83]

An arbitrator's view of his function in reviewing discipline may vary according to the nature of the offense. For instance, Arbitrator Robert G. Howlett has stated that an arbitrator should be more hesitant to overrule penalties where the offense is directly related to the company's product than where it involves primarily the personal behavior of the employee and is only indirectly related to production.[84] Also, where the safety of the public is a direct factor in a discharge, another arbitrator would require the union to "show that the decision was arbitrary, made in bad faith, or clearly wrong."[85]

An approach offered by Arbitrator Carroll R. Daugherty involves the use of "a set of guide lines or criteria" to be applied in any given case to determine whether the arbitrator should "substitute his judgment for that of the employer."[86]

Finally, it should be recognized that while arbitrators do not lightly interfere with management's decisions in discharge and discipline matters, this by no means suggests that they fail to act firmly

---

[82]Riley Stoker Corp., 7 LA 764, 767 (1947). The Platt view was quoted with approval by Arbitrator Boyer in 76 LA 1187, 1190; Newmark in 76 LA 946, 952; Roumell in 73 LA 707, 709; Hayes in 56 LA 924, 926. Arbitrator Platt's continued adherence to his view is apparent from his statement in Ludington News Co., 78 LA 1165, 1167 (1982). In Indianapolis Chair Co., 20 LA 706, 709 (1953), Arbitrator W. Howard Mann stated that in reviewing discharge, "The Arbitrator must accept the responsibility of making an actual determination."

[83]See Arbitrator Frank in 81 LA 385, 386; Gerber in 73 LA 1185, 1192; Coffey in 48 LA 1349, 1353; Klein in 46 LA 974, 977; Volz in 45 LA 968, 970–971; Doyle in 44 LA 522, 526–527; Hebert in 41 LA 745, 750 (denying that the arbitrator is merely to determine whether management's action was capricious or arbitrary and declaring that he has a responsibility to determine whether the punishment fits the crime); Turkus in 39 LA 823, 825; Teple in 37 LA 85, 90; Thompson in 36 LA 537, 539. In Capital Packing Co., 36 LA 101, 102 (Seligson, 1961), the arbitrator stated that "a discharge case in arbitration is a hearing in equity, permitting of a flexibility and assessment of mitigating circumstances and factors not available under the more rigorous common law rules."

[84]Valley Steel Casting Co., 22 LA 520, 524–525 (1954).

[85]United Air Lines, 19 LA 585, 587 (McCoy, 1952). While also expressing strong concern for public safety, a somewhat broader scope of review nonetheless was exercised by Arbitrator Abrams in 79 LA 729, 732–733; Dolson in 46 LA 1161, 1165; Lennard in 30 LA 830, 834–835.

[86]Enterprise Wire Co., 46 LA 359, 362–365 (1966), where he also stated, however, that frequently "the facts are such that the guide lines cannot be applied with precision." For examples of arbitral use of the Daugherty criteria, see Arbitrator Role in 78 LA 236. 238; Saracino in 76 LA 1058, 1061; Keltner in 70 LA 1028, 1030; Chockley in 69 LA 1192, 1194; Forsythe in 68 LA 369, 371; Hon in 68 LA 151, 154. Also see the more detailed statement of criteria by Arbitrator McBrearty in 70 LA 458, 463–465, and the criteria stated in a public-sector decision by the Connecticut State Bd. of Mediation & Arbitration in 69 LA 985 at 985.

when management's decisions are found to be unjust or unreasonable under all the circumstances.[87] In this regard, Arbitrator Charles B. Spaulding replied as follows where an employer cited awards allegedly to the effect that arbitrators should not interfere with discipline assessed by management where the agreement permits it to exercise judgment:

> "Three answers to this line of argument seem appropriate. The first is that arbitrators very frequently do step in and upset the decisions of Management. The second is that, if arbitrators could not do so, arbitration would be of little import, since the judgment of management would in so many cases constitute the final verdict. Finally, the more careful statement of the principle would probably run to the effect that where the contract uses such terms as discharge for 'cause' or for 'good cause' or for 'justifiable cause' an arbitrator will not lightly upset a decision reached by competent careful management which acts in the full light of all the facts, and without any evidence of bias, haste or lack of emotional balance. Even under these conditions, if the decision is such as to shock the sense of justice of ordinary reasonable men, we suspect that arbitrators have a duty to interfere. Since the acts of Management in this case do shock our sense of justice, and since they do seem to have occurred in a situation of emotional tension, in haste, and without a very careful weighing of the facts, we find ourselves inevitably driven to overthrow the decision of this Management."[88]

Authority of Arbitrator to Modify Penalties

Many agreements give the arbitrator express authority to modify penalties found to be improper or too severe.[89] Also the agreement may give the arbitrator such authority by implication.[90] Some agreements expressly limit the arbitrator's authority to modify penalties. Under such agreements arbitrators sometimes have sustained discharge where they probably would have reduced the penalty but for

---

[87]Many arbitrators are likely to agree with the following statement of Arbitrator William J. LeWinter:

"The arbitrator must be fully cognizant that he is taking into his hands the Employer's personnel policies. The arbitrator does not live with the parties, he has not actually experienced the problems management may have which might require strong disciplinary measures. * * * At the same time, while he must use great restraint, an arbitrator must do essential justice and take the actions necessary to achieve it."

Werner-Continental, 72 LA 1, 9–11 (1978), where Arbitrator LeWinter quoted both McCoy and Platt without stating a preference for the view of either; he found discharge excessive and in reducing the penalty to suspension, he stated that "the arbitrator must sustain a suspension of such length that would not shock his conscience whether he would have suspended for that period or not."

[88]Fruehauf Trailer Co., 16 LA 666, 670 (1951). Also see Arbitrator Stix in 70 LA 75, 78 (the agreement expressly denied him authority to substitute his "discretion" for that of the company—he construed the agreement to give the company discretion in the disciplinary matter in question and he concluded that he could not review the exercise of that discretion unless it was "exercised arbitrarily or in bad faith"); Autrey in 45 LA 117, 119–120.

[89]For example, see Sundstrand Corp., 46 LA 346, 349 (Larkin, 1966). The parties clothed the arbitrator with this power at the hearing in Dayton Malleable Iron Co., 17 LA 666 at 666 (Hampton, 1951).

[90]See McInerney Spring & Wire Co., 21 LA 80, 82 (Smith, 1953).

the limitation upon their authority;[91] but in other instances the denial of arbitral authority to modify penalties has resulted in the reinstatement of employees with no penalty at all even though the employee was guilty of misconduct justifying some punishment.[92]

In one case a party expressed serious doubt as to the wisdom of placing "the arbitrator in a position of making a 'black or white' decision,"[93] and it is not surprising that arbitrators have sometimes considered that any restriction upon their authority to modify penalties must be clearly and unequivocally stated and have narrowly construed contractual provisions purporting to restrict that authority.[94]

Where the agreement fails to deal with the matter, the right of the arbitrator to change or modify penalties found to be improper or too severe may be deemed to be inherent in the arbitrator's power to decide the sufficiency of cause, as elaborated by Arbitrator Harry H. Platt:

> "In many disciplinary cases, the reasonableness of the penalty imposed on an employee rather than the existence of proper cause for disciplining him is the question an arbitrator must decide. This is not so under contracts or submission agreements which expressly prohibit an arbitrator from modifying or reducing a penalty if he finds that disciplinary action was justified, but most current labor agreements do not contain such limiting clause. In disciplinary cases generally, therefore, most arbitrators exercise the right to change or modify a penalty if it is found to be improper or too severe, under all the circumstances of the situation. This right is deemed to be inherent in the arbitrator's power to discipline and in his authority to finally settle and adjust the dispute before him."[95]

---

[91]See Arbitrator Flannagan in 74 LA 481, 486; Strasshofer in 69 LA 1108, 1111; Eaton in 53 LA 1274, 1278; Williams in 52 LA 957, 958; Jones in 48 LA 1092, 1093–1094; Granoff in 40 LA 686, 688–689; Seinsheimer in 39 LA 580, 584. In Hayes Intl. Corp., 81 LA 99, 103–104 (1983), Arbitrator Van Wart concluded that he lacked authority to disturb the discharge penalty assessed for conduct which violated the requirements of a "last chance" agreement which had been signed by the employer, union, and employee. Similarly, see Arbitrator Blum in 79 LA 34, 36.

[92]See Arbitrator Gootnick in 73 LA 908, 910–911; Bellman in 47 LA 899, 902; McDermott in 46 LA 985, 989; King in 43 LA 940, 945–946.

[93]Luce Press Clipping Bureau, 40 LA 686, 688 n. 6 (Granoff, 1963). Arbitral power to modify penalties was generally supported by labor and management representatives in a survey conducted by Eaton, "Labor Arbitration in the San Francisco Bay Area," 48 LA 1381, 1386–1387 (1967).

[94]See Arbitrator Kossoff in 76 LA 300, 308; Volz in 50 LA 600, 603; Gilbert in 45 LA 580, 584; Dworkin in 36 LA 124, 128. Also see Amoco Oil Co. v. Atomic Workers, 94 LRRM 2518, 2521, 2524–2525 (CA 7, 1977). For discussion of other court cases on this aspect, see Fogel, "Court Review of Discharge Arbitration Awards," 37 Arb. J. No. 2. pp. 22, 32 (1982). Even a clear restriction upon the arbitrator's authority was stated to be inapplicable under the circumstances in Consolidated Paper Co., 33 LA 840, 846–847 (Kahn, 1959).

[95]Platt, "The Arbitration Process in the Settlement of Labor Disputes," 31 J. Am. Jud. Soc. 54, 58 (1947). To similar effect as to inherent authority to modify penalties, Arbitrator Rothschild in 75 LA 32, 35; Feller in 54 LA 1231, 1246; Goetz in 54 LA 546, 550; Koven in 49 LA 190, 193; Autrey in 47 LA 327, 330; Dolson in 46 LA 1161, 1165; Strasshofer in 44 LA 644, 646; Wren in 41 LA 1020, 1023; Sembower in 41 LA 631, 636; Williams in 36 LA 333, 341–342; Levy in 28 LA 65, 69; Wyckoff in 25 LA 634, 637–638; Hebert in 25 LA 439, 442; Hepburn in 9 LA 345, 348. Indeed, the fact that most arbitrators do modify penalties found to be excessive, evidences their general belief that authority exists. For an informative collection and discussion of court decisions concerning arbitral authority to modify penalties, see Fogel, "Court Review of Discharge Arbitration Awards," 37 Arb. J. No. 2, p. 22 (1982). Some of Arbitrator Fogel's statements, based upon his study of many court decisions, are quoted here:

•   "Where the contract contains only language that specifies the employer's broad right to

Regarding the federal sector, it has been held that "an arbitrator hearing a case under the CSRA *must* consider issues of mitigation unless the parties' contract lawfully provides otherwise."[96]

Leniency

Modification by an arbitrator of a penalty found to be too severe should not be confused with the exercise of leniency (or clemency). The distinction between these actions was emphasized by Arbitrator Whitley P. McCoy when he recognized the power of arbitrators to modify penalties found on the basis of mitigating circumstances to be too severe for the offense, but at the same time declared that arbitrators have no authority to grant clemency where the penalty assessed by management is not found too severe.[97]

The fact that an arbitrator considers that he has no power of leniency or clemency, and accordingly that he must sustain management's disciplinary action where just cause is found, does not prevent him from *recommending* leniency when he personally feels that it should be considered by management.[98] Implicit in such recommenda-

---

discipline or discharge, the courts have long held that an arbitrator may judge whether the penalty assessed by management fits the behavior that is alleged to be cause for a penalty, as well as establish whether the alleged behavior in fact occurred. If the punishment is found to be excessive, the arbitrator can reduce it, thereby modifying the assessed penalty." Id. at 24. Some examples are Local 53 v. Sho-Me Power Corp., 114 LRRM 2177, 2179–2180 (CA 8, 1983); IAM v. San Diego Marine Constr. Corp., 104 LRRM 2613, 2614 (CA 9, 1980); International Union of Dist. 50, UMW v. Bowman Transp., 421 F.2d 934, 936 (CA 5, 1970).

● "A number of court decisions have vacated arbitral modifications of discharges where the discharges were assessed under contract clauses specifying certain causes for discharge. When such clauses exist, the courts fairly consistently rule that arbitrators do not have the authority to judge whether discharge is an excessive penalty for the violation committed." 37 Arb. J. No. 2 at p. 27. Some examples are St. Louis Theatrical Co. v. Local 6, 114 LRRM 2097, 2098–2099 (CA 8, 1983); Firemen & Oilers Local 935-B v. Nestle Co., 105 LRRM 2715, 2717 (CA 6, 1980); Mistletoe Express Serv. v. Motor Expressmen, 96 LRRM 3320, 3322 (CA 10, 1977). But cf., Kane Gas Light & Heating Co. v. Firemen & Oilers, 111 LRRM 2094, 2098 (CA 3, 1982); Vulcan-Hart Corp. v. Local 110, 109 LRRM 2993, 2994–2995 (CA 8, 1982); Norfolk Shipbuilding Corp. v. Local 684, 109 LRRM 2329, 2330 (CA 4, 1982), stating that a relevant consideration is "whether there was any custom or practice in the plant which had been integrated into the contract giving the arbitrator authority to modify the penalty imposed by" the employer. In the latter regard, also see F.W. Woolworth Co. v. Local 781, 104 LRRM 3128, 3135–3136 (CA 7, 1980).

● "In a numerical sense, at least, the Trilogy decisions for court review of arbitration awards have been followed with respect to discharge awards. Only a tiny percentage of these awards are challenged in court and only one in four of the challenged awards is vacated. The discharge awards of arbitration are final with very rare exceptions." 37 Arb. J. No. 2 at p. 33.

[96]Local 2578, AFGE v. General Servs. Admin., 711 F.2d 261, 265 (D.C. Cir., 1983), emphasis added.

[97]Chattanooga Box & Lumber Co., 10 LA 260, 261 (1948). Also stating that arbitrators have no leniency power, Arbitrator Williams in 79 LA 464, 467–468; Madden in 78 LA 1290, 1294; O'Connell in 72 LA 175, 179; Hebert in 70 LA 20, 27; Chockley in 69 LA 1192, 1195; Dolnick in 53 LA 990, 991–992; Abernethy in 50 LA 1194, 1198; Daugherty in 50 LA 83, 90; Larkin in 45 LA 156, 159–160; Hughes in 42 LA 307, 310. But see Kleeb in 69 LA 987, 989; Cahn in 44 LA 1043, 1044. In Hiram Walker & Sons, 75 LA 899, 900–901 (1980), Arbitrator William Belshaw questioned whether any valid distinction exists between arbitral power to modify penalties found to be too severe, and arbitral exercise of leniency. The present Authors believe that the distinction stated by Arbitrator McCoy is valid for most cases, although it also appears that in very close cases there possibly may be some overlap between the two concepts or that they may be separated only by a thin line.

[98]See Arbitrator Evenson in 74 LA 939, 945; Paradise in 74 LA 509, 513; Nigro in 70 LA 574, 575; Bothwell in 51 LA 1076, 1080; Stouffer in 47 LA 443, 448; Abersold in 24 LA 1251, 1255; Mueller in 36 LA 965, 969; Rosenfarb in 24 LA 674, 675–676; Dworkin in 23 LA 696, 702; Miller in 22 LA 620, 623; Marshall in 22 LA 573, 576; Howlett in 22 LA 520, 527; Kelliher in 21 LA 444, 446; Seward in 17 LA 334, 335.

tions is silent recognition by arbitrators that powers of leniency or clemency reside in management.[99]

In certain cases the arbitrator in upholding the penalty assessed by management, either (1) explained in detail why the arbitrator nonetheless urged the use of leniency by management,[100] or (2) explained in detail why the arbitrator did understand management's determination not to risk a less severe penalty.[101]

Factors in Evaluating Penalties

Numerous factors may be relevant in the review or evaluation of penalties assessed by management for misconduct of employees. The more prominent of these factors are considered briefly below.

Nature of the Offense: Summary Discharge Versus Corrective Discipline

It is said to be "axiomatic that the degree of penalty should be in keeping with the seriousness of the offense."[102] In this regard, Arbitrator Whitley P. McCoy explained:

---

[99]Arbitrators also have expressly recognized this power in management. See Arbitrator Evenson in 74 LA 939, 945; Dolnick in 53 LA 990, 991–992; Luckerath in 48 LA 182, 183; Daugherty in 45 LA 515, 517; Hughes in 42 LA 307, 310; Abernethy in 36 LA 1092, 1096; McCoy in 12 LA 1190, 1192; Gorder in 9 LA 73, 77.

[100]In upholding all but one of the many discharges that resulted from a prohibited work stoppage in Clinton Corn Processing Co., 71 LA 555, 571 (1978), Arbitrator Stanford C. Madden stated:

"I agree with the Union that the Company has established its point many times over and to the extent any further suffering can be ameliorated by leniency it should be done. This is particularly true in the light of the fact that some facts became apparent to the Company for the first time in the hearing. To fear to approach negotiations on this subject from this point forward for fear of weakening its position will certainly be counter productive as an employer can enjoy the long run effects of good labor relations only when employees can be assured that its judgments are fair and just. Too much severity in the matter of assessing discipline, even though legal, may not be in the best interest of the harmonious relations which make best for an efficient work force.

"The Union's point that more harmonious and fruitful Company-Union relations would result from greater leniency is well taken. But leniency is not within the arbitrator's province * * *."

Also see Arbitrator Marlatt in 77 LA 721, 725 (upholding discharge and stating that the "employer may properly consider whether more lenient discipline may serve the desired purpose of correction so that the employment relationship may be salvaged"); O'Connell in 72 LA 175, 178–179 (stating that the "granting of leniency in individual situations cannot act to prevent the invocation of the proscribed penalty if management finds this the desirable course of action," and that while the arbitrator must uphold the discipline in the present case and "is unable to substitute his judgment for that of management," it would appear "that as an internal personnel problem * * * some degree of leniency might have been considered").

[101]See Brooks Foundry, 75 LA 642, 644 (1980), where Arbitrator William P. Daniel stated: "This employee is so highly thought of by the company that it would not be surprising that the company would have, if it could, moderated the discipline but it is clear to this arbitrator that the company feels so strongly the necessity of maintaining a firm rule and consistent enforcement that it did so even when such was contrary to its own interests. It would be improper for this arbitrator where a violation has been found and where, particularly the employee has attempted to cover up the facts, to disregard the judgment of the company in assessing the penalty. The company knows its business and its operations and the manner in which it must deal with its employees. This arbitrator cannot deny that a firm and absolute approach to penalties in such cases may very well discourage numerous other instances by other employees in the future. For this reason it would be inappropriate to disturb the penalty selected in this case."

For related discussion, see subtopics entitled "Lax Enforcement of Rules" and "Unequal or Discriminatory Treatment" below.

[102]Capital Airlines, 25 LA 13, 16 (Stowe, 1955).

"Offenses are of two general classes: (1) those extremely serious offenses such as stealing, striking a foreman, persistent refusal to obey a legitimate order, etc., which usually justify summary discharge without the necessity of prior warnings or attempts at corrective discipline; (2) those less serious infractions of plant rules or of proper conduct such as tardiness, absence without permission, careless workmanship, insolence, etc., which call not for discharge for the first offense (and usually not even for the second or third offense) but for some milder penalty aimed at correction."[103]

As to the less serious offenses, the concept of corrective or progressive discipline has been recognized by arbitrators. Arbitrator M.S. Ryder, for instance, stated:

"Further, if the employer so chooses, and it is common practice in industry, the employer may adopt a corrective approach toward penalty, by making second and third offenses of the same nature, or of another nature, cumulative in terms of the degree of severity of penalty imposed for each of the subsequent proven offenses so as to dissuade any further commissions."[104]

However, Arbitrator Robert S. Thompson cautioned:

"In industrial practice discipline is often 'progressive' or 'corrective' in nature. Warning is tried before suspension; suspension before discharge. Penalties are designed to correct if possible. While theories and practices of 'progressive' or 'corrective' discipline may be in wide use, it does not follow that every Company must, in the absence of contract provisions, adopt such views. Every business and industry has its own peculiar conditions. An Arbitrator should be slow to substitute his own judgment as to the appropriateness of penalties on the basis of theories which seem to have wide appeal."[105]

In fact, there appears to be considerable diversity of arbitral thought in respect to corrective discipline. Without attempting to distinguish or reconcile any cases which appear to conflict, the Authors merely note some of the various views or actions by arbitrators concerning corrective discipline:

---

[103]Huntington Chair Corp., 24 LA 490, 491 (1955). Also see statement by Arbitrator Roberts in 70 LA 1110, 1117. For other cases recognizing the propriety of summary discharge for serious offenses, see Arbitrator Nicholas in 80 LA 891, 893; Cantor in 74 LA 1084, 1090 (threatening a foreman); Axon in 73 LA 164, 166 (disloyalty to employer by using contacts and information obtained on the job "to turn a personal profit at their employer's expense"); Laybourne in 71 LA 148, 151 (extorting $20 as condition for allowing truck to be unloaded); Fitch in 70 LA 1088, 1091 (false statements concerning safety maliciously made to regulatory agency); Glendon in 70 LA 696, 699; Duff in 70 LA 625, 627–628 (refusal of public-sector employee to work overtime in an emergency); Powell in 70 LA 146, 149 (striking a foreman); Kaufman in 69 LA 776, 779 (possession of marijuana and giving it to fellow employee at work); Turkus in 68 LA 351, 352 ("openly defiant and egregiously insubordinate" conduct); Schmidt in 52 LA 1019, 1021–1022; Keefe in 52 LA 709, 713; Daugherty in 50 LA 83, 90; Livengood in 47 LA 1170, 1175; Tsukiyama in 43 LA 1218, 1223–1224; Jaffee in 27 LA 768, 772–773; McCoy, Schedler & Alexander in 25 LA 270, 276; Stowe in 25 LA 13, 16; Marshall in 22 LA 573, 576; Seward in 19 LA 210, 212; Updegraff in 17 LA 224, 225. In some of these cases the arbitrator expressly stated that summary discharge is permissible even though the employee has long seniority with a good record.

[104]Michigan Seamless Tube Co., 24 LA 132, 133–134 (1955). Also see statements by Arbitrator Platt in 25 LA 733, 735; McCoy in 24 LA 490, 492. For further discussion see comments by Arbitrator Alexander in Management Rights and the Arbitration Process, 76, 79–82 (BNA Books, 1956), quoted in significant part by Arbitrator Howlett in 48 LA 283, 287.

[105]Niagara Frontier Transit Sys., 24 LA 783, 785 (1955), reducing the penalty on the basis of grievant's long seniority. Also see Arbitrator Nelson in 77 LA 927, 933–934.

1. There are cases in which management was held obligated to use corrective discipline although there was no indication that management had ever approved its use either by the agreement or by unilaterally instituting corrective discipline in the past.[106]

2. It has been said that the formalization of a corrective discipline program is a matter for negotiations by the parties, not for the arbitrator.[107] It also has been said that it "is one thing to determine whether or not a contract permits discharging an employee under given circumstances," but that it "is entirely another matter for an arbitrator to conclude that an employee's discharge violated a contract because of something not in the contract," i.e., because of the absence of a corrective discipline program where none is specified by the agreement.[108]

3. There are cases in which discharge was upset where the company had a corrective discipline system but failed to abide by it.[109]

4. Where an employer was reluctant to suspend the employee and used counseling and warnings instead (as predischarge measures), this demonstrated a desire to help rather than hurt the employee, an arbitrator said, and for this the employer should not be criticized.[110]

---

[106]See Arbitrator Yarowsky in 69 LA 1173, 1178; Heilbrun in 56 LA 884, 887; Zack in 55 LA 987, 989–990; Teple in 50 LA 541, 544; Nichols in 50 LA 249, 251; Wallen in 48 LA 19, 23; Duff in 45 LA 538, 540; Prasow in 44 LA 669, 672; Dworkin in 40 LA 1052, 1059. Also see Szollosi in 71 LA 928, 929; Dyke in 70 LA 1103, 1110.

[107]Union Carbide Corp., 46 LA 195, 196–197 (Cahn, 1966), where some corrective discipline had in fact been used.

[108]Aro, Inc., 47 LA 1065, 1070 (Whyte, 1966). Also see Arbitrator Nutt in 76 LA 1278, 1280; Goodstein in 74 LA 171, 175. In Fruehauf Corp., 47 LA 618, 621 (Levin, 1966), the arbitrator said that until the union approves the three-step disciplinary procedure unilaterally instituted by management, the ultimate test for reviewing discipline must be its "reasonableness."

[109]See Arbitrator Welch in 81 LA 96, 98; Marcus in 72 LA 1310, 1313; Brooks in 72 LA 865, 870–871; Fitzsimmons in 70 LA 1099, 1101–1102; Belshaw in 49 LA 573, 576–577; Morgan in 45 LA 280, 283; Kates in 43 LA 1031, 1034–1035, and in 39 LA 286, 290–292 (the established sequence should be adhered to in the absence of compelling circumstances otherwise); Dworkin in 41 LA 862, 866. Agreeing that the established sequence should be adhered to, Arbitrator Dawson J. Lewis explained: "The imposition of a penalty in the progressive discipline system, i.e., an oral warning, a written warning, one day suspension, five days suspension, creates an expectancy. That expectancy is destroyed, not only for that employee, but for all others as well if a suspension is followed by a mere warning for a similar offense." Troy Dept. of Pub. Works, 77 LA 153, 159 (1981). But the need for flexibility in the administration of corrective discipline systems was recognized by Arbitrator George S. Bradley in TRW Metals Div., 52 LA 538, 544 (1969). Also see Arbitrator Cox in 81 LA 459, 460 (stating that the "principles of progressive discipline do not require a lock step approach"); Schroeder in 70 LA 199, 201; Krislov in 48 LA 634, 636. Regarding complete abandonment of a progressive discipline program, it was held in Portec, Inc., 72 LA 804, 806–807 (Ellmann, 1979), that the progressive discipline feature of a plant rule had become a binding past practice and could not be abandoned by the employer without bargaining. For related discussion, see Chapter 12, topic entitled "Custom and Practice as Part of the Contract," and subtopic entitled "Regulation, Modification, or Termination of Practice as Implied Term of Contract"; Chapter 13, topic entitled "Plant Rules."

[110]American Cyanamid Co., 51 LA 181, 184–185 (Stouffer, 1968). Similarly, see Arbitrator Ross in 79 LA 523, 528; Strasshofer in 69 LA 1108, 1111; Stouffer in 51 LA 688, 691. For one company's program, see Huberman, "Discipline Without Punishment," 66 Harv. Bus. Rev. 62 (1977). But see Arbitrator House in 72 LA 712, 719; High in 72 LA 510, 513; Jones in 68 LA 1068, 1070–1071; Duff in 52 LA 101, 104 (management's continued reliance upon gentle verbal rebukes that were not effective did not adequately warn the employee that his conduct would not continue to be tolerated).

5. Where there were "no circumstances to suggest that corrective discipline would rehabilitate the grievant into a satisfactory employee," discharge without corrective discipline was upheld.[111]
6. In adopting a corrective discipline program a company was held not to have surrendered its right to invoke summary discharge for serious offenses warranting such action.[112] Also, the mere fact that an agreement specified the use of corrective discipline for some offenses did not necessarily mean that it must be used for all offenses.[113]
7. In sustaining discharge, arbitrators sometimes have stressed the fact that corrective discipline had been used without avail.[114]

Due Process and Procedural Requirements

Discharge and disciplinary action by management has been reversed where the action violated basic notions of fairness or due process. This was true, for instance, where the employer gave employees no chance to be heard but discharged them summarily upon learning that they had been convicted of larceny by a court.[115] In other situations, too, the failure of management to make a reasonable inquiry or investigation before assessing punishment was a factor (sometimes the sole factor) in the arbitrator's refusal to sustain the discharge or discipline as assessed by management.[116] An unusual

---

[111]International Tel. & Tel. Corp., 54 LA 1110, 1113 (King, 1970).
[112]Inland Steel Prods. Co., 47 LA 966, 970 (Gilden, 1966). Accord, Arbitrator Glendon in 70 LA 696, 699. Also see statement by Arbitrator Bradley in 52 LA 538, 544. In Woman's Gen. Hosp., 74 LA 281, 288–289 (Klein, 1980), a series of offenses in rapid succession made it impossible for the employer to administer progressive discipline, and the employee's acts "were, *when considered as a whole*, acts of sufficient gravity to justify a discharge penalty for a first offense under the specific facts and circumstances of" the case.
[113]Alliance Mach. Co., 48 LA 457, 462–463 (Dworkin, 1967), upholding the propriety of summary discharge for serious offenses not listed in the corrective discipline schedule. Similarly, see Arbitrator Cantor in 74 LA 1084, 1090.
[114]See Arbitrator Moats in 76 LA 607, 611; Sinicropi in 72 LA 1006, 1009; Daniel in 72 LA 591, 594; Spencer in 70 LA 1168, 1171; O'Shea in 70 LA 41, 49; Altrock in 48 LA 1224, 1227; Cahn in 47 LA 747 at 747; Stouffer in 47 LA 464, 468; Dworkin in 47 LA 266, 268; Tsukiyama in 45 LA 1124, 1133.
[115]United States Steel Corp., 29 LA 272, 277–278 (Babb, 1957), citing other cases also recognizing the obligation of management to make appropriate inquiry before discharging employees in such situations. Also see Arbitrator Maggs in 16 LA 829, 834. Cf., Arbitrator Sembower in 49 LA 439, 441–442.
[116]See Arbitrator Roumell in 80 LA 516, 520; Modjeska in 79 LA 166, 170; Dunn in 78 LA 1309, 1310; Allen in 78 LA 542, 544; Axon in 77 LA 820, 829; Nelson in 77 LA 661, 666–667; Raymond in 77 LA 309, 312; Atwood in 73 LA 367, 370–371; White in 72 LA 1069, 1072; High in 72 LA 510, 512; Lauritzen in 70 LA 1026, 1028; Fox in 70 LA 707, 717–718; Helburn in 70 LA 504, 513–514 (stating that the award "is based solely on procedural deficiencies and is not meant to imply satisfactory performance" by grievant); Strasshofer in 69 LA 766, 769; King in 69 LA 721, 725; Harter in 69 LA 414, 418; Beck in 68 LA 1146, 1151–1152; Edes in 68 LA 931, 932; O'Connell in 68 LA 26, 30; Erbs in 55 LA 197, 209 (only one side of the matter was investigated); Solomon in 54 LA 1, 6–7; Howlett in 52 LA 375, 381–382 (management's failure to make objective investigation did not exonerate the employees but the penalty was reduced); Bernstein in 50 LA 1263, 1265–1266; Summers in 48 LA 1278, 1279–1280; Karlins in 44 LA 609, 613–614; Daugherty in 42 LA 555, 557; Dworkin in 36 LA 124, 128. Also see Local 878 v. Coca-Cola Bottling Co., 103 LRRM 2380, 2383–2384 (CA 8, 1980). But see Cahn in 19 LA 674, 676. In Equitable Gas Co., 75 LA 853, 857–858 (1980), Arbitrator James C. Duff found it necessary to determine whether the wording of

approach was taken by Arbitrator Otis H. King, who refused to require reinstatement of a discharged employee but nonetheless required back pay up to the time when a proper investigation had been conducted establishing just cause for the discharge.[117]

One of the factors leading to a reduction of the penalty assessed by management in one case was the failure to give the employee or union an opportunity, either at the suspension hearing or in the prearbitral grievance procedure, to question the foreman who was the employee's accuser.[118] Likewise, procedural unfairness was found where the employer selected certain employees for discharge out of a group of illicit strikers without telling the union or the discharged employees the reason for their being selected until the arbitration hearing.[119] In another case a discharge was set aside where delay in notifying the employee of his discharge made it difficult for him to obtain witnesses in his own behalf (due to the fact that intoxication was the offense charged).[120]

Many agreements specify procedural requirements for discharge or discipline. In many cases arbitrators have refused to uphold management's action in discharging or disciplining an employee where management failed to fulfill some procedural requirement specified by the agreement, such as a required statement of charges against the employee, or a notice or investigation requirement, or a requirement for a hearing or joint discussion prior to the assessment of punishment.[121]

However, in many other cases compliance with the spirit of such procedural requirements was held to suffice where the employee had

---

a preinvestigation letter from the employer merely "charged" certain named employees with having engaged in a prohibited work stoppage, or "whether the letter itself implicitly amounted to the imposition of discipline by revealing managerial predisposition with respect to the underlying issue of the named individual's participation."

[117]Southwest Airlines, 80 LA 628, 631 (1983). Similarly, Arbitrator Melvin Leonard stated that such "back pay without reinstatement" remedy was in order where the employee clearly was guilty of a serious offense but had been denied a pretermination hearing specified by the agreement. Kaiser Steel Corp., 78 LA 185, 190–191 (1982). Also see Arbitrator Kossoff in 75 LA 1266, 1272.

[118]Pittsburgh Steel Co., 47 LA 923, 926 (McDermott, 1966). Also see Arbitrator Cutler in 72 LA 1313, 1317; Merrill in 19 LA 417, 419–420 (discharge on the basis of a finding by the company physician without giving the employee opportunity to present countervailing medical testimony was held improper). But see Buckeye Cellulose Corp., 111 LRRM 2502, 2504 (CA 6, 1982).

[119]Ross Gear Tenn. Plant, 45 LA 959, 963–964 (Sanders, 1965), the agreement expressly permitting selective discipline of such strikers.

[120]National Carbide Co., 27 LA 128, 130 (Warns, 1956). Also see Arbitrator Kanner in 72 LA 179, 183.

[121]See Arbitrator Dobry in 80 LA 321, 325; Dallas in 78 LA 647, 649; Leahy in 78 LA 291, 292, 294–295; Youngblood in 78 LA 243, 247; Smith in 71 LA 452, 453–454; Gorsuch in 70 LA 1036, 1040; Marcus in 68 LA 204, 211; McDaniel in 56 LA 694, 696–697; Davis in 55 LA 764, 767; Wolff in 55 LA 677, 679–680; Porter in 54 LA 361, 362–363 (contract gave employee right to present evidence before being discharged); Gershenfeld in 52 LA 184, 187; Dolnick in 48 LA 273, 276; Krimsly in 48 LA 257, 261; Sembower in 47 LA 910, 913–914; Griffin in 47 LA 257, 258 (duty to notify union *prior* to discharge); Larkin in 46 LA 1214, 1216; Rohman in 44 LA 417, 420; Kates in 44 LA 389, 391, and in 43 LA 977, 980; Howlett in 40 LA 660, 663 (oral notice did not suffice where contract required written notice); Stouffer in 38 LA 882, 885 (oral notice similarly did not suffice); Merrill in 24 LA 522, 524–526; Platt in 17 LA 412, 417–418. Regarding the scope of the arbitrator's authority in federal-sector cases to interpret contractual clauses specifying procedural requirements for the assessment of discipline, see Devine v. White, 697 F.2d 421, 439–444 (D.C. Cir., 1983).

not been adversely affected by the failure of management to accomplish total compliance with the requirements.[122] In a few cases the employer's failure to comply even with the spirit of procedural requirements did not lead the arbitrator to disturb the disciplinary action.[123] Also, in one case a contractual procedural requirement was held waived by the failure to make a timely objection to the fact that the specified procedure was not followed precisely, the arbitrator also noting that no prejudice resulted to the grievant from the manner in which the discharge was handled.[124]

Postdischarge Conduct or Charges

Some agreements require that all reasons for discharge action be given to the employee at the time of discharge. Under such provisions it has been held that only evidence bearing on the charges made at the time of discharge should be considered in determining the existence of cause for punishment.[125] Even without such specific contractual provision, arbitrators have held that discharge, to use the words of Arbitrator Paul N. Guthrie, "must stand or fall upon the reason given at the time of discharge"; other reasons may not be added when the

[122]See Arbitrator Everitt in 81 LA 243, 245; Mead in 76 LA 1137, 1139 (stating that the procedural defect was "technical in nature and has not deprived the grievant of due process"); Lubic in 75 LA 1158, 1163; Williams in 74 LA 362, 364; Johannes in 72 LA 966, 968; Roumell in 68 LA 41, 43; Schurke in 56 LA 973, 976; Jaffee in 55 LA 1102, 1103–1104; Kamin in 55 LA 118, 128; Kreimer in 53 LA 342, 344 (oral notice sufficed although contract specified written notice); Dykstra in 52 LA 1213, 1215–1217; Willingham in 52 LA 951, 953; Kates in 52 LA 818, 820; Eaton in 50 LA 807, 808–810 (requirement of notice to union *after* discharge need not be complied with as strictly as must be a predischarge notice requirement); Buckwalter in 50 LA 177, 179; Block in 49 LA 810, 816–817 (violation was merely technical and did not work to employee's disadvantage); Seidenberg in 49 LA 620, 624–625; Stouffer in 46 LA 654, 657–658; Wren in 41 LA 1020, 1021; Daugherty in 34 LA 83, 85. For cases in which the employer first failed to fulfill a procedural requirement but then acted to rectify the omission, see Arbitrator Nicholas in 76 LA 315, 318; Kaufman in 69 LA 776, 777–778; Murphy in 36 LA 1071, 1073.

[123]In Marquette Inn, 79 LA 1259, 1263–1264 (1982), certain procedural requirements were not complied with even in spirit, but Arbitrator John J. Flagler refused to disturb the discharge since the employee clearly was guilty of a serious offense and had not been prejudiced by the procedural defects. Also see Arbitrator Flagler in 80 LA 219, 225 (stating that the "deference arbitrators pay to due process is to vacate any result that is *substantially* tainted and *irreversible* because of procedural defects"). In Cameron Iron Works, 73 LA 878, 881–882 (1979), the employer "totally ignored" a contract procedural requirement but discharge was sustained since the employee clearly was guilty of a serious offense and had not been prejudiced by the procedural defect, Arbitrator Ernest E. Marlatt stating:

"Constitutional due process is based on the enormous disparity in power between the State and the accused individual * * *. But employers and unions meet in bargaining session on approximately equal terms, and their contracts speak of 'just cause' rather than 'due process.' The distinction is significant. The essential question for an arbitrator is not whether disciplinary action was totally free from procedural error, but rather whether the process was fundamentally fair. He must find in order to overturn the employer's action on procedural grounds, that there was at least a possibility, however remote, that the procedural error may have deprived the grievant of a fair consideration of his case."

In Dorsey Trailers, 73 LA 196, 200 (Hamby, 1979), a contractual notice requirement was held inapplicable where the employer had "no opportunity to give notice" and the employee was not prejudiced by the absence of notice.

[124]United Eng'g. & Foundry Co., 37 LA 1095, 1097 (Kates, 1962). A waiver of a procedural requirement similarly was found by Arbitrator Talent in 78 LA 859, 865; Nicholas in 76 LA 315, 318; Howell in 75 LA 217, 220–221; McDermott in 69 LA 339, 343; Fleischli in 62 LA 1107, 1110–1111.

[125]See Bethlehem Steel Co., 29 LA 635, 640–643 (Seward, 1957); Forest Hill Foundry Co., 1 LA 153, 154 (Brown, 1946).

case reaches arbitration.[126] Arbitrator James T. Burke reasoned in one of these cases that: "The only relevant evidence are the facts which the person making the discharge was in possession of at the time he acted. A discharge cannot be based upon conjecture, surmise, suspicion, or anything but hard, material, and known facts."[127]

In some other cases the arbitrator did consider postdischarge misconduct or predischarge misconduct of which the company was unaware until after the discharge;[128] in some of these cases the arbitrator purported to qualify such consideration by stating that the misconduct could not be used to justify the discharge but could be used in determining the extent to which the penalty should be modified, if at all.[129] It should also be noted that the discovery of new information or the postdischarge actions of the grievant may equally be considered in the grievant's favor.[130]

Finally, it should be noted that there is a line of cases in which the company's evidence was held inadequate to establish the offense for which the employee had been disciplined but was held to be adequate to establish a related lesser offense for which an appropriate penalty

---

[126]West Virginia Pulp & Paper Co., 10 LA 117, 118 (1947). To similar effect, Arbitrator Killion in 80 LA 765, 769–770; Witney in 73 LA 663, 666; Gerhart in 73 LA 556, 560–561; Christopher in 70 LA 308, 318; Ray in 51 LA 1019, 1022; Roberts in 49 LA 1207, 1210; Williams in 49 LA 210, 213; Summers in 48 LA 188, 190; Jones in 44 LA 175, 181–182; McKelvey in 38 LA 586, 593; Morvant in 35 LA 205, 209; Larson in 32 LA 71, 73; Brecht in 29 LA 451, 457; Healy in 12 LA 108, 115; Burke in 3 LA 607, 608. Also see Alutto in 71 LA 828, 831–832; Somers in 45 LA 655, 658, 661; Kates in 43 LA 1031, 1034; Abersold in 37 LA 62, 70; Dworkin in 33 LA 735, 740; Abernethy in 30 LA 1039, 1042–1043. Cf., Mueller in 71 LA 56, 58; Peck in 48 LA 953, 956. In Nickles Bakery, 73 LA 801, 802 (Letson, 1979), a witness who testified at the grievant's discharge hearing was later threatened by him; the employer's motion to reopen the hearing to permit consideration of this factor was denied. Cf., Arbitrator Gibson in 81 LA 365, 366.

[127]Borden's Farm Prods., 3 LA 607, 608 (1945). In San Gamo Elec. Co., 44 LA 593, 600 (1965), Arbitrator Sembower concluded that an employer may investigate further in an effort to buttress the action already taken, but not to add an entirely new ground for action or to enlarge the penalty; he also concluded that in the present case the postdisciplinary investigation was well within the employer's original "theory of the case." Also indicating that additional evidence as to the facts may be obtained and relied upon by the company after discharge, Arbitrator Eaton in 80 LA 1225, 1231; Peck in 72 LA 1075, 1078; High in 70 LA 100, 103; Seitz in 41 LA 823, 830–831.

[128]See Arbitrator Madden in 80 LA 238, 242 (considering the grievant's postdischarge misconduct to be the decisive factor against him in that it served to discredit his denial of the original dishonesty charge); Knowlton in 74 LA 607, 608–609; Chaffin in 69 LA 307, 311; McKenna in 53 LA 909, 918; McCoy in 47 LA 752, 753 (ordinarily a discharge made for one explicit reason cannot be justified in arbitration for an entirely different reason, but this rule does not apply where the employee has fair opportunity to defend against the additional grounds and the grounds would be reason for another discharge immediately following a reinstatement by the arbitrator); Merrill in 46 LA 1044, 1048 (additional offense at time of discharge formed "part of one connected whole"); Davis in 44 LA 193, 193–194; Daugherty in 39 LA 183, 187; Seitz in 36 LA 706, 709; Simkin in 26 LA 836, 839; McCoy, Schedler & Alexander in 25 LA 270, 274–277; Alexander in 24 LA 353, 355; Updegraff in 17 LA 224, 226–227, and in 14 LA 745, 747. Also see Lubow in 77 LA 219, 222. For related matters, see Chapter 8, topic entitled " 'New' Evidence at Arbitration Hearing"; Chapter 7, topic entitled "Extent of Permissible Deviation From Prearbitral Discussion of Case."

[129]Making this qualified use of postdischarge misconduct, Arbitrator Kates in 44 LA 507, 513–514; Volz in 43 LA 849, 852; Alexander in 40 LA 935, 936; Gorsuch in 40 LA 641, 651 (saying that postdischarge misconduct may be considered in judging the appropriateness of the penalty just as the employee's past record may be considered); McCoy in 33 LA 807, 808. Also see Weitzman in 69 LA 839, 841–842. Making this qualified use of predischarge misconduct of which the employer was unaware, Arbitrator Gibson in 81 LA 365, 366; Levin in 55 LA 1061, 1068–1069.

[130]See Arbitrator Cocalis in 78 LA 562, 563; Finan in 74 LA 969, 972; Prasow in 42 LA 408, 411; Thompson in 21 LA 58, 58–59. Sometimes less leeway has been recognized for such consideration of the grievant's postdischarge actions than for consideration of new predischarge information in the grievant's favor. See Mobil Oil Corp. v. Oil Workers Local 8-831, 110 LRRM 2620, 2623–2624 (CA 3, 1982); Sharon Steel Corp., 71 LA 737, 740 (Klein, 1978).

(either as assessed by the employer or as reduced by the arbitrator) was in order.[131] In one such case where an employee was disciplined for sleeping on duty, management failed to prove conclusively that the employee was asleep; but Arbitrator Whitley P. McCoy nonetheless upheld the penalty assessed by management since the evidence did establish a related offense:

> "The Association argues that since the Company made no contention that the penalty was imposed for any other reason than being asleep, the Board has no right to justify the penalty unless it finds that he was asleep. I cannot agree with that contention. The penalty was imposed as a result of the facts. * * * Giving a name to those facts is not important. There was a time when the criminal law was so technical that on a given set of facts a conviction of larceny would be set aside on the ground that those facts constituted embezzlement, and vice versa. Arbitration should not be tied up with such technicalities. Cambre did certain things—leaned back in his swivel chair, put his feet on the desk, closed his eyes, relaxed his muscles, leaned his head back against the wall, and assumed the position and appearance of sleeping. Those facts constitute an offense, and I do not think the Board is bound to set a penalty aside merely because the facts fail to prove conclusively that Cambre was asleep."[132]

Double Jeopardy

By application of "double jeopardy" concepts it has been held that once discipline for a given offense has been imposed and accepted it cannot thereafter be increased.[133] The same result has been reached where the original penalty had not been accepted by the employee.[134]

The double-jeopardy concept (or something akin thereto) also has been held applicable where management unduly delays the assessment or enforcement of discipline.[135] But in some cases delays ranging

---

[131]See Arbitrator Wilmoth in 80 LA 546, 547; Hanes in 77 LA 526, 530; Davies in 76 LA 194, 197; Mewhinney in 73 LA 1066, 1068–1069; Brisco in 72 LA 1022, 1025–1026; Rose in 72 LA 774, 775; Bernhardt in 69 LA 411, 413; Roberts in 69 LA 286, 290; Turkus in 50 LA 616, 620; Hughes in 50 LA 133, 136; Volz in 45 LA 968, 970; Davey in 42 LA 840, 842; Roberts in 35 LA 939, 943; McCoy in 19 LA 495, 497–498. Also see Arbitrator Flaten in 69 LA 1071, 1074; Sembower in 51 LA 391, 396 (insufficient evidence to support the charged offense but back pay was withheld because grievant at the investigation did not make forthright denial of charge but fostered suspicion against himself); Feinberg in 36 LA 839, 841 (similar result where grievant failed to cooperate at the investigation); Maggs in 36 LA 179, 185. But see Coyle in 73 LA 912, 914.

[132]Esso Standard Oil Co., 19 LA 495, 497–498 (1952).

[133]See Arbitrator McCrary in 76 LA 758, 760; Gundermann in 43 LA 907, 910; Sembower in 41 LA 1083, 1085–1086; Dworkin in 40 LA 87, 90; Livengood in 24 LA 356, 358; McCoy in 16 LA 616, 616–617. Cf., Schedler in 81 LA 564, 567–568 (holding that the same incident involved two "misconducts," for which two separate penalties were proper). For other situations in which the double jeopardy concept was applied, see Arbitrator Boals in 80 LA 1090, 1096; Conant in 72 LA 1089, 1092; Simons in 55 LA 447, 449 (employee who was discharged and then reinstated after full investigation could not then be discharged again for the same incident); Keefe in 48 LA 910, 914; Ryder in 24 LA 132, 134. Any right to assert the double jeopardy rule was held waived under the circumstances in Kisco Co., 56 LA 623, 636 (Witney, 1971).

[134]United Parcel Serv., 51 LA 462, 463 (Turkus, 1968); R. Munroe & Sons Mfg. Corp., 40 LA 1300, 1302–1303 (Duff, 1963). Cf., Arbitrator Lubic in 75 LA 1158, 1162.

[135]See Arbitrator Hawkins in 72 LA 544, 557; Bowles in 69 LA 574, 579; Lehoczky in 53 LA 75, 78; Keefe in 52 LA 663, 666; Hill in 39 LA 203, 206; Schedler in 37 LA 1003, 1006–1007; McCoy in 37 LA 860, 861; Bradley in 28 LA 874, 878 ("Holding the threat of the penalty over the employee for approximately four months is something of a penalty in itself"). Also see Pollard in 8 LA 234, 245. But see Rockwell in 77 LA 229, 232 (stating that there "is no acceptable reason for a delay of approximately nine weeks in imposing a suspension against any employee," but that the "contract in effect at that time had no provision that actions be completed within a certain number of days and therefore there is no violation of the contract").

from several weeks up to a year, or even longer, were permitted under the existing facts and circumstances.[136]

The double-jeopardy concept has been held inapplicable where the preliminary action taken against the employee may not reasonably be considered final.[137] In one case where employees were first suspended for participating in an unauthorized work stoppage and later discharged on the basis of subsequently obtained evidence indicating that they had led the stoppage (a dischargeable offense under the contract), Arbitrator W. Willard Wirtz would not honor a plea of double jeopardy. He stated that the rule of double jeopardy presupposes a full hearing before the first penalty is imposed; since a full hearing of the type assumed by the rule is not customary in industrial disciplinary procedures and was not had in this case when the suspension penalty was imposed, the rule was inapplicable.[138]

The fact that an employee has paid a fine or served a jail sentence for acts committed in connection with his employment does not preclude an arbitrator from taking the acts into account in deciding whether the employer had just cause for disciplining the employee, despite the claim that this amounts to double jeopardy.[139] On the other hand, the mere fact that an employee has been acquitted of criminal charges based upon the incident for which management has assessed discipline likewise does not preclude an arbitrator from upholding management's action where adequate evidence is presented to convince him of the employee's guilt of misconduct.[140]

---

[136]See Arbitrator Hewitt in 80 LA 806, 807–808 (delay in discharge was attributed not to the employer but rather to the grievant's actions in appealing his court conviction); Lane in 80 LA 65, 75; Flagler in 79 LA 645, 649 (delay of six months was not unreasonable where grievant was not prejudiced and the delay resulted from employer's objective of not impeding grievant's recovery from injuries); Witney in 76 LA 26, 30 (the three-week "delay in the discharge did not harm the Grievant or prejudice his rights"); Nitka in 74 LA 780, 785; Yarowsky in 70 LA 1208, 1209; Roumell in 68 LA 848, 852 (while agreeing that "prompt disciplinary action and notice thereof is a procedural requirement to the validity of any disciplinary action," he found no "impermissible" investigative delay in the present case, in which employees had called in sick in large numbers and the delay was caused by the employer's "thorough investigation into each individual's allegation of illness"); Strong in 43 LA 31, 31–32; Seward in 12 LA 344, 345.

[137]See Arbitrator Nelson in 81 LA 318, 323 (suspension pending investigation followed by discharge); Goodman in 78 LA 956, 962; Richman in 71 LA 954, 959; Emerson in 37 LA 1112, 1115 (suspension pending investigation followed by discharge); Schmidt in 35 LA 293, 296 (employee was sent home with instructions to return the next morning for final disposition of his case); Hebert in 35 LA 95, 101; Smith in 32 LA 581, 586. Also see Bailey in 69 LA 1224, 1226; Tucker in 69 LA 150, 155 (no double jeopardy where grievant was reinstated on probation, violated probation, and was then discharged).

[138]International Harvester Co., 13 LA 610, 613–614 (1949). Accord, Arbitrator Bowles in 74 LA 1012, 1016.

[139]Westinghouse Elec. Corp., 26 LA 836, 846 (Simkin, 1956), where the arbitrator also stated, however, that he could consider the previous punishment in determining the severity of the penalty assessed. Agreeing that the employer may punish the employee even if the latter has been punished under the criminal law, Arbitrator Ward in 74 LA 949, 951–952; Stutz in 45 LA 350, 351; Scheiber in 45 LA 366, 374; Schmidt in 40 LA 1169, 1173; Mueller in 36 LA 965, 968–969. Also see Seinsheimer in 50 LA 725, 732. But see Dunn in 74 LA 33, 36.

[140]See Arbitrator Simon in 76 LA 387, 391; Kramer in 76 LA 133, 140; Kornblum in 69 LA 344, 349; Lubow in 67 LA 861, 866–867; Alexander in 53 LA 1279, 1282; Turkus in 50 LA 616, 618–619; Block in 49 LA 810, 814–815; Gershenfeld in 49 LA 606, 608 (the arbitration hearing must be de novo, but the court acquittal may be introduced as evidence in support of the employee); Prasow in 39 LA 614, 617; Wyckoff in 38 LA 93, 96, 99; Simkin in 32 LA 44, 47. Also see Ott in 77 LA 765, 767. Cf., Malinowski in 79 LA 1327, 1333; Florey in 72 LA 149, 153; Gomberg in 45 LA 490, 493.

Arbitrators have rejected the claim that consideration of prior offenses in determining the propriety of the penalty assessed for a later offense constitutes double jeopardy.[141]

Grievant's Past Record

Some consideration generally is given to the past record of any disciplined or discharged employee. An offense may be mitigated by a good past record and it may be aggravated by a poor one. Indeed, the employee's past record often is a major factor in the determination of the proper penalty for his offense.

In many cases arbitrators have reduced penalties in consideration, in part, of the employee's long good past record.[142] On the other hand, an arbitrator's refusal to interfere with a penalty may be based in part upon the employee's poor past record.[143] In one case Arbitrator Morris J. Kaplan held that although neither the incident at the time of discharge nor any other single incident cited by the employer was sufficient to warrant discharge, the general pattern of the employee's unsatisfactory conduct and performance, as established by a series of incidents over an extended period, was preponderant evidence justifying discharge.[144] In similar "last straw" situations other arbitrators have also reached similar results.[145]

But there are limitations in the consideration of past offenses. For instance, a distinction should be made between rule infractions that have been proved and mere past "charges." Thus, it has been held that while an employer may have the right to post notations alleging rule infractions on employee records, the failure of the employer to notify

---

[141]See Arbitrator Rule in 71 LA 1077, 1081; Davey in 51 LA 127, 134; Sembower in 46 LA 737, 740–741; Porter in 41 LA 890, 892; Pollack in 24 LA 401, 407; Bernstein in 20 LA 331, 334. Prior offenses are often considered in evaluating the propriety of penalties. See this Chapter, subtopic entitled "Grievant's Past Record."

[142]E.g., Arbitrator Newmark in 79 LA 1225, 1236; Winton in 79 LA 76, 78–79; Goodman in 78 LA 956, 961; Gerhart in 73 LA 556, 561; Cohen in 72 LA 824, 828; Hawkins in 72 LA 544, 558; Roberts in 70 LA 278, 284; Yarowsky in 69 LA 1173, 1178; Cahn in 67 LA 869, 869–870; Kesselman in 54 LA 145, 151; Scheiber in 50 LA 487, 495; Levin in 47 LA 937, 940; Lee in 46 LA 297, 302; Young in 35 LA 428, 430; Seitz in 33 LA 257, 259; Hebert in 29 LA 604, 608; Dunlop in 28 LA 668, 672; Haughton in 28 LA 394, 398; Thompson in 26 LA 575, 577.

[143]E.g., Arbitrator Traynor in 80 LA 1313, 1320; Kaufman in 74 LA 1281, 1284; O'Shea in 70 LA 41, 49; Simon in 68 LA 1010, 1015; Howlett in 55 LA 288, 290; Teple in 53 LA 933, 939; Bothwell in 51 LA 1076, 1080; Stouffer in 51 LA 181, 183; Dworkin in 47 LA 266, 270; Wallen in 46 LA 246, 248; Davis in 44 LA 193, 194; Gilden in 43 LA 753, 756; Porter in 41 LA 890, 892; Sembower in 30 LA 948, 950; Guthrie in 27 LA 358, 361.

[144]Electronic Corp. of Am., 3 LA 217, 218–220 (1946).

[145]See Arbitrator Hewitt in 81 LA 449, 452; Penfield in 74 LA 889, 895; Herrick in 72 LA 765, 768; Rule in 71 LA 1077, 1081; Spencer in 70 LA 1168, 1171; Griffin in 69 LA 439, 456, 459; Scheiber in 57 LA 981, 992; Howlett in 55 LA 288, 290; Williams in 52 LA 1254, 1257–1258; Koven in 52 LA 448, 450, 451, and in 44 LA 412, 415–416; Dunne in 51 LA 945, 950; McNaughton in 48 LA 1201, 1202, 1204; Singer in 47 LA 948, 951; Sembower in 46 LA 737, 739; Tsukiyama in 45 LA 1124, 1129, 1133; Seward in 45 LA 612, 614; Cahn in 41 LA 887, 888; Oppenheim in 39 LA 652, 653–654; Turkus in 36 LA 639, 640, 643; Hepburn in 32 LA 485, 486; Roberts in 20 LA 274, 275. Cf., Arbitrator Teple in 78 LA 603, 611–612, and in 48 LA 558, 562; Belshaw in 49 LA 573, 577; Davey in 37 LA 605, 616–619; Schmidt in 35 LA 12, 14; Pollard in 8 LA 234, 245. Where there was no present offense, discharge was reversed by Arbitrator Kelman in 75 LA 805, 808; Stone in 72 LA 981, 986; J. Dworkin in 70 LA 1299, 1303; Sembower in 69 LA 201, 210; McCoy in 45 LA 254, 255; Fallon in 39 LA 855, 858; H. Dworkin in 29 LA 305, 311. Cf., Winton in 77 LA 428, 432; O'Shea in 70 LA 41, 44–45.

employees of alleged infractions at the time of occurrence precludes him from using the notations to support disciplinary action at a later date, since employees should not be required to disprove stale charges.[146] Nor would an arbitrator consider past rule infractions for which the employee was in no way reprimanded,[147] or past warnings which had not been put in such form as to make them subject to a grievance.[148]

If an employee is given notice of adverse entries in his record and does not file a grievance where able to do so, an arbitrator may subsequently accept the entries on their face without considering their merits.[149]

Collective agreements sometimes limit consideration of an employee's record to a specified period.[150] The need for some time limitation in the consideration of past offenses may also be recognized even where the agreement does not expressly impose one. Thus, Arbitrator John Day Larkin, while emphasizing the need to consider and weigh a grievant's past record, observed:

> "In general we should say that in discharge cases the past conduct of the employee in question is of concern to the arbitrator called upon to review Management's disciplinary action. If the employee has an excel-

---

[146]Consolidated Vultee Aircraft Corp., 10 LA 907, 909 (Dwyer, 1948). Of similar substance, see Arbitrator Cohen in 75 LA 1092, 1095–1096; Lehoczky in 51 LA 540, 545; Sembower in 49 LA 1100, 1109; Lee in 46 LA 175, 180; Block in 46 LA 154, 159; Miller in 42 LA 568, 570–571 ("Past incidents, for which no formal disciplinary action was taken and no official records maintained, and which cannot at a later date be adequately investigated, cannot be accepted" to support discharge); Belkin in 32 LA 86, 88; Scheiber in 24 LA 538, 541. Cf., Jones in 78 LA 313, 318–319.

[147]Western Air Lines, 37 LA 130, 133 (Wyckoff, 1961). Similarly, see Arbitrator Oppenheim in 48 LA 251, 255.

[148]Duval Corp., 43 LA 102, 106 (Myers, 1964). The recording of warnings given to employees has been held to be a form of discipline which may require proper cause. Federal Labor Union v. American Can Co., 21 LA 518 (N.J. Super. Ct., 1953). Also see Arbitrator Seitz in 54 LA 1185, 1187; Louisell in 20 LA 826, 831.

[149]See Arbitrator Abrams in 70 LA 1174, 1175–1176; Bothwell in 51 LA 1076, 1080; Stouffer in 50 LA 1118, 1121. Cf., Dworkin in 70 LA 1299, 1302; Gould in 50 LA 1127, 1129–1131. In Purex Corp., 38 LA 313, 316–317 (1962), the employee had not been given written notice of the entries on his record but did know of them and it was company policy that employees were invited to inspect their personnel records; while Arbitrator Milton T. Edelman stated that the company should use written notices, he refused to "rule that its records are so secret that they cannot be used to establish an employee's past conduct." In proper cases arbitrators have ordered the removal of matter from an employee's personnel file or have permitted matter to remain with the understanding that it not be used against the employee in the future. See Arbitrator Roberts in 81 LA 497, 502; Kaye in 68 LA 160, 163; Sembower in 54 LA 839, 844; Jenkins in 50 LA 115, 125; Leach in 48 LA 299, 304; Stark in 47 LA 91, 94–96; Meyers in 43 LA 102, 106; Stouffer in 41 LA 315, 317. On the other hand, where three employees claimed to be ill rather than participants in a "sick-out," Arbitrator William Ray Forrester stated that he was ruling in their favor "on the basis of the weight of the evidence rather than on a firm conviction that he knows the actual facts," and for this reason his award expressly provided that: "The records of these proceedings may be retained, or referred to, in the personnel record of each grievant so that the records will be available for consideration in the event any one of these grievants is involved in absenteeism in the future at a time when concerted job action of an illegal nature occurs, such as a 'sick-out.'" Federal Aviation Admin., 72 LA 761, 765 (1979). Also see Arbitrator Bell in 69 LA 682, 686. Concerning management's right to place material in employee personnel files and the right of employees to be apprised of and to have access to the file material, also see Chapter 14, subtopic entitled "Merit Rating Plans."

[150]For example, see Arbitrator Kanner in 69 LA 787, 789; Dybeck in 53 LA 124, 126 (employer was obviously penalized for submitting evidence in violation of such provision); Scheiber in 50 LA 487, 495 (such provision did not prevent consideration of *good* record prior to the limitations period); Kates in 48 LA 833, 834–835 (such provision was narrowly construed); Bradley in 47 LA 994, 999; Aaron in 10 LA 119, 128. As to a provision forbidding the "pyramiding" of penalties, see Arbitrator Shister in 52 LA 1263, 1266.

lent record in the Company's service, the Union is sure to emphasize this. No arbitrator can fail to take note of a good record, the absence of prior warning notice, and other factors which may pertain to the employee's fitness to be continued on his job.

"By the same token, if an employee's past performance has been one of increasing disregard of his responsibilities to his job and to the employer who is paying him, no arbitrator can rightly sweep this sort of evidence under the rug and confine himself to technical evidence pertaining to a particular incident on a particular day. To do so would not add to the cause of good industrial relations. It might do irreparable harm to the arbitration process.

"However, this does not mean that we are to consider everything that is introduced as having equal weight and significance. We sympathize with the position often taken by unions that there should be some limitation on how far back in the record one should be permitted to go in the matter of digging up old scores. Such historic incidents should be close enough in their relation to the problem involved in the immediate case to warrant consideration."[151]

Also emphasizing the need to consider an employee's past record, and rejecting a union request for a contractual clause to prohibit the employer or any arbitrator "from considering any previous warning notices and/or disciplinary actions which were issued more than 12 months prior to consideration of new disciplinary action," interest Arbitrator Stanley M. Block offered this explanation:

"As an experienced arbitrator, the undersigned feels that the proposal here made could seriously hamper the City's efforts to develop and maintain a workforce which is cooperative, dependable, and loyal to management and other employees. In an arbitration case, the Union always refers to the length of service of the Grievant as a factor deserving mercy. But if the arbitrator is not free to consider the *entire record* of an employee, he is unable to distinguish between a 10-year employee with a nearly perfect record and another 10-year employee with a very black record of violations and disciplines, holding onto his job only because the City and Arbitrator are barred from considering the constant repetitions of violations."[152]

Evidence of past acts showing a course of conduct has sometimes been considered relevant in some types of cases as indicating some likelihood that the employee committed the specific act with which he was charged.[153]

---

[151]Borg-Warner Corp., 22 LA 589, 596 (1954). Also regarding "digging up" past matters, see Arbitrator Reynolds in 17 LA 737, 740. In Consolidated Foods Corp., 43 LA 1143, 1148–1150 (Klein, 1964), reduced weight was given to discipline assessed before the union came to the plant. But in rejecting the union's contention that the employee's record prior to establishment of the bargaining unit should not be considered in Central Blood Bank of Pittsburgh, 69 LA 1031, 1036 (1977), Arbitrator Amis stated that the employee's "employment record will be considered and it will be given what weight it deserves"; and in fact that record was a significant factor in the decision.

[152]City of Quincy, Ill., 81 LA 352, 359 (1982).

[153]See Arbitrator Sweeney in 41 LA 1061, 1062; Pedrick in 12 LA 262, 264–265; Gorder in 3 LA 455; Wolff in 3 LA 285. Also see Koven in 48 LA 264, 267. But see Bowles in 69 LA 351, 356; Alexander in 46 LA 184, 186; Sembower in 30 LA 948, 950. For discussion, see Fleming, The Labor Arbitration Process, 168–170 (U. of Ill. Press, 1965); Wirtz, "Due Process of Arbitration," Proceedings of the 11th Annual Meeting of NAA, 1, 20–21 (BNA Books, 1958), noting that caution obviously should be exercised in using evidence of past acts for this purpose.

Length of Service With Company

Long service with the company, particularly if unblemished, is a definite factor in the employee's favor when his discharge is reviewed through arbitration.[154] Arbitrators have recognized that the loss of seniority may work great hardship on the employee,[155] and that it is not conducive to the improvement of relations between other workers and management.[156]

In one case the fact that a long-service employee was nearing eligibility for retirement was an additional factor in support of reinstatement,[157] but in another case the arbitrator refused to give weight to the fact of approaching retirement.[158]

Knowledge of Rules; Warnings

It has been reported, on the basis of examining over 1000 discharge cases, that one of the two most commonly recognized principles in arbitration of such cases is that there must be reasonable rules or standards, consistently applied and enforced and widely disseminated.[159] Concerning notice of rules, Arbitrator William M. Hepburn stated: "Just cause requires that employees be informed of a rule, infraction of which may result in suspension or discharge, unless conduct is so clearly wrong that specific reference is not necessary."[160] In the latter regard it has been held, for instance, that employees need not be notified of rules against threatening others with loaded firearms, for "Common sense alone would dictate that a weapon such as a

---

[154]For instances where this factor was given weight, see Arbitrator Boyer in 76 LA 1187, 1190; Abrams in 74 LA 847, 853; Gerber in 73 LA 1185, 1192; Heinsz in 71 LA 989, 992; Roumell in 71 LA 653, 658–659; Kanner in 69 LA 787, 789; Hershenfeld in 49 LA 1262, 1264; Abernethy in 47 LA 184, 192; Drake in 44 LA 234, 237; Prasow in 42 LA 408, 411; Altrock in 41 LA 460, 463–464; Gilden in 29 LA 464, 466; Dunlop in 28 LA 668, 672; Simkin in 24 LA 606, 609.

[155]See Arbitrator Roumell in 68 LA 1160, 1166; Kates in 46 LA 365, 368; Jones in 45 LA 972, 974–975; McCoy in 37 LA 704, 706; Simkin in 24 LA 606, 609; Shipman in 2 LA 194, 195–196.

[156]Argonne Worsted Co., 4 LA 81, 83 (Copelof, 1946). Nonetheless, even long service with the company will not save the job if other factors strongly justify discharge. See Arbitrator Odom in 79 LA 802, 807; Krimsly in 51 LA 745, 747; Porter in 47 LA 104, 105–106. Furthermore, in one case the arbitrator stated that better performance reasonably could have been expected of the grievant as a long-service employee, and thus that "this factor weighs against the Grievant as well as for him." Hayes-Albion Corp., 70 LA 696, 698 (Glendon, 1978). Similarly, see Arbitrator Johnson in 77 LA 1125, 1127.

[157]Brown & Bigelow Co., 44 LA 237, 241 (Graff, 1964).

[158]American Welding & Mfg. Co., 47 LA 457, 463 (Dworkin, 1966).

[159]"Arbitration Awards in Discharge Cases," 28 LA 930, 931–932 (1957).

[160]Lockheed Aircraft Corp., 28 LA 829, 831 (1957). For other cases requiring clear notice of rules and of the possible penalties for their violation (particularly where discharge is one of the penalties), see Arbitrator Dunn in 74 LA 33, 35; Rentfro in 72 LA 513, 516–517 (company's case was "flawed by failure to properly notify employees * * * that the instant offense meant outright discharge for first offenders"); Millious in 71 LA 802, 805 (stating that the employer "is under an obligation to properly notify all affected employees, not just Union officials"); Beck in 71 LA 314, 320; Witney in 48 LA 395, 399–400; Cahn in 48 LA 349, 350; Neville in 48 LA 120, 123; Autrey in 45 LA 117, 119; Maggs in 21 LA 676, 679; Reid in 21 LA 322, 325; Prasow in 5 LA 109, 111. For related material, see Chapter 13, subtopic entitled "Posting of Rules." In Phillips Petroleum Co., 47 LA 372, 374 (Caraway, 1966), the company was required to establish that the employee had actual knowledge of the rule he was charged with violating. In Metromedia, Inc., 46 LA 161, 165–167 (Dworkin, 1965), employees could be disciplined for refusing to sign a statement acknowledging receipt of a certain plant rule.

loaded firearm would not be permitted on the premises of any employer except in the possession of a duly authorized plant protection man."[161]

In regard to warnings, evidence as to whether warnings of unsatisfactory conduct were given prior to discharge or discipline generally is relevant in determining whether the penalty was justified.[162] Where an employee continues prohibited conduct after having been warned, the fact that he was warned stands against him.[163] In one case the employee had been warned repeatedly about leaving his place of duty, so discharge was upheld even though progressive discipline had not been used; the arbitrator said that the warnings had apprised the employee of the seriousness of his misconduct and that there was no reason to believe that "one more chance" would improve his conduct.[164] On the other hand, failure to give prior warnings may be one of the reasons for the refusal by an arbitrator to sustain disciplinary action (particularly discharge).[165]

Arbitrators have emphasized that no warning is required where the offense is legally and morally wrong.[166]

Lax Enforcement of Rules

Arbitrators have not hesitated to disturb penalties, assessed without clear and timely warning, where the employer over a period of time had condoned the violation of the rule in the past—lax enforcement of rules may lead employees reasonably to believe that the

---

[161]Brown & Williamson Tobacco Corp., 50 LA 403, 412 (Willingham, 1968). Also see Arbitrator Ross in 78 LA 1032, 1037; High in 76 LA 643, 648 (formal rule not required in order to make sleeping on the job an offense); Paradise in 74 LA 509, 511; Dworkin in 70 LA 1299, 1301; Keeler in 45 LA 437, 441 ("a Company does not have to establish that it had, or that it had communicated specific rules for certain well-recognized proven offenses such as drunkenness, theft, or insubordination"); Schmidt in 35 LA 293, 296. But see Forsythe in 68 LA 369, 374–375.

[162]Warnings ordinarily need not be in writing unless required by contract. See Glenn L. Martin Co., 6 LA 500, 507 (Brecht, 1947). Also see Arbitrator Modjeska in 72 LA 520, 522. Cf., Milentz in 80 LA 713, 716–717. Where the contract does require warnings to be written, the requirement may be firmly enforced. See Arbitrator Eaton in 53 LA 85, 87–88; Cantor in 46 LA 1041, 1044. In Covington Furniture Mfg. Corp., 75 LA 455, 456, 461–462 (Holley, 1980), the agreement specified that "Warning notices and reprimands shall be given to the employee in writing," but written warning was held not to be required for the "serious matter" of insubordination.

[163]See Arbitrator Modjeska in 72 LA 520, 522; Abernethy in 40 LA 582, 585–586; Scheiber in 9 LA 765, 766–767, 770; Bowles in 9 LA 447, 449.

[164]Potash Co. of Am., 40 LA 582, 585–586 (Abernethy, 1963). Similarly, see Arbitrator Nutt in 76 LA 1278, 1280. But see Greer Limestone Co., 40 LA 343, 349 (Lugar, 1963), where repeated warnings followed by repeated noncompliance without discipline was said to have lulled the employee into believing the warnings were not serious.

[165]See Arbitrator Brown in 56 LA 725, 727; Robertson in 56 LA 512, 514; Volz in 50 LA 600, 604; Teple in 48 LA 558, 562–563; Dunlop in 45 LA 535, 537; Wyckoff in 44 LA 552, 553; Spaulding in 39 LA 58, 63; Jones in 37 LA 520, 527–528; Dworkin in 35 LA 17, 23–24; Levy in 28 LA 65, 69; McCoy in 27 LA 160, 162; Wyckoff in 25 LA 634, 637; Marshall in 24 LA 555, 559. In Standard Shade Roller Div., 73 LA 86, 90 (undated), warning was given but Arbitrator William A. Dawson concluded (1) that insufficient time elapsed between the warning and discharge to have given the employee "opportunity for sober reflection," and (2) that the warning "was given too casually to qualify as a formal warning." Regarding the time element, also see Arbitrator Goetz in 78 LA 915, 919; regarding the "casual" quality, also see Anderson in 80 LA 13, 15, and Dallas in 70 LA 28, 32–33.

[166]Kroger Co., 50 LA 1194, 1198 (Abernethy, 1968); Glenn L. Martin Co., 27 LA 768, 772–773 (Jaffee, 1956).

conduct in question is sanctioned by management.[167] Of course, the employer must have known of the prior violations by employees in order to be held to have waived the right to punish an employee who is detected.[168] Another qualification is illustrated by an arbitrator's holding that past condonation of the taking of small quantities of scrap metal did not immunize the attempted theft of large quantities.[169]

Although previously having been lax, an employer can turn to strict enforcement after giving clear notice of the intent to do so.[170] Moreover, the arbitration of a case involving discharge for violation of a rule serves clear notice to the employees for the future that the particular type of misconduct is deemed by the employer to be a dischargeable offense.[171]

Unequal or Discriminatory Treatment

It is generally accepted that enforcement of rules and assessment of discipline must be exercised in a consistent manner; all employees who engage in the same type of misconduct must be treated essentially the same unless a reasonable basis exists for variations in the assessment of punishment (such as different degrees of fault or mitigating or aggravating circumstances affecting some but not all of the employees).[172] In this regard, Arbitrator Benjamin Aaron declared: "Abso-

---

[167]See Arbitrator Greco in 78 LA 129, 137; Kaufman in 75 LA 1081, 1086; LeWinter in 72 LA 1, 10–11; Hall in 70 LA 1066, 1072; Jacobs in 55 LA 1274, 1277; Springfield in 54 LA 281, 286; Kelliher in 53 LA 428, 429–430; Sembower in 52 LA 1296, 1300; Williams in 49 LA 210, 212; Somers in 48 LA 98, 100–101; Cantor in 46 LA 1041, 1043; Gross in 46 LA 882, 884; Volz in 46 LA 248, 251; Duff in 45 LA 538, 540; Larkin in 45 LA 517, 521; Dworkin in 40 LA 87, 90. But see Stouffer in 53 LA 45, 55–56. In Great Atl. & Pac. Tea Co., 77 LA 278, 283 (Seidenberg, 1981), employees had the impression that supervisors had been violating with impunity a rule against eating company merchandise, the employees not having been informed that the rule did not apply to supervisors; this appearance of laxity toward supervisors with respect to the rule led the arbitrator to reduce to suspension the discharge penalty which had been assessed against an employee for violating the rule.

[168]See Arbitrator Richman in 71 LA 954, 959; Laybourne in 71 LA 148, 151; Greenwald in 44 LA 921, 923. But where supervisors or other management representatives knew of rule violations in the past, their knowledge was imputed to the employer by Arbitrator Sloane in 71 LA 302, 306 (here the management representatives either knew or under the facts should have known of the past rule violations); Moore in 68 LA 1048, 1053; Dworkin in 40 LA 87, 90. For related discussion, see Chapter 10, topic entitled "Agency Principles."

[169]United States Steel Corp., 48 LA 1114, 1118 (Mittenthal, 1967). In Hilo Coast Processing Co., 74 LA 236, 240 (1980), Arbitrator Tamotsu Tanaka stated that the grievant's offense was so serious that "it would be unreasonable for any employee to believe" it to be one of "those types of acts which would ever be condoned by management."

[170]See Arbitrator Doering in 70 LA 667, 669; Dyke in 48 LA 681, 683; Fisher in 47 LA 224, 226.

[171]Universal Match Corp., 42 LA 184, 186 (Coffey, 1963). In Grand Rapids Die Casting Corp., 63 LA 995, 996 (1974), Arbitrator M. David Keefe concluded that for the purpose of establishing order out of chaos in the plant, his award would order (1) that the employer must clear all employee records of all disciplinary entries prior to the date of his award, and (2) that thereafter the employees shall have a responsibility to obey the employer's plant rules and the employer shall have a responsibility to actively enforce them. Regarding management's responsibility to maintain order, also see statement by Arbitrator Edmund A. Cyrol in F S Servs., 73 LA 610, 614 (1979).

[172]Arbitrators have frequently refused to uphold variations in punishment where not supported by reasonable basis. For many cases see page 644 of the Third Edition of this book. For later cases, see Arbitrator Galambos in 80 LA 1283, 1286; Bard in 80 LA 1161, 1171; Woolf in 80 LA 969, 980; Milentz in 80 LA 344, 351; Gould in 78 LA 1109, 1112; Conner in 78 LA 644, 647; Tsukiyama in 78 LA 592, 597; Shanker in 77 LA 289, 295 (stating that "even assuming that a Company should be permitted to exercise discretion to give favored treatment to one employee in order to assure his full cooperation and truthful testimony, nevertheless * * * the discrepancy

lute consistency in the handling of rule violations is, of course, an impossibility, but that fact should not excuse random and completely inconsistent disciplinary practices."[173]

Where reasonable basis for variations in penalties does exist, they will be permitted notwithstanding the charge of disparate treatment.[174] That variations in penalties assessed do not necessarily mean that management's action has been improper or discriminatory was persuasively elaborated by Arbitrator J. Charles Short:

> "The term 'discrimination' connotes a distinction in treatment, especially an unfair distinction. The prohibition against discrimination requires like treatment under like circumstances. In the case of offenses the circumstances include the nature of the offense, the degree of fault and the mitigating and aggravating factors. There is no discrimination, or no departure from the consistent or uniform treatment of employees, merely because of variations in discipline reasonably appropriate to the variations in circumstances. Two employees may refuse a work assignment. For one it is his first offense, there being no prior warning or misconduct standing against his record. The other has been warned and disciplined for the very same offense on numerous occasions. It cannot be seriously contended that discrimination results if identical penalties are not meted out."[175]

Particularly in cases involving illicit strikes or slowdowns, management may vary discipline on the basis of the degree of fault and is not required to assess uniform punishment against all participants; also, management may punish those who bear greater fault while not punishing other participants at all.[176] Nor is management prohibited

---

between the handling of Helper and the Grievant in this case is too wide to be permitted"); Brooks in 75 LA 478, 485; Watkins in 72 LA 975, 981; Grabb in 72 LA 486, 490; Daniel in 69 LA 424, 426; Kaufman in 69 LA 62, 63; Dunsford in 69 LA 39, 43–44; Warren in 68 LA 693, 697. But see Cahn in 28 LA 355, 356. In Lukens Steel Co., 42 LA 849, 850 (1964), Arbitrator Donald A. Crawford recognized that discipline of supervisors "is the sole prerogative" of management, but the failure to punish a supervisor as severely for similar misconduct was a factor in ordering reinstatement of a discharged employee. Also see Arbitrator Roberts in 70 LA 278, 283–284. In John Deere Tractor Co., 9 LA 73, 77 (Gorder, 1947), the power of leniency was recognized in management "if the leniency shown is not for sinister, malicious, or discriminatory purposes." For related discussion, see subtopic entitled "Leniency," above.

[173]Aaron, "The Uses of the Past in Arbitration," Arbitration Today, 1, 10 (BNA Books, 1955). Also see Arbitrator Sisk in 48 LA 1286, 1290; Simkin in 26 LA 836, 844.

[174]See Arbitrator Mayer in 78 LA 1012, 1016; Gray in 76 LA 1251, 1253; Robins in 73 LA 1048, 1049 (stating that the "Union talks of inequitable treatment, but nothing can be more inequitable than to ignore an employee's length of service, past record with the employer or prior disciplinary record"); Silver in 72 LA 626, 628; Foster in 71 LA 779, 781; Barsamian in 67 LA 45, 51; Larkin in 49 LA 1253, 1256–1257; Block in 48 LA 1118, 1120; Teple in 46 LA 265, 273; Porter in 45 LA 1007, 1009; Small in 45 LA 257, 258, Pedrick in 15 LA 308, 313. Many other instances are cited hereinbelow in the discussion of penalties for illicit work stoppages.

[175]Alan Wood Steel Co., 21 LA 843, 849 (1954). Regarding Arbitrator Short's reference to "variations in discipline reasonably appropriate to the variations in circumstances," also see Keenan in 78 LA 516, 527, stating that "an essentially proportionate relationship must be maintained."

[176]See Arbitrator Laybourne in 74 LA 748, 751–752; McDonald in 73 LA 9, 12; Madden in 71 LA 555, 559, 565–566; Murphy in 56 LA 880, 882; McDermott in 56 LA 340, 348; Holly in 55 LA 667, 670; Oppenheim in 52 LA 1047, 1049–1050; Turkus in 51 LA 1228, 1235; Altrock in 48 LA 1224, 1227; Roberts in 48 LA 855, 860–861; Krimsly in 48 LA 257, 261–263 (employer can classify degrees of participation and punish different employees on that basis); Hilpert in 47 LA 129, 137; Malkin in 46 LA 982, 984; Duff in 46 LA 120, 124; Stouffer in 45 LA 943, 952–954 (employer may select certain strikers for discipline if basis for selection is reasonable); Autrey in 45 LA 585, 589–590; Wolff in 42 LA 951, 953; Pollack in 42 LA 142, 143–144 (employer may discharge strike leaders and need not prove extent of leadership); Markowitz in 41 LA 732, 735–736; Kelliher in 41 LA 110, 112; Schedler in 40 LA 1209, 1211; Davey in 38 LA 1144, 1148–1149; Pigors in 37 LA 977,

from punishing the known leaders of a stoppage or those employees detected in overt activities in connection with the stoppage merely because the company is unable to identify other participants who may have been equally guilty.[177]

Arbitrators have emphasized that in illicit strike or slowdown situations the company need not deprive itself of the services of all participants but may use selective discipline on the basis of relative fault.[178] Arbitrator Marlin M. Volz commented about this:

> "[I]t is unreasonable to require a Company to discharge all the workers participating in a slowdown and thereby lose its experienced work force when selective disciplinary action against one or more key leaders of the slowdown will restore production."[179]

Where all employees on a given shift refused to perform certain work it was held that management was not required to punish all equally if doing so would impair production. In permitting management to order individual employees to perform the work and to send them home for refusing, Arbitrator Louis Yagoda explained:

> "It is my opinion that management is not under an obligation to apply equal punishment to all transgressors, if to do so would cause injury to the operations. Discrimination may be validly charged only when there is either [a] a demonstrated inconsistency of posture towards the violations and the violators (such as is present when management tolerates, condones or ignores a series of mis-acts by some and then punishes others for committing the same improprieties); or [b] when the Employer is responding to an improper ulterior motive or animus, using the alleged wrongdoing as a pretext or subterfuge."[180]

980; Volz in 37 LA 401, 406; Horlacher in 36 LA 660, 663–664 (union declined to identify the strike leaders and employer used fairest method available in selecting employees for discipline); Teple in 33 LA 194, 198 (employer not permitted to "pick and choose" but could single out for punishment those who had lead roles); Smith in 25 LA 663, 674; Short in 21 LA 843, 849–850; Updegraff in 19 LA 601, 602; Morrissey in 15 LA 829, 830; Wirtz in 13 LA 610, 613. Many arbitrators, including some of those just cited, have recognized that union leaders have a special responsibility to promote use of the grievance procedure in lieu of self-help. For discussion of this special responsibility, along with discussion of the important question whether failure to fulfill the responsibility is proper basis for discipline or for variations in discipline (both under the collective agreement as viewed by arbitrators and under the NLRA), see Chapter 5, subtopic entitled "Use of Grievance Procedure v. Self-Help."

[177]See Arbitrator Scheiber in 50 LA 487, 494 (it is inevitable that some of the guilty "get away with it"); Garrett in 50 LA 472, 475–476; Crawford in 49 LA 383, 388; Wallen in 41 LA 1240, 1244.

[178]See Arbitrator Turkus in 51 LA 1228, 1235; Malkin in 46 LA 982, 984; Stouffer in 45 LA 943, 953; Horlacher in 36 LA 660, 663 (to require a uniform penalty against all strikers would make a nullity of the no-strike clause). Also, as a means of protecting itself management is permitted to stagger suspensions, for it cannot be expected to suspend all guilty employees for the same period and thus make a shutdown of operations the price for taking disciplinary action. United States Steel Corp., 40 LA 598, 600 (Seitz, 1963); Bethlehem Steel Co., 39 LA 686, 688 (Valtin, 1962).

[179]American Radiator & Standard Sanitary Corp., 37 LA 401, 406 (1961). Even where the agreement provided that disciplinary action taken against employees for illicit strike "shall be applied with equality and impartiality to all employees," management could punish those who had greater part in the strike although not punishing all participants. Drake Mfg. Co., 41 LA 732, 735–736 (Markowitz, 1963).

[180]Interchemical Corp., 48 LA 124, 131 (1967). Cf., Arbitrator McCoy in 37 LA 593, 598–599. In United States Steel Corp., 49 LA 1236, 1241–1242 (McDermott, 1968), management could punish those employees who engaged in slowdown after formal warning had been given while not punishing violators prior to the warning, the arbitrator stating that management was engaged in a rational plan to halt the slowdown. In Midland Ross Corp., 65 LA 1151, 1154 (Dallas, 1975), the employer's imposition of a more severe penalty for succeeding incidents involving a dangerous form of horseplay was held justified as a means of stopping the activity.

Finally, it may be noted that arbitrators themselves have sometimes reduced the penalties of some employees where management had assessed uniform discipline against all participants but where the arbitrator found different degrees of fault.[181] In one such case Arbitrator Sylvester Garrett stated that "equality of penalties does not represent equal justice" where management assessed identical penalties against the victim as well as the aggressor in a fight.[182]

Charges of Antiunion Discrimination

One arbitrator stated that a charge of discrimination because of union activities cannot rest upon mere "surmise, inference or conjecture."[183] Numerous other arbitrators appear to agree, requiring clear proof to sustain such charges.[184]

However, Arbitrator Ted T. Tsukiyama cautioned that arbitrators have an obligation to examine the evidence with special care where antiunion animus may be involved:

"Whenever an employee who holds a high union office is discharged, there is always raised the question of a real possibility that the discharge is discriminatory or undertaken in bad faith, that the Company is ridding itself of a zealous unionist under the guise of 'just cause' discharge. In these cases, the arbitrator is obliged to make a thorough search and examination of the entire record to ascertain and satisfy

---

[181]See Arbitrator Garrett in 51 LA 546, 548; Kates in 36 LA 857, 859–860; McIntosh in 36 LA 280, 285–286.

[182]United States Steel Corp., 51 LA 546, 548 (1968). In upholding the different penalties assessed by management against fight participants Arbitrator Block commented: "The wisdom of a rule calling for identical penalties to all employees involved in a fight, without regard to culpability, is certainly open to question." Kaiser Steel Corp., 48 LA 1118, 1120 (1967).

[183]New York Racing Assn., 43 LA 129, 135 (Scheiber, 1964). Similarly, see Arbitrator Guenther in 73 LA 651, 654; Willingham in 49 LA 509, 511.

[184]See Arbitrator Nelson in 81 LA 318, 324 (stating that to support a charge of antiunion discrimination "there must be evidence and/or powerful inferences reasonably drawn from the evidence); Armstrong in 77 LA 849, 852 (stating that a charge of antiunion discrimination "requires clear proof," and that such proof existed in the statement of grievant's supervisor that he was mad because grievant went to the union and that he intended to harass grievant "right out of here"); Hearne in 77 LA 32, 37 (the charge of antiunion discrimination "was based on unsupported hearsay"); O'Connell in 72 LA 175, 179 (mere "coincidence" of discipline and assumption of union office, "standing alone," is insufficient to establish antiunion discrimination); Comey in 71 LA 977, 978, 980; Gentile in 71 LA 762, 769; Kossoff in 67 LA 1230, 1233–1234; Kotin in 49 LA 731, 735 (sharp conflicts in negotiations and a strike do not by themselves constitute prima facie evidence of subsequent discrimination in treatment of union leader); Livengood in 45 LA 495, 498 (that grievant was an active union member is not enough to make out a case of antiunion discrimination); Dworet in 43 LA 1070, 1072; McNaughton in 43 LA 529, 537; Davis in 42 LA 710, 712; Gilden in 39 LA 1131, 1134; Berkowitz in 38 LA 705, 708; McCoy in 33 LA 206, 207, and in 1 LA 447, 448–449; Carmody in 23 LA 38, 39; Maggs in 21 LA 676, 678; Bailer in 20 LA 7, 9; Doyle in 19 LA 111, 122; Scarborough in 2 LA 520, 521. Cf., comments of Arbitrator Lipson in 79 LA 1035, 1040; Ruben in 73 LA 335, 341–342; Remington in 69 LA 1157, 1158–1159; Kamin in 55 LA 118, 129; Wallen in 48 LA 19, 23; Block in 44 LA 889, 895, in which cases the arbitrator found either that antiunion animus caused or that it contributed to management's action against the employee. In the latter regard it may be noted that in NLRB v. Transp. Management Corp., 103 S.Ct. 2469, 2473-2475, 113 LRRM 2857 (1983), the U.S. Supreme Court upheld, as an "at least permissible" construction of the NLRA, the NLRB's 1980 *Wright Line* rule for cases involving "mixed motives." Under this rule the NLRB General Counsel has the burden of proving that protected conduct was "a substantial or motivating factor" in the discharge; if this burden is met the discharge will be held to violate the Act unless the employer proves as an affirmative defense that the employee would have been discharged for other (valid) reasons even if the protected conduct had not been involved.

himself that Management has not violated the collective bargaining agreement in this manner."[185]

Management Also at Fault

Where an employee is guilty of wrongdoing but management (ordinarily the supervisor) is also at fault in some respect in connection with the employee's conduct, the arbitrator may be persuaded to reduce or set aside the penalty assessed by management.[186] However, the mere fact that a supervisor was not entirely without fault in an incident was held not to excuse or justify physical assault by an employee, so the employee's discharge was sustained.[187]

Arbitral Remedies in Discharge and Discipline Cases

The more common remedies utilized by arbitrators in upsetting managerial actions in discharge and discipline cases have been summarized previously by the Authors as follows:[188] If a penalty of discharge is upset through arbitration, the award often will order reinstatement either with back pay, without back pay, or with partial back pay, and often will further order that other rights and privileges shall remain unimpaired; or the discharge may be commuted to suspension for a specified period, or even to a reduced penalty of only a reprimand or warning. Where a penalty of suspension assessed by management is upset through arbitration, the award usually will either void the suspension completely (sometimes substituting a reprimand or warning), or will simply reduce the length of time the employee is to be deemed suspended—in either event back pay will be ordered consistent with the shortened or eliminated period of suspension.

There are other remedies which, by comparison with those just noted, are less frequently used (some only rarely). Some of these variations in arbitral remedies are:

   a. *Loss of seniority*. Some employees have been ordered reinstated on the basis that they not be credited with any seniority

---

[185]Arden Farms Co., 45 LA 1124, 1130 (1965), where the charge of antiunion motivation was found to be without substance. For a similar statement as to an arbitrator's obligation, see Arbitrator Wallen in 48 LA 19, 23.

[186]Many cases are cited at p. 647 of the Third Edition of this book. For later cases see Arbitrator Muessig in 81 LA 1051, 1054; Kossoff in 76 LA 300, 307–308; Maloney in 75 LA 747, 750; McDonnell in 74 LA 875, 877; Seidenberg in 73 LA 535, 538; Randall in 71 LA 70, 73; Nicholas in 69 LA 1084, 1088; Smoot in 69 LA 671, 673–674; Draznin in 69 LA 191, 192–193; Kornblum in 68 LA 223, 225. But see Schmidt in 52 LA 1019, 1022.

[187]Gerber Prods. Co., 46 LA 956, 959 (Howlett, 1966).

[188]Elkouri & Elkouri, "Arbitral Review of Discipline: Variations in Penalties," Symposium on Labor Relations Law, 458 at 458 (Symposium edited by Ralph Slovenko and published by Claitor's Bookstore, 1961). The commonly utilized remedies are encountered in many of the cases listed in the present Chapter's Table of Offenses, below.

for the period between discharge and reinstatement.[189] Loss of some seniority that had accrued prior to the discharge is also a possibility.[190]

b. *Loss of other benefits under the agreement.* In denying seniority credit for the period between discharge and reinstatement, arbitrators often have prohibited the accumulation of other agreement-provided benefits during said period.[191]

c. *Probation or final warning.* Some discharged employees have been reinstated on a probationary basis (the probation conditions varying from award to award and the probationary periods often ranging from 1 to 12 months),[192] or with a final warning that any repetition of the offense will justify immediate discharge.[193]

d. *Reinstatement conditioned upon some special act or promise by employee.* Reinstatement has been ordered on the condition that the employee resign his outside job,[194] that he furnish an indemnity bond required by the employer,[195] that he sign an agreement by which he promises to apply and comply consci-

---

[189]Many cases are cited at p. 648 of the Third Edition of this book. For later cases, see Arbitrator Ruben in 80 LA 815, 825; Dobry in 80 LA 321, 326; Weizenbaum in 79 LA 977, 978; Sloane in 79 LA 689, 693; Winton in 79 LA 76, 79; Daniel in 76 LA 379, 386; Hart in 74 LA 953, 958; Wyman in 71 LA 1090, 1095; Kates in 71 LA 1082, 1084; Ross in 71 LA 710, 716; Bailey in 71 LA 538, 543; G. Smith in 71 LA 452, 454; Gorsuch in 70 LA 1036, 1041; Marcus in 68 LA 1300, 1305; Krislov in 68 LA 72, 75; LaCugna in 68 LA 66, 67; J. Smith in 65 LA 1177, 1182. In Warner & Swasey Co., 71 LA 158, 161 (Siegel, 1978), the employee lost seniority but it could be regained by meeting a specified condition. Under a strike settlement agreement in Reden Corp., 50 LA 413, 414 (Roberts, 1968), economic strikers did not acquire any seniority for the period of the strike.

[190]See Arbitrator Copelof in 19 LA 437, 439; Hilpert in 10 LA 324, 335; Cheney in 6 LA 211, 213. Also see Merrill in 21 LA 560, 565. Cf., Jaffee in 15 LA 715, 725. Contra, Kelliher in 30 LA 519, 527. Temporary loss of accrued seniority was ordered in Pennsylvania Greyhound Lines, 3 LA 880, 884 (Brandschain, 1946).

[191]Arbitrators cited in note 189 above who did this are Ruben, Dobry, Sloane, Winton, Daniel, Wyman, Kates, Ross, Bailey, G. Smith, Gorsuch, Marcus, and J. Smith, as did Arbitrator Hunter in 79 LA 640, 645; Schedler in 32 LA 677, 680; Wolff in 24 LA 549, 554, and in 19 LA 221, 231. Cf., Fearing in 9 LA 505, 509.

[192]See Arbitrator Abrams in 81 LA 333, 338; Dobry in 80 LA 321, 326; Morgan in 74 LA 208, 210; Carter in 73 LA 817, 819; Fogelberg in 71 LA 445, 449; Smoot in 69 LA 671, 674; Roumell in 68 LA 1160, 1166–1167; Mullin in 45 LA 560, 565; Kelliher in 30 LA 519, 528; Simkin in 24 LA 606, 610; Lehoczky in 17 LA 283, 285; Copelof in 15 LA 505, 509; Komaroff in 12 LA 233, 238; Scheiber in 10 LA 57, 61; Wardlaw in 8 LA 248, 250; Pollard in 8 LA 234, 245; Cole in 6 LA 958, 960; Updegraff in 3 LA 242, 245. Probationary reinstatement also has been ordered for employees discharged for subnormal production. See Arbitrator Lehoczky in 27 LA 55, 57; Updegraff in 7 LA 191, 195.

[193]See Arbitrator Hart in 74 LA 953, 958; Gerber in 73 LA 1185, 1193; Foster in 73 LA 819, 825; Bothwell in 72 LA 350, 351; Hall in 70 LA 1066, 1073; Draznin in 69 LA 939, 941; Seidenberg in 69 LA 884, 887; Kornblum in 69 LA 344, 351; Harkless in 68 LA 1245, 1248; Seinsheimer in 53 LA 1197, 1202–1203; Gordinier in 52 LA 731, 733; Cahn in 44 LA 1043, 1044; Kesselman in 44 LA 289, 294. In General Elec. Co., 32 LA 637, 640 (LaCugna, 1959), an employee who had been discharged for absenteeism was reinstated on the condition that the employer could discharge her should she be absent more than 20 working days in any succeeding year. Where parties had agreed to reinstatement of an employee on probation or with a final warning, such agreement was strictly enforced (i.e., subsequent discharge for breach of the probation or final warning conditions was sustained) by Arbitrator Blum in 79 LA 34, 36; Randall in 73 LA 956, 958; Dash in 73 LA 896, 898–899; Burwell in 69 LA 589, 594.

[194]Kansas City Star Co., 12 LA 1202, 1206 (Ridge, 1949). Also see John Deere Tractor Co., 4 LA 161, 163, 166 (Updegraff, 1946).

[195]Robert Hall Clothes, 50 LA 840, 845 (Davis, 1968).

entiously with company safety rules,[196] that he reduce his weight from 340 to 215 pounds and quit smoking cigarettes,[197] that he accept counseling from his pastor or some competent social agency,[198] or that the employee comply with some other specified condition.[199]

e. *Written waiver required.* Where the collective agreement arguably might have required back pay in the event of reinstatement after discharge, a condition to reinstatement was imposed in the form of a requirement that the employee agree in writing to waive back pay.[200]

f. *Reinstatement conditioned upon proof of mental or physical fitness.* Employees discharged for misconduct somehow connected with physical or psychological disability sometimes have been ordered reinstated on the condition that they be physically and/or mentally fit for the job as determined by physicians or psychiatrists, as the case may be.[201]

g. *Reinstatement conditioned upon the employee's not holding union office.* Under the circumstances of some cases the arbitrator has concluded that the discharged employee should be reinstated, but only on the condition that he not hold union office for a stated period (in some cases the disqualification was to be permanent).[202]

---

[196]Bunker Hill Co., 43 LA 1253, 1256 (Luckerath, 1964). Also see Arbitrator Rutherford in 71 LA 22, 27. In International Harvester Co., 53 LA 1197, 1202–1203 (Seinsheimer, 1969), the condition required two employees to sign an agreement stating that they would not threaten or molest each other or any other employee, and that violation of the agreement would subject them to immediate discharge.

[197]Taystee Bread Co., 52 LA 677, 680 (Purdom, 1969), where the arbitrator was given broad latitude as to the remedy. Also see Arbitrator Bothwell in 71 LA 1099, 1102.

[198]Charleston Naval Shipyard, 54 LA 145, 151 (Kesselman, 1970).

[199]See Arbitrator Ruben in 80 LA 815, 825 (must sign payroll deduction authorization enabling employer to recoup sum received by employee without right); Meyers in 80 LA 663, 669 (must successfully complete rehabilitation program); Miller in 80 LA 646, 648 (must attend special training course); Herrick in 76 LA 417, 420 (must successfully complete rehabilitation program); Rehmus in 68 LA 171, 177 (must state willingness to work full shifts as scheduled when needed for essential production—the employer had made reasonable accommodation for the employee's religious observances but she had been absent additionally to attend bible study meeting).

[200]International Harvester Co., 2 LA 158, 163 (Gilden, 1946). To similar effect is an award by Arbitrator Kelliher subsequently cited and quoted by him in Lone Star Steel Co., 30 LA 519, 528 (1958). For other attached conditions in the general nature of a waiver, see Arbitrator McAllister in 78 LA 836, 842 (employee must affirm in writing his understanding that the award holds that a certain work procedure is not unsafe); Roumell in 70 LA 614, 620 (reinstatement was conditioned upon retention of information in the employee's file for a longer period than permitted by the literal language of the agreement); Kornblum in 69 LA 344, 350–351 (employee must waive in writing his right as a peace officer to carry firearms while off duty).

[201]See Arbitrator Ruben in 80 LA 815, 824–825; Martin in 77 LA 123, 127–128; Daniel in 76 LA 753, 757–758; Howlett in 72 LA 1065, 1069; Keefe in 48 LA 1369, 1372–1374; Sembower in 46 LA 1014, 1018; Solomon in 42 LA 1, 14; Wallen in 33 LA 788, 791; Stouffer in 32 LA 686, 689–690; Wolff in 26 LA 295, 300. Also see Schedler in 32 LA 677, 680; Pollard in 19 LA 405, 408. Sometimes reinstatement has been similarly conditioned where the employee had been discharged for alleged physical disability (see Arbitrator Teple in 53 LA 334, 338) or for poor workmanship connected with the employee's physical condition (see Arbitrator Kates in 46 LA 365, 368–369).

[202]See Arbitrator Shime in 66 LA 812, 818; Crowley in 54 LA 488, 492; McGury in 46 LA 220, 224; Hayes in 33 LA 103, 107–108; Phelps in 32 LA 690, 695 (the award was modified by a state court in 33 LA 292, 293, by striking the condition against holding union office); Miller in 10 LA

h. *Reinstatement to a different job.* In disciplinary discharge cases where the arbitrator concludes that the grievant should be reinstated but that some strong reason exists for denying him his former job (such reason may involve his physical condition, or a need to screen him from contacts with the public, or personality conflicts, or the like), reinstatement may be ordered to some other job which does not involve the conditions or impediments that disqualify him for his former job.[203] In one case an employee who had been discharged for engaging in a slowdown was ordered reinstated but with the proviso that the company could place him on any job it might wish.[204]

i. *Other variations in remedies.* Yet other infrequently used remedies have been tailored by arbitrators to fit the circumstances of the particular discharge or discipline case. Some of these variations include forced apologies,[205] unrecorded suspension,[206] and treating the grievant's mental anguish as a penalty.[207]

Table of Offenses

Many types of conduct have been the "just cause" basis of industrial discipline—discharge or a lesser penalty. Detailed analysis of each individual type of conduct is beyond the scope of this volume.[208] However, to review the more usual grounds for industrial discipline,

79, 83; Klamon in 7 LA 422, 424; Whiting in 6 LA 965, 968. In Kankakee Elec. Steel Co., 53 LA 178, 184 (1969), Arbitrator Sembower stated that he lacked authority to tell the union whom it might choose as representatives but he did "recommend that the Grievant not be given further duties as a grievanceman." Arbitrator Dudley E. Whiting twice imposed the disqualification from holding union office, once for which he was commended and once for which he was castigated. See comments of Arbitrator Whiting in discussion of the remedy power, Proceedings of the 16th Annual Meeting of NAA, 70, 73 (BNA Books, 1963). Use of this remedy is questioned by Crane, "The Use and Abuse of Arbitral Power," Proceedings of the 25th Annual Meeting of NAA, 66, 75 (BNA Books, 1973); Kearns, "Comment," id. at 88–89.

[203]See Arbitrator Gershenfeld in 49 LA 606, 608; Dworkin in 47 LA 457, 463, in 40 LA 1054, 1058–1060 (personality conflicts), and in 36 LA 491, 495; Keefe in 45 LA 986, 989–990; Tsukiyama in 44 LA 218, 222–223; Stix in 43 LA 824, 825 (discharge converted to suspension and leave of absence until a vacancy occurs in a job which would be proper for grievant); Leary in 10 LA 814, 817–818. Also see Brown in 69 LA 555, 563. Cf., Mueller in 36 LA 965, 969. In ordering reinstatement in Corns Truck & Tractor, 63 LA 828, 831 (Cowan, 1974), the Arbitrator specified that the grievant be "demoted" to the next lower classification. For related material see Chapter 13, topic entitled "Demotion of Employees."

[204]Dirilyte Co. of Am., 18 LA 882, 884 (Ferguson, 1952). Cf., Arbitrator Ralston in 18 LA 544, 548–550.

[205]See Arbitrator Winton in 79 LA 76, 79; LaCugna in 78 LA 780, 783; Rezler in 75 LA 819, 822; Erbs in 59 LA 1147, 1150; Rauch in 20 LA 823, 826; Kramer in 19 LA 475, 481–482. But some arbitrators have spoken strongly against forced apologies. See Arbitrator Jensen in 38 LA 781, 784; Dworet in 35 LA 381, 383; Klamon in 22 LA 528, 534. Also see Imundo in 81 LA 201, 213–214; Aronin in 80 LA 46, 53.

[206]Fort Pitt Bridge Works, 30 LA 633, 635 (Lehoczky, 1958), in which suspension was upheld but all reference to it was ordered striken from the employees' personnel records. Also see Ironite Inc., 28 LA 394, 398 (Haughton, 1956).

[207]Dayton Steel Foundry Co., 29 LA 137, 142 (Young, 1957); Ashland Oil & Ref. Co., 28 LA 874, 878–879 (Bradley, 1957).

[208]Such detailed analysis is provided by Redeker, Discipline: Policies and Procedures (BNA Books, 1983); Stessin, Employee Discipline (BNA Books, 1960).

and to make numerous cases quickly available to the reader, the following table is offered. Two considerations should be emphasized. First, in some cases the arbitrator considers the misconduct sufficiently serious to justify the employer in discharging for the first offense and even in the face of mitigating circumstances. Second, in the vast majority of cases there is no such "automatic" basis for discharge; in these cases all factors relevant to industrial discipline may be considered by the arbitrator in determining whether the employee deserved discharge, some lesser penalty, or no penalty at all—each case is thus decided largely on the basis of its own facts and circumstances.

Included in the table are selected cases. Some of the cases were selected because they discuss one or more of the following: elements of the offense, proof or evidence required, mitigating or aggravating factors. Some were selected because they are especially thoroughly reasoned and/or cite numerous other cases involving the same type of offense. Still other cases were selected because they are relevant to the possible scope of the offense, or because they contain some other aspect of special interest. On the other hand, cases sometimes were selected without regard to the above factors, there being relatively few reported cases on the offense or for the given column in the table. Finally, *it is emphasized that these tables include only a part of the many relevant and useful cases* that have been published in the arbitration reports.

Table of Offenses

Offense	Discharge Upheld	Lesser Penalty Upheld (as assessed by employer)	Penalty Reduced by Arbitrator	No Penalty Permitted
Absenteeism[a]	81 LA 403	74 LA 205	81 LA 333	81 LA 56
	80 LA 1286	73 LA 1279	80 LA 286	79 LA 433
	80 LA 1086	73 LA 649	77 LA 1049	77 LA 889
	80 LA 735	67 LA 1	77 LA 585	
	80 LA 365	66 LA 1317	77 LA 28	
	79 LA 837	66 LA 674	76 LA 160	
	79 LA 299	65 LA 919	74 LA 847	
	78 LA 1323	64 LA 1283	73 LA 1193	
	78 LA 673	62 LA 280	72 LA 1285	
	78 LA 233	61 LA 464	72 LA 809	
	77 LA 146		72 LA 541	
	74 LA 641		72 LA 350	
	74 LA 623		72 LA 1	
	74 LA 531		71 LA 653	
	71 LA 919		71 LA 195	
	71 LA 737		71 LA 1	

[a]Earlier "absenteeism" cases are similarly charted at p. 652 of the Third Edition of this book. For related material, see Chapter 13 of the present edition, subtopic entitled "Excessive Absences Due to Illness."

TABLE OF OFFENSES—CONT'D.

Offense	Discharge Upheld	Lesser Penalty Upheld (as assessed by employer)	Penalty Reduced by Arbitrator	No Penalty Permitted
Absenteeism, cont'd.	69 LA 1123 69 LA 388 69 LA 128 63 LA 618 62 LA 882 61 LA 464		63 LA 1315 62 LA 779	
Tardiness[b]	81 LA 297 78 LA 809 77 LA 947 74 LA 290 65 LA 1028 62 LA 882 59 LA 1235 58 LA 303	76 LA 1066 72 LA 1266 66 LA 127 63 LA 739	80 LA 1021 80 LA 797 78 LA 1165 76 LA 994 72 LA 510 71 LA 828 67 LA 1047 66 LA 127	80 LA 720 71 LA 802 71 LA 744 69 LA 145 66 LA 1245 63 LA 54 61 LA 125
Loafing[b]	81 LA 816 72 LA 211	73 LA 1092 64 LA 91	77 LA 443 71 LA 710 71 LA 1 65 LA 1122 64 LA 77 63 LA 1135	74 LA 365 71 LA 1041 62 LA 1195
Absence From Work[b]	81 LA 259 81 LA 243 81 LA 56 80 LA 513 79 LA 802 76 LA 958 74 LA 1185 74 LA 362 74 LA 37 73 LA 1159 73 LA 651 72 LA 1217 72 LA 133 70 LA 963 70 LA 696 70 LA 651 69 LA 170 66 LA 1071 66 LA 933 63 LA 1262 62 LA 958 62 LA 245 61 LA 1	81 LA 564 69 LA 325 67 LA 431 66 LA 674 62 LA 280	74 LA 860 72 LA 1262 72 LA 531 72 LA 133 71 LA 70 69 LA 193 68 LA 651 64 LA 1274 62 LA 1023 62 LA 616 62 LA 245	80 LA 1124 79 LA 1320 79 LA 911 79 LA 433 77 LA 889 75 LA 1040 69 LA 191 66 LA 239 64 LA 940

[b]Earlier "tardiness" and "loafing" cases are similarly charted at p. 652 of the Third Edition of this book, "absence from work" cases at 653.

Table of Offenses—cont'd.

Offense	Discharge Upheld	Lesser Penalty Upheld (as assessed by employer)	Penalty Reduced by Arbitrator	No Penalty Permitted
Leaving Post (Includes early quitting)c	81 LA 241	75 LA 1051	78 LA 956	79 LA 697
	81 LA 198	75 LA 847	78 LA 915	77 LA 1069
	79 LA 539	73 LA 141	78 LA 857	76 LA 1139
	78 LA 320	72 LA 536	77 LA 838	75 LA 805
	76 LA 723	71 LA 771	77 LA 478	75 LA 722
	76 LA 62	69 LA 831	76 LA 994	74 LA 359
	74 LA 481	67 LA 690	75 LA 122	64 LA 1216
	73 LA 1256		74 LA 137	
	68 LA 171		73 LA 641	
	67 LA 346		73 LA 578	
	65 LA 1200		70 LA 600	
	64 LA 595		70 LA 458	
	63 LA 157		70 LA 278	
			69 LA 792	
			62 LA 917	
			61 LA 389	
Sleeping on Jobc	80 LA 1313	76 LA 18	72 LA 1230	81 LA 1009
	79 LA 738	69 LA 901	66 LA 702	80 LA 1
	79 LA 732		64 LA 734	78 LA 893
	78 LA 978		61 LA 686	77 LA 1200
	77 LA 1143			71 LA 1041
	76 LA 643			69 LA 721
	76 LA 232			
	74 LA 115			
	73 LA 705			
	72 LA 1275			
	72 LA 1006			
	70 LA 121			
Assault and Fighting Among Employeesc	79 LA 1259	78 LA 148	80 LA 742	79 LA 847
	79 LA 650	75 LA 258	80 LA 544	79 LA 409
	79 LA 464	74 LA 1113	79 LA 1225	78 LA 937
	78 LA 1290	73 LA 993	79 LA 650	78 LA 148
	77 LA 1217		78 LA 644	77 LA 978
	75 LA 12		78 LA 267	76 LA 1192
	75 LA 1		78 LA 17	76 LA 1095
	74 LA 537		77 LA 139	70 LA 572
	73 LA 1248		76 LA 1249	68 LA 581
	71 LA 886		76 LA 244	66 LA 471
	71 LA 884		74 LA 835	
	70 LA 1010		73 LA 908	
	65 LA 1233		73 LA 493	
	64 LA 386		71 LA 1084	
	63 LA 1217		71 LA 883	
	63 LA 952		68 LA 1160	
	63 LA 3		68 LA 931	

cEarlier "leaving post" cases are similarly charted at p. 653 of the Third Edition of this book, "sleeping on the job" and "assault and fighting" cases at p. 654.

TABLE OF OFFENSES—CONT'D.

Offense	Discharge Upheld	Lesser Penalty Upheld (as assessed by employer)	Penalty Reduced by Arbitrator	No Penalty Permitted
Assault and Fighting Among Employees, cont'd.			66 LA 471 66 LA 1005 65 LA 487 64 LA 304 63 LA 1217 63 LA 731 63 LA 94 63 LA 3 62 LA 248	
Horseplay[d]	76 LA 339 75 LA 305 75 LA 290 74 LA 785 59 LA 337	75 LA 592 65 LA 1151	76 LA 946 75 LA 673 73 LA 817 71 LA 1049 69 LA 1227 69 LA 884 66 LA 796 60 LA 909 59 LA 1153 59 LA 1097 58 LA 1038	77 LA 19 73 LA 912 58 LA 421
Insubordination[e]	81 LA 241 80 LA 509 80 LA 693 80 LA 465 79 LA 674 78 LA 363 78 LA 313 75 LA 281 75 LA 32 74 LA 281 74 LA 163 71 LA 1148 71 LA 1077 69 LA 307 68 LA 1123 67 LA 1310 67 LA 1305 67 LA 1181 67 LA 878 62 LA 789	81 LA 368 80 LA 1140 80 LA 601 78 LA 557 76 LA 421 76 LA 1 75 LA 455 75 LA 295 74 LA 947 74 LA 158 74 LA 58 74 LA 15 73 LA 1092 72 LA 1015 72 LA 564 72 LA 314 69 LA 919 68 LA 1305 65 LA 769 62 LA 348 62 LA 161 61 LA 1103	80 LA 1133 80 LA 611 80 LA 584 79 LA 953 79 LA 640 79 LA 76 78 LA 784 78 LA 687 78 LA 516 78 LA 49 76 LA 1120 76 LA 467 76 LA 118 75 LA 574 74 LA 1276 74 LA 338 74 LA 208 72 LA 1047 71 LA 1199 71 LA 977 71 LA 619 69 LA 286 68 LA 291 68 LA 151 64 LA 849	80 LA 1126 78 LA 469 77 LA 694 76 LA 921 74 LA 946 72 LA 1248 72 LA 437 75 LA 6 69 LA 901 68 LA 1284 67 LA 1178 64 LA 1051 64 LA 498 64 LA 117 62 LA 1164 61 LA 594

[d]Earlier "horseplay" cases are similarly charted at p. 655 of the Third Edition of this book.
[e]Earlier "insubordination" cases are similarly charted at p. 655 of the Third Edition of this book. Some of the cases listed in the present edition's chart for "refusal to accept job assignment," below, also involve an "insubordination" aspect.

TABLE OF OFFENSES—CONT'D.

Offense	Discharge Upheld	Lesser Penalty Upheld (as assessed by employer)	Penalty Reduced by Arbitrator	No Penalty Permitted
Racial Slur	68 LA 770	71 LA 1252	79 LA 1236	
	68 LA 706	71 LA 342	79 LA 12	
	66 LA 1020		75 LA 1220	
	64 LA 15		71 LA 1021	
	61 LA 162		62 LA 248	
			56 LA 623	
Threat or Assault of Management Representative[f]	81 LA 553	81 LA 371	81 LA 569	81 LA 634
	81 LA 230	80 LA 642	81 LA 176	79 LA 185
	80 LA 806	79 LA 403	80 LA 273	73 LA 1057
	79 LA 1122	79 LA 44	77 LA 1272	73 LA 297
	78 LA 347	78 LA 148	76 LA 1187	71 LA 847
	78 LA 185	75 LA 284	75 LA 673	70 LA 1026
	76 LA 1086	73 LA 250	75 LA 366	63 LA 917
	76 LA 761	70 LA 796	74 LA 1101	61 LA 587
	76 LA 526	69 LA 917	74 LA 969	
	76 LA 480	68 LA 41	74 LA 664	
	75 LA 764	63 LA 244	74 LA 601	
	75 LA 468		73 LA 959	
	75 LA 321		73 LA 711	
	74 LA 1084		73 LA 111	
	74 LA 558		69 LA 1084	
	74 LA 210		67 LA 505	
	74 LA 42		66 LA 702	
	73 LA 610		64 LA 700	
	72 LA 1254		62 LA 1103	
	72 LA 966		61 LA 10	
	72 LA 960			
	71 LA 96			
	70 LA 1289			
	70 LA 146			
	67 LA 861			
	67 LA 426			
	66 LA 206			
	65 LA 1119			
	65 LA 694			
	62 LA 387			
	61 LA 1292			
	61 LA 536			

[f]Earlier "threat or assault of management representative" cases are similarly charted at p. 656 of the Third Edition of this book.

TABLE OF OFFENSES—CONT'D.

Offense	Discharge Upheld	Lesser Penalty Upheld (as assessed by employer)	Penalty Reduced by Arbitrator	No Penalty Permitted
Abusive Language to Supervision[g]	81 LA 722 78 LA 985 78 LA 806 73 LA 1244 73 LA 764 69 LA 839 68 LA 770 68 LA 706 68 LA 669	81 LA 865 81 LA 158 78 LA 566 75 LA 907 75 LA 858 73 LA 887 73 LA 561 72 LA 654 71 LA 771 71 LA 571 71 LA 164 69 LA 1220 69 LA 124 68 LA 1279 61 LA 1301	81 LA 821 80 LA 1061 80 LA 1038 80 LA 344 78 LA 391 76 LA 1058 76 LA 782 76 LA 195 75 LA 1220 75 LA 819 74 LA 881 74 LA 7 71 LA 889 69 LA 339 67 LA 835 65 LA 25	80 LA 1126 77 LA 1080 75 LA 733 73 LA 663 72 LA 1030 69 LA 737
Profane or Abusive Language (Not toward supervision)[g]	75 LA 288 69 LA 1031	79 LA 551 77 LA 1259 66 LA 149	80 LA 940 80 LA 352 74 LA 875 72 LA 1065 71 LA 1021 64 LA 866 60 LA 1343 59 LA 661 58 LA 1139	80 LA 1046 75 LA 553 72 LA 276 71 LA 314
Falsifying Employment Application[g]	81 LA 158 79 LA 816 76 LA 520 74 LA 354 74 LA 176 73 LA 512 72 LA 351 71 LA 1126 70 LA 167 65 LA 797 64 LA 1260 62 LA 389 61 LA 1113		77 LA 569 73 LA 367 66 LA 96 65 LA 801	80 LA 250 72 LA 1171 71 LA 1168 71 LA 100 69 LA 985 68 LA 217 67 LA 1042 64 LA 1129 64 LA 194 61 LA 929

[g]Earlier "abusive language to supervision" cases are similarly charted at p. 656 of the Third Edition of this book, "profane or abusive language" cases at 657, and "falsifying employment application" cases at 658.

Table of Offenses—cont'd.

Offense	Discharge Upheld	Lesser Penalty Upheld (as assessed by employer)	Penalty Reduced by Arbitrator	No Penalty Permitted
Falsifying Company Records (Including time records, production records)h	81 LA 736	79 LA 1157	81 LA 165	80 LA 1005
	81 LA 579	74 LA 710	80 LA 1283	79 LA 1103
	81 LA 393	70 LA 1249	79 LA 351	79 LA 61
	79 LA 147	69 LA 887	78 LA 647	78 LA 287
	78 LA 208		75 LA 40	74 LA 1095
	76 LA 1245		70 LA 750	73 LA 1278
	76 LA 1197		67 LA 1098	73 LA 756
	76 LA 953		66 LA 758	66 LA 736
	76 LA 735		65 LA 1091	
	76 LA 714		64 LA 1167	
	76 LA 213		63 LA 843	
	75 LA 154		63 LA 837	
	75 LA 45		63 LA 79	
	74 LA 739		62 LA 677	
	74 LA 498		62 LA 493	
	73 LA 387			
	71 LA 142			
	70 LA 1017			
	70 LA 696			
	68 LA 1232			
	67 LA 231			
	63 LA 768			
	62 LA 14			
	61 LA 363			
Disloyalty to Government (Security risk)	30 LA 642	22 LA 709	28 LA 810	39 LA 1280
	27 LA 548		22 LA 751	35 LA 315
	27 LA 265			30 LA 636
	26 LA 792			29 LA 567
	26 LA 609			28 LA 668
	24 LA 852			24 LA 567
	23 LA 715			21 LA 1
	21 LA 532			
	19 LA 40			
	19 LA 39			
	16 LA 234			

hEarlier "falsifying company records" cases are similarly charted at p. 657 of the Third Edition of this book.

TABLE OF OFFENSES—CONT'D.

Offense	Discharge Upheld	Lesser Penalty Upheld (as assessed by employer)	Penalty Reduced by Arbitrator	No Penalty Permitted
Theft[i]	81 LA 577	76 LA 373	79 LA 473	80 LA 280
	81 LA 268		78 LA 236	79 LA 102
	80 LA 617		77 LA 648	79 LA 24
	80 LA 65		78 LA 1109	78 LA 454
	79 LA 1045		78 LA 780	77 LA 864
	79 LA 1040		78 LA 665	77 LA 530
	79 LA 833		78 LA 409	77 LA 11
	79 LA 468		75 LA 473	76 LA 857
	79 LA 191		74 LA 714	76 LA 96
	79 LA 79		73 LA 1050	75 LA 659
	78 LA 1153		71 LA 1080	75 LA 588
	78 LA 368		71 LA 989	75 LA 562
	77 LA 133		70 LA 304	74 LA 1163
	76 LA 1245		68 LA 1245	71 LA 1202
	76 LA 1216		67 LA 869	71 LA 1109
	76 LA 939		66 LA 1313	70 LA 1097
	76 LA 592		65 LA 1157	67 LA 982
	75 LA 439		64 LA 1186	66 LA 216
	75 LA 217		64 LA 252	64 LA 1167
	74 LA 1293		61 LA 250	63 LA 648
	74 LA 509			61 LA 1180
	73 LA 878			61 LA 803
	73 LA 702			
	72 LA 175			
	71 LA 1224			
	70 LA 865			
	70 LA 100			
	69 LA 1192			
	66 LA 1165			
	66 LA 1051			
	62 LA 1253			
	61 LA 663			
Dishonesty[i]	81 LA 393	74 LA 710	81 LA 864	80 LA 75
	80 LA 879	62 LA 952	81 LA 165	79 LA 1327
	80 LA 577		80 LA 1161	76 LA 44
	80 LA 373		80 LA 815	74 LA 1095
	80 LA 238		80 LA 725	72 LA 223
	79 LA 633		80 LA 546	70 LA 909
				Cont'd.

[i]Earlier "theft" cases are similarly charted at p. 659 of the Third Edition of this book and earlier "dishonesty" cases at 658.

TABLE OF OFFENSES—CONT'D.

Offense	Discharge Upheld	Lesser Penalty Upheld (as assessed by employer)	Penalty Reduced by Arbitrator	No Penalty Permitted
Dishonesty, cont'd.	79 LA 523		80 LA 321	69 LA 766
	77 LA 576		79 LA 1181	67 LA 27
	77 LA 386		79 LA 689	64 LA 1099
	76 LA 714		77 LA 1113	64 LA 803
	76 LA 347		77 LA 526	63 LA 849
	76 LA 133		75 LA 1292	62 LA 1015
	75 LA 1201		75 LA 1062	
	74 LA 1052		74 LA 1300	
	74 LA 785		71 LA 1090	
	73 LA 722		68 LA 858	
	72 LA 956		66 LA 1295	
	72 LA 490		64 LA 1186	
	72 LA 281		63 LA 20	
	71 LA 148		62 LA 293	
	70 LA 1017			
	66 LA 1331			
	66 LA 189			
	66 LA 140			
	65 LA 623			
	64 LA 934			
	64 LA 110			
	62 LA 958			
	62 LA 732			
	61 LA 933			
Disloyalty to Employer (Includes competing with employer, conflict of interests)[j]	78 LA 1032	69 LA 582	75 LA 1092	80 LA 302
	76 LA 1197		75 LA 1033	77 LA 161
	76 LA 714		75 LA 868	76 LA 44
	74 LA 1066		73 LA 335	75 LA 640
	73 LA 164		70 LA 719	74 LA 1034
	72 LA 855		68 LA 1224	74 LA 349
	70 LA 1088		68 LA 13	69 LA 201
	67 LA 985		62 LA 225	68 LA 223
	67 LA 632			67 LA 1261
	63 LA 412			65 LA 1042
	62 LA 732			61 LA 1125
	58 LA 773			61 LA 279
	57 LA 1267			59 LA 69
				58 LA 1296
				58 LA 385

[j]Earlier "disloyalty to employer" cases are similarly charted at p. 660 of the Third Edition of this book.

TABLE OF OFFENSES—CONT'D.

Offense	Discharge Upheld	Lesser Penalty Upheld (as assessed by employer)	Penalty Reduced by Arbitrator	No Penalty Permitted
Moonlighting (Excluding competing with employer)[k]	79 LA 802		76 LA 770	65 LA 394
	67 LA 606		76 LA 140	64 LA 856
	58 LA 827		66 LA 177	62 LA 779
	57 LA 1267		63 LA 941	59 LA 47
	49 LA 400		52 LA 918	54 LA 381
	41 LA 1126		52 LA 818	51 LA 421
				43 LA 1106
				42 LA 446
				37 LA 1095
				33 LA 902
Unsatisfactory Performance (Includes incompetence, low productivity, and poor or improper job performance)[l]	81 LA 621	81 LA 463	80 LA 902	81 LA 808
	81 LA 573	80 LA 1235	80 LA 176	81 LA 772
	79 LA 569	80 LA 186	80 LA 145	80 LA 1070
	79 LA 564	77 LA 1191	78 LA 928	79 LA 582
	78 LA 394	74 LA 303	78 LA 172	78 LA 799
	78 LA 227	74 LA 274	78 LA 4	72 LA 1009
	77 LA 60	73 LA 385	77 LA 409	72 LA 981
	76 LA 7	72 LA 787	75 LA 1158	71 LA 396
	74 LA 1008	71 LA 515	73 LA 697	70 LA 799
	74 LA 896	70 LA 1050	72 LA 1310	70 LA 216
	74 LA 806	70 LA 809	70 LA 1103	66 LA 311
	74 LA 705	70 LA 216	70 LA 816	64 LA 159
	74 LA 578	69 LA 71	70 LA 195	62 LA 672
	73 LA 901	68 LA 485	69 LA 132	62 LA 305
	73 LA 857	68 LA 444	67 LA 687	
	73 LA 771	66 LA 55	67 LA 154	
	71 LA 1205	65 LA 1182	64 LA 346	
	71 LA 1044	65 LA 987	63 LA 293	
	71 LA 192		62 LA 965	
	65 LA 1148			
	65 LA 535			
	65 LA 405			
	65 LA 380			
	65 LA 270			
	64 LA 885			
	64 LA 248			
	62 LA 272			

[k]For discussion of moonlighting, see Chapter 17, topic entitled "'Moonlighting' and Outside Business Interest."

[l]Earlier "unsatisfactory performance" cases are similarly charted at p. 661 of the Third Edition of this book. For related material, see Chapter 13 of the present edition, topic entitled "Production Standards, Time Studies, and Job Evaluation."

Table of Offenses—cont'd.

Offense	Discharge Upheld	Lesser Penalty Upheld (as assessed by employer)	Penalty Reduced by Arbitrator	No Penalty Permitted
Refusal to Accept Job Assignment[m]	81 LA 83	81 LA 564	81 LA 385	81 LA 486
	80 LA 1349	80 LA 926	80 LA 297	79 LA 697
	80 LA 1034	78 LA 627	78 LA 716	79 LA 587
	79 LA 1200	75 LA 170	78 LA 642	77 LA 309
	79 LA 769	74 LA 1131	77 LA 759	77 LA 300
	79 LA 327	73 LA 1273	77 LA 239	75 LA 808
	78 LA 1012	72 LA 405	75 LA 879	72 LA 747
	77 LA 927	70 LA 1058	74 LA 441	72 LA 417
	76 LA 1178	69 LA 732	73 LA 819	71 LA 513
	72 LA 215	68 LA 841	70 LA 325	71 LA 56
	71 LA 192	68 LA 481	69 LA 320	69 LA 39
	70 LA 1013	65 LA 34	65 LA 101	68 LA 297
	70 LA 574	63 LA 854	61 LA 773	67 LA 970
	68 LA 386	63 LA 251	61 LA 613	64 LA 901
	68 LA 351	62 LA 605		63 LA 1258
	68 LA 114	62 LA 286		63 LA 1111
	67 LA 1031	61 LA 14		63 LA 653
	67 LA 820			63 LA 267
	67 LA 682			61 LA 821
	67 LA 78			61 LA 813
	66 LA 90			61 LA 607
	65 LA 852			
	63 LA 773			
	62 LA 1148			
Refusal to Work Overtime[n]	81 LA 198	81 LA 829	80 LA 1321	80 LA 435
	78 LA 1067	80 LA 926	78 LA 74	78 LA 1077
	78 LA 74	78 LA 566	74 LA 1020	76 LA 153
	78 LA 70	78 LA 74	73 LA 86	74 LA 967
	73 LA 1048	77 LA 698	71 LA 721	73 LA 864
	73 LA 250	73 LA 1235	71 LA 222	73 LA 135
	72 LA 591	73 LA 1140	69 LA 414	64 LA 458
	70 LA 625	73 LA 256	68 LA 1264	63 LA 608
	65 LA 1101	72 LA 759	65 LA 748	61 LA 360
	67 LA 364	72 LA 668	62 LA 779	
	63 LA 474	70 LA 999	61 LA 443	
	62 LA 1246	70 LA 876		
		67 LA 1152		
		63 LA 794		

[m]Some of the cases listed on this chart also involve an "insubordination" aspect. Earlier "refusal to accept job assignment" cases are similarly charted at p. 662 of the Third Edition of this book. For related material, see Chapter 5 of the present edition, subtopic entitled "Use of Grievance Procedure v. Self-Help."

[n]Earlier "refusal to work overtime" cases are similarly charted at p. 662 of the Third Edition of this book. For related material, see Chapter 13 of the present edition, subtopic entitled "Right to Require Overtime."

TABLE OF OFFENSES—CONT'D.

Offense	Discharge Upheld	Lesser Penalty Upheld (as assessed by employer)	Penalty Reduced by Arbitrator	No Penalty Permitted
Negligence°	81 LA 644 77 LA 1125 77 LA 73 76 LA 582 73 LA 707 71 LA 954 68 LA 732 66 LA 1342 66 LA 805 64 LA 382	81 LA 747 76 LA 315 70 LA 1078 69 LA 879 63 LA 753 61 LA 140	79 LA 929 79 LA 717 79 LA 597 78 LA 278 74 LA 793 70 LA 587 68 LA 593 63 LA 828	81 LA 227 76 LA 1134 74 LA 752 73 LA 1042 61 LA 1174
Damage to or Loss of Machine or Materials°	80 LA 873 80 LA 393 77 LA 33 74 LA 814 72 LA 81 68 LA 132 65 LA 829 64 LA 7 61 LA 831	80 LA 229 79 LA 172 79 LA 1	81 LA 537 74 LA 257 71 LA 27 70 LA 1056 69 LA 555 67 LA 565 61 LA 952	81 LA 659 73 LA 760 70 LA 988 68 LA 1341 61 LA 573
Prohibited Strike°	81 LA 179 76 LA 487 74 LA 748 73 LA 9 72 LA 326 72 LA 84 71 LA 555 69 LA 966 69 LA 459 69 LA 103 69 LA 93 68 LA 618 66 LA 682 66 LA 626 63 LA 678 61 LA 896	73 LA 1140 71 LA 174 69 LA 1182 69 LA 816 68 LA 805 62 LA 90	78 LA 593 78 LA 129 76 LA 487 75 LA 1107 73 LA 551 73 LA 9 72 LA 326 69 LA 459 69 LA 103 69 LA 93 67 LA 1250 66 LA 446 65 LA 15 63 LA 678 61 LA 148	78 LA 129 76 LA 487 75 LA 836 74 LA 877 72 LA 761 71 LA 555 71 LA 174 69 LA 1024 69 LA 459 68 LA 805 63 LA 678 62 LA 90

°Earlier "negligence" cases are similarly charted at p. 660 of the Third Edition of this book, earlier "damage to or loss of machine or materials" cases at 661, and earlier "prohibited strike" cases at 663.

Table of Offenses—cont'd.

Offense	Discharge Upheld	Lesser Penalty Upheld (as assessed by employer)	Penalty Reduced by Arbitrator	No Penalty Permitted
Misconduct During Strike[p]	80 LA 717	76 LA 587	80 LA 606	79 LA 601
	69 LA 351	65 LA 1077	79 LA 601	77 LA 483
	68 LA 706		79 LA 391	74 LA 726
	66 LA 1020		77 LA 83	69 LA 351
			75 LA 929	69 LA 223
			72 LA 838	
			70 LA 985	
			69 LA 351	
			67 LA 1044	
			64 LA 1061	
Refusal to Cross Picket Line (Usually another union's picket line)[q]	79 LA 1017 R	80 LA 1151	78 LA 189	76 LA 228
	62 LA 1264	79 LA 783 R	69 LA 399	72 LA 706
	49 LA 261	79 LA 1189	64 LA 1210	72 LA 169 R
	47 LA 1065	75 LA 36	61 LA 727	72 LA 73
	45 LA 826	67 LA 45	61 LA 693	70 LA 752 R
		64 LA 1210	53 LA 154	60 LA 842
		60 LA 1167	32 LA 994	37 LA 847
		54 LA 41		
		53 LA 154		
Union Activities[r]	76 LA 723	74 LA 1271	81 LA 569	80 LA 201
	76 LA 273	73 LA 636	78 LA 148	78 LA 148
	74 LA 675	69 LA 831	77 LA 1272	77 LA 172
	73 LA 1244	69 LA 582	77 LA 1008	74 LA 916
	72 LA 583	68 LA 517	76 LA 499	74 LA 261
	65 LA 165	67 LA 887	74 LA 601	73 LA 663
	64 LA 428	67 LA 788	71 LA 255	72 LA 865
	61 LA 933	64 LA 1046	67 LA 1203	72 LA 118
		64 LA 698	67 LA 1001	70 LA 664
		64 LA 521	67 LA 729	70 LA 257
		61 LA 1103	63 LA 892	68 LA 124
			61 LA 981	68 LA 26
				67 LA 1261
				63 LA 449
				61 LA 750

[p]Earlier "misconduct during strike" cases are similarly charted at p. 663 of the Third Edition of this book.

[q]The letter "R" following a citation in this chart signifies that permanent or temporary replacement rather than discharge or discipline had been effected by management and was upheld by the arbitrator (cases in "upheld" columns) or was not permitted (cases in "no penalty" column).

[r]Earlier "union activities" cases are similarly charted at p. 664 of the Third Edition of this book.

TABLE OF OFFENSES—CONT'D.

Offense	Discharge Upheld	Lesser Penalty Upheld (as assessed by employer)	Penalty Reduced by Arbitrator	No Penalty Permitted
Slowdowns	78 LA 612 74 LA 675 58 LA 69	80 LA 375	81 LA 183 66 LA 812 64 LA 425 62 LA 1289 61 LA 246	81 LA 183 79 LA 885 64 LA 56 62 LA 305 58 LA 977
Possession or Use of Intoxicants	81 LA 344 80 LA 875 80 LA 851 78 LA 302 77 LA 1180 77 LA 1064 76 LA 163 75 LA 699 74 LA 641 73 LA 228 73 LA 191 68 LA 421 67 LA 1296 67 LA 1145	71 LA 329	77 LA 775 77 LA 289 72 LA 198 71 LA 445 67 LA 847 66 LA 965	76 LA 1005 74 LA 972 69 LA 1143 69 LA 811 65 LA 159 64 LA 743
Possession or Use of Drugs	81 LA 174 80 LA 419 78 LA 1334 78 LA 1104 73 LA 868 72 LA 1075 72 LA 11 70 LA 1110 70 LA 318 70 LA 75 68 LA 792 67 LA 828 65 LA 1233 62 LA 200 58 LA 1299 58 LA 1015	80 LA 1173 73 LA 1133 72 LA 1107 65 LA 1271	80 LA 1261 80 LA 1243 80 LA 663 78 LA 1299 78 LA 1147 74 LA 1103 74 LA 1032 73 LA 1066 72 LA 513 71 LA 685 71 LA 585 71 LA 82 68 LA 72 66 LA 286 65 LA 1271 64 LA 721 59 LA 709	80 LA 1074 79 LA 1185 72 LA 780 72 LA 517 65 LA 386 62 LA 709 60 LA 125

sEarlier "slowdown" cases are similarly charted at p. 664 of the Third Edition of this book, earlier "intoxicant" cases at 665, and earlier "drug" cases at 664. For an intensive examination of arbitration decisions reviewing discharge and discipline for intoxicant and drug offenses, see Denenberg & Denenberg, Alcohol and Drugs: Issues in the Workplace (BNA Books, 1983).

Table of Offenses—cont'd.

Offense	Discharge Upheld	Lesser Penalty Upheld (as assessed by employer)	Penalty Reduced by Arbitrator	No Penalty Permitted
Distribution of Drugs	76 LA 387		69 LA 987	78 LA 1311
	74 LA 299			70 LA 1208
	69 LA 965			69 LA 214
	69 LA 776			
	69 LA 379			
	68 LA 697			
	64 LA 880			
	64 LA 826			
	64 LA 404			
	60 LA 613			
Obscene or Immoral Conduct[t]	81 LA 99	81 LA 459	80 LA 1091	75 LA 377
	80 LA 1225	78 LA 1049	80 LA 19	
	80 LA 891		78 LA 1060	
	80 LA 509		78 LA 1049	
	78 LA 985		78 LA 652	
	75 LA 288		73 LA 1167	
	74 LA 1281		73 LA 523	
			72 LA 540	
			71 LA 54	
Gambling	45 LA 1007	51 LA 707	49 LA 1262	78 LA 937
	45 LA 646	29 LA 442	44 LA 1174	68 LA 1048
	45 LA 350		37 LA 188	59 LA 370
	40 LA 1323		28 LA 97	52 LA 945
	40 LA 262		22 LA 851	45 LA 247
	39 LA 154		22 LA 210	41 LA 823
	33 LA 174			39 LA 621
	32 LA 44			28 LA 97
	32 LA 26			18 LA 938
	31 LA 191			
	29 LA 778			
	21 LA 788			
	17 LA 150			
	16 LA 727			
	16 LA 461			

[t]Earlier "obscene or immoral conduct" cases are similarly charted at p. 665 of the Third Edition of this book.

TABLE OF OFFENSES—CONT'D.

Offense	Discharge Upheld	Lesser Penalty Upheld (as assessed by employer)	Penalty Reduced by Arbitrator	No Penalty Permitted
Attachment or Garnishment of Wages[u]	77 LA 1132 71 LA 832 63 LA 1157 60 LA 924 58 LA 1029	72 LA 850	71 LA 538 59 LA 947	78 LA 799 65 LA 1101 63 LA 912
Abusing Customers (Includes abuse of public agency clientele)[u]	80 LA 628 80 LA 496 79 LA 422 77 LA 144 76 LA 350 75 LA 957 75 LA 409 72 LA 723 72 LA 206 71 LA 942 71 LA 805 70 LA 432 59 LA 1235		79 LA 665 78 LA 1127 78 LA 217 76 LA 595 75 LA 1205 70 LA 614 70 LA 97 69 LA 939 63 LA 892 62 LA 25 61 LA 1047 60 LA 741	80 LA 1046 77 LA 210 72 LA 1313 70 LA 572 66 LA 633 63 LA 514 60 LA 1326
Abusing Students, Patients, or Inmates	81 LA 306 79 LA 1154 76 LA 1133 64 LA 96	80 LA 1065 76 LA 412 61 LA 1159	79 LA 977 76 LA 595 72 LA 1240 69 LA 1173 69 LA 671 68 LA 713 65 LA 389 64 LA 346 62 LA 1281	75 LA 1177 74 LA 830 73 LA 918 72 LA 276 68 LA 369 60 LA 688
Sexual Harassment[v]	82 LA 921 82 LA 640 78 LA 985 78 LA 690 78 LA 417 74 LA 1281 62 LA 1272	81 LA 459 80 LA 133 78 LA 120 75 LA 592	80 LA 940 80 LA 19 79 LA 940 73 LA 522 72 LA 540 71 LA 54 60 LA 1343 58 LA 1139	81 LA 730 75 LA 377

[u]Earlier "attachment or garnishment" cases and earlier "abusing customers" cases are similarly charted at p. 666 of the Third Edition of this book.

[v]For related material, see Chapter 17, topic entitled "Protection Against Sexual Harassment."

Chapter 16

Safety and Health

Safety and health considerations may arise directly or indirectly out of many labor-management concerns, such as crew size,[1] the physical or mental condition of an employee, refusal of an employee to obey an order, requirements for special protective clothing or equipment, and the like. Moreover, unions sometimes have contested management's right to require employees to observe a safety rule, and they have grieved that management has not adequately protected the safety and health of the employees. In such cases, arbitrators have generally applied the test of "reasonableness." Indeed, the reader will observe that the golden thread of "reasonableness" runs throughout arbitration decisions on safety and health matters.

Management Rights and Obligations in Safety and Health Matters

Initially, it may be noted that when the agreement is silent on the subject, arbitrators have held or recognized that management has the right to promulgate and enforce reasonable rules and regulations to insure the safety and health of its employees.[2]

However, many agreements do contain safety and health provisions, and the typical clause may state that management will exert a reasonable effort to protect the safety and health of its employees.[3]

---

[1]See Chapter 13, topic entitled "Determination of Size of Crews."

[2]See Arbitrator Gibson in 71 LA 457, 460; Conant in 68 LA 912, 915; Hnatiuk in 50 LA 985, 986; Jenkins in 48 LA 1094, 1096; Logan in 30 LA 252, 253; Yeager in 29 LA 487, 489; Kelliher in 29 LA 367, 368; Morvant in 24 LA 453, 457; Brecht in 24 LA 199, 209; Seward in 19 LA 210, 211–212; Short in 18 LA 671, 673–675; Shipman in 10 LA 113, 116. Also see Chapter 13, topic entitled "Plant Rules."

[3]See, for example, Arbitrator Madden in 75 LA 50, 51; Hayes in 73 LA 1100 at 1100; Eaton in 73 LA 267, 268; Rutherford in 71 LA 22, 23; Wolf in 47 LA 425, 426; Welch in 47 LA 83, 84; Luckerath in 43 LA 1253, 1255; Duff in 43 LA 583, 585; Barrett in 41 LA 211, 212; Dworkin in 40 LA 1285, 1290; Valtin in 39 LA 40, 42. Also see Griffin in 61 LA 1154, 1156 (recognizing a right of management to "change standing practices whenever appropriate with respect to safety and other rules" where the agreement gave it the right to establish, maintain, and enforce reasonable rules to assure orderly plant operations).

SAFETY AND HEALTH 709

Under such a clause, arbitrators have ruled that while management must make a reasonable effort toward safety, it is not required to eliminate all possible hazards or to utilize all possible safety precautions.[4]

Another contract clause requiring the company to make every reasonable effort to provide necessary and practicable safety measures was construed as constituting the *minimum* obligation which the company had assumed for the safety and health of its employees; but the company could do more toward that end so long as it acted reasonably.[5] Similarly, where the contract called for safety rules or devices as should be agreed upon by the joint safety committee, one arbitrator held that the company had an obligation to make, and could enforce by discipline, reasonable provision for the safety and health of the employees even beyond the agreed-upon rules;[6] and another ruled that such a clause did not bar the company from "acting on its own in carrying out its responsibility to provide the employees with a safe place to work," nor did the clause "limit or block the Company's continuing right to take such reasonable safety measures" as would provide for the safety and health of its employees.[7]

Interpreting a "reasonable effort" clause, Arbitrator Harry J. Dworkin listed five specific employer obligations which he reasoned derived from the clause:

"Under the terms of the contract, it might be reasoned that a specific duty is imposed on the employer to provide (1) a safe place to work; (2) safe machinery, tools, and equipment; (3) competent fellow employees; (4) instructions and warnings as to the dangers involved; and (5) rules for the conduct of the work."[8]

OSHA Considerations

The Federal Occupational Safety and Health Act of 1970 requires employers to comply with specific safety and health standards, and under its "general duty" provisions it requires employers to furnish a

---

[4]See Arbitrator Wolf in 47 LA 425, 428; Murphy in 37 LA 501, 503; Dworkin in 36 LA 902, 912.

[5]See Bethlehem Steel Co., 41 LA 211, 212 (Barrett, 1963); Bethlehem Steel Co., 39 LA 40, 43 (Valtin, 1962).

[6]Bunker Hill Co., 43 LA 1253, 1256 (Luckerath, 1964).

[7]Giant Portland Cement Co., 63–1 ARB ¶8261 (Williams, 1963). In United States Steel Corp., 69 LA 1215, 1219–1220 (1977), a dispute over a new safety rule was remanded to the parties by Arbitrator Margery Gootnick in order to give the contractual safety committee a fair opportunity to fulfill its function. Also see Arbitrator Wolff in 79 LA 242, 247–248 (safety aspects of a grievance were remanded for consideration by safety committee). For a discussion of the proper role or scope of activity of safety committee members, see Newport News Shipbuilding & Dry Dock Co., 77 LA 364, 367–368 (Garrett, 1981). For cases involving removal or other actions against safety committee members for alleged abuse of responsibility, see Arbitrator Ruben in 78 LA 473, 478–479; Ipavec in 71 LA 257, 260; Hebert in 70 LA 20, 23–24, 27; Clarke in 69 LA 679, 681–682; Perry in 68 LA 720, 727–728.

[8]Erie Mining Co., 36 LA 902, 912 (1961). Also see Arbitrator Dworkin in 76 LA 339, 343; Wolf in 47 LA 425, 428; Murphy in 37 LA 501, 503; Williams in 63–1 ARB ¶8261. In the absence of such contractually derived obligation, it may be noted that while the common law does not impose an affirmative requirement on the employer to take these safety measures, he may be liable for damages if an employee sustains physical injury due to the employer's failure to do so. Of course workers' compensation legislation goes even further in giving relief to injured workers.

place of employment free of hazards likely to cause death or serious physical harm to employees. The Act empowers the Secretary of Labor, through the Occupational Safety and Health Administration, to promulgate standards that are "reasonably necessary or appropriate to provide safe or healthful employment and places of employment." The Act provides for enforcement by means of: inspections and investigations of work facilities; citations by the Secretary of Labor against employers for safety and health violations, such citations ordering abatement of the violation and stating any proposed assessment of penalty; employer opportunity to contest citations or proposed penalties before the Occupational Safety and Health Review Commission and the courts; injunction proceedings to remedy imminently dangerous conditions; civil penalties assessed by the Review Commission; criminal penalties for certain violations.[9]

The Act often has been a factor (sometimes a particularly strong factor) in the arbitration of safety and health issues. It was a factor supporting the employer's position in a number of cases, for instance, where the protested employer action had been prompted directly or indirectly by a current or past OSHA citation.[10] The Act also was a

---

[9]29 U.S.C. §§ 651 et seq. In Industrial Union Dept. v. American Petroleum Inst., 100 S.Ct. 2844, 2864, 2866, 2869 (1980), the U.S. Supreme Court concluded that the Act "was intended to require the elimination, as far as feasible, of significant risks of harm," that "Congress was concerned, not with absolute safety, but with the elimination of significant harm," and that "the Act empowers the Secretary to promulgate health and safety standards only where a significant risk of harm exists." For more on the Act, see Gellens, "Resolving Industrial Safety Disputes: To Arbitrate or Not to Arbitrate," 34 Lab. L.J. 149 (1983); Wolfson, "Arbitration and OSHA," 38 Arb. J. No. 3, p. 12 (1983); Britton, "Courts, Arbitrators, and OSHA Problems: An Overview," Proceedings of the 33rd Annual Meeting of NAA, 260 (BNA Books, 1981); Schwartz, "Comment," id. at 276; Alesia, "Practice Before the United States Occupational Safety and Health Review Commission," 86 Case & Com. 34 (1981); Nothsetei, The Law of Occupational Safety and Health (1981); The Job Safety and Health Act of 1970 (BNA Books, 1971). The Federal Coal Mine Health and Safety Act of 1969 prescribes mandatory health and safety standards for the protection of coal miners and requires the Secretary of the Interior to conduct continuing surveillance of mines to detect imminently dangerous conditions and violations of the mandatory standards, procedures being specified for abating the dangerous conditions and violations of standards. 30 U.S.C. §§ 801 et seq. A summary of the Act and its procedures is provided in National Indep. Coal Operator's Assn. v. Kleppe, 96 S.Ct. 809, 811–812 (1976); Kleppe v. Delta Mining, Inc., 96 S.Ct. 816 (1976). Under Executive Order 12196 issued by President Carter in 1980 federal agencies "generally must: (1) comply with the same safety and health standards followed by private industry; (2) abate hazards promptly or develop abatement plans; (3) agree not to take any action against an employee for reporting accidents or participating in agency safety programs." A Survey of Safety and Health Provisions in Federal Labor Agreements, 1 (OPM, 1981), where it is indicated that a high percentage of collective agreements in the federal sector deal expressly with safety.

[10]See Arbitrator Robertson in 77 LA 495, 498; Ipavec in 73 LA 1025, 1027; Carter in 72 LA 702, 703; Sloane in 71 LA 302, 305; Johannes in 70 LA 1269, 1271–1272; Conant in 68 LA 912, 913, 916; Crane in 68 LA 82, 84; Larkin in 64 LA 24, 27; Griffin in 61 LA 1154, 1155; Chalfie in 61 LA 400, 408 (OSHA citations with costly penalties for failure to meet time limitations on compliance "created unusual circumstances which gave rise to abnormal rather than normal operating conditions" within the meaning of the agreement). Also see Kaufman in 76 LA 579, 580–581; Dyke in 59 LA 912, 918–919. Cf., Jones in 78 LA 682, 684–685; Eischen in 72 LA 795, 800. In Monsanto Co., 77 LA 495, 497–498 (1981), a safety rule was upheld where the union's evidence did not establish that the employer's action in adopting and applying the rule was arbitrary or capricious and where the employer had been fined by OSHA several years earlier, Arbitrator Francis J. Robertson stating that "it is not unreasonable for this Company to seek to avoid any potential questioning of its safety procedures by OSHA so as not to have to litigate questionable practices." In Mrs. Baird's Bakeries, 68 LA 773, 777–778 (1977), Arbitrator Mildren J. Fox, Jr., responded as follows to a union assertion that the employer's action was not required by OSHA: "Regulations set forth by OSHA are the minimum standards that an employer must meet. These regulations, or standards, do not say that an employer cannot use greater safety standards than those specified * * *." Also see Arbitrator Hunter in 69 LA 727, 731. On the other hand, in Allied

factor supporting the employer's position in other cases where the arbitrator found that the employer, without having been cited for any OSHA violation, had met OSHA standards or had acted for the purpose of meeting them.[11]

Employee Obligations in Safety Matters

The union and employees have a correlative duty in safety and health matters. This duty may be imposed by contract, usually in the form of an agreement to cooperate in promoting safety.[12] It may be imposed by a state safety code,[13] and it is imposed by OSHA. Of course, it also may be imposed upon the employee by safety rules promulgated under management's right to issue such rules.[14] Moreover, employees have an inherent obligation to protect their own safety and to cooperate in promoting safety.[15] An employee's obligation to comply with safety rules may carry an obligation to bear or share the cost of safety apparel.[16]

Safety Rules

While, as noted above, management has the right to issue reasonable safety rules, certain fundamental principles of labor-management relations are pertinent to the question of the reasonableness of such rules. Thus, a safety rule must bear a reasonable

---

Chem. Corp., 74 LA 412, 416–417 (1980), Arbitrator Dana E. Eischen refused to uphold a safety rule which he found to be unreasonable notwithstanding that a factor in its adoption was the employer's "understandable desire to avoid further legal difficulties with OSHA"; Arbitrator Eischen believed that "upon careful analysis" the OSHA citation against the employer could not "be deemed a mandate for" the employer's action. Also see Arbitrator Tripp in 60 LA 90, 92–93.

[11]See Arbitrator Newmark in 76 LA 421, 424; Hardin in 75 LA 214, 215–216; Fishgold in 74 LA 921, 922; Markowitz in 74 LA 58, 62; Flannagan in 73 LA 644 at 644; Livengood in 73 LA 201, 205–206; Dash in 71 LA 879, 880, 882; May in 71 LA 535, 536–537; Dyke in 70 LA 596, 599; McKone in 68 LA 841, 844 (stating that in addition to other evidence negating grievant's claim that a health hazard existed, "OSHA has frequently inspected the full range of manufacturing operations at the plant and made no citations with respect to" the operation in question); Gentile in 62 LA 511, 512–513; Doyle in 61 LA 448, 449; Nicholas in 59 LA 72, 74–75. Also see Wolff in 80 LA 649, 657.

[12]See 54 LA 1084, 1086–1087; 51 LA 156 at 156; 50 LA 115, 118; 48 LA 1094, 1095; 47 LA 425, 426; 43 LA 583, 585; 42 LA 1206, 1207; 39 LA 40, 42; 36 LA 970, 971; 32 LA 103 at 103.

[13]As in United States Borax & Chem. Corp., 36 LA 970, 973 (Keeler, 1961).

[14]As in United States Plywood-Champion Papers, 50 LA 115, 121 (Jenkins, 1968); Rome Kraft Co., 61–3 ARB ¶8792 (Hawley, 1961).

[15]See General Elec. Co., 31 LA 386, 389 (Sutermeister, 1958). As a corollary, employees should not be penalized for protesting hazards. Reserve Mining Co., 55 LA 648, 652 (Sembower, 1970). Cf., Arbitrator Schedler in 75 LA 682, 688–689.

[16]See Arbitrator Ipavec in 73 LA 1025, 1027–1028 (employees rather than employer had the obligation to pay for safety shoes required by OSHA, Arbitrator Ipavec stating that the agreement did not specifically impose such obligation upon the employer, that the employer was supported by bargaining history, and that the employer was "not bound to purchase safety shoes for employees by a past practice of supplying employees with safety equipment such as glasses, aprons and gloves"); Johannes in 70 LA 1269, 1272 (contract language and bargaining history supported employer); Harr in 70 LA 194, 195; Ray in 69 LA 828, 830–831 (stating that "the question of who pays for safety shoes is to be resolved * * * at the bargaining table," and that both past practice and bargaining history supported the employer as to this item of apparel); Richman in 69 LA 751, 754–755; Crane in 68 LA 82, 84; Eyraud in 61 LA 1286, 1289. Cf., Seidman in 79 LA 921, 922–923.

relationship to its purpose, i.e., safety and health considerations.[17] Moreover, it must be reasonable in application as well as in content.[18] In this regard, a rule was held to be reasonably and non-discriminatorily applied where the company required employees working in hazardous areas to wear "hard hats" and safety glasses while it exempted others who worked in an enclosure protecting them from the hazard.[19]

As is true of other plant rules, safety rules must be adequately communicated to the employees in some manner.[20] Finding that adequate notice of a safety rule had been given and that the rule had been violated, an arbitrator may uphold suspension of the offending employee.[21] Discharge may be justified where an employee has persistently disobeyed safety regulations in spite of progressive discipline, and sometimes it may be found justified without having been preceded by progressive discipline.[22] In the absence of a contractual restriction on reclassifying employees for safety reasons, violation of safety rules may be a controlling factor in the demotion of an employee.[23]

It would appear that when a rule is in furtherance of safety, there is an even stronger than usual reason to require strict compliance by the employee, with the right to file a grievance instead of resorting to self-help.[24] This is especially so where the company operations are hazardous in themselves.[25] In some cases, too, arbitrators have found contractual violations by management in changing or in itself not complying with safety rules or regulations.[26]

---

[17]See Arbitrator Strasshofer in 73 LA 443, 445–447; Black in 42 LA 1206, 1208; Barrett in 41 LA 211, 212, cited and followed by Strongin in 48 LA 765, 766; McDermott in 62–1 ARB ¶8051. Also see Wallen in 47 LA 1135, 1141. A safety rule is not unreasonable merely because its benefits are minor. United States Steel Corp., 40 LA 205, 207 (Florey, 1963).

[18]See Arbitrator Carter in 74 LA 400, 407; Eischen in 74 LA 412, 416–417; Kaufman in 69 LA 62, 63; Tripp in 60 LA 90, 93; Jenkins in 48 LA 1094, 1096; Kates in 48 LA 861, 863; Strongin in 48 LA 765, 767; Black in 42 LA 1206, 1208; Barrett in 41 LA 211, 213. Also see Seitz in 39 LA 1140, 1142.

[19]Bethlehem Steel Co., 41 LA 213, 214 (Barrett, 1963).

[20]Oral communication was sufficient where the parties had a history of oral safety rules in Reserve Mining Co., 38 LA 443, 449 (Sembower, 1962).

[21]See Arbitrator Kaufman in 76 LA 579, 580–581; Carter in 72 LA 702, 703; Sloane in 71 LA 302, 305; Miller in 64–1 ARB ¶8356; Stouffer in 64–1 ARB ¶8018; Duff in 63–2 ARB ¶8675. Arbitrator Bothwell reduced a penalty of discharge to disciplinary suspension due to mitigating circumstances in 36 LA 898, 901, as did Rohman in 45 LA 772, 775, and Marshall in 40 LA 247, 254. Similarly, Arbitrator Dworkin in 47 LA 457, 463, where he gave the company the option to restore grievant to his job or to negotiate with the union on placement in another job.

[22]Discharge followed progressive discipline in Vulcan-Hart Corp., 78 LA 59, 62 (Ghiz, 1982); American Potash & Chem. Corp., 64–1 ARB ¶8356 (Miller, 1963). Discharge was upheld without any indication that progressive discipline had been utilized by Arbitrator Klaiber in 78 LA 226, 226–227 (the union stressed that progressive discipline had not been used); Nutt in 76 LA 1278, 1280 (expressly holding progressive discipline not required); Ferguson in 72 LA 164, 167 (persistent and insubordinate refusal to wear type of clothing required by safety rule); Brown in 64 LA 511, 513–514; Rutherford in 62 LA 139, 143, 145 (discharge for first safety violation was upheld "based upon the severity of the safety hazard created").

[23]United States Borax & Chem. Corp., 36 LA 970, 972–973 (Keeler, 1961).

[24]See situations confronting Arbitrator Murphy in 44 LA 459, 462; Boles in 44 LA 385, 388–389; Bothwell in 36 LA 898, 901; Daugherty in 34 LA 83, 85.

[25]See Arbitrator Murphy in 44 LA 459, 462; Daugherty in 34 LA 83, 85; Sutermeister in 31 LA 386, 388–389. Insurance may be a factor as in Solar Chem. Corp., 62–2 ARB ¶8651 (Taft, 1962).

[26]See Arbitrator Kubie in 78 LA 1331, 1333 (employer permitted supervisors who are subject to same risks as line employees to ignore safety rules that line employees must observe); Goodstein in 75 LA 849, 853 (contractual requirement for rotation of duty was violated by federal agency employer's order); Leventhal in 72 LA 44, 47.

Arbitrator Alexander B. Porter ruled that employees may not exercise individual discretion regarding the need to comply with safety rules. He stated: "Obviously, a safety program based upon permitting thousands of employees to decide when they may safely remove their [safety] glasses would be doomed to fail from the outset."[27]

Safety rules may not only require observance of certain procedures and practices by employees but they may also impose a duty upon the employee to refrain from working under potentially unsafe conditions.[28]

Refusal to Obey Orders—The Safety Exception

It is a well-established principle that employees must obey management's orders and carry out their job assignments, even if believed to violate the agreement, then turn to the grievance procedure for relief.[29] An exception to this "obey now—grieve later" doctrine exists where obedience would involve an unusual or abnormal safety or health hazard.[30] But this exception has been held inapplicable where the hazard is inherent in the employee's job.[31] Moreover, when the exception is invoked, the union must show that a safety or health hazard was the real reason for the employee's refusal.[32]

The exception has been held to apply as well where the employee asserts that if he were to perform as ordered the safety of others would be in jeopardy.[33] However, even assuming that there is a safety hazard sufficient to justify an employee in refusing to do the work, this right of refusal applies only to the employee assigned to do the work; other employees not assigned the work (and not affected by the unsafe condition) would not be justified in resorting to self-help, such as walking off the job, instead of using the grievance procedures.[34]

A contract clause may expressly deal with the right of an employee to refuse to do work in abnormally hazardous conditions. Such a clause may give the employee the right, after reporting the

---

[27]Bethlehem Steel Co., 41 LA 1152, 1153 (1963). Similarly, see Arbitrator Bothwell in 53 LA 627, 628, and in 36 LA 898, 901; Hale in 39 LA 385, 389.

[28]See Arbitrator Roberts in 73 LA 1133, 1139; Rutherford in 62 LA 139, 143, 145; McCoy in 45 LA 293, 295; Sembower in 38 LA 443, 449; Hawley in 61–3 ARB ¶8792.

[29]See Chapter 5, subtopic entitled "Use of Grievance Procedure v. Self-Help."

[30]See Arbitrator Bard in 79 LA 953, 961–962; Clark in 79 LA 697, 702; McCollister in 79 LA 587, 590; Ness in 77 LA 1080, 1084; Wahl in 71 LA 513, 515; Rohman in 51 LA 709, 711; Jenkins in 50 LA 115, 123–124; Epstein in 49 LA 429, 430; Hopson in 48 LA 788, 793–795; Dworkin in 48 LA 457, 461; Abernethy in 47 LA 184, 191–192; McCoy in 45 LA 293, 295, and in 8 LA 647, 651–652; Roberts in 44 LA 919, 920; Meyers in 43 LA 102, 105; Barrett in 27 LA 523, 526–530; Parker in 22 LA 624, 626; Shipman in 21 LA 335, 337–338; Elson in 8 LA 826, 831.

[31]See Arbitrator Kelly in 71 LA 238, 240, 243; House in 48 LA 1082, 1084; Dworkin in 48 LA 457, 461; Meyers in 43 LA 102, 105; Porter in 41 LA 1323, 1326; Anrod in 38 LA 375, 378; Duff in 26 LA 915, 917. Cf., Rohman in 45 LA 772, 775; Gilden in 5 LA 300, 302–304.

[32]See Arbitrator House in 48 LA 1082, 1084–1085; Rohman in 48 LA 963, 965, and in 48 LA 457, 461; Yagoda in 48 LA 124, 131; Mullin in 47 LA 848, 854.

[33]A.M. Castle & Co., 41 LA 666, 670 (Sembower, 1963).

[34]Metal Specialty Co., 43 LA 849, 853–854 (Volz, 1964), citing and quoting from Ford Motor Co., 41 LA 608, 615 (Platt, 1963).

alleged hazard to his supervisor, to file a grievance at an advanced step for preferred handling, or to be relieved of the job and, at management's discretion, to be assigned to another available position.[35]

The Range of Arbitral Reasoning

Many grievances have arisen out of discharge or discipline assessed for refusal to obey an order or perform an assignment because of alleged safety or health hazards. Such allegations, countered by management's assertion that no unusual hazard existed, have led arbitrators on a merry chase after an elusive standard or formula for determining when an employee's refusal is justified.[36]

Arbitration decisions are couched in such language as: an "employee's reasonable belief" that unusual danger is involved is enough;[37] the employee "sincerely and genuinely" feared for his life;[38] the "employee's good faith belief of the existence of a hazard does not suffice," but the "hazard must be demonstrated to exist";[39] the employee erroneously but "actually entertained" the fear of danger to his life;[40] if the employee "is sincere in his belief of danger" and "makes a 'reasonable' appraisal of the potential hazards, he is protected in his decision not to act, regardless of whether later on, in fact, it should be established that no hazard existed";[41] the "standard to be applied is not the cowardice or bravery of anyone";[42] "although their fears were based on misconceptions, they were nonetheless real";[43] the employee must obey the order unless there is a "real and imminent danger to life and limb";[44] the fact that a fellow employee is an unsafe driver was "ample reason" for grievant's fears and therefore "valid and reasonable grounds for refusing the assignment";[45] considering the grievants' inadequate training and experience, "the work assignment constituted *for them* an abnormal hazard";[46] although there

---

[35]See, for example, Arbitrator Strongin in 49 LA 1203 at 1203; Jenkins in 48 LA 1094, 1095; Dworkin in 46 LA 43, 50; Garrett in 45 LA 426, 428; Duff in 43 LA 583, 585. Also see Odom in 74 LA 946, 947.

[36]By definition, a "hazard" is "potential," and determining when the "potential" is sufficient to justify an employee in refusing to obey an order depends upon the facts.

[37]Hercules, Inc., 48 LA 788, 794–795 (Hopson, 1967).

[38]Lone Star Steel Co., 48 LA 1094, 1097 (Jenkins, 1967). Also see Arbitrator Crawford in 69 LA 320, 324.

[39]Wilcolator Co., 44 LA 847, 852 (Altieri, 1964). Also see Arbitrator Kelly in 71 LA 238, 241; McKone in 68 LA 841, 845, stating that "When * * * a claim of health hazard has been made, the one expecting the benefit of that defense must accept the burden of establishing it."

[40]Allied Chem. Corp., 47 LA 686, 688 (Hilpert, 1966).

[41]A.M. Castle Co., 41 LA 666, 671 (Sembower, 1963). Cf., Dodge Mfg. Corp., 49 LA 429, 430–431 (Epstein, 1967).

[42]Goodyear Tire & Rubber Co., 45 LA 772, 775 (Rohman, 1965).

[43]New York Shipbuilding Co., 39 LA 1186, 1188 (Crawford, 1963). Also see Arbitrator Wagner in 49 LA 325, 330.

[44]Pennsylvania R.R., 45 LA 522, 523 (Seidenberg, 1965). Also see Arbitrator Lubow in 70 LA 1013, 1016; Turkus in 61 LA 607, 609 (stating that unless imminent danger to life or limb is satisfactorily demonstrated at the arbitration hearing, an "honest belief and fear of imminent bodily harm" does not immunize the employee from discipline although it may be a mitigating factor relevant "to the quantum of the disciplinary penalty").

[45]United States Plywood-Champion Papers, 50 LA 115, 123–124 (Jenkins, 1968).

[46]Bethlehem Steel Corp., 49 LA 1203, 1206 (Strongin, 1968), emphasis added. Also see Arbitrator Crawford in 69 LA 320, 323–324.

were some conditions "which required correction and attention in order to maintain the required standards of safety," nevertheless "there were no imminently dangerous conditions which presented a hazard to their safety and health so as to justify them in refusing to work";[47] although the employee "honestly believed" that there would be unnecessary danger if he complied with the work order, "it was not so clearly and evidently unsafe" that he could disobey after failing to protest through the grievance procedure;[48] the hazards were "neither so compelling nor the opportunities for their correction so hopeless as to require nothing less than an abandonment of the grievance procedure";[49] grievant was "entirely sincere" in questioning the safety of the crew, but his concern was not "well founded";[50] there must be "a reasonable basis" for the allegation that the assignment is dangerous and "at least *prima facie* evidence" that the work is unsafe, but the evidence should be "more than a mere presumption."[51] Even where a personnel manual was binding on the parties and permitted delay in performance of an assignment if the "employee believes" its performance "cannot be carried out without unreasonably endangering his health or safety," the arbitrator declared that "the belief of the employee must be a reasonable one and have a rational basis," and that it "cannot be fanciful or contrary to all known fact."[52]

Thus, arbitral reasoning appears to range from the purely subjective test of what the particular employee "honestly" or "sincerely" believed as to the presence of a hazard, to the "cold facts" approach of requiring a showing of actual danger with a "real and imminent" hazard to life and limb, and all the shadings between these two extremes.

The "Reasonable Person" Approach

The greatest number of arbitrators appear to take some form of the "reasonable person" approach, i.e., an approach which attempts to ascertain whether the facts and circumstances known to the employee at the time of the incident would have caused a "reasonable person" to fear for his or her safety or health. This view was stated succinctly by Arbitrator Ralph Roger Williams under a contract which required the employee to establish "positively" the claimed health hazard in order to avoid discipline for refusal to obey an order:

> "* * * Hence, if the grievant actually believed that the performance of the assigned task would have created a serious health hazard to him, and if a 'reasonable man' would have reached the same conclusion under

[47]International Salt Co., 40 LA 1285, 1291–1292 (Dworkin, 1963).
[48]Duval Corp., 43 LA 102, 105 (Meyers, 1964).
[49]New York Tel. Co., 42 LA 1217, 1223 (Stockman, 1964).
[50]W.P. Fuller & Co., 30 LA 545, 547 (Cobb, 1959).
[51]Marble Prods. Co., 40 LA 247, 253 (Marshall, 1963).
[52]United States Customs Serv., 68 LA 297, 301–302 (Nicholau, 1977). Also see Arbitrator Dunsford in 69 LA 39, 42–43.

the same circumstances, the requirement [of the contract] is met * * *."[53]

Arbitrator Wilber C. Bothwell summarized the prevailing view as follows:

> "The principle * * * is that an employee may refuse to carry out a particular work assignment if, at the time he is given the work assignment, he reasonably believes that by carrying out such work assignment he will endanger his safety or health. In such an instance the employee has the duty, not only of stating that he believes there is a risk to his safety or health, and the reason for believing so, but he also has the burden, if called upon, of showing by appropriate evidence that he had a reasonable basis for his belief. In the case of dispute, as is the case here, the question to be decided is not whether he actually would have suffered injury but whether he had a reasonable basis for believing so."[54]

Must Employees Explain Their Refusal?

Ordinarily, employees express their fear of danger and thus no question is presented as to whether the burden is on management to elicit or on employees to express the reasons for refusing to perform an assigned task. The question has been raised in a few cases, however. In the language just quoted, Arbitrator Bothwell appears to place the burden upon employees to state not only their fears but also their reasons for being fearful and to be prepared to substantiate their statements with evidence.[55]

Another arbitrator apparently would be more demanding of the employer in some circumstances. Thus, where the employee requested additional help for an assigned task but apparently could not articulate his fear, Arbitrator Dan Hopson took the approach that while ideally the duty to speak up should be equal, it does "not seem unreasonable" to impose a slightly higher standard upon the company to ask the uncommunicative employee why he refused to work.[56] However, Arbitrator John F. Sembower pointed out that the failure of management to ask employees for an explanation does not "excuse them forever from making one."[57]

The burden to explain or clarify may shift from employee to employer as a situation develops. For instance, where the company safety rules provided that employees should go to their supervisor "If special conditions arise which make [them] think it necessary to violate any safety rule in order to do [their] work," it was held that,

---

[53]Jefferson City Cabinet Co., 50 LA 213, 216 (1968).
[54]Laclede Gas Co., 39 LA 833, 839 (1962). For some of the later cases utilizing the "reasonable person" approach, see Arbitrator McCollister in 79 LA 587, 590; McAllister in 78 LA 836, 840–841; Ness in 77 LA 1080, 1084; Volz in 74 LA 620, 623; Foster in 73 LA 819, 824–825.
[55]Laclede Gas Co., 39 LA 833, 839 (1962). Accord, Arbitrator Stouffer in 41 LA 755, 759.
[56]Hercules, Inc., 48 LA 788, 795 (1967). Cf., Eaton, Yale & Towne, 50 LA 517, 521 (Levy, 1968), where the employee did not express his fears and the company did not inquire; held: insubordination justified the suspension.
[57]A.M. Castle & Co., 41 LA 667, 671 (1963).

after the employee raises a question as to the safety of the assignment, it then becomes the supervisor's responsibility to initiate any discussion and to give such advice and explanation as might be required.[58]

The Statutory Picture: OSHA, NLRA § 7, LMRA § 502

The U.S. Supreme Court in its 1980 *Whirlpool* decision upheld a regulation which was issued under the Occupational Safety and Health Act and which provided in substance that it "is the right of an employee to choose not to perform his assigned task because of a reasonable apprehension of death or serious injury coupled with a reasonable belief that no less drastic alternative is available."[59] Stating that the regulation "does not conflict with the general pattern of federal labor legislation in the area of occupational safety and health," the Court pointed out that the NLRA and the LMRA give "workers a right, under certain circumstances, to walk off their jobs when faced with hazardous conditions."[60]

Although the U.S. Supreme Court has recognized a statutory right to strike over safety issues, the Court also has recognized that the right may be waived by a contractual no-strike obligation. In its 1974 *Gateway Coal* decision, involving the enjoinability of a strike rather than any question of employee discipline, the Supreme Court held both that a collective agreement's broad arbitration clause covered safety disputes and that it gave "rise to an implied no-strike obligation."[61] The Court thus reached the question whether an exception to the no-strike obligation existed under § 502 of the Labor Management Relations Act. The latter Section provides that "the quitting of labor by an employee or employees in good faith because of abnormally dangerous conditions for work at the place of employment of such employee or employees [shall not] be deemed a strike." The Supreme Court held that § 502 "provides a limited exception to an express or implied no-strike obligation," but that "a union seeking to justify a contractually prohibited work stoppage under § 502 must

---

[58]Rome Kraft Co., 61–3 ARB ¶8792 (Hawley, 1961).

[59]Whirlpool Corp. v. Marshall, 100 S.Ct. 883, 886 (1980), where the regulation literally stated (1) that "an employer would not ordinarily be in violation of [OSHA] by taking action to discipline an employee for refusing to perform normal job activities because of alleged safety or health hazards"; but, (2) that such discipline would violate OSHA "If the employee, with no reasonable alternative, refuses in good faith to expose himself to the dangerous condition," provided that the condition "must be of such a nature that a reasonable person, under the circumstances then confronting the employee, would conclude that there is a real danger of death or serious injury and that there is insufficient time due to the urgency of the situation, to eliminate the danger through resort to regular statutory enforcement channels." The Court cautioned that "any employee who acts in reliance on the regulation runs the risk of discharge or reprimand in the event a court subsequently finds that he acted unreasonably or in bad faith." 100 S.Ct. at 895.

[60]100 S.Ct. at 893, where the Court explained (1) that under NLRA § 7 "employees have a protected right to strike over safety issues," the Court citing Washington Aluminum Co., 82 S.Ct. 1099, 60 LRRM 2235 (1962), and (2) that the effect of LMRA § 502 "is to create an exception to a no-strike obligation in a collective-bargaining agreement," the Court citing its *Gateway Coal* decision.

[61]Gateway Coal Co. v. United Mine Workers, 94 S.Ct. 629, 635–639, 85 LRRM 2049 (1974).

present 'ascertainable, objective evidence supporting its conclusion that an abnormally dangerous condition for work exists.' "[62]

Other important aspects of this subject are treated in the Supreme Court's 1984 *City Disposal Systems* decision. There in regard to the right of employees under NLRA § 7 to engage in "concerted activities for the purpose of collective bargaining or other mutual aid or protection," the Supreme Court (1) upheld the NLRB's *Interboro* doctrine under which an individual employee's assertion of a right grounded in a collective agreement is regarded as "concerted" activity,[63] but also the Court (2) indicated that even though the employee's action may qualify as "concerted," in some circumstances it nonetheless may be unprotected.[64]

---

[62]294 S.Ct. at 640–641, the Supreme Court rejecting the Court of Appeals view that "an honest belief, no matter how unjustified, in the existence of 'abnormally dangerous conditions for work' necessarily invokes the protection of § 502"; the Supreme Court stated that "If the courts require no objective evidence that such conditions actually obtain, they face a wholly speculative inquiry into the motives of the workers."

[63]NLRB v. City Disposal Sys., Inc., 104 S.Ct. 1505, 1510, 1514, 115 LRRM 3193 (1984), where an employee had been discharged for refusing to drive an allegedly unsafe truck. The Court noted the NLRB's rationale that an individual employee's assertion of a contractual right is an extension of the concerted action that produced the agreement and affects the rights of all employees covered by the agreement. In upholding the *Interboro* doctrine, the Supreme Court stated:

"As long as the employee's statement or action is based on a reasonable and honest belief that he is being, or has been, asked to perform a task that he is not required to perform under his collective-bargaining agreement, and the statement or action is reasonably directed toward the enforcement of a collectively bargained right, there is no justification for overturning the Board's judgment that the employee is engaged in concerted activity, just as he would have been had he filed a formal grievance."

It should be noted that shortly before the Supreme Court issued its *City Disposal Systems* decision, the NLRB itself had held in Meyers Indus., 115 LRRM 1025, 1029 (NLRB, 1984), that in order for action by an individual employee to qualify as "concerted," the action must "be engaged in with or on the authority of other employees, and not solely and on behalf of the employee himself"; but in so holding, the NLRB distinguished its *Interboro* doctrine on the basis that it applies to action taken by an employee in attempting to enforce an existing collective agreement, whereas in *Meyers* "there is no bargaining agreement, much less any attempt to enforce one." Id. at 1028.

[64]104 S.Ct. at 1514–1516, the Supreme Court cautioning that the fact that an activity is concerted "does not necessarily mean that an employee can engage in the activity with impunity," that an employee "may engage in concerted activity in such an abusive manner that he loses the protection of § 7," and that "if an employer does not wish to tolerate certain methods by which employees invoke their collectively bargained rights, he is free to negotiate a provision in his collective-bargaining agreement that limits the availability of such methods" (the Court mentioning no-strike provisions as one possible type of limitation). In *City Disposal Systems* the collective agreement expressly provided that the employer "shall not require employees to take out * * * any vehicle that is not in safe operating condition" and that it "shall not be a violation of the Agreement where employees refuse to operate such equipment unless such refusal is unjustified." The Supreme Court stated that because the employee "reasonably and honestly invoked his right to avoid driving unsafe trucks, his action was concerted," but the Court stated further:

"It may be that the collective-bargaining agreement prohibits an employee from refusing to drive a truck that he reasonably believes to be unsafe, but that is, in fact, perfectly safe. If so, Brown's action was concerted but unprotected."

The Supreme Court pointed out that the only issue before it, and the only issue passed upon by the NLRB or the Court of Appeals, was whether the employee's action was "concerted," not whether it was unprotected. The Supreme Court remanded the case for further proceedings, "including an inquiry into whether" the employee's action "was unprotected, even if concerted." Id. at 1516. In Irvin H. Whitehouse & Sons v. NLRB, 108 LRRM 2578, 2582 (CA 7, 1981), it was held that an arbitration provision created an implied no-strike obligation as to safety issues and permitted the discharge of two employees who quit work to protest allegedly unsafe conditions. Another case held unprotected an employee's refusal to perform a hazardous operation where he was aware, prior to taking the job, that the job was inherently dangerous. Daniel Constr. Co., 111 LRRM 1321 at 1321 (NLRB, 1982).

In view of the requirement under OSHA of "reasonable person" apprehension under the circumstances, and the requirement under LMRA § 502 of "ascertainable, objective evidence," it seems clear that the objective rather than subjective test applies under both statutes. On the other hand as concerns NLRA § 7, if nothing in the collective agreement is found to restrict an employee from refusing to work because of an alleged safety hazard, or if there is no collective agreement at all, and assuming that the refusal qualifies as "concerted," the NLRB may apply the subjective test (it thus sufficing that the particular employee acted in a good faith belief of danger) and find the employee to be protected against punishment by the employer.[65]

Compatibility of Award With Employee Rights Under Statute

It seems apparent that an award construing employee rights under a collective agreement will not be incompatible with employee rights under a statute unless the award holds the employee to a stricter standard than does the statute. We have observed the views of arbitrators under the collective agreement as concerns the safety exception to the "obey now—grieve later" rule. Arbitrators at one end of the spectrum apply the purely subjective test of what the particular employee believed, while arbitrators at the other end apply the objective test of what a "reasonable person" would have believed under the existing circumstances. We have also observed that under U.S. Supreme Court decisions both OSHA and LMRA § 502 utilize the objective test in determining applicability of the safety exception. Thus, whether the arbitrator utilizes the objective test or the subjective test, it appears that the award would be compatible with employee

---

[65]For an illustrative case in which the subjective test was used or arguably used, see Tamara Foods, Inc., 108 LRRM 1218, 1219 (NLRB, 1981), where the NLRB stated that:

"Inquiry into the objective reasonableness of employees' concerted activity is neither necessary nor proper in determining whether that activity is protected. * * * Whether the protested working condition was actually as objectionable as the employees believed it to be * * * is irrelevant to whether their concerted activity is protected by the Act."

The Board stated that the fact that the employees were not represented by a union or covered by a collective agreement containing a no-strike clause was of "particular significance." The Board also stated that the fact that OSHA had found the employer in compliance with its regulations could not negate rights of employees under NLRA § 7. The Board's order was enforced in NLRB v. Tamara Foods, Inc., 111 LRRM 3003 (CA 8, 1982). Another illustrative case is NLRB v. Modern Carpet Indus., 103 LRRM 2167, 2169 (CA 10, 1979), where the Court in enforcing the NLRB's reinstatement order agreed that the employees in good faith believed that working with radioactive lead was dangerous and, therefore, their refusal to work was protected by § 7. For other discussions of OSHA, § 502, and/or § 7 standards, see Smith, "Arbitrating Safety Grievances: Contract or Congress?" 33 Lab. L.J. 238 (1982); Backer, "Refusals of Hazardous Work Assignments: A Proposal for a Uniform Standard," 81 Colum. L. Rev. 544 (1981), proposing at p. 569 that other labor law standards "should be modified to conform to the standard established in the OSHA regulation," which "most clearly resolves the conflicting interests of employees and employers"; Drapkin & Davis, "Health and Safety Provisions in Union Contracts: Power or Liability?" 65 Minn. L. Rev. 635 (1981); McDonough, "Safety in the Workplace: Employee Remedies and Union Liability," 13 Creighton L. Rev. 955 (1980); Summa, "Criteria for Health and Safety Arbitration," 26 Lab. L.J. 368 (1975).

rights under OSHA and § 502, since the objective test meets the statutory standards while the subjective test simply implies that the collective agreement gives employees rights beyond those accorded by statute. But we also have observed that the less demanding subjective test has been utilized in certain NLRA § 7 cases not involving any express or implied no-strike obligation. Discipline assessed in such a case is not likely to reach an arbitrator (the absence of an implied no-strike obligation connotes the absence of any arbitration clause); but if such a case does reach arbitration and if the arbitrator utilizes the more demanding objective test, an award against the employee may possibly be held incompatible with NLRA § 7 rights unless the employee action otherwise constitutes unprotected conduct.[66]

Employee Complaints of Specific Hazards

Employee claims of safety and health hazards have been based upon many different circumstances, such as, complaints that plant temperature was too cold,[67] that ventilation was poor and the temperature too high,[68] that it was too drafty,[69] that fumes or dust produced unsafe working conditions,[70] that tobacco smoke produced a health hazard,[71] that employees were endangered by exposed or airborne asbestos,[72] and that excessive noise was detrimental to health.[73] In such cases, arbitrators attempt to distinguish between mere discomfort or displeasure and the situation in which a real threat

---

[66]Unless the Supreme Court or Congress at some point makes clear that the subjective test is or is not applicable to safety refusals to work under § 7, it will remain possible that an arbitration award utilizing the objective test may be held incompatible with the statute in certain cases.

[67]See 79 LA 231, 235–236 (involving federal guideline on 65–68 degree temperature); 73 LA 267, 268, 271 (complaint that temperature varied from too cold to too hot); 47 LA 332, 335; 46 LA 1131, 1135; 46 LA 920, 922; 41 LA 895, 898; 38 LA 1105, 1108–1109; 38 LA 655, 657; 37 LA 1101, 1103; 34 LA 678, 681; 22 LA 841; 22 LA 835, 837. Also see 41 LA 1144, 1146, where the employee was required to work outside in cold weather. For related discussion, see Mills, "The Energy Crisis and Labor Relations," 35 Arb. J. No. 4, p. 3 (1980).

[68]Wilcolator Co., 44 LA 847, 852 (Altieri, 1964).

[69]See 48 LA 1343, 1344; 47 LA 332, 335.

[70]See 81 LA 390, 392; 48 LA 1291, 1295–1296; 38 LA 375, 378; 61–2 ARB ¶8394; 31 LA 699, 701. Also see 49 LA 429, 430–431.

[71]See 78 LA 865, 867; 75 LA 308, 312; 55 LA 61, 62–64. In United States Steel Corp., 55 LA 61, 62–64 (Dybeck, 1970), an employee could not be punished for refusing to remove a dust respirator while attending a required safety meeting, there being tobacco smoke in the room. Employer rules prohibiting or restricting smoking were upheld under the circumstances by Arbitrator Clarke in 78 LA 865, 870; Grabb in 75 LA 308, 312; Yarowsky in 72 LA 258, 261. Such rules were found unreasonable under the circumstances by Arbitrator Koven in 79 LA 193, 195–196; Roberts in 69 LA 930, 932, 937–939; Lubow in 66 LA 928, 930. Also see Johns-Manville Sales v. IAM Local 1609, 621 F.2d 756 (CA 5, 1980). For court cases recognizing that employers who expose employees to tobacco smoke in the workplace possibly may be liable for breach of the common-law duty to provide a safe place to work, see Smith v. Western Elec. Co., 643 S.W.2d 10, 13 (Mo. Ct. App., 1982); Shrimp v. New Jersey Bell Tel. Co., 368 A.2d 408, 410, 413–416 (N.J. Super. Ct., 1976). For discussion, see Reynolds, "Extinguishing Brushfires: Legal Limits on the Smoking of Tobacco," 53 U. Cin. L. Rev. 435 (1984); Cochran, "The Worker's Right to a Smoke-Free Workplace," 19 U. Dayton L. Rev. 275 (1984).

[72]See 75 LA 988, 990 (exposed asbestos-covered wall); 73 LA 644 at 644 (airborne asbestos).

[73]Gallis Mfg. Co., 46 LA 75, 79 (Wood, 1966).

to employee health or safety is present, the result in any event being dependent upon the facts of the given case.[74]

Where the employee has refused to cross a picket line of another union due to alleged fear of harm, arbitrators have held such refusal unjustified unless based upon a "reasonable fear of violence."[75]

Defective equipment is another source of employee claims of safety or health hazard.[76] In this regard, it has been observed that the mere fact that defective equipment is operated without accident for some period of time does not mean that there was actually no danger at all; the arbitrator further noted that "any insurance actuarian will state that a hazard which persists long enough has an ever-increasing curve of expectation as to whether a loss will occur."[77]

Lack of experience or training on a job has been another basis for employee complaints of hazard. Thus, it has been held that while an assignment would not normally constitute an unsafe condition for those employees who were trained and experienced in the work, the task could be unsafe and an abnormal hazard where the employees are untrained or inexperienced.[78]

The co-worker's carelessness has been advanced as a reason for refusal of an assignment; an arbitrator's finding that a fellow employee was an unsafe driver was held to be justification for the grievant's refusal to ride with him.[79]

Physical or Mental Condition as a Safety Hazard

Physical or mental conditions giving rise to employer action on safety grounds are varied, including, for example, epilepsy,[80] Parkin-

---

[74]See, for example, Arbitrator Eaton in 73 LA 267, 270–271 (the agreement required the employer "to provide a safe and healthful working environment," and in denying a grievance protesting varying temperatures Arbitrator Eaton stated that while the union had "shown a feeling of discomfort on the part of many employees," it had not met its burden of proving "by a preponderance of the evidence that a truly unhealthful or unsafe work environment exists"); Stouffer in 53 LA 45, 55; Kallenbach in 48 LA 1291, 1295–1296; Duff in 46 LA 920, 922; Anrod in 38 LA 375, 378; Stutz in 22 LA 841; Smith in 22 LA 835, 837. Where the plant was in fact too cold to work in safety, the employees could not be punished for walking off the job. See Arbitrator Di Leone in 47 LA 332, 335–336; Goldberg in 46 LA 1131, 1136; Cabe in 38 LA 655, 657. For related discussion see the preceding subtopics.

[75]Gulf Coast Motor Lines, 49 LA 261, 262–263 (Williams, 1967). Similarly, Arbitrator Maniscalco in 67 LA 438, 441–442; Seidenberg in 45 LA 522, 523. In Phillips Pipe Line Co., 54 LA 1019, 1024 (Davey, 1970), a contractual safety clause was construed only to cover safety on the job—it did not apply to a picket line situation. A contractual safety clause similarly was held inapplicable to a racial conflict situation in Board of Educ. of City of Buffalo, 60 LA 357, 365 (McKelvey, 1973). In an "interest" case, the arbitrator prescribed protection to be afforded by a telephone company to its employees assigned to work in designated urban areas in which they reasonably fear they are in personal danger of criminal or physical attack. New York Tel. Co., 50 LA 21, 23–24 (McFadden, 1968).

[76]See Arbitrator Hayes in 73 LA 1100, 1103–1104 (stating that the mere fact of limited use of equipment does not minimize or negate a safety violation); Hopson in 48 LA 788, 796; Garrett in 45 LA 426, 429; Sembower in 41 LA 666, 670–671; Luskin in 34 LA 504, 506.

[77]A.M. Castle & Co., 41 LA 666, 671 (Sembower, 1963).

[78]Bethlehem Steel Corp., 49 LA 1203, 1206 (Strongin, 1968).

[79]United States Plywood-Champion Papers, 50 LA 115, 123–124 (Jenkins, 1968). Cf., Arbitrator Van Pelt in 72 LA 677, 681–682; Cobb in 32 LA 545, 547–548.

[80]See Arbitrator Edes in 77 LA 708, 709–710; Seibel in 74 LA 1154, 1161–1162; Cohen in 67

son's disease,[81] heart condition,[82] obesity,[83] fainting spells,[84] visual problems,[85] mental disability,[86] diabetes,[87] physical incapacity,[88] and pregnancy.[89] Arbitral disposition of such cases depends mainly upon medical evidence and evidence concerning safety aspects of grievant's condition as it relates to his work.

Management Action: Transfer, Demotion, Layoff, Leave of Absence, or Termination

The prevailing view of arbitrators would appear to be that management has not only the right but also the responsibility to take corrective action when an employee has a physical or mental disability which endangers his own safety or that of others. Such action may take the form of transfer, demotion, layoff, leave of absence, or even termination, depending upon the extent and nature of the employee's disability as well as upon other factors such as the availability of another job which he would be capable of performing.[90]

Thus, where an employee sustained a handicap which created a hazard to himself and others in his work, the arbitrator upheld the company's action in transferring him to a different job which he was capable of performing without undue hazard.[91] Such action has been upheld even though the transfer was tantamount to a demotion.[92] As indicated below, however, some arbitrators appear reluctant to

---

LA 706, 707–708; Yeager in 63 LA 56, 59; Moberly in 61 LA 1115, 1118–1119; Morris in 53 LA 578, 583; Gorsuch in 45 LA 616, 620; Murphy in 44 LA 1252, 1263; Hale in 40 LA 18, 26–28; May in 38 LA 1049, 1054; Petree in 38 LA 829, 838; Roberts in 38 LA 826, 828–829; McCoy in 37 LA 503, 505–506. For a discussion of earlier cases, see Florey, "Medical Separation of Epileptics," 17 Arb. J. 175 (1962).

[81]See Arbitrator Tripp in 64–1 ARB ¶8026; Stouffer in 38 LA 156, 160–161.

[82]See Arbitrator Boles in 43 LA 734, 739–740; Rubin in 41 LA 337, 339; Valtin in 39 LA 918, 920–921; Cahn in 62–3 ARB ¶8803, and in 61–3 ARB ¶8747.

[83]See Arbitrator Cohen in 79 LA 1100, 1102; Block in 48 LA 2, 9–10; Kates in 43 LA 61, 63–64; Scheiber in 41 LA 278, 284; Donnelly in 37 LA 456, 458.

[84]See Hughes Aircraft Co., 41 LA 535, 541–544 (Block, 1963).

[85]See Arbitrator Dworkin in 66–3 ARB ¶8999; Scheiber in 41 LA 278, 284; Lande in 40 LA 799, 804–805; Williams in 61–3 ARB ¶8657.

[86]See Arbitrator Roumell in 76 LA 355, 357, 362–363; Roomkin in 76 LA 167, 169; Traynor in 66 LA 533, 537–538; Dworkin in 45 LA 377, 383, and in 45 LA 384, 387; Guthrie in 38 LA 297, 299–300; Mueller in 37 LA 629, 633–634; Kelliher in 37 LA 175, 176.

[87]See E.W. Bliss Co., 43 LA 217, 223–224 (Klein, 1964).

[88]See Arbitrator Emery in 49 LA 403, 404–405 (leg injury); Luskin in 48 LA 649, 650–653 (back trouble); Florey in 41 LA 597, 598 (impaired sight, hearing, and balance after having had meningitis); Reid in 37 LA 126, 128 (one leg amputated as a result of diabetes).

[89]See Arbitrator Brown in 64 LA 511, 513–514; Wallen in 47 LA 1135, 1141; Sembower in 38 LA 632, 638–639. Also see Bailey in 78 LA 1276, 1283.

[90]See cases cited in this topic hereinbelow. An important aspect of physical or mental disability cases is the evidence adduced at the hearing. In this regard, see Chapter 8, topic entitled "Medical Evidence." For other related discussion, see Chapter 13, topic entitled "Disqualifying Employees for Physical or Mental Reasons."

[91]American Zinc Co., 46 LA 645, 652–654 (Abernethy, 1966); United States Steel Corp., 64–1 ARB ¶8026 (Tripp, 1963). Also upholding transfers required by the employer for safety or health reasons, Arbitrator Kates in 79 LA 895, 897–899; Dyke in 70 LA 596, 599.

[92]See Arbitrator Jaffe in 78 LA 1160, 1162–1163; Murphy in 44 LA 1252, 1263; Tripp in 64–1 ARB ¶8026. Also see Blackmar in 79 LA 419, 421–422 (safety was a factor in upholding termination of trial period on better job); Aronin in 79 LA 357, 362 (desired assignment was denied as carrying special risk to grievant); Seinsheimer in 77 LA 773, 775; Evensen in 76 LA 1233, 1236 (safety considerations limited grievant to job paying less); Abernethy in 46 LA 645, 654. For related discussion, see Chapter 13, topic entitled "Demotion of Employees."

require management, where not obligated by the contract, to offer a disabled employee another, less hazardous job even if it is available,[93] or to create one for the employee.[94]

An employer may be upheld in placing an ailing employee on medical leave of absence where justified by safety considerations. In one such case, Arbitrator Samuel S. Perry rejected the view that the only relevant consideration is whether the employee can give a fair day's work on the assigned job:

> "Management has a right to look further than 'a fair day's work.' It has a right and an obligation to look to the physical well-being of its employees and the condition of the firm's physical plant. The true test is whether it appears to management that the employee can *safely* give a fair day's work on the job assigned to him without endangering either his own health or safety, the health and safety of his fellow employees, or the physical plant of the Company."[95]

Also, when an employee has been on medical leave of absence, the arbitrator may on safety grounds uphold the company's refusal to recall him; but the arbitrator may also rule that if the employee's condition improves in the future so that there would no longer be a safety hazard, he may then seek return to work.[96] For example, in a case involving an employee seeking reinstatement following extended sick leave because of recurrence of his mental illness, Arbitrator Harry J. Dworkin stated:

> "* * * An employee who is mentally ill to the point that his employment presents abnormal risks to management and to his fellow employees is obviously not entitled to be returned to his job. A determination that such conditions exist does not foreclose reconsideration and reappraisal upon subsequent change in the employee's condition. An employee who is physically or mentally ill may not be forever condemned to be deprived of the right to employment; when the conditions have changed so as to require re-evaluation of the existence of a legitimate reason or basis for denial of employment, he is entitled to further consideration."[97]

---

[93]See cases cited below in note 99. Also see Arbitrator Doyle in 49 LA 535, 540; Scheiber in 41 LA 279, 284; Platt in 14 LA 444, 446.

[94]See Arbitrator Rule in 75 LA 1154, 1158; Belcher in 52 LA 1152, 1154; Rubin in 41 LA 337, 339; Feinberg in 40 LA 1254, 1258; Hale in 40 LA 18, 26–28. Also see Short in 38 LA 1076, 1083–1084.

[95]Auer Register Co., 62 LA 235, 238–239 (1974). Also upholding compulsory medical leave for safety reasons, Arbitrator Wray in 79 LA 110, 116–117; Doyle in 49 LA 535, 539–540. For cases holding that medical leave rather than discharge should have been utilized, see Arbitrator Roomkin in 76 LA 167, 169; Klein in 69 LA 922, 928 (employer had the right and obligation to sever mentally ill employee "from active employment," but the proper means of accomplishing the severance was a medical leave of absence rather than discharge for the employee's unprovoked assault upon another employee).

[96]See Arbitrator Gibson in 62 LA 558, 561; Kates in 43 LA 61, 64–65; Florey in 41 LA 597, 598; Stouffer in 38 LA 156, 160–161. Also see Stern in 71 LA 161, 164.

[97]Ashtabula Bow Socket Co., 45 LA 377, 383 (1965), where he directed further examination of the grievant by an "impartial" psychiatrist; in a supplemental award, 45 LA 384, 387, he reinstated the grievant following such examination but retained jurisdiction of the case for an additional six months "during which period he will be authorized to consider any problems which may arise concerning grievant's employment following his reinstatement." Also see Arbitrator Katz in 79 LA 590, 592–593; Seibel in 74 LA 1154, 1161–1162 (airline unreasonably refused to return to flight attendant duty an epileptic "who had been seizure free for some two and one-half years"); Cohen in 67 LA 706, 707–708; Traynor in 66 LA 533, 537–538 (holding mentally ill employee entitled to a six-month trial period, termination to be permitted if trial period is unsuccessful).

Similarly, where an employee has been laid off because there is no available work which he could safely perform due to his physical condition, the arbitrator may approve the continuation of his layoff status subject to his being recalled to a job which may become available in the future and which his seniority and ability may warrant.[98]

Many arbitrators are in accord with the view that an employee's physical or mental disability may constitute just cause for his termination "if the disability is of such kind and degree as to make unduly hazardous to himself or to others his employment in any job in his employer's facility which he is qualified to fill and which is available to be assigned to him."[99]

Protecting the Employee Himself

In some cases, a prime objective in denying an employee's request for reinstatement in his former job was to protect the employee himself from possible danger even though he was willing to undertake the risk.[100] But in others, the arbitrator stated either that he lacked the authority or that the employer lacked the right to prevent the employee from endangering his life.[101]

---

[98]Glass Container Mfrs. Inst. 66–3 ARB ¶8999 (Dworkin, 1966); Hughes Aircraft Co., 41 LA 535, 541–544 (Block, 1963).

[99]Stauffer Chem. Co., 40 LA 18, 26 (Hale, 1963). Also permitting termination on the basis of physical or mental disability, Arbitrator Stonehouse in 79 LA 943, 946; Edes in 77 LA 708, 709–710; Roomkin in 76 LA 167, 169; Rule in 75 LA 1154, 1157–1158; Duff in 75 LA 12, 14; Jacobs in 73 LA 228, 231–232; Stashower in 68 LA 69, 72, and in 45 LA 464, 465–466; Yaeger in 53 LA 56, 59; Moberly in 61 LA 1115, 1118–1119; Rentfro in 59 LA 726, 729; Davis in 59 LA 200, 201; Doyle in 58 LA 764, 767; Luskin in 48 LA 649, 650–653; Block in 48 LA 2, 9–10; Boles in 43 LA 734, 739; Rubin in 41 LA 337, 339; May in 38 LA 1049, 1054; Roberts in 38 LA 826, 828–829; Mueller in 37 LA 629, 633–634; McCoy in 37 LA 503, 505–506; Kelliher in 37 LA 175, 176; Reid in 37 LA 126, 128, and in 34 LA 681, 685; Merrill in 20 LA 480, 481. Three gradations may be observed in the foregoing cases upholding termination: (1) in many of the cases it was expressly indicated that no job was available for which the disabled employee was qualified and which he could fill safely; (2) in a fair number of the cases no reference was made to any need to consider the possibility of another job for the employee instead of termination; (3) such consideration was expressly held not required in a few of the cases. On the other hand, there are cases in which termination has been overruled on the basis that the employer failed to take steps to place the employee on a job he could handle. See Arbitrator Welch in 81 LA 486, 488; Nichols in 66 LA 86, 90; Hayes in 60 LA 674, 676; Rentfro in 59 LA 722, 725; McNaughton in 50 LA 1277, 1279; Black in 43 LA 1225, 1228; Donnelly, Curry & Clark in 20 LA 266, 268. For related discussion, see Wolkinson, "Arbitration and the Employment Rights of the Physically Disadvantaged," 36 Arb. J. No. 1, pp. 23, 30 (1981), comparing results reached in arbitration with those produced by the Office of Federal Contract Compliance Programs under the Rehabilitation Act of 1973. The impact of the latter Act in some cases is illustrated by United Technologies Corp., 80 LA 92 (Bloch, 1982).

[100]See Arbitrator Abrams in 73 LA 1269, 1273; Rakas & Garrett in 68 LA 785, 788; Luskin in 48 LA 649, 653; Abernethy in 46 LA 645, 653; Block in 41 LA 535, 543; Hale in 40 LA 18, 26–28; Roberts in 38 LA 826, 828–829; Reid in 37 LA 126, 128. In Warner & Swazey Co., 53 LA 643, 644–645 (High, 1969), the arbitrator upheld an employer's refusal to permit an employee to come to work with a splint on his finger because the condition created a safety hazard to the employee. Also see Aronin in 79 LA 357, 362; Garrett in 70 LA 171, 172–173.

[101]See Arbitrator Cohen in 79 LA 1100, 1102–1103; Seinsheimer in 50 LA 1171, 1175–1176 (where he ruled, however, that the company could properly discharge the employee, afflicted with silicosis, and rehire him in a nonunit job in order to protect itself from increased insurance premiums); Valtin in 39 LA 918, 920–921 (where he decided that the evidence did not support a finding that termination of grievant, who had had four attacks, was necessary in the best interests of the company, and that under the contract neither the arbitrator nor the company could decide for the grievant whether he should risk shortening his life by return to work). Also see Bernstein in 66 LA 211, 215. Cf., Cahn in 61–3 ARB ¶8747.

Chapter 17

Employee Rights and Benefits

Over the years, the give and take between management and employees has resulted in the establishment of certain employee rights and benefits (such as paid vacations and paid holidays) which are covered by the agreement or which evolved out of a well-established practice. Other rights may be asserted by employees which are more personal in nature and which are less firmly established or not recognized at all in labor-management relations. These asserted personal rights often are indirectly brought to the fore when management enforces a plant rule (such as one dealing with personal appearance), or when management disciplines an employee for refusing to obey a management directive issued pursuant to some contractual right (such as a work-scheduling clause under which the company schedules Sunday work), or when a grievance is filed charging that management has violated some provision of the agreement (such as a maintenance-of-practices clause).

Many employee rights are reflected and sometimes extensively treated in other chapters of this book. Various other employee rights or asserted rights not dealt with elsewhere are collected and discussed in the present chapter. By the same token, not all subjects in this chapter involve employee rights alone. Management, too, has rights and privileges pertaining to these subjects.

As can be readily recognized, in any given area of labor-management relations there may be claim and counterclaim of rights. However, it must also be recognized that many of the asserted employee rights relate more to "the area of traditional and conventional management discretion" concerning operations and production than to "employee rights not so intimately connected with the production process."[1] Thus, while discussion of employee rights in this chapter necessarily includes a discussion of management rights, all of the subjects involve considerations which may be of great personal interest to individual employees.

---

[1]Eastern Air Lines, 44 LA 1034, 1040 (Yagoda, 1965).

Vacations

Employees have no inherent right to vacations; rather, vacation rights arise out of the contract.[2] Employees, of course, are interested in vacations not only for the rest and relaxation derived from such periods away from work but also for the pay received. The company is also said to have an interest, aside from immediate production needs, in employee vacations. Thus, as stated by Arbitrator Marlin M. Volz:

> "Vacations are for the mutual benefit of employees and employers. The employee who returns to work after a period of rest and relaxation and who has had some free time with his family and to tend to personal affairs is a more valuable man to his employer. * * * A vacation is also one of the economic attractions which a Company offers to its employees to remain on the payroll or to become employees. While a vacation may be regarded as earned or deferred compensation, it may also be considered as an investment by the Company in promoting the longevity of service of its employees and a more productive working force."[3]

Scheduling Vacations

From the employee's standpoint, his right to take his vacation "at a time personally selected is a valuable right";[4] but it is a right that is limited by considerations of business needs. Herein lies the conflict that is reflected in the great number of arbitration cases on scheduling vacations.

It is said that "one of the prerogatives of management [is] to schedule vacations at such time as best meets the needs of the business," and that "in doing so the employer will very often and perhaps wherever possible also try to do his utmost to meet the wishes of employees."[5] Arbitrator Harold W. Davey elaborated:

> "Absent specific contract language, it is generally understood in industrial relations practice that a vacation is an earned equity and is generally to be taken in terms of the employee's preference, subject to the exigencies of the Company's production and maintenance requirements. Where the contract is silent on the specific policy or procedure to be followed, it must be assumed that the employee will request his vacation at a time suitable to his own preferences and that his preferences will be honored to the degree that Company requirements will permit. How-

---

[2]See Arbitrator R. Williams in 66 LA 160, 161; C. Williams in 65 LA 745, 747; Volz in 59 LA 1245, 1247, and in 48 LA 965, 968; Jaffee in 44 LA 1045, 1049.

[3]Dover Corp., 48 LA 965, 969 (1966). Similar language was used in Blue Box Co., 61 LA 754, 755 (Gibson, 1973). Also see Ajax Rolled Ring Co., 71 LA 460, 461 (Daniel, 1978), noting the increasing importance of time off with or without pay because of "economic security, social and family commitments and * * * personal items of lifestyle that frequently put money in second place to doing one's own thing."

[4]Welch Grape Juice Co., 48 LA 1018, 1021 (Altrock, 1967). The length of permitted vacation may be affected by the time when it is taken. See R.D. Werner Co., 55 LA 303, 305 (Kates, 1970), holding that increased vacation benefits under a new contract were not retroactive where the new contract did not expressly provide for retroactivity for employees who had already taken their vacation for the year.

[5]Sinclair Ref. Co., 12 LA 183, 189 (Klamon, 1949). Arbitrator Klamon reiterated (as dictum) this inherent right in Heil Packing Co., 36 LA 454, 458 (1961). Also see Tenneco Chems., 51 LA 699, 701 (Williams, 1968).

ever, where the contract is silent, it must also be assumed that managerial discretion is greater than in those cases where contract language puts the burden on management to show need for the employee to take his vacation at a particular time, or not to take vacation at a particular time."[6]

Operational Needs—Whether management is given the right by the agreement or possesses it as a residual power, the right to schedule vacations should be exercised with certain considerations in mind. The needs of the business and the maintenance of production are important considerations in vacation scheduling.[7] For instance, under an agreement permitting employees to select their vacation dates whenever practicable, management was permitted to schedule vacations at such times as would not interfere with its operations or increase its costs.[8] Similarly, under a clause providing that "the vacation period shall be selected by the employees by departments in the order of their seniority," but where the contract also reserved exclusively to management the "disposition and number of the working forces," it was held that the vacation desires of the employees should be honored to the extent that this would not unreasonably interfere with orderly plant operations.[9]

However, management may be required to justify denying an employee his preferred vacation time.[10] Thus, under a contract providing that "Vacations will, so far as possible, be granted at times most desired by employees," reserving to the company "the final right to allot vacation periods * * * in order to insure the orderly operation of the plants," it was held that the grievant was improperly denied his choice of vacation time since, contrary to management's contentions, there was available another employee who had been trained to fill the position, and hence there would have been no interference with the "orderly operation of the plants."[11]

Justification was shown under a similar contract clause with the result that the employer could deny the right to take vacations during summer months where business forecasts indicated that work would be at its "peak."[12]

---

[6]Hubinger Co., 29 LA 459, 461 (1957).

[7]See Arbitrator Pittoco in 70 LA 149, 150; Hedges in 64 LA 906, 911; Rill in 61 LA 958, 961; Kelliher in 48 LA 1000, 1004. For cases dealing with the special problems involved in scheduling extended vacations, see Arbitrator Altrock in 61 LA 1061, 1063; McDaniel in 53 LA 264, 265–266; Strongin in 46 LA 702, 704; Kates in 45 LA 120, 124–125; Tongue in 44 LA 475, 478–479; C. McDermott in 44 LA 906, 909–910; Garrett in 43 LA 790, 795–797 (listing 7 factors to be considered in scheduling EVs); T. McDermott in 42 LA 1002, 1007–1008.

[8]Sinclair Ref. Co., 12 LA 183, 190 (Klamon, 1949); National Tube Co., 19 LA 330, 331 (Garrett, 1952). Also see Arbitrator Erbs in 73 LA 813, 815–816; Taylor in 73 LA 687, 690; Livengood in 30 LA 225, 229; McKelvey in 25 LA 94, 98. Cf., Emory in 17 LA 461, 462.

[9]Carling Brewing Co., 46 LA 715, 717–718 (Kates, 1966). Cf., Arbitrator Denson in 73 LA 906, 908. The employee must submit his request by the stated contract date in order for his vacation preference to be given "consideration." MacMillan Bloedel, 65 LA 1252, 1254–1255 (King, 1976).

[10]See Arbitrator Tongue in 44 LA 475, 477, citing many cases; Gill in 36 LA 488, 490; Valtin in 30 LA 899, 900.

[11]United States Steel Corp., 53 LA 222, 224 (McDermott, 1969). Similarly, New York Ship-Building Corp., 43 LA 854, 855–856 (Crawford, 1964). But it has been held that management is not required to recall laid-off employees in order to accommodate vacation preferences. Bethlehem Steel Co., 39 LA 673, 675 (Gill, 1962).

[12]Westinghouse Elec. Corp., 40 LA 972, 974 (Cahn, 1963). Also see Arbitrator Manos in 66 LA 64, 65.

Under an employee preference clause, one arbitrator ruled that management could not reserve certain weeks exclusively for foremen's vacations since the presence of such preference clause in the contract "obligates the Company to give priority to employees' preferences over the foremen's choices where the two conflict, so long as there is no problem about the 'orderly and efficient operation of the plant.' "[13]

In another case, the parties had a practice of having a one-week vacation shutdown, but the grievant was entitled by contract to a second week of vacation. The parties had no established practice and the company had no policy in regard to the second week. Although the contract was silent as to the scheduling of vacations, the arbitrator stated that the company's discretion was limited by the vacation clause according grievant two weeks, which clause could not be "frustrated by arbitrary and unreasonable denial of employee preferences," and that grievant's preference for his second week of vacation should be granted unless an "adequate reason relating to the operational and production needs of the Company" could be shown.[14]

Where operational needs have been established, arbitrators have permitted management to limit the number of employees who could be on vacation at the same time.[15] But another arbitrator rejected both the company's limit and the union's demand—rather he stated a procedure for determining in a flexible manner the number of employees to be on vacation at a given time.[16]

Vacation Shutdown—Umpire Harry Shulman pointed out that some correlation between vacations and what otherwise would be layoffs is not only permissible but also desirable.[17] Under an agreement giving management the right to schedule vacations, the scheduling of vacations to coincide with temporary shutdowns was permitted.[18] There are limitations, however. For instance, where an agreement gave management the right to schedule vacations subject to the requirement that "due consideration" be given to employees' wishes, Umpire Shulman, distinguishing temporary and indefinite

---

[13]Air Reduction Chem. & Carbide Co., 42 LA 1192, 1195 (Kesselman, 1964), distinguishing Armstrong Cork Co., 37 LA 21, 23 (Williams, 1961), on the basis of strong contract language giving management the right to designate vacation time.

[14]National Lock Co., 48 LA 588, 590–591 (Volz, 1967).

[15]See Arbitrator Gilden in 46 LA 887, 890; Seward in 36 LA 584, 585–586. In Reynolds Metals Co., 44 LA 475, 476–477 (Tongue, 1965), the company's limit was raised by the arbitrator. In Laclede Steel Co., 54 LA 506, 507–508 (Kelliher, 1970), management could schedule vacations on an equal basis over the full year and thus eliminate the "summer bulge" of vacations.

[16]Carling Brewing Co., 46 LA 715, 717–718 (Kates, 1966). Also see Mansfield Tire & Rubber Co., 32 LA 762, 766–767 (Shaw, 1959), where the arbitrator was requested to and did formulate a procedure to be followed in scheduling vacations.

[17]Ford Motor Co., 3 LA 829, 831 (1946).

[18]Sefton Fibre Can Co., 12 LA 101, 105 (Townsend, 1948). Also permitting vacation shutdowns, see Arbitrator Feller in 52 LA 257, 259; Williams in 51 LA 699, 700–701 (involving a vacation clause giving management strong rights in the final allocation of vacation periods), and in 39 LA 659, 660–661; Whitton in 39 LA 149, 150–151 (emphasizing the necessity of showing production requirements); Jaffee in 37 LA 458, 464; Livengood in 30 LA 225, 231. Cf., Continental Can Co., 35 LA 836, 840 (Miller, 1960). In Wyman-Gordon Co., 51 LA 561, 565 (Rauch, 1968), past practice strongly supported the two-week vacation shutdown.

layoff, ruled that management could not require employees to take their vacations during a period of indefinite layoff where to do so would destroy the substantive features of a vacation. He reasoned:

> "A vacation is a period of rest between periods of work. A layoff is a period of anxiety and hardship between periods of work. The tremendous difference lies in the assurance of the vacationer that he will return to work at the end of his vacation and the equal assurance of the employee on layoff that he does not know when he will return to work. The basic difference, with its financial, emotional, and psychological implications, is not obliterated by a form of words or by the receipt of income for a part of the indefinite period of layoff."[19]

Other arbitrators have held that, where the contract provides that the employer is to consider the requests of individual employees for particular vacation times, the company may not order a vacation shutdown, since to schedule such a vacation would be to fail to take into account the desires of individual employees as required by contract.[20] However, under "clear, precise, unequivocal" contract language simply stating that "Vacations are to be granted as designated by the Management of the Company," with no reservations, restrictions, or limitations in favor of employee desires, it was held that the company had the right to designate a two-week vacation shutdown.[21] In another case the contract granted employees preference as to vacation dates, but it reserved to management the "final right to allot vacation periods and to change such allotments" and (with the required notice) to schedule regular vacations during a shutdown period in lieu of previously scheduled vacations; it was held that management had the right to schedule two separate vacation shutdowns during the year.[22]

A vacation shutdown does not necessarily exclude the performance of all work in the plant. Thus, where the contract permitted a two-week vacation shutdown, it was held that the shutdown need not be "total" but that the employer could work employees on essential maintenance, limited receiving and shipping, and limited clerical payroll functions.[23]

---

[19]Ford Motor Co., 3 LA 829, 831 (1946). Cf., Westinghouse Elec. Corp., 45 LA 131, 140 (Hebert, 1965). As to scheduling vacations for employees who are already on layoff, see United States Steel Corp., 36 LA 603, 615–616 (Garrett, 1961). In Kentile Floors, 55 LA 808, 812–813 (Cyrol, 1970), the employees had started applying for unemployment compensation during plant shutdown periods, thus adding to costs; the arbitrator upheld management's right to schedule vacations during plant shutdown. Cf., Arbitrator Williams in 65 LA 745, 747–748.

[20]See Arbitrator Altrock in 48 LA 1018, 1021 (opinion reinforced by past practice); Nichols in 42 LA 1321, 1325–1326; Sembower in 38 LA 389, 392–395 (distinguishing the Shulman award in 3 LA 829); Manson in 35 LA 921, 923–924; Valtin in 35 LA 535, 538–539, and in 33 LA 772, 774; Eckhardt in 32 LA 913, 916–917; Wolff in 32 LA 776, 781; Seward in 30 LA 992, 994; Kelliher in 18 LA 934, 935. Also see Howlett in 59 LA 613, 616–621 (discussing many cases). Cf., Taylor in 81 LA 254, 258; Smith in 15 LA 568, 572–573. But see Williams in 39 LA 1108, 1111; Schmidt in 34 LA 693, 697–698; Garrett in 19 LA 330, 331.

[21]Wisconsin Bridge & Iron Co., 46 LA 993, 1004–1005 (Solomon, 1966). A like result was reached in Vogt Mfg. Corp., 44 LA 488, 489–490 (Sarachan, 1965), where the contract had no provision as to scheduling vacations.

[22]United States Steel Corp., 59 LA 195, 196 (McDermott, 1972). Cf., Arbitrator Larkin in 54 LA 501, 503, where the contract specified a shutdown for a "two-week period during the summer."

[23]General Cable Corp., 48 LA 1000, 1004 (Kelliher, 1967). Also see United States Steel Corp., 69 LA 719, 721 (Edwards, 1977), where the union argued unsuccessfully that retention of a junior employee to service other operations violated seniority provisions of the agreement.

Vacation Period Fixed by Contract—Where the agreement fixes the period for taking vacations, the employer has been held not entitled to designate in addition any other vacation period.[24] Employees, too, have been confined to the fixed vacation period. Thus, under a contract which entitled employees with a year's service to a paid vacation, the employee who completed his year's service after the end of the vacation period fixed by contract was required to wait until the following vacation season to take his vacation.[25]

The contract may state specific requirements for the posting of vacation schedules. Strictly construing such a contract, one arbitrator held improper a notice posted two days after the deadline date and reached the "equitable" solution of setting the vacation period to be the same as in prior years.[26]

Remedy for Forced Vacations—While forced vacations are not always improper,[27] the question sometimes arises as to what remedy can be applied by the arbitrator when the company has improperly scheduled and "forced" vacations. One arbitrator awarded "damages" by requiring the company to give the grievants another week's vacation with pay;[28] another refused to duplicate vacation pay but awarded another week's vacation.[29] Another arbitrator, finding that he could not "assign a monetary value to grievants' mental discomfort," refused to grant additional pay in view of the company's good-faith belief that the agreement permitted its action (which apparently had been unchallenged by the union in previous years); but he warned that the company was now on notice and could in the future be required to give the aggrieved employee "either a further vacation on the proper dates or pay-in-lieu thereof."[30]

Vacation Benefits: Deferred Wages or "Refresher"?

Perhaps the confusion of theories as to whether vacations are refreshers or deferred wages can best be approached from the histor-

---

[24]Cone Mills, 29 LA 346, 350 (McCoy, 1957). Cf., General Am. Transp. Co., 15 LA 481, 484 (Kelliher, 1950). Nor may the employer pay vacation pay to laid-off employees prior to the contractually agreed vacation period, in view of the practical impact of such action upon the employees' entitlement to unemployment compensation, S.U.B. benefits, and vacations within the agreed period as required by contract. See United States Steel Corp., 36 LA 113, 116 (Garrett, 1961). Also see Arbitrator McIntosh in 70 LA 186, 190; Greco in 62 LA 149, 154–155.

[25]Kent of Grand Rapids, 18 LA 160, 162–163 (Platt, 1952); General Cable Corp., 18 LA 44, 45–46 (Cahn, 1952). Also see Victor Metal Prods. Corp., 66 LA 333, 336–337 (Ray, 1976). For a "split vacation" case, see Riverdale Plating & Heat Treating Co., 71 LA 43, 46–47 (Petersen, 1978).

[26]Interstate Indus., 46 LA 879, 881 (Howlett, 1966).

[27]See, for example, Arbitrator Moore in 65 LA 572, 576–577; Render in 64 LA 1021, 1027–1028 (involving U.S. Army civilian employees); Kaye in 68 LA 160, 162–163, holding that where employees returned late from a coffee break the Social Security Administration's action of charging the time against annual leave (vacation) was nondisciplinary and permissible under a contract permitting enforced leave when an employee is not "ready, willing and able to work."

[28]Scovil Mfg. Co., 31 LA 646, 651 (Jaffee, 1958). Also see Arbitrator Valtin in 37 LA 821, 824; Gill in 37 LA 134, 139 (also involving unemployment benefits); Garrett in 33 LA 82, 84.

[29]Chrysler Corp., 32 LA 776, 781 (Wolff, 1959). Also see Arbitrator Howlett in 59 LA 613, 621; Sembower in 38 LA 389, 395; Fleming in 31 LA 37, 41.

[30]Bethlehem Steel Co., 31 LA 857, 858 (Seward, 1958). Also see Arbitrator Williams in 39 LA 1051, 1057; Valtin in 33 LA 772, 775.

ical view, namely, that originally a vacation was a gratuity "awarded" to faithful employees for past services and to "refresh" them for future service. As the collective bargaining process has evolved, vacations and vacation benefits (while still providing rest and relaxation) have become more and more the subjects of bargaining and as such are considered and included in the "wage package," or are at the least bargained against higher wages or other employee benefits. Indeed, vacation provisions often are included in the wage section of the agreement.[31] The so-called trend in decisions toward considering such benefits deferred wages which vest in the employee is the result of recognition of the industrial-relations fact that the parties themselves have bargained for and made vacation benefits a part of the agreement. It is therefore, as usual, to the contract and its bargaining history that one must turn in order to ascertain the status of vacation benefits.[32] In this connection, the U.S. Supreme Court has noted that generally the presence of a work requirement in the contract is strong evidence that the vacation benefit was intended as a form of deferred compensation for work actually performed.[33]

Even though vacation rights may vest in the employee, entitlement to such rights is not absolute but may require compliance with conditions of the agreement such as a minimum length of service (for example, requiring 52 full weeks of employment),[34] or being on the payroll as of a particular date.[35]

The question of vesting of vacation rights has been raised in situations of plant closure or sale of the business,[36] voluntary quit or

---

[31]See, for example, Infant Socks, 51 LA 400, 402 (Moberly, 1968).

[32]For discussion of various aspects of these and other related concepts and/or collections of cases, see Arbitrator Talmadge in 81 LA 489, 492–493; Jackson in 66 LA 745, 749; White in 64 LA 791, 792–794; Warns in 60 LA 1200, 1201; Murphy in 52 LA 837, 839–840; Moberly in 51 LA 400, 402–403; Doyle in 51 LA 349, 350–351; Cox in 49 LA 837, 838–839; Volz in 48 LA 965, 968–969, and in 34 LA 170, 172; McDermott in 43 LA 860, 862; Larkin in 41 LA 513, 514; Cheney in 38 LA 737, 739; Brown in 35 LA 560, 565; Hogan in 34 LA 158, 163–165; Reid in 33 LA 316, 318; Wirtz in 32 LA 156, 168–169; Feinberg, "Do Contract Rights Vest?" Proceedings of the 16th Annual Meeting of NAA, 194–205 (BNA Books, 1963).

[33]Foster v. Dravo Corp., 95 S.Ct. 879, 884–885, 89 LRRM 2988 (1975). The Court concluded that since the returning veteran had not met the work requirement in the agreement, § 9 of the Military Selective Service Act did not guarantee him full vacation benefits for the year in question.

[34]Great Atl. & Pac. Tea Co., 43 LA 1, 2 (Turkus, 1964). Also see Arbitrator Beckman in 67 LA 641, 643; Owen in 67 LA 1265, 1267; Moberly in 51 LA 400, 403; Singer in 49 LA 895, 897; Cox in 49 LA 837, 838; Doyle in 39 LA 489, 491; Cheney in 38 LA 737, 739–740; Brown in 35 LA 560, 565; Ross in 33 LA 837, 840.

[35]See Arbitrator Gershenfeld in 69 LA 431, 434; Bradley in 61 LA 342, 346–347; Seitz in 53 LA 692, 692–693. Also see Gilden in 49 LA 646, 648; Davis in 48 LA 938, 940; Turkus in 42 LA 1332, 1334; Doyle in 39 LA 489, 491; Jaffee in 28 LA 838, 841 (who found that because of the plant closure, employees' failure to be at work on the eligibility date was not attributable to them). For examples of cases viewing the "eligibility date" simply as a "cut-off date" for computing vacation pay and not as condition precedent for entitlement to vacation benefits, see Murphy in 52 LA 837, 840; Moberly in 51 LA 400, 403; Cox in 49 LA 837, 838; Markowitz in 38 LA 912, 915; Brown in 35 LA 560, 565; Hogan in 34 LA 158, 163.

[36]In these cases, arbitrators speak in terms of vacation rights as deferred earnings which have vested in the employee; in some instances they point out that vacation pay is by contract based upon the employee's earnings. See Arbitrator Kates in 58 LA 1111, 1116–1117; Moberly in 51 LA 400, 403; Doyle in 51 LA 349, 350; Reid in 49 LA 421, 422; Markowitz in 38 LA 912, 915; Brown in 35 LA 560, 564–565; Hogan in 34 LA 158, 163–165; Wirtz in 32 LA 156, 168–169. For discussion of "successor employer" doctrine (NLRB and court cases) as applied to vacation rights see A.B.A. Diesel Parts & Serv. Co., 62 LA 660, 663–667 (Harter, 1974). Also see Arbitrator Speroff in 74 LA 861, 863–864; Wahl in 70 LA 1157, 1158; Turkus in 61 LA 26, 28–31. For related discussion see Chapter 14, subtopic entitled "Merger or Sale of Company."

retirement by the employee,[37] or death of the employee.[38] In such cases, where the vacation has been fully earned and the employee has fully met all the conditions required by the contract, arbitrators are in general agreement that vacation benefits must be held to have vested in the employee; but where he has not met such conditions, he has been denied vacation benefits.[39]

Strikes as Affecting Vacation Benefits

In the absence of contract language requiring a different result, arbitrators are disinclined to permit employees to benefit in the accrual of vacation credits during time spent on strike, since vacation benefits as deferred wages are part of the pay received for *working* for the company. Arbitrator Marion Beatty has stated:

> "The employer does not reward employees for being absent on strike, but if the Union's position is upheld in this case, the employers will be required to accord these employees vacation pay for time they did not work. The employers here feel aggrieved for being asked, in effect, to subsidize the strike."[40]

The effect of strikes on vacation credits is rarely treated in the contract[41] and is seldom directly covered in the strike settlement agreement. Unions have argued that the denial of vacation credits violates strike settlement agreements which require that no penalty be assessed against anyone participating in the strike. Arbitrators, however, have held that the denial of vacation credits where the contract relates such credits to time worked is not to be considered a

---

[37]Where the employee has met contractual requirements prior to quit or retirement, he is entitled to vacation benefits. See Arbitrator Petrie in 76 LA 611, 616–619; Hellman in 63 LA 965, 968; Murphy in 52 LA 837, 839–841; Cox in 49 LA 837, 838–839; Altieri in 42 LA 1209, 1211–1213. But where the employee has not met contractual requirements, such as employment on a particular date, he is not entitled to vacation pay. See Gershenfeld in 69 LA 431, 433–434; Lieberman in 67 LA 128, 130; Warns in 60 LA 1200, 1202–1203; Seitz in 53 LA 692, 692–693; Gilden in 49 LA 646, 648; Doyle in 39 LA 489, 491. Also see Kabaker in 54 LA 66, 68; Volz in 48 LA 965, 969.

[38]Where the employee has met contractual requirements before death, there is no forfeiture of vacation benefits. See Arbitrator Feinberg in 46 LA 1129, 1130–1131; T. McDermott in 43 LA 860, 862–863; Larkin in 41 LA 513, 515; C. McDermott in 40 LA 1308, 1310–1311; Crane in 38 LA 479, 481. The result was different where strict contract language required employment on an entitlement date. See Arbitrator Erbs in 54 LA 232, 235–236; Davis in 48 LA 938, 940; Seward in 47 LA 258, 259–260; Turkus in 42 LA 1332, 1333–1334. Cf., Kreimer in 44 LA 126, 127.

[39]See citations in notes 37 and 38 above. For cases involving pro rata vacation pay, see Arbitrator Conant in 68 LA 663, 668 (voluntary quit); LeBaron in 67 LA 735, 740–741 (company made voluntary adjusted vacation payments to laid-off employees); White in 64 LA 791, 792–794 (employee not eligible for pro rata vacation pay due to illness); Cox in 62 LA 185, 187–188 (voluntary quit); Volz in 59 LA 1246, 1249 (retirement).

[40]Motor Car Dealers Assn. of Kan. City, 49 LA 55, 57 (1967), cited with approval by Arbitrator Gorsuch in 53 LA 784, 791. Similarly, Arbitrator Jackson in 66 LA 745, 749. Where it was established to the arbitrator's satisfaction that under past practice vacation credits had been given in all prior strike situations, full vacation time was allowed in Mobil Oil Co., 42 LA 102, 105–106 (Forsythe, 1963), upheld in Local 7-644 OCAW v. Mobil Oil Co., 45 LA 512, 59 LRRM 2938 (CA 7, 1965). Similarly, see Arbitrator Nitka in 79 LA 1294, 1300–1301. Past practice may also deny vacation credits. See Arbitrator Gottlieb in 70 LA 636, 639–640; Larkin in 42 LA 247, 249; Ross in 33 LA 837, 839.

[41]See Evening News Assn., 53 LA 170, 176 (Casselman, 1969).

penalty but is simply an application of the vacation provisions of the contract.[42]

Many cases turn on the question whether a strike is an "excused absence" so as to deprive (or not to deprive, depending upon contract language) employees of vacation credits. For instance, where the contract provided that vacation pay was to be computed on the basis of the employee's earnings for the year and allowed credit for time lost due to illness or other excused absence, it was held that a strike is not an excused absence.[43] Another arbitrator, where the contract provided for prorating vacation pay in case of sick leave or leave of absence, held that a strike "should be treated the same" as a leave of absence.[44] Both arbitrators thus reached the same end result of denying vacation credits for the strike period. The reluctance of arbitrators to credit strike time for vacation benefits in these cases is explained by Arbitrator Russell A. Smith:

> "It would seem anomalous that the parties, had they specifically considered the matter, would have intended that working time lost because of direct participation in a strike would be credited as service time whereas [the contract provides that] time lost on authorized leave of absence was not to be credited."[45]

Other cases have involved contracts basing vacation pay on some qualifying phrase such as "hours worked" or "time worked,"[46] or "years of service,"[47] or "continuous service,"[48] or "employment" by the company,[49] or being "in the employ" of the company,[50] or "scheduled working days."[51] These phrases have been interpreted as requiring the actual rendition of services for vacation eligibility, and as excluding time spent on strike. Thus, a distinction must be made between the bare retention of employment status and the actual performance of services which fulfill the eligibility requirements.[52]

---

[42]See Arbitrator Kates in 47 LA 319, 322; Larkin in 42 LA 247, 249; Smith in 27 LA 251, 255. But see Koven in 52 LA 169, 171, where the strike settlement agreement provided for "retroactivity" of fringe benefits. The Company's formula for loss of vacation credits due to strike may be "even-handed" but its application may result in unpermitted inequities. See Arbitrator Gottlieb in 70 LA 636, 640.

[43]Motor Car Dealers Assn. of Kan. City, 49 LA 55, 58 (Beatty, 1967). Also see Arbitrator Wolk in 74 LA 1061, 1063; Wolf in 49 LA 1182, 1185 (discussing the nature of a strike); Smith in 27 LA 251, 254–255. Cf., Ford Motor Co., 33 LA 638, 639–640 (Platt, 1959), involving a somewhat unusual "company policy statement."

[44]Richland Shale Brick Co., 49 LA 113, 117 (Seinsheimer, 1966). Similarly, Arbitrator Smith in 48 LA 213, 217–219; Kates in 47 LA 319, 322; Seligson in 42 LA 929, 930–931. But see Dworkin in 40 LA 689, 696, and Wood in 34 LA 428, 431, both involving different contract language. For the other side of the coin, see Ordman in 242 AAA 5, and Seligson in 42 LA 929, 930–931, holding that in computing vacation benefits, the company may not deduct work time lost due to a lockout.

[45]Vindicator Printing Co., 48 LA 213, 219 (1966).

[46]Givaudan Corp., 68 LA 337, 342 (Brent, 1977); Modecraft Co., 38 LA 1236, 1239 (Dall, 1961).

[47]Reichhold Chems., 66 LA 745, 749 (Jackson, 1976); Great Atl. & Pac. Tea Co., 43 LA 1, 2 (Turkus, 1964).

[48]Ohio Power Co., 63 LA 1235, 1240–1241 (Chockley, 1974); Evening News Assn., 53 LA 170, 175 (Casselman, 1969). Cf., Arbitrator Wood in 34 LA 428, 431.

[49]Union Carbide Corp., 49 LA 1180, 1181 (Cahn, 1967); Vickers, Inc., 27 LA 251, 254–255 (Smith, 1956).

[50]San Bruno Sportservice, 33 LA 837, 838–839 (Ross, 1959).

[51]Lord Mfg. Co., 47 LA 319, 321 (Kates, 1966). Also see Hawaii Dept. of Educ., 62 LA 415, 418–420 (Kanbara, 1974). Cf., Arbitrator Platt in 33 LA 638, 639–640.

[52]See San Bruno Sportservice, 33 LA 837, 838 (Ross, 1959), citing and quoting from Safeway Stores, 22 LA 466, 469 (Hildebrand, 1954); Vickers, Inc., 27 LA 251, 254–255 (Smith, 1956).

Layoff as Affecting Vacation Benefits

Similar reasoning has been applied in layoff cases. Thus, where employees have met eligibility requirements and their vacations have been earned prior to layoff, they have been held to be entitled to vacation benefits in full if fully earned,[53] or on a pro rata basis if partially earned,[54] the rationale being that vacation pay is in the nature of additional wages. However, where the laid-off employees were found not to have met the contract's eligibility requirements, they were held not entitled to any vacation benefits.[55]

Sick Leave as Affecting Vacation Benefits

Where the two benefits arose under different contract provisions and were separate and distinct, it was held that the employee should receive both his vacation pay and his sick pay.[56] Similarly, under a contract providing for both vacation and sickness benefits, employees who were on sick leave when the employer closed the plant for a vacation period were held entitled to receive their sickness benefits and to select a different time for their vacations.[57]

The earning of vacation credits during time spent on sick leave is another matter, however. Thus, it has been held that an employee who was on paid sick leave for a month was not entitled to vacation credits for the sick leave period, since vacation pay is earned by service; the "test should not be merely whether an employee is receiving payments from the employer," because all payments are "not necessarily 'pay' for the purpose of earning or accruing" vacation credits.[58]

Maternity Leave as Affecting Vacation Benefits

It has been held that time spent on maternity leave is not to be included in computing vacation pay since such leave is directed to job

---

[53]See Arbitrator Cohen in 80 LA 680, 684; Cooley in 68 LA 67, 68; Lugar in 40 LA 129, 131–135, citing and discussing many cases; Reid in 33 LA 316, 318–319; Howlett in 32 LA 278, 282–283, relying in part on principles of equity.

[54]See Arbitrator Barone in 61 LA 468, 472–473; Cheney in 38 LA 737, 739–740; Volz in 34 LA 170, 172, citing cases; Knowlton in 33 LA 428, 431, permanent layoff. Also see Turkus in 43 LA 1, 2.

[55]See Arbitrator Wolff in 79 LA 340, 344; LeBaron in 67 LA 735, 740–741 (but the company voluntarily made adjusted vacation payments to laid-off employees); Yarowsky in 65 LA 1249, 1250–1252, citing and relying upon Foster v. Dravo Corp., 95 S.Ct. 879, 89 LRRM 2988 (1975); King in 64 LA 641, 642; McCoy in 39 LA 1240, 1241–1242; Cheney in 38 LA 737, 740; Caraway in 35 LA 717, 720–721; Pollack in 33 LA 477, 481–482 (permanent layoff).

[56]Airco, Inc., 62 LA 1056, 1058 (Eyraud, 1974); International Paper Co., 37 LA 1026, 1028–1029 (Bothwell, 1962). But see Auer Register Co., 62 LA 235, 240 (Perry, 1974), where there was no contract provision for medical leave of absence.

[57]See Arbitrator Brown in 64 LA 993, 995; McKelvey in 25 LA 94, 99–100; Donnelly, Mannino & Mottram in 21 LA 745 at 745. Cf., Cantor in 64 LA 737, 739–740.

[58]San Francisco Newspaper Publishers Assn., 46 LA 260, 262–264 (Burns, 1965). Also see Arbitrator Jaffee in 44 LA 1045, 1049; Reid in 37 LA 126, 129.

security and is not intended to extend to vacation eligibility.[59] For related discussion which now should be considered in cases involving this subject, see subtopic entitled "Maternity or Maternity-Related Leave," below in this Chapter.

Holidays

Collective bargaining agreements customarily provide for pay for named holidays not worked.[60] The primary purpose of holiday pay provisions is to insure the employee against the possible loss in earnings when he does not work because of a holiday occurring during the workweek.[61] Some contracts explicitly or by clear implication also include pay for holidays which fall on days when the employee would not have been scheduled to work, such as his regular day off or Saturday.[62]

It is clear that "there is no inherent right to holiday pay, and none exists except as it may be set forth in the labor agreement."[63] As elaborated by Arbitrator Harry J. Dworkin:

> "The right to holiday pay is a creature of contract; it does not exist as a matter of law. To the extent that the parties have seen fit through the orderly process of collective bargaining to stipulate holiday benefits, employees that are covered are entitled to the full measure of the benefits that were bargained for in the contract. It necessarily follows that employees are not entitled to more than the contract provides, nor can contract benefits be expanded beyond the meaning warranted by the language used."[64]

---

[59]American Enka Corp., 48 LA 989, 992 (Pigors, 1966). Also see Arbitrator Mullin in 58 LA 159, 161; Witney in 47 LA 272, 277; Gundermann in 39 LA 1270, 1273. Cf., Davis in 58 LA 1338, 1340; Geissinger in 38 LA 1085, 1088, where ambiguous contract language and past practice resulted in a different award.

[60]For a checklist of various aspects of holiday pay which may be covered in the contract, see Rothschild, Merrifield & Edwards, Collective Bargaining and Labor Arbitration, 690–691 (2d Ed., 1979). Additional discussion of holidays is provided by Abrams & Nolan, "Resolving Holiday Pay Disputes in Labor Arbitration," 33 Case W. Res. L. Rev. 380 (1983). A distinction has been drawn between governmentally designated "legal holidays" and "observed holidays" for holiday pay purposes under private industry contracts. See Stein, Inc., 71 LA 124, 127 (Klein, 1978).

[61]Anaconda Aluminum Co., 48 LA 219, 223 (Allen, 1967). Similarly, see Arbitrator Dworkin in 51 LA 724, 728; Hill in 39 LA 500, 503; Updegraff in 37 LA 1009, 1010, and in 20 LA 323, 324; Pollack in 33 LA 477, 483. For discussion of the history of holiday pay provisions, see Arbitrator Killion in 37 LA 934, 940; Howard in 24 LA 667, 670–672 (also giving examples of types of clauses as well as discussion of work requirements). In R. Herschel Mfg. Co., 35 LA 826, 827 (Ruckel, 1960), the contract stated that the purpose of holiday pay is that no employee shall be deprived "of income he would have been able to earn."

[62]See Arbitrator Dworkin in 53 LA 1165, 1166; Kates in 45 LA 905, 907 (an "interests" arbitration); Goldstein in 43 LA 676, 677; Myers in 42 LA 269, 272; Koven in 40 LA 577, 581; Stark in 35 LA 788, 791–792; Caraway in 33 LA 494, 496; Howard in 24 LA 667, 671; Donnelly in 21 LA 325, 326. Cf., Anderson in 23 LA 392, 394; Seligson in 22 LA 806, 807; Jones in 21 LA 120, 122; Stutz in 21 LA 59, 60. For a case involving the right of the company to *require* employees to work on a holiday, see Georgia-Pacific Corp., 59 LA 417, 418–420 (Hilpert, 1972).

[63]Gregory Galvanizing & Metal Processing, 46 LA 102, 105 (Kates, 1966). In Wallace Murray Corp., 71 LA 877, 878–879 (Gibson, 1978), pay was denied when the holiday fell during a hiatus period between contracts.

[64]Lewall Sportswear Co., 53 LA 1165, 1169 (1969). To similar effect, see Arbitrator Goetz in 72 LA 840, 842–843; Gibson in 71 LA 1039 at 1039, and in 71 LA 877, 878; Johnston in 69 LA 604, 607; Hunter in 41 LA 991, 993, citing Shapiro in 25 LA 341, 342–343 (both discussing the background and purpose of holiday pay provisions).

Moreover, it has been declared that "A holiday pay provision is not a guarantee of additional earnings unless it contains specific language to that effect."[65]

When the contract does provide for holiday pay (which, as noted, is the usual practice), it is recognized that such pay is a "fringe benefit" earned by the employee; however, "it is conceived of as being earned by his working a specified qualifying period and also by working specified shifts at agreed time proximate to" the holiday as required by the contract.[66] Thus, while it is recognized as an earned benefit, holiday pay is usually conditioned upon the employee's compliance with contractually stated work requirements.

Work Requirements

Typical of holiday pay provisions are the work requirements upon which such pay is conditioned.[67] Thus, in order for the employee to be eligible for holiday pay, contracts commonly require both a stipulated minimum period of service and work on designated days surrounding the holiday. In the latter regard, the contract may require the employee to work *his* last scheduled day before and *his* first scheduled day after the holiday,[68] or the last *regularly* scheduled day before and the first *regularly* scheduled day after the holiday,[69] or the last *scheduled* workday before and the first *scheduled* workday after the holiday,[70] or the day before *and* the day after the holiday,[71] or the day before *or* the day after the holiday,[72] or the *scheduled full* workday of the plant before and after the holiday,[73] or a specified number of workdays during the period before and after the holiday.[74]

The precise language used in the particular contract applied to the facts of a given case ordinarily determines whether holiday pay

---

[65]Sealtest Foods, 47 LA 868, 869 (Krinsky, 1966). Holiday pay was "guaranteed" by contract in Marmon Group, 73 LA 607, 608–609 (Marshall, 1979).

[66]Kennecott Copper Corp., 36 LA 507, 510 (Updegraff, 1960). Also see Arbitrator Klein in 48 LA 1101, 1102; Kelliher in 47 LA 582, 583; Dworkin in 36 LA 517, 521; Tischler in 33 LA 919, 921 (and cases cited); Tatum in 24 LA 517, 520.

[67]By far the greatest number of holiday pay arbitration cases are concerned with the various aspects of eligibility for such pay—compliance with work requirements, part day absence or tardiness before or after a holiday, and the effect on eligibility of layoff, leave, vacation, or strike.

[68]See Arbitrator Carson in 72 LA 607, 609; Shaffer in 67 LA 638, 639; Jones in 53 LA 477, 478; Keefe in 52 LA 745, 746; Roberts in 48 LA 1281, 1283.

[69]See Arbitrator Morgan in 75 LA 801, 804–805 (absence for religious reasons was not a specified exception to the work requirements clause); Warns in 70 LA 1273, 1274; Teple in 69 LA 599, 603–604, and in 51 LA 481, 482; Lieberman in 67 LA 128, 130 (retired employee); Davis in 51 LA 1309 at 1309; Klein in 48 LA 1101 at 1101.

[70]See Arbitrator Kelliher in 47 LA 582, 583; Larson in 41 LA 83, 84; Anderson in 33 LA 890, 891. The contract may make a distinction between "scheduled" and "regularly scheduled" work. See Corhart Refractories Co., 47 LA 648, 649 (McCoy, 1966).

[71]See Arbitrator Hertz in 57 LA 167 at 167; Belsky in 44 LA 910 at 910; Larson in 38 LA 746, 747; McIntosh in 28 LA 693 at 693.

[72]See Arbitrator Kabaker in 71 LA 74, 75; Hunter in 41 LA 991, 993.

[73]See Price-Pfister Brass Mfg. Co., 25 LA 398, 400 (Prasow, 1955).

[74]See Arbitrator Goetz in 72 LA 840, 844; Allen in 48 LA 219, 220 ("actually works during the payroll week in which the holiday falls"); House in 47 LA 567, 568 (three scheduled workdays out of five scheduled workdays before and after the holiday); Updegraff in 36 LA 507, 508 (a minimum of two shifts during the workweek in which the holiday occurs).

should be awarded. To illustrate, in the situation where the employee had been in layoff before and after a holiday, Arbitrator Clarence M. Updegraff drew a distinction between (1) contract language requiring the employee to work on *his* last scheduled day before and *his* first scheduled day after the holiday, and (2) contract language requiring the employee to work on *the* last scheduled day before and *the* first scheduled day after the holiday. Under the first type of clause the employee "would seem to become entitled to the holiday pay upon the showing that he worked faithfully up to the time of the lay-off in which the holiday occurred and returned promptly to work in the first day after the end of the lay-off," while under the second type of clause "obviously he cannot work those days while he is on lay-off" and thus would not be entitled to holiday pay.[75]

In a similar vein, Arbitrator Harry J. Dworkin distinguished the phrase "regular workday" (which appeared in the holiday pay provision under consideration) from "scheduled workday," holding that employees who worked their regular workdays of Friday and Tuesday (surrounding Labor Day) were eligible for holiday pay even though they were scheduled for but did not work overtime on Saturday before the holiday.[76] But where the contract required the employee to work the last "scheduled" workday before and the first "scheduled" workday after the holiday, it was held that Saturday overtime falls within the "scheduled workday" clause as used in the contract and employees who refused to work as scheduled on Saturday were not entitled to holiday pay.[77]

It is generally agreed that the purpose of "surrounding days" work requirements is to prevent employees from "stretching" holidays[78] and to assure a full working force on the day before and the day after a holiday.[79] For these reasons, contractual exceptions to the "surrounding days" work requirements have been strictly construed.[80] A significant consequence of the work requirements clauses

[75]Hemp & Co., 37 LA 1009, 1010 (1962), with many citations. Similarly, see Arbitrator Creo in 80 LA 1289, 1292; Tanaka in 72 LA 528, 530. Also see Ruben in 69 LA 944, 953–954. In Baggett Transp. Co., 71 LA 609, 612 (Marcus, 1978), the contract required the employee to work *his* last scheduled day before and *the* first scheduled day after the holiday.

[76]A.O. Smith Corp., 47 LA 654, 660–661 (1966). Similarly, see Arbitrator McCoy in 47 LA 648, 649; Kelliher in 47 LA 582, 584; McCormick in 22 LA 505, 508. Also see Arbitrator Davis in 51 LA 1309, 1310.

[77]Youngstown Steel Door Co., 46 LA 323, 324 (Marshall, 1966). Similarly, see Arbitrator Mallet-Prevost in 67 LA 1287, 1289; Begley in 44 LA 1212, 1214–1215; Larson in 38 LA 746, 748–749; Crane in 35 LA 389, 390.

[78]See Arbitrator Koven in 81 LA 196, 197–198; Mueller in 73 LA 777, 780; Kabaker in 71 LA 74, 76; Erbs in 70 LA 814, 816; Cantor in 69 LA 189, 190; Hill in 53 LA 1206, 1209; Seinsheimer in 49 LA 468, 470; Klein in 48 LA 1101, 1102; Larkin in 41 LA 414, 415; Sembower in 38 LA 632, 634; Cheit in 28 LA 390, 393; Davey in 26 LA 322, 324; Simkin in 21 LA 686, 689; Updegraff in 20 LA 323, 324. Also see General Cable Corp., 37 LA 934, 942 (Killion, 1961), discussing the initial (historical) function and the present day function of the work requirement clauses in the parties' former and present contracts.

[79]See Arbitrator Lewis in 70 LA 1288, 1289; Griffith in 65 LA 795, 796; Meiners in 58 LA 1122, 1123–1124; Kates in 46 LA 102, 105; Reid in 40 LA 673, 675; Kleinsorge in 32 LA 769, 771; Cheit in 28 LA 390, 393.

[80]See Arbitrator Warns in 70 LA 1273, 1274–1275; Erbs in 70 LA 814, 816; Cantor in 69 LA 189, 190.

is that the "failure of an employee to comply with * * * [them] as a condition precedent to holiday pay operates to disqualify him from receiving such benefit."[81]

Part Day Absence or Tardiness on Surrounding Day

Contracts requiring the employee to work the surrounding days in order to qualify for holiday pay are ordinarily interpreted as requiring full days of work so that a part day absence[82] or tardiness[83] may serve to defeat an employee's right to such pay. However, if the part day absence[84] or tardiness[85] is contractually or otherwise excused, holiday pay may be awarded. The theory behind the "excused" cases is that the reason for the work requirement is to prevent "stretching" the holiday, and since the employees in these cases demonstrated that they did not try to stretch the holiday they are entitled to holiday pay.[86] A similar rationale has been applied where the work time

---

[81]Motch & Merryweather Mach. Co., 51 LA 723, 730 (Dworkin, 1968). Also see Arbitrator Foster in 66 LA 416, 419.

[82]See Arbitrator Griffith in 69 LA 1129, 1131–1132 (permission to attend union meeting was not an "excused absence"); Meiners in 58 LA 1122, 1123–1124 (unexcused absence of ill employee who left work early on day after holiday); Keefe in 52 LA 745, 749 ("excused" pass obtained by deception); Dworkin in 51 LA 723, 729–730 (unexcused absence after lunch period); Koven in 43 LA 885, 887 (employee had a legitimate excuse but refused to state more than "personal reasons"); Reid in 40 LA 673, 675 (wildcat strike); Marshall in 35 LA 117, 120 (union meeting was a form of strike). For cases where the employee left early without permission, see Seinsheimer in 49 LA 468, 470; Bauder in 46 LA 712, 713–714; Kelliher in 34 LA 478, 478–479; Kleinsorge in 32 LA 769, 771. In C.G. Conn, 66 LA 195, 196 (Davis, 1976), properly scheduled "overtime became a part of the full scheduled work shift within the meaning" of the contract so that employees who left at the end of their regular eight-hour preholiday shift "became ineligible for holiday pay."

[83]See Arbitrator Lewis in 70 LA 1288, 1289; Keefe in 70 LA 935, 936; Simkin in 21 LA 686, 690; Fulda in 14 LA 201, 203.

[84]For cases where permission was granted to leave early, see Arbitrator Thomson in 73 LA 415, 417–418 (but other employees were not excused); Ruben in 69 LA 944, 957–959 (many cases cited at 954–955); Kesselman in 54 LA 112, 116–117; Kabaker in 53 LA 431, 432; Nichols in 48 LA 321, 322; Sembower in 38 LA 632, 635. For other situations, see Arbitrator Kuhn in 69 LA 437, 438–439 (employee, given permission to visit doctor, returned to finish her shift); Summers in 45 LA 1149, 1151–1152 (twenty-year practice of short shift on the day before Thanksgiving); Belsky in 44 LA 910, 911 (contractual exception for illness); Autry in 38 LA 400, 403 (permission granted ten days in advance); Cheit in 28 LA 390, 393 (employee left early on the day after the holiday in response to a subpoena); Davey in 26 LA 322, 323 (contractual exception for illness); Copelof in 23 LA 476, 481 (employee had to take his father to the hospital). In one case, Arbitrator Edwin R. Teple held that under the contract language and past practice the company was justified in paying proportional holiday pay on the basis of the number of hours actually worked on the surrounding days. See Trabon Eng'g. Corp., 49 LA 220, 222–223 (1967), also citing many cases.

[85]See Arbitrator Johnston in 69 LA 604, 606–607 (company upheld when it excused employees who were late because of weather conditions but denied holiday pay to employee who did not appear for work at all); Larkin in 41 LA 414, 415–416 (one employee had car trouble and was one hour late; another missed her usual ride, walked to work, and was twenty-six minutes late—the arbitrator said that these employees did not extend the holiday); Cheit in 28 LA 390, 393 (car pool driver did not appear and employee took a bus); Hayes in 25 LA 753, 754–755 (employee was thirty-six minutes late on the day after the holiday); Copelof in 23 LA 476, 481 (employee's husband was ill and needed to be given medicine on time). Arbitrator William E. Simkin set out guidelines to aid the parties in future cases involving tardiness before and after a holiday in Crucible Steel Co., 21 LA 686, 691 (1953).

[86]See Arbitrator Larkin in 41 LA 414, 415; Sembower in 38 LA 632, 634–635; Cheit in 28 LA 390, 393; Fulda in 14 LA 201, 204. Also see Koven in 81 LA 196, 197–198 (full day excused absence did not constitute "deliberate" stretching of holiday). But absence before a holiday for "personal reasons" (see Arbitrator McDermott in 55 LA 1098, 1101), and a part day absence for "illness" (see Thomson in 73 LA 415, 418), both without adequate explanation have been held insufficient reasons to qualify for holiday pay.

missed was minimal, even though the contract required "full" work-days before and after the holiday.[87]

Holidays Falling During Layoff

As stated above, the primary purpose of holiday pay is to protect the earnings of the employee when a holiday occurs on a day on which he otherwise would have worked. Therefore, since the employee in layoff is not working and would have no earnings, it is said that he would not be entitled to holiday pay in the absence of a contract provision extending such benefits to laid-off employees.[88]

A threshold question may be the status of employees in layoff. In one case, the company argued that the grievants failed to achieve a "fundamental standing" for holiday pay since they were not in "active status" on the date of the holiday; it was held, however, that the word "employee" as used in the holiday pay eligibility provisions of the contract "must be given its literal meaning to include both employees actively at work and inactive employees on layoff who retain seniority status."[89]

Most cases involving holidays during layoff have been decided on the basis of the work requirements clause[90] or the excused absence clause of the holiday pay provision, the latter excusing the employee from complying with the work requirements in the event of specified circumstances (such as illness) and sometimes adding such language as "or other valid excuse." Thus, in some cases where the contract did not provide for holiday pay for laid-off employees, the arbitrator, basing his opinion upon the excused absence clause[91] or upon the work requirements clause[92] of the holiday pay provision, reasoned that the

---

[87]Vertex Sys., 68 LA 1099, 1101 (Marcus, 1977), where the employee was only three minutes late because of an ice storm and the company previously had made some exceptions to "the rigid rule" by excusing employees. But where an employee was one and three-tenths hours late, missing a "substantial portion" of the scheduled half day prior to a holiday, the company was upheld in denying holiday pay in Van Dyne-Crotty, 70 LA 1288, 1289 (Lewis, 1978). Cf., Columbus Show Case Co., 57 LA 167, 168 (Hertz, 1971), holding that the contract language "worked the day" before and after the holiday could just as reasonably mean "worked *on* the day" as "worked the *full* day."

[88]See Hemp & Co., 37 LA 1009, 1010 (Updegraff, 1962). Similarly, see Arbitrator Leach in 44 LA 481, 484–487 (discussing many awards); Hunter in 41 LA 991, 993–994; Scheiber in 40 LA 152, 154–155; Pollack in 33 LA 477, 483; Dworkin in 27 LA 507, 510; Shapiro in 25 LA 341, 343; Ralston in 23 LA 49, 51. Cf., Arbitrator Tener in 75 LA 651, 653, and Dworkin in 22 LA 601, 604, both involving broad holiday pay provisions with no qualifying factors for eligibility.

[89]Allis-Chalmers Corp., 72 LA 840, 844–845 (Goetz, 1979), awarding holiday pay to one group of employees who met the contractual requirement of working in the week containing a holiday and to another group who met the "substitute" requirement of a "letter of understanding" regarding a multiple holiday week.

[90]See examples and discussion of work requirements above in subtopic entitled "Work Requirements."

[91]Layoff was considered an excused absence by Arbitrator Kates in 42 LA 111, 116 (discussing many cases pro and con); Tischler in 33 LA 919, 923 (citing many cases on various aspects of holiday pay at 921–924); Updegraff in 20 LA 323, 324–325.

[92]For cases in which the employee was found to have complied with the contract requiring work on *his* scheduled workday before and after the holiday, see Arbitrator Wood in 37 LA 103, 106; Prasow in 31 LA 449, 451; Parkman in 28 LA 1, 4; Tatum in 24 LA 517, 519–520. A like result obtained where the plant was closed for short periods surrounding the holidays and the contract required work on *the* scheduled day before and after the holidays in question. See George Otto Broiler Co., 37 LA 57, 60 (Garmon, 1961). Similarly, see Arbitrator Rossman in 77 LA 691, 692;

employee had met the basic conditions of the contract and consequently qualified for holiday pay; in some of these cases the arbitrator noted the additional fact that the layoff was of "reasonably" short duration before and after the holiday. However, in other cases the arbitrator rejected the argument that layoff was an excused absence and refused to award holiday pay.[93] Likewise, where the employee in layoff was found not to have complied with the work requirements clause, he was denied holiday pay.[94]

It should be noted that arbitrators would disapprove of the situation in which the facts indicate that the layoff was made in bad faith or was contrived as a means of avoiding the payment of holiday pay.[95]

Of course, the contract may specifically deny holiday pay to employees in layoff,[96] or it may specifically provide for such pay for employees in layoff within a specified time of the holiday.[97]

Vacation or Leave as Affecting Holiday Pay

Where the contract specifically provides for holiday pay in addition to vacation pay when the holiday happens to occur during an employee's vacation period, arbitrators are in agreement that holiday pay must be allowed.[98] This is so even though the employee reported back to work a day or more late after his vacation,[99] or was guilty of an

---

Blackmar in 66 LA 835, 836. In Premiere Corp., 67 LA 376, 380–381 (Fieger, 1976), bad faith was found in laying off the employees precipitously on the day before Thanksgiving and pay was awarded for that holiday; but recognizing a 90-day "reasonable time" rule as applicable, the arbitrator denied holiday pay to employees in layoff for five to seven months even though the employee may have worked "his" scheduled workday before and after the holidays included in the layoff period. In R. Herschel Mfg. Co., 35 LA 826, 829 (1960), Arbitrator Ruckel would have had "no hesitancy in finding for the Union" on the basis of the scheduled workday clause but for another clause stating that the purpose of the holiday pay provision was that no employee should be deprived of income he would have been able to earn; employees in layoff did not lose the opportunity to work as a result of the holiday.

[93]See Arbitrator Marcus in 71 LA 609, 611–612, citing with approval Scheiber in 40 LA 152, 155–156 (discussing many cases at 154–158); Pollack in 33 LA 477, 483 ("To say that being laid off is to be excused by the company from the necessity of meeting the conditions precedent is preposterous"); Prasow in 25 LA 398, 403; Cahn in 22 LA 18, 19–20.

[94]See Arbitrator Tanaka in 72 LA 528, 530; Leach in 44 LA 481, 487 (discussing many cases at 484–486); Updegraff in 37 LA 1009, 1010 (past practice also involved); Williams in 37 LA 273, 274–275 (past practice also involved); Pollack in 33 LA 477, 482–483; Prasow in 25 LA 398, 402–403; Ralston in 23 LA 49, 51 (past practice also involved). In all of these cases the contract required the employee to work on *the* scheduled workdays surrounding the holiday.

[95]See comments of Arbitrator Fieger in 67 LA 376, 380–381; House in 47 LA 567, 571; Hunter in 41 LA 991, 994; Williams in 37 LA 273, 274; Parkman in 28 LA 1, 4–5; Shapiro in 25 LA 341, 343.

[96]See Flintkote Co., 26 LA 526, 527 (Morvant, 1956); Price-Pfister Brass Mfg. Co., 25 LA 398, 400 (Prasow, 1955).

[97]See contract provisions in 73 LA 1129, 1130; 70 LA 1200, 1201; 70 LA 79 at 79; 66 LA 938, 940; 57 LA 742, 746 (involving also a conflict between the "mandates of" the holiday pay provisions and an act of God clause); 53 LA 477, 478; 51 LA 400, 405; 48 LA 915, 917; 47 LA 86, 87; 46 LA 132, 135; 44 LA 817 at 817; 31 LA 449 at 449; 29 LA 173, 175; 27 LA 507, 508; 23 LA 400, 401. In Norris Indus., 73 LA 1129, 1131–1132 (Roumell, 1979), the decision rested on the issue of whether the effective date of the layoff was the last day the employees worked or the first day they were off work (citing arbitration and court cases in support of the latter). Also see ITT, 75 LA 729, 731–732 (Howlett, 1980), discussing many cases.

[98]Brooks Foods, 45 LA 249, 251 (Larkin, 1965), where holiday pay was awarded to employees who had elected to take their vacations during a layoff period, since they satisfied contractual requirements for such pay.

[99]See Arbitrator Suagee in 41 LA 621, 624; Sembower in 39 LA 104, 105–106; Autry in 36 LA 204, 206–207. Also see Reynard in 24 LA 116, 120–121.

unexcused absence prior to the vacation period,[100] and even though the contract contained surrounding days work requirements. In the latter regard, the rationale used by arbitrators is that such requirements are intended to meet the employer's manning problems when a holiday occurs during a regular workweek and have no application when a holiday occurs during a vacation week.[101]

A vacation shutdown clause may affect the employees' entitlement to holiday pay as it did in a case where the contract also stated that the intent of the holiday pay clause was to pay wages for holidays not worked to employees "who are scheduled to work on the day on which the holiday falls." The employer there scheduled a vacation shutdown during the week when a holiday fell, and the arbitrator refused to award holiday pay, resting his decision "squarely on the restrictive terms of the contract."[102] In another situation, concerned with pay in lieu of vacation, the arbitrator held that an employee on leave of absence who received pay in lieu of vacation could not also receive holiday pay for a holiday occurring during the leave since "a payment in lieu of vacation does not cover any particular time."[103]

The holiday pay issue is also complicated when both layoff and vacation are involved at the same time. Under a contract provision granting holiday pay to employees on vacation in the payroll period in which the holiday occurs, one arbitrator resolved the problem by ruling that a laid-off employee is entitled to pay for a holiday falling within his scheduled vacation period if the vacation is scheduled prior to the layoff, or if the employee is on layoff at the time the vacation is scheduled but returns to work and remains at work until he takes his scheduled vacation; an employee who is not working at the time his vacation is scheduled or prior to the time his vacation occurs is not eligible for pay for a holiday occurring within the vacation period.[104] Another arbitrator, taking the view that vacation pay benefits are deferred earnings, ruled that employees, who were in layoff status but who were eligible for vacation during the scheduled vacation shutdown, had met the basic holiday pay eligibility requirement that the "individual employee received any earnings from the Company during the pay period in which the holiday in question falls."[105]

---

[100]See Bethlehem Steel Co., 27 LA 801, 802 (Seward, 1956); Miami Copper Co., 16 LA 191, 193 (Prasow, 1951), stating also that the arbitrator believed that the employee is "subject to appropriate disciplinary penalty for his unexcused absence."

[101]See Arbitrator Suagee in 41 LA 621, 623; Sembower in 39 LA 104, 105–106; Autry in 36 LA 204, 207; Prasow in 16 LA 191, 193.

[102]Geeco, Inc., 29 LA 658, 662 (Walsh, 1957). Also denying holiday pay because of restrictive contract language in a vacation shutdown situation, see Arbitrator Epstein in 64 LA 538, 539; Townsend in 12 LA 101, 104–106. Denying holiday pay because of past practice, see Griffith in 65 LA 795, 796–797.

[103]TRW Metals Div., 48 LA 414, 416 (Laybourne, 1967). Still another facet of holiday pay was presented in a "productivity leave" issue decided by Arbitrator Ables in 65 LA 285, 286–287.

[104]United States Steel Corp., 36 LA 603, 616 (Garrett, 1961). Similarly, Arbitrator Garrett in 36 LA 385, 388; Platt in 14 LA 552, 560. Under contract language identical to that in the Garrett opinion in 36 LA 603, Arbitrator Alexander B. Porter held that the contract applied to employees on sick leave as well as layoff even though the holiday pay provision was "couched in layoff language." Bethlehem Steel Co., 41 LA 624, 627 (1963).

[105]Lectromelt Corp., 58 LA 463, 467–468 (McDermott, 1972). Also involving holiday pay for employees in layoff during vacation shutdown, see Aladdin Indus., 18 LA 581, 583–584 (Hampton, 1952).

The contract may be unclear regarding payment for holidays falling during leaves of absence. If this is the case, the determination of eligibility for holiday pay may turn on such contract provisions as the surrounding days work requirements,[106] or other requirements such as being a "regular" employee, or working during the pay period in which the holiday occurs,[107] or the justifiable absence clause.[108]

In the absence of a specific contract provision for pay for holidays occurring during sick leave or other leaves of absence, arbitrators have been reluctant to award such pay.[109] Even where the contract does provide for holiday pay for employees on leave, it has been strictly interpreted. For example, a provision for holiday pay for the employee on sick leave "if his absence due to sickness begins no earlier than the second workday preceding or begins no later than the first work day following the holiday" was strictly applied to deny holiday pay to an employee whose sick leave began earlier than the second workday preceding the holiday.[110]

In some cases where the contract contains no explicit provision on sick leave as affecting holiday pay, the issue may involve the "justifiable excuse" exception to the surrounding days work requirements clause. For instance, where the contract provided that an employee would be ineligible for holiday pay if he was absent on either of the surrounding days "unless such absence is for justifiable cause," the arbitrator held that "an employee on sick leave must be regarded as excused from work or absent for 'just cause,'" thus qualifying for holiday pay.[111] However, although the contract was silent on the

---

[106]See Mattel, Inc., 23 LA 383, 387 (Warren, 1954).

[107]See Femco, Inc., 50 LA 1146, 1148 (McDermott, 1968); Republic Steel Corp., 21 LA 317, 319–320 (Shipman, 1953).

[108]See Arbitrator Gibson in 60 LA 990, 992–993; Dworkin in 46 LA 9, 10. In Lithonia Lighting Co., 74 LA 30, 32–33 (Rimer, 1980), an employee, absent on the day after a holiday because of an ill stepchild, had a "valid excuse" within the meaning of the holiday pay provision.

[109]See Femco, Inc., 50 LA 1146, 1148 (McDermott, 1968), where the contract provided holiday pay for the "regular" employee, defined as "one having worked in the pay period in which the holiday falls"; the arbitrator said that this provision excluded from holiday pay eligibility employees like the grievant who were on extended leaves of absence. In San Francisco Publishers Assn., 46 LA 260, 265 (1965), Arbitrator Burns held that if the parties had intended to provide holiday pay for employees on sick leave they could have done so just as they provided pay for holidays occurring during regular days off or vacations. Also see Arbitrator McGilligan in 64 LA 762, 764–765; Prasow in 32 LA 336, 340, involving past practice.

[110]See Columbus & S. Ohio Elec. Co., 45 LA 1021, 1023 (Schmidt, 1965). Also strictly applying a sickness exception, see Arbitrator Woy in 71 LA 1067, 1068; Gibson in 71 LA 1039, 1040; Hadlick in 64 LA 625, 627 (doctor's certificate required); Maniscalo in 63 LA 982, 986; Hilgert in 62 LA 837, 841–842; Teple in 42 LA 75, 76–77; Shipman in 21 LA 317, 320; Aaron in 15 LA 204, 207. For cases in which the sickness exception contained no restrictive language, see Lipson in 69 LA 1195, 1200; Dunsford in 67 LA 97, 100; Kadish in 29 LA 424, 426–427; Sherman in 24 LA 694, 965.

[111]Wooster Sportswear Co., 46 LA 9, 10 (Dworkin, 1965). Similarly, see Arbitrator Eckhardt in 68 LA 928, 930 (involving disability leave of absence); Schaffer in 67 LA 638, 640; Roumell in 63 LA 544, 545–548, citing many cases; Donnelly, Curry & Mottram in 24 LA 815, 817; Kaplan in 18 LA 777, 779–780. Cf., Arbitrator Warns in 32 LA 516, 521–522. Nor did the employer's obligation to make sick leave payments to the Union's Welfare Fund limit his obligation regarding holiday pay, since the contract expressly provided that the welfare payments shall not be deemed "wages due to the workers." See Wooster Sportswear Co., 46 LA 9, 11 (Dworkin, 1965). Regarding receipt of both workers' compensation and holiday pay, see Penthouse Furniture Ltd., 81 LA 494, 495 (Roberts, 1983), stating that "whether or not Grievant received workman's compensation for the holiday in question is irrelevant to whether or not Grievant was entitled to holiday pay under the contract." In Printing Indus. of N.Y., 44 LA 124, 125 (Kornblum, 1965), it was held that payment of sick leave pay did not necessarily preclude the requirement of proof of illness to qualify for holiday pay.

matter, the arbitrator held further that it would be "practical and reasonable" and not in conflict with any of the terms of the agreement to "imply a limitation that an employee on sick leave would be entitled to not more than two paid holidays occurring during a three month period of sick leave, providing the employee returns to work upon cessation of her illness."[112]

An established practice of denying holiday pay to employees on sick leave may lead the arbitrator to deny such pay.[113] Or a practice, or prior settlements reached by the parties, may require holiday pay to employees on sick leave.[114]

Holidays Falling on Nonworkdays

Arbitrators appear to be in disagreement on the issue of pay for holidays falling on a nonworkday Saturday where the contract designates certain paid holidays without distinguishing between holidays falling within or outside the regular workweek.

Thus, on one hand, many arbitrators have held that under such a contract employees are entitled to pay for holidays that fall on Saturdays even though the regular workweek is Monday through Friday;[115] they base their rulings upon the lack of ambiguity and upon "the clear, plain and explicit" language of the contract which is "not limited or restricted by any qualifying provision."[116]

On the other hand, many other arbitrators have denied pay for holidays falling on nonworkday Saturdays; they have held that while the contract language is unrestricted, it is ambiguous in that it does not contain an express provision that holiday pay should be granted regardless of the day upon which the holiday falls.[117] Some of these arbitrators felt compelled to turn to the "conduct of the parties" or their past practice which gave meaning to the contract; and finding a previously unchallenged practice of not paying for Saturday holidays, these arbitrators refused to grant such pay.[118]

---

[112]Wooster Sportswear Co., 46 LA 9, 11 (Dworkin, 1965).

[113]See Arbitrator Elkouri in 38 LA 1061, 1064; Warns in 32 LA 516, 521–522; Prasow in 32 LA 336, 340. For cases involving past practice regarding eligibility for holiday pay when the employee is receiving disability pay, see Arbitrator Beatty in 26 LA 206, 208; Boles in 25 LA 100, 104.

[114]See Arbitrator Brown in 62 LA 1025, 1026–1027; Koven in 44 LA 1010, 1014–1015; Rubin in 35 LA 680, 681.

[115]See Arbitrator Goldstein in 43 LA 676, 677–678; Myers in 42 LA 269, 272; Caraway in 33 LA 494, 496; Howard in 24 LA 667, 670–671; Donnelly, Curry & Mottram in 21 LA 325, 326; Anderson in 20 LA 910, 911; Gaffey in 20 LA 734, 737; Phillips in 12 LA 43, 45; Albert in 7 LA 824, 826. In two of these cases the arbitrators awarded holiday pay in spite of consistent past practice of not paying for Saturday holidays. See Myers in 42 LA 269, 272; Donnelly, Curry & Mottram in 21 LA 325, 326.

[116]International Paper Co., 43 LA 676, 677 (Goldstein, 1964).

[117]See Arbitrator Seligson in 22 LA 806, 807; Cheit in 21 LA 98, 101–104; Grant in 18 LA 74, 75–76; Seward in 13 LA 983, 984–985; Trotta in 12 LA 417, 418; Rosenfarb in 11 LA 635, 636–638; Feinberg in 8 LA 334, 336–337; Wallen in 7 LA 745, 746; Scheiber in 7 LA 663, 664–665. Also see Arbitrator Stein in 11 LA 970, 970–971.

[118]See Arbitrator Grant in 18 LA 74, 75–76; Trotta in 12 LA 417, 418; Rosenfarb in 11 LA 635, 637–638; Feinberg in 8 LA 334, 336–337.

The contract may specifically exclude Saturday holidays which are not workdays from the holiday pay clause;[119] or it may specifically include holidays which fall on nonworkday Saturdays;[120] or the contract may contain a qualifying clause granting pay for named holidays provided they fall on regularly scheduled workdays.[121] In the latter event, no holiday pay ordinarily would be allowed for holidays occurring outside the regular workweek;[122] nor would the employees under such a contract be entitled to have the Friday preceding a Saturday holiday considered as a paid holiday off.[123]

Strikes as Affecting Holiday Pay

Arbitrators have been generally reluctant to award pay to employees for holidays occurring while they are on strike unless the contract provides otherwise.[124] Thus, in a number of cases where work was available and scheduled during a strike and the contract contained a surrounding days work requirements clause, it was held that employees on strike were not entitled to pay for holidays falling during the strike period.[125] As for holidays falling during a strike occurring in a hiatus period between contracts, the result ordinarily is the same.[126] The rulings of the arbitrators are based upon the lack of compliance with the contractual conditions for entitlement,[127] or, in a

---

[119]As in American Can Co., 33 LA 809 at 809 (Bothwell, 1959); Western Union Tel. Co., 20 LA 756 at 756 (Shipman, 1953).

[120]As in Lewall Sportswear Co., 53 LA 1165, 1166 (Dworkin, 1969); Foster Wheeler Corp., 35 LA 788, 789 (Stark, 1960). For cases involving holiday "bumping" see Arbitrator Barone in 71 LA 1034, 1037–1038 (discussing other cases); Scanlon in 71 LA 599, 601; Klein in 71 LA 124, 128–129; Jones in 69 LA 806, 807; Murphy in 61 LA 58, 61–64; Cohen in 60 LA 737, 738; Altrock in 59 LA 581, 582; Allen in 58 LA 973, 975–976; Stix in 58 LA 123, 124; McIntosh in 66–1 ARB ¶8320.

[121]As in cases decided by Arbitrator Cayton in 42 LA 843, 844; Anderson in 23 LA 392, 393; Jones in 21 LA 120 at 120; Stutz, Mottram & Mannino in 21 LA 59 at 59; Pigors in 18 LA 356, 357; Gooding in 12 LA 165 at 165.

[122]See cases cited in note 121 above. In Vulcan-Mold & Iron Co., 21 LA 7, 8–9 (Kelliher, 1953), the employer was required to pay for a Saturday holiday despite the contract where there was a past practice of regularly scheduling Saturday work.

[123]Printing Indus. of Wash., D.C., 42 LA 843, 844 (Clayton, 1964). Similarly, see Arbitrator Dworkin in 53 LA 1165, 1169.

[124]See Arbitrator Hill in 53 LA 1206, 1209; Wolff in 50 LA 921, 924; Stieber in 46 LA 967, 970; Kates in 46 LA 102, 104–105; Crawford in 43 LA 213, 214; Forsythe in 42 LA 102, 107; Teple in 42 LA 75, 78–79; Reid in 40 LA 673, 675; Trotta in 24 LA 560, 562–563. But where the contract has no surrounding days work requirements, the result may be different, as in Hellenic Lines, Ltd., 38 LA 339, 341–343 (Yagoda, 1962).

[125]See Arbitrator May in 65 LA 189, 192 (holiday fell during vacation which was encompassed by strike period); Seinsheimer in 57 LA 1217, 1219–1220 (wildcat strike); Kates in 46 LA 102, 104–105; Teple in 42 LA 75, 78–79; Reid in 40 LA 673, 675 (wildcat strike); Marshall in 35 LA 117, 120 (wildcat strike). Also see Goldberg in 62 LA 681, 683 (work stoppage for alleged safety reasons); Klamon in 25 LA 841, 844. Cf., Keefe in 52 LA 512, 514–515; Davis in 51 LA 1309, 1310.

[126]See Arbitrator Feldman in 74 LA 1058, 1060; Traynor in 43 LA 539, 545; Kerrison in 37 LA 3, 4; Updegraff in 36 LA 507, 510; Seitz in 33 LA 681, 682–683; Hepburn in 30 LA 671, 674; Trotta in 24 LA 560, 562–563. Also see Sugarman in 36 LA 1276, 1278. But see Universal-Cyclops Steel Corp., 36 LA 1237, 1240–1241 (Crawford, 1961), where a strike settlement agreement extended the old contract.

[127]See Arbitrator Rutledge in 62 LA 785, 788; Kates in 46 LA 102, 105; Teple in 42 LA 75, 78–79; Reid in 40 LA 673, 675; Kerrison in 37 LA 3, 4; Marshall in 35 LA 117, 120; Kadish in 24 LA 149, 152; Brecht in 19 LA 73, 75. In Packaging Corp. of America, 62 LA 1214, 1216 (1974), Arbitrator Gibson held that, although the strike settlement agreement "reinstated" provisions of the expired contract, employees had failed to satisfy the surrounding days work requirements because they were on strike.

hiatus period strike, upon the reasoning that the right to holiday pay is a creature of contract and such right does not exist when there is no contract.[128]

Moreover, where the strike had been settled but not all of the employees had been recalled when the holiday occurred, the contractual eligibility requirements were held to apply to disqualify those who had not yet returned to work.[129] In this regard, Arbitrator Samuel S. Kates has stated that despite the original purpose of the surrounding days work requirements "to encourage full staffing of the plant before and after a holiday and to prevent stretching of holiday periods," nevertheless "when a contract states in absolute terms that holiday pay will be allowed only if" such requirements are met, it would be adding to the contract to disregard such requirements.[130]

Where agreements contain a holiday pay clause providing pay for employees on layoff within a certain period of time surrounding the holiday, unions have argued that employees awaiting recall after a strike has ended are entitled to pay under such clause. Arbitrators have ruled both ways on the issue of whether such employees are "laid-off" within the meaning of the contract. Thus, where the contract stated that an otherwise eligible employee who is "laid off for lack of work" will be eligible for holiday pay "if his layoff begins or ends during the holiday week," one arbitrator ruled that employees who after the strike ended were idle while waiting to be recalled "were not laid off for 'lack of work' nor had the Company laid them off in the first instance," but their idle time resulted from the strike; and they were not eligible for holiday pay for a holiday occurring during the waiting period.[131] However, under a contract clause providing that "employees on layoff two weeks prior to the holiday or two weeks after the holiday shall" be eligible for holiday pay, another arbitrator held that the term "layoff" was broad enough to include employees waiting to be called back to work after a strike; and the employees therefore were held entitled to pay for Labor Day (the strike having ended on August 31st).[132]

Regarding employees laid off because operations were suspended due to another union's strike, it has been held that no holiday pay was due where the contract did not provide for such pay for holidays falling

[128]See Arbitrator Feldman in 74 LA 1058, 1060; Gibson in 71 LA 877, 879; Traynor in 43 LA 539, 545; Teple in 42 LA 75, 78; Kerrison in 37 LA 3, 4; Seitz in 33 LA 681, 682–683.

[129]See Arbitrator Taylor in 70 LA 190, 193–194; Kates in 46 LA 102, 105; Updegraff in 36 LA 507, 509–510; Klamon in 25 LA 841, 844.

[130]Gregory Galvanizing & Metal Processing, 46 LA 102, 105 (1966), where he also emphasized that this was so whether the last scheduled workday was "one day or three days or one week or two weeks or other period before the holiday." In this case it was the day the strike began, which was two weeks before the holiday.

[131]E.J. Lavino & Co., 43 LA 213, 214 (Crawford, 1964). Also see Arbitrator Kadish in 26 LA 149, 151–153; Klamon in 25 LA 841, 844. In Mobil Oil Co., 42 LA 102, 107 (Forsythe, 1963), a past practice of not granting holiday pay to employees awaiting recall was held controlling.

[132]St. Regis Paper Co., 46 LA 967, 969–970 (Stieber, 1966); the arbitrator took note of the surrounding days work requirements but found that the exception in the clause noted above applied to the employees in the instant case. Similarly, Arbitrator Michelstetter in 62 LA 455, 459; Camp in 12 LA 211, 212.

within a layoff period.[133] Moreover, where the contract excused
employees from complying with the surrounding days work requirements for certain named reasons or "similar good cause," it was held
that employees did not have a "similar good cause" excuse when they
did not work the day before a holiday because an illegal strike by other
employees forced the employer to shut down the plant.[134] However,
where one employee managed to report to work but was told that no
work was available and other employees were unable to enter the
plant because of picket lines of employees on unauthorized strike, they
were held eligible for holiday pay, the arbitrator stating that "whether
grievants were stopped at the gate or actually got into the plant, they
did all that reasonably could have been required of them and thus
their failing to work was because of a 'similar good cause.'"[135]

Another aspect is presented when employees voluntarily honor
the picket line of another union. In such cases holiday pay has been
denied, one arbitrator commenting that "when employees voluntarily
absent themselves from work in order to honor the picket line of fellow
employees from another union, loss of holiday pay, like loss of wages,
is part of the price which they must pay for choosing that course of
action."[136]

Loss of Holiday Pay as Penalty for Misconduct

It is generally held that it is improper for the employer to deny
holiday pay to an employee as punishment for misconduct or for
violation of plant rules if the employee is otherwise eligible for such
benefit (but the employee could be properly disciplined).[137] However,
if the employee by his misconduct or by his violation of plant rules fails
to comply with the work requirements of the contract, he disqualifies

---

[133]See Arbitrator Turkus in 40 LA 140, 142; Hill in 39 LA 500, 503–504; Wolff in 36 LA 1232, 1235. In Rockwell Mfg. Co., 33 LA 77, 79–80 (Scheiber, 1959), an established practice of not paying holiday pay to laid-off employees was held controlling. Where the contract had no eligibility requirements for holiday pay, the arbitrator held that the company had an absolute obligation to pay without regard to the company's operations. See Turkus in 61 LA 1216, 1217; Walsh in 25 LA 91, 93–94.

[134]Phoenix Steel Corp., 44 LA 927, 928 (Crawford, 1965). Similarly, Schlage Lock Co., 30 LA 105, 107–109 (Ross, 1958), noting that the weight of arbitral decisions declines holiday pay under such circumstances, with citation of cases on both sides of the question at 108–109. Also see Arbitrator Whitton in 25 LA 687, 689–691.

[135]United States Steel Corp., 46 LA 473, 477 (McDermott, 1966). Similarly, United States Steel Corp., 45 LA 509, 511 (Altrock, 1965). Also awarding holiday pay, see Arbitrator Shipman in 36 LA 99, 100; McIntosh in 32 LA 30, 32–33; Seward in 23 LA 141, 143; in all of these cases the employees reported for work and were sent home or were notified not to report for work because of a strike by other employees, and the contract in the Seward case had a "similar good cause" exception while the contracts in the other two cases contained language to the effect that an employee's absence with company approval or permission was an exception to the work require-ments clause.

[136]Lucky Stores, Inc., 57 LA 149, 153 (Eaton, 1971), discussing other cases at 151–152. Similarly, Arbitrator Caraway in 70 LA 930, 934–935; White in 68 LA 220, 221–222; Bauder in 54 LA 754, 756–757.

[137]See Arbitrator Tripp in 54 LA 947, 950; Dworkin in 51 LA 723, 728, and in 36 LA 517, 520–522; Reid in 40 LA 673, 674; Sembower in 39 LA 104, 106–107; Anderson in 33 LA 890, 892; Schedler in 32 LA 865, 867–868; Platt in 16 LA 317, 319, and in 13 LA 126, 131–132. Cf., Arbitrator Schmidt in 31 LA 558, 560–561; Smith in 11 LA 1195, 1198–1199; in both of which cases the contract contained language justifying denial of holiday pay as a disciplinary action.

himself for holiday pay. This was the ruling in a case in which the employees by their wildcat strike on the day before a holiday failed to comply with the surrounding days work requirements clause and thus did not qualify for holiday pay.[138]

Other Holiday Issues

Other holiday issues which have been arbitrated include the right of the employer to determine the day to be observed as the holiday named in the contract;[139] various issues relating to employee birthday holidays;[140] the question of straight time or overtime pay for unworked holidays;[141] the question of premium pay for working on a holiday;[142] the basis for computation of holiday pay;[143] the issue of holiday pay entitlement when the employee is receiving workers' compensation;[144] holiday issues involving probationary employees.[145]

Leaves of Absence

"Ordinarily, in industrial relations parlance 'leave', when 'granted', connotes absence from work without the imposition of penalties that might otherwise be suffered for failing to report * * * when scheduled for work."[146]

While a leave of absence status may have important immediate benefits to the employee in terms of pay for time lost and freedom from penalty when absent briefly from work, it may be even more important in terms of future job security (keeping his job open for him and retention of seniority) and future major benefits (disability pensions or retirement benefits) when he must be absent for an extended period of

---

[138]American Brake Shoe Co., 40 LA 673, 675 (Reid, 1963). Similarly, Arbitrator Belshaw in 71 LA 321, 322, where an employee, because of misconduct on the job, was sent home early on the day after a holiday; Mallet-Prevost in 67 LA 1287, 1290, where an employee was absent on his scheduled (overtime) Saturday shift before a holiday because he was "fed up" with job irritations; Dworkin in 51 LA 724, 730. Cf., Marshall in 73 LA 607, 609–610, where a new contract "guaranteed pay" for named holidays.

[139]See Arbitrator Shister in 72 LA 408, 410 (practice of observing Memorial Day on last Monday in May); Drotning in 70 LA 1283, 1285; Ipavac in 69 LA 115, 119–123 (past practice controlled); Kelly in 66 LA 192, 193; Gratz in 59 LA 730, 732; Gould in 51 LA 445, 448–449; Fallon in 45 LA 85, 88–90. Also see Hatcher in 69 LA 665, 669–670 (a "floating" holiday issue).

[140]See Arbitrator Cohen in 74 LA 1276; Potter in 72 LA 534; Grooms in 68 LA 992; Perry in 68 LA 835; Dworkin in 67 LA 723; Bardwell in 65 LA 1217; Greene in 57 LA 177.

[141]See Arbitrator Lovell in 74 LA 199; Shearer in 73 LA 547 (commission employees); Levy in 70 LA 1296 (Saturday holiday "pushed back" to Friday); Hadlick in 70 LA 653; Murphy in 61 LA 58; Kleinsorge in 56 LA 1239; Carson in 56 LA 1033; McKenna in 56 LA 652; Farinholt in 55 LA 992.

[142]See Arbitrator Gowan in 74 LA 345; Lubow in 73 LA 342; Richman in 71 LA 813; Charm in 71 LA 676; McIntosh in 62 LA 540; Dunne in 57 LA 140.

[143]See Arbitrator Handsaker in 73 LA 1305 (shift differential); Glushein in 73 LA 172; Fox in 66 LA 1183; Daniel in 66 LA 586.

[144]See Arbitrator Gundermann in 71 LA 1118, 1122; Dallas in 61 LA 627, 630.

[145]See Arbitrator Brown in 62 LA 1202; Neas in 67 LA 666; Sloane in 60 LA 128.

[146]Publishers' Assn. of N.Y. City, 32 LA 513, 515 (Seitz, 1959). Also see Menasco Mfg. Co., 71 LA 696, 698 (Gowan, 1978), where a distinction is drawn, based on contract language, between "leave of absence" and "excused absence."

time.[147] From management's standpoint, its interest is not only in the cost of monetary benefits to the employee but also in production problems which may result from the absence of an experienced employee who may be difficult or impossible to replace.[148] Thus, management has a natural interest in promoting regular attendance by employees and in preventing abuse of leave of absence privileges.[149]

It has been held that except as restricted by the agreement, the granting or denial of leaves of absence is a prerogative of management, and the judgment of management will not be disturbed so long as the action taken is not unreasonable or discriminatory.[150] In some cases past practice and custom concerning leaves of absence have determined whether management's action should be upheld.[151] Where leaves of absence were provided for in the contract, with the right reserved to the company to judge the cause for the requested leave, the "arbitrary or discriminatory" test was applied by the arbitrator in determining whether leave had been properly denied.[152]

An employee is not automatically entitled to a leave of absence since this right or privilege exists by virtue of provision in the collective bargaining agreement or a leave plan unilaterally instituted by management or by reason of past practice. For example, one arbitrator held that although the contract provided for sick leave of absence, such leave was not automatic in view of the contractual requirement, not

---

[147]See Joyce-Cridland Co., 35 LA 133, 136–137 (Schmidt, 1960). Also see Nashville Gas Co., 79 LA 802, 804 (Odom, 1982). The seniority date of an employee and the grant of an extended leave of absence can adversely affect the seniority rights of fellow employees. See Allied Roll Builders, 72 LA 609, 613 (Leahy, 1979), where the contract was silent on leave of absence and the arbitrator held that the six-month leave "was not justified under the Management Rights Clause" and that "the integrity of the Seniority system should be maintained."

[148]See Hudson Pulp & Paper Co., 35 LA 581, 583 (Hill, 1960). Also see Arbitrator Odom in 79 LA 802, 804; Leeper in 78 LA 8, 11; Gowan in 71 LA 696, 698; Greer in 63 LA 1093, 1096.

[149]In a case involving discipline for excessive absences, Arbitrator Vernon L. Stouffer stated, "Arbitrators have consistently held that one of the obligations of employment is that the employee report for work inasmuch as successful operation of a plant depends upon regular attendance." Insley Mfg. Corp., 52 LA 59, 73 (1968).

[150]See Arbitrator Slade in 79 LA 973, 977; Odom in 79 LA 802, 805; Foster in 76 LA 626, 631–632; Gowan in 71 LA 696, 697–698; Roberts in 48 LA 1166, 1167–1168; Dworkin in 45 LA 667, 670; Fallon in 43 LA 670, 673; Waite in 12 LA 661, 662; Wardlaw in 3 LA 108, 110. Also see Dugan in 71 LA 674, 676; Elson in 21 LA 502, 511; Tyree in 19 LA 604, 607; Aaron in 15 LA 928, 933. Cf., Leahy in 72 LA 609, 613. An implied limitation on management was found in contract provisions by Arbitrator Schmidt in 35 LA 133, 136–137.

[151]See Arbitrator Hebert in 45 LA 621, 627–628; Tatum in 44 LA 373, 376; Elkouri in 38 LA 1061, 1063–1064; Levinson in 23 LA 277, 280; McCraw in 19 LA 709, 710; Lesser in 18 LA 528, 531. Also see Cahn in 52 LA 176, 177. For a case involving an attempted but unsuccessful discontinuance of a past practice regarding leaves of absence, see Hillbro Newspaper Printing Co., 48 LA 1166, 1167–1168 (Roberts, 1967). In Saydel Consol. School Dist., 76 LA 673, 676 (Nathan, 1981), past practice supported a broad construction of a "business leave" provision, significantly reducing management's right to deny leave requests. But where there was insufficient evidence of a past practice, the employer was not required to pay an employee who was absent from work due to an Act of God, in Columbia Gas of W. Va., 77 LA 990, 993–994 (Beilstein, 1981), where the union also relied in part on an alleged practice of another corporate entity which was a signatory to the contract. For related discussion, see Chapter 12, topic entitled "Custom and Practice as Part of the Contract."

[152]Hudson Pulp & Paper Co., 35 LA 581, 583 (Hill, 1960), holding that denial of leave (requested for the purpose of serving a jail sentence) was not improper. Also see Arbitrator Anderson in 76 LA 566, 568 (unqualified contract language gave complete discretion to the employer); Nathan in 74 LA 934, 937–939 (the quota established by the employer was held "arbitrary on its face"). Cf., Yarowsky in 77 LA 701, 704.

complied with by the grievant, for the submission of a written request.[153] Another arbitrator, noting that "The contract language should not be construed or applied so as to defeat its substantive purpose, namely, to make provision for necessary sick leave," held not only that the contract did not require that sick leave requests be granted automatically even though the employee presents a statement from his doctor that sick leave is necessary, but also that the company could "evaluate the factual basis of a sick leave request" and deny the request if it is frivolous and not supported by the facts.[154]

Sick Leave

Provision for sick leave may be negotiated into the contract,[155] or a sick leave plan or policy may be instituted unilaterally by management.[156] In any event, management has a legitimate concern in preventing abuse of sick leave claims and in so doing it may formulate reasonable rules for the documentation of illness,[157] prescribe forms to be filled out by the employee and his doctor,[158] or develop a system for the policing of a sick benefits plan,[159] so long as it is not arbitrary, discriminatory, or unreasonable.[160] As stated by Arbitrator Russell C. Neas:

> "Although there may not be an abuse of its discretion in such matters and absent any contractual restrictions, the Company has the right to require proof of illness in order to avoid fraud, invalid claims or other abuses of the system. Such rights include the privilege of requiring a

---

[153]Doering's Super Valu, 47 LA 364, 368–369 (Lee, 1966). Cf., Arbitrator Teple in 48 LA 615, 618, where the contract provided for six months sick leave as a matter of right without formal application or approval.

[154]The Magnavox Co., 45 LA 667, 669–670 (Dworkin, 1965). Also see Hormel Fine Frozen Foods, 75 LA 1129, 1141 (Neas, 1980).

[155]As in 78 LA 221, 223; 76 LA 875, 876; 76 LA 46, 47–48; 75 LA 862, 864; 74 LA 1254, 1255; 45 LA 667, 668.

[156]As in Socony Mobil Oil Co., 45 LA 1062, 1063 (Kadish, 1965); Block Drug Co., 58 LA 1197, 1198, 1200 (Trotta, 1972). In J.H. Day Co., 62 LA 909, 912–913 (Paradise, 1974), the company was held bound by a long-standing "practice of paying for time spent on off-premises doctor's visits for the treatment of job-related injuries."

[157]See Arbitrator Neas in 75 LA 1129, 1141; Brown in 69 LA 980, 983–984; Greer in 63 LA 1093, 1096; Williams in 41 LA 1063, 1064; Corsi in 40 LA 386, 388. Also see Oppenheim in 48 LA 554, 557–558.

[158]See Arbitrator Ipavec in 75 LA 21, 25; Marshall in 52 LA 593, 596; Ryder in 41 LA 1133, 1135; McGury in 38 LA 419, 422.

[159]See Socony Mobil Oil Co., 45 LA 1062, 1065 (Kadish, 1965). For some cases involving abuse of sick leave and the various means used by employers to combat abuse, see Arbitrator Boken in 76 LA 624, 625; Fitzsimmons in 76 LA 46, 53–54; Sherman in 75 LA 623, 624–625; Ables in 72 LA 125, 126; Hutcheson in 67 LA 606, 608 (contract restriction); Edelman in 63 LA 928, 930.

[160]The reasonableness test was applied in National Airlines, 43 LA 1169, 1171 (1964), where Arbitrator Black held that even though the contract permitted the company to require a physician's certificate to confirm a sick claim, it could do so only when it has reasonable doubts as to the employee's sick claim. Also see Arbitrator Eisler in 76 LA 1267, 1272 (stating that the "rule of reasonableness must be applied to the facts of each case" and that management "has the right to curb and correct abuses of sick leave when they are found to exist"); Hays in 71 LA 1064, 1066; Curry in 69 LA 375, 378 (common sense and reasonableness must be applied); Taylor in 62 LA 77, 82. Where the company's right to require a medical certificate had been the subject of bargaining in the past and had been negotiated out of the agreement, the arbitrator nevertheless ruled that "If the Company has *reasonable* grounds for believing an employee is abusing sick leave the Company has the right to request proof of illness." Galloway Co., 49 LA 240, 242–243 (Gundermann, 1967).

doctor's certification, questioning the claimant and the attending physician, requiring submission of additional medical documentation, and to generally conduct a thorough investigation of any questionable claim when there is reasonable cause."[161]

Indeed, it is said that the company has an obligation to guard against fraudulent sick pay claims.[162] Thus, Arbitrator John P. McGury stated that the company has both "the right and the duty to make reasonable inquiries concerning the basis for a sick benefit claim and it would be extremely impractical if not impossible for these legitimate inquiries to be made without the Company having the right to request the necessary information."[163]

Documentation may also be required under suspicious circumstances, such as absence before a vacation,[164] or mass absences on a holiday,[165] or other suspicious circumstances.[166] Moreover, it has been stated that "where there is a claim under suspicious circumstances * * * the documentation required may be more exacting than otherwise might be the case."[167]

Contract provisions vary as to documentation requirements. The contract may, as in one case, specify detailed requirements for sick leave, such as a written application on a specified form, submission of a medical certificate (showing date of disability, physician's personal

---

[161]Hormel Fine Frozen Foods, 75 LA 1129, 1141 (1980). The NLRB ruled in Womac Indus., 99 LRRM 1185 (NLRB, 1978), that the employer violated the NLRA when, without notifying or bargaining with the union, it established a new rule that employees must furnish a doctor's excuse for all absences due to illness; the Board explained that plant rules "clearly affect conditions of employment and are mandatory bargaining subjects" and the new rule was a "significant change" from the employer's prior practice.

[162]Lloyd Noland Found., 74 LA 1236, 1243 (Griffin, 1980); Curtiss-Wright Corp., 36 LA 842, 845 (Seitz, 1961). Also see Arbitrator Talmadge in 74 LA 189, 191.

[163]Cities Serv. Petroleum Co., 38 LA 419, 422 (1961), holding that the company acted reasonably in requiring the employee to sign a "medical waiver" authorizing the disclosure of information by his doctor to the company. Accord, Gillette Co., 79 LA 953, 958 (Bard, 1982), emphasizing (at 960, 962) that the company must act reasonably in its requirement of medical certificates. Also see Arbitrator Ipavec in 75 LA 21, 25–27; Griffin in 74 LA 1236, 1244. But see Arbitrator Richman in 74 LA 923, 926.

[164]See Marion Power Shovel Co., 43 LA 507, 509–510 (Dworkin, 1964), where the contract did not require medical proof when absence due to illness did not exceed three days and the past practice of the company had been to accept an oral statement by the employee, but the employee "acted improperly in refusing to cooperate" by providing management with information which he had to verify his illness. The arbitrator held that grievant was properly disciplined for his refusal to cooperate.

[165]See Arbitrator Roumell in 68 LA 848, 852–854; Platt in 28 LA 897, 899. Cf., Bethlehem Steel Co., 42 LA 851, 852 (Hill, 1964), where the arbitrator ruled that although grievant's explanation of an absence was open to "suspicion, if not downright disbelief," the company could not condition payment for a holiday upon the employee's proving his preholiday claim of illness at home since there was no practice at the plant of making an employee prove that he had been absent for medical reasons.

[166]See Arbitrator Feldesman in 76 LA 705, 711–714 (company upheld in requiring "personal" notice of illness even though such notice was not required by contract, company rules, or past practice); Boken in 76 LA 624, 625; Garman in 76 LA 441, 445–446; Caraway in 73 LA 1235, 1236; Edelman in 63 LA 928, 930; Zimring in 54 LA 1107, 1109. A "sick-out" was involved in Federal Aviation Admin., 72 LA 761, 764–765 (Forrester, 1979), but three grievants "presented the stronger proof" that they were actually ill; the award was based on "the weight of the evidence rather than on a firm conviction" regarding the actual facts. In another "sick-out" case disciplinary action was upheld where abuse of sick leave provisions was found. City of Hartford, 67 LA 1107, 1108–1109 (Mellon, 1976).

[167]Cities Serv. Oil Co., 62 LA 77, 82 (Taylor, 1974). To similar effect, Lloyd Noland Found., Inc., 74 LA 1236, 1243 (Griffin, 1980). Requirement of documentation must be reasonable even though "circumstances were suspect," as in Kansas City Area Transp., 76 LA 1267, 1272 (Eisler, 1981).

attendance or treatment, nature of illness or injury, date of first treatment and date physician predicts employee will be able to resume work), and, in addition, examination of the employee by a physician selected by the company.[168] Or the contract may be less demanding, as in another case, requiring merely that notice could be by "registered mail, telegram, telephone, or in person within 5 days of the last day worked," but even such notice would be waived if it was "impossible to notify the Company."[169]

In the absence of a formal procedure set up by the contract or by company rules, what kind of proof of illness must the employee offer and what kind of proof can the company demand? In one case, the parties had an informal practice of many years whereby the employee ordinarily told his foreman whether his absence was due to "sickness" and the foreman accepted the explanation if he had no reason to doubt the employee's truthfulness. The parties had no desire to change this practice or to introduce any new rigid requirements. However, Arbitrator Harry H. Platt said that the practice does not mean that the company may never ask for proof of "sickness," and he provided the following guidelines:

> In most cases, it would suffice for the employee to provide an explanation in sufficient detail to enable the supervisor to make a judgment as to whether sick leave is justified.
>
> Some cases require more, but the proof need not be in any particular form, nor must it be the strongest and best proof possible. Verification could be in the following forms:
>
> (a) A doctor's letter would be appropriate but should not be an absolute requirement since there may be illness without the attention of a doctor;
> (b) A druggist's prescription might be adequate; or
> (c) A written statement from the employee's wife, neighbor, or fellow worker might suffice.
>
> The nature of the proof must ultimately depend upon the facts and circumstances of each case.[170]

Other issues involving sick leave which have been arbitrated include: whether an absence should be charged to sick leave or other

---

[168]Birmingham-Jefferson County Transit Auth., 78 LA 221, 223–224 (Shaeffer, 1982). In federal-sector employment, the statutes, FPM, and agency regulations are relevant along with the contract in the resolution of sick leave issues. See Scott AFB, 76 LA 46, 47–48, 54 (Fitzsimmons, 1980).

[169]Eaton Corp., 67 LA 1065, 1066 (Cantor, 1976). Also see Arbitrator Beilstein in 64 LA 540, 541.

[170]Republic Steel Corp., 28 LA 897, 899 (Platt, 1957), a "mass absences" case, cited with the recommendation that the parties follow these guidelines in Laclede Gas Co., 63 LA 628, 630 (Edelman, 1974). This approach using the above kinds of proof was taken by the company in another "mass absences" case. See Phoenix Steel Co., 51 LA 357 at 357 (Cahn, 1968). Cf., Bridgeport Gas Co., 31 LA 253, 255–256 (Stutz, 1958).

leave,[171] whether sick leave benefits accumulate during a strike or layoff or when an employee is on worker's compensation,[172] whether employees may use sick leave during a strike or picketing or layoff,[173] whether employees may use sick leave to tend to an ill family member,[174] and whether employees are entitled to receive payment for unused accumulated sick leave upon retirement or termination.[175] Awards in such cases depend variously upon explicit contract language, interpretation of the contract by the arbitrator, past practice, or bargaining history, or some combination of these factors.

Maternity or Maternity-Related Leave

Prior to 1973, when the Equal Employment Opportunity Commission issued pregnancy leave guidelines under Title VII of the Civil Rights Act, arbitration decisions generally recognized a right to maternity or maternity-related leave only to the extent that such right was provided for by the collective agreement or existed by past practice.[176]

During the period from the 1973 adoption of EEOC pregnancy leave guidelines until their use was sidetracked by the U.S. Supreme

[171]See Dubuque Community School Dist., 75 LA 862, 868 (C. Smith, 1980); Naval Ordnance Station, 62 LA 610, 614–616 (Cabe, 1974). Also see next subtopic entitled "Maternity or Maternity-Related Leave."

[172]See Arbitrator Rubin in 73 LA 899, 900–901 (layoff); Rule in 72 LA 776, 778–780 (honoring picket line); Gundermann in 71 LA 1118, 1122 (worker's compensation).

[173]See Arbitrator Penfield in 78 LA 1056, 1059 (layoff); Neas in 75 LA 1129, 1135–1144 (layoff); Kanes in 73 LA 981, 984–985 (strike); Brent in 68 LA 337, 341–342 (strike); Koven in 65 LA 992, 995–996 (strike); Stamm in 58 LA 1376, 1378–1379 (picketing); Sembower in 57 LA 337, 339–340 (strike). For views of NLRB Chairman and Members regarding the effect of strike and picketing on sick benefits, see Emerson Elec. Co., 103 LRRM 1073 (1980).

[174]See Arbitrator Gallagher in 83 LA 66, 68–69; Coyle in 73 LA 885, 887; Teple in 72 LA 229, 233–234; Ferguson in 69 LA 1245, 1246–1247; Jenkins in 64 LA 45, 48–50; Griffin in 59 LA 1114, 1115–1116; Purcell in 57 LA 1242, 1243–1244.

[175]For retirement cases see Arbitrator Mayer in 82 LA 970, 972–973; Kramer in 71 LA 1051, 1053–1054; Block in 58 LA 623, 626–627. For termination cases see Caraway in 69 LA 541, 544–546; McKone in 65 LA 373, 375–376.

[176]See cases cited at page 708 of the Third Edition of this book, subtopic entitled "Maternity Leave." In entitling the present subtopic "Maternity or Maternity-Related Leave," the Authors sought a title sufficiently broad to encompass the various leave situations and results reached in the cases and statutory materials cited in the subtopic. Leave nomenclature or terminology may vary in scope and meaning from case to case. For example, the broad scope that sometimes may be given to the term "maternity leave" is illustrated by the case in which a female employee who adopted a three-month-old girl was held entitled to a leave under a contractual "maternity leaves" provision; Arbitrator Carl F. Stoltenberg noted that the agreement did not restrict "maternity" to pregnancy or, as did another agreement, to "childbirth leave," and he declared that "no such distinction can be made that a mother adopting an infant is any less a mother or parent who requires a maternity leave than a natural mother." Ambridge Borough, 81 LA 915, 917 (1983). Similarly, see Arbitrator Seidenberg in 71 LA 93, 95–96. On the other hand, see Arbitrator Gruenberg in 64 LA 1132, 1134, and Belshaw in 64 LA 531, 532–533, in both of which cases maternity leave did not include leave for child care, as was also the result in Arbitrator Hardy's decision discussed below in this subtopic. And note the following statement in Ankeny Community School Dist., 77 LA 860, 861 (Nathan, 1981): The grievant "was pregnant with her first child. She applied for a year of parental leave pursuant to * * * the parties' Agreement. Parental leave, which differs from sick leave due to pregnancy (i.e., maternity leave), is intended to permit a new parent to spend full time with a newborn child." In West Side Credit Union, 77 LA 622, 626 (Ellmann, 1981), the dispute resulted because the agreement used (without adequately distinguishing or indicating the extent of overlap in the terms) "parental and/or infant care leave," "maternity leave," and "sick leave," all of which terms were used in reference to employees who become pregnant.

Court's 1976 decision in *General Electric Company v. Gilbert,* diverse approaches were pursued by arbitrators concerning consideration of statutory law in resolving pregnancy disability issues involved in maternity leave cases.[177]

In its *General Electric* decision the Supreme Court held that the employer's disability benefits plan did not violate Title VII because of its failure to cover pregnancy-related disabilities, absent any indication that the exclusion of pregnancy disability benefits was a pretext for discriminating against women; the Court stated that "gender-based discrimination does not result simply because an employer's disability benefits plan is less than all inclusive."[178]

However, the Pregnancy Discrimination Act of 1978 amended Title VII of the Civil Rights Act to expressly prohibit discrimination "because of or on the basis of pregnancy, childbirth, or related medical conditions."[179] The Equal Employment Opportunity Commission then issued updated guidelines in 1979, providing in part that:

---

[177]Different schools of thought and the arbitration decisions reflecting them during this period are discussed by Wolkinson & Liberson, "The Arbitration of Sex Discrimination Grievances," 37 Arb. J. No. 2, pp. 35, 41–42 (1982), where it is explained that "when resolving grievances over the denial of benefits for pregnancy-related illness or disabilities," among other approaches: some arbitrators relied upon saving clauses (making the agreement subject to statutory law and regulations) to justify use of EEOC guidelines as an implied part of the agreement; at least one arbitrator believed that EEOC guidelines must be applied even without such a saving clause; some arbitrators rejected the concept that EEOC guidelines may be referred to when adjudicating contractual disputes. For related discussion, see Chapter 10, topic entitled "Range of Views as to Application of 'Law' "; subtopic entitled "Title VII of the Civil Rights Act."

[178]General Elec. Co. v. Gilbert, 97 S.Ct. 401, 408–409, 413, 13 FEP Cases 1657 (1976). In so holding, the Supreme Court pointed to its decision in Geduldig v. Aiello, 94 S.Ct. 2485, 8 FEP Cases 97 (1974), where a state's exclusion of pregnancy from disability insurance coverage did not violate the Fourteenth Amendment. However, in Cleveland Bd. of Educ. v. LaFleur, 94 S.Ct. 791, 798–800, 6 FEP Cases 1253 (1974), the Supreme Court held invalid under the Fourteenth Amendment public school rules requiring pregnant public school teachers to take maternity leave five months before the expected birth of their child, the Court reasoning that arbitrary cut-off dates had no valid relationship to the state's interest in preserving continuity of teaching and amounted to a conclusive presumption that every pregnant teacher who has reached such date of pregnancy is physically incapable of continuing even when the medical evidence as to an individual woman's physical status might be wholly to the contrary. It has been explained that during the period between issuance of the Supreme Court's *General Electric* decision and enactment of the Pregnancy Discrimination Act of 1978, some arbitrators, "relying on saving clauses, continued to require employers to extend maternity benefits to pregnant women where there was in effect state legislation requiring pregnancy to be viewed as a disability," but that some other arbitrators relied on *General Electric* "to rule that pregnancy was not a compensable illness unless there was evidence that the contractual provisions on sick pay, leave, and disability had been specifically intended to cover pregnancy." Wolkinson & Liberson, "The Arbitration of Sex Discrimination Grievances," 37 Arb. J. No. 2, pp. 35, 42 (1982.)

[179]42 U.S.C. § 2000e(k), which is § 701(k) of the Civil Rights Act. This section, which became effective Oct. 31, 1978 (except that it became effective 180 days later as to any fringe benefit program or fund that was in effect on Oct. 31, 1978), states in part that:

"(k) The terms 'because of sex' or 'on the basis of sex' include, but are not limited to, because of or on the basis of pregnancy, childbirth, or related medical conditions; and women affected by pregnancy, childbirth, or related medical conditions shall be treated the same for all employment-related purposes * * * as other persons not so affected but similar in their ability or inability to work * * *."

In Newport News Shipbuilding & Dry Dock Co. v. EEOC, 103 S.Ct. 2622, 2631, 32 FEP Cases 1 (1983), the U.S. Supreme Court stated: "The Pregnancy Discrimination Act has now made clear that, for all Title VII purposes, discrimination based on a woman's pregnancy is, on its face, discrimination because of her sex." The actual holding in this case was that a health insurance plan which provided female employees benefits for pregnancy-related conditions to the same extent as for other medical conditions but which provided less extensive pregnancy benefits for spouses of male employees, discriminated "against male employees because of *their* sex"; the Court held the plan "unlawful, because the protection it affords to married male employees is less comprehensive than the protection it affords to married female employees." 103 S.Ct. at 2627.

"Written or unwritten employment policies and practices involving matters such as the commencement and duration of leave, the availability of extensions, the accrual of seniority and other benefits and privileges, reinstatement, and payment under any health or disability insurance or sick leave plan, formal or informal, shall be applied to disability due to pregnancy, childbirth or related medical conditions on the same terms and conditions as they are applied to other disabilities."

"Where the termination of an employee who is temporarily disabled is caused by an employment policy under which insufficient or no leave is available, such a termination violates the Act if it has a disparate impact on employees of one sex and is not justified by business necessity."[180]

In an arbitration case decided after the 1978 amendment became effective, the employer's maternity leave policy was challenged by the union both under the collective agreement and under the Civil Rights Act. In considering the challenge under the Civil Rights Act, Arbitrator J. Hazen Hardy, Jr., quoted at length from the amendment's legislative history, a portion of which is noted here to give some indication of what may now be required by the Act:[181]

"(a) Disability Benefits
" * * * Benefits need to be paid only on the same terms applicable to other employees—that is, generally, only when the employee is medically unable to work. For example, if a pregnant woman wishes, for reasons of her own, to stay at home to prepare for childbirth, or, after the child is born, to care for the child, no disability or sick leave benefits need be paid * * * . Since the period of disability for a normal pregnancy is 4–8 weeks, benefits will normally be paid for only that period. Of course, if there are medical complications of pregnancy or childbirth which prevent a woman from working for more than the normal period, the entire disability period, up to any time or dollar limit otherwise applicable would have to be covered."
"c. Leaves and Other Policies
" * * * Under this bill, employers will no longer be permitted to force women who become pregnant to stop working regardless of their ability to continue; employers will not be permitted to set arbitrary time limits within which disabled women must return to work, or before they may not return to work, if no such limits exist for other employees * * * ."

The challenged employer policy in the case being considered by Arbitrator Hardy limited unpaid maternity leave after childbirth to six weeks, an extension being available upon submission of a physician's certification that the pregnancy-related disability had continued and prevented a return to work. The employer's policy was supported by medical evidence that leave of six weeks after childbirth is adequate for normal pregnancy, which includes about 95 percent of

---

[180]The just-quoted sections, respectively, are 29 C.F.R. §§ 1604.10(b) and 1604.10(c). The discharge of a pregnant, unmarried employee was held to violate Title VII in Jacobs v. Martin Sweets Co., 14 FEP Cases 687, 691–692 (CA 6, 1977). Regarding "business necessity," in Harriss v. Pan Am. World Airways, 24 FEP Cases 947, 949–951 (CA 9, 1980), an airline's policy of requiring a pregnant stewardess to take maternity leave immediately upon learning of her pregnancy was held justified both as a business necessity and as a bona fide occupational qualification (BFOQ), the Court explaining when each of the two defenses becomes applicable.
[181]Saint Joseph Hosp., 73 LA 482, 487–488 (1979).

all pregnancies. In upholding the employer's policy, Arbitrator Hardy (1) stated that to the extent that child care was claimed by the union as an aspect of maternity leave, the "Maternity Leave" clause in the agreement contained language which would disallow such a claim, and (2) regarding the Civil Rights Act, he cited materials in the legislative history which he stated "support the conclusion that child care is not included in maternity leave."[182]

In some other arbitration cases which likewise were decided after the 1978 amendment became effective and in which there was an issue concerning maternity or maternity-related leave, the arbitrator expressly considered the Civil Rights Act (or, in some instances, considered an antidiscrimination statute of the state), examining the statute's requirements at least sufficiently to satisfy the arbitrator that the award was compatible with the statute.[183] Often in these cases the question of compliance with the statute was specifically raised by a party; or the agreement contained some provision such as a saving or legality clause requiring compliance with statutory law; or the employer, or both the employer and the union, had taken some step

---

[182]Id. at 492–493. Additional cases are cited above in this subtopic on the question of whether child care is included in maternity leave.

[183]See Arbitrator Shister in 80 LA 225, 229 (employee was not entitled to use sick leave bank to cover postdelivery care of her child under contract allowing use of bank if employee is incapacitated by severe sickness or injury); Neas in 75 LA 1129, 1136–1137, 1144 (noting that the agreement "was obviously revised in order to comply with the Pregnancy Discrimination Act," he stated that the Act requires that an employer with a sick benefit plan must treat an employee with a pregnancy-related disability the same as an employee with any other type of disability; he found "no evidence the Company has in any manner violated the Act," and found also that neither the agreement nor past practice had been violated by denial of disability benefits for pregnancy-related partial disability which occurred during layoff); Cabe in 74 LA 1288, 1290–1293 (relying on EEOC guidelines, he held that an employee who already was on unpaid pregnancy leave on the effective date of the Pregnancy Discrimination Act, became entitled to paid sick leave from that date, notwithstanding the employer's contention that the employee had become an inactive employee when she obtained pregnancy leave under the agreement and that inactive employees had not been considered eligible for sick leave benefits); Kossoff in 74 LA 604, 606–607 (here the situation and the arbitrator's view are similar to those just noted in the preceding citation, except that Arbitrator Kossoff deferred final decision pending submission by the employee of medical verification of disability); Davis in 72 LA 358, 359 (contract providing for advance sick leave "for serious disability or illness" did not require advance sick leave for normal pregnancy, the arbitrator stating that while pregnancy can bring about serious disability and illness, in this instance "it did not and most times it doesn't"; nor did the amended Civil Rights Act require the employer to grant the grievant's application for advance sick leave "to take care of impending pregnancy," the arbitrator stating that her application was not denied "because of sex, pregnancy or childbirth," the grievant having been "treated like all other women who experience normal childbirth"); Drotning in 71 LA 1219, 1221, 1223 (although not mentioning the federal statute, he stated that "employment policies which treat pregnancy and childbirth differently than other physical disabilities is prohibited by" the New York statute, and he concluded that both under the statute and under the employer's past practice of allowing female teachers to use up accumulated sick leave before using unpaid leave for childbearing and child rearing purposes, the employer improperly required grievant to elect between paid sick leave and unpaid leave rather than to permit her to utilize a combination of the two); Shister in 71 LA 1102, 1106 (this case involves the same New York statute and a contract issue and ruling similar to those just noted in the decision by Arbitrator Drotning, except that the facts in the Shister decision did not involve past practice but did involve an express contract clause requiring conformance with legal requirements); Barnhart in 71 LA 1178, 1179–1180 (until the EEOC pregnancy leave guidelines were issued in 1973 the collective agreement expressly excluded pregnancy disability from entitlement to sickness and accident benefits, but the express exclusion was deleted in reponse to the EEOC guidelines; Arbitrator Barnhart construed the agreement not to require sickness benefits during the period between the Supreme Court's *General Electric* decision and the effective date of the Pregnancy Discrimination Act, since the employer had made it clear that the employer's willingness to delete the express exclusion of pregnancy disability "arose from obedience to the law rather than from an obligation stemming from negotiation with the Union").

reflecting an intention to comply with the requirements of the amended Civil Rights Act.

In still other maternity or maternity-related leave cases decided after the 1978 amendment became effective, the arbitrator made no mention of the Civil Rights Act or any state statute in resolving the case, the arbitrator looking only to the agreement and any past practice.[184]

Leave for Union Business

Contract provisions for leaves of absence for union business vary greatly, and whether such leave should be granted depends not only upon the particular contract clause but also upon the facts and circumstances involved in each case, with particular reference to the good faith of both parties.[185] While internal affairs of the union and union

---

[184]See Arbitrator Winton in 80 LA 41, 44–45 (where contract provided that leave not exceeding 30 days for "any valid reason" other than sickness or injury "shall" be granted to employees, grievant was entitled to leave to nurse her new baby since the word "valid" had been liberally interpreted under past practice); Cyrol in 79 LA 1070, 1074–1075 (employee who had had two previous miscarriages was entitled to sickness disability benefits for period that physician certified that she was pregnant and should not do any work that involved lifting, pulling, pushing, or straining of any kind); Nathan in 77 LA 860, 861, 863–864 (where contract provided that "parental leave shall be without salary and shall be granted for a period not to exceed one year," the parties' intent being to permit a new parent to spend full time with a newborn child, the employer improperly denied a request for one year of parental leave for such purpose—the employer had failed to give individual and objective consideration to the grievant's request and the denial actually had resulted from the employer's general dissatisfaction with long leaves of absence); Ellmann in 77 LA 622, 626 (the dispute concerned the possible total number of months of leave that employees who become pregnant are entitled to under contract clauses which were poorly drafted and which spoke of "prenatal and/or infant care leave," "sick leave," and "the maternity leave," all in reference to such employees—the dispute was resolved by a decision which the arbitrator felt was a "reasonable and reasoned interpretation of the contract"); Hannan in 76 LA 241, 244 (past practice controlled the disposition of an issue concerning continuation of insurance coverage during unpaid maternity leave which commenced after paid sick leave had expired).

[185]See C. & D. Batteries, 32 LA 589, 594 (Jaffee, 1959), where criteria were discussed in regard to granting leave for union business. For other discussions which may serve to provide criteria, see Arbitrator Cloke in 80 LA 201, 204–205; Thornell in 78 LA 969, 972–973 (this case upheld the employer's right to place a union officer on unpaid leave of absence without the consent of the union where absence from work on union business for nearly one-half of work time was found to "seriously interfere with" the individual's "ability to perform his job with the employer"); Gentile in 76 LA 648, 652; Howlett in 75 LA 66, 73–76; McDermott in 71 LA 349, 354; Hazelwood in 58 LA 253, 254. As to a second leave at the end of a first leave where the contract provides for "leave of absence for six months" for union business, see Wallingford Steel Co., 54 LA 1130, 1133–1134 (Sherman, 1970). Where an agreement expressly specified the duration of leaves of absence, it was held that the grant or denial of "leaves for a shorter period of time [than specified in the agreement] lies within the discretion of the Company." Minnesota Mining & Mfg. Co., 55 LA 539, 542 (Karlins, 1970). Similarly, see Arbitrator Gowan in 71 LA 696, 698. In Davis Cabinet Co., 80 LA 1055, 1057–1058 (Williams, 1983), the agreement provided that a leave of absence "will" be granted to employees elected to union office; under this provision the employer was required to grant a leave to a laid-off employee who was elected to union office seven days before she otherwise would have lost her seniority because of continuous layoff for 12 months, notwithstanding the employer's contention that her sole reason for requesting the leave was to extend her recall and seniority rights. The employee's apparent expectation here was that the employer-employee relationship would continue by virtue of the leave of absence and that valuable contractual rights accordingly would be retained. For other cases illustrating the possibility that important consequences may result from continued employer-employee relationship during leave of absence for union business, see Arbitrator McDermott in 68 LA 618, 624–625 (upholding discharge of union president for leading illicit work stoppage while on leave as full time union officer receiving pay from union); Dworkin in 64 LA 709, 718–720 (holding that for purpose of determining pension benefits the employee could include as credited years of service with the employer his 22-year leave of absence while serving as union officer; as part of his discussion, Arbitrator Dworkin stated that the "concept of 'leave of absence' implies that some form of employee-employer relationship continues in effect").

"secrets" need not be divulged, the employer is entitled to enough information regarding the nature of the union business involved and the probable duration of the absence to permit an intelligent choice as to granting or denying leave.[186]

Leave for "union business" has been held to encompass organizational activity outside the bargaining unit at a plant affiliated with the employer,[187] but it does not include union *political* activity.[188]

Under some contracts, arbitrators have approved the action of management in granting leave on a conditional basis.[189] In some cases involving leave for union business, past practice of the parties and industry practice have influenced or determined the arbitrator's decision.[190]

Leave for Jury Duty

The vast majority of reported decisions deal not with the right to leave of absence for jury duty but with the resultant pay problems under pertinent contract language on jury duty pay differential. In the absence of such a provision, it has been held that the company is not required to pay jury duty benefits to its employees.[191]

---

[186]See Arbitrator Leeper in 78 LA 8, 14; Porter in 50 LA 1140, 1144; Anderson in 42 LA 632, 636; Kinyon in 35 LA 873, 881; Jaffee in 32 LA 589, 593–594; Hilpert in 11 LA 569, 572. Also see Levy in 69 LA 831, 838; Rule in 64 LA 1274, 1278. Arbitrator Jaffee drafted a written form (at the parties' request) to be used in requesting leave for union business, in 32 LA 589, 594.

[187]See Arbitrator Porter in 50 LA 1140, 1144; Fallon in 43 LA 670, 675; Anderson in 42 LA 632, 635–636; Kinyon in 35 LA 873, 878–879. Also see Cox in 74 LA 916, 917–918. Another activity for which leave has been requested is collective bargaining. In one case under an agreement which included "union business" as a ground for excusing absences, the employer improperly denied the request by two union officials for a half-day's leave to attend a bargaining session at the plant of a competitor. Hurd Millwork Corp., 58 LA 253, 254 (Hazelwood, 1972). Cf., Arbitrator O'Neill in 64 LA 975, 977–978. Concerning the right of union representatives in the federal sector to administrative leave for time spent in collective bargaining, including leave for time spent attending classes on collective bargaining, see Department of the Air Force, 80 LA 403, 408–412 (Wann, 1983); Marine Corps Logistics Base, 74 LA 396, 398–399 (Mazurak, 1980). Also see Arbitrator Gentile in 74 LA 501, 503–504.

[188]See Husky Oil Co., 37 LA 249, 251–252 (Simpson, 1961); Anchor Duck Mills, 5 LA 428, 430 (Hepburn, 1946). Cf., Arbitrator Updegraff in 8 LA 350, 354. Regarding picketing as "union business," in Jackson Public Schools, 64 LA 1089, 1092 (1975), the employer was not obligated to pay teachers for time spent picketing another school under a contract entitling union delegates to up to 25 days' pay per year for "union business," Arbitrator M. David Keefe declaring it to be "incontrovertibly clear that payment by any Management to its Employees for engaging in strike-activities elsewhere, even though involving another Employer, is incompatible with Management's natural philosophy and repugnant to its material interests, inasmuch as proliferation of such arrangements could eventually result in a paid-for stranger-pickets closing down the home activity of the original Employer." Also see Arbitrator Gentile in 76 LA 648, 652.

[189]See Husky Oil Co., 37 LA 249, 252 (Simpson, 1961); United States Indus. Chems. Co., 36 LA 400, 404 (Teple, 1961). Cf., Arbitrator Klein in 41 LA 739, 743–744; Stutz in 37 LA 475, 483.

[190]See Arbitrator Bowles in 76 LA 1273, 1276–1278; Howlett in 75 LA 66, 75; Felice in 70 LA 887, 889–891; Barnhart in 70 LA 664, 667; Fallon in 43 LA 670, 675; Donnelly in 15 LA 611, 612; Martin in 14 LA 574, 591 (interest arbitration); Hilpert in 11 LA 569, 573; Dwyer in 11 LA 1074, 1075.

[191]See Ryder Truck Lines, 38 LA 113, 115 (Williams, 1961). In Ziegler Steel Serv. Corp., 69 LA 1102, 1103 (Tsukiyama, 1977), a contractual provision for jury pay was held inapplicable to service as a witness. It may be noted that apart from contractual rights, jury duty rights against the employer may be provided by statute. For example, an Alabama statute requiring employers to pay workers excused for jury duty their regular pay "less the fee or compensation" received for serving as a juror, was upheld as to constitutionality in Dean v. Gadsen Times Publishing Corp., 93 S.Ct. 2264 (1973). The Jury System Improvements Act of 1978 prohibits employers from discharging, threatening to discharge, coercing, or intimidating permanent employees because they are serving or are scheduled to serve on a federal jury. In NLRB v. Merrill & Ring, Inc., 116 LRRM 2221 (CA 9, 1984), pay for jury duty was held to be a mandatory subject of bargaining under the NLRA.

It has been said that the object of such provisions is to "provide competent jurors through the removal of the monetary loss that would otherwise accompany jury service."[192] Thus, employees who are called for jury duty while on vacation[193] or in layoff status[194] have been held not to be entitled to jury duty pay.

The key words in many contracts are "time lost," and where the employee was called to jury service but excused early, the arbitrator held that he had an obligation to return to work since "he could readily have returned to his home, changed to appropriate clothing, and reported for work" for the last half of his shift.[195]

Reconciling jury duty pay provisions to situations in which shift schedules did not coincide precisely with hours of jury duty, Arbitrator Clare B. McDermott held that the "rule of reason" must be applied; and when the hours of jury service come so close before or after the employee's scheduled shift as to give him justifiable grounds for missing that shift, he should be excused and paid jury allowance.[196]

Under a contract providing for pay "If an employee is required to absent himself from the job" for jury service, the employee's need for rest was cited as justification for jury duty pay to an employee who was scheduled to work on the night shift. The arbitrator stated that it was "clear that the Grievant was 'required' to absent herself from the job" in order to obtain needed rest.[197]

The question sometimes arises as to whether time spent in jury service should be included as time worked for purposes of other provisions of the contract. In the absence of a provision specifically covering the issue, it has been held that jury duty does not count as time worked for purposes of computing weekly overtime.[198] One arbitrator, however, held that time spent on jury duty was to be included in computing the employee's vacation time.[199]

---

[192]Greenleaf Mfg. Co., 32 LA 1, 2 (Edelman, 1959). Also see Arbitrator Dahl in 76 LA 170, 171; Freund in 49 LA 901, 905; Mills in 40 LA 1195, 1197. Cf., Hutchison in 74 LA 865, 867, where past practice controlled the result.

[193]Columbus Auto Parts Co., 51 LA 1288, 1292 (Klein, 1968).

[194]American Airlines, 39 LA 500, 503–504 (Hill, 1962). Also see Arbitrator Dahl in 76 LA 170, 171 (employer not obligated to pay jury duty pay for two scheduled off days that fell during 10-day period of jury duty); Warns in 65 LA 264, 267 (employee who was on jury duty on days when plant operation was suspended due to snowfall was not entitled to jury pay from the employer for those days). Cf., General Elec. Co., 50 LA 852, 860 (Seinsheimer, 1967), involving jury duty performed by employees during a strike called by another union.

[195]Continental Can Co., 47 LA 683, 685–686 (Dash, 1966), awarding the employee compensation for only one half of each of the five days he was released early from jury duty. Also see Arbitrator Volz in 39 LA 763, 766. Cf., Bernstein in 72 LA 1057, 1059; D'Angelo in 65 LA 867, 868.

[196]United States Steel Corp., cases at 36 LA 590, 595; 36 LA 595, 597; 36 LA 597, 599 (1961). Arbitrator Ralph T. Seward, while noting that these cases are not binding upon the parties in Bethlehem Steel Corp., 49 LA 334, 336–337 (1967), was "particularly impressed" by Arbitrator McDermott's analysis and wrote that he "joins Arbitrator McDermott * * * in holding that the rule of reason should govern application of the jury pay provision." In United States Pipe & Foundry Co., 55 LA 856, 858–859 (1970), it was held that the grievants should not have been expected to report for work before reporting for jury duty since only a maximum of one to two hours could have been worked; Arbitrator F. Fred Holly stated that "the Company's position is entirely unreasonable since it places a heavy burden on the employee-juror, and the Company cannot hope to receive any significant amount of productive work from the employee."

[197]Hunt Foods & Indus., 36 LA 929, 931 (McNaughton, 1961). To similar effect, see Arbitrator Holly in 33 LA 508, 511–512; Schedler in 27 LA 189 at 189.

[198]See Arbitrator Ray in 52 LA 575, 577; Carter in 52 LA 357, 360; Mills in 40 LA 1195, 1197.

[199]Goodyear Aerospace Corp., 51 LA 540, 546 (Lehoczky, 1968).

Funeral Leave

Cases involving funeral leave provisions have turned upon the precise wording of the funeral leave or "bereavement" pay clause, and arbitrators appear to be inclined toward strict construction of such clauses. Thus, where the contract specifically stated that a certain number of days of paid leave would be allowed to attend the funeral of a member of the employee's immediate family, arbitrators have held that such leave provision includes attendance at the funeral and necessary travel time but does not contemplate absences to aid bereaved relatives or to attend to the estate.[200] Moreover, where the language used is "pay for time lost" or "paid leave of absence" while attending the funeral of a family member, arbitrators generally have denied such pay when the employee was already on vacation or otherwise not scheduled to work.[201] However, in some instances (but not always) the arbitrator may favor a somewhat broader construction with regard to that portion of the funeral leave clause which specifies the family members or relatives for whose funeral the leave provisions become applicable. For example, where the contract listed "brother" among other members of the family, the arbitrator, emphasizing the closeness of the relationship between the employee and his stepbrother, held that "the latter must be deemed his brother within the meaning of that term as used in the agreement."[202]

---

[200]See Arbitrator Hon in 70 LA 830, 833; Williams in 61 LA 510, 512; Caraway in 53 LA 1108, 1109; Edelman in 53 LA 974, 975; Hill in 48 LA 351, 352; Teple in 47 LA 438, 440; Daugherty in 45 LA 494, 495; Luskin in 42 LA 59, 61; Sweeney in 40 LA 223, 224–225; Wolff in 36 LA 1077, 1078; Hays in 34 LA 300, 301. Also see Berns in 73 LA 115, 117; Rule in 73 LA 96, 98. But see Cantor in 80 LA 1305, 1309; Gamser in 59 LA 768, 769; McIntosh in 44 LA 739, 740. One arbitrator held that the company could issue a rule requiring the employee to furnish evidence of attendance at the funeral. See Borg-Warner Corp., 47 LA 691, 697–698 (Bradley, 1966). Similarly, see Arbitrator Penfield in 67 LA 536, 540. Also see Dolnick in 57 LA 951, 954. Cf., Jones in 70 LA 693, 695–696.

[201]See Arbitrator Gibson in 79 LA 82, 84; Williams in 75 LA 1076, 1077; McIntosh in 51 LA 517, 518; Tsukiyama in 46 LA 849, 851–852; McCoy in 46 LA 11, 14; Lockhart in 45 LA 644, 645; Roberts in 45 LA 291, 292–293; Davis in 44 LA 937, 939; Turkus in 36 LA 1330, 1332; Updegraff in 33 LA 629, 632; Lanoue in 27 LA 362, 363. Also see Strongin in 62 LA 771, 772; O'Connell in 61 LA 382, 383; Payne in 58 LA 706, 707; Garrett in 57 LA 421, 426; Volz in 55 LA 437, 440. Cf., Raymond in 75 LA 845, 847; Ipavec in 70 LA 950, 953–954; Cyrol in 68 LA 165, 170; Midonick in 32 LA 385, 386. But where contract language is ambiguous or less specific, or where a conflicting practice is a factor, a different result may obtain. See Arbitrator Raymond in 75 LA 845, 847; Brown in 58 LA 852, 854; Yaffee in 49 LA 768, 769–770; Seitz in 37 LA 1034, 1035–1037 (where he discussed two of his earlier awards); Kahn in 37 LA 151, 154–155. In Conoco, Inc., 78 LA 381, 383 (Foster, 1982), a clause which specified funeral leave pay for "time actually lost" was held applicable to time which would have been worked as voluntary overtime but for attendance at a funeral. Also see Arbitrator Kreimer in 68 LA 1206, 1207–1208. Cf., Mewhinney in 76 LA 603, 606. For cases upholding an employee's claim for two separate allowances of paid funeral leave where the deaths of two relatives occurred at about the same time, see Arbitrator Dworkin in 72 LA 337, 340; Teple in 65 LA 787, 789–790.

[202]Foremost Dairies, 43 LA 616, 617 (Greenwald, 1964), citing Arbitrator Cahn in 28 LA 469, 469–470, and Shister in 26 LA 108, 110. For other cases in which the arbitrator favored a somewhat *broad construction* of the provision specifying the relationship requirement, see Arbitrator Cohen in 63 LA 163, 164 (term "close relatives" in contract was held not to be limited to relatives by consanguinity but rather would include relatives by affinity to whom employee factually is "close"); Petrie in 62 LA 447, 451 (term "parents" included stepmother even though natural mother was still living); Teple in 61 LA 1224, 1226 (term "brother-in-law" included employee's husband's sister's husband); Berkowitz in 54 LA 56, 58–59; Thompson in 43 LA 467, 469–470; Marshall in 40 LA 1230, 1234; Kornblum in 38 LA 1029, 1031; Klamon in 31 LA 603,

Of course, past practice may affect the arbitrator's decision. Thus, in one case where the contract contained no funeral leave clause but did provide for maintenance of working conditions, the arbitrator ruled that the employer was required to continue an established practice of granting up to three days funeral leave.[203] In another case, an existing funeral leave policy, recognized by both parties, of not including payment of such benefits during any period of paid absence from work (such as vacations) was deemed by the arbitrator to have carried over into the new contract provision dealing with paid funeral leave.[204]

Leave for "Personal Business"

As with other leaves of absence, arbitrators have held that management's determination to grant or deny leaves for "personal business" must be reasonable and nondiscriminatory.[205] Management must have some information in order to make that determination intelligently, and it is not enough for the employee to state merely "personal business" as his reason for requesting such leave. Thus, Arbitrator Maurice H. Merrill held that the employer has the right to require the employee to give a reasonably explicit statement of rea-

---

606–607. But Arbitrator Dworkin refused to extend the meaning of "brother-in-law" to include the employee's wife's sister's husband. Consumers Power Co., 49 LA 595, 601–603 (1967). For other cases in which the arbitrator was inclined toward *strict construction* of the provision specifying the relationship requirement, see Arbitrator Rybolt in 77 LA 1127, 1128–1129 (husband of employee's sister ceased to be employee's brother-in-law when sister died); Dworkin in 76 LA 1107, 1111–1112; Eyraud in 73 LA 1144, 1145–1146 (stating that "the relationship of husband and wife is one of affinity, not consanguinity," and stating that "a relationship of affinity is broken by death or divorce," he held that the term "brother-in-law" in funeral leave clause "does not encompass the brother of a deceased wife"); O'Shea in 71 LA 1071, 1072 (father of grievant's wife ceased to be his father-in-law when grievant and his wife were divorced); Chapman in 71 LA 874, 876; Yarowsky in 71 LA 473, 475; Hunter in 69 LA 1080, 1083; Teple in 64 LA 1078, 1080 (term "immediate family" did not include brother of employee's deceased wife, where employee had remarried, even though employee may have retained at least part of his emotional ties with in-laws by his first marriage); Rimer in 63 LA 1036, 1039 (absent bargaining history or past practice expanding meaning of term "father," it did not include stepfather); Teple in 61 LA 1224, 1226 (term "grandparent" did not include grandmother of employee's husband); Bradley in 61 LA 79, 86; Kates in 57 LA 959, 962; Berkowitz in 52 LA 768, 769 (wife's uncle would not qualify as employee's uncle); Davis in 51 LA 289, 290 (stepfather-in-law would not qualify as employee's "immediate family").

[203]Commercial Motor Freight, 34 LA 592, 595 (Stouffer, 1960). Also see Arbitrator Dybeck in 53 LA 1215, 1216.

[204]Food Employers Council, 45 LA 291, 292–293 (Roberts, 1965).

[205]See Arbitrator Nathan in 76 LA 673, 675–676; Belcher in 75 LA 953, 957; Merrill in 47 LA 531, 535; Hill in 35 LA 581, 583; Jaffee in 12 LA 95, 97; Wardlaw in 3 LA 108, 110. Also see Berman in 75 LA 131, 134–135; Dyke in 74 LA 1284, 1287–1288. Particular language in the agreement may significantly affect the arbitrator's conclusion regarding the scope of management's right or discretion in determining whether to grant the requested leave. For instance, see Arbitrator Daniel in 80 LA 513, 515 (where agreement provided that leave "shall" be granted for certain specified purposes and that "Personal Leave" and certain other categories of leave "may be granted by the discretion of the Employer," the employer's discretion in denying personal leave was upheld since it was not arbitrary or capricious); Smith in 72 LA 1135, 1142 (also note the discussion at 1143–1144 concerning what constitutes "personal business"); Brisco in 71 LA 1026, 1028–1029 (involving contractual clause on leave for "personal necessity"); Smith in 70 LA 555, 558 (discussing what constitutes "personal business"); Kossoff in 64 LA 1155, 1163–1164 (contractual provision for leave "for personal reasons" was declared to be "very broad language"). For a case dealing with the question of whether the employer must grant an employee's request to terminate leave before its term is completed, see Ringgold School Dist., 75 LA 1216, 1219 (Duff, 1980).

sons rather than simply stating "personal business."[206] He noted that this may result in a conflict between the employee's right to privacy with respect to his personal life and the employer's interest in discouraging unnecessary absences and insuring efficient operations. However, he found support in the contract for his conclusions, not only in a general leave of absence clause requiring presentation of evidence by the employee to substantiate his request, but also in specific leave clauses relating to jury duty, voting time, and funeral leave, all of which also indicated the necessity of presenting information concerning the employee's personal affairs.[207]

"Moonlighting" and Outside Business Interest

Employees sometimes engage in "moonlighting," i.e., holding a second job during off hours (part time or full time); or they may carry on an outside business interest.[208] In cases involving such "off hours" activity, unions argue for the asserted right of the employee to do what he pleases during his off hours and to use his knowledge and skill to augment his income.[209] It is recognized that the employee may engage in work during his off hours within the limits noted hereinbelow. As stated by Arbitrator Thomas P. Whelan:

> "It is well established that the time of an employee outside his regular hours of work and outside the overtime sometimes incidental thereto belongs to him and may be used for recreation and work, provided the employee does not engage in practices or occupations that are detrimental or clearly prejudicial to the business and interests with which his duties in the service of his regular employer are connected."[210]

In light of this, the bare fact that an employee holds a second job would not necessarily be grounds for discipline or discharge. Thus, if the primary employer has no set policy forbidding outside employment and it is not shown that the employee's work for that employer has suffered, or if it is not shown that the employee (in a competitive

---

[206]Union Carbide Corp., 47 LA 531, 534–535 (1966). Accord, Arbitrator Brisco in 71 LA 1026, 1028; Griffin in 51 LA 1121, 1124. Also see Concepcion in 78 LA 890, 893. Cf., Yaffe in 79 LA 1209, 1214–1215, where special contract provisions significantly affected the result.

[207]Union Carbide Corp., 47 LA 531, 533 (Merrill, 1966).

[208]Broadly, the term "moonlighting" may be considered to encompass all remunerative activity engaged in during off hours, whether a second job or a business interest.

[209]For example, these arguments were presented (but to no avail because of the facts involved) in Firestone Retread Shop, 38 LA 600, 601 (McCoy, 1962), and Capital-Chrysler Plymouth, 53 LA 1247, 1250 (Sembower, 1969), respectively. For related discussion, see Chapter 13, topic entitled "Plant Rules," and Chapter 15, topic entitled "Conduct Away From Plant."

[210]Janitorial Serv., 33 LA 902, 907–908 (1959). Similarly, see statement by Arbitrator Kelliher in 66 LA 177, 180. In Armstrong Rubber Co., 58 LA 827, 829 (1972), Arbitrator Ralph Roger Williams stated in reference to the employee's weekend work as an ambulance driver, that "the Company cannot forbid an employee to work at a second job during his off-duty hours, so long as it does not impair his job performance for the Company"; but in reference to the employee's full-time work as a private-duty nurse for another employer, Arbitrator Williams upheld discharge since this work violated the agreement's express prohibition against "working on another job while on leave of absence."

situation) had access to trade secrets, discipline or discharge may be set aside or the penalty may be reduced by the arbitrator.[211]

Balanced against the arguments of the union are the primary employer's right to receive a full measure of productiveness during the employee's hours of work for him[212] and the primary employer's right to loyalty free from the employee's competitive activity or other activity resulting in a conflict of interest.[213] Thus, it has been held that if the employee's second job adversely affects his attendance or work performance or otherwise detrimentally affects his employer, disciplinary action (or discharge in appropriate cases) may be deemed proper.[214]

Moreover, off hours activity may be in indirect competition with the primary employer if the employee works for a competing company, or in direct competition if he himself carries on a business of the same nature as that of his employer. Even where the activity is not competitive, it may result in a conflict of interests.[215] In this regard, where the employee's second job or business interest is prohibited by the contract or by clear company policy and is in direct competition with his employer, or creates a conflict of interest, it is likely that the arbitrator will uphold his discharge,[216] especially where trade secrets are involved.[217]

---

[211]As in cases decided by Arbitrator Kossoff in 63 LA 941, 945; Keefe in 52 LA 1290, 1296 (grievant refused to work overtime so that he could meet the obligations of his second job—penalty reduced because of extenuating circumstances); Kates in 52 LA 818, 820–821, and in 51 LA 1098, 1101–1102 (in both cases, leave of absence was obtained by deceit and the employee went to work for his other employer—reinstated without back pay); Lee in 46 LA 175, 179 (no detriment to the employer was shown—employee reinstated with back pay); Kates in 37 LA 1095, 1098 (employee reinstated with back pay); Whelan in 33 LA 902, 908, and Pigors in 31 LA 547, 551 (in both cases, there was a somewhat competitive situation but there was no rule and no detriment shown to the employer—employee reinstated with back pay); Smith in 17 LA 179, 182–183 (somewhat competitive situation and grievant "did not exhibit the fidelity to his employer which his job required"—reinstated without back pay). Also see Koven in 76 LA 770, 771; Levitan in 76 LA 140, 141; Whyte in 64 LA 856, 858; Boals in 62 LA 779, 780, 784; Rodio in 59 LA 47, 51.

[212]See, for example, Safeway Stores, 49 LA 400, 402 (Caraway, 1967).

[213]See Arbitrator Taylor in 74 LA 1066, 1072; Shanker in 68 LA 13, 16 (upholding employer rule which requires employees to reveal outside employment so that employer "can investigate to determine whether such employment raises conflict of interest possibilities, or the potentiality for competitive disadvantage to it"); Caraway in 47 LA 372, 374; Teple in 43 LA 338, 340; Dworkin in 39 LA 404, 409; Gorsuch in 34 LA 636, 642. Also see Ross in 78 LA 1032, 1037; Koven in 59 LA 69, 71.

[214]See Arbitrator Kates in 52 LA 818, 820–821, and in 51 LA 1098, 1101–1102; Dworkin in 39 LA 404, 409; Keller in 26 LA 401, 403. Also see Arbitrator Hon in 38 LA 965, 971; Jaffee in 37 LA 254, 257–258.

[215]As in Tribune Publishing Co., 42 LA 504, 506–507 (Kagel, 1963), where a drama critic for a newspaper obtained outside work as a press agent for a summer theater. Also see Arbitrator Friedman in 62 LA 225, 227 (newspaper sports reporter accepted part ownership of a horse that raced at tracks on his reportorial beat, "which patently conflicts with his ability to do his job properly").

[216]See Arbitrator Taylor in 74 LA 1066, 1072; Axon in 73 LA 164, 165–166; Whyte in 54 LA 942, 946–947; Sembower in 53 LA 1247, 1251–1252; Karasick in 53 LA 1176, 1180; Caraway in 49 LA 400, 401–402; Kagel in 42 LA 504, 506–507; Jenkins in 40 LA 1293, 1295; Gorsuch in 34 LA 636, 642–643. Also see Arbitrator Darrow in 67 LA 985, 988; Matten in 67 LA 632, 635; Wyckoff in 44 LA 552, 553. Cf., Hildebrand in 68 LA 1224, 1229; Rohman in 58 LA 1296, 1299. For cases holding that the company may promulgate a rule prohibiting outside work in competition with it, see Whyte in 54 LA 942, 945–946; Teple in 43 LA 338, 340–341; Dworkin in 39 LA 404, 409; Gorsuch in 34 LA 636, 642–643; Kates in 27 LA 540, 542; Keller in 26 LA 401, 403. In upholding the reasonableness of such rules, arbitrators have pointed out that the prohibition did not apply to work in other areas of endeavor. See Arbitrator Caraway in 47 LA 372, 374; Jenkins in 40 LA 1293, 1295; Gorsuch in 34 LA 636, 642; Keller in 26 LA 401, 403.

[217]See Arbitrator McCoy in 46 LA 1009, 1010–1011, stating that "the Company had the right

Arbitrator Whitley P. McCoy commented upon some aspects of an employee's competitive activity which are "intolerable" to the employer:

> "But this is not a mere case of 'moonlighting', that is, holding down another job. It is a case of going into business in competition with his employer, thus creating a conflict of interest. He was in the position of competing in the purchase of * * * [raw materials], and competing in the sales of * * * [the finished product]. At the same time he was in a position to learn of any improvements in materials or processes developed by * * * [the Company], and to adopt them himself. * * * The whole thing created an intolerable situation. I think there was a breach by the grievant of an implied condition of employment.
>
> "I do not consider this discharge as disciplinary. His ownership of a competing business was not, strictly speaking, an offense. But it was a condition, created by him, that made his continued employment by the Company intolerable."[218]

Regarding situations involving a conflict of interest, it has been emphasized that there is no need to prove an actual detriment to the primary employer:

> "[I]t is not necessarily required that the employer convincingly establish that a business detriment or financial loss has in fact resulted; it is sufficient if the off-duty relationship is such as would reasonably suggest that the outside employment would lead to a disclosure to the competitor of information and skills acquired by the employee * * *."[219]

Personal Appearance: Hair and Clothes

Employees have the right to decide what their personal appearance will be in private life, away from their place of employment, so long as no harm results to the employer.[220] While the employee's personal appearance in private life may in some circumstances

---

to lock the stable door before the horse was stolen," and in 38 LA 600, 601; Dworkin in 39 LA 404, 409–410; Updegraff in 3 LA 113, 115. Also see Caraway in 47 LA 372, 375, where the grievant was reinstated because he had not known of the rule prohibiting outside activity which conflicts with the company's best interest, but he was required to refrain from such activities in the future; Kates in 27 LA 540, 542–543, where the company's right to discharge for violating a rule against working for a competitor was upheld, but the grievant was reinstated (without back pay) because he gave two weeks notice of resignation to his second employer the day the rule went into effect.

[218]Firestone Retread Shop, 38 LA 600, 601 (1962). The employee here was warned and later given an opportunity to sell his business before being discharged. Other aspects of competitive work by employees are discussed by Arbitrator Dworkin in 39 LA 404, 410; Gorsuch in 34 LA 636, 641–642; Keller in 26 LA 401, 403.

[219]Ravens-Metal Prods., 39 LA 404, 409–410 (Dworkin, 1962). Similarly, see Arbitrator Gorsuch in 34 LA 636, 643; Keller in 26 LA 401, 403. Cf., Shister in 79 LA 1129, 1133; Calhoon in 75 LA 640, 642; Christopher in 65 LA 1042, 1046.

[220]See material in Chapter 15, topic entitled "Conduct Away From Plant." The Authors do not consider any constitutional law aspects of the present topic, nor do they consider Title VII of the Civil Rights Act in relation to employer dress and grooming policies (except that the Authors do deal briefly with such policies as possible religious discrimination under the Act). For discussion of court and EEOC decisions relating to the possibility that such policies in certain cases may constitute sex, race, or religious discrimination in violation of the Act, see Annotation, "Employer's Enforcement of Dress or Grooming Policy as Unlawful Employment Practice Under § 703(a) of the Civil Rights Act of 1964," 27 ALR Fed. 274 (1976); McGuckin, "Employee Hair

adversely affect the employer, it is primarily the employee's assertion of the aforementioned right at work with which we are concerned here.

Employees tend to resist broad company prohibitions or requirements which they feel may infringe upon their personal right to dress and to wear their hair or beards as they please. On the other hand, management historically has been concerned with the personal appearance of its employees, both from the standpoint of the company's public "image" and from the standpoint of such safety and health factors as may be involved.[221]

Recognizing expressly or implicitly the right of employees to determine their clothing or hair style, arbitrators nonetheless point out that such right may be limited by the nature of the employment.[222] On balance, arbitrators recognize both the "image" and the safety and health arguments of the employer and the right to regulate the personal appearance of employees for those purposes, but not for the purpose of requiring conformity to the employer's preference on such matters.[223]

It has been noted that "the prevailing theory is that the Company has the right to require its employees to cut their hair and shave when long hair and beards can reasonably threaten the Company's relations with its customers or other employees, or a real question of safety is involved."[224] With regard to the image presented by employees to the public, Arbitrator Philip Neville elaborated:

> "The arbitrator holds to the view that an employer should be free, reasonably to regulate, and to prescribe standards of, personal appearance for its employees so as to require of them a certain degree of

---

Styles: Recent Judicial and Arbitral Decisions," 26 Lab. L.J. 174 (1975). A U.S. Supreme Court decision upholding dress and hair rules for county police officers against challenge under the Fourteenth Amendment is Kelley v. Johnson, 96 S.Ct. 1440 (1976). The latter decision was discussed and applied in City of Cincinnati, 75 LA 1261, 1264–1265 (Seifer, 1980). For other arbitration decisions touching on constitutional questions, see Arbitrator Hilgert in 77 LA 953, 959 (leaving constitutional questions to the courts); Denson in 76 LA 532, 535; Jacobs in 60 LA 1191, 1196–1197; Kleinsorge in 55 LA 1020, 1025; Volz in 55 LA 663, 667; Eaton in 55 LA 459, 460; Elson in 54 LA 816, 819; Stutz in 54 LA 439, 441 (leaving constitutional questions to the courts); Steese in 52 LA 1282, 1284. For general discussion of arbitration decisions in dress and grooming cases, see Tucker, "Arbitration of Labor Disputes Involving Hair," 10 Willamette L.J. 258 (1974); discussions by Valtin, McDermott & Cohen, "Changing Life Styles and Problems of Authority in the Plant," Proceedings of the 25th Annual Meeting of NAA, 235–255, 266–281 (BNA Books, 1973).

[221]Weighing these respective positions, Arbitrator Volz recognized the reasonableness and clarity of one company's grooming regulations, stating further that they represented "a middle ground between the concern of the Company to protect and improve its image with the public and the preference of an employee for self-expression and individuality through hair styling." Pepsi Cola Bottlers, 55 LA 663, 666 (1970). Of course, safety, health, and "image" considerations are not necessarily the only possible justifications for employer dress and grooming requirements. For example, in Greater Harlem Nursing Home, 76 LA 680, 684 (Marx, 1981), male and female employees could be required to wear differing uniforms to provide ready identification for nursing home patients, who, the Arbitrator stated, are entitled to know the sex of the nursing attendant by whom they are being served. Similarly, see Arbitrator Denson in 77 LA 1027, 1029, where the employer specified different colors of clothing "to help patients and others identify various levels of " nursing home personnel.

[222]See Arbitrator Kreimer in 73 LA 605, 606–607; Volz in 55 LA 663, 666; Elson in 54 LA 816, 819–820; Stutz in 54 LA 439, 440; Krinsky in 50 LA 901, 908–909; Johnson in 49 LA 867, 868.

[223]See Arbitrator Richman in 70 LA 266, 269; Schoenfeld in 68 LA 473, 475; Krimsly in 54 LA 604, 605; Stutz in 54 LA 439, 441; Bothwell in 53 LA 627, 628; Kotin in 52 LA 1068, 1069; Steese in 52 LA 1282, 1284; Bradley in 51 LA 983, 988–989; Neville in 48 LA 120, 123.

[224]Dravo-Doyle Co., 54 LA 604, 606 (Krimsly, 1970).

conventionality and approximate conformation to the norm. The employer should be permitted, for instance, to prohibit extra long shoulder-length hair or extreme clothing on male employees, full beards on younger men, scanty or sexually exciting dress on the part of female employees. It should be able to expect that its employees will practice personal hygiene and will clothe themselves in a neat manner, at least where the employees meet the public."[225]

However, there must be a showing of a reasonable relation between the company's image or health and safety considerations and the need to regulate employee appearance.[226] Thus, management's right to regulate in this area is not absolute. As stated by Arbitrator Leo Kotin:

> "Companies providing a service to the public still have the right to protect their image. To the degree that that image is based upon the appearance of its employees dealing with the public, the company has the right to establish rules and standards of personal appearance. This right has long been recognized by unions. The right, however, is not absolute. Its exercise in any specific manner may be challenged as arbitrary, capricious or inconsistent with the objective for which the right is being exercised."[227]

The Employer's "Image"

The employer's public "image" is a matter of particular concern where the company offers services to the public (as, for example, an airline) or where the employee comes in contact with the company's customers (as a clerk in a store).[228] It has been emphasized that "an

---

[225]Northwest Publications, 48 LA 120, 122 (1966). Also see detailed statement by Arbitrator Clair V. Duff in Southern Bell Tel. & Tel. Co., 74 LA 1114, 1116 (1980).

[226]See Arbitrator Killion in 80 LA 765, 770; Murphy in 73 LA 850, 856–857; Eaton in 55 LA 459, 463; Elson in 54 LA 816, 820; Stutz in 54 LA 439, 441; Krinsky in 50 LA 901, 908–909 (particularly where rules "infringe on an individual's personal life"). It must also be established that company rules were adequately communicated to the employees and uniformly enforced. See Arbitrator Neblett in 55 LA 531, 535; Neville in 48 LA 120, 123; Davis in 28 LA 83, 87. Also see Belshaw in 74 LA 918, 920 (employer, objecting to long fingernails which impede production, must clearly indicate to employee how long they reasonably may be). In Hillview Sand & Gravel, 39 LA 35, 40 (Somers, 1962), there were no company rules prohibiting beards, but the arbitrator stated that if the employee's actions caused the company loss, it "would be well within its rights" in suspending him for continual refusal to shave off his beard. Also see Arbitrator Kreimer in 73 LA 605, 607; Kaufman in 71 LA 200, 203.

[227]United Parcel Serv., 52 LA 1068, 1069 (1968). The points made in this statement apply as well with respect to management's right to regulate for health and safety purposes. Also see Arbitrator Kotin in 53 LA 126, 128, where for the same parties he set forth standards clarifying company rules as to what constitutes satisfactory appearance for employees. In Pacific Gas & Elec. Co., 55 LA 459, 464 (1970), Arbitrator Eaton formulated rules to supplant company rules about permissible facial hair.

[228]The employees themselves may recognize this fact. For example, the New York Times Service reported in March 1971 that TWA's pilots had embarked upon a program to help restore the company's earning power; the first step of the program was for the pilots to avoid "extreme styles of personal appearance" and to dress so that "any potential customer" is not offended. The pilots thus expressed recognition that employee appearance and mode of dress can produce an adverse public reaction detrimental to the employer's operations. Even apart from the interest which employees share with the employer for successful operations, employees may have strong interests of their own in making a favorable public impression. For example, see the explanation by Arbitrator Clair V. Duff in Federal Aviation Admin., 70 LA 226, 229 (1978), stating in part that if the grievants there "cling to their goal of using clothing to express their individuality by working in casual attire," they may not violate the collective agreement "but they will bear the costly risk that those people who observe them will not be impressed by the important nature of the air traffic control function they perform."

employee who deals with the public or who solicits sales has an added responsibility for presenting a pleasing appearance."[229]

There are many arbitration cases in which protection or advancement of the employer's public image was a significant and sometimes controlling factor in upholding dress and grooming policies imposed upon employees by the employer.[230] For example, where a stewardess arrived late for her scheduled flight and was disheveled in appearance, the arbitrator noted that passengers judge the airline primarily by the stewardess who is the main contact between the airline and a "fickle public"; he held that "the appearance of a tardy and disheveled Stewardess on the ramp is conduct prejudicial to the Carrier."[231] Another arbitrator likewise stressed the company's image and upheld its right to protect its image of giving better service through its neat, clean employees; under the mores prevailing at that time, he accepted that the "vast majority of the public" associated long hair and beards with irresponsibility.[232]

---

[229]Pepsi Cola Bottlers, 55 LA 663, 666 (Volz, 1970). Similarly, see Arbitrator Kleinsorge in 55 LA 1020, 1024. Customer disapproval or complaints regarding the personal appearance of employees may be a significant factor supporting the employer's position before an arbitrator. For example, see Arbitrator Wolff in 78 LA 819 at 819; Fogelberg in 74 LA 1017, 1019; Williams in 72 LA 1055, 1056; Kaufman in 71 LA 200, 202. Cf., Beitner in 79 LA 993, 997–998.

[230]See, e.g., Arbitrator Christopher in 80 LA 1104, 1105 (in keeping with a restaurant's image of fine European dining, waitresses could be required to wear gowns of Roman or Grecian mode and to wear their hair blond and upswept); Larkin in 79 LA 835, 836–837 (no-beard rule newly adopted to enhance company's image was upheld, Arbitrator Larkin recognizing employer's right "to issue new rules dealing with old matters not prohibited by some language of " the agreement); Wolff in 78 LA 819 at 819 (hotel could require employees working in lobby to wear clean shirt, tie, jacket, trousers, and shoes, instead of more casual dress such as jeans, sweatshirts, and sneakers); Hilgert in 77 LA 953, 958–959 (although finding the employer's dress and grooming policies "rather conservative by today's contemporary standards," Arbitrator Hilgert upheld a "no facial hair" rule that the employer had uniformly enforced for many years in order to project a favorable image to its customers and where the penalized grievant fully understood the rule and the consequences of not complying with it); Hulsey in 77 LA 705, 706 (upholding a well-established no-beard rule for drivers who have contact with the public while making deliveries to retail stores); Duff in 74 LA 1115, 1116–1117 (telephone company in Florida could prohibit its coin telephone collectors from wearing shorts while on duty in an effort to project an attractive company image to the public, Arbitrator Duff concluding that the "minor inconvenience of a Collector being less comfortable than he desires is overbalanced by his duty to his employer to project an acceptable appearance"); Fogelberg in 74 LA 1017, 1019 (supplier of food products upheld in barring driver from working until he removed beard); Sembower in 74 LA 729, 732 (upholding grocery store no-beard rule since the employer seeks "maintenance of a reasonable image," Arbitrator Sembower commented that "Under other circumstances, such as perhaps in staging a rock band, the very opposite might be desired, and beards indeed might be required"); Kaufman in 71 LA 200, 202–203 (upholding grocery store no-beard policy); Rinaldo in 69 LA 141, 144 (upholding an airline's no-beard rule, but also recognizing that "As fashion styles and public concerns change, rules and regulations such as these will continue to be tested," and that "each case will have to be determined on the facts peculiar to it"). In the latter regard, other arbitrators also have stressed that in reviewing the reasonableness of employer dress and grooming policies, each case must be considered on the basis of its particular facts and circumstances. For example, see Arbitrator Duff in 74 LA 1115, 1116; Christopher in 73 LA 1209, 1213.

[231]Western Air Lines, 37 LA 130, 133–134 (Wyckoff, 1961), holding, however, that discharge was too severe and reducing the penalty to seven months suspension without pay. In Trans World Airlines, 46 LA 611, 612 (Wallen, 1965), it was held that "management must be accorded the right to verify compliance with clothing, hair length and appearance regulations in a manner which imposes no unreasonable or undignified demands on the employee," and that requiring "such verification is neither improper nor unreasonable"; therefore the airline had the right to require a hostess to demonstrate that she was not wearing a wig.

[232]Western Air Lines, 52 LA 1282, 1284 (Steese, 1969), upholding discharge for refusal to comply with rule prohibiting long hair and beards. Also upholding discharge, Arbitrator Dugan in 57 LA 994, 995; Daly in 57 LA 453, 456; Kleinsorge in 55 LA 1020, 1025; Volz in 55 LA 663, 666–667; Johnson in 49 LA 867, 868 (supermarket employee wore his hair long for his second job in a rock and roll band). Also see Casselman in 57 LA 789, 794–795. Upholding or assessing a

However, there are also many arbitration cases in which the "image" factor was recognized as a valid factor but was not shown to be sufficiently strong under the facts to justify the employer's interference with employee free choice as to dress and grooming.[233] For example, where an employee refused to cut his long hair and shave his beard to comply with a company rule, the arbitrator found that the employee worked in an isolated area where contact with customers and other employees was extremely rare, and he further noted that at the hearing the grievant's general appearance was one of "cleanliness and neatness," although his hair was long and he had sideburns and a short van dyke beard. Stating that the rule "as it applied to this grievant working in this location is not reasonable," the arbitrator held that the grievant could maintain the hair style he desired so long as it did not affect his work or that of other employees, or the company's relations with its customers.[234]

The concern of management with its image is keyed to public acceptance of the clothing and hair styles adopted by its employees. As mores change and the acceptability of given attire and hair styles is no

lesser penalty for refusal to comply with appearance regulations, Arbitrator Caraway in 52 LA 1117, 1118; Turkus in 51 LA 292 at 292, and in 47 LA 1182 at 1182.

[233]See, e.g., Arbitrator Beitner in 79 LA 993, 997–998 (grievants had limited contact with the public and there was inadequate proof "that the Company's image was adversely affected by allowing employees to wear hair nets instead of cutting their hair," as formerly had been permitted); Maniscalco in 77 LA 973, 977 (no-beard policy held unreasonable and arbitrary where utility employer failed to show "any reasonable relationship between its announced 'New Public Image Policy' and the real attitudes of the public it serves"); J. Jones in 77 LA 807, 813–814 (stating that transportation employer had not adequately established that its "prohibition against mirror-type sun glasses is related to its legitimate objectives of increasing ridership," and finding "substantial evidence of community acceptance of the type of sun glasses in issue"); Madden in 75 LA 798, 801 (grocery store discharged employee who refused to shave beard prohibited by store's grooming standards—the discharge was overruled because the employee suffers from a skin condition that becomes worse if any type of razor is used to shave beard); Christopher in 73 LA 1209, 1213–1215 (refusing to uphold an airline's absolute prohibition on beards for flight attendants where the airline failed to produce convincing evidence that a neatly trimmed beard would damage its "public image or otherwise have a detrimental effect on its business activities"); Dallas in 70 LA 28, 32 (overruling discharge for refusing to cut long hair, he stated that grievant's hair style "is similar to the hair styles worn by a large proportion of young men in his age group throughout the country," and "in the arbitrator's opinion should not be detrimental to the Company's image or sales"). In Hughes Air Corp., 72 LA 588, 590–591 (1979), Arbitrator Richard I. Bloch collected many cases reflecting "great diversity among arbitral responses" to the "sensitive issue" of beards, mustaches, and hair length, and he reviewed his own previous decision which had upheld an airline no-beard rule; he refused to uphold a similar rule in the present case but explained that "the decision in this case is limited to the finding that, in light of changes effected by deregulation, one may no longer assume, absent proof, that passengers' preferences concerning beards will be of demonstrable import in their choice of carrier." In Department of Health, Educ. & Welfare, 69 LA 44, 48 (1977), Arbitrator Arnold M. Zack found that most government and private business offices do not require employees to wear neckties, so he held that the Employer may encourage do not require the wearing of neckties under an agreement specifying that mode of dress "shall be consistent with accepted standards of business offices dealing with the public."

[234]Dravo-Doyle Co., 54 LA 604, 605–607 (Krimsly, 1970). Similarly, Badger Concrete Co., 50 LA 901, 908 (Krinsky, 1968), but also holding that the company can enforce the rule as to some classes of employees or employees performing certain jobs, for safety or other reasons connected with the company's operations. Id. at 909. Also see Hillview Sand & Gravel, 39 LA 35, 39–40 (Somers, 1962), observing that an employee can look neat and shave daily (in compliance with a company rule) and still retain a beard. For additional cases in which the arbitrator refused to uphold the employer's rule or assessment of discipline as to long hair, see Arbitrator Murphy in 73 LA 850, 856–857 (but cautioning grievants "that upon their return to their job that their hair must be kept clean and neat and orderly and well combed"); Forsythe in 57 LA 1017, 1019 (employee could use wig to cover long hair); Jacobs in 57 LA 963, 969–970; Leonard in 57 LA 821, 824; Somers in 57 LA 410, 414; Strong in 57 LA 197, 199.

longer questioned by the general public, industry has likewise accepted changes. This is effectively illustrated by the evolution of acceptability of certain attire of female employees: in the 1930s women were not permitted to wear slacks in some plants because of a possible production hazard in distracting male employees;[235] in the 1940s many plants *required* women to wear slacks to avoid danger involved in working around industrial machinery;[236] in the 1950s and 1960s, slacks for women gained wide acceptability; by 1970 slacks, often in the form of "pant suits" or "pant dresses," came to be viewed by many employers as the preferable attire, gaining approval not only in industrial plants but also in many other business concerns (offices— even some government offices—and retail establishments), hospitals, and airlines (for stewardesses).[237]

One arbitrator has urged: "Custom and fashion in dress and behavior change from time to time, and employees should be permitted to conform reasonably with these changes."[238] So long as no detriment results to the company and no safety or health hazard is involved, conformity to current fashion should not be objectionable if the style followed is not extreme—one can be "in fashion" without resorting to the extremes of fads.[239]

Safety and Health Considerations

Safety, health, and sanitation reasons also have been advanced in imposing restrictions on employees' apparel, hair, or beards.[240] Questions of safety may be raised where loose fitting clothing, dangling jewelry, and long unprotected hair are worn while operating machinery. Management may be expected to object when an employee

---

[235]See comments in Mitchell-Bentley Corp., 45 LA 1071, 1073 (Ryder, 1965), involving the wearing of shorts by women workers.

[236]Also required for reasons of modesty when women worked, for instance, as welders on elevated platforms. The issue faced in an early case by one arbitrator (decided in the negative) was whether *red* slacks constituted a production hazard because of a tendency to distract male employees. Shulman, Opinions of the Umpire (Ford Motor Co.), Opinion A-117 (1944).

[237]Admittedly, many employers found the pant suits or pant dresses preferable to the "mini" dress which, for instance, led many employers to feel compelled to add "modesty shields" at the front of secretary desks. In School Dist. of Kingsley, 56 LA 1138, 1145 (Howlett, 1971), a school board's notice prohibiting teachers from wearing pant suits was held to be "null and void." Stating that "pant-suits [for women] now are an acceptable mode of dress in many of our medical care facilities," another arbitrator required a nursing home to modify its dress code "so as to permit the wearing of dresses or pant-suits." Oxford Nursing Home, 75 LA 1300, 1301–1302 (Wolff, 1980).

[238]Springday Co., 53 LA 627, 629 (Bothwell, 1969).

[239]A discharged shipping clerk was described as "wearing boots, tight clinging orange-brown pants (with a wide oversized belt and buckle) and a flowing hirsute cranial adornment characteristic of the Beatles." But since his past record was good and since he demonstrated a willingness to cooperate by appearing at the hearing "shorn of his flowing locks, and presenting the very epitome of the more mundane accepted norm," he was reinstated without back pay on condition that he continue to maintain such appearance. American Export-Isbrandten Lines, 47 LA 1182 at 1182 (Turkus, 1967).

[240]See Arbitrator Mount in 78 LA 630, 631; Ferguson in 72 LA 164, 167–168; Rutherford in 71 LA 22, 25–26; Mattice in 57 LA 1036, 1038; Elson in 54 LA 816, 819–820; Stutz in 54 LA 439, 441; Bothwell in 53 LA 627, 628–629; Bradley in 51 LA 983, 988–990; Krinsky in 50 LA 901, 908. Also see Fishgold in 74 LA 921, 922; Davis in 28 LA 83, 87. For general considerations of safety and health matters, see Chapter 16, Safety and Health.

operating machinery wears a loose shirt with the tail hanging out, or a dangling bracelet or necklace (even a wedding ring may be a hazard in some situations[241]), or long hair, any of which may become caught or entangled in the machinery. In a case involving a safety rule regarding loose apparel and long unprotected hair, management was upheld in refusing to permit an employee to continue work unless he trimmed his beard, Arbitrator Wilber C. Bothwell ruling:

> "It is properly the function of management personnel who directly supervise employees to determine the conditions under which a beard constitutes a safety hazard. The individual employee cannot decide how safety rules are to apply to him, or whether or not he should obey a particular safety rule in a particular situation. * * *
> * * *
> "The arbitrator cannot determine whether a particular beard constitutes a safety hazard. This must be done on a day to day basis by supervision in the industrial plant. Only if such decisions by supervision are clearly unreasonable should the arbitrator intervene."[242]

He stated further: "The employee is not being unreasonably restrained in his conduct or dress so long as there is a reasonable relation between what is required and safety."[243]

In regard to the reasonable relation requirement, arbitrators have upheld rules restricting the wearing of beards or other facial hair where the restriction is necessary for proper functioning of respirators needed for safety purposes;[244] but such rules have not been upheld as to employees who have no real need for the use of a respirator or whose need is too remote and conjectural.[245]

A reasonable relation likewise must be shown where health reasons are argued. Thus, an arbitrator found that it was unreasonable of the company to apply a general rule against growing beards to the grievant where the health reasons urged by the company—that

---

[241]See General Foods Corp., 76 LA 532, 535 (Denson, 1981); Bethlehem Mines Corp., 48 LA 765, 766 (Strongin, 1967). Also see Arbitrator Strasshofer in 73 LA 443, 447.

[242]Springday Co., 53 LA 627, 628–629 (1969), where the company did not prohibit the wearing of beards but only regulated them for safety purposes. Another arbitrator would not lay down guidelines as to the point where "face hair becomes hirsute and unacceptable" from a safety standpoint, stating that "each mustache and each pair of sideburns * * * will have to be measured against the safety factor and treated accordingly." City of Waterbury, 54 LA 439, 441 (Stutz, 1970).

[243]Springday Co., 53 LA 627, 629 (1969). A reasonable relationship was found where facial hair, often treated with tonics, salves, or sprays which contain inflammable materials, "may well ignite if touched by a very hot spark" of the type present in the work of the employees. Phoenix Forging Co., 71 LA 879, 882 (Dash, 1978). A reasonable relationship was not found where the employee (operating machinery) wore a protective cap over his long hair. Challenge-Cook Bros., 55 LA 517, 520–521 (Roberts, 1970). For a statement regarding "reasonableness" in finding the existence of a safety hazard, and reasonableness in determining whether a perceived safety hazard necessitates the restriction upon employee choice as to dress or grooming, see statement of Arbitrator Clare McDermott as quoted by Arbitrator Strasshofer in Babcock & Wilcox, 73 LA 443, 445 (1979).

[244]See Arbitrator Light in 78 LA 327, 330; E. Jones in 77 LA 320, 329–330; Teple in 76 LA 841, 843–844; Johnston in 75 LA 770, 774; Hutcheson in 69 LA 824, 826; Conant in 68 LA 912, 915–916. Also see Riceland Foods v. Carpenters Local 2381, 116 LRRM 2948 (CA 8, 1984); Bhatia v. Chevron U.S.A., 34 FEP Cases 1816 (CA 9, 1984), discussed below in this subtopic; Arbitrator Markowitz in 74 LA 58, 62–63. Cf., Arbitrator H. Jones in 78 LA 682, 685–686.

[245]See Union Carbide Corp., 82 LA 1084, 1087–1088 (Goldman, 1984); E. & J. Gallo Winery, 80 LA 765, 770 (Killion, 1983).

beards contributed to dermatitis caused by handling the company's product—were found not to apply to the grievant who was a mechanic and had little or no contact with the product.[246]

Employers may attempt to combat employee hirsuteness for sanitation reasons. In one case, the arbitrator recognized that "The maintenance of a [supermarket] meat department, so as to give a clean and sanitary appearance, is essential to its proper operation." But he concluded that sideburns "even somewhat fuzzier" than those worn by the grievant at the hearing did not present a reasonable basis for concern.[247] However, another arbitrator emphasized that "Although hair styles have changed, sanitation needs have not"; and he upheld the discharge of an employee who wore sideburns longer than permitted by the company rule, which the arbitrator held was directed at protecting the company's products from hair contamination rather than at regulating employees' appearance.[248]

Wigs and hair pieces may likewise be the subjects of company rules. In one case, the arbitrator held that for sanitation reasons a meat packing company could prohibit the wearing of wigs and hair pieces in the plant; he placed such items in the same category as hats and other "street clothing" which were barred from the plant by a company rule (the company providing dressing rooms for changing) and by a U.S. Department of Agriculture regulation, such "street clothing" being considered a source of contamination.[249]

Sometimes dress or grooming policies adopted for safety, health, or sanitation reasons are opposed by individual employees on religious grounds. In one such case a safety rule required employees to wear pants but an employee was prevented from doing so by her religion, which had a tenet against women wearing men's clothing. She insisted upon wearing a dress or skirt and was discharged when she refused to wear pants as required by the safety rule. In this case Arbitrator William T. Rutherford explained his conclusion that it is permissible for an employer "to give greater weight to safety considerations than to religious preferences" in certain circumstances:

"The Arbitrator must let safety considerations prevail if the Employer has made an objective determination that a certain rule is necessary based on demonstrated facts and reasonable inferences. This is not to say that Freedom of religion/or religious expression is ignored or not a part of the total fabric of the so-called "common law of the shop." There are other places to express religious preferences but there is no other place to practice on the job safety except the work site. Safety rules affect and

[246]Badger Concrete Co., 50 LA 901, 908 (Krinsky, 1968).

[247]Economy Super Mart, 54 LA 816, 820 (Elson, 1970).

[248]Kellogg Co., 55 LA 84, 88 (Shearer, 1970).

[249]Marhoefer Packing Co., 51 LA 583, 588–590 (Bradley, 1968), with much discussion of evidence comparing natural hair with wigs, and noting in particular that in contrast with natural hair wigs become brittle and break and that dust and dirt settling on a wig can fall off or be blown away more easily. Safety rather than sanitation was involved in Babcock & Wilcox, 73 LA 443, 444, 447 (Strasshofer, 1979), where "the evidence did not prove the alleged safety hazards"; it was not "proven that there is any particularly significant increase in safety risks to the employee or anyone else created by a wig under a hard hat, as opposed to natural hair under a hard hat."

inure to the benefit of all employees. The fact that the rules are most frequently originated by the Employer does not destroy the benefit which flows to employees. In any event, safety on the job is a lawfully mandated federal requirement under the Occupational Safety and Health Act, and, in this specific case safety is also a contractually mandated requirement under Article XIII."[250]

In another case a hospital employer transferred an operating room technician who refused to wear pants, which her religion forbade her to wear but which were required under the hospital's program to lower the incidence of infection in the operating room. The collective agreement contained a clause expressly prohibiting "discrimination as to * * * creed," and, looking to Title VII of the Civil Rights Act for aid in construing the intent of the clause, Arbitrator George T. Roumell concluded that the employer must show that no acceptable alternative existed which would accomplish the same purpose as the employee's transfer out of the operating room. The award specified steps to be taken for designing an operating room uniform that would conform to the infection control program without violating the employee's religious beliefs.[251] It then developed, however, that the employee rejected for the same religious reason the alternative uniform that was designated pursuant to the award. In subsequent proceedings Arbitrator Roumell ruled that the employer could transfer her "to a job which she is able to perform and not be required to wear slacks."[252]

Safety interests are not the only interests that may clash with those of individual employees under their religious faith. The next topic deals with other areas of conflict and the need to make reasonable accommodations for employee religious beliefs.

---

[250]Colt Indus., 71 LA 22, 25 (1978). The employer made the required showing of necessity and the discharge was held to be for just cause, but the award provided that "in view of the delicate balance between safety considerations and religious beliefs which the case presents," the employee "should be allowed to return to work without any back pay but without any loss of seniority whenever she decides that she will comply with the Employer's safety related dress code." Id. at 26. In Alameda-Contra Costa Transit Dist., 75 LA 1273, 1282 (Randall, 1980), the employee's belief in the particular religious tenet upon which she relied was found not to be sincere and her discharge for violating the employer's dress code was upheld. In Louisville Water Co., 80 LA 957, 962 (Hunter, 1983), the employee's belief in the particular religious tenet upon which she relied was found to be sincere but her discharge for refusing to wear a jumpsuit uniform nonetheless was upheld on the basis of estoppel—she had accepted the jumpsuit requirement as a condition of employment for several years until she adopted a religion whose beliefs prevented her from wearing men's clothing. The Arbitrator stated that his jurisdiction was limited to the contract and that the question "Whether or not she is estopped under the Civil Rights Act of 1964" was not before him.

[251]Hurley Hosp., 70 LA 1061, 1063–1066 (1978).

[252]Hurley Hosp., 71 LA 1013, 1015 (1978), the award providing also that "She shall be paid the rate of said new job." An employer's adherence to a safety policy was upheld over an employee's adherence to a tenet of his religion in Bhatia v. Chevron U.S.A., 34 FEP Cases 1816 (CA 9, 1984), where the employer was held to have reasonably accommodated the employee under Title VII in transferring him to a lower paying job after the employee's religion resulted in his refusal to shave as required for wearing a gas mask needed on the job. The court said the employer would suffer undue hardship by retaining the employee on the job: to subject the employee to toxic fumes would render the employer liable under state law, and to relieve the employee of the duties involving exposure to toxic fumes would necessitate revamping an entire system of duty assignments and would require co-workers to assume the employee's share of potentially hazardous work.

Accommodation of Employee Religious Beliefs

We observed in the preceding topic that dress and grooming policies adopted by the employer for health or safety reasons sometimes have been opposed by individual employees on religious grounds. Sometimes employees also have complained that their freedom of religion was violated by the scheduling of work on the Sabbath or on other religious holidays. They have urged that they were discriminated against when the employer required them to work on such days or disciplined them for their failure to work. However, until 1972, when Title VII of the Civil Rights Act was amended to impose an obligation upon management to make reasonable accommodations for employee religious beliefs, arbitrators generally had held that the employer was not required to accommodate individual requests for scheduling work so that the employee could observe religious holidays; and discharge or discipline had been upheld where the employee had refused for such reason to work as scheduled.[253] Arbitrators emphasized the company's right to maintain efficient industrial operations, and they noted the disruption (one arbitrator labeling it "industrial chaos") which would result if the company were required to accommodate the religious beliefs of individual employees.[254]

Another aspect of the problem was the need to avoid discrimination against other employees.[255] In one case, a foreman discontinued a special schedule for one employee when other employees complained that such arrangement was discriminatory; the employee grieved when he was told that he would have to work his regular schedule or become subject to discipline. Ruling for the company, the arbitrator stated: "This simply is not a case involving discrimination *against* grievant because of his religious beliefs. Rather, it is he who seeks a special privilege which is not accorded to other employees."[256]

Another question which arose was whether an employer could require employees of the same faith to take time off on religious days,

---

[253]See Arbitrator Turkus in 52 LA 707, 708; Walt in 50 LA 375, 380; Daugherty in 49 LA 204, 206; Garrett in 48 LA 1340, 1342–1343; Cahn in 48 LA 619, 620–621; Summers in 39 LA 374, 378–379 (stating that "In spite of the high value placed on religious freedom in our society, employers have commonly scheduled work on days which are the sabbath for various employees and are generally considered entitled to dismiss employees who refuse to work for religious reasons"); Stark in 29 LA 77, 79; Kelliher in 15 LA 121, 123.

[254]See Arbitrator Turkus in 52 LA 707, 708; Walt in 50 LA 375, 380; Daugherty in 49 LA 204, 206; Cahn in 48 LA 619, 621. Also see Stark in 29 LA 77, 79. Cf., Spiegel, Inc., 55 LA 653, 657 (Luskin, 1970) (involving a de minimis situation).

[255]Thus, where the contract contained a provision prohibiting discrimination, it was observed that to treat an employee differently for religious reasons would be to discriminate against other employees in violation of the contract. Avco Lycoming Div., 52 LA 707, 708 (Turkus, 1969); Combustion Eng'g., 49 LA 204, 206 (Daugherty, 1967). Also, a company argument in United States Steel Corp., 56 LA 694, 695 (McDaniel, 1971), was that should the company permit such differential treatment for religious reasons it might be subject to a charge of "reverse discrimination" or favoritism. The contract in this case, however, contained a requirement that the joint Committee on Civil Rights "shall review matters involving Civil Rights" and the arbitrator set aside the discharge pending such review. Id. at 696–697.

[256]United States Steel Corp., 48 LA 1340, 1341, 1343 (Garrett, 1967). But in another case, discipline of an employee for refusal to work on Sunday for religious reasons was held to constitute discrimination in violation of the contract where the company had habitually shown consideration for the religious scruples of other employees in the plant. Goodyear Tire & Rubber Co., 1 LA 121, 122–123 (McCoy, 1945). Also see Arbitrator Klamon in 2 LA 201, 205–206.

imposing upon them the same degree of observance he finds proper for himself. Arbitrator Eva Robins answered in the negative, ruling that to do so would be an arbitrary use of the contractual right to relieve employees from duty.[257]

Even prior to the amendment of Title VII of the Civil Rights Act of 1964, the Equal Employment Opportunity Commission guidelines stated that the duty imposed by Title VII not to discriminate on religious grounds "includes an obligation on the part of the employer to make reasonable accommodations to the religious needs of employees * * * where such accommodations can be made without hardship on the conduct of the employer's business." In *Dewey v. Reynolds Metals Company* the discharge of an employee who refused to work on Sundays or to induce others to work in his place was upheld, the court ruling that the employer had made "reasonable accommodation" to the employee's religious needs when it gave him the opportunity to secure replacements for his Sunday overtime assignments.[258]

Under Title VII of the Civil Rights Act as amended by the Equal Opportunity Act of 1972, employers must make reasonable accommodations for employee religious beliefs in the scheduling of work and the like, unless the employer demonstrates that doing so would result in "undue hardship on the conduct of the employer's business."[259]

---

[257]Eagle Elec. Mfg. Co., 31 LA 1038, 1039 (1957). Also see Eagle Elec. Mfg. Co., 29 LA 489, 491 (Gamser, 1957) (finding a violation of the seniority provisions under like circumstances).

[258]429 F.2d 324 (CA 6, 1970), affirmed by a 4–4 decision of the Supreme Court, 91 S.Ct. 2186 (1971).

[259]Sec. 701(j), which provides in full that:

"The term 'religion' includes all aspects of religious observance and practice, as well as belief, unless an employer demonstrates that he is unable to reasonably accommodate to an employee's or prospective employee's religious observance or practice without undue hardship on the conduct of the employer's business."

As analyzed in the Congressional Record, March 6, 1972, this subsection requires employers to make reasonable accommodations for religious practices "which differ from the employer's or potential employer's requirements regarding standards, schedules, or other business-related employment conditions." That source also states that "The purpose of this subsection is to provide the statutory basis for EEOC to formulate guidelines on discrimination because of religion such as those challenged in Dewey v. Reynolds Metals Company." The EEOC's "Guidelines on Discrimination Because of Religion" are published in 29 C.F.R. Part 1605. For discussion of what constitutes a "religious belief," see Hill, "Reasonable Accommodation and Religious Discrimination Under Title VII: A Practitioner's Guide," 34 Arb. J. No. 4, pp. 19, 20, 24–25 (1979). Also note the statement in Edwards v. School Bd., City of Norton, 21 FEP Cases 1375, 1377 (USDC, 1980), that:

"A religious belief excludes mere personal preference grounded upon a non-theological basis, such as personal choice deduced from economic or social ideology. Rather, it must consider man's nature or the scheme of his existence as it relates in a theological framework. Furthermore, the belief must have an institutional quality about it and must be sincerely held by plaintiff."

In Building Owners & Managers Assn., 67 LA 1031, 1033–1034 (1976), a Roman Catholic employee's discharge for refusing to work on Sunday was upheld since the employer had the right to assign Sunday work and the Roman Catholic religion does not forbid its faithful to work on Sunday but rather maintained schedules which would have permitted the employee to fulfill his obligations both to his job and to his Church; Arbitrator J. J. Griffin stated that the employee "has the unfettered personal right to impose his own standards regarding Sunday work, even when those individual standards exceed those required by the faith he professes," but "the exercise of that right is not without possible peril." In this case Arbitrator Griffin did not expressly mention Title VII, but he did state his conclusion that the employee's discharge "was violative of neither his contractual, nor religious/civil rights." For other cases drawing a distinction between personal preference or the individual's conscience on the one hand, and the actual requirements of the Catholic Church on the other, see Arbitrator Kanner in 71 LA 937, 941, and Arbitrator

The U.S. Supreme Court's 1977 decision in *Trans World Airlines v. Hardison* considered both the provision for reasonable accommodation of religious beliefs under § 701(j) of the Act, and the protection of bona fide seniority systems under § 703(h). In this case an employee had insufficient seniority to avoid working on Saturdays and thus not violate a tenet of his religion—he eventually was discharged for refusing to work on Saturdays. Accepting the District Court's view that TWA had done all that could reasonably be expected within the bounds of the seniority system, the Supreme Court held that "absent a discriminatory purpose, the operation of a seniority system cannot be an unlawful employment practice even if the system has some discriminatory consequences."[260]

The Court of Appeals had believed that TWA could have accommodated the employee without undue hardship on the business (1) by permitting him to work a four-day week, utilizing in his place a supervisor or another worker on duty elsewhere, (2) by filling his shift with another employee at premium overtime pay, or (3) by arranging a "swap between Hardison and another employee either for another shift or for the Sabbath days." The Supreme Court disagreed, and in doing so the Court explained its rejection of alternative (3) first:

> "TWA cannot be faulted for having failed itself to work out a shift or job swap for Hardison. Both the union and TWA had agreed to the seniority system; the union was unwilling to entertain a variance over the objections of men senior to Hardison; and for TWA to have arranged unilaterally for a swap would have amounted to a breach of the collective-bargaining agreement."[261]

Yarowsky in 68 LA 1056, 1060, both cases involving the construction of contractual leave provisions. Also see Fox in 70 LA 707, 714 (employee failed to establish either that the asserted religious belief was sincerely held or that the action requested by the employer would violate any tenet of the asserted religious faith); High in 63 LA 157, 159 (employee "indicated that there would be no serious impairment of the fulfillment of his religious obligations to arrive" late at religious meetings, "but that he personally felt it important to be punctual"); Simon in 60 LA 525, 532 (stressing that it was the grievant's "own *personal* conviction that one should not perform work on Sunday"). In Social Security Admin., 79 LA 449, 449–455 (1982), a statute provided that federal employees "whose personal religious beliefs require the abstention from work during certain periods of time, may elect to engage in overtime work for time lost for meeting those religious requirements"—Arbitrator Eugene Mittelman concluded that "neither the statute nor the constitution precludes an employer from making a reasonable inquiry to ascertain whether an employee in fact has a personal religious belief which requires him or her to refrain from work."

[260]Trans World Airlines v. Hardison, 97 S.Ct. 2264, 2273, 2275, 14 FEP Cases 1697 (1977), referred to below in this topic as the *TWA* decision. The Supreme Court noted TWA's actions to accommodate as had been summarized by the District Court:

"It held several meetings with plaintiff at which it attempted to find a solution to plaintiff's problems. It did accommodate plaintiff's observance of his special religious holidays [which could reasonably be done since they fell on days that most other employees preferred to work]. It authorized the union steward to search for someone who would swap shifts, which apparently was normal procedure."

97 S.Ct. at 2273. The Supreme Court also noted that "TWA itself attempted without success to find Hardison another job." Ibid. Furthermore, the Court considered that the seniority system "itself represented a significant accommodation to the needs, both religious and secular, of all of TWA's employees"—it "represents a neutral way of minimizing the number of occasions when an employee must work on a day that he would prefer to have off"; and "recognizing that weekend work schedules are the least popular, the company made further accommodation by reducing its work force to a bare minimum on those days." Id. at 2274.

[261]97 S.Ct. at 2274, where the Court said it did "not believe that the duty to accommodate requires TWA to take steps inconsistent with the otherwise valid agreement." The Court did believe that "the strong congressional policy against discrimination in employment argues

Then the Supreme Court explained its rejection of alternatives (1) and (2):

> "Both of these alternatives would involve costs to TWA, either in the form of lost efficiency in other jobs or as higher wages.
>
> "To require TWA to bear more than a *de minimis* cost in order to give Hardison Saturdays off is an undue hardship. Like abandonment of the seniority system, to require TWA to bear additional costs when no such costs are incurred to give other employees the days off that they want would involve unequal treatment of employees on the basis of their religion. * * *
>
> " * * * [T]he paramount concern of Congress in enacting Title VII was the elimination of discrimination in employment. In the absence of clear statutory language or legislative history to the contrary, we will not readily construe the statute to require an employer to discriminate against some employees in order to enable others to observe their Sabbath."[262]

It may be noted that the lower courts have expressed differing views on the question of what showing an employer must make to demonstrate a reasonable accommodation of employee religious beliefs under § 701(j) and the Supreme Court's *TWA* decision: some courts require an employer to show that it took active steps, though unsuccessful, to accommodate the employee, whereas other courts do not require active steps and rather allow an employer to fulfill its obligation by arguing that any proposed or possible accommodation would create an undue hardship.[263]

Also to be noted is a court's explanation that the term "reasonable accommodation" is a relative term and cannot be given a hard and fast meaning; that each case "involving such a determination necessarily depends upon its own facts and circumstances"; and that the "trier of fact is in the best position" to make the determination.[264]

Subsequent to the 1972 amendment of the Civil Rights Act, court decisions (particularly the Supreme Court's *TWA* decision) and/or EEOC guidelines often have been given serious consideration by arbitrators in deciding issues concerning accommodation of employee religious beliefs.[265] In some of these cases the arbitrator found that

---

against interpreting the statute to require the abrogation of the seniority rights of some employees in order to accommodate the religious needs of others."

[262]Id. at 2276–2277. In City of Auburn Police Dept., 78 LA 537, 541 (Chandler, 1982), the *TWA* decision was cited in connection with the Arbitrator's conclusion that the employer had improperly discriminated against one employee in order to accommodate the religious needs of another.

[263]Court of Appeals decisions supporting each of these views are cited in Edwards v. School Bd., City of Norton, 21 FEP Cases 1375, 1377–1378 (USDC, 1980). In this case the court rejected the view that "active steps" are required, but still held for the employee, a teacher's aid who had been discharged for missing work to attend a religious convocation; the school employer relied upon opinion testimony that the aide's absence resulted in great harm to students' educational progress and that other school personnel might complain because of the special treatment she would receive, but the court concluded that this is "mere opinion and speculation," and insufficient to establish undue hardship. Id. at 1379.

[264]Redmond v. GAF Corp., 17 FEP Cases 208, 212 (CA 7, 1978), citing other cases in general accord.

[265]For related discussion see Chapter 10, subtopic entitled "Title VII of the Civil Rights Act." For articles discussing arbitration decisions concerning accommodation of employee religious beliefs, see Helburn & Hill, "The Arbitration of Religious Practice Grievances," 39 Arb. J. No. 2, p. 3 (1984); Wolkinson, "Title VII and the Religious Employee: The Neglected Duty of Accommodation," 30 Arb. J. 89 (1975).

the employer had demonstrated a reasonable accommodation and/or an undue hardship.[266] In other of the cases in which court decisions and/or EEOC guidelines were considered, the arbitrator found that the employer had not shown either a reasonable accommodation or an undue hardship.[267]

Some arbitrators since 1972 have mentioned Title VII doctrine relating to accommodation of religious beliefs but have deemed their

---

[266]See Arbitrator Belkin in 79 LA 299, 303–306 (sustaining discharge for absences due to inability to work weekends because of religion, Arbitrator Belkin found reasonable accommodation by the employer's willingness to permit the employee to bid another job although at significantly lower wages, and found also that the accommodation proposed by the employee would involve scheduling difficulties, would subject the employer to greater than de minimis increase in costs, and would disregard resentment expressed by other employees against any preferential scheduling, which consequences create undue hardship under teachings of the *TWA* decision); Greene in 77 LA 838, 843–845 (relying extensively upon the *TWA* decision, he concluded that the employer did not discriminate against grievant in discharging him for failing to make a necessary delivery on Friday afternoon and leaving work five hours early that day to prepare for Sabbath before sundown as required by his religion; but in light of mitigating factors the award left a possibility open for the employee to obtain reinstatement); Conant in 72 LA 505, 509–510 (the parties requested a determination of grievant's rights under the agreement and the Civil Rights Act—Arbitrator Conant pointed to special needs of the business and concluded that the employer's decision to transfer the grievant to another department where she could be scheduled off on Sundays and thus accommodate her religion, "was the most sensible option" under all of the circumstances, although it meant her loss of "a preferred kind of work"); Shearer in 70 LA 1123, 1126–1127 (although not discussing the *TWA* decision, which was relied upon by the employer, Arbitrator Shearer pointed to the employer's offer to transfer the employee to other departments where he would not be required to work on Saturday, his Sabbath; and, upholding the employee's discharge for absenteeism on Saturdays, Arbitrator Shearer stated that "under the circumstances the Company acted reasonably with respect to trying to accommodate Grievant's religious need with the Company's operating realities"); Oppenheim in 69 LA 325, 327–329 (the employee was inflexible in requesting the particular accommodation which was denied him and the employer, supported by the *TWA* decision, "demonstrated that it was unable reasonably to accommodate" the employee's "religious practice without undue hardship in the conduct of its business"); Rehmus in 68 LA 171, 174–176 (finding that the employer did make reasonable accommodation for the employee's religious needs by allowing her time off to attend bible study meetings when production was not essential, but that the employee herself "made no attempt to make any accommodation to her employer's needs for her regular production" by taking advantage of other available steps by which "she could have satisfied the needs of her conscience" without imposing undue hardship upon the employer; although her discharge was held justified, reinstatement was ordered on the condition that she "offers to work full shifts as scheduled when needed for essential production by the Company"). Also see Gregg in 74 LA 1131, 1132; Greco in 73 LA 1146, 1148 (stating that the Title VII reasonable accommodation provision "does not go to the extent of requiring" the employer to provide leave with pay, he held that paid leave for religious holidays was not required where not required by the agreement); Gentile in 70 LA 936, 939 (citing the *TWA* decision, he concluded that the employer could have asserted undue hardship and thus need not have granted the request of 36 percent of the work force for religious leave on Good Friday—granting such request resulted in a shortage of personnel which led to the layoff of the remaining work force without being given the contractually required 48-hour notice).

[267]See Arbitrator Clarke in 79 LA 1320, 1325–1326 (the agreement prohibited discrimination on the basis of "creed," and an EEOC guideline provided that "where there is more than one means of accommodation which would not cause undue hardship, the employer * * * must offer the alternative which least disadvantages the individual"—Arbitrator Clarke held that "under the facts of this case giving the Grievant an opportunity to take a personal or sick leave" rather than giving him an excused absence on the day of his absence to preach at a funeral was not a reasonable accommodation); Dunsford in 70 LA 1131, 1135–1138 (noting that the parties had agreed that Title VII standards would control his decision, and having analyzed and distinguished the *TWA* decision, he stated that the "reasonable accommodation of which the Act speaks refers not only to efforts to satisfy the employee's religious needs within the confines of his present job, but also a serious examination of whether there are alternative positions which the employee might fill without violating the terms of " the collective agreement); Jacobs in 65 LA 650, 653–654 (noting that this case "involves the breaking of an employee's seniority on recall because he could not accept a job which was available on the swing shift because of his religious convictions," and finding that the employer could have made reasonable accommodation since there were other laid-off employees who were qualified to perform the work on the swing shift, Arbitrator Jacobs declared that the agreement's recall/forfeiture provision "cannot * * * be construed in such fashion as to violate rights guaranteed by Title VII").

jurisdiction to be limited to consideration of the collective agreement alone.[268]

It appears that most arbitration decisions at least mention the Civil Rights Act where the case involves religious accommodation and arose subsequent to the 1972 amendment of the Act.[269]

Protection Against Sexual Harassment

Preliminary understanding of what is or may be involved in "sexual harassment" in the workplace is aided by the 1981 MSPB Report prepared by the Merit Systems Protection Board at the request of Congress. The Report is based upon an extensive survey of the views of federal employees, along with an intensive study of literature and case law on the subject of sexual harassment.[270]

The MSPB survey of federal employees indicated general agreement by men and women respondents that the following behaviors, ranked in order of agreement, constitute sexual harassment: (1) letters, phone calls, or materials of a sexual nature; (2) pressure for sexual favors; (3) touching, leaning over, cornering, or pinching; and, deemed less severe than the aforementioned behaviors, (4) pressure

---

[268]See Arbitrator Morgan in 75 LA 801, 804–805 (he noted the *TWA* decision's statement that to require the employer to incur more than de minimus cost constitutes an undue hardship, but refusing to determine whether undue hardship existed in the present case, he held for the employer solely on the basis of his finding that the employer had not violated the agreement in refusing holiday pay to an employee who failed to work the last scheduled workday before the holiday because that workday fell on his Sabbath); Larkin in 66 LA 933, 935 (employee who was also a minister was discharged for unauthorized absence from job while attending a religious conference—upholding the discharge, Arbitrator Larkin stated that his role was to administer the agreement rather than the statute, but he did point out that "the grievant was not asking for time off to attend religious services," the purpose of the conference being to raise funds for a church-affiliated college); Simon in 60 LA 525, 531–533 (he stated that his role was only to interpret the agreement, but he did find that the employer had "tried to accommodate the employee's request but could not do so").

[269]Even where the Act is not mentioned, the result reached by the arbitrator may not be too far out of line, if at all, with the Act's requirements. For instance, see Reynolds & Reynolds Co., 63 LA 157, 159 (1974), where an employee was discharged for leaving the job before completing scheduled overtime work in order to attend religious services. In upholding the discharge, Arbitrator Theodore K. High stressed that (1) this occurred during the employer's busy season requiring regularly scheduled overtime, (2) the conflict between job and religious needs occurred "on a regular, twice-a-week basis," (3) to excuse the employee "would have discriminated against the other employees," and (4) "it is far from clear that Grievant had done all he could to accommodate his personal obligations to those he had as an employee to the company." Also see Arbitrator May in 62 LA 1246, 1248–1249. In Charles Todd Uniform Rental Serv. Co., 77 LA 144, 146 (1981), an employee was discharged for his practice of preaching his religious beliefs to customers, some of whom had ceased dealing with the employer. In upholding the discharge Arbitrator Kent Hutcheson did not mention Title VII, but he did state that:

"The Constitution does not * * * require that an employer finance the religious activities of its employees. Nor is an employer required to permit an employee to use paid Company hours and Company financed facilities * * * [in order to] practice his religious beliefs.
    * * *
"It is not unreasonable for an employer to require that an employee quietly and unobtrusively practice his faith or lack of faith in such a manner that the employer's economic venture will not be damaged or destroyed."
An employee's compulsion to preach on the job also may severely antagonize his co-workers, as in United Parcel Serv., 76 LA 244, 247 (Darrow, 1981).

[270]MSPB Report, Sexual Harassment in the Federal Workplace: Is It a Problem? (MSPB, 1981).

for dates. But general agreement was not found concerning (5) sexually suggestive looks or gestures, or (6) sexual teasing, jokes, remarks, or questions. Concerning behaviors (5) and (6) the survey indicated that "men were less likely to think that 'sexual looks' and 'sexual comments,' the more ambiguous and prevalent forms of sexual behavior on the job, were sexual harassment, particularly when perpetrated by a coworker." In the latter regard, "men and women were more likely to think that a behavior was sexual harassment if the perpetrator was a supervisor rather than a coworker."[271]

Concerning the underlying nature of sexual harassment, the Report found to be "valid under some circumstances" (1) the view that "sexual harassment is a form of power that is exercised by those in control, usually men, over low-status employees, usually women" (referred to also in the Report as an "abuse of power"); the Report found similarly valid (2) the view that "individuals with certain low-power characteristics, such as youth and low salaries, are more subject to sexual harassment than others"; but the Report rejected (3) the view that "sexual harassment is an expression of personal attraction between men and women that is widespread and cannot and should not be stopped."[272]

The MSPB Report stated the belief, among other conclusions, that "sexual harassment is a problem encountered by a significant number of women," and that the "experience frequently has a negative emotional and physical effect on the victim and may diminish job performance."[273]

---

[271]The source of all information included above in this paragraph is MSPB Report, p. 4. The Report states at page G-4 that writers and researchers seem to agree that "sexual harassment is nonreciprocal behavior and does not include mutually satisfactory, no-job-related-strings-attached relationships in the office." Also regarding what does *not* constitute sexual harassment, consider the statement in Heelan v. Johns-Manville Corp., 20 FEP Cases 251, 255 (USDC, 1978), that under the Civil Rights Act

"A cause of action does not arise from an isolated incident or a mere flirtation. These may be more properly characterized as an attempt to establish personal relationships than an endeavor to tie employment to sexual submission. Title VII should not be interpreted as reaching into sexual relationships which may arise during the course of employment, but which do not have a substantial effect on that employment. In general, we would limit Title VII claims in this area, as suggested by one commentator, to 'repeated, unwelcome sexual advances' which impact as a term or condition of employment."

[272]MSPB Report, p. 101.

[273]MSPB Report, pp. G-8 and G-9, where a portion of the Report's "Conclusion" states:

"What has been established is that sexual harassment is a problem encountered by a significant number of women. The most common forms of harassment are comments and nonverbal behaviors such as gesturing and touching; far less common are instances of attempted or actual rape or sexual assault. It is not uncommon for harassment to be in the form of demands tied to negative job consequences if rejected or to positive consequences if accepted.

"Victims often are young and working in low-status occupations, but it is clear that women of all ages, both married and unmarried and working at all levels in a range of jobs, experience harassment. Victims respond in a variety of ways, most often by ignoring the behavior, attempting to avoid the harasser, and/or asking the harasser to stop; some leave the situation altogether by transferring or quitting. Few victims report the incidents or file formal complaints; those who do get little help and sometimes suffer negative consequences as a result. The experience frequently has a negative emotional and physical effect on the victim and may diminish job performance.

"Little is known about the harassment of men or same-sex harassment. Nor is much known about the way different factors in the workplace influence the incidence and nature of harassment."

It is now established that under certain conditions sexual harassment constitutes a type of sex discrimination prohibited by Title VII of the Civil Rights Act of 1964. However, it must be stressed that case law in the area of sexual harassment is still developing, and that there has been diversity of thought and of results on some of the important issues in sexual harassment litigation.

The most favorable approach to sexual harassment as a violation of the Act, from the viewpoint of the victimized employees, appears to be that taken in guidelines which the Equal Employment Opportunity Commission adopted in 1980. In this regard, it was stated by one analysis that "For the most part, the EEOC's guidelines follow the court decisions that are favorable to employees"; it was also stated that "Except perhaps for its suggestion that employees who are disadvantaged by another worker's submission to sexual advances may have a claim of their own, it does not appear that the Commission has gone beyond the most liberal of the pro-employee [court] rulings."[274] However, while the EEOC guidelines may serve to persuade, they are not binding on any court.[275]

The cornerstone provision of the EEOC sexual harassment guidelines states that:

"(a) Harassment on the basis of sex is a violation of Sec. 703 of Title VII. Unwelcome sexual advances, requests for sexual favors, and other verbal or physical conduct of a sexual nature constitute sexual harassment when (1) submission to such conduct is made either explicitly or implicitly a term or condition of an individual's employment, (2) submission to or rejection of such conduct by an individual is used as the

---

[274]"EEOC's Adoption of Guidelines Forbidding Sexual Harassment in the Workplace," 105 Analysis 21, 24, LRR Yearbook 395, 398 (1980). The EEOC guidelines are published in 29 C.F.R. §1604.11 (1983). For discussion of court decisions, the EEOC guidelines, and other aspects of sexual harassment as a violation of Title VII, see Burge, "Employment Discrimination—Defining an Employer's Liability Under Title VII for On-the-Job Sexual Harassment: Adoption of a Bifurcated Standard," 62 N.C.L. Rev. 795 (1984); Cohen & Vincelette, "Notice, Remedy, and Employer Liability for Sexual Harassment," 35 Lab. L.J. 301 (1984); Note, "Sexual Harassment Claims of Abusive Work Environment Under Title VII," 97 Harv. L. Rev. 1449 (1984); Conte & Gregory, "Sexual Harassment in Employment: Some Proposals Toward More Realistic Standards of Liability," 32 Drake L. Rev. 407 (1983); Lindenberger, "What Behavior Constitutes Sexual Harassment?" 34 Lab. L.J. 238 (1983); Rasnic, "The Evolvement of an Action for Sexual Harassment Under Title VII," 26 St. Louis U.L.J. 875 (1982); Adams, "Sexual Harassment and the Employer-Employee Relationship," 84 W. Va. L. Rev. 789 (1982); BNA Editorial Staff, Sexual Harassment and Labor Relations (BNA Books, 1981); Martin, "EEOC's New Sexual Harassment Guidelines: Civility in the Workplace," 5 Nova L.J. 405 (1981); Greenbaum & Fraser, "Sexual Harassment in the Workplace," 36 Arb. J. No. 4, p. 30 (1981); Hill & Behrens, "Love in the Office: A Guide for Dealing with Sexual Harassment Under Title VII of the Civil Rights Act of 1964," 30 De Paul L. Rev. 581 (1981); Meier, "Expanding Title VII to Prohibit a Sexually Harassing Work Environment," 70 Geo. L.J. 345 (1981); Murphy, "Arbitration of Discrimination Grievances," Proceedings of the 33rd Annual Meeting of NAA, 285, 290–294 (BNA Books, 1981); MacKinnon, Sexual Harassment of Working Women (1979); Seymour, "Sexual Harassment: Finding a Cause of Action Under Title VII," 30 Lab. L.J. 139 (1979); Backhouse & Cohen, The Secret Oppression: Sexual Harassment of Working Women (1978); Lawrence, Sex Discrimination in the Workplace (Center for Compliance Information, 1978); Note, "Sexual Harassment and Title VII: The Foundation for the Elimination of Sexual Cooperation as an Employment Condition," 76 Mich. L. Rev. 1007 (1978); Weisel, "Title VII: Legal Protection Against Sexual Harassment," 53 Wash. L. Rev. 123 (1977); Rhodin, "Employment Discrimination—Sexual Harassment and Title VII," 51 N.Y.U. L. Rev. 148 (1976).

[275]The EEOC guidelines of course may be persuasive upon arbitrators as well as courts. For cases in which arbitrators utilized the guidelines, see Arbitrator Madden in 82 LA 921, 925; Heinsz in 80 LA 19, 21; Cohen in 78 LA 690, 695; Yarowsky in 78 LA 417, 422.

basis for employment decisions affecting such individual, or (3) such conduct has the purpose or effect of unreasonably interfering with an individual's work performance or creating an intimidating, hostile, or offensive working environment."[276]

For employment in the federal public sector the Office of Personnel Management issued a Government-wide policy statement describing sexual harassment both as a prohibited personnel practice and as a form of employee misconduct.[277] Sexual harassment should be and probably is equally subject to censure in the state public sector.[278]

---

[276]29 C.F.R. § 1604.11(a). The EEOC guidelines also state that:

- The determination by EEOC of the illegality of alleged sexual harassment "will be made from the facts, on a case by case basis." 29 C.F.R. § 1604.11(b).
- The employer "is responsible for its acts and those of its agents and supervisory employees with respect to sexual harassment regardless of whether the specific acts complained of were authorized or even forbidden by the employer and regardless of whether the employer knew or should have known of their occurrence." 29 C.F.R. § 1604.11(c), which states also that as used in the guidelines the term "employer" applies to an employer, employment agency, joint apprenticeship committee, or labor organization. One of the various questions upon which court decisions are in conflict is whether the doctrine of *respondeat superior* is applicable so as to make the employer liable for a supervisor's sexual-harassment conduct regardless of whether the employer has knowledge of that conduct. See the writings cited above in this topic.
- With respect to sexual harassment by fellow employees, the employer "is responsible for acts of sexual harassment in the workplace where the employer (or its agents or supervisory employees) knows or should have known of the conduct, unless it can show that it took immediate and appropriate corrective action." 29 C.F.R. § 1604.11(d).
- Under certain circumstances an employer may "be responsible for the acts of non-employees, with respect to sexual harassment of employees." 29 C.F.R. § 1604.11(e).
- An employer "should take all steps necessary to prevent sexual harassment from occurring." 29 C.F.R. § 1604.11(f).
- An employer may be liable for sex discrimination against an employee who is denied an employment opportunity or benefit which was granted instead to another employee because of "submission to the employer's sexual advances or requests for sexual favors." 29 C.F.R. § 1604.11(g). This provision, which apparently was not based upon any actual court decision, has been described as "noble in theory but only empty words in application" because of proof problems. Martin, "EEOC's New Sexual Harassment Guidelines: Civility in the Workplace," 5 Nova L.J. 405, 416 (1981).

For cases illustrating that illegal sexual harassment may be found where an employee is subjected to conduct creating a hostile working environment for the employee, see Katz v. Dole, 31 FEP Cases 1521 (CA 4, 1983), where the Federal Aviation Agency was held responsible for the sexual harassment of a female air traffic controller who had been subjected to extremely vulgar and offensive sexually related epithets by fellow controllers and supervisory personnel; Bundy v. Jackson, 24 FEP Cases 1155 (D.C. Cir., 1981), the court ruling that the victim of sexual harassment did not have to prove that she resisted the harassment or that any resistance caused a loss or denial of tangible job benefits; Continental Can Co. v. State of Minn., 22 FEP Cases 1808 (Minn. S.Ct., 1980), where, among other abuses, male co-workers had made sexually derogatory statements and verbal sexual advances to a female employee, a violation of the Minnesota Human Rights Act being found by application of principles developed under Title VII of the Civil Rights Act of 1964. In Goodwin v. Circuit Court of St. Louis County, 34 FEP Cases 347 (CA 8, 1984), a judge's derogatory statements about women in the workplace, *even if made in jest*, were weighty evidence in finding that a female hearing officer was discriminatorily transferred.

[277]MSPB Report, Sexual Harassment in the Federal Workplace: Is It a Problem?, p. F-1 (MSPB, 1981), where it is also noted that OPM (1) defined sexual harassment as "deliberate or repeated unsolicited verbal comments, gestures, or physical contact of a sexual nature which are unwelcome," and (2) declared that "sexual harassment is unacceptable conduct in the workplace and will not be condoned." In United States Army Signal Center, 78 LA 120, 128 (1982), Arbitrator Malcolm J. Hall declared that "Sexual harassment should not be tolerated any place"; in this case he upheld the discipline of a male instructor who was charged by female soldiers with touching their breasts in a manner which each thought to be more than accidental while giving instructions.

[278]For example, see University of Missouri, 78 LA 417, 423–424 (Yarowsky, 1982), upholding discharge of a supervisor for putting his arm around the waist of one female employee, looking and smacking his lips and commenting on the attractiveness of a second employee, and casting

In the private sector, too, sexual harassment is considered to be a form of employee misconduct. In this regard, the arbitration of sexual harassment cases in the private sector generally involves grievances challenging the discharge or discipline of an employee for misconduct based in whole or in part upon alleged sexual harassment of another employee.[279] This contrasts sharply with sexual harassment litigation instituted under the Civil Rights Act, for the latter actions will be brought by an employee who allegedly has been the victim of sexual harassment by another individual.

Many arbitrators have upheld discharge or discipline as assessed by the employer against employees for behavior of types which constitute sexual harassment under views noted above in this topic.[280]

In other cases misconduct in the form of sexual harassment was found but the penalty as assessed by the employer was refused by the arbitrator on the basis of mitigating factors or as having been excessive under the circumstances of the offense.[281] Under the circumstances or because of the quality of proof in some cases no penalty was permitted against the employee charged with sexual harassment.[282]

---

penetrating looks at a third employee to the point that the employee imagined herself "undressed"; this conduct of the supervisor created stress and anxiety among the female employees that affected their mental health and interfered with their job performance.

[279]In addition to the coverage of such cases below, see discussion by Marmo, "Arbitrating Sex Harassment Cases," 35 Arb. J. No. 1. p. 35 (1980). For one of the rather rare arbitration cases in which the grievant alleged that she was the *victim* of sexual harassment, see Hopemen Bros., 75 LA 944, 946–948 (Fogel, 1980), where the grievant alleged that the situation for which she was discharged had resulted dually from sexual harassment against her by supervision and from an antifemale work environment. Also see Braniff Airways, 66 LA 421, 427 (Lieberman, 1976), where the grievant was the victim of sexual ostracism.

[280]For cases upholding discharge, see Arbitrator Madden in 82 LA 921, 922–923, 925 (male employee with poor work record made persistent and continued advances to several female co-workers, creating offensive working environment and causing loss of work time in their efforts to avoid him); Daughton in 82 LA 640, 641–642 (grabbing, hugging, and kissing co-worker on three separate occasions—the grievant, a leadman, had an unblemished work record but he knew prior to engaging in this behavior that company policy did not tolerate sexual harassment); Neas in 78 LA 985, 998–999 (calling female supervisor an obscene name and making obscene gesture toward her—grievant had a poor disciplinary record and he had failed to respond to corrective discipline); Cohen in 78 LA 690, 694–696 (grievant relentlessly harassed female co-worker about twice his age through obscene gestures and demeaning slurs); Kaufman in 74 LA 1281, 1282–1284 (threat to rape co-worker—there had been prior incidents involving physical touching of females by grievant and his record afforded "virtually no mitigating factors"); Larkin in 62 LA 1272 at 1272, 1274 (grievant made sexual advances to co-employee in elevator on two successive days and he was guilty of similar conduct toward another female employee on a previous occasion). For cases upholding a lesser penalty as assessed by the employer, see Arbitrator Cox in 81 LA 459, 460 (grievant boasted to co-worker of having touched the co-worker's girlfriend, another co-worker, on the breast and rump); Abrams in 80 LA 133, 134–135 (breast touching incident); Penefield in 75 LA 592, 596 (physical restraint of female employee by grievants). It may be noted that discharge for sexual harassment of customers has also been upheld. See Nabisco Foods Co., 82 LA 1186, 1191–1192 (Allen, 1984), citing other cases also upholding discharge for such misconduct.

[281]See Arbitrator Heinsz in 80 LA 19, 21–22 (incident involving touching of breast and making kissing sounds—discharge reduced to seven-month suspension); Stoltenberg in 79 LA 940, 942–943 (entering women's bathhouse—discharge reduced to 60-day suspension without accrual of seniority); Flannagan in 73 LA 520, 522 (entering women's restroom—discharge was too severe for the offense and was reduced to suspension for period from discharge until reinstatement); Cocalis in 71 LA 54, 56 (sexually offensive words and gesture—discharge reduced to suspension for period from discharge until reinstatement).

[282]See Louisville Gas & Elec. Co., 81 LA 730, 733 (Stonehouse, 1983); Godchaux-Henderson Sugar Co., 75 LA 377, 380 (Barnhart, 1980).

Fraternization, Intermarriage of Employees, Employment of Relatives, Married Employees

Management sometimes promulgates rules prohibiting fraternization among its employees, intermarriage of employees, employment of relatives of its employees, and employment after marriage of certain employees. Arbitrators appear to subject such rules to close scrutiny, but uphold them when justification is shown.[283]

In one case, a company promulgated a rule prohibiting male and female employees from fraternizing after a "love triangle" of employees ended in a shooting incident. Upholding the discharge of an employee who likewise became involved in a love triangle situation, the arbitrator held that the rule was reasonable under the facts.[284] Similarly, discipline was upheld when an airline pilot violated a rule prohibiting dating between male crew members and hostesses, the arbitrator stating that the company has a right to establish and enforce regulations, prohibiting practices "which could reasonably result in detriment, damage, and even disaster" in the areas of safety and comfort of passengers in flight, the company's good name, and the reputation of its hostesses.[285]

As to a company policy against hiring or continuing the employment of relatives, it has been held that in the absence of special circumstances or a showing that intermarriage of employees created a particular problem or had an adverse effect upon the operation of the plant, a rule requiring the resignation or termination of one of the employees could not stand.[286] But another arbitrator upheld a com-

---

[283]5 U.S.C. § 7202(a) authorizes the President to "Prescribe rules which shall prohibit, *as nearly as conditions of good administration warrant*, discrimination because of marital status" in federal employment (emphasis added). The ambivalence with which Congress thus approached the matter of "marital status" discrimination often may be equaled by that of arbitrators called upon to decide private-sector cases involving intermarriage of employees, employment of relatives, and the like, since arbitrators also recognize that company rules on such matters hold the potential both for good and for bad. In the present topic the Authors discuss arbitration decisions only. The body of court decisions and statutory law, both federal and state, bearing on the types of matters treated in the topic appears to be fairly extensive but also fairly fragmented. For discussion of the court decisions and statutory provisions, see Edelman, "Marital Status Discrimination: A Survey of Federal Case Law," 85 W. Va. L. Rev. 347 (1983); Wexler, "Husbands and Wives: The Uneasy Case for Antinepotism Rules," 62 B.U.L. Rev. 75 (1982); Kovarsky & Hauck, "The No-Spouse Rule, Title VII, and Arbitration," 32 Lab. L.J. 366 (1981).

[284]Alterman Foods, 45 LA 459, 460–461 (Woodruff, 1965).

[285]Braniff Airways, 29 LA 487, 489 (Yeager, 1957).

[286]Hayes Indus., 44 LA 820, 823 (Teple, 1965), stating that the policy was not clearly stated or consistently followed. For other instances in which the arbitrator sustained a grievance protesting some type of adverse treatment of the grievant based upon company policy restricting the hiring or continued employment of relatives, see Arbitrator Seidman in 83 LA 163, 165 (overruling discharge of employee for marrying co-worker with whom he had lived for six months—rule prohibiting employment of relatives was unjustly applied in the particular case since both employees had been with the company for about six years during which time they "clearly demonstrated that they were capable employees, had no attendance problems, were loyal to the Company, presented no problems with respect to the scheduling of work, and demonstrated maturity in their personal relationships with fellow employees," Arbitrator Seidman declaring that the inchoate threat that they would become entirely different employees the day after their marriage was not a sufficient basis for discharge in the face of this actual record of service, attendance, and loyalty to the employer); Peterschmidt in 74 LA 886, 888 (employer could not bar senior employee's bid for a job because he would be reporting directly to a relative—the policy asserted by the employer had not been posted or communicated to the employees, and the

pany policy not to hire the spouse of an incumbent employee (male or female) in the interest of a harmonious working relationship in the bargaining unit and to maintain order and efficiency; he placed the burden upon the union to show the unreasonableness of the policy.[287]

In the latter regard, Arbitrator F. Jay Taylor upheld a company's policy prohibiting relatives from working on the same shift in the same department, but he placed the burden on the company to justify application of the policy in the specific instance:

> "The Company has made a strong case to demonstrate that its so-called 'Relative Policy' is based on sound practice. Certainly it is recognized that actual conflicts can result when employees have to make a decision concerning their relatives. Favoritism, disharmony, etc., among relatives could prove disruptive to the working force. That is why I believe that an anti-nepotism rule, as long as it is consistently and fairly applied, is a proper exercise of sound management.
>   * * *
> "[T]he Company is not proscribed from promulgating such a policy even though it was unilaterally adopted by Management. Invoking the rule,

---

collective agreement established seniority and qualifications as the only factors limiting the right to bid for jobs); Roberts in 74 LA 650, 657–658 (employer's recently adopted policy against hiring spouses could not be reasonably interpreted to apply to employees who subsequently marry, nor did the employer establish that the policy is related to its business needs so as to justify intrusion into the personal lives of employees after hire); Ross in 71 LA 959, 962–963 (company policy against employment of a relative in the same department or under the supervision of a relative was improperly applied to grievant since the policy had not been adequately communicated to the employees and had been inconsistently applied, but apart from these deficiencies Arbitrator Ross inferred that the policy probably could be justified by business needs); Springfield in 70 LA 788, 791–792 (company rule stated that "should any two employees become married, either the husband or wife will be required to resign"—Arbitrator Springfield stressed that this rule was adopted "before the changing life-style of the next decade gave rise to a more general acceptance of living together," and he held that the rule accordingly should not "be construed to include 'cohabitation' as being equivalent to 'becoming married'"); Steese in 64 LA 276, 278; Wyckoff in 53 LA 1238, 1240. Also see Roberts in 70 LA 719, 724–725 (discharge of union representative who married company president's daughter was improper, the daughter having resigned her position in personnel office thus removing possibility of conflict of interest in making available to grievant confidential information to which she had access); Rule in 69 LA 290, 293 (company admitted that one reason for denying grievant a promotion as senior employee was his father's managerial position with the company—Arbitrator Rule found that the company had no general policy against the employment or promotion of relatives, and he stated that without such a policy uniformly enforced, the company's action in the present case "must be considered an unreasonable action if not a discriminatory one," notwithstanding the possibility that some employee "might complain or even grieve about nepotism if the Grievant were promoted").

[287]Studebaker Corp., 49 LA 105, 110 (Davey, 1967). For other cases upholding the employer's policy regarding relatives, see Arbitrator Kossoff in 73 LA 512, 516 (upholding discharge for falsely answering "no" to question in employment application asking whether applicant had relatives employed by the company, Arbitrator Kossoff stated that the company "had a rational policy which made the hiring of relatives the exception rather than the rule," that it "is a policy which, although not uniformly followed in industry, is not uncommon among employers," and that the management rights clause expressly reserved the company's right to manage the business "according to its best judgment"); Kelliher in 69 LA 509, 511 (retail company had right to transfer clerk in one store to another store located four miles away following his marriage to co-worker, the policy against relatives working in same store being "based upon prior experiences and problems encountered in the management of the stores" such as the unlikelihood of one spouse testifying against another where removal of company product is involved, scheduling problems when both spouses need to be off at the same time, and the possibility that marital disharmony might be carried over onto store premises); Novak in 68 LA 1309, 1314 (finding that "the Company has experienced problems with married couples taking simultaneous sick leaves and concomitant personal leaves leaving vacancies on the production line," he concluded "that the Company was completely within its rights to establish the rule that they will not hire a spouse of a present employee or a partner living with an employee").

however, must be demonstrably related to the efficient operation of the plant or necessary to the management of the business. And this is what the Company has failed to prove [in the present instance]."[288]

A no-marriage policy for airline stewardesses and women employees in other industries has been the subject of many arbitration cases. While upheld as reasonable in earlier cases, arbitrators have been reluctant to uphold such policy in later years. They cite the fact that "times have changed and views have been altered by experience."[289] In holding such a rule unreasonable in an airline stewardess case, Arbitrator Saul Wallen found that its justification as a safety measure is minimal, its value as a sales promotion device is doubtful, and it is not in conformity with modern attitudes and trends of thought.[290] Even where the contract gave the company the right to terminate six months after marriage, the right was held to be limited to exercising the option by using good faith judgment and discretion (with respect to individual stewardesses) to determine whether the employee's performance of her duties was adversely affected by her marriage.[291]

In another industry, the contract in the case specified certain grounds for the termination of employees but did not include marriage or pregnancy. The arbitrator held that marriage or pregnancy per se was not cause for discharge. However, as a matter of safety and health, management may "promulgate certain rules relating to layoff when pregnancy is advanced to a point where hazards arise to the employee, the unborn infant, and perhaps other employees."[292]

Privacy, Dignity, and Peace of Mind

In management's direction of the enterprise, situations sometimes occur in which employees allege an invasion of their right of privacy or an infringement upon their dignity or peace of mind. Employees have invoked such rights in attempts to protect personal aspects of their industrial life in such diverse situations as a safety

---

[288]Temple-Eastex Inc., 69 LA 782, 786 (1977), where Arbitrator Taylor also stated: "I have found no showing * * * that the transfer [requested by grievant] would have had an adverse effect on the operations of the business or that the performance of his duties would have been adversely affected. He would not have been working in such close proximity to his brother as to create a legitimate Company concern. There was no evidence that one would exercise supervisory functions over the other. Quite simply, there were no insurmountable difficulties. Thus, my reasoning is not to invalidate the rule, only that I find that it is not enforceable in this particular instance."
[289]Southern Airways, 47 LA 1135, 1141 (Wallen, 1966). Also see Braniff Airways, 48 LA 769, 770 (Gray, 1965).
[290]Southern Airways, 47 LA 1135, 1141 (1966). Also see Arbitrator Gray in 48 LA 769, 770; Kelliher in 48 LA 734, 737–738. Cf., Arbitrator Kahn in 48 LA 727, 733–734.
[291]American Airlines, 48 LA 705, 723–724, 727 (Seitz, 1967).
[292]Alwin Mfg. Co., 38 LA 632, 638–639 (Sembower, 1962). Also finding that marriage is not proper cause for discharge, Tennessee Coal, Iron & R.R. Co., 11 LA 1062, 1065 (Seward, 1948). Where the contract provided that marriage would not disqualify a stewardess from employment with the company but that pregnancy would, the employer properly discharged a stewardess who had concealed her pregnancy and falsely secured sick leave in Western Air Lines, 54 LA 600, 603 (Wyckoff, 1970).

rule prohibiting the wearing of finger rings,[293] rules against fraternization or intermarriage of employees,[294] the regulation of employees' personal appearance,[295] requirements for giving reasons for leave of absence,[296] and the situations discussed hereinbelow.

Arbitrators have attempted to strike a balance between the personal rights of the employee and the rights of the company in the conduct of the business, considering such factors as whether there was a legitimate business need for management's action or rule,[297] whether there were reasonable safeguards for employee rights,[298] and whether management's action resulted in a substantial change in working conditions.[299]

The observations of some arbitrators in regard to claimed rights of privacy, dignity, and peace of mind are noted below in the setting of the particular situations to which they apply.

Disclosure of Information to Employer

Employees sometimes have claimed a right of privacy in resisting the employer's requirement to disclose certain information for company records. However, where such information was reasonably necessary for the proper conduct of the business, management could require the disclosure.

Thus, a company was upheld when it required an employee to disclose his unlisted phone number so that he could be contacted for necessary overtime assignments, the arbitrator stating:

> "It is my opinion that it is not an invasion of privacy for the Company to have an employee's phone number, any more than it could be considered an invasion of privacy to have his home address, or for that matter, to talk to the employee. If being able to call an employee on the telephone could be considered an invasion of his privacy, then so could just talking to him be so considered, and this is obviously just plain unadulterated nonsense."[300]

---

[293]Bethlehem Mines Corp., 48 LA 765, 766 (Strongin, 1967), where the arbitrator found the rule to be reasonable, rejecting the union's claim that the rule, as it pertains to wedding bands, infringes upon the employee's religious and moral beliefs.

[294]See this Chapter, topic entitled "Fraternization, Intermarriage of Employees, Employment of Relatives, Married Employees."

[295]See this Chapter, topic entitled "Personal Appearance: Hair and Clothes."

[296]See this Chapter, topic entitled "Leaves of Absence."

[297]For example, see Arbitrator Karlins in 78 LA 505, 507–508; Mueller in 77 LA 233, 236; Stutz in 55 LA 910, 915–916; Keefe in 53 LA 525, 530; Scheiber in 53 LA 312, 317–320; Seinsheimer in 52 LA 755, 758; Shister in 50 LA 65, 67–68; Mittenthal in 46 LA 335, 338; Delany in 44 LA 563, 564.

[298]For example, see Arbitrator Roberts in 73 LA 34, 45–48; Griffin in 51 LA 1121, 1124; Kelliher in 51 LA 469, 470.

[299]For example, see Arbitrator Karlins in 78 LA 505, 508; Fleischli in 66 LA 19, 24; Stutz in 55 LA 910, 914–916 (safety and health clause); Keefe in 53 LA 525, 530 (maintenance of working conditions clause); Delany in 44 LA 563, 564 (maintenance of working conditions clause).

[300]Wyandotte Chems. Corp., 52 LA 755, 758 (Seinsheimer, 1969). In Amoco Oil Co., 64 LA 511, 513–514 (1975), company policy regarding exposure to toxic substances required female employees of childbearing age to notify the company doctor without delay when they had reason to believe they were pregnant. Arbitrator Leo C. Brown noted several important interests of the company served by the policy and he stated that the "crucial question is whether those interests can be adequately protected in some manner less invasive of an employee's privacy than that embodied in" the policy. There being "no showing in the record that they can be so protected," he upheld the policy and the discharge of an employee who had violated it.

Another case involved a conflict of interest situation in which a broadcasting company was held entitled to require members of its news staff to fill out a questionnaire regarding financial interests. Regarding the claimed right of privacy, the arbitrator stated:

> "The litmus test of a careful examination makes it clear that the right of privacy is, at best, a limited right which, in general, protects the individual from having his name, picture, actions and statements commercially made public and exploited without his consent. This right, however, only safeguards him from the publication of his private statements or actions."[301]

It was held that the rule was a reasonable method of supervising employees and did not trespass upon their right of privacy since there was no public disclosure of private facts and the information was sought for the legitimate and limited business reason of insuring the absence of bias in reporting the news.[302]

On the other hand, in ordering the reinstatement of employees who had been discharged for refusing to complete a fidelity bond application form which would require them to reveal their indebtedness, sources of income, and property owned, Arbitrator George R. Fleischli declared:

> "The requirement that the employes complete and sign the fidelity bond application form constituted a substantial intrusion into their privacy and caused them to assume obligations which are greater than those otherwise imposed by law on employes who are accused of dishonesty. It was more than a mere work rule. It constituted a substantial change in the conditions of employment in the very real sense that their continued employment hinged on their willingness to complete and sign the form."[303]

In another case an employee was held justified in refusing to sign a form authorizing the release of medical records (which the employer sought in order to check the truthfulness of the employee's employment application), the arbitrator finding the form "so lacking in specificity and so broad in its application and coverage" as to be "a license for a fishing expedition into his private affairs."[304]

Name Tags

In two cases, arbitrators considered the question of whether management can require employees to wear their surnames on their uniforms. One case involved city police while the other involved ser-

---

[301]National Broadcasting Co., 53 LA 312, 317 (Scheiber, 1969).

[302]Id. at 317–320, where the question of self-incrimination was also discussed. Also see Scheiber, "Tests and Questionnaires in the Labor-Management Relationship," 20 Labor L.J. 695, 697–702 (1969).

[303]Pilgrim Liquor, 66 LA 19, 24 (1975).

[304]Bondtex Corp., 68 LA 476, 478 (Coburn, 1977). Also see Arbitrator Gibson in 71 LA 457, 459–460. Where an employee had used her diary to refresh her recollection prior to testifying, the company "was entitled to see those entries in the diary that were relevant to the proceedings and presumably reviewed by" the employee but the company "was not entitled to insist on inspection of the full diary by its own counsel." Pacific Nw. Bell Tel. Co., 81 LA 297, 300 (Gaunt, 1983).

vice employees of a gas company. In both, the union argued that adding the employee's surname to his uniform was a change in working conditions and that the employer was required to bargain on the issue. In both cases, the union also argued that the wearing of surnames on their uniforms would subject the employees (and their families) to harrassment and an invasion of their privacy. The arbitrator in the police case found (1) that the duty to bargain had been complied with, (2) that while individual officers and their families had received harrassing, threatening, and indecent phone calls, the evidence did not support a conclusion that increased harrassment resulted from the use of name tags, and (3) that there was a reasonable basis for issuing the name tag order (i.e., to improve the police-community relationship).[305]

The arbitrator in the gas company case, finding no legitimate business need, stated:

> "The protested surname display constitutes a recognizable and material change in the working conditions of employees which can believably be expected, under entirely plausible and predictable circumstances, to have adverse reactions on the peace-of-mind, personal security and family privacy of at least certain individuals, thereby subjecting them to unjustifiable and avoidable hardship and inconvenience—if not outright personal hazard."[306]

Observing Employees at Work

It has been said that "Management is properly concerned with the employee's work performance, what he does on the job and whether he obeys the plant's rules and regulations."[307] Such matters are regularly noted by supervisors. However, employees have sometimes alleged that management has gone beyond the proper limits of its right to observe them for the aforementioned purposes.[308]

Thus, in one case employees complained that intensive observations by a production engineer in cooperation with the foreman created undue "alarm and annoyance" and "fear and apprehension." The arbitrator found that the engineer was performing a proper management function, and he noted that "Although emotional tranquility is a

---

[305]City of Boston, 55 LA 910, 915–916 (Stutz, 1970), where the arbitrator, notwithstanding such findings, stated that if harassment should increase, and the increase can be attributed to the name tags, the union would have a sound basis for demanding that the use of name tags be abandoned. The *City of Boston* decision was stated to be "persuasive authority" and was quoted with clear approval in City of Minneapolis, 78 LA 504, 509 (Karlins, 1982), where a requirement that police officers wear name tags on their uniforms was upheld. In Briggs & Stratton Corp., 77 LA 233, 236 (Mueller, 1981), the company had the right to institute an employee identification program requiring the employee's picture, social security number, and date of birth; legitimate business interests (computerized payroll and clocking in and out procedures) were served by including the social security number and date of birth on identification cards, which interests "outweigh the alleged potential harm and inconvenience that may befall an employee" if the card is lost.

[306]Michigan Consol. Gas Co., 53 LA 525, 529 (Keefe, 1969).

[307]FMC Corp., 46 LA 335, 338 (Mittenthal, 1966).

[308]For related discussion, see Chapter 8, topic entitled "Evidence Obtained by Allegedly Improper Methods."

condition much to be desired in labor relations, it is not one of the rights guaranteed by law or by the contract between the parties."[309]

In two cases involving the installation of closed circuit television to observe workers arbitrators reached opposite conclusions. In one, where there had been loss of material and equipment, the company was upheld, Arbitrator Richard Mittenthal stating:

> "One of the supervisor's principal functions is to observe employees at work. Surely, such supervision cannot be said to interfere with an employee's right of privacy. The same conclusion should apply in this case. For all the Company has done is to add a different method of supervision to the receiving room—an electronic eye (i.e., the television camera) in addition to the human eye. Regardless of the type of supervision (a camera, a supervisor, or both), the employee works with the knowledge that supervision may be watching him at any time. He has a much better chance of knowing when he is being watched where there is no camera. But this is a difference in degree, not a difference in kind. For these reasons, I find there has been no interference with the employee's right of privacy."[310]

A maintenance of working conditions clause was crucial to the other case, in which there was no indication of any need to supplement the already adequate supervision.[311] Ruling that the television cameras must be removed, Arbitrator Hubert T. Delany stated:

> "While I do not base my opinion on the Union's argument of the employees' legal 'right of privacy,' nor on the argument advanced by it on unlawful 'surveillance' and 'spying,' I do agree that this argument cannot be totally overlooked since I find that the TV equipment does vitally affect the employees' working conditions."[312]

Secret surveillance has been upheld in two cases, one of which involved the right of the employer to hire private checkers (whose identity need not be revealed) to follow and check the work performance of delivery truck drivers.[313] The other case involved a tele-

---

[309]Picker X-Ray Corp., 39 LA 1245, 1246 (Kates, 1962). Similarly, F & M Schaefer Brewing Co., 40 LA 199, 200–201 (Turkus, 1963), upholding management's right to conduct time studies and finding that in doing so management was "neither 'spying on employees' nor improperly 'maintaining them under surveillance.'"

[310]FMC Corp., 46 LA 335, 338 (1966), emphasizing that an individual's right of privacy serves to protect him against the publication of his *private* statements or *private* actions and that an employee's actions during working hours are not private actions. The *FMC* decision was quoted with approval in Cooper Carton Corp., 61 LA 697, 699–700 (Kelliher, 1973), upholding the employer's right to install two television cameras to enable its vice president and production manager, both of whom had heart conditions, to observe operations being run by foremen; Arbitrator Kelliher pointed to the broad management clause, to the absence of any provision requiring the maintenance of conditions that are beneficial to employees, and to the fact that "No employee has been disciplined based on these T.V. observations." In Colonial Baking Co., 62 LA 586, 591 (1974), Arbitrator Alex Elson noted the company's statement that the TV camera installation there was for security and not for disciplinary purposes, and he limited his holding to approving the surveillance system for security purposes only.

[311]EICO, Inc., 44 LA 563, 564 (1965).

[312]Id. at 563, and he found that while the company must have a good deal of discretion in carrying on its operations, use of the TV system imposed an "appreciable and intolerable burden" on the employees.

[313]Kroger Co., 40 LA 316, 317–318 (Reid, 1963). The union had argued that the "secret agents" following the drivers in unmarked cars on unfrequented highways at night put the drivers under an "intolerable strain." Id. at 317. For discussion on the evidential use of "spotters," see Chapter 8, topic entitled "Right of Cross-Examination."

phone company's use of remote listening devices to monitor secretly the telephone operators' performances. There, the union argued that "policy reasons" exist "for preventing any information gathered by secret and remote observations to be used for disciplinary purposes," explaining that such use would produce tensions upon the subject employees and that their performance would vastly improve if they were assured that such surveillance would not be so used. However, Arbitrator Russell A. Smith stated that such considerations "are more pertinent for collective bargaining than to the arbitral forum," and he commented:

> "I do not mean to suggest that 'policy considerations' will under no circumstances be relevant to a determination of the extent of management's right to make use of techniques for keeping employees under surveillance. Modern electronics has produced a variety of possibilities which, if used to the fullest extent, could disclose, surreptitiously, an employee's every move and every conversation while in the plant, whether directly work related or not. This could, allegedly, be the 'Brave New World' of Huxley or Orwell's world of 1984! Some of these developments in employee surveillance might well raise the important question whether there is not, indeed, a 'right of privacy' which employees may invoke to protect some, at least, aspects of their industrial life."[314]

But he said that in the case before him no such issue was actually presented for decision and he made no determination as to the existence or extent of the grievant's right of privacy.[315]

Checking Out

It has been held that the right of employees to absent themselves from their work area to use restrooms or for rest periods was not violated by the employer's requirement that they sign a "check-out" list; the arbitrator found that the rule was not unreasonable and that the evidence did not establish that management had invaded the employees' privacy by using the lists as a basis for improper questions regarding personal habits of individual employees.[316] Similarly, a requirement that employees sign a slip to be placed in a special box when their foreman is unavailable to give them permission to leave was held reasonable since it implemented a long-standing rule that employees must obtain permission to leave their work places.[317]

While the company may require "clocking out and in" when an employee leaves his (or her) work station for personal reasons, the

---

[314]Michigan Bell Tel. Co., 45 LA 689, 695 (1965).
[315]Id. at 696.
[316]Elgin Instrument Co., 37 LA 1064, 1068 (Roberts, 1961), where employees had abused the rest period privilege. In Cagle's Poultry & Egg Co., 73 LA 34, 48 (Roberts, 1979), it was held that management had the right to install a special time clock outside restrooms and to require employees to punch their time cards on entering and leaving, under guidelines instituted to prevent abuse of emergency use of restrooms; also, the number of emergency visits could be generally limited to 20 times in any four-week period. In this case it was also found, however, that the guidelines had not been administered in a reasonable manner, and this was ordered to be corrected.
[317]Certain-Teed Prods. Corp., 38 LA 46, 48 (Sembower, 1962).

application of such rule must be reasonable and nondiscriminatory. So stated Arbitrator John W. Teele, who found the rule before him to be unreasonable to the extent that it was a "source of embarrassment" to female employees who were required to have their male foremen note the reason for the "clock-out." He also found the rule to be discriminatory in that it was applied unevenly in different parts of the plant.[318] While the company was ordered to revoke the rule, it was given an opportunity (after a waiting period of 30 days) to devise an alternate method of accounting for restroom time or to reinstate the "clock-out" method but with proper safeguards to eliminate discrimination, protect the individual's privacy, and avoid undue embarrassment.[319]

Another arbitrator likewise did not quarrel with the company's right to issue a check-out rule directed at abuse of relief privileges, but he found the rule before him to be unreasonable in that it was vague and imprecise in several important respects; he stated further that even if the rule could be assumed to achieve its objective of eliminating abuses, "it does so at a considerable price in terms of actual or threatened invasion of modesty and the ordinary amenities."[320]

Inspecting Employee Lockers, Purses, or Briefcases

In several cases, where management had serious problems with thefts or where it had other reasonable cause, a rule or practice requiring employees to submit purses, briefcases, or lockers for inspection was upheld.[321] The arbitrator in a purse case emphasized that

---

[318]Gremar Mfg. Co., 46 LA 215, 219 (1965). Concerning the invasion of privacy issue, he stated: "Whether the routine involved an invasion of personal privacy probably boils down to a matter of degree, and it is sufficient, perhaps, to find affirmatively as to embarrassment." He cited other cases dealing with check-out rules and drew certain general conclusions from them. Id. at 218–219.

[319]Id. at 220. In Schmidt Cabinet Co., 75 LA 397, 400 (1980), the employer adopted a rule requiring employees to "punch out before entering restroom (except at breaks and noon) and punch back in before returning to" the job. The rule cautioned that "Excessive trips or too long trips may cause disciplinary action." Pointing out that there were no female supervisors in the plant and that monitoring of the rule by male supervisors resulted in embarrassment of female employees, Arbitrator Harry Berns struck the rule down as being unreasonable. In doing so he declared that while "no one can blame the Company for wanting to curb the wasteful practices of a small number of loiterers," other "Methods can surely be found to reduce the incidence of loitering without loading on all employees an onerous and humiliating timekeeping procedure which is seldom used in industrial practice."

[320]Detroit Gasket & Mfg. Co., 27 LA 717, 722 (Crane, 1956). In one case, the employer approached the problem of loitering in restrooms and defacing of toilet doors by removing the doors to the toilets, later agreeing to replace them when the union agreed to cooperate in trying to prevent such loitering and defacing. The case went to arbitration when a modest employee, who felt the doorless toilets were "not decent or proper," was discharged for leaving his department to use the restroom (with doors intact) in another department. He was reinstated without back pay (a loss of 6½ months). See Chris-Craft Corp., 45 LA 117, 118–119 (Autry, 1965).

[321]See Arbitrator Griffin in 83 LA 27, 30; Sergent in 76 LA 249, 253; Oppenheim in 70 LA 326, 329 (upholding the company's right to inspect lockers, he stated that "as long as the employee is notified that an inspection will take place and he will not be taken by surprise and that a Union representative is present as a member of the inspection team, there is no necessity for the locker holder to be present"); Martin in 68 LA 811, 816–817; Kelliher in 51 LA 469, 470; Shister in 50 LA 65, 67–68; Williams in 39 LA 934, 936–937. But see Emerson in 66 LA 480, 481. In Fruehauf Corp., 49 LA 89, 90–91 (Daugherty, 1967), a past practice of inspecting outgoing employees' lunch buckets for possible pilfered company property was found to support the company in searching incoming employees' buckets for liquor on a preholiday shift where

employees are entitled to reasonable safeguards but have a duty to cooperate. He found that the company took all reasonable procedural precautions to protect the employee's privacy and dignity when the security guard exhibited her badge and asked the employee to come to a closed room where the inspection would be made only by the female security guard.[322]

Another arbitrator cautioned that the company must not act in a discriminatory, capricious, arbitrary, or unreasonable fashion but must have a reasonable basis for its search of employee lockers—in this case, the company's search for missing company property was a reasonable basis and the manner of conducting the search was proper.[323]

Use of Personal Radios

It has been stated that "Absent any privilege on the part of the employees which would amount to a contractual right to bring radios into the shop and using them in an unrestricted manner," the company can promulgate rules absolutely or partially restricting employee use of personal radios in the plant so long as such rules are not arbitrary, unreasonable, or discriminatory.[324] Thus, a company restriction on use of radios may be found proper if it is based upon adequate reasons such as insuring the quality and quantity of production and promoting safety in the shop.[325]

---

drinking on the job had been a problem on such shifts in the past. For cases involving other security or search measures taken by management, see Arbitrator Keefe in 80 LA 693, 696–697 (employee suspected of selling drugs possibly prevented discovery of evidence by violating direct order not to flush toilet—discharge upheld); Kossoff in 80 LA 413, 417–418 (upholding metal detector and random inspection procedures adopted to guard against theft and violence—employees had been informed of the procedures and this "removes any likelihood that any employee will be forced to incriminate himself"); Keefe in 74 LA 163, 165 (upholding discharge for insubordination in refusing to produce newspaper in which grievant had folded plastic bag suspected of containing narcotics); Martin in 73 LA 396, 398 (upholding discharge of employee who refused to raise pants leg to reveal nature of bulges that guard had observed); Bode in 69 LA 217, 222–223 (upholding ban on use of large drink coolers as lunch boxes since such use could facilitate bringing alcohol into plant and removing employer's property from plant); Simon in 68 LA 797, 803–804 (upholding rule requiring warehouse employees to wear slacks and to place shirt inside belt waist before entering and leaving warehouse, the rule being justified to remedy a serious theft problem); Ross in 66 LA 307, 310–311 (upholding discharge for refusing to allow search of box-shaped bulge on back of leg while leaving plant); Lipson in 65 LA 1295, 1298–1299. For related discussion, see Chapter 8, subtopic entitled "Failure of Grievant to Testify," and topics entitled "The Lie Detector" and "Evidence Obtained by Allegedly Improper Methods." Also see Craver, "The Inquisitorial Process in Private Employment," 63 Cornell L. Rev. 1 (1977).

[322]Alden's, Inc., 51 LA 469, 470 (Kelliher, 1968). Regarding privacy for female employees, cf., Arbitrator Martin in 68 LA 811, 816–817.

[323]International Nickel Co., 50 LA 65, 68 (Shister, 1967). Also see Arbitrator Kossoff in 80 LA 413, 418–419. For cases involving demands to be paid for time lost by employees in connection with employer searches, see Arbitrator Fitch in 74 LA 1055, 1058; Allen in 73 LA 103, 106–107; King in 65 LA 59, 61–62.

[324]Anaconda Aluminum Co., 51 LA 281, 283–284 (Dolson, 1968), finding no established practice to support the alleged right and finding that the company's restrictions were reasonable and proper, but also finding that the rules were discriminatorily applied.

[325]See Arbitrator Lynch in 76 LA 561, 562; Johnson in 75 LA 1226, 1231–1232 (bus company could prohibit drivers from using radios while performing their duties after it received passenger complaints about loud volume causing them to miss their stops); Lewis in 53 LA 1024, 1026–1027; Dolson in 51 LA 281, 283–284. Also see Yagoda in 44 LA 1034, 1040. Cf., Ables in 71 LA 963, 968–969 (federal agency employer did not have right to require employee to discontinue watching her battery-powered TV at desk in her work station during lunch break).

Management's right in this regard may be limited somewhat where there is a well-established practice of allowing employees to play their radios. Thus, it has been held that in the absence of misuse of the radios or adverse effect on the employees' work, the company was not justified in discontinuing a long-time practice of playing radios although it could promulgate reasonable rules to control the type of program as well as the volume of sound.[326]

While one arbitrator ruled that the company was unreasonable in imposing an absolute ban on radios in a plant which had a "well established traditional right of employees to play radios," he also ruled that the company has "ULTIMATE authority to ban employee radios when such a ban appears to be—after suitable alternatives have been tried—the only practical ('reasonable') solution."[327]

In another case where permission had always been required to bring in radios, the arbitrator held that "the practice existed only subject to management permission, modification, or prohibition," and that the employer could properly refuse to permit it to spread to a newly opened building.[328] That arbitrator stated that "it is relevant that the use of personal radios seems to come closer to the area of traditional and conventional management discretion concerning productive factors and influences, than to that of employee rights not so intimately connected with the productive process."[329]

Coffee Making by Employees; Free Coffee

As to employee use of coffee-making equipment in work areas, management has been held entitled to prohibit such use in the absence of an express recognition of the privilege in the agreement or a showing of a well-established practice.[330] In a case where the contract had a maintenance of practices clause and there was an established practice of employees brewing their coffee, it was held that the company violated the contract by installing coffee vending machines and requiring the removal of employees' coffee-making equipment; but the

---

[326]Minnesota Mining & Mfg. Co., 49 LA 332, 334 (Jensen, 1967), where there was a 20-year practice of permitting radios during nonworking time; Bangor Punta Operations, 48 LA 1275, 1276 (Kates, 1967), where the practice of playing radios during working time was recognized but the company could also substitute "piped-in" music or company-provided radios at reasonable locations. In FWD Corp., 71 LA 929, 931–932 (Lynch, 1978), it was held that the employer improperly discontinued a past practice of allowing employees to play their radios; the employer was directed to reinstate the prior practice and to bargain with the union to agreement or impasse prior to changing the practice.

[327]Square D Co., 66–1 ARB ¶8134, p. 3493 (Kahn, 1963), finding that a "reasonable procedure" would include efforts by supervision to discuss the problem of objectionable radio playing with the offending employee, and if that failed, to discuss it with the union.

[328]Eastern Air Lines, 44 LA 1034, 1038, 1040 (Yagoda, 1965), where the contract contained a clause maintaining privileges so long as they are not abused.

[329]Id. at 1040.

[330]Benson Mfg. Div., 52 LA 571, 574 (Belcher, 1968), finding that the alleged practice was not approved but was intermittent and sometimes surreptitious; Ohio Power Co., 50 LA 501, 504 (Teple, 1967), stating that "The kind of equipment which can be brought onto the Company's premises, and the use of Company time to operate such equipment, would appear to be well within the general authority and control of management" unless the agreement expressly recognizes the particular privilege.

company could impose requirements for "orderly and reasonable use of the equipment for coffee and related beverage making" and could require employees using this equipment to be responsible for "orderly housekeeping practices and any abuses of excessive time use on the equipment."[331]

Where there is an established practice of supplying free coffee to employees during coffee breaks and/or lunch periods, arbitrators have held that the employer may not unilaterally discontinue such practice,[332] but that the company may change the manner in which it supplies the coffee.[333]

Dangerous Weapons on Company Property

The company has a duty to protect the health and safety of its employees, which duty includes "maintaining the right kind of environment where employees can be trusted not to commit acts of violence against other employees."[334] To this end it may promulgate and enforce rules dealing with dangerous weapons.[335] Thus, discharge or discipline has been upheld when an employee was guilty of infraction of a no-weapons rule.[336]

Even where there is no express written rule prohibiting firearms or knives on company premises, the company can prohibit them and can discipline employees for bringing such weapons to company premises. "Some conduct is so obviously contrary to good sense, notice of that fact by all employees may be assumed."[337] But where "conditions of permissiveness" existed, the arbitrator reduced discharge to five

---

[331]Sheridan Mach. Co., 37 LA 831, 832–833 (Gomberg, 1961), also holding that management could "protect itself against the erosion of its rights" by employee extension of the coffee-making privilege to using sandwich grills and frying and cooking pans. A binding practice was also found by Arbitrator Abrams in 72 LA 470, 474–475 (practice allowing employees to drink coffee in work area during working hours); Lynch in 71 LA 929, 931 (practice allowing employees to use their personal coffee pots).

[332]Beech-Nut Life Savers, 39 LA 1188, 1191 (Handsaker, 1962); Cushmans Sons, 37 LA 381, 383, 385 (Scheiber, 1961).

[333]Pillsbury Co., 34 LA 615, 616 (McIntosh, 1960).

[334]Albritton Eng'g. Corp., 46 LA 857, 859 (Hughes, 1966). Also see Michigan Standard Alloy, 53 LA 511, 513 (Forsythe, 1969).

[335]See Brodie Indus. Trucks, 50 LA 112, 114 (Teele, 1968); Campbell Soup Co., 2 LA 27, 31 (Lohman, 1946).

[336]See Arbitrator Flagler in 79 LA 645, 648–649; Staudter in 79 LA 508, 511–512; Ryder in 53 LA 1028, 1029–1030; Williams in 53 LA 545, 546–547; Willingham in 50 LA 403, 412 (many cases cited); Teele in 50 LA 112, 114–115; Larson in 61–3 ARB ¶8665. But the evidence of such infraction must be convincing. See Michigan Standard Alloy, 53 LA 511, 513 (Forsythe, 1969). In Navy Exch., 52 LA 1142, 1144 (Williams, 1969), it was found that grievant was not the aggressor but drew a knife in a "defensive posture."

[337]Ross-Meehan Foundries, 55 LA 1078, 1080 (King, 1970), nevertheless holding that discharge was too severe under the peculiar circumstances (grievant's son had been shot by a fellow employee), and reinstating grievant with only two days disciplinary suspension. In accord with the above-quoted statement, Brown & Williamson Tobacco Corp., 50 LA 403, 412 (Willingham, 1968). Discharge was upheld in International Harvester Co., 50 LA 766, 767–768 (Doyle, 1968), citing many cases; Inland Container Corp., 28 LA 312, 314 (Ferguson, 1957). Discharge was reduced to a long suspension in the absence of a rule in Owens-Corning Fiberglas Corp., 54 LA 419, 420 (Reed, 1970); American Synthetic Rubber Corp., 46 LA 1161, 1163–1165 (Dolson, 1966), involving other charges as well. For cases where the company alleged a work-related incident occurring off the company premises, see International Paper Co., 52 LA 1266, 1269 (Jenkins, 1969); Bird & Son, 30 LA 948, 950–951 (Sembower, 1958).

months disciplinary suspension, emphasizing that if the company had warned the employees about a new rule prohibiting firearms and if there had been a "line of demarcation between the * * * permissiveness and a new strict policy," discharge would have been upheld.[338]

Company Liability for Employee's Damaged or Stolen Property

When an employee's equipment or personal property is damaged or stolen while on company premises (most cases have involved tools), the employee sometimes claims entitlement to recompense from the company. In some cases the company was held liable for all or part of the loss.[339] In many other cases the company was not held liable.[340] The elements argued by the parties or considered by the arbitrator in these cases included: (1) whether the contract's safety and health provision was applicable, (2) whether a bailment relationship existed between the parties, (3) whether the company had exercised reasonable care or had been negligent in regard to the employee's property, (4) whether the contract contained language express or implied to impose liability upon the company, and (5) whether there had been contract negotiations on the subject.

Most arbitrators have rejected the contention that the safety and health provision of the contract applies in cases where an employee's equipment or personal property is stolen or damaged while on company premises. Arbitrator Edwin R. Teple stated that such provision "clearly relates to the employees themselves, and not to their equipment or personal possessions."[341] Arbitrator Marion Beatty felt that "to apply provisions of the working agreement to issues here is reaching way out, for it would take an extremely liberal interpretation of

---

[338]Bright-O, Inc., 54 LA 498, 500 (Mullin, 1970).

[339]See Arbitrator Williams in 79 LA 487, 491–493 (employer ordered to reimburse employees for stolen tools "Based purely upon its failure to communicate" to employees its policy that they could take their tools home or leave the tools on company premises at their own risk); Goodman in 79 LA 153, 157–158; Bard in 75 LA 615, 621–623; Ruben in 72 LA 568, 576–578; Tyer in 70 LA 994, 995–996; Ipavec in 67 LA 358, 360–361 (employer must reimburse employees for vandalism damage to their vehicles parked near job site, the employer having failed to provide adequate parking on job site as required by the agreement); Richman in 61 LA 1245, 1248–1249; Amis in 54 LA 430, 432; Lennard in 49 LA 76, 79–80; Cohen in 43 LA 114, 115; Handsaker in 22 LA 482, 483–484; Luskin in 14 LA 641, 644. For two cases in which the arbitrator mentioned the matter of insurance carried by the employee, neither arbitrator considering this to be a relevant factor in determining the employer's obligation, see Arbitrator O'Connell in 75 LA 724, 727, and Ipavec in 67 LA 358, 361. Also see Roumell in 77 LA 57, 57–58.

[340]See Arbitrator Neyland in 81 LA 224, 227; Allen in 79 LA 179, 180; Griffin in 77 LA 1145, 1150–1151; Dennis in 74 LA 525, 528; Mewhinney in 71 LA 852, 855–856; Cohen in 71 LA 679, 683–684; Harrison in 70 LA 584, 586–587 (employee not entitled to reimbursement for cost of protective jacket stolen from locker, the determining factor being that the garment, though "a quite desirable piece of protective clothing," was not required by the employer); Whaley in 63 LA 76, 78; McDaniel in 59 LA 826, 828; Teple in 55 LA 700, 703–704; Kesselman in 54 LA 240, 242–243; Jenkins in 53 LA 963, 964; Gorsuch in 69–2 ARB ¶8750; Cahn in 51 LA 636, 638; Hampton in 50 LA 348, 350–351; Leonard in 66–1 ARB ¶8362; Block in 47 LA 574, 575; Beatty in 41 LA 727, 729; Valtin in 37 LA 195, 196, and in 32 LA 124, 125–126; Crawford in 36 LA 1136, 1137.

[341]Standard Prods. Co., 55 LA 700, 704 (1970). Accord, Arbitrator Ruben in 72 LA 568, 574; Kesselman in 54 LA 240, 243; Stouffer in 46 LA 106, 108. Also see Hampton in 50 LA 348, 350.

the working agreement to read into it a duty of the Company to insure against loss of the personal effects of an employee under any circumstances."[342] Arbitrator Rolf Valtin stated that it "would be a strained interpretation" of the safety clause to hold the company responsible for the safekeeping of all personal belongings stored in company-provided lockers.[343] And Arbitrator Donald A. Crawford wrote: "Nor do safety clauses as used in labor agreements generally provide for damage suits unless there is a specific provision to that effect."[344]

However, Arbitrator Melvin Lennard stated: "While I believe that it is true general safety clauses are designed primarily to safeguard the health and personal security of employees, such clauses should not be held to exclude *all* items of personal property." He postulated that eyeglasses, hearing aids, and items of clothing actually being worn by the employee while at work "seem almost to be extensions of the employee's person," that such items as well as tools the employee is required to furnish make possible the proper performance of the employee's work, and that management and employee interests in having the job well done "form one of the bases for interpreting" the safety clause to cover such personal effects and employee-owned tools. On this basis he concluded: "* * * I believe that when the present employer agreed [in the contract] to 'make reasonable provision for the safety and health of its employees at the plant,' it undertook to do that for both the personal health and safety of employees and also for their clothing being worn, their eyeglasses, hearing aids, etc., and also for tools which the employer requires the employee to bring in and work with."[345] However, he cautioned that nothing in his decision "should be construed as holding or even suggesting that this employer is, or must become, an insurer of employees' tools," but that his decision was directed to the company's obligation to observe an adequate standard of care where locked tool boxes were left on the plant premises in the exclusive custody of the employer while their owners were away from the plant.[346]

The applicability of bailment concepts is sometimes considered by arbitrators in determining the responsibility of the company for the safekeeping of employee property left or stored on plant premises. In this regard Arbitrator Louis C. Kesselman noted two schools of thought, with arbitrators of one school suggesting that "a bailment relationship for the mutual benefit of both parties has been created by

---

[342]Trans World Airlines, 41 LA 727, 729 (1963), where the union argued for the application of the safety and health provision and a general provision requiring cooperation between the company and the union.

[343]Bethlehem Steel Co., 32 LA 124, 126 (1959). Accord, Arbitrator Bard in 75 LA 615, 620.

[344]Curtiss-Wright Corp., 36 LA 1136, 1137 (1961), where an employee claimed damages for the cost of replacing eyeglasses broken because of the company's alleged negligence regarding defective machinery. Similarly, Arbitrator Neyland in 81 LA 224, 227 (concluding that the safety and health clause did not "either directly or implicitly" contemplate that the arbitrator "is to engage in the resolution of claims for damages based on negligence theories brought by employees against the Company").

[345]Sargent-Fletcher Co., 49 LA 76, 78 (1967).

[346]Id. at 80.

the Company's requirement that the mechanics furnish their own hand tools for the Company's benefit and by the Company's awareness of and acquiescence to having the tools stored on its premises due to the physical problem of removing them each night." Under this rationale, he said that if a bailment relationship does exist in a given case, it is then proper for the arbitrator to determine whether the company has been negligent in safeguarding the property in question. Arbitrators of the other school of thought, which Arbitrator Kesselman endorsed, reason as follows: (1) The arbitrator's duty is to interpret the parties' agreement, which is the law in every case before him. (2) A bailment relationship is a legal one which may or may not be incorporated into the contract—if it is, it should be enforced by the arbitrator. (3) If a bailment relationship is not a part of the contract, the arbitrator has no authority to enforce it or to rule on the question of negligence because such a ruling cannot be enforced by him.[347]

Some arbitrators have cited the company's negligence in ruling for the employee,[348] while other arbitrators have found for the company since it had made a reasonable effort to protect the employee's property.[349] Arbitrators have also looked to the contract and, finding nothing there to impose liability on the company, have denied the grievance or found it nonarbitrable (some referring the grievant to a civil court of law).[350] In some cases it was emphasized either that

---

[347]Commercial Motor Freight Co., 54 LA 240, 243–244 (1970), citing arbitrators for both lines of reasoning. For later cases finding bailment, negligence, and consequent employer liability, see Arbitrator Bard in 75 LA 615, 620–622; Ruben in 72 LA 568, 576–577. In Arden Mayfair Co., 63 LA 76, 78 (1974), Arbitrator W. Paul Whaley stated that "as an arbitrator, my concern is with the language in the contract between the parties, not with whether a bailment existed between" the employee and the company.

[348]See Arbitrator Tyer in 70 LA 994, 996; Lennard in 49 LA 76, 79–80 (company did not provide a locked area for tool boxes or a system to safeguard tool box keys left with the guard); Cohen in 43 LA 114, 115 (others had access to locked storage area); Handsaker in 22 LA 482, 483–484; Luskin in 14 LA 641, 644. In Sharpe-Saunders Constr., 79 LA 153, 155, 157 (Goodman, 1982), the agreement required the employer to "provide an adequate tool house or storage room for the safekeeping of the employee's tools," and this was held to "impose a higher standard than that of reasonable care"; the employer was liable for loss of employee tools by theft where it "did not take every reasonable precaution," as evidenced by the fact that it provided greater security for its own tools than for those of the employee. In Plough, Inc., 54 LA 430, 432 (Amis, 1970), the contract required the company to furnish and maintain satisfactory lockers, and while grievants were out on strike the company emptied their lockers (piling the contents in boxes) to make lockers available for employees hired to replace the strikers. The arbitrator held that the company failed to exercise reasonable care and therefore was required to compensate the grievants for damage to and loss of their property. Arbitrators Lennard in 49 LA 76, 79, and Cohen in 43 LA 114, 115, commenting on the advantage to the company from the presence of employee tools on the premises, noted that the company's obligation varies from exercising greater care when the employee's property is in its exclusive custody to exercising lesser care when the custody is shared or is almost exclusively in the employee himself.

[349]See Arbitrator Allen in 79 LA 179, 180; Griffin in 77 LA 1145, 1150; Dennis in 74 LA 525, 528; Teple in 55 LA 700, 704 (fence with barbed wire on top, locked gate, guards); Gorsuch in 69–2 ARB ¶8750; Stouffer in 46 LA 106, 108; Valtin in 37 LA 195, 196 (new locks on locker-room doors, janitors instructed to keep doors locked, employees invited to report suspicious behavior, locker rooms included in rounds of plant guards); Valtin in 32 LA 124, 125–126. In Fruehauf Corp., 50 LA 348, 350–351 (Hampton, 1968), where a company rule held employees responsible for 50 percent of the value of company tools lost while in their possession, it was ruled that since the employer and employees each took reasonable security precautions neither was required to compensate the other for loss of tools by theft.

[350]See Arbitrator Neyland in 81 LA 224, 227; Allen in 79 LA 179, 180; Teple in 55 LA 700, 703 (stating that he "firmly believes that the Company cannot properly be held to be an insurer of property of employees left or stored upon the plant premises unless the collective agreement contains express terms imposing such broad liability"); Kesselman in 54 LA 240, 243–244;

contract language protecting the employees was sought unsuccessfully by the union in negotiations or that the problem of tool thefts was so widely recognized in the industry that the parties would have provided protection if they had so intended.[351]

Union Bulletin Boards

Collective bargaining agreements often contain clauses stating that the company will provide a bulletin board for the posting of union notices, usually specifying notices of union meetings, elections, social activities, and general union business (or "official" union business).[352] Such clauses also may contain a proviso that the notices must be "approved," or "signed," or "notated" by the company. In some cases disagreement has arisen between company and union as to whether company approval was wrongly withheld or whether the notices the union sought to post were proper notices within the meaning of the contract.

In fact, the issue before the arbitrator in contractual "bulletin board" cases ordinarily does concern the *content* of the employee communication, as distinguished from the *time* or *place* of the communication. If the content is proper there ordinarily will be no issue as to time or place.[353] This contrasts with cases involving employee com-

---

Jenkins in 53 LA 963, 964; Cahn in 51 LA 636, 637–638 (finding a bailment relationship and a possible *legal* obligation on the company, but no contract violation); Stouffer in 46 LA 106, 108; Crawford in 36 LA 1136, 1137; Beatty in 41 LA 727, 729 (rejecting the union's bailment argument).

[351]See Arbitrator Whaley in 63 LA 76, 78; Jenkins in 53 LA 963, 964; Yagoda in 48 LA 1040, 1043–1044 ("Silence on this subject has significance here as an absence of intent, because of the fact that the subject of protection of employees of this kind against loss of tools is a well-known one to negotiators in this industry. It has been dealt with in other contracts by the same Union bargainers"); Block in 47 LA 574, 575; Leonard in 66–1 ARB ¶8362 (contract provision obligating the company to replace employee tools that "have been broken, lost or worn out in the performance of work for the Company" held not to apply to stolen tools in view of union's unsuccessful attempt in two previous negotiations to have the term "stolen" inserted in the clause). Also see Cohen in 71 LA 679, 683–684.

[352]Even where the agreement did not contain a bulletin board clause, the union had a right under the NLRA to use the plant bulletin board since the employer had discriminatorily denied its use to the union while permitting it for personal messages of employees and for group notices by other organizations. NLRB v. Honeywell, Inc., 114 LRRM 3658 (CA 8, 1983). In another case, a union's action was in a sense a discriminatory denial of bulletin board use, where the union whose collective agreement gave it the right to use a bulletin board for official union business violated the NLRA by removing material that a dissident member had posted criticizing union actions and policies. Helton v. NLRB, 107 LRRM 2819 (D.C. Cir., 1981), the court holding, in disagreement with the NLRB, that the union's action did "restrain or coerce" the employee in violation of § 8(b)(1)(A) of the Act.

[353]There should be no place issue, the place of the communication being the contractually provided bulletin board. There could be a time issue if the employer seeks to regulate even the minimal use of time required for the physical act of posting or seeks to restrict the time for bulletin board viewing. Where the communication is achieved not by use of the bulletin board but by some other method, such as distribution of handbills, a stronger possibility exists for the arbitrator to be confronted with a time and/or place issue. For example, see Arbitrator King in 81 LA 311, 317–318 (federal-sector employees have "no statutory right to distribute literature in work areas during work time, and absent agreement by an agency and bargaining representative, an agency may validly prohibit such distribution"); O'Connell in 74 LA 1270, 1272; O'Neill in 74 LA 99, 104 (upholding discharge of employee who distributed literature during working time); Seidman in 71 LA 999, 1003; Koven in 67 LA 323, 326; Hutcheson in 62 LA 1219, 1220.

munications under the NLRA, where the issue very well may be concerned with *time, place,* and/or *content*.[354]

In regard to the content of bulletin board notices, in arbitration the employer has been upheld in refusing approval of a list of wages paid at another of the company's plants and at a rival company's plant (the bulletin including some controversial and political material which the company alleged would involve it in an unfair labor practice suit),[355] an announcement of the terms of a strike settlement at another company,[356] and a letter which praised and defended the union's activity but derogated and maligned the company.[357]

The company has also been upheld in disciplining employees who have deliberately disobeyed an order of management not to post cer-

---

[354]Regarding *time* and *place* of employee communications under the NLRA, the U.S. Supreme Court has upheld the NLRB's rule that, absent special circumstances, an employer's restriction on employee solicitation during nonworking time and distribution during such time in nonworking areas is presumptively an unreasonable interference with employee rights under the Act. Beth Israel Hosp. v. NLRB, 98 S.Ct. 2463, 2469–2470, 98 LRRM 2727 (1978), holding that a hospital improperly prohibited distribution of an employee publication in its cafeteria, which was patronized primarily by employees. The publication was objectionable to the employer because it disparaged the hospital's ability to provide adequate patient care due to understaffing, but the content of the publication was not the question considered by the Court in this case. For other cases dealing with time and place of employee communications under the NLRA, see NLRB v. Baptist Hosp., 99 S.Ct. 2598, 101 LRRM 2556 (1979); Republic Aviation Corp. v. NLRB, 324 U.S. 793, 16 LRRM 620 (1945). Regarding plant access by nonemployee union organizers for the purpose of communicating with employees, see Hudgens v. NLRB, 96 S.Ct. 1029, 91 LRRM 2489 (1976), holding that it is under the NLRA rather than the First or Fourteenth Amendments that labor may have a right of access to the private property of another person; NLRB v. Babcock & Wilcox Co., 76 S.Ct. 679, 38 LRRM 2001 (1956). Regarding the *content* of employee communications under the NLRA, the U.S. Supreme Court did deal directly with the matter of *content* in Eastex, Inc. v. NLRB, 98 S.Ct. 2505, 98 LRRM 2717 (1978). In this case the employer prohibited distribution of a union newsletter in nonworking areas of the plant because the newsletter contained material (making appeals in respect to right-to-work and minimum wage legislation) which the employer found objectionable and which the employer said was unrelated to the employer-union relationship. The Court found "no warrant for the [employer's] view that employees lose their protection under the 'mutual aid or protection' clause of [NLRA § 7] when they seek to improve terms and conditions of employment or otherwise improve their lot as employees through channels outside the immediate employee-employer relationship." 98 S.Ct. at 2512. In holding the employer's prohibition improper the Court stressed that the employer did not show that management interests would be prejudiced by distribution of the literature. The Court would not attempt to delineate precisely the boundaries of the "mutual aid or protection" clause, a task for the NLRB to perform in the first instance as it considers the wide variety of cases that come before it. The Court did indicate, however, that distribution of literature could be prohibited if its content is inflammatory to the point of threatening disorder or interruption of the normal functioning of the business, and also the Court noted that the NLRB had accepted employer disallowance of "purely political" literature even though the election of any political candidate may have an ultimate effect on employment conditions. In Auto Workers Local 174 v. NLRB, 106 LRRM 2561 (D.C. Cir., 1981), the NLRB's view that purely political literature is not protected activity under § 7 was upheld. In Timpte, Inc. v. NLRB, 100 LRRM 2479 (CA 10, 1979), the court upheld the discharge of an employee for refusing to stop distributing union campaign literature containing "vulgar and indecent" language; in denying enforcement of an NLRB order, the court held that the "combination of profanity and filthy language" in the employee's disparagement of co-workers, union stewards, and management was "indefensible" and unprotected by NLRA § 7.

[355]Reynolds Metals Co., 13 LA 278, 280 (Kleinsorge, 1949).

[356]Danly Mach. Co., 13 LA 499, 500–501 (Luskin, 1949), finding that "the announcement contained material that is not customarily and generally considered an official Union announcement of the kind and character usually posted on bulletin boards where the bulletin boards are controlled by the Company." Also see Arbitrator Oppenheim in 66 LA 449, 451–452 (posting of newspaper advertisement concerning strike by another union against another company could be prohibited by employer based upon its objection that the appeal was inflammatory); McCormick in 63 LA 588, 593 (employer could remove poster urging boycott of another employer's product).

[357]General Elec. Co., 31 LA 924, 925 (LaCugna, undated). The contract provided that company approval would "not be unreasonably withheld," and the arbitrator found that the company's refusal to approve the letter was not unreasonable in view of its controversial and derogatory tone. Also see Arbitrator Eisenberg in 61 LA 750, 753.

tain materials on the union bulletin board, such as materials of a political and controversial nature.[358] In another case discharge was upheld when an employee (after being warned) repeatedly posted on the union bulletin board items which were "inflammatory and defamatory," such as a notice charging that the company practiced favoritism and nepotism in job promotions. To the employee's contention that his right of free speech was being violated, the arbitrator stated:

> "In my opinion, although an employee while at work in his employer's plant may not be muzzled, he nevertheless has no unhampered right to voice opinions about his employer at the plant during his working time of such kind and in such manner as clearly to tend to disrupt employee morale or interfere with the orderly and efficient operation of the plant."[359]

In two cases where the contracts provided for union bulletin boards for the posting of "official" notices but did not require company approval, it was held that the company could remove or require the union to remove a notice containing the names of nonunion employees of the company. The arbitrator in one of these cases considered the notice as detrimental to work discipline and likely to create an inflammatory response.[360] The arbitrator in the second case found that the list of names was not "official business" of the union, and he found further:

> "[T]he postings tended to incite prejudice, animosity, hatred, discrimination and intimidation against certain employees of the Company because of their Non-Union affiliation. * * * Such conclusion is not predicated on a baseless assumption—any ordinary, reasonable man could predict such a resulting effect."[361]

However, in a third case where the contract provided for union bulletin boards but did not expressly require company approval of notices, Arbitrator John J. Flagler found that the company had been unsuccessful in its attempt to negotiate a contractual restriction on the subject matter of bulletin board notices, the company having obtained only a commitment during negotiations that the union would "try to cooperate." He declared that there "is nothing in the words 'try to cooperate' which binds the Union to accept the Company's determination of what is an appropriate or inappropriate subject of a notice

---

[358]Cyprus Gardens Citrus Prods., 50 LA 1183, 1186 (Christon, 1968), stating that "The substance of the particular material which the Union posted was completely unrelated to the plant's operations, or to the Union's activities, either in or out of the plant." Also see Arbitrator Brown in 59 LA 513, 515 (upholding suspension of union president who did not seek permission from employer before posting notice urging boycott of employer's product—the notice, which was posted at request of another union engaged in a strike at another plant of the employer, was contrary to the interest of the employer and did not pertain to normal union business); Seward in 53 LA 228 at 228 (where, after express warning, an employee deliberately violated a long-standing company rule barring the posting of notices without management's permission). Cf., Calhoon in 64 LA 593, 595.

[359]Beaver Precision Prods., 51 LA 853, 854–855 (Kates, 1968), where there was no express contractual provision pertaining to bulletin boards, but the company as a matter of practice provided some for the union's use. Also finding no denial of the right of free speech, Union Carbide Corp., 44 LA 554, 561 (Stouffer, 1965).

[360]Quaker Oats Co., 64–3 ARB ¶8986 (Bauder, 1964).

[361]Union Carbide Corp., 44 LA 554, 561 (Stouffer, 1965).

to be posted on the bulletin board." Stating that the union argued convincingly that another union's strike "does raise the issue of trade union solidarity," making it fall within "the legitimate business interests" of the union in the present case "to communicate with its members concerning a constituent policy position that the local union has taken to support the striking members of another union," Arbitrator Flagler held that the company acted improperly in removing from the bulletin board a notice urging union members to support a strike by another union against another employer.[362]

Furthermore, even though the contract provided for company approval of notices to be posted, it has been held that the company does not have "an unrestricted right to edit and reject" union notices, and it may not arbitrarily, unreasonably, or capriciously withhold its approval; the arbitrator stated, however, that the company can "reject and refuse to approve for posting notices which contain statements that are derogatory to it and its Supervision, those containing obscene or immoral statements, and those which are patently detrimental or disloyal to the Company, its Management and/or its business." The notice in this case announced a meeting to hear a report of contract negotiations at another plant of the employer, and the arbitrator noted that while the company may have considered the purpose of the meeting to be adverse to its interests, it was not warranted in rejecting the notice.[363]

Another arbitrator, ruling on a company approval clause, stated that "The Company cannot be arbitrary or capricious in making its determination of whether to post a particular notice * * * but has the right to exercise some judgment concerning its approval or willingness for posting a notice."[364] The case before him resulted from the return of two supervisors to the bargaining unit (contributing to the layoff of unit employees). The notice in question charged that such action violated the agreement and further charged that the action was taken by the company in order to cause a wildcat strike so that it could discharge strike participants, thereby breaking the union. However, the notice advised that the union had not authorized a wildcat strike and would fight the employer's action through legal means. The company's reason for not posting the notice was that it was inflammatory, but it offered to post it if objectional portions were omitted. The arbitrator, commenting that the notice had some "rather harsh words" concerning the company's action, held that the notice was union business within the meaning of the union bulletin board provision and that its "main purpose seemed to be to avert a work stoppage." He concluded that the company should have posted the notice, noting that

---

[362]Wisconsin Tissue Mills, 73 LA 271, 273–274 (1979). In Warren City Mfg. Co., 7 LA 202, 206 (Abernethy, 1947), the new contract dropped the company approval requirement and the arbitrator interpreted the bulletin board provision strictly, stating that the contract does not give the company authority to refuse to post "union material submitted by the union" or to remove from bulletin boards "union material posted there by the authorized officials of the union."
[363]Conn Organ Corp., 42 LA 1198, 1200 (Stouffer, 1964).
[364]Fruehauf Corp., 54 LA 1096, 1098 (Marshall, 1970).

the company could have posted a notice of its own to the effect that it was not encouraging a wildcat strike.[365]

In other cases, it has been held improper to reject a notice of a meeting at which a strike vote would be taken,[366] a union version of the plant seniority list,[367] campaign material promoting union membership and characterizing management as being an unfair exacting overseer,[368] and a notice requiring union members to report any management contacts with respect to promotion out of the unit;[369] all of which were viewed as union business.

Thus, the cases noted above indicate that notices for posting on union bulletin boards (1) may not stray in subject matter from the reasonable concept of what constitutes union business at the particular plant, (2) may not be of such a nature as to have a detrimental effect upon employee morale, or of such nature as to inflame employees against each other or against the employer, (3) may not contain statements which defame the employer or are patently detrimental or disloyal to him, and (4) may not be rejected if the notices clearly are matters of "union business" even though they approach being inflammatory or adverse to the company's interests.

It seems reasonable to expect that similar results would also be reached in arbitration cases concerning employee communications by handbills, newsletters, and other methods not involving the use of bulletin boards.[370]

Finally, as concerns constitutional rights, it should be noted that (1) public-sector employees have freedom of speech rights against their employer under the First and Fourteenth Amendments,[371] but (2) a contrary situation exists for private-sector employees, since, as the U.S. Supreme Court has held, "the First and Fourteenth Amendments safeguard the rights of free speech and assembly by limitations on *state* action, not on action by the owner of private property used nondiscriminatorily for private purposes only."[372]

---

[365]Id. at 1098–1099. For another case in which an employer omission was a factor in holding for the union even though its notice "was in poor taste," see Bureau of Prisons, 65 LA 1240, 1244–1245 (Hall, 1975).

[366]Fairchild Engine & Airplane Corp., 16 LA 678, 681 (Jaffee, 1951).

[367]Lennox Furnace Co., 20 LA 788, 789 (Johannes, 1953).

[368]Wisconsin Dept. of Transp., 63 LA 588, 590, 593 (McCormick, 1974).

[369]Walker Mfg. Co. of Wis., 31 LA 80, 81–82 (Luskin, 1958).

[370]For some of the relatively few arbitration cases involving such other methods of employee communications, see Arbitrator Wolff in 78 LA 812, 813–815 (discussing criteria relevant to the wearing of union buttons); Weiss in 76 LA 273, 278 (upholding discharge for distributing purely political literature in plant after being warned); Roumell in 75 LA 83, 96–97 (upholding discharge for distribution of inflammatory literature); Morris in 70 LA 342, 344; Nicholas in 68 LA 1170, 1173–1174 (employer improperly prohibited wearing of T-shirts with slogan urging repeal of state's right-to-work law); Rose in 67 LA 249, 250, 254 (union leaflet maligned management official); Block in 59 LA 219, 223 (employer could prohibit protest signs on toolboxes which were of such nature as to create an unfavorable impression upon customers in the plant).

[371]See Givhan v. Western Line Consol. School Dist., 99 S.Ct. 693, 695–696, 18 FEP Cases 1424 (1979), citing other Supreme Court decisions on such rights. Also see Arbitrator King in 81 LA 311, 318; Sembower in 62 LA 1098, 1101–1102. Cf., Arbitrator Rule in 73 LA 274, 276–277.

[372]Hudgens v. NLRB, 96 S.Ct. 1029, 1036, 91 LRRM 2489 (1976), the Supreme Court quoting its earlier *Tanner* decision. Also see Arbitrator Weiss in 76 LA 273, 276; Roumell in 75 LA 83, 90–91, and in 63 LA 378, 382; Maslanka in 72 LA 968, 971; Morris in 70 LA 342, 343.

Change in Time or Method of Pay

Changes in the time or method of payment of wages sometimes lead to disputes between unions and employers. However, arbitrators agree that unless restricted by the contract the employer may change the time of payment of wages. Thus, arbitrators have upheld a change from weekly to biweekly paydays even though paydays had been weekly for many years.[373] Likewise, the employer was upheld in changing the day of the week on which employees were paid despite the fact that employees had been paid on a particular day for many years.[374]

In cases where the company changed the method of payment from cash to checks (with arrangements to permit employees to cash their checks), and where there was no contractual restriction, arbitrators permitted the company's action even though payment had been in cash for many years.[375] However, in another case, past practice was found to be the decisive factor in denying the company the right to change from hand delivery on company premises to mail delivery of payroll checks. The arbitrator said that this function was not one which fell within the scope of the management rights clause as it was not a question of scheduling production or determining processes of manufacturing. He concluded: "As to their pay fully accrued, employees have rights as creditors, so that decision as to the place where check delivery is to be made is not the exclusive function of management."[376]

---

[373]See Arbitrator Roberts in 50 LA 125, 127–128; Florey in 66–1 Arb ¶8323 (not a local working condition protected by contract); Barrett in 30 LA 100, 104.

[374]See Arbitrator McCoy in 51 LA 577, 578–579 (payday held not to be a "condition of employment" within the meaning of the contract provision requiring bargaining on all conditions of employment); Dugan in 46 LA 1007, 1008 (finding no binding past practice); Gorsuch in 40 LA 417, 422; Kadish in 30 LA 964, 966.

[375]United States Steel Corp., 36 LA 220, 221–222 (McDermott, 1961); Diamond Alkali Co., 38 LA 1055, 1057 (Rubin, 1962), stating: "Nor is the method of wage payment, whether in cash or by check, a type of benefit guarded by the principle of accepted past practice."

[376]Manitowac Shipbuilding, 39 LA 907, 909 (Kovenock, 1962). Also see Peoples Gas Light & Coke Co., 39 LA 224, 225–226 (Davis, 1962), where a "firmly established" past practice was "created" based upon a grievance settlement under which the employer agreed to pay "cash supper allowance," thus precluding the employer from changing to check payments for the period of the current contract. In Union Oil Co. of Cal., 65 LA 1278, 1280 (Coburn, 1976), the company was not liable for late receipt of wages where "the delay was caused solely by the untimely delivery of the paycheck by the U.S. Postal Service and not through any negligence of the Company." However, in National Automatic Sprinkler Assn., 80 LA 800, 803 (Wright, 1983), the agreement expressly provided for eight hours pay when a paycheck is received late and this provision was strictly enforced where delayed payment resulted from a computer breakdown. Also see Arbitrator Christopher in 76 LA 1203, 1211. Cf., Sharnoff in 69 LA 1100, 1101.

Chapter 18

Standards in Arbitration of Interest Disputes

Do Standards Exist?

The nature and proper scope of interest arbitration, as well as the function of the arbitrator in such arbitration, are discussed in Chapter 3. There it is also noted that one of the important reasons why arbitration of interest issues is viewed with suspicion by many persons is the belief that there is an absence of definite criteria or standards to govern the arbitrator. But there are, in fact, a number of standards that can be used and often are used. Many of these standards were used by the National War Labor Board. Not only did the Board give a great impetus to the process of arbitration, but it gave also an impetus to the use of many of these standards.

Sometimes the parties will specify, in their stipulation for arbitration, the standards to be observed.[1] Even if the parties do not stipulate the standards to be observed, the arbitrator generally will make an award based upon one or several of the commonly accepted standards. In such case the selection of the standards used is still determined by the parties, though less directly, since an arbitrator generally will not apply any given standard unless evidence has been introduced to support its application.

The standards used by arbitrators are not pulled out of the air—nor are they artificially created. They are, generally speaking, the very same ones that are used by the parties in their negotiations. But

---

[1]As in 77 LA 667, 674; 65 LA 997, 997–998, 1001; 63 LA 824, 825; 16 LA 933, 935; 12 LA 608,609–610; 11 LA 118, 120. For discussion of the pros and cons of this practice, see Handsaker, The Submission Agreement in Contract Arbitration (U. of Pa. Press, 1952). It has been emphasized that only the parties, not an arbitrator, should place limitations in the collective agreement concerning the standards that may be observed by future interest arbitrators. United Traction Co., 27 LA 309, 317–318 (Scheiber, 1956). Also see Arbitrator Cornsweet in 15 LA 263, 273. For standards (some particularly interesting and unique) specified by collective agreement for use in baseball salary arbitration, and standards prohibited by the agreement, see Grebey, "Another Look at Baseball's Salary Arbitration," 38 Arb. J. No. 4, pp. 24, 26 (1983).

if the arbitrator and the parties all use the same bargaining criteria, how can arbitration successfully resolve disputes where the parties' bargaining has failed? It can do so because the arbitrator is much more likely to be objective and to weigh impersonally the evidence adduced with respect to the various criteria.

Admittedly, most of the criteria are nebulous; but they are equally so whether applied by the parties or by the arbitrator. They are still the same standards regardless of who applies them, and in no case is it possible to determine whether their application is entirely correct. In this regard, one Emergency Board stated:

> "This Board does not believe that there is any mechanical formula by which wages can be determined by these parties in collective bargaining or recommended by an Emergency Board seeking to encourage a settlement. But the Board does believe there are a number of wage standards, many of which have been discussed by the parties, which may be applied to facilitate and to check the judgment of neutrals."[2]

Since a certain amount of risk of misapplication of standards cannot be avoided in any case, it may be better for the parties to resort to arbitration when an impasse is reached in negotiations than for them to pay the price of a strike which would be costly to labor, to management, and also to the public.

Without question the most extensively used standard in interest arbitration is "prevailing practice." This standard is applied, with varying degrees of emphasis, in most interest cases. In a sense, when this standard is applied the result is that disputants indirectly adopt the end results of the successful collective bargaining of other parties similarly situated. The arbitrator is the agent through whom the outside bargain is indirectly adopted by the parties. That the parties may thus indirectly adopt the collective bargain of others is well illustrated by the statement of one arbitration board, which, in applying the "pattern" standard, said through its Chairman, Clark Kerr:

> "There is no magic formula for wage adjudication. Consequently one of the compelling considerations must be what has happened in free and successful collective bargaining. This indicates how experienced bargainers have evaluated the wage influencing factors which have evidenced themselves, and what they consider to be 'just.'
>
> "Arbitration of primary disputes over the terms of a new contract is a substitute for successful bargaining, and the 'pattern' or 'package' indicates what might have evolved from successful bargaining had the parties acted like others similarly situated. Attention to the 'pattern' or 'package,' rather than adherence to any rigid formula, also reduces the risks of parties entering wage arbitration, but also should encourage their own free settlement. It tends to afford equality of treatment for persons in comparable situations. It also provides a precise, objective figure, rather than an artificially contrived rate."[3]

---

[2]Railroads v. Nonoperating Unions, 34 LA 517, 524 (Dunlop, Aaron & Sempliner, 1960).

[3]Pacific Gas & Elec. Co., 7 LA 528, 534 (1947). Also see statement by Arbitrator Roumell in 56 LA 209, 216; Edes in 53 LA 372, 374–375; Gundermann in 39 LA 249, 253. For broader discussion, see Chapter 3, topic entitled "Arbitrator's Function in Interest Disputes."

The existence of standards lends a degree of predictability to interest arbitration, but the arbitrator is anything but a mere automaton. Even with points of reference agreed upon, his discretion is quite broad. He must determine the weight to be given to each of the standards applied in the given case, since rarely is the number of standards under consideration limited to one. His freedom to weigh the standards, to "mix the porridge," so to speak, means that the results will depend upon the way he applies the standards.[4] It may not often be possible or desirable for the arbitrator to make a strict application of the standards. Rather, they must be applied with the end in view of providing a solution that will be satisfactory enough to both sides to be workable. The circumstances of the parties must always be kept in mind. The arbitrator's task is to determine what the parties, as reasonable persons, should have agreed upon by negotiations.[5]

No single standard is available for universal application in all industries and under all circumstances. Arbitrators generally apply a combination of standards, the combination varying from case to case. Each party will advance standards believed to support its position in the given case. Standards that may be applicable in times of prosperity or inflation might be of little value during depressions. The number of standards entitled to be given consideration, and possibly some weight, varies from only one in some cases[6] to as many as 10 or 12 in other cases.[7]

---

[4]"While there are familiar objective wage criteria to guide an arbitrator in a task of this kind, there is an area of discretion left to him in deciding which criteria are most appropriate or controlling. And persons with equal intelligence and integrity might of course differ as to the applicability of any one or number of criteria or as to the weight to be given to them." Houston Chronicle Publishing Co., 56 LA 487, 491 (Platt, 1971). For affirmance of the arbitrator's right to decide which standards are to be accorded weight in the given case, see In re Hopkins; 13 LA 716 (N.Y. Sup. Ct., 1949). Where the submission limited him to consideration of five specified factors and required him to indicate how each of the factors affected his award, Arbitrator I. Robert Feinberg explained his authority as follows: "As the arbitrator reads the stipulation, he is required to determine whether a wage increase is justified by considering only the factors listed therein. On the other hand, it does not appear that all of the factors must necessarily be considered of the same or equal importance. Rather, their relative importance is for the Arbitrator to determine. He is merely cautioned not to consider any other factors." H. Boker & Co., 12 LA 608, 610 (1949). Where the New Jersey Public Utilities Disputes Act provided that decisions should be based on the five standards set forth in the Act, so far as applicable to the matter in dispute, a decision could not be based on consideration of only one of the five standards. In re New Jersey Bell Tel. Co., 15 LA 238, 244 (N.J. Sup. Ct., 1950). For views concerning the extent of consideration which must be given to the various standards listed in statutes covering public-sector disputes, see topic entitled "Standards in Public-Sector Disputes," below.

[5]The arbitrator's freedom to fulfill this task will be restricted if final-offer arbitration is being utilized, and even more so where it is the "total package" rather than "issue-by-issue" variety of final-offer arbitration. For related discussion, see Chapter 2, subtopic entitled "Interest Arbitration Statutes." Sometimes the parties themselves, as reasonable persons and aided by discussions and arguments made in the course of arbitration proceedings on an interest issue, may be able to dispose of the issue themselves. For example, see Air N.Z. Ltd., 77 LA 667, 670 (Feller, 1981). In the course of the proceedings in the latter case the parties were also able to agree upon the disposition of other issues, as Arbitrator David E. Feller explained: "As the meetings progressed, and with some assistance from me when I indicated how I would probably decide, the parties were able to negotiate settlement of most of " the approximately 30 disputed issues. Id. at 669.

[6]As in Waterfront Employers Assn. of Pac. Coast, 5 LA 758, 759 (Kerr, 1946).

[7]See Los Angeles Examiner et al., 20 LA 30, 31–32 (Kerr, 1952); San Francisco Employers Council, 7 LA 35, 38 (Wyckoff, 1946).

Sometimes no indication will be given as to the standards considered in arriving at the award.[8] At other times it is difficult to tell from an award the weight given by the arbitrator to any particular standard. Only a few of the standards can be said to be basically objective. The weighing and balancing process is illustrated by the statement of Arbitrator Benjamin S. Kirsh, who, in speaking of the case before him, said:

> "The adjudication of the various factors which are material to this determination have been carefully and conscientiously weighed by the arbitrator. This case involves a just and equitable evaluation of the totality of the considerations herein described and requires that each material factor be given its proper weight, with the final award representing a fair determination of the entire issue."[9]

Whether this process leads to an award based upon "compromise" is problematical. Often an arbitrator will consciously strive to avoid such a result, and he may deny specifically that the award involves "splitting the difference."[10] In the final analysis, the weight to be accorded a standard in any given case is, or should be, the result of the evidence submitted by the parties in respect to its application. The burden is upon the parties to submit evidence which is both factual and material, for arbitrators can be expected to be "unwilling to enter into the field of speculation."[11]

The remainder of this Chapter is largely devoted to a consideration of each of the standards used with some frequency in interest arbitration. Many of the standards to be considered are of greatest value in the arbitration of disputes involving wages or other "financial" issues. In this regard, the reported arbitration awards indicate that a high percentage of interest arbitrations involve wage or related matters, although other types of issues have also been submitted to interest arbitration.[12]

Arbitrators tend to apply those standards which are sufficiently recognized in practice to warrant acceptance by the parties. The fact that a given standard is advanced in collective bargaining or arbitration does not of itself mean that the standard has been accepted without disagreement or qualification by economists. It is not the arbitrator's function to set forth a systematic theory of wages or working conditions. This does not mean, however, that arbitrators do

---

[8]See Town of Manchester, 68 LA 1097 (Post, 1977); American Overseas Airlines, 6 LA 226 (Lewis, 1947).

[9]Baker & Co., 7 LA 350, 353 (1947). Also see statement by Arbitrator Eisele in 78 LA 1119, 1124; Winton in 72 LA 190, 196; Block in 55 LA 568, 579; Seinsheimer in 54 LA 1069, 1074; Schmidt in 52 LA 1301, 1304; Florey in 51 LA 994, 996; Platt in 50 LA 1103, 1115; Dworkin in 42 LA 548, 553–554; Ross in 29 LA 96, 100; Shipman in 26 LA 651, 659; Kerr in 20 LA 30, 32.

[10]See Billings Contractors' Council, 33 LA 451, 454 (Heliker, 1959); Reliable Optical Co., 7 LA 257, 258 (Rosenfarb, 1947).

[11]St. Louis Pub. Serv. Co., 8 LA 397, 405 (Holland, Anderson & Hollingsworth, 1947). Also see Arbitrator Seinsheimer in 54 LA 1069, 1072; Feinsinger in 16 LA 501, 504.

[12]For an enumeration of some of these other issues and for citation of cases in which they were submitted to arbitration, see Chapter 3, topic entitled "Purpose and Subjects of Interest Arbitration."

not at times consider the theoretical economic effects that may result from the application of a standard.

Prevailing Practice—Industry, Area, Industry-Area

In giving effect to the prevailing practice, an arbitrator relies upon precedent, adopting for the parties that which has been adopted by other parties through collective bargaining or, as sometimes is the case, as a result of arbitration awards. An award based upon application of this standard is not likely to be too far from the expectations of the parties, since most persons in the business community have long accepted the idea that there should be no basic inequalities among comparable individuals or groups.[13]

If the terms of employment of a given employer are below the standard set by the prevailing practice of comparable employers and if no basis exists for a differential, an arbitrator may conclude that an inequality exists. Many arbitration awards have undertaken to reduce or eliminate inequalities, such as inequalities between related industries,[14] inequalities within an industry,[15] inequalities between comparable firms or work within a specific area,[16] and inequalities within the plant itself.[17]

---

[13]See Ross, Trade Union Wage Policy, 74 (1948). Also see Arbitrator Roumell in 78 LA 153, 154–155, quoting Professor Ervin Bernstein. From an arbitrator's viewpoint and as stated by Arbitrator Carlton J. Snow, "comparisons provide valuable insight into the reasonableness of a party's wage demand." City of Havre, Mont., 76 LA 789, 791–792 (1981), where he also recognized certain limitations upon the use of comparisons.

[14]See Arbitrators Cole, Aaron & Wirtz in 19 LA 76, 83; Sullivan in 18 LA 599, 608; Jackson, Healy & Dennis in 7 LA 630, 641; Feinberg in 7 LA 30, 32–33; Wallen, Cahn & Donahue in 4 LA 251, 259–260; Strong, Wolfe & Borgmann in 3 LA 41, 81–84.

[15]See Arbitrator Nicholas in 73 LA 223, 226–227; Gill in 62 LA 654, 657–659; Platt in 56 LA 487, 491; Wallen in 43 LA 1094, 1099; Shipman in 26 LA 651, 665; Whiting, Dash & Larkin in 25 LA 506, 521; Hogan in 25 LA 23, 27; Howard in 23 LA 429, 435–436; Colby in 23 LA 422, 426; Cole in 22 LA 371, 375–376; Hays in 20 LA 75, 80–81. Parties sometimes seek to avoid inequalities within an industry by adoption of "most favored nation" clauses designed to equalize benefits within the industry. For cases dealing with the interpretation and application of such clauses, see Arbitrator Cole in 49 LA 551; Scheiber in 49 LA 557; Brecht in 42 LA 1097.

[16]See Arbitrator Winton in 72 LA 190, 197; Eckhardt, Cross & Jackson in 71 LA 113, 115; Golob in 68 LA 163, 164; Rule in 65 LA 1009, 1015; Barstow in 54 LA 981, 987; Zack in 54 LA 492, 493; Kane in 13 LA 255, 260; Stein in 11 LA 1115, 1115–1116; Cole in 9 LA 577, 578–579; Bitker, Arps & Runge in 8 LA 961, 963–964; Wolff in 4 LA 800, 802.

[17]See Arbitrator Sherman in 65 LA 557, 560; Mueller in 63 LA 824, 827–828 (narrowing an existing differential to a more justifiable spread); Platt in 56 LA 487, 491; Young in 51 LA 1134, 1138; Wallen in 43 LA 1094, 1099–1100; Dworet in 27 LA 343, 346; Shipman in 26 LA 651, 661; Kleinsorge in 23 LA 733, 743; Copelof in 10 LA 133, 138; Jacobs, Clothier & Meyer in 8 LA 9, 16; Strong in 7 LA 673, 677; Cahn, Snyder & Forge in 5 LA 590, 597; Fly in 4 LA 689, 693. In City of Philadelphia, 79 LA 372, 375 (DiLauro, Felix & McNally, 1982), it was stated that by the award, "economic parity has been reestablished between uniformed Fire Department employees and uniformed Police Department employees," and it was further stated that:

"If during the term of this Award such parity is destroyed by final decision of the highest court of competent jurisdiction or an arbitrator or board of arbitrators having jurisdiction over the City of Philadelphia, the City shall immediately restore parity for the duration of the Award."

Also regarding maintenance of parity between police and firefighters, see Arbitrator Rauch in 63 LA 126, 132. Where the salary structure within a hospital had been established by careful study and with the advice of experienced consultants, an arbitrator would not lightly undertake to restructure the salary relationships within the hospital. Palo Alto-Stanford Hosp. Center, 50 LA 700, 705 (Mann, 1968), where the arbitrator stated, however, that under the evidence he was unable to find an imbalance in the internal salary structure. Also see Arbitrators Eckhardt, Cross & Jackson in 71 LA 113, 115.

Application of the prevailing-practice standard may involve difficulties. First, what is to be the basis of comparison? For instance, is it to be the entire industry, the particular industry within the area, or industry in general within the area? After it is decided which prevailing practice is to be used, then just what that practice is must be determined. Finally, there remains the problem of applying the practice to the particular company involved in the case. While difficulties may be encountered, they are not insuperable. The application generally can be made.[18]

In many cases strong reason exists for using the prevailing practice of the same class of employers within the locality or area for the comparison. Employees are sure to compare their lot with that of other employees doing similar work in the area; it is important that no sense of grievance be thereby created.[19] Unions have found, for instance, that the imposition of different wage scales upon the same class of employers in the same locality causes trouble both from employers and union members.[20] Sometimes, however, one party will insist upon industrywide terms while the other party insists upon an area comparison.

If the parties cannot reach agreement as to the basis of comparison, the responsibility is that of the arbitrator to determine, from the facts and circumstances of the case as indicated by the evidence, the appropriate basis for comparison. In the final analysis it may well be that the prevailing practice which properly should be used for the comparison is that of the employer's competitors, whether within or without the area, or that of other firms or industries so situated that there is a sufficient similarity of interests between them and the employer in question for it to be reasonable to use their practice as the standard; comparison with others similarly situated within the industry or area thus may be the crux of the matter.[21]

In the newspaper industry several arbitrators have made some use of comparisons with newspaper operations in other comparable

---

[18]For an illustration both of (1) the difficulties that sometimes are involved in utilizing the prevailing-practice standard, and (2) the fact that the application can be made even in very complex situations or comparisons, see Air N.Z. Ltd., 77 LA 667, 674–680 (Feller, 1981). On the other hand, in League of Voluntary Hosps., 67 LA 293, 294–295 (1976), Arbitrator Margery Gootnick, not relying significantly upon the comparability factor, stated that comparability "is an issue pregnant with difficulty," that she was confronted "with a plethora of information," but that the "comparability evidence standing by itself points in both directions."

[19]Condé Nash Publications, 1 ALAA ¶67,168 p. 67,355 (1942). Also see statement of Arbitrator Deibler as quoted in Houston Chronicle Publishing Co., 56 LA 487, 490 (1971).

[20]Slichter, Basic Criteria Used in Wage Negotiations, 28 (1947).

[21]In this regard, see, generally, Cummins Sales, 54 LA 1069, 1070–1071 (Seinsheimer, 1970). Also see Arbitrator Eisele in 78 LA 1119, 1123; Nathanson in 77 LA 1300, 1302, 1304; Goldberg in 72 LA 90, 92. In University of Chicago Hosps., 63 LA 824, 826 (1974), the employer was a 654-bed hospital, the employer's list of assertedly "comparable" hospitals included those ranging in size from 982 beds to 52 beds, and the union's list of assertedly "comparable" hospitals included those ranging in size from 2173 beds to 216 beds; Arbitrator Robert J. Mueller proceeded as neutrals often do where neither party's list reasonably "fits" the case under consideration—from the two lists submitted by the parties, he compiled a list of the more truly comparable employers (which in this instance included "only those hospitals within approximately 200 beds of " the employer's 654-bed operation). Also see Arbitrator Holden in 67 LA 384, 386. In Kent Nursing Home, 69 LA 771, 771–772 (Sabghir, 1977), the parties agreed to utilize for comparison purposes the employment terms of a single comparable employer, other comparable employers having refused to provide the data requested by the parties for use in the arbitration proceedings.

cities across the nation, this "national comparable cities" approach being said by one arbitrator to be relevant in view of the widely recognized similarities in newspaper operations across the nation.[22]

In public-sector disputes the comparison often has been made with similar occupational groups in comparable cities within the area (this standard is specified in many of the interest arbitration statutes for the public sector).[23] Also as concerns public-sector employees, it should be noted that by no means will their terms of employment always be compared only with those of other public-sector employees.[24]

As to whether the comparison ordinarily should be limited to similar occupational groups, one arbitration board expressed the following view:

> "It should be emphasized that in determining appropriate salaries the basis for comparison is what is paid for work in a particular profession. If the school district were hiring Engineers, Accountants, Physicists, and the like, salaries paid for those professions would presumably apply. Thus a comparison of starting salaries for teachers, who have traditionally been several thousand dollars behind the average of the other professions, may indicate the disadvantageous position of the profession in attracting competent college graduates, but it does not control in determining what should be the proper rate for entry into that profession.
>
> "The same theory holds true in the Association's argument that teachers' starting salaries should be competitive with those of other professions such as Child Welfare Supervisors, or even callings such as

---

[22]Houston Chronicle Publishing Co., 56 LA 487, 491 (Platt, 1971). For a collection of other newspaper cases in which greater or lesser use was made of the "national comparable cities" standard, see Dallas Publishers, 50 LA 367, 369–370 (Elkouri, 1968), where some problems involved in the use of the standard are also noted. In A.S. Abell Co., 45 LA 801, 804 (Cluster, Gallagher & Kraushaar, 1965), the standard was used for news and editorial employees but comparisons with local wage rates were used for other employees of the newspaper. The "national comparable cities" standard has also been used in the local transit industry. See Arbitrator Platt in 50 LA 1103, 1105, 1113; Kates in 45 LA 905, 910; Crawford in 45 LA 58, 60–61. But area comparisons were utilized in Des Moines Transit Co., 38 LA 666, 672 (Flagler, 1962). Regarding the newspaper and local transit industries, also see discussants Platt, Sternstein, Dash, Adair, Bacheller, McLellan & Zingman, "Arbitration of Interest Disputes in the Local Transit and Newspaper Publishing Industries," Proceedings of the 26th Annual Meeting of NAA, 8-61 (BNA Books, 1974).

[23]E.g., see Arbitrator Roumell in 78 LA 153, 155–157, and in 55 LA 716, 722–723; Weizenbaum in 75 LA 268, 274; Winton in 72 LA 190, 196–197; Silver in 70 LA 850, 852–853; O'Brien in 70 LA 154, 158–159; Gruenberg in 68 LA 1258, 1262; Witney in 68 LA 454, 459; Dorsey in 67 LA 1034, 1035; Sherman in 65 LA 557, 562–563; Barstow in 54 LA 981, 986; Young in 51 LA 1134, 1136; Saltonstall in 51 LA 208, 209–210; Seigel in 50 LA 1036, 1041–1042. In City of Renton, 71 LA 271, 273–274 (Snow, 1978), the determination of what cities were "comparable" for purposes of arbitral resolution of a dispute between the City and its police officers was made on the basis of the following factors: (1) proximity to a large city, (2) population, (3) size of the police force, and (4) size of the police department budget.

[24]For example, see the standards specified in the Michigan Police and Firemen's Arbitration Act, quoted below in the topic entitled "Standards in Public-Sector Disputes." For examples from the federal sector, see Arbitrator Keltner in 73 LA 429, 432–434; Bloch in 73 LA 1, 3–4, 6. On the other hand, where multiple issues were submitted to interest arbitration under a Texas public-sector statute which permitted comparisons only with private-sector employment, and where as to some of the issues evidence submitted concerning private-sector comparability was insufficient, Arbitrator John A. Bailey's apparent frustration was revealed by his declaration that: "It must be kept in mind that, under the governing statute, our sole standard for decision is comparability of wages and benefits for similar work in the private sector in the same labor market area, an extremely restrictive standard for a case of this nature." City of Beaumont, Tex., 65 LA 1048, 1057 (1975).

police privates, police sergeants, bricklayers, or plumbers. Each occupation has its own rationale for wage determination, not least of which is supply and demand and control thereover.

"It is not the duty of this Panel to rectify years of inequity among various callings, or to impose its judgment as to the relative worth of one trade or profession over another."[25]

However, in another case the arbitrator stated that an appropriate guide in judging the pay of municipal police officers assigned to and paid directly by private concerns "are wage rate comparisons with other skilled craftsmen and semi-professionals employed to render highly responsible and skilled services in the private sector of the economy."[26]

If the case involves the setting of terms for an entire industry, the comparison may be with a similar industry. In determining whether a significant and close relationship exists between two industries a wide variety of factors may be considered. Such relationship has been found to exist between two industries on the basis of the following factors: "Both are engaged in handling essentially the same products. There is a marked similarity of operations, job titles, job classifications, job duties, and products handled. There is considerable overlapping of union representation * * *. There is competition between the two industries for raw materials as well as for employees. The products of one industry are used almost exclusively by the other."[27] The telephone industry was found related to the telegraph industry on the basis of the following factors: their products were similar, frequently interdependent, and partially competitive; skills required in key jobs were similar; and requirements in many auxiliary occupations, such as clerical and accounting, were virtually identical.[28]

---

[25]Arlington Educ. Assn., 54 LA 492, 494 (Zack, FitzGerald & Cohen, 1970). Also see Arbitrator Snow in 76 LA 789, 792. In Air N.Z. Ltd., 77 LA 667, 676, 678 (1981), Arbitrator David E. Feller resolved an important pay issue between Air New Zealand and its pilots by use of the prevailing-practice standard, utilizing the rates of pay for United Air Lines pilots as a guideline. He refused to follow the lead of another neutral in an earlier case who had compared increases requested by New Zealand pilots "with the salaries paid to the Chief Justice of New Zealand, the Prime Minister and other senior civil servants," Arbitrator Feller stating that he did "not think that the relativity between the pay of airline pilots and that of the Prime Minister and other government officials is meaningful."
[26]Town of Tiverton, R.I., 52 LA 1301, 1303 (Schmidt, 1969). Moreover, the mere fact that an occupational group across the public sector has been underpaid in the past does not mean that interest arbitrators will disregard the occupation's claim to fair and equitable recognition for the future. For example, see Arbitrators McDermott, Zollner & Hutskow in 52 LA 233, 234–235; Florey in 51 LA 994, 995–996; Handsaker in 51 LA 879, 882; Seitz in 47 LA 1036, 1039. In this general regard, it also may be noted that some public-sector statutes clearly are not intended to restrict comparisons absolutely to the same occupational group. See the Michigan statute quoted below in the topic entitled "Standards in Public-Sector Disputes." Under the limited evidence presented in one case subject to the latter statute, Arbitrator Harry H. Platt found it "difficult if not impossible" to make a comparison between Detroit police and police in other communities for purposes of resolving the "residency requirement" issue involved in the proceedings; on the other hand, he stated that "Of special significance * * * are the residency requirements contained in the recent collective bargaining agreements negotiated between the City" and unions representing its firefighters. City of Detroit, 65 LA 293, 312 (1975).
[27]Yakima Cement Prods. Corp., 3 LA 793, 795 (Prasow, 1946).
[28]Western Union Tel. Co., 4 LA 251, 259–260 (Wallen, Cahn & Donahue, 1946). For guides developed by the National Wage Stabilization Board (1946) for determining whether industries were related, see Policy Statement of that Board at 2 LA XIII.

In any use of area practice, the geographical limits of the appropriate area must be determined.[29] Also, if the prevailing practice of industry in general within the area is to be used, there is the task of selecting the firms whose practice is to be considered in determining the prevailing area practice.[30] Arbitrators frequently use for the comparison the prevailing practice of the particular industry (or public sector occupational group) in question, as opposed to industry in general, within the area.[31]

Where each of various comparisons had some validity, an arbitrator concluded that he should give the greatest weight to those comparisons which the parties themselves had considered significant in free collective bargaining, especially in the recent past.[32]

The selection of the employers whose practices are to determine the standard must, in wage cases, be followed by an analysis of jobs for comparability. Mere job titles often are not reliable and are by no means conclusive. "The range of duties assigned to a single worker has not been as standardized among plants as is widely assumed. The varying ages and types of equipment, the differing scales of operation between large and small plants, and the different techniques of various managers are factors making for different job contents among firms producing roughly similar goods."[33] It is incumbent upon the parties to supply reliable job descriptions in order to establish a basis for comparison.[34]

After the prevailing practice has been determined, it must be applied to the particular company involved in the case. This is not difficult where issues involve matters other than wage rates, as, for example, where the issue is the number of paid holidays. But the application of prevailing wage rates is not so simple. There may be reasons why the employer in question should not pay the prevailing rates. These reasons, which for the sake of convenience the Authors choose to call the "minor" standards, include such matters as relative general differentials of skill and training, responsibility, steadiness of

---

[29]Frequently the metropolitan area or the state is used. In consideration of national wage stabilization policy the National War Labor Board favored area comparison for the establishment of wage rates. Basic Steel Cos., 19 War Lab. Rep. 568 (1944).

[30]Comparison with rates for industry in general within the area may be deemed of relatively little value unless adequate data are submitted with respect to the kind of industries being cited and the skill levels of the employees involved. See Florida E. Coast Ry., 41 LA 1001, 1008–1009 (Platt, Bok & Guthrie, 1963). For other considerations that may be relevant in making interindustry comparisons, see Railroads v. Nonoperating Unions, 34 LA 517, 530–532 (Dunlop, Aaron & Sempliner, 1960).

[31]See Arbitrator Roumell in 56 LA 209, 214, and in 55 LA 716, 722; Barstow in 54 LA 981, 987; McCoy in 29 LA 7, 11; Howard in 23 LA 429, 432–434; Stutz in 20 LA 718, 719; Feinberg in 18 LA 55, 59; Warren in 17 LA 353, 354–355.

[32]Rochester Transit Corp., 15 LA 263, 270 (Cornsweet, 1950). Also see Arbitrator Feller in 60 LA 1, 7–8; Horlacher in 27 LA 295, 296; Donnelly in 22 LA 192, 195; Gilden in 16 LA 539, 541. But see Platt in 56 LA 487, 489–491. For related discussion, see topic entitled "Past Practice and Bargaining History," below.

[33]Dunlop, "The Economics of Wage-Dispute Settlement," 12 Law & Contemp. Probs. 281, 283 (1947). Also see Arbitrator Hepburn in 26 LA 381, 382–383.

[34]Illustrating that a misleading picture may result in wage comparisons where job descriptions are incorrect, City of Marquette, 54 LA 981, 986–987 (Barstow, 1970).

employment, hazards of the employment, and fringe benefits, as well as established geographical differentials and wage leadership (these "minor" standards are discussed below).

Consideration of some of the numerous types of issues which have been resolved on the basis of prevailing practice indicates the very broad application that is given to the standard by arbitrators, emergency boards, and fact-finding boards in private-sector and public-sector disputes alike. In addition to basic wage rates, the following types of issues have been resolved in some cases largely (and sometimes entirely) on the basis of the prevailing-practice standard: holidays,[35] vacations,[36] sick leave,[37] hospitalization benefits,[38] pensions and retirement,[39] meal periods,[40] rest periods,[41] union security provisions,[42] length of workday or workweek,[43] shift differentials,[44] work schedules and shifts,[45] overtime provisions,[46] premium pay for Sundays and holidays,[47] length of contract term.[48] In addition to issues such as those just enumerated, a variety of other interest issues in the public sector have been resolved with the aid of the prevailing-practice standard.[49]

Differentials and the "Minor" Standards

As stated above, there may be reasons why a differential should exist between the wage terms of an employer and those of other employers (or between different groups of employees within the same company) with whom a comparison is made in applying the prevailing-practice standard.[50] In this regard, the arbitrator in one public sector dispute commented:

[35]See 71 LA 271; 65 LA 557; 55 LA 716; 53 LA 372; 52 LA 1301; 21 LA 494; 17 LA 353; 16 LA 933; 11 LA 1037; 9 LA 540; 4 LA 780.

[36]See 68 LA 628; 65 LA 938; 63 LA 71; 55 LA 716; 53 LA 372; 47 LA 482; 24 LA 835; 18 LA 415; 17 LA 353; 9 LA 666; 6 LA 98; 5 LA 170.

[37]See 65 LA 557; 53 LA 372; 21 LA 356; 17 LA 152; 11 LA 450; 7 LA 845; 2 LA 95.

[38]See 71 LA 271; 54 LA 796; 21 LA 356; 11 LA 450; 2 LA 624.

[39]See 25 LA 54; 19 LA 538; 13 LA 813; 13 LA 46.

[40]See 17 LA 353; 4 LA 548.

[41]See 17 LA 353; 7 LA 845; 2 LA 227.

[42]See 65 LA 248; 57 LA 613; 55 LA 671; 54 LA 901; 53 LA 372; 45 LA 801; 18 LA 112; 17 LA 833; 16 LA 611; 6 LA 567.

[43]See 68 LA 628; 52 LA 1301; 49 LA 1229; 47 LA 482; 27 LA 343; 19 LA 358; 18 LA 903; 9 LA 566; 5 LA 504; 2 LA 582.

[44]See 71 LA 271; 54 LA 901; 53 LA 372; 50 LA 700; 9 LA 865; 8 LA 488; 5 LA 71; 4 LA 489.

[45]See 43 LA 875; 9 LA 282; 5 LA 781.

[46]See 72 LA 916; 68 LA 1258; 66 LA 992; 65 LA 557; 52 LA 1301; 4 LA 604; 4 LA 548.

[47]See 8 LA 700; 6 LA 269; 2 LA 227.

[48]See 68 LA 1064; 56 LA 209; 50 LA 700; 47 LA 482; 45 LA 58; 27 LA 468.

[49]For example, see Arbitrator Sembower in 72 LA 916, 918, 925–927; Snow in 71 LA 271, 276; Roumell in 55 LA 716, 723–726; Schmidt in 52 LA 1301, 1302–1304; Duff in 51 LA 1072, 1074. The standard has been utilized, too, in awarding "rights" arbitration provisions for public employees. See Arbitrator St. Antoine in 55 LA 671, 672; Barstow in 54 LA 981, 984; Wolf, Feinberg & Stockman in 49 LA 1212, 1226–1228; Wallen in 48 LA 1044, 1049; Dunlop in 42 LA 1114, 1118–1119.

[50]Economist Sumner H. Slichter classified wage differentials as follows: "1. Differentials which equalize the attractiveness of jobs in different occupations, industries, and places. 2. Differentials which reflect the efficiency of men in different occupations and of individuals within an occupation." Slichter, Basic Criteria Used in Wage Negotiations, 41 (1947).

"What happens in one community is not necessarily going to follow in another community. It depends on many circumstances. Wages are only one part of bargaining. There may be fringe benefits. Certainly, the financial situation varies from community to community and should be considered in each instance. There may be a question of working conditions. It is noted for example that in [the present case] the working conditions [of firemen] do leave something to be desired because the department is undermanned causing a potential safety hazard. This may not be the situation in other communities. Such a situation may justify more of an increase than normally."[51]

Sometimes an arbitrator is asked to institute a new differential, and sometimes to perpetuate a differential that has existed in the past. Differentials serve a constructive purpose when supported by sound reasons.

Skill and Training—Arbitrators recognize that wages should be to some degree responsive to the general level of skill and experience required in the plant. For instance, where an employer had a "young shop," composed of workers with relatively less experience and therefore less skill as compared with the average in the industry, the factors of skill and training were given consideration as a proper basis for some differential.[52] In another case it was held that a differential should be reduced but not entirely eliminated where a lesser degree of skill was required to produce a tannery company's product than was required in other tanneries; the quality of leather and the consequent skill required to produce it were found to be superior in the other tanneries to the quality and skill prevailing in the company's plant.[53]

Emphasizing that a differential may be warranted for employees whose work requires special skill or responsibility, an Emergency Board for the railroad industry stated that the single wage rate in each craft resulted in an inequity in pay among mechanics with reference to the performance of the more skilled and responsible assignments. The Board recommended the negotiation of a wage differential for the latter assignments, and thus a "move in the direction of removing a pay inequity in the existing wage structure which will otherwise become more serious with continuing technological change."[54]

---

[51]City of Southgate, 54 LA 901, 913 (Roumell, 1970).

[52]Reliable Optical Co., 7 LA 257, 259 (Rosenfarb, 1947). Also see Arbitrator McCoy in 20 LA 610, 613; Reynolds in 16 LA 933, 937. Differentials between different groups within the same company are justified by differences in skill required. See Arbitrator Kagel in 28 LA 600, 604–605; Feinsinger, Dunlop, Aaron & Coman in 17 LA 68, 70; Townsend in 16 LA 53, 56. In City of Tucson, 71 LA 113, 115 (Eckhardt, Cross & Jackson, 1978), the Arbitrators explained as follows their recommendation that a 6 percent across-the-board increase be granted rather than a $70 across-the-board increase:

"The Union's proposal for a $70 across-the-board increase, if adopted, would reduce the percentage differences between the ranges and steps in the existing salary schedule. Existing percentages attempt to compensate for knowledge and abilities, complexity and variety of duties, and responsibilities. To the extent possible, the existing salary schedule is equitable in its differing rates for differing jobs. It is concluded that it is inadvisable to disturb the existing relationships between ranges and steps as set forth in the existing salary schedule. A flat dollar increase would compress the pay plan by reducing the relative differences between salary ranges."

[53]Moench Tanning Co., 8 War Lab. Rep. 54, 60 (National War Lab. Bd., 1943).

[54]National Ry. Lab. Conference, 53 LA 555, 561 (Seward, Howlett & Livernash, 1969).

Responsibility—Differentials have been justified, in part at least, on the basis of greater responsibility placed upon one group of employees as compared with that placed upon another.[55]

Steadiness of Employment—Differences in the steadiness of employment may justify differences in wage rates. Wage rates for seasonal workers and workers who otherwise have limited job security frequently are set above those of workers with steady employment.[56] This principle was held to justify a rate differential in favor of construction workers as against utility workers even though both were employed on the same work project, weight being given to the fact that utility workers have much greater continuity of employment.[57]

Hazards and Other Undesirable Conditions of Work—Differentials often justifiably exist in favor of employees who perform hazardous work or who work outside during inclement weather or under other undesirable conditions.[58]

Geographic Differentials—Although the individual worker does not always understand why higher wages should be paid to another worker doing the same work but in a different area, there is believed to be sound reason for geographic differentials, as simply stated by one arbitration board: "* * * [E]veryone knows our country cousins, workmen, professional men, all, on the average, earn less than urbanites; and need less. They get on the whole more comforts, services, and commodities for their dollars."[59]

The existence of past wage uniformity between components of a given industry in adjoining areas and the fact that the two areas may tend to constitute a single labor market for that industry may be held insufficient reason for requiring employers in the industry in one of the areas to grant the same wage adjustment granted in the other area if differences in the economies of the two areas far outweigh the similarities.[60]

Even if the cost of living were the same in all places, geographic differentials could still be justified on the ground that they cause labor and capital to flow into areas where they are most needed. Employment opportunities are diminishing in many rural regions and increasing in the cities, and movement of labor from rural to urban

---

[55]See Arbitrator Black in 41 LA 372, 375 (a difference in the number of duties that employees have may justify a difference in wage rates); Dworet in 27 LA 343, 347; Ross in 22 LA 226, 227–228; Blair in 13 LA 454, 455. Also see Healy in 17 LA 636, 637; Stauffer Chem. Co., 15 War Lab. Rep. 264 (1944).

[56]See Arbitrator Rubin in 23 LA 4, 5; Simkin in 6 LA 860, 865; Taylor in 6 LA 830, 834; Prasow in 3 LA 793, 796.

[57]Consolidated Edison Sys. Cos. of N.Y., 6 LA 830, 834–835 (Taylor, 1947).

[58]See Arbitrator Blair in 13 LA 454, 455; Prasow in 3 LA 793, 796; Fly, Black & Harper in 3 LA 165, 170–171. Also see Bloch in 73 LA 1, 7–8; Sabghir in 69 LA 771, 773 (the work in question required "much more constant and acute attention from employees" than did the work of employees whose terms were being utilized for comparison purposes); Gill in 62 LA 654, 657; Hepburn in 26 LA 381, 382.

[59]Chesapeake & Potomac Tel. Co. of Baltimore, 7 LA 630, 641 (Jackson, Healy & Dennis, 1947).

[60]Associated Gen. Contractors, 9 LA 201, 221 (Aaron, 1947).

areas may be stimulated by relatively high urban wage rates. Capital, on the other hand, often needs to be encouraged to move from a high- to a low-wage area.[61] In a number of cases arbitrators have recognized the need for geographic differentials and have ordered their institution or continuance.[62]

Fringe Benefits—Basic wages are not the only "money" benefits that employees may receive. Terms of employment include other pecuniary benefits, such as pensions, holidays and vacations with pay, sick leave, shift premiums, social and health insurance, and bonuses. These fringe benefits must be taken into account in making wage comparisons.[63] If the fringe benefits offered by an employer are substantially more favorable to employees than those of the employers whose prevailing practice is being used for comparative purposes and if these favorable provisions are not counterbalanced by other provisions which are less favorable than the prevailing practice, a differential in basic wage rates may be justified in favor of the employer who offers the superior fringe benefits.[64]

In one public-sector case a school board asserted that the smaller class sizes and fewer clerical duties of its teachers constituted working conditions "sufficiently preferable to offset any difference in salary compared to other communities." The arbitrators stated, however, that it was unrealistic to attach a specific dollar figure to the value of such working conditions and that, in any event, such working conditions did not justify the employer in asking its teachers to absorb increases in the cost of living for which other teachers in the area had received adjustments.[65]

Wage Leadership—A differential which has existed in the past by virtue of the employer's position as a wage leader may be the basis of an award of wage rates higher than those paid by prevailing prac-

---

[61]Slichter, Basic Criteria Used in Wage Negotiations, 37 (1947).

[62]See Arbitrator Feinberg in 18 LA 46, 53; Hays, Cole & Stein in 11 LA 276, 284; Leiserson, Bushnell & Wirtz in 9 LA 865, 877; Aaron in 9 LA 201, 221; Hepburn in 8 LA 691, 694; Jacobs, Clothier & Meyer in 8 LA 9, 14–15. However, geographic differentials have been reduced or eliminated where changed conditions justified such action. See Basic Steel Indus., 18 LA 112, 117–118 (W.S.B., 1952); New Jersey Bell Tel. Co., 14 LA 574, 588 (Martin, Lewis & Lesser, 1950).

[63]That fringes should be included was emphasized in Des Moines Transit Co., 38 LA 666, 672–673 (Flagler, 1962), where data pertaining to nine selected fringe benefits were secured from each of the 10 companies with which comparison was being made. Also see Arbitrator Gill in 62 LA 654, 657. However, fringe benefits were disregarded where the parties failed to provide evidence about the comparability of the benefits. Cummins Sales, Inc., 54 LA 1069, 1072 (Seinsheimer, 1970). In City of Marquette, 54 LA 981, 987 (Barstow, 1970), the arbitrator noted that many fringe benefits "are extremely difficult to translate into dollar terms," but he was "unable to determine any clear evidence of imbalance among fringes" of similar occupational groups in the area, and he concluded that the fringe benefits being compared were "roughly similar in total value" although "differences in detail abound." In City of Providence, 47 LA 1036, 1038 (Seitz, 1966), the arbitrator found that there was such a "wide diversity of working conditions and fringes among the cities ranked" that the prevailing practice standard itself was rendered of little utility.

[64]See Arbitrator Eisele in 78 LA 1119, 1124; Kliensorge in 23 LA 733, 742; Kerr in 7 LA 528, 535; Simkin in 6 LA 860, 867, 881. Cf., Randle in 18 LA 280, 281.

[65]Arlington Educ. Assn., 54 LA 492, 494–495 (Zack, FitzGerald & Cohen, 1970).

tice.[66] Companies which in the past have set the prevailing wage may be looked to for further leadership when the trend is toward a higher level of wages.[67] It has been emphasized, however, that the lead occasionally passes from one company to another and that wage adjustments need not always wait upon agreement of the parties who usually provide the lead.[68]

In a case involving employees of Dallas, Texas, newspapers the union declared that Dallas is a dynamic city whose explosive economic and industrial progress in recent years had benefited the Dallas publishers; the arbitrator agreed that in view of Dallas' economic growth and vitality, the union was not totally unjustified in looking to the publishers for wage leadership.[69]

Historical Differentials—Arbitrators are sometimes reluctant to eliminate historical differentials[70] or those which initially were established by collective bargaining.[71] This reflects a hesitancy to disturb a stabilized situation except on compelling grounds.[72]

Economist Sumner H. Slichter pointed out that some may argue that long-established relationships between wages in several occupations, plants, or localities should be maintained because the quality of labor tends to adjust itself to the wage structure, which means that employers who pay wages above the prevailing rate attract a better class of workers, and the retention of customary differentials merely serves to compensate those with superior ability. He pointed out further, however, that in a rapidly changing world the argument that traditional wage relationships should be preserved has very limited

---

[66]See Arbitrator Snow in 71 LA 271, 281; Donnelly in 26 LA 904, 907; Whiting in 11 LA 1023, 1033; Cornsweet in 8 LA 597, 606. Also see Gill in 62 LA 654, 658. But see Goldberg in 72 LA 90, 93; Kerr in 7 LA 528, 532. A related question arising out of wage leadership is whether the leader's rate should be included in the sample used for determining the prevailing rate.

[67]But the leader may be relieved of this responsibility if its ability to pay becomes weak. Des Moines Transit Co., 38 LA 666, 674 (Flagler, 1962).

[68]Tribune Publishing Co., 28 LA 477, 480 (Ross, 1957).

[69]Dallas Publishers, 50 LA 367, 373 (Elkouri, 1968).

[70]See Arbitrator Feller in 77 LA 667, 674; Snow in 71 LA 271, 280–281; Crawford in 45 LA 58, 61; Seibel in 43 LA 410, 411, 414; Ross in 29 LA 96, 99; Pierson in 17 LA 152, 158; Kerr in 14 LA 111, 112, and in 11 LA 458, 461; Dwyer in 5 LA 513, 515–516; Cahn in 3 LA 729, 732. Also see United States Smelting Co., 18 LA 676, 677 (Wage Stabilization Bd., 1952). Cf., Arbitrator Cheney in 5 LA 220, 222; Wasservogel in 4 LA 548, 575.

[71]See Arbitrator Dworkin in 42 LA 548, 555; Holly in 39 LA 207, 212; Donnelly in 26 LA 904, 907; Cornsweet in 15 LA 263, 270–271; Horvitz in 3 LA 318, 320. Also see McCoy in 20 LA 610, 613.

[72]Newark Call Printing & Publishing Co., 3 LA 318, 320–321 (Horvitz, 1946). In Houston Chronicle Publishing Co., 56 LA 487, 490–491 (Platt, 1971), the importance of not making too large an award (though such award be otherwise justified to fully eliminate an intercity or interemployer inequity) was stressed in view of the need to protect "intra-plant harmony." Similarly, see Arbitrator Elkouri in 50 LA 367, 368–369. In Area Educ. Agency 12, 72 LA 916, 919 (1979), Fact-Finder John F. Sembower rejected a union wage proposal which could not be adopted "without distorting the comparability picture" of the area education group in question "in relation with the other" state area education groups "and in relationship generally with the education community." Also see Arbitrator Block in 81 LA 352, 357 (refusing to increase certain wages where "a sudden increase of these wages could easily throw these jobs out of line with other jobs"); Hamby in 78 LA 352, 357 (refusing to grant the full increase requested where to grant it "would create more of a margin * * * than is justified by past practice," in favor of these employees over those of comparable companies).

validity.[73] Nonetheless, where a historical parity had existed between the pay of policemen and firemen, an arbitrator acted firmly to maintain it.[74]

If There Is No Prevailing Practice

The question sometimes arises as to how arbitrators should treat demands for contract terms sufficiently unprecedented that no "prevailing practice" is available. It might be urged that demands for improved contract terms should not be rejected on the sole ground that they are unprecedented, since the adoption of a contrary principle would seriously impair the usefulness of arbitration as a method of settling labor disputes. It is clear, however, that arbitrators will require a party seeking a novel change to justify it by strong evidence establishing its reasonableness and soundness. Moreover, the absence of prevailing practice may be taken to show that a demand has not yet been adequately justified by labor within the industry or area.[75] Arbitrators generally agree that demands for unusual types of contract provisions preferably should be negotiated. This view was elaborated by Arbitrator Whitley P. McCoy, speaking as Chairman of a board of arbitration:

> "We believe that an unusual demand, that is, one that has not found substantial acceptance in other properties, casts upon the union the burden of showing that, because of its minor character or its inherent reasonableness, the negotiators should, as reasonable men, have voluntarily agreed to it. We would not deny such a demand merely because it had not found substantial acceptance, but it would take clear evidence to persuade us that the negotiators were unreasonable in rejecting it."[76]

New provisions, however, are often included in the recommendations of fact-finding boards. These agencies frequently enter upon policy considerations and considerations of public interest, and they recognize the need for leadership in the introduction of innovations.[77]

Cost of Living

The cost-of-living standard is frequently advanced in collective bargaining and arbitration during periods characterized by pronounced changes in living costs.

---

[73]Slichter, Basic Criteria Used in Wage Negotiations, 40 (1947). Also see Arbitrator Goldberg in 72 LA 90, 93 (stating that "the principle of equal pay for equal work is entitled to more weight than that of maintaining historic disparities"). Where the validity which a historical differential once had has disappeared, the situation may be viewed as a present inequity. Atlanta Newspapers, 43 LA 1094, 1100 (Wallen, 1964).

[74]City of Southgate, 54 LA 901, 910–911 (Roumell, 1970). To similar effect, Arbitrator Gillingham in 53 LA 361, 363.

[75]See Fifth Ave. Coach Co., 4 LA 548, 579 (Wasservogel, 1946).

[76]Twin City Rapid Transit Co., 7 LA 845, 848 (1947). Also see Arbitrator Cole in 11 LA 450, 453–454; Hepburn in 3 LA 194, 196.

[77]For instance, see Minnesota State Highway Patrol, 56 LA 697, 699 (Gleeson, 1971); General Motors Corp., 1 LA 125, 137 (Garrison, Eisenhower & Stacy, 1946).

The use of this standard has an obvious appearance of fairness, but it is not without criticism. For instance, it is said that a rising cost of living means that the demand for goods at existing prices is outrunning the supply and that increases in wages would simply aggravate the problem except as they reflect increased production through improvements in technique or in employee efficiency.[78] One answer given to this criticism is that the readjustment of wages has been the result rather than the primary cause of increased living costs. Price rises, it is said, are due to many complex causes.[79] A criticism which labor registers against the cost-of-living standard is that its rigid application would result in a stationary real wage rather than a higher standard of living.[80] But in spite of these criticisms, the very frequent use of this standard is strong evidence that it is generally regarded to be of much value, and in recent decades it has held an important place in the national economy.[81]

In applying the cost-of-living standard arbitrators rely heavily upon the Consumer Price Index (CPI) issued by the Bureau of Labor Statistics of the United States Department of Labor. As the result of a major revision which was commenced in 1970 and completed in 1978, the Consumer Price Index in fact is now a group of separate indexes.[82]

---

[78]Slichter, Basic Criteria Used in Wage Negotiations, 15 (1947).

[79]Satter, "Principles of Arbitration in Wage Rate Disputes," 1 Indus. & Lab. Rel. Rev. 363, 367 (1948). A thought-provoking statement concerning the causes and effects of a related phenomenon, inflation, was offered by Arbitrator Bruce R. Boals:

"Inflation is a tremendously complicated subject, but perhaps some of the primary reasons for the predicament should be mentioned. Prices in general have increased primarily because of government deficit financing, a rapid increase in the supply of money and credit. Politicians seem to have caught on to a unique technique: With inflation, they have an automatic way to increase taxes without passing tax laws, as the income tax takes a larger percentage of higher money incomes. This is a cruel but hidden tax on savings. In turn, they have more money which they can dispense to programs that can please their constituency. The result is that few in Congress are unseated nowadays. Other reasons for general inflation include: rising energy and raw material costs; over-regulation of business by EEOC, OSHA, ICC, EPA and other such agencies; slow increases of late in man-hour productivity; and high-prices administered by firms with market power and import cartels. There are many other reasons, and the inflationary process is dynamic and complex, involving *anticipated* price changes by all sellers, buyers and employees. In addition, many have the incorrect belief of a long-run trade-off between unemployment and inflation."
Celotex Corp., 68 LA 672, 674–675 (1977), where Arbitrator Boals also made a detailed statement specifically concerning the inflationary spiral of costs in the medical care and health insurance fields.

[80]The criticism led one arbitrator to largely disregard the cost-of-living standard, the arbitrator stating that the "uncritical use of the cost-of-living formula often involves the false assumption that all is well when real wages remain constant." 195 Broadway Corp., 7 LA 516, 519 (Meyer, 1947).

[81]The case in its favor was strengthened in 1951 by the Wage Stabilization Board's adoption of it as a ground for wage increases without the need of official approval.

[82]The sole national index prior to the revision was the "Consumer Price Index for Urban Wage Earners and Clerical Workers." The revision replaced this index with two national indexes: (1) the "Consumer Price Index for All Urban Consumers (CPI-U)," and (2) the "Consumer Price Index for Urban Wage Earners and Clerical Workers (Revised series) (CPI-W)." The Consumer Price Index Revision–1978, p. 1 (Bureau of Lab. Statistics, 1978), which provides a detailed comparison of the old index and each of its two replacements. Among other features common to each of the three indexes is the fact of monthly issuance and the use of the same base period, i.e., 1967 = 100. The need for broader population coverage than was provided by the old index, was explained as follows:

"The previous index represented only wage earners and clerical workers and therefore was, strictly speaking, appropriate for only that group. A more comprehensive consumer price index was needed to reflect expenditures for the many population groups other than wage earners and clerical workers whose income payments are now being escalated and to

Where the particular separate index to be utilized for the given arbitration case has not been mutually specified by the parties, the arbitrator will decide which index best serves the case.[83]

The Consumer Price Index (which will be referred to below merely as the index) reflects the cost of living as of a date about six weeks prior to its issuance.[84] By use of the index it is possible to measure changes in retail costs of services and commodities and the resulting effect upon the purchasing power of the income of workers in the larger cities. Essentially, the index is the ratio of the current cost of a specified market basket of goods and services to the average cost of the same market basket during some designated past period. The base period for the index is the average for the year 1967 (1967 = 100), but it should be noted that the base period is updated periodically.[85]

The Bureau of Labor Statistics does not hold that its index is an exact measurement of changes in the cost of living, but arbitrators can be expected to give it considerable weight. For example, it was held in one instance to be an appropriate measure of the change in living costs although the union claimed that it underestimated the change and the company claimed that it overestimated the change; neither party presented sufficient evidence to support an adjustment of the index figures, which the arbitrator said at least carried apparent and official certitude.[86]

---

measure inflation and guide monetary and fiscal policy for the Nation as a whole."
The Consumer Price Index: Concepts and Content Over the Years, Report 517, p. 6 (Bureau of Lab. Statistics, 1977), which also explains (at p. 5) that along with the new Index for All Urban Consumers, the revision increased the number of city indexes, and also established regional indexes:

"(1) A new index representing all urban consumers—80 percent of the population—has been issued in addition to the index for wage earners and clerical workers which represents roughly half of the urban population; (2) monthly or bimonthly indexes are published for 28 cities compared with 24 monthly or quarterly indexes formerly published; (3) regional indexes are available for urban areas of different population sizes * * *."

But it is also significant that "Although many changes in scope, coverage, frequency, and publication format have occurred over the years, the index has continued to measure changes in the price of a fixed market basket of goods and services." Id. at 3.

[83]For example, in Commonwealth Edison Co., 72 LA 90, 94 (1978), Arbitrator Stephen B. Goldberg noted data from the Chicago metropolitan area index and data from the national index, and he explained why he chose the former: "Inasmuch * * * as all * * * employees live in or near the Chicago metropolitan area, Chicago data are more meaningful than nation-wide data." Also see Fact-Finder Dorsey in 67 LA 1034, 1035–1036.

[84]For one type of interpretative problem that this time gap can produce, see Duriron Co., 54 LA 124, 127–128 (Kates, 1969).

[85]For current and some historical CPI data see BNA's Labor Relations Reporter, LRX 161 et seq. Historical data based upon prior base periods is available from the Bureau of Labor Statistics. For an explanation that it is possible to continue the use of indexes utilizing earlier base periods than the 1967 = 100 index, and that "the percentage increases shown by each Index would be identical," see National Cleaning Contractors, 70 LA 917, 920–921, 925 (Dworkin, 1978), explaining also that "current information is still collected and made available for former Indexes, all the way back * * *."

[86]R.H. Macy & Co., 9 LA 305, 308 (Shulman, 1947). In City of Havre, Mont., 76 LA 789, 793 (1981), Arbitrator Carlton J. Snow stated:

"The difficulty with the Consumer Price Index is that it provides no insight concerning differences in cost of living from one city to another in Montana. Consequently, one does not know what the Consumer Price Index is for Havre, Montana. Nor does the Index give us insight into the standard of living that particular individuals can sustain on a given income. The point is that such price indices do not provide the precision many want to give them credit for providing. But the Employer offered no rebuttal to the Association's contention [concerning the increase in cost of living reflected by the Consumer Price Index]."

Also regarding index shortcomings, see comments of Arbitrator Bloch in 73 LA 1, 5. Sometimes

The latest index available at the time of the arbitration is ordinarily used in determining the cost-of-living adjustment to be paid employees until the next wage review; this is so even though such review is not expected to take place until several months later. Thus, in setting wages for a six-month period, one arbitrator stated that "greater emphasis must obviously be placed on known facts than on guesses" as to the index level during the next six months.[87] But a wage increase in excess of that indicated to be justified by the index may be awarded where the amount granted does not exceed "the amount which the Arbitrator finds on the record as a whole is presently justified to offset increases in living costs * * *."[88] Moreover, in one case the arbitrator declared that the employees (teachers) were entitled to "an increase that will both maintain their present real income and afford them some protection against the continuing rise in the cost of living, which appears likely to occur during the period of the next agreement."[89]

Many arbitration awards have granted wage improvements on the basis, in part at least, of the application of the cost-of-living standard.[90] Often, however, its effect has been modified by the application at the same time of other standards. In the latter regard one arbitration board refused to guarantee that the employees would be "insulated in toto" against all of the rise in cost of living, the board stating:

> "To rest wage rate raises upon cost of living rises as the sole measuring rod means wages will rise with commodity rises as the thermometer goes up on a hot day. If wages are to be raised solely because commodity prices go up, wages should go down with falling commodity prices, as the mecury goes down to zero in a freeze; unless, like the human elbow joint, the system is created to flex upward, and only upward."[91]

errors occur in the index. For cases permitting recoupment of overpayment caused by BLS error in the index, see Arbitrator Platt in 69 LA 52, 59, and Roberts in 68 LA 970, 973; for a case not permitting recoupment, see Karasick in 64 LA 862, 864.

[87]Waterfront Employers Assn. of Pac. Coast, 5 LA 758, 761 (Kerr, 1946). To similar effect, Arbitrator Feinberg in 18 LA 55, 58–59. In Yaun Welding & Mach. Works Co., 73 LA 223, 227 (Nicholas, 1979), the burden of proof was placed upon the union "to justify a further wage increase," and the Arbitrator concluded that the union had "failed to show conclusively that inflation will more than consume the" increase which had been offered by the company.

[88]Waterfront Employers Assn. of Pac. Coast, 9 LA 172, 181 (Miller, 1947). Also see Arbitrator Dworet in 27 LA 343, 346.

[89]Worcester Teachers' Assn., 54 LA 796, 800 (Seidenberg, 1970). Also see Arbitrator Platt in 63 LA 1189, 1195 (stating that in his "judgment, a reasonable 'guestimate' at this time would be that the Consumer Price Index will rise at or near a 12 percent rate" during a specified future period). Where an arbitrator awarded a "firm two year contract" the wage increase he granted was based in part upon "anticipated increases in living costs." The New York Times, 15 LA 332, 333 (Dunlop, 1950).

[90]E.g., Arbitrator Block in 81 LA 352, 356–357; Nathanson in 77 LA 1300, 1304; Keltner in 73 LA 429, 435; Bloch in 73 LA 1, 6; Winton in 72 LA 190, 196; Rule in 65 LA 1009, 1015; Sater in 65 LA 938, 941; Mueller in 63 LA 824, 826–827; Roumell in 56 LA 209, 216; Barstow in 54 LA 981, 988 ("governmental units have a responsibility to cushion their employees to the extent possible against short term cost-of-living changes"); Seidenberg in 54 LA 796, 799–800; Elkouri in 50 LA 367, 374; House in 43 LA 29, 30; Ross in 29 LA 96, 98; McCoy in 29 LA 7, 10; Kagel in 28 LA 600, 606; Dworet in 23 LA 629, 640; Shulman in 22 LA 297, 299; Platt in 18 LA 686, 690; Marshall in 15 LA 878, 880; Sonnenschein in 13 LA 40, 44; Hays in 11 LA 276, 280.

[91]Chesapeake & Potomac Tel. Co. of Baltimore, 7 LA 630, 640 (Jackson, Healy & Dennis, 1947). In City of Burlington, Iowa, 68 LA 454, 457–458 (1977), the union urged that its wage proposal should be selected "because it reflects most closely the * * * per cent increase in the

An appropriate base period must be selected in applying the cost-of-living standard. The base period that is selected determines the real wage that is to be maintained by the standard. Generally the date of the last arbitration award or of the parties' last wage negotiations is used as the base date.[92]

The determination of any adjustment to be made on the basis of a change in the cost of living requires a comparison of the percentage of change in the cost of living with the percentage of change in wages between the base period and the date of the wage adjustment.[93]

In determining whether wages have kept pace with the cost of living, basic wage rates, rather than take-home pay, are generally used for the comparison.[94] The use of take-home pay for the comparison would lead to a distortion of the normal relationship of earnings to hours worked.[95] In making the comparison some changes in wages have been held not to be material. Among these are increases resulting from increased skill and effort,[96] increases granted for the sole purpose of eliminating inequities within the industry,[97] and pay raises for length of service or promotions.[98] The following, on the other hand, may be taken into consideration in making the comparison: Increased earnings of incentive workers which result from a simplification of the work or any other increase not the result of increased efforts of the workers;[99] reclassification adjustments general enough to affect the whole wage structure and thus to be considered general increases instead of merit increases.[100] The use of basic wage rates instead of take-home pay for the comparison eliminates from consideration vacation, holiday, and other fringe benefits granted to employees since the base date.[101]

The cost-of-living standard may be expected to be used much less generally as a basis for wage reductions than as a basis for wage

Consumer Price Index." Arbitrator Fred Witney's response took note of "the financial plight" of the employer, and also explained that additional insurance benefits offered by the employer would in a sense be "even more beneficial" to the employees "because they would not be required to pay income taxes on the additional insurance benefits as they would be required if an equivalent amount would be paid in a salary increase."

[92]See Los Angeles Transit Lines 11 LA 118, 130 (Aaron, 1948); New York City Omnibus Corp., 7 LA 794, 802 (Cole, 1947). But a date other than that of the last negotiations may be selected as the base period. For some years after World War II, for instance, January 1, 1941, was often used by arbitrators. The use of this date was initiated by the National War Labor Board of World War II. Bethlehem Steel Corp., 1 War Lab. Rep. 325 (1942). The 1941 date was deemed clearly outmoded in Publishers Assn. of N.Y. City, 22 LA 35, 41–42 (Seward, Slocum & Meany, 1954), a later date having been established under a subsequent governmental wage control program.

[93]Regarding the determination and application of the percentage increase in cost of living, see Arbitrator Dworkin in 70 LA 917, 921–922; Sembower in 70 LA 223, 225–226; Elkouri in 50 LA 367, 374.

[94]Waterfront Employers Assn. of Pac. Coast, 5 LA 758, 761 (Kerr, 1946); Bee Line, Inc., 1 ALAA ¶67,161 (1946).

[95]Waterfront Employers Assn. of Pac. Coast, 9 LA 172, 177 (Miller, 1947), and in 5 LA 758, 761 (Kerr, 1946).

[96]McGlynn Hays Indus., 10 LA 360, 361 (Lesser, 1948).

[97]Atlantic & Gulf Coast Shippers, 6 LA 700, 704 (Kleinsorge, 1947).

[98]Trans World Airlines, 19 LA 308, 323 (Wenke, Boyd & Sharfman, 1952); Fifth Ave. Coach Co., 1 ALAA ¶67,423 (1946). Also see Arbitrator Stutz in 20 LA 718, 719–720; Lesser in 17 LA 914, 916.

[99]Associated Dress Mfrs. Assn., 6 LA 24, 27 (Copelof, 1946).

[100]Puget Sound Navigation Co., 11 LA 1100, 1107 (Haughton, 1948).

[101]See Bee Line, 1 ALAA ¶67, 161 (1946).

increases.[102] In one contract, for instance, the parties provided for adjustments to maintain the relative purchasing power of the employees against rises in the cost of living, but they provided that "In no event will a decline in the Index * * * cause a reduction in the scale of wages."[103] The social and ethical reasons that can be used to support the application of the standard in times of rising costs are not so readily applicable when costs are on the decline. Rather, these considerations support the constant efforts of labor to attain a higher standard of living. At least, "insofar as a drop in the cost of living is the result of technological progress, it does not furnish a sound reason for wage cuts"; it calls, instead, for a rise in real wages.[104]

However, a governmental wage stabilization agency did require that escalator clauses negotiated after January 25, 1951, provide for downward as well as upward revision of wage rates. It is also interesting to note that a fact-finding board for the basic steel industry, in refusing to recommend a general wage increase, cited, as one of the factors given consideration, the fact that in the prior year the cost of living had declined slightly.[105] Thus, while a decrease in the cost of living may not be strong reason for wage reductions, it may have a greater relevance in determining whether new wage increases are justified.

Escalator and Wage Reopening Clauses

Many collective agreements contain "escalator" clauses which provide for automatic changes in wage rates in response to specified changes in the cost of living.[106] The use of such a clause may justify a longer basic term for the agreement.[107]

An alternative to use of escalator clauses is to provide for wage reopening during the term of the agreement.[108] A wage reopening

---

[102]See Puget Sound Navigation Co., 13 LA 255, 258–259 (Kanes, 1949).

[103]Koppel Photo Co., 56 LA 1085, 1086 (Zack, 1971).

[104]Slichter, Basic Criteria Used in Wage Negotiations, 18 (1947).

[105]Basic Steel Indus., 13 LA 46, 79 (Daughterty, Cole & Rosenman, 1949).

[106]For example, see Arbitrator Bothwell in 72 LA 1214, 1215 (here the provision included a "cap" limiting the adjustment in hourly rate to no more than 15 cents each year); Grabb in 70 LA 765 at 765; Sembower in 70 LA 223, 224. Another possibility is to provide for automatic wage adjustments at specified intervals. For example, see Arbitrator Katz in 81 LA 274, 274–275; Shearer in 81 LA 272, 272–273; Moski in 71 LA 1186, 1187; Zack in 56 LA 1085, 1086. For the matters that should be covered in escalator clauses, see Tile Contractors Assn. of N. Cal., 25 LA 9, 11 (Ross, 1955). Also see Arbitrator Gill in 62 LA 654, 658–659; Platt in 50 LA 1103, 1111. Regarding "rounding off" fractions to the nearest cent in making adjustments, see Arbitrator Moski in 71 LA 1186, 1187–1188; Grabb in 70 LA 765, 766–767.

[107]See Port Auth. of Allegheny County, 45 LA 58, 62 (Crawford, 1965).

[108]See City of Marquette, 54 LA 981, 988 (Barstow, 1970). Also see Arbitrator Gootnick in 67 LA 293, 299 (awarding a "reopener on wages" with provision for use of interest arbitration if needed). Of 1717 contracts examined in one survey, nearly 500 contained provisions for renegotiation of economic issues during the contract term and about 15 percent of these provided for arbitration should negotiations fail. Major Collective Bargaining Agreements: Arbitration Procedures, 101 (U.S. Dept. Labor Bull. No. 1425–6, 1966), indicating also that demands for general wage changes were the predominant issues subject to arbitration. For other statistics as to use of reopening (and escalator) clauses, see Stieber, "Voluntary Arbitration of Contract Terms," Proceedings of the 23rd Annual Meeting of NAA, 71 (BNA Books, 1970). In State of Conn., 77 LA 729, 746–747 (1981), Fact-Finders Healy and Seibel explained that in the public sector a significant number of retirement programs "have some form of COLA [cost of living adjustment] protection

clause may provide for the negotiation of new wage terms when the cost of living changes by a specified percentage, when there has been a "substantial" change,[109] or simply at specified intervals.[110]

In the arbitration of contract reopening disputes the cost-of-living standard is relevant in many instances. Furthermore, in some reopening disputes the arbitrator asserted the authority to consider all relevant standards, unless restricted by the agreement or the submission, all wage determining factors being deemed equally applicable whether it be a reopening or a new contract dispute.[111] However, in other instances the arbitrator recognized the limitation that weight may be given only to those factors for which the evidence indicates there has been a change since the agreement was signed (this sometimes has been called the "erosion doctrine," limiting the function of reopening to "restoring the bargain" which the parties made when the agreement was signed).[112]

Living Wage

The living-wage standard is related to, but not the same as, the cost-of-living standard. The living-wage standard is in some respects based upon the ideal that the standard of living of American workers should be raised to the highest level possible,[113] but a more realistic basis for it is the belief that "employees are entitled to wages and salaries sufficient to enable them, through the exercise of thrift and reasonable economy, to maintain themselves and families in decency and comfort and to make reasonable provision for old age."[114] In advancing the living-wage theory, a union may be expected to insist

---

despite its high cost"; that the programs "generally do not fully adjust pension benefits to keep pace with inflation"; but that a "significant number of states provide a method for some ad hoc COLA increases in addition to any guaranteed COLAs provided for in their retirement programs." They explained further that the ad hoc "type of protection becomes particularly important in periods of high inflation during which one may also assume that the earnings from the assets of the retirement program will exceed the assumed rate of return."

[109]Concerning what might be considered "substantial," see Arbitrator Lesser in 17 LA 914, 916; Justin in 17 LA 31, 33; Granoff in 16 LA 944, 949.

[110]See Major Collective Bargaining Agreements: Arbitration Procedures, 101 (U.S. Dept. Labor Bull. No. 1425–6, 1966).

[111]See Arbitrator Platt in 56 LA 487, 491; Wallen in 43 LA 1094, 1099 (stating that a "de novo" wage determination was permitted); Dworkin in 42 LA 548, 553; Shipman in 26 LA 651, 659; Shulman in 22 LA 297, 298–299; Lesser in 17 LA 114, 116. Also see Ross in 35 LA 185, 187–188; Dash in 14 LA 662, 669–670. In Rose-Derry Ohio, 49 LA 40, 43 (Kates, 1967), a clause permitting wage reopening when the cost-of-living index changes 2.5 percent was deemed to specify the time of reopening but not to specify how much of a wage adjustment may be negotiated when a reopening is triggered.

[112]See Arbitrator Roberts in 36 LA 171, 177; Dworet in 23 LA 629, 639–640; Gray in 21 LA 13, 14; Livingston in 9 LA 632, 636; Miller in 9 LA 172, 175–176; Kerr in 5 LA 758, 759. Also see Luskin in 36 LA 201, 203–204; Hogan in 25 LA 23, 24, 29; O'Connell in 20 LA 437, 439. An objective similar to that of "restoring the bargain" was found in connection with a clause for automatic wage adjustments at specified intervals in Auburn Foundry, 81 LA 274, 276 (1983), Arbitrator Jonas B. Katz stating that "based on the purpose of such clauses, absent specific language limiting the right to decrease cost of living allowances, the allowance should increase or decrease depending on the Consumer Price Index." Similarly, see Arbitrator Shearer in 81 LA 272, 274.

[113]Atlantic & Gulf Coast Shippers, 6 LA 700, 702 (Kleinsorge, 1947).

[114]San Francisco Employers Council, 7 LA 35, 38 (Wyckoff, 1946). Similarly, see Arbitrator Singer in 47 LA 482, 486.

that no privately owned industry should be permitted to insure its solvency or to consider a return upon its investment at the expense of its employees nor to require them to subsidize its investment by compelling them to accept wages or working conditions below normal standards of decency.[115] A similar position may be advanced in public-sector disputes.[116]

An important difference exists between the cost-of-living and the living-wage standards. While the cost-of-living standard is used to keep the standard of living of employees in status quo, the living-wage standard (which is not directly tied to changes in the cost of living) is invoked to raise the wages of employees to the point that will allow them a decent standard of living. Application of the living-wage standard may well result in a wage increase greater than that which is indicated by the change in cost of living.

The "budget approach" is sometimes used by parties advancing the living-wage standard. A similar approach underlies the state and federal minimum wage laws. Generally speaking, budgets have been used primarily as background and supplementary material rather than as a specific criterion in the formulation of wage demands.[117] But in some cases unions have relied directly upon the budget approach. A board of inquiry for the meatpacking industry, for instance, was asked to give serious consideration to the "City Worker's Family Budget" issued by the Bureau of Labor Statistics. The board stated that a budget approach to wage determination was not invalid or unprecedented and that the union could properly offer it for consideration as a criterion for resolving the dispute. The board concluded, however, that a proper application of the budget approach to that dispute would require more information than the parties had supplied or could supply from their limited study of the subject up to that date, and more than the board could obtain from governmental or other sources.[118]

This illustrates a major disadvantage of the living-wage standard; namely, its indefiniteness.[119] What may be considered a decent standard of living is largely dependent upon time and circumstances. The aforementioned board also concluded that even with the necessary information, a number of broad policy decisions would have to be made by agreement of the parties. The most important of these decisions were said to be:

---

[115]Such a position was taken by the union in St. Louis Pub. Serv. Co., 8 LA 397, 402 (1947).

[116]See Arbitrators Zack, FitzGerald & Cohen in 54 LA 492, 494; McDermott, Zollner & Hutskow in 52 LA 233, 234–235; Florey in 51 LA 994, 995–996.

[117]See Meat Packing Indus., 9 LA 978, 998 (Feinsinger, Davis & Schaefer, 1948). Also see Arbitrator Snow in 71 LA 271, 279; Kleinsorge in 24 LA 38, 43.

[118]Meat Packing Indus., 9 LA 978, 992, 998–999 (Feinsinger, Davis & Schaefer, 1948).

[119]In Port Auth. of Allegheny County, 50 LA 1103, 1112–1113 (Platt, 1968), the parties referred to the City Worker's Family Budget but the arbitrator deemed it of little significance to the case. He commented: "To properly evaluate this criterion would involve consideration of many collateral questions to which there are no answers in the record. Indeed, as Professor Alfred Kuhn observed in his monograph on Arbitration in Transit, the living wage criterion, because of its vagueness and intangibility, provides a sort of glittering generality which 'has never been and does not seem destined to become an important wage determinant in the transit industry.' " Also see comments of Arbitrator Goldberg in 72 LA 90, 95.

"(1) whether the size of the family alone * * * or the composition of the family, including size and other characteristics, should be used; (2) whether the necessary income should come only from earnings of the employee or whether income from all sources should be considered; (3) whether income from earnings should be computed on the basis of 2,080 hours (52 × 40 hours) at straight-time, without incentive earnings or 'fringe' benefits, * * * or on the basis of earnings from overtime plus incentive earnings and 'fringe' benefits, as well as straight-time earnings; (4) whether the resulting increase should be related only to the job performed or should also vary with number of dependents of individual employees."[120]

It is recognized that budgetary experts are not in agreement as to the composition of an adequate budget. One arbitrator declared that the particular budget submitted to him had "served the purpose more of a goal to be attained over a period of time than the next step in the improvement of the living standards" of America's wage earners, and that the actual attainment of the budget could be had "through full and efficient production and distributive justice." He concluded that the budget could not, at that time, "serve as the sole, or even a significant, basis for wage adjudication."[121] Similarly, where teachers asserted that their salaries should be "commensurate with the standard of living" in their community, the arbitration tribunal stated that this "should be a goal rather than a controlling criterion."[122]

It can be expected that as long as the living-wage argument is presented only in general terms, giving arbitrators no specific basis of application to the concrete problems before them, the standard will be given little effect in awards.[123] However, there are public-sector cases in which the arbitrator did find the presentation adequate to give some weight to the living-wage standard.[124]

Ability to Pay

Although it is a generally recognized principle that large profits do not alone justify demands for wages substantially higher than those which are standard within an industry and that small profits do not justify the payment of substandard wages,[125] the ability-to-pay criterion is of great importance in the determination of wage rates and other contract benefits. This importance lies largely in the fact that, while an employer's ability to pay is not, in and of itself, a sufficient

---

[120]Meat Packing Indus., 9 LA 978, 998–999 (Feinsinger, Davis & Schaefer, 1948).

[121]Pacific Gas & Elec. Co., 7 LA 528, 530 (Kerr, 1947). Also see Arbitrator Kleinsorge in 24 LA 38, 43.

[122]Arlington Educ. Assn., 54 LA 492, 494 (Zack, FitzGerald & Cohen, 1970).

[123]See Atlantic & Gulf Coast Shippers, 6 LA 700, 702 (Kleinsorge, 1947). Also see Arbitrator Coke in 12 LA 870, 884.

[124]See Arbitrators McDermott, Zollner & Hutskow in 52 LA 233, 234–235 (police); Florey in 51 LA 994, 996 (police); Singer in 47 LA 482, 486 (sanitarium employees).

[125]See Third Ave. Transit Corp., 1 LA 321, 325 (Hays, 1946). Galveston Model Laundry, 26 War Lab. Rep. 224 (1943). Cf., Arbitrator Blum in 65 LA 997, 1001–1002. In City of Southfield, 78 LA 153, 155 (1982), Arbitrator Roumell quoted Arbitrator Charles C. Killingsworth to the effect that "the employer's ability to pay may probably be taken into consideration only within the limits of a 'zone of reasonableness.' "

basis for a change in wages, it is a significant element properly to be taken into account in determining the weight to be attached to other criteria.[126]

The ability-to-pay standard has been advanced more frequently by management than by labor. For this reason, it has been suggested that perhaps it should be called the "inability-to-pay" standard.[127] Regardless of title, however, the standard has been advanced by management to resist wage demands on the ground of inability to pay, and it has been advanced by labor to support demands for higher wages on the ground of ability to pay. In advancing this criterion, labor may argue that, when the trend is toward higher wage levels, leadership should be taken by employers best able to afford it.[128]

To determine wages exclusively on the basis of ability to pay would lead to wage scales that vary from company to company, and would require a new determination of the wage scale with each rise or fall in profits. The existence of unequal wage levels among different companies would be incompatible with union programs for the equalization of wage rates among companies in the same industry or area. If inability to pay were used as the sole or absolute basis for wage cuts, inefficient producers would receive the benefit of having a lower wage scale than that of efficient ones, regardless of the fact that the value of the services rendered by the employees of each is the same.[129] Indeed, arbitrators have expressed the view that to use the ability-to-pay standard as the sole basis for a wage increase would in effect involve a decision by the arbitrator as to how business revenues should be distributed among stockholders, employees, and the consuming public; arbitrators do not feel themselves competent to rule on such a broad issue of social and economic policy.[130]

One board of arbitration indicated three different degrees of weight which may be given to the ability-to-pay factor. Speaking through its Chairman, John T. Dunlop, that board outlined the three situations as follows: (1) "In the case of properties which have been highly profitable over a period of years, the wage rate would normally be increased slightly over the levels indicated by other standards"; (2) "in the case of persistently unprofitable firms, the wage rate would normally be reduced slightly from the levels indicated by other standards"; (3) "in the case of the companies whose financial record over a period of years falls between these extremes, the wage rate level would be determined largely by other standards."[131]

---

[126]General Motors Corp., 1 LA 125, 145 (Garrison, Eisenhower & Stacy, 1946). Also see statement by Arbitrator Prasow in 27 LA 468, 473.
[127]Slichter, Basic Criteria Used in Wage Negotations, 25 (1947).
[128]A General Motors fact-finding board considered the earning capacity and the good prospects for high profits of the corporation as one basis for its taking leadership in the establishment of a wage pattern for American industry. General Motors Corp., 1 LA 125, 137–138 (Garrison, Eisenhower & Stacy, 1946).
[129]The employer paying lower scales would, of course, ultimately tend to get less efficient labor.
[130]International Harvester Co., 1 LA 512, 517 (Marshall, Spencer & Holly, 1946).
[131]Twin City Rapid Transit Co., 10 LA 581, 594 (1948).

Another board, serving as fact-finders in a public-sector dispute, stressed that the employer's "ability to pay cannot be the starting point of any analysis." The following explanation by that board's members, James J. Healy and Laurence E. Seibel, was made in response to the State of Connecticut's plea of inability to pay increased retirement benefits for teachers whose representatives contended that "significant pools of income" remain untapped and available to finance the benefits:

> "The State argued that the increasing budget deficits, the need to maintain a lower tax burden than New York and Massachusetts so as to maintain and attract business, the loss of substantial federal revenues under the new Reagan federalism, the competing demands for limited State resources, and the political climate precluding the introduction of new taxes, taken together, result in the State's inability to maintain the present retirement system, much less to increase benefits as requested by the Bargaining Groups.
>
> "The Bargaining Groups countered that Connecticut is a wealthy State with a high per capita income, that there are significant pools of income that presently are undertaxed in relation to other states, and that a State income tax would provide more than adequate revenue for the continuation and needed improvements in the * * * retirement programs.
>
> "A claim of inability to pay ordinarily is a type of affirmative argument that would be applicable only if it were initially determined that, on the merits, the arguments of the Bargaining Groups were valid, i.e., that the present retirement system should be continued and improved. A state's ability to pay cannot be the starting point of any analysis; the fact that a state may have a large budget surplus, in and of itself, would not justify an improvement in fair and adequate retirement benefits. Similarly, budgetary problems, in and of themselves, would not justify reducing retirement benefits, as opposed to social programs or other state services, if those retirement benefits were found to be reasonable and appropriate in light of all relevant circumstances.
>
> "Accordingly, the reasonableness and appropriateness of the present retirement programs must be examined to determine whether the State has sustained its burden of persuading us that a different and more limited retirement program is justified * * *."[132]

There have been many instances where the "unfavorable" financial condition of the employer resulted in the granting of smaller increases (or none at all) than otherwise would have been allowed had there been no inability to pay.[133] In one instance a reduction in wages was granted because of the employer's precarious financial position,

---

[132]State of Conn., 77 LA 729, 732 (1981). Although the quoted statement may have its broadest applicability in the public sector, the thought which the statement carries may be relevant also in many private-sector cases.

[133]See Arbitrator Sabghir in 69 LA 771, 774 (finding some limitation on ability to pay and stating that the employer, as a private enterprise nursing home rather than a nonprofit institution, is "entitled to some reasonable level of net income"); Gootnick in 67 LA 293, 296–297; Sembower in 65 LA 839, 843–844; Mueller in 63 LA 824, 828; Kelliher in 62 LA 897, 898; Platt in 50 LA 1103, 1114–1115; Singer in 48 LA 289, 291; Stutz in 40 LA 282, 284; Flagler in 38 LA 666, 673–674; Fallon in 37 LA 270, 272; Bothwell in 34 LA 398, 402; Jones in 28 LA 40, 43; Scheiber in 27 LA 309, 315; Hogan in 25 LA 247, 251; Abruzzi in 23 LA 334, 336; Stein in 10 LA 813, 814; Albert in 10 LA 18, 19; Taylor in 9 LA 666, 683–684; Rosenfarb in 7 LA 257, 259; Brissenden in 6 LA 639, 643; Blair in 3 LA 370, 371, and in 3 LA 245, 248.

even though there had been a large increase in the cost of living since the last wage increase. In ordering the reduction, the arbitrator said:

> "The Arbitrator is mindful of the fact that the recommendation of a reduction in wage rates at this time, while the general trend is towards the granting of increases, is a very serious and unpopular recommendation. However, the Arbitrator is convinced that, if the property can be saved, it should result in long-range benefits to the employees and that the seniority accumulated by many of the present employees of the Company will be conserved, enabling them to reap the benefits thereof when profitable operations are again resumed."[134]

An arbitrator may give recognition to an employer's weak financial position by ordering that a needed increase be made gradually.[135] Sometimes an arbitrator will award an increase but will recognize the inability-to-pay factor at least to the extent of limiting or denying retroactivity,[136] or of ordering a review of the employer's financial situation after a specified period.[137] Thus, appropriate relief can be granted to the employer based on operations under the award during the specified period.[138] But mere temporary inability to pay generally is not sufficient to cut down an increase warranted by other criteria. Moreover, consideration generally will not be given to short-run variations in profits.[139] Thus, for example, extensive nonrecurring losses charged to current operations were rejected as the basis for a lower wage adjustment.[140] A probable future decline in ability to pay sometimes will be taken into account by arbitrators "as a moderating influence on the amount of the increase recommended."[141]

Inability to pay may be given slight consideration where the employer's rates are substandard or inequitable in comparison with

---

[134]Trailways of New Eng., 7 LA 319, 321 (Copelop, 1947). The decision appears to have been well advised, for a few months later the arbitrator found the Company's financial position to be sufficiently improved to permit a restoration of the prior wage rate. Trailways of New Eng., 8 LA 363, 365 (Copelof, 1947). A wage reduction was ordered because of the employer's precarious position in Tynan Throwing Co., 20 LA 614, 615 (Bailer, 1953).

[135]See Arbitrator Roumell in 56 LA 209, 218; Brecht in 21 LA 356, 359; Lesser in 17 LA 914, 917; Justin in 9 LA 468, 471.

[136]See Florida E. Coast Ry., 41 LA 1001, 1014 (Platt, Bok & Guthrie, 1963); Felt Cos., 16 LA 881, 883 (Lesser, 1951). The National War Labor Board considered ability to pay in determining retroactivity of its orders, James L. Whitaker, 14 War Lab. Rep. 401 (1944), and it also considered this factor in certain special cases, such as where an employer was unable to pay because of inability to get sufficient oil to operate profitably, Consumers Oil & Ref. Co., 9 War Lab. Rep. 407 (1943).

[137]International Braid Co., 6 LA 911, 913 (Brown, 1947).

[138]Associated Food Shops, 7 LA 870, 872–873 (Baskind, 1947).

[139]Florida E. Coast Ry., 41 LA 1001, 1011–1013 (Platt, Bok & Guthrie, 1963); Twin City Rapid Transit Co., 10 LA 581, 594 (Dunlop, 1948). A railroad emergency board explained the "interaction between wages and ability to pay," stating in part that: "Financial distress or high profits do not tend in large-scale industry to affect wages in the very short period. The relationship between wages and financial conditions in large-scale industry is typically more gradual. Erosion of financial conditions and the decline in long-run prospects, or a series of profitable years with continuing good prospects, influence wage setting. The financial experience of the railroads over a series of recent years and their prospects for the next several years are most significant to current decisions on wages." Railroads v. Nonoperating Unions, 34 LA 517, 534 (Dunlop, Aaron & Sempliner, 1960).

[140]United States Sugar Co., 5 LA 314, 319 (France, 1946).

[141]Greyhound Bus Co., 1 LA 596, 609 (Simkin, Freidin & Wallen, 1946). To similar effect, Arbitrator Murray in 11 LA 1132, 1134–1135.

other rates in the industry or area.[142] While there is a duty to stockholders to make profits, there is also a duty to employees to pay "fair" wages.[143] It has been said that a company "does not expect price concessions from suppliers because of inability to pay, and must recognize its duty to its employees to pay them fair wages."[144] If, however, an increase in wage rates would put the rates above the industry or area standard, the inability-to-pay factor will be given considerable weight.[145]

Sometimes an increase in wage rates, if granted, would endanger the solvency of the employer. While the basic risk of business belongs to management, not to the employees,[146] "high wage rates have no value to employees when layoffs are caused thereby."[147] Arbitrators give consideration to the reason for the absence of profits. If the reason is managerial inefficiency, the employees are not likely to be penalized by the denial of wage increases to which they are entitled.[148] The theory here is that if the employer goes out of business new management may put the company on a paying basis.[149] But, if the reason lies in causes beyond the control of management or if it is a matter of strong competition by large firms against small firms, the arbitrator will be less likely to risk the possibility of bankruptcy of the employer. In making a wage award, one arbitration board said: "We assume, without deciding, that any wage increase will put the company out of business." Then the board explained its severe but interesting view as follows:

> "On the record before us, the employer has no better claim to continue in business upon the basis of a subnormal payroll than the employees have to seek wage increases upon the basis of the size of the employer's past profits or the amount of his assets.
> "Never have the wages of the employees of this company been related to profit or loss contingencies. The company and its employees have never been partners or joint venturers in this enterprise. Over the many years when the company made sustained and substantial profits, the employees were not offered a share in the benefits. And now, when it

---

[142]See Arbitrator Donnelly in 27 LA 85, 87; Brecht in 21 LA 356, 359; Meyers in 20 LA 258, 259; Cole in 9 LA 577, 580; Frankenthaler in 8 LA 478, 480. Also see Raines in 19 LA 464, 466.

[143]See Arbitrator Stutz in 40 LA 282, 284 ("employees should not be expected to underwrite the employer's losses"); Donnelly in 27 LA 85, 87; Strong in 7 LA 673, 676; Meyer in 4 LA 604, 634. In Textile Maintenance Assn., 63 LA 197, 202 (1974), the employers argued that "the employees must suffer because they are in a declining industry [laundry and dry cleaning]," to which argument Arbitrator Anthony V. Sinicropi responded that "Likewise the employers must suffer."

[144]Birmingham Elec. Co., 7 LA 673, 676 (Strong, 1947). To similar effect, Arbitrator Kleinsorge in 23 LA 733, 740.

[145]Western Union Tel. Co., 4 LA 251, 263 (Wallen, Cahn & Donahue, 1946).

[146]Capital Transit Co., 9 LA 666, 684 (Taylor, 1947); Atlantic City Transp. Co., 9 LA 577, 580 (Cole, 1948).

[147]Prairie DuChien Woolen Mills Co., 10 LA 73, 75 (Rauch, 1948). To similar effect, Arbitrator Gootnick in 67 LA 293, 303; Hogan in 25 LA 247, 250–251; Abruzzi in 23 LA 334, 336; Bailer in 20 LA 614, 615; Simkin in 18 LA 631, 645; Brown in 11 LA 984, 990–991.

[148]See Western Union Tel. Co., 4 LA 251, 264 (Wallen, Cahn & Donahue, 1946). Also see Arbitrator Hamby in 78 LA 352, 356–357; Donnelly in 27 LA 85, 87.

[149]See discussion in Centinela Valley Taxicab Co., 28 LA 40, 42–43 (Jones, 1957). But consider the U.S. Supreme Court *Bildisco* decision discussed in note 150 below.

is claimed that the company faces losses, it is not perceived why the employees should be asked to share any of the burden.

"We therefore conclude that these wages should be fixed without regard to the financial condition of the company or its ability to continue in business."[150]

Some arbitrators, however, take the view that "a clear showing that proposed increases would destroy a business or cause the discontinuance of a service would ordinarily be an important and perhaps a controlling factor in an arbitration decision."[151]

Proof of Inability to Pay

Employers who have pleaded inability to pay have been held to have the burden of producing sufficient evidence to support the plea. The alleged inability must be more than "speculative,"[152] and failure to produce sufficient evidence will result in a rejection of the plea.[153] The payment of reasonable dividends to stockholders and of reason-

---

[150]California Street Cable Ry., 7 LA 91, 94 (Wyckoff, 1947). The National War Labor Board sometimes granted increases despite employer contentions that any increase would force the company out of business. Title Guarantee & Trust Co., 9 War Lab. Rep. 457 (1943). On the other hand, the possibility exists than an employer may be able to escape burdensome collective agreement obligations through reorganization in bankruptcy. In its 1984 *Bildisco* decision the U.S. Supreme Court stated that the "fundamental purpose of reorganization [under the Bankruptcy Code] is to prevent a debtor from going into liquidation, with an attendant loss of jobs and possible misuse of economic resources," and the Court held that while the employer remains "obligated to bargain in good faith under NLRA §8(a)(5) over the terms and conditions of a possible new contract, it is not guilty of an unfair labor practice by unilaterally breaching a collective-bargaining agreement before formal Bankruptcy Court action" on allowing rejection of the collective agreement as an "executory contract" under the Bankruptcy Code, or before having reached an impasse in bargaining. NLRB v. Bildisco & Bildisco, 104 S.Ct. 1188, 115 LRRM 2805, 2813, 2815–2816 (1984). The Court stated that before acting on a petition to modify or reject a collective agreement, "the Bankruptcy Court should be persuaded that reasonable efforts to negotiate a voluntary modification have been made and are not likely to produce a prompt and satisfactory solution"; the Court also stated that rejection should not be permitted without a finding that the policy of the Bankruptcy Code to permit successful rehabilitation of debtors "would be served by such action," and that this determination "involves balancing the interests of * * * the debtor, creditors, and employees." 115 LRRM at 2812-2813. Soon after the *Bildisco* decision was issued, Congress enacted legislation which overrules it to some extent. In this regard, it has been explained that the Bankruptcy Amendments and Federal Judges Act of 1984 contains a "provision which requires bankruptcy court approval before a debtor can reject a collective bargaining agreement, and permits the court to approve rejection only if the union has rejected the debtor's contract modifications 'without good cause' and the balance of equities 'clearly favors' rejection of the union contract." "Approval of Bankruptcy Reform Bill," 116 LRR 181, 182 (1984), where it is also explained that under the Act

"it is possible for a debtor to unilaterally implement contract changes if the bankruptcy court fails to act on its application to reject the union contract in timely fashion. A debtor can also make 'interim changes' in a union contract with court approval 'if essential to the continuation of the debtor's business or in order to avoid irreparable damage to the estate.' "

[151]Georgia Power Co., 8 LA 691, 695 (Hepburn, 1947). To similar effect, Arbitrator Tyree in 13 LA 384, 386. Again, consider the material in note 150 above.

[152]Restaurant-Hotel Employers' Council of San Diego, 11 LA 469, 477 (Aaron, 1948).

[153]See Arbitrators Platt, Bok & Guthrie in 41 LA 1001, 1013; Justin in 7 LA 241, 243; Feinberg in 6 LA 636, 639; Copelof in 3 LA 437, 442. Also see Winton in 72 LA 190, 196 (proceeding on the assumption that the municipal employer was "in reasonably good financial condition," since "No evidence to the contrary was presented"); Sinicropi in 63 LA 197, 201 (pointing to certain inadequacies of income tax returns as evidence of the employer's economic status). From the standpoint of the duty to bargain under the National Labor Relations Act, substantiating evidence to support a plea of inability to pay need not always be furnished, but refusal to furnish such evidence on request is one of the factors which may be considered in determining whether the employer has refused to bargain in good faith. Truitt Mfg. Co. v. NLRB, 76 S.Ct. 753, 38 LRRM 2042 (1956).

able salaries to top management has been held to render invalid a plea of inability to pay.[154] Management should be prepared to disclose its profit and loss statements in support of a plea of inability to pay. Arbitrators should provide any safeguards needed to protect the confidential nature of such evidence. Failure of management specifically to plead inability to pay may be considered sufficient to establish ability to pay up to the maximum demanded by the union.[155]

Public Utility Ability to Pay

Special considerations are involved in the application of the ability-to-pay standard in public utility disputes. It is recognized that, since a public utility produces a basic necessity of life and since the public regulatory body must assure the opportunity for a fair return, capacity to pay generally will exist, potentially at least, and that almost any conceivable level of wages could be paid and a "fair profit" still returned to the stockholders. However, not only "fair wages" and "fair profits" are involved—a "fair price" to the consumer also enters the picture—thus, ability to pay should not be made the primary consideration in determining public utility wage rates.[156]

An arbitrator may give some weight to the fact that a company is unable, under the terms of its franchise, to seek an increase in the price of its service to the public. This was done by one arbitrator despite the contention of the union that it should not be made a party to the "straightjacket" in which the company had placed itself.[157] On the other hand, an arbitrator may refuse to grant the request of a public utility that any wage increase awarded should be conditioned on the company's securing a rate increase for its services. Arbitrator John T. Dunlop, speaking as Chairman of a board of arbitration, explained the view behind such refusal:

"In public utilities, including the railroads, there appears to be a long tradition of separation of wage and rate setting. This does not mean that rates and prices are irrelevant to wage setting, but rather that wage rates have tended to be fixed with some general reference to financial capacity and then these costs in turn have been taken into account by the rate or fare making body. Such has been the actual relation between collective bargaining or emergency boards determining wage rates and the Inter-State Commerce Commission setting railroad rates and fares. The transit industry has tended to follow an analogous practice.

---

[154]Employees Transit Lines, 4 LA 748, 752 (Copelof, 1946). In City of Havre, Mont., 76 LA 789, 794–797 (1981), Arbitrator Carlton J. Snow stated it to be "his obligation to test the basic proposition of the Employer that 'severe financial hardships' prevent the City from funding what the arbitrator has concluded is a reasonable wage demand." Pointing to recent equipment acquisitions and capital improvements, which were nice but not imperative, and noting that the City had not taken advantage of the full potential of revenue sources, he concluded that the City had failed to meet its burden of proving financial hardship in relation to the reasonable wage demand of the employees. Also see comments of Arbitrator Block in 81 LA 352, 357.

[155]Oil Indus., 1 LA 168, 176 (Graham, Eliel & Beyer, 1946).

[156]Pacific Gas & Elec. Co., 7 LA 528, 531 (Kerr, 1947). Also see Arbitrator Eisele in 78 LA 1119, 1122–1124 (note the company's position and its discussion by the Arbitrator); Sembower in 65 LA 839, 844; Platt in 63 LA 1189, 1196.

[157]New York City Omnibus Corp., 7 LA 794, 809 (Cole, 1947).

"The majority of the Arbitration Board believes it can follow no other precedent in this case.* * * When the Arbitration Board has fixed the wage rates, the appropriate fare making body should then set fares, in accordance with proper standards, including the wage rates set by this Arbitration Board as costs. No other procedure in the fixing of wages and fares, which are necessarily interdependent, by different bodies can be workable."[158]

Public Sector Ability to Pay

Special considerations are likewise involved in the application of the ability-to-pay standard in public sector cases. In these cases the employer often does not have sources of revenue apart from the taxing power, which has various limitations including the need for public support.[159]

Where a city-owned hospital did have sources of revenue over and above the taxing power, Fact-Finder George T. Roumell specified that a recommended wage increase should be made gradually in consideration of the hospital's "somewhat dismal" financial picture, but he explained his refusal to give greater weight to the hospital's plea of inability to pay:

"The point is that we are in a period of inflation. Public employees have made great strides in attempting to bridge the gap in their wages between those of private sector and themselves. Such an attempt becomes even more dramatic in a city like Flint where a large percentage of the work force is employed by an employer paying very substantial wages, namely the General Motors Corporation. What private employers have been finding is that because of increased wage demands they have been faced with a profit squeeze. It has caused reappraisals in management techniques in order to continue to produce profits. Such an approach should also occur in public employment. This is particularly so when dealing with a hospital that does have sources of revenues over and above taxing powers. Bluntly put, Hurley Hospital must act like any other employer in recognizing inflationary trends and the normal request for wage increases that are occurring all over the country and

---

[158]Indianapolis Rys., 9 LA 319, 330 (1947). In recognition of the problem implied here, it has sometimes been suggested that the whole job should be done by the same agency; i.e., that the rate-making body should also have jurisdiction to determine wage rates. It has also sometimes been suggested that wage awards should bind the utility commission. In any event, one arbitrator in effect asked that the regulatory commission grant a rate increase to accommodate the wage increase granted by his award. See Twin City Rapid Transit Co., 16 LA 749, 760 (Platt, 1951).

[159]For discussion of various special considerations that may be involved, see Miscimarra, "Inability to Pay: The Problem of Contract Enforcement in Public Sector Collective Bargaining," 43 U. Pitt. L. Rev. 703 (1982); Mulcahy, "Ability to Pay: The Public Employee Dilemma," 31 Arb. J. 90 (1976). In Hamtramck Bd. of Educ., 54 LA 162, 162–163 (Gould, 1969), the dispute was submitted by the parties with the understanding that the neutral should not make any recommendations which would result in a deficit budget for the public employer. In City of N. Las Vegas, Nev., 75 LA 784, 789 (1980), Fact-Finder James A. Sullivan stated that by statute his recommendations or award must be based upon "facts" in evidence, and that "anticipated, but not yet appropriated, certain or guaranteed" federal revenue sharing funds accordingly could not be considered in determining the public-sector employer's financial ability to pay the full increase demanded by the union. For discussion of interest arbitration and state "cap" laws limiting increases in public spending, see articles by Minami, Clark, and Fallon, "Interest Arbitration: Can the Public Sector Afford It? Developing Limitations on the Process," Proceedings of the 34th Annual Meeting of NAA, 241–272 (BNA Books, 1982).

meet the increases by a review of its labor needs and its management techniques."[160]

In another case Fact-Finder Richard I. Bloch noted the dilemma of a Board of Education, as employer, which was confronted by wage demands from teachers in spite of recent defeats of tax proposals for school purposes:

"The Board of Education is placed squarely in the middle in all these financing problems. On the one hand, they must provide for the citizenry the best possible education for the children of the area. On the other hand, they must answer to those same citizens for the use of the tax dollars. Unfortunately, millage issues seem to be the area where already-overtaxed voters get their revenge. Unless the Oscoda area constituents soon realize the importance of their support, their children will have no classrooms in which to learn. The burden of supporting the capital expenditures of a school system should not fall totally upon the teachers, although some restraint in wage demands is advisable."[161]

In granting a wage increase to police officers to bring them generally in line with police in other communities, an arbitration board recognized the financial problems of the city resulting from temporarily reduced property valuations during an urban redevelopment program; but the board stated that a police officer should be treated as a skilled employee whose wages reflect the caliber of the work expected from such employees, and the board declared that it "cannot accept the conclusion that the Police Department must continue to

---

[160]Hurley Hosp., 56 LA 209, 219 (1971). Also see statements by Arbitrator Edes in 53 LA 372, 383; Cahn in 52 LA 971, 972. In Palo Alto-Stanford Hosp. Center, 50 LA 700, 716 (Mann, 1968), the arbitrator spoke in terms of balancing and giving fair recognition to the interests of the employees and the hospital employer, and also to the interests of the public "in high quality, economical, and essential hospital care."

[161]Oscoda Area Schools, 55 LA 568, 578 (1970). Also see statements by Arbitrator Witney in 68 LA 454, 457 (stating that the municipal employer was "faced with serious financial problems resulting from economic conditions over which it has no control," and that while the Arbitrator's observations concerning the employer's financial situation "will not comfort" the employees, "they are economic realities"); Holden in 67 LA 384, 387; Bychinsky in 66 LA 249, 250; Oppenheim in 63 LA 621, 624–625; Rauch in 63 LA 126, 131–132; Seidenberg in 54 LA 796, 799 ("the salaries must come from public revenues which are not limitless, and while teachers should not be expected to subsidize the community in its efforts to obtain quality education, their salary requests must be viewed in light of the total county demands for public funds"); Zack in 54 LA 492, 495; Kerrison in 52 LA 1169, 1176 (noting budget limitations and the fact that the budget had been approved at the polls); Teple in 52 LA 800, 802 (community refused to support higher levy needed for teacher salary increase—the arbitrator recommended no increase for balance of school year since the employer had no source of revenue for payment of any increase, the arbitrator rejecting a suggestion that an increase be paid even if the school must close early for lack of funds). Legislation enacted to implement California's Proposition 13 was involved in County of Humbolt, 72 LA 63, 66 (Henderson, 1978), where the award merely stated that "the County is *not* in a position to finance the economic request of the Sheriff's Department, even though based upon the [Consumer Price Index] and other factors a salary increase may well be justified." For other examples of statutory obligation imposed upon neutrals to give substantial or controlling weight to the public-sector employer's inability to pay, see City of N. Las Vegas, Nev., 75 LA 784, 785 (Sullivan, 1980), involving a Nevada statute providing that a finding must first be made regarding financial ability to pay, and that if ability to pay is found, then the neutral "shall use normal criteria for interest disputes"; Gershenfeld & Gershenfeld, "Significant Developments in Public Employment Disputes Settlement During 1978," Proceedings of the 32nd Annual Meeting of NAA, 215, 221–222 (BNA Books, 1980), discussing the Financal Emergency Act for the City of New York as amended in 1978 to require neutrals to accord substantial weight to the factor of ability to pay—the amendment defined ability to pay as the "financial ability * * * to pay the cost of any increase in wages or fringe benefits without requiring an increase in the level of city taxes existing" when the impasse proceeding commenced.

suffer until the redevelopment program is completed."[162] However, the board did give definite weight to the city's budget limitations by denying a request for improved vacation benefits, additional insurance, a shift differential, and for a cost-of-living escalator clause.[163] In another case, involving police officers and firemen, an arbitrator awarded a 6 percent wage increase (which he recognized as the prevailing pattern in private industry) in spite of the city's financial problems; he did limit the increase to this figure, though a larger increase was deserved, in order to keep the city within the statutory taxing limit and in light of the impact of the award upon the wages of other city employees.[164]

In some cases neutrals have expressly asserted an obligation of public employers to make added effort to obtain additional funds to finance improved terms of employment found to be justified.[165] Also, in another case the neutral refused to excuse a public employer from its obligation to pay certain automatic increases which the employer had voluntarily contracted to pay, the neutral ordering the employer to "take all required steps to provide the funds necessary to implement" his award in favor of the employees.[166]

Finally, we may note that where one city submitted information regarding its revenues and expenditures to support its claim of inability to pay an otherwise justified wage increase, Arbitrator Stanley M. Block responded that the "information is interesting, but is not really relevant to the issues," and he explained:

> "The *price of labor* must be viewed like any other commodity which needs to be purchased. If a new truck is needed, the City does not plead poverty and ask to buy the truck for 25% of its established price. It can

---

[162]Borough of Turtle Creek, 52 LA 233, 235 (McDermott, Zollner & Hutskow, 1968). Also see statement of Arbitrator Gabriel Alexander quoted by Arbitrator Roumell in 78 LA 153, 155.

[163]Id. at 235, 237. In City of Uniontown, 51 LA 1072, 1074 (Duff, 1968), some improved fringe benefits were awarded to police department employees in lieu of awarding a salary increase larger than that necessary to place them "on parity with salaries paid by municipalities of comparable size."

[164]City of Easton, Pa., 51 LA 879, 881–882 (Handsaker, 1968). In City of Mount Vernon, 49 LA 1229, 1232–1233 (McFadden, Gould & Karow, 1968), involving police and firemen, fact-finders would "not ignore" the city's ability to pay, but they declared that they must make recommendations that are fair and equitable to the employees, the public employer, and the public itself, and they added: "In the final analysis, the City * * * must raise whatever revenues are necessary in the manner which it deems best. The electorate must then pass on these decisions and, inferentially, this Board's recommendations." The fact-finders construed the New York public employee statute as contemplating budgetary action subsequent to fact-finding and they suggested that the budgetary action already taken by the city should not be deemed so final as to preclude implementation of the board's recommendations. For another case where the neutral balanced the interests of the employees (firemen), the city (particularly as to financial resources), and the public, see Arbitrator Dunlop in 42 LA 1114, 1118–1119. Also see DiLauro in 79 LA 372, 373.

[165]See Arbitrator Rule in 65 LA 1009, 1015 (outlining several steps that the employer might consider for the purpose of financing the full wage increase recommended for teachers); Gleeson in 56 LA 697, 699 (the parties should urge the Legislature to appropriate funds); Roumell in 54 LA 901, 908–910; Seitz in 47 LA 1036, 1040. In Amphitheater Pub. School Bd. of Trustees, 75 LA 268, 274–275 (1980), Arbitrator Sharon K. Weizenbaum's wage recommendation was made with due recognition that it was "a time when careful planning and paring of dollars from the budget is essential," but the door was left ajar for possible additional benefits, her award stating that the parties "agree to reopen negotiations if the Arizona legislature makes changes in school finance after an agreement is reached."

[166]City of Cleveland, 57 LA 781, 787–789 (Dworkin, 1971). Cf., Fact-Finder Gentile in 67 LA 654, 657–658.

shop various dealers and makes of truck to get the best possible buy. But in the end the City either pays the asked price or gets along without a new truck."

It should be recognized that the employer was a "home rule" city and that Arbitrator Block did not indicate the existence of any legal debt limitation upon the city.[167]

Competition

A factor which often must be given consideration in interest arbitration is the competitive nature of the employer's business. In some respects this is related to the ability-to-pay standard. In other respects it is related to the prevailing-practice standard. For these reasons it is generally not considered as an independent standard. Where, however, an employer is engaged in a highly competitive business or is faced with special competitive problems, the arbitrator may specifically point out the competitive nature of the employer's business as a factor to be given special consideration in setting contract terms (sometimes even justifying a wage reduction).[168]

Wage "Patterns"

The "pattern" may be defined as a particular kind of solution of collective bargaining issues which has been used on a wide enough scale to be distinctly identified. The pattern standard is obviously closely related to the prevailing-practice standard and could reasonably be considered merely as one of its aspects. However, it is often spoken of as if it were a distinct criterion.

A "pattern" in wage arbitrations is often stated in terms of a specific number of cents per hour, or it may be stated as a percentage wage increase. For instance, the pattern standard would recognize that where companies or industries A, B, and C have granted general wage increases of 10 cents per hour, related company or industry D should grant a 10 cent increase also. In the application of this standard stress is placed upon the granting of the same amount or percentage of increase granted by others, rather than upon the granting of the same total wage that is paid by comparable employers.

A limited number of key wage bargains, or even only one, might set a pattern for a large part of American industry. Recognition of this

---

[167]City of Quincy, Ill., 81 LA 352, 356–357 (1982). As a "home rule" city under the State Constitution, the city was permitted to "exercise any power and perform any function pertaining to its government and affairs; and to protect the general health, morals, safety and welfare of its citizens." Id. at 353.

[168]See Arbitrator Stout in 66 LA 158, 160; Gill in 62 LA 654, 655; Black in 41 LA 372, 375; Gundermann in 39 LA 249, 253; Kleinsorge in 24 LA 38, 44; Donnelly in 23 LA 843, 844; Hogan in 23 LA 762, 773; Knowlton in 22 LA 653, 654; Bailer in 20 LA 614, 615; Gellhorn in 18 LA 774, 775; Simkin in 18 LA 631, 644–645; Singer in 9 LA 567, 569; Wolff in 8 LA 194, 195; Kirsh in 7 LA 350, 353; Whiteacre in 6 LA 749, 750–751.

fact was one of the factors which strongly influenced a fact-finding board for the Basic Steel Industry to refuse to grant a general wage increase; it was felt that any increase granted would probably be urged as a pattern to be followed in other industries, which, considering the best interests of the general economy at that time, would not have been desirable.[169]

Among other possibilities, the pattern observed may be a national pattern for industry in general,[170] or a national pattern for the particular industry or for related industries,[171] or it may be the pattern for general industry in the area,[172] or for the particular industry in the area.[173] The national pattern may be rejected where a grant of the national figure would upset the trend set by the local area pattern.[174]

Arbitrator Clark Kerr stated that arbitrators should give great weight to "patterns" or "packages" of wage increases, such as those established during the various rounds of increases after World War II, since "rightly or wrongly" such patterns had been established and widely applied in free collective bargaining.[175] While in many cases the full amount of the pattern figure has been granted, in others the pattern factor has been just one of several considered, with the result that the increase granted was not the exact pattern figure.[176] Then, too, under the circumstances of some cases the "pattern" may be rejected entirely.[177]

"Patterns" do not always call for wage increases. Rather, the "pattern" may be for wage decreases,[178] or, when the economy so justifies, for maintenance of the status quo.

---

[169]Basic Steel Indus., 13 LA 46, 52 (Daugherty, Cole & Rosenman, 1949). Illustrating that a pattern may be accepted on its face value, one emergency board, in applying the established pattern, said that "we need not consider the multiple factors in wage determination that entered into the establishment thereof." New York Harbor Carriers v. Railroad Marine Harbor Council, 35 LA 628, 632 (Whiting, Roberts & Coburn, 1960). In Pacific Maritime Assn., 35 LA 185, 189 (Ross, 1960), it was emphasized that there are some bargaining topics which are affected by variations in local conditions and cannot be satisfactorily handled by a blanket, industrywide approach.

[170]As where an arbitrator recognized a "pattern of increases" of about 6 percent to have been "widespread in American industry." City of Easton, Pa., 51 LA 879, 880 (Handsaker, 1968). Also see Arbitrator Platt in 50 LA 1103, 1104.

[171]See railroad emergency boards in 53 LA 555; 41 LA 1001; 35 LA 628; 34 LA 517; 28 LA 110; 17 LA 236; 6 LA 334. Also see 26 LA 14. In Iowa Beef Processors, 62 LA 654, 657–658 (1974), an express objective of Arbitrator Lewis M. Gill's award was *to establish a pattern* for the industry.

[172]Viloco Mach. Co., 3 LA 867, 870–871 (Ziegler, 1946). A settlement by a large employer in a given area may have strong impact upon other industries within that area, as did a General Motors settlement. Hurley Hosp., 56 LA 209, 213–215 (Roumell, 1971).

[173]See Arbitrator Platt in 63 LA 1189, 1196; Ross in 29 LA 96, 99; Howard in 23 LA 429, 434; Haughton in 14 LA 655, 660–661. Also see Feller in 60 LA 1, 6–7. It could even be a pattern for one company only, as where a pattern resulting from agreements between an employer and several unions was applied to some of his employees represented by still another union. Memphis Publishing Co., 26 LA 381, 382 (Hepburn, 1956). Similarly, see Arbitrator Goldberg in 72 LA 90, 92; Williams in 68 LA 1064, 1066–1067; Joseph in 48 LA 425, 428–429. In United States Postal Serv., 83 LA 1120, 1122 (1985), arbitration board Chairman Marlin M. Volz spoke of the "need to stay within, or close to, the monetary benefits" awarded to other employees of the same employer by another arbitration board in United States Postal Serv., 83 LA 1105 (Kerr, Simon, Kheel, Nash & Mahon, 1984).

[174]Jamaica Buses, 4 LA 225, 227 (Cahn, 1946).

[175]Pacific Gas & Elec. Co., 7 LA 528, 534 (1947).

[176]See Arbitrator Roumell in 56 LA 209, 213–214; Healy in 8 LA 124, 126–127; Pollard in 8 LA 134, 136; Kirsh in 7 LA 350, 353. In Labor Standards Assn., 36 LA 171, 178 (Roberts, 1960), departure from the "pattern" was denied lest an inequity be created.

[177]See E. Cummings Leather Co., 25 LA 247, 250 (Hogan, 1955).

[178]As in Cheney Bros., 21 LA 159, 163–165 (Scheiber, 1953). Also see Arbitrator Kleinsorge in 24 LA 38, 44.

In one railroad emergency board proceeding the use of the industry "pattern" was vigorously challenged by the railroad shopcrafts, which insisted that their wage claims should be considered on their merits regardless of the terms to which other railroad unions had agreed. The emergency board responded:

> "Again, as earlier stated, this Board is trapped in the 'pattern' dilemma faced by the parties and by many previous Emergency Boards. The Organizations are asked to accept a general wage increase which was established at bargaining tables at which they were not represented, a wage increase agreement which is thus not of their making. The frustration of the Organizations at being locked into an established pattern is understandable, but, equally understandable is the Carriers' unwillingness to break and upset * * * a wage agreement voluntarily negotiated in good faith at an earlier date. Late settlements above a pattern earlier established penalize employees involved in the earlier voluntary negotiations. This is destructive of the broader system of collective bargaining in the industry. Until and unless the structure of bargaining is modified in the industry there can be no improved approach to this difficult problem. Under these circumstances this Board cannot recommend departure from the wage pattern already in effect for some 77 percent of all railroad employees."[179]

However, the board did say that special increases could be given, without breaking the "pattern," based upon factors peculiar to the shopcrafts:

> "To the extent and degree mutually satisfactory modifications of [work] rules are negotiated, appropriate wage adjustments could be made. Wage increases justified by modifications in rules which, through improved organization of work, contribute to efficiency, productivity, and cost reduction would not be incompatible with earlier wage settlements. On the contrary, the Board is of the opinion that negotiations of this character should be encouraged in the industry."[180]

Productivity

The productivity standard is frequently advanced for consideration by arbitrators of wage disputes. Proponents of this standard urge that increases in productivity should be reflected by increases in wages. It has been recognized that there is a close relationship between the general level of productivity and the general level of

---

[179]National Ry. Lab. Conference, 53 LA 555, 559–560 (Seward, Howlett & Livernash, 1969). In Arizona Pub. Serv. Co., 63 LA 1189, 1196 (1974), Arbitrator Harry H. Platt stated:
"In a wage dispute, a Board of Arbitration is bound to an important degree by evidence of a developing or established pattern of wage adjustments in the industry or area under consideration, especially when the adjustments have been reached through collective bargaining. For, as the Chairman has had occasion to note in previous cases, it is almost axiomatic that, if arbitration is to function successfully as a dispute-settling process, it must not yield substantially different results than could be obtained by the parties through bargaining."
For a vigorous effort by an employer to escape the "pattern," see Florida E. Coast Ry., 41 LA 1001, 1010–1013 (Platt, Bok & Guthrie, 1963). Though historically following the prevailing "pattern," the employer escaped it in Franklin Woolen Mills, 37 LA 270, 272 (Fallon, 1961).
[180]National Ry. Lab. Conference, 53 LA 555, 560 (Seward, Howlett & Livernash, 1969).

wages,[181] and that both an increase in wage rates and a reduction in hours may be warranted by increased productivity measured in terms of added output per man-hour.[182]

There is a question, however, as to the extent to which increases in productivity in specific industries should be used as the basis of wage increases within those industries. In one case the union advanced figures to show that productivity had been rising over an extended period of time within the plant, and argued that real wages should be increased commensurately. The arbitration board considered productivity to be an "influential but not decisive" factor, and speaking through its Chairman, Clark Kerr, said:

> "Normally wages rise somewhat more rapidly in those industries where productivity is rising rapidly and less rapidly where productivity is rising slowly or not at all or even declining. Thus productivity is an influential but not controlling factor. For the whole economy it is of more significance, perhaps, than for the individual plant or industry. Real wages can rise significantly in the long run only as physical productivity increases. To tie wages rigidly in each minor segment of the economy to changes in physical productivity in that segment would, however, cause greater distortion as between and among progressive, static and regressive industries than could be sustained."[183]

In another case a fact-finding board for the Basic Steel Industry stated the belief that wage rates in a particular industry should not be tied directly to productivity in that industry but rather should be related to the general industrial rise in productivity; moreover, the board said that any excesses of productivity in any one industry over the general average should provide primarily the means of reducing the prices of the products of that industry.[184]

Increases in productivity can result in increased wages, decreased prices, increased profits, or some combination of the three. If the increase in output per man-hour is due to greater effort and greater skill, there would appear to be no doubt that the gain should accrue to

---

[181]Slichter, Basic Criteria Used in Wage Negotiations, 21 (1947). In a December 1970 speech to the National Association of Manufacturers, Secretary of Labor Hodgson noted the growing interest in improving what might be termed the quality of life and he suggested that the problem is whether this can be achieved without sacrificing something in the quantity or quality of goods and services; in his view, increased productivity or production efficiency is the answer.

[182]General Motors Corp., 1 LA 125, 130 (Garrison, Eisenhower & Stacy, 1946).

[183]Pacific Gas & Elec. Co., 7 LA 528, 530 (1947). Some weight was also given to productivity by Arbitrator Snow in 76 LA 789, 793–794 (finding that there were fewer employees than formerly, he stated that it "is not simply a matter of the same number of employees performing more work, but fewer employees are accomplishing the job for the Employer"); Bloch in 73 LA 1, 4–5; Platt in 63 LA 1189, 1192, 1196; Kagel in 28 LA 600, 606; Hogan in 23 LA 762, 774; Cole in 22 LA 371, 378; Shulman in 22 LA 297, 299; Gilden in 20 LA 219, 223–224; Guthrie in 20 LA 93, 98–99; Coke in 12 LA 870, 883–884; Bushnell in 3 LA 687, 704. Also see Platt in 56 LA 487, 488. No weight was given to this factor where the evidence was skimpy. Atlanta Newspapers, 39 LA 207, 209 (Holly, 1962).

[184]Basic Steel Indus., 13 LA 46, 50 (Daugherty, Cole & Rosenman, 1949). Also see Arbitrator Hays in 20 LA 75, 82–83. Cf., Basic Steel Indus., 18 LA 112, 117 (W.S.B., 1952). In Railroads v. Nonoperating Unions, 34 LA 517, 533 (Dunlop, Aaron & Sempliner, 1960), the Board stated: "The relevance of increases in productivity to wage rates in a particular industry depends in part upon the ratio of labor costs to total costs; the competitive character of the industry, which influences whether such gains are transmitted rapidly into price and quality changes; the methods of wage payment; and other factors."

the benefit of the employees. But if the increase is the result of technological progress or better management, several considerations must be taken into account.

It was pointed out by Economist Sumner H. Slichter that changes in wages affect the attitude of employees toward the productivity of the enterprise in which they work and that they will be more likely to cooperate with management to increase productivity if some of the gains of that increase are passed on to them. On the other hand, he recognized two disadvantages of directly passing such gains to the employees: (1) Increase in wages in such cases would introduce unjustified inequalities into the wage structure of the community; and (2) industry as a whole would be prevented from producing the largest possible product, since the rise of wages in the industries where labor productivity is increasing most rapidly would tend to prevent them from reducing their prices to consumers and thus from expanding output and employment. However, he concluded that between raising wages and lowering prices, both of which are likely to follow technological change, the adjustment of the economy to technological progress through higher wages is more favorable to employment and to technological advance than adjustment through falling prices.[185]

While arbitrators may give weight to the productivity factor when increased production is used as the basis of a demand for an increase, it appears that they are not likely to give the factor much consideration when an employer defends against an increase by alleging that his employees have a lower per capita output than is standard. For instance, low productivity has been held not to justify the denial of a pattern increase, for the reasons that employees' efficiency and output are largely within the control of the employer and that the employer should be able, by extending the incentive system, to put the business on a "reasonable competitive basis" in relation to production costs.[186]

A board of arbitration held that an allegedly great reduction in labor efficiency, which the board found to be true to some extent, did not justify the denial of a cost-of-living increase where the inefficiency and high costs in the industry were caused by a variety of factors, including out-of-date technology, high cost of materials, and a shortage of skilled craftsmen.[187] In another case the arbitrator granted a

---

[185]Slichter, Basic Criteria Used in Wage Negotiations, 22–23, 43, 48 (1947). Compare the view of Professor J.E. Isaac as quoted in Air N.Z. Ltd., 77 LA 667, 675 (Feller, 1981). In a 1979 report to Congress the Council on Wage and Price Stability spoke of the possibility of making an exception to wage-price guidelines which would allow larger pay increases to groups of employees "if it can be clearly demonstrated that the additional pay is solely the result of additional work effort," while productivity improvements resulting from new equipment or technology "not tied to workers' diligence" would not be eligible for the exception. 101 LRR 241 (1979).

[186]Watson Elevator Co., 8 LA 386, 389 (Copelof, 1947). In Dallas Publishers, 50 LA 367, 373 (Elkouri, 1968), the employees failed to establish any special claim to a wage increase based upon their productivity, but the arbitrator acknowledged the economic vitality of the city in which they work to be another type of productivity that had some relevance, under the facts, to the request for increased wages.

[187]Associated Gen. Contractors, 9 LA 201, 226–227 (Aaron, 1947). Also see Arbitrator Abernethy in 22 LA 88, 93.

cost-of-living increase without giving weight to the employer's complaint that productivity was low, on the ground that there was a failure to establish a decline in productivity after the execution of the contract.[188]

Numerous reasons exist for the refusal of arbitrators to make productivity a decisive factor in wage determination. The rate of change in productivity varies from firm to firm and even from department to department within a plant. Thus, exclusive use of the productivity standard for wage adjustments would soon lead to a chaotic wage structure within a single plant or industry.[189] Moreover, the measurement of productivity presents highly difficult problems of economic analysis and statistical measurement,[190] although assistance may be available under the U.S. Department of Labor productivity measurement program (which issues industry indexes of output per man-hour).[191] Even after a change in productivity has been measured, the problem still remains of determining whether it was caused by increased skill and effort of employees or by better management or improved technology. The arbitrator also must face the problem of assigning a value to the change in productivity—evidence of changes in productivity is not readily transformed into cents-per-hour wage adjustments.[192]

A powerful factor giving impetus to consideration of productivity as an element in determining wage increases came into being with the agreement of General Motors Corporation in 1950 to grant an annual "improvement factor" increase, amounting to four cents per hour. The figure was based on an estimated three percent annual improvement in productivity throughout all industry, a figure which the company stated it expected to surpass.[193] The 1979 General Motors agreement

---

[188]Waterfront Employers Assn. of Pac. Coast, 9 LA 172, 178 (Miller, 1947). But declining productivity was one of the factors considered by Arbitrator Samuel J. Nicholas, Jr., in refusing to award a greater wage increase than that offered by the company in Yaun Welding & Mach. Works Co., 73 LA 223, 227 (1979), stating that "In the face of such declining productivity, Management may rightly demand evidence that an additional increase will prove worthwhile." In this case Arbitrator Nicholas did note and agree with the union's view that "low wages undoubtedly serve to generate high turnover costs, especially among skilled employees, lowering the productivity of labor." But he also noted that the union had rejected management's effort to meet the problem by use of a percentage rather than across-the-board dollar increase (a percentage increase would have meant a larger dollar increase for skilled employees and thus would reduce their turnover rate).

[189]Dunlop, "The Economics of Wage-Dispute Settlement," 12 Law & Contemp. Probs., 281, 286–287 (1947).

[190]Id. at 287–288. For an example of the difficulty involved in proving productivity changes, see Waterfront Employers Assn. of Pac. Coast, 9 LA 172, 177–178 (Miller, 1947). Also see Arbitrator Horlacher in 27 LA 295, 299; Fact-Finders Platt, Gemrich & Arsulowicz in 18 LA 686, 690.

[191]See Productivity Indexes for Selected Industries, 1977 Edition (Bureau of Lab. Statistics Bull. No. 1983, 1977); Indexes of Output per Man-Hour, Selected Industries, 1939 and 1947–66 (Bureau of Lab. Statistics Bull. No. 1572, 1967). A guide for productivity measurement in individual companies is provided by Greenberg, A Practical Guide to Productivity Measurement (BNA Books, 1973).

[192]Dunlop, "The Economics of Wage-Dispute Settlement," 12 Law & Contemp. Probs. 281, 288 (1947). Also see New York Shipping Assn., 20 LA 75, 82–83 (Hays, 1952); San Diego Gas & Elec. Co., 12 LA 245, 255–256 (Aaron, 1949).

[193]Regarding the influence elsewhere of this General Motors step, see Union R.R., 20 LA 219, 224 (Gilden, 1953). While granting an increase partly on the basis of the "annual improvement factor," an arbitrator emphasized that an increase on the basis of this factor is not due automati-

specified improvement factor increases (ranging from 25 cents to 45 cents per hour depending on the employee's wage rate) and stated: "The improvement factor provided herein recognizes that a continuing improvement in the standard of living of employees depends upon technological progress, better tools, methods, processes and equipment, and a cooperative attitude on the part of all parties in such progress. It further recognizes the principle that to produce more with the same amount of human effort is a sound economic and social objective." This type of "improvement factor" increase at General Motors apparently fell victim to the economic recession which confronted the country in 1982, for no "fixed cost" improvement factor provision was included in the 1982 agreement.[194] Nonetheless, the 1982 agreement did offer the employees a special incentive for improving productivity, in that the agreement provided for possible profit sharing by employees.[195]

Take-Home Pay

Maintenance of take-home pay emerged at the end of World War II as a means of "cushioning the shock" of the transition from an economy of war to one of peace.[196] Sudden and extensive reductions in weekly earnings throughout industry as a result of reduction of hours, especially overtime, became a matter of national concern at the end of the war while living costs were still rising. Labor demanded wage increases to maintain take-home pay as hours of work were reduced. In considering these demands, arbitrators and fact-finding boards were guided by the national wage-price policy laid down in executive orders, regulations under the Wage Stabilization Act, and an address by the President to the nation. This national wage-price policy recognized that wage increases were necessary as a means of cushioning the shock of the war-peace conversion but that wage increases which would necessitate price increases would have dangerous inflationary tendencies. On the other hand, the policy recognized that business as a whole was in a very favorable earning position and thus could, and

---

cally in every case, but that the factor is one of the considerations to be taken into account along with other factors. Printing Indus. of Ind., 29 LA 7, 11 (McCoy, 1957). In Labor Standards Assn., 36 LA 171, 178 (Roberts, 1960), the union sought to introduce a productivity factor which had been adopted in other industries, but the arbitrator stated that "it has never been integrated into the wage bargain of these parties and should not be imposed by an arbitrator."

[194]Regarding that recession, a BNA special report indicated that in the first three months of 1982 some 350,000 U.S. workers lost their jobs either temporarily or permanently because of production cutbacks or shutdowns, and the report discussed the phenomenon of concession bargaining that characterized several major settlements at that time, including the UAW agreements with both General Motors and Ford. Labor Relations in an Economic Recession: Job Losses and Concession Bargaining (BNA Books, 1982).

[195]See 109 LRR 264–266, 321.

[196]Another type of situation in which need may exist to "cushion the shock" concerns automation. For example, see New York Shipping Assn., 36 LA 44 (Stein, 1960), which was an interest arbitration to determine whether and to what extent royalties should be paid by ship owners to cushion the labor displacement impact of the use of cargo containers.

should, make substantial wage increases without seeking price increases.[197]

The maintenance of take-home pay standard has been given consideration in numerous cases. Although it generally has not been the only one considered, it has been responsible at least for a part of the increase granted in those cases.[198] In the application of this standard, potential[199] or probable[200] loss of take-home pay may be considered as well as present loss.

Application of other standards may preclude the maintenance of take-home pay. For instance, lack of ability to pay was deemed a sufficient reason for permitting the discontinuance of overtime work without at the same time granting a wage increase to maintain take-home pay.[201]

Several arguments may be advanced against use of this standard. Since a reduction in hours means that less labor is being sold, should not the total amount paid for labor drop accordingly? If the principle of relating total wages to the number of hours worked is sound when hours are increasing, is it not sound when hours are decreasing? Moreover, should not workers be encouraged to leave rather than remain in industries and places where a labor surplus exists?[202]

It has been suggested that the heavy penalty rates required for overtime work by the Fair Labor Standards Act and by most collective agreements will keep such work to a minimum in time of peace, and hence that the maintenance of take-home pay will not often need to be considered.[203] It may be reasonable to expect, however, that the standard will be given consideration in any instance where, in the absence of a wage increase, a sudden and extensive reduction in earnings within a specific industry or within a large segment of industry generally would result from a reduction of hours.

This, for instance, was the situation where a railroad emergency board was asked to recommend a 40-hour week in lieu of the then existing 48-hour week for approximately one million nonoperating railway workers. The board recognized 40 basic hours per week with time and a half for overtime to be the prevailing practice in American industry, a practice which had been put into effect not only in industries covered by the Fair Labor Standards Act but to a steadily increasing extent in industries excluded from the Act. The board recommended the adoption of a 40-hour week, and, in connection therewith, it recommended that all basic rates of pay then in effect be

---

[197]General Motors Corp., 1 LA 125, 127–128 (Garrison, Eisenhower & Stacy, 1946).

[198]See Arbitrator Yarowsky in 68 LA 628, 631–632; McCoy in 29 LA 7, 10–11; Gooding, Fitzgibbon & Slavney in 21 LA 307, 309; Tolley, McKelvey & Turkus in 19 LA 538, 551–553; Payne in 15 LA 524, 525–526; Cole, Horovitz & Edwards in 12 LA 507, 515; Dunlop in 10 LA 581, 596; Gellhorn, Paley & Miller in 4 LA 502, 506; Copelof in 3 LA 566, 569; Wallen in 3 LA 639, 645; Witte, Kerr & Starr in 1 LA 333, 338–339; Garrison, Eisenhower & Stacy in 1 LA 125, 130, 133.

[199]F.W. Woolworth Co., 4 LA 502, 506 (Gellhorn, Paley & Miller, 1946).

[200]General Motors Corp., 1 LA 125, 133 (Garrison, Eisenhower & Stacy, 1946).

[201]Roberts Pressure Valve Co., 8 LA 665, 667 (Singer, 1947). Also see Railroads v. Operating Unions, 14 LA 688 (McDonough, O'Malley & Watkins, 1950).

[202]Slichter, Basic Criteria Used in Wage Negotiations, 20–21 (1947).

[203]Id. at 19.

increased by 20 percent to provide the same basic earnings for 40 hours of work as had been received for 48 hours.[204]

Past Practice and Bargaining History

The past practice of the parties has sometimes, although infrequently, been considered to be a standard for interest arbitration. This standard is of special significance when parties are engaged in their initial negotiations. It was stated in one instance by Arbitrator Clark Kerr:

> "The arbitrator considers past practice a primary factor. It is standard form to incorporate past conditions into collective bargaining contracts, whether these contracts are developed by negotiation or arbitration. The fact of unionization creates no basis for the withdrawal of conditions previously in effect. If they were justified before, they remain justified after the event of union affiliation. It is almost axiomatic that the existing conditions be perpetuated. Some contracts even blanket them in through a general 'catch-all' clause."[205]

Arbitrators may require "persuasive reason" for the elimination of a clause which has been in past written agreements.[206] Moreover, they sometimes order the formalization of past practices by ordering that they be incorporated into the written agreement.[207]

In arbitrating the terms of a renewal contract, one arbitrator would consider seriously "what the parties have agreed upon in their past collective bargaining, as affected by intervening economic events * * *."[208] The past bargaining history of the parties, including the criteria that they have used, has provided a helpful guide to other interest arbitrators.[209]

---

[204]Railroads v. Nonoperating Unions, 11 LA 752, 761–763 (Leiserson, Cole & Cook, 1948). A subsequent board recommended a reduction in the workweek of certain operating railroad employees but did not recommend a requested 20 percent wage increase to maintain take-home pay. The board noted the award for the nonoperating employees but distinguished the cases on the following grounds: (1) the rates of the operating employees were already higher than those of employees in other industries, whereas the nonoperating rates had been lower; (2) the requested increase was not justified in view of the railroads' financial condition. The board did, however, believe an increase of 18 cents an hour to be justified. Railroads v. Operating Unions, 14 LA 688, 707–708 (McDonough, O'Malley & Watkins, 1950).

[205]Luckenbach S.S., 6 LA 98, 101 (1946). Also see St. Paul Dept. Stores, 2 LA 52 (Johnston, Gydeson & Harmon, 1946).

[206]Minneapolis-Moline Power Implement Co., 2 LA 227, 230, 240 (Van Fossen, Humphrey & Prifrel, 1946). Similarly, see Arbitrator Sembower in 72 LA 916, 925–927; Holden in 69 LA 1041, 1043–1045. Also see Fact-Finders Healy and Seibel in 77 LA 729, 743.

[207]Sosna Bros., 6 LA 846, 850 (Rosenfarb, 1947); F.W. Woolworth Co., 4 LA 502, 508 (Gellhorn, Paley & Miller, 1946). Also see Arbitrator Roumell in 54 LA 901, 914; Singer in 47 LA 482, 486 (ordering continuation of an unwritten practice); Sanders, Begley & Gilden in 28 LA 182, 196.

[208]United Traction Co., 27 LA 309, 315 (Sheiber, 1956).

[209]This aid was used, as specified by a public-sector statute, in Hurley Hosp., 56 LA 209, 212–215 (Roumell, 1971). In other public-sector cases it was used by Arbitrator Gruenberg in 68 LA 1258, 1263; Holden in 67 LA 384, 386. It was used in private-sector arbitration by Arbitrator Goldberg in 72 LA 90, 95; Holden in 69 LA 1041, 1048; Williams in 68 LA 1064, 1067–1068; Griffin in 65 LA 1016, 1018–1019; Blum in 65 LA 997, 1002; Feller in 60 LA 1, 7; Elkouri in 50 LA 367, 370; Gunderman in 39 LA 249, 251; Flagler in 38 LA 666, 671; Luskin in 36 LA 201, 202–203; Abernethy in 22 LA 88, 92. In Volunteer Elec. Coop., 78 LA 352, 356 (1982), Arbitrator Hamby

Prearbitration Negotiations

It has been said that the award in a wage dispute seldom falls outside the area of "probable expectancy" and that this area is the normal resultant product of the parties' negotiations and bargaining prior to submitting their differences to arbitration.[210] In this regard, too, one arbitration board concluded:

> "An examination of the wealth of evidence submitted in this matter in conjunction with the provisions of settlement worked out by the parties indicates that the most satisfactory award which the Board could render would be one in general agreement with those terms on which the parties were able at one time to substantially agree. Obviously, these terms are not what either party wanted. They represent compromise by both parties. However, since the general terms indicate a meeting of the minds, the Board considers that they hold the basis of a just award."[211]

While observing that an interest arbitrator usually can make a more useful award if he has knowledge of the bargaining positions of the parties prior to the arbitration stage, one group of arbitrators suggested that if at least one of the parties wishes to exclude consideration of prearbitral offers it may be sound policy for the arbitrator to do so lest future bargaining be inhibited.[212] However, the members of one board of inquiry declared that type of tribunal to be of such nature that tentative agreements, as well as offers and counteroffers, of the parties during the negotiation stage could not be ignored completely by the board even though one of the parties protested any consideration of such matters.[213]

Public Interest

The question arises as to how far arbitrators should go in considering the public-interest aspects of interest disputes. The public,

---

refused to disturb certain contractual obligations which had been initially negotiated by the parties and subsequently perpetuated by another interest arbitrator. In Bonneville Power Admin., 73 LA 429, 435 (1979), the wage increase awarded was determined on "the basis of the historical tandem relationships" existing between the employer and eight other utilities in the area, Arbitrator Keltner stating that "the rate of increase should be consistent with the past practice of paying the average of the prevailing rates." Also see Arbitrator Bloch in 73 LA 1, 4.

[210]Justin, "Arbitrating a Wage Dispute Case," 3 Arb. J. (n.s.) 228 (1948). Also see Arbitrator Simkin in 18 LA 631, 643. It is also said that parties sometimes agree upon contract terms but for political reasons want an arbitrator to order them. Current Problems of Arbitration, American Unionism, 29 LA 880, 883 (1958).

[211]Durso & Geelan Co., 17 LA 748, 749 (Donnelly, Curry & Clark, 1951). Also see Arbitrator Siegel in 50 LA 1036, 1042–1043; Black in 41 LA 372, 375–376. In "many instances intangible factors such as the indicated bids or offers by the parties in private bargaining * * * will be of considerable importance" in the arbitrator's consideration of the case. Backman, Economic Data Utilized in Wage Arbitration 3 (1952). In Palo Alto-Stanford Hosp. Center, 50 LA 700, 701 (Mann, 1968), the submission agreement expressly confined the arbitrator to the limits of the parties' original proposals. Similarly, see Arbitrators Cluster, Gallagher & Kraushaar in 45 LA 801, 806. In Eastalco Aluminum Co., 70 LA 793, 795 (1978), Arbitrator Whyte acknowledged the limitation without clearly indicating that it was imposed by the submission agreement.

[212]Guides for Labor Arbitration, 9–10 (1953), by a group of arbitrators in the Philadelphia area. Also see Arbitrator Sembower in 65 LA 839, 842.

[213]Rochester Transit Corp., 19 LA 538, 541–542 (Tolley, McKelvey & Turkus, 1952). In Cummins Sales, 54 LA 1069, 1072 (Seinsheimer, 1970), the arbitrator gave significant weight to the employer's offer in negotiations.

although not a direct party, has a vital interest in the settlement of some disputes. Fact-finding boards do give strong consideration to the public welfare in making recommendations. For instance, a fact-finding board for General Motors Corporation would recommend only such wage increases as it believed would not have inflationary price consequences.[214] A fact-finding board for the Basic Steel Industry considered the public interest to be one of the two major inquiries which should be made in determining whether a wage increase should be granted. In denying any increase, the board placed strong emphasis on its belief that a wage increase for the steel industry would be used as a pattern for other industries and might well cause price dislocations with adverse effects on the general economy.[215]

The public interest is an important consideration in public utility disputes (see subtopic entitled "Public Utility Disputes" below), and equally so in disputes directly involving the public sector.[216] For example, the "interest and welfare of the public" is a factor specified by state statute to be given consideration by arbitrators of interest disputes in the public sector.[217]

Public Utility Disputes

The public-interest standard is often invoked for public utility disputes. Several considerations are generally involved. The first is that services of public utilities, being constantly consumed necessities of life, should be made available to consumers at a fair price. Since wages paid by a utility will directly affect the cost of its services to the public, the amount of any wage increase granted may be affected by the arbitrator's conclusion about the probable effect of the increase upon the price of the service involved. The arbitrator will keep in mind the needs of the consumers.[218]

---

[214]General Motors Corp., 1 LA 125, 128 (Garrison, Eisenhower & Stacy, 1946). Also see Arbitrator Bloch in 73 LA 1, 6.

[215]Basic Steel Indus., 13 LA 46, 52 (Daugherty, Cole & Rosenman, 1949). In Chesapeake & Potomac Tel. Co. of Baltimore, 7 LA 630, 640 (Jackson, Healy & Dennis, 1947), an increase sufficient to offset the full rise in the cost of living would not be granted where to do so would contribute further to inflation. Cf., Bonneville Power Admin., 73 LA 429, 434–435 (Keltner, 1979); Basic Steel Indus., 18 LA 112, 136 (W.S.B., 1952). In League of Voluntary Hosps., 67 LA 293, 294, 303 (1976), a factor taken into consideration was the possible curtailment of hospital services, Arbitrator Margery Gootnick stating that "at some point increases in wages and benefits would result in layoffs, closing and reduction of services," which "would be tragic."

[216]See this Chapter, subtopic entitled "Public Sector Ability to Pay" and topic entitled "Standards in Public-Sector Disputes." It has been stated that public policy must be considered much more in public-sector disputes than in those in the private sector. Jones, "The Role of Arbitration in State and National Policy," Proceedings of the 24th Annual Meeting of NAA, 42, 60 (BNA Books, 1971).

[217]See Arbitrator Witney in 68 LA 454 at 454, 456; Platt in 65 LA 293, 303, 306–308, 312; Roumell in 55 LA 716, 721; Schmidt in 52 LA 1301, 1302, 1304.

[218]See Arbitrators Platt, Gemrich & Arsulowicz in 18 LA 686, 690; Holland, Anderson & Hollingsworth in 8 LA 397, 402; Kerr in 7 LA 528, 530–531; Taylor in 6 LA 830, 836. Cf., Volunteer Elec. Coop., 78 LA 352, 357 (1982), where Arbitrator Horace Hamby, Jr., stated that "although the plight of [the public utility's] customers whose incomes are below the so-called 'poverty level' is regrettable, it is the opinion of the arbitrator that this consideration is not a valid one on which to base less than reasonable wage rates" for the utility's employees.

The second consideration recognizes that the public has a paramount interest in continuity of operations of public utilities. The public expects utilities to provide uninterrupted service. Indeed, in one case the arbitrator stated that "most of the unions and most of the employees engaged in the essential public utilities" had "long recognized that their responsibilities required uninterruped service to the public."[219]

Since public utility employees are under a very strong obligation not to strike, there has been considerable public discussion of the need for a wage policy which will assure equitable treatment to these employees, and emphasis usually has been placed upon the desirability of assuring them rates and conditions of work which are as good as or better than those available for comparable work anywhere in the area.[220]

In recognizing these several considerations, Arbitrator George W. Taylor stated that, while a meritorious argument is presented, it is difficult to put them into practice in specific terms.[221] But Arbitrator Clark Kerr declared that an effort should be made to assure utility workers "both as high or higher absolute levels and as favorable or more favorable relative changes in wages as other workers generally in the community."[222] Another arbitrator expressed preference for the view that utility employees should expect to enjoy substantially the same wages, hours, and working conditions—no better and no worse— as those enjoyed by other workers living in the area; thus, utility employment should be made to conform to local conditions, not to blaze new trails.[223]

As noted in Chapter 1, some states have enacted antistrike laws for their public utilities (some of these laws have subsequently been repealed and/or merged into broader statutes including public-sector coverage). In some instances these states have also specified standards to be observed in the compulsory arbitration of public utility disputes, the objective appearing to be to insure that utility employees shall have the same wages, hours, and working conditions as those prevailing for comparable workers.

The Nebraska provisions are of interest in this regard. The Nebraska Act (the coverage of which was expanded in 1969 to include disputes involving governmental service) provides for a Court of Industrial Relations, which is empowered to establish or alter the scale of wages, hours of work, or conditions of employment. In respect to the standards to be applied by the Court, the following is provided by the Act:

---

[219]Capital Transit Co., 9 LA 666, 679 (Taylor, 1947).
[220]Consolidated Edison Sys. Cos. of N.Y., 6 LA 830, 834 (Taylor, 1947).
[221]Ibid.
[222]Pacific Gas & Elec. Co., 7 LA 528, 531 (1947). To similar effect, Consumers Power Co., 24 LA 581, 584 (Smith, Howlett & Sorensen, 1955).
[223]Cleveland Elec. Illuminating Co., 8 LA 597, 600, 605 (Cornsweet, 1947). While this view had been advanced earlier by Lee H. Hill, a management spokesman, in the instant case it was approved, but interpreted differently, by both the labor and employer arbitrators.

"In making such findings and order or orders, the Court of Industrial Relations shall establish rates of pay and conditions of employment which are comparable to the prevalent wage rates paid and conditions of employment maintained for the same or similar work of workers exhibiting like or similar skills under the same or similar working conditions. In establishing wage rates the court shall take into consideration the overall compensation presently received by the employees, having regard not only to wages for time actually worked but also to wages for time not worked, including vacations, holidays, and other excused time, and all benefits received, including insurance and pensions, and the continuity and stability of employment enjoyed by the employees. Any order or orders entered may be modified on the court's own motion or on application by any of the parties affected, but only upon a showing of a change in the conditions from those prevailing at the time the original order was entered."[224]

This Nebraska statutory requirement for the use of the prevailing-practice standard (including the recognition of appropriate differentials) illustrates again the standard's value and acceptability.

Governmental Wage Stabilization

In times of wage stabilization interest arbitrators, emergency boards, and fact-finders must take cognizance of governmental stabilization regulations that may apply to the parties.[225] In some cases awards or recommended terms have been made subject to approval by wage stabilization authorities.[226] Sometimes arbitrators have ordered one party to join the other in seeking such approval.[227] Then, too, the arbitrator might examine stabilization regulations and reach his own conclusion as to the permissibility of requested increases.[228]

---

[224]Nebraska Revised Statutes 1943, Reissue of 1978, § 48-818 as amended in 1969. The Wisconsin statute provides that the specific enumeration of standards shall not be construed as precluding the consideration of other factors normally taken into consideration in the determination of wages, hours, and working conditions through voluntary collective bargaining or arbitration. See West's Wisconsin Statutes Annotated, § 111.57.

[225]Another aspect of governmental wage stabilization programs concerns their possible lingering effect after the regulatory agency ceases to be viable. In Colorado Contractors Assn., 63 LA 702, 707 (Elkouri, 1974), the union argued that in no event can any agreement entered into by parties under government compulsion continue to bind them after the government power to coerce has terminated, while the employers argued that the purpose of wage and price controls is to stabilize the economy and reduce inflation, and that this purpose "would be almost completely nullified" if the parties after termination of the program's legal authority "were able to return to the same level which they would have been at had the Act [which established the program] never been in effect." For discussion of governmental wage stabilization programs, see articles by Weber, Aaron, Davey, McKenna, and Pollara, "Labor-Management Relations in a Controlled and Rationed Economy," Proceedings of the 27th Annual Meeting of NAA, 163–188 (BNA Books, 1975); Bloch, "Wage Controls and Interest Arbitration in the Public Sector," 52 J. Urb. L. 203 (1974); Tiernan, "The Pay Board," Proceedings of the 25th Annual Meeting of NAA, 229 (BNA Books, 1973). Coverage of state and local government employees by the Economic Stabilization Act of 1970 was upheld as to constitutionality in Fry v. United States, 95 S.Ct. 1792, 22 WH Cases 284 (1975).

[226]See Los Angeles Standard Rubber, 17 LA 353, 354, 361 (Warren, 1951); Felt Cos., 16 LA 881, 882 (Lesser, 1951).

[227]See Durso & Geelan Co., 17 LA 748, 750–751 (Donnelly, 1951). Also see Arbitrator Hays in 20 LA 75, 76.

[228]See Frederick Loeser & Co., 16 LA 399, 404 (Justin, 1951). In one case the arbitrator did this at the request of the parties after they had agreed as to increases. City of Cheboygan, Mich., 57 LA 1090, 1091 (Keefe, 1971). Also see Macy's N.Y., 57 LA 1115, 1118 (Stark, 1971), where the arbitrator ruled as to the permissibility under wage stabilization regulations of certain automatic wage increases. But see Arbitrator Markowitz in 58 LA 191, 193.

Where the parties in submitting a case to interest arbitration specified that the arbitration board should seek wage stabilization approval (if necessary) of any increase ordered, the arbitrators stated that the wage stabilization program was just one factor to be considered along with others in determining the amount of any wage adjustment.[229] Another arbitrator declared that while wage stabilization regulations should be taken into account in determining wage adjustments, the influence of wage stabilization on an arbitrator's decision should vary "in direct ratio to the certainty, clarity and stage of its evolution."[230] It may also be noted that at times the President has adopted wage guidelines and has urged their observance by industry to aid the control of inflation.[231]

Standards in Public-Sector Disputes

The standards or criteria utilized by neutrals for interest cases in the private sector also have been utilized for interest cases in the public sector.[232] Indeed, the general utility of using private-sector

---

[229]North Am. Aviation, 19 LA 76, 77 (Cole, Aaron & Wirtz, 1952).

[230]Merchants Bank of N.Y., 16 LA 901, 904 (Rosenfarb, 1951). In San Francisco Elec. Contractors Assn., 60 LA 1, 2 (1972), Arbitrator David E. Feller offered the following explanation in issuing his award essentially independent of governmental stabilization considerations:

"I do not regard it as my function to predict what the Construction Industry Stabilization Committee will permit. My function as an arbitrator is to determine the appropriate package increase * * *. If that amount should be less than the maximum permissible under government regulations, I should award that lesser amount. If I believe the amount to be larger than that which is argued to be permissible under government regulations, I should similarly award that larger amount and allow the parties to determine if that larger amount is permissible. I believe that this is correct as a matter of principle. It is, in any case, a conclusion which I would necessarily come to in view of the grave uncertainty as to the precise application of the guidelines to particular cases. It is by no means clear to me, or I believe to anyone, what the determinants of a permissible increase under the applicable regulations are."

For related discussion, see Chapter 10, topic entitled "Statutory Law."

[231]See Arbitrator Tamoush in 72 LA 1180, 1185; Sembower in 72 LA 916, 919 (stating that the given guidelines were "of great importance" but that other factors were more significant in that particular case); Winton in 72 LA 190, 194–195 (stating that he had weighed the given guidelines "as one important factor alongside three or four others"); Crawford in 45 LA 58, 59 (rejecting use of the given guidelines, and stating that "There is no evidence that the national guidelines for wage increases have ever been applied in collective bargaining or arbitration in this industry, and this is not the time for innovation"). Also see Keltner in 73 LA 429, 433; Bloch in 73 LA 1, 4.

[232]Many of the more recent citations for standards discussed elsewhere in this Chapter are public-sector cases. For other writings which give some consideration to standards for public-sector cases, see articles by Minami, Clark & Fallon, "Interest Arbitration: Can the Public Sector Afford It? Developing Limitations on the Process," Proceedings of the 34th Annual Meeting of NAA, 241–272 (BNA Books, 1982); articles by Ellman, Gershenfeld, Loihl & Torosian, "Decision-Making in Public-Sector Interest Arbitration," Proceedings of the 31st Annual Meeting of NAA, 291–350 (BNA Books, 1979); Morris, "The Role of Interest Arbitration in a Collective Bargaining System," The Future of Labor Arbitration in America, 197, 227–250 (AAA, 1976); Berkowitz, "Arbitration of Public-Sector Interest Disputes: Economics, Politics, and Equity," Proceedings of the 29th Annual Meeting of NAA, 159–191 (BNA Books, 1976), including comments of Morse & Zwerdling followed by group discussion; articles by Anderson, Loewenberg, Rehmus & Stern, "Lessons From Interest Arbitration in the Public Sector: The Experience of Four Jurisdictions," Proceedings of the 27th Annual Meeting of NAA, 59–105 (BNA Books, 1975); Klapper, "Legislated Criteria in Arbitration of Public Safety Contract Disputes," 29 Arb. J. 115 (1974); Doering, "Impasse Issues in Teacher Disputes Submitted to Fact Finding in New York," 27 Arb. J. 1 (1972); Block, "Criteria in Public Sector Interests Disputes," Proceedings of the 24th Annual Meeting of NAA, 161 (BNA Books, 1971); Jones, "The Role of Arbitration in State and National Policy," id. at 42; Garber, "Compulsory Arbitration in the Public Sector: A Proposed Alternative," 26 Arb. J. 226 (1971); Bain, "Third-Party Settlements in Education," 26 Arb. J. 41 (1971); Drotning & Lipsky, "The Outcome of Impasse Procedures in New York Schools Under the Taylor Law," 26 Arb. J. 87

standards for interest disputes in the public sector is underscored by the action of various states which have expressly ordered the use of such standards for public-sector disputes. The Michigan Police and Firemen's Arbitration Act provides, for example:

> "Sec. 9. Where there is no agreement between the parties, or where there is an agreement but the parties have begun negotiations or discussions looking to a new agreement or amendment of the existing agreement, and wage rates or other conditions of employment under the proposed new or amended agreement are in dispute, the arbitration panel shall base its findings, opinions and order upon the following factors, as applicable:
>
> "(a) The lawful authority of the employer.
>
> "(b) Stipulations of the parties.
>
> "(c) The interests and welfare of the public and the financial ability of the unit of government to meet those costs.
>
> "(d) Comparison of the wages, hours and conditions of employment of the employees involved in the arbitration proceedings with the wages, hours and conditions of employment of other employees performing similar services and with other employees generally:
>
> "(i)   In public employment in comparable communities.
>
> "(ii)   In private employment in comparable communities.
>
> "(e) The average consumer prices for goods and services, commonly known as the cost of living.
>
> "(f) The overall compensation presently received by the employees, including direct wage compensation, vacations, holidays and other excused time, insurance and pensions, medical and hospitalization benefits, the continuity and stability of employment, and all other benefits received.
>
> "(g) Changes in any of the foregoing circumstances during the pendency of the arbitration proceedings.
>
> "(h) Such other factors, not confined to the foregoing, which are normally or traditionally taken into consideration in the determination of wages, hours and conditions of employment through voluntary collective bargaining, mediation, fact-finding, arbitration or otherwise between the parties, in the public service or in private employment."[233]

(1971); Wollett & Chanin, The Law and Practice of Teacher Negotiations (BNA Books, 1970); Loewenberg, "Compulsory Arbitration and the Arbitrator," 25 Arb. J. 248 (1970).

[233]Michigan SLL 32:262c; MCL 423.239. In Detroit v. Police Officers Assn., 105 LRRM 3083, 3092, 3095 (Mich. S.Ct., 1980), the court upheld the constitutionality of the § 9 standards as being "at least as reasonably precise as the subject matter requires or permits." The court added that other jurisdictions "have sanctioned their compulsory interest arbitration schemes even though presented with less precise or even non-explicit standards for decision." Id. at 3096. Pointing to the § 9 mandate that "the arbitration panel shall base its findings, opinions and order upon" the factors listed in § 9, the court stated that the statutory factors constitute a "compulsory checklist," and the court then explained:

> "Since the §9 factors are not intrinsically weighted, they cannot of themselves provide the arbitrators with an answer. It is the panel which must make the difficult decision of determining which particular factors are more important in resolving a contested issue under the singular facts of a case, although, of course, all 'applicable' factors must be considered."

Id. at 3102–3103. In the latter regard, the court believed that the failure of the parties to submit evidence on a given factor "did not excuse the panel's inattention to the factor." Id. at 3108. In City of Boston, 70 LA 154, 154–155, 160 (1977), Arbitrator Robert M. O'Brien in applying the Massachusetts statute agreed that all statutory standards must be considered but that their respective weight in the given case is to be determined by the neutral. In City of Winter Haven, 65 LA 557, 558–559, 562 (1975), Arbitrator James J. Sherman considered the Florida statute, which lists various standards and emphasizes the use of comparisons with recognition of appropriate

Note that one of the criteria listed in the Michigan statute is the "lawful authority of the employer." This consideration has special relevance to the public sector. Other considerations which likewise are not normally relevant in private-sector cases will no doubt be recognized for special application in public-sector cases in the course of the fuller development of that area in the future. A few of the possibilities as to special considerations are reflected, for instance, in the following statements or actions by neutrals in public-sector cases already decided.

As to police officers, Arbitrator Peter Seitz stated that:

"* * * if the exacting requirements of police work are to be met in the near and more distant future, at least two conditions must be recognized: the level of pay must be high enough to attract able and promising young people who will be able to withstand the lure of higher wages at less dangerous work in plants in the surrounding communities in the general labor market and the compensation system should be one that will maintain the highest possible morale and esprit de corps in the present force."[234]

Another arbitrator "adopted the principle that Police Department personnel should receive compensation which is sufficient to maintain reasonable standards of health and decency without the necessity to hold alternate employment."[235]

In reference to firemen, Arbitrator John T. Dunlop pointed out that "The City has a fiscal interest in maintaining the quality and morale of its firefighting forces since the fire insurance rates to business and the attractiveness of doing business in Providence are influenced in part by the costs of fire protection."[236]

---

differentials, and he stated that the statutory standards in his opinion "are intended to be applied only selectively depending upon the circumstances of each case," that the standards "are not to be given equal weight in every case," and that "Indeed in some cases particular standards probably have no applicability and should not even influence the decision." The New Jersey police and firefighter statute lists standards generally similar to the Michigan standards quoted above and calls for "giving due weight to those" statutory standards "that are judged relevant for the resolution of the specific dispute." See 34 N.J.S.A. §§ 13A–16g. As to the New Jersey statute also see Arbitrator Silver in 70 LA 850, 851. For some other sets of statutory standards, see Arbitrator Snow in 76 LA 789, 791 (Montana), and in 71 LA 271, 272 (Washington); Sullivan in 75 LA 784, 785 (Nevada); Henderson in 72 LA 63, 64 (California); Winton in 70 LA 1258, 1259 (Iowa); Bailey in 65 LA 1048, 1049 (Texas); Rauch in 63 LA 126, 131 (Wisconsin); Schmidt in 52 LA 1301, 1302 (Rhode Island statute emphasizing the "comparable practice" standard with recognition of appropriate differentials). For general discussion of state statutes relating to interest arbitration in the public sector, see Chapter 2, subtopic entitled "Interest Arbitration Statutes."

[234]City of Providence, 47 LA 1036, 1039 (1966). Also see comments of Arbitrator Silver in 70 LA 850, 855. In City of Birmingham, 55 LA 716, 723 (Roumell, 1970), the arbitrator stated that police officer compensation "should receive relative improvement as compared to other types of employees because of the changing duties and responsibilities of their jobs."

[235]City of Uniontown, 51 LA 1072, 1073 (Duff, 1968). However, this arbitrator could find no compelling reason to classify police department employees as a special group entitled to more holidays or vacation time than other city employees. Id. at 1075. Agreeing that "moonlighting" by police officers should be discouraged by an adequate police wage, Arbitrator Seitz in 47 LA 1036, 1039.

[236]City of Providence, 42 LA 1114, 1119 (1963). Similarly as concerns fire insurance rates, see Arbitrator Witney in 68 LA 454, 456. Also regarding firefighters, see Arbitrator O'Brien in 70 LA 154, 157 (speaking of the public's "interest in a well-trained, efficient and motivated fire suppression force," and recognizing the great hazards "inherent in this profession"); Sembower in 66 LA 992, 998.

Considerations underlying a fact-finder's recommendations for increases in teacher salaries were to keep the school district in a competitive position to recruit new teachers, to attract competent experienced teachers, to hold valuable teachers now serving the school district, to give recognition to advanced degrees and training, and to recognize the constantly increasing costs of advanced training to the teacher.[237]

The need to keep public-sector employers competitive to obtain and keep well-qualified employees likewise has been a consideration in other cases.[238]

---

[237]Whitesboro Teachers Assn., 51 LA 58, 61 (Bickal, 1968). Also see Arbitrator Young in 51 LA 1134, 1135–1138.

[238]See Arbitrator Shaw in 62 LA 1310, 1312 (mechanical employees); McDermott, Zollner & Hutskow in 52 LA 233, 234–235 (police); Young in 51 LA 1134, 1135–1136 (teachers); Florey in 51 LA 994, 995 (police); Singer in 48 LA 289, 291 (nursing home).

Chapter 19

Arbitration's Place As an Industrial and Public-Employment Institution

Arbitration in practice is a distinct institution, the product of a collectively bargained compromise between the alternatives of resort to courts of law, which are not well adapted to the needs of labor-management relations, and resort to work stoppages, which are wasteful and costly not only to both parties but to the public as well. While arbitration is a distinct institution, however, it would be totally unrealistic to deny the close relationship now existing between it, especially "rights" arbitration, and our formal legal system. Indeed, labor arbitration has drawn heavily from the standards and techniques of that system. In this connection, the Authors believe that on the whole sound judgment has been exercised by arbitrators in effectively utilizing established legalisms without paying slavish deference thereto.

Arbitration is an avenue traveled by thousands, indeed millions, of industrial and public-employment disputants. It is a vital force in establishing confidence and minimizing confusion at all levels of the labor-management relationship and is a major constructive force in the collective bargaining process itself. Arbitration should not, however, be expected or totally relied upon to create either good contracts or cooperative human relationships—it is a supplement to, rather than a substitute for, conscientious grievance processing and genuine collective bargaining.

Finally, the Authors desire to emphasize their firm conviction that not only has arbitration been an exceedingly useful social and industrial institution but that it will become even more so in the future, both in the private sector and in the public sector.

Titles of NAA Proceedings
1948–1984

The Profession of Labor Arbitration, Selected Papers From the First Seven Annual Meetings of the National Academy of Arbitrators, 1948–1954 (BNA Books, 1957).

Arbitration Today, Proceedings of the 8th Annual Meeting, National Academy of Arbitrators (BNA Books, 1955).

Management Rights and the Arbitration Process, Proceedings of the 9th Annual Meeting, National Academy of Arbitrators (BNA Books, 1956).

Critical Issues in Labor Arbitration, Proceedings of the 10th Annual Meeting, National Academy of Arbitrators (BNA Books, 1957).

The Arbitrator and the Parties, Proceedings of the 11th Annual Meeting, National Academy of Arbitrators (BNA Books, 1958).

Arbitration and the Law, Proceedings of the 12th Annual Meeting, National Academy of Arbitrators (BNA Books, 1959).

Challenges to Arbitration, Proceedings of the 13th Annual Meeting, National Academy of Arbitrators (BNA Books, 1960).

Arbitration and Public Policy, Proceedings of the 14th Annual Meeting, National Academy of Arbitrators (BNA Books, 1961).

Collective Bargaining and the Arbitrator's Role, Proceedings of the 15th Annual Meeting, National Academy of Arbitrators (BNA Books, 1962).

Labor Arbitration and Industrial Change, Proceedings of the 16th Annual Meeting, National Academy of Arbitrators (BNA Books, 1963).

Labor Arbitration: Perspectives and Problems, Proceedings of the 17th Annual Meeting, National Academy of Arbitrators (BNA Books, 1964).

Proceedings of the 18th Annual Meeting of the National Academy of Arbitrators, 1965 (BNA Books, 1965).

Problems of Proof in Arbitration, Proceedings of the 19th Annual Meeting, National Academy of Arbitrators (BNA Books, 1967).

The Arbitrator, the NLRB, and the Courts, Proceedings of the 20th Annual Meeting, National Academy of Arbitrators (BNA Books, 1967).

Developments in American and Foreign Arbitration, Proceedings of the 21st Annual Meeting, National Academy of Arbitrators (BNA Books, 1968).

Arbitration and Social Change, Proceedings of the 22nd Annual Meeting, National Academy of Arbitrators (BNA Books, 1970).

Arbitration and the Expanding Role of Neutrals, Proceedings of the 23rd Annual Meeting, National Academy of Arbitrators (BNA Books, 1970).

Arbitration and the Public Interest, Proceedings of the 24th Annual Meeting, National Academy of Arbitrators (BNA Books, 1971).

Labor Arbitration at the Quarter-Century Mark, Proceedings of the 25th Annual Meeting, National Academy of Arbitrators (BNA Books, 1973).

A full listing of NAA titles is given here for the reader's reference to supplement the abbreviated titles used in footnotes of this Edition.

Arbitration of Interest Disputes, Proceedings of the 26th Annual Meeting, National Academy of Arbitrators (BNA Books, 1974).

Arbitration—1974, Proceedings of the 27th Annual Meeting, National Academy of Arbitrators (BNA Books, 1975).

Arbitration—1975, Proceedings of the 28th Annual Meeting, National Academy of Arbitrators (BNA Books, 1976).

Arbitration—1976, Proceedings of the 29th Annual Meeting, National Academy of Arbitrators (BNA Books, 1976).

Arbitration—1977, Proceedings of the 30th Annual Meeting, National Academy of Arbitrators (BNA Books, 1978).

Truth, Lie Detectors, and Other Problems in Labor Arbitration, Proceedings of the 31st Annual Meeting, National Academy of Arbitrators (BNA Books, 1979).

Arbitration of Subcontracting and Wage Incentive Disputes, Proceedings of the 32nd Annual Meeting, National Academy of Arbitrators (BNA Books, 1980).

Decisional Thinking of Arbitrators and Judges, Proceedings of the 33rd Annual Meeting, National Academy of Arbitrators (BNA Books, 1981).

Arbitration Issues for the 1980s, Proceedings of the 34th Annual Meeting, National Academy of Arbitrators (BNA Books, 1982).

Arbitration 1982: Conduct of the Hearing, Proceedings of the 35th Annual Meeting, National Academy of Arbitrators (BNA Books, 1983).

Arbitration—Promise and Performance, Proceedings of the 36th Annual Meeting, National Academy of Arbitrators (BNA Books, 1984).

Arbitration 1984: Absenteeism, Recent Law, Panels, and Published Decisions, Proceedings of the 37th Annual Meeting, National Academy of Arbitrators (BNA Books, 1985).

Topical Index